The Penguin Dictionary of the
THEATRE

Market House Books Ltd

PENGUIN BOOKS

PENGUIN BOOKS

Published by the Penguin Group
Penguin Books Ltd, 80 Strand, London WC2R 0RL, England
Penguin Group (USA) Inc., 375 Hudson Street, New York, New York 10014, USA
Penguin Books Australia Ltd, 250 Camberwell Road, Camberwell, Victoria 3124, Australia
Penguin Books Canada Ltd, 10 Alcorn Avenue, Toronto, Ontario, Canada M4V 3B2
Penguin Books India (P) Ltd, 11 Community Centre, Panchsheel Park, New Delhi – 110 017, India
Penguin Group (NZ), cnr Airborne and Rosedale Roads, Albany, Auckland 1310, New Zealand
Penguin Books (South Africa) (Pty) Ltd, 24 Sturdee Avenue, Rosebank 2196, South Africa

Penguin Books Ltd, Registered Offices: 80 Strand, London WC2R 0RL, England

www.penguin.com

First published 1988
This revised and enlarged edition published 2001
Reprinted as *The Penguin Dictionary of the Theatre* 2004
1

Copyright © Market House Books Ltd, 1988, 2001
All rights reserved

The moral right of the author has been asserted

Typeset in ITC Stone
Typeset by Market House Books Ltd
Printed in England by Clays Ltd, St Ives plc

This dictionary is a comprehensive guide to the theatre; its 5000 articles include entries on actors, playwrights, directors and producers, plays, venues and companies, genres, technical terms, organizations, and other related topics. In selecting the entries, the editors have taken into account their significance in the history of the theatre, their interest to the general reader, and their usefulness to theatre students. Thus, such entries as **Sir Henry Irving**, *Much Ado Nothing*, **Royal National Theatre**, and the **unities** will be found interspersed with articles on **fires**, **ghosts**, **make-up**, **taboos**, **vamp trap**, etc. The dictionary explores the theatre of all eras, nations, and styles but pays special attention to that of Britain, Ireland, and North America.

A particular feature of the book is the inclusion of entries for most of the important plays in the history of Western drama. These provide information concerning the author, first performance, alternative titles, brief plot summary, initial reception, and original cast. In addition, the principal dramatic works of major playwrights are listed separately, at the end of their entries.

An effort has been made to include a selection of entries relating to the contemporary stage, especially those performers and writers who may be expected to have a lasting influence. Because the choice of these entries has to be subjective, the editors take full responsibility for inclusions and omissions.

Entries are arranged in strict alphabetical order. The extensive use of cross references has made the book virtually self-indexing. The use of SMALL CAPITALS indicates that further information relevant to the entry being read will be found in the article so highlighted. In the case of entries for plays, we have generally given the title by which the work is best known in the English-speaking world (usually the English title), followed by alternative titles in parentheses. A date given in parentheses after a play title indicates either the date of its first performance or the date of the performance relevant to the context in which it is being discussed.

DHP
JL

Editors

Jonathan Law
David Pickering
Richard Helfer (US and Canadian consultant)

Contributors

Deborah Chapman
Hazel Egerton
Rosalind Fergusson
Kurt Ganzl
Ann Hoffmann
Lawrence Holden
Tony Jackson
Richard O'Donoghue
William Packard
Kate Reddick
Charlotte Savidge
Barry Sloan

A

Abba, Marta *See* Pirandello, Luigi.

Abbey Theatre A theatre founded in Dublin in 1904. Established as a permanent home for the IRISH NATIONAL DRAMATIC SOCIETY of W B Yeats and Lady Gregory, the theatre was the gift of Annie HORNIMAN, who also provided a subsidy. The main aim was to provide a platform for contemporary Irish drama. As well as Yeats and Lady Gregory themselves, writers who had their work presented there included J M Synge, AE, and Sean O'Casey. The most famous production in the early years of the theatre was Synge's *The Playboy of the Western World*, which caused riots in 1907. The resident company soon established itself internationally with eventful tours of the US and elsewhere, despite the need for strict economy in production after Miss Horniman withdrew her support in 1910. Subsequently, under the management of Lennox ROBINSON, the theatre was acknowledged as Ireland's national theatre, becoming the first state-subsidized theatre in the English-speaking world in 1924. There was a new surge of interest in the 1920s when the plays of Sean O'Casey were first presented there and the company included such celebrated performers as Sara ALLGOOD, Barry FITZGERALD, and F J MCCORMICK. The theatre was badly damaged by fire in 1951 but later restored (1966); it continues to produce a predominantly Irish programme in the main auditorium and experimental drama in the smaller **Peacock Theatre** (first opened in 1925 and reopened in 1967).

Abbot of Misrule *See* Misrule, Lord of.

Abbots Bromley Horn Dance *See* Horn Dance.

Abbott, George (1887–1995) US playwright and director, also famous as a 'play doctor' for works in trouble before opening. His first successful play, *The Fall Guy* (1925), was written in collaboration with James Gleason. In 1938 he wrote the successful *The Boys From Syracuse*, a musical based on Shakespeare's *The Comedy of Errors* (with music by Rodgers and Hart). His other works, most of which were collaborations, include *Broadway* (1926), *Coquette* (1927), *Three Men on a Horse* (1935), *Where's Charley?* (1948), *The Pajama Game* (1954), *Damn Yankees!* (1955), and *Fiorello* (1959). He directed his own plays and many other comedies and musicals including *Twentieth Century* (1932), *Room Service* (1937), *On the Town* (1944), and *A Funny Thing Happened on the Way to the Forum* (1962: Tony Award). Works he produced range from *Twentieth Century* to the 1954 revival of *On Your Toes*. He remained actively involved in projects after his 100th year.

Abbott, William (1789–1843) British actor, who appeared at the Haymarket and from 1813 was at Covent Garden. He was the original Appius Claudius in Sheridan Knowles's *Virginius* and played Romeo to Fanny Kemble's Juliet in 1830. Appearances in the US in 1836 were not successful.

abele spelen The earliest vernacular plays of the Netherlands, which evolved in the 13th century alongside the liturgical drama and were based upon chivalric romances. Three 14th-century examples have survived, the most notable of which is the tragedy *Lanseloet van Denemarken*.

Abell, Kjeld (1901–61) Danish playwright and artist, whose plays rejected naturalism in favour of experimentalism. His first work, *Melodien der blev vock* (The Melody that got Lost), was produced in Copenhagen in 1931 and the following year at the Arts Theatre, London. His other plays include *Anna Sophie Hedvig* (1939), often regarded as his finest, *Den blå pekineser* (The Blue Pekingese; 1954), and *Skriget* (The Scream; 1961), which was first performed posthumously.

Abington, Frances (Frances Barton; 1737–1815) British actress, who made her stage debut in 1755 at the Haymarket. In 1756 she moved to Drury Lane, where she remained for three years. Her marriage to the musician James Abington did not last, but as Mrs Abington she was much acclaimed during the next five years in Dublin. Garrick then persuaded her back to Drury Lane, where her leading parts included the first Lady Teazle in *The School for Scandal* (1777). She moved to Covent Garden in 1782 and retired in 1799.

above *See* stage direction.

Absurd, Theatre of the The works of a loosely associated group of dramatists writing in the 1950s and 1960s, whose plays are characterized by a broadly similar view of the futility of existence. The term itself was derived from an essay by Camus, in which he first described the human condition as 'absurd'. Beckett, Ionesco, Albee, Adamov, Pinter, and other leading Absurdists allowed the philosophical ideas behind a play to dictate its dramatic structure. Despite their dislocated language, illogical plots, and intellectual seriousness, the plays are often comic, reflecting the irrationality of real experience. By the 1960s Albee and Ionesco had turned to a more allegorical form, Pinter to high comedy, and Adamov to the epic theatre of Brecht, while Beckett's works grew steadily shorter and more austere.

Accesi An Italian company that presented plays of the *commedia dell'arte* in the early 17th century. Founded in about 1590, the company was led by Pier Maria Cecchini and Tristano Martinelli and twice visited France. Actors with the company included Flamineo Scala and Silvio Fiorillo.

Accidental Death of an Anarchist (*Morte accidentale di un anarchico*) A farce by Dario FO. First performance: Varese, 1979. A black satire, the play was based upon the investigation following the death of the railway worker Guiseppe Pinelli, who fell from the window of a Milan police station in mysterious circumstances. The play enjoyed a major success in the West End in 1980–81.

Accius, Lucius (170 BC–86 BC) Roman playwright, whose numerous tragedies (of which only fragments and about 40 titles survive) established him as one of the leading writers of his time. Many of his works were translations from earlier Greek plays and tackle subjects from mythology as well as, occasionally, themes taken from Roman history. Some belong to the *praetexta* tradition; all were notable for their forceful rhetoric and violent plots. His critical writings included the *Pragmatica*, an examination of the techniques then open to the dramatist.

Achard, Marcel (Marcel-Auguste Ferréol; 1899–1974) French playwright, who made his reputation in 1923 with *Voulez-vous jouer avec moâ?*, produced by Dullin. Several later plays, including *Marlborough s'en va-t'en guerre* (1924), *Domino* (1931), and *Le Corsaire* (1938), were produced by Louis Jouvet. His plays are sentimental love stories, often derived from the *commedia dell'arte*.

Acharnians, The A comedy by ARISTOPHANES. First performance: Athens, 425 BC. The earliest surviving comedy by Aristophanes, the play satirizes the Peloponnesian War through the activities of Dicaepolis, an old farmer who makes his own peace treaty with the Spartans.

Achurch, Janet (Janet Sharp; 1864–1916) British actress, who appeared in the earliest British productions of Ibsen. After appearing at the Adelphi Theatre, she toured with Benson before joining Tree's company. In 1889 she attracted attention as Nora in *A Doll's House* directed by her husband at the Novelty Theatre. She subsequently played two of Shaw's heroines, Candida (which he wrote for her) and Lady Cicely Wayneflete in *Captain Brassbound's Conversion*.

Ackermann, Konrad Ernst (c. 1710–71) German actor-manager, who established the first German National Theatre. He began his acting career as a member of Schönemann's company and toured Europe before marrying Sophie SCHRÖDER and eventually settling in Hamburg in 1765. Here he built a small theatre; quarrels with his stepson, however, severely hampered this enterprise despite the support of Lessing and others.

His daughters, **Dorothea Ackermann** (1752–1821) and **Charlotte Ackermann** (1757–75), both became distinguished actresses at the theatre, appearing in plays by Lessing, Goethe, and Shakespeare until their careers ended with Dorothea's marriage and Charlotte's early death.

Ackland, Joss (Sidney Edmond Jocelyn Ackland; 1928–) British actor, who made his West End debut in *The Hasty Heart* in 1945. Subsequently he spent several years working as a tea planter in central Africa before joining the Old Vic company in 1958. His earlier parts ranged from Caliban to Brecht's Galileo and Eustace in *The Madras House* (1977) at the National Theatre. Subsequent roles have included Falstaff at the opening of the Barbican Theatre in 1982, Captain Hook and Mr Darling in *Peter Pan* (1982, 1985–86), Clarence Darrow in *Never the Sinner* (1990), and Ill in *The Visit* (1995). His roles in musicals have included Fredrik in *A Little Night Music* (1975) and Juan Perón in *Evita* (1978); he has also appeared in numerous films and television productions.

acoustics The quality of sound transmission in a particular building. In the theatre it is commonly affected by such factors as the design of the auditorium, the carpeting, the distance from the stage to the back row of seats, and the presence of a proscenium arch. Devices designed to improve the acoustical properties of an auditorium have included the PERIAKTOI of the ancient Greeks, which when correctly angled may have helped to deflect sound towards the audience, the use of a small roof over the stage in the Elizabethan theatre to aim sound downwards, and – to a limited extent – modern electrical amplification equipment.

act A major structural division of a play, usually ranging from one to five in number. Division of a tragedy into five acts was introduced in ancient Greece and first stipulated as a formal requirement by Horace in his *Ars Poetica* (68–65 BC). Shakespeare's tragedies were not originally written in five acts but were so arranged by his editors after Jonson introduced the convention into the English theatre. Comedies of the period frequently favoured a three-act structure, while the 19th century saw a short-lived fashion for division into four acts. Much recent drama has favoured a more flexible structure, often opting for two or three acts and thus limiting intervals to one or two during a performance.

act drop *See* curtain.

acting The performing of a role before an audience. The practice of acting is thought to have its roots in childhood games and social ritual but first emerged as a disciplined art in Greece in the 5th century BC. THESPIS was the first to perform separately from the chorus and subsequently a second actor was added (by Aeschylus) and then a third (by Sophocles). Euripides in turn emphasized the importance of the actor by reducing the role of the chorus; actors in his day still relied, however, solely upon their voices and static physical presence to achieve their effects.

In the Roman theatre the emphasis was upon a livelier coarser style, incorporating stock characters as well as slapstick and acrobatics; eventually this unfettered form of entertainment offended the Church and in the 6th century AD virtually all theatrical activity ceased. Acting was then confined to Church ritual and the peripheral traditions of the JONGLEURS, GOLIARDS, and MINSTRELS until the later medieval period, when members of trade guilds and other amateurs began to present entertainments in their own localities.

The Renaissance saw the return of the professional actor and a renewal of interest in classical acting techniques; these were absorbed into the highly stylized yet lively and improvizational *commedia dell'arte*, among other new forms. All female roles on the professional stage were played by men, as they had been since Roman times.

Such celebrated companies as the Comédie-Française acquired their own distinctive styles and gradually the actors themselves became the dominant force in the theatre, plays being chosen and even rewritten to suit their particular strengths. Despite the provocative and witty ease of Restoration comedy, acting styles became increasingly artificial and emotionally extravagant during the 17th and 18th centuries, leading ultimately to the rant and shallowness of MELODRAMA in the 19th-century theatre. Nonetheless, the partial reforms and natural brilliance of such performers as David Garrick, Edmund Kean, the Kembles, and Macready in Britain and Edwin Forrest, the Booths, and the Jeffersons in the US transformed often mediocre material into highly effective theatre.

The foundation of the Duke of Saxe-Meiningen's troupe (in which all the members were considered equal) foreshadowed the decline of the theatre of the stock companies and actor-managers (of whom Sir Henry Irving was one of the best-known) and the emergence of the modern director-controlled drama. STANISLAVSKY codified modern acting theory through his work with the Moscow Art Theatre and his ideas have since been developed in many countries, notably in the US by the GROUP THEATRE and the ACTORS' STUDIO, famous for its METHOD acting. The contemporary actor is encouraged to draw upon inner motivations but is also expected to be able to apply to both tragedy and comedy such wide-ranging skills as mime, acrobatics, singing, and dance, whether he is acting under naturalistic or non-naturalistic direction.

More formalized acting techniques continue to be observed, however, in various forms of traditional theatre outside Europe and the US. Notable examples of these survivals include the *Nō* theatre of Japan and some Indian drama, in which a precise range of gestures and movements is rigidly adhered to.

Acting Company A US repertory company formed in 1972 by graduates of the Juilliard School under the direction of John Houseman; its declared mission was to train young actors and to build a nationwide theatre-going public. Though administratively based in New York, it tours to colleges, regional theatres, and other venues across the US.

actor A performer in a dramatic entertainment; the term was previously limited to male performers but is now frequently applied to females, in preference to ACTRESS. The earliest actors were probably performers in dumb shows and participants in religious ceremonies. The first actor whose name is known to us was Thespis, in whose honour all subsequent performers have often been dubbed Thespians; professional actors, however, did not appear until the 16th century. The Roman actor Quintus Roscius set high standards of acting in the ancient world and similarly lent his name to distinguished actors of subsequent eras, being commemorated by the African Roscius, the Ohio Roscius, the Scottish Roscius, the Young Roscius, and various others. Richard Burbage is generally recognized as the first great English actor, while notable acting dynasties over the years have included the Kembles, the Terrys, and the Redgraves in England and the Barrymores in the US. In ancient Greece actors enjoyed an elevated status; in Rome, however, they were ranked alongside the lowest in society – a position in which they remained until the 19th century when those at the top of their profession became eligible for knighthoods and other forms of public recognition.

actor-manager An actor who also runs the company in which he appears. The great age of the actor-managers was the 19th century, when they included Sir Henry Irving and Sir Herbert Beerbohm Tree.

Actor Prepares, An A treatise on drama theory by STANISLAVSKY, published in 1926. The most widely-known of his studies of naturalism, it discusses the psychology of acting and was subsequently used as the basis of the METHOD theory in the US. His later writings, however, balanced this emphasis upon the actor's importance with his interest in technique and his belief in the need for a production to adopt a particular 'style' to which individual actors may be harnessed.

Actors' Company *See* McKellen, Sir Ian.

Actors' Equity Association *See* American Actors' Equity Association; British Actors' Equity Association; Canadian Actors' Equity Association.

Actors Fund of America A US charitable organization for those in the theatre, founded in 1881. It is funded partly by benefit performances of Broadway shows given on off-nights, thus allowing other working actors to attend.

Actors' Studio A theatre workshop founded in 1947 in New York by Elia Kazan and Lee Strasberg. It exercized enormous influence as a place where professional actors could study and experiment with the METHOD acting technique.

Actors' Theatre A production company founded in New York in 1939 for the training of young actors and as a testing ground for new plays. The company, which functioned until 1947, produced notable plays by Ibsen, Shaw, and others at the Provincetown Playhouse in Greenwich Village.

Actors Theatre of Louisville A theatre in Louisville, Kentucky, founded in 1964 and now the State Theatre of Kentucky. It moved into its two permanent homes – the Pamela Brown Auditorium, where classical and modern plays are performed, and the Victor Jory Theatre, where an off-Broadway series is shown – in 1972. The company's Humana Series of New American Plays is well-known. Several of its plays have moved to Broadway, D L Coburn's *The Gin Game* and Beth Hensley's *Crimes of the Heart* (1982) winning Pulitzer Prizes.

actress A female performer in a dramatic entertainment, usually a play. The presence of women on the stage was prohibited in early times and only began to become generally acceptable in Europe in the 17th century. Notable early actresses who established strong reputations in defiance of prejudice against their sex included Isabella Andreini in Italy, Carolina Neuber in Germany, and Madeleine Béjart in France; the first woman to grace the stage in England was Margaret Hughes, who first appeared in *The Moor of Venice* in 1660 to enthusiastic applause. Many actresses now prefer to be known as ACTORS.

Acts of the Apostles (*Actes des Apôtres*) A mystery play written between 1452 and 1478 by Simon GRÉBAN, possibly in collaboration with his brother Arnoul Gréban. The play deals with the travels, preaching, and martyrdom of Christ's apostles.

act-tune A piece of music played between the acts of a play. Act-tunes were an accepted feature of the Elizabethan theatre; composers of such music in the Restoration theatre included Purcell.

Adam de la Halle (Adam le Bossu d'Arras; c. 1240–c. 1288) French poet and musician, traditionally acknowledged as the founder of secular drama in France. Born in Arras, he travelled to Italy in the service of Count Robert II of Artois. His first dramatic work, *Jeu de la feuillée*, performed in Arras in about 1276, is a licentious satirical fantasy; *Jeu de Robin et Marion*, performed in Naples in about 1283, is sometimes regarded as a predecessor of the comic opera.

Adamov, Arthur (1908–70) French playwright, born in Russia. He moved to Paris in 1924 but did not begin writing for the theatre until the late 1940s, when he drew inspiration from the plays of Strindberg. The recurring themes of futility and alienation in such early plays as *Le Professeur Taranne* (1953 Lyons; translated as PROFESSOR TARANNE, 1962) and *Le Ping-Pong* (1955) led to his association with the Theatre of the Absurd. His later plays, including *Paolo Paoli* (1957) and *Le Printemps '71* (1961; translated as SPRING '71), contain more explicit social and political comment.

Adams, Maude (1872–1953) US actress. Born into a theatrical family, she had her first success at the age of five in *Fritz, Our German Cousin*. In the same year, she appeared as Little Eva in *Uncle Tom's Cabin*. She first appeared in New York in 1888 and later played in several works by J M Barrie, the first being *The Little Minister* (1897) as Little Babbie, a part the author enlarged for her. After playing the lead in Rostand's *L'Aiglon*, she toured in *The Merchant of Venice* (1931) and *Twelfth Night* (1934).

ADC *See* Amateur Dramatic Club.

Adding Machine, The An Expressionist drama by Elmer RICE. First performance: New York, 1923. The protagonist, a book-keeper named Mr Zero, is an Everyman figure attempting to survive in a dehumanized world of extreme mechanization.

Addison, Joseph (1672–1719) English essayist, poet, and playwright, who also served as an under-secretary of state. In 1713 his neoclassical blank verse tragedy *Cato* was successfully staged at Drury Lane, the title role being created by Barton Booth. An attempt to write a moral comedy, *The Drummer*, in 1715 met with failure. His critical writings on the theatre appeared in *The Spectator* and *The Tatler*.

Ade, George (1866–1944) US humorist and playwright, whose career in the theatre began with the New York production of his light opera *The Sultan of Sulu* (1902). This was followed by such comedies as *The County Chairman* (1903) and *The College Widow* (1904), which established his reputation as a leading contemporary playwright.

Adelphi Theatre One of the most popular London theatres in the 19th century, home of the celebrated 'Adelphi dramas'. The present building is the fourth on the site, the theatre having been known in turn as the **Sans Pareil** (1806–19), Adelphi (1819–29), Theatre Royal New Adelphi (1829–67), **Royal Adelphi** (1867–1901), **Century** (1901–02), and Royal Adelphi (1902–40). 'Royal' was dropped from the name in 1940. Well known in the mid-19th century for its burlettas and dramatized versions of Sir Walter Scott's novels, it became (1834) the first theatre in England to have a sinking stage installed. The 'Adelphi dramas', mostly written by J B Buckstone, were produced under the management of Madame Céleste and Ben Webster in the years 1844–53. After being rebuilt in 1858 to resemble the Opéra Comique in Paris, the Adelphi became noted for its romantic melodramas; in 1897 the popular actor William Terriss was shot dead outside the theatre by a madman. Rebuilt again in 1900, it was then used for modern poetic drama and Shakespeare. A period of musical comedy followed from 1908 and then, after further reconstruction in 1930, C B Cochran took over as manager, staging spectacular revues. Marie Tempest made her final stage appearance at the Adelphi in 1940, while Ivor Novello's *The Dancing Years* enjoyed a long run from 1942. After the war Cochran returned to present revues by A P Herbert, including the popular *Bless the Bride* (1947). Subsequent musical successes have included the long-running *Charlie Girl* (1965) and *Me and My Girl* (1985), *Sunset Boulevard* (1993), and the much-acclaimed *Chicago* (1998).

Adler, Jacob (1855–1926) US actor, born in Russia, who became the best-known and most respected actor of New York's Yiddish theatre. He produced plays for his own company at the Grand Theatre on the Lower East Side, and also acted in English, most famously as Shylock in London in 1906.

His daughter, **Stella Adler** (1902–1992), made her first appearance on stage in 1906 for her father's company, for which she acted throughout her youth. In the late 1920s she played over 100 parts in countries in Europe and South America as well as the US. She joined the Group Theatre in 1931. From 1949, while continuing to take occasional acting roles, she directed and taught at her Stella Adler Conservatory of Acting, which became one of the best-known in the US.

Jacob's son, **Luther Adler** (1903–1984), also grew up in the Yiddish theatre, making his adult debut in 1921 with the Provincetown Players. In the 1930s he was active with both the Theatre Guild and the Group Theatre, playing Dr Gordon in *Men in White* (1934) and Joe Bonaparte in *Golden Boy* (1937), which he also performed in London. Other roles include Mr Rochester in *Jane Eyre* (1942), Shylock (1956), Teyve in *Fiddler on the Roof* (1965), and Gregory Solomon in Miller's *The Price* (1970).

ad lib To improvise lines not in the script, either on impulse or to cover for some emergency on stage, often inability to remember the original words.

Admirable Crichton, The A comedy by J M BARRIE. First performance: London, 1902. The play examines questions of social status and natural ability. In the story an upper-class family are shipwrecked on an island along with Crichton, their butler; he assumes leadership in this emergency only to revert to his inferior position when rescue arrives.

Admiral's Men An English company, formed in 1585 and named in honour of its patron, Admiral Lord Howard, that presented original performances of many major plays of the period. In 1590 the company occupied the Theatre, subsequently moving to the Rose Theatre under Henslowe and Edward Alleyn. Members of the company produced several of Marlowe's plays and then transferred to the Fortune Theatre, being renamed **Prince Henry's Men** in 1603. In 1612 they changed their name to **Palsgrave's Men**; they finally disbanded in 1631.

Adolph, Johann Baptist (1657–1708) Austrian playwright, who was a major writer of Jesuit drama. His play *Philemon et Apollonius* was based on a work by Avancini, whose post at the royal court he inherited; other plays were based on the writings of Calderón and Gryphius.

Adrian, Max (Max Bor; 1903–73) British actor, born in Ireland, who first established his reputation playing in *Troilus and Cressida* and *The Doctor's Dilemma* at the Westminster Theatre in 1938. After appearances at the Old Vic and the Haymarket Theatre, he won acclaim as a performer in revue in the 1940s and 1950s and also ventured into musicals and farce. Subsequently he was for several seasons with the Royal Shakespeare Company and contrived one-man shows on Shaw (1966) and on Gilbert and Sullivan (1969).

Advent play *See* liturgical drama.

advertisement curtain *See* curtain.

AE (George William Russell; 1867–1935) Irish poet and playwright. His single play, *Deirdre* (1902), was performed by the Irish National Dramatic Society. He was also one of the founders of the Abbey Theatre, alongside W B Yeats and Lady Gregory.

Aerial Gardens Theatre *See* New Amsterdam Theatre.

Aeschylus (c. 525 BC–456 BC) Greek playwright, born at Eleusis, near Athens, and generally considered to be the earliest important writer of the Western theatrical tradition. Initially a soldier in the Persian Wars, he became the first playwright to achieve official recognition in ancient Greece, establishing himself as a writer, performer, and director and winning three contests, the first in 484 BC. Of his 90 plays only seven survive; they all tackle themes of guilt and its expiation and were written for the Dionysia, usually as parts of connected trilogies.

The only complete trilogy to survive is THE ORESTEIA, comprising *Agamemnon*, the *Choephori*, and the *Eumenides*. This late work shows Aeschylus's theatrical innovations, which included using a reduced chorus (possibly as few as 12 performers) and more than one actor, at their most advanced. His plays seem to have been presented with rudimentary props against painted backcloths. With his mastery of poetic language, complex structure, and psychological analysis, Aeschylus has inspired numerous writers of both classical and modern times, including Sophocles, Euripides, Seneca, Shelley, Voltaire, Eugene O'Neill, and Jean-Paul Sartre.

As well as being a master of tragedy, Aeschylus was also the author of many satyr-plays, of which only fragments are known. According to tradition he died after an eagle mistook his bald head for a rock and dropped a tortoise on it in an attempt to break its shell. His son was the playwright Euphorion.

Principal works:

THE PERSIANS: 472 BC.
SEVEN AGAINST THEBES: 469 BC.
PROMETHEUS BOUND: C. 460 BC.
THE SUPPLIANT WOMEN: C. 460 BC.
Agamemnon: 458 BC.
Choephori: 458 BC.
Eumenides: 458 BC.

Aesopus, Claudius (1st century BC) Roman tragic actor, who was admired by both Horace and Cicero. When the latter was exiled Aesopus made appeals on stage for his return. His identification with his roles was so great that he was said to have accidentally killed another actor during a performance.

affective memory An aspect of the METHOD theory of acting. The technique involves the invocation of past experiences in an actor's life in order to help him to recreate genuine emotion on stage.

Afinogenov, Alexander Nikolaevich (1904–41) Soviet playwright, whose dramas won popular success and official approval in his own country as well as an audience in the West. He started writing in the 1920s, producing his first play, *Robert Tim*, in 1924; this was followed by (amongst others) *Fear* (1931) and *Distant Point* (1934), which are regarded as two of his finest works. His last play, *On the Eve* (1941), dealing with the German invasion of the USSR, was first performed after his untimely death in an air raid.

Afranius, Lucius (2nd century BC) Roman playwright, considered the leading writer of the *togata* tradition. Of his 44 or more works fragments survive; he was noted for his handling of complex plots and may have been the first to tackle the theme of homosexuality on stage.

African Roscius *See* Aldridge, Ira.

afterpiece A short play, usually a comedy, presented as light relief after a full-length tragedy. Such afterpieces were a common feature of British drama in the 18th century.

After the Fall A psychological drama by Arthur MILLER. First performance: Washington Square Theatre, New York, 1964. The play takes place in a courtroom where Quintin, a lawyer, reviews his life and examines his relationships with ex-wives Maggie and Louise and his friend Lou. It is usually considered semi-autobiographical, although Miller himself has discouraged this view.

Agate, James (1877–1947) British theatre critic, who was drama critic for *The Sunday Times* from 1923 until his death. Notorious for his belief that no actor had achieved greatness since Irving and Bernhardt, he also published nine volumes of diaries under the general title *Ego* (1935–47).

His sister was the actress **May Agate** (1892–1960), who studied with Bernhardt and appeared with her in Paris and London. After working with Miss Horniman's company in Manchester, she appeared regularly in the West End. In 1945 she published *Madame Sarah*, a book about her former mentor.

Agathon (d. c. 400 BC) Greek playwright, who developed the function of choral odes, making them musical interludes within a play and thus paving the way for the division of a play into separate acts. He won two dramatic contests (the first in 416 BC) and was mourned after his death by Aristophanes.

agent An intermediary who performs various matters of business connected with the theatre. The first professional literary agents appeared in the 19th century and, also known as author's agents or play agents, commonly assist writers in finding producers for their work; frequently they combine these tasks with those of a talent agent, seeking out unknown actors and actresses and listing themselves under the generic term of theatrical or dramatic agent. Actors' agents negotiate contracts on behalf of actors as well as finding suitable parts for them, while casting agents are employed to find suitable actors for a particular production; many agents combine these two roles. Advance agents handle the business arrangements ahead of touring companies while booking agents organize the tours. Press agents look after all publicity matters connected with a production. Ticket agents buy tickets on behalf of theatre-goers (for a small extra fee), usually acting independently of the theatres themselves.

Aggas, Robert (c. 1619–79) English scene painter and landscape artist. He worked at several major theatres, including the Blackfriars Theatre, the Dorset Garden Theatre, and for Killigrew at Drury Lane. He was the first artist in England to paint movable scenery.

agon An ancient Greek term taken to signify the fundamental conflict essential to classical tragedy. The word may have been derived from that used for gladiatorial contests in which two men fought to the death.

Ainley, Henry (1879–1945) British actor, who achieved immediate success when he was selected by George Alexander to play Paolo in Stephen Phillips's *Paolo and Francesca* at the St James's Theatre in 1902; he subsequently became highly popular in romantic parts. After acclaim in several Shakespearean roles, he later developed as a powerful character actor, with *Hassan* (1923), *Macbeth* (1926), and St John Ervine's *The First Mrs Fraser* (1929) among his triumphs.

Aitken, Maria (1945–) British actress and director, who was the first woman to be elected to the OUDS. Her professional career began with an appearance in *A Streetcar Named Desire* at Coventry in 1967. Subsequently she toured the Far East as Viola in *Twelfth Night* and Hermione in *A Winter's Tale* and played Countess Charlotte Malcolm in *A Little Night Music* (1975). She is now particularly associated with the work of Noël Coward, having starred in *Blithe Spirit* (1976) at the National Theatre, *Private Lives* (1980) at the Duchess Theatre, *The Vortex* (1989) at the Garrick Theatre, and *Hay Fever* (1992) at the Albery. Her work as a director includes *Sister Mary Ignatius* (1984), in which she also took the title role, *The Rivals* (1985), and *As You Like It* (1992).

Akimov, Nikolai Pavlovich (1901–68) Russian scene designer and director, who became famous for his radical designs for productions at Leningrad's Theatre of Comedy and at the Vakhtangov Theatre in Moscow in the 1920s and 1930s. His most controversial production as a director was his *Hamlet* (1932), in which Hamlet invented his father's ghost and a drunk Ophelia died during an orgy. In 1936 Akimov returned to the Theatre of Comedy, where he staged new Soviet comedies.

Akins, Zoë (1886–1958) US poet and playwright, whose best-known work for the stage was the highly popular *The Greeks Had a Word for It* (1930). Subsequently she won a Pulitzer Prize for her adaptation for the stage of Edith Wharton's novel *The Old Maid* (1935).

Alarcón y Mendoza *See* Ruiz de Alarcón y Mendoza, Juan.

Albanesi, Meggie (Margharita Albanesi; 1899–1923) British actress, whose early death cut short a career of singular promise. After winning the Bancroft Gold Medal at the Royal Academy of Dramatic Art she attracted admiration over the next five years in such roles as Sonia in Heijeerman's *The Rising Sun* (1919), Jill Hillcrest in Galsworthy's *The Skin Game* (1920), Sydney Fairfield in Clemence Dane's *A Bill of Divorcement* (1921), and Daisy in Maugham's *East of Suez* (1922).

Albee, Edward (1928–) US playwright, the adopted grandson of a theatre manager of the same name who ran an early vaudeville circuit and built several theatres during the 1880s. Albee's works deal primarily with the conflict between reality and illusion and the plight of humanity in a decaying world. His first work, the one-act *The Zoo Story*, won him attention, although it was his first success on Broadway, the award-winning WHO'S AFRAID OF VIRGINIA WOOLF?, that established his reputation. Subsequent works proved less accessible, although both *A Delicate Balance* and *Seascape* received Pulitzer Prizes. He has produced and directed a number of his own plays as well as works by other writers. After a period of neglect in the 1980s, there was revival of interest in his work in the 1990s, leading to the award of a third Pulitzer Prize for *Three Tall Women* in 1994, the Kennedy Center Honors in 1996, and the US National Medal of Arts in 1997.

Principal works:
The Zoo Story: 1959.
The Death of Bessie Smith: 1960.

THE AMERICAN DREAM: 1961.
Who's Afraid of Virginia Woolf?: 1962.
The Ballad of the Sad Café: 1963.
Tiny Alice: 1964.
A Delicate Balance: 1966.
All Over: 1970.
Seascape: 1975.
The Lady from Dubuque: 1980.
The Man Who Had Three Arms: 1983.
Marriage Play: 1986.
Three Tall Women: 1990.
The Play About the Baby: 1996.

Alberti, Rafael (1902–99) Spanish poet and playwright. He is best known for such popular plays as *El hombre deshabitado* (The Deserted Man; 1930) and *El adefesio* (The Odd One; 1914) and for the collection of poetry *Sobre los angeles* (Concerning the Angels; 1929).

Albery, James (1838–89) British playwright, whose best known work was *Two Roses* (1870), in which Henry Irving achieved great success as Digby Grant. He was for many years connected with the Criterion Theatre, whose leading lady, Mary Moore (later Lady WYNDHAM), he married in 1878.

Their son was the theatre manager **Sir Bronson James Albery** (1881–1971), who took over the Criterion Theatre and subsequently also the New Theatre and Wyndham's Theatre, running them in collaboration with Howard Wyndham. After his death the New Theatre was renamed the Albery in his memory.

Albery Theatre A theatre in St Martin's Lane, London, formerly the New Theatre. It was opened in 1903 by Charles Wyndham and from 1905 to 1913 saw regular appearances by Fred Terry and Julia Neilson. Other successes included performances by Katharine Cornell and, in 1924, the triumph of Sybil Thorndike in the title role of G B Shaw's *St Joan*. From 1944 to 1950 the theatre was the home of the Old Vic Company, whose own theatre had been bombed; during this period there were many outstanding Shakespeare productions, the players including Edith Evans, John Gielgud, Laurence Olivier, Michael Redgrave, and Ralph Richardson. Subsequently the Lionel Bart musical *Oliver!* (1960–66) ran for a record 2618 performances; it was revived in 1977 for a further three-year run while another departure was the successful rock musical *Joseph and the Amazing Technicolour Dreamcoat* (1973). The theatre was renamed the Albery in 1973 in honour of the former director, Sir Bronson Albery, and to avoid confusion with the New London Theatre. Subsequent successes have included the long-running musical *Blood Brothers* (1988).

Alcano, Cielo d' (13th century) Italian playwright, born in Sicily. He was the author of the first Italian dialect play, written in the CONTRASTO tradition.

Alchemist, The A satirical comedy by Ben JONSON. First performance: Globe Theatre, London, 1610. The plot revolves around the machinations of the servant Face, who conspires with the fraudulent alchemist Subtle and Dol Common, a whore, to dupe a series of gullible visitors to his master's house while the latter is absent. Face eventually placates his outraged master by arranging his marriage to Dame Pliant.

Aldrich, Louis (Louis Lyon: 1843–1901) US actor, who became a celebrated child actor in major Shakespearean roles. Known as the **Ohio Roscius**, he excelled in such parts as Richard III and Home's Young Norval; later in life he appeared regularly opposite Mrs John Drew in Philadelphia and won praise in Bartley Campbell's *My Partner* (1879) and Edward J Swartz's *The Kaffir Diamond* (1888).

Aldridge, Ira (1804–67) British actor, born in the US, who was recognized as the first of the great Black actors. He made his London debut in 1826, playing Othello at the Royalty Theatre and billed as the **African Roscius**. During his subsequent successful career, he played Lear, Macbeth, and other major roles all over Europe. He was particularly popular in Germany and in Russia, where he played Lear with a pale face and black hands.

Aldwych Theatre A theatre in London that is still best known for the farces it staged before World War II; it was also the former headquarters in the capital of the Royal Shakespeare Company. Built as a companion theatre to the Strand, the Aldwych Theatre was opened in 1905 by Seymour Hicks and the US impresario Charles Frohman. It opened with a new version of Hicks's musical play *Blue Bell in Fairyland*, starring Hicks and his wife Ellaline Terriss. Marie Dressler appeared at the theatre in 1909 and in 1911 the first English performance of a Chekhov play, *The Cherry Orchard*, was staged there. During World War I the theatre became a club for Australian soldiers. C B Cochran took over in 1919, introducing among others Sacha Guitry and Yvonne Printemps; later managers included Viola Tree and Donald Calthrop. In 1924 *It Pays to Advertise*, presented by Tom Walls and Leslie Henson, ran for 598 performances. There followed the celebrated series of 'Aldwych farces', written by Ben Travers and performed by a cast headed by Tom Walls and Ralph Lynn; these included *A Cuckoo in the Nest* (1925), *Rookery Nook* (1926), *Thark* (1927), and *A Cup of Kindness* (1929). Subsequent successes included Lillian Hellman's *Watch on the Rhine* (1942); Daphne Du Maurier's *September Tide* (1948), starring Gertrude Lawrence; and Tennessee Williams's *A Streetcar Named Desire* (1949), with Vivien Leigh. In 1960 the theatre became the London home of the Royal Shakespeare Company, until the latter's move to the Barbican in 1982. During the RSC's occupancy such modern plays as Anouilh's *Becket* (1961) and Pinter's *The Homecoming* (1965) were interspersed with Shakespeare, and in 1980 the eight-and-a-half-hour production of *Nicholas Nickleby* was much acclaimed. Now under US ownership, the theatre's more recent successes have included Stoppard's *Hapgood* (1988), *The Rise and Fall of Little Voice* (1992), and the Lloyd Webber musical *Whistle Down the Wind* (1998).

Alecsandri, Vasile (1811–90) Romanian statesman, poet, and playwright, who was the author of a number of successful social comedies. *Iórgu de la Sadagúra* (1844), *The Tyrannic Prince* (1897), and *Ovid* (1885) were all produced at the theatre in Jassy, which Alecsandri had helped to establish in 1840.

Aleichem, Sholom (Solomon Rabinowitz; 1859–1976) Russian-born Jewish writer, whose sympathetic and humorous accounts of everyday life in the Jewish communities of the Ukraine proved enormously popular. A number of his novels and stories were adapted for the stage, including the series of comic tales entitled *Tevye the Milkman*, which as the musical FIDDLER ON THE ROOF enjoyed successes on Broadway (1964) and in London (1967).

Aleotti, Giovanni Battista (1546–1636) Italian theatre designer, usually remembered as the architect of the TEATRO FARNESE in Parma. Important for its incorporation of a proscenium arch, the theatre originally contained a set of wings probably also designed by Aleotti.

Alexander, Sir George (George Alexander Gibb Samson; 1858–1919) British actormanager, who was for many years associated with the ST JAMES'S THEATRE. Having worked as an actor with Irving, Kendal, and Hare, he went into management in 1889 with the aim of building up a prestigious theatre using British plays. Among the authors who had never written for the stage, he put on plays by Thomas Hardy, Arnold Bennett, and John Galsworthy. He was responsible for the production of Oscar Wilde's, *Lady Windermere's Fan* (1892) and *The Importance of Being Earnest* (1893), and for a number of Pinero's works. As an actor he was suited to fashionable drawing-room comedy. His most successful appearances, however, were in Anthony Hope's *The Prisoner of Zenda* (1896), in which he played the dual leading role. He was knighted in 1911.

Alexander, Jane (1939–) US actress, who first appeared on stage as a child in her native Boston. In 1966 she joined the Arena Stage company, for whom she played many roles, including Elanor in *The Great White Hope*, which made her reputation when it opened in New York in 1968. Her work ranges from Shakespeare to O'Neill and includes both light comedy (*Six Rms Riv Vu*: 1974) and serious comedy (*The Sisters Rosensweig*: 1993). In 1993 she became chairperson of the US National Endowment for the Arts.

Alexandra Theatre A theatre in Birmingham, founded in 1901. First known as the Lyceum, it was used for productions of pantomime, melodrama, music hall, and revue before becoming a repertory theatre in 1927. Gradually, however, touring companies took over and since 1976 it has housed touring productions only; it was refurbished in 1979 and now seats 1562.

Several other theatres of the same name have also existed in London – in Highbury Barn (1861–71), Camden (1873–81), and Stoke Newington (1897–1940) – but none now survive.

Alexandre le Grand A tragedy by Jean RACINE. First performance: Paris, 1665, produced by Molière. Two weeks after its opening at the Palais-Royal, Racine transferred the play to the rival Hôtel de Bourgogne, causing a rift between the two playwrights. The plot concerns the conflict between Alexander the Great and the Indian kings Porus and Taxile, rivals for the love of Axiane.

Alexandrinsky Theatre *See* Pushkin Theatre.

Alexis (c. 375 BC–c. 275 BC) Greek playwright and uncle of Menander, who wrote numerous examples of both Middle and New Comedy. Of the 245 plays attributed to him, only fragments survive.

Alfieri, Vittorio Amedeo, Conte (1749–1803) Italian poet and playwright, who wrote a number of notable verse tragedies, many of which were bitter condemnations of tyranny. Influenced by Voltaire, Rousseau, and Montesquieu, he scored his first success with *Cleopatra* in 1775, after which he wrote a further 20 or so tragedies, of which his masterpiece *Saul* (1782) and *Mirra* (1784) were particularly well received. His other dramatic writings include the comedy *Il Divorzio* (1802).

Alhambra A celebrated music hall in Leicester Square, London, opened in 1854 as an exhibition centre called the **Royal Panopticon of Science and Art**. Seating 3500 people and decorated with a facade in the Moorish style, it became a music hall in 1860 and saw the first appearances in England of the acrobat Léotard (1861), performances of the can-can (which caused the temporary loss of the theatre's licence), drama, ballet, and – after rebuilding in 1883 following a fire – popular revues. Diaghilev's company performed there in 1919 and 1922; subsequent performers, before the building's demolition in 1936, included Gracie Fields. The Odeon cinema now occupies the site.

alienation effect A technique developed by Brecht as part of his EPIC THEATRE, sometimes referred to as the **A-effect** or the *Verfremdungseffekt*. It stipulates the emotional detachment of both the audience and the actors from the drama, in order to emphasize the intellectual significance of what is happening. It suggests the use of various artificial devices, including placards, masks, and third-person narration, to help to achieve this effect.

Alizon (fl. 1610–48) French actor, who became famous for his interpretation of female roles. At his best in farce, he appeared at the Faubourg Saint-Germain before transferring to the Hôtel de Bourgogne in 1634.

Allen, Chesney *See* Crazy Gang.

Allen, William (d. 1647) English actor, who joined Lady Elizabeth's Men. His major roles included Grimaldi in Massinger's *The Renegado* and Captain Lanby in Shirley's *The Wedding*. In 1626 he joined the King's Men.

Alleyn, Edward (1566–1626) English actor and manager. After appearances with the Earl of Worcester's company (1583–87), he became a leading actor with the Admiral's Men. Through his marriage to Joan Woodward, stepdaughter of Philip Henslowe, he became closely associated with his father-in-law's theatrical ventures, sharing with him the ownership of the Rose and Fortune theatres. He played leading roles in plays by Marlowe, Greene, Dekker, and Chapman, retiring from the stage around 1604. He then devoted himself to the support of charities and the foundation of Dulwich College.

Alley Theatre *See* Nina Vance Alley Theatre.

All for Love; or, the World Well Lost A tragedy in blank verse by John DRYDEN. First performance: London, 1678. Sharing the same plot as Shakespeare's *Antony and Cleopatra*, the play concentrates on the last hours of the two central characters. While never achieving the grandeur of the earlier version, it focuses effectively and movingly on the conflict between love and honour.

All God's Chillun Got Wings A play by Eugene O'NEILL. First performance: New York, 1924. The plot depicts the relationship between a Black boy, Jim Harris, and a White girl, Ella Downey, who fall in love, marry, but see their lives gradually disintegrate around them. O'Neill received many angry letters in response to the first production, which provoked racist demonstrations.

Allgood, Mollie *See* O'Neill, Maire.

Allgood, Sara (1883–1950) Irish actress, who made her London debut in 1904 as Cathleen in Synge's *Riders to the Sea*. She appeared regularly at the Abbey Theatre, Dublin, in such plays as *The Playboy of the Western World* (1907) and Yeats's *Cathleen ni Houlihan* (1913). She also toured Australia in *Peg o' My Heart* (1916) before returning to the Abbey where she appeared in *Juno and the Paycock* (1924), *The Plough and the Stars* (1926), and other plays.

Allio, René (1921–) French theatre designer, who did much to encourage the adoption of flexible staging in the modern theatre. He argued for the involvement of the technical aspects of a production in the process of COLLECTIVE CREATION and the use of variable stage shapes. As well as work in France, he designed productions for the National Theatre in Britain. Later successes included designs for Marivaux's *Infidelities* (1987) at London's Lyric Theatre, Hammersmith.

All My Sons A play by Arthur MILLER. First performance: New York, 1947. The story revolves around Joe Keller, a factory owner who sells defective engines to the government, resulting in the deaths of many US pilots during World War II and causing his own sons to turn against him.

All-Russian Theatrical Society (VTO) Russian theatre organization founded in 1883 to defend actors' interests. The subsidiary Union of Stage Workers acted on behalf of playwrights and composers. After 1917 the society did much to improve acting standards throughout the USSR and promoted works by contemporary Russian writers; its president from 1916 to 1964 was Alexandra Yablochkina.

All's Well That Ends Well A tragicomedy by William SHAKESPEARE, written 1603–04. First performance: date unknown. Considered one of the so-called 'problem plays' because of its sombre tone and mainly unattractive characters, the play focuses upon the unrequited love of the worthy Helena for the arrogant Bertram; the comic subplot centres upon the cowardly Parolles. The play lacks the romantic fantasy of the earlier comedies but is notable for the intensity of Helena's soliloquies and for her somewhat enigmatic personality. Virtue, age, and free will are among the themes discussed.

Alma-Tadema, Sir Lawrence (1836–1912) British artist, born in Holland, who designed sets for Irving and Tree. His designs were noted for their scrupulous archaeological and architectural accuracy. He was knighted in 1899.

Almeida Theatre A 350-seat theatre in Islington, London, which has been the home of the Almeida Theatre Company since 1981; the building (1830s) was previously a warehouse. The company, which was founded in 1979, quickly established a reputation for stylish and innovative work with an international flavour. However, the Almeida's current standing as perhaps the most dynamic theatre in London dates from 1990, when Jonathan KENT and Ian MCDIARMID became joint artistic directors. Their many acclaimed productions have included *Hamlet* (1995), which transferred to Broadway, Molière's *Tartuffe* (1996), Chekhov's *Ivanov* (1997), which travelled to Moscow, and Racine's *Phèdre* (1998). In 2000 the theatre closed for refurbishment.

Aloni, Nissim (1926–) Israeli playwright and director, who first established his reputation as one of Israel's leading dramatists with the much-acclaimed *Bigdey*

Ha'melech (The Emperor's New Clothes; 1961), which he directed himself. His other works include *Ha'anesiha H'amerikait* (The American Princess), which was performed by the newly established Theatre of the Seasons (1963), and *Doda Liza* (Aunt Liza; 1969), which marked a departure from his hitherto complex and fantastic style inspired by the Theatre of the Absurd.

alternative theatre *See* collective creation; community theatre; fringe theatre.

Altona A play by Jean-Paul SARTRE, which has also been translated as *Loser Wins* and *The Condemned of Altona*. First performance: Paris, 1959. Set in Germany, the play explores the guilt of those who cooperated with the Nazis; its main characters are the industrialist Von Gerlach and his elder son Frantz, who has lived in isolation since the war.

Altwiener Volkstheater A form of comic play that developed in Vienna during the early 18th century, chiefly under Stranitsky and Prehauser. A variation of the HAUPT-UND STAATSAKTIONEN, it relied heavily upon comic improvisation and gave free rein to the character Hanswurst. The tradition was suppressed by the authorities in the mid-18th century but later re-emerged in the fairy-tale plays and farces that were eventually amalgamated into the operetta.

Álvares, Afonso (16th century) Portuguese playwright, who developed the early Portuguese tradition of the SAINT PLAY. His dramas, which were much influenced by the works of Vicente, combined religious sentiments with comic elements; four of them, notably his *Auto de Santo António* (1531), survive.

Álvarez Quintero, Serafín (1871–1938) Spanish playwright, who collaborated with his brother, **Joaquin Álvarez Quintero** (1873–1944), on about 200 light-hearted comedies based largely on life in their native Andalusia. The first, *Esgrima y amor* (1888), was produced while the brothers were still in their teens. Some of their works, translated by Helen and Harley Granville-Barker, were subsequently performed in London and New York; these included *Fortunato* (1928), and *The Lady from Alfaqueque* (1928).

Alvin Theatre *See* Neil Simon Theatre.

Amadeus A play by Peter SHAFFER. First performance: 1979. The play explores the jealousy of the composer Salieri for his rival Mozart and speculates upon the circumstances surrounding the latter's death. It provided fine roles for Paul Scofield and Frank Finlay in London and subsequently Ian McKellen and John Wood in New York (1980). An Oscar-winning film version appeared in 1983.

Amateur Dramatic Club (ADC) An amateur theatre group established in Cambridge by F C Burnand in 1855. Drawing upon undergraduates from Cambridge University, the club continues to produce many actors for the professional stage and has won acclaim for productions directed by George Rylands.

amateur theatre Any form of drama in which those involved do not expect payment for their work. Most modern professional theatre has its roots in the amateur tradition; amateur drama is now primarily the province of university groups (*see* university drama departments) and local amateur theatre societies, which present a wide range of productions – occasionally in their own theatres (known as Little Theatres)

– and often take part in major drama festivals. Amateur groups are particularly valued for their role in the fringe theatre, as training grounds for future professionals, and in maintaining a theatrical tradition in areas infrequently visited by professional companies. The International Amateur Theatre Association, based at The Hague, was founded in 1952 under E Martin Browne. *See also* National Youth Theatre; Theatre in Education; British Theatre Association; National Operatic and Dramatic Association.

Ambassadors Theatre A small London theatre celebrated for staging the longest-running production in theatre history, Agatha Christie's *The Mousetrap*. It was designed as one of a pair (with St Martin's Theatre) by W G R Sprague and opened in 1913. Alice Delysia appeared here in revues during World War I, while Ivor Novello made his debut here in 1921 and Vivien Leigh her first West End appearance in *The Mask of Virtue* (1935). During World War II the Ambassadors remained open throughout the Blitz with daytime performances by the Ballet Rambert. *The Mousetrap* opened on 25 November 1952 and transferred to St Martin's on 25 March 1974. Successes since then have included the Royal Shakespeare Company's *Les Liaisons dangereuses* (1987) by Christopher Hampton and Lee Hall's *Spoonface Steinberg* (1998). The venue was renamed the **New Ambassadors Theatre** in 1999.

Ambassador Theatre A 1121-seat theatre in New York, situated on West 49th Street between Broadway and 8th Avenue. It opened in 1921 under the management of the Shubert brothers with the musical *The Rose Girl*. The theatre housed radio and television programmes for a period before returning to straight plays in 1956. Since then notable successes have included an adaptation of Forster's *A Passage to India* (1962) and plays by Peter Weiss, Robert Anderson, and Molière, as well as the musical *Your Arms Too Short to Box With God* (1980), a revival of Maugham's *The Circle* (1989), and the tap musical *Bring in 'da Noise, Bring in 'da Funk*, which transferred from the Public Theatre in 1996.

Ambigu, Théâtre de l' A theatre on the Boulevard du Temple in Paris, which opened in 1769. For some years it was restricted to performances of puppet shows and children's theatre; after the Revolution, however, it became a popular venue for melodrama. It was then burnt down (1822) and rebuilt in the Boulevard Saint-Martin, where further melodramas – especially those of Dumas *père* and Hugo – were highly successful. It was finally demolished in 1971.

Ameipsas (5th century BC) Greek playwright, who wrote a number of examples of Old Comedy. He is known to have defeated Aristophanes in a contest in 414 BC and to have ridiculed Socrates in another of his plays. Fragments of his work survive.

American Academy of Dramatic Arts A leading US drama school, founded in New York in 1884 as the Lyceum Theatre School of Acting. It now has campuses in New York and Hollywood offering a two-year programme with a third-year academy.

American Actors' Equity Association A trade union for professional actors; founded in 1913, it consolidated its power in a bitter strike in 1919. Unlike the BRITISH ACTORS' EQUITY ASSOCIATION, it is only for the stage; there are other unions for the cinema and television and for variety actors. It is affiliated to the American Federation of Labor and has done much to protect performers' interests and secure improvements in pay.

American Airlines Theatre A New York theatre, mainly on West 43rd Street but with an entrance from 42nd Street. It opened in 1918 as the **Selwyn Theatre**. Noted productions included Ferber and Kaufman's *The Royal Family* (1927), Cole Porter's *Wake Up and Dream* (1929), and Sophocles's *Electra* (1932) before it became a cinema in 1932. In 2000 it was renovated for the ROUNDABOUT THEATRE COMPANY and renamed after their major corporate sponsor.

American Buffalo A play by David MAMET. First performance: Chicago, 1975. The play deals with three not-very-smart men who plan to steal a valuable coin, the theft being less important to the plot than their shifting relationships and struggle for power.

American Company A US theatre company, which was assembled in Charleston under David Douglass in 1763–64 and comprised former members of the elder Hallam's troupe. Successively managed by John Henry and Lewis Hallam (in partnership), Hodgkinson, and lastly – from 1796 – Dunlop, the company was housed at the John Street Theatre and – from 1798 – the Park Theatre. The elder Joseph Jefferson was among its distinguished players between 1795 and 1803. Presenting a wide range of successful productions the group was rivalled only by Wignell's company in Philadelphia and was the first professional US company to stage a play by an American – Thomas Godfrey's *The Prince of Parthia*. It was disbanded in 1805.

American Conservatory Theatre (ACT) A theatre in Geary Street, San Francisco, which opened in 1910 as the Columbia. In the 1920s it was known as both the Wilkes and the Lurie and, in 1928, was renamed the Geary Theatre. Since 1967 the theatre has housed the American Conservatory Theatre Company, which was founded by William Ball in Pittsburgh in 1965 and run by him until 1986. The ACT is one of the largest and most important regional theatre in the US, producing both classical and modern plays. The theatre was damaged in the earthquake of 1989 and only recently reopened.

American Dream, The A one-act play by Edward ALBEE. First performance: New York, 1961. The play, an Absurdist satire, reveals the destructive forces beneath the superficial harmony of middle-class US family life.

American Laboratory Theatre A drama school and production company founded in New York in the 1920s by **Richard Boleslavsky** (1889–1937) and **Maria Ouspenskaya** (1876–1949) of the Moscow Art Theatre. The group became the most important channel for the communication of Stanislavsky's ideas in the US and included amongst its pupils Lee Strasberg and Harold Clurman.

American Museum A theatre on Broadway, New York, which was originally opened as a museum by Phineas Taylor Barnum in 1841. It became a theatre in 1849 with its own company and, refurbished in 1850, reopened with Sedley-Smith's melodrama *The Drunkard*. Sold by Barnum in 1855 but under his management again from 1860, it was used to present his shows of extraordinary phenomena until 1865 when it burnt down. Later that year Barnum opened his **New American Museum** also on Broadway in what was formerly the Chinese Rooms, which sometimes staged plays. It burnt down in 1868 during a performance of Harriet Beecher Stowe's *Uncle Tom's Cabin*.

American Music Hall *See* American Theatre.

American National Theatre and Academy (ANTA) A non-commercial theatre organization founded by Congress in 1935. It became the US centre of the International Theatre Institute in 1948 and, two years later, took over New York's Guild Theatre (*see* Virginia Theatre) – renaming it the Anta Theatre – as a venue for experimental drama. It also provided the Washington Square Theatre for Vivian Beaumont's company (1963) and, in 1968, under the National Council on the Arts, became a centre for non-profit-making theatre groups. In recent years it has suffered a decline and is currently moribund.

American Negro Theatre A theatre organization founded in 1940 in consultation with the writer Abram Hill. The group produced plays on Broadway and in London and Europe, its greatest success being Philip Yordan's *Anna Lucasta* (1944); it ceased operations in the mid-1950s.

American Opera House *See* Chatham Theatre.

American Place Theatre A US company set up in 1964 by Wynn Handman and Sydney Lanier, the pastor of St Clement's Church, New York, where it initially performed. In 1971 it moved into a new theatre incorporated into an office structure on West 46th Street, between 6th and 7th Avenues. Important productions have included Robert Lowell's *The Old Glory* (1964), Ed Bullin's *The Electronic Nigger* (1968), Sam Shephard's *Killer's Head* (1975) and *Action* (1975), and John Leguizamo's *Mambo Mouth* (1991).

American Repertory Theatre A theatre company at Harvard University, in Cambridge, Massachusetts, founded in 1979 by Robert BRUSTEIN. It uses the school's Loeb Drama Center, which opened in 1960. The company specializes in classics (frequently in avant garde stagings), in neglected older works, and in new plays, including Marsh Norman's Pulitzer-Prize-winning *'night, Mother* (1982) and the musical *Big River*, which went to Broadway in 1985.

American Shakespeare Theatre A theatre in Stratford, Connecticut, which is the home of a celebrated annual summer festival. Originally called the American Shakespeare Festival Theatre, it seats 1534 and opened in 1955 with *Julius Caesar*; its octagonal design echoes that of the Elizabethan theatre. Such stars as Christopher Plummer, Katharine Hepburn, and James Earl Jones have appeared there in plays by Shakespeare, Chekhov, and Tennessee Williams among others. By the early 1980s a decline in business led to the festival closing; there are various plans for its rebirth.

American Theatre A theatre on West 42nd Street, New York, that opened in 1893 with Pettit and Augustus Harris's *The Prodigal Daughter*. In 1908 the name was changed to the **American Music Hall** and in 1929 it became a burlesque house. The theatre was demolished after a fire in 1932 but another of the same name was opened two years later on East 55th Street with a production of Sedley-Smith's *The Drunkard*. *See also* Chambers Street Theatre.

American Theatre Association (ATA) A US theatre organization, which was formerly the American Educational Theatre Association. It supported educational and noncommercial theatre in US colleges and communities before going bankrupt in 1986.

American Theatre Wing A US theatre organization, founded in 1939, which does much work providing scholarships and organizing seminars; however, it is best known for its Antoinette Perry Awards (the TONY AWARDS).

American Theatrical Commonwealth Company *See* Ludlow, Noah Miller; Smith, Sol(omon) Franklin.

amphitheatre A circular, semicircular, or elliptical auditorium surrounded by raised seating, which was developed in ancient times originally as a venue for gladitorial contests and similar events, but later for theatrical performances. The Colosseum in Rome, built by 80 AD, could seat 87 000 people.

Amphitruo A comedy by PLAUTUS. First performance: date unknown. The play, which is based on the Greek legend of Amphitryon and Alcmene, is remarkable for its parody of mythological themes and characters. It inspired imitations by Molière, Dryden, Giraudoux, and others.

Amphitryon 38 A play by Jean GIRAUDOUX. First performance: Paris, 1929. It was adapted for the English stage by S N BEHRMAN and opened in London in 1938. The play is based on the Greek legend of the seduction of Alcmena by Jupiter; Giraudoux claimed his to be the 38th version of the legend – hence the title.

Amy's View A play by David HARE. First performance: Royal National Theatre, London, 1996. The play presents the conflict between Esme, a somewhat over-the-top actress of the old school, and her son-in-law Dominic, a fashionable pundit who denies the relevance of theatre in an age of electronic media. Caught between the two is Amy, who tries her best to promote mutual understanding. Judi Dench gave one of her most memorable ever performances in the role of Esme.

Anatomist, The A play by James BRIDIE. First performance: Edinburgh, 1930. Based on the true story of the Edinburgh anatomist who conspired with bodysnatchers Burke and Hare, it established the author as a leading British playwright.

Ancey, Georges (Georges Mathevon de Curnieu; 1860–1917) French playwright, born in Paris. His explicit and bitter comedies (*comédies rosses*) in the style of Henry Becque, including *Les Inséparables* (1889) and *L'Écoles des veufs* (1889), were produced at the Théâtre-Libre by Antoine, but are not now very popular.

Anderson, John Murray (1886–1954) Canadian-born director, author, and lyricist, who contributed to the development of revue and musical comedy in the US. He was involved with the eight editions of the *Greenwich Village Follies*, which began in 1919. He went on to produce and stage musical comedies and revues including Ziegfeld's *Follies*.

Anderson, Dame Judith (Frances Margaret Anderson-Anderson; 1898–1992) Australian actress, who made her first stage appearance in Sydney in 1915. In 1917 she went to the US, having her first big success in 1924 in Martin Brown's *Cobra*. Subsequently she won acclaim in plays by O'Neill and Pirandello and as Gertrude to Gielgud's Hamlet (1936); other roles included Lady Macbeth opposite Laurence Olivier (1937), Medea (1947), Madame Arkadina in *The Seagull* (1960), Hamlet (1970), at the age of 71, and the Nurse in a revival of *Medea* (1982). She was appointed DBE in 1960.

Anderson, Lindsay (1923–94) British director and theatre critic, who also enjoyed a successful career as a film director. In 1957 he joined the Royal Court Theatre, where he directed realistic productions of plays by Arden and other contemporary playwrights, including Keith Waterhouse and David Storey. He later (1969–74) became a director of the Royal Court and worked at the National Theatre and the Chichester Festival Theatre. Notable stage productions included *Serjeant Musgrave's Dance* (1959), *Home* (1970), and *The March on Russia* (1989).

Anderson, Maxwell (1888–1959) US playwright whose works, many of which were written partly in verse, reflect his contention that great drama relies upon great poetry. His first play, *White Desert* (1923), was followed by one of Anderson's more successful plays, *What Price Glory?* (1924). Written in collaboration with Lawrence Stalling, the play focused on a soldier in action during World War II. His 'serious comedy' *Saturday's Children* (1927) also met with great success. After *Night Over Taos* (1932) and *Mary Queen of Scots* (1933), he wrote *Both Your Houses* (1933), a play attacking political corruption that won a Pulitzer Prize. Other plays include *Winterset* (1936), *Key Largo* (1939), and *Anne of the Thousand Days* (1948).

Anderson, Miles (1947–) British actor, whose many appearances for the Royal Shakespeare Company have included Poins in *Henry IV Part I*, Orsino in *Twelfth Night*, and Eilif in Brecht's *Mother Courage*. In 1982 he became the first man to play the part of Peter Pan. At Stratford again in 1988 he played the title role in *Macbeth* and Dorimant in Etherege's *The Man of Mode*.

Anderson, Robert (1917–) US playwright, who began his theatrical career while at Harvard. While serving in the US Naval Reserve he won critical acclaim with his play *Come Marching Home* (1945). Many of his later plays deal with family relationships; they include *Tea and Sympathy* (1953), which caused some controversy with its allusions to homosexuality, *Silent Night, Lonely Night* (1959), *I Never Sang for My Father* (1968), *Solitaire/Double Solitaire* (1971), and *Free and Clear* (1981).

Andreini, Francesco (1548–1624) Italian actor-manager and playwright, who founded and led the Gelosi *commedia dell'arte* company. As an actor he appeared as young lovers with Flamineo Scala's company; later he excelled as Il Capitano. Under him the Gelosi visited France several times between 1571 and 1604.

His wife, **Isabella Andreini** (Isabella Canali; 1562–1604), became the leading actress with the Gelosi company, which she helped to found. Formerly with Scala's company, she was the subject of great adulation both for her acting and for her poetry. Upon her early death, her husband retired from the stage.

Their son, **Giovann Battista Andreini** (c. 1579–1654), also played *commedia dell'arte* roles and was probably one of the cofounders of the Fedeli troupe. Popularly known as **Lelio**, he subsequently toured Italy and visited Paris; he was also the author of several plays, including *L'Adamo* (1613) and *La Centaura* (1622).

Andrews, Harry (1911–89) British actor, who appeared at the Liverpool Playhouse before coming to London as Tybalt in *Romeo and Juliet* (1935) and accompanying Gielgud to New York in the following year. Subsequently he played numerous classical parts at the Old Vic and at Stratford as well as the title role in Bond's *Lear* at the Royal Court in 1971. His few appearances in other modern plays included Casanova in

Tennessee Williams's *Camino Real* (1957), Allenby in Rattigan's *Ross* (1960), and the General in Osborne's *A Patriot for Me* (1983).

Andreyev, Leonid Nikolaivich (1871–1919) Russian novelist and playwright, who was a friend of Gorky and enjoyed considerable success with a number of pessimistic dramas before the Revolution of 1917. *Life of Man* (1906) and *He Who Gets Slapped* (1914) won him considerable popularity; after the Revolution, however, he fell from official favour and died in exile.

Androcles and the Lion A play for children by G B SHAW. First performance: Berlin, 1912. Androcles, a kindly and witty Greek slave, removes a thorn from a lion's paw; subsequently the animal spares him when he is thrown to the lions in the Colosseum.

Andromaque A tragedy by Jean RACINE. First performance: Paris, 1667, with Racine's mistress Mlle Du Parc in the title role. The play is set at the end of the Trojan War: Hector's widow, Andromaque, is forced to marry her captor Pyrrhus. The union arouses the jealousy of Hermione, who has Pyrrhus killed and then commits suicide over his body.

Andronicus, Lucius Livius (c. 284 BC–c. 204 BC) Roman playwright, who was the first great writer of Latin drama and poetry. Originally a slave, he produced a translation of a Greek play for the Ludi Romani (*see ludi scaenici*) in 240 BC (the first dramatic performance to be given in Rome), after which he wrote further plays based on Greek originals, usually competing with Naevius. Of his nine tragedies and three comedies only fragments survive.

angel *See* impresario.

Angel, Edward (fl. 1660–73) English actor, who was engaged as a boy by John Rhodes. Later, under Davenant at the Dorset Garden Theatre, he was highly acclaimed as a low comedian. Wycherley describes him as "a good fool" in *The Gentleman Dancing-Master* (1671).

Angels in America A play in two parts by Tony Kushner. First New York performance: 1993, after earlier versions at the Mark Taper Forum in Los Angeles and (Part I) at the Royal National Theatre in London. In two full evenings, *Millennium Approaches* and *Perestroika*, it offers a phantasmagorical vision of the intersection of AIDS, morality, and politics in Ronald Reagan's America, mixing fictional and real characters.

Anglin, Margaret (1876–1958) US actress, born in Canada, who began her career under Charles Frohman in 1894. She attracted attention in Rostand's *Cyrano de Bergerac* (1898) and subsequently in plays by Henry Arthur Jones, Shaw, and Dumas *fils*, as well as in numerous classical works and in Shakespearean roles.

animal impersonator An actor or other performer who dresses as an animal, thus following in a tradition that dates from the earliest primitive rituals and the accompanying animal sacrifices. Examples in folk theatre of such impersonation include the HOBBY HORSE of the mummers' play and the Mascarade and the reindeer of the HORN DANCE. In the classical theatre Aristophanes made considerable comic use of animal impersonation, while later instances have included the cats, cows, and horses of English pantomime.

Animation Culturelles, Centres d' *See Décentralisation Dramatique.*

Anna Christie A play by Eugene O'NEILL. First performance: New York, 1921. The plot, which is partly based on Theodore Dreiser's *Sister Carrie* (1900), concerns Anna, a prostitute, who is shown searching for and eventually finding her sailor father. She then falls in love with an Irish stoker, who reacts violently when he learns of her past.

Annie Get Your Gun A musical by Herbert and Dorothy Fields that is based on the life of the sharpshooter Annie Oakley. First performance: New York, 1946. The music and lyrics by Irving BERLIN include some of his most popular songs, including 'There's No Business Like Show Business' and 'Anything You Can Do I Can Do Better'. Ethel Merman played the title role in the original production.

Annunzio, Gabriele D' *See D'Annunzio, Gabriele.*

Anouilh, Jean (1910–87) French playwright, born in Bordeaux, who began his theatrical career in 1931, when he became secretary to Louis Jouvet. He made his name in France with *Le Voyageur sans bagage*; after World War II, helped by the success of *Antigone*, his popularity spread to the English-speaking world.

   Anouilh's plays are conventionally divided into the light *pièces roses*, the melancholy *pièces noires*, the witty *pièces brillantes*, the bitter *pièces grinçantes*, and the historical *pièces costumées*. Recurring themes include the loss of innocence, the relationship between reality and make-believe, and the inevitability of compromise. His later works became increasingly whimsical in nature.

Principal works:

   L'Hermine: 1932; translated as *The Ermine*.
   Le Voyageur sans bagage: 1937; translated as THE TRAVELLER WITHOUT LUGGAGE.
   La Sauvage: 1938; translated as *The Restless Heart*.
   Le Bal des voleurs: 1938; translated as THIEVES' CARNIVAL.
   Léocadia: 1940; translated as *Time Remembered*.
   Le Rendez-vous de Senlis: 1941; translated as *Dinner With the Family*.
   Eurydice: 1942; translated as *Point of Departure* (or *Legend of Lovers*).
   Antigone: 1944.
   L'Invitation au château: 1947; translated as RING ROUND THE MOON.
   Ardèle ou la Marguerite: 1948.
   La Répétition ou l'Amour puni: 1950; translated as *The Rehearsal*.
   La Valse des toréadors: 1952; translated as THE WALTZ OF THE TOREADORS.
   Médée: 1953; translated as *Medea*.
   L'Alouette: 1953; translated as THE LARK.
   Pauvre Bitos, ou le Dîner de têtes: 1956; translated as *Poor Bitos*.
   Becket, ou L'Honneur de Dieu: 1959; translated as BECKET, OR THE HONOUR OF GOD.
   Le Nombril: 1981; translated as *The Navel*.

Ansky (Solomon Zainwil Rappoport; 1863–1920) Jewish ethnologist and man of letters, born in Russia. Ansky's writings include folk and Hasidic tales and poetry, but he is remembered for the play *The Dybbuk, or between Two Worlds* (1920), which draws its supernatural theme of possession from Hasidic doctrine, and provided a major success for the Vilna Troupe and the Habimah company in Moscow.

Anspacher Theatre *See* New York Shakespeare Festival.

ANTA *See* American National Theatre and Academy.

ANTA Theatre *See* Virginia Theatre.

Anthony Street Theatre A theatre in Worth Street, New York, which opened as the Olympic Theatre in 1812 with a Philadelphian company headed by Mrs Melmoth and Thomas Twaits. The mixed programme included circus acts as well as straight drama: the US premiere of M G Lewis's *Timour the Tartar* took place there the same year. In 1813, after refurbishment, the theatre was reopened as the Anthony Street Theatre with a new company including Mrs Beaumont and Placide. Successive managements during 1814 renamed the theatre the **Commonwealth Theatre** and later the **Pavilion Theatre**. The theatre's popularity peaked in 1820 when Edmund Kean made his first appearance in New York as Richard III; after Kean's company left for the Park Theatre in 1821 the Anthony Street Theatre was demolished.

Antigone A tragedy by SOPHOCLES. First performance: Athens, c. 442 BC. Set against a background of civil war, the play concentrates upon Antigone's defiance of a law forbidding her to bury her brother Polynices for political reasons. She is condemned to death by her kinsman Creon, but commits suicide first. With its theme of private conscience versus public duty, the play has inspired imitations by numerous subsequent writers, including ANOUILH. In Anouilh's wartime version (1944) Antigone is depicted as a martyr to purity while Creon rejects the guilt suffered by his counterpart in Sophocles's play.

anti-masque A brief interlude, usually a dance, performed before or during masques as a contrast to the main performance. The first such piece was presented by Jonson in 1609.

Antoine, André (1858–1943) French actor, director, and theatre manager, who founded the THÉÂTRE LIBRE in Paris in 1887 to promote naturalistic drama. Using mostly amateur actors, he pioneered the naturalistic movement in France and fostered numerous innovations in set design and acting, using real furniture and properties. He presented French premieres of works by such authors as Ibsen, Strindberg, Tolstoy, and Hauptmann. The Théâtre Libre closed in 1894, after which Antoine founded his own Théâtre Antoine in 1897 then went on to become director of the Odéon, where he presented many more influential but financially unsuccessful dramas between 1903 and 1916. Among those profoundly influenced by him were Jacques Copeau, Otto Brahm, and Grein.

Antonelli, Luigi (1882–1942) Italian playwright, who became a leading exponent of the *teatro del grottesco*. His best-known plays, which express a generally gloomy view of life, include *L'Uomo che incontrò se stesso* (The Man Who Met Himself; 1918), *L'Isola delle scimmie* (The Island of Monkeys; 1922), *La bottega dei sogni* (The Dream Shop; 1927), and *Il maestro* (1933).

Antony and Cleopatra A tragedy by William SHAKESPEARE, written c. 1606. First performance: c. 1607. Based upon the writings of Plutarch, the drama places the history of the doomed lovers Antony and Cleopatra against a vast imperial canvas. Later scenes contain some of the most moving love poetry in Shakespeare's dramatic works. Dryden's *All for Love* displaced Shakespeare's play for many years; it was not until 1849 that the latter was revived in its original form.

Anvil Productions *See* Oxford Playhouse.

Anything Goes A musical with score and lyrics by Cole PORTER and book by Guy Bolton, P G Wodehouse, Howard LINDSAY, and Russel Crouse. First performance: New York, 1934. A lighthearted story about a series of romances on a steamliner, it scored a major hit with Ethel Merman in the leading role.

Anzengruber, Ludwig (1839–89) Austrian playwright and novelist, who became famous for his realistic depictions of life in peasant communities. Most of his plays, in which he made some attempt to represent peasant dialect, were witty comedies – notably *Die Kreuzlschreiber* (1872) and *Der Doppelselbstmord* (1876); others included the antireligious drama *Der Pfarrer von Kirchfeld* (1870), the tragedy *Der Meineidbauer* (1871), and the problem play *Das vierte Gebot* (1877).

Apollodorus of Carystos (3rd century BC) Greek playwright, author of several examples of New Comedy. Of his works, which influenced Terence, only fragments survive.

Apollo Theatre The third oldest theatre in London's Shaftesbury Avenue, opened in 1901. Early successes included *The Girl from Kays* (1902), *Véronique* (1904), and *Tom Jones* (1907), in which Cicely Courtneidge made her London debut. In 1908 the Apollo became the home of the popular *Pélissier Follies*. In 1913 the policy of musical comedy was discontinued and since that date stage play successes have included Ian Hay's *Tilly of Bloomsbury* (1919) and *Housemaster* (1936), a series of plays (including *Hyde Park Corner*, *Espionage*, *The Fugitives*, and *London After Dark*) written by Walter Hackett for his actress wife Marion Lorne in the years 1934–37, and Patrick Hamilton's *Gaslight* (1939). Outstanding wartime productions were Rattigan's *Flare Path* (1942) and Coward's *Private Lives* (1944). In the post-war period, John Dighton's farce *The Happiest Days of Your Life* ran for 605 performances (1948), Hugh Hastings's *Seagulls Over Sorrento* (1950) for 1551 performances, and Marc Camoletti's *Boeing, Boeing* (1962) for 2035 performances. Now under the management of Stoll Moss Theatres, the Apollo's more recent productions have included Peter Shaffer's *Lettice and Lovage* (1987), starring Maggie Smith, Keith Waterhouse's *Jeffrey Bernard is Unwell* (1989) and *Our Song* (1992), both of which starred Peter O'Toole, and a revival of Coward's *Fallen Angels* (2000).

The **Apollo Theatre** on 42nd Street, between 7th and 8th Avenues in New York, opened in 1910 as the **Bryant Theatre** and was used for films and vaudeville. In 1920 it became the Apollo Theatre, housing musical comedies until 1924. From 1924 to 1931, George White's *Scandals* were staged there; but in 1933 it again became a cinema. It was renovated and reopened in 1979 as the **New Apollo**, to avoid confusion with the theatre in Harlem. Shows seen there included *On Golden Pond* (1979) and Lanford Wilson's *The Fifth of July* (1980). With the renovation of Times Square in the 1990s, it was torn down, its space and some of its decorations being used for the FORD THEATRE CENTER.

The **Apollo Theatre** on West 125th Street, in the Harlem area of New York, was opened in 1913 as a Whites-only burlesque house. By 1934 it was reopened to a Black audience and rapidly became the most prestigious house in the US for Black musical and variety talent. After a period of neglect from the mid-1970s, it is currently used both as a theatre and a media studio.

Apollo Victoria Theatre A theatre in Wilton Road, London, which opened in 1980 as a concert hall. Formerly a cinema, it housed a revival of *The Sound of Music* in 1981 and subsequently staged Lloyd Webber's *Starlight Express* (1984), which was still running in 2000.

Appia, Adolphe (1862–1928) Swiss stage designer, who did much to develop staging techniques in the early 20th century. He was particularly noted for his use of lighting to suggest three-dimensional scenery and for his settings for the plays of Shaw and Ibsen, as described in his treatise *Die Musik und die Inscenierung* (1899).

Apple Cart, The A political comedy by G B SHAW. First performance: Warsaw, 1929. Set in England in the late 20th century, the play analyses the relationship between monarchy and democracy and raises questions about political morality. The more immediate target of the play was Ramsay MacDonald's socialist government.

apron That part of the stage in front of the proscenium arch, often considerably enlarged in modern theatres. In some theatres the apron, also called the **forestage**, can be extended over the pit.

Aquarium Theatre *See* Imperial Theatre.

aquatic drama A theatrical entertainment, developed in the circuses of Paris, in which much, or all, of the action takes place on water. During the 18th and 19th centuries many major theatres in London were altered to facilitate the performance of such dramas, including Drury Lane, Covent Garden, and Sadler's Wells.

Aquatic Theatre *See* Sadler's Wells Theatre.

Arbuzov, Alexei Nikolayevich (1908–86) Russian playwright, whose works were also performed in the West. He began writing in the 1920s and achieved his first notable success with *Tanya* (1939). Among his works to have been produced outside Russia were *It Happened In Irkutsk* (1959), a study of small-town life that was staged in Paris in 1961 and in Sheffield in 1967, and *The Promise* (1965), which was seen in London and New York. *Old World* was premiered in Poland in 1975 and a year later was performed by the Royal Shakespeare Company; it was then produced in Paris and New York.

arc *See* carbon arc spotlight.

Arcadia A comedy by Tom STOPPARD. First performance: Royal National Theatre, London, 1993. Set in an English country house, the play alternates scenes from the 1800s and the 1990s. Farcical elements are interwoven with discussions of chaos theory, landscape gardening, and the nature of historical enquiry.

Archer, William (1856–1924) British critic and playwright, born in Scotland. In London from 1879, he was dramatic critic successively for *Figaro*, *The World*, *The Tribune*, *The Nation*, and *The Star*. His translation of *Samfundets Støtter* as *The Pillars of Society* was the first version of one of Ibsen's plays to be performed in England (1880); translations of all of Ibsen's other plays followed. His own melodrama *The Green Goddess* had a long run at the St James's Theatre in 1921.

Archetringle A festival of folk theatre that takes place annually on New Year's Eve at Laupen in Switzerland. It culminates in a mock battle between masked performers.

Arch Street Theatre A theatre in Philadelphia, which was opened by William B Wood in 1828. It survived the financial crisis of 1829, brought about by competition from other theatres in the city, and, under Mrs John Drew from 1860 to 1892, became a great success both commercially and artistically.

Arden, John (1930–) British playwright, who emerged as a significant writer for the theatre with several plays presented by the Royal Court Theatre in the 1950s. *Live Like Pigs* (1958) was followed by the much-acclaimed Brechtian drama SERJEANT MUSGRAVE'S DANCE (1959), which nonetheless failed in its initial production. Subsequent plays of the 1960s included *The Happy Haven* (1960), *The Workhouse Donkey* (1963), *Armstrong's Last Goodnight* (1964), and *Left-Handed Liberty* (1965). He has also written several plays (notably *The Island of the Mighty* in 1972) in collaboration with his wife, the Irish writer **Margaretta D'Arcy**. Following an acrimonious dispute with the Royal Shakespeare Company in 1972, the couple concentrated upon producing strongly Marxist drama with amateur groups. Arden published several novels in the 1980s and 1990s but has never returned to the mainstream theatre.

Arden of Faversham An Elizabethan prose tragedy, written c. 1592. First performance: c. 1592. Based on a murder case of 1551, it has sometimes been attributed to Thomas KYD and, incorrectly, to Shakespeare.

arena An open acting area in the centre of an auditorium, as used in theatre-in-the-round.

Arena Stage A theatre in Washington DC, which was designed by Harry Weise in 1961 as a theatre-in-the-round. The theatre opened with a production of Brecht's *The Caucasian Chalk Circle*. The resident company, founded in 1950 by Zelda Fichandler, had previously played in a converted burlesque house and an old brewery. It has since established a strong reputation with both modern and classic drama. Plays it has sent to Broadway include Howard Sackler's *The Great White Hope* (1968), Arthur Kopit's *Indians* (1969), and Michael Weller's *Moonchildren* (1971). A proscenium theatre was opened in 1971.

Aretino, Pietro (1492–1556) Italian poet, prose writer, and playwright, author of a number of major works in the *commedia erudita* tradition. Although he wrote one good tragedy, *Orazio* (1546), he was better known for his five comedies, of which the most successful was *La Cortigiana* (1526).

Argent, Théâtre de l'Hôtel d' The second oldest theatre in Paris, opened in 1598 under licence from the Confrérie de la Passion, who ran the rival Théâtre de l'Hôtel de Bourgogne. The theatre was run by the father of Marie Venier, who herself appeared there as the leading lady opposite her husband. In 1610 all the Paris theatres were deserted following the assassination of Henry IV; when the actors returned a new company under Lenoir and Montdory took over the Hôtel d'Argent, remaining there until 1634, when the Théâtre du MARAIS opened.

Argyll Rooms *See* Trocadero Palace of Varieties.

Arion of Lesbos (c. 625 BC–585 BC) Greek poet and musician, author of the earliest Greek verse drama. His works helped to establish the dithyramb and the satyr-play as serious literary forms. Legend has it that he escaped from pirates by being carried to safety by a dolphin, which was entranced by his singing.

Ariosto, Lodovico (1474–1533) Italian poet and playwright, author of the epic poem *Orlando Furioso*. He was the author of four major comedies of the *commedia erudita* tradition, which were performed under the patronage of the d'Este family in a theatre in Ferrara with scenery designed by Raphael. They included *La Cassaria* (1508) and *I suppositi* (1509), which subsequently influenced Shakespeare's *The Taming of the Shrew*.

Aristophanes (c. 448 BC–380 BC) Greek playwright, author of the only intact surviving examples of OLD COMEDY. Of the 11 of his 40 or so plays that are still in existence, the earlier works are bawdy and outspoken satirical dramas, while the later ones, notably *Ecclesiazousae* and *Plutus*, are written in the more restrained style of MIDDLE COMEDY. The early plays usually took their titles from the role played by the disguised chorus and were based on little more than a skeleton plot, used to satirize such targets as contemporary politicians, fellow-playwrights, and foreigners. The more subdued later works probably reflect the increasingly unsettled political atmosphere in Athens at that time. After centuries of relative neglect, many of his plays were successfully revived in the 20th century.

Principal works:
  THE ACHARNIANS: 425 BC.
  The Knights: 424 BC.
  THE CLOUDS: 423 BC.
  The Wasps: 422 BC.
  THE PEACE: 421 BC.
  THE BIRDS: 414 BC.
  LYSISTRATA: 411 BC.
  Thesmaphoriazousae: 410 BC.
  THE FROGS: 405 BC.
  Ecclesiazousae: 392 BC.
  Plutus: 388 BC.

Aristotle (384 BC–322 BC) Greek philosopher, scientist, and theatre critic, whose theoretical writings represent a detailed analysis of certain types of contemporary drama. Although his writings on comedy are now lost, his theories upon tragedy – laid down in the *Poetics* (c. 330 BC) – countered those of Plato and Socrates and attempted to define the purpose and form of such drama, as exemplified for him in the plays of Sophocles. In order to achieve the ultimate aim of CATHARSIS, he approved the use of extreme situations and the manipulation of the audience's emotions; this was usually to be realized through the inevitable downfall of the hero as the consequence of some tragic mistake. In the 17th and 18th centuries, when playwrights began to look to classical works for guidance as to the function and structure of tragedy, Aristotle's theories were further developed into the concept of the three UNITIES.

Arlecchino A character of the *commedia dell'arte*, capable of both great stupidity and cunning, who gradually evolved from being one of the *zanni* into the more refined English HARLEQUIN. He was conventionally dressed in a multi-coloured patched suit and wore a small black mask; in the French tradition he was known as Arlequin. Noted interpreters of the role, which required some skill as an acrobat and dancer, included Tristano Martinelli and Giuseppe Biancolelli.

Arliss, George (Augustus George Andrews; 1868–1946) British actor, who became a popular film actor. His first stage success was in *The Second Mrs Tanqueray* (1901), in which play he went to the US where he remained for 20 years, playing many leading roles. Back in London he spent over a year in Archer's *The Green Goddess* (1921), making his last stage appearance in 1928 as Shylock in New York.

Armin, Robert (c. 1568–c. 1611) British actor and writer, who began as a pupil of Tarleton and probably made his debut as a clown at the Globe. In 1610 he was in the first production of *The Alchemist*; in the 1623 Folio he was also listed as one of the actors in Shakespeare's plays. His own play *The Two Maids of More Clacke* was produced in 1609.

Arms and the Man A play by G B SHAW. First performance: London, 1894. A mercenary soldier, Bluntschli, breaks into the bedroom of Raina Petkoff and disrupts her idyllic romance with Sergius Saranov. The play mocks the idealism of both love and war. It was later made into a musical by Oscar Straus, as *The Chocolate Soldier*.

Armstrong, William (1882–1952) British actor and director, who first appeared at Stratford-on-Avon in 1908, then toured widely and worked in several repertory companies before becoming director and producer at the Liverpool Playhouse (1922). When the theatre closed in 1941, he directed several London productions before returning to repertory at Birmingham in 1945 under Barry Jackson.

Arnaud, Yvonne Germaine (1892–1958) French actress, who became one of the leading actresses upon the London stage. After training as a pianist as a child, she made her debut in musical comedy in 1911 at the Adelphi Theatre and won immediate acclaim. Subsequently she triumphed in further musical comedies and farces by Will Evans and Ben Travers among others. Her greatest performances included Mrs Pepys in Fagan's *And So To Bed* (1926) and Mrs Frail in Congreve's *Love for Love* (1943). The Yvonne Arnaud Theatre was opened in 1965 in Guildford, where she lived.

Arne, Susanna Maria (1714–66) British actress and singer. Her career as a tragic actress began in 1736, but was immediately interrupted by a scandal. This was the result of the machinations of her husband Theophilus CIBBER, who had forced her into an affair with her friend William Sloper and then brought an action against him. Eventually she returned to the stage in Dublin, and from then on divided her time between Drury Lane and Covent Garden.

Arnold, Matthew (1822–88) British poet and theatre critic, son of the headmaster of Rugby School. He stressed the cultural importance of theatre and wrote dramatic criticism for the *Pall Mall Gazette*. He also wrote the poetic dramas *Empedocles on Etna* (1852) and *Merope* (1858).

Aronson, Boris (1900–80) Russian-born stage designer, who left Kiev to come to New York in 1923. A year later he designed his first stage production, *Day and Night* (1924), for the Unser Theatre in the Bronx. His innovations included the use of projections in suggesting scenery. Among the shows he designed scenery for were *Fiddler on the Roof* (1964), *Cabaret* (1966), *Company* (1970), *Follies* (1971), and *Pacific Overtures* (1976).

Arrabal, Fernando (1932–) Spanish-born French playwright, who settled in Paris in 1955, publishing his first collection of plays in 1958. Although usually associated with the Theatre of the Absurd, Arrabal labelled his works *Théâtre Panique*; often grotesque, violent, and blasphemous (*La Cimetière des voitures* parodies the Crucifixion), they depict a fantasy world of horror and betrayal. Childhood memories of the Spanish Civil War dominate the plays: *Et ils passèrent des menottes aux fleurs*, which was banned in 1969, attacks political oppression. His more experimental works include *Orchéstration théâtrale* (1959), which has no dialogue at all.

Principal works:
  Pique-nique en campagne: 1959; translated as *Picnic on the Battlefield*.
  Fando et Lis: 1961; translated as *Fando and Lis*.
  La Cimetière des voitures: 1966; translated as *The Car Cemetery*.
  L'Architecte et l'empereur d'Assyrie: 1967; translated as *The Architect and the Emperor of Assyria*.
  Et ils passèrent des menottes aux fleurs: 1969; translated as *And They Put Handcuffs on the Flowers*.
  Le Jardin des délices: 1969.
  La Ballade du train fantôme: 1974.
  Théâtre Bouffe: 1978.
  Baal Babylone: 1980.
  La Traversée de l'Empire: 1988.

Arsenic and Old Lace A comedy-thriller by Joseph Kesselring. First performance: New York, 1941. The plot revolves around two old ladies who invite men to their home in Brooklyn, only to poison them with elderberry wine. The bodies are quietly buried by their brother, who thinks he is Teddy Roosevelt, until a homicidal nephew arrives with his own corpse to conceal. The play was filmed by Frank Capra in 1942.

Art A play by Yasmina REZA. First performance, 1994; first English-language performance, Wyndhams Theatre, London, 1996. The relationship between two old friends is threatened when one of them buys an expensive avant-garde painting which the other regards as completely worthless; a third friend tries to hold things together. The London production, which originally starred Tom Courtenay, Albert Finney, and Ken Stott, was still running in 2000. The play has now enjoyed success worldwide, having been translated into 35 languages.

Art, Théâtre d' A French theatre, founded by Paul Fort in 1891 for the performance of poetic drama. In 1893 it was taken over by Lugné-Poë and renamed the **Théâtre de l'Oeuvre**.

Artaud, Antonin (1896–1948) French actor, director, poet, and playwright, born in Marseilles. Artaud entered the theatre as an actor in the early 1920s and became involved with the Surrealist movement. With the Théâtre Alfred Jarry, which he co-founded with Roger Vitrac, he produced works by Strindberg, Vitrac, and himself. Artaud's own plays made little impact (*Les Cenci* had only a fortnight's run in 1935); his major contribution to the world of drama was his conception of the Theatre of CRUELTY, expounded in the essays collected in *Le Théâtre et son double* (1938; *The Theatre and Its Double*, 1958). Despite the fact that he spent the years between 1937 and 1946 in various psychiatric hospitals, Artaud profoundly influenced many subsequent directors, including Barrault, Blin, and Peter Brook.

Artists of Dionysus Organizations of actors and other members of the theatre in ancient Greece. Dating from the 4th century BC, these guilds ruled on questions relating to performers' wages and acted as governing bodies for the profession as a whole.

Arts Councils The four major funding bodies for the arts in the UK. The original Arts Council of Great Britain was established in 1946 by Royal Charter, as a development of the earlier **Council for the Encouragement of Music and the Arts** (CEMA). Its purpose was to promote high standards in the arts and increase their accessibility throughout Britain. Receiving its grant directly from government, the Council contributed to the abolition of weekly repertory, the maintenance of relatively low-priced seats, the development of new writing, and investment in new buildings. In the 1980s most of its responsibility for small scale, community, and young people's theatre was devolved to regional arts associations. Independent Arts Councils for England, Scotland, and Wales were created in 1994 (that for Northern Ireland having always been separate). Since 1995 the Councils have been responsible for allocating National Lottery funding for the arts.

Arts Laboratory A theatre in Drury Lane, London, opened in 1968. Founded by Charles Marowitz and Jim Haynes, it was much used by a number of theatre companies, including the PIP SIMMONS THEATRE GROUP and other fringe theatre organizations before its closure in late 1969.

Arts Theatre A small theatre in Great Newport Street, London, established in 1927 for the staging of unlicensed and avant-garde plays. Seating 337 people, it began as a club theatre with a number of productions that subsequently transferred to major commercial venues before Alec CLUNES took over in 1942. One of its early successes was John Van Druten's *Young Woodley* (1928), a play banned by the Lord Chamberlain. Clunes (and then Campbell Williams) encouraged the performance there of new plays by such playwrights as Christopher Fry, Samuel Beckett, Jean Anouilh, Harold Pinter, and Edward Albee, memorable premieres including *Waiting for Godot* (1955) and *The Caretaker* (1960). The Royal Shakespeare Company took a six-month lease of the theatre for experimental drama (1962), after which (from 1967) the Unicorn Theatre of Caryl Jenner staged entertainments for children. More recent successes by visiting companies have included Stoppard's *Dirty Linen* (1976), John Godber's *Teechers* (1988), and a revival of Julian Mitchell's *Another Country* (2000).

Asch, Sholom (1880–1957) Jewish novelist and playwright, born in Poland, who made an important contribution to Yiddish literature with such works as *Dos Schottl* (The Village; 1904), a novel about the life of Jews in rural Poland. His best-known work, *Der Got fun Nikome* (The God of Vengeance; 1907), was a widely-performed play with a religious theme and was first produced by Reinhardt in Berlin.

Asche, Oscar (John Stanger Heiss; 1871–1936) British actor, manager, and playwright, born in Australia of Norwegian descent. He appeared in Benson's company and with Tree before assuming the management of Her Majesty's Theatre in 1902 and presenting numerous Shakespearean productions in which he frequently appeared himself. After creating Hajj in Knoblock's *Kismet* in 1911, he went on to write the popular fantasy CHU CHIN CHOW (1916). His plays *Mecca* (1920) and *Cairo* (1921) were, however, failures.

His wife, **Lily Brayton** (1876–1953), appeared alongside him in many productions.

Ashcroft, Dame Peggy (Edith Margaret Emily Ashcroft; 1907–91) British actress, who first appeared at the Birmingham Repertory Theatre in 1926 as Margaret in Barrie's *Dear Brutus* and made her London debut in Feuchtwanger's *Jew Süss* at the Duke of York's Theatre in 1929. She was Desdemona to Paul Robeson's Othello in 1930 and subsequently played a series of Shakespearean heroines at the Old Vic. At the New Theatre she triumphed as Juliet in Gielgud's 1935 production and as Nina in Komisarjevsky's production of *The Seagull* in 1936. She played leading roles in Gielgud's classical seasons at the Queen's Theatre (1939–40) and at the Haymarket (1944–45) and was a sensation as Hedda Gabler in 1954, which she played in London and Oslo. Her contemporary roles included the title part in *The Heiress* (1949), a Henry James adaptation, Hester in Rattigan's *The Deep Blue Sea* (1952), and Miss Madrigal in Enid Bagnold's *The Chalk Garden* (1956). She was a founder member of the Royal Shakespeare Company, of which she later became a director, and frequently appeared with them in Stratford and London, notably as Queen Margaret in *The Wars of the Roses* (1963–64). Her later successes included roles in Ibsen's *Ghosts* (1967) and *John Gabriel Borkman* (1975), Beckett's *Happy Days* (1975), Hellman's *Watch on the Rhine* (1980), and *All's Well that Ends Well* (1981). A 700-seat theatre in Croydon was named after her in 1962.

Ashley, Elizabeth (1939–) US actress, who made her professional debut in 1959 as Louise in *Marcus in the High*. Subsequent roles have included Mollie Michaelson in *Take Her, She's Mine* (1961), Carrie Bratter in *Barefoot in the Park* (1963), Margaret in *Cat on a Hot Tin Roof* (1974), Dr Livingstone in *Agnes of God* (1982), and Mrs Venable in *Suddenly Last Summer* (1992).

Ashman, Howard *See* Menken, Alan.

Ashwell, Lena (Lena Pocock; 1872–1957) British actress, who established her reputation in Arthur Jones's *Mrs Dane's Defence* (1900) and took over the Kingsway Theatre in 1907. During World War I she organized overseas companies; afterwards she produced new plays at the Century Theatre (later the Bijou Theatre) in Bayswater, including her own versions of *Crime and Punishment* and *Dr Jekyll and Mr Hyde*.

aside A line or, sometimes, a whole speech addressed by an actor directly to the audience rather than to the other characters, who are assumed not to be able to hear.

ASM *See* stage manager.

Asolo State Theatre A theatre company based in Sarasota, Florida, which grew out of the summer festival of 18th and 19th century comedies produced by the Division of Theatre at Florida State University in 1960. The plays were given in a rebuilt 1798 theatre transported from Asolo, Italy. This became the State Theatre of Florida with a fully professional repertory company in 1966.

Asphaleian system An early mechanical system by means of which various parts of the stage floor might be raised or lowered. First developed in 1884 in Austria-Hungary, it was constructed largely of iron, thus reducing the risk of fire.

Assembly Theatre *See* Princess Theatre.

assistant stage manager *See* stage manager.

Association of Community Theatres (ACT) An organization of professional theatrical groups established in New Zealand during the 1970s. It includes the Court Theatre in Christchurch, the Centrepoint Theatre in Palmerston North, and the Fortune Theatre Company in Dunedin.

Astley's Amphitheatre A theatre established by a former cavalry officer, Philip Astley (1742–1814), as a forerunner of the modern circus. A noted rider himself, Astley staged equestrian dramas there as well as various acrobatic entertainments from 1769. The original building (the stage was uncovered until 1784) was based on Roman designs and was subsequently destroyed by fire a number of times before it emerged as the **Royal Amphitheatre of Arts** in 1804. Equestrian dramas, which remained popular under the management of Andrew Ducrow (1793–1848), were then alternated with melodrama until another fire in 1841; regular visitors included Charles Dickens. Rebuilt as Batty's Amphitheatre it was taken over by Dion Boucicault (as the **Theatre Royal, Westminster**) and saw premieres of plays by himself and Sir Walter Scott. From 1864 Adah Isaacs Menken starred in the highly successful *Mazeppa*, adapted from a poem by Byron, after which the theatre was enlarged and reverted to its former use as a circus (renamed **Sanger's Grand National Amphitheatre**). It was demolished in 1895.

Another Astley Amphitheatre was opened in Paris in 1782.

Aston, Anthony (d. 1753) Irish actor, popularly known as **Matt Medley**. He became well known (as Tony Aston) while touring the English provinces presenting his *Medley*, a farrago of scenes taken from different plays. Earlier in his career he appeared at Drury Lane and was one of the first professional actors to perform in the US (c. 1703). He was also the author of the pamphlet *Lives of the Late Famous Actors and Actresses by Anthony, vulgo Tony, Aston* and several plays.

Astoria Theatre A theatre in Charing Cross Road, London, built as a cinema in 1927 and popularly known as the 'Jam Factory'. In 1977 it was adapted for the theatre and staged the musical *Elvis*. Since coming under new management in July 1987 it has been a live music venue.

Astor Place Opera House A theatre off Broadway, New York, which opened in 1847. Between opera seasons its actors included Charlotte Cushman, Julia Dean, and George Vandenhoff. Its reputation suffered irrecoverable damage when the anti-British Astor Place riot (in which 22 people died) took place there in May 1849 as a result of the rivalry between Macready (who was appearing there) and the US actor Edwin Forrest. The theatre reopened later that year but its blighted reputation led to its final closure in 1850.

Astor Theatre A theatre on Broadway in New York, which opened in 1906 with *A Midsummer Night's Dream*. In 1913 George M Cohan's dramatization of Earl Bigger's novel *Seven Keys to Baldpate* was seen there. The theatre became a cinema in 1925.

As You Like It A comedy by William SHAKESPEARE, written c. 1599. First performance: date unknown. Based on Thomas Lodge's *Rosalynde*, the play juxtaposes the two worlds of Frederick's court and the pastoral Forest of Arden; the plot concerns the romantic trials of Rosalind and Orlando and three other couples. Other characters include the enigmatic Jaques. The play provided major roles for Macklin, Kitty Clive, Peg Woffington, Charles Kean, and Mrs Siddons in the 18th century and Laurence Olivier, Edith Evans, and Vanessa Redgrave in more recent times.

ATA *See* American Theatre Association.

Atelier, Théâtre de l' A theatre close to the Montmartre area of Paris, founded in 1822. As the Théâtre des Élèves, it was originally a venue for melodrama and vaudeville and then a cinema before Charles Dullin took it over in 1922. Subsequently it became a focus of the avant-garde movement, with plays by Achard, Pirandello, and others; it was also recognized as a leading training ground for young actors. From 1940 André Barsacq (and later his son) continued to stage serious drama there.

atellana A form of early Roman FABULA, named after the town of Atella, near Capua. With its stock of clown characters – Bucco, Dossennus, Maccus, Manducus, and Pappus – it was distinguished by its coarse humour and rustic settings and made extensive use of masks and disguises. Few scripts survive and the emphasis seems to have been upon improvisation; ultimately the *atellana* gave way to mime entertainments.

Athalie A tragedy by Jean RACINE. First performance: Versailles, 1691, by Madame de Maintenon's school for young ladies (for whom the play was written). The plot revolves around the Old Testament story of Athaliah, whose attempt to destroy the house of David is thwarted by the survival of Joash. The play, Racine's last, reflects his Jansenist religious views.

Athénée, Théâtre de l' A theatre in Paris, that first became well known (called the Athénée-Comique) as a venue for light entertainment, including melodrama. In 1934 Louis Jouvet transformed its reputation with numerous influential productions of serious drama until his death in 1951, after which it declined.

Athenian drama Greek theatre of the 4th and 5th centuries BC, sometimes referred to as the classical period. This era saw the evolution of both TRAGEDY and COMEDY from choral lyrics and the rituals connected with Dionysus and the emergence through the various drama contests of the great tragic poets, AESCHYLUS, SOPHOCLES, and EURIPIDES, and the comic poet ARISTOPHANES. Early tragedy and OLD COMEDY tackled such universal issues as justice and suffering but gradually became more interested in character analysis and looser in structure, employing more actors and relying less upon the chorus. Rudimentary scenery and props were in use towards the end of this period, which also saw the building of the first stone theatres. In the 4th century BC the rules of drama were codified by Aristotle and MIDDLE COMEDY and NEW COMEDY developed, ultimately bridging the gap between Athenian and Roman drama. *See also* Hellenistic drama.

Atkins, Eileen (1934–   ) British actress and writer, who started in repertory at Bangor in Ireland in 1952 before appearing at the Open Air Theatre, Stratford-on-Avon, and Bristol. Subsequently she played Shakespearean leads with the Old Vic company and was highly acclaimed in Frank Marcus's *The Killing of Sister George* (1965) and as Elizabeth I in Bolt's *Vivat! Vivat Regina!* (1970). Other celebrated performances of the 1970s and 1980s included roles in the plays of Marguerite Duras, G B Shaw, and Peter Nichols. In 1988 she won an Olivier award for playing the Queen in *Cymbeline*. Her own play *Vita and Virginia*, about the friendship of Virginia Woolf and Vita Sackville-West, was produced in 1994 with herself and Vanessa Redgrave in the title roles.

Atkins, Robert (1886–1972) British actor-manager, who first established himself as an excellent Shakespearean actor when engaged by Ben Greet at the Old Vic in 1915. Between 1920 and 1925 he proceeded to stage every Shakespearean play except for *Cymbeline* there. He also directed the first London production of *Peer Gynt*, founded the **Bankside Players**, directed at Stratford, and for over 30 years ran the Open Air Theatre, Regent's Park.

Atkinson, (Justin) Brooks (1894–1984) US theatre critic, who was the drama critic for the *New York Times* from 1926 to 1960. He received a Tony Award for distinguished achievement in the theatre and, upon his retirement, the Mansfield Theatre in New York was renamed the BROOKS ATKINSON THEATRE in his honour.

Atta, Titus Quintius (d. 77 BC) Roman playwright, author of plays in the *togata* tradition. Very little of his work survives; he was noted in his own time especially for his depiction of women.

Aubignac, François Hédelin, Abbé d' (1604–76) French critic and playwright, born in Paris. His *Pratique du théâtre* (1657; translated as *The Whole Art of the Stage*, 1684), commissioned by Cardinal de Richelieu, emphasizes the strict observance of the three unities. Aubignac also wrote critical commentaries on the works of Corneille and others.

Auckland Theatre Trust *See* Mercury Theatre.

Auden, W(ystan) H(ugh) (1907–73) British poet, who wrote several verse dramas during the 1930s. His plays written in collaboration with Christopher Isherwood include *The Dog Beneath the Skin* (1935), *The Ascent of F6* (1936), and *On the Frontier* (1938); other dramatic contributions include opera libretti.

Audiberti, Jacques (1899–1965) French poet, novelist, and playwright, born in Antibes. He moved to Paris in 1925, becoming involved with the Surrealist movement; it was not until the mid-1940s, however, that he made his name as a playwright with such plays as *Quoat-Quoat* (1946), *Le Mal court* (1947), and *La Fourmi dans le corps* (1962). The next two decades saw the performance of almost 30 of his plays, which characteristically depict the conflict between good and evil against a background of the supernatural.

audition A competitive test at which an actor or other performer is invited to demonstrate his aptitude for a particular role, usually in the presence of the director of the planned production. Where the choice of actor is difficult, more than one audition may be held.

auditorium The area of a theatre in which the audience sits, formerly called the auditory or spectatory (in the 19th century). In the Greek open-air theatre the auditorium was usually cut into a hillside and consisted of a horseshoe of tiered stone or wooden seats rising up from the stage itself; such auditoriums held as many as 17 000 spectators and provided excellent acoustic effects. Roman theatres were based on fundamentally the same design, although the semicircular auditorium (or *cavea*), which was often elaborately decorated and sometimes equipped with an awning to shelter the audience, was usually specially built rather than incorporated into a natural feature. The colossal amphitheatres used for chariot racing and gladiatorial contests usually formed a complete circle.

When the theatrical tradition was revived during medieval times audiences generally stood in front of temporary stages or booths to watch a play, often moving from one small stage to another to follow the action. In England such booth stages eventually developed into the circular Elizabethan playhouse, in imitation of the innyards used by travelling players.

The introduction of the proscenium arch in Italy during the Renaissance prompted the revival of the Greek horseshoe design, although elsewhere the conversion of tennis courts into theatres meant that many early auditoriums comprised deep rectangles. Court theatres, however, followed Italian models, with the addition of a Royal Box. In England and France typical auditoriums of the time consisted of tiered **galleries** overlooking a central area known as the **pit**, which was sometimes open to the sky and usually offered the cheapest seats. Seating for the most ostentatious members of the audience, who wished to be seen as much as to see, was also provided on stage, to the detriment of acting standards.

From the late 17th century onwards English auditoriums adopted elements of the Italian tradition, while remaining plainer than most Continental models. By the 1830s a standard plan had emerged; this consisted of the **orchestra pit** (where the musicians performed), a pit containing expensive **stalls** at the front and cheaper seats further back, a small number of **boxes** on either side, and then an arrangement of balconies known as **circles** (often divided into the **dress circle** and **upper circle**) and, higher up still, the **galleries** (the topmost of which was traditionally called the **gods**).

Elsewhere in Europe, however, architects created increasingly ornate auditoriums and, by the 19th century, were adding impressive colonnades and porticos to the exterior as well in imitation of the opera houses. The building of Richard Wagner's Opera House in Bayreuth in 1876 signalled a revolution in theatre design with its rejection of boxes and galleries in favour of a single sloping tier of seats facing the stage and its austerity in matters of decoration. The orchestra was hidden and the auditorium darkened. A similar spirit of reform and simplicity has characterized most new auditoriums in the last 100 years. This has been combined, however, with a new eclecticism, so that modern seating plans may range from versions of the Victorian norm to arrangements involving a single tier of seats, seating on all sides (as in theatre-in-the-round), or some other grouping made possible by flexible staging.

Auditorium Theatre A theatre in Chicago, whose Louis Sullivan design is considered a masterpiece of the First Chicago School of architecture. Opened in 1890 as an opera house and famous for its acoustics, it suffered a long period of neglect, but is now used for dance and large musical productions.

auditory *See* auditorium.

Audrey, Robert (1908–80) US playwright, whose best-known play was the allegorical drama set in a lighthouse, THUNDER ROCK (1939). Other works included *How To Get Tough About It* (1938) and *Shadow of Heroes* (1958).

Augier, Emile (1820–89) French playwright. Born in Valence, he began with a number of mediocre verse plays, such as *Gabrielle* (1849). His reputation rests on such prose comedies as *Le Gendre de Monsier Poirier* (1854; translated as *Monsieur Poirier's Son-in-law*, 1915), which depict the social life and moral issues of the middle classes, a reaction against the Romantic movement.

Augustan drama English neoclassical drama written during the earlier 18th century, an era known as the Augustan Age after a distinguished period of Roman writing (27 BC–14 AD). Augustan drama includes the solemn tragedies of Rowe, Addison, and Dr Johnson, very few of which have been revived.

Augustus Druriolanus *See* Harris, Sir Augustus Glossop.

aulaeum *See* curtain.

Aureng-Zebe A heroic tragedy by John DRYDEN. First performance: 1675. Remotely based on contemporary events in India, the play depicts the downfall of an exemplary hero when surrounded by anarchy and vice. It is written in rhyming pentameters.

Ausoult, Jeanne (1625–62) French actress, wife of the actor André Baron and mother of Michel Baron. The daughter of strolling players, she excelled in Desjardin's *Manlius* at the Hôtel de Bourgogne, but died before she could act a part Corneille had written for her.

author's night A BENEFIT performance, traditionally the third night of a production, the proceeds of which – in the 17th and 18th centuries – went to the playwright.

auto sacramental The early LITURGICAL DRAMA of Spain, the origins of which date back to about 1200. Strongly allegorical, the plays were performed on temporary stages or waggons at major religious festivals (especially during the feast of Corpus Christi), and gradually developed as a powerful tool for Catholic propaganda, notably in the expert hands of Lope de Vega and Calderón. Often seen as the Spanish equivalent of the mystery play in other countries, the genre was eventually prohibited by royal command in 1765.

Avancini, Nikolaus (1611–86) Austrian playwright, who held high posts at the court of Leopold I and was a leading writer of Jesuit drama. His plays, which were noted for their spectacular effects, combined religious sentiment with propaganda in support of the House of Habsburg, as in *Pietas victrix sive Flavius Constantinus Magnus de Maxentio tyranno victor* (1659), in which Leopold I was hailed as a successor to Constantine.

avant-garde A loosely defined movement in modern drama that reacted against realism and favoured a more imaginative approach to the theatre, often stressing the role of the director as an interpreter of a playwright's ideas. Initiated in France in the 1920s, it developed under Jouvet, Dullin, and others (*see* Cartel) into the experimental drama of post-World War II theatre.

Avignon Festival A major theatre festival founded by Jean Vilar at Avignon in France in 1947. The festival, held in the open air in July, grew rapidly following the foundation of the Théâtre National Populaire in 1951, significant productions including plays by Shakespeare, Corneille, and Kleist. After Vilar's death in 1971 the festival continued to expand, acquiring a lively fringe tradition, which included performances by the controversial Living Theatre. In more recent years the huge numbers of groups attending the festival has arguably weakened its identity as well as fragmenting audiences; nevertheless, it is still regarded as perhaps France's leading cultural event. Peter Brook's epic production of THE MAHABHARATA was premiered at the festival in 1985.

Avon Theatre *See* Klaw Theatre; Stratford (Ontario) Festival.

Awake and Sing! A play by Clifford ODETS. First performance: Group Theatre, 1935. The play revolves around a Jewish family, and in particular the domineering mother. Toughened by poverty, she forces her daughter to marry someone she does not love, while breaking up her son's relationship with an orphan girl. The awakening occurs when the daughter defiantly elopes with a racketeer.

Axer, Erwin (1917–) Polish director, regarded as one of the leading theatrical figures in 20th-century Poland. He is best known for his presentation of numerous modern Polish dramas, including works by Kruczkowski, Mrożek, and Witkiewicz, although he has also directed plays by Brecht, Chekhov, Ibsen, Shakespeare, and others with great success. He founded his own company in Łódź in 1945 and later (1949) established the Contemporary Theatre in Warsaw, which he continued to direct until 1981. He has also directed plays at the National Theatre in Britain and in several other countries, as well as writing prolifically on the theatre.

Ayala, Adelardo López de *See* López de Ayala, Adelardo.

Ayckbourn, Sir Alan (1939–) British playwright and director, whose many commercially successful farces are characterized by his bleak view of the frustration and futility he perceives in British middle-class society. *Relatively Speaking* was his first major London success and set the tone for most of the plays that followed with its suburban setting and underlying bitterness. His plays are notable also for their technical inventiveness: the widely performed *The Norman Conquests* comprises a trilogy of comedies using the same locale and basic plot, *Sisterly Feelings* provides a choice of endings, while the plays *House* and *Garden* are written to be staged simultaneously in separate auditoriums. His more recent works have been distinguished by their increasingly black outlook. In 1975 he had five plays running at once in London's West End. Since 1970 Ayckbourn has been artistic director of the Stephen Joseph Theatre at Scarborough, where most of his plays have been given their first performance. He was knighted in 1997.

Principal works:
  Mr Whatnot: 1964.
  Relatively Speaking: 1967.
  How the Other Half Loves: 1970.
  Time and Time Again: 1972.
  Absurd Person Singular: 1973.
  The Norman Conquests: 1974.
  Absent Friends: 1975.
  Confusions: 1976.
  BEDROOM FARCE: 1977.
  Just Between Ourselves: 1977.
  Ten Times Table: 1978.
  Joking Apart: 1979.
  Sisterly Feelings: 1980.
  Suburban Strains: 1981.
  Way Upstream: 1982.
  Intimate Exchanges: 1982.
  Making Tracks: 1983.
  A Chorus of Disapproval: 1985.
  A Small Family Business: 1987.
  Woman in Mind: 1988.
  Body Language: 1990.
  The Revengers Comedies: 1991.
  Wildest Dreams: 1993.
  Haunting Julia: 1994.
  Things We Do For Love: 1998.
  House and Garden: 2000.

Aylmer, Sir Felix (Sir Felix Edward Aylmer-Jones; 1889–1979) British actor, who began his career with Seymour Hicks at the Coliseum before joining the first Birmingham Repertory Company and appearing in plays by Shakespeare and Shaw. After World War I he resumed his career in both London and New York, becoming identified with roles of dry humour and authority; his most notable parts included Walter Harrowby in Charles Morgan's *The Flashing Stream* (1938) and Sir Joseph Pitts in Bridie's *Daphne Laureola* (1949).

Aymé, Marcel (1902–67) French novelist, short-story writer, and playwright. Aymé's first play, *Lucienne et le boucher*, was produced in 1948; his dramatic works are marked by coarse and sometimes cruel humour and by a blending of fantasy, reality, and the absurd.

Aynesworth, Allan (E Abbot-Anderson; 1865–1959) British actor, director, and manager, whose long career began with Tree's company at the Haymarket in 1887. A handsome gentlemanly actor, he created a number of important roles, including Algernon in *The Importance of Being Earnest* (1895) and Lord Porteous in Maugham's *The Circle* (1921). He was also involved in the management of the New, Garrick, and Criterion theatres.

Ayrenhoff, Cornelius von (1733–1819) Austrian playwright, author of several influential dramas. His plays, written in an attempt to counteract the prevailing light comedies popular in Vienna at the time, were successfully presented at the Burgtheater by Joseph von Sonnenfels.

Ayrer, Jakob (1543–1605) German playwright, who incorporated many of the features of Elizabethan drama in his plays of the *Fastnachtsspiel* tradition. A pupil of Hans Sachs, Ayrer was much influenced by the English Comedians; his 100 or more works include spectacular comedies, tragedies, and histories as well as examples of the *Singspiele* tradition, which he popularized.

B

Babanova, Maria Ivanovna (1900–82) Russian actress, who became the leading actress at the Theatre of the Revolution. She appeared under Komisarjevsky and Meyerhold early in her career and was later directed by Popov and Okhlopkov among others; her most celebrated roles included Juliet and the title role in Arbuzov's *Tanya*.

Bacchae, The A tragedy by EURIPIDES. First performance: Athens, 406 BC. The most frequently revived of all his works, the play was first produced (by his son) after the author's death and revolves around the contrasting figures of the licentious god Dionysus and the prudish Pentheus. It ends in frenzied violence.

Bacchus *See* Dionysus.

backcloth A large curtain or painted canvas hung at the back of the stage, usually in conjunction with flats and often with a gauze. In the US it is referred to as a **backdrop**.

backdrop *See* backcloth.

backing flat A flat positioned behind a door or window in order to mask off the backstage area from the audience's view.

backstage That part of a theatre behind the proscenium arch or stage area. It includes the wings, workshops, storerooms, and dressing-rooms.

Back to Methuselah A play by G B SHAW. First performance: Theatre Guild, 1922. Consisting of five plays in one, it covers the whole of human history and discusses the acquisition of wisdom through longevity; it was considered by Shaw his finest play but is rarely revived. Its first London production was given by Barry Jackson's company, having transferred from the Birmingham Repertory Theatre.

Baddeley, Angela (1904–76) British actress, who appeared on stage as a child and made her first adult appearance in *The Beggar's Opera* at the Lyric Theatre, Hammersmith in 1920. Subsequent successes included the title role in Allen Harker's *Marigold* (1927), *The Greeks Had a Word for It* (1934) by Zoë Akins, in which she appeared with her sister, Dodie Smith's *Dear Octopus* (1938), and Rattigan's *The Winslow Boy* (1946). She also appeared in Shakespearean productions and several musicals. She was married to Glen Byam Shaw.

Her sister, **Hermione Baddeley** (1906–86), began as an actress in such acclaimed revues as *On With the Dance* (1925) and *Still Dancing* (1926) before appearing in straight drama. She then went on to perform in such plays as *When Crummles Played* (1927) by Nigel Playfair, Wycherley's *The Country Wife* (1940), Greene's *Brighton Rock* (1943), and Coward's *Fallen Angels* (1949). Successes in the US included Shelagh Delaney's *A Taste of Honey* (1961) and *The Milk Train Doesn't Stop Here Anymore* (1964) by Tennessee Williams.

Baddeley, Robert (1732–94) British actor, who appeared regularly at Drury Lane. Prior to his stage debut in 1760 he was a gentleman's gentleman, touring the Continent and so acquiring a firsthand knowledge of foreign accents. A noted character actor, he created the part of Moses in *The School for Scandal*. The last actor habitually to wear the Royal Livery off the stage, he left a capital sum to provide a cake and wine to be consumed annually on Twelfth Night by the company at Drury Lane. His wife was the actress Sophia SNOW.

Badel, Alan (Firman) (1923–82) British actor, who played numerous classical roles at the Old Vic and at Stratford, including Romeo to Claire Bloom's Juliet (1952), Lovborg in *Hedda Gabler* (1954), and Hamlet (1956). Subsequently he both directed and acted in *The Public Prosecutor* (1957) at the Arts Theatre and *Ulysses in Nighttown* (1959). In 1971 he was much admired in Sartre's *Kean*.

Bagnold, Enid (Lady Jones; 1889–1981) British playwright and novelist, whose best-known work for the stage was *The Chalk Garden* (1955), in which Peggy Ashcroft and Edith Evans both appeared. Other plays included adaptations of her novels *Serena Blandish* (1929), in which Vivien Leigh performed, *Lottie Dundass* (1943), and *National Velvet* (1946), and the three later plays *The Last Joke* (1960), *The Chinese Prime Minister* (1964), and *Call Me Jacky* (1967).

Bahr, Hermann (1863–1934) Austrian writer, whose literary output encompassed a wide range of critical works and essays and almost 80 naturalistic plays. Of these the most notable were *Das Tschaperl* (1898) and the polished urbane farce *Daz Konzert* (1910); he became director at the Deutsches Theater in Berlin in 1906.

Bailey, Pearl (1918–90) US actress, who began her career in vaudeville in 1933. She made her Broadway debut 13 years later as Butterfly in *St Louis Woman*; subsequent roles include Madam Fleur in *House of Flowers* (1954) but she remained best known for her cabaret work. Her Dolly in the all-Black *Hello Dolly!* (1967) is credited with creating a new interest in Broadway among the Black community.

Baird, Dorothea (1875–1933) British actress, who made her first appearance in 1894. She won instant fame in 1895 in the title role of Du Maurier's *Trilby* at the Haymarket; she was married to Henry Brodribb IRVING.

Bajazet A tragedy by Jean RACINE. First performance: Paris, 1672. The play is set in Constantinople in 1638; Bajazet, the sultan's brother, is obliged to marry the powerful Roxane in order to win the throne. When Roxane learns of Bajazet's love for the young princess Atalide, she has him killed.

Baker, George Pierce (1866–1935) US theatre scholar, who did much to promote new writing for the US theatre. His pupils at Harvard, where he also founded the influential '47 Workshop, included Edward Sheldon and Eugene O'Neill; subsequently (from 1925) he continued his important work at Yale.

Baker, Sarah (c. 1736–1816) British actress and manager. After her husband's death in 1769, she developed her own touring circuit in Kent, with her three children – one of whom married the actor William Dowton – all taking part. She presented both comedies and tragedies and built 10 theatres to present them in.

Bakst, Léon (Lev Samoylovich Rosenberg; 1866–1924) Russian artist, who had a profound effect upon both costume and scenery design in the early 20th century. He executed his earliest works for the theatre in 1900 and later won fame for his non-naturalistic designs for Diaghilev's ballets; later he also designed productions of the tragedies of D'Annunzio and plays presented at the Paris Opéra.

Balanchine, George (1904–83) US choreographer; although best known for classical ballet, he worked extensively on Broadway in the 1930s and 1940s. With *On Your Toes* (1936) he was the first person listed as 'choreographer' for a musical comedy.

balcony *See* auditorium.

Balcony, The (*Le Balcon*) A play by Jean GENET. First performance: London, 1957. The play collapses the distinction between illusion and reality, as the roles played by the clients of a brothel are suddenly translated to the outside world.

Bald Prima Donna, The (*La Cantatrice chauve*) A one-act play by Eugène IONESCO. First performance: Paris, 1950. It was staged in London in translation in 1956 and in New York, as *The Bald Soprano*, in 1958. A pioneering work in the Theatre of the Absurd, the play depicts the meaningless existence of two married couples.

Bale, John (1495–1563) English playwright, who became Bishop of Ossory in Ireland. He wrote 21 plays in defence of Protestantism and established a company of travelling actors. He employed the interlude for propaganda purposes and presented moral abstractions alongside specific figures from history in his major work, *Kynge Johan* (c. 1538), which was probably the first historical play in English.

Balieff, Nikita (1877–1936) Russian director, who produced a number of celebrated revues in Paris in the early 20th century. His elaborate shows began with *Le Chauve-Souris* (The Bat) in 1908 and included humorous sketches and songs as well as highly popular appearances by Balieff himself. From 1921 his shows were staged in London by C B Cochran and from 1922 also in New York but closed shortly after Balieff's death.

Ball, William (1931–91) US actor and director, who made his stage debut in *Uncle Vanya*, *Candida*, and *Hamlet* (1948). He toured with Margaret Webster and later appeared at various Shakespeare Festivals and elsewhere, directing and acting in plays by Molière, Pinero, Arthur Miller, Chekhov, and many others. In 1965 he founded the AMERICAN CONSERVATORY THEATRE, which he managed till 1986.

ballad opera A form of musical drama, popular in the 18th century, in which spoken dialogue was interspersed with songs set to contemporary tunes. Gay's *The Beggar's Opera* (1728) was the most celebrated example and was typical of the genre in having a distinctly satirical air, originally intended as a parody of Italian opera but also lampooning various political targets. Garrick, Fielding, Colly Cibber, Sheridan, and Thomas Jevon all composed such works, Jevon's *The Devil to Pay* (1731) when performed in Germany inspiring the development of the parallel *Singspiele* tradition there.

Ballard, Sarah   *See* Terry, Benjamin.

Balsam, Martin (1919–96)   US actor, who made his professional debut in *The Play's the Thing* (1941). After World War II, he toured as Norman in *Wedding Breakfast* (1955) and, in 1961, appeared in *The Iceman Cometh*. He also won awards for his performance in *You Know I Can't Hear You When the Water's Running* (1967).

Bałucki, Michał (1837–1901)   Polish playwright, author of several bourgeois comedies influenced by Aleksander Fredro. His plays include *Big Shots* (1881) and *The Bachelors' Club* (1890), both of which owed much to Fredro's *Ladies and Hussars* (1825).

Balzac, Honoré de (1799–1850)   French novelist and playwright, born in Tours. Balzac is remembered chiefly for his prose works: his plays had little success. *Vautrin* (1840), which was based on his novel *Le Père Goriot*, was banned after its first performance; *Les Ressources de Quinola* (1842) and *Paméla Giraud* (1843) both had relatively short runs. *La Marâtre*, forced to close by the Revolution of 1848, showed more potential, and *Mercadet* (1851), produced after Balzac's death, has received critical acclaim.

BAM   *See* Brooklyn Academy of Music.

Banbury, Frith (1912–)   British actor, director, and manager, who made his first appearance in *If I Were You* at the Shaftesbury Theatre in 1933, then appeared in numerous modern comedies and revues, including *Goodness, How Sad!* (1938), *New Faces* (1940), and *Uncle Vanya* (1943). He subsequently directed productions by Rattigan, Nichols, and many others in London, New York, and other parts of the world.

Bances Candamo, Francisco Antonio (c. 1662–1704)   Spanish playwright, author of the *Teatro de los teatros de los pasados y presentes siglos*, an early account of the Spanish theatre. His plays, notably *Por su Rey y por su dama* (1685), were influenced by Calderón.

Bancroft, Anne (1931–)   US actress, who trained at the American Academy of Dramatic Arts and the Actors' Studio before winning awards in *Two for the See-Saw* (1958). In 1959 she was acclaimed in *The Miracle Worker*; but has subsequently worked mainly in film. Later stage roles include Mother Courage (1963), Regina Giddens in Lillian Hellman's *The Little Foxes* (1967), and Golda Meir in *Golda* (1977). She is married to the film director Mel Brooks.

Bancroft, Sir Squire (1841–1926)   British actor-manager who made his first stage appearance in Birmingham in 1861. After four years touring he went into partnership with **Marie Effie Wilton** (1839–1921), reopening the old Queen's Theatre in 1865 as the Prince of Wales's (*see* Scala Theatre). In 1867 they married and went on to enjoy a long period of success, particularly with the naturalistic plays of T W Robertson. They did much to raise the status of the profession, paying higher salaries and insisting upon improved standards of acting. They retired in 1885 after five years at the Haymarket. Squire Bancroft also became president of the Royal Academy of Dramatic Art, where his name is commemorated by the Bancroft Gold Medal. He was knighted in 1897.

Bandbox Theatre A theatre on East 57th Street, New York, which originally opened as the Adolph Phillip Theatre in 1912 and was renamed the Bandbox Theatre in 1914. It was the New York venue for the Washington Square Players from 1915 until 1917, when it closed.

Bankhead, Tallulah (Brockman) (1902–68) US actress, well known for her eccentric private life as well as for her stage performances. She made her first New York appearance in *The Squab Farm* (1918), then went to London and remained there until 1930. Back in the US she was admired in a wide variety of roles, including Sadie Thompson in *Rain* (1935), Cleopatra in *Antony and Cleopatra* (1937), Regina Giddens in *The Little Foxes* (1939), Sabina in *The Skin of Our Teeth* (1942), Queen in *The Eagle Has Two Heads* (1947), and Blanche du Bois in a revival of *A Streetcar Named Desire*.

Bankrupt, The (*Bankrot*) A play by Alexander OSTROVSKY. First performance: 1849. Written when the author was 25 years old, the play exposed fraudulent practices involving bogus bankruptcies among the traders of Moscow. This resulted in Ostrovsky's dismissal from the Civil Service and the banning of the play for 13 years.

Banks, Leslie (1890–1952) British actor, who first appeared with Benson's company in 1911. Later he was at the Birmingham Repertory Theatre and also with the Lena Ashwell Players (1919–20). A versatile actor, his parts ranged from Captain Hook in New York (1924) to Petruchio opposite Edith Evans (1937); he also appeared in Gielgud's classical season at the Haymarket (1944–45) and directed several plays. From the early 1930s he also appeared in films.

Bankside Players *See* Atkins, Robert.

Bannister, Jack (1760–1836) British actor, son of the comedian Charles Bannister (1741–1804). He appeared for the first time at his father's benefit at the Haymarket in 1778. He then moved to Drury Lane, where he became a leading comedy actor. Sir Anthony Absolute and Tony Lumpkin were two of his most celebrated roles. He also collaborated with George Colman the Younger on his one-man show *Bannister's Budget*. In 1783 he married **Elizabeth Harper** (1757–1849), principal singer at the Haymarket until 1793.

Banvard's Museum *See* Daly's Theatre.

Baptiste *See* Deburau, Jean-Gaspard.

Baraka, (Imamu) Amiri (Leroi Jones; 1934–) US playwright and poet, who was active in the development of Black theatre. His plays, mostly in the agit-prop tradition, include *Dante* (1962), *Black Mass* (1966), *The Great Goodness of Life (A Coon Show)* (1968), *Sidnee Poet Heroical* (1975), which he also directed, and *The Motion of History* (1977).

Barbican Centre A public entertainments complex in the City of London, named after part of the capital's Roman fortifications. Built on a bombsite from World War II, it was opened in 1982. The Centre includes an art gallery, a concert hall, three cinemas, and two theatres – the **Barbican Theatre**, seating 1166, and a smaller studio theatre, **The Pit**, seating 200. The Barbican is the London home of the Royal Shakespeare Company; productions are given in repertory throughout the year, many of them transferring from Stratford-on-Avon.

Barbican Nursery *See* nurseries.

Barbieri, Niccolò (1576–1641) Italian actor and playwright, who probably created the character of Scapino in the *commedia dell'arte*. Using the stage name **Beltrame**, he appeared with the Gelosi and the Fideli before finally joining the Confidenti; his play *L'Inavertito* (1629) influenced Molière's *L'Étourdi*.

Bard, Wilkie (William Augustus Smith; 1874–1944) British music hall comedian, who made his London debut at Collins's Music Hall in 1895. He was famous for his tongue-twisting songs, notably 'She Sells Sea-Shells on the Sea-Shore', and played Pantaloon in pantomime harlequinades.

Barefoot in the Park A comedy by Neil SIMON. First performance: 1963. The play concerns a newlywed couple who rent an apartment in New York but then undergo marital strain as the result of overwork and visits from eccentric neighbours and relations. The play was filmed starring Robert Redford and Jane Fonda in 1967.

barker A person employed by a theatrical company performing at a fair or other similar event to attract an audience to a show. Such barkers were employed in classical times and subsequently became a common feature of fairgrounds throughout Europe and the US.

Barker, Harley Granville- *See* Granville-Barker, Harley.

Barker, Howard (1946–) British playwright, who established his reputation as a prominent writer for the fringe theatre while associated with the Royal Court Theatre during the 1970s. His plays, many of which have historical settings, are preoccupied with violence and corruption; his style is deliberately rhetorical and antinaturalistic. *Cheek* and *No One Was Saved* were his first plays to reach the stage (1970); subsequent works have included *Claw* (1975), *The Love of a Good Man* (1980), *The Poor Man's Friend* (1981), which was written for an enormous cast, *The Castle* (1985), *Scenes from an Execution* (1989), and *A Hard Heart* (1992).

Barkworth, Peter (1929–) British actor, who made his London debut in Dodie Smith's *Letter from Paris* (1952). Since then his parts have included Captain Mortlock in Coward's *South Sea Bubble* (1956), Edward VIII in Royce Ryton's *Crown Matrimonial* (1972), and Headingly in Michael Frayn's *Donkeys' Years* (1976). In 1987 he had a great success in a solo performance as Siegfried Sassoon, presented in the West End and on a national tour. More recent work has included Rattigan's *The Winslow Boy* (1994).

Barlach, Ernst (1870–1938) German sculptor and playwright, who was the author of several notable Expressionist dramas. His mystical Gothic plays, which included *Der tote Tag* (The Dead Day; 1919), *Der arme Vetter* (The Poor Cousin; 1919), and *Der Findling* (The Foundling; 1922), tackled such themes as the tension between God and the world and the relationship shared by a father and son.

barn door shutters A pair (or more) of spotlight shutters, used to adjust the size and shape of the beam thrown onto the stage.

Barnes, Clive Alexander (1927–) British theatre and dance critic, writing for the *New York Times* from 1965 to 1978 and the *New York Post* since 1978. His hugely influential reviews have often proved controversial, notably for his supposed prejudice against commercial Broadway productions. He has also written for *Dance and Dancers* and *The Spectator*.

Barnes, Sir Kenneth *See* Royal Academy of Dramatic Art.

Barnes, Peter (1931–) British playwright, who first attracted attention with the eccentric comedy *The Ruling Class* in 1968. Since then he has written further unconventional comedies, including *Leonardo's Last Supper* (1969), *The Bewitched* (1973), *Laughter!* (1978), *Red Noses* (1985), and *Sunset and Glories* (1990). He has also adapted works by Jonson, Feydeau, and others, as well as writing widely for radio, television, and the cinema.

Barnes, Thomas (1785–1841) British journalist and theatre critic. Prior to his appointment as editor of *The Times* in 1817, he wrote theatre criticism for the *Examiner*, using the pen-name Criticus; his most important review was that of Kean's Shylock at Drury Lane in 1814.

Barnes Theatre A theatre in the Barnes district of London, opened in 1925. Early productions that attracted comment included Hardy's *Tess of the D'Urbervilles* (1925) and Chekhov's *Uncle Vanya* (1926), which were rapidly followed by a series of Russian dramas in which Gielgud, Laughton, and other leading actors appeared under the direction of Komisarjevsky. After diversifying with two of Drinkwater's plays, the theatre closed in late 1926.

barnstormer An actor who performs in a noisy declamatory style. The name comes from the touring companies who performed in barns and other makeshift theatres during the 19th century.

Barnum, Phineas Taylor (1810–91) US showman and impresario, founder of a famous circus and the AMERICAN MUSEUM in New York. He publicized the midget Charles Stratton, known as General Tom Thumb, while other attractions included a fake mermaid. His appreciation of the value of publicity foreshadows much of modern culture. The popular musical *Barnum* (1981) was based on his career.

Baron, André (c. 1601–55) French actor, who appeared at the Théâtre du Marais with Montdory's company before moving in 1641 to the Hôtel de Bourgogne. He excelled in both comedy and tragedy; his death, according to tradition, was caused by a wound from his own prop sword during a performance of Corneille's *Le Cid*.

His son by Jeanne Ausoult, **Michel Baron** (1653–1729), was also an actor, who first appeared on the stage in a boy company with Raisin and Jean de Villiers. Subsequently he was taken on by Molière, until a quarrel with the playwright's wife caused him to leave for a time. After Molière's death, Michel moved to the Hôtel de Bourgogne and appeared in plays by Racine. With his wife, the daughter of La Thorillière, he later joined the Comédie-Française and became the leading actor there. His own plays include *Le Rendez-vous de Tuilleries* (1685) and the comedy *L'Homme à bonne fortune* (1686). He was in retirement from 1691 to 1720, but then returned to repeat many of his most celebrated roles.

Barraca, La A Spanish theatre company, founded in 1931 to present classical works to audiences in the provinces. Properly called the Teatro Universitario, the company was led by García Lorca until the Spanish Civil War, after which it was disbanded.

Barrault, Jean-Louis (1910–94) French actor, director, and manager, who was first recognized as a leading theatrical figure after World War II. Having trained under Charles Dullin, he began his career at the Théâtre de l'Atelier in 1931 and subsequently assisted Antonin Artaud. He also studied mime under Étienne Decroux, employing this skill to good effect in his first independent production – an adaptation (with Camus) of Faulkner's *As I Lay Dying* – in 1935.

Subsequently he studied Molière and married the actress Madeleine Renaud, whom he met on joining the Comédie-Française under Copeau in 1940. There he appeared in several classic French dramas by Corneille, Racine, and others before founding his own company (the Compagnie Renaud-Barrault) in 1946 and moving into the Théâtre Marigny, where he remained for the next 10 years. As well as such classics as *Hamlet*, the company became famous for productions of plays by Claudel (notably *Christophe Colomb* in 1953), Feydeau, Marivaux, and many others, before eventually moving (1956) to the Théâtre Sarah Bernhardt, the Palais-Royal, and then the Odéon, where further notable productions included plays by Beckett, Genet, and Ionesco.

In 1968 Barrault's sympathetic attitude to the student riots led to his dismissal from the Odéon. He returned to the independent theatre and found immediate success with an extravaganza based on the novels of Rabelais; it was subsequently staged in Britain and the US to equal acclaim. He transferred to a new venue in 1972 and again in 1980, when he moved to the Théâtre du Rond Point, where he presented both new plays and revivals of earlier successes. His most famous performance as a mime actor was in the film *Les Enfants du Paradis* (1945), in which he impersonated DEBURAU.

barrel *See* batten.

Barrett, George Horton (1794–1860) US actor, who first attracted attention as a child on the New York stage in such roles as Home's Young Norval. Subsequently he excelled in the comedies of Sheridan, becoming known as Gentleman George on account of his refined manner.

Barrett, Lawrence (1838–91) US actor and producer, who was much admired in numerous classical roles, both in the US and in Britain, where he managed the Lyceum Theatre for a time. His greatest successes included Sheridan Knowles's *The Hunchback* (1857) and the part of Cassius in *Julius Caesar*.

Barrett, Wilson (1846–1904) British actor-manager, who, after some years in the provinces, established himself in London as a leading actor of melodrama. He became lessee of the Royal Court Theatre in 1879, staging successful productions by Henry Arthur Jones, before taking over the Princess's Theatre, where he remained for five years. His greatest success came in 1882 with the melodrama *The Silver King*. In 1895, he was acclaimed as Marcus Superbus in the pseudo-religious play *The Sign of the Cross*, which he wrote himself while in the US.

Barretts of Wimpole Street, The A play by Rudolf Besier. First performance: 1930. The plot is based on events that occurred in the house of Edward Moulton-Barrett, dominant father of the invalid poet Elizabeth, and culminates in her elopement with Robert Browning. The play enjoyed a huge success in the US, where Elizabeth was played by Katherine Cornell.

Barrie, Sir J(ames) M(atthew) (1860–1937) Scottish playwright and novelist, whose earliest theatrical successes were *The Professor's Love Story* (1894) and *The Little Minister* (1897), which was adapted from his own novel. His most famous work, PETER PAN (1904), is a whimsical fantasy; a similar note of sentimentality recurs in such plays as *A Kiss for Cinderella* (1916), *Dear Brutus* (1917), and *Mary Rose* (1920). His other works include the social comedies THE ADMIRABLE CRICHTON and WHAT EVERY WOMAN KNOWS, the period romance QUALITY STREET, and the mystery play *Shall We Join the Ladies?* (1922).

Barry, Elizabeth (1658–1713) English actress, who became Betterton's leading lady, appearing at Drury Lane, the Haymarket, and Lincoln's Inn Fields. Her numerous original roles included Belvidera in Otway's *Venice Preserv'd*, Isabella in Southerne's *The Fatal Marriage*, and Lady Brute in *The Provoked Wife*. She was the first English actress to receive a benefit performance and retired in 1710. Although never married, she was the subject of numerous scandals.

Barry, Philip (1896–1949) US playwright, whose first professional production, *You and I*, illustrated a father's attempt to live out his artistic dreams through his son. He followed this with *Cock Robin* and *Holiday* (both 1928), *Hotel Universe* (1930), *The Animal Kingdom* (1932), and *Here Come the Clowns* (1938). His play *The Philadelphia Story* was extremely popular and was successfully adapted for the screen. Later plays included *Liberty Jones* (1941), *Without Love* (1942), and *The Foolish Notion* (1945).

Barry, Sebastian (1955–) Irish playwright and author. His first play, *The Pentagonal Dream* (1986), was followed by *Boss Grady's Boys* (1988) and *Prayers of Sherkin* (1990), both of which were staged at the Abbey Theatre. In 1995 *The Steward of Christendom* was presented at London's Royal Court Theatre to universal acclaim; the play explores the Irish 'Troubles' of 1919–23 through the anguished memories of a Catholic policeman, now a psychiatric patient. Barry's most recent plays are *The True History of Lizzie Finn* (1995) and the lyrical *Our Lady of Sligo* (1998), which was premiered at the Royal National Theatre. He has also written novels and poetry.

Barry, Spranger (1719–77) Irish actor, who repeated his first success as Othello (at the Smock Alley Theatre, Dublin, 1744) when he came to Drury Lane in 1746. When he and Garrick appeared together they proved a highly popular attraction. In 1750, however, Barry transferred to Covent Garden and the two great actors became rivals, appearing in simultaneous productions of such plays as *Romeo and Juliet* and *King Lear*. A disastrous investment by Barry in a new Dublin theatre in 1758 forced him to move to the Haymarket; in 1766 he was again engaged by Garrick. Two years later he married Ann DANCER.

Barrymore, Maurice (Herbert Blythe; 1847–1905) British actor, born in India, who made his London debut in 1875. As well as his London appearances, notably at the Haymarket, he worked in the US, later especially in vaudeville, until forced to give up through mental instability. He was also the author of several plays. By his marriage to Georgina DREW he was the father of the famous Barrymore trio, Lionel, Ethel, and John.

Lionel Barrymore (1878–1954) was the eldest child and made his stage debut at the age of 15. Subsequently he was much admired in New York in plays by George

Du Maurier and others although he failed as Macbeth. After 1925 he abandoned the stage for a successful film career.

Lionel's sister, **Ethel Barrymore** (1879–1959), established her reputation as as an excellent US actress with her performance in Clyde Fitch's *Captain Jinks of the Horse Marines* (1901) in New York. This was followed by the lead in *Cousin Kate* (1903) by H H Davies and the role of Nora in *A Doll's House*, in which her brother also appeared. Her Shakespearean roles included Juliet, Ophelia, and Portia, while beauty and intelligence also ensured her success in plays by Pinero, Dumas *fils*, and many others. In 1928 the ETHEL BARRYMORE THEATRE opened with a performance by her in Martínez Sierra's *The Kingdom of God*; roles late in life included Gran in *Whiteoaks* (1938) by Mazo de la Roche and Miss Moffat in Emlyn Williams's *The Corn Is Green* (1940).

Lionel's younger brother, **John Barrymore** (1882–1942), first appeared as an as actor in 1903 as Max in *Magda*. After success in J M Barrie's *Pantaloon* (1905) and W S Gilbert's *The Fortune Hunter* (1909) he became highly popular, although it was not until 1916, when he played Falder in Galsworthy's *Justice*, that he was recognized as a serious actor. Subsequent major roles included the lead in George Du Maurier's *Peter Ibbetson* (1917), Fedor in *The Living Corpse* (1918), Giannetto Malespini in *The Jest* (1919), and, from 1922, Hamlet, which was considered his finest part and provided him with a record-breaking run of 101 performances. Later in life he appeared in films but suffered from alcoholism.

Barrymore, Richard Barry, Earl of (1760–93) British theatre enthusiast, who owned a small puppet theatre in Savile Row, London. He built the first indoor private theatre in England at his house in Wargrave, Berkshire but the upkeep ruined him financially and the theatre was demolished in 1792.

Barrymore, William (1759–1830) British actor and author of several melodramas. His *Trial by Battle; or, Heaven Defend the Right* was the first play presented at the Old Vic (then the Royal Coburg) in 1818.

Barsacq, André (1909–73) French director and manager, born in the Crimea, who began his career under Dullin at the Théâtre de l'Atelier. After attracting attention with such productions as Jonson's *Volpone* (1928), he founded (1937) a travelling company, the Compagnie des Quatre Saisons, with Jean Dasté and went on to produce almost all the works of Jean Anouilh by 1953. After World War II he succeeded Dullin at the Atelier, where he presented numerous works by new playwrights as well as many Russian classics.

Bart, Lionel (Lionel Begleiter; 1930–99) British composer and lyricist, whose first musical, *Wally Pone* (1958), was written for the Unity Theatre. The following year he wrote the lyrics for the musical *Lock Up Your Daughters* and the songs for *Fings Ain't Wot They Used t'Be* before achieving international success with OLIVER!, which was based on Dickens. After further success with *Blitz!* (1962) and *Maggie May* (1964), his career foundered with the failure of *Twang!!* (1965) and *La Strada* (1969).

Barter Theatre A theatre in Abingdon, Virginia, which was founded during the Depression, opened in 1933. The name comes from the theatre's original practice of trading tickets for services and meals for the actors. Seating 380, it became the official state theatre of Virginia in 1946. A second theatre, the Barter Playhouse, was built in 1971 to house both classical and contemporary plays. The company offers extensive theatrical services to a rural area not usually considered sympathetic to the stage.

Bartholomew Fair A prose comedy by Ben JONSON, written to be acted at court on St Bartholomew's Day. First performance: 1614. A kaleidoscope of brief scenes, the play presents numerous characters in the crowd at the Smithfield Fair and satirizes the extravagant behaviour of traders, showmen, gamblers, and the hypocritical Puritan Zeal-of-the-land Busy.

Barton, John (1928–) British director and playwright, who became famous for his interpretations of Shakespeare's historical dramas at Stratford-on-Avon in the 1960s. Previously a director with the Marlowe Society and the Amateur Dramatic Club at Cambridge, he won great acclaim for such RSC productions as *The Taming of the Shrew* (1964), *The Wars of the Roses* cycle (1963), and *Henry IV* as *When Thou Art King* (1969). Later productions have included *The Greeks* cycle (1979) from the plays of Euripides and others, *The Vikings at Helgeland* at Den Nationale Scene in Berlin in 1983, and a small-scale *Peer Gynt* (1993). He was an associate director of the RSC from 1964 to 1991 and is now an advisory director.

Barton's TANTALUS, an epic cycle of plays based on the legends of the Trojan Wars that had been many years in gestation, was finally staged in the USA in 2000.

Bassermann, August (1848–1931) German actor and manager, who excelled in the tragedies of Schiller and others. He became manager of the Manheim Theatre in 1886 and later ran a theatre in Karlsruhe and visited New York to further acclaim.

His nephew, **Albert Bassermann** (1867–1952), was also an actor and became one of the leading interpreters of naturalistic drama. He made his debut at Mannheim and later appeared under Max Reinhardt and Otto Brahm in Berlin, where he excelled in the plays of Ibsen. He was also highly successful in works by Goethe, Schiller, and Shakespeare, notably as Lear and Shylock. He emigrated to the US in the 1930s, appearing in films before returning to Europe in 1945.

Batalov, Nikolai Petrovich (1899–1937) Russian actor, who established his reputation in comic roles with the Moscow Art Theatre, which he joined in 1916. Subsequently he also showed a talent for satire, his most successful parts including Beaumarchais's Figaro and roles in the plays of Ivanov, notably Vasska Okorka in *Armoured Train 14–69*.

Bateman, Hezekiah Linthicum (1812–75) US impresario, who was the head of a notable theatrical family. Having married the daughter of Joseph Cowell, he did much to further the careers of his daughters and, while lessee of the Lyceum Theatre in London, presented Henry Irving in *The Bells* with enormous success.

His eldest daughter, **Kate Josephine Bateman** (Mrs George Crowe; 1842–1917), first acted as a child under her father in 1847. Subsequently she toured the US and Britain in many Shakespearean parts and plays by other authors, most notably in Daly's *Leah the Forsaken* (1863) in which she appeared opposite Henry Irving. Successes at the Lyceum included *Othello*, *Richard III*, and Tennyson's *Queen Mary*.

Hezekiah Bateman's second daughter, **Virginia Frances Bateman** (1843–1940), made her adult debut as an actress at the Haymarket in 1868. Later she also appeared at the Lyceum, married (1882) Edward COMPTON, and helped to run the Compton Comedy Company.

Hezekiah's third daughter, **Isabel Emilie Bateman** (1854–1934), first appeared on stage as an adult under her father at the Lyceum Theatre in 1871. She was much admired in such intense roles as Ophelia and Desdemona, both opposite Henry Irving, despite her dislike for theatre in general. Subsequently she ran the Sadler's Wells Theatre for a time before eventually retiring in 1898 to become a nun.

Bates, Alan (1934–) British actor, who established his reputation in 1956 as Cliff Lewis in *Look Back in Anger* at the Royal Court. Subsequently he appeared in plays by O'Neill, Pinter (notably as Mick in *The Caretaker* in 1960), and Storey and acted in films and on television. Other successes have included various Shakespearean roles, Solness in Ibsen's *The Master Builder* (1995) and performances in *Butley* (1971), *Otherwise Engaged* (1975), *Stage Struck* (1979), *Melon* (1987), and *Life Support* (1997) – all by Simon Gray.

Bathyllus (1st century BC) A celebrated writer and *pantomimus* of ancient Rome. Together with Pylades he contributed greatly (as a performer of comic roles) to the popularity of the mime dance tradition.

batten A length of wood or metal used to strengthen a flat or to hang lighting or scenery from. A metal batten may also be referred to as a **barrel** or **spot bar** in Britain and as a **pipe** (**pipe batten**) in the US. Light battens, when comprising a number of lights mounted in a row of compartments, are known as **compartment battens** or **magazine battens** in Britain and as **strip lights** or **border lights** in the US. Positioned immediately behind the proscenium arch, they are used primarily for colour mixing.

Baty, Gaston (1885–1952) French director and playwright, who established his reputation with a series of plays in which great emphasis was placed upon the pictorial aspects of the production. Having opened a theatre in his own name in 1930, he staged a combination of both new plays and classics, of which the most notable included Dostoevsky's *Crime and Punishment* (1938) and plays by Jean-Jacques Bernard. He joined the Comédie-Française in 1936; of his own plays the most successful was *Dulcinée* (1938), which was loosely based on *Don Quixote* by Cervantes.

Bauer, Wolfang (1941–) Austrian playwright noted for his brutal comedies, several of which revive the traditions of the German folk-play. One of a number of young Graz-based writers in the local dialect to emerge in the late 1960s, he won attention with such plays as *Sylvester oder das Massaker im Hotel Sacher* (Sylvester or the Massacre in Hotel Sacher; 1971), *Film und Frau* (1971), which was performed in London in 1972 as *Shakespeare the Sadist*, and *Magnetic Kisses* (1976).

Bäuerle, Adolf (1786–1859) Austrian playwright, who introduced the character STABERL to the Viennese stage in the play *Die Bürger in Wien* (1813). Inspired by the popularity of Staberl when played by Ignaz Schuster, Bäuerle went on to write a further four plays around him as well as numerous other plays based on fairy tales.

Bauernfeld, Eduard von (1802–90) Austrian playwright, whose numerous light comedies depicting Viennese society dominated the Vienna Burgtheater for many years. A friend of Grillparzer and Schubert, he discussed social and political issues in such successful plays as *Das Liebes-Protokoll* (1834) and *Aus der Gesellschaft* (1867).

Bausch, Pina (1940–) German choreographer and director, famous for her experimental works combining dance with theatre. After training at the Juilliard School in New York and working as a dancer, she returned to Germany and established the Wuppertal Dance Theatre in 1973. Her work for the company has included radical adaptations of classic plays and ballets, as well as a series of original pieces that explore themes of emotional disturbance and isolation. These include *Bluebeard* (1977), *Nelken* (1982), and *Nur Du* (1996).

Baxter, Anne (1923–85) US actress, who made her New York debut in 1936. From 1940 onwards she worked mainly in the cinema. Later she toured the US with Raymond Massey in *John Brown's Body* (1953) and appeared on Broadway in *The Square Root of Wonderful* (1957) and *Applause* (1971).

Baylis, Lilian (1874–1937) British theatre manageress, who founded the Old Vic and new Sadler's Wells theatres and became famous for her devotion to the London stage between the wars. She first appeared on stage as a child and later toured in South Africa; in 1912 she established the Old Vic (originally a temperance music hall run by her aunt, Emma Cons) as a leading venue for Shakespearean productions, subsequently presenting the whole canon between 1914 and 1923, including uncut versions of *Hamlet*. Her productions of Shakespeare were acclaimed for their simplicity and, especially in later years, for the high standard of acting; other playwrights whose work was performed there included Ibsen. In 1931 she reopened the old Sadler's Wells Theatre as a venue for ballet, the companies under her charge eventually becoming the Royal Ballet and the English National Opera.

Bayreuth A town in Bavaria, Germany, in which Richard Wagner established his famous Festspielhaus in 1876. Based on designs by the architect **Gottfried Semper** (1803–79), the starkly simple layout of the auditorium had a profound effect upon subsequent theatre building.

Beale, Simon Russell (1961–) British actor. Born in Malaysia, he trained as a singer before moving into fringe theatre in the 1980s. From 1986 to 1996 he performed with the Royal Shakespeare Company, making his reputation in roles that included Konstantin in *The Seagull* (1990), Ariel in *The Tempest* (1993), and Oswald in *Ghosts* (1994). Subsequently he joined the Royal National Theatre Company, for whom he gave award-winning performances as Iago in *Othello* (1997) and Pangloss in *Candide* (1999). His Hamlet, given at the National in 2000, was hailed as one of the best interpretations of recent times.

Bear Gardens Museum A theatre museum in Bankside, London, founded close to the site of the Globe Theatre by Sam Wanamaker in 1972. The museum specializes in the drama of Shakespeare and his contemporaries.

Beaton, Sir Cecil (1904–80) British stage designer and photographer, who was knighted in 1972. Having produced designs for a number of ballets and revues, he designed the costumes and scenery for numerous London productions, including Gielgud's production of *Lady Windermere's Fan* (1945) and Coward's *Quadrille* (1952). After 1954 he worked chiefly for the New York stage, achieving his greatest success with his designs for the musical *My Fair Lady* (1956), which also appeared in the film version.

Beaubour, Pierre Tronchon de (1662–1725) French actor, who succeeded Baron as a member of the Comédie-Française in 1691. He was criticized for his inclination to rant in tragedy and, according to contemporary sources, would probably have been more successful as a comic actor.

Beauchâteau (François Chastelet; d. c. 1665) French actor, who acted at the Hôtel de Bourgogne until 1634 and then appeared at the Théâtre de Marais before returning to the Bourgogne in 1642. He and his wife, **Madeleine de Pouget** (1615–83), were later satirized by Molière in *L'Impromptu de Versailles* (1664) and criticized by others for their sentimental performances.

Beaumarchais, Pierre-Augustin Caron de (1732–99) French playwright, born in Paris. The son of André-Charles Caron, a clockmaker, Beaumarchais acquired his new surname and a position at the court of Louis XV through his first marriage. Having served for a time as music teacher to the king's daughters, he was able to buy himself into higher office as a result of successful financial speculations, which ultimately led to litigation and scandal. He subsequently undertook secret diplomatic missions for the king, sold arms to American revolutionaries, published the first complete edition of Voltaire's works, and faced exile and imprisonment during the Revolution.

His earliest dramatic works, a series of *parades* (sketches), were followed by the unremarkable *Eugénie* and *Les Deux Amis*. His comedies of intrigue, *The Barber of Seville* and THE MARRIAGE OF FIGARO, were extremely successful, however, and were used as bases for libretti by Rossini and Mozart, respectively.

Principal works:

Eugénie: 1767.
Les Deux Amis ou le Négociant de Lyon: 1770.
Le Barbier de Séville: 1775; translated as *The Barber of Seville*.
Le Mariage de Figaro ou la Folle Journée: 1874; translated as *The Marriage of Figaro*.
La Mère coupable: 1792.

Beauménard, Rose-Petronelle le Roy (1730–99) French actress, wife of the actor Bellecour. She excelled in plays by Molière while with the Comédie-Française from 1749 and became highly popular; she also appeared in plays by Marivaux, Favart, and Beaumarchais with varying success. An attempted comeback after she was ruined financially by the Revolution was a failure.

Beaumont, Sir Francis (1584–1616) English playwright, who is usually remembered for his successful collaboration on several plays with John Fletcher. Before meeting Fletcher in 1605, he had already achieved success with *The Woman Hater* (1606), repeating it with the satirical THE KNIGHT OF THE BURNING PESTLE. With Fletcher he wrote at least half a dozen plays, including *Philaster; or, Love Lies Bleeding* (1609), *The Maid's Tragedy* (1610), and *A King and No King* (1611). Beaumont retired as a playwright on his marriage in 1613.

Beauval (Jean Pitel; c. 1635–1709) French actor, who appeared with Molière's company in such plays as *Le Malade Imaginaire*. Never regarded as a particularly gifted actor himself, his wife – the daughter of Filandre – was nevertheless a popular comic actress. When Molière died husband and wife moved to the Hôtel de Bourgogne and later became part of the Comédie-Française.

Beaux' Stratagem, The A comedy by George FARQUHAR. First performance: 1707. The plot revolves around two young gentlemen, Archer and Aimwell, who pretend to be master and servant in the hope of furthering their fortunes in love and money. The play, which introduced the character Lady Bountiful, has been frequently revived.

Beazley, Samuel (1786–1851) British architect and playwright. He was responsible for the Lyceum Theatre, St James's Theatre, the Adelphi frontage, and the colonnade of Drury Lane. He was also author of several farces and short comedies.

Beccari, Agostino (d. 1598) Italian playwright, noted for his pastoral *Il Sacrifizio* (c. 1544). Performed before the royal court at Ferrara, it may have had a strong influence upon the subsequent works of Tasso.

Beck, Heinrich (1760–1803) German actor, who made early appearances in Ekhof's company before transferring to Mannheim in 1778. There he performed in plays by Schiller and ventured into theatre management with Iffland.

Beck, Julian *See* Living Theatre.

Becket, or the Honour of God (*Becket ou l'Honneur de Dieu*) A *pièce costumée* by Jean ANOUILH. First performance: Paris, 1959. The play is based on Thomas à Becket's relationship with Henry II, culminating in Becket's martyrdom and Henry's penitence.

Beckett, Samuel (1906–89) Irish playwright and novelist, who in 1927 moved to Paris where he worked for James Joyce and began writing poetry and novels. He remained an inhabitant of Paris for most of the rest of his life – indeed, some of his best-known works were written in French. In his first performed play, WAITING FOR GODOT, and its successor, ENDGAME, he attempted to explore a genuinely new territory for the theatre, abandoning such basic elements as plot, action, and character in his examination of the human predicament.

Regarded as the leading writer for the Theatre of the Absurd, he became widely known for his unique combination of nihilism and humour, his characters being torn between the pointlessness of their lives and their seemingly inexhaustible instinct to keep going. The later works (including several radio plays) show a progression towards a far more private and more confined world in which the characters are barely capable of communication. *Not I*, *Footfalls*, and *Rockaby* are all monologues for women. Beckett was awarded a Nobel Prize in 1969.

Principal dramatic works:
En attendant Godot: 1953; translated as *Waiting for Godot*.
Fin de partie: 1957; translated as *Endgame*.
KRAPP'S LAST TAPE: 1958.
HAPPY DAYS: 1961.
Play: 1963.
Breath: 1969.
Not I: 1971.
That Time: 1976.
Footfalls: 1976.
Ghost Trio: 1976.
…But the Clouds…: 1977.
A Piece of Monologue: 1980.

Rockaby: 1980.
Ohio Impromptu: 1981.
Quad: 1982.
Catastrophe: 1982.
Nacht und Traüme: 1983.
What Where: 1983.

Becque, Henry François (1837–99) French playwright, associated with naturalism. Becque's plays, produced at André Antoine's Théâtre Libre, were not fully appreciated by their first audiences. *Les Corbeaux* (1882; translated as *The Vultures*, 1913) is a powerful drama of greed and opportunism, while the comedy *La Parisienne* (1885; translated as *The Woman of Paris*, 1955) centres on the amorality of the heroine.

Bedford Music Hall A theatre in Camden, London, that was opened in 1861 and enjoyed a long career as a venue for music hall entertainments. Seating 1168, it saw appearances by George Leybourne and Marie Lloyd among many others; it was later used for revivals of popular plays for a time before being demolished in 1969.

bedroom farce A broad comedy in which much of the action centres about one or more bedrooms. Such farces commonly exploit mistaken identity, lost clothing, and sexual innuendo for comic effect and have proved an important part of the staple diet of the commercial theatre in the 20th century.

Bedroom Farce A farce by Alan AYCKBOURN. First performance: National Theatre, London, 1977. A bleak suburban comedy, the action revolves around three married couples and takes place in their respective bedrooms, which are presented simultaneously on the stage.

Beekman Street Theatre *See* Chapel Street Theatre.

Beerbohm, Sir (Henry) Max(imilian) (1872–1956) British playwright and theatre critic, who succeeded G B Shaw as drama critic for the *Saturday Review* in 1898. He wrote vividly about a wide range of dramatic productions and was the author of several successful plays, notably *The Happy Hypocrite* (1900), a novel, and short stories. His drama criticism was collected in *Around Theatre* (1953) and *More Theatres* (1968). In 1908 he married the actress Florence Kahn; Herbert Tree was his half-brother.

Beeston, Christopher (c. 1570–1638) English actor and manager, who was a member of Strange's Men at the outset of his career and, possibly, also appeared with the Chamberlain's Men. He was at the Rose Theatre in 1602, but gave up acting when he became manager of the Cockpit in 1616. He remained there until the company, known as Queen Henrietta's Men from 1625, disbanded in 1636. He then formed a company of young players called Beeston's Boys.

Following his death his son, **William Beeston** (c. 1606–82), took over, but was imprisoned for staging an unlicensed play. After the closure of the theatres during the Commonwealth he re-established the young training company at Salisbury Court, but was forced by the army to close in 1649. He reopened the theatre in 1660, thus providing a link between Elizabethan drama and that of the Restoration.

Beggar's Opera, The A ballad opera by John GAY. First performance: 1728. The plot follows the rivalry between Polly Peachum and Lucy Lockit over the philandering highwayman Macheath. Highly successful in its own time, when it was widely understood as a satire on the prime minister Sir Robert Walpole, it was adapted in the 20th century by Benjamin Britten and inspired THE THREEPENNY OPERA.

Behan, Brendan (1923–64) Irish playwright, whose early experiences as a member of the IRA were reflected in his richly ironic and inventive plays. He was imprisoned twice and eventually died an alcoholic, his tumultuous life story providing the material for the autobiography *Borstal Boy* (1958). THE QUARE FELLOW established his reputation in the theatre when presented by Joan Littlewood in 1958, while the tragicomedy THE HOSTAGE was seen in New York and London as well as Dublin and reflected the influence of Brecht. Behan's third play, *Richard's Cork Leg*, was unfinished as his death but was later adapted for performance (1972) at the Abbey Theatre; his only other dramatic work was *The Big House* (1957), a television play.

Behn, Aphra (1640–89) English playwright and novelist. She was employed as a spy in the Netherlands and imprisoned for debt – being released according to tradition on the intervention of Killigrew – before becoming the first professional female writer in England in the 1670s. She wrote more than a dozen lively and often coarse plays, of which the most famous was THE *Rover*; others included the comedies *The Lucky Chance* (1686) and *The Emperor of the Moon* (1687), which was inspired by the *commedia dell'arte* and influenced the early development of the English pantomime. A friend of Dryden, Etherege, Otway, and other leading literary figures, she recalled her early years in Surinam in her novel *Oroonoko, or the History of the Royal Slave*, adapted for the stage by Southerne in 1695.

Behrman, S(amuel) N(athaniel) (1893–1973) US playwright, who was the author of many popular sophisticated light comedies as well as several less successful tragedies and serious dramas. He established his reputation with the comedy of manners *The Second Man* (1927); many of his subsequent works were adaptations of plays by other authors, of which the best known included *Amphitryon '38* (1938), based on Giraudoux, *The Pirate* (1942), from a play by Ludwig Fulda, and *I Know My Love* (1949), based on Achard's *Auprès de ma blonde* – all starring the Lunts. His other original works numbered amongst them *No Time for Comedy* (1939), and *The Cold Wind and the Warm* (1958), which both had a strong autobiographical element.

Beil, Johann David (1754–94) German actor, who was a member of Ekhof's company in Gotha and later transferred to Mannheim where he appeared in comedy and in plays by Schiller. He also performed in works by his friend Iffland; after his early death Iffland inherited several of his roles.

Béjart, Joseph (1616–59) French actor, the eldest member of a theatrical family closely associated with Molière. He was with Molière in the Illustre-Théâtre company and subsequently created parts in the celebrated playwright's *L'Étourdi* and *Dépit amoureux*.

His sister, **Madeleine Béjart** (1618–72), was an actress and had a profound influence upon the young Molière. She was a cofounder with him of the Illustre-Théâtre and eventually accompanied him to Paris in 1658. She excelled in classical tragedy and in the soubrette roles that Molière wrote for her in such plays as *Les Précieuses ridicules* and *Tartuffe*.

Her sister, **Geneviève Béjart** (1624–75), was also an actress with Molière's company, appearing chiefly in tragedy under her mother's maiden name, as Mlle Hervé.

Another sister, **Armande-Grésinde-Claire-Élisabeth Béjart** (1641–1700), became the target of malicious gossip upon her marriage to Molière in 1662, through the suggestion that she was in fact the playwright's daughter by Madeleine. The scandal was eventually defused by Louis XIV, who acted as godfather to their first child. The marriage was less than happy, despite the fact that Armande, who was trained as an actress by her husband, went on to create several major roles in Molière's plays, including Célimène in *Le Misanthrope* and Elmire in *Tartuffe*. When Molière died, she oversaw the troupe's amalgamation with the company from the Théâtre du Marais and subsequently the formation of the Comédie-Française.

Belasco, David (David Valasco; 1859–1931) US actor-manager and playwright, of Portuguese-Jewish parentage, who was a dominant figure in US theatre in the early 20th century. Popularly known as the 'Bishop of Broadway' and famous for his flamboyant personality, he successfully linked the sentimentalism of Victorian drama with the new naturalism of modern European writers, directing or producing over 300 plays on Broadway alone.

He began his career in San Francisco, subsequently working briefly with Boucicault and then moving to New York, where he eventually became stage manager under Daniel Frohman at the Madison Square Theatre (1882). He was soon recognized as a prolific playwright and adaptor of old plays and novels in both New York and London, his most successful works including *The Heart of Maryland* (1895), *Madame Butterfly* (1900), and *The Girl of the Golden West* (1905), of which the latter two have survived in operatic versions by Puccini.

In 1902 he acquired the Republic Theatre and renamed it the Belasco Theatre, subsequently staging many of his own plays there with such performers as David Warfield and George Arliss. Later he also built and opened the Stuyvesant Theatre (again renamed the Belasco Theatre in 1910), which remained his base until his death.

Belasco Theatre A 1008-seat theatre on West 44th Street, New York, which was opened as the **Stuyvesant Theatre** in 1907. The name was changed three years later in honour of its manager, David Belasco, and the theatre reopened with Belasco's *The Lily*. From 1935 to 1941 it housed the Group Theatre, whose production of *Trio* (1944) by Dorothy and Howard Baker aroused controversy with its discussion of lesbianism and led to the theatre's closure. For a period of four years from 1949 to 1953 it was used for broadcasting but subsequently reverted to live drama; the theatre is now owned by the Shubert Organization. Recent productions seen there include *The Rocky Horror Picture Show* (1975), *Ain't Misbehavin'* (1981), *Hamlet* (1995) with Ralph Fiennes, and *A Doll's House* (1997) with Janet McTeer.

Belcari, Feo (1410–84) Italian playwright, author of several early *sacra rappresentazione*. A native of Florence, he collaborated with Antonio Meglio upon an influential play depicting the Last Judgement.

Belfast Civic Arts Theatre A theatre in Belfast, Northern Ireland, opened in 1944 as the **Mask Theatre** in a converted loft. Early plays included performances of major European dramas; as the Belfast Arts Theatre it then added plays by leading US writers before moving in 1961 to Botanic Avenue. Civil unrest caused the theatre's closure from 1971 to 1976, when it prospered once more (seating 500) with a wide variety of productions, from work by native writers to musicals and plays for children.

Bel Geddes, Norman (1893–1958) US scene designer, who paved the way for THE-ATRE-IN-THE-ROUND in 1915 when he initiated the idea of a theatre without a proscenium. His designs for Volmöller's *The Miracle* in 1923 earned him recognition and, in 1935, he employed COMPOSITE SETTING for a production of Kingsley's *Dead End*.

His daughter, **Barbara Bel Geddes** (1921–), made her stage debut in 1940. After making her New York debut in *Out of the Frying Pan* (1941), she enjoyed success in 1945 in d'Usseau and Gow's *Deep Are the Roots*. Later roles included Margaret in *Cat on a Hot Tin Roof* (1955) and Katherine Johnson in *Silent Night, Lonely Night* (1959); in the 1980s she became still more widely known for her portrayal of Miss Ellie in the *Dallas* television series.

Belgrade Theatre A theatre in Coventry, opened in 1958 and named in recognition of a gift of timber for its erection sent from Belgrade in Yugoslavia. The first of the CIVIC THEATRES, the building includes accommodation for the resident company (which also presents the annual Coventry mystery play cycle) and space for exhibitions. Major productions that have been staged there include plays by Wesker and Bond and numerous acclaimed plays for children. Under the successive managers Brian Bailey and Warren Jenkins the company has maintained an extremely varied programme, while experimental drama has also flourished in a smaller studio theatre, the Belgrade Venue. The main auditorium seats 866 people.

Belgravia Theatre *See* Royal Court Theatre.

Bell, John (1745–1831) British publisher and journalist. He brought out an acting edition of Shakespeare, based on the prompt books of the patent theatres and edited by Francis Gentleman, in 1773. *Bell's British Theatre* is a valuable selection of plays and prefaces.

Bell, John Joy (1871–1934) Scottish playwright, who specialized in writing in the Scottish vernacular. His one-act comic plays include *Courtin' Christina*, *The Pie in the Oven*, and *Wee MacGregor's Party*, while his most famous work is a tense thriller, *Thread o'Scarlet* (1923).

Bell, Marie (Marie-Jeanne Belon; 1900–85) French actress and manager, who became a leading performer in tragedy at the Comédie-Française, which he joined in 1921. She excelled in dramas by Racine as well as in modern works by Claudel, Félicien Marceau, and Jean Genet; she was manager of the Théâtre du Gymnase from 1959.

Bellamy, George Anne (c. 1727–88) British actress, who acquired her Christian names by mistake; she should have been christened Georgiana. The illegitimate daughter of Lord Tyrawley, she was engaged by Christopher Rich at Covent Garden, where she played opposite James Quin. Garrick subsequently engaged her at Drury Lane, casting her as Juliet to his Romeo. She was never a great actress and was involved in numerous scandals. She retired in 1785, publishing an unreliable six-volume autobiography.

Bellecour (Jean-Claude-Gilles Colson; 1725–78) French actor and playwright, who was one of the best-known comic actors of the Comédie-Française. He began as an artist but excelled in comedy after joining the Comédie-Française in 1750 at the urging of Richelieu, soon relinquishing his tragic roles to Lekain. His wife was the actress Rose-Petronelle le Roy Beauménard.

Belleroche (Raymond Poisson; c. 1630–90) French actor, who was much admired in comic roles at the Hôtel de Bourgogne, despite his slight stutter. He was particularly identified with the role of CRISPIN, who appeared in several of his own comedies. His son was the actor Paul POISSON.

Bellerose (Pierre le Messier; c. 1592–1670) French actor-manager, who became leader of Valleran-Lecomte's company on the latter's death and subsequently took over the combined troupe at the Hôtel de Bourgogne in 1634. He was popular in both comedy and tragedy and excelled as the central character in Corneille's *Le Menteur*, amongst other roles.

Belleville *See* Turlupin.

Bell Inn An inn in Gracechurch Street in London, where plays were staged in the late 16th century. Companies that performed there included the Queen's Men.

Belloy, Pierre Laurent Buirette de (1727–75) French playwright. De Belloy's reputation rests on the patriotic tragedy *Le Siège de Calais*, first performed in Paris in 1765, which appealed to the rising spirit of nationalism in France at the time; his other plays are of little worth.

Bells, The An adaptation by Leopold LEWIS of *Le Juif Polonais* by ERCKMANN-CHATRIAN. First performance: Lyceum Theatre, 1871. Sir Henry IRVING's performance as the burgomaster, haunted by his guilt for an undiscovered murder that he has committed, established him as the leading actor of his day and restored the theatre's fortunes.

Bellwood, Bessie (Elizabeth Ann Katherine Mahoney; 1857–96) British music hall performer, formerly a rabbit-skinner in Bermondsey. She developed a notorious line in suggestive songs and was idolized by her audiences; she was also successful in New York.

Belmont Theatre A theatre on West 48th Street, New York, which was opened as the Norworth Theatre in 1918. Later that year the name was changed to the Belmont; plays staged there included the Pulitzer Prize-winning *Miss Lulu Bett* (1920) by Zona Gale and Philip Barry's *You and I* (1923). The theatre was turned into a cinema in 1936 and was finally demolished in 1951.

below *See* stage direction.

Beltrame *See* Barbieri, Niccolò.

Benavente y Martínez, Jacinto (1866–1954) Spanish playwright and critic, noted for his many satirical comedies. These include *La noche del sabado* (1903), *Los intereses creados* (1907), which as *The Bonds of Interest* was the first play performed by the Theatre Guild in New York in 1919, and *La Malquerida* (The Passion Flower; 1913), which was presented in New York in 1920 and in London in 1926. His enormous output included over 150 original plays, as well as translations of Molière and Shakespeare. He was awarded a Nobel Prize in 1922.

benefit A special performance of a play, the proceeds of which go to a specified member or members of the cast (customarily on their retirement) or to a particular worthy cause.

Benelli, Sem (1875–1949) Italian playwright, noted for his historical dramas written in blank verse. Most renowned of these was *La cena della beffe* (1909), which as *The Jest* was produced in New York in 1919. His other works include *Tignola* (The Bookworm; 1908), *L'amore dei tre rei* (The Love of the Three Kings; 1910), and his last major work, *Orfeo e Proserpina* (1928).

Benfield, Robert (d. 1649) English actor, who appeared with Lady Elizabeth's Men in plays by Beaumont and Fletcher and later with the King's Men, appearing as Antonio in *The Duchess of Malfi* (1619) and in major roles in plays by Massinger. He is in the 1623 Folio list of actors in Shakespeare's plays and was a shareholder in the Globe and Blackfriars theatres.

Benger, Sir William (d. 1572) English court official, who was appointed Master of the Revels in 1559. His period in office saw the reduction of the role to that of censorship only.

Bennett, Alan (1934–) British actor and playwright, who first attracted attention as a member of the *Beyond the Fringe* revue in 1960. His first play, the satirical *Forty Years On* (1968), established his reputation as a playwright with a particularly acute ear for ordinary speech and the pathos and ironies of everyday life; the London cast included John Gielgud. Subsequent successes in the theatre have included *Getting On* (1971), the farce *Habeas Corpus* (1973), in which Bennett himself appeared, *The Old Country* (1977), dealing with the state of mind of an exiled spy, *Enjoy* (1980), *Kafka's Dick* (1986), the double bill *Single Spies* (1988), *The Madness of George III* (1991, later filmed), and *The Lady in the Van* (1999). He has also written two celebrated series of monologues for television under the general title *Talking Heads* (1987; 1998).

Bennett, (Enoch) Arnold (1867–1931) British novelist and playwright, who had some success with such plays as *Milestones* (1912) – which was written in collaboration with Edward Knoblock and inspired Coward's *Cavalcade* – and *The Great Adventure* (1913), which was based on one of his novels. His later dramatic works, which were less successful, include *London Life* (1924) and *Mr Prohack* (1927).

Bennett, Hywel (1944–) British actor, born in Wales, who first appeared in London as Ophelia in a youth production of *Hamlet* (1959). He then trained at RADA and worked in the provinces before performing at the Mermaid Theatre as Prince Hal in *Henry VI Parts I and II* (1970) and Antony in *Julius Caesar* (1972) at the Young Vic. Subsequently he played Simon in Simon Gray's *Otherwise Engaged* (1977), Andreas Capodistriou and Inspector Bowden in Anthony Shaffer's *The Oily Levantine* (1979), and won praise in Chekhov's *Three Sisters* (1987). He has also worked as a guest director at leading repertory theatres and made numerous television appearances.

Bennett, Jill (1931–90) British actress, who began her career at Stratford in 1949. Subsequently she participated in Olivier's season at the St James's Theatre in 1951, appearing in *Antony and Cleopatra* and *Caesar and Cleopatra*, and excelled as Isabelle in Anouilh's *Dinner with the Family* (1957). She also appeared in several plays by John OSBORNE (to whom she was married 1968–77), including his version of *Hedda*

Gabler (1976). Later work for the stage included Gertrude in the Royal Court production of *Hamlet* (1980), *The Little Foxes* (1981), and *Dance of Death* (1983).

Bennett, Michael (1943–87) US choreographer and director. He danced in the chorus of Broadway shows before making his choreographic debut with *A Joyful Noise* (1966) and enjoying success with *Promises, Promises* (1968). After important work for Stephen Sondheim with *Company* (1970) and *Follies* (1971), he found his greatest success with A CHORUS LINE (1975), which he developed through extensive workshops – a now much-imitated technique. He enjoyed a second hit, *Dreamgirls* (1981), before his early death.

Bennett, Richard (1872–1944) US actor, who became highly popular in romantic leading roles. His many successes, achieved in spite of his own unpredictable nature and occasional criticisms of the audience delivered from the stage, included plays by Barrie, Brieux, O'Neill, and Shaw as well as Maxwell Anderson's *Winterset* (1935).

Benserade, Isaac de (1613–91) French poet and playwright. His literary output consisted chiefly of poetry and libretti for the royal ballets, on which he collaborated with Molière. *Cléopâtre* (1636) is generally considered to be the best of his mediocre dramatic works.

Benson, Sir Frank Robert (1858–1939) British actor-manager, who first appeared on the professional stage (at the Lyceum) in 1882. A year later he led his own company on tour in the provinces, presenting plays by Shakespeare – notably the first production of *Hamlet* in its entirety (1899) – at Stratford-on-Avon at an annual summer festival from 1886 to 1916. He was knighted in 1916 by George V at Drury Lane, becoming the only actor to be thus honoured actually inside a theatre.

His wife was the actress **Constance Featherstonhaugh** (1860–1946), who was a leading lady with his celebrated company for many years.

Benthall, Michael (1919–74) British theatre director, who was a prominent member of the Oxford University Dramatic Society and subsequently codirector with Tyrone Guthrie of *Hamlet* at the Old Vic in 1944. He was noted for his Shakespearean and classical productions and was director of the Old Vic from 1953 to 1959.

Bentley, Eric Russell (1916–) British-born US critic, director, and playwright. A tireless supporter of avant-garde and left-wing causes, Bentley did much to popularize the plays of Brecht, whose work he began to translate in the 1940s. In 1950 he was coproducer with Brecht of *Mother Courage* in Munich; he also directed plays by O'Neill, Lorca, and cummings. His own plays include *Are You Now Or Have You Ever Been...?* (1972), *The Recantation of Galileo Galilei* (1973), and *Expletive Deleted* (1974). Books of criticism include *The Life of the Drama* (1964) and *Thinking About the Playwright* (1987).

Beolco, Angelo (c. 1502–42) Italian actor and playwright, who had an early influence upon the development of the *commedia dell'arte*. He became popularly known as **Il Ruzzante**, after the talkative character he created, and was the author of several plays (written in his native Paduan dialect) that have enjoyed revivals in the last 100 years.

Bérain, Jean (1637–1711) French theatrical designer, who executed elaborate stage designs for plays by Molière. He succeeded Vigarani at the Salle des Machines and worked at the Paris Opéra, subsequently designing influential exotic costumes and decorations for performances at the royal court.

Bérard, Christian (1903–49) French artist and designer, who became famous for his romantic and historical designs for both ballets and plays in the 1930s and 1940s. He was particularly noted for his work on productions of Molière and Marivaux under Jouvet and Barrault as well as for his collaborations with Jean Cocteau in both the theatre and the cinema; their works together included *La Machine infernale* (1934) and *L'Aigle à deux têtes* (1946).

Bergbom, Kaarlo (1842–1906) Finnish theatre manager, who established the Finnish National Theatre in 1872. Members of his company presented many of Ibsen's plays, including the first performance of *John Gabriel Borkman* (1897).

Bergerac, Cyrano de *See* Cyrano de Bergerac, Savinien.

Berghof, Herbert (1909–90) Austrian-born actor, director, and teacher who came to New York in 1939 to direct *From Vienna* at the Music Box Theatre. He made his New York stage debut in *Reunion*, which he also codirected. In 1964, with his wife Uta Hagen, he founded the Herbert Berghof Studio in New York, where he taught acting.

Bergman, Hjalmar (1883–1931) Swedish novelist, playwright, and short-story writer, who is regarded as one of Sweden's most important writers after Strindberg. His earliest stage successes were the one-act plays, *Dödens Arlekin* and *Herr Sleeman Kommen* (both 1917); later works included the comedy *Swedenhjelms* (1925), *Petrasket* (The Baron's Will; 1928), and adaptations of two of his own novels – *Hans Nåds Testamente* and *Makurells i Wadköping* (God's Orchid; 1919) – which were both produced in 1930.

Bergman, (Ernst) Ingmar (1918–) Swedish director. Although best known as one of the foremost 20th-century directors for the cinema, Bergman has also won acclaim for his work in the theatre. He led an amateur theatre group while still at university and later took over theatres in Halsingborg (1944–46) and Gothenburg (1946–49); his early stage successes included his own play *Kaspers död* (Kasper's Death; 1942) and Camus's *Caligula* (1946). Subsequently he worked at Malmö (1952–60) and at the Kungliga Dramatiska Teatern (1963–66), specializing in intense psychological dramas by Strindberg, Chekhov, Brecht, Ibsen, and others. In 1977–78 he transferred to Munich after an argument with the Swedish tax authorities. His production of *Hamlet* with the Stockholm Royal Dramatic Theatre was seen at the National Theatre in 1987.

Bergner, Elisabeth (1900–86) Austrian actress, who became a leading performer in Berlin in the 1920s and later in London (from 1933) and New York. She established her reputation under Reinhardt as Shaw's St Joan in 1924 and subsequently excelled in Shakespeare in such roles as Portia and Juliet. Other celebrated successes included plays by Strindberg, O'Neill, and Giraudoux; in London and New York she appeared in plays by Barrie, Webster, Rattigan, and others, as well as repeating her interpretation of St Joan.

Bergopzoomer, Johann Baptist (1742–1804) Austrian actor, who was a friend of Friedrich Schröder. He began his career in Vienna, appearing in conventional Viennese comedies but later was much admired for his performances in tragedy in both Vienna and in Germany with Kurz's company.

Bergstrøm, Hjalmar (1868–1914) Danish playwright, whose dramas often tackled the social and political problems of his day. The class struggle was discussed in *Lynggaard and Co* (1905) and the emancipation of women in *Karen Bornemann* (1907).

Berkoff, Steven (1937–) British playwright, actor, and director, noted for his highly physical style of theatre; he founded the London Theatre Group to present his own work in 1968. His plays include *Metamorphosis* (1969), from Kafka; *The Fall of the House of Usher* (1974), from Edgar Allan Poe; *East* (1975), which applied the language of high tragedy to life in London's East End; *Greek* (1979), based on the Oedipus story; *West* (1983), an adaptation of the Beowulf legend; *Sink the Belgrano!* (1986), which was a parody of *Henry V*; *Kvetch* (1987); and *Massage* (1997), in which he appeared in drag.

Berlin, Irving (Israel Baline; 1888–1989) Russian-born US songwriter, who also wrote several major Broadway musicals. His first full Broadway score was *Watch Your Step* (1914); subsequent successes included patriotic reviews in both World War I (*Yip, Yip, Yaphank*) and World War II (*This is the Army*), several editions of both Ziegfeld's *Follies* and *The Music Box Revue* (staged at his own MUSIC BOX Theatre), *As Thousands Cheer* (1933), ANNIE GET YOUR GUN, and CALL ME MADAM. He is regarded as one of the creators of US popular music.

Berliner Ensemble A German theatre company, founded by Bertolt BRECHT and Helene WEIGEL in 1949. Based in East Berlin, it moved from the Deutsches Theater to the Theater am Schiffbauerdamm in 1954 and established a strong reputation for its productions of Brecht's works. After his death it was led by Weigel until 1971 and then by their daughter, Barbara Brecht-Schall, and her actor husband Ekkerhard Schall until 1992. By this time the Ensemble was generally seen as being in serious decline, despite attempts to diversify with plays by Shaw and Wedekind among others. A group of five leading West German directors were placed in charge in the early 1990s.

Bernadon A comic character of the Viennese theatrical tradition, developed by Joseph Kurz from HANSWURST. In the course of his adventures he frequently finds himself embroiled in struggles against the supernatural.

Bernard, Tristan (Paul Bernard; 1866–1947) French playwright. His light comedies, in which good use is made of such devices as disguise, intrigue, and mistaken identity, include *L'Anglais tel qu'on le parle* (1899), *Triplepatte* (1905; translated as *Toddles*, 1907), and *Le Petit Café* (1911).

His son, **Jean-Jacques Bernard** (1888–1972), was also a playwright. His dramas of the Theatre of SILENCE include *Le Feu qui reprend mal* (1921, translated as *The Sulky Fire*, 1926), *Martine* (1922; translated 1927), and *Le Printemps des autres* (1924; translated as *The Springtime of Others*, 1934).

Bernhardt, Sarah (1844–1923) French actress, one of the most admired performers ever to appear on the French stage. Noted for her distinctive voice and romantic looks, she began her career at the Comédie-Française in 1862 and subsequently established an international reputation as a fine as well as eccentric and tempestuous actress in tragedy. In 1880 she also ventured into theatre management. Her greatest performances included the title roles in Shakespeare's *Hamlet*, Racine's *Phèdre*, and Scribe's *Adrienne Lecouvreur*, Doña Sol in Hugo's *Hernani*, Marguerite Gautier in *La Dame aux camélias* by Dumas *fils*, the King of Rome in Rostand's *L'Aiglon*, and various characters in the melodramas of Sardou. After her right leg was amputated in 1915 she continued to appear to undiminished acclaim in parts written specially for her until her death.

Bernini, Giovanni Lorenzo (1598–1680) Italian sculptor, architect, and artist, noted for his development of stage effects for use in the theatres of Rome. His spectacular scenery and stage machinery, including storm effects and transformation scenes, influenced many later designers, notably Inigo Jones.

Bernstein, Aline (Aline Frankau; 1881–1955) US scene designer, whose first work was for the Indian play *The Little Clay Cart* (1924). She also worked on productions of Moeller's *Caprice* (1928), Chekhov's *The Seagull* (1929), *Romeo and Juliet* (1930), Molnár's *Liliom* (1932), Barry's *The Animal Kingdom* (1932), Elmer Rice's *Judgement Day* (1934), Hellman's *The Children's Hour* (1934) and *The Little Foxes* (1939), and Cocteau's *The Eagle Has Two Heads* (1949).

Bernstein, Henry (1876–1953) French playwright, born in Paris. Bernstein's early successes were powerful melodramas; he subsequently turned to psychological themes, notably in *Le Secret* (1913) and *La Galérie des glaces* (1924). The son of a Jewish banker, he attacked anti-Semitism in *Samson* (1907) and *Israël* (1908) and Nazism in *Elvire* (1940).

Bernstein, Leonard (1918–90) US composer, conductor, and pianist. One of the few composers successfully to blend the classical and the popular, he brought a new urban energy into the US musical with the scores for *On the Town* (1944), *Wonderful Town* (1953), *Candide* (1956), and *West Side Story* (1957), as well as composing ballets and a one-act opera, *Trouble in Tahiti*. He also wrote incidental music for Barrie's *Peter Pan* (1950).

Bersenev, Ivan Nikolaievich (Ivan Nikolaievich Pavlishchev; 1889–1951) Russian actor and director, who was the leading figure at the Lenkom Theatre from 1938. He began his career in Kiev under Mardzhanov and appeared at the Moscow Art Theatre from 1928 to 1938; his most successful productions included Simonov's *And So It Will Be* (1944) and other contemporary Soviet plays.

Bertinazzi, Carlo (1713–83) Italian actor of the *commedia dell'arte*, who specialized in the role of Arlequin. Popularly known as **Carlin**, he was one of the few Italian actors still performing with the Comédie-Italienne in the early 18th century, having succeeded Tommaso Vicentini at the Hôtel de Bourgogne in 1741.

Bertolazzi, Carlo (1870–1916) Italian playwright, author of several notable plays written in the Milanese dialect. *El nost' Milan* (Our Milan; 1893) was revived by Strehler in 1955; other plays include *L'egoista* (1900) and *Lulù* (1903).

bespeak performance A special performance given during the 19th century at which a single patron, or group of patrons, bought all the tickets and chose the play to be performed. The proceeds from the evening were shared amongst the cast.

Bessenyi, György (c. 1746–1811) Hungarian playwright, regarded as the most influential writer for the early Hungarian theatre. His plays include the comedy *The Philosopher* (1777) and a number of historical tragedies.

Besson, Benno (1922–) Swiss director and actor, who became a leading member of Brecht's Berliner Ensemble. He began his career under Serreau in Paris and with Brecht worked on several notable adaptations of Molière, Farquhar, and others. Subsequently he produced dramas at the Deutsches Theater (1961–69), where his successes included works by Aristophanes and Offenbach, at the Volksbühne (1969–79), where his productions included *Spectacles I and II* and Müller's *Die Schlacht*, and at the Théâtre de la Comédie in Geneva (1980s). He also mounted several acclaimed productions at the Avignon Festival.

Betterton, Thomas (c. 1635–1710) English actor, son of a cook in Charles I's household. He began acting for John Rhodes at the Cockpit, then joined Davenant at Lincoln's Inn Fields. When Davenant died in 1671, Betterton took over his company, moving to Dorset Garden. When his company amalgamated with Killigrew's in 1682, he became the leading actor at Drury Lane, confirming his reputation in plays by Shakespeare and contemporary playwrights. Unable to put up with Christopher RICH's management, he returned to Lincoln's Inn Fields in 1695, opening with the first performance of *Love for Love*. 10 years later he moved to the Haymarket, where he made his final appearance in 1710. The foremost figure of the Restoration stage, he was buried in Westminster Abbey. His wife was the actress Mary SAUNDERSON.

Betti, Ugo (1892–1953) Italian playwright, poet, and short-story writer, often regarded as Italy's most outstanding dramatist since Pirandello. A judge by profession, Betti wrote over 20 plays, many of which have a courtroom setting or are in the form of a legal investigation, including *Delitto all'isola delle capre* (Crime on Goat Island; 1948) and *Corruzione al Palazzo di Giustizia* (Corruption in the Palace of Justice; 1949), which number among his most important plays. His other works include *I nostri sogni* (Our Dreams; 1937), a charming light comedy, *Frano allo scala Nord* (Landslide; 1936), *Ispezione* (The Inquiry; 1947), and *L'aiuola bruciata* (The Burnt Flowerbed; 1952).

Betty, William Henry West (1791–1874) British boy actor brought up in Ireland. Hailed initially as the Minor Roscius, he was publicized by his father, hoping for long-term exploitation, as the **Young Roscius**. This publicity led to engagements at Covent Garden and Drury Lane in the 1804–05 season. Playing the great Shakespearean tragedies, he evoked near hysteria with his performances. Two years later, however, he was hissed off the stage while playing Richard III. He retired at the age of 17.

Beverley, William Roxby (c. 1811–89) British scene painter, who studied with Clarkson Stanfield. He worked first as an actor and scene painter for his father, who managed the Theatre Royal, Manchester. In 1853 he was appointed scenic director at Covent Garden; a year later he moved to Drury Lane, where he remained for 30 years. He was famous, in particular, for his pantomime designs and sets for Charles Kean's Shakespearean productions.

Beyond the Horizon A play by Eugene O'NEILL. First performance: Broadway, 1920. Set in New England, it revolves around the Mayo brothers, Robert and Andrew, a farmer and a seaman; Robert proves to be the real adventurer though he fails as a farmer. The play reaches a climax when Ruth, who married Robert, confesses her love for Andrew. The play won a Pulitzer Prize.

Bharata (fl. 500 AD) Indian sage, who established the basic rules for early Indian drama in his treatise *Natyashastra*. He defined theatre as a means of achieving spiritual peace and laid down the various gestures and eye movements available to the actor, as well as giving guidance on dance, playwriting, and theatre architecture.

Bhāsa (2nd century AD) Indian playwright, author of the earliest known Sanskrit drama. His 13 surviving plays, notably *Svapnavasavadatta*, were heroic romances based on prose epics and had a profound influence upon the writings of Kālidāsa and on the popular anonymous play *The Little Clay Cart*.

Biancolelli, Giuseppe Domenico (c. 1637–88) French actor, born in Italy, who became famous for his interpretation of Arlequin, the French version of Arlecchino in the *commedia dell'arte*. Popularly known as **Dominique**, he played an important part in persuading Louis XIV to allow him and his fellow-players to perform in French rather than Italian. One of his daughters married the son of Françoise La Thorillière.

His youngest son, **Pietro Francesco Biancolelli** (1680–1734), was also an actor. Known as Dominique le Jeune, he appeared as Arlequin, Pierrot, and subsequently in straight plays with Riccoboni's company.

Bibiena, Ferdinando (1657–1743) Italian theatrical designer, who – with his brother **Francesco Bibiena** (1659–1739) – established the Bibiena family (originally called **Galli**) as leading architects of baroque theatres throughout Europe. Ferdinando contributed towards the building of the Teatro Farnese in Parma and subsequently moved to Vienna, where he collaborated upon further theatrical designs with Francisco and his own sons.

Ferdinando's eldest son **Alessandro Bibiena** (1686–1748) became an architect, while his other sons **Giuseppe Bibiena** (1695–1756), **Antonio Bibiena** (1697–c. 1774), and **Giovanni Maria Bibiena** (1700–74) all worked on theatre design.

Giuseppe's son **Carlo Bibiena** (1721–87) contributed to the design of the Bayreuth opera-house and, together with other members of the family, helped to develop the use of the perspective scene.

Bible-history *See* mystery play.

Bickerstaffe, Isaac (1735–1812) British playwright, born in Ireland, who wrote or collaborated on numerous comedies and ballad operas. *Thomas and Sally; or, the Sailor's Return* was staged at Covent Garden in 1760 and was followed by such pieces as *Love in a Village* (1762), *The Maid of the Mill* (1765), and *Lionel and Clarissa* (1768). In 1772 he was accused of sodomy, at that time a capital offence, and fled to the Continent where he died in penury.

Biddles, Adelaide Helen (1837–1921) British actress, who first appeared as a child in Charles Kean's company. In 1856 she married the actor-manager Charles Calvert (1828–79). She played leading parts in his company and, after his death, toured extensively. Her son was the actor Louis CALVERT.

Bidermann, Jakob (1578–1639) German playwright and priest, an important writer of Jesuit drama. His best known play, *Cenodoxus* (1602), depicts the founding of the Carthusian order and was revived in Munich in 1958.

Bijou Theatre A theatre in Bayswater, London, which was a regular venue for performances presented in order to protect an author's copyright. Plays by Shaw and Wilde were among those produced there in the late 19th century; in 1925 Lena Ashwell renamed the theatre the **Twentieth Century Theatre** and appeared there in numerous plays by Masefield, Dostoevsky, and others. After 1933 the building was only sporadically used as a theatre and finally became a warehouse.

An earlier **Bijou Theatre** opened in the Haymarket in 1862, staging both plays and concerts; it was burnt down in 1876.

Another **Bijou Theatre** opened on Broadway, New York, in 1878 as the **Brighton Theatre**. Later renamed the **Broadway Opera House**, it became the Bijou in 1880 and prospered with appearances by Lillian Russell. Rebuilt in 1883, it saw the adult debut of Julia Marlowe and many musicals before demolition in 1915.

The **Bijou Theatre** on West 45th Street, New York, opened in 1917. Plays staged there included works by Barrie, Ibsen, and Benn Levy; it then became a cinema (1931–45). Russel Crouse and Howard Lindsay's *Life With Father* was staged there from 1945 to 1947; later successes included O'Neill's *A Moon for the Misbegotten* (1957) and – after another period as a cinema (1962–72) – the pantomime *Mummenschanz* (1977). The theatre was abolished in 1982.

A smaller **Bijou Theatre** opened on West 48th Street, New York, in 1970 as part of the Playhouse Theatre.

Bill-Belotserkovsky, Vladimir Naumovich (1884–1970) Russian playwright, who worked in the US from 1911 to 1917, acquiring there the nickname Bill, which he tacked on to his surname. Although his first play, *Echo* (1924), was set in the US, his best-known play, *Hurricane* (1925), was set in Russia during the Civil War; it was first staged at the Mossoviet Theatre and subsequently performed in many other East European countries.

Billetdoux, François (1927–91) French playwright and actor, born in Paris. A student of Charles Dullin, Billetdoux made his name in 1959 with the tragicomedy *Tchin-Tchin*. Noted for their unconventional plots, his plays include *Le Comportement des époux Bredburry* (1960) and *Va donc chez Törpe* (1961), in which a series of suicides takes place at the same inn, and *Il faut passer par les nuages* (1969). After a lengthy period during which he wrote mainly for television, he returned to the stage with *Wake Up! Philadelphia!* (1988), in which a teenage girl finds herself trapped in the body of an old woman.

Billinger, Richard (1890–1965) Austrian novelist, playwright, and poet, whose first play, *Das Perchtenspiel*, was produced by Max Reinhardt in 1928. Others include *Die Hexe von Passau* (The Witch of Passau; 1935), which was used by Ottmar Gerster as the basis for an opera (1941), *Das nachte Leben* (1953), and *Menschen nennen es Schicksal* (1962).

Billington, Michael (1939–) British drama critic, whose reviews have appeared regularly in *The Guardian* since 1971. An advocate of the social and political role of the theatre, he has written books on Ayckbourn, Stoppard, and Pinter.

Bill of Divorcement, A The first play by Clemence DANE. First performance: London, 1921. Written in the style of Pinero, it argued that insanity is sufficient grounds for divorce and caused considerable controversy. The play's success in London and New York encouraged Dane to become a full-time writer.

Billy Liar A comedy by Willis HALL and Keith WATERHOUSE, based on the latter's novel. First performance: London, 1960. The play revolves around 19-year-old Billy, who relieves the boredom of his life in northern England with a series of fantasies, which inevitably lead to trouble.

Billy Rose Theatre *See* Nederlander Theatre.

Biltmore Theatre A 994-seat theatre on West 47th Street, between Broadway and 8th Avenue, New York, which opened in 1925. It attracted attention early on with Mae West's notorious *Pleasure Man* (1928), which was banned by the authorities, and appearances by the Federal Theatre Project (1936). Later in 1936 it was taken over by Warner Brothers and, from 1952 to 1962, it was used as a broadcasting studio. In 1963 it reopened for live drama with Neil Simon's *Barefoot in the Park*. Other productions of the 1960s and 1970s included *Hair* (1968) and William Douglas Home's *The Kingfisher* (1978). It has subsequently seen a period of neglect and a legal dispute over ownership, and is currently in an unsafe condition. There are various plans for renovation, perhaps including a hotel to be built over it.

Bio-Mechanics An approach to the direction and training of actors developed by MEYERHOLD as a reaction against Stanislavsky's ideas. The theory called for the suppression of all emotion by the actors and the complete domination of a production by the director. In order to achieve this stark detachment it stipulated precise attention to movement and gesture and the removal of almost all items of scenery; the theory failed to have any lasting influence.

Bird, Robert Montgomery (1806–54) US novelist, playwright, and poet, whose popular dramas used classical settings to explore topical issues. *The Gladiator* (1831), which had over 1000 performances, focuses upon slavery and the fight for liberty. Other works included *Ordalloossa* (1832) and *The Broker of Bogota* (1934); all of his plays were produced by the actor Edwin Forrest.

Bird, Theophilus (1608–64) English actor, whose father, **William Bird** (d. 1624) was one of the Admiral's Men. Theophilus joined Queen Henrietta's Men at the Cockpit as a player of female roles, appearing in plays by Massinger, Heywood, and Thomas Nabbes. Subsequently he married Christopher Beeston's daughter, Anne, and served as his father-in-law's agent in the purchase of Salisbury Court. Later he also appeared under Killigrew at Drury Lane.

Birds, The A comedy by ARISTOPHANES, often considered his best. First performance: Athens, 414 BC. The play revolves around the attempt of two Athenians to create a fantasy utopia between heaven and earth with the help of the birds. It is the origin of the phrase 'Cloud Cuckoo Land'.

Birman, Serafima Germanovna (1890–1976) Soviet actress and director, who began her career at the Moscow Art Theatre and later became one of the leading figures at the Lenkom Theatre, which she joined in 1938. There she directed notable versions of plays by Rostand, Simonov, and Tolstoy as well as making numerous successful personal appearances.

Birmingham Repertory Theatre A theatre in Birmingham, opened in 1913 at the instigation of Barry JACKSON, who also provided much of the necessary finance. After the first production, *Twelfth Night*, the theatre presented a number of plays by John Drinkwater and Shaw until the theatre was forced to close temporarily in 1924. After its reopening a series of commercial successes – notably Jackson's innovative modern-dress *Hamlet* (1925) and *Macbeth* (1928) – secured the theatre's future and it became respected for its staging of foreign works and for its training of young actors, including Olivier, Paul Scofield, and Albert Finney. Numerous productions transferred to London and New York and in 1971 the company moved into a new theatre, seating 900, in the centre of Birmingham. Since then the theatre has been used for largely commercial productions, although experimental drama is still performed in the smaller studio theatre, seating 160.

Bíró, Lajos (1880–1948) Hungarian playwright, best known for the satirical play *The Family Circle* (1909), which exposes hypocrisy in bourgeois society. Other works, which were seen throughout Europe and the US, included *The Yellow Lily* (1910), *Patricia's Seven Houses* (1946), which was loosely based on Shaw's *Widowers' Houses*, and *Our Katie* (1946).

Birthday Party, The Harold PINTER's first full-length play. First performance: Arts Theatre, Cambridge, 1958. Peter Wood directed and Richard Pearson played Stanley, the central figure. Stanley's delusions and fears are played upon by sinister visitors who, under the pretext of celebrating his birthday, proceed to destroy his identity.

Bjørnson, Bjørnstjerne (1832–1910) Norwegian poet, playwright, and novelist, who became Ibsen's successor at the Bergen Theatre in 1857 and went on to establish an international reputation as a writer and public figure, winning a Nobel Prize in 1903. The son of a pastor, he was a fervent patriot and in his early dramatic works (1857–64) drew heavily upon Norwegian folklore and history. Later, however, he adopted Socialist ideals and became widely-known for the social dramas *En fallit* and *Redaktøren*; other plays discussed religious intolerance and contemporary social evolution. The most highly regarded of these later works is *Over Ævne I*, in which he examines the position of the individual in society. From 1865 to 1867 he was artistic director of the Kristiana Theater, where his son – Bjørn Bjørnson (1859–1942) – was director from 1885 to 1893 before taking over the Nationaltheatret in 1899.

Principal dramatic works:
Mellen Slagene: 1857; translated as *Between the Battles*.
Halte-Hulde: 1858; translated as *Lame Hulda*.
Kong Sverre: 1861; translated as *King Sverre*.
Sigurd Slembe: 1862.
Maria Stuart i Skotland: 1864.
De Nygifte: 1865; translated as *The Newly-Marrieds*.
Sigurd Jorsalfar: 1872.
Kong Eystejn: 1872.
Redaktøren: 1874; translated as *The Editor*.
En fallit: 1875; translated as *The Bankrupt*.

Kongen: 1877; translated as *The King*.

Det ny system: 1879; translated as *The New System*.

En Handske: 1883; translated as *A Gauntlet*.

Geografiog Kjœlighed: 1885; translated as *Love and Geography*.

Over Ævne I: 1883; translated as *Pastor Sang*.

Paul Lange og Tora Parsberg: 1893.

Over Ævne II: 1895; translated as *Beyond Human Power*.

Laboremus: 1901.

Daglannet: 1904.

Når den ny vin blomstrer: 1909; translated as *When the New Wine Blooms*.

Black, George (1890–1943) British impresario, who presented a series of revues in London during and after World War II, with his sons George and Alfred. Their successes included *Apple Sauce* (1940), *Piccadilly Hayride* (1946), and *Take It From Us* (1950).

Black Crook, The A production usually considered the first musical comedy. First performance: New York, 1866. In that year Niblo's Gardens theatre was preparing a melodrama in which a young huntsman makes a deal with a mysterious stranger (the devil) to win the hand of his love. At the same time, a troupe of French ballet dancers found themselves stranded in New York when their theatre burned down. The two groups were combined, music was hastily composed, and the resulting mélange became the US theatre's biggest success of the century.

Black-Ey'd Susan A nautical drama by Douglas JERROLD. First performance: 1829. The lovely Susan remains faithful to William, her absent sailor-husband; William, however, catches his own captain attempting to seduce her, strikes him, and is sentenced to death. Sentiment and excitement mount until a last-minute reprieve.

Blackfriars Theatre A theatre erected in the grounds of an old monastery in London. It was first adapted as a private theatrical venue by Richard Farrant, master of the choirboys at Windsor, in 1576. After his death in 1581 a combined boy company appeared there briefly until 1584. In 1596 James Burbage attempted to revive another part of the monastery as a theatre but met with official opposition and it was not until 1600, when his son Richard Burbage leased the theatre to the Children of the Chapel Royal, that performances were again undertaken there. From 1608 to 1642 the King's Men were the resident company, presenting plays by Shakespeare, Jonson, and others and the venue became highly popular with the English nobility; productions there were notable for their use of scenery and music. The theatre was demolished in 1655.

blackout The extinguishing of all stage lighting, either suddenly (a **snap blackout**) or gradually, to allow for a scene change, suggest a break in the action, or achieve some other stage effect.

Blacks, The (*Les Nègres*) A play by Jean GENET. First performance: Paris, 1959. It explores the theme of racial conflict through a troupe of Black actors who perform a play within a play, in which a White woman is ritually murdered.

Blagrove, Thomas (d. 1603) English court official, who was appointed clerk to the MASTER OF THE REVELS in 1560. He was in charge of censorship in English drama for many years, subject to the Lord Chamberlain, but never became Master himself.

Blakely, Colin (1930–87) British actor, born in Ireland, who first attracted attention in O'Casey's *Cock-a-Doodle-Dandy* at the Royal Court in 1959. Subsequently he appeared with the Royal Shakespeare Company, the National Theatre, and in films. His finest roles included Pizarro in Shaffer's *The Royal Hunt of the Sun*, Kite in *The Recruiting Officer*, and Joe Keller in Miller's *All My Sons*.

Blakemore, Michael (1928–) Australian-born director, who worked as an actor in Britain before becoming a codirector of the Glasgow Citizens' Theatre in 1966–68. He was associate artistic director at the National Theatre (1971–76) but has subsequently worked freelance. Among modern playwrights he is particularly associated with the work of Peter NICHOLS, having directed the first productions of *A Day in the Death of Joe Egg* (1967), *The National Health* (1969), and *Privates on Parade* (1977). Other work includes Michael Frayn's *Noises Off* (1982) and Peter Shaffer's *Lettice and Lovage* (1987), as well as plays by O'Neill, Chekhov, and Ibsen. In 1998 he received two Tony awards for his Broadway productions of Frayn's *Copenhagen* and the musical *Kiss Me Kate*.

Blanchar, Pierre (1896–1963) French actor, who began his career at the Odéon in 1919. He excelled in numerous plays by contemporary authors, including Achard, Salacrou, Montherlant, and Camus; he also enjoyed a successful career in films. He appeared at the Comédie-Française from 1939 to 1946.

Blanchard, Kitty *See* Rankin, Arthur McKee.

Blanchard, William (1769–1835) British actor, born at York. His early attempts to run several northern theatres failed; in 1800 he arrived at Covent Garden as Bob Acres in *The Rivals* and stayed there for 34 years, except for a brief visit to the US in 1832. He was particularly noted for comedy character parts.

Blanchard's Amphitheatre *See* Chatham Theatre.

Bleasdale, Alan (1946–) British playwright, best-known for his television series *The Boys From the Blackstuff* (1983) and *GBH* (1991). His works for the stage include *Having a Ball* (1981), *Are You Lonesome Tonight?* (1985), a musical about the life of Elvis Presley, and *On the Ledge* (1993).

Blin, Roger (1907–84) French actor and director, who became famous as a director of notable works of the Theatre of the Absurd. Having previously worked with Artaud and Barrault, he won high praise in the 1950s for directing the first production of *En attendant Godot* (1953), in which he played Pozzo, and other works by Beckett. He also directed new plays by Adamov and Genet and became known for always designing his own sets.

Blithe Spirit A comedy by Noël COWARD. First performance: London, 1941. It centres on the activities of Madame Arcati, a medium, and Elvira, a troublesome ghost who returns to haunt her late and recently remarried husband Charles. The play enjoyed lengthy runs in both London and New York and has frequently been revived.

Bliziński, Józef (1827–93) Polish playwright, author of several comedies much influenced by the plays of Aleksander Fredro. His other dramatic works include such problem plays as *The Wrecks* (1877), which tackle various moral issues.

blocking The process of deciding at rehearsal the basic movement of the actors on the set, usually written down for later reference.

Blok, Alexandr Alexandrovich (1880–1921) Russian poet and playwright, who was a major figure of the Russian Symbolist movement. Such poetic dramas as *The Puppet Show* (1906) and *The Rose and the Cross* (eventually staged in Britain in 1941) exhibit the mixture of romance and despair that characterized his poetry.

Blondel *See* minstrel.

Blondin, Charles (Jean-François Gravelet; 1824–97) French tightrope walker, who became a popular star of British music hall. Best-known for his tightrope crossings of the Niagara Falls, he was much admired for his high wire act at the Crystal Palace in London from 1861 and made his last appearance in 1896.

Blood Brothers A musical by Willy RUSSELL. First performance: Liverpool, 1983, and subsequently in London. A West End revival opened in 1988 and was still running at the Phoenix Theatre in 2000. The plot, which is loosely adapted from Boucicault's THE CORSICAN BROTHERS, concerns the intertwining fates of twins parted at birth.

blood tub *See* gaff.

Blood Wedding (*Bodas de sangre*) A tragedy by GARCÍA LORCA. First performance: Madrid, 1933. The first part of a famous trilogy of folk tragedies (it was followed by YERMA and THE HOUSE OF BERNARDA ALBA), the play was based on an actual news item. It concerns the rivalry and eventual deaths of two suitors for the same gypsy woman; at the heart of the play is the conflict between passion and honour. It has also been translated as *Marriage of Blood*.

Bloom, Claire (1931–) British actress, who established her reputation in 1949, when she appeared in Fry's *The Lady's Not for Burning*. Subsequently she appeared at the Old Vic alongside Gielgud and others in various Shakespearean productions and began a successful film career. She returned to the stage with acclaimed performances in Ibsen's *Hedda Gabler* and *A Doll's House* (both 1971). Other successes have included Bolt's *Vivat! Vivat Regina!* (1972), *A Streetcar Named Desire* (1974) by Tennessee Williams, Chekhov's *The Cherry Orchard* (1981 and 1994), and *Electra* (1998). She has also toured with the one-woman show *These are Women*, a study of several Shakespearean heroines.

blue *See* border.

boards The constituent parts of a stage floor, variously supported by vertical posts, tie-bars, or bracing. Hence the phrase 'tread the boards', meaning acting in general.

Boar's Head Inn An inn in the Whitechapel district of London, where plays were staged in the 16th century. In 1595 the stage and galleries were roofed over and improved; the inn remained in use as a theatrical venue as late as 1616.

boat truck A movable platform, upon which a component part of the set can be wheeled onto the stage or, alternatively, raised up to it from below.

Bobèche (Antoine Mandelot; 1791–c. 1840) French actor, who specialized in farce, making many appearances in parades with **Galimafré** (Auguste Guérin; 1790–1870) at the Boulevard du Temple. Jokes at Napoleon's expense, however, obliged Bobèche to go into exile for a time before making a shortlived comeback, while Galimafré retired as a performer in 1814.

Bobo A comic character of the early Spanish theatre. A rustic clown, he appeared in the plays of Lope de Rueda and others. The GRACIOSO figure may have inherited some of his traits.

Bocage (Pierre-François Tousez; 1797–1863) French actor, who appeared for many years at the Odéon after failing to be accepted at the Comédie-Française. He became especially popular in melodrama and was eventually invited to join the Comédie-Française but quickly returned to the Odéon, becoming its director in 1845.

Bock, Jerry (1928–) US composer, who enjoyed a series of hits in the 1960s with the lyricist **Sheldon Harnik** (1924–); their *Fiddler on the Roof* (1964) was a world-wide triumph and set the record for the longest run for a Broadway musical. Other shows include *Fiorello!* (1959), *She Loves Me* (1963), *The Apple Tree* (1966), and *The Rothchilds* (1970).

Bodel, Jean (c. 1165–c. 1210) French poet and playwright, whose *Jeu de Saint Nicolas*, first performed at Arras in 1200, was the first French miracle play. The plot concerns a Saracen king's conversion to Christianity after the restoration of his stolen treasure by Saint Nicholas. Bodel's poetic works include a *chanson de geste* and a moving farewell to his friends.

Boeck, Johann Michael (1743–93) German actor, who appeared with his wife as a member of the troupe at Mannheim. His greatest success was as Karl Moor, a part which he was the first to create, in Schiller's *Die Räuber* in 1782.

Bogdanov, Michael (1938–) British director, who was an associate director for the National Theatre from 1980 to 1988 and cofounded the ENGLISH SHAKESPEARE COMPANY with Michael PENNINGTON in 1986. Earlier in his career he attracted attention working with Peter Brook, Barrault, and other leading figures on plays by Shakespeare and Molière with the Royal Shakespeare Company, the Young Vic, and other groups. His productions for the National Theatre included Brenton's *The Romans in Britain* (1980) and Chekhov's *Uncle Vanya* (1982). For the English Shakespeare Company he directed the massive cycle of seven history plays *The Wars of the Roses* (1987–89). His exuberant populist style has often proved controversial, as with a much-criticized production of Goethe's *Faust* (1996).

Bogusławski, Wojciech (1757–1829) Polish actor, director, and playwright, often regarded as the father of Polish theatre. He wrote more than 80 plays, of which the most important was the comic opera *Cracovians and Highlanders* (1794). As an actor, he was the first Polish Hamlet, appearing in his own version of Shakespeare's play; from 1783 to 1814 he was the director of the Polish National Theatre in Warsaw.

Boileau-Despréaux, Nicolas (1636–1711) French critic, a friend of Racine, La Fontaine, and Molière. In his influential critical writings he argued for the observance of classical standards in both drama and poetry.

Boisrobert, François le Métel, Seigneur de (1592–1662) French playwright. He found favour with Cardinal de Richelieu and exploited his position to assist other writers. A founder member of the Académie Française, he wrote several plays, of which the comedy *La Belle Plaideuse* (1654) is the only one of any lasting merit.

Boleslavsky, Richard *See* American Laboratory Theatre.

Bolt, Robert (Oxon) (1924–95) British playwright, who had his first West End success with *Flowering Cherry* (1957), a Chekhovian study with Ralph Richardson in the leading role. In 1960 A MAN FOR ALL SEASONS was an enormous success with Paul Scofield and Leo McKern as Sir Thomas More and Henry VIII; the play was notable for its use of Brechtian devices. Another historical drama, *Vivat! Vivat Regina!*, depicting the relationship of Elizabeth I and Mary Queen of Scots, was similarly successful in 1970. Other works included *The Tiger and the Horse* (1960), starring Michael and Vanessa Redgrave, *Gentle Jack* (1963), starring Edith Evans, the children's play *The Thwarting of Baron Bolligrew* (1965), and *State of Revolution* (1977), as well as several screenplays.

Bonarelli della Rovere, Guidobaldo (1563–1608) Italian playwright, whose pastoral *Filli di Sciro* (1607) was the most successful of the 17th century. English translations were also executed and presented before the royal court at London.

Bond, Edward (1934–) British playwright, whose first play, *The Pope's Wedding*, was presented at the Royal Court Theatre in 1962. Throughout his career Bond has maintained an uncompromising commitment to socialism. His earlier plays use parable-like forms, emphasizing the unjust nature of capitalist societies through violent and often stunning stage imagery (notably the stoning of a baby in SAVED). His plays of the 1970s and 1980s were premiered by the National Theatre, the Royal Shakespeare Company, and various politically active fringe groups. Subsequently, however, his didactic style fell out of favour and few of his recent works have reached the London stage.

Principal works:
  The Pope's Wedding: 1962.
  Saved: 1965.
  Early Morning: 1968.
  Narrow Road to the Deep North: 1968.
  Lear: 1971.
  The Sea: 1973.
  Bingo: 1973.
  The Fool: 1975.
  The Woman: 1978.
  The Bundle: 1978.
  The Worlds: 1979.
  Restoration: 1981.
  Summer: 1982.
  Restoration: 1988.
  In the Company of Men: 1989.
  September: 1990.
  Coffee: 1994.

Bonfils Theatre *See* Denver Performing Arts Center.

Bonstelle, Jessie (Laura Justine Bonesteel; 1872–1932) US actress and manager, who was a pioneer of civic theatre in the US. Known as the 'Maker of Stars', she worked with Augustin Daly for some years before taking up management and eventually establishing an important civic theatre in Detroit in 1928; performers who benefited from her support included Katharine Cornell.

Bontempelli, Massimo (1978–1960) Italian writer, who had a very active and varied literary career as playwright, poet, novelist, short-story writer, and critic. He is remembered chiefly for such novels as *Il figlio di due madri* (The Son of Two Mothers; 1930) and such plays as *La guardia della luna* (1920), *Nostra Dea* (1925) and *Minnie la candida* (1929).

Bon Ton Theatre *See* Koster and Bial's Music Hall.

book In a musical, the words which serve to advance the plot, as opposed to those which serve as an individual song. These are usually, but not always, spoken words. Thus, even a totally sung work can have a book; in an opera, it is called the **libretto** (Italian for 'little book').

book ceiling A hinged ceiling made from a pair of flats, formerly an integral part of a box set.

book flat A hinged flat, capable of standing without any other means of support. In the US such a flat is usually called a **two-fold**.

book-holder An Elizabethan term for the PROMPTER. Traditionally the book-holder was also in charge of all the props.

book-keeper A member of the Elizabethan acting company, who served as its librarian, copying play scripts and being responsible for them when they were not in use. In the Restoration theatre he was also sometimes employed as a prompter.

book wing An arrangement of attached wings, usually four in number, capable of being revolved so as to present a different scene, turning like the pages of a book.

boom A vertical batten in the wings or a horizontal batten suspended across the stage upon which lighting equipment is mounted; the lights themselves thus mounted may also be referred to as booms.

booth A temporary theatre, consisting of a sturdy platform and sometimes equipped with rudimentary items of scenery and props, in which travelling acting troupes formerly presented theatrical performances at fairs throughout Europe. The more elaborate booths consisted of a large tent (in which the stage and auditorium were housed) and had a smaller platform at the entrance that was used to attract an audience from (*see* parade). Flourishing until the 19th century, such booths provided venues for a wide variety of entertainments, from popular comedies and tragedies to melodramas and, in a reduced form, Punch and Judy shows.

Booth, Barton (1681–1733) British actor, who worked in Dublin before joining Betterton at the Lincoln's Inn Fields Theatre in 1700. His performance in *The Distressed Mother* (1712) brought fame, and in 1713 his interpretation of Cato in Addison's play confirmed him as the leading tragedian of the day. He was renowned for his habit of striking and holding dramatic attitudes during a play. For a time he also partnered Cibber and Wilks in the management of Drury Lane.

Booth, Junius Brutus (1796–1852) US actor, born in England, who was the head of a famous US theatrical family. He appeared regularly at Covent Garden and, from 1820, Drury Lane in leading Shakespearean roles and became a rival of Edmund Kean. In 1821, however, he left his wife and emigrated to the US with a flowerseller, Mary Ann Holmes, whom he married in 1851 and by whom he had 10 children. He was particularly admired as Richard III and Shylock, to which his grand style of acting was well suited, but suffered increasingly from melancholia and eventually madness.

His son **Junius Brutus Booth** (1821–83) began his acting career in 1835 on tour with his father and, in 1852, played Iago to his father's Othello. A member of the Bowery Theatre stock company, his best part was Dan Lowrie in *The Lass o' Lowrie's* (1878) by Frances Hodgson Burnett. His younger son, **Sydney Barton Booth** (1873–1937), was also an actor and star in vaudeville.

Edwin Thomas Booth (1833–93), another son of Junius Brutus Booth senior, was the first US actor to establish a major reputation as a tragedian in European theatrical circles. He first appeared in one of his father's productions and, at the age of 18, played the title role in *Richard III*. His most acclaimed tragic roles included Shylock in *The Merchant of Venice*, Hamlet, and the title role in Bulwer-Lytton's *Richelieu*. He also built Booth's Theatre in New York, opening it in 1869 playing Romeo to his second wife Mary McVicker's Juliet. After bankruptcy in 1873 he toured internationally and appeared alongside Irving in London. In 1888 he became associated with the Players' Club, although his later years were marred by melancholia.

Edwin's younger brother **John Wilkes Booth** (1839–64) was also an actor but is usually remembered as the assassin of President Lincoln, whom he shot at Ford's Theatre on 14 April, 1865 during a production of *Our American Cousin*. It has been suggested that he was jealous of Edwin Booth's success and hoped the crime would make him equally famous.

Booth, Shirley (Thelma Booth Ford; 1907–92) US actress, who made her first stage appearance in *The Cat and the Canary* (1919). Six years later she made her New York debut, going on to appear in major roles in *The Philadelphia Story* (1939), *My Sister Eileen* (1940), and *The Time of the Cuckoo* (1952). She received awards as Grace Woods in Fay Kanin's *Goodbye, My Fancy* (1948) and as Lola in William Inge's *Come Back, Little Sheba* (1950). She also appeared in musicals and on television and radio.

Booth's Theatre A large theatre built for Edwin Booth on 23rd Street, New York. Its features included a hydraulic lift system for lowering three-dimensional scenery to the cellar and a stage with no rake. It opened in 1869 with *Romeo and Juliet* starring Booth and Mary McVicker. Booth gave many of his best performances here in subsequent seasons, supported by such players as Lawrence Barrett and Charlotte Cushman. It was also the venue for the first New York appearance of Adelaide Neilson and the last appearances of Kate Bateman, the younger James Wallack, and Charles Thorne. Other famous performers to appear included Joseph Jefferson III, Janauschek, and Minnie Maddern (later Mrs Fiske).

By 1874, following Booth's bankruptcy in 1873 and his elder brother Junius Brutus Booth's failure as manager, the theatre had passed out of the family's control. Subsequent successes included *Henry V* and Byron's *Sardanapalus*, both directed by Louis Calvert. Boucicault took over the theatre in 1879 but the building was demolished after *Romeo and Juliet*, with Modjeska and Maurice Barrymore, was staged in 1883.

Booth Theatre A 766-seat theatre on West 45th Street, New York, which opened in 1918 with Arnold Bennett's *The Great Adventure*. Productions staged there have included Kaufman and Hart's *You Can't Take It With You* (1936), which ran for two years, William Saroyan's *The Time of Your Life* (1934), Inge's *Come Back, Little Sheba* (1950), Bernard Pomerance's *The Elephant Man* (1979), and Stephen Sondheim's award-winning *Sunday in the Park with George* (1985).

Borchert, Wolfgang (1921–47) German playwright, short-story writer, and poet, whose single drama, *Draussen vor der Tür* (1947), reflected his experiences as a soldier and prisoner during World War II and its aftermath. The play expressed the despair he felt at the desolation of Germany in the immediate post-war years.

border A narrow strip of curtain or other material hung across the stage behind the proscenium arch. Formerly called a **top drop**, it is used to conceal lighting and other equipment from the audience's view. If painted as foliage it is usually referred to as a **tree border**; if painted as sky it is called a **sky border** or **blue**.

border lights *See* batten.

Borisova, Yulia Konstantinovna (1925–) Russian actress, who became famous in plays by contemporary Soviet authors at the Vakhtangov Theatre, where she first appeared in 1949. She was highly acclaimed in works by Arbuzov and in Dostoevsky's *The Idiot* (1958).

Bottomley, Gordon (1874–1948) British poet and playwright, whose poetic dramas *King Lear's Wife* (1915), *Britain's Daughters* (1922), *Gruach* (1923), and *Laodice and Danae* (1930) reflect the influence both of Shakespeare and of Japanese *Nō* plays. His other works include *The Acts of St Peter* (1933), written for the Exeter Cathedral Festival.

Boublil, Alain (1941–) French playwright and author, who with the composer Claude-Michel Schönberg (1944–) enjoyed huge international success with the musicals LES MISÉRABLES (1980) and MISS SAIGON (1989); a third collaboration, *Martin Guerre* (1996), proved rather less successful. His other work includes the straight play *Le Journal d'Adam et Eve* (1994).

Boucicault, Dion(-ysius) Lardner (c. 1822–90) Irish playwright, actor, and director, born in Dublin, who was the author of roughly 250 popular plays, including adaptations of other plays, melodramas, and musical extravaganzas. After beginning as an actor, under the name Lee Morton, he established his reputation with LONDON ASSURANCE – one of the most popular plays of the century – and subsequently worked with Ben Webster at the Adelphi Theatre. Later he joined Charles Kean at the Princess's Theatre, where his most notable success was his adaptation of THE CORSICAN BROTHERS. *The Poor of New York* (later retitled after whichever city the play was being performed in) made his name in the US, while *The Octoroon*, in which – as in several other of his plays – his lover Agnes Robertson (by whom he had four children) appeared, broke new ground in seriously examining the lot of US Blacks.

His other works include a series of Irish plays, of which *The Colleen Bawn* – about the murder of an Irish girl by a British officer – was the most successful, melodramas based on horse-racing, and dramatizations of stories by Dickens and Washington Irving. He also ran a school for young actors, pressed for copyright protection (despite his own transgressions), and pioneered the matinée performance and use of the box set.

Principal works:
  London Assurance: 1841.
  The Corsican Brothers: 1852.
  The Poor of New York: 1857.
  Jessie Brown; or, the Relief of Lucknow: 1858.
  The Octoroon; or, Life in Louisiana: 1859.
  Dot: 1859.
  The Colleen Bawn; or, the Brides of Garryowen: 1860.
  Arrah-na-Pogue; or, The Wicklow Wedding: 1864.
  Hunted Down: 1866.
  The Flying Scud; or, Four-Legged Fortune: 1866.
  Babil and Bijou; or, the Lost Regalia: 1872.
  The Shaughraun: 1874.

Boucicault, Dot (Darley George Boucicault; 1859–1929) British actor-manager and playwright, son of Dion Boucicault, who appeared in his father's company before becoming director at the Duke of York's Theatre in London (1901–15). His finest roles included Sir William Gower in Pinero's *Trelawny of the 'Wells'*; his wife was the actress Irene VANBRUGH.

Boucicault, Nina (1867–1950) British actress, daughter of Dion Boucicault. She began her career in her father's company, appearing in *The Colleen Bawn* in 1885. Later successes included *Charley's Aunt* by Brandon Thomas and *The Light that Failed*, based on Kipling's story; she was best-known, however, as the first to play the title role in Barrie's *Peter Pan* (1904).

Bouffes du Nord, Théâtre des *See* International Centre of Theatre Research.

Boulevard du Temple A fairground in Paris, where a number of notable BOOTHs formerly existed. Of these small theatrical venues, the most significant included the permanent stages of the AMBIGU, the FUNAMBULES, and the GAÎTÉ; authors for these theatres included Dumas *père* and Pixérécourt. The site was destroyed when Paris was extensively redesigned in 1862.

Boulevard plays A form of popular French drama of the late 19th and 20th centuries, equivalent to that presented in the West End in London and on Broadway in New York. Traditionally encompassing farce and domestic drama, the genre developed from the plays performed in the fairground booths of Paris and reached its peak before World War I; it has since declined. Successful playwrights of *Boulevard* plays have included Feydeau, Labiche, and Achard.

Bourchier, Arthur (1863–1927) British actor-manager. A founder-member of the Oxford University Dramatic Society, he left Oxford to join Lillie Langtry's company in 1889. He was manager of the Garrick Theatre from 1900 to 1906 and appeared frequently with his wife, Violet VANBRUGH. In 1910 he transferred to Her Majesty's Theatre, where he appeared with Tree.

Bourdet, Édouard (1887–1945) French playwright and administrator of the Comédie-Française (1936–40). His plays are social satires, characterized by sharp psychological insight. *La Prisonnière* (1926) deals with lesbianism and *La Fleur des pois* (1932) with homosexuality; *Vient de paraître* (1927) attacks the commercial world of publishing and literature.

Bourgogne, Théâtre de l'Hôtel de The first permanent theatre to be built in Paris, erected in the ruins of the palace of the dukes of Burgundy by the CONFRÉRIE DE LA PASSION in 1548. Long and narrow in shape, with a small stage, the theatre was hired out to travelling companies until about 1610, when the King's Players, run by Valleran-Lecomte, were installed there. The Hôtel de Bourgogne then remained the most important venue in the city until the opening of the Théâtre du Marais in 1634 and the emergence of Molière; in 1680 the resident company was absorbed into the Comédie-Française. Subsequently the theatre was used for performances of the Comédie-Italienne until 1783.

Boursault, Edmé (1638–1701) French playwright, chiefly remembered for *Le Portrait du peintre* (1663), an attack on Molière prompted by the latter's CRITIQUE DE L'ÉCOLE DES FEMMES; the two men were later reconciled. Boursault's finest plays were written during the last two decades of his life: *Le Mercure galant* (1683) satirized a periodical of that name, whose editor's objections led to the adoption of the play's alternative title *La Comédie sans titre*.

Bouschet, Jan *See* Sackville, Thomas, First Earl of Dorset.

Bouwmeester, Louis (1841–1925) Dutch actor, who became a leading figure of the first Dutch national theatre. He appeared, often alongside his sister **Theo Bouwmeester** (1850–1939), in plays by Dumas *fils*, Sardou, and others and was much admired as Shakespeare's Shylock.

Bowery Theatre A theatre in New York, which opened in 1826 as the New York Theatre, Bowery and enjoyed early success with appearances by Edwin Forrest. In 1828 the theatre was burned down but reopened later the same year and had further success under the management of Hamblin before being burned down again in 1836. It reopened in 1837, burned down in 1838, reopened in 1839, burned down in 1845, and reopened again four months later. Edward Eddy made his first appearance there in 1851 and became a great favourite, briefly working as manager there. In 1858 it became a home of pantomime and, as the **Old Bowery Theatre**, melodrama and burlesque. The theatre closed in 1878 and reopened a year later as the **Thalia Theatre**, housing German-language plays. After further fires in 1923 and 1929, it was closed and not rebuilt.

Another **Bowery Theatre**, later called the **Stadt Theatre**, opened as a venue for circus acts in 1835 and subsequently staged both plays and German opera.

A **New Bowery Theatre** was opened by the managers of the Bowery Theatre in 1859. Run by George L Fox, it staged a variety of shows until being destroyed by fire in 1866.

box *See* auditorium.

box office The area, customarily in the foyer of a theatre, where tickets may be purchased for current or future performances. It is usually run by the box office manager and his assistants.

box set A naturalistic set of a room, consisting of three walls (and sometimes a ceiling) constructed from flats, usually with working doors and windows. The box set was introduced to Britain by Madame Vestris in 1832 but has been less widely used in modern drama.

Boy Bishop A boy chosen to oversee the merrymaking at an annual festival observed at various choir schools and other religious establishments throughout Europe in medieval times. Nominally a religious occasion, the festival provided an opportunity for the performance of plays in Latin until the practice was ended during the Reformation. The tradition was often amalgamated with the festivities associated with the Feast of Fools.

boy companies (or children's companies) Theatrical companies first organized in the 16th century from the choirboys at the Chapels Royal in London and Windsor and from those at St Paul's cathedral. Under such Masters as Richard Farrant, William Cornish, Sebastian Westcott, Nathaniel Giles, and Philip Rosseter, the companies acquired a fine reputation for their performances of masques and disguisings at Court before being introduced to the professional theatre. Regularly on stage at the Blackfriars Theatre from 1576 and later at the Whitefriars Theatre and elsewhere, members of the companies acted in first performances of major plays by Lyly, Jonson, Chapman, and many others and several of them, including Ezekiel Fenn, Nathan Field, William Ostler, John Rice, and Richard Robinson, went on to become popular adult actors. The fashion for child actors, which attracted the scorn of Shakespeare and other writers of serious drama, died out, however, by 1615.

Boy Friend, The A musical written and composed by Sandy WILSON. First performance: Players' Theatre, London, 1953. A gentle spoof of the musical comedies of the 1920s, the show ultimately transferred to Wyndham's Theatre for a run of more than five years and provided the basis of a successful film.

Boyle, Roger See Orrery, Lord.

Boyle, William (1853–1923) Irish playwright, whose works were performed in the Abbey Theatre, Dublin. *The Building Fund* (1905) is a comic exploration of avarice, while *The Eloquent Dempsey* (1906) satirizes political duplicity and *Family Failing* (1912) deals with indolence. *The Mineral Workers* (1906) and *Nic* (1916) both examine the impact of modern values on traditional Irish life.

bozze An early form of stage lighting, first developed in Italy in the 17th century. It consisted of a glass globe fitted with handles and a wick and could be used to achieve colour effects when placed behind bottles of coloured liquid.

Bracco, Roberto (1862–1943) Italian playwright and progenitor of the Theatre of SILENCE. A versatile dramatist, Bracco wrote such comedies as *Il frutto acerbo* (Bitter Fruit; 1904), dramas in the vein of Ibsen, notably *Fantasmi* (Ghosts; 1906), and naturalistic studies of Neapolitan life, including *Don Pietro Caruso* (1895). His most important play was *Il piccolo santo* (The Little Saint; 1909). Because he actively opposed Fascism, Bracco's work suffered a long period of neglect and only in recent decades has there been a renewed interest in his once popular plays.

brace A length of wood used to support a flat, usually held in place by a weight and attached to the flat by means of a hook and eye.

Bracegirdle, Anne (c. 1663–1748) British actress, who began her stage career under Betterton. Despite the murder of William MOUNTFORT in a quarrel over her favours, she enjoyed a chaste reputation, although she was the mistress of Congreve for several years. She is credited with creating Congreve's Angelica in *Love for Love* (1695) and Millamant in *The Way of the World* (1700). She is also thought to have been the first woman to play Portia in *The Merchant of Venice*.

Brady, William Aloysius (1863–1950) US actor, producer, and manager, who produced many successful plays in the Manhattan, 48th Street, and Playhouse theatres of New York. These included Du Maurier's *Trilby* and Harriet Beecher Stowe's *Uncle Tom's Cabin*. He made his acting debut in 1882 and by 1888 had formed his own touring company; he was also manager to Helen Hayes, Douglas Fairbanks, Grace George (his wife), and Alice Brady (his daughter).

Brahm, Otto (Otto Abrahamsohn; 1856–1912) German director and critic, who did much to encourage the development of Realism in the early 20th century. Under the influence of André Antoine, he founded the FREIE BÜHNE in Berlin in 1889, where he presented plays by Ibsen and Tolstoy. Subsequently he directed the Deutsche Theater in Berlin and trained actors in the naturalistic style of Stanislavsky. Later he took over the Lessing Theater in Berlin.

Braithwaite, Dame (Florence) Lilian (1873–1948) British actress, who first appeared as a professional in South Africa and subsequently with Benson's company, finally joining Alexander's company at the St James's Theatre in 1901. Acclaimed as a performer of long-suffering heroines, she also triumphed as the mother in Coward's *The Vortex* in 1924 and later appeared in light comedies, notably *Arsenic and Old Lace* (1942).

Branagh, Kenneth (1961–) British actor and director, born in Northern Ireland. After winning the Bancroft Gold Medal at RADA he made an outstanding London debut as Judd in Julian Mitchell's *Another Country* (1982). In 1984 he joined the Royal Shakespeare Company and enjoyed huge acclaim as a youthful Henry V. In 1986 he founded the **Renaissance Theatre Company**, starred in his own play *Tell Me Honestly*, and directed *Twelfth Night*. His company, which was seen as reviving the tradition of the actor-manager, went on to present a season of Shakespeare in 1988 and several productions directed by leading actors, including Judi Dench. Since 1988 he has worked mainly in films, including several self-directed Shakespearean productions. More recent stage work has included *Look Back in Anger* (1989), and *Hamlet* for the RSC (1992).

Brand A verse tragedy by Henrik IBSEN, published in 1866. First performance: Stockholm, 1885. Initially composed as a narrative poem but later rewritten in Italy, the play is an ironic exploration of the bleakness Ibsen perceived in the Norwegian character. It concerns Brand, a fanatical pastor whose refusal to compromise with the world brings destruction on all those around him. The play was an immediate success and secured Ibsen's reputation in Europe.

Brandane, John (John MacIntyre; 1869–1947) Scottish playwright and doctor, who wrote for the Scottish National Players and later became one of their directors. His humorous and carefully observed plays, notably *The Glen is Mine*, employ Highland settings. He was also influential in encouraging James Bridie to become a dramatist.

Brandão, Raul (1867–1930) Portuguese novelist and playwright, who was the author of a number of naturalistic plays tackling the issues of poverty and oppression. *Jesus Cristo em Lisboa* is typical, depicting the arrival of Christ in the slums of Lisbon.

Brandes, Georg (1842–1927) Danish theatre critic and scholar, who did much to reform Scandinavian literature in the late 19th century. Encouraged by Ibsen, he argued for the increased use of naturalistic styles in his many lectures, collected as *Hovedstrømninger* (Main Currents in Nineteenth-Century Literature; 1872–90). He also supported such notable playwrights as Bjørnson, Kielland, and Strindberg and was a champion of Nietzsche; his writings include biographies of Shakespeare, Goethe, and Voltaire.

Brandes, Johann Christian (1735–99) German actor and playwright, who became popular as a writer of monodramas during the 1770s. He had little success as an actor, appearing with the companies of Schönemann, Schuch, and subsequently Iffland.

His wife was the actress **Esther Charlotte Henrietta Koch** (1746–84), who was much acclaimed in tragedy; his daughter **Minna Brandes** (1765–88) also appeared on the stage.

Brando, Marlon (1924–) US actor, born in Nebraska. After being expelled for indiscipline from acting school in New York, Brando attended the Actors' Studio, where he studied with Elia Kazan. He first appeared on Broadway in *I Remember Mama* (1944). Subsequent theatre performances included *Truckline Cafe* (1946), *Candida* (1946), and *The Eagle Has Two Heads* (1946). *A Streetcar Named Desire* (1947) made Brando's reputation on Broadway and four years later in the cinema. Thereafter he largely confined himself to the cinema, as a leading exponent of METHOD acting.

Branner, Hans Christian (1903–66) Danish novelist, short-story writer, and playwright, who first achieved success in the theatre with a dramatization of his novel *Rytteren* (1949). This was followed by the comedy *Søskende* (1951), *Thermopyloe* (1957), which was set during the Occupation, and several radio plays.

Brasseur, Pierre (Pierre Espinasse; 1905–72) French actor, who first appeared on stage as a child and later became one of the leading actors in Paris, following initial success in *Le Sexe faible* (1929). He was praised in strong romantic roles in plays by Claudel, Sartre, Anouilh, Montherlant, and Shaw, being particularly admired as Edmund Kean in Sartre's adaptation of Dumas *père's Kean*. His film roles included a celebrated impersonation of Frédéric Lemaître in Carné-Prevert's *Les Enfants du paradis* (1944).

Brayton, Lily *See* Asche, Oscar.

Bread and Puppet Theatre A US theatre company, which was founded by Peter Schumann in 1961 to present large-scale popular theatre on socialist principles. Typical productions involve the use of massive puppets; noted successes have included *The Cry of the People for Meat* (1969). The company has been based in Vermont since 1974.

Brecht, (Eugen) Bertolt (1898–1956) German playwright, director, and poet, who is recognized as one of the most important figures in 20th century drama. Brecht wrote his first works for the theatre – much influenced by Expressionism – while studying medicine in Munich after World War I; these ultimately led to appointments at the Munich Kammerspiele (1921) and then as assistant to Reinhardt at the Deutsches Theater in Berlin in 1924.

Mann ist Mann marked the beginnings of his theory of EPIC THEATRE and the introduction of the controversial ALIENATION EFFECT, ideas later codified in his treatise *Kleines Organon für das Theater* (1949). After marrying (1928) his second wife, Helene WEIGEL, who appeared in many of his plays, Brecht collaborated with Kurt WEILL on a series of didactic musical dramas, many of which featured Weill's wife Lotte LENYA. Other influences at that time included that of oriental drama, notably through the translations of Arthur Waley.

In 1933 Brecht and his wife fled Nazi Germany, finally arriving in the US in 1941. During this unsettled time he wrote most of his best-known plays, in which he studies the human condition with great sensitivity while encouraging his audience to maintain a coolly intellectual detachment from the events being portrayed, often in highly poetic terms. A fervent critic of capitalism and totalitarianism, his Marxist leanings led eventually to his examination (1947) by the notorious Committee for Un-American Activities, before which he defended himself with great skill.

In 1949 he and his wife returned to East Germany, founding the BERLINER ENSEMBLE at the Theater am Schiffbauerdamm to present many of Brecht's early works as well as his adaptations of plays by Shakespeare and others. All his dramas after 1928 were distinguished by an increasingly overt Marxist element. This has contributed greatly to the controversy that his plays have continued to arouse in the years since his death, despite a general acceptance of his brilliance as a writer and theorist for the stage.

Principal works:

Baal: 1923 (written 1918).
Trommeln in der Nacht: 1922; translated as *Drums in the Night*.
Im Dickicht der Städte: 1923; translated as *In the Jungle of the Cities*.
Edward II: 1924.
Mann ist Mann: 1926; translated as *A Man's a Man*.
Die Dreigroschenoper: 1928; translated as THE THREEPENNY OPERA.
Aufstieg und Fall der Stadt Mahagonny: 1927; translated as *The Rise and Fall of the City of Mahagonny*.
Happy End: 1929.
Der Jasager und der Neinsager: 1929–30.
Die sieben Todsünden: 1933; translated as *The Seven Deadly Sins*.
Die heilige Johanna der Schlacthöfe: 1959 (written 1930s); translated as *St Joan of the Stockyards*.

Mutter Courage und ihre Kinder: 1941; translated as MOTHER COURAGE AND HER CHILDREN.

Leben des Galilei: 1943; translated as GALILEO.

Der gute Mensch von Sezuan: 1943; now usually translated as THE GOOD PERSON OF SETZUAN.

Schweik in the Second World War: 1943.

Der kaukasische Kreidekreis: 1954 (written 1945); translated as THE CAUCASIAN CHALK CIRCLE.

Herr Puntila und sein Knecht Matti: 1948; translated as *Herr Puntila and his servant Matti*.

Die Tage der Kommune: 1949; translated as *The Days of the Commune*.

Die Gesichte der Simone Machard: 1957; translated as *The Vision of Simone Machard*.

Der aufthaltsame Aufstieg des Arturo Ui: 1958; translated as THE RESISTIBLE RISE OF ARTURO UI.

Brécourt, Guillaume Marcoureau, Sieur de (1638–85) French actor and playwright. Brécourt performed with the Théâtre du Marais and with Molière's company before joining the Hôtel de Bourgogne in 1664. Forced into exile for a time after he killed a coachman in a quarrel, he ended his career with the Comédie-Française. He excelled both in comic roles and in the tragedies of Racine; as a playwright he was less successful.

Bredero, Gerbrand Adriaansz (1585–1618) Dutch poet and playwright, born in Amsterdam, who was the author of three celebrated late medieval farces, notably the *Farce of the Cow* (1612). Together with his comedies set against a background of cosmopolitan Dutch life, the best of which was *The Spanish Brabanter* (1617), these effectively established the Dutch comic tradition. His work was characterized by the realism with which he contrasted the conflicting worlds of the gentry and the common people.

breeches part A role in which an actress plays a male character, a common feature of English comedies of the early 18th century. Noted performers of such parts included Peg Woffington, Mrs Bracegirdle, and Mrs Mountfort. Subsequently the tradition was maintained on the Victorian stage by such distinguished actresses as Madame Vestris and Sarah Bernhardt (who was famous for her Hamlet) and by various music hall performers. More recently it has survived primarily in cabaret and pantomime, in which the PRINCIPAL BOY is conventionally played by an actress. *Compare* female impersonator.

Brenton, Howard (1942–) British playwright best known for the controversial play THE ROMANS IN BRITAIN. His early plays were performed in the late 1960s at the Royal Court's Theatre Upstairs and subsequently he became resident dramatist at the Royal Court (1972–73). His most significant plays have included *Brassneck* (with David Hare, 1973), *The Churchill Play* (1974), and *Epsom Downs* (1977). Many of his plays present disturbing images, ranging from male rape to urban terrorism, to criticize postwar British society. His more recent plays have included *Pravda* (with David Hare, 1985), a satire on tabloid journalism, *Berlin Bertie* (1992), and several topical satires written with the journalist Tariq Ali. He has also translated works by Brecht and Büchner.

Bresselau, Menahem Mendel (1760–1827) Jewish playwright, whose plays were heavily influenced by Moses Luzzato. His play *Yaldut Ubahrut* (1786) was written for a bar mitzvah.

Bretón de los Herredos, Manuel (1796–1873) Spanish poet and playwright, who was the author of over 180 original plays and adaptations of Spanish, French, and German dramas. He established his reputation with his first play, *A la vejez, viruelas* (1824), and went on to write numerous gently satirical bourgeois comedies, including the well-known *Marcela, o ¿cual de los tres?* (1831).

Brice, Fanny (Fannie Borach; 1891–1951) US actress and singer, married to Billy Rose, who began her long career with Ziegfeld's *Follies* in 1910. In 1931 she appeared in the play *Crazy Quilt*, written by her husband. Her life was dramatized in Styne's *Funny Girl*.

bridge An extension of the flies, capable of being raised and lowered in order to facilitate work on lighting and scenery. In the US it is often referred to as an **elevator**. *See also* catwalk.

Bridges, Dr John *See* Stevenson, William.

Bridges-Adams, William (1889–1965) British director, who worked at various provincial repertory theatres before being appointed director of the theatre in Stratford-on-Avon as successor to Frank Benson. He directed 29 of Shakespeare's plays there before the fire of 1926 and subsequently oversaw the opening of the new theatre in 1932; in 1934 he left to work for the British Council.

Bridie, James (Osborne Henry Mavor; 1888–1951) Scottish doctor, playwright, and founder of the Glasgow Citizens' Theatre. His success with THE ANATOMIST launched him upon a prolific writing career. His plays are somewhat loosely constructed, but the dialogue is engaging and vital. Many explore Scottish themes, especially the conflict between puritanism and worldliness; others range from comedies and biblical plays to historical dramas and ballad operas. His greatest success came in 1949 when Edith Evans was much acclaimed in the leading role of *Daphne Laureola*.

Principal works:
The Anatomist: 1930.
Tobias and the Angel: 1930.
Jonah and the Whale: 1932.
A SLEEPING CLERGYMAN: 1933.
Susannah and the Elders: 1937.
What Say They?: 1939.
Mr Bolfry: 1943.
It Depends What You Mean: 1944.
Doctor Angelus: 1947.
Daphne Laureola: 1949.
Mr Gillie: 1950.
The Queen's Comedy: 1950.

Briers, Richard (1934–) British actor, who began his career with the Liverpool Playhouse company and made his West End debut in 1959. Acclaimed as a comedy and farce actor, he is particularly well-known for his television appearances but has also been praised for stage performances in such plays as Stoppard's *The Real Inspector Hound* (1968), Ayckbourn's *Absurd Person Singular* (1973), and Ibsen's *The Wild Duck* (1980). Since 1986 he has been a member of BRANAGH's Renaissance Theatre Company, starring as Malvolio in 1987 and Lear on a world tour in 1990. He has also appeared in Branagh's Shakespearean films.

Brieux, Eugène (1858–1932) French playwright, born in Paris. His plays deal with social evils – the unethical behaviour of a magistrate in *La Robe rouge* (1900), venereal disease in *Les Avariés* (1902; translated as *Damaged Goods*, 1911) – and were praised by G B Shaw. Other plays include *Le Trois Filles de M Dupont* (1897).

Brigadoon A musical fantasy by Alan Jay LERNER and Frederick Loewe. First performance: Broadway, 1947. This story of the accidental intrusion of two modern Americans into a bewitched Scottish village reached London in 1949 and was successfully filmed in 1954.

Brighella A character of the *commedia dell'arte*, one of the *zanni*. Formerly depicted as a thieving rogue, he gradually diminished into a scheming but sentimental servant.

Brighouse, Harold (1882–1958) British novelist and playwright, who became associated with the 'Manchester School' of playwrights (*see* New Drama). He wrote over 50 one-act and 16 full-length plays, many for the newly established repertory theatres before World War I. His plays, which were frequently set in his native Lancashire, included *Dealing in Futures* (1909), *The Northerners* (1914), *Zack* (1916), *Garside's Career* (1914) and the still-performed HOBSON'S CHOICE.

Brighton Beach Memoirs A play by Neil SIMON. First performance: New York, 1983. The first of a semi-autobiographical trilogy (with *Biloxi Blues* and *Broadway Bound*), it shows Eugene Jerome (Simon) and his family dealing with the stresses of the Depression. While still very funny, the play has a seriousness seen as marking a new phase in Simon's career.

Brighton Theatre *See* Bijou Theatre.

bristle trap A trap by means of which an actor appears through overlapping bristles or foliage.

Bristol Hippodrome A theatre in Bristol, opened in 1912 as a home of variety. Seating 1975, the original theatre contained a large water tank and was used for circuses and musical as well as dramatic productions. In 1948 a fire destroyed the building; it was subsequently rebuilt as a venue for leading touring companies, including the National Theatre.

Bristol Old Vic A theatre in Bristol, reconstructed (1941–43) from the old **Theatre Royal**. The oldest working theatre in England (founded in 1766), it reopened under its present name with *She Stoops to Conquer* by Oliver Goldsmith and later acquired its own respected resident company (founded by Hugh HUNT in 1946). Successful productions since then have included the musical *Salad Days* (1954), *Love's Labour's Lost* (1964), and *Born in the Gardens* (1979) by Peter Nichols. The theatre was extensively altered and enlarged in the 1970s and now seats 650; it also includes a smaller studio theatre, the New Vic, seating 150, and a theatre school.

Britannia Music Hall *See* Rotunda.

Britannia Theatre A theatre in Hoxton, London, which opened in 1841 as the Britannia Saloon, providing free entertainment for diners. After a period as a music hall it became a venue for plays under Sam LANE – who ran it until 1871 – in 1843, being considerably enlarged in 1850. Sam Lane's wife Sara took over the management on her husband's death and the theatre prospered, its pantomimes being particularly successful. Closed for a time in 1903, the theatre later reverted to its use as a music hall and then became a cinema; it was destroyed by bombs during World War II.

British Actors' Equity Association A trade union for professional actors in Britain, established in 1929 to oversee matters relating to actors' salaries, conditions of employment, etc. Equity was originally set up under the guidance of Ben Webster and replaced earlier models, including H B Irving's and Seymour Hicks's Actors Union. It now regulates radio, film, and television drama as well as stage performances and defends the rights of its members against actors from outside the association; it also helps to subsidize ailing professional companies. The rival **Variety Artists Federation**, founded in 1906, merged with Equity in 1968.

British Council A British organization dedicated to the promotion of British culture abroad. It established a specialist drama department in 1939, amalgamating it with dance in 1980, and helps to organize overseas tours by British companies as well as offering publicity and advice and arranging visits to Britain by distinguished theatrical figures from other countries.

British Drama League *See* British Theatre Association.

British Theatre Association (BTA) A British theatre organization, which helps to coordinate amateur drama throughout Britain. Originally called the **British Drama League**, it was founded in 1919 by Geoffrey Whitworth (1883–1951) and fosters contact between amateur groups (as well as some professional companies), runs a library service, and stages a national drama festival annually. Parallel organizations elsewhere in the British Isles include the Scottish Community Drama Association, founded in 1926, the Amateur Drama Association in Wales, founded in 1965, and the Amateur Drama Council in Ireland, founded in 1952. The **International Amateur Theatre Association**, based in The Hague, was established by E Martin Browne in 1952.

British Theatre Museum Association *See* Theatre Museum.

Britton, Nellie *See* Lang, (Alexander) Matheson.

Brizard, Jean-Baptiste (1721–91) French actor, who became noted as a player of elderly characters after joining the Comédie-Française in 1756. His roles included Henry of Navarre in Colle's *La partie de chasse d'Henri IV* (1774) and the first French King Lear (1782).

Broadhurst, George Howells (1866–1952) US playwright, born in England, who wrote such comedies as *What Happened to Jones* (1897) before winning acclaim with such dramas as *The Man of the Hour* (1906) and *Bought and Paid For* (1911). From 1917 he presented plays at his own Broadhurst Theatre.

Broadhurst Theatre A 1185-seat theatre on West 44th Street, New York, which was opened in 1917 by George Broadhurst with the New York premiere of G B Shaw's *Mis-*

alliance. Since then both musicals and straight plays have been staged there, including *Broadway* (1926), *Men In White* (1933), a famous revival of *Pal Joey* (1952), *Cabaret* (1966), *More Stately Mansions* (1967), *Amadeus* (1980), *Kiss of the Spider Woman* (1993), and *The Tempest* (1995) with Patrick Stewart.

Broadway An avenue in New York City that runs the length of Manhattan from Battery Park in the south to Inwood Hill at the northern end. More generally, the term is used to refer to the theatre district in Manhattan, through which Broadway runs, and the commercial theatre throughout New York. Theatres have clustered close to Broadway since before 1800, gradually moving to the northern ('uptown') end as Manhattan Island became more populated. Broadway reached its peak in the 1920s, when it boasted 80 theatres and was known as The Great White Way because of its brilliant lighting.

Most 'Broadway' theatres do not have a Broadway address, but are on the side streets between Broadway and 8th Avenue. The actual distinction between Broadway and so-called OFF-BROADWAY theatres lies in the size of the house, the various unions having different wage scales for different sizes, 'Broadway' being the largest. Owing mainly to changes in the audience caused by the rise of world tourism since the 1970s, Broadway has come to specialize in musicals and star revivals, with new straight plays being presented mainly off-Broadway.

Broadway Alliance An agreement (1990) between unions, producers, and theatre owners whereby certain of the smaller Broadway houses are allowed to pay reduced salaries and royalties to increase the chance of making a profit from serious drama. The first plays produced on these terms were financial failures, but success was achieved with Terrence McNally's *Love! Valour! Compassion!* in 1992.

Broadway Music Hall *See* Wallack's Lyceum.

Broadway Opera House *See* Bijou Theatre.

Broadway Theatre There have been several theatres in New York with this name since 1837, when the former **Euterpean Hall** on Broadway adopted this title.

In 1847 another theatre of this name opened on Broadway with Sheridan's *The School for Scandal*, starring Henry Wallack. Based on London's Haymarket Theatre, it became the home of the former Park Theatre company in 1848; performers who appeared there included Edwin Forrest, Charlotte Cushman, and the Bateman family. It collapsed in 1855, was rebuilt, but closed for good in 1859.

A third **Broadway Theatre** was opened on Broadway in 1880 as the **Metropolitan Casino** with Fanny Davenport in Sardou's *Tosca*. Subsequent successes included *Ben Hur* (1899), pantomime, and Frances Hodgson Burnett's *Little Lord Fauntleroy* (1907). It was turned into a cinema in 1913 and demolished in 1929.

The current 1759-seat **Broadway Theatre** on Broadway and 53rd Street, was opened as a cinema in 1924. It has been used for live productions since 1930. From 1930 to 1935 it housed Earl Carroll's *Varieties* and other vaudeville shows; it was then used as a cinema until 1943, when Moss Hart's *Lady in the Dark* was staged there. Other productions seen there have included the musicals *Gypsy* (1959), *Cabaret* (1968), *Candide* (1974), *The Wiz* (1977), *Evita* (1979), *Les Misérables* (1987), and *Miss Saigon* (1991).

Brockmann, Johann Franz Hieronymus (1745–1812) German actor, who was a leading member of Schröder's company at Hamburg. His roles there included Hamlet (1776); subsequently he was equally acclaimed at the Burgtheater in Vienna.

Bródy, Sándor (1863–1924) Hungarian novelist and playwright, who wrote a number of influential naturalistic dramas. Best known for his non-dramatic prose, he had his biggest stage success with a dramatization of his novel *Snow White* (1901).

Brody Singers Performers of Yiddish entertainments in Russia during the 19th century. Named after the town of Brody (then in Poland), these performers specialized in comic and sentimental music, sketches, and dance and provided the basis for the early Yiddish theatre in Russia.

Broken Jug, The (*Der zerbrochene Krug*) A one-act comedy by Heinrich von KLEIST. First performance: Weimar, 1808. The plot revolves around a village magistrate who finds himself presiding at the trial of an innocent man accused of a crime he himself has committed; the play failed when first produced by Goethe but was later recognized as a comic masterpiece.

Brome, Richard (c. 1590–1653) English playwright, who is thought to have been a servant of Ben Jonson and established his reputation as a writer of comedy with *The Lovesick Court*, a parody of heroic tragedy. Subsequent successes included *The Northern Lass* (1629) and *A Jovial Crew, or, the Merry Beggars* (1641), which was performed by Christopher Beeston's company shortly before the closing of the theatres. Other plays – of which 15 survive – provided material for works by Aphra Behn and Dryden among others.

Bronnen, Arnolt (1895–1959) German playwright and theatre critic, who wrote a number of radical plays in the Expressionist tradition. He established his reputation with *Vatermord* (1922), which dealt with incest and patricide; subsequent works, including *Die Geburt der Jugend* (1922) and *Reparationen* (1926) reflected his sympathy for the Nazi cause. His few works after World War II included *Die jungste Nacht* (1958).

Brook, Peter (1925–) British director and stage designer, widely recognized as one of the most innovative directors for the contemporary stage. He produced his first play, Marlowe's *Dr Faustus*, in 1943 at the Torch Theatre in London at the age of 18, and attracted immediate attention with his eye for the essentials of a production and his challenging approach.

After producing *Love's Labour's Lost* (1946) at Stratford-on-Avon for Sir Barry Jackson, Brook then won great acclaim with such plays as Anouilh's *Ring Round the Moon* (1950) and Otway's *Venice Preserv'd* (1953), in both of which he directed Paul Scofield to great effect. In 1955 his *Hamlet* was staged as far away as the USSR and in 1962 he was appointed codirector of the newly formed Royal Shakespeare Company. Celebrated productions with the RSC included *King Lear* (1962), Weiss's *Marat/Sade* (1964), Seneca's *Oedipus* (1968), an enormously admired *A Midsummer Night's Dream* (1970), famous for its acrobatics and all-white set, and *Antony and Cleopatra* (1978). In more recent years he has been based in Paris, where he founded the INTERNATIONAL CENTRE OF THEATRE RESEARCH in 1970. Works for this experimental multiracial company have included a stage adaptation of the Hindu MAHABHARATA, which lasted 10 hours, and radical reworkings of *Carmen* (1989) and *Hamlet* (1995).

Brooke, Gustavus Vaughan (1818–66) British actor, born in Dublin and known as the **Dublin Roscius** or **Hibernian Roscius**. After touring the provinces, he appeared at the Olympic Theatre in 1848, and was acclaimed as Othello, Hamlet, Richard III, and in other roles associated with Edmund Kean. He was drowned when his ship foundered in the Bay of Biscay while returning from an Australian tour.

Brooklyn Academy of Music A theatre complex with four stages at 30 Lafayette Avenue, Brooklyn, New York, originally built as an opera house in 1859 and moved to its present location in 1903. After decades of neglect it was rebuilt in the mid-1970s. Popularly called BAM, it has since offered a wide range of music, dance, theatre and performance art, becoming the most prestigious venue in New York for the avant garde. In 1987 a nearby vaudeville house, the **Majestic**, was renovated and added to the complex, opening with Peter Brook's *The Mahabharata*.

Brooklyn Theatre A small theatre in New York, opened in 1871 and run by the family of F B Conway until 1875 when under Palmer it had a short, but successful season. Burnt down during a performance of Oxenford's *The Two Orphans* in 1876, it was never rebuilt.

Brooks Atkinson Theatre A 1088-seat theatre on West 47th Street, between Broadway and 8th Avenue, New York, which opened as the **Mansfield Theatre** in 1926. It was used for broadcasting before reopening in 1960 as the Brooks Atkinson, named after the celebrated critic. Productions have included Ansky's *The Dybbuk* (1926), Connelly's *Green Pastures* (1930), Neil Simon's *Come Blow Your Horn* (1961), Tennessee Williams's *The Milk Train Doesn't Stop Here Anymore* (1964), Joseph A Walker's *The River Niger* (1973), Bernard Slade's *Same Time, Next Year* (1975), Lanford Wilson's *Talley's Folly* (1980), Michael Frayn's *Noises Off* (1985), and O'Neill's *The Iceman Cometh* (1999) with Kevin Spacey.

Brooks Theatre *See* Cleveland Play House.

Brough, Lionel (1836–1900) British actor, born in Pontypool. He began as an actor in a play by his brother **William Brough** (1826–70), produced at Covent Garden in 1854; later he developed his own one-man show. In 1864 Lionel was engaged at Liverpool; subsequently he established himself as a fine comedian, especially in the plays of Sheridan and Goldsmith.

His daughter was the actress **Mary Brough** (1863–1934), who made her stage debut in 1881 in Brighton and later appeared alongside Lillie Langtry in London. She was particularly successful as a comic actress in the farces of Ben Travers at the Aldwych Theatre.

Mary's cousin was the actress **Fanny Whiteside Brough** (1854–1914), who first appeared on stage in 1869 in pantomime. She too excelled in comic roles, being the first to play such parts as Mary Melrose in H J Byron's *Our Boys* (1875) and frequently appearing at Drury Lane.

Brown, Pamela (1917–75) British actress, who first attracted attention in Shakespearean parts at Stratford-on-Avon. Subsequent roles included Nina in *The Seagull*, Gwendolen in *The Importance of Being Earnest*, and – with Gielgud's company – Millamant in Congreve's *The Way of the World* and Aquilina in Otway's *Venice Preserv'd*. In Shakespeare, she was particularly admired as Juliet, Ophelia, and Goneril; she also appeared in plays by Aldous Huxley, Christopher Fry, Wycherley, and Shaw.

Browne, Coral (1913–91) Australian actress, who came to London in 1934 after appearances in Australia and made her British debut in Philip Johnson's *Lover's Leap*. She soon emerged as a leading actress in such plays as Maugham's *Lady Frederick* (1946) and later won acclaim with the Old Vic company as Lady Macbeth (1956) and Gertrude in *Hamlet* (1958). Her many other roles included Mrs Warren in Shaw's *Mrs Warren's Profession* (1970) at the National Theatre.

Browne, E(lliot) Martin (1900–80) British actor and director, who was associated with the revival of poetic and religious drama in England. He directed all of T S Eliot's plays, including the first production of *Murder in the Cathedral*, and directed the **Pilgrim Players** from 1939 to 1948. In 1951 he produced the York Cycle of mystery plays, which had not been acted since 1572. *See also* British Theatre Association.

Browne, Maurice (1881–1955) British actor, playwright, and theatre manager, who established his reputation in the US and effectively founded the Little Theatre movement when he opened the Chicago Little Theatre in 1912. After directing on Broadway, he moved to London, taking over the Savoy Theatre in 1929 and subsequently acquiring control over the Globe and Queen's theatres. His London productions included *Othello* (1929), with Paul Robeson, Peggy Ashcroft, and himself in the main roles, *Hamlet* (1930), with Gielgud, and plays by Fagan and others.

Browne, Robert (fl. 1583–1620) English actor, who belonged to Worcester's Men before becoming a well-known comedian on the Continent, where he spent a lot of time between 1590 and 1620. He and his companies toured Holland and Germany with a selection of plays, jigs, and biblical pieces; in 1595 they were appointed players and musicians to the Landgrave of Hesse-Cassel, proceeding thence to Heidelberg, Frankfurt, and Strasbourg.

Browne, W Grahame *See* Tempest, Dame Marie.

Browning, Robert (1812–89) British poet and playwright, author of three verse dramas. *Strafford* (1837) was produced by Macready at Covent Garden with scant success, *A Blot on the 'Scutcheon* (1843) was staged at Drury Lane with Phelps in the lead, while *Colombe's Birthday* was performed at the Haymarket in 1844. The closet drama *Pippa Passes* has occasionally been staged.

Browning Version, The A one-act play by Terence RATTIGAN. First performance: London, 1948. It is an intense study of an unpopular classics master, Andrew Crocker Harris, and his relationships with his unfaithful wife, one of her lovers, and an unexpectedly sympathetic schoolboy.

Bruckner, Ferdinand (Theodor Tagger; 1891–1958) Austrian playwright, who established his reputation with the controversial *Krankheit der Jugend* (Malady of Youth; 1926). Subsequent successes included *Die Verbrecher* (The Criminals; 1928) and *Elizabeth von England* (1930), which both tackled contemporary themes of justice in a historical context, and a reinterpretation of Shakespeare's *Timon of Athens* (1933) as a criticism of Nazi Germany. Working in the US from 1936 to 1951, he also wrote modern equivalents of classical tragedy and adapted an old Indian play as *Das irdine Wägelchen* (The Little Clay Cart; 1957).

Brückner, Johannes (1730–86) German actor, who was a pupil of both Lessing and Ekhof and became a much-admired member of Koch's company. He excelled in tragedy; his most famous role was the central character of Goethe's *Götz von Berlichingen*.

Brueys, David-Augustin de (1640–1723) French playwright. Brueys wrote several plays for the Comédie-Française in collaboration with Jean PALAPRAT; his own works, with the exception of *L'Avocat Pathelin* (1706), were less successful.

Brun, (Johan) Nordahl (1745–1816) Norwegian playwright, poet, bishop, and statesman, who was the author of the stirring patriotic tragedy *Zarine* (1772). Based in Copenhagen, he also wrote the first Norwegian national anthem, hymns, and a further tragedy, *Einer Tanbeskielver* (1772).

Brunelleschi, Filippo *See paradiso.*

Bruno, Giordano (1548–1600) Italian philosopher, scientist, and playwright, who was burnt at the stake as a heretic by the Inquisition. A friend of Sir Philip Sidney, he was the author of a single play, *Il Candelaio* (The Candlemaker; c. 1582), which attacked corruption and was banned; it was revived in 1965. *The Heretic* (1970), by Morris West, was based upon his life.

Brunton, Anne *See* Merry, Anne.

Brunton, Elizabeth *See* Yates, Frederick Henry.

Bruscambille (Jean Deslauriers; fl. 1610–34) French actor, who established his reputation in the Paris fairs. Subsequently he accompanied Jean Farine to the Hôtel de Bourgogne where he demonstrated his facility in farce and his control over unruly audiences.

Brustein, Robert (1927–) US actor, director, and critic, who founded the Yale Repertory Theatre, where he also worked as a director, in 1966. Subsequently he moved (1980) to Harvard, where he directed the professional **American Repertory Theatre** company in performances of Shakespeare, Brecht, and many others. His many books about the modern theatre are highly admired.

Bryan, Dora (Dora Broadbent; 1924–) British actress, who appeared as a child in pantomime at Manchester in 1935. She came to London in Coward's *Peace in Our Time* (1947), had a two-year run as Eva in Arthur Macrae's *Traveller's Joy* (1948), and subsequently established herself as an engaging comedienne in numerous revues and musicals. In her later years she has appeared in such classics as Goldsmith's *She Stoops to Conquer* (1985) and Pinter's *The Birthday Party* (1994), both at the National Theatre.

Bryant, Michael (1928–) British actor, whose first appearance was in Tennessee Williams's *A Streetcar Named Desire* at Brighton (1951). He went on to establish his reputation in Peter Shaffer's *Five Finger Exercise* (1958) at the Comedy Theatre and in Rattigan's *Ross* (1961) at the Haymarket. He was acclaimed as Teddy in Pinter's *The Homecoming* (1965) while with the Royal Shakespeare Company and later joined the National Theatre (1977), appearing in numerous roles, from Sir Paul Plyant in Congreve's *The Double Dealer* (1978) to Enobarbus in *Antony and Cleopatra* (1987) and the Fool in *King Lear* (1997). In the 1990s he appeared in all three parts of David Hare's trilogy *Racing Demon* (1990), *Murmuring Judges* (1991), and *The Absence of War* (1993).

Bryant's Opera House *See* Koster and Bial's Music Hall.

Bryant Theatre *See* Apollo Theatre.

Bryden, Bill (1942–) Scottish director and playwright, who was associated with the National Theatre from 1975 to 1985. Previously with the Belgrade Theatre in Coventry, the Royal Court Theatre, and Edinburgh's Lyceum Theatre, he won praise at the National Theatre for such productions as Synge's *The Playboy of the Western World* (1975). In 1978–80 he took over the National's Cottesloe Theatre, where he staged several influential promenade productions ranging from mystery plays to works by Eugene O'Neill. After leaving the National he worked mainly in opera and television drama before returning to live theatre with such productions as his own *The Big Picnic* (1994), staged in a Glasgow shipyard.

BTA *See* British Theatre Association.

Bucco A character of the Roman *atellana*, probably a fat clown. He was the main character in two plays by Pomponius.

Buchanan, Jack (1890–1957) Scottish actor-manager and director, who made his first London appearance in a comic opera, *The Grass Widow*, in 1912, and went on to become a star of revue and musical comedy. Outstanding in *A to Z* at the Prince of Wales's Theatre in 1921, he subsequently appeared in a memorable series of musical shows, including *Sunny* (1926), *Wake Up and Dream* (1929), and *This'll Make You Whistle* (1936). His work in straight comedy included Lonsdale's *Canaries Sometimes Sing* (1947) and Alan Melville's *Castle in the Air* (1949).

Büchner, Georg (1813–37) German playwright and doctor, who was the author of three plays anticipating the Expressionist movement of the 20th century. Büchner was a political radical and his works betray his inner pessimism and sympathy for the oppressed. His first play, DANTON'S DEATH, was a gloomy assessment of the French Revolution and was not acted until 1903; *Leonce und Lena* – not acted until 1895 – similarly criticized Romanticism. Büchner's last play WOYZECK found many admirers in the 20th century, despite being unfinished at the time of his early death from typhoid fever.

Buck, Sir George (d. 1623) English historian and poet, who succeeded his uncle, Sir Edmund Tilney, as MASTER OF THE REVELS in 1610 but was removed from office in 1622 due to his mental infirmity. Unfortunately, his records concerning the Elizabethan theatre were destroyed by fire.

Buckingham, George Villiers, Second Duke of (1628–87) English playwright and statesman, best known for his burlesque of heroic drama THE REHEARSAL (1671), which lampooned Dryden and provided the basis for Sheridan's *The Critic*. A leading political force during the Restoration, he was also the author of an adaptation of Fletcher's *The Chances* (1623).

Buckley's Olympic *See* Olympic Theatre.

Buckstone, John Baldwin (1802–79) British actor, playwright, and manager, who ran the Haymarket Theatre from 1853 until his death. As a comic actor he was encouraged by Edmund Kean, appearing as the original Gnatbrain in *Black-Ey'd Susan* (1829). His many farces and melodramas include *Luke the Labourer* (1826), *The Green Bushes* (1845), *The Flowers of the Forest* (1847), and *Leap Year* (1850). *See also* ghosts.

Buero Vallejo, Antonio (1916–2000) Spanish dramatist, best known for his sociohistorical plays, which include *Un soñador para un pueblo* (1958) and *Las meniñas* (1960). His first play *Historia de una escalera* (1949) was written while he was a political prisoner and represented a Spanish expression of Socialist Realism. Later works include *Dialogo secreto* (1984) and *Las Trampas del Azar* (1994).

Buffalo Bill *See* Cody, William Frederick.

Bugaku A form of early Japanese musical dance, which had a strong influence upon the *Nō* drama. Usually based upon Chinese religious texts, such pieces were performed by dancers wearing masks both at Court and before audiences at religious festivals from the 7th century AD onwards.

built stuff Any piece of three-dimensional scenery specially constructed for use on stage, including rostra, items of furniture, and landscape features.

Bulandra, Lucia Sturdza- *See* Sturdza-Bulandra, Lucia.

Bulgakov, Mikhail Afanaseyev (1891–1940) Russian playwright and novelist, who established his reputation with a dramatization of his novel *The White Guard* as *The Days of the Turbins* in 1926. Presented by Stanislavsky at the Moscow Art Theatre, it later fell foul of the Bolsheviks; other works for the Moscow Art Theatre included *The Flight*, *The Cabal of Saintly Hypocrites* (1936), which depicted Molière's struggle with the censors, and a version (1941) of *Don Quixote* by Cervantes. He also adapted Gogol's *Dead Souls* for the stage with great success in 1930; several of his works have been revived since his death.

Bull, Ole (1810–80) Norwegian violinist, who oversaw the establishment of the first Norwegian national theatre. Det Norske Teatret (*see* Nationale Scene), which opened in Bergen in 1850, employed a Norwegian rather than a Danish staff, including Ibsen and Bjørnson among its members.

Bull Inn An inn at Bishopsgate in London, where a number of plays were staged between 1576 and c. 1600. Companies that appeared there included the Queen's Men, who visited it in 1583.

Bullins, Ed (1935–) US playwright, who became a leading figure in the Black theatre of San Francisco and Harlem. Author of such plays as *Clara's Ole Man* (1965), *The Duplex* (1970), *The Fabulous Miss Marie* (1971), and *The Taking of Miss Janie* (1975), he has had works regularly produced at the New Lafayette and American Place theatres.

Bulwer-Lytton, Edward, Lord (1803–73) British novelist, playwright, and statesman, who took to writing to augment his income and achieved success with a number of novels and three highly acclaimed plays. *The Lady of Lyons; or, Love and Pride* (1838), *Richelieu; or, the Conspiracy* (1839), and *Money* (1840) provided Macready, Irving, and others with good parts and were all revived several times.

Bunn Hill Nursery *See* nurseries.

Bunraku The best known form of Japanese puppet theatre, in which almost lifesize dolls act out a dramatic narrative set to music (*see Jōruri*). Until the 18th century the three operators needed for each puppet remained hidden behind a screen; since then, however, they have appeared behind the puppets themselves, the assistants being dressed entirely in black and wearing black hoods. The tradition had its roots in the Asian puppet theatre imported in the 11th century and reached its peak in the 18th century after which the genre declined until only one *Bunraku* theatre remained, at Osaka.

Buontalenti, Bernardo (c. 1536–1608) Italian stage designer and theatre architect, known as *delle Girandole* after his firework displays. Employed by the Medici family in Florence, he organized numerous entertainments incorporating lavish stage effects and elaborate costumes.

Burbage, James (c. 1530–97) English actor and manager, who began as a joiner and actor with Leicester's Men. He lived in Shoreditch and in 1576 acquired a 21 year lease of nearby land, on which he erected the THEATRE. Later he converted part of a former monastery into the Blackfriars Theatre, but died before it opened.

His elder son, **Cuthbert Burbage** (c. 1566–1636), was also an actor in his earlier years and jointly inherited the theatres with his brother, becoming involved in disputes over the land at Shoreditch. The Burbages eventually dismantled the Theatre and reconstructed it as the GLOBE THEATRE on Bankside, forming a syndicate with Shakespeare and others.

Cuthbert's brother, **Richard Burbage** (c. 1567–1619), who made his acting debut as a boy at the Theatre, became the leading player at both the Globe and Blackfriars theatres. The first great English actor, he created the parts of Hamlet, Lear, Othello, Richard III, and other Shakespearean characters; he also appeared in plays by Webster, Jonson, and Beaumont and Fletcher.

Bürgerliches Trauerspiel A theatre movement in Germany, which had its origins in the domestic dramas of Lessing. The genre was notable chiefly for making middle-class characters the central figures in tragedy for the first time; writers connected with the movement included Schiller and Hebbel.

Burgoyne, John (1722–92) British general and playwright, author of the popular comedy *The Heiress*, which was staged at Drury Lane by Sheridan in 1786. Remembered for his defeat at Saratoga in the US War of Independence, he was later depicted by G B Shaw in THE DEVIL'S DISCIPLE.

Burgtheater A theatre in the Imperial Palace in Vienna, built in 1741. Originally used by French and German companies it came to the fore in 1776, when Emperor Josef II decreed that it was to become the home of serious drama in Austria in opposition to the tradition of the ALTWIENER VOLKSTHEATER. Under the management of Sonnenfels and Schreyvogel the theatre soon acquired a considerable reputation, actors there – including Schröder – appearing in both established classics and plays by contemporary European writers. Subsequently Heinrich Laube (1806–84) brought a new impetus to the Burgtheater and staged popular performances of well-made plays from France as well as installing early examples of the box set. In 1888 the resident company moved to a new theatre, where Anton WILDGANS staged significant Expressionist productions after World War I; this theatre was later rebuilt in 1955 after suffering severe damage during World War II. Reopened by Berthold VIERTEL, the company – although now presenting little experimental drama – established a high reputation for spectacle and high standards of performance in classical plays.

Burk, John Daly (c. 1775–1808) Irish-born playwright, who emigrated to the US in 1796. His patriotic play *Bunker Hill; or, the Death of General Warren* (1797) was a favourite with US audiences for many years. He died in a duel with a Frenchman, who had challenged him for insulting Napoleon.

Burke, Billie *See* Ziegfeld, Florenz.

burla A comic scene interpolated into *commedia dell'arte* performances. Not usually a part of the plot itself, the *burla* provided minor characters with an opportunity to indulge in slapstick humour. The word *burla* later gave rise to the terms BURLETTA and BURLESQUE.

burlesque In English drama, a type of comedy that developed in the late 17th century as a spoof of more serious plays. Examples include Buckingham's *The Rehearsal* (1671), which lampooned heroic drama, and Sheridan's *The Critic* (1779), which parodied sentimental plays. Gay's *The Beggar's Opera* (1728) similarly ridiculed the conventions of opera. Subsequently burlesque lost its satirical edge in the 19th century, when H J Byron's parodies of contemporary melodrama became popular. Manifestations of the tradition in 20th-century British theatre were confined largely to REVUE.

   The **burlesque** tradition in the US theatre is unrelated to the British form and was first devised by Michael Leavitt (1843–1935) in the 1860s. Combining songs, sketches, and variety acts, US burlesque can be thought of as a salacious cousin of vaudeville – at its worst tasteless, but at its best having a rowdy vitality which produced many high-quality low comedians. The distinguishing feature of these shows was always their erotic content, notably with the **striptease**, which was first incorporated in the 1920s and quickly became the prime event starring such performers as Gypsy Rose Lee (1914–70). Owing to this sexual element, burlesque survived longer than vaudeville in the face of competition from radio and talking pictures, but it had nevertheless lost its vitality as a genre by the 1940s.

burletta Originally a farce with music and subsequently a form of production developed as a means of evading the restrictions on drama outside the patent theatres during the 19th century. In the latter context, many straight dramas, including those of Shakespeare, were embellished with songs and dances in order to be regarded outside the scope of the licensing laws.

Burnaby, Davy *See* pierrot troupes.

Burnand, Sir Francis Cowley (1836–1917) British playwright and founder of the AMATEUR DRAMATIC CLUB at Cambridge. He wrote numerous burlesques and adaptations from the French.

burnt-cork minstrels *See* minstrel show.

Burton, Richard (Richard Walter Jenkins; 1925–84) British actor, son of a Welsh miner, who made his stage debut in 1943 in *The Druid's Rest* by Emlyn Williams. After service with the RAF he appeared in several plays by Christopher Fry, including *The Lady's Not For Burning* (1949); in the 1950s he played numerous Shakespearean roles at Stratford and the Old Vic before concentrating upon his film career. Occasional stage appearances after that included the musical *Camelot* (1960) and *Hamlet* (1964), directed by John Gielgud. He also appeared on Broadway in Shaffer's *Equus* (1976) and in *Private Lives* (1983) with Elizabeth Taylor.

Burton, William Evans (1804–60) British actor and manager, who was engaged in 1831 as an actor at the Haymarket, where he appeared with Edmund Kean. Subsequently he moved to the US, acting under his own management in Philadelphia and, in 1848, opening his own theatre, Burton's (*see* Chambers Street Theatre), in New York. There he appeared in a variety of comic parts, including Dickensian and Shakespearean characters. His move to the Metropolitan Theatre in 1856, however, brought little success at a time of financial crisis, and he was forced to close.

Bury, John (1925–2000) British stage designer, who was head of design at the National Theatre from 1973 to 1985. Previously in charge of design with Joan Littlewood's Theatre Workshop and with the Royal Shakespeare Company (1964–71), he became well known for his use of authentic materials and his three-dimensional sets for plays by such authors as Ibsen, Behan, Dürrenmatt, Shakespeare, and Pinter. His most notable successes included designs for the RSC's *Wars of the Roses* (1963), *Hamlet* (1975), and Peter Shaffer's *Amadeus* (1979). In the 1980s and 1990s he worked increasingly in opera.

Busch, Charles (1954–) US actor and playwright, who first attracted attention with the long-running off-Broadway production *Vampire Lesbians of Sodom* (1985). His shows, in which he usually stars in drag, show a witty appreciation of popular culture. He has lately had success with plays written for others, *The Tale of the Allergist's Wife* (2000) offering a much-admired star part for Linda Lavin.

Busch, Ernst (1900–80) German actor, who began his career in cabaret in Germany in the 1920s and appeared at the Deutsches Theater in Berlin after World War II. He became a leading member of Brecht's company in 1950, appearing in such celebrated works as *Mutter Courage und ihre Kinder* (1954).

Bush Theatre A fringe theatre in the Shepherd's Bush area of London, established in the upstairs room of a pub in 1972. It is dedicated to the production of new plays by little-known authors. Plays first staged at the Bush include Doug Lucie's *Progress* (1984), Sharman McDonald's *When I Was a Girl I Used to Scream and Shout* (1984), and Conor McPherson's *St Nicholas* (1998). The theatre, which seats about 100 in rather cramped conditions, was badly damaged by fire in 1987 but subsequently refurbished.

busker A street performer, typically a musician, juggler, or other entertainer who performs to passers-by or theatre-goers as they queue to enter the theatre. Derived from the word *buskin* (*see* cothurnus), the term is also sometimes used for performers of Punch and Judy.

Butti, Enrico Annibale (1868–1912) Italian playwright, whose social dramas depict the futility of the struggle of the individual against society. Influenced by Ibsen, his plays include *Il vortice* (The Vortex; 1892), *L'Utopia* (1894), *La corsa al piacere* (The Pursuit of Pleasure; 1900), and *La tempesta* (1901).

Byam Shaw, Glen Alexander (1904–81) British actor and director, who appeared in London, Oxford, and New York during the 1920s before joining Gielgud's company at the Queen's Theatre (1937–38). After World War II he concentrated on direction, beginning with Rattigan's *The Winslow Boy* in 1946. Subsequently he worked at both the Old Vic and the Young Vic before becoming codirector with Anthony Quayle at the Shakespeare Memorial Theatre in 1953; he was sole director there from 1956 to 1959. Later successes included Rattigan's *Ross* (1959); he took over the Sadler's Wells Opera company in 1962.

Byrne, John (1940–) Scottish playwright and designer. Born in Paisley, Byrne studied art in Glasgow and Italy before starting a career as a designer and graphic artist. He began to design for the theatre in 1971. His best-known play *The Slab Boys* (1978) is based on his early experiences in the Paisley carpet industry; it was followed by two sequels *Cuttin' a Rug* (1979) and *Still Life* (1982). Other work for the stage includes his first play *Writer's Cramp* (1977) and *Colquhoun and Macbryde* (1988). He has also found success writing for television.

Byron, George Gordon, Lord (1788–1824) British poet and author of a number of verse dramas. In 1815 he became a member of the committee at Drury Lane, where his *Marino Faliero* was produced in 1821. After his death, Macready appeared in *Werner* (1830), *Sardanapalus* (1834), and *The Two Foscari* (1838); his closet drama *Manfred* was staged at Covent Garden in 1834.

Byron, Henry James (1834–84) British playwright and actor, noted for his many burlesques and extravaganzas. His comedies *War to the Knife* (1865) and *A Hundred Thousand Pounds* (1866) were amongst those produced at the Prince of Wales Theatre (later the Scala Theatre) where he was associated with the Bancrofts in management. The most successful of all his works was, however, *Our Boys*, which began a record-breaking run at the Vaudeville Theatre in 1875.

cabaret A form of entertainment combining music and various forms of theatre at a club or other venue with an intimate atmosphere. Having its origins in music hall, cabaret includes at one extreme solo acts presented in small bars and at the other spectacular revues staged at famous restaurants and even theatres. During the 1930s, cabaret became one of the liveliest areas of German theatre, attracting such major figures as Brecht and acquiring a strong political identity; subsequently it flourished in Britain and the US during the 1950s and 1960s. A tradition of anti-establishment satirical cabaret arose in Britain in the 1960s and again in the 1980s.

Cabaret A musical by the team of John Kander and Fred Ebb, based on I AM A CAMERA, the stage version of Isherwood's *Goodbye to Berlin*. First performance: New York, 1966. Its staging, by Hal Prince, was a landmark in its use of musical numbers as commentary on the action and themes rather than strictly for plot and character development. The production, which won the Tony Award for Best Musical, starred Lotte Lenya as cabaret singer Sally Bowles.

Caecilius Statius (c. 219 BC–c. 166 BC) Roman playwright, who translated many Greek works for the Latin stage. Originally a slave, he adapted about 40 comedies, many by Menander; only titles and fragments survive.

Caen, Compagnie de *See Décentralisation Dramatique.*

Caesar and Cleopatra A history play by G B SHAW. First performance: Berlin, 1906. Unlike Shakespeare's Cleopatra, Shaw's queen is depicted as little more than a spoilt girl; by contrast, the character of Caesar is used to represent Shaw's concept of the Life Force that stimulates man's progress.

Café La Mama *See* La Mama Experimental Theatre Club.

Caffé Cino A theatre and coffee house on Cornelia Street, New York, which opened in 1958 and became the first venue for plays of the off-off-Broadway theatre movement. Plays were produced here from 1961 to 1967 and included many new US works.

Calderón, Maria (17th century) Spanish actress, popularly known as La Calderona. She performed in *autos sacramentales* and *comedias* before retiring to enter a convent; she was also the mistress of Philip IV of Spain.

Calderón de la Barca, Pedro (1600–81) Spanish playwright, regarded as the most important successor to Lope de Vega. Born in Madrid, he was the author of approximately 120 religious and secular plays, including tragedies, comedies, histories, and philosophical dramas. Of his secular plays, *La vida es sueño* – a depiction of the state of mind of a prince who is released after having been locked up all his life in prison – is regarded as the best; other notable works include *La alcade de Zalamea*, a study of seduction and revenge. His plays on religious themes include *La cena de Baltasar*, *El gran teatro del mundo*, and *El mágico prodigioso*, which is set in the time of Diocletian. In 1651 he was ordained as a priest, becoming chaplain of honour to the king in 1663; from this date he concentrated upon the writing of numerous *autos sacramentales* noted for their poetic power and masterly theatricality. His works inspired many later writers to make adaptations and translations, notably Killigrew and Wycherley in the English tradition, Tuke in the French, and Schlegel and Tieck in the German.

Principal works:

El segreto a voces: 1626.

Casa con dos puertos mal es de guarda: 1629; translated as *It is Difficult to Guard a House with Two Doors*.

El príncipe constante: 1629.

La dama duende: c. 1629; adapted as *The Parson's Wedding*.

La devocion de la cruz: c. 1633.

El mayor monstruo, los celos: c. 1634; translated as *No Monster Like Jealousy*.

La cena de Baltasar: c. 1634; translated as *Belshazzar's Feast*.

A secreto agravio, secreta venganza: 1635; translated as *Secret Vengeance for Secret Insult*.

El medico de su honra: 1635; translated as *The Surgeon of His Honour*.

El mágico prodigioso: 1637; translated as *The Wonder-Working Magician*.

El pintor de su deshonra: 1637; translated as *The Painter of His Dishonour*.

La vida es sueño: c. 1638; translated as *Life's a Dream*.

El alcalde de Zalamea: c. 1640; translated as *The Mayor of Zalamea*.

El gran teatro del mundo: c. 1645; translated as *The Great World Theatre*.

La hija del aire: 1653.

Caldwell, Zoë (1934–) Australian actress, who was one of the original members of the Union Theatre Repertory Company in Melbourne. She appeared with the Shakespeare Memorial Theatre Company at Stratford-on-Avon in 1958 and later performed at the Royal Court Theatre, the Stratford (Ontario) Festival, the Tyrone Guthrie Theatre, and elsewhere in numerous acclaimed parts; her roles have included Millamant in Congreve's *The Way of the World* (1965), Shakespeare's Cleopatra (1967), Jean Brodie in Muriel Spark's *The Prime of Miss Jean Brodie* (1968), Mary Tyrone in O'Neill's *Long Day's Journey Into Night* (1976), Medea (1982), and Lillian Hellman in William Luce's *Lillian* (1986).

California Suite A series of short comedies by Neil SIMON. First performance: 1976. The plot concerns the guests at a Beverly Hills hotel and their various adventures. The play was filmed in 1978 starring Alan Alda, Jane Fonda, Walter Matthau, Maggie Smith, Michael Caine, and Elaine May.

call board A noticeboard situated in the backstage area, upon which messages for the cast and stage crew are displayed.

call boy A former member of the stage crew, who was responsible for making sure that actors were ready to take their cue to go on stage.

call doors *See* proscenium doors.

Call Me Madam A musical by Howard LINDSAY and Russel Crouse, with music and lyrics by Irving BERLIN. First performance: New York, 1950. A Washington hostess, Sally Adams, is appointed ambassador to Lichtenberg and falls in love with the foreign minister. The play was filmed in 1953 with Ethel Merman, who starred in the original production.

Callow, Simon (1949–) British actor and director, who first appeared in London with the Edinburgh Traverse Theatre in 1974. Subsequent parts have included several with the Joint Stock Company, Mozart in Peter Shaffer's *Amadeus* (1979) at the National Theatre, Tony Perrelli in Edgar Wallace's *On the Spot* (1984), the title role in Goethe's *Faust* (1988), Oscar Wilde in *The Importance of Being Oscar* (1997), and Falstaff in *Chimes at Midnight* (1998). In *The Mystery of Charles Dickens* (2000) he impersonated over 40 of Dickens's characters. As well as appearing in films, he has directed productions of *Amadeus* (1986), *Shirley Valentine* (1988, 1989), a stage adaptation of *Les Enfants du Paradis* (1996) for the Royal Shakespeare Company, and several operas and musicals.

Calmo, Andrea (1509–71) Italian playwright, actor, and gondolier, who appeared in early *commedia dell'arte* productions. As an actor he specialized in playing elderly men.

Calvert, Louis (1859–1923) British actor, son of the provincial actor-manager **Charles Calvert** (1828–79). Louis Calvert worked with Irving at the Lyceum and in the companies of Ben Greet and Frank Benson before becoming a leading actor for the Vedrenne-Barker management at the Royal Court Theatre, where he was the original Broadbent in Shaw's *John Bull's Other Island* (1904) and William in a revival of *You Never Can Tell* (1905). A forceful actor, whose range encompassed Sir Peter Teazle and Andrew Undershaft in Shaw's *Major Barbara*, he was a respected manager and ran his own touring company.

Câmara, João da (1852–1908) Portuguese playwright, author of several notable historical dramas and comedies. He also encompassed realism in *Os Velhos* (The Old Ones; 1893) and symbolism in *Meia Noite* (Midnight; 1900).

Cambridge Festival Theatre A theatre in Cambridge, which became a focus of development in stage design under the management of Terence GRAY (1926–33). Formerly known as the Barnwell Theatre, it was totally reorganized by Gray, who removed the proscenium arch and explored the possibilities of a flexible split-level acting area as well as experimenting with innovative lighting arrangements. After 1933 the theatre was run on a less adventurous commercial basis and was finally taken over by the Cambridge Arts Theatre as a workshop and store.

Cambridge Theatre A theatre in the Seven Dials district of London, opened in 1930. The opening production was *Charlot's Masquerade*, starring Beatrice Lillie. Seasons of plays, ballets, and films were presented for some years, and later Sunday concerts; in 1934 the theatre played host to the Comédie-Française. For two years from 1946 the Cambridge was the headquarters of the newly founded New London Opera

Company. Since 1952 a policy of plays and musicals has been maintained, the most successful including William Douglas Home's *The Reluctante Debutante* (1955), Keith Waterhouse's *Billy Liar* (1960–62), Tommy Steele in *Half a Sixpence* (1963–64), Ingmar Bergman's version of Ibsen's *Hedda Gabler* (1970), Jonathan Miller's production of Chekhov's *Three Sisters* (1976), the US musical *Chicago* (1979) and the long-running *Return to the Forbidden Planet* (1990–93). In 1988 it became the home of the newly reconstituted D'Oyly Carte opera company.

Cameri Theatre A theatre company established in Palestine in 1944 in reaction to the formalized realism favoured by other contemporary theatre groups. Presenting plays by such authors as Goldoni, the Čapek brothers, and García Lorca, the company established a strong reputation; after the founding of Israel in 1948 it also staged naturalistic works by leading contemporary writers in Hebrew as well as continuing to present plays by Brecht, Pinter, and other foreign playwrights. In 1961 it moved to Tel Aviv, becoming the city's official resident theatre company in 1970.

Cameron, Beatrice *See* Mansfield, Richard.

Caminelli, Antonio (1436–1502) Italian playwright, also known as **Il Pistoia**. His play *Filostrato e Panfile* (1499) was influenced by the tragedies of Seneca and by the tradition of the *sacra rappresentazione*.

Camões, Luís Vaz de (c. 1524–80) Portuguese poet and playwright, usually remembered for the epic poem *Os Lusíadas*. He spent much of his life in the Portuguese colonies and was the author of three plays based on classical themes. *Os Anfitriões*, *El-Rei Seleuro*, and *Filodemo* (his best play) were all influenced by the works of Vicente.

Campbell, Herbert (1846–1904) British music hall comedian. He started in minstrel shows and even appeared as an actor at Drury Lane in 1882. From 1891, by which time he weighed 19 stone, he partnered the diminutive Dan Leno in 14 consecutive Drury Lane pantomimes.

Campbell, Ken (1941–) British playwright and director, who took over the Everyman Theatre, Liverpool, in 1980 after establishing a strong reputation with his leadership of the **Science Fiction Theatre of Liverpool** and the anarchic Ken Campbell Roadshow. Earlier successes included the *Illuminatus* (1976) cycle of five plays, cowritten with Chris Langham, and Neil Oram's *The Warp* (1979); at the Everyman Theatre in the 1980s Campbell presented a series of experimental dramas, many aimed at young audiences. His own works include the children's entertainment *Old King Cole* (1969), *Stungpoonery* (1975), *War With the Newts* (1981), and *Recollections of a Furtive Nudist* (1990). He presented a pidgin version of *Macbeth* at the Cottesloe Theatre in 1998 and *Ken Campbell's History of Comedy, Part One: Ventriloquism* in 2000.

Campbell, Mrs Patrick (Beatrice Rose Stella Tanner; 1865–1940) British actress, who became one of the most famous actresses of her day on account of her exceptional stage presence and biting wit. She made her debut in Liverpool in 1888 and subsequently appeared in melodrama at the Adelphi Theatre in London; in 1893 she was selected to create Paula in *The Second Mrs Tanqueray* (1893), the part that established her reputation. Later she triumphed in the title role of Pinero's *The Notorious Mrs Ebbsmith* (1895), in numerous Shakespearean parts while joint-manager of the Lyceum, and alongside Bernhardt in Maeterlinck's *Pelléas et Mélisande* (1904). She also excelled in the plays of Shaw, who wrote *Pygmalion* for her and with whom she entered into a long and celebrated correspondence.

Campen, Jacob van (1595–1657) Dutch architect, who designed the first theatre to be built in Amsterdam (c. 1638). The **Schouwburg** shared many features with Palladio's Teatro Olimpico; a proscenium arch was subsequently added by Jan Vos. The theatre was destroyed by fire in 1772.

Campion, Thomas (1567–1629) English poet, musician, and doctor, who wrote a number of masques for the court of James I. He may also have contributed pieces for the public stage through his friend Philip Rosseter.

Campistron, Jean Galbert de (1656–1723) French playwright, born in Toulouse. Sent to Paris by his father in 1673, he found a friend in the actor Jean-Baptiste Raisin and later entered the service of Louis XIV. Campistron's dramatic output consisted largely of tragedies in the style of Racine and Corneille, notably *Andronic* (1685), *Alcibiade* (1685), and *Tiridate* (1691).

Camus, Albert (1913–60) French novelist, playwright, and essayist, born in Algeria. Although better known for his novels, Camus wrote several plays that anticipate the Theatre of the ABSURD. He also produced successful stage adaptations of novels by William Faulkner and Dostoevsky. His own works include *Le Malentendu* (1944), *Caligula* (1945), *L'État de siège* (1948; translated as *State of Siege*, 1958), and *Les Justes* (1949; translated as *The Just Assassins*, 1958). He died in a car crash.

Canadian Actors' Equity Association A trade union for professional actors in Canada, established in 1955 as a branch of the American Actors' Equity Association and becoming independent in 1976. Based in Toronto, it maintains close links with its US counterpart; it also has an office in Vancouver.

Candida A play by G B SHAW. First performance: South Shields, 1895. Arguably Shaw's best constructed play, it explores the conflict between common sense and poetry through the relationship between Candida and the young poet Marchbanks. In the end Candida, torn between Marchbanks and her conventional Christian Socialist husband, chooses the latter.

Candide A musical by Leonard Bernstein, with a book by Lillian HELLMAN, and lyrics by (among others) Richard Wilbur and John Latouche. First performance: New York, 1956. Based on VOLTAIRE's satirical novella, it was an initial failure owing to what was felt to be a heavy-handed book, although the high quality of the music made a lasting impression. A 1974 version with the book rewritten by Hugh Wheeler ran for almost two years.

Candler Theatre *See* Harris Theatre.

Cane, Andrew (fl. 1620–44) English actor, originally a goldsmith, often referred to as **Cane the Clown**. He was with Lady Elizabeth's Men in 1622, then with Princes Charles's Men at the Fortune Theatre. After the closure of the theatres in 1642 he continued to appear at the Red Bull Theatre; during the Civil War, however, he resumed his former trade.

Cañizares, José de (1676–1750) Spanish playwright. Several of his plays were largely derived from the works of Lope de Vega.

Cankar, Ivan (1876–1918) Czech playwright, who emerged as the most important figure in his country's theatre in the early 20th century. Much influenced by Ibsen and subsequently by Symbolism, he was the author of six plays – the first being *Jakob Ruda* (1900) – notable for their poetic intensity.

Canterbury Music Hall A theatre in Lambeth, London, opened as a music hall in 1852 by Charles MORTON close to his Canterbury Tavern. The venue was so successful that Morton soon rebuilt it as the larger New Canterbury Music Hall, seating 1500 people. After Morton gave up his interest in the theatre, it was redesigned in three tiers, remaining one of the most popular of all music halls – with several royal patrons – until the genre died out in the 20th century. It was destroyed by bombs in World War II.

Cantor, Eddie (Isidore Itzkowitz; 1892–1964) US singer and actor, who first attracted attention as a jumpy, pop-eyed, often blackfaced, music-hall act. He then turned to musical comedy and revue and was associated for many years with Ziegfeld's *Follies*. Film versions of his Broadway hits (notably *Whoopee!*, 1929) made him one of the biggest Hollywood stars of the 1930s; he but made a final Broadway appearance in *Banjo Eyes* (1941).

capa y espada, comedia de *See comedia.*

Čapek, Karel (1890–1938) Czech playwright, novelist, and travel-writer, whose early plays, notably RUR (1921), and *Ze života hymzu* (THE INSECT PLAY; 1921), deal with the underlying discord between man and his universe. The latter play, written with his brother **Josef Čapek** (1887–1945), who died in Belsen, was followed by such works as *Bílá nemoc* (The White Scourge; 1937) and *Matka* (The Mother; 1938), which expressed his concern about the rise of Fascism in Europe, as well as *Adam the Creator* (1927), which was a sequel to *The Insect Play*.

Capitano, Il A character of the *commedia dell'arte*, a pretentious but cowardly soldier. He probably inherited much of his character from that of Plautus's MILES GLORIOSUS.

Capon, William (1757–1827) British architect and painter, born at Norwich, the son of an artist. In 1794 John Philip Kemble engaged him as scenic director at Drury Lane, where he produced painstakingly accurate historical sets. After Drury Lane burnt down in 1808, he accompanied Kemble to Covent Garden where his magnificent Shakespearean settings were universally acclaimed.

Captain Brassbound's Conversion A play by G B SHAW. First performance: London, 1900. Originally written for Ellen Terry, the play suffers from its reliance upon contrived situations. The plot revolves around the shrewd Lady Cicely Waynflete, who successfully 'tames' the vengeful pirate Brassbound. It was published as one of Shaw's *Three Plays For Puritans* (1901).

Capuana, Luigi (1839–1915) Italian Realist novelist, playwright, and critic, who wrote several notable dramas in the *verismo* tradition. Generally considered the first Italian writer to adopt the ideals of naturalism, he wrote several plays in the Sicilian dialect, of which *Malia* (1895) and *Lu Cavalieri Pidagna* were the most successful.

Caragiale, Ion Luca (1852–1912) Romanian playwright and short-story writer, who is generally considered Romania's greatest writer for the theatre. His satirical comedies, notably *O noapte furtunoasă* (A Stormy Night; 1879) and *O scrisoare pierdută* (The Lost Letter; 1884), mocked political and social pretensions and were all staged at the National Theatre in Bucharest, of which he was briefly director-general (1888–89).

carbon arc spotlight A spotlight with two carbon electrodes, formerly widely used for its brilliant, though flickering, beam before the introduction of the electric incandescent bulb. It was informally referred to as an **arc**.

Caretaker, The A play by Harold PINTER. First performance: Arts Theatre Club, 1960, with Alan Bates, Peter Woodthorpe, and Donald Pleasence in the cast. The play's action is a struggle for power between two brothers and the devious tramp, Davies, who tries to ingratiate his way into their house. The production established Pinter as an important new dramatist.

Carey, Joyce (1898–1993) British actress, daughter of Gerald LAWRENCE and Lilian BRAITHWAITE. She was chiefly associated with comedies, particularly those of Coward; she also excelled in such roles as Lady Markby in Wilde's *An Ideal Husband* (1966) and as Agatha Christie's Miss Marple. Under the name Jay Mallory she wrote the successful play *Sweet Aloes* (1934).

Carl, Karl (Karl Andreas von Bernbrunn; 1789–1854) Austrian actor, playwright, and director, who managed theatres in Munich and Vienna with great success. Noted himself as an actor in romantic parts, he popularized STABERL in Germany and later wrote numerous farces in collaboration with Nestroy for the Viennese stage. He also oversaw the building of a new Leopoldstädter Theater in 1847.

Carlin *See* Bertinazzi, Carlo.

Carmines, Al (1936–) US composer, one of the creators of the OFF-OFF BROADWAY movement. Works include *In Circles* (1967), based on the writings of Gertrude Stein, *Promenade* (1969), an Obie-winning version of Aristophanes's *Peace* (1969), and *The Faggot* (1973), one of the first open depictions of homosexuality on the US stage. An Episcopalian minister, he has premiered many of his works at the Judson Memorial Church in New York's Greenwich Village.

Carmontelle (Louis Carrogis; 1717–1806) French artist and playwright. He wrote light comedies, published in the collections *Proverbes dramatiques* (1768–81) and *Théâtre de campagne* (1775); the former created a genre that was subsequently developed by Alfred de Musset.

Carney, Kate (1868–1950) British music hall singer. She began her career singing Irish ballads, but later established herself as the 'Cockney Queen', performing songs of East London life.

Carnival play *See* Fastnachtsspiel.

Carnovsky, Morris (1897–1992) US actor, who made his New York debut in 1922 in *The God of Vengeance* by Sholom Asch. He then appeared with the Theatre Guild (1923–30) and subsequently with the Group Theatre, starring in Paul Green's *The House of Connelly* (1931) and *Awake and Sing!* (1935) and *Golden Boy* (1937) by Clifford

Odets. His performances with other companies included Ibsen's *An Enemy of the People* (1950). In the 1950s and 1960s he made regular appearances at the American Shakespeare Festival in Stratford, Connecticut, most famously as King Lear.

Caroline drama English drama of the reign of Charles I (1625–42). The period saw many elaborate masques and pastorals, notably those of Milton, Jonson, and Inigo Jones, and the domestic comedies of James Shirley and Richard Brome; John Ford was the foremost writer of tragedy. There was little theatre outside London during this period, which came to an end with the closure of all theatres by Parliament on the outbreak of the Civil War (*see* Interregnum).

Carousel A musical by RODGERS and HAMMERSTEIN. First performance: New York, 1945. Based on Ferenc Molnár's play *Liliom*, the plot concerns a fairground barker who is killed during an attempted robbery but is given a last chance to make amends on earth. With its masterly integration of music, plot, and lyric, the work is often considered Rodgers and Hammerstein's best.

carpenter's scene A scene that takes place at the front of the stage before the curtain, thus enabling the stage crew to change the set unnoticed by the audience and without a break in the action. It remains a common device in pantomime and musical comedy.

carpet cut A slot in the stage in which a carpet or other stage cloth is secured by means of hinged flaps.

Carretto, Galleotto del (d. c. 1530) Italian playwright. His plays *Timon* (1497) and *Sofonisba* (1502) were heavily influenced by the tragedies of Seneca and by the tradition of the *sacra rappresentazione*.

carriage-and-frame system A method of effecting a rapid change of scenery, developed in Italy in the 17th century. Also called the **chariot-and-pole system**, it consisted of pairs of flats mounted on wheeled platforms, which were drawn beneath the stage by ropes on a network of rails so that as one flat disappeared into the wings another automatically took its place.

Carroll, Earl (1893–1948) US impresario, who built and ran the EARL CARROLL THEATRE. In 1923 he staged the first of a series of his own revues, *Earl Carroll's Vanities*. Among the straight plays be produced was Leon Gordon's *White Cargo* (1923).

Carroll, Paul Vincent (1900–68) Irish playwright. From 1945 he lived in England, where he wrote film and television scenarios as well as plays on Irish themes. Heavily influenced by Ibsen, he won an Abbey Theatre prize for *Things That Are Caesar's* in 1932. His most successful play was *Shadow and Substance* (1934), which won a New York Drama Critics Circle Award, a success which he repeated with *The White Steed* (1939). Other works include two lively satirical comedies.

Cartel A loosely-defined association of four leading French actor-managers in the 1920s, which aimed to create a new theatrical impetus. The combined efforts of the various members of the Cartel – Baty, Dullin, Jouvet, and Pitoëff, who in 1936 shared the directorship of the Comédie-Française – triggered the AVANT-GARDE movement.

Carton, Richard Claude (Richard Claude Critchett; 1856–1928) British playwright and actor, whose career as a writer blossomed with the success of *Liberty Hall* in 1892. He then embarked upon a series of farcical comedies, which often starred his wife, Katherine Mackenzie COMPTON, the best-known being *Lord and Lady Algy* (1898).

Cartoucherie de Vincennes *See* Soleil, Théâtre du.

Cartwright, William (c. 1606–c. 1687) English actor, presumed to be the son of William Cartwright (fl. 1590–1622), who at one time leased, in partnership, the Fortune Theatre. The younger Cartwright was a member of Prince Charles's Men at Salisbury Court and joined Killigrew at Drury Lane after the Restoration. His most notable roles included Corbaccio in Jonson's *Volpone* (1663).

Casarés, Maria (1922–96) Spanish actress, who moved to France during the Spanish Civil War and did not return until 1975. She established her reputation in Synge's *Deidre of the Sorrows* (1942) and in existentialist dramas by Camus, Sartre, and Anouilh; her classic roles included Racine's Phèdre at the Comédie-Française (1952–54) and Lady Macbeth at the Avignon Festival (1954). She joined the Théâtre National Populaire in 1955, subsequently appearing in intense modern dramas by such authors as Genet, Brecht, and Bond.

Casino Theatre A theatre on Broadway, New York, which opened in 1883 and became the leading musical-comedy theatre in New York. The theatre closed after the production of *The Desert Song* (1926) and was demolished in 1930.

Casona, Alejandro (Rodríguez Álvarez; 1900–65) Spanish playwright, who wrote humorous plays for performance by a travelling theatre, El Teatro del Pueblo. His most successful plays include *La sirena varada* (1934) and *Prohibido suicidarse en primavera* (1937).

Casson, Sir Lewis (1875–1969) British actor and director, who began with the Vedrenne-Barker management and then the Horniman company in Manchester. The husband of Sybil Thorndike, he acted with her and directed her in many plays, touring widely with her at home and abroad. He also directed and appeared in classical productions at the Old Vic and other theatres; contemporary roles included Gertler in *I Have Been Here Before* (1937) and the Professor in *The Linden Tree* (1947) by J B Priestley. He was knighted in 1945.

Caste A play by T W ROBERTSON. First performance: 1867. The play, an attack on class prejudice, centres upon Esther Eccles, a girl from the ballet who marries into the aristocracy. Her husband, falsely reported killed in battle, returns to rescue her from the effects of social snobbery.

CAS Theatre *See* Community Arts Service.

Castro y Bellvís, Guillén de (1569–1631) Spanish playwright, author of *La mocedades del Cid* (c. 1599), a play in two parts upon which Corneille based *Le Cid* in 1637. A friend of Lope de Vega, he was also the author of several comedies and stage adaptations of *Don Quixote* by Cervantes.

catharsis A concept formulated by Aristotle in his *Poetics*. It denotes the emotional purification of the audience ideally achieved at the end of a tragedy.

Cathleen Ni Houlihan A one-act play by W B YEATS, with Lady GREGORY as an un-credited collaborator. First performance: Dublin, 1902, by the Irish National Dramatic Society. With its theme of patriotic sacrifice, the play was rapturously welcomed by Irish nationalists. Based in part on an old ballad, the plot concerns a peasant, Michael Gillane, who abandons his family to fight for a wronged old woman, later revealed as the mystical Queen of Ireland.

Cat on a Hot Tin Roof A drama by Tennessee WILLIAMS. First performance: New York, 1955. The plot concerns a wealthy but dysfunctional Southern family. Maggie (the 'cat' of the title) wants a child but cannot have one by Brick, her alcoholic hus-band, because her infidelity has made him impotent. Brick's father, the bullying pa-triarch Big Daddy, desperately wants a grandson because he is dissatisfied with his two sons. The play won a Pulitzer Prize.

Cats A musical by Andrew LLOYD WEBBER. First performance: New London The-atre, London, 1981. Based on the poems in T S Eliot's *Old Possum's Book of Practical Cats*, the show is constructed around a series of dance numbers. The London pro-duction, which was created by Trevor Nunn, became the longest-running musical in history in 1996 (and is still running in 2001). The Broadway production also ran for a record-breaking 18 years.

catwalk A narrow bridge above the stage from which scenery and lighting equip-ment can be manhandled.

Caucasian Chalk Circle, The (*Der Kaukasische Kreidekreis*) A play by Bertolt BRECHT, written in 1943–45. First performance: Minnesota, 1948. First performed in German by the Berliner Ensemble in 1954, it revolves around a peasant woman's attempts to retain custody of a small child against its biological mother and her final appeal for justice at the court of a mysterious judge. The moral is that things rightly belong to those who will use them constructively, not to the legal owners.

cauldron trap A square trap positioned upstage; so-called from its use in the witches scene in *Macbeth*.

Cavalcade A play by Noël COWARD. First performance: Drury Lane, 1931. The play, which requires a huge cast, presents a panoramic and highly patriotic view of British life from 1899 to 1930 through the history of the Marryot family. Subsequently it was successfully turned into a film.

Cave, Joe (Joseph Arnold Cave; 1823–1912) British music hall comedian, who was the first performer to work a black-faced comedy act. Later he became manager of the Marylebone Music Hall.

Cawarden, Sir Thomas (d. 1559) English court official, appointed MASTER OF THE REVELS in 1545. During his time the involvement of this office in censorship became more profound; Cawarden did, however, live just long enough to supervise the rev-els for the coronation of Queen Elizabeth I.

Cecchi, Giovanni Maria (1518–87) Italian playwright, author of numerous come-dies, notably *Assiulo* (1550), and religious plays. His use of various additional comic characters in biblical stories was a significant development in the foundation of an Italian secular theatrical tradition.

Cecchini, Pier Maria (1575–1645) Italian actor and playwright of the *commedia dell'arte*, who was known on stage as **Fritellino**. He became leader of the Accesi troupe in 1600 and often appeared with his wife Orsola, who was known as **Flaminea** and later moved with him to join the Fedeli company.

ceiling-cloth A cloth used to provide the ceiling of a box set as an alternative to a rigid book ceiling.

Céleste, Céline (1814–82) French actress, noted for her expressive performances in both dance and pantomime. After visiting New York she played in London in 1830 and later appeared at Drury Lane and elsewhere in speaking parts in such plays as *A Tale of Two Cities* (1860) by Dickens. She also managed the Adelphi Theatre with Ben Webster for a time.

Celestina, La A dialogue novel by Fernando de ROJAS, regarded as the most important piece of Spanish dramatic writing of the 15th century. A popular and frequently humorous study of tragic love, it was also highly successful in English, Italian, and French adaptations, including that of John RASTELL.

cellar The area directly beneath the stage, used for storage, the operation of stage equipment, and for access to the stage through traps.

Celle castle A castle in the town of Celle in Germany, which is also the home of one of the oldest theatres in Europe. Completed by 1674, it was designed in the baroque style and seated 330 people; numerous balls and dramatic entertainments were staged there in front of the Hanoverian Court. Many years later Schröder appeared there, although the theatre fell into disuse for long periods. It was restored in 1935 and the resident company was revived in 1950.

Celtis, Conradus (Conrad Pickel; 1459–1508) German scholar, who did much to promote the study of classical drama in Cologne, Heidelberg, and as a professor at the university of Vienna. He published the plays of Hroswitha in 1501 and was himself the author of two dramatic works, the masques *Ludus Dianae* (1501) and *Rhapsodia, laudes et victoria Maximiliani de Boemannis* (1504).

CEMA *See* Arts Councils.

Cenci, The A verse tragedy by Percy Bysshe SHELLEY, published in 1819. First performance: 1886. It recounts the true story of a 16th-century Italian noblewoman, Beatrice Cenci, who murdered her father after he developed an incestuous passion for her.

censorship *See* Lord Chamberlain.

Centaur Theatre The main English-speaking theatre company in Montreal, Canada, and one of the most important in the country. Established in 1969 in an auditorium in the Old Stock Exchange, it was able to buy and renovate the whole building by 1974. It has two theatres which present both classic and new Canadian plays.

Centlivre, Susannah (1667–1723) English playwright and actress, who established herself as a successor to Aphra Behn with her play *The Gamester* in 1705. As an actress she appeared predominantly in male roles; of her many comedies of intrigue the most celebrated were *The Busie Body* (1709), *The Wonder: a Woman Keeps a Secret*

(1714), and *A Bold Stroke for a Wife* (1718). Some of David Garrick's most popular roles were in Centlivre's plays.

Central School of Speech and Drama A drama school in London, founded in 1906 by the actress **Elsie Fogerty** (1866–1945). Initially concerned chiefly with the performance of poetic drama, it was based in the Albert Hall before moving to the Embassy Theatre.

Central Theatre of the Soviet Army *See* Red Army Theatre.

Centre 42 *See* Round House.

Centres Dramatiques *See Décentralisation Dramatique.*

centrestage *See* stage direction.

Century Grove *See* Century Theatre.

Century Theatre A theatre on 62PPnd Street, New York, which opened in 1909 as the **New Theatre**. It reopened as the Century in 1911, housing musicals and some acclaimed Shakespearean productions. Other successes were Vollmöller's *The Miracle* (1924) and Reinhardt's version of *A Midsummer Night's Dream* (1927). The theatre closed in 1929 and was demolished, together with the **Cocoanut Grove** or **Century Grove** theatre on its roof, in 1930.

Another **Century Theatre** opened on 7th Avenue, New York, as the **Jolson Theatre** in 1921. The theatre was named the Century in 1944 and housed visiting companies from Britain, France, and the USSR, including Stanislavsky's Moscow Art Theatre in 1923. Known as the **Venice Theatre** from 1934 to 1937, it housed several other companies (including the Federal Theatre Project and the Old Vic company) before demolition in 1961.

See also Adelphi Theatre; Bijou Theatre.

Cervantes (Saavedra), Miguel de (1547–1616) Spanish novelist and playwright, who turned to literature after service in the army, having lost the use of his left hand as the result of a wound received at the battle of Lepanto (1571) and having been imprisoned for five years after his capture by pirates. His romance *Don Quixote de la Mancha* has provided numerous subsequent writers with material for their own plays, including an adaptation by W G Wills in which Irving appeared. Of his works written specifically for the stage 16 survive; the best include the *comedia Pedro de Urdemalas*, the full-length play *El cerco de Numancia*, and *El trato de Argel*.

Césaire, Aimé (1913–) West Indian poet and playwright, whose plays reject European influences and make extensive use of African rhythms and history. His best-known works, written in French, include *La Tragédie du roi Christophe* (1963) and *Une saison au Congo* (1967), both of which discuss the problems faced by newly independent African states, and a version of *The Tempest* (1969) highlighting racial themes. He also followed a political career, representing Martinique in the French Constituent Assembly from 1946 to 1993.

Český Krumlov A castle in the Czech Republic, site of one of the oldest existing theatres in Europe. Built in 1766 in the baroque style, it contains 10 unique sets of scenery (by Viennese artists) notable for their use of perspective effects and much original stage machinery. The theatre is still occasionally used for dramatic presentations.

Chaikin, Joseph (1935–) US actor, director, and producer, who made his New York debut in *Dark of the Moon* (1958), then joined the Living Theatre, acting in Jack Gelber's *The Connection* (1959, revived 1963). In 1964 he founded the OPEN THEATRE, which he ran on the principles set down in his book *The Presence of the Actor* (1972). He has also directed in Los Angeles, New York, and Israel.

Chaillot, Palais de A theatrical venue in Paris, close to the Eiffel Tower, which contains several stage areas and exhibition spaces. The original building was the home of Gémier's Théâtre National Populaire from 1920 to 1934; after rebuilding in 1937 it became the base of a second Théâtre National Populaire led by Vilar and Wilson before extensive reorganization in the 1970s (*see Décentralisation Dramatique*).

chairman The master of ceremonies in a music hall. The post had been largely dropped by the 1890s.

Chairs, The (*Les Chaises*) A play by Eugène IONESCO. First performance: Paris, 1952. The chairs of the title, assembled to seat the invisible guests of an elderly married couple, dominate the stage: the two old people finally commit suicide.

Chamberlain's Men An English theatrical company founded in 1594. Including Shakespeare amongst its members, the company, for which Shakespeare wrote the majority of his plays, performed at the Theatre until 1599 and then at the Globe Theatre, led by Richard Burbage. They also appeared at the court of Elizabeth I and were ultimately renamed the KING'S MEN after the accession of James I in 1603. Apart from Shakespeare, other playwrights who had their work performed by the company included Jonson, Dekker, and Beaumont and Fletcher.

Chambers of Rhetoric Associations of rhetoricians, first organized in both northern France and the Low Countries (where they were known as **Rederykers**) in the 12th and 13th centuries. These groups of writers staged drama festivals and developed various Continental equivalents of the mystery, miracle, and morality plays, notably the allegorical *spel van sinne*. Their reputation eventually declined and the last such chambers were disbanded in the early 17th century.

Chambers Street Theatre A theatre in Chambers Street, New York, which opened as Palmo's Opera House in 1844. From 1848 to 1856 it was known as Burton's Chambers Street Theatre under the management of William E Burton, who successfully staged Shakespeare as well as plays based upon novels by Dickens. Subsequently Edward Eddy presented a popular season of farce and melodrama. Renamed the **American Theatre** under E L Davenport in 1857 it was closed within a month.

Champagne Charlie *See* Leybourne, George.

Champion, Harry (1866–1942) British music hall comedian, who abandoned his early negro act to become a cockney comic. He had a long career singing, sometimes at tremendous speed, such songs as 'Any Old Iron', 'Boiled Beef and Carrots', and 'I'm Henry the Eighth I am, I am'.

Champmeslé, Charles Chevillet (1642–1701) French actor and playwright, who performed in the provinces before appearing at the Théâtre du Marais, the Hôtel de

Bourgogne, and, ultimately, the Comédie-Française. He excelled in tragedy, notably in Racine's *Bérénice* (1670). His own plays include the comedy *Crispin Chevalier* (1673), *Le Florentin* (1685), and *La Coupe enchantée* (1688).

His wife was the celebrated actress **Mlle Champmeslé** (Marie Desmares; 1643–98), who eventually became the leading tragic actress with the Comédie-Française. She established her reputation while at the Théâtre du Marais and inspired Racine, who became her lover, to write such parts as Bérénice, Roxane, and Phèdre for her. She became famous for her musical intonation and subsequently attracted large audiences to the Hôtel de Bourgogne, where she was from 1670, and the Comédie-Française, where she remained from 1680 until her death, often playing opposite Michel Baron.

Champs-Élysées, Comédie des *See* Comédie des Champs-Élysées.

Chancerel, Léon (1886–1965) French playwright and director, noted for his production of plays for young audiences. He founded Le Théâtre de L'Oncle Sebastien for this purpose in Paris in 1935 and served as head of both the Société d'Histoire du Théâtre and the Centre Dramatique. A prize in his name is awarded biannually for outstanding plays for children.

Changeling, The A tragedy by Thomas MIDDLETON and William ROWLEY. First performance: London, 1622. The play concentrates on the relationship between the ugly servant De Flores and the headstrong aristocrat Beatrice, who incites him to commit a murder. The grotesque subplot concerns two young men who pose as lunatics to woo the wife of the doctor in a madhouse.

Channing, Carol (1921–) US actress and singer, who first appeared in New York in 1941. Her most successful roles were Lorelei Lee in *Gentlemen Prefer Blondes* (1949), and (her greatest triumph) Dolly Gallagher Levi in *Hello Dolly!* (1964, 1978, 1980, 1985).

Chantilly, Mlle (Marie-Justine-Benoiste Duronceray; 1727–72) French actress, who was married to the playwright Charles Simon FAVART. She became an important member of the Comédie-Italienne and was responsible for introducing more realistic costumes in productions there.

Chapel Street Theatre A small theatre in Chapel Street, New York, which was also later known as the **Beekman Street Theatre**. Opened by David Douglass in 1761, it staged the first New York performance of *Hamlet*, with the younger Hallam as Hamlet. Douglass's company left in 1762, after which amateurs and members of the British garrison used the building until 1766, when a mob burst in during a performance and damaged the building; it was never used again.

Chapman, George (1560–1634) English poet, playwright, and translator of the works of Homer. After spending some years elsewhere in Europe (1585–91) he returned to London to write for Philip Henslowe. He is best known for the comedy *Eastward Ho!* (1605), for which he was imprisoned with his collaborators Marston and Jonson, the tragedy *Bussy d'Ambois* (1604), and its sequel *The Revenge of Bussy d'Ambois* (c. 1610).

Chappuzeau, Samuel (1625–1701) French writer. His *Le Théâtre français* (1674), containing information about contemporary drama, is a valuable work of reference on

17th-century French theatre. He also wrote a number of comedies, collected in *La Muse enjouée ou le Théâtre comique*.

Charing Cross Music Hall *See* Gatti's.

Charing Cross Theatre A theatre in King William Street, London, which was initially known as the Polygraphic Hall. It became a notable venue in 1872 when Fanny STIRLING appeared with great success as Mrs Malaprop in *The Rivals* for the first time; subsequent productions included numerous burlesques as well as a few plays and early comedies by Pinero. It closed in 1895 and was demolished to make way for the rebuilding of Charing Cross Hospital.

chariot-and-pole system *See* carriage-and-frame system.

Charke, Charlotte (c. 1710–60) British actress, daughter of Colley CIBBER. Noted for her eccentricities, she appeared at the Haymarket, Drury Lane, and Lincoln's Inn Fields. She also worked as a puppeteer and a conjuror's assistant. Her autobiography appeared in 1755.

Charles Hopkins Theatre *See* Punch and Judy Theatre.

Charleson, Ian (1949–90) British actor, born in Edinburgh, where he made his debut with the Young Vic company at the 1972 Festival. Subsequently he played Hamlet (1975) with the Cambridge Theatre Company and important parts with the Royal Shakespeare Company; among his leading roles at the National Theatre were Sky Masterson in *Guys and Dolls* (1982), Brick in Tennessee Williams's *Cat on a Hot Tin Roof* (1988), and Hamlet (1990), in which he triumphed shortly before his death from AIDS. He also starred in the film *Chariots of Fire* (1981).

Charley's Aunt A farce by Brandon THOMAS. First performance: London, 1892. It ran for four years at the Royalty Theatre with W S Penley as Lord Fancourt-Babberley, who is persuaded to impersonate the aunt of his scheming friend, Charles; various complications ensue when the real aunt returns from Brazil. The play was subsequently made into a highly successful musical, *Where's Charley?*, with songs by Frank Loesser.

Charlot, André (1882–1956) British impresario, who organized numerous celebrated musical entertainments in London during the 1920s and 1930s. Before World War I he presented revues at the Alhambra featuring such stars as Jack Buchanan; after the war *Charlot's Revue* (seen in both London and New York in two editions, 1924 and 1925) established Noël Coward in such shows and also featured Gertrude Lawrence and Beatrice Lillie.

Charon, Jacques (1920–75) French actor and director, who became a leading director of farce and vaudeville at the Comédie-Française. Previously he worked with Gaston Baty before winning praise for such productions as Feydeau's *Un Fil à la patte* (1964), which was also seen in London.

Chatham Theatre A theatre between Duane and Pearl streets, New York, which was opened in 1823, as the **Pavilion Theatre**, by Barrière – a pastry cook who held a licence to provide entertainments at Chatham Gardens nearby. Seating 1300 persons, it was the first theatre in New York to be lit by gas and housed a talented company that included Joseph Jefferson I (who made his final New York appearance there in 1825), Joseph Jefferson II, Henry Wallack, and James Hackett. Upon Barrière's death in 1826 Wallack and Hackett took over the theatre with limited success, renaming it the **American Opera House** in 1829. From 1830 Blanchard presented a mixed bill of straight and equestrian drama until, under Hamblin, the theatre (known as **Blanchard's Amphitheatre**) was closed down in 1832.

Another **Chatham Theatre** was opened on Chatham Street, New York, in 1839. Seating 2200, it was managed for a time by Charles Thorne and then (as the **New National Theatre**) by Frank Chanfrau. Under Purdy's management Edwin Booth made his first New York appearance there in 1850, large crowds came to see Beecher Stowe's *Uncle Tom's Cabin* (1853), and Adah Isaacs Menken made her New York debut (1859). After a fire in 1860 it became the **Union Theatre**, the **National Concert Hall**, and finally the **National Music Hall** before being demolished in 1862.

Chauve-Souris A revue produced by the Russian theatre director Nikita BALIEFF. First performance: Chauve-Souris Club, Paris, 1908. The highly successful *Chauve-Souris* consisted of sketches, burlesques, songs, and pantomime and was first seen in London in 1921 and in New York in 1922.

Chayefsky, Paddy (1923–81) US playwright and screenwriter, whose best-known work for the stage is *The Tenth Man* (1959). Other plays include *Middle of the Night* (1956), *The Passion of Josef D* (1964), about Stalin and the Russian Revolution, *Gideon* (1966), and *The Latent Heterosexual* (1968). He won three Oscars for his film screenplays.

Cheek by Jowl A British touring company specializing in scaled down versions of classic plays, founded in 1981. Under the leadership of artistic director Declan DONNELLAN, the company gained a reputation for the freshness and simplicity of its approach in such productions as *Andromache* (1985), *Twelfth Night* (1987), and *Measure for Measure* (1994). Although it disbanded in 1998, this is intended as a temporary pause for reflection. Meanwhile Donnellan and designer Nick Ormerod continue to work as a team.

Cheeseman, Peter (1932–) British director who, after managing Stephen Joseph's Studio Theatre Company, became (1962) director of Joseph's VICTORIA THEATRE in Stoke-on-Trent. There he staged a series of local documentary plays and oversaw (1986) the company's move to the larger New Victoria Theatre.

Chekhov, Anton (Pavlovich) (*or* Tchehov, Tchekhov; 1860–1904) Russian playwright and short-story writer, whose enormously influential plays are regarded as classics of the modern theatre. Of a humble background, Chekhov made his first attempts at dramatic writing – the successful one-act comedies *The Bear*, *The Proposal*, and *The Wedding* – after studying medicine in Moscow. After the less successful IVANOV, however, he experienced total failure with the full-length play *The Wood Demon*; when THE SEAGULL also failed in 1896 Chekhov nearly abandoned the theatre. Nemirovich-Danchenko and Stanislavsky, however, revived the play at the Moscow Art Theatre in 1898 with great success and Chekhov went on to follow it with a series of increasingly accomplished works that only ended with his early death.

His plays, of which THE CHERRY ORCHARD is usually considered the masterpiece, place great emphasis on ensemble playing and express a profound awareness of both the comic and tragic aspects of daily life; although not tightly plotted, they are now accepted as brilliantly atmospheric portrayals of the tensions inherent in prerevolutionary Russia.

Suffering from tuberculosis, Chekhov spent the last years of his life at Yalta in the Crimea. He married Olga KNIPPER, an actress with the Moscow Art Theatre, in 1901. The first English translations of his plays were performed within five years of his death.

Principal dramatic works:
The Bear: 1888.
The Proposal: 1889.
Ivanov: 1889.
The Wedding: 1890.
The Seagull: 1896.
UNCLE VANYA: 1899.
THREE SISTERS: 1901.
The Cherry Orchard: 1904.

Chelidonius, Benedictus (16th century) Austrian humanist and churchman, abbot of the Schottenkloster in Vienna. He was the author of the religious drama *Voluptatis cum virtute disceptatio* (1515), which discusses the nature of virtue and vice.

Chelsea Theatre *See* Royal Court Theatre.

Chelsea Theatre Center A US off-off-Broadway company, which was founded in 1965 in order to stage new plays and rarely performed classics. It was named after its original home in Chelsea, New York, but three years later moved to the Brooklyn Academy of Music. Among the works produced before the company folded in 1981 were Imamu Barak's *Slaveship* (1969), Gay's *The Beggar's Opera* (1972), Allen Ginsberg's *Kaddish* (1972), Voltaire's *Candide* (1973), and Kleist's *The Prince of Homburg* (1976).

Chénier, Marie-Joseph(-Blaise) de (1764–1811) French playwright and politician, born in Constantinople. Brother of the poet André de Chénier and a member of the Convention, he wrote patriotic songs and historical tragedies, which provided excellent parts for Talma and others. Fired by the spirit of the Revolution, such plays as *Charles IX* (1789) and *Caius Gracchus* (1792) were very popular in their time.

Cherkassov, Nikolai Konstantinovich (1903–66) Russian actor, who established his reputation in comedy acts in music hall but later won acclaim in classical roles. He made his debut at the Leningrad Theatre of Young Spectators in 1926, subsequently appearing at the Puskhin Theatre in Leningrad from 1933 in both modern and classic roles. He also starred in several films by Eisenstein.

Cherry Lane Theatre A 180-seat theatre on Commerce Street, New York. The building, part of which dates back to the late 18th century, was converted into a theatre in 1924. In 1927 it was taken over for a year by the New Playwrights Theatre, who reopened it with Paul Sifton's *The Belt*. Since then it has been used by a number of companies, although it currently presents shows on a rental basis. Successful productions have included plays by Albee, Beckett, Ionesco, and Pinter.

Cherry Orchard, The The last play of Anton CHEKHOV. First performance: Moscow Art Theatre, 1904. Regarded by many as Chekhov's masterpiece, the play revolves around a country family's doomed attempts to save their estate, including a much loved cherry orchard, from bankruptcy. It constitutes a sensitive but critical portrayal of the landowning class in prerevolutionary Russia. Stanislavsky's production of the play as an essentially melancholic tale has proved widely influential but displeased Chekhov himself, who emphasized the humour in the piece.

Chess A musical written by Tim RICE, with music by Bjorn Ulvaeus and Benny Andersson (formerly of Abba). First performance: Prince Edward Theatre, London, 1986. The plot revolves around the romantic entanglement of a Soviet chess champion with the former lover of his US opponent.

Chestnut Street Theatre A theatre in Philadelphia, Pennsylvania, built in 1793 for an English company hired by Thomas Wignell and later known as **'Old Drury'**. It was the first US theatre to be built in the English proscenium style, being a direct copy of the Theatre Royal at Bath. Seating 2000, it was subsequently (from 1803) managed by William Wood and the elder William Warren, who successfully maintained the theatre's virtual monopoly of acting in Philadelphia until the Walnut Street Theatre opened in 1811. A stock company took over until 1820 when, damaged by fire, it was closed until 1822. It was again destroyed in 1855 and not rebuilt until 1863; it closed finally in 1910.

Chettle, Henry (1560–1607) English playwright and printer, of whose many plays only the revenge tragedy *Hoffmann* (1603) survives. As a printer he was responsible for the publication of *A Groatsworth of Wit* by Robert Greene.

Chevalier, Albert (1861–1923) British music hall performer, who became immensely popular as a singer of cockney songs. Before beginning his music hall career he appeared as an actor in comedy, burlesque, and melodrama; as a music hall artist he first performed at the London Pavilion in 1891. His songs included 'Knocked 'Em in the Old Kent Road' and 'My Old Dutch'.

Chevalier, Maurice (1888–1972) French singer, who became a leading performer of revues and musical comedies both on stage and in films. He became highly popular as Mistinguett's partner in Paris before World War I, sporting a straw hat and cane and adopting an exaggerated French accent.

Chiado, António Ribeiro (d. 1591) Portuguese playwright. His loosely-plotted plays, set in Lisbon, are notable for their realistic characterization and naturalistic dialogue.

Chiarelli, Luigi (1884–1947) Italian playwright, whose plays are characterized by the grotesque humour and violent realism of the *Teatro* GROTTESCO. His most successful play, a farcical comedy entitled *La maschera e il volta* (The Mask and the Face; 1916), satirizes modern society and has been widely translated and performed throughout Europe. His other plays include the comedy *Una più due* (One Plus Two; 1935) and *Il cerchio magico* (The Magic Circle; 1937).

Chicago A musical by John Kander and Fred Ebb, based on a 1926 play of the same name by Maurine Dallas Watkins. First performance: New York, 1975. The plot, which is unusually cynical for a musical, centres on Roxie Hart, who has shot her faithless lover and hopes to turn her notoriety into a career on the vaudeville stage. The show itself takes the form of a vaudeville performance, with each twist in the

plot being marked by a different type of number. The original production was a triumph for director-choreographer Bob FOSSE, while the late 1990s saw highly successful revivals in New York and London.

Chicano Theatre   A group of Mexican-American theatre companies, which perform
in both Spanish and English throughout the US. Their productions rely heavily upon
improvisation and focus on such social problems as unemployment, housing, education, drug abuse, racism, and low wages. The first Chicano group was the **Teatro
Campesino** (Fieldworkers' Theatre), which was formed in 1965 in California from
striking vineyard workers. Later groups – most of which are concentrated in the SW
US – were made up of college and university students; the most important companies have included the **Teatro de los Barrios** in Texas (founded in 1969), the **Teatro
del Piojo** (founded in Seattle in 1970), the **Teatro de la Gente** (founded in San José
in 1970), and the **Teatro de la Esperanza** (founded in Santa Barbara in 1971). Their
activities include annual festivals and conferences.

Chichester Festival Theatre   A theatre in Chichester, built in 1962 as the site for
an annual summer drama festival on the lines of that presented at the Stratford (Ontario) Festival in Canada. Seating 1394 in its hexagonal auditorium, it was directed
by Laurence Olivier from 1962 to 1966 and saw the early development of the company that later became the National Theatre. Plays presented at the festival have included those of Chekhov, Arden, Shaffer, Brecht, Bolt, and Ibsen. John Clements
succeeded Olivier as director in 1966 and was himself replaced by Keith Michell in
1974. Subsequent directors have included Peter Dews (1978–80), who staged notable revivals during his stay, and Michael Rudman (1989–91). A new studio theatre,
the **Minerva Theatre**, was opened in 1988 with the young Sam Mendes as its first
director.

Chicken Soup with Barley   The first play in a trilogy by Arnold WESKER. First performance: Belgrade Theatre, Coventry, 1958. The three acts follow the lives of the
Kahns, a Jewish family in the East End of London, from the mid-1930s to the mid-
1950s. Their socialist beliefs are tested by post-war disillusion, but the ideals of
Sarah, the matriarch, remain unextinguished.

Chikamatsu Monzaemon (Sugimori Nobumori; 1653–1724)   Japanese playwright,
who is widely regarded as the greatest writer for the theatre that Japan has produced.
He began his career writing for the puppet theatre alongside Takemoto Gidayū in
Osaka, establishing the distinctive 'Gidayū music' style of the *Jōruri* tradition. Subsequently he spent 15 years writing *Kabuki* drama, before returning to the puppet theatre in 1703, after which he wrote many of his finest plays. These included such
domestic tragedies as *Sonezaki Shinjū* (The Love Suicides at Sonezaki; 1703) and such
historical romances as *Kokusenya kassen* (The Battles of Coxinga; 1715).

Children of a Lesser God   A play by Mark Medhoff. First performance: Los Angeles,
1979, New York, 1981. The plot deals with the love affair between a deaf woman and
a hearing man. Apart from the play's intrinsic quality, it was important in making
the general theatre world aware of the large number of excellent hearing-impaired
actors. A successful film version appeared in 1986.

children's companies   *See* boy companies.

Children's Hour, The Lillian HELLMAN's first play. First performance: New York, 1934. The plot concerns two teachers falsely accused of lesbianism and culminates in the closure of the school and a suicide. The underlying theme is prejudice and its destructive power.

children's theatre Theatrical productions presented specifically for a young audience. A feature predominantly of 20th-century drama, children's theatre has flourished in various Communist states, often with propagandist aims in mind, as well as in several European countries. Important organizations founded to cater for children's theatre have included Chancerel's Théâtre de l'Oncle Sebastien (1935–39) in France and the National Youth Theatre in Britain. *See also* amateur theatre; boy companies; Jesuit drama; school drama; Westminster Play; Young Vic Theatre.

Chionides (5th century BC) Greek poet. In 486 BC he became the winner of the first competition for comedy in the City Dionysia.

Chips with Everything A play by Arnold WESKER. First performance: Royal Court Theatre, London, 1962, directed by John Dexter. The play dramatizes the training undergone by Royal Air Force recruits and highlights the damage that class divisions and heirarchical institutions can do to individuals.

Chirgwin, George H (1854–1922) British music hall performer, who first appeared on stage as a child in 1861. Later he became famous for his solo minstrel performances as 'The White-eyed Kaffir' (so-called because of his bizarre eye make-up).

Chodorov, Jerome *See* Fields, Joseph.

Choerilus (6th century BC) Greek playwright, who succeeded Thespis as the earliest major figure in classical drama. He is thought to have been the author of about 160 plays, the first of which was presented in approximately 520 BC.

choregus A patron of theatrical productions in ancient Greece. Responsible for managing and paying the CHORUS, the *choregi* were chosen in rotation from among the wealthiest citizens and competed against each other. In return for their involvement, the *choregi* were excused payment of taxes during that year.

choreography The planning and execution of stage dances, usually directed by a specialist choreographer.

chorus A group of actors who support those who undertake the main roles (the principals) in a production. The chorus was important in ancient Greek drama, when its members – who danced and sang dithyrambs – numbered 50. Later, however, the size of the chorus was reduced and it was redeveloped as a passive commentator upon the main action. In Elizabethan times the role was frequently undertaken by a single actor, who delivered a prologue. In modern musical shows the chorus is employed chiefly for crowd scenes and song-and-dance routines.

Chorus Line, A A musical by Marvin HAMLISCH, with book by James Kirkwood and Nicholas Dante and lyrics by Edward Klebin. First performance: New York, 1975. The plot, which follow dancers as they undergo a gruelling audition for a Broadway show, was based largely on actual experiences and developed by choreographer-director Michael Bennett in a series of workshops (a method now widely imitated). It won a Pulitzer Prize and set a record for longest Broadway run (till 1990; the record was broken by *Cats* in 1997).

Christiania Theatre *See* Kristiania Theater.

Christie, Dame Agatha (1890–1976) British novelist and playwright, whose play THE MOUSETRAP became the longest running production in commercial theatre. She adapted several of her crime novels for stage, among them *Ten Little Niggers* (1943), *Murder on the Nile* (1946), and *The Hollow* (1951); her other plays include *Witness for the Prosecution* (1953), *The Spider's Web* (1954), and *The Unexpected Guest* (1958). Some of her novels have also been adapted by other writers, notably *Murder at the Vicarage* (1950) by Moie Charles and Barbara Toy and *A Murder is Announced* (1977) by Leslie Darben.

Chronegk, Ludwig (1837–91) German actor-manager and director, who became the director of the Meininger company in 1871. He began as an actor in comedy in Berlin but later appeared successfully in Shakespearean parts. He became manager of the company in 1877 and subsequently superintendent of the Court theatres (1884) under the Duke of Saxe-Meiningen himself.

Chu Chin Chow A musical comedy by Oscar ASCHE, with music by Frederic Norton. First performance: His Majesty's Theatre, London, 1916. A retelling of *Ali Baba and the Forty Thieves*, it was staged with Asche himself playing the robber chief and enjoyed a record-breaking run of nearly five years.

Churchill, Caryl (1938–) British playwright, who first attracted attention for her work with the Joint Stock Theatre Company, notably the historical play *Light Shining in Buckinghamshire* (1976). Her plays since then have included *Cloud Nine* (1978), TOP GIRLS (1982), *Fen* (1983), the highly successful SERIOUS MONEY (1987), about the City of London during the mid-1980s boom, *Lives of the Great Poisoners* (1991), *The Skiker* (1994), a play with music, the experimental double bill *Blue Heart* (1997), and *Far Away* (2000). Her works combine great formal inventiveness with a concern for sexual politics.

Churchill, Frank *See* Lewes, George Henry.

Cibber, Colley (1671–1757) British actor-manager and dramatist. The son of a sculptor, he joined Betterton's company in 1690. As an actor he excelled as Sir Novelty Fashion in his own play *Love's Last Shift* (1696), which was later acknowledged as the first sentimental comedy, and as Lord Foppington in *The Relapse*. Amongst his subsequent successes as a writer were *She Would and She Would Not; or, the Kind Imposter* (1702) and *The Careless Husband* (1704), as well as adaptations of Molière and Fielding. His adaptation of *Richard III* held the stage for more than a century.

In 1711 he became part of the celebrated triumvirate management of Drury Lane in which role, despite his innate tactlessness, he contributed much to the theatre's prosperity. In 1730 he was appointed poet laureate; he was also author of the autobiography *Apology for the Life of Mr Colley Cibber, Comedian* (1740).

His son, **Theophilus Cibber** (1703–58) was also an actor at Drury Lane, where he became notorious for his dissolute behaviour. Continually at odds with Quin and Macklin, he eventually fled abroad to escape his creditors. Cleared by his second wife, Susanna Arne, he brought two scandalous actions against her friend, William Sloper, and his popularity declined. He was living in penury when invited to Dublin in 1758 and lost his life in a shipwreck after setting sail from Holyhead. *See also* Charke, Charlotte.

Cicognini, Giacinto Andrea (1606–60) Italian playwright, author of over 40 plays. His writing was heavily influenced by the works of Lope de Vega and Calderón, which were performed by various Spanish touring companies in Naples, where he lived. He was the author of the earliest Italian version of the Don Juan story.

Cid, Le A drama by Pierre CORNEILLE. First performance: Paris, 1636 or early 1637. Based on *Las mocedades del Cid* by Guíllen de CASTRO Y BELLVÍS, it is usually considered the first masterpiece of the French stage. To avenge a mortal insult to his father, Rodrigo kills the father of Chimène, his beloved. Although she believes that he was justified, and still loves him, she must then seek vengeance on him. The end is ambiguous, but allows for their marriage after a year of mourning. The play is not really a tragedy, but rather a dramatic meditation on the relationship between self-image, public image, and love. Disagreement over its merits led to a battle of pamphlets known as the *querelle du Cid*, which, in its turn, led to the codification of the rules for what would become NEOCLASSICAL DRAMA.

cieco d'Adria, Il *See* Groto, Luigi.

Cincinnati Playhouse in the Park A theatre, housing two auditoriums, which opened in Cincinatti, Ohio, in 1959. It is the professional playhouse for the Ohio River Valley area, producing both classical and modern plays as well as many world premieres, some found through an annual play competition.

Cinquevalli, Paul (Paul Kestner; 1859–1918) British music hall performer, born in Poland. After a trapeze accident he took up juggling as a therapy and developed it to a standard never surpassed. Billed as 'The Human Billiard Table', he was a star of the halls for over 20 years.

Cinthio, Il *See* Giraldi, Giovanni Battista.

Circa Theatre A theatre in Wellington, New Zealand, opened in 1976 and run independently of the state subsidized theatre system. Run on a co-operative basis, it was founded by members of the Downstage Theatre company and has enjoyed commercial success with a number of comedies.

circle *See* auditorium.

Circle, The A comedy by W Somerset MAUGHAM. First performance: London, 1921. Often considered Maugham's finest play, *The Circle* concerns a young married woman's decision to elope with her lover, a rubber planter from Malaya, and the attempts of her estranged parents to dissuade her.

Circle-in-the-Square A theatre-in-the-round in Sheridan Square, New York, which opened in 1951 as the home of José Quintero's Loft Players. In 1954 the theatre was closed as a fire hazard but reopened in 1956 with a famous production of O'Neill's *The Iceman Cometh*. It was demolished in 1960 and the company moved to the New Stages Theatre on Bleeker Street, now the Circle-in-the-Square Downtown. In 1972 the company moved to the new Joseph E Levine Theatre, in the basement of the same mid-town office block that holds the **Gershwin Theatre**. Subsequent productions have included the musical *I'm Getting My Act Together and Taking It on the Road* (1978), *As Is* (1981), one of the first plays to deal with AIDS, and Tina Howe's *Coastal Disturbances* (1987).

Circle Repertory Company A New York Theatre company founded in 1969 by Marshall Mason, housed in a 160-seat theatre in Greenwich Village. It has a special relationship with Lanford WILSON, most of whose plays have premiered there.

circuit A group of theatres in the same geographical area that are regularly visited in turn by touring companies. The circuit system was developed in the 18th century and played a crucial role in the training of young actors. Some of the most important British circuits were those named after Aberdeen, Exeter, Kent, Manchester, Newcastle, Norfolk and Suffolk, Norwich, Winchester, and York.

circus A public entertainment, featuring animals, clowns, acrobats, and the like, often performed in a large tent. The name originally referred to the gladiatorial shows and festivals of ancient Rome, and the arenas in which they were held. The modern circus developed in Britain and the US at the end of the 18th century. Its links to the central dramatic tradition can be seen most clearly in the melodramas, dog dramas, equestrian dramas, and music hall of the 19th century. Concern about the use of performing animals led to a reduction of this element in the late 20th century, when a tradition of 'alternative' circus entertainment also developed.

Cirque du Soleil A Montreal-based company founded in 1984, which brings to traditional circus entertainment (without animal acts) a sense of narrative and visual experiment drawn from the alternative theatre. Following success at home and several tours of Europe and the US, it has established new permanent companies in several tourist centres. The most important of these are in Las Vegas, where two theatres with many unusual technical devices have been built especially for them.

Citizens' Theatre *See* Glasgow Citizens' Theatre.

City Center of Music and Drama A theatre on West 55th Street, New York, which opened in 1943 with the New York Philharmonic Orchestra. Seating 2935, it served as the home of the New York City Ballet and the New York City Opera until 1960, when they both moved to the Lincoln Center. Today it mainly hosts dance companies and foreign troupes.

City Dionysia *See* Dionysia.

City of London Theatre A theatre in Norton Folgate, London, designed by Samuel BEAZLEY and opened in 1837. It enjoyed early success with dramatizations of the works of Charles Dickens and then prospered (1848–68) under the experienced managers Nelson Lee and Johnson with productions featuring leading performers. Subsequently the theatre's reputation declined and it became a home of melodrama; it was destroyed by fire in 1871.

City Pantheon *See* City Theatre.

City Theatre A theatre in Grub Street (later Milton Street), London, opened in 1829. Formerly a chapel, it was run first by the comic actor John Bedford (who renamed it the **City Pantheon**) and then by John Kemble Chapman (1830–31), who attracted leading performers of the day, including Edmund Kean and Ellen Tree, to the theatre. From 1831 to 1836 the theatre shared companies with the Royal Coburg (*see* Old Vic Theatre), after which the building was used as a warehouse.

The first **City Theatre** in New York opened on Warren Street in 1822 as an amateur venue. It closed a year later during a yellow fever epidemic.

Another **City Theatre** in New York opened as part of the City Saloon on Broadway in 1837. It enjoyed considerable success with appearances by Joe Cowell before closing later the same year.

A third **City Theatre** in New York opened on East 14th Street in 1910. It soon became a home of vaudeville and housed the Yiddish Art Theatre for a time before becoming a cinema in 1929 and being demolished in 1952.

Ciulei, Liviu (1923–) Romanian director, actor, and designer, who succeeded Lucia Sturdza-Bulandra as artistic director of the Municipal Theatre in 1961. He appeared there under his own direction in a number of acclaimed productions, including Dürrenmatt's *Play Strindberg* (1972), before moving to the Guthrie Theatre in Minneapolis in 1980 (again as artistic director), where his successes included several of Shakespeare's plays and premieres of new US dramas. Since leaving Minneapolis in 1984 he has worked as a freelance director and taught at Columbia University. He has also directed films and operas.

Civic Repertory Company *See* Le Gallienne, Eva.

civic theatre (*or* **municipal theatre**) A system by which certain theatres in Britain are funded by local government on the principle that there should be active civic support for the cultural life of the community. The first such theatres were often erected by a city council and then leased to an independent theatre trust, as was the case with the first in the field, the Belgrade Theatre, Coventry (1958). Alternatively, they were sometimes funded by a partnership between local government, the Arts Council, and other organizations (as with the Nottingham Playhouse) or even (uniquely in the case of Manchester's Library and Forum Theatres) wholly owned and operated as fully-fledged repertory theatres by a city council. More recently civic authorities have purchased and refurbished some of the old touring theatres as prestigious regional centres for the arts, thus contributing to the revival of large-scale touring by national companies; notable examples include Bradford's Alhambra Theatre and Nottingham's Theatre Royal. *See also* Repertory Theatre Movement.

Cixous, Hélène (1937–) French playwright, feminist, and literary theorist. Although best known for her works of feminist theory, Cixous found success in the theatre with *Portrait de Dora* (1976) and *La Prise de l'Ecole de Madhubaï* (1983). Her historical epics *L'Histoire...de Norodom Sihanouk* (1985), about modern Cambodia, and *L'Indiade* (1987), about the partition of India, were produced by Ariane MNOUCHKINE's Théâtre du Soleil.

Clairon, Mlle (Claire-Josèphe-Hippolyte Léris de la Tude; 1723–1803) French actress, who became a leading member of the Comédie-Française. Earlier in her career she performed in minor parts at the Comédie-Italienne, attracting the praise of Garrick before appearing in such major tragic roles as Racine's *Phèdre* (1743). Under the guidance of Marmontel and Diderot she successfully tempered her declamatory style and encouraged the introduction of more historically-accurate costume. In 1765, however, she was imprisoned over a dispute involving another actor; upon her release she found shelter with Voltaire, in whose plays she had acted, and confined her activities to writing her *Mémoires* (1779) and to private theatricals, dying in poverty after the Revolution.

Clandestine Marriage, The A comedy by George COLMAN the Elder and David GARRICK. First performance: 1766. Fanny Sterling and Lovewell have secretly married, but she has difficulty fending off more eligible suitors, including Lord Ogleby. The play was enormously popular but led to a dispute between the two authors after Garrick refused to appear in it.

Clark, John Pepper (1935–) Nigerian poet and playwright, who is the author of a number of plays based on African myth. A trilogy, consisting of *Song of a Goat* (1962), *The Masquerade* (1964), and *The Raft* (1964), evoked Greek tragedy and established his reputation; later works include *Ozidi* (1966) and *The Bikoroa Plays* (1985).

Clarke, Austin (1896–1974) Irish poet, playwright, and novelist, born in Dublin. Although his reputation rests primarily on his poetry, in his youth he was inspired by W B Yeats and the work of the Abbey Theatre. This is reflected in his own verse plays, the first of which was *The Son of Learning* (1927), and in his work with the Dublin Verse-Speaking Society and the Lyric Players.

Claudel, Paul (1868–1955) French poet, playwright, and diplomat. Claudel's conversion to Catholicism in 1886 had a profound effect on his literary work: his plays present the conflict of good and evil, the quest for salvation, and other Christian themes. Despite recognition in Germany and elsewhere in the 1920s, it was not until 1943, with Jean-Louis Barrault's production of *Le Soulier de satin*, that Claudel's plays began to receive attention in France.

Principal works:

Tête d'or: 1919 (published 1890).
La Ville: 1955 (published 1893); translated as *The City*.
Partage de midi: 1948 (published 1906); translated as *Break of Noon*.
L'Annonce faite à Marie: 1912; translated as THE TIDINGS BROUGHT TO MARY.
L'Échange: 1914; translated as *The Exchange*.
L'Ôtage: 1914; translated as *The Hostage*.
Le Pain dur: 1949 (published 1918).
Le Soulier de satin: 1943 (published 1929); translated as THE SATIN SLIPPER.

Claus, Hugo (1929–) Belgian (Flemish) poet, novelist, and playwright, who has dominated Belgian theatre since World War II. Influenced by Artaud while in Paris, he won acclaim for such plays as *A Bride in the Morning* (1953), *Sugar* (1958), *Friday* (1969), and *Leopold II* (1970), which treat themes ranging from family relationships to colonialism. Later works for the stage include *Orestes* (1976), which was derived from Euripides. In more recent decades he has concentrated on prose fiction.

Clements, Sir John (Selby) (1910–88) British actor-manager, who became well-known for his revivals of classic plays. He founded his own repertory company at the Intimate Theatre in north London in 1935 and subsequently directed 42 plays, playing leads in 36 of them. In a revival of *Private Lives* in 1944 he played opposite **Kay Hammond** (Dorothy Katharine Standing; 1909–80), whom he married and with whom he enjoyed a long stage partnership. As actor-manager his triumphs included seasons at the St James's and Saville theatres and a record-breaking run of *The Beaux' Stratagem* at the Phoenix Theatre (1949). In 1964 he succeeded Olivier as director of the Chichester Festival Theatre, stepping down in 1973; he virtually retired after his wife's death.

Cleveland Play House A theatre in Cleveland, Ohio, which was founded in 1915 and became the home of the first resident professional theatre company in the US. It has one small and two large auditoriums and has staged many US and world premieres, including Paul Zindel's *The Effect of Gamma Rays on Man-in-the-Moon Marigolds* (1969). It collaborates with Case Western Reserve University on a three-year training programme.

Clifton, Harry (1832–72) British music hall singer, who sang such sentimental moralistic songs as 'Paddle Your Own Canoe' and 'Pretty Polly Perkins of Paddington Green'.

Clive, Kitty (Catherine Raftor; 1711–85) British actress, who was engaged by Colley Cibber to sing at Drury Lane. Her merit as an actress was discovered when she played Nell in the farce *The Devil to Pay*, by Coffey. Throughout her career, spent mostly at Drury Lane, she hankered to play tragedy, although her real strength lay in high comedy and farce. In consequence, she and Garrick quarrelled constantly although they admired each other's work. She retired in 1769 to a house at Twickenham given to her by Horace Walpole.

cloak-and-sword play *See comedia.*

Close Studio Theatre *See* Glasgow Citizens' Theatre.

closet drama A play written for reading as opposed to actual performance. Works of this type include the plays of Seneca and much Victorian poetic drama.

cloth A length of canvas or other material suspended from the flies and used for scenic purposes. It was formerly called a **drop** in Britain and is still referred to by that name in the US. When coloured blue to represent the sky it is called a **sky cloth**.

clouding A border, sometimes movable, painted to resemble a cloudy sky. Such borders were in common use in masques.

Clouds, The A comedy by ARISTOPHANES. First performance: Athens, 423 BC. The play, in which Socrates and the Sophists became the butt of the author's satire, seeks to ridicule contemporary education and morality.

clown A comic character of both the theatre and the circus, distinguished by his outlandish appearance and boisterous comedy. The modern clown is descended from the clowns of Shakespeare and his contemporaries, which were derived in turn from the medieval Fool or Jester. The attributes of such early clowns combined with features from the characters of the *commedia dell'arte* until the familiar clown of the pantomime and modern circus had evolved. Joseph GRIMALDI is universally recognized as one of the greatest exponents of the role.

Clunes, Alec (Sheriff de Moro) (1912–70) British actor, director, and manager, who ran the Arts Theatre in London from 1942 to 1950, presenting acclaimed productions of such plays as *Awake and Sing!* by Clifford Odets and *The Lady's Not For Burning* by Christopher Fry. He also appeared many times at Stratford and elsewhere in plays by Shakespeare, Shaw, and others.

Clurman, Harold Edgar (1901–80) US director, manager, author, and theatre critic. After studying under Boleslavsky he appeared in 1924 at the Greenwich Village Playhouse. In 1925 he joined the Theatre Guild; subsequently, in 1931, he founded the Group Theatre with Lee Strasberg and Cheryl Crawford. There he produced plays by Odets before the group broke up in 1940, after which he went on to direct works by such writers as Inge, Anouilh, O'Neill, Arthur Miller, Lillian Hellman, Giraudoux, and Chekhov.

Coal Hole *See* song-and-supper rooms.

Coates, Robert (1772–1848) British amateur actor, born in Antigua, who hired theatres at Bath, Brighton, and Richmond to promote himself as Romeo. Dubbed 'Romeo' Coates, he ignored public ridicule and performed at the Haymarket to universal scorn, after which he retired into obscurity.

Cobb, Lee J (Leo Jacoby; 1911–76) US actor, who began his career at Pasadena Playhouse in 1929, made his New York debut in *Crime and Punishment* (1935), and later joined the Group Theatre. His roles included Mr Carp in Clifford Odets's *Golden Boy* (1937) and Lammanawitz in Irwin Shaw's *The Gentle People* (1933). His most famous part was Willy Loman in Arthur Miller's *Death of a Salesman* (1949).

Coborn, Charles (Colin Whitton McCallum; 1852–1945) British music hall performer, who introduced Albert Chevalier to the halls. Of his own songs the most popular were 'Two Lovely Black Eyes' and 'The Man Who Broke the Bank at Monte Carlo'.

Coburg Theatre *See* Old Vic Theatre.

Coburn, Charles (1877–1961) US actor-manager, who – with his wife Ivah Wills (1882–1937) – founded the Coburn Shakespearean Players. Although he also played such well-established roles as Hamlet, Othello, and Shylock, his greatest success was as Old Bill in Bruce Bairnsfather and Arthur Eliot's *The Better 'Ole* (1918). After his wife died he embarked on a long film career, but returned to the stage as Falstaff in *The Merry Wives of Windsor* (1946) and won acclaim as Grandpa Vandenhoff in Kaufman and Hart's *You Can't Take It with You*.

Coburn Theatre *See* Daly's 63rd Street Theatre.

Cochran, Sir Charles Blake (1872–1951) British impresario, noted for his production of revues, comedies, and musicals. After experience as an actor and agent, he produced Ibsen's *John Gabriel Borkman* in New York in 1897. Subsequent productions included Reinhardt's *The Miracle* (1911), celebrated series of revues at the Ambassadors and then the London Pavilion (featuring a chorus of 'Young Ladies'), and several plays by Noël Coward. He also imported to Britain plays by O'Casey, O'Neill, and many others and arranged Sacha Guitry's first appearance in London (1920). After World War II he scored his greatest commercial success with the musical comedy *Bless the Bride* (1947).

Cockpit A theatre in Drury Lane, London, originally opened as a venue for cock-fighting in 1609. Adapted by Christopher Beeston in 1616, it was destroyed in a riot in 1617 and rebuilt as the Phoenix, which housed a number of companies in succession. Floridor's company opened there in 1635 and Beeston's Boys were installed in 1637. Davenant then took over, staging illegal performances after the closure of the theatres in 1642; in 1660 the theatre was reopened by John Rhodes, who was himself succeeded by George Jolly. The theatre was closed in 1665 after audiences defected to Drury Lane.

Another theatre of the same name was opened in Gateforth Street, London, in 1970 for use by schools and youth theatre groups.

Cockpit-in-Court A theatre in Whitehall, London, which was converted from a cockpit around 1604. Performances were given there before the Court and subsequently the public by the King's Men and other companies intermittently until 1664.

Cocktail Party, The A poetic drama by T S ELIOT. First performance: Edinburgh Festival, 1949. Based in part on *Alcestis* by Euripides, the play revolves around the god-like psychiatrist Sir Henry Harcourt-Reilly, who exposes the illusions of the four main characters.

Cocoanut Grove *See* Century Theatre.

Cocteau, Jean (1889–1963) French poet, novelist, playwright, film director, and critic. In response to a challenge from Diaghilev at the Ballets Russes, he began writing ballets and plays in his early twenties. His dramatic works range from classical tragedy to romantic melodrama. After World War II, Cocteau devoted himself to the cinema and it is in this role that he is usually remembered.

Principal dramatic works:
  Antigone: 1922.
  Orphée: 1926; translated as *Orpheus*.
  La Voix humaine: 1930; translated as *The Human Voice*.
  La Machine infernale: 1934; translated as *The Infernal Machine*.
  Les Chevaliers de la Table Ronde: 1937.
  Les Monstres sacrés: 1940; translated as *The Holy Terrors*.
  La Machine à écrire: 1941.
  L'Aigle à deux têtes: 1946; translated as *The Eagle Has Two Heads*.

Cody, William Frederick (1846–1917) US showman, known as **Buffalo Bill**, who was a rider for the Pony Express and a scout in the US Civil War. In 1872 he began appearing in plays written for him and, in 1883, went on to create his own Wild West Show featuring sharpshooter **Annie Oakley** (1860–1926). The pair became famous worldwide and were depicted in Irving Berlin's *Annie Get Your Gun* (1946).

Coffey, Charles (d. 1745) British playwright, noted for his ballad operas. Such pieces as *The Beggar's Wedding* (1729) and *The Devil to Pay* (1731), adapted from a play by Thomas Jevon, greatly influenced the development of the *Singspiele* form of ballad opera in Germany.

Coghill, Neville (1899–1980) British theatre scholar, who founded the Friends of the OUDS group in Oxford in 1940. The organization presented much-admired productions of plays by such authors as Ibsen, often touring widely; its last production was in 1946. Previously, in 1936, Coghill had founded the Oxford University Experimental Theatre Club to present new and little-performed works by both British and foreign writers with casts and crews consisting solely of undergraduates.

Coghlan, Rose (1850–1932) US actress, born in Britain, who spent most of her career on the New York stage. She was highly acclaimed at Wallack's Theatre and elsewhere in such roles as Lady Teazle in Sheridan's *The School for Scandal* and in a variety of modern parts as well as in Shakespeare. Other successes included her starring appearance in the premiere of Wilde's *A Woman of No Importance* (1893).

Cohan, George M(ichael) (1878–1942) US actor, playwright, composer, and manager, who first appeared on stage with his family as the Four Cohans. He wrote for the vaudeville stage and made his New York debut in his own play, *The Governor's Son*, in 1901. After playing in *Little Johnny Jones* (1904) and *George Washington, Jr* (1906), which gave new energy to the developing US musical, he opened (1911) the GEORGE M COHAN THEATRE, where he continued to appear in his own plays. Although he personally was a considerate employer, he opposed the new Actors' Equity union in a famous 1919 strike, leading to a decade of strained relations with the theatrical community. By the 1930s he had success in works by other authors, including O'Neill's *Ah, Wilderness!* (1933).

Cohan and Harris Theatre *See* Harris Theatre.

Cohen, Gustave (1879–1958) French theatre historian, who devoted his career to the study and revival of ancient liturgical drama. His *Histoire de la mise en scène dans le théâtre religieux français du moyen age* (1906) was an authoritative account of the medieval tradition of religious drama. Cohen also formed his own amateur group at the Sorbonne – Les Théophiliens – to present various examples of the genre, including Adam de la Halle's *Jeu de Robin et de Marion* and other works.

Coleridge, Samuel Taylor (1772–1834) British poet and critic, whose blank verse tragedy *Remorse* was successfully produced at Drury Lane in 1813. He wrote two other plays, neither of which was acted, *The Fall of Robespierre* (1794) and *Zapolya* (1817), and translated Schiller's *Wallenstein*. He also lectured brilliantly on Shakespeare.

Coliseum *See* London Coliseum.

Collé, Charles (1709–83) French playwright and songwriter. He wrote *parades* (sketches) for fairground theatres and several comedies. *La Partie de chasse de Henri IV* (1774) was banned by Louis XV for depicting the king in informal conversation with his subjects, which was regarded as disrespectful; it was later performed under Louis XVI.

collective creation The development of a new production through the collaboration of a whole company, who work on the project from beginning to end. Drawing heavily upon such techniques as improvisation, the process became popular in alternative theatre during the 1960s, although it is thought that the much earlier *commedia dell'arte* troupes and Elizabethan companies may have operated in a similar way. Notable exponents of the system in modern times have included the Living Theatre, the Open Theatre, the San Francisco Mime Troupe, and the Performance Group in the US and the People Show, Welfare State International, and the Pip Simmons Theatre Group in Britain.

Collier, Constance (1878–1955) British actress, who began her career on stage as a child before becoming a Gaiety Girl. Subsequently she played leading roles with Tree's company from 1901 to 1908 – notably in Shakespeare – and appeared in the US. She played Gertrude to John Barrymore's Hamlet in 1925 and, with Ivor Novello, wrote the play *The Rat*, which ran for a year. Other successful roles included Nancy in *Oliver Twist*, and Anastasia in *The Matriarch* by G B Stern.

Collier, Jeremy (1650–1726) British pamphleteer, best known for his *Short View of the Immorality of the English Stage* (1698), in which he castigated the plays of Dryden, Congreve, Vanbrugh, and others, and protested against the ridiculing of clergymen on the stage. The pamphlet provoked a number of retaliatory essays but also found wide public support, hastening the end of the licentious Restoration drama.

Collier, John Payne (1789–1883) British literary critic, who falsified documents from various sources and published an edition of Shakespeare's plays based on his forgeries. In 1852 he claimed to have bought a copy of the second Folio extensively annotated in a 17th-century hand. His forgeries were exposed some years later.

Collin d'Harleville, Jean-François *See* Harleville, Jean-François Collin d'.

Collins, Lottie (1866–1910) British music hall performer. She first appeared as a skipping-rope dancer, then worked with her two sisters and became a solo act in 1881. In 1891 she became an overnight success with the song 'Ta-Ra-Ra-Boom-De-Ay'.

Collins, Sam (1827–65) British music hall performer and manager, formerly a chimney-sweep. Although born in London, he usually appeared as a genial Irishman. He was one of the first stars of the Canterbury Music Hall; in 1863 he opened the famous COLLINS'S MUSIC HALL in Islington.

Collins, Wilkie (1824–89) English novelist and playwright, author of dramatizations of both of his famous detective novels, *The Woman in White* and *The Moonstone*, which were produced at the Olympic Theatre in 1871 and 1877 respectively. He also collaborated with Charles Dickens on various plays, notably *No Thoroughfare*, which was staged at the Adelphi Theatre in 1867.

Collins's Music Hall A theatre on Islington Green, London, opened in 1851 as part of the Lansdowne Arms public house. A purpose-built theatre was erected there in 1863, seating 600, by Sam COLLINS and became extremely popular as a music hall. Enlarged in 1897, it later staged repertory before declining as a venue for striptease and comedy. It was demolished after a fire in 1958.

Colman, George (1732–94) British playwright and theatre manager, usually called the Elder to distinguish him from his son. He was encouraged to write for the theatre by Garrick, who produced his first play, *Polly Honeycombe*, at Drury Lane in 1760. After the success of *The Jealous Wife* in 1761, he collaborated with Garrick in writing THE CLANDESTINE MARRIAGE and took over Covent Garden; seven years later he succeeded Foote at the Haymarket. In all, he wrote or adapted some 30 plays, as well as editing the works of Beaumont and Fletcher, and executing translations of Terence and Horace.

His son, **George Colman** (1762–1836), was known as the Younger and made his name as a playwright with *Inkle and Yarico* (1787), eventually succeeding his father as manager of the Haymarket. His many plays included, at the Haymarket, *The Bat-*

tle of Hexham (1789), *Sylvester Daggerwood* (1795), and *The Heir-at-Law* (1797); at Drury Lane, the tragedy *The Iron Chest* (1796); and, at Covent Garden, *John Bull; or, the Englishman's Fireside* (1803). Despite his reputation for recklessness, he was appointed Examiner of Plays in 1824, in which capacity he proved unexpectedly censorious.

Colon, Jenny (1808–42) French actress, who began at the Opéra-Comique and later appeared elsewhere in Paris and in Britain. She was highly popular for her lively, good-humoured performances until her career was ended by her early death.

Colonial Theatre *See* Hampden, Walter.

Colosseum A theatre in Regent's Park, London, opened in the 1830s. Plays were staged there under Braham and Frederick Yates until about 1840.

Colosseum Theatre *See* Herald Square Theatre.

colour wheel A metal disc fitted with small circles of coloured gel, which when rotated in front of a spotlight produces a succession of differently coloured beams.

Colum, Padraic (1881–1972) Irish playwright, poet, and novelist. His most important contribution to drama belongs to the early part of his career when he became a member of the Irish National Dramatic Society, a signatory of the original Abbey Theatre charter, and the author of three of the company's earliest plays. *Broken Soil* (1903) and *The Land* (1905) explore the preoccupation of small farmers with the land they work; *Thomas Muskerry* (1910) examines small-town society. After 1914 he lived mostly in the US, where he worked on a series of *Nō* plays.

Columbine One of the central figures of the harlequinade. The daughter of Pantalone and the lover of Harlequin, she originally began as one of the *zanni* of the *commedia dell'arte*, a servant girl named Columbina.

Columbus Circle Theatre *See* Majestic Theatre.

Comden and Green The performing and writing team of Betty Comden (1919–) and Adolph Green (1915–), who after a start in nightclubs and revues enjoyed a long series of musical successes as lyricists and bookwriters, often with plots set in New York City. Their hits include *On the Town* (1944), *Wonderful Town* (1953), *Bells Are Ringing* (1956), *Do Re Mi* (1960), *Applause* (1971), *On the Twentieth Century* (1978), and *Will Rogers Follies* (1991).

comedia A general term for Spanish plays of the 17th century, usually subdivided into the MACHINE PLAY and the COMEDY OF INTRIGUE. The latter category included the popular *comedia de capa y espada* (or **cloak-and-sword play**), which – written by such writers as Torres Naharro, Lope de Vega, and Tirso de Molina – dealt with the various romantic adventures of young courtiers and exercised a strong influence upon playwrights of the 19th century.

comedia a fantasía *See* Torres Naharro, Bartolomé de.

comedia a noticia *See* Torres Naharro, Bartolomé de.

Comedians A play by Trevor GRIFFITHS. First performance: Nottingham Playhouse, 1975. The play follows a group of budding stand-up comedians who have to put their newly learnt craft to the test at a local bingo hall. In the process Griffiths presents a disturbing and theatrically riveting debate about the relationship between comedy, prejudice, and social change.

comédie-ballet A form of musical play popular at the court of Louis XIV during the 17th century. Combining elements of dance, music, and dialogue and involving the participation of the courtiers themselves, the *comédie-ballet* was transformed by MOLIÈRE, who placed the emphasis upon the dialogue in such pieces as *Le Bourgeois gentilhomme* (1671). Ultimately the genre gave way to opera and operetta.

Comédie-Canadienne, Théâtre de la *See* Gélinas, Gratien.

Comédie des Champs-Élysées A theatre in the Avenue Montaigne, Paris, opened in 1912. Productions there by Gémier during the 1920s made the theatre a focus of the avant-garde movement; subsequent directors included the Pitoëffs, Jouvet, and Giraudoux. Anouilh took the theatre over in the 1950s, staging *boulevard* plays as well as his own works.

Comédie-Française The French national theatre, also called the **Théâtre-Français** and **La Maison de Molière**, which was formed in 1680 by the combination of the companies from the Théâtre du Marais (with which Molière's troupe had already merged) and the Théâtre de l'Hôtel de BOURGOGNE. After appearing at various venues with a virtual monopoly of the theatre in Paris, the company split during the Revolution, the more reactionary actors remaining where they were under Molé (as the **Théâtre de la Nation**) and the others being installed by Talma (as the **Théâtre de la République**) in what was to become the permanent home of the Comédie-Française, now in the Place de Théâtre-Française in the Rue de Richelieu. In 1803 the two halves reunited and in 1812 Napoleon set down the rules by which the company would be run. These established the holding of shares in the company, following a probationary period, by the actors themselves (as *pensionnaires* or the more senior *sociétaires*) and the granting of pensions to long-serving members. The Comédie-Française underwent some reorganization in 1945 and 1959; actors with the company in the 20th century included Sarah Bernhardt and Jean-Louis Barrault.

Comédie-Italienne The name by which the companies presenting the Italian *commedia dell'arte* in France were known after 1680, in order to distinguish them from the indigenous COMÉDIE-FRANÇAISE. Italian companies first appeared in France in the 16th century and gradually absorbed many native French elements; important venues in Paris associated with the Comédie-Italienne included the Salle du Petit-Bourbon and the Palais-Royal, both of which were shared with Molière until 1680, when the Comédie-Italienne moved to the Hôtel de Bourgogne. In 1697, however, the Comédie-Italienne companies were banished from France, allegedly for offending Madame de Maintenon; after their return in 1716 they became increasingly distant from their Italian origins and gradually turned to comic opera; the remaining group (known as the **Théâtre Favart**) amalgamated with a rival troupe (the **Théâtre Feydeau**) to form the new **Opéra-Comique** in 1801. Leading figures of the Comédie-Italienne included Fiorillo, Biancolelli, Costantini, Riccoboni, and Bertinazzi; writers linked to the tradition included Dufresny, Regnard, Palaprat, and Marivaux.

comédie larmoyante A form of sentimental comedy that became popular in France during the 18th century. Leading practitioners of plays of the genre, which usually carried a strong moral message, included La Chaussée; the style is generally considered as prefiguring the plays of the more realistic DRAME.

comédie rosse *See* Ancey, Georges.

comedy A form of drama distinguished by its humorous content and happy ending. Taking its name from the Greek words for 'revel-song', comedy is thought to have developed from fertility rituals and other rustic festivities. The oldest surviving comedies are the bawdy satires of Aristophanes. With his successors, most notably Menander, he established the tradition that comedy should be written in simple language and deal mainly with the lower classes and with affairs of the day. During the Roman era comedy typically revolved around the obstacles faced by young lovers and was frequently boisterous and coarse in nature. These traditions were eventually revived in the *commedia dell'arte*, following the disappearance of comedy as a form in itself during the Middle Ages. Subsequently comedy was taken to new heights by Shakespeare, Jonson, Molière, and others, who drew their characters from all levels of society and used sophisticated language capable of conveying the deepest truths about human nature.

Subdivisions of the form include the COMÉDIE LARMOYANTE, the COMEDY OF HUMOURS, the COMEDY OF INTRIGUE, the COMEDY OF MANNERS, the COMEDY OF MORALS, and SENTIMENTAL COMEDY. Following the apotheosis of sophisticated wit in the comedies of Oscar Wilde and Noël Coward, the 20th century saw a return to the earlier bawdy and more physical tradition in the revival of FARCE and the frequent combination of comedy and tragedy. *See also* satire.

Comedy of Errors, The An early comedy by William SHAKESPEARE, written c. 1592–93. First performance: London, 1594. Revolving around a series of mistaken identities involving two sets of identical twins, the plot is derived from *Menaechmi* by Plautus, which was itself based on an earlier Greek model. The addition of a second set of twins demonstrates Shakespeare's early mastery of structure and complex plotting.

comedy of humours A form of comedy in which the focus is placed upon a particular trait of personality of one or more of the characters. The genre – which was named after the medieval concept of the body holding four liquids (or humours), the balance of which decided a person's character – found full expression in the plays of such English writers as FLETCHER and JONSON.

comedy of intrigue A form of comedy in which the action revolves around various complicated and highly farcical situations. Ultimately deriving from a Roman tradition, the comedy of intrigue was later developed in Spain and subsequently taken up by writers of the 17th and 18th centuries, examples being written by Shakespeare (notably *The Comedy of Errors*) and Molière among others.

comedy of manners A form of witty and often daring comedy in which various social shortcomings are satirized by being made to appear ridiculous. Descended from the NEW COMEDY of Menander, the comedy of manners was revived by Molière in such plays as *Les Précieuses ridicules* (1658) and *Le Médecin malgré lui* (1666) and later developed by such writers as Jonson, Etherege, Vanbrugh, Wycherley, Congreve, Farquhar, Goldsmith, and Sheridan. In more recent times the tradition, distinguished by the elegance and sophistication of its humour, has been continued by Wilde, Coward, and other critics of the affectations of society. *See also* Restoration drama.

comedy of morals A form of comedy in which the playwright condemns socially unacceptable behaviour. The supreme example of the genre, which was an extreme version of the comedy of manners, is Molière's *Tartuffe*.

Comedy Theatre A theatre in London's West End that has a long-standing reputation for both drama and comedy. Intended originally as the home of comic opera, it was built in Panton Street, off the Haymarket, and opened in 1881 with Audran's *The Mascotte*. Violet Melnotte, on becoming lessee in 1885, introduced dramas to the theatre. In 1887 Beerbohm Tree produced *The Red Lamp* by W Outram Tristam, while under Charles Hawtrey's management (1888–92 and 1896–99) straight comedy was alternated with farce. The first real success of the early 1900s, Lonsdale and Messager's *Monsieur Beaucaire*, ran for over 400 performances. Marie Tempest appeared in several plays in 1907–09, Gerald Du Maurier in 1910, and Marie Löhr the following year. John Hartley Manners's *Peg o' My Heart* (1914) ran for 710 performances, and in later years, under various managements, a mixed policy of plays, revues, and musicals was adopted. From 1956 to 1959 the Comedy became the headquarters of the New Watergate Theatre Club, which presented such plays as Tennessee Williams's *Cat on a Hot Tin Roof* (1958) and Peter Shaffer's *Five Finger Exercise* (1959), both refused a licence by the Lord Chamberlain. Later successes included the Alan Ayckbourn comedy *Time and Time Again* (1972), Nell Dunn's *Steaming* (1981), and Hugh Whitemore's *A Letter of Resignation* (1997). It also hosts frequent transfers from other theatres.

Another **Comedy Theatre** was built by the Shuberts on West 41st Street, New York, and opened in 1909 with Zangwill's *The Melting Pot*. In 1937 it was renamed the **Mercury Theatre** and housed numerous productions directed by Orson Welles, including Shaw's *Heartbreak House* and Buchner's *Danton's Death*. In 1938 it was also the focus of national alarm when Welles's company broadcast H G Wells's *The War of the Worlds* from it, convincing many that an actual Martian invasion was taking place. The building was demolished in 1942.

The **Comedy Theatre** in St Petersburg was founded in 1929. It is famous chiefly for the productions of Nikolai AKIMOV, staged from the 1920s onwards. He became art director of the theatre in 1936.

Comella y Villamitjana, Luciano Francisco (1751–1812) Spanish playwright, who was the author of more than 100 plays. He was highly popular in his own day but was ridiculed in the plays of Fernández de Moratín.

command performance A performance of a play or other entertainment given in response to a request by a member of a royal family or national leader. In Britain such performances are held annually and usually have a charitable purpose.

commedia dell'arte A comic theatrical tradition that evolved in Italy during the 16th century and later exerted a profound influence upon drama throughout Europe. Improvised about basic three-act skeleton plots, the *commedia dell'arte* (also known as the *commedia a soggetto*) featured a variety of stock characters, including PANTALONE, Il CAPITANO, Il DOTTORE, and the ZANNI, all of whom had their own distinctive costumes and masks.

The genre was derived ultimately from Greek theatre, via the Roman *atellana*, and incorporated numerous theatrical disciplines, including acrobatics, mime, and comic slapstick routines. Leading Italian companies of the *commedia dell'arte*, which performed at various courts or travelled with their own portable stage, included the GELOSI, the DESIOSI, the CONFIDENTI, the UNITI, the ACCESI, and the FEDELI. These companies subsequently toured Europe, inspiring the foundation of *commedia dell'arte* troupes elsewhere, notably in France where the COMÉDIE-ITALIENNE flourished. Fiorillo played an important role in bringing the *commedia dell'arte* to London in the late 17th century, where elements of the Italian tradition were readily absorbed into the English theatre, most lastingly in the HARLEQUINADE and, subsequently, the PANTOMIME. By the end of the 18th century the tradition had largely fallen from fashion, although the 20th century has seen a widespread revival of interest in the form. *See also burla; lazzo.*

commedia erudita An Italian theatrical form of the 16th century, a more scholarly counterpart to the *commedia dell'arte*. Unlike the *commedia dell'arte*, the *commedia erudita* was based upon written scripts (derived largely from the comedies of Plautus and Terence) and was intended for performance before educated audiences. Among those who wrote for the *commedia erudita* were Aretino, Ariosto, Della Porta, and Machiavelli.

Commonwealth Theatre *See* Anthony Street Theatre.

Community Arts Service (CAS) A theatre company in Auckland, New Zealand, which toured productions throughout North Island from 1947 to 1962. Connected to Auckland University, it presented numerous classics as well as the first production in New Zealand of Beckett's *Waiting for Godot* (1958).

community theatre Theatre that has as its primary aim the performance of plays for and within specific communities – as opposed to the theatre-for-all approach of most commercial and repertory theatres. Whereas in the US such theatre is synonymous with amateur theatre, in Britain there are numerous professional companies set up with the express purpose of reaching communities that rarely if ever go to the theatre, either because of the distance involved or because there is no tradition of doing so. The plays performed by such groups usually focus upon issues of immediate concern (sometimes adopting a high political profile) or upon the community's own history (often researched with the help of local people) and are toured to community centres, church and school halls, and labour clubs. Many companies combine community work with THEATRE IN EDUCATION; others target their work at specific groups, typically those that are in some way underprivileged.

Compagnia Dei Giovani An Italian theatre company, founded in 1954 by Romolo Valli and Giorgio de Lullo. Subsequently renamed I Giovani del Teatro Elisio, it toured internationally with plays by Fabbri and Pirandello.

Compagnia Reale Sarda An Italian theatre company, founded in Turin in 1821. It established its reputation with old-fashioned dramas by Goldoni and his contemporaries but later diversified with productions of well-made plays; actors with the company included Salvini and Ristori. It was disbanded in 1855 when its official grant was withdrawn.

Compagnie des Quinze A French theatre company, founded by actors from Copeau's company in 1929. Led by Michel Saint-Denis, it excelled with productions of the plays of André Obey before breaking up in 1934.

Company A musical by Stephen SONDHEIM. First performance, New York: 1970. The first of Sondheim's musicals to show his mature qualities, it follows Bobby, a New York bachelor, both attracted to and wary of emotional commitment, as he observes his married friends.

compartment batten *See* batten.

Complicite An international touring company based in North London; it was founded (as **Théâtre de Complicité**) in 1983 by **Simon McBurney**, who remains its artistic director. Since its inception the company has staged nearly 30 productions in over 40 countries, winning numerous international awards. It has become celebrated for its intensely physical style of acting and its use of austere but imaginative staging techniques. Notable productions have included a revival of Dürrenmatt's *The Visit* (1990), starring Kathryn Hunter, *The Three Lives of Lucie Cabrol* (1994), one of several collaborations with the writer John Berger, a new version of *The Caucasian Chalk Circle* (1997), which was seen at both the Royal National Theatre and the Berliner Ensemble, and *Light* (2000).

composite setting A stage setting, formerly called a **multiple setting** and first developed in medieval drama, in which three or more different locations are presented simultaneously upon the stage. In the US it is called a **simultaneous-scene setting**.

Compton, Henry (Charles Mackenzie; 1805–77) British actor, born in Huntingdon. After 11 years in the provinces, he reached Drury Lane in 1837, where he became a noted character actor and exponent of Shakespeare's clowns. He transferred to the Haymarket in 1853.

His daughter, **Katherine Mackenzie Compton** (1853–1928), became an actress and excelled in the comedies of her husband, Richard CARTON.

His son, **Edward Compton** (1854–1918), acted in the provinces and was the author of two plays. In 1881 he organized the Compton Comedy Company, which toured successfully for over 30 years.

He married Virginia Frances BATEMAN in 1882 and became the father of the actress **Fay Compton** (Virginia Lillian Emmeline Compton; 1894–1978), who established her reputation in the plays of J M Barrie and Somerset Maugham. Subsequently Fay was acclaimed in plays by Dodie Smith, Noël Coward, and Ibsen as well as in numerous Shakespearean roles, notably as Ophelia to the Hamlets of John Barrymore (1925) and John Gielgud (1939). Later performances included Lady Bracknell in *The Importance of Being Earnest* and appearances in pantomime.

concert party A summer show comprising songs, dances, and sketches, of the type popular at British seaside resorts in the early 20th century.

Concert Theatre *See* John Golden Theatre.

Condell, Henry (d. 1627) English actor, who was recorded as a member of the Chamberlain's Men in 1598. He remained with the company until his death, although he gave up acting in about 1616. He appeared in several of Jonson's plays and probably in supporting Shakespearean roles. He was a shareholder in the Globe and Blackfriars theatres and, with Heminge, edited the First Folio of Shakespeare's plays.

Confidenti An Italian *commedia dell'arte* company, founded in 1574. Led by Pellesini, the company toured Europe for many years until, under the patronage of Giovanni de' Medici, it returned to Italy led by Flamineo Scala. When it was disbanded in 1621 some of its members joined the Fedeli.

Confrérie de la Passion An amateur theatre company founded in Paris in 1402. Drawing its actors from the merchants and craftsmen of the city, the company became highly respected for its performances of mystery plays and in 1518 was given a monopoly of theatre in Paris. Subsequently, however, the Church took exception to the company's increasingly liberal attitudes and in 1548, as the company was moving into its new home at the building that later became the Théâtre de l'Hôtel de Bourgogne, it was prohibited from presenting religious works. In the years that followed the Confrérie de la Passion ceased to present its own productions and leased the theatre to other companies, retaining its restrictive control over all theatrical activity in Paris until 1595; the company was finally disbanded in 1676.

Congreve, William (1670–1729) English playwright, regarded as the foremost exponent of the English comedy of manners during the Restoration. He achieved sufficient success in 1692 with his comedy THE OLD BACHELOR at Drury Lane, with Betterton and Mrs Bracegirdle in the cast, to persuade the management to produce his satire *The Double Dealer* the following year. LOVE FOR LOVE, with which Betterton opened the new Lincoln's Inn Fields Theatre in 1695, confirmed his reputation and won him a share in the theatre. His tragedy *The Mourning Bride* was publicly acclaimed in 1697 but is now largely forgotten. Conversely, THE WAY OF THE WORLD, coldly received at that time, is now considered his most brilliant work. His comedies have been frequently revived in the last hundred years.

Principal works:
> *The Old Bachelor*: 1692.
> *The Double Dealer*: 1694.
> *Love for Love*: 1695.
> *The Mourning Bride*: 1697.
> *The Way of the World*: 1700.

Connection, The A play by Jack GELBER. First performance: Living Theatre, 1959. The plot concerns a group of drug addicts who are waiting for someone to arrive with a fresh supply of narcotics. It caused considerable controversy and virtually created the off-Broadway theatre.

Connelly, Marc(us) Cook (1890–1980) US playwright, who also directed and acted in a number of productions. He began his career as a theatrical journalist and collaborated as a writer with George Kaufman before winning a Pulitzer Prize in 1930 with his play *The Green Pastures*, which he also directed with a Black cast. His other plays include *The Farmer Takes a Wife* (1934), *Everywhere I Roam* (1938), and *The Flowers of Virtue* (1942).

Conquest, George Augustus (1837–1901) British actor, playwright, and theatre manager, son of the actor-manager **Benjamin Conquest** (Benjamin Oliver; 1805–72).

Educated in France, he translated and adapted several French plays, which were produced under his father's management, and wrote numerous successful pantomimes and melodramas. He managed the Grecian Theatre with his father, and, in 1881, took over the Surrey Theatre. His three sons also appeared regularly in pantomime.

Conservatoire National d'Art Dramatique A drama school in Paris, founded in 1786 and closely linked to the Comédie Française. Opened as the École de Déclamation, it has produced such leading performers as Talma, Mlle Rachel, Sarah Bernhardt, and Constant Coquelin. It underwent some reorganization in 1968.

Constant Wife, The A comedy by W Somerset MAUGHAM. First performance: New York, 1926. The play depicts a long-suffering wife's achievement of independence from her profligate husband and eventual triumphant elopement to Italy with her lover.

Constructivism *See* Meyerhold, Vsevolod Emilievich.

Contact Theatre Company A theatre company based in Manchester, founded in 1973 at Manchester University. It was established by Hugh Hunt and aims to bring drama into the surrounding community.

Contat, Louise (1760–1813) French actress, who excelled as a comic actress at the Comédie-Française, which she joined in 1776. A pupil of Préville, she was particularly admired in the plays of Beaumarchais and Marivaux.

Contemporary Theatre, A A theatre company founded 1965 in Seattle, Washington. It has two main stages and a cabaret, offering classics and modern works as well as a popular annual production of *A Christmas Carol*.

Conti, Italia (1874–1946) British actress, who – at the instigation of Charles Hawtrey – founded the Italia Conti School for dancers, singers, and actors. From 1929 to 1938 she herself appeared annually as Mrs Carey in *Where the Rainbow Ends* at the Holborn Empire. Pupils at her school included Gertrude Lawrence.

Contrast, The A comedy by Royall TYLER. First performance: John Street Theatre, New York, 1787. The first play by an American to be professionally produced in the US, it contrasts the Old World duplicity of Dimple, who abandons his fiancée in favour of a wealthy coquette, with the New World honesty of Dimple's brother.

contrasto A form of early Italian theatrical entertainment, related to the LAUDA. Dating from the 13th century, it usually revolved about a central dispute, usually with a religious or domestic theme.

Conway, William Augustus (1789–1828) British actor, born in Ireland, who made his London debut in 1813 at Covent Garden, where he played classic leads for two years. Upset by adverse criticism after appearances at the Haymarket, he then went to New York, opening as Hamlet. He subsequently appeared alongside Thomas Cooper and with Macready (1826–27). Suffering a mental breakdown, he finally drowned himself in Charleston harbour.

His son, **Frederick Bartlett Conway** (1819–74), became a leading figure on the New York stage in the 1860s, opening the first theatre in Brooklyn in 1863. Subsequently he opened the Brooklyn Theatre also and assembled an admired stock company there.

Cook, Barbara (1927–) US actress, whose purity of voice and radiant stage presence made her the reigning musical ingenue of the 1950s and 1960s. After making her New York debut in *Flahooley* (1951), major roles included Hilda in *Plain and Fancy* (1955), Cunegonde in *Candide* (1956) – in which she hit a strong E above high C eight times a week – Marian in *The Music Man* (1957), and Amalia in *She Loves Me* (1963). She retired from musical theatre in the 1970s but has continued to star in cabaret.

Cook, Peter (1937–95) British comedy actor and writer. He wrote the revues *Pieces of Eight* (1959) and *One Over the Eight* (1960) while still at Cambridge University and was co-author of the celebrated satirical revue *Beyond the Fringe*, in which he appeared at the Edinburgh Festival and elsewhere in 1960. He subsequently toured widely with Dudley MOORE in *Behind the Fridge* and appeared frequently on television.

Cooke, George Frederick (1756–1812) British actor, greatly admired by Edmund Kean. He arrived at Covent Garden in 1800 after many years in the provinces. He made his successful London debut as Richard III and went on to play Shylock and Iago with equal acclaim, despite his dependence upon alcohol. He was also one of the first British actors to tour the US; his alcoholism, however, gradually alienated his audience and probably contributed to his death later in the tour.

Cooke, Thomas Potter (1786–1864) British actor, popularly known as Tippy. He became known as an actor of engaging nautical characters but achieved particular fame as William in *Black-Ey'd Susan* at the Surrey Theatre in 1829.

Cooney, Ray(mond) (1932–) British playwright, director, producer, and actor. His numerous popular farces include *One for the Pot* (1961, with Tony Hilton), *Not Now Darling* (1967, with John Chapman), *Move Over Mrs Markham* (1969), *Run for Your Wife* (1981), and *Funny Money* (1996). He directed his own Theatre of Comedy company at the Shaftesbury Theatre from 1983 to 1989 and bought the Playhouse in 1992.

Cooper, Dame Gladys (1888–1971) British actress, who made her London debut in *The Belle of Mayfair* (1906) and subsequently established herself as an outstanding actress in both comedy and straight drama. She was much admired in plays by such authors as Maugham, Pinero, and Shaw, often appearing under her own joint-management with Frank Curzon at the Playhouse. In 1934 she made her New York debut in Keith Winter's *The Shining Hour* and from then on appeared regularly on both sides of the Atlantic. Later roles included performances in plays by Shakespeare, Bagnold, and Coward, as well as numerous film appearances.

Cooper, Thomas Abthorpe (1776–1849) US actor, born in Britain, who was one of the first British actors to transfer permanently to the US. Having won acclaim on the London stage in Shakespearean and other major roles, he went to the US in 1796 to appear at the Chestnut Street Theatre; later he joined the American Company and toured the eastern states in such roles as Macbeth.

Co-Optimists *See* pierrot troupes.

Copeau, Jacques (1879–1949) French actor, director, and critic, who was a prominent figure in the reaction against Realism in the early 20th century. Advocating attention to the play itself rather than to sets and costume, he took over the Théâtre du Vieux-Colombier in 1913, staging influential productions of classic plays by Molière, Shakespeare, and Claudel among others. The theatre itself echoed the Elizabethan stage with no proscenium arch or wings and little scenery, the emphasis being thrown instead upon lighting and the acting of the company (which included Charles Dullin and Louis Jouvet).

In 1924 Copeau founded a company of young actors – known as '*les Copiaus*' – in Burgundy, training them in his techniques (which included the extensive use of mime); many of these actors subsequently appeared in the innovative Compagnie des Quinze of Copeau's nephew and assistant Michel Saint-Denis. In 1936 Copeau was recognized as a major reformer of French stage practice when he was made a director of the Comédie-Française.

Copenhagen A play by Michael FRAYN. First performance: Royal National Theatre, London, 1998. The play explores the moral responsibilities of science by examining the wartime careers of the nuclear physicists Niels Bohr and Werner Heisenberg. Michael Blakemore's production transferred to the West End, where it is still running (2000), and also to Broadway, where it earned Tony Awards for Best Play and Best Director.

Coppin, George Selth (1819–1906) Australian theatre manager and actor, born in Britain, often called the 'father' of Australian theatre. He sailed to Australia in 1843 and in due course he formed his own company and built six theatres, to which he lured leading performers from Britain and the US.

copyright The legal entitlement of the owner of a dramatic work to claim a fee (known as a **royalty**) in exchange for his permission for its performance or publication. Although a form of theatrical copyright developed during the 19th century through the efforts of Planché, Bulwer-Lytton, and others, it remained a somewhat ambiguous legal concept; therefore it became customary for many playwrights – including G B Shaw – to stage special 'copyright performances' of their plays prior to publication in order to feel certain that their rights were legally protected. The Berne Conventions of 1886 and later years did much to bring the various copyright laws of different countries into line and to extend protection into the fields of film, radio, and television; other international agreements on the subject include the Universal Copyright Convention of 1952 and the harmonization of practices throughout the EU in the 1990s. Copyright in most countries is generally recognized as lasting for at least 50 years following the author's death (70 years in EU countries and 95 years in the US). Any infringement of copyright amounts to a civil offence and can give rise to actions for damages and injunctions. Prior to the development of modern copyright law, playwrights either sold their plays outright or relied upon proceeds from publication or special benefit performances (*see* author's night); more fortunate writers drew on other sources of income or survived on the generosity of their patrons.

Coquelin, Constant-Benoît (1841–1909) French actor, known as Coquelin *aîné*, who is usually remembered as the first actor to create Rostand's Cyrano de Bergerac (1897). He was, with his brother, **Ernest-Alexandre-Honoré Coquelin** (1848–1909) or Coquelin *cadet*, a leading member of the Comédie-Française and later toured with Sarah Bernhardt throughout Europe and the US, being particularly admired in the plays of Molière. Coquelin *cadet* died insane shortly after his brother's sudden death.

Coriolanus A tragedy by William SHAKESPEARE, written c. 1607–08 and therefore probably his last. First performance: date unknown. Although successful in battle, the aristocratic hero Coriolanus reveals his contempt for the common masses and is banished. In a fury, he joins his former enemies and beseiges Rome. Eventually, at the entreaties of his mother Volumnia and his wife Virgilia, he spares the city, leading to his death at the hands of his new Volscian allies. As Shakespeare's most overtly political play it has provoked much speculation about his own sympathies.

Corneille, Pierre (1606–84) French playwright, born in Rouen; one of the most important figures in the history of French drama. After studying with the Jesuits, Corneille followed his father and grandfather into the legal profession and held office in Rouen for some 20 years. He began writing for the theatre in the late 1620s; encouraged by the success of MÉLITE, he produced four more comedies and a tragicomedy (*Clitandre*) before turning to tragedy, the genre in which he made his greatest contribution to French literature. His classical tragedies (including LE CID and HORACE), in which the portrayal of the moral conflicts and emotional sufferings of the central characters takes precedence over the representation of action, heralded a new era in French drama.

He also produced *Psyché*, a *comédie-ballet*, written in collaboration with Molière and Philippe Quinault, while the tragedy *Andromède* pioneered the 17th-century tradition of the MACHINE PLAY. After 1650 Corneille's popularity began to decline and in the 1660s he was gradually eclipsed by Racine; the plays of his latter years enjoyed limited success but proved to be of no lasting merit.

He also encouraged his younger brother, **Thomas Corneille** (1625–1709), who produced some 40 plays – largely comedies in the Spanish style and romantic tragedies, such as *Timocrate* (1656) – before abandoning the theatre in favour of lexicography.

Principal works:

Mélite: 1629.
Clitandre: 1631.
La Veuve: 1631–32.
La Galerie du palais: 1632.
La Suivante: 1633.
La Place royale: 1633–34.
Médée: 1635.
L'Illusion comique: 1635–36.
Le Cid: 1636–37.
Horace: 1640.
Cinna: 1641.
Polyeucte: 1641–42.
La Mort de Pompée: 1642–43.
Le Menteur: 1643.
Rodogune, princesse de Parthes: 1645.
Héraclius: 1646–47.
Don Sanche d'Aragon: 1649.
Andromède: 1650.
Nicomède: 1651.
Oedipe: 1659.

La Toison d'or: 1660.
Sertorius: 1662.
Psyché: 1671.

Cornell, Katharine (1893–1974) US actress, who made her London debut with great success in Louisa Alcott's *Little Women* (1919) and her New York debut as Sydney in Clemence Dane's *A Bill of Divorcement* in 1921. She went on to become the leading actress of her day, playing such parts as Shaw's Candida (1924) and Elizabeth in Rudolf Besier's *The Barretts of Wimpole Street* (1934). She was usually directed by her husband, Guthrie McClintic; her later appearances included the Countess in Fry's *The Dark Is Light Enough* (1955) and Mrs Patrick Campbell in Jerome Kilty's *Dear Liar* (1960).

corner trap A small square trap positioned downstage, through which actors may make entrances.

Corn is Green, The A comedy by Emlyn WILLIAMS. First performance: London, 1938. The play revolves around Miss Moffat, an indomitable schoolteacher in the Welsh valleys; in the original production Williams himself played the miner Morgan Evans and Sybil Thorndike played Miss Moffat.

Cornish, William (fl. 1509–23) English Gentleman of the Chapel Royal, who organized the choirboys of the Chapel Royal into a boy company. The company entertained regularly at court, often in elaborate disguisings.

Cornish Rounds Ancient open-air theatres in Cornwall, once used for performances of mystery plays. In use until the 17th century, these were usually cut into a slope and were circular in shape; other features included a trench from which actors could make sudden entrances.

Coronet Theatre *See* Eugene O'Neill Theatre.

Corpus Christi play *See* mystery play.

Corrie, Joe (1894–1968) Scottish playwright and actor, who was the author of a number of celebrated one-act plays on Scottish themes. Such pieces as *The Shillin'-a-Week Man* were performed in music halls throughout Scotland and northern England in the late 1920s; longer plays included *In Time o'Strife* (1930) and *Master of Men* (1944).

Corsican Brothers, The A melodrama by Dion BOUCICAULT. First performance: 1852. An adaptation of an earlier French play, this tale of duelling and revenge was immensely successful in a production by Charles Kean and was subsequently revived many times.

Corsican trap *See* ghost glide.

Cort Theatre A theatre on West 48th Street, between 6th and 7th Avenues, New York, which opened in 1912 with Laurie Taylor's famous performance in John Hartley Manners's *Peg o' My Heart*. Early productions included Chekhov's *Uncle Vanya* (1930), Anouilh's *Antigone* (1946), and Goodrich and Hackett's *The Diary of Anne Frank* (1955). The theatre was used for television productions between 1969 and 1974, when it reopened with Doug Henning's musical *The Magic Show*, which ran for 1920 performances. Though its east-of-Broadway location is considered problematic, recent successes have included Zoë Caldwell in *Medea* (1982) and the Steppenwolf Theatre's production of *The Grapes of Wrath* (1990).

Cosmopolitan Theatre *See* Majestic Theatre.

Cossa, Pietro (1830–81) Italian playwright, author of a number of verse tragedies based on classical models. His more successful plays include *Nerone* (1872), a version of the life of Nero, and the antireligious *Cola di Rienzo* (1874) but all his works were marred by the poor quality of his poetry and by his interest in Realism, which did not combine well with the demands of classical tragedy. Other plays include *Pushkin* (1870) and *Messalina* (1876).

Costa, Francisco da (1533–91) Portuguese playwright, who wrote a number of poems and seven plays during his long imprisonment in Morocco, where he died. Some of his plays on biblical subjects were first performed by his fellow-prisoners.

Costantini, Angelo (c. 1655–1729) Italian actor of the *commedia dell'arte*, who appeared chiefly as Messetino with the Comédie-Italienne in Paris. In 1697, when the company was exiled, he moved to Brunswick where he was imprisoned for 20 years after becoming involved in a love triangle with the Duke there. He was also the author of a biography (1695) of Tiberio Fiorillo.

Coster, Samuel (1579–1665) Dutch physician and playwright, who was a friend of many of the leading playwrights in the Netherlands at that time. In 1617 he opened the first Dutch Academy in Amsterdam in order to promote study of the theatre and learning in general.

costume The clothing worn on stage by an actor or other performer. The Greeks and Romans developed specific costumes for tragedy and comedy and used simple devices to identify stock characters. The Renaissance period saw the fabulous costumes of the masques, as well as the more formalized outfits of the *commedia dell'arte*; otherwise most actors seem to have appeared in contemporary dress. There was a gradual movement towards more elaborate clothing in the early 18th century until Garrick and others led a return to more simple styles. The 19th century saw the first authentically costumed versions of Shakespeare and, with the advent of realism, a demand for historical accuracy. In the 20th century designs have ranged from the completely naturalistic to the highly symbolic; another development was the linking of costume with lighting and other aspects of theatrical design so that it was no longer considered in isolation. *See also* wardrobe.

cothurnus A thick-soled shoe worn by the tragic actor in the classical Greek and Roman theatre. Also known as a *buskin*, it was adopted in order to differentiate the principals from the chorus, who wore low shoes. *See also soccus*.

Cottesloe Theatre One of the three theatres comprising the ROYAL NATIONAL THEATRE in London, opened in 1977. Seating 400, it was named after the chairman of the South Bank Theatre Board and has been used for a wide variety of serious dramas, notably US works and PROMENADE productions. Successful plays there, which have featured many leading performers, have included the promenade productions *Lark Rise* and *The Mysteries* (1978), O'Neill's *The Iceman Cometh* (1980), Miller's *The*

View from the Bridge (1987), Stoppard's *The Invention of Love* (1997), and Frayn's *Copenhagen* (1998).

Couldock, Charles Walter (1815–98) US actor, born in Britain, who appeared regularly in the US and Canada from 1849. Closely associated with most of the leading players of his day, he was particularly successful in Kotzebue's *The Stranger* (1849), Tom Taylor's *Our American Cousin* (1858), and Steele Mackaye's *Hazel Kirke* (1880).

Council for the Encouragement of Music and the Arts *See* Arts Councils.

Counsell, John (1905–87) British actor, who established a repertory company at the Theatre Royal, Windsor, in 1938 and made the theatre there an important provincial venue. Although there is no company now resident at Windsor, the theatre continues to present both new works and revivals.

counterweight system An arrangement of lines and weights that enables the raising and lowering of heavy pieces of scenery. A theatre equipped with such a system is occasionally described as a counterweight house. *See also* hand-worked house.

Country Girl, The A play by Clifford ODETS. First performance: New York, 1950. The plot concerns a woman who blossoms, despite her alcoholic husband, when she becomes a singer. It was seen in Britain as *Winter Journey* in 1952. The play was filmed in 1954 with Bing Crosby and Grace Kelly.

Country Wife, The A comedy by Sir William WYCHERLEY. First performance: 1674. The play concerns the libertine Horner, who spreads a rumour that a disease has made him impotent, thus allowing foolish husbands to trust him with their wives. The chief of these is Mrs Pinchwife, the title character – young, innocent, eager, and married to a much older jealous man. The play was later successfully adapted by Garrick as *The Country Girl* (1766).

Courteline, Georges (Georges-Victor-Marcel Moineaux; 1858–1929) French playwright, short-story writer, and journalist, born in Tours. His comedies are lively farces satirizing military life, as in *Les Gaîtes de l'escadron* (1896), the legal profession, and a variety of other contemporary targets.

Courtenay, Sir Tom (1937–) British actor, who made his professional debut as Konstantin in *The Seagull* in Edinburgh in 1960 and then transferred to the Old Vic. Subsequently he was acclaimed in the title role of *Billy Liar* (1961), played Andrei in Frisch's *Andorra* (1964) with the National Theatre company, and appeared in major Shakespearean roles with the 69 Theatre Company, Manchester. Other successes have included Lord Fancourt Babberley in *Charley's Aunt* (1971), Norman in Ayckbourn's *The Norman Conquests* (1974), the title part of *The Dresser* by Ronald Harwood (1980), Molière's *The Hypochondriac* (1987) and *The Miser* (1991), the one-man show *Moscow Stations* (1993, 1994), and *Art* (1996). He has also appeared in films.

Court Fool A performer, also known as the **King's Jester**, who was retained by a royal court in the late medieval period to amuse members of the court with stories, music, and his wit. Dressed in a parti-coloured suit after the fashion of the FOOL of folk drama, from which tradition that of the Court Fool was quite distinct, he enjoyed special licence in satirizing the follies of noble society. It was from this tradition that Shakespeare's Fools were derived.

Courtneidge, Dame Cicely (1893–1980) British actress, who played Peaseblossom in *A Midsummer Night's Dream* as a child and later appeared in her actor-manager father's shows. In one of these she met her future husband, the actor **Jack Hulbert** (1892–1978), thus beginning a famous stage partnership in revues and musical comedies, from *By the Way* at the Apollo (1925) to *Under Your Hat* at the Palace (1938). In later years she appeared in straight comedy roles in such plays as Ronald Millar's *The Bride and the Bachelor* (1956) and Cooney and Chapman's *Move Over, Mrs Markham* (1971). Jack Hulbert's brother, **Claude Hulbert** (1900–64), also appeared in revue.

Court Street Theatre *See* Milwaukee Repertory Theatre.

Court Theatre *See* Royal Court Theatre.

Covent Garden (Royal Opera House) England's national opera house, home of the Royal Opera and the Royal Ballet. The present building, currently the subject of a controversial extension scheme, is the third theatre on the site. The first, known as the **Theatre Royal, Covent Garden**, was designed for the pantomimist John Rich and opened in 1732, in rivalry to the Theatre Royal, Drury Lane; David Garrick acted at both theatres and Peg Woffington made her debut at Covent Garden in 1740.

At first plays alternated with opera, George Frederick Handel composing several operas and oratorios specially for the theatre; the piano was played for the first time in public here in 1767. Subsequent milestones included the first performances of Oliver Goldsmith's *She Stoops to Conquer* (1773) and Sheridan's *The Rivals* (1775). John Kemble bought a share in the management in 1803 but in 1808 the theatre was destroyed by fire.

A new theatre, modelled on the Temple of Minerva at Athens, opened in 1809 but an increase in the price of seats brought about the infamous **Old Price Riots**, which lasted for 61 days. Mrs Siddons made her farewell appearance at Covent Garden in 1812 and Macready his debut there in 1816. The following year John Kemble was succeeded in management by his brother Charles, who in 1823 staged an innovatory revival of *King John* with costumes designed by Planché.

Carl Maria von Weber was musical director from 1824 to 1826, but the theatre went into decline and was only revived by the popularity of Fanny Kemble, who first appeared there in 1829. Edmund Kean made his final appearance at Covent Garden in 1833, while in 1837 Macready inaugurated the use of limelight in the theatre.

In 1847 the theatre was reopened as The Royal Italian Opera House but was again burned down in 1856. Rebuilt with a portico featuring the Flaxman reliefs salvaged from the previous building, Covent Garden reopened in 1858 and prospered with appearances by Adelina Patti and the burning down of Her Majesty's Theatre in 1867. Augustus Harris's management (1888–96) marked one of the theatre's most successful periods, with the installation of electric light and performances by all the leading singers of the day. Sir Thomas Beecham was musical director in 1919–20 and artistic director from 1933 until the outbreak of World War II.

Used as a dance hall during the war, the theatre was reopened in 1946 as the national opera house, home of the Royal Opera Company and from 1956, the Sadler's Wells Ballet Company (later the Royal Ballet). Since then virtually all the world's greatest singers, dancers, and conductors have performed at Covent Garden, which is celebrated for its lavish presentations. The theatre was closed for refurbishment in 1997–99; the 1990s also saw severe financial problems.

Coward, Sir Noël (1899–1973) British actor, playwright, and composer, who is considered the foremost writer of the English comedy of manners since Wilde. He made his stage debut at the age of 10 in a Christmas play at the Crystal Palace and, by 1920, was playing juvenile leads in West End comedies and writing songs, sketches, and plays. He sang and danced through the revue *London Calling* (1923), having contributed to the book and score, and, in 1924, caused a sensation as actor and author with his play THE VORTEX. Subsequently he exhibited wit, glamour, and impeccable comedy acting in a succession of revues, plays, and romantic musicals opposite such stars as Gertrude Lawrence and the Lunts. During World War II he wrote the song 'London Pride', and scripted, directed, and starred in the film *In Which We Serve*. His post-war plays never repeated his earlier success but he triumphed as a cabaret star in London and the US and was acclaimed as King Magnus in Shaw's *The Apple Cart* (1953) at the Haymarket. His farewell appearance was in his triple bill, *Suite in Three Keys*.

Principal works:

The Vortex: 1924.
FALLEN ANGELS: 1925.
HAY FEVER: 1925.
On With the Dance: 1925.
This Year of Grace: 1928.
Bitter Sweet: 1929.
PRIVATE LIVES: 1930.
CAVALCADE: 1931.
DESIGN FOR LIVING: 1933.
Tonight at 8.30: 1936.
BLITHE SPIRIT: 1941.
PRESENT LAUGHTER: 1943.
THIS HAPPY BREED: 1943.
Relative Values: 1951.
Nude With Violin: 1956.
LOOK AFTER LULU: 1959.
Waiting in the Wings: 1960.
Suite in Three Keys: 1966.

Cowell, Joseph Leathley (1792–1863) British actor, born in Devon. He appeared at Drury Lane and toured the Lincoln circuit in an entertainment called *Cowell Alone; or A Trip to London* before making his US debut as a comic actor in 1821. He was most successful as Crack in Knight's *The Turnpike Gate*.

His son, **Samuel Houghton Cowell** (1820–64), also played Crack successfully and toured the US, where he was popularly known as the **Young American Roscius**. Subsequently, in London, he made such a hit singing at the Grecian Theatre that he took to the music halls, in which he became a popular performer.

Cowl, Jane (1884–1950) US actress and playwright, who began her career under Belasco in 1903. Subsequently she won particular acclaim in such Shakespearean roles as Juliet and Viola and in the plays of Coward, Dumas *fils*, Shaw, Robert Sherwood, and Thornton Wilder. Her own plays included *Hervey House*, directed in London by Tyrone Guthrie in 1935.

Cowley, Abraham (1618–67) English poet and playwright, whose most successful play was the comedy *The Guardian* (1642), presented at Lincoln's Inn Fields as *Cutter of Coleman Street* in 1661. A precocious writer who had his first works published at the age of 15, Cowley's other dramatic pieces include the Latin play *Naufragium Jaculare* (1638) and the pastoral drama *Love's Riddle* (1638). A Royalist, he was imprisoned during the Civil War.

Cowley, Hannah (1743–1809) British playwright, whose first play, *The Runaway*, was successfully produced by Garrick in 1776. She followed it with twelve others, including *Who's the Dupe?* (1779), *The Belle's Stratagem* (1780), which was her most popular work and has been frequently revived, *A Bold Stroke for a Husband* (1783), and *The Town before You* (1794).

Cowley, Richard (d. 1619) English actor, who appeared with Strange's Men before joining the Chamberlain's Men in about 1594. He is in the 1623 Folio list of actors in Shakespeare's plays and is known to have appeared as Verges to the Dogberry of Kempe.

Cox, Brian (1946–) British actor and director. He made his London debut in 1967 and established his reputation in a series of plays at the Royal Court, including *Hedda Gabler* (1972) and *Cromwell* (1973). Award-winning work of the 1980s included O'Neill's *Strange Interlude* (1984), *Rat in the Skull* (1984), and *Titus Andronicus* for the RSC (1987). He played Richard III and Lear at the Royal National Theatre in 1990–91, but thereafter worked mainly in the US, where he starred in the Broadway production of *Art* (1998). In 2000 he appeared in Conor McPherson's *Dublin Carol* at the re-opened Royal Court.

Cox, Robert (d. 1655) English comic actor, who developed the DROLL during the suppression of the theatre in the 1640s. He combined scenes from Shakespeare and others with original pieces by himself and such varied entertainments as rope-dancing and juggling. In 1653, while performing at the Red Bull Theatre, he was arrested and imprisoned.

Crabtree, Charlotte (1847–1924) US actress, who began her career as a child and became a leading performer of burlesque and extravaganza. Popularly known as Lotta, she toured mining camps before first appearing in New York in 1865.

Craig, Edith (1869–1947) British actress and stage director, daughter of Ellen Terry and E W Godwin. After stage appearances with both her mother and Sir Henry Irving and stage management for Ellen Terry's 1907 tour of the US, Edith Craig left the theatre and studied music in London and Berlin. On returning to London she directed the Pioneer Players in some 150 plays between 1911 and 1921.

Her brother, **Gordon Craig** (1872–1966), worked as a stage director, designer, and theorist and had an immense influence on the theatre both in Europe and the US. After a time as an actor, he directed several plays – including *The Vikings at Helgeland* and *Much Ado About Nothing*, which both had his mother in the cast – between 1901 and 1903 before concentrating upon stage design and dramatic theory. Although he contributed designs for *Venice Preserv'd* (1904), *Rosmersholm* (1906), *Ham-*

let (1911), and *The Pretenders* (1926), he was most influential for his many ideas about nonrepresentational settings and atmospheric effects, as detailed in his book *On the Art of the Theatre* (1911).

Craig Theatre *See* George Abbott Theatre.

Crane, Ralph (c. 1550–c. 1632) English public official, who executed copies of several contemporary plays for actors, prompters, and authors. He was employed as scrivener to the King's Men from time to time between 1615 and 1625 and is known to have taken down plays by Fletcher, Massinger, and Middleton.

Crates (fl. 450 BC–470 BC) Greek actor and playwright, author of some of the earliest examples of Old Comedy. As an actor he appeared in plays by Cratinus; as a playwright he won his first contest in 450 BC and was highly praised by Aristophanes and Aristotle. Fragments of his works survive.

Cratinus (c. 520 BC–c. 423 BC) Greek playwright, author of several major examples of Old Comedy. Lampooned as a drunkard by Aristophanes in *The Knights*, he defeated Aristophanes in a contest a year later (424 BC) with his play *The Bottle*, which also took his drunkenness as its subject. Fragments of his plays survive.

Craven, Lady Elizabeth (Margravine of Anspach; 1750–1828) British playwright and amateur actress. She married Lord Craven in 1767 and presented her plays in a privately built theatre at their house at Newbury. After Craven's death in 1791 she married the Margrave of Anspach and continued to stage her plays at the private theatre that they built at Brandenburgh House, Hammersmith.

Craven, Hawes (Henry Hawes Craven Green; 1837–1910) British scene painter, who studied stage design at the Britannia Theatre. He attracted attention at the Olympic, then worked at Covent Garden, Drury Lane, and the Theatre Royal, Dublin, before going to the Lyceum. There he painted scenery for nearly all of Henry Irving's productions, beginning with *The Bells* in 1871.

Crawford, Cheryl (1902–86) US actress, director, and producer, who began her career in 1923 with the Theatre Guild. She was one of the three founders of the Group Theatre (1930), joined with Eva Le Gallienne and Margaret Webster to found the **American Repertory Theatre** (1946), and helped to establish the Actors' Studio in 1947. Plays she produced include *One Touch Of Venus* (1943), *Brigadoon* (1948), and Tennessee Williams's *The Rose Tattoo* (1951) and *Sweet Bird of Youth* (1959). She was also Joint-General Director of the play series produced by the American National Theatre and Academy (ANTA), presenting plays by Tennessee Williams, Brecht, Arbuzov, and many others.

Crawford, Michael (Michael Dumbell Smith; 1942–) British actor, who began his stage career in Coventry at the age of 16. His talent for comedy was revealed in Neil Simon's *Come Blow Your Horn* (1962) and subsequently he became well known as a television performer. In 1971 he returned to the stage in Anthony Marriott and Alastair Foot's *No Sex Please, We're British* (1971). He then went to enjoy outstanding success in the musicals *Billy* (1974), *Barnum* (1981, 1983, 1985), and Andrew Lloyd Webber's *The Phantom of the Opera* (1987), in which he also triumphed in New York.

Crazy Gang A group of seven British comedians, immensely popular on the London stage (especially at the Palladium and the Victoria Palace) from the 1930s to the 1960s. Specializing in revues featuring their own distinctive style of boisterous farcical humour, the Gang consisted of **Bud Flanagan** (Robert Winthrop; 1896–1968) and **Chesney Allen** (William Allen; 1894–1982); **Jimmie Nervo** (James Holloway; 1897–1975) and **Teddy Knox** (Albert Edward Cromwell-Knox; 1896–1974); **Charlie Naughton** (1887–1976) and **Jimmy Gold** (James McConigal; 1886–1967); and 'Monsewer' **Eddie Gray** (1897–1969).

Crébillon, Prosper Jolyot de (1674–1762) French playwright, born in Dijon. Crébillon was highly acclaimed in the 18th century – his admirers compared him with Racine – but his plays, which include *Idoménée* (1705) and *Rhadamiste et Zénobie* (1711), are generally considered to be too crudely melodramatic to rank among the great tragedies of French theatre. Elected to the Académie Française in 1731, he became court censor in 1735, a position that provoked the enmity of his rival Voltaire.

Creditors, The (*Fordringsägare*) A tragicomedy by August STRINDBERG. First performance: 1890. Written in the same year as *Miss Julie*, the play again tackles the battle of the sexes, this time through the relationship of Tekla and her husband Adolf. Tekla is portrayed as a destructive character who drains the strength from the men around her.

crepidata *See palliata.*

Crepuscolari, I A theatrical movement in Italy during the early 20th century. Distinguished by its subdued, melancholic tone, it found its best expression in the plays of Martini and Lodovici, among others.

cresset A knot of tarred rope, usually enclosed in a small iron cage, that when burning produced rudimentary stage lighting in the Elizabethan theatre.

Crispin A character of traditional French comedy, derived from SCARAMUCCIA and Il CAPITANO from the *commedia dell'arte*. A cunning valet, he was a prominent figure in the plays of Scarron, Lesage, and Regnard.

Criterion Theatre A theatre in London's West End, which was originally built entirely underground. Situated in Regent (now Piccadilly) Circus on the site of an old inn, it opened in 1874 with the comedy *An American Lady* by the theatre's first manager H J Byron. Charles Wyndham was manager from 1875 to 1899 and lessee from 1879 until his death in 1919. His leading lady and wife from 1916, Mary Moore (Mrs James Albery), inherited the Criterion on her husband's death; in 1931 it passed to her son, Sir Bronson Albery. In 1883 the theatre was closed for reconstruction, which included the installation of electricity; it was further remodelled in 1902. Early productions ranged from light comedy and farce to more serious plays by Henry Arthur Jones. During World War I the Walter Ellis farce *A Little Bit of Fluff* (1915) ran for 1241 performances. Marie Tempest appeared in several plays in 1926–29. Outstanding productions of the 1930s were Ivor Novello's comedy *Fresh Fields* (1933) and Terence Rattigan's immensely popular *French Without Tears* (1936), which ran for 1039 performances. The theatre was used as a studio by the BBC during World War II. Samuel Beckett's *Waiting for Godot* was transferred from the Arts Theatre in 1955, while in more recent years the Criterion has staged successful plays by such writers as Alan Ayckbourn, Simon Gray, David Mercer, and Tom Stoppard. Ray Cooney's *Run for your Wife!*, with Ernie Wise, passed its 2000th performance in 1988. The theatre was closed from 1989 to 1992. Since 1995 it has presented the Reduced Shakespeare Company's version of all 37 plays by Shakespeare in 97 minutes.

The **Criterion Theatre** on Broadway, New York, opened in 1895 (as the Lyric Theatre) as part of the Oscar Hammerstein Olympia complex. The theatre was renamed the Criterion in 1899 and saw appearances by Julia Marlowe, John Hare, Irene Vanbrugh, and Lionel Barrymore before being converted into a cinema. It was demolished in 1935.

critic One who is paid to write reviews and similar articles on the theatre. The earliest influential commentator upon the theatre was Aristotle; of his successors the most distinguished have included Sir Richard Steele (who was the first to outline the role of the modern critic), William Hazlitt (who was noted for his reviews of Edmund Kean), Leigh Hunt, G B Shaw, Max Beerhohm, James Agate, and Kenneth Tynan in Britain, Victor Hugo in France, and James Huneker (remembered as a champion of Ibsen and Shaw) and George Nathan in the US. Some of the most famous criticisms over the years have included Shaw's notorious "there is no eminent writer ... whom I despise as entirely as I despise Shakespeare", the anonymous review of *Oklahoma!* "no legs, no jokes, no chance", and Penelope Gilliatt's memory of *Waiting for Godot*, which she said "arrived in London ... like a sword burying itself in an over-upholstered sofa".

Critic, The A farce by SHERIDAN. First performance: 1779. Dangle, an amateur critic, Sneer, a malicious wit, and Sir Fretful Plagiary, attend a rehearsal of a tragedy by Puff; their comments provide a scathing satire upon the contemporary theatre and literary criticism.

Critique de l'École des femmes, La A comedy by MOLIÈRE, written in response to criticism of *L'École des femmes* (*see School for Wives, The*). First performance: Paris, 1663. It consists of a conversation in which the central characters discuss the original play. *See also Impromptu de Versailles, L'*.

Croft, Michael *See* National Youth Theatre.

Crommelynck, Fernand (1888–1970) Belgian playwright, writing in French, who established his reputation in 1920 with Lugné-Poë's production in Paris of the savage tragicomedy *Le Cocu magnifique*. His early works were influenced by Maeterlinck but never met with the success of his masterpiece upon the theme of marital infidelity, which was subsequently seen in London and Moscow with great acclaim; later works, chiefly imitations of his most famous play, included *Tripes d'or* (1925) and *Une Femme qui a le couer trop petit* (1934).

Cronyn, Hume (1911–) Canadian actor, who made his debut in 1931 with the National Theatre Stock Company. After success on Broadway in such plays as *She Stoops to Conquer* (1935) and Chekhov's *Three Sisters* (1937), he married Jessica Tandy, with whom he appeared in Jan de Hartog's *The Fourposter* (1951) and other plays. Subsequent roles included Jimmie Luton in *Big Fish, Little Fish* (1961), Polonius in Gielgud's *Hamlet* (1964), the title roles in Peter Luke's *Hadrian VII* (1969) and Beckett's *Krapp's Last Tape* (1972), and Shylock and Bottom at Stratford, Ontario (1976). From 1980 to 1982 he toured as Hector Nations in *Foxfire*, ending with a New York run.

Crooked Mirror, Theatre of the A theatre in St Petersburg, founded in 1908. It soon established itself as a centre of satirical drama with works by Evreinov, Andreyev, and Gogol, whose play *The Government Inspector* was one of its greatest successes. Closed from 1918 to 1922, it continued without attracting great attention until 1931.

Cross Keys Inn An inn in Gracechurch Street in London, where plays were staged by such companies as Strange's Men during the late 16th century. It ceased to operate as a theatrical venue in about 1596.

Crothers, Rachel (1878–1958) US playwright and theatre scholar, who wrote and produced her own plays very successfully from 1906, when her first play *The Three of Us* appeared on Broadway, until 1937. Her subjects ranged from the frustrated position of women in contemporary US society, as in *A Man's World* (1909), to the problems of the younger generation, as in *Nice People* (1921). Her most important play was *Susan and God* (1937), in which a woman becomes absorbed in a religious cult.

Crouse, Russel *See* Lindsay, Howard.

Crowder's Music Hall *See* Greenwich Theatre.

Crowe, Mrs George *See* Bateman, Hezekiah Linthicum.

Crowne, John (c. 1640–c. 1703) English playwright, who wrote a masque and a number of plays for performance at the court of Charles II. The most memorable character in his first comedy, *The Country Wit* (1675), was later developed into the central figure of his play *Sir Courtly Nice* (1685). His other dramatic works include 11 tragedies and the heroic drama *The Destruction of Jerusalem by Titus Vespasian* (1676–77).

Crow Street Theatre A theatre in Dublin, opened in 1758 by Spranger Barry and Henry Woodward in competition with the Smock Alley Theatre. With a companion theatre of the same name in Cork, the Crow Street Theatre finally closed in 1820.

Crucible, The A drama by Arthur MILLER. First performance: New York, 1953. Ostensibly a play about the Salem witch trials that took place in 1693, resulting in the deaths of 20 people, it was intended as a veiled criticism of the anti-communist purge instituted in the US by Senator McCarthy.

Crucible Theatre A theatre in Sheffield, opened in 1971 and inheriting the repertory company of the Sheffield Playhouse, which it replaced. Seating 1000 people, the theatre includes a studio theatre as well as the main auditorium and has built a reputation for performances of contemporary plays and local documentaries as well as for taking drama out into the surrounding communities. Recent years have seen successes with US musicals as well as the staging of numerous major snooker tournaments. In 1998 it enjoyed its biggest-ever hit with a stage version of the film *Brassed Off*.

Cruelty, Theatre of A theatrical genre of the mid-20th century, based on the ideas of Antonin ARTAUD, as expressed in his treatise *Le Théâtre et son double* (1938). It advocated the use of the primitive, ritualistic, and violent in an attempt to shock the audience into a new awareness; writers associated with the Theatre of Cruelty included Genet, Arrabal, Orton, and Weiss.

Cruger's Wharf Theatre A theatre in New York, otherwise known as the **Wharf Theatre**, built in 1758 by David Douglass. It opened with Rowe's *The Tragedy of Jane Shore* and closed a few months later with *Richard III*. Its talented company included the widow of Lewis Hallam and her three children.

Cruz Cano y Olmedilla, Ramón Francisco de la (1731–94) Spanish playwright, who wrote a number of distinctive SAINETES, sketches, and libretti. His realistic depiction of the lower classes of Madrid foreshadowed much Spanish drama of the 19th century.

Csiky, Gergely (1843–91) Hungarian playwright, who introduced Realism into the Hungarian theatre. His satirical bourgeois dramas include *The Parasites* (1880), *Glittering Misery* (1881), *The Stomfay Family* (1883), and *The Grandmother* (1891).

Csokor, Franz Theodor (1885–1969) Austrian playwright, whose early works reflected the influence of Büchner and Expressionism. His most admired plays included *Die rote Strasse* (1918), *Gesellschaft der Menschenrechte* (1929), and *Dritter November 1918* (1937), which depicted the defeated Austro-Hungarian army at the close of World War I. His later works included two trilogies on religious themes – of which the most notable single play was *Cäsars Witwe* (1952) – and *Das Zeichen an der Wand* (1962).

Cuckoo in the Nest, A A farce by Ben TRAVERS. First performance: Aldwych Theatre, London, 1925. The first of the Aldwych farces, the play established the author's reputation. It was filmed in 1933.

cue A signal, commonly the closing words of an actor's speech, which notifies another actor or a member of the stage crew that the time for him to deliver a line or perform some other prearranged action is imminent.

Cueva, Juan de la (c. 1543–1610) Spanish playwright and poet, an important predecessor of Lope de Vega. Much influenced by Seneca, he wrote plays based upon Spanish history and the tragedy *Los Siete infantes de Lara* (The Seven Princes of Lara), as well as such comedies of manners as *Comedia del viejo enamorado* (Comedy of the Infatuated Old Man) and *El Infamador* (The Backbiter).

Cumberland, Richard (1732–1811) British playwright, whose numerous pieces for the stage exemplified the prevailing style of sentimental comedy. His most successful play was *The West Indian*, produced by Garrick in 1771; others include *The Brothers* (1769), *The Fashionable Lover* (1772), and *The Jew* (1794). He was caricatured by Sheridan as Sir Fretful Plagiary in *The Critic*. His *Memoirs* (1806–07) are a useful source of information on 18th-century theatre.

Cummings, Constance (1910–) British actress, born in the US, who spent most of her career on the London stage. She appeared in various works by her husband, **Benn Wolfe Levy** (1900–73), while her most celebrated classic roles included Shakespeare's Juliet and Shaw's St Joan. Other successes included plays by Albee and Robert Sherwood and, with the National Theatre, Chekhov and O'Neill; her later performances included parts in Shaw's *Mrs Warren's Profession* (1982), Bagnold's *The Chalk Garden* (1982, 1992), and *Uncle Vanya* (1996).

cup-and-saucer drama A drawing-room drama in which issues of contemporary social relevance are treated in a sober, realistic way, albeit via sometimes artificial plots. The term was first used to describe the plays of T W Robertson.

curtain The heavy cloth used to screen the stage from the audience's view before, after, and sometimes at points during a performance. Curtains were first used, as the *aulaeum* and *siparium*, by the Romans and were reintroduced in the 16th and 17th centuries; Irving was the first to lower a curtain during scene changes. Also known as the **act drop**, **tabs**, or house curtain, it is usually augmented by a safety curtain and, formerly, by an **advertisement curtain** bearing details of the theatre's sponsors.

curtain call The reappearance on stage of members of the cast to take a bow at the end of a performance in response to the audience's applause. *See also* proscenium doors.

curtain-music Music played while the curtain is closed, usually before a performance begins. Formerly, music was also often played between acts.

curtain-raiser A one-act play or other brief entertainment presented before the main drama. Curtain-raisers, usually short farces, were a common feature of theatre in the 19th century.

curtain set An arrangement of curtains, including borders and backcloth, which comprises the entire setting, usually without the use of flats. It is known in the US as a **drapery setting**.

Curtain Theatre A theatre in Shoreditch, London, opened in 1577 close to the Theatre. Little is known of the construction of the building, which housed the Chamberlain's Men and several other companies over the years. *Romeo and Juliet* and *Henry V* may have had their first performances there and Jonson's *Every Man in His Humour* was given its premiere at the Curtain in 1598. The building itself was still standing possibly as late as 1666.

The **Curtain Theatre** in Glasgow was a small company that presented productions from 1932 in a Victorian terraced house in the city, eventually moving into the Lyric Theatre in 1935. The group presented works by Scottish writers until 1940, when it closed (although similar productions continued until the opening of the Pitlochry Festival Theatre in 1949).

Cusack, Cyril (1910–93) Irish actor, who joined the Abbey Theatre company in 1932 and gave his first London performance as Richard in O'Neill's *Ah, Wilderness!* in 1936. He established a fine reputation in plays by such Irish writers as Shaw, Synge, and O'Casey, while his classical roles included Romeo (1945) and Hamlet (1957) at the Gaiety Theatre, Dublin, which he managed for a time after leaving the Abbey in 1945. He was also highly acclaimed in France in *Krapp's Last Tape* by Samuel Beckett (1960). Parts with the Royal Shakespeare Company included Cassius in *Julius Caesar* (1963); subsequently he joined The National Theatre, excelling as Antonio in *The Tempest* (1974) and Fluther Good in O'Casey's *The Plough and the Stars* (1977). Later roles included the lead in Hugh Leonard's *A Life* (1980) with the Abbey Theatre company.

His daughter, **Sinéad Cusack** (1948–), made her stage debut at the age of 12 at the Olympia Theatre, Dublin and later played juvenile leads at the Abbey. In 1972 she played Juliet at the Shaw Theatre in London and subsequently took over as Grace Harkaway in Boucicault's *London Assurance*. She joined the Royal Shakespeare Company in 1979 and has since appeared as Portia, Beatrice, and Lady Macbeth among other roles, while also winning admiration in plays by O'Keeffe, Beaumont and Fletcher, and Aphra Behn. She is married to the actor Jeremy IRONS. Her sisters **Niamh** and **Sorcha Cusack** are also actresses.

Cushman, Charlotte (1816–76) US actress, who intended to be an opera singer but turned to acting and made her debut in New York as Lady Macbeth in 1836. She went on to win acclaim in such roles as Meg Merrilies in Scott's *Guy Mannering* and Lady Gay Spanker in Boucicault's *London Assurance*, as well as playing Shakespearean heroes and heroines in both the US and the UK. Among her controversial male portrayals were Romeo, Cardinal Wolsey, and Claude Melnotte in Bulwer-Lytton's *The Lady of Lyons*.

cut-cloth A cloth cut so that scenery behind it is partially revealed. Such a cloth is usually termed a cut-out drop in the US.

Cwmni Theatr Cymru *See* Theatr Gwynedd.

cyclorama A curved curtain or other barrier positioned so as to screen both the rear of the stage and part of the wings from the audience's view and to create an impression of space. Some theatres have permanent domed cycloramas made of cement. In Germany, where the cyclorama was first developed, it is known as a *Rundhorizont*.

Cyder Cellars *See* song-and-supper rooms.

Cymbeline A romance by William SHAKESPEARE, written c. 1610. First performance: Globe Theatre, London, 1611. One of Shakespeare's last dramatic works, the play combines elements of fairytale with British and Roman history in telling the story of the restoration of Imogen to her father, King Cymbeline. Shakespeare's plot, derived in part from Boccaccio's *Decameron*, culminates in a series of revelations in the final scene.

Cyrano de Bergerac A heroic comedy by Edmond ROSTAND. First performance: Paris, 1897. The eponymous hero, embarrassed by his long nose, nobly refrains from declaring his love for Roxane and encourages her romance with his rival Christian. The play has enjoyed lasting success, not only in France but also in Britain and the US, there have been several adaptations for stage and screen.

Cyrano de Bergerac, Savinien (1619–55) French writer, born in Paris. In 1641 he abandoned his military career in favour of philosophy, literature, and science. He produced just two plays, the tragedy *La Mort d'Agrippine* (1653) and the comedy *Le Pedant joué* (1654), and is better known for his stories. Thanks to Edmond Rostand's play CYRANO DE BERGERAC and other semihistorical accounts, he is also remembered for his extremely large nose.

D

Dada A deliberately irrational and nihilistic movement in art and literature that had a marked effect upon drama in the early 20th century. It began simultaneously in New York and Zürich in 1916 and flourished in Paris and elsewhere during the 1920s.

Dadié, Bernard Binlin (1916–) African novelist, playwright, poet, and statesman, who became minister of culture for the Ivory Coast (now Côte d'Ivoire) after independence. His early plays included *Les Villes* (1933) and the historical play *Assémien Déhylé, roi du Sanwi* (1936); later more satirical works influenced by the Theatre of the Absurd include *Monsieur Thôgô-gnini* (1969) and *Les Voix dans le vent*.

Dagerman, Stig (1923–54) Swedish playwright, novelist, and short-story writer, whose Expressionist plays treat such themes as fear, anxiety, death, and destruction. His best plays, *Den Dödsdömde* (The Condemned; 1947), in which a condemned man faces the terror of death, and *Skuggan av Mart* (The Shadow of Mart; 1948), are dominated by a sense of overwhelming evil and seem to foreshadow Dagerman's eventual suicide.

Dagmarteatret A theatre in Copenhagen, founded in 1883. Under Bjørn Bjørnson the theatre enjoyed a strong reputation during the 1890s and challenged the Kongelige Teater as the chief theatrical venue in the capital. It closed in 1937 and was demolished.

Dalberg, Wolfgang Heribert, Baron von (1750–1806) German theatre manager, who ran the National Theatre at Mannheim from 1778. His achievements there included the first German translation of Shakespeare's *Julius Caesar* and the production of Schiller's *Die Räuber* in 1782.

Daldry, Stephen (1961–) British director, who was artistic director at the Royal Court Theatre, London, from 1994 to 1998. After training in Italy, Daldry directed plays for the Crucible Theatre, Sheffield (1984–88) and the Gate Theatre, London (1989–92). He made his name with an Expressionistic production of J B Priestley's *An Inspector Calls* at the Royal National Theatre in 1992; this won several awards and transferred to the West End, where it is still running (2001). Other memorable productions have included Sophie Treadwell's *Machinal* (1993) and a revival of Wesker's *The Kitchen* (1994). As director of the Royal Court he oversaw the theatre's rebuilding in 1997–2000. His first film, *Billy Elliot*, was released to high acclaim in 2000.

Dalin, Olof von (1708–63) Swedish poet, playwright, and essayist, who played a crucial role in introducing Swedish writers and audiences to the classical French plays of Molière and others. He was editor of the influential *Savanska Argus* weekly newspaper and the author of several plays.

Dallas Theatre Center A theatre, designed by the architect Frank Lloyd Wright, which opened in Dallas, Texas, in 1959. The centre consists of the large **Kalita Humphreys Theatre**, which shows classical plays as well as contemporary works, a smaller cabaret theatre, and two flexible areas.

Daly, (John) Augustin (1839–99) US theatre manager and playwright, who presided over the emergence of a new independent US theatre in the late 19th century. As manager of the 5th Avenue Theatre and then of his own DALY'S THEATRE in New York, he led a distinguished company (including John Drew and Ada Rehan) and presented many plays either written or adapted (sometimes needlessly) by himself. He also opened Daly's Theatre in London, where his productions were equally well received.

Daly's 63rd Street Theatre A theatre on West 63rd Street in New York, which was originally a children's cinema (called the **Davenport Theatre**). It opened as Daly's in 1922 and was later renamed the **Coburn Theatre** (1928), the **Recital Theatre** (1932), the **Park Lane Theatre** (1932), and **Gilmore's Theatre** (1934). In 1936 the Federal Theatre Project took it over (as the **Experimental Theatre**) for the New York premiere of Shaw's *On the Rocks*. The theatre was demolished in 1957.

Daly's Theatre A theatre on Broadway, New York, which opened as **Banvard's Museum** (later renamed **Wood's Museum**) in 1867. The majority of the productions seen here were burlesque and variety shows with the occasional straight play after 1872; the theatre was remodelled in 1879 and, under the management of Augustin Daly, became one of the most successful playhouses in New York, featuring such stars as Ada Rehan. The theatre was a cinema from 1915 to 1920, when it was demolished.

Daly opened another **Daly's Theatre** off Leicester Square, London, in 1893 in conjunction with George EDWARDES. The theatre quickly established itself as an important venue for musicals as well as the plays of Shakespeare, Dumas *père*, and others featuring such leading performers as Violet Vanbrugh and Eleonora Duse. Subsequent successes included *The Merry Widow* (1907) and the musical *The Maid of the Mountains* (1917) before a series of failures led to a decline and the theatre's closure in 1937; the Warner Cinema now stands on the site.

dame A comic female character of the English pantomime, traditionally played by a man. Celebrated exponents of such roles as Widow Twankey, Mother Goose, Dame Trot, and the two Ugly Sisters have included Dan Leno and George Robey.

D'Amico, Silvio (1887–1955) Italian theatre scholar and theatre critic, who was the author of numerous authoritative accounts of the history of the stage. He is best known for his massive *Enciclopedia dello Spettacolo* and for the academy of dramatic art founded by him in 1935 and now named in his honour; other writings included numerous theatrical reviews.

Dancer, Ann (Ann Street; 1734–1801) British actress, born at Bath. After nine years at the Crow Street Theatre in Dublin, she accompanied Spranger Barry to the Haymarket in 1766. A year later she played Juliet to his Romeo there, after which they transferred to Drury Lane. In 1762 they were married; on Barry's death in 1778, she married again, appearing as Mrs Crawford. She excelled in both high comedy and tragedy.

Danchenko, Vladimir Nemirovich- *See* Nemirovich-Danchenko, Vladimir Ivanovich.

Dancing at Lughnasa A play by Brian FRIEL. First performance: Abbey Theatre, 1990. The play deals poignantly with the circumscribed lives of a family of sisters in 1930s Donegal, as recalled in the present day by Michael, the illegitimate son of the youngest girl. It transferred to the Royal National Theatre, London, and then to the West End and Broadway, being widely hailed as a masterpiece.

Dancourt, Florent Carton (1661–1725) French actor and playwright. Dancourt abandoned his legal studies for a career on the stage after marrying into a theatrical family. He acted with the Comédie-Française for some 33 years and wrote many witty comedies of manners depicting contemporary society and village life, notably *Le Chevalier à la mode* (1687) and *La Maison de campagne* (1688).

His daughters, **Marie-Anne-Armande Dancourt** (1684–1745) and **Marie-Anne-Michelle Dancourt** (1685–1780), made many successful stage appearances as Manon and Mimi respectively. As children they performed in plays by their father; subsequently they joined the Comédie-Française, Manon retiring a year later (1702).

Dandy Dick A farce by PINERO. First performance: 1887. The plot centres on the fortunes of the Reverend Augustin Jedd and his family, each of whom has bet on the eponymous racehorse to achieve particular ends.

Dane, Clemence (Winifred Ashton; 1888–1965) British novelist and playwright, whose drama A BILL OF DIVORCEMENT (1921) established her reputation. Her other plays include *Will Shakespeare* (1921), *Naboth's Vineyard* and *Granite* (both 1926), *Wild Decembers* (1932), which is about the Brontë family, and *Eighty in the Shade* (1958), which was written for Sybil Thorndike and Lewis Casson.

Dangerous Corner A play by J B PRIESTLEY. First performance: London, 1932. One of Priestley's so-called 'Time Plays', it traces a series of events resulting from a chance remark at a dinner party and culminates in a suicide.

Dangeville, Mlle (Marie-Anne Botot; 1714–96) French actress, who was much admired in comic roles with the Comédie-Française, which she joined in 1730. She excelled in the plays of Marivaux, in which she appeared with Préville, and was highly popular with her fellow-players; Collé's banned play *La Partie de chasse d'Henri IV* was given its first performance in her garden.

Daniel, Samuel (1563–1619) English poet and playwright, who wrote a number of works for the court of James I. His tragedy *Philotas* (1604) led some to believe that its author sympathized with the rebellion of the Earl of Essex in 1600 and caused a decline in his popularity. His other plays include the tragedy *Cleopatra* (1594), pastorals, and masques.

D'Annunzio, Gabriele (Gabriele Rapagnetta; 1863–1938) Italian poet, playwright, and novelist, whose writing for the stage is distinguished by intense passion and highly poetic language. His plays, which enjoyed the enthusiastic support of Eleonora Duse, include the tragedies *La Città morta* (1898) and *La Gioconda* (1899) and the

French mystery play *Le Martyre de Saint Sébastien* (1911). His most outstanding play is generally considered to be *La figlia di Jorio* (1904), a poetic expression of his delight in the natural world; other important works for the stage included *Francescala Rimini* (1902). In 1919 D'Annunzio became a national hero for his capture of the port of Fiume for Italy; subsequently, however, his reputation has suffered from the identification of his turbulent idealism with Fascist philosophy.

Danske Skueplads A theatre in Copenhagen, opened in 1722. Over the next five years it was used for the presentation of 28 comedies specially written by Ludvig Holberg, effectively laying the foundation of the Danish theatrical tradition. In 1748 the resident company transferred under royal patronage to a new theatre, which was named the KONGELIGE TEATER in 1770.

Danton's Death (*Dantons Tod*) A play by Georg BÜCHNER, written in 1835. First performance: Berlin, 1903. A pessimistic account of the conflict between Robespierre and Danton during the French Revolution, the play was influenced by Büchner's disenchantment with contemporary politics.

D'Arcy, Margaretta *See* Arden, John.

Darlington, W(illiam) A(ubrey) (1890–1979) British theatre critic and playwright, who was drama critic for *The Daily Telegraph* from 1920 to 1968. Also a writer for *The New York Times* from 1936 to 1960, he was the author of the play *Alf's Button* (1924), based on one of his own novels, and biographies of Sheridan (1932) and J M Barrie (1938).

Dasté, Jean (1904–94) French actor and director, who began his career with Copeau's company in Burgundy. Later he joined Saint-Denis's Compagnie des Quinze and assisted Barsacq with the newly established Compagnie des Quatre Saisons before moving to Grenoble and then to St Étienne (1947) to take over the local dramatic centre founded under the *décentralisation dramatique* policy. This centre became famous for his productions of both classics and new plays, including works by Brecht, until his resignation in 1970.

Daubeny, Sir Peter Lauderdale (1921–75) British impresario and manager, whose achievements included visits to Britain by many leading foreign companies and the management of the annual World Theatre Season from 1964 to 1973. Early in his career he worked at the Liverpool Playhouse and presented acclaimed productions in London; later successes included Henry James's *The Aspern Papers* (1959) and the controversial play *The Connection* (1961) by Jack Gelber.

Dauvilliers (Nicolas Dorné; c. 1646–90) French actor, who was regarded as a brilliant performer of the great tragic roles. With his wife, the daughter of Raymond Poisson, he appeared with Molière's company until the playwright's death; subsequently he was briefly with the troupe led by Molière's widow before joining the Comédie-Française in 1680. According to legend his genius in tragedy eventually caused him to go mad during one of his performances and to attempt to kill himself with a property sword; he died in an asylum.

Davenant, Sir William (1606–68) English playwright, sometimes alleged to be the illegitimate son of William Shakespeare. His early work for the theatre included masques for the court of Charles I and his comic masterpiece *The Wits* (1633). In 1656 he evaded the Puritans' restrictions on drama by presenting *The Siege of Rhodes*, a play with music that is generally regarded as the earliest English opera. After the Restoration he obtained a royal patent to open the Lincoln's Inn Fields Theatre; subsequently he built the theatre at Dorset Garden. He became poet laureate in 1638 and executed several adaptations of Shakespeare's plays.

Davenport, Edward Loomis (1815–77) US actor, who was a popular performer of leading Shakespearean and other roles in both Britain and the US. He became a member of Mrs John Drew's troupe in 1843 and subsequently won acclaim on both sides of the Atlantic in such parts as Hamlet, Othello, and Richard III and in Boucicault's *The Corsican Brothers*, working for some years with Mrs Mowatt. Back in the US he formed his own company and toured widely, several other members of his family also appearing with his troupe.

His daughter, **Fanny Lily Gipsy Davenport** (1850–98), played her first adult role in 1865 and subsequently appeared with Augustin Daly's company in New York. Later she led her own touring company, continuing to appear in a wide variety of Shakespearean and other roles, notably in the plays of Sardou.

Davenport, Jean Margaret *See* Lander, Mrs.

Davenport, Lizzie *See* Mathews, Charles.

Davenport Theatre *See* Daly's 63rd Street Theatre.

Davidson, Gordon *See* Mark Taper Forum.

Davies, Hubert Henry (1869–1917) British playwright, whose plays include *Cousin Kate* (1903), in which Ethel Barrymore played the leading role, *Mrs Gorringe's Necklace* (1903), and *The Mollusc* (1907). His most commercially successful work was his last play *Outcast* (1914), which explored double standards of morality.

Davies, Robertson (1913–95) Canadian playwright and novelist, the author of a number of plays written in collaboration with Tyrone Guthrie for the Stratford (Ontario) Festival and of several books on Shakespeare. Other works for the theatre included *Fortune My Foe* (1949), *A Masque of Aesop* (1952), *Love and Libel* (1960), which adapts one of his own novels, and such comedies as the satirical *Question Time* (1975). He is now best known for his novels, several of which are set in the world of the theatre.

Davis, Fay *See* Lawrence, Gerald.

Davis, Hallie Flanagan *See* Flanagan, Hallie.

Davis, John (1822–75) British-born playwright, actor, and manager, who worked in the British theatre before emigrating to the US in 1855. He successfully ran a theatre in New Orleans until the city's capture during the Civil War; his plays included *The Roll of the Drum* (1861), which was performed throughout the Confederate South.

Davis, Ossie (1922–) Black US actor and writer, who made his Broadway debut in 1948 with the title role in *Jeb*. During a tour (1946–47) in *Anna Lucasta* he met his wife, Ruby DEE, with whom he has frequently performed. Other roles include Walter in *A Raisin in the Sun* (1959), Purlie in his own play *Purlie Victorious* (1961), and Midge in Herb Gardner's *I'm Not Rappaport* (1981).

Day, John (c. 1574–c. 1640) English playwright, who collaborated on numerous plays with Dekker, Rowley, Chettle, and many others. His own plays include the allegorical *The Parliament of Bees* (c. 1607) and the *Isle of Gulls* (1606), which caused considerable controversy on account of its satirical view of Anglo-Scottish relations.

Dean, Basil (1888–1978) British actor, playwright, and director, who became a leading director on the London stage. He began his career with Miss Horniman's company in Manchester and later worked at the Liverpool Playhouse before reaching London in 1919. Significant productions under his direction included Clemence Dane's *A Bill of Divorcement* (1921), James Elroy Flecker's *Hassan* (1923), and J B Priestley's *Johnson Over Jordan* (1939). Having presented entertainment for the troops in World War I, he controlled the many productions organized by ENSA during World War II. Later productions included Priestley's *An Inspector Calls* (1946).

Death of a Salesman A play by Arthur MILLER. First performance: New York, 1949. The play concerns Willy Loman, a salesman, who is obsessed with materialistic success and the desire to be personally popular; when he is demoted by his company at the age of 60, he decides to kill himself to raise insurance money for his family. The play won a Pulitzer Prize. Famous revivals have starred Dustin Hoffman (1984) and Brian Denehy (1998).

Deathwatch (*Haute Surveillance*) A play by Jean GENET. First performance: Paris, 1949. Lefranc and Maurice, minor criminals, aspire to the glory of their cellmate Yeux-Verts, a murderer: Lefranc finally kills Maurice in a futile attempt to gain Yeux-Verts's prestige.

De Brie, Mlle (Catherine Leclerc de Rozet; c. 1630–1706) French actress, who played many major roles in the plays of Molière. She joined Molière's company in 1650 and was highly popular in such roles as Agnès in *L'École des femmes*; subsequently she was one of the founder members of the Comédie-Française.

Deburau, Jean-Gaspard (Jan Kašpar Dvořák; 1796–1846) French pantomimist, born in Bohemia, who – under the stagename **Baptiste** – redeveloped the character of PIERROT. Around 1811 he became involved with the Théâtre des Funambules on the Boulevard du Temple, where he inherited the role of Pierrot and transformed him into the melancholy but hopeful lover who became one of the most popular figures of the harlequinade.

His son, **Charles Deburau** (1829–73), eventually succeeded him in the role before going on to open the first Théâtre Marigny in 1858.

De Camp, Maria Theresa (1773–1838) British actress, wife of Charles KEMBLE. She was engaged at the Haymarket in 1786 and achieved fame as Macheath six years later. She accompanied the Kembles to Covent Garden in 1806 and in 1808 was successful in her own play *The Day After the Wedding*.

Décentralisation Dramatique In France, the government-backed policy of encouraging new theatre companies outside Paris that began in 1945. The awarding of state subsidies to regional groups had a fundamental effect upon the French theatre. Regional organizations, or **Centres Dramatiques**, cover each area of France; of these the most significant have included André Calvé's group and Jean Dasté's **Comédie de Saint-Étienne** in eastern France, the **Grenier de Toulouse** in the south-west, the **Comédie de l'Ouest** based in Rennes, the **Centre Dramatique de Sud-Est** in the south-east (later renamed Action Culturelle du Sud-Est), the Théâtre de la Commune d'Aubervilliers, the Théâtre des Amandiers based at Nanterre, and the **Compagnie de Caen**, founded in 1968. As well as the Centres Dramatiques, which organize regular theatrical productions and tours, other institutions established under the policy include the **Maisons de la Culture**, which foster the development in the provinces of the arts in general, the **Centres d'Animation Culturelle**, and the **Troupes Permanentes**, comprising touring companies based on their own theatre. In addition to all these organizations, the state also subsidizes the **Théâtres Nationaux**, which include the Comédie-Française and other leading national theatre companies.

Dee, Ruby (1924–) Black US actress, who made her New York debut in 1941 with the American Negro Theatre. She met her husband, Ossie DAVIS, while touring (1946–47) in *Anna Lucasta*. Other roles include Ruth in *A Raisin in the Sun* (1959) and Lena in Athol Fugard's *Bosman and Lena* (1970). Revivals include Cordelia and Kate with the American Shakespeare Festival in 1965, Gertrude for the New York Shakespeare Festival in 1975, and Amanda in *The Glass Menagerie* in 1989 in Washington DC.

Deep Blue Sea, The A drama by Terence RATTIGAN. First performance: London, 1952. The play is a moving portrayal of the plight of a judge's wife whose affair with a dissolute ex-fighter pilot leads to her attempted suicide. It has provided a fine role for such leading actresses as Peggy Ashcroft, Celia Johnson, Googie Withers, and Penelope Keith. The film version starred Kenneth More and Vivien Leigh.

Deevy, Teresa (1894–1963) Irish playwright, born in Waterford. Her portrayals of ambition and Irish rural life include *Temporal Powers* (1931), which won an Abbey Theatre prize. Her best-known play was *Katie Rooke* (1936); her later contributions were primarily for the radio.

de Filippo, Eduardo (1900–84) Italian actor-manger and playwright, who wrote a number of plays strongly influenced by the *commedia dell'arte* tradition. He and other members of his family earned a high reputation for their presentation of his plays at their own theatre in Naples. The most successful included the comedy *Filumena Marturano* (1946) – later filmed as *Marriage Italian Style*, *Grande magia* (Grand Magic; 1948), *Le voci di dentro* (Voices from Within; 1948), seen at London's National Theatre in 1983, and *Il figlio di Pulcinella* (The Son of Pulcinella; 1959). *Saturday, Sunday, Monday* (1959) was also well received in a National Theatre production starring Laurence Olivier and Joan Plowright.

Defresne *See* Dufresne.

Deirdre of the Sorrows A tragedy by J M SYNGE. First performance: Abbey Theatre, Dublin, 1910. Unfinished at the time of Synge's death, the play is based on the legendary tale of Deirdre and Naisi's fatal relationship and is notable for its poetic intensity.

Déjazet, Pauline-Virginie (1798–1875) French actress, who became highly popular for her performances in male roles. She began her career in vaudeville, moving to the Palais-Royal in 1831 and establishing herself as a major actress of both male and female characters. Subsequently she appeared at the Variétés and the Gaîté before taking over the Folies-Nouvelles (as the Théâtre Déjazet) in 1859. Her most famous roles included Voltaire, Napoleon, and one of the men in Sardou's *Monsieur Garat*.

Dejmek, Kazimierz (1924–) Polish director, who succeeded Leon Schiller as head of the New Theatre in Łódź in 1949. He established his reputation with productions of contemporary Polish plays, moving to the National Theatre in Warsaw in 1962 and then working abroad and back in Łódź. He was appointed general manager of the Polish Theatre in Warsaw in 1980 and served as minister of culture and art from 1993 to 1996. His most celebrated successes have included plays by Mickiewicz and Mrożek as well as classics by Shakespeare, Chekhov, and Euripides.

Dekker, Thomas (c. 1570–c. 1632) English playwright, who wrote or collaborated on at least 40 plays. Among the most celebrated of his collaborations were *Satiro mastix* (1601), written with Marston, *The Honest Whore* (1604) and *The Roaring Girl* (1610), written with Middleton, *The Virgin Martyr* (1620), written with Massinger, and *The Witch of Edmonton* (1621), written with both Rowley and Middleton. Of his own plays the most important was THE SHOEMAKER'S HOLIDAY.

Delacorte Theatre *See* New York Shakespeare Festival.

de la Motte, Houdar *See* Houdar de la Motte, Antoine.

Delane, Dennis (d. 1750) British actor, born into an Irish family. After appearances at the Smock Alley Theatre, he transferred (1734) to the Goodman's Fields Theatre, where he played Shakespearean leads for four years. Later he also appeared at Covent Garden and Drury Lane.

Delaney, Shelagh (1939–) British playwright, who established her reputation at the age of 17 with A TASTE OF HONEY (1958). A calculated counter to the sophisticated theatre of Terence Rattigan and others, it was highly acclaimed for its uncomprising realism on its premiere by Joan Littlewood's Theatre Workshop. A second play, *The Lion in Love*, about a failing marriage, was first presented in 1960; since then she has concentrated upon the television and cinema. Her only other work for the stage has been *The House That Jack Built* (1978).

de la Tour, Frances (1944–) British actress, who first appeared with the Royal Shakespeare Company in 1965 as a beggar in *Timon of Athens* and remained until 1971, when she played Helena in Peter Brook's *A Midsummer Night's Dream*. She played the title role in *Hamlet* in 1979, won three prestigious awards for her performance in Tom Kempinski's *Duet for One* in 1980, and was a memorable St Joan (1984) in the National Theatre revival of Shaw's play. More recent successes have included William Luce's *Lillian* (1986), Cocteau's *Les Parents terribles* at the Royal National Theatre (1994), *Antony and Cleopatra* for the Royal Shakespeare Company (1999), and Noël Coward's *Fallen Angels* (2000).

Delaunay, Louis-Arsène (1826–1903) French actor, who had a long career as a performer of young lovers. He began at the Odéon before transferring to the Comédie-Française in 1848; many of his finest parts were in plays by de Musset, Hugo, Marivaux, and Regnard.

Delavigne, Casimir (1793–1843) French playwright and poet, born in Le Havre. His tragedies, influenced in style both by neoclassicism and by Romanticism, treat historical subjects rather than classical legend, as in *Les Vêpres siciliennes* (1819). Delavigne also wrote comedies, notably *L'École des vieillards* (1823).

Della Porta, Giambattista (1538–1615) Italian scientist, philosopher, and playwright, author of a number of major plays of the *commedia erudita* tradition. His comedies, most of which drew on works by Plautus and other earlier writers, included *Il due fratelli rivali*, which influenced Shakespeare's *Much Ado About Nothing*, *La fantesca*, and *La trappolaria*.

de Loutherbourg, Philip James *See* Loutherbourg, Philip James de.

Delysia, Alice (Alice Lapize; 1889–1979) French actress and singer, who was highly popular in revue, notably under C B Cochran. She began her career in 1903 at the Moulin Rouge in Paris as a chorus girl, subsequently attracting attention with Yvonne Printemps at the Folies-Bergère and elsewhere. She joined Cochran in London in 1914 and appeared in many of his revues, including *Odds and Ends* (1914) and *On With the Dance* (1925). She also performed in several light comedies in the 1930s and toured during World War II.

DeMille, Agnes (1905–93) US choreographer and director. Her first show on Broadway, a 1929 revival of *The Black Crook*, was not a success. Following work in London, she returned to the US and became known for her work with the new American Ballet Theatre, especially her 1942 ballet, *Rodeo*. This led to her being hired by the Theatre Guild to provide the dances in OKLAHOMA!, for which her fusion of folk and classical ballet proved perfect. Moreover, her dances furthered plot and character development and were not mere decorative interludes in the forward movement of the play. Further work included *Bloomer Girl* (1946), *Brigadoon* (1947) – sometimes called her masterpiece – *Allegro* (1949), with which she became the first woman to direct a Broadway musical, *Paint Your Wagon* (1951), *Kwamina* (1961), and 110 in the Shade (1963). Her extensive writings on dance and theatre were also influential.

Dench, Dame Judi (1934–) British actress, who made her professional debut as Ophelia with the Old Vic company in 1957. After excelling there as Juliet in 1960, she worked with the Royal Shakespeare Company, at the Oxford Playhouse, and at Nottingham and made her musical debut in *Cabaret* at the Palace Theatre in 1968. Subsequent successes with the Royal Shakespeare Company have ranged from Grace Harkaway in Boucicault's *London Assurance* (1970) to Imogen in *Cymbeline* (1979) and Brecht's Mother Courage at the Barbican (1984). At the National Theatre she has played Wilde's Lady Bracknell (1982), Shakespeare's Cleopatra (1987), in which role she completed a record 100 performances, Desirée in *A Little Night Music* (1995), and Esme in Hare's *Amy's View* (1997). In 1988 she directed *Much Ado About Nothing* for Kenneth Branagh's Renaissance Theatre Company. She was married to the actor Michael WILLIAMS.

Denison, Michael (1915–98) British actor. He first appeared in *Charley's Aunt* at Frinton in 1938, then took part in the London Mask Theatre season at the Westminster Theatre, where his roles included Paris in *Troilus and Cressida* (1938) and Lexy in *Candida* (1939). After World War II he featured in West End comedies and thrillers and toured South Africa with his wife, Dulcie GRAY, with whom he often appeared. Subsequent performances included roles in the plays of Shakespeare, Ibsen, Wilde, Shaw, and Barrie.

Dennis, John (1657–1734) English theatre critic and playwright, who wrote nine moderately successful plays, the best known being the tragedy *Rinaldo and Armida* (1699), *Liberty Asserted* (1704), and *Appius and Virginia* (1709), which was ridiculed by Pope in his *Essay on Criticism*. He also produced adaptations of plays by Shakespeare, a number of pamphlets defending the theatre, as well as a considerable amount of neoclassical literary criticism.

Denver Performing Arts Center A US arts complex in Denver, Colorado. It was created in 1972 around the nucleus provided by the **Bonfils Theatre**, which was founded (as the University Civic Theatre) in 1929. Completed in 1980, the present **Helen Bonfils Theatre Complex** has four main auditoriums and a resident company. The Center, which claims to be the largest performing arts complex in the US, also includes cabaret spaces, a concert hall, and a ballroom. The founder and chairman is Donald R Seawell (1912–), who also provided most of the finance. In 2000 the Center achieved a major coup by staging the world premiere of Barton and Hall's TANTALUS.

Derwent, Clarence (1884–1959) British actor, who went to the US in 1915, made his first New York appearance as Undershaft in Shaw's *Major Barbara*, and remained to play important supporting roles for the next 31 years. In 1945 he established the annual Clarence Derwent Awards in New York and London for the best supporting performances.

Desclée, Aimée-Olympe (1836–74) French actress, who excelled as heroines in the plays of Dumas *fils*, who did much to encourage her. Early appearances at the Gymnase were not successful but after Dumas saw her with a touring company he arranged her return to Paris, where she triumphed in several of his plays before her sudden death.

Deseine, Mlle *See* Dufresne.

designer One who undertakes the design of the costumes, scenery, lighting, and other technical aspects of a particular production, usually working in close collaboration with the director. The earliest designers included Giacomo Torelli and Philippe James de Loutherbourg. Celebrated 20th-century designers included Adolphe Appia, Gordon Craig, and Josef Svoboda.

Design for Living A comedy by Noël COWARD. First performance: New York, 1933. The plot revolves around a *ménage à trois*, whose members reject conventional values. Coward himself appeared with the Lunts in the original production.

Desiosi An Italian *commedia dell'arte* company, possibly founded by Diana da PONTI in about 1581. Actors with the Desiosi included Tristano Martinelli, who appeared as Arlecchino; when the company disbanded after several years many of its members joined the Accesi.

Desire Under the Elms A tragic drama by Eugene O'NEILL. First performance: New York, 1924. The play examines the relationship between the New England farmer Ephraim Cabot and his wife, Abbey Putnam, who becomes involved with Ebon, the son of Ephraim's first marriage. The depiction of incest and infanticide led the New York police to raid the first production.

Desjardins, Marie-Catherine-Hortense (Mme de Villedieu; 1632–83) French writer, originally a member of Molière's company. After an adventurous youth she produced many fashionable short novels and a number of plays, of which the best-known is the tragedy *Manlius Torquatus* (1662).

Desmares, Nicolas (c. 1645–1714) French actor and playwright, brother of Mlle Champmeslé. After appearing with a French troupe at Copenhagen and in the provinces, he joined the Comédie-Française where he was praised in peasant roles.

His daughter was the actress **Charlotte Desmares** (1682–1753), who was trained by Mlle Champmeslé and, with Mlle Duclos, inherited many of her roles at the Comédie-Française. Her greatest successes included Voltaire's *Oedipe*.

Desmarets de Saint-Sorlin, Jean (1595–1676) French poet and playwright. A protégé of Cardinal de Richelieu and a founder member of the Académie Française, he wrote plays of varying quality: the witty comedy *Les Visionnaires* (1637), which satirized polite society and anticipated Molière, was an immense success. His only other work of note was *Mirame* (1641).

Desœillets, Mlle (Alix Faviot; 1621–70) French actress, who was much admired in tragedy at the Hôtel de Bourgogne despite her lack of striking looks. She first appeared in Paris after many years in the provinces and excelled in plays by Corneille and Racine; she retired immediately, however, upon seeing Mlle Champmeslé act in one of her roles for the first time.

Destouches (Philippe Néricault; 1680–1754) French playwright, born in Tours. A member of a troupe of strolling players in his youth, he worked for several years at the French embassy in London, returning in 1723. His most successful comedies, *Le Philosophe marié* (The Married Philosopher; 1727) and *Le Glorieux* (The School for Arrogance; 1732), were influenced both by Molière and by English Restoration drama.

detail scenery Small items of scenery, generally BUILT STUFF, that are introduced during a performance on a formal stage or other stage setting.

deus ex machina In a play, the sudden and unexpected appearance of a new character, who immediately resolves the complications of the plot. The term comes from ancient Greek tragedy, in which the *deus ex machina* would be a god lowered mechanically onto the stage to settle all disputes.

deuteragonist *See* protagonist.

Deutsch, Ernst (1890–1969) German actor, born in Prague, who became a leading performer of Expressionist drama. He established his reputation in Hasenclever's *Der Sohn* (1916) and subsequently appeared under Reinhardt with great success until moving to the US (1933); after his return to Germany in 1947 he won further praise in plays by Hauptmann, Lessing, Schnitzler, and others.

Deutsches Theater A theatre group founded in Berlin in 1883 to promote the performance of new works. Led by Adolf L'Arronge, Josef Kainz, and Agnes Sorma, the group first performed popular historical dramas. It subsequently won new fame under

Max Reinhardt and, after World War I, Heinz Hilpert. It became the National Theatre of East Berlin in 1946 and was run by Benno Besson from 1961 to 1969. In the 1990s the Deutsches Theater underwent major reorganization following the re-unification of Germany.

de Villiers, Claude Deschamps *See* Villiers, Claude Deschamps de.

Devils, The A historical drama by John WHITING. First performance: London, 1961. Based on Aldous Huxley's novel *The Devils of Loudon*, it was first presented by the Royal Shakespeare Company. The play, which bears the influence of Brecht, concerns the outbreak of mass hysteria in a 17th-century French nunnery.

Devil's Disciple, The A comedy by G B SHAW. First performance: New York, 1897. Set during the American War of Independence, the play satirizes the conventions of romantic melodrama. Despite his reputation as a villainous disgrace to his family, Dick Dudgeon cannot help himself from taking the place of a condemned clergyman on the gallows, driven by his own innate virtue.

Devine, George (1910–66) British actor and theatre director, who was president of OUDS before appearing in Gielgud's London seasons. He became director and manager of Saint-Denis's London Theatre Studio (1936–39), taught at the Old Vic school, played Tesman to Peggy Ashcroft's Hedda Gabler (1954), and directed Gielgud in a curious Japanese-designed *King Lear* (1955). In 1956 he founded the English Stage Company at the Royal Court Theatre in London, where he presented the work of such innovative playwrights as Osborne, Pinter, and Bond.

Devrient, Ludwig (1784–1832) German actor, who was judged the greatest performer of tragedy of the Romantic era in Germany. Appearing with Iffland's company from 1814, he caused a sensation in such passionate roles as King Lear and Franz Moor in Schiller's *Die Räuber*. Later in his career he was confined to comedy roles only and, frustrated as a serious actor, he abandoned himself to alcohol.

His eldest nephew, **Karl August Devrient** (1797–1872), was also an actor, who played many leading roles at the Court Theatre in Dresden. His greatest successes included major parts in plays by Schiller, Goethe, and Shakespeare.

Another nephew, **(Philipp) Eduard Devrient** (1801–77), began as an opera singer but later worked at the Court Theatre in Dresden and the Court Theatre at Karlsruhe as an actor and director. He also published the first history of the German stage (1848–74) and translations of Shakespeare (1873–76).

A third nephew, **(Gustav) Emil Devrient** (1803–72), was also a much-acclaimed actor at the Court Theatre in Dresden and elsewhere. He was particularly admired in the tragedies of Goethe, Schiller, and Shakespeare.

Eduard's son, **Otto Devrient** (1838–94), was active as an actor, playwright, and director and was the author of three tragedies. He worked at the Karlshruhe Court Theatre and later at Weimar, where his production of Geothe's *Faust* (1876) in the style of a mystery play was much discussed.

Karl's son, **Max Devrient** (1857–1929), made his acting debut in Drésden in 1878 and later appeared throughout Germany and in Vienna in plays by Goethe, Schiller, and Shakespeare. Although admired chiefly as a tragedian, he was also highly successful in comic roles.

Dewhurst, Colleen (?1926–91) Canadian actress, who made her professional debut in the ANTA revival of *Desire Under the Elms* (1952). She performed in the New York Shakespeare Festival from 1956 to 1959, playing Tamora in *Titus Andronicus*, Katherine in *The Taming of the Shrew*, Lady Macbeth in *Macbeth*, and Cleopatra in *Antony and Cleopatra*. Other successes have included Albee's *Who's Afraid of Virginia Woolf?* (1965), Brecht's *The Good Woman of Setzuan* (1970), and *Hamlet* (1972). She was especially known for her performances in the works of Eugene O'Neill, including another revival of *Desire Under the Elms* (1963), as well as the parts of Josie in *A Moon for the Misbegotten* (1973) and Mary Tyrone in *Long Day's Journey Into Night* (1987). She was president of American Actors' Equity in the 1980s.

Dexter, John (1925–90) British actor and director, who first attracted attention with his productions for the English Stage Company at the Royal Court Theatre in the 1950s. Following success with a trilogy of Wesker's plays, he scored further successes with plays by Lillian Hellman, G B Shaw, and Shakespeare among others, several of which were presented by the National Theatre (1963–66). Actors who have appeared under his direction have included Laurence Olivier, who played Othello with the National Theatre, and Alec Guinness; his later productions included a number of operas at New York's Metropolitan Opera House, Brecht's *Life of Galileo* (1980), the musical *Gigi* (1985), and Henry Hwang's *M Butterfly* (1988).

Diary of Anne Frank, The A play by Frances Goodrich and Albert Hackett. First performance: New York, 1955. The play is based on the well-known diary of Anne Frank, a 13-year-old Jewish girl, who lived in hiding with her parents and family friends for three years during World War II before being found and sent to a concentration camp, where she died. A 1998 revival used a revised script, said to be closer to the original diary.

Dias, Baltasar (16th century) Portuguese playwright, who lived in Madeira. Despite his blindness, he wrote a number of popular though inconsequential plays influenced by the works of Vicente.

Dibdin, Charles (1745–1814) British actor, playwright, and songwriter, noted for his ballad operas. He established his reputation as an actor in Bickerstaffe's *The Padlock* in 1768, after which he appeared in a series of one-man shows (1788–93).

His illegitimate children by the actress Harriet Pitt included Charles PITT and **Thomas John Dibdin** (1771–1841), who was also an actor, playwright, and songwriter. He first appeared on stage (at the age of four) at Drury Lane as Cupid to the Venus of Mrs Siddons. After experience in the provinces he achieved fame as the author of such stirring naval dramas as *The Mouth of the Nile* (1798), *Naval Pillar* (1799), and *Nelson's Glory* (1805). His pantomimes, notably *Mother Goose* (1806), were also highly acclaimed. He speculated disastrously with the Surrey Theatre and briefly managed the Haymarket.

Dickens, Charles (1812–70) British novelist, who was an enthusiastic amateur actor and, with his friends, gave performances in his private theatre at TAVISTOCK HOUSE, his home in London. As an actor he was praised for his portrayal of comic roles and for his many solo dramatic readings of his works both in Britain and the US. Early in his career he wrote several pieces for performance at the St James's Theatre, chiefly operatic burlettas and farces; later he collaborated with Wilkie Collins on *No Thoroughfare*, which was produced by Ben Webster in 1867. More influential, however, have been the numerous stage adaptations of his prose works, including versions of *The Cricket on the Hearth*, *The Old Curiosity Shop*, *Great Expectations*, *The Pickwick Papers*, and *A Tale of Two Cities*. Successful adaptations in the later 20th century included Bart's OLIVER!, the Royal Shakespeare Company's *Nicholas Nickleby*, and *The Mystery of Edwin Drood*.

didascalia A teacher of drama in ancient Greece, or a production itself. The term was also used of various catalogues relating to dramatic entertainments, of which fragments survive.

Diderot, Denis (1713–84) French philosopher, encyclopedist, novelist, essayist, playwright, and critic. The son of a cutler, he led a bohemian existence in the company of Rousseau and others before devoting himself seriously to writing. The *Encyclopédie* (1751–72) is Diderot's major work: his plays, such sentimental bourgeois dramas as *Le Fils naturel* (published 1757; performed 1771 Paris), *Le Père de famille* (published 1758; performed 1761 Paris), and *Est-il bon? Est-il méchant?* (written 1781), form only a small part of his literary output. His dramatic theories, however, contained in such works as *Le Paradoxe sur le comédien* (published 1830; written in the 1770s), strongly influenced European theatre over the next 100 years.

Digges, Dudley (1879–1947) US actor, born in Ireland, who remained in the US after a visit with the Abbey Theatre company in 1904. He joined the newly formed Theatre Guild in 1919, working with them both as actor and director for 11 years. His parts ranged from Mr Zero in Elmer Rice's *The Adding Machine* (1932) to Andrew Undershaft in Shaw's *Major Barbara* (1928). His final performance was as Harry Hope in O'Neill's *The Iceman Cometh* (1946).

Digges, Dudley West (1720–86) British actor. The first actor to play Young Norval in Home's *Douglas* (1756), he was highly acclaimed at the Haymarket as Cato, Wolsey, and in other classic roles.

Dikie, Alexei Denisovich (1889–1955) Russian actor and director, who studied under Stanislavsky at the Moscow Art Theatre. Later he worked at various theatres, attracting attention for his direction of plays by Faiko, Ostrovsky, Sofronov, and others as well as for his acting in such works as Korneichuk's *Front* (1942) at the Vakhtangov Theatre.

Dillingham, Charles Bancroft (1868–1934) US theatre manager, who became a noted associate of Charles Frohman in New York. As well as fostering the US careers of many leading performers, he presented the first US production of Shaw's *Man and Superman* (1905), opened the Globe Theatre (later the Lunt-Fontanne Theatre), and managed vaudeville at the Hippodrome Theatre.

dimmer An electrical or mechanical means of dimming stage lighting, controlled in the modern theatre from a central computerized dimmer board.

Dionysia The religious festivals held annually in ancient Greece in honour of DIONYSUS. Initially the festivals involved simple rites and processions; subsequently, however, a tradition of dramatic presentations developed, most notably at the **City Dionysia** or **Great Dionysia** (held in late March and early April), where the daily entertainment included three tragedies and a satyr-play all by the same author.

Such festivals usually concluded in contests for DITHYRAMBS. Key figures in the development of the early Greek festivals included Thespis and Pisistratus. *See also* Lenaea; Rural Dionysia.

Dionysus (*or* Bacchus) The Greek god of nature and wine, whose worship gave rise to the earliest Greek drama (*see* Dionysia). The rites associated with Dionysus included the wearing of the symbolic phallus, a custom which passed directly into the comic tradition. The legendary attendants of Dionysus, half man and half animal, appear in the SATYR-PLAY. *See also* dithyramb.

diorama A type of PANORAMA, which makes use of special lighting, cut-out scenery, and transparencies to create three-dimensional effects and an impression of movement.

Diphilus of Sinope (d. 290 BC) Greek playwright, author of several important examples of New Comedy. Only titles and fragments of his plays, which influenced Terence and Plautus, survive.

director The person in overall charge of a production; in Britain such a person was called the producer until 1956, when it was officially agreed that the British theatre would adopt the US usage. The director co-ordinates all aspects of a show and is responsible for deciding how a particular script is to be interpreted. Until the 20th century the role was variously undertaken by the author, the stage manager, the prompter, or the leading actor. Madame Vestris and David Belasco were among the first to fulfil the role; their successors have included such notable figures as Stanislavsky, Granville-Barker, Copeau, Jouvet, Baty, Dullin, Pitoëff, Piscator, Jessner, Taïrov, Okhlopkhov, Vakhtangov, Saint-Denis, Eva Le Gallienne, Strasberg, Kazan, Clurman, Peter Brook, Peter Hall, Joan Littlewood, Giorgio Strehler, and Peter Zadek.

disguising A form of dramatic entertainment presented at the English Court during the 15th and 16th centuries. Participants in disguisings, which often included music, dancing, and the exchanging of gifts, included the nobility themselves; by the mid-16th century such entertainments were generally referred to as **masks**.

Disney, Walt This worldwide entertainment organization had no significant involvement in live theatre until the 1990s. However, when critics noted that its 1991 animated film *Beauty and the Beast* had a better score than most of the shows on Broadway, the company experimented with a live version, which opened to great success in 1994. An equally successful version of *The Lion King*, with music by Elton John and lyrics by Tim Rice, opened in New York in 1996 and London in 1999. Disney has also become a major player in the renovation of New York's Times Square area, purchasing and renovating the NEW AMSTERDAM THEATRE and thereby sparking the revival of 42ND STREET.

dithyramb A hymn sung in honour of DIONYSUS during festivals or banquets in ancient Greece. Performed by a chorus of 50 actors dressed as satyrs and led by the PROTAGONIST, the earliest dithyrambs, which were improvised, were presented in the 7th century BC; the form acquired literary status later through the efforts of Arion of Lesbos and became a part of the Dionysia, during which poets would compete against each other in the form. Lasus of Hermione was the most celebrated composer of dithyrambs; fragments by other writers survive. Ultimately the form was supplanted by tragedy.

Dmitrevsky, Ivan Afanasyevich (1733–1821) Russian actor and administrator, who dominated the St Petersburg theatre. He began as an amateur with Volkov and later performed with Sumarokov's company before visiting Paris to study the French theatre. He excelled in plays by Molière, Sumarokov, and Fonvizin.

Dmitriev, Vladimir Vladimirovich (1900–48) Russian stage designer, who established a strong reputation for his work at the Moscow Art Theatre and the Vakhtangov Theatre before his early death. He was particularly acclaimed for his settings for plays by Ostrovsky and Gorky and for Virta's *Our Daily Bread* (1947).

Dmitri of Rostov (Daniel Tuptalo; 1651–1709) Russian churchman and playwright, who became a bishop and was canonized in 1757. He was the author of six verse plays on religious themes, notably *The Nativity Play*, *The Penitent Sinner*, and *The Resurrection of Christ*.

Döbbelin, Karl Theophil (1727–93) German actor-manager, who began as a strolling player and later led his own troupe in Berlin. His company, established after encouragement from Gottsched, was noted for its production of plays by Lessing, including a much-acclaimed *Minna von Barnhelm* (1768) and a less successful *Nathan der Weise* (1783), in which Döbbelin played the leading role in his customary ranting style.

Dockstader, Lew (George Alfred Clapp; 1856–1924) US minstrel and vaudeville performer, who appeared with amateur blackface troupes in Hartford, Connecticut before turning professional and eventually teaming up with the Dockstader Brothers Minstrels in 1876. 10 years later his attempt to run his own theatre in New York failed, but he continued in partnership with George Primrose (1952–1919), working the vaudeville circuit and revitalizing the act by introducing topical satire.

Dock Street Theatre A theatre in Dock Street, Charleston, South Carolina, the first building in America to be built solely for presenting drama. It opened in 1736 with Farquhar's *The Recruiting Officer*, but closed only a year later.

A second **Dock Street Theatre** on the same site opened in 1937 with the same opening bill, presented by the resident **Footlight Players**. Currently, the theatre is used by the Charlestown Stage Company, which produces 120 performances a year.

Docteur amoureux, Le A partly improvised farce by MOLIÈRE, in the Italian style. The play had already been seen by provincial audiences when it was staged before Louis XIV in 1658, following a performance of Pierre Corneille's *Nicomède* by Molière's troupe: its success earned the company the patronage of the king.

Doctor's Dilemma, The A tragicomedy by G B SHAW. First performance: Royal Court Theatre, London, 1906. Sir Colenso Ridgeon has the choice of treating either a dissolute artist or a fellow general practitioner; his decision is complicated by his love for the artist's wife. The play attacks contemporary medical ethics.

documentary drama A form of theatre, also known as the **Theatre of Fact**, in which productions are closely based upon historical records. It developed as a recognizable theatrical form in the 1950s and 1960s, notably in Germany with the drama of Hochhuth and Weiss among others. Subsequently it became a major feature of contemporary drama, often concentrating upon local history. *See also* Living Newspaper.

Dodd, James (1734–96) British actor, who served a long provincial apprenticeship before Garrick engaged him at Drury Lane in 1765. He established himself as the natural successor to Colley Cibber in playing foppish roles, creating the role of Sir Benjamin Backbite in *The School for Scandal* and being acclaimed as Aguecheek in *Twelfth Night*.

Dodsley, Robert (1703–64) English playwright and bookseller. In 1735, through Pope's influence, his play *The Toy Shop* was staged at Covent Garden with great success, after which he set up as a publisher. He continued to write plays, including *The King and the Miller of Mansfield* (1737), *The Blind Beggar of Bethnal Green* (1741), and the tragedy *Cleone*, which was well received in 1758. As a publisher his list contained works by Dr Johnson, Goldsmith, and others.

dog drama A form of drama popular in the 19th century, in which live dogs appeared on stage as part of the cast. In Britain dog drama was a huge success when presented at Drury Lane; plays written specially to include canine performers included Pixérécourt's celebrated *Le Chien de Montargis, ou la Fôret de Bondy* (1814).

Doggett, Thomas (c. 1670–1721) British actor, who was the most original comedian of his day. Ben in *Love for Love* (1695) and Fondlewife in *The Old Bachelor* (1693) were both written for him by Congreve. In 1710 he joined Colley Cibber and Wilks as managers of Drury Lane, but resigned in protest on the admission of Barton Booth as fourth shareholder. His name is remembered in Doggett's Coat and Badge, a sculling prize he founded on the accession of George I; it is still competed for by Thames watermen on 1 August.

Doherty, Brian *See* Shaw Festival.

Dolce, Lodovico (1508–68) Italian playwright, noted for the violence of his plays. His notoriously bloody tragedies, most of which were derived from classical subjects, include *Giocasta*; other more sophisticated works include *Marianna* (1565).

Doll's House, A (*Et Dukkehjem*) A drama by Henrik IBSEN. First performance: Copenhagen, 1879. The central character, Nora Helmer, comes to realize that her husband will never take her seriously as a responsible human being. In the play's final scene, which caused deep shock at the time, she rejects his pleas and walks out in an attempt to establish her own independence.

Dominion Drama Festival A major theatre festival founded in Canada in 1933. Presented at different locations each year, the festival did much to stimulate the native Canadian theatre before finally coming to an end in 1978.

Dominion Theatre A theatre in Tottenham Court Road, London; one of the West End's largest venues, it seats 2082 with room for a further 100 standing. Built by the Milburn brothers in 1928, it converted to a cinema in 1930. In 1957 it presented the Judy Garland Show, and from the 1960s until the 1980s it hosted a mixed bill of music, film, dance, and some theatre. In recent years it has housed blockbuster musicals such as *Grease* (1993–96), *Scrooge* (1996–97), and Disney's *Beauty and the Beast* (1997–).

Dominique *See* Biancolelli, Giuseppe Domenico.

Don Carlos, Infant von Spanien A romantic tragedy by Friedrich von SCHILLER. First performance: 1789. Set in the time of Philip II of Spain, *Don Carlos* was Schiller's first historical drama and also his first written in blank verse.

Don Juan A stock character of the Spanish theatrical tradition, an arrogant aristocratic libertine descended from various legendary figures. Don Juan was first introduced to the stage in Tirso de Molina's *El Burlador de Sevilla y Convidado de Piedra* (1630). In this piece Don Juan is punished for his wrongdoing by a statue that accepts his mocking invitation to share supper with him. Don Juan has subsequently appeared in the theatrical traditions of many different countries, inspiring works by Molière, Goldoni, Rostand, Shaw, Tennessee Williams, and other playwrights, as well as Mozart's opera *Don Giovanni* (1787).

Donmar Warehouse A small theatre in Earlham Street, Covent Garden, London, originally the vat room of a large brewery, and later a banana warehouse. It was converted by Donald Albery, who named it after himself and the dancer Margot Fontaine, whom he managed. From 1977 until their move to the Barbican in 1982 the Donmar was the London studio theatre of the Royal Shakespeare Company. During the later 1980s it staged mainly touring productions by fringe companies and presented an annual 'best of' the Edinburgh Fringe. After a period of closure (1990–92) it reopened under the energetic leadership of Sam MENDES, who has presented a mixed repertoire of classic revivals, new plays, and musicals to great acclaim. Outstanding productions have included Sondheim's *Assassins* (1992), Tennessee Williams's *The Glass Menagerie* (1995), and David Hare's *The Blue Room* (1998), in which the Hollywood actress Nicole Kidman appeared nude. It has an open stage and seats 250 people (with some extra standing room).

Donnellan, Declan (1953–) British director, who founded the touring company CHEEK BY JOWL in 1981. His successes with the company, which presented scaled-down versions of the classics, included adaptations of Racine's *Andromache* (1985) and Ostrovsky's *A Family Affair* (1987), as well as several works by Shakespeare. In 1989 he became an associate director of the Royal National Theatre, where his productions have included the two parts of *Angels in America* (1991, 1993). He has subsequently directed the West End musical *Martin Guerre* (1996) and an award-winning version of *The Winter's Tale* with the Maly Theatre of St Petersburg (1998).

Doone, Rupert *See* Group Theatre.

Dorset Garden Theatre A theatre on the bank of the Thames, off Fleet Street in London, opened in 1671 by Henry Harris and Thomas Betterton. Originally an idea of Sir William Davenant, the theatre (initially called the **Duke of York's House**) may have been the work of Sir Christopher Wren but was somewhat flawed by its peculiarly narrow auditorium. Early productions there included the plays of Dryden and Davenant's version of *Macbeth* (1673), which established the theatre as a venue for opera. Betterton triumphed in several works by Shadwell and Mrs Barry was acclaimed in plays by Otway, notably *Venice Preserv'd* (1681); other writers connected with the theatre included Aphra Behn, Sir George Etherege, and Sir William Wycherley. Financial considerations, however, led to the amalgamation of the resident company with that at Drury Lane in 1682 and the virtual end of productions at Dorset

Garden. Renamed the Queen's Theatre in 1687, it was later used for circus-type entertainments before demolition in 1709.

Dorst, Tankred (1925–) German playwright, who began his career in puppet theatre but later developed as a leading writer in the tradition of Brecht. *Grosse Schmährede an der Stadtmauer* (Great Vituperation at the City Wall; 1961) was acclaimed for its use of Brechtian techniques, while *Toller* (1968) was based on events in the life of the playwright Ernst Toller. *Eiszeit* (Ice Age; 1973) explored the life of Knut Hamsun, the Norwegian author and Nazi collaborator. Later plays, which include *Merlin Oder das würste Land* (1981), are less political. He has also written screenplays and opera libretti.

Dorval, Marie-Thomase-Amélie (1798–1849) French actress, who first appeared on stage as a child and later achieved fame when she appeared as Amélie in *Trente Ans, ou la Vie d'un joueur* (1827) alongside Frédérick. In 1835 she arrived at the Comédie-Française in *Chatterton* by Vigny, who was her lover; shortly after, however, she she left the company, partly due to the hostility of Mlle Mars. In 1847 she had a further success in Racine's *Phèdre* at the Odéon but subsequently died in poverty.

Dossenus A stock character of the Roman *atellana*. He was probably a hunchback and shared some of the traits of character of MANDUCUS.

Dostoevsky, Fyodor Mikhailovich (1821–81) Russian novelist, whose celebrated novels dealing with both moral and political themes have also had some success in stage adaptations. Of these the most notable have included *The Idiot* (acclaimed at the Old Vic in 1970 in a version by Simon Gray), *The Brothers Karamazov*, and *Crime and Punishment*.

Dotrice, Roy (1925–) British actor, born in Guernsey, who spent 10 years in provincial repertory companies before joining the Stratford-on-Avon company in 1958. He remained for seven years, during which he also appeared at the Aldwych Theatre in roles ranging from Caliban to John of Gaunt. He has since given numerous solo performances in many countries, most notably as Aubrey in *Brief Lives*.

Dottore, Il A character of the *commedia dell'arte*, often appearing as a counterpart to PANTALONE. Conventionally portrayed as a verbose physician or lawyer called Graziano, Il Dottore could be played with or without a mask and usually appeared dressed in black with a white ruff. The character did not pass into the English harlequinade but was further developed in the French theatre in the plays of Molière.

double masque *See* masque.

Douglass, David (d. 1786) US actor-manager, who founded the celebrated AMERICAN COMPANY in New York. He installed the troupe successively in Cruger's Wharf, the Chapel Street Theatre, and in John Street before erecting for them the first permanent theatre in the US – the Southwark Theatre in Philadelphia. His productions included Thomas Godfrey's *The Prince of Parthia* (1767), the first native US tragedy; his actors included John Henry.

Downes, John (fl. 1662–1710) British stage prompter and writer. When the Lincoln's Inn Fields Theatre opened in 1661, Downes was engaged as prompter. In 1708 he published *Roscius Anglicanus or an Historical Review of the Stage*, a valuable source of information about early Restoration drama.

downstage *See* stage direction.

Downstage Theatre A theatrical company based in Wellington, New Zealand. Founded in 1964 by a group of playwrights and actors, it presented works by local writers as a café-theatre before moving into the **Hannah Playhouse** in 1970. Designers with the company have contributed greatly to the development of stage design in New Zealand.

Dowton, William (1764–1851) British actor, who abandoned his apprenticeship as an architect to become a strolling player. After several years spent touring, he made his debut at Drury Lane as Sheva in *The Jew* by Richard Cumberland. He soon became a respected character-actor, playing parts like Hardcastle in *She Stoops to Conquer* and Sir Hugh Evans in *The Merry Wives of Windsor*. He was also critically acclaimed for performances as Falstaff.

D'Oyly Carte, Richard (1844–1901) British impresario. As a concert agent he produced Gilbert and Sullivan's *Trial by Jury* at the Royal Theatre in 1875; the success of this and other Gilbert and Sullivan works enabled him to build the SAVOY THEATRE and to become involved in the management of several provincial theatres. He also built the Royal English Opera House (now the Palace Theatre).

Drabinsky, Garth (1950–) Canadian entrepreneur who, after producing plays and building theatres in his native Toronto, founded the production company **Livent**. This represented a unique attempt to produce plays not by raising money show by show, but by creating a large permanent fund to be used for development as a manufacturing company might. Livent built the FORD THEATRE CENTERS in Toronto, New York and Chicago and had artistic successes with several very large-scale productions – *Show Boat* (1993) and *Ragtime* (1998) among them – but they were overproduced and not profitable. The company has since gone bankrupt amidst charges of Drabinsky's misuse of its funding.

Drachmann, Holger Henrik Herholdt (1846–1908) Danish poet, novelist, and playwright, who is usually remembered for his passionate lyrical poetry, which was initially influenced by Georg Brandes but later extolled patriotism and romanticism. Of his dramatic works the most significant is the fantasy *Der var en Gang* (Once Upon a Time; 1885), for which Peter Lange-Muller wrote the music; others include several melodramas and the plays *Brav Karl* (1888) and *Der gronne Haab* (Green Hope; 1903).

drag artist *See* female impersonator.

Drake, Alfred (Alfred Caparro; 1914–92) US actor whose virile baritone and stage presence made him the era's premier romantic lead in musical comedies. In 1943 he was acclaimed as Curly in *Oklahoma!*; other famous roles included Fred/Petruchio in *Kiss Me Kate* (1948), Hajj in *Kismet* (1953), and Shakespearean parts.

Drama and Comedy, Theatre of *See* Taganka Theatre.

drama school An institution at which persons intending to pursue a career in the theatre receive training. Formerly, all training in the theatre was acquired through actual experience, the first specialist schools only being founded in the late 18th century. The CONSERVATOIRE NATIONAL D'ART DRAMATIQUE, established in Paris in 1786, was among the first great schools; leading establishments of the same kind founded since then have included the LUNACHARSKY STATE INSTITUTE OF THE-ATRE ART in Russia, the LONDON ACADEMY OF MUSIC AND DRAMATIC ART, the ROYAL ACADEMY OF DRAMATIC ART, and the CENTRAL SCHOOL OF SPEECH AND DRAMA in Britain, and the AMERICAN ACADEMY OF DRAMATIC ARTS in the US. Alternatively, aspiring actors and directors can receive an education in drama at various UNIVERSITY DRAMA DEPARTMENTS.

dramatis personae The members of the cast in a particular production, or – more commonly – the characters they portray.

Dramatists' Guild, The A US professional association of playwrights, stage composers and lyricists, founded in 1920 to protect their rights and improve conditions. Its headquarters are in New York City.

drame A form of French drama in which elements of comedy and tragedy were combined in the dramatization of middle-class issues and concerns. First defined by Diderot, the *drame* was descended from the *comédie larmoyante* and the ***tragédie-Bourgeoise*** of Voltaire; other writers of the genre included Sedaine and Mercier.

Draper, Ruth (1884–1956) US monologist, who wrote and performed what were, in essence, entire plays for a solo performer (something now quite common). Initial work in the US was followed by extensive world touring from 1918, including great success in England in 1920. Her best-known monologues included 'Showing the Garden', 'Three Generations', 'Mr Clifford and Three Women', and 'An English House Party'.

drapery setting *See* curtain set.

drawing-room drama A play that takes place largely in a genteel domestic setting, typically examining middle-class values.

Dream Play, A (*Ett drömspel*) A play by August STRINDBERG, written in 1902. First performance: 1907. Written during Strindberg's brief third marriage, the play is an elaborate poetic fantasy requiring a cast of 46. This passionate debate upon the unreality of existence is often quoted for its conclusion "Mankind's to be pitied".

dress circle *See* auditorium.

dressing-room One or more rooms situated in the backstage area of a theatre where actors may put on their costumes and make-up; they also rest in their dressing rooms between appearances and after performances.

Dressler, Marie (Leila Koeber; 1871–1934) US star of vaudeville, best remembered for the song 'Heaven Will Protect the Working Girl' from the musical *Tilly's Nightmare* (1894). In 1914 she left the theatre to work in films.

dress rehearsal A rehearsal at which members of the cast appear in full costume and make-up as though for an actual performance; it is usually the final rehearsal before the opening night.

Drew, Mrs John (Louisa Lane; 1820–97) US actress and manager, born in London into an acting family, who was taken to the US by her mother and made her debut as the Duke of York in *Richard III* at the Walnut Street Theatre, Philadelphia, in 1827. Subsequently she appeared throughout the US alongside such notable actors as the elder Edwin Booth, Joseph Jefferson, and Edwin Forrest in such roles as Lady Macbeth. Her most celebrated role was Mrs Malaprop in Sheridan's *The Rivals* in which part she frequently toured, but her chief claim to fame was her forceful management of Philadelphia's Arch Street Theatre from 1869 to 1892, during which time she produced a consistently high standard of classic and contemporary drama.

Her son, **John Drew** (1853–1927), took to the stage, somewhat reluctantly, at his mother's theatre in Philadelphia in 1873. Invited to New York by Augustin Daly, he made his debut in 1875 and subsequently became well-known as a comedian and was referred to as 'the first gentleman of the stage'. He appeared several times in London and was much admired as Petruchio in *The Taming of the Shrew*. Later he worked for Charles Frohman, his parts including the title role in Maugham's *Jack Straw* (1908) and Major Arthur Pendennis in a version of Thackeray's novel (1916).

Mrs John Drew's daughter, **Georgiana (Emma) Drew** (1856–92), made her debut at her mother's Arch Street Theatre in 1872. She later joined Daly's company in New York, opening as Mary Standish in his play *Pique*. In 1876 she married fellow-actor Maurice BARRYMORE and became the mother of the three famous Barrymores – Ethel, John, and Lionel. She continued to act in Modjeska's and Charles Frohman's companies until her premature death.

Dr Faustus, The Tragical History of A tragedy in blank verse by Christopher MARLOWE. First performance: London, c. 1588. Based upon the German Faust legend, the play focuses on the aspiration and subsequent downfall of Dr Faustus, who sells his soul to the Devil in exchange for magical powers.

Drinkwater, John (1882–1937) British poet, playwright, actor, and manager, a founder member of the Birmingham Repertory Theatre. His early poetic dramas, of which the most successful was *X=O; a Night of the Trojan War* (1917), were followed by such plays as *Abraham Lincoln* (1919) and the comedy *Bird in Hand* (1927) as well as several historical dramas.

droll A short comic entertainment that developed in England during the Commonwealth, when more elaborate drama was difficult to present without attracting the hostile attention of the Puritan authorities. It often consisted of an extract from a longer play and usually included a dance; the most famous performer of drolls was Robert COX.

drop *See* cloth.

Drottningholm Theatre A theatre, now also run as a museum, in the royal palace near Stockholm, built in 1766. Originally used by a French company, it enjoyed a considerable reputation under Gustaf III from 1772 to 1792, when productions there were designed by Louis-Jean Desprey. It was little used in the 19th century and restored in 1921, since when it has been an occasional venue for opera. It contains well-preserved items of stage machinery and scenery.

drum-and-shaft system An arrangement of lines attached to a central drum above the stage, enabling several heavy pieces of scenery to be moved at the same time. Widely used in the Renaissance and Baroque theatre, the system was gradually superseded by machinery capable of moving items of scenery simultaneously but independently of each other.

Druriolanus, Augustus *See* Harris, Sir Augustus Glossop.

Drury Lane (Theatre Royal) The oldest and most famous of London's theatres. Opened in 1663, the theatre is (with Covent Garden) one of Britain's two PATENT THEATRES, having been granted its charter by Charles II in 1662. The original theatre was built by Thomas Killigrew and saw the first stage appearance of Nell Gwynn in 1665 before being burnt down seven years later. Rebuilt to a design by Sir Christopher Wren in 1674 and with John Dryden as resident playwright, the theatre was plagued by rifts in the management (notably during the tenure of Christopher Rich) but achieved stability in 1711 under the celebrated management of Colley Cibber, Thomas Doggett, and Robert Wilkes. David Garrick first appeared there in 1742 and took over in 1746. During the following 30 years he presided over many notable productions; in 1776 Sheridan succeeded him, beginning his term by staging the first production of *The School for Scandal*. Sarah Siddons became a firm favourite at Drury Lane, as did John Kemble, who first appeared there in *Hamlet* in 1789.

Rebuilt in 1791–94, burnt down in 1809, and again reopened in 1812, the theatre staged increasingly varied productions, from classic plays and melodrama to pantomime and concerts. Despite successful seasons by Edmund Kean (1814–20) and William Macready (1841–43), the theatre's fortunes declined until 1880 when the impresario Augustus Harris and his successor Arthur Collins revived interest with large-scale productions of opera and ballet and spectacular melodramas. Since the 1930s the theatre has been the venue for a number of successful musicals, notably Ivor Novello's *Glamorous Night* (1935) and *The Dancing Years* (1939), *Oklahoma!* (1947–51), *South Pacific* (1951–53), *The King and I* (1953–58), *My Fair Lady* (1958–63), *A Chorus Line* (1976–79), *42nd Street* (1984–88), and *Miss Saigon* (1989–99). *See also* ghosts.

Druten, John Van *See* Van Druten, John.

Dryden, John (1631–1700) English poet, critic, and playwright, the most important exponent of the English heroic drama. The author of nearly 30 plays in a variety of styles, he is remembered as a dramatist for the tragedy ALL FOR LOVE and for such elegant comedies as MARRIAGE À LA MODE; his critical writing on the theatre is also historically important. His heroic drama *Almanzor and Almahide* was satirized by Buckingham in *The Rehearsal*. Several of his works were successfully revived in the 20th century.

Principal dramatic works:
  The Wild Gallant: 1663.
  The Rival Ladies: 1664.
  The Indian Queen: 1664 (with Sir Robert Howard).
  The Indian Emperor: 1665.
  Secret Love; or, the Maiden Queen: 1667.
  Sir Martin Mar-All; or, the Feign'd Innocence: 1667.
  An Evening's Love; or, the Mock Astrologer: 1668.
  Tyrannic Love; or, the Royal Martyr: 1669.
  Almanzor and Almahide; or, the Conquest of Granada: 1670–71.
  Marriage à la Mode: 1671.
  The Assignation; or, Love in a Nunnery: 1672.

Amboyna; or, the Cruelties of the Dutch to the English Merchants: 1673.
AURENG-ZEBE: 1675.
All for Love; or, the World Well Lost: 1677.
Amphitryon: 1690.

Držić, Marin (1508–67) Croatian playwright, author of several pastorals and comedies written in the vernacular. Such comedies as *Uncle Maroje* (1550) were produced at Dubrovnik and have been revived in the 20th century.

Dubé, Marcel (1930–) French-Canadian playwright, whose most successful works include adaptations in French of major contemporary US dramas, notably the plays of Arthur Miller. His own plays range from *Le Bal triste* (1950), and *Zone* (1953), which were both influenced by socially-aware US drama, to the poetic *Florence* (1961), the musical comedy *Il est une saison* (1965), and the tragedy *Au Retour des oies blanches* (The White Geese; 1966), which is regarded as his finest work. He was closely associated for some years with the Théâtre du Nouveau Monde.

Dublin Roscius *See* Brooke, Gustavus Vaughan.

Dublin Theatre Festival A major theatre festival founded in Dublin in 1957. Taking place in October each year, the festival involves all of Dublin's theatres and includes a healthy fringe; notable productions have included plays by O'Casey, Synge, Wilde, Tennessee Williams, and Yeats. The festival of 1958 was cancelled due to the controversy over plans to present O'Casey's *The Drums of Father Ned*; in more recent years the emphasis has been upon new Irish drama.

Duchess of Malfi, The A tragedy in blank verse by John WEBSTER. First performance: London, c. 1619. The play explores the predicament of the widowed Duchess, who secretly marries her steward in defiance of her two brothers. The brothers arrange her imprisonment and sadistic murder at the hands of the malcontent Bosola, who then turns on his employers.

Duchess Theatre A Tudor Gothic style theatre in Catherine Street, off the Strand in London. It opened in 1929 under the joint management of Jack de Leon and his sister Delia; a year later theatre history was made here when the curtain was rung down before the close of the first performance of *The Intimate Revue* – the shortest run of any London production. J B Priestley became associated with the theatre in the 1930s with the presentation of such plays as *Eden End* (1934) and *Time and the Conways* (1937). In 1935 Emlyn Williams appeared in his own play *Night Must Fall*, which ran for over a year, while T S Eliot's *Murder in the Cathedral* received its first West End production at the Duchess in 1936. The outbreak of World War II interrupted the run of Emlyn Williams's *The Corn is Green*; the major success of the war years was Noël Coward's *Blithe Spirit* (1942), first produced at the Piccadilly Theatre. Later successes included plays by Rattigan, Agatha Christie, and William Douglas Home. The nude revue *Oh, Calcutta!* transferred from the Royalty Theatre in 1974 and ran until 1980. Marc Camoletti's comedy *Don't Dress for Dinner* ran from 1991 until 1997.

Ducis, Jean-François (1733–1816) French playwright, remembered for his adaptations of Shakespeare. Working from inferior translations, he restyled such plays as *Hamlet* (1769) and *Othello* (1792) to conform with the rules of classical tragedy and the tastes of his audience. Ducis's own tragedies, which include *Oedipe chez Admète* (1778) and *Abufar* (1795), are of little worth.

Duclos, Mlle (Marie-Anne de Châteauneuf; 1668–1748) French actress, who inherited many of the great tragic roles formerly played by Mlle Champmeslé at the Comédie-Française. Renowned for her tempestuous character, she made many enemies amongst the troupe, especially over her vindictive treatment of Adrienne Lecouvreur.

Du Croisy (Philibert Gassot; c. 1625–95) French actor, who began his career in the provinces before joining Molière's company at the Petit-Bourbon in 1659. A large man, he appeared in several of Molière's plays, notably as the first Tartuffe (originally called Panulph) in 1667.

Ducrow, Andrew (1793–1842) British equestrian performer, who was chief equestrian and rope dancer at ASTLEY'S AMPHITHEATRE. In 1823 he played in Planché's *Cortez* at Covent Garden; the following year he appeared at Drury Lane. He became joint owner of Astley's in 1825 and never recovered from its destruction in 1841.

Duel of Angels (*Pour Lucrèce*) Jean GIRAUDOUX's last play, written in 1944. First performance: Paris, 1953. The play was produced in London in 1958, in a translation by Christopher Fry; Vivien Leigh played Paola, who tricks the virtuous Lucille into believing that she has committed adultery, driving her ultimately to suicide.

Duenna, The A comedy by SHERIDAN, with songs by his father-in-law, Thomas Linley. First performance: Covent Garden, 1775. The play, which proved a huge success, revolves around the attempts of Donna Louisa to escape an undesired match.

Duff, Mrs (Mary Ann Dyke; 1794–1857) US actress, born in London, who began her career as a dancer in Dublin. In 1810, with her second husband – John Duff (1787–1831) – she went to Boston where they opened as Romeo and Juliet. In 1812 they went to Philadelphia where she also achieved some distinction, but never attracted the same popularity in New York when she made her debut there as Hermione in Philips's *The Distressed Mother* in 1823. She toured extensively after her husband's death, remarried twice, and appeared in New Orleans in 1836 in the title role of Rowe's *The Tragedy of Jane Shore* and as Portia in *The Merchant of Venice*.

Dufresne (Abraham-Alexis Quinault; 1693–1767) French actor, sometimes called **Defresne**, who was the most important member of a family of actors who appeared at the Comédie-Française. Dufresne joined the company in 1712 and excelled in heroic roles, eventually succeeding Beaubour in such roles in 1718. His most celebrated parts included the title role in *Oedipe* (1718) by Voltaire and the central character in *Le Glorieux* (1732) by Destouches.

His wife, **Mlle Deseine** (1705–67), was also a popular actress but retired in 1736 due to ill health.

Dufresne, Charles (c. 1611–c. 1684) French actor-manager, whose company – regarded as one of the best in France – combined with the Illustre-Théâtre of Molière in about 1644. Dufresne subsequently handed over the leadership of the amalgamated troupe to Molière but continued to appear as an actor until 1659.

Dufresny, Charles (1648–1724) French playwright, a great-grandson of Henri IV. Dufresny's first plays were produced by the Comédie-Italienne; his best comedies, however, were those written for the Comédie-Française in the early 18th century, notably *L'Esprit de contradiction* (1700), *Le Double Veuvage* (1702), and *La Coquette du village* (1715).

Dugazon (Jean-Baptiste-Henri Gourgaud; 1746–1509) French actor, who excelled in comic roles at the Comédie-Française, which he joined in 1771. One of the first members of the acting school that became the Conservatoire in 1793, he was particularly successful in the plays of Scarron.

Duke of York's House *See* Dorset Garden Theatre.

Duke of York's Theatre The first theatre to be built in St Martin's Lane, London. It opened in 1892 as the **Trafalgar Square Theatre**, the name being changed to the Duke of York's in 1895. From 1897 it came under the management of Charles Froham; Marie Tempest, Gerald Du Maurier, and Irene Vanbrugh all appeared here in the early 1900s. Frohman also presented several plays by J M Barrie, notably *The Admirable Crichton* (1902) and *Peter Pan*, which was staged every Christmas from 1904 to 1914. He was less successful in his attempt to introduce the repertory system to London in 1910; among the plays he staged that year were G B Shaw's *Misalliance*, John Galsworthy's *Justice*, Granville Barker's *The Madras House*, and a revival of Pinero's *Trelawny of the 'Wells'*. In 1916 Jean Webster's *Daddy Long-Legs* ran for 514 performances. Under Violet Melnotte's management (1923–28) there followed the successful revue (written mainly by Noël Coward) *London Calling*. Roland Pertwee's *Is Your Honeymoon Really Necessary?* (1944) provided the theatre with the longest run; later productions have included Frank Marcus's *The Killing of Sister George* (1965), Arthur Miller's *The Price* (1969), and Alan Ayckbourn's *How the Other Half Loves* (1988). The Duke of York's was purchased by Capital Radio in 1978 and reopened as a theatre in 1980. It played host to the Royal Court company from 1997 to 2000.

Dukes, Ashley (1885–1959) British playwright, theatre critic, and manager, who founded the Mercury Theatre in Notting Hill Gate, London, where he presented many important new British and foreign plays. He adapted many foreign works himself, notably Fernando de Rojas's *La Celestina* as *The Matchmaker's Arms* (1930), Sternheim's *Die Marquise von Arcis* as *The Mask of Virtue* (1935), and Machiavelli's *Mandragola* (1939); of his own plays the most successful was *The Man With a Load of Mischief* (1924). His wife was the ballet dancer Marie Rambert.

Duke's Theatre *See* Holborn Theatre Royal.

Dullin, Charles (1885–1949) French actor and producer, who founded a famous experimental company in 1919 and subsequently installed it at his own Théâtre de l'Atelier in Paris. He began his career under Copeau at the Vieux-Colombier and later won acclaim for his productions of both French classics and experimental dramas by such authors as Pirandello and Cocteau. He became a director at the Comédie-Française in 1936 and his pupils included Jean-Louis Barrault; as an actor he triumphed over his own physical deformity in such roles as Harpagon in Molière's *L'Avare*.

Dumas, Alexandre (Dumas *père*; 1802–70) French novelist and playwright, son of a Napoleonic general. Dumas made his name with *Henri III et sa cour* (1829), the first of a series of spectacular melodramas on historical and romantic themes, which included *Antony* (1831), *La Tour de Nesle* (1832), and *Kean, ou Désordre et génie* (1836). In retrospect, however, Dumas *père* is more widely admired for his novels, notably *Les Trois Mousquetaires* (The Three Musketeers; 1844) and *Le Comte de Monte Cristo* (The Count of Monte Cristo; 1844–45), both of which were adapted for the theatre.

His illegitimate son, **Alexandre Dumas** (Dumas *fils*; 1824–95) was also a playwright and novelist, best known for the play *La Dame aux camélias* (1852; translated as THE LADY OF THE CAMELLIAS or *Camille*). His subsequent plays were moralizing social dramas in which he preached against such evils as the destruction of marriage and family life by illicit liaisons and prostitution. *Le Fils naturel* (1858) and *Un père prodigue* (1859) are exposés of the shame and misery caused by the stigma of illegitimacy and give some insight into Dumas's attitude to his father.

Du Maurier, Sir Gerald (1873–1934) British actor-manager, son of the artist and writer George Du Maurier and father of the novelist Daphne du Maurier. After appearances with Tree's company he first came to public attention in 1902 in *The Admirable Crichton* at the Duke of York's Theatre and went on to appear in many of Barrie's other plays. He achieved lasting fame as Raffles, the gentleman cracksman, in 1906; in 1910 went into management with Frank Curzon at Wyndham's Theatre, specializing in light comedy. Subsequently he moved to the St James's Theatre where he played in *The Last of Mrs Cheyney* (1925).

dumb show *See* mime.

Dumb Waiter, The A one-act play by Harold PINTER. First performance: Hampstead Theatre Club, 1960. About two hired gangsters waiting for their orders to kill an as yet unknown victim, the play is a simple yet powerful study of a relationship under pressure, genuinely a comedy of menace.

Dumesnil, Mlle (Marie-Françoise Marchand; 1713–1803) French actress, who was highly regarded for her passionate performances in the tragedies of Corneille, Racine, and Voltaire. She joined the Comédie-Française in 1737; her greatest successes there included the title role in Voltaire's *Mérope* (1743). Late in life she published her memoirs in reply to criticisms by Mlle Clairon.

Dunlap, William (1766–1839) US playwright and manager, who was one of the first dominant figures to emerge in the early development of US theatre. He studied art in London and wrote his first play (in New York) in 1787; his second, *The Father; or, American Shandyism* (1789) established his reputation while the tragedy *Leicester* (1794) indicated his versatility. He became a manager of the American Company in 1796 and opened the Park Theatre – with Hodgkinson – in 1798, productions there including his *André*, which was the first US tragedy on strictly native themes. Disruption caused by yellow fever epidemics and financial pressures led to his bankruptcy in 1805, but he remained assistant manager at the Park Theatre until 1812; subsequently he organized a US tour by George Fredericke Cooke and wrote a *History of the American Theatre* (1832).

Dunlop, Frank (1927–) British director, who founded the Young Vic in 1970 and remained as its director and guiding light until 1974, when the company became wholly independent of the National Theatre. From 1984 until 1991 he was director of the Edinburgh Festival. Productions for which he won particular acclaim at the

Young Vic included Molière's *Scapino*, *The Comedy of Errors*, and *Joseph and his Amazing Technicolour Dreamcoat*. He also worked at the Nottingham Playhouse (1963–64), at the National Theatre, and with the Royal Shakespeare Company.

Dunnock, Mildred (1900–91) US actress, who studied with Lee Strasberg and Elia Kazan and mader her New York debut in 1932. She had her first big success in 1949 as Linda Loman in *Death of a Salesman*; subsequent roles included Gina in *The Wild Duck* (1951) and Big Mama in *Cat on a Hot Tin Roof* (1955), as well as parts in *The Milk Train Doesn't Stop Here Anymore* (1962) and *The Glass Menagerie* (1966). She worked at the Williamstown Festival and at the Long Wharf Theatre until 1975.

Dunsany, Edward John Moreton Drax Plunkett, Lord (1878–1957) Irish playwright. His first play, *The Glittering Gate* (1907), was written for the Abbey Theatre at the request of W B Yeats; several of his later plays were also staged there. His many other plays include *The Gods of the Mountain* (1911) and *If* (1921).

Dunville, Thomas Edward (1870–1924) British music hall comedian, who, after his London debut at Gatti's in 1890, became famous as an eccentric comedian. Sporting ludicrous clothes and clownish make-up, he sang such equally ludicrous songs as 'Dinky Doo'. Successful in variety and pantomime for 30 years, he drowned himself in a fit of depression after his popularity had waned.

duologue A short theatrical presentation or single scene in which only two actors deliver lines (although they may be supported by other silent performers). The form became popular in Germany during the late 18th century as part of triple bills and remains a common feature of modern drama.

Du Parc, Mlle (Marquise-Thérèse de Gorla; 1633–68) French actress, who appeared with Molière's troupe before transferring to the Hôtel de Bourgogne. There she excelled in the tragedies of Racine, notably as Andromaque (1667). She joined Molière's company in 1653 after marrying the comic actor René Berthelot (c. 1630–64), who – known as **Gros-René** due to his bulk – had been with Molière since 1648. She died in childbirth; scurrilous rumours had it that she was in fact poisoned by Racine, her lover.

Durang, Christopher (1949–) US playwright, who has established a strong reputation with his satirical and surrealistic comedies. His best-known works include *The Vietnamization of New Jersey* (1977), *Beyond Therapy* (1981), and *Laughing Wild* (1988). His *Sister Mary Ignatius Explains It All For You* (1979), in which four former students exact their revenge upon the dictatorial nun who taught them, created some controversy with its attack on the Catholic Church.

Durante, Jimmy (James Francis Durante; 1893–1980) US actor and singer, familiarly known as 'Schnozzle' or 'Schnozzola', who started as a honky-tonk pianist in 1910, eventually forming a crazy musical trio that appeared in musicals up to 1931. He continued on his own in such shows as *Strike Me Pink* (1933) and became increasingly famous in films and cabarets.

Duras, Marguerite (1914–96) French novelist, playwright, and screenwriter, who made her name with the film script for *Hiroshima mon amour* (1959). Born in Indochina, she moved to Paris in 1932. Her plays explore a variety of themes – solitude, futility, lack of communication, crime – and are generally associated with the Theatre of the Absurd. *Savannah Bay*, in which an ageing actress reflects upon her daughter's death by drowning, was written for Madeleine Renaud.

Principal dramatic works:

Le Square: 1956.

Les Viaducs de la Seine-et-Oise: 1960; translated as *The Viaduct*.

Les Eaux et les forêts: 1965.

Des Journées entières dans les arbres: 1965; translated as *Days in the Trees*.

L'Amante anglaise: 1968; translated as *A Place Without Doors* (or *The Lovers of Viorne*).

India Song: never performed (written 1973).

L'Eden Cinéma: 1977.

Savannah Bay: 1984.

D'Urfey, Thomas (1653–1723) English playwright, who wrote numerous songs, satires, melodramas, and farces; many of his dramatic works were adaptations of earlier pieces. He was prosecuted for profanity in 1698.

Dürrenmatt, Friedrich (1921–90) Swiss playwright and novelist, who is regarded, as one of the most important post-war German-language dramatists. His satirical and often experimental black comedies, noted for their grotesque humour and rapid changes of mood, ridicule hypocrisy, greed, and the inhumanity of post-war bourgeois society. The deliberate formlessness of several of his absurdist dramas, which he justified in his essay *Theaterprobleme* (1955), reflected his concern with the breakdown of moral values and social responsibility. His most successful plays include *The Visit* (1956), a black comedy that deals with an old woman's revenge against the money-worshipping villagers of her native town, and *The Physicists* (1962) – a bitter tragicomedy which tackles the theme of the abuse of power. He also wrote numerous radio plays, published in the collection *Gesammelte Hörspiele* in 1961, and adapted plays by Strindberg and Shakespeare.

Principal works:

Es steht geschrieben : 1946.

Der Blinde: 1948.

Romulus der Grosse: 1949.

Die Ehe des Herrn Mississippi: 1952; translated as *Mr Mississippi's Marriage*.

Ein Engel kommt nach Babylon: 1953.

Der Besuch der alten Dame: 1956; translated as *The Visit*.

Die Oper einer Privatbank: 1960.

Die Physiker: 1962; translated as *The Physicists*.

Der Meteor: 1966; translated as *The Meteor*.

Porträt eines Planeten: 1971.

Du Ryer, Pierre (c. 1605–58) French playwright, born in Paris. Du Ryer's early dramatic works consisted largely of tragicomedies and comedies, notably *Les Vendanges de Suresne* (1633); he subsequently wrote tragedies on biblical and classical themes, influenced by Pierre Corneille. *Scévole* (1644), set in ancient Rome, is generally considered to be his masterpiece.

Duse, Eleonora (1859–1924) Italian actress, who was regarded by G B Shaw and others as superior even to Sarah Bernhardt as a performer of tragedy. Unlike her rival,

Duse was capable of great subtlety in her acting, and was ideal as the intense and enigmatic heroines of Ibsen, notably Ellida in *The Lady from the Sea*, Rebecca West in *Rosmersholm*, and Hedda Gabler. She established her reputation in Italy in 1878 with her interpretation of Zola's *Thérèse Raquin* and later toured France and South America and subsequently the world with her own company. In 1894 she fell in love with the poet Gabriele D'Annunzio, who wrote several plays for her, including *La Gioconda* (1898), *La Città morta* (1898), and *Francesca da Rimini* (1902). Other major successes included passionate performances in the plays of Sardou and Dumas *fils*. Internationally acclaimed, she died after coming out of retirement to tour the US.

Dust Hole *See* Scala Theatre.

Dutch Courtesan, The A comedy by John MARSTON. First performance: London, c. 1605. Through the relationship of the earnest Freewell and the cynical Malheureux, both of whom become involved with Franchesina, the courtesan of the title, Marston examines the conflict between reason and desire typical of the Renaissance man.

Dybwad, Johanne (1867–1960) Norwegian actress, who became famous for her interpretation of roles in the plays of Ibsen. The leading actress with the Nationaltheatret from 1899, she toured widely in such parts as Nora in *A Doll's House* and Rebecca West in *Rosmersholm*.

Eagle Theatre *See* Standard Theatre.

Earl Carroll Theatre A theatre on 50th Street and 7th Avenue, New York, which was the home of Earl Carroll's *Vanities* in the 1920s. Another theatre of the same name opened on the site in 1931. Seating 3000, it closed due to financial difficulties during the Depression, reopening briefly in 1932 as the Casino and in 1938 as the Casa Mañana. It was closed and partially demolished in 1939 and completely demolished in 1990.

Earth Spirit (*Erdgeist*) A play by Frank WEDEKIND, written in 1893. First performance: 1902. Taking as its main theme the dangers of repressed sexuality, the play introduces the beautiful and sensual Lulu, who eventually turns to prostitution; her story was continued in PANDORA'S BOX.

Easmon, Raymond Sarif (c. 1930–) African playwright, who became a dominant figure in the theatre of Sierra Leone. Such anticolonial satires as *Dear Parent and Ogre* (1964) have enjoyed enormous popularity throughout Africa.

East, John Marlborough (1860–1924) British actor, manager, and director. After working as an actor he became manager of the Lyric Theatre in Hammersmith in 1892. His productions there of pantomime and melodrama, in which he often appeared himself, established a strong local following; he later worked on productions at the Britannia in Hoxton and at Crystal Palace.

East London Theatre *See* Royalty Theatre.

East Lynne Any of several plays adapted from the 1861 novel by Mrs Henry Wood. The plot concerns the sufferings and eventual redemption of Isabel, a good woman who makes one mistake. The story's extreme emotionalism made it popular in its time, especially in the US. Today it is seen as the epitome of melodramatic excess.

East 74th Street Theatre *See* Phoenix Theatre.

Eastside Playhouse *See* Phoenix Theatre.

Eberle, Oskar (1902–56) Swiss director, who became famous for his revivals of liturgical drama and other theatrical works of the 16th century. His greatest successes included Calderón's *El gran teatro del mundo* in Einsiedeln and the Lausanne Passion Play as well as his close involvement with various leading drama festivals.

ecclesiastical drama *See* liturgical drama.

Echegaray, José (1832–1916) Spanish playwright, who received a Nobel Prize in 1905. Such plays as *El locos dios* (The Divine Madman; 1900) and *El gran Galeoto* (1881) employ verse forms to great effect and treat such controversial themes as social tensions and inherited disease.

Eckenberg, Johann Carl (1685–1748) German actor, who was also a talented acrobat and juggler. He was the leader of a company of actors with similar skills and presented entertainments of the most varied kind throughout Europe, offering a popular alternative to the classical repertory of Caroline Neuber and others.

Eddington, Paul (1927–95) British actor, who made his London debut in *The Tenth Man* (1961) at the Comedy Theatre. He was associated for many years with the Bristol Old Vic company as actor and director, his numerous roles including Palmer Anderson in Iris Murdoch and J B Priestley's *A Severed Head*, which he also played in London and New York. In addition to much television work, he appeared regularly in the West End in such plays as Frayn's *Noises Off* (1982) and Rattigan's *The Browning Version* (1988).

Eden Theatre *See* Phoenix Theatre.

Edgar, David (1948–) British playwright, who began with such topical works as *Dick Deterred* (1973), based on the career of Richard Nixon. His works of the mid-1970s and 1980s, which were mainly political in inspiration, included the highly acclaimed *Destiny* (1976), an attack on racism in British culture, *Wreckers* (1977), *Maydays* (1983), an epic exploring the changes in British society over 30 years, the community play *Entertaining Strangers* (1985), and *That Summer* (1987). More recently he has written *The Shape of the Table* (1990), *Pentecost* (1994), and *Albert Speer* (1999), a powerful work about Hitler's architect. He also achieved a huge popular and critical success with his adaptation (1980) of *Nicholas Nickleby* for the Royal Shakespeare Company.

Edinburgh Civic Theatre Company *See* Lyceum Theatre.

Edinburgh Festival A leading international festival of music and drama that takes place annually in Edinburgh, for three weeks during August and September. Founded in 1947, the festival includes a wide variety of productions by British and foreign companies, including the Royal Shakespeare Company. T S Eliot's *The Cocktail Party* and *The Confidential Clerk*, Thornton Wilder's *The Matchmaker*, Ray Lawler's *The Unshaven Cheek*, and Tom Stoppard's *Rosencranz and Guildenstein are Dead* all had their first performances at the Edinburgh Festival. Since the 1950s an unofficial Fringe has developed, featuring miscellaneous and often bizarre theatrical works by both professional and amateur groups.

Edison Theatre A 499-seat theatre on West 47th Street, New York, which opened in 1970 with the musical *Show Me Where the Good Times Are*. The theatre has also housed such contemporary productions as Kurt Vonnegut's *Happy Birthday, Wanda June* (1970) and the revue *Oh, Calcutta!* (1976). It is currently a nightclub connected with the adjoining Edison Hotel.

Edouin, Willie (William Frederick Bryer; 1846–1909) British actor, who began as a child-actor in pantomime. As an adult, his greatest success was in burlesque, in which he appeared in both Britain and the US. He was also manager of the Strand Theatre for some time.

Edward II A history play by Christopher MARLOWE. First performance: London, 1593. The play explores the relationship between the weak king and his favourite, Gaveston, and culminates in the former's violent death; it was a major influence upon Shakespeare's *Richard II*.

Edwardes, George (1852–1915) British theatre manager, of Irish parentage, who worked at the Gaiety Theatre, Dublin, before transferring to the Savoy Theatre in 1881. Having gone into partnership with Hollingshead at the old GAIETY THEATRE in London in 1885, he became sole manager a year later and began a series of musical comedies featuring a handpicked chorus of 'Gaiety Girls'. He opened Daly's Theatre in 1893 and a new Gaiety Theatre in 1903.

Edwards, Hilton (1903–82) British actor and director, noted for his performances in the plays of Shakespeare. After numerous appearances at the Old Vic, he founded the Gate Theatre in Dublin with Micheál MacLiammóir in 1927, directing many plays there and at the Gaiety Theatre himself. He presented *Hamlet* at Elsinore in 1937 and subsequently toured widely with the Gate Theatre company.

Edwards, Richard (c. 1523–66) English playwright and poet. His tragicomedy of devoted friendship, *Damon and Pithias*, was performed before Elizabeth I by the Children of the Chapel Royal, of which he was Master, probably at Christmas 1565. His other plays include *Palamon and Arcite* (1566).

Edwin, John (1749–90) British actor, who succeeded to the comedy parts formerly played by Ned Shuter at Covent Garden and excelled in the comic light operas and burlesques of O'Keeffe. Although a heavy drinker, he was also acclaimed in a number of Shakespearean character roles.

His son, **John Edwin** (1768–1803), was also an actor, who appeared with his father at the Haymarket and later organized productions for the Earl of Barrymore's private theatre. His wife was the actress **Elizabeth Rebecca Richards** (c. 1771–1854), who appeared at Drury Lane.

eidophusikon A dioramic display presented by Philip James de Loutherbourg in London in 1781. With a stage just six feet wide, it was used for the demonstration of various atmospheric lighting effects, chiefly those produced by transparencies, and foreshadowed the interest of designers in lighting during the 19th century.

Eisenhower Theatre *See* Kennedy Center.

Ek, Anders (1916–79) Swedish actor, noted for his strong performances in both classical and modern works. He began his career in Gothenburg after World War II and later appeared with the Kungliga Dramatiska Teatern and in Stockholm, excelling in plays by authors as diverse as Shakespeare, Strindberg, and O'Neill. He was often directed both on stage and on the screen by Ingmar Bergman.

Ekhof, Konrad (1720–78) German actor and director, who played a crucial role in the foundation of a German theatrical tradition. In 1739 he joined Schönemann's company and over the next 17 years evolved a new naturalistic style of acting, appearing in leading roles in German adaptations of French plays. In 1753 he established an Academy of Acting; after it closed he remained with Schönemann's troupe for a time before spending five years with Ackermann's company and then touring with Abel Seyler and becoming a friend of Goethe at Weimar. Subsequently he took over the theatre at Gotha, inviting Iffland to join his company and making his final appearance as the Ghost in *Hamlet*. His greatest acting successes included roles in the domestic dramas of Lillo, Lessing, Diderot, and Edward Moore.

ekklykema An item of stage machinery used in the ancient Greek theatre. It consisted of some type of wheeled platform, upon which actors could be brought on stage.

Ekman, Gösta (1890–1938) Swedish actor, director, and manager, who was noted for his idiosyncratic interpretation of major tragic roles in the plays of Ibsen, Shakespeare, and Shaw. He ran the Svenska Teater in Stockholm from 1913 until it was burnt down in 1925, after which he moved to the Oscarsteater and the Vasateater with equal success.

Electra There are several plays with this title, the earliest being versions by SOPHOCLES (c. 415 BC) and EURIPIDES (c. 413 BC); the story of Electra's desire for revenge on her mother for the killing of her father, and its eventual attainment through the return of her lost brother Orestes, is also treated in the middle section of Aeschylus' *Oresteia* (458 BC). A comparison of these plays shows how freely myth could be treated in Greek tragedy to support individual views of life. There are famous later treatments of the same material by many others, including Hofmannsthal (1903), O'Neill (1931), and Giraudoux (1937).

Elen, Gus (Ernest Augustus Elen; 1862–1940) British music hall singer, who achieved fame as a cockney comedian at the Middlesex Music Hall in 1891. His popular sentimental songs included 'If It Wasn't For the 'Ouses In Between' and 'It's A Great Big Shame'.

Elephant and Castle Theatre A theatre built on the site of the NEWINGTON BUTTS THEATRE in Newington, London in 1872. It was used primarily for pantomime and melodrama before eventually becoming a cinema.

elevator *See* bridge.

Eliot, T(homas) S(tearns) (1888–1965) Anglo-American poet, playwright, and critic, who wrote several successful poetic dramas. His first major play, often considered his best, was MURDER IN THE CATHEDRAL, which reveals the influence of the medieval *Everyman* as well as that of Greek tragedy and church ritual. In his subsequent plays he moved closer to the language and settings of contemporary West End drama, THE COCKTAIL PARTY in particular being commercially successful. His last plays now seem failures and are very rarely revived. He won a Nobel Prize in 1948. The light verse in his *Old Possum's Book of Practical Cats* (1939) formed the basis for the hugely successful musical CATS (1981).

Principal dramatic works:
  Murder in the Cathedral: 1935.
  THE FAMILY REUNION: 1939.
  The Cocktail Party: 1949.
  The Confidential Clerk: 1953.
  The Elder Statesman: 1958.

Elizabethan drama English drama from the reign of Elizabeth I (1558–1603). The Elizabethan age saw a great flowering in the English theatre, culminating in the works of William SHAKESPEARE. As the effects of the Renaissance made themselves felt, English playwrights absorbed the influence of the classical world. The plays of Seneca (translated between 1559 and 1581) and others had a profound influence on such writers as Shakespeare, John Lyly, Christopher Marlowe, Robert Greene, Thomas Kyd, and George Peele, although all of them were prepared to reject classical models for the sake of theatricality.

The first classically based English comedy, *Ralph Roister Doister*, was written in 1552 and the first true English tragedy, *Gorbuduc*, in 1562; other forms of drama that developed significantly during the period included REVENGE TRAGEDY. In the early years of Elizabeth's reign, during which the mystery play and other types of religious theatre were curtailed, drama was largely confined to the royal court (*see* masque) and private venues, including inn courtyards. In 1576, however, James Burbage opened the Theatre, which was the first permanent public theatre in England; it was soon followed by the Curtain Theatre (1577), the Rose Theatre (1587), the Swan Theatre (1594), and, ultimately, the Globe Theatre (1599), where so many of Shakespeare's plays were first performed.

In response to the new popularity of the theatre, and with the support of influential patrons, the number of acting companies also increased dramatically during this period; among them were such celebrated groups as the rival Chamberlain's Men and Admiral's Men, and various BOY COMPANIES. As well as the Burbages, actors with these companies (who often acquired a personal financial interest in the theatres in which they appeared) included Edward Alleyn, William Kempe, and the young Ben Jonson, who was destined to become the dominant figure of JACOBEAN DRAMA. *See also* Renaissance drama.

Elizabethan Stage Society A British theatre organization established by William Poel in 1894 to specialize in production of plays from the Elizabethan period. The group revived the techniques and scenery of the theatre of Shakespeare's day: its productions of such works as *Twelfth Night* (1895), *Everyman*, and *Romeo and Juliet* (1905) – although not profitable – proved highly influential.

Elizabethan Theatre Trust, Australian A theatre organization founded in Australia in 1955 and named in honour of a visit by Elizabeth II in 1954. Based in the Majestic Theatre in Melbourne under Hugh Hunt, it promoted national tours by professional companies and encouraged new Australian writing as well as running a successful company, which included such stars as Judith Anderson. The company was eventually disbanded and the trust's work taken over by the Australian Council.

Elliott, Denholm (1922–92) British actor, who made his West End debut in Chetham-Strode's *The Guinea Pig* (1945) and then won an award for his performance in Fry's *Venus Observed* (1950). The same year he appeared on Broadway in Anouilh's *Ring Round the Moon*, after which he featured in a number of successful London productions and seasons at Stratford-on-Avon as well as in the US. In 1949 he began a highly successful film career. His last appearance on stage was in Mamet's *A Life in the Theatre* (1989).

Elliott, G(eorge) H(enry) (1884–1962) British music hall singer, billed as the 'Chocolate Coloured Coon'. Originally a minstrel singer, he became the leading singer of 'coon' songs in the style of Eugene Stratton, reviving many of his successes.

Elliott, Maxine (Jessie Dermot; 1868–1940) US actress, noted for her looks and stage presence, who first appeared in H A Jones's *The Middleman* in New York in 1890. She teamed up with the comedian Nat Goodwin, whom she later married, in 1895, and appeared with him in such parts as Lydia Languish in Sheridan's *The Rivals* (1897) and Mrs Weston in Clyde Fitch's *The Cowboy and the Lady* (1899). After divorce she opened her own theatre in 1908, retiring in 1911 but making a successful comeback in the 1920s.

Her sister, **Gertrude Elliott** (1874–1950), also attracted praise in the plays of Clyde Fitch and later worked under Forbes-Robertson, marrying him in 1900. Their daughter was the actress Jean FORBES-ROBERTSON.

Elliott, Michael (1931–84) British director, who began his professional career with an acclaimed production of *Brand* for the 59 Theatre Company at the Lyric Theatre, Hammersmith, in 1959. Seasons followed at Nottingham, Glasgow, Stratford, the Old Vic, and the National Theatre before, in 1968, he founded the 69 Theatre Company in Manchester, which in 1976 became the ROYAL EXCHANGE THEATRE Company. His sensitive productions of Ibsen and Shakespeare gained him an international reputation.

Elliston, Robert William (1774–1831) British actor-manager, who made his London debut in 1796 under George Colman the Younger. Widely admired in the great tragic roles, he also appeared in works by Sheridan, O'Keeffe, and others. In 1819, having held the lease of the Surrey Theatre for several years, he took over Drury Lane. There, known as The Great Lessee, he engaged such popular actors as Kean, Vestris, and Macready. Within seven years, however, he was bankrupt and had to return to the Surrey Theatre.

Elsinore Shakespeare Festival A festival of Shakespearean drama, devoted exclusively to productions of *Hamlet*, that takes place annually at Kronberg Castle, Elsinore, in Denmark. The traditional location for the story of Hamlet, Elsinore has seen visits by many leading foreign companies, including the Old Vic company at the first festival in 1937 and the Prospect Theatre company in 1978.

Eltinge, Julian (William Dalton; 1883–1941) US actor, who became famous for his impersonation of glamorous young women. After his debut in such a role in the musical *Mr Wix of Wickham* (1905), he toured with a minstrel show for two years, and then, for the next four years, played Hal Brooke, a character who disguises as a woman, in the musical comedy *The Fascinating Widow* (1911). He went on to appear in the musicals *The Crinoline Girl* (1914) and *Cousin Lucy* (1915) and to star in vaudeville throughout the 1920s.

Eltinge Theatre *See* Empire Theatre.

Elton, Ben (1959–) British comedian, scriptwriter, playwright, and novelist. After studying drama at Manchester University, Elton emerged as a stand-up comic and television scriptwriter in the mid-1980s. His first West End play, the environmentalist satire *Gasping*, was staged successfully in 1990. Subsequent work for the stage has included *Popcorn* (1996) and *Blast from the Past* (1998). He also wrote book and lyrics for the Lloyd Webber musical *The Beautiful Game* (2000).

Embassy Theatre A theatre in Hampstead, London, opened in 1928. Several new plays, including *The Dominant Sex* (1934) by Michael Egan, transferred successfully from here to the West End. It survived damage in World War II and was run for a time by Anthony Hawtrey before being taken over by the Central School of Speech and Drama in 1957.

Emery, John (1777–1822) British actor, born into a theatrical family in Sunderland. He established his reputation at an early age and in 1798 joined the company at Covent Garden. He excelled in the portrayal of comic rustics in Shakespeare, although Tyke in Thomas Morton's *School of Reform* was his most famous role.

His son, **Samuel Anderson Emery** (1817–81), was also an actor. After provincial tours, he won much acclaim for his portrayals of Dickensian characters at the Lyceum. He continued to play in London for upwards of 30 years, performing numerous parts associated with his father.

Sam's daughter, **(Isabel) Winifred Maud Emery** (1862–1924), began her acting career at the age of eight and made her adult debut in London at the Imperial Theatre in 1879. She later went with Henry Irving to the US and established herself in a number of Shakespearean roles. In 1888 she married Cyril MAUDE and appeared under his management at the Haymarket in a variety of parts.

Emmet, Alfred *See* Questors Theatre.

Emney, Fred (1900–80) British comedian, son of the music hall star **Fred Emney** (1865–1917). He first appeared on stage in Edward Sheldon's *Romance* (1915), then toured the US in vaudeville for more than 10 years, returning to England to become a major personality in revues and musical comedies. He also appeared in such legitimate comedies as Pinero's *The Schoolmistress* (1950) and Priestley's *When We Are Married* (1970).

Emperor Jones, The An early play by Eugene O'NEILL. First performance: 1920. The play depicts a Black emperor regressing to his aboriginal roots after he sees how he has oppressed and exploited his own people. Paul Robeson won great acclaim in the title role.

Empire A theatre in Leicester Square, London, opened in 1884. After being used as a venue for various light satirical entertainments, it became a popular music hall in 1887 under George Edwardes and Augustus Harris. Audiences flocked to the Empire both for its magnificent ballets and its promenade, which was a haunt of prostitutes. After World War I it became a home of revues and musical comedies, of which those by George Gershwin were the most significant. In 1927 the building was demolished; a cinema now occupies the site. *See also* Grand Theatre.

Empire Theatre A theatre in Liverpool, opened in 1866 as the New Prince of Wales (later renamed the Alexandra). With its large auditorium, seating 2312, it has been a venue for all types of theatrical entertainment; it was much altered in 1979 when it was taken over by the local council.

The **Empire Theatre** on Broadway and 40th Street in New York opened in 1893 with Belasco's *The Girl I Left Behind Me*. Subsequently it was used by the companies of Charles Frohman, John Drew, and Maude Adams. Among the theatre's many successes were Barrie's *Peter Pan* (1905), Kester's *When Knighthood was in Flower* (1901), and Shaw's *Captain Brassbound's Conversion*, starring Ellen Terry. Julia Marlowe,

Ethel Barrymore, and Jane Cowl all won acclaim at the theatre before the controversy caused by Bourdet's *La Prisonnière* resulted in temporary closure in 1926. Katharine Cornell appeared there in 1928, 1931, and 1937, while Gielgud played Hamlet there in 1936. Crouse and Lindsay's *Life With Father* ran from 1939 to 1945; the theatre finally closed and was demolished in 1953.

The **Empire Theatre** on West 42nd Street, New York, opened in 1912 as the **Eltinge** (after Julian ELTINGE) with Jane Cowl in the melodrama *Within the Law*, her first starring role. Several successful productions followed and by 1930 it had become a celebrated venue for burlesque. With the city crackdown on Burlesque in 1942, it was converted into a cinema and renamed in 1954 after the previous Empire Theatre has been demolished. In 1998 the entire theatre was moved 50 m (168 ft) to the west and renovated as the entrance for a large cinema complex opened in 2000.

Encina, Juan del (1469–c. 1539) Spanish playwright, poet, and composer, who was the author of several influential pastorals, set to his own music. A priest, he worked as a dramatist at the court of the Duke of Alba from 1492, writing early examples of Spanish secular drama. Subsequently he travelled to Italy, where his play *Égloga de Plácida y Vitoriano* is known to have been performed in 1513.

Endgame (*Actes sans paroles*) A one-act play by Samuel BECKETT, written in French, 1954–56. First performance: Royal Court Theatre, London, 1957. The play is a bleak drama in which the two main characters – the blind Hamm and his servant Clov – eke out their remaining days in a decaying world, with Hamm's legless parents dying in nearby dustbins. The play's ironic humour gives it much of its humanity.

Enemy of the People, An (*En folkefiende*) A play by Henrik IBSEN. First performance: Oslo, 1882. The play centres on the predicament of Dr Stockmann, whose discovery of pollution in the waters of the spa town in which he lives brings only hostility from his fellow citizens. Stockmann is shown as arrogant and undiplomatic but right. Written in the wake of the hostility aroused by *Ghosts*, the play seems to reflect Ibsen's own feelings about the public's response to his work.

English Aristophanes *See* Foote, Samuel.

English Comedians Troupes of English actors who toured the German states during the late 16th and early 17th centuries, when the native drama was comparatively undeveloped. The first of these companies, all of which relied upon visual comedy or the services of an interpreter to communicate with their audiences, appeared in Holland and Denmark in the 1580s. The most famous of the early troupes was that led by Robert Browne, who began with Worcester's Men but left to produce plays in Leiden in 1591 and subsequently toured widely until 1619. Numerous other groups, presenting jigs, short comedies, and versions of works by Shakespeare, Kyd, and other contemporaries, followed – some establishing permanent bases in German theatres.

The most popular actors included Thomas Sackville, who led a company at Wolfenbüttel and was the creator of the comic character Jan Bouschet, and Robert Reynolds, upon whose character Pickelhering the German clowns Hanswurst and Thaddädl were later modelled. By 1630 the troupes were presenting an ever-increasing number of native German works and ultimately the tradition was absorbed into the indigenous theatre (*see Haupt- und Staatsaktionen*). The last reference to a troupe of English Comedians still touring was in 1659.

English Shakespeare Company A British touring company founded in 1986 by the director Michael BOGDANOV and the actor Michael PENNINGTON. The aim was to bring lively and accessible productions of Shakespeare to provincial audiences. The company's populist style and trademark use of modern dress and other deliberate anachronisms was seen in its cycle of history plays *The Wars of the Roses* (1987–89). Subsequent productions, many of which have toured internationally, include *Coriolanus* (1990) and *Timon of Athens* (1997).

English Stage Company A British theatre company founded by George Devine in 1955 to promote new and experimental drama. The company eventually made its permanent home at the Royal Court Theatre, becoming highly influential with premieres of works by Arden, Osborne (notably *Look Back in Anger* in 1956), Wesker, and others from the 1950s onwards.

Ennius, Quintus (239 BC–169 BC) Roman poet and playwright, who became the leading tragic writer after Andronicus and Naevius. Many of his 20 or so tragedies (of which only titles and fragments survive) were based on Euripides and were notable for their sympathy with the characters and their poetic language. Despite the fact that his highly rhetorical style was lampooned by Plautus and that he failed in his attempts to write comedy, he remained much admired after his death, his poetry creating for him a lasting reputation as the father of Roman literature.

ENSA *See* Entertainments National Service Association.

enter *See* stage direction.

Entertainer, The A play by John OSBORNE. First performance: Royal Court Theatre, 1957, with Laurence Olivier as Archie Rice. The decline of the music hall and the once-popular comic Archie Rice is presented as a metaphor for the decline of England. The action moves constantly between music hall and family scenes.

Entertaining Mr Sloane A comedy by Joe ORTON. First performance: London, 1964. With a plot featuring murder, blackmail, and various sexual perversions, the play is remarkable for Orton's use of bland, even elegant, language to express his incongruous subject matter. At the centre of the play is a young murderer who attempts to blackmail a woman and her brother but then finds himself under their control.

Entertainments National Service Association (ENSA) A British theatre organization established just before World War II to provide a variety of entertainments for troops and other war workers serving both at home and overseas. It was managed by Basil Dean from Drury Lane and operated on all the war fronts.

Enthoven, Gabrielle (1868–1950) British theatre historian, who donated her own huge collection of theatrical artefacts to the Victoria and Albert Museum in London in 1924. Herself an amateur actress and playwright, she administered the collection for many years and became the first president of the Society for Theatre Research.

entremé A brief entertainment presented during the course of a banquet in Spain. Originally a feature of Corpus Christi processions in Catalonia, it was later adapted for use during lengthy plays and often concluded in a dance. Writers of such pieces included Quiñones de Benavente, Lope de Vega, and Cervantes.

Epicharmos (C. 530 BC–C. 440 BC) Greek poet and playwright, who wrote important early examples of Old Comedy. Only titles and fragments of his comic plays, which tackled mythological themes and influenced Plautus, survive.

epic theatre A form of political theatre based on an appeal to the intellect rather than to the emotions, as developed in Germany during the late 1920s. As formulated by Brecht and Piscator, the theory of epic theatre derived ultimately from Aristotle; it advocated disregard for the unity of time and other structural conventions while emphasizing the need for political relevance. This tradition of political drama was continued by many playwrights of the 1970s and 1980s. *See also* alienation effect.

Epidaurus The earliest surviving example of an ancient Greek theatre, built during the 4th century BC. Designed by the architect Polycleitus, it seated 14 000 spectators and included a circular orchestra, a raised stage, and an elaborate *skene* building; the theatre, which has been much restored, is still in use.

epilogue A brief scene or speech given at the end of a performance, often encapsulating the underlying significance of what has preceded it.

Epiphany play *See* liturgical drama.

equestrian drama A form of theatre, popular in London in the early 18th century, in which spectacular displays of horsemanship were an integral feature of a production. The most important venues included Astley's Amphitheatre, Covent Garden, and Drury Lane; plays presented included equestrian versions of Shakespeare and *Mazeppa* (1823), which was based on a poem by Lord Byron. Leading performers of equestrian drama included Edward Alexander Gomersal and Andrew Ducrow.

Equity *See* American Actors' Equity Association; British Actors' Equity Association; Canadian Actors' Equity Association.

Equus A play by Peter SHAFFER. First performance: 1973. Revolving around a psychiatrist's exploration of the mental state of a stable-boy who has blinded a number of horses, the play was highly praised as a reflection upon the conflict between rationality and instinct. It was subsequently filmed with Richard Burton, Peter Firth, and Jenny Agutter.

Erckmann-Chatrian (Émile Erckmann; 1822–99 *and* Alexandre Chatrian; 1826–90) French writers, who collaborated on several popular novels and plays, set in Alsace, notably *Le Juif polonais* (1869; adapted as THE BELLS, 1871). Their association ended in litigation in 1889.

Erlanger's Theatre *See* St James Theatre.

Ernst, Paul (1866–1933) German playwright, critic, and prosewriter, best-known for his historical hero-tragedies modelled on Aristotelian ideals. His writing for the stage developed from such early naturalistic dramas as *Lumpenbagasch* (1898) to neoclassical tragedies, notably *Demetrios* (1905) and *Canossa* (1908), in which he extols a heroic conception of life. Other major works include *Manfred und Beatrice* (1912), *Preussengeist* (1914), and the comedy *Der heilige Crispin* (1910).

Ervine, St John Greer (1883–1971) Irish playwright, born in Belfast. As a young man he became acquainted with G B Shaw, whose biography he wrote (1956). In 1915 he was appointed manager at the Abbey Theatre for one disastrous season. His early plays, notably *Jane Clegg* (1913), discussed various social problems; later he wrote drawing-room comedies for the London stage.

Escamilla, Antonio de (Antonio de Vazquez; d. 1695) Spanish actor and manager, who led his own company and excelled in *Gracioso* parts. He specialized in the presentation of *zarzuelas* and in the plays of Calderón.

Esmond, Henry Vernon (Henry Vernon Jack; 1869–1922) British actor-manager and playwright. He began writing plays when he was in Alexander's company at the St James's Theatre, where he was admired in *The Second Mrs Tanqueray* (1893). With his wife, **Eva Moore** (1870–1955), he toured in many of his own plays, which included the sentimental comedy *Eliza Comes to Stay* (1913).

Espert I Romero, Núria (1936–) Spanish actress and director, who has appeared in many major Spanish works at the head of her own company, which she founded in 1959. Her most celebrated roles include Claire in Genet's *Les Bonnes* (1969) and the title role in García Lorca's *Yerma* (1971), under the direction of Victor García. In 1986 she won acclaim for her direction of García Lorca's *The House of Bernarda Alba* in London. She has also directed operas at Covent Garden and elsewhere.

Espy, L' *See* L'Espy.

Esslair, Ferdinand (1772–1840) German actor and manager, who took over the Court Theatre in Munich in 1820. He began his career in the provinces and later excelled in passionate roles in the plays of Schiller.

Estcourt, Richard (1668–1712) English actor, who began as a strolling player at Worcester. He reached Drury Lane in 1704 where Christopher Rich engaged him to play comedy roles. He was an incorrigible mimic and the friend of Addison, Steele, and other distinguished contemporaries.

Estébanez, Joaquín *See* Tamayo y Baus, Manuel.

Est Parisien, Théâtre de l' A theatre in Paris, formerly a cinema, which opened in 1963. It was founded as the home of the La Guilde company of Guy Rétoré, which established its reputation with a mixed programme during the 1950s and acquired a wide popular following. The theatre was given a state subsidy in 1964.

Ethel Barrymore Theatre A 1096-seat theatre on West 47th Street, New York, which was opened by Lee Shubert in 1928 with Ethel Barrymore (after whom it was named) in *The Kingdom of God* by Martínez Sierra. Notable productions that followed included Coward's *Design for Living* (1933), Elsie Schauffler's *Parnell* (1935), Emlyn Williams in his own play *Night Must Fall* (1936), and Clare Boothe's *The Women* (1936). Among its distinguished players have been Marlon Brando and Jessica Tandy in the prizewinning *A Streetcar Named Desire* by Tennessee Williams (1947), John Wood in Stoppard's *Travesties* (1975), and Alec McCowen in Christopher Hampton's *The Philanthropist* (1971). Other modern productions have included Peter Shaffer's double-bill *Black Comedy* and *White Lies* (1967), David Mamet's *American Buffalo* (1977), Bernard Slade's *Romantic Comedy* (1979), and Wendy Wasserstein's *The Sisters Rosensweig* (1992).

Etherege, Sir George (1634–91) English playwright, who wrote the first of the English comedies of manners. His first play, the verse drama *The Comical Revenge; or, Love in a Tub* (1664), contained a comic element that he went on to develop in the highly successful comedies SHE WOULD IF SHE COULD and THE MAN OF MODE, his finest play.

Ethiopian opera A feature of the MINSTREL SHOW, in which parodies of Shakespeare and opera were performed by actors in blackface make-up. Many of these burlesques were based on works by T D Rice.

Euclid-77th Street Theatre *See* Cleveland Play House.

Eugene O'Neill Theatre A 1075-seat theatre on West 49th Street, New York, which opened as the **Forrest Theatre** in 1925 and was home to the famous run (1934–41) of *Tobacco Road*. Known as the **Coronet Theatre** from 1945, it offered Arthur Miller's *All My Sons* in 1947 and was renamed after Eugene O'Neill in 1959, when his play *The Great God Brown* was seen there. More recent productions have included a number of plays by Neil Simon, who owned the theatre from the late 1960s until 1982, among them *The Prisoner of Second Avenue* (1971), *California Suite* (1976), *Chapter Two* (1979), and *I Ought To Be In Pictures* (1980). Notable shows since then have included the musical *Big River*, Henry Hwang's *M Butterfly*, and a long-running revival of *Grease*.

Eugene O'Neill Theatre Center An organization based at O'Neill's former estate in Waterford, Connecticut. It hosts the **National Playwrights Conference**, which has met here every summer since 1966 under the direction of Lloyd Richards, providing housing and support services for eight to 12 playwrights and professionally staged readings of their works-in-progress. The Center also holds conferences on criticism and puppetry as well as sponsoring a year-round outreach programme, the National Theatre Institute.

Euphorion (5th century BC) Greek playwright, the son of Aeschylus. Although none of his work survives, he is known to have defeated both Euripides and Sophocles in drama contests.

Eupolis (c. 446 BC–411 BC) Greek playwright, regarded as one of the masters of Old Comedy. His 18 plays, the first of which was produced in 424 BC, won several contests and were notorious for their frankness and satirical content. Many fragments, notably of *The Demes*, survive.

Euripides (484 BC–406 BC) Greek playwright, probably born at Salamis, who became the third major tragedian of the ancient Greek theatre, alongside Aeschylus and Sophocles. The author of possibly as many as 92 plays (of which 17 tragedies and one satyr-play survive), he suffered in his own lifetime from unpopularity with the audience in Athens; he was lampooned by Aristophanes and won only five contests at the Dionysia. This was probably on account of his individualistic stance on several topics, notably the role of women (the central characters in several of his plays) and the horror of war – an unpopular view at a time when Athens was in conflict with Sparta. These unorthodox opinions may have contributed to his departure from Athens as an old man.

The characters in his plays, which deal almost exclusively with mythological subjects, are depicted with greater realism than was attempted by his contemporaries;

in this respect he foreshadowed the tragedies of Seneca and the New Comedy of Menander. Using straightforward language, he tackled such themes as incest, revenge, madness, and repression. He was also responsible for such innovations as the PRO-LOGUE and the DEUS EX MACHINA and did much to broaden the range of tragedy, adding elements of sentimentalism, romance, and even comedy (notably in *Alcestis, Ion,* IPHIGENIA IN TAURIS, and *Helen*). THE BACCHAE, in particular, has been revived many times in the last hundred years on account of its psychological intensity.

Principal works:
  Alcestis: 438 BC.
  MEDEA: 431 BC.
  Hippolytus: 428 BC.
  Children of Heracles: c. 428 BC.
  Hecuba: c. 426 BC.
  THE TROJAN WOMEN: 415 BC.
  Iphigenia in Tauris: c. 414 BC.
  ELECTRA: 413 BC.
  Helen: 412 BC.
  Phoenician Women: 411 BC.
  Orestes: 408 BC.
  The Bacchae: date unknown.
  Ion: date unknown.
  Iphigenia in Aulis: date unknown.
  Madness of Heracles: date unknown.
  THE SUPPLIANT WOMEN: date unknown.

Euston Palace *See* Regent Theatre.

Euterpean Hall *See* Broadway Theatre.

Evans, Dame Edith (1888–1976) British actress, who began her career as Shakespeare's Cressida directed by William Poel for the Elizabethan Stage Society in 1912. Particularly admired in comedy, she became one of the most distinguished actresses of her time, playing many of the great Elizabethan and Restoration roles, including Millamant in Congreve's *The Way of the World* (1924 and 1927), Shakespeare's Cleopatra, Rosalind, and the Nurse (1926), and Mrs Sullen in Farquhar's *The Beaux' Stratagem* (1930). She also excelled in portrayals of such Shavian characters as Lady Utterword in *Heartbreak House* (1921) and Orinthia in *The Apple Cart* (1929).

At the New Theatre in 1935 she was again the Nurse in Gielgud's *Romeo and Juliet* and, in 1937, Rosalind in *As You Like It*. In 1939, again with Gielgud, she appeared in her most famous role, Lady Bracknell in *The Importance of Being Earnest*. In addition to classical parts, she starred in many modern plays by such authors as James Bridie, N C Hunter, and Enid Bagnold. In the 1959 Stratford-on-Avon season she was acclaimed as the Countess of Roussillon in *All's Well That Ends Well* and as Volumnia in *Coriolanus*. After being directed by Coward in his own play *Hay Fever* for the National Theatre Company in 1964, she tended to work more in films and television, but returned to the stage for a final appearance in *Edith Evans... and Friends* in 1974.

Evans, Maurice Hubert (1901–89) US actor and manager, born in Britain, who began his career in Cambridge and then joined the Old Vic company, playing

Shakespearean roles. He made his New York debut as Romeo in 1935 and toured widely in the so-called 'G. I. *Hamlet*', his own adaptation of Shakespeare's plays, during World War II. His other roles included John Tanner in his own production of *Man and Superman* (1947), Hjalman Ekdal in *The Wild Duck* (1951), and King Magnus in *The Apple Cart* (1956). Among his subsequent successes were the musical *Tenderloin* (1960) and *On Golden Pond* (1981), as well as several films.

Evans, Will (1875–1931) British music hall comedian, who made his stage debut at Drury Lane while still a child. He appeared in clown make-up and presented slapstick sketches and monologues, performing in every Drury Lane pantomime from 1911 to 1919. He was also part author of *Tons of Money*, the first of the famous Aldwych farces.

Evans's A SONG-AND-SUPPER ROOM in Covent Garden, London, established in the cellar of a hotel around 1820. It became famous under the management of the comic actor W C Evans, who presented such leading performers as Charles Sloman and Sam Cowell as well as early minstrel shows in the 1840s. In 1856 the building was enlarged and Evans's became a popular music hall before finally closing in 1880 as a result of the rivalry of other venues. The PLAYERS' CLUB took over the building in 1934.

Everyman An English morality play by an unknown author, probably based upon a Dutch original, *Elckerlyc* (c. 1495). First performance: c. 1500. The play depicts the desertion of the hero by all his friends except Good Deeds when death approaches. It was revived in 1901 by William Poel; Hugo von Hofmannsthal wrote a German version, *Jedermann*, in 1920.

Every Man in his Humour A comedy by Ben JONSON. First performance: London, 1598. First performed by the Chamberlain's Men, with Shakespeare in the cast, the play draws its comedy from the differing 'humours' or fixed personality traits of its characters; these include the jealous Kitely, the vainglorious Bobadil, and the blunt Downright. Jonson followed it with *Everyman Out of His Humour* (1599).

Everyman Theatre A theatre in Liverpool, opened by Terry HANDS and others in 1964. It quickly established a reputation as an important venue for the performance of new works, including plays by Bond and Pinter, as well as for entertainments with a local flavour, notably the musical *John, Paul, Ringo... and Bert* (1974) and other plays by Willy Russell, and dramas by Alan Bleasdale and John McGrath. The theatre was rebuilt in the 1970s and taken over by Ken Campbell, who presented influential experimental drama, in 1980. Owing to cuts in local-authority funding in 1995, the number of in-house productions has been much reduced in recent years.

Another **Everyman Theatre** opened in Hampstead, London, in 1920 and over the next six years prospered under Norman MACDERMOTT. Plays by Shaw were regularly performed there; other successes included works by Bjørnson, Coward, Ibsen, and Pirandello. After 1926 Raymond Massey managed the theatre for a time; it was converted into a cinema in 1947.

Evita A musical by Tim RICE and Andrew LLOYD WEBBER. First performance: London, 1978. Based on the career of the glamorous Eva Perón, who rose to become the wife of the leader of Argentina before her early death, the story is told mainly in flashbacks by the cynical Che Guevara. *Evita*'s enormous international success reinforced the West End's gathering reputation as a focus of the musical stage to rival Broadway.

Evreinov, Nikolai Nikolaivich (1879–1953) Russian playwright, who became a leading writer of Symbolist drama. He expressed his opposition to the naturalistic theories of Stanislavsky in the comic satires *Revisor* (1912) and *The Fourth Wall* (1915); other notable works included the monodrama *The Theatre of the Soul* (1912), in which he defined his own understanding of the theatre, and *The Chief Thing* (1921). His career was ended by the enforcement of Socialist Realism.

Ewald, Johannes (1743–81) Danish poet and playwright, whose historical drama *Rolf Krage* (1770), which was inspired by his reading of Shakespeare and Ossian, was the first true Danish tragedy. Of his other dramatic writings the operetta *Fiskerne* (The Fishermen; 1780) is the best known.

exit *See* stage direction.

Experimental Theatre *See* Daly's 63rd Street Theatre.

Expressionism A movement in the theatre and the arts in general that developed in Germany around 1910. Its exponents, who included Georg Kaiser and Ernst Toller, sought to probe the innermost thoughts and feelings of their central chacters, who were often depicted in anguished conflict with the world around them. What is seen on stage is generally a representation of the hero's inner life, rather than any outer reality, and frequently has a dreamlike or nightmarish aspect. Forerunners of the movement, which can be seen as a revolt against realism in the theatre, included Strindberg and Wedekind. After World War I the movement was enlivened by the support of the Dadaists, who emphasized the symbolic element in Expressionist drama while also adopting a more extreme philosophical stance. Eventually, during the 1920s, the movement succumbed to its own mannerisms, although its influence remained strong upon such writers as Brecht and O'Neill.

extravaganza A lavish theatrical entertainment popular in England in the 19th century. Combining music, satire, and elaborate costumes and sets, most extravaganzas were based on myths or folk-stories and resembled pantomime; leading writers of the genre included J R Planché and H J Byron.

Eyre, Sir Richard (1943–) British director, who succeeded Sir Peter Hall as director of the National Theatre (subsequently the Royal National Theatre) in 1988; he is noted especially for his productions of contemporary drama and musicals. Eyre first achieved national recognition while artistic director of the Nottingham Playhouse (1973–78). His hugely successful revival of *Guys and Dolls* (1982) is widely credited with rescuing the National Theatre from its financial difficulties. Subsequent productions at the National included an acclaimed series of plays by David Hare, including *Racing Demon* (1990) and *Amy's View* (1997), Tennessee Williams's *Sweet Bird of Youth* (1994), and Ibsen's *John Gabriel Borkman* (1996). He stepped down in 1997.

Eysoldt, Gertrud (1870–1955) German actress, who was much admired in the plays of Ibsen, Maeterlinck, Wedekind, and other modern authors. She began her career with the Meninger company in 1890; subsequently she acted under Reinhardt and performed in the controversial first production of Schnitzler's *Reigen* in Berlin (1921).

F

Fabbri, Diego (1911–80) Italian playwright, whose Roman Catholic upbringing is reflected in all his plays. *The Knot* (1935), his most famous play, incurred the disapproval of the Fascist authorities and was rewritten as *The Swamp* (1942). After World War II, however, Fabbri emerged as the leading Italian writer of poetic drama with such plays as *Inquisizione* (Inquisition; 1950), *Processo di famiglia* (Family Trial; 1955), and *Processo a Gesù* (The Trial of Jesus; 1955).

Fabre d'Églantine (Philippe-François-Nazaire Fabre; 1750–94) French playwright, actor, and poet, who played an important role in the French Revolution and died on the guillotine. He wrote satirical comedies inspired by contemporary politics, notably *Le Philinte de Molière ou la Suite du Misanthrope* (1790).

fabula The Latin term for a play. It was used of works of various different types, including those of the ATELLANA, PALLIATA, PRAETEXTA, RHINTHONICA, RICINIATA, SALTICA, TOGATA, and TRABEATA.

Fact, Theatre of *See* documentary theatre.

Fagan, James Bernard (1873–1933) Irish-born playwright, director, and actor, who began his stage career in Frank Benson's company in 1895. Later he became manager of the Royal Court Theatre and in 1923 the Oxford Playhouse. The productions staged there employed several young actors and actresses destined to become leading performers of their generation. He became director of the Festival Theatre in Cambridge in 1929. His own plays include *The Wheel* (1922), *And So to Bed* (1926), and *The Improper Duchess* (1931).

Faiko, Alexei Mikhailovich (1893–1978) Russian playwright, whose best-known play was *The Man with the Portfolio* (1928), which depicted the dilemma of a careerist academic who disapproves of the new Soviet government but keeps his opposition to himself. Other works included *Lake Lyul* (1923), which was produced by Meyerhold, and the comedy *Don't Set Yourself up as God!* (1957).

fair A public festivity, originally asociated with market trading, held at regular intervals in towns and villages throughout Europe since medieval times. The early fairs provided ample opportunities for the presentation of theatrical entertainments, which varied from solo performances by jugglers and acrobats to full-scale plays presented in a temporary theatre (*see* booth). Eventually some of these sites became the homes of permanent theatrical enterprises, notably in the case of the **Saint-Germain** and **Saint-Laurent fairgrounds** in Paris, and witnessed the emergence of many significant theatrical figures in the 17th and 18th centuries despite opposition from other established theatrical companies. In England such fairs as those held at Saint Bartholomew and Southwark in London included puppet shows, drolls, and performances of complete plays, while those held in Germany and elsewhere on the Continent provided venues for troupes of travelling English players (*see* English Comedians). Similar gatherings in Italy and Spain in particular also contributed to the development of the *commedia dell'arte*.

Fairbrother, Sydney (Sydney Parselle; 1872–1941) British actress, who made both her first (1889) and her last (1938) appearances at the Haymarket. She excelled as Wally in *Two Little Vagabonds* (1896) by G R Sims and Arthur Shirley, Proserpine in Shaw's *Candida* (1904), partnered the elder Fred Emney in a music hall sketch (1912–14), and played Mahbubah in Asche's *Chu Chin Chow* (1916–20). Latterly, she played numerous character parts.

Falckenberg, Otto (1873–1947) German director, who became famous for his work in contemporary drama at the Munich Kammerspiele (1915–44). Having first attracted attention with Strindberg's *Spöksonaten* in 1915, he subsequently won acclaim for his evocative production of plays by Barlach, Brecht, and Shakespeare among others.

Fallen Angels A comedy by Noël COWARD. First performance: London, 1925. It deals with two married women nervously awaiting the reappearance of their former lover, drinking heavily as they do so.

falling flap A hinged flat, formerly much used to execute rapid changes of scene. When the hinged section is released the flat presents an entirely different view.

false proscenium An arrangement of flats or cloths by means of which the opening of the proscenium arch is reduced in size. In the US the false proscenium is usually referred to as a **portal opening**.

Falsettos A musical by William Finn, with a book by Finn and James Lapine. First performance as a full-length work: New York, 1992 (several sections were performed earlier as one-act pieces). The play follows Marvin, a gay Jewish man, through relationships with both men and women, and explores homosexual life in the years before and during the AIDS epidemic.

Family Reunion, The A poetic drama by T S ELIOT. First performance: London, 1939. The play draws upon THE ORESTEIA of Aeschylus with its pursuing Furies, to explore the guilt of Harry Monchensey over the mysterious death of his wife. Although sometimes revived, it suffers from the uneasy combination of classical convention and contemporary subject matter.

fan effect *See* transformation scene.

Fanny's First Play A play by G B SHAW; his first commercial success. First performance: London, 1911. The plot concerns the son and daughter of two respectable families who, after serving a term in jail, marry totally unconventional spouses. As well as satirizing middle-class values the play also lampoons several contemporary drama critics.

Fantastics, The An off-Broadway musical by Harvey Schmidt, with words by Tom Jones. First performance: New York, 1960. Based on Rostand's *Les Romanesques*, the plot deals with two young lovers whose fathers pretend to be enemies to pique their children's interest in each other. It was still playing in 2000, being by far the longest-running show in US history.

farce A form of drama characterized by its broad humour and complicated plots. Farce relies heavily upon stereotypes and slapstick comedy and is in its modern form descended from the plays of such writers as Labiche, Feydeau, and Pinero, written in the 19th and early 20th centuries. In its ancient form it had its roots in satyr-plays and ritual celebrations and played an important role in the plays of Plautus, Terence, and others. It was also a characteristic feature of much medieval and religious drama and, through the *commedia dell'arte*, had an influence upon the plays of Molière and his contemporaries. Short farces were often performed during the 18th and 19th centuries as part of an evening's entertainment alongside full-length tragedies. The term is now mainly applied to the subgenre known as BEDROOM FARCE, which emerged in the early 20th century.

Farine, Jean (fl. 1600–35) French actor, who appeared at Paris fairgrounds before moving to the Hôtel de Bourgogne. Thought to have begun as a quack doctor, he was popular in improvised farces, appearing with Bruscambille.

Farjeon, Herbert (1887–1945) British critic, author, and revue librettist, whose *Nine Sheep* (1938) and *The Little Revue* (1939) were highly successful. He also collaborated with his sister Eleanor on such musical plays as *The Glass Slipper* (1944).

Farquhar, George (1678–1707) Anglo-Irish playwright and actor. Farquhar's friendship with Robert Wilks led to his first play, *Love and a Bottle*, being produced at Drury Lane in 1698; the following year, *The Constant Couple; or, a Trip to the Jubilee*, met with a brilliant reception, the hero (played by Wilks) later providing a famous breeches part for Peg Woffington. After its sequel, *Sir Harry Wildair* (1701), and several less successful works he went on to write THE RECRUITING OFFICER and THE BEAUX' STRATAGEM, which are considered among the finest of all Restoration comedies.

Principal works:
  Love and a Bottle: 1698.
  The Constant Couple; or, a Trip to the Jubilee: 1699.
  Sir Harry Wildair: 1701.
  The Inconstant; or, the Way to Win Him: 1702.
  The Twin Rivals: 1703.
  The Stage Coach: 1704.
  The Recruiting Officer: 1706.
  The Beaux' Stratagem: 1707.

Farr, Florence (1860–1917) British actress and director, who popularized the plays of Ibsen, Yeats, and Shaw on the London stage. She acted in *Widower's Houses* (1892), the first of Shaw's plays to be staged in London, and produced *The Land of Heart's Desire* (1894), the first of Yeats's plays to be given in the capital. Subsequently she collaborated with Granville-Barker on revivals of plays by Euripides before emigrating to Ceylon as a teacher.

Farren, Elizabeth (1759–1829) British actress, the daughter of strolling players. She played at Wakefield and Liverpool before her Haymarket debut as Kate Hardcastle in *She Stoops to Conquer* in 1777. She also appeared at Covent Garden and Drury Lane, becoming the natural successor to Mrs Abington. She married the Earl of Derby in 1797 and retired from the stage.

Farren, William (1725–95) British actor, who played important parts at Drury Lane and Covent Garden. He was the original Careless in *The School for Scandal* (1777) and Leicester in *The Critic* (1779). In 1784 he transferred to Covent Garden.

His son, **William Farren** (1786–1861), made his Covent Garden debut as Sir Peter Teazle in *The School for Scandal* in 1818 and was subsequently acclaimed in numerous Shakespearean parts. He suffered a stroke in 1843 but continued to act, becoming for a time manager of the Strand and Olympic theatres.

His grand-daughter, **Ellen Farren** (1848–1904), known as as Nellie, first appeared at the Olympic in 1864. For 30 years she was a leading star at the Gaiety Theatre, where she first appeared in 1868.

Fastnachtsspiel (*or* Carnival play) A form of German medieval drama that developed separately from the liturgical theatrical tradition during the 15th century. The plays, generally episodic ribald farces, were usually performed in the open air by amateur companies and combined elements of both the morality play and liturgical drama with some satirical comment. Writers of such Carnival plays included Hans Rosenplüt and Hans Sachs; the central comic character was that of the NARR.

fate drama *See Schicksaltragödie.*

Father, The (*Fadren*) A play by August STRINDBERG. First performance: 1887. The first of Strindberg's famous analyses of sexual conflict, the play depicts the descent of an army captain into madness at the hands of his merciless wife, Laura. The misogyny of the play reflects Strindberg's own unhappy marriage.

Faucit, Helen (1817–98) British actress, daughter of theatrical parents, who made her debut at Covent Garden in 1836 in *The Hunchback* by Sheridan Knowles. She remained at the theatre when Macready took over, then went with him to the Haymarket and Drury Lane. In 1838 she created Pauline in Bulwer-Lytton's *The Lady of Lyons*; she also excelled in Shakespeare.

Faust A verse play by GOETHE, written in two parts (1770–1808) and generally considered to be his masterpiece. First performance (of complete work): Weimar, 1876. Although the play draws upon Marlowe's celebrated version (*see Dr Faustus, The Tragical History of*), its theme is not the damnation of a soul so much as modern man's capacity for endless restless aspiration. Goethe's initial inspiration is said to have been a puppet-play that he saw as a young man. Owing to its vast length and philosophical complexity, the play is rarely staged in full.

Faust, Johann (c. 1480–1540) German conjuror, who became the central character of numerous plays and other theatrical entertainments following the publication of his biography in 1587. Marlowe's *The Tragical History of* DR FAUSTUS (c. 1589–92) combined Faust's life with the medieval legend of a man who sold his soul to the devil; subsequent dramatic versions included plays by Lessing, Goethe, Grabbe, and Stephen Phillips as well as a puppet drama and several operas.

Favart, Charles Simon (1710–92) French playwright, librettist, and director of the Opéra-Comique, Paris. He wrote various comic operas and sentimental or pastoral comedies, sometimes in collaboration with his wife, the actress Mlle CHANTILLY.

Favart, Théâtre *See* Comédie-Italienne.

Faversham, William (1868–1940) US actor, born in London, where he first appeared in John Oxenford's *Retained for the Defence* (1885). Stranded in New York after the failure of *Pen and Ink* (1887), he went on to enjoy a successful career, spending many years in Charles Frohman's company in parts ranging from Romeo to Algernon in Wilde's *The Importance of Being Earnest*. In management on his own he won particular acclaim in Stephen Phillips's *Herod* (1909), as Mark Antony in *Julius Caesar* (1912), and as Iago in *Othello* (1914).

Fay, Frank J (1870–1931) Irish actor, who – with his brother **William George Fay** (1872–1947) – worked tirelessly for the Irish National Theatre movement and assisted in the creation of the Abbey Theatre company in 1904. They were in most of the Abbey productions, including *The Playboy of the Western World* (in which William played Christy Mahon), until 1908, when they went to the US to stage a repertory of Irish plays. On returning, Frank became a speech teacher in Dublin, while William went on to direct plays at Nottingham (1920–21) and Birmingham (1925–27) and appeared in many London productions.

Feast of Fools A New Year's festivity common to many European churches and other religious establishments during medieval times. Possibly descended from ancient Roman traditions, the Feast of Fools emerged in France during the 12th century and conventionally included the performance of a dramatic entertainment. The festivity, which provided ample opportunity for feasting and merriment, was nominally under the control of an elected temporary king, or BOY BISHOP, chosen from the lower ranks of the clergy; the post eventually evolved into that of the Abbot of MISRULE. Due to the scandalous nature of the custom, it had generally died out in England by 1500 and in France by 1700.

Featherstonhaugh, Constance *See* Benson, Frank Robert.

Fechter, Charles Albert (1824–79) French actor, who became popular throughout Europe and the US as a performer of tragic and melodramatic roles, which he could deliver in both English and French. He first appeared at the Comédie-Française in 1840 but later toured extensively in works by Dumas *fils*, Hugo, and others. His passionate character made him a great success with audiences but caused offence with many fellow-actors. Later in his career he managed the Lyceum in London for a time and opened a theatre in his own name.

Fedeli An Italian *commedia dell'arte* company, founded by Giovann Andreini c. 1601. After acquiring actors from the Gelosi and Accesi, the company toured extensively before disbanding around 1650. Actors with the Fedeli included Tristano Martinelli.

Federal Theatre Project A nationwide theatre scheme, initiated in the US in 1935 as part of President Roosevelt's New Deal programme. Its purpose was to provide employment for out of work actors, directors, designers, stage hands, vaudeville artists, circus entertainers, and puppeteers, and at the same time to boost national morale. Under Hallie Flanagan, it quickly established itself as a pioneer of socially concerned theatre. Its most controversial productions were the LIVING NEWSPAPERS, but of equal interest were the plays for children, new dramas, revivals of the classics, large-scale pageants, tours, vaudeville entertainments, and special programmes for ethnic communities. Tickets were either free or very low-priced. The Project was abruptly closed down in 1939 following alleged communist infiltration.

Fehling, Jürgen (1885–1968) German director, who became a leading figure of the Realist tradition in the theatre of Berlin. Trained initially under Reinhardt, he took an Expressionist approach in his earlier work, presenting notable dramas by Brecht and Barlach among others at the Staadstheater (1922–32). Later, he revived the use of the box set and came to favour sparse scenic detail. His most famous productions included several plays by Shakespeare featuring such actors as Kortner, Krauss, and Gründgens.

female impersonator A male actor who performs female roles, in modern times usually for comic effect. The tradition has its roots in the Greek and Elizabethan theatre, in which boys or men performed all female roles (as was also the case in the Chinese and Japanese theatre). In the modern theatre female impersonators (or **drag artists**) conventionally appear as DAMES in pantomime and in their own speciality acts; leading contemporary exponents of such roles include Danny La Rue and Barry Humphries. *Compare* breeches part.

Fenton, Lavinia (1708–60) British actress, who made her debut at the Haymarket in 1726 in Otway's *The Orphan*, subsequently playing Cherry in *The Beaux' Stratagem*. In 1728, at the Lincoln's Inn Fields Theatre, she created Polly Peachum in *The Beggar's Opera*. In 1751 she married the Duke of Bolton.

Ferber, Edna *See* Kaufman, George S.

Fernández, Lucas (c. 1474–1542) Spanish playwright and musician, who wrote six plays notable for their simple comedy and use of music. Much influenced by the plays of his rival Encina, his works comprise three religious dramas, notably the *Auto de la Passíon*, and three secular comedies, which anticipated the development of the *zarzuela*.

Fernández de Moratín, Nicolás *See* Moratín, Nicolás Fernández de.

Ferrari, Paolo (1822–89) Italian playwright, who established his reputation with *Goldoni e le sue sedici commedie* (1853), which took Goldoni as its subject. His later works, in which he adopted conservative views on a number of social issues, included *Il duello* (1868), *Il suicido* (1875), and *La satira e Parini* (1865), based on the life of the poet Giuseppe Parini.

Ferreira, António (1528–69) Portuguese playwright and poet, author of the celebrated *Tragédia de Dona Inêz de Castro* (c. 1558), which inspired numerous imitations. His other works include the two comedies *O Gioso* and *Bristo*.

Ferrer, José (1912–92) US (Puerto Rican) actor, who made his debut in 1934 on a showboat on the Long Island Sound. He then joined Joshua Logan's Stock Company, making his New York debut in 1935. After success in Maxwell Anderson's *Key Largo* (1939) and Brandon Thomas's *Charley's Aunt* (1940), he played Iago to Paul Robeson's Othello (1943) to great acclaim; other roles included Cyrano de Bergerac, Volpone, and Richard III. From the 1950s onwards his work was mainly in film.

Festival Theatre *See* Cambridge Festival Theatre.

Feuchtwanger, Lion (1884–1958) German novelist and playwright, who is usually remembered for *Jew Süss* (1925), a historical drama derived from his own novel. He became associated with Expressionist circles in the 1920s and worked on several plays in collaboration with Brecht, notably *Eduard II* (1924), *Kalkutta* (1927), and *Die Gesichte der Simone Machard* (1942). Other important dramatic works include *Drei Angelsächsische Stücke* (Three Anglo-Saxon Plays; 1927).

Feuillère, Edwige (1907–98) French actress, who established her reputation at the Comédie-Française in the 1930s. Trained at the Conservatoire, she appeared initially in lightweight romantic roles but was recognized as a leading tragic actress with her performance in Becque's *La Parisienne* (1937) and subsequently Dumas *fils's La Dame aux camélias* (1940 and 1952). At the same time she began a distinguished career in French films. She went on to play in the premieres of Giraudoux's *Sodome et Gomorrhe* (1943), Cocteau's *L'Aigle à deux têtes* (1946), and Claudel's *Partage de midi* (1948), among other important works. Later successes included Arbuzov's *Old World* (1977).

Feydeau, Georges (1862–1921) French playwright, who began writing for the theatre in the 1880s and produced some 40 farces during his career. The plays owe their success to well-structured plots, witty dialogue, improbable situations, and the skilful manipulation of traditional comic devices. His reputation has grown stronger since his death, partly through revivals at the Comédie-Française.

Principal works:
 Tailleur pour dames: 1887.
 Un Fil à la patte: 1894; adapted as *Cat among the Pigeons*.
 L'Hôtel du Libre Échange: 1894; translated as HOTEL PARADISO.
 Le Dindon: 1896.
 La Dame de chez Maxim: 1899; translated as *The Girl from Maxim's*.
 La Puce à l'oreille: 1907; adapted as *A Flea in Her Ear*.
 Occupe-toi d'Amélie: 1908; translated as *Keep an Eye on Amélie*; adapted as LOOK AFTER LULU.
 On purge bébé: 1910.

Feydeau, Théâtre *See* Comédie-Italienne.

Ffrangcon-Davies, Gwen (1891–92) British actress, who had her first London success as Etain in Rutland Boughton's opera *The Immortal Hour* (1920). During her long career she played many important roles, including Eve in Shaw's *Back to Methuselah* (1923), Elizabeth Moulton-Barrett in Rudolf Besier's *The Barretts of Wimpole Street* (1930), and Lady Macbeth, opposite John Gielgud (1942). She appeared in South Africa for several years from 1943 but was at Stratford-on-Avon in 1950 to play Queen Katharine in *Henry VIII* and Regan among other parts. Later interesting performances included Miss Madrigal in Enid Bagnold's *The Chalk Garden* (1957), Amanda in Tennessee Williams's *The Glass Menagerie* (1965), and Madame Voynitsky in *Uncle Vanya* (1970).

fiabe A form of drama developed in Italy in the 18th century by Carlo GOZZI. A derivative form of the *commedia dell'arte*, the *fiabe* retained the traditional elements of comic improvisation and stock characters while adding a new strain of fantasy; most examples of the genre took mythological subjects as their theme.

Fiddler on the Roof A musical by Jerry Bock, with lyrics by Sheldon Harnick and book by Joseph Stein. First performance: New York, 1964. The story is based on Sholom Aleichem's *Tevye the Milkman*. The plot deals with Tevye, a dairyman in a small Jewish village who must deal with his five marriageable daughters as well as the general problem of anti-Semitism. Though seeming to be specifically about the Jewish experience, the musical tapped into wider concerns about the loss of old traditions. The Broadway production (staged by Jerome Robbins) ran for a record 3242 performances. The London production of 1967 starred TOPOL, as did the celebrated film version.

Field, Nathan (1587–c. 1620) English actor and playwright, who began as a boy actor with the Children of the Chapel Royal, appearing in plays by Jonson at the Blackfriars Theatre. In 1604 he was particularly acclaimed in Chapman's *Bussy d'Ambois*. He wrote the plays *A Woman is a Weathercock* (1609) and *Amends for Ladies* (1611) and collaborated on others with Massinger and Fletcher.

Field, Sid (1904–50) British performer in music hall, who was popular as the comic character Slasher Green. He appeared in the provinces before reaching London in 1943 and appearing in revues; he retired from the stage in 1949.

Field Day Theatre Company An Irish touring company founded in 1980 by the playwright Brian FRIEL and the actor Stephen Rea. Although its base is in Londonderry, it tours throughout the North and South of Ireland, receiving funds from both governments. It specializes in presenting contemporary Irish work (including several plays by Friel), but has also staged new versions of the European classics. The Field Day organization also publishes poetry and other literary works.

Fielding, Henry (1707–54) British novelist and playwright, author of a number of comedies and burlesques. His first real success was *The Author's Farce* (1730), which ridiculed contemporary fashions, as did TOM THUMB THE GREAT, which was a resounding triumph. In 1731 he daringly depicted royalty on the stage in *The Welsh Opera; or, The Grey Mare the Better Horse*, after which he satirized the government in *Quixote in England* (1734), *Pasquin* (1736), and *The Historical Register for the Year 1736* (1737), which he produced when he became manager of the Haymarket. The Licensing Act of the same year was in part a response to his satirical writing and effectively ended his association with the theatre.

Fields, Gracie (Grace Stansfield; 1898–1979) British actress and singer, born in Rochdale, where she first appeared at the Hippodrome in 1910. She topped the bills at all the major music halls and was much loved for her lively delivery of such songs as 'The Biggest Aspidistra in the World'.

Fields, Joseph (1895–1966) British playwright, who collaborated with **Jerome Chodorov** (1911–) on such plays as *My Sister Eileen* (1940), *Wonderful Town* (1953), and *Anniversary Waltz* (1954). He also assisted Anita Loos in the stage adaptation of her novel *Gentlemen Prefer Blondes* (1949) and worked with Oscar Hammerstein.

Fields, Lew *See* Weber and Fields.

Fields, W C (William Claude Dukenfield; 1879–1946) US actor, originally a comic juggler, who became a celebrated comedian and appeared in many editions of Ziegfeld's *Follies*. Throughout the 1920s he played haughty gravel-voiced misanthropic characters in musicals, including Eustace McGargle in *Poppy* (1923) and Q Q Quayle in *Ballyhoo* (1930), and appeared in vaudeville throughout the US and Europe. He then embarked on an immensely successful career in films.

Fierstein, Harvey (1954–) US playwright and actor, who has established a reputation for his plays on homosexual themes. *Torch Song Trilogy* (1982) was highly successful as a series of off-off-Broadway one-acts and then as a full evening on Broadway, while the musical *La Cage aux folles* (1983) was acclaimed in New York and London. Other works include *Safe Sex* (1987), another evening of one-acts.

5th Avenue Theatre A theatre on Broadway, New York, which opened in 1867 and specialized in minstrel shows, but was shut down after a brawl in the auditorium in which a man was killed. In 1869 it reopened with John Brougham starring in one of his own plays. Daly became manager later that year; his own version of *Frou-Frou* by Meilhac and Halévy was a great success as was Bronson Howard's *Saratoga* in 1870. Refurbished in 1872, it was destroyed by fire in 1873.

A second 5th Avenue Theatre was opened by Daly in 1874 with a loss-making production of *Love's Labour Lost*. Daly's own play *The Big Bonanza* (1875) restored the theatre's finances and saw the first New York appearance of John Drew. Subsequently Georgiana Drew make her New York debut there in H J Byron's *Our Boys*. In 1878, under Stephen Fiske, Mary Anderson and Helen Modjeska also played their first New York roles there. The theatre was eventually demolished in 1908 after several changes of name.

58th Street Theatre *See* John Golden Theatre.

51st Street Theatre *See* Mark Hellinger Theatre.

54th Street Theatre *See* George Abbott Theatre.

Filandre (Jean-Baptiste Monchaingre; 1616–91) French actor-manager, also known under the names Jean Mathée and Paphetin. He spent most of his acting career in the provinces and the Low Countries, although he did appear at the Théâtre du Marais as Floridor's successor from 1647 to 1648.

Filippo, Eduardo de *See* de Filippo, Eduardo.

Finlay, Frank (1926–) British actor. He first attracted attention in new plays at the Royal Court Theatre, playing such roles as Harry Kahn in Wesker's *Chicken Soup with Barley* (1958) and Private Attercliffe in Arden's *Serjeant Musgrave's Dance* (1960). On joining the National Theatre company in 1964, he set the seal on his reputation with an impressive Iago to Olivier's Othello. Subsequently he played Jesus Christ in Dennis Potter's *Son of Man* at the Round House (1969), Peppino in de Filippo's *Saturday, Sunday, Monday* (1973–74), and Salieri in Shaffer's *Amadeus* (1981). In 1985 he appeared as Captain Bligh in the musical *Mutiny* at the Piccadilly Theatre. More recent work has included the supernatural chiller *The Woman in Black* (1993) and *Peter Pan* (1994), in which he played Captain Hook and Mr Darling.

Finney, Albert (1936–) British actor. After starting his career at the Birmingham Repertory Theatre he appeared in London in Jane Arden's *The Party* (1958) and at Stratford-on-Avon. He triumphed in the title roles of *Billy Liar* (1960) and Osborne's *Luther* (1961) and went on to demonstrate his range with the National Theatre, playing roles as diverse as Jean in Strindberg's *Miss Julie*, Poche in the Feydeau farce *A Flea in Her Ear*, and Armstrong in Arden's *Armstrong's Last Goodnight*. He was an associate artistic director at the Royal Court from 1972 to 1975 and, when the National company moved onto the new Lyttelton and Olivier stages, excelled as Hamlet (1975) and in the title role in Marlowe's *Tamburlaine the Great* (1976). In 1983 he was back at the Old Vic directing and starring in a revival of *Armstrong's Last Goodnight*. In 1986 he won several awards in Lyle Kessler's *Orphans*. Subsequent work has ranged from the musical *Chicago* (1991) to Yasmina Reza's three-hander *Art* (1996), which earned him an Evening Standard Award. He has also enjoyed success in films.

Fiorillo, Silvio (d. c. 1633) Italian actor of the *commedia dell'arte*, who was famous for his interpretation of Il Capitano and was probably the first to play Pulcinella. He ran his own company in Naples and visited France with the Accesi; he was also the author of several plays and scenarios.

He is thought to have been the father of **Tiberio Fiorillo** (1608–94), who was born in Naples and eventually appeared with *commedia dell'arte* companies in Paris. Appearing at the Petit-Bourbon and the Palais-Royal, he excelled as Scaramuccia, in which role he appeared without a mask. He also made successful appearances in London and wrote an autobiography; he continued acting into his old age.

Another of Silvio's sons, **Battista Fiorillo** (fl. 1614–51), also appeared as Scaramuccia.

Fire-Raisers, The (*Biedermann und die Brandstifter*) A black comedy by Max FRISCH, regarded as a major example of the Theatre of the Absurd. First performance: Zürich, 1958. Written originally as a radio play in 1953, it condemns the passive attitude of complacent citizens to fire-raisers and reflects Frisch's lack of faith in human responsibility.

fires Although stringent safety precautions have reduced the risk of fire in the modern theatre, a great many theatres have been destroyed in this way over the years. Casualties in the days of candles and gas lighting included such celebrated venues as Shakespeare's Globe Theatre (1613), Drury Lane (1672 and 1809), and Covent Garden (1782 and 1808). The worst fire in British theatre history was however, in 1887 at the Theatre Royal in Exeter, when 186 people died. In the US, a fire at the Brooklyn Theatre in 1876 cost 300 lives, while a fire at the Iroquois Theatre in Chicago in 1903 caused 600 deaths, despite the fact that the building was allegedly fireproofed. Elsewhere, even worse disasters occurred at Karlsruhe in 1847, when 631 people died, and at St Petersburg in 1836, when fire killed 800. The most tragic theatre fire of all time, however, happened in China in 1845 when 1670 people lost their lives. The introduction of electricity has done much to improve safety standards and has thankfully put an end to the many tales of actors' costumes being ignited by dangerous stage lighting.

Fisher, Clara (1811–98) British actress, who made a sensational debut at Drury Lane at the age of six, appearing in Garrick's *Gulliver* and impersonating Richard III. She moved with her family to the US in 1827, where she played light comedy roles.

Fiske, Minnie Maddern (Marie Augusta Davey; 1865–1932) US actress, of theatrical parentage, who began on stage at the age of three under her mother's name, Maddern. By the time she was five she had made her New York debut and within 10 years was a star. She retired on her marriage to Harrison Grey Fiske (1861–1942), but soon reappeared in her husband's *Hester Crewe* (1893) and as Nora in Ibsen's *A Doll's House* (1894), the first of a number of modern socially provocative roles; among others were parts in Hardy's *Tess of the D'Urbevilles* and Ibsen's *Hedda Gabler* and *Rosmersholm*. For a time she and her husband also managed the Manhattan Theatre (1901–07), where she directed a series of distinguished plays in opposition to the Theatrical Syndicate. She was seen subsequently in many light comedies, notably as Mrs Malaprop in Sheridan's *The Rivals*.

Fitch, (William) Clyde (1865–1909) US playwright, whose prolific output began with *Beau Brummell* (1890), which was written for Richard Mansfield. Subsequently he enjoyed considerable success with such plays as *Nathan Hale* (1898), *Barbara Frietchie* (1899), and *Captain Jinks of the Horse Marines* (1901), in which Ethel Barrymore appeared. Other works, which did much to make Broadway the focus of US commercial drama, included melodramas, *The Girl with Green Eyes* (1902) – on the theme of jealousy, and *The Truth* (1907), which is regarded as one of his finest plays. His last play, *The City* (1909), was an impassioned protest against urban values.

Fitzball, Edward (1792–1873) British playwright, whose vast output of melodramas, adaptations, and nautical dramas were performed at the minor London theatres. They included *The Pilot; or, a Tale of the Sea* (1825), a spectacular version of *The Flying Dutchman* (1827), *The Red Rover; or, the Mutiny on the Dolphin* (1829), *Jonathan Bradford; or, the Murder at the Wayside Inn* (1833), which was based on a true murder case, and *Paul Clifford* (1835).

Fitzgerald, Barry (William Joseph Shields; 1888–1961) Irish actor, who was for many years at the Abbey Theatre, Dublin and established his reputation as Captain Boyle, a part written for him by O'Casey in *Juno and the Paycock* (1924). He came to London in the same author's *The Silver Tassie* (1929) and thereafter appeared regularly in both cities. From the late 1930s he played numerous 'stage Irish' roles in Hollywood films.

Fitzmaurice, George (1877–1963) Irish playwright, who spent most of his life in Dublin. His first play, *The Country Dressmaker* (1907), was a conventional peasant comedy, but later he created such bizarre and fanciful tragi-comedies as *The Dandy Dolls* (1908) and *The Magic Glasses* (1913). His early work was extremely popular at the Abbey Theatre, but from 1923 until his death none of his plays was staged there.

Fitzroy Theatre *See* Scala Theatre.

Five Finger Exercise The first play by Peter SHAFFER. First performance: Comedy Theatre, London, 1958. This examination of the underlying tensions within a middle-class family was enormously successful in its first production, directed by John Gielgud, and established the author's reputation.

Flaminia *See* Cecchini, Pier Maria.

Flanagan, Bud *See* Crazy Gang.

Flanagan, Hallie (1890–1969) US theatre scholar and director, who controlled the Federal Theatre Project from 1935 to 1939. A pioneer of experimental drama and the Living Newspaper technique, she presided over more than 1000 productions under the project and published several authoritative accounts dealing with contemporary US theatre.

Flanders, Michael (1922–75) British actor and lyric writer, who first appeared in Shaw's *You Never Can Tell* at Oxford in 1941. Later, crippled by poliomyelitis, he collaborated with the musician **Donald Swann** (1923–94) on *At the Drop of a Hat* (1956) and other revues.

Flare Path A play by Terence RATTIGAN. First performance: Apollo Theatre, London, 1942. Drawing on Rattigan's own experiences in the RAF, it depicted the strain suffered by both pilots and their families during the Battle of Britain and attracted enormous wartime audiences in both Britain and the US.

flat A rectangular wooden frame, covered in canvas or some other material, painted, and used as a constituent part of a box set. Usually supported by weights and braces, flats were first introduced in the 17th century and are still used in a variety of adaptations.

Flavio *See* Scala, Flamineo.

Fleck, Johann Friedrich Ferdinand (1757–1801) German actor, who was much admired in plays of the *Sturm und Drang* movement. At the National Theatre in Berlin he distinguished himself with passionate – though unpredictable – performances in the plays of Schiller and Shakespeare and his early death was much regretted.

Flecker, James Elroy (1884–1915) British poet and playwright, whose two poetic dramas were staged posthumously. HASSAN, an oriental melodrama, was acclaimed for its combination of extravagant spectacle, impressive poetry, and incidental music by Delius; his other play, *Don Juan* (1926), however, suffered from weak characterization.

Fleetwood, Charles (d. 1745) British theatre manager, who – having bought the Drury Lane patent – went into partnership there with Theophilus Cibber and then Macklin. A notorious gambler and spendthrift, he was disgraced and forced to give up in 1744. His tenure was notable for the first engagement of Garrick at Drury Lane, Macklin's sensational Shylock, and a walk-out by the company.

Fleschelles *See* Gaultier-Garguille.

Fletcher, John (1579–1625) English playwright, who met Francis Beaumont in 1605 and subsequently worked with him on several plays before Beaumont's retirement in 1613. He then became playwright for the King's Men, working on his own and collaborating with Shakespeare, Massinger, and others. Fletcher's own plays include *The Faithful Shepherdess* (1608), the tragedy *Bonduca* (1613), and the comedies *Wit Without Money* (1614), *The Wild Goose Chase* (1621), and *The Chances* (1625). His plays with Beaumont include *Philaster; or, Love Lies Bleeding* (1609), *The Maid's*

Tragedy (1610), and *The Scornful Lady* (1613). With Shakespeare he worked on *The Two Noble Kinsmen*, *Henry VIII*, and (probably) a lost play called *Cardenio*.

Fleury (Abraham-Joseph Bénard; 1750–1822) French actor, who was highly popular as a comic actor with the Comédie-Française. A protégé of Voltaire, he joined the company in 1778 and was its leader until 1818, surviving imprisonment during the Revolution and being much admired in the plays of Molière, especially as Alceste in *Le Misanthrope*.

flexible staging Any system of staging that can be readily adapted to provide a variety of acting areas. Most modern theatres have favoured such systems rather than conventional proscenium arch designs.

flies The area above the stage, from which scenery, lighting, and other equipment can be suspended.

flipper A small extension to a flat, usually attached by a hinge at right angles in order to give added support.

float *See* footlight.

floodlight A lighting unit capable of illuminating a large area of the stage with a diffuse beam, sometimes referred to simply as a flood.

Florence, William Jermyn (or James) (Bernard Conlin; 1831–91) US actor, who made his New York debut in 1850 as Hallagan in John Brome's *Home*. For 12 years he played mostly Irish parts, often acting with his wife, **Malvina Pray** (1831–1906), and also appeared at London's Drury Lane in the farce *The Yankee Housekeeper* (1856). Subsequently he was highly successful in such parts as Bob in Tom Taylor's *The Ticket-of-Leave Man*, George D'Alroy in T W Robertson's *Caste* (produced in New York without permission), and as Bardwell Slote in Woolf's *The Mighty Dollar* (1876). In his last years he also played Sir Lucius O'Trigger in Sheridan's *The Rivals* and Zekiel Homespun in Colman the Younger's *The Heir-at-Law* for Joseph Jefferson.

Floridor (Josias de Soulas, Sieur de Primefosse; c. 1608–71) French actor, who became leader of the company at the Hôtel de Bourgogne. Much admired in the plays of Corneille and Racine, he led a strolling company in the provinces before joining the Théâtre du Marais in 1638 and then moving to the Hôtel de Bourgogne in 1647. He was noted for his restrained acting style.

Flower Drum Song An unsuccessful musical by Richard RODGERS and Oscar HAMMERSTEIN II. First performance: New York, 1958. Set amongst the immigrants of San Francisco's Chinatown, the plot depicts several romantic entanglements. Despite its failure with both critics and the public, *Flower Drum Song* was made into a film in 1961.

fly gallery An elevated platform in the flies, running parallel to the side of the stage, where ropes used to hang scenery and stage equipment can be secured.

flying effect The practice, first developed in the ancient Greek theatre, of lowering scenery or actors to the stage by means of ropes or wires (to which a performer is attached by a harness) in order to create the illusion of flight.

Fo, Dario (1926–) Italian playwright and actor-manager, noted for his controversial revues and plays on political themes. A skilled mime artist, he and his wife Franca RAME established a popular cabaret act in the 1950s and subsequently attacked such targets as Fascism and organized religion in such plays as *Gli arcangeli non giocano al flipper* (Archangels Don't Play the Pin-Tables; 1959) and *Settimo; ruba un po'meno* (Seventh: Thou Shalt Steal a Little Less; 1964). In 1969 he first appeared in the one-man show *Mistero Buffo*, which he has frequently revived. *Morte accidentale di un anarchico* (ACCIDENTAL DEATH OF AN ANARCHIST; 1970) was written for the La Commune company and enjoyed long runs in London and elsewhere; subsequent successes have included *Can't Pay? Won't Pay!* (1974), *Trumpets and Raspberries* (1982), and *The Open Couple* (1987). He received the Nobel Prize for literature in 1997.

focus lamp A unit of lighting, also called a **lens spot**, the beam of which is adjusted by a lens. Generally replaced by the Fresnel spot, it is still used in Germany, where it is known as a *Linsenscheinwerfer*.

Foersom, Peter (d. 1817) Danish actor, noted for his early translations into Danish of the plays of Shakespeare. His translations included *Hamlet* (1813), in which he played the title role.

Fogerty, Elsie *See* Central School of Speech and Drama.

Folies-Bergère A music hall in Paris, opened in 1869 as a venue for pantomime and opera. Popular for its long and fashionable promenade, it became widely known under the management of Paul Derval from 1919 to 1966 for its shows featuring large numbers of scantily clad beautiful young women. Mistinguett and Maurice Chevalier also appeared here.

Folies Dramatiques, Théâtre des A theatre on the Boulevard du Temple in Paris, opened in 1831 on the site of the Théâtre de l'Ambigu. It was a home of melodrama and saw the early success of Frédérick in one of his own plays. Demolished in 1867, a new theatre of the same name was erected in the rue de Bondy. *See also* Kingsway Theatre.

Folies-Marigny *See* Marigny, Théâtre.

Folies-Nouvelles, Théâtre des A theatre in Paris, opened in 1852 as a venue for pantomime and opera. Subsequently it staged various unsophisticated dramas before being renamed the Théâtre Déjazet in 1859 in honour of the actress Pauline-Virginie DÉJAZET, who appeared there over several years.

folk theatre A form of early rural drama, usually linked to specific festivals in the agricultural calendar. Common to most European countries with a strong agricultural tradition, folk theatre includes various ritual dances, notably the HORN DANCE and MORRIS DANCE in Britain, as well as entertainments with a stronger dramatic element. Well-known examples of folk theatre elsewhere include the ARCHETRINGLE of Switzerland, the antics of the Bavarian Wild Men, and the MASCARADE of France. The early forms of folk theatre influenced the mummers' play and contributed to the development of liturgical drama. *See also* Plough Monday; Robin Hood play.

Follies A musical by Stephen SONDHEIM, with a book by James Goldman. First performance: New York, 1971. Two couples meet again at a religious service held before the demolition of the theatre in which the women were showgirls. As the couples become enmeshed in present events, we see 'ghost' versions of the characters act out events in the past. The score includes pastiche versions of music from the heyday of lavish revues.

follow spot A spotlight that can be directed by hand so that its powerful beam can be kept trained upon an actor or other mobile object on the stage.

Folz, Hans (c. 1435–1513) German poet, playwright, and publisher, who was the author of early examples of the *Fastnachtsspiel*. Based in Nuremberg from about 1459, he also influenced the development of the *meistersänger* tradition.

Fontanne, Lynn *See* Lunt, Alfred.

Fonvizin, Denis Ivanovich (1744–92) Russian playwright, noted for his plays satirizing the pretensions of the upper classes. His successful comedy, *Brigadir* (The Brigadier-General; 1766–69), lampooned those members of the nobility who sought to imitate French manners; it was followed by his masterpiece, *Nedorosl* (The Minor; 1782), in which he took up wholly Russian themes concerning land ownership and serfdom. In 1783, however, Fonvizin fell from favour with Catherine the Great on account of his interest in social issues and his plays were banned.

Fool A clown who appeared in the medieval FEAST OF FOOLS and in various festivities associated with folk theatre. He wore a brightly-coloured suit (called motley) with a hood to which bells, horns, or ass's ears were attached and played an important comic role in both the morris dance and the mummers' play. He was armed with a *marotte* or bauble, comprising a miniature Fool's head mounted on a short stick, or a wooden sword. *See also* Court Fool.

Fools, Feast of *See* Feast of Fools.

Foote, Horton (1916–) US playwright and screenwriter, who has produced a long series of works dealing mainly with his native Texas. His first New York production was *Wharton Dance* in 1940. Other works include *The Trip to Bountiful* (1953) and *The Young Man From Atlanta* (1995), which won the Pulitzer Prize.

Foote, Samuel (1720–77) British actor-manager and playwright, who became an actor in 1744 and was often called the **English Aristophanes**. Taking over the Haymarket Theatre in 1747, he exhibited a talent for biting caricature in a series of plays that he wrote and performed. The Haymarket having no play licence, Foote evaded the law by claiming to hold lectures or tea parties at which any entertainment was free. His first successful play, *The Englishman in Paris*, was produced at Drury Lane in 1753; his most celebrated play, *The Minor*, ridiculed the Methodist movement and was staged at the Crow Street Theatre, Dublin, then at the Haymarket in 1760. In 1766 he obtained a limited patent through the Duke of York's influence; this was compensation for the loss of a leg through a practical joke in which the duke had been involved.

footlight A lighting unit positioned at floor level at the front of the stage, usually one of a strip of such lights, in order to illuminate the stage area from a low angle. In Britain such lights are sometimes referred to as **floats**.

Footlight Players *See* Dock Street Theatre.

Footlights Club A theatre group in Cambridge, founded in 1883. Comprising members of Cambridge University, it presents an annual revue, which tours nationally and has brought to light a long line of comic talents. Women have been admitted since 1957.

footlights trap A long narrow opening across the front of the stage of older theatres, into which the footlights sank when a dimming of the stage lighting was desired.

fops' alley An area of the pit or forestage in the Restoration theatre. Visible from the rest of the auditorium, the area was popular with dandies of the day as a place to show off their dress and broadcast opinions of the play being presented.

Forbes-Robertson, Sir Johnston (1853–1937) British actor-manager who was a pupil of Samuel Phelps. Having made his debut in 1874, he became a member of Irving's company at the Lyceum in 1882. After touring the US with Mary Anderson he returned to the Lyceum under his own management to play Romeo to the Juliet of Mrs Patrick Campbell. In the same season he appeared as Hamlet, an outstanding performance. He also excelled in works by Pinero and Henry Arthur Jones, and was especially successful in an adaptation of Jerome K Jerome's *The Passing of the Third Floor Back* (1908).

  He married Gertrude ELLIOTT; their daughter, **Jean Forbes-Robertson** (1905–62), came to prominence as an actress as Sonia in Komisarjevsky's production of *Uncle Vanya* in 1926. She followed it with equally acclaimed performances as Juliet, Peter Pan (which she played for eight consecutive seasons), and numerous classical roles. Her modern parts included Tessa in Margaret Kennedy's *The Constant Nymph* (1928) and Kay in Priestley's *Time and the Conways* (1937); more unusually, she also appeared as Oberon, Everyman, and Jim Hawkins in *Treasure Island*.

Ford, John (1586–1639) English playwright, who wrote his first plays in 1628, after training as a lawyer. Of the plays he wrote alone the most significant was 'TIS PITY SHE'S A WHORE; the others include *Love's Sacrifice* (1627), *The Lover's Melancholy* (1628), and *The Broken Heart* (1629), all of which tackle various self-destructive obsessions. He probably collaborated with William Rowley and Dekker on *The Witch of Edmonton* (1621) and with Dekker on *The Sun's Darling* (1624).

Forde, Florrie (Florence Flanagan; 1876–1940) Australian-born music hall singer, whose career began in Sydney in 1894. She came to London in 1897 and became famous for leading the audience in such rousing songs as 'Hold Your Hand Out, Naughty Boy' and 'Down at the Old Bull and Bush'.

Ford's Theatre A theatre in Washington DC, which opened in 1862 as Ford's Atheneum in a former church. The theatre was later rebuilt, opening in 1863 as Ford's Theatre. It closed, however, after President Lincoln's assassination there by John Wilkes Booth on 14 April, 1865, during a performance of Tom Taylor's *Our American Cousin*. In 1932 it became a museum. The original auditorium was subsequently restored and the theatre reopened for performances in 1968; since then productions have included the musicals *Don't Bother Me, I Can't Cope* and *Your Arms Too Short to Box With God*. The theatre currently hosts a company specializing in small-scale musicals and plays dealing with the African-American experience.

Ford Theatre Center The name of three theatres built by Garth DRABINSKY's Livent productions, with additional funding from the Ford Motor Co, the first of which was opened in 1993 in North Toronto. The second, a 1786-seat theatre on West 43rd Street, New York, with an entrance on 42nd, opened in 1997 with *Ragtime*. This was built on the site of the APOLLO and LYRIC theatres, elements of which were saved and incorporated in the new structure. In 1998 Livent created another theatre of the same name in Chicago, when it renovated the Oriental Theatre, previously a vaudeville and cinema house.

Foreman, Richard (1930–) US playwright and director who, with his Ontological Hysterical Theatre, has created a series of works for off-off Broadway noted for their dreamlike visuals and avoidance of linear plot. The plays are marked by tight control, slow pace, and, until recently, untrained actors speaking with a deliberately flat inflection.

forestage *See* apron.

Formalism A theatre movement that emerged in the USSR shortly after the Revolution of 1917. Championed by such directors as Meyerhold and Akimov, it advocated the subjection of an actor's individuality to the intentions of the director alone; it soon lost favour with audiences and had to be abandoned.

formal stage A stage setting in which a simple arrangement of scenic features remains basically unchanged throughout a performance, apart from alterations to the DETAIL SCENERY.

Formby, George (George Hoy Booth; 1904–61) British music hall singer, who became popular with comic songs delivered in a Lancashire accent to high-speed banjulele accompaniment. Famous for such songs as 'Mr Wu' and 'When I'm Cleaning Windows', he starred in numerous film comedies.

Fornés, María Irene (1930–) US playwright, born in Cuba, who has been influential in the off-off Broadway movement. Her plays, such as *Fefu and Her Friends* (1977), *Mud* (1983), and *The Conduct of Life* (1985), are frequently abstract and show a concern with feminist and Hispanic issues. She has also been active in workshops and the development of new talent.

Forrest, Edwin (1806–72) US actor, who made his first appearance at the age of 10 in an amateur production. In 1820 he appeared as Young Norval in Home's *Douglas*, after which he gradually built up a reputation as the finest player of tragic roles in the US, noted for his resonant voice and grand style. He played many Shakespearean roles, including King Lear, Hamlet, Macbeth, Othello, and Mark Antony. He also excelled as Spartacus in Bird's *The Gladiator* (1831), a part which was written for him, and the title role in Stone's *Metamora* (1829). He appeared with success in London but became involved in public rivalry with Macready, which culminated in the famous riot (1849) at the Astor Place Opera House. In 1872 he made his last performance, in Bulwer-Lytton's *Richelieu*.

Forrest Theatre *See* Eugene O'Neill Theatre.

Fort, Paul (1872–1960) French poet, director, and manager, who founded the Théâtre d'Art in 1890 as a centre of the French Symbolist movement. Previously he ran the Théâtre Mixte, where he developed his theories of abstract theatre; he abandoned drama altogether in 1892 after failing to reconcile his abstract ideals with the physical reality of the actors.

Fortune Theatre A theatre in Cripplegate, London, which opened in 1600 as the home of the ADMIRAL'S MEN. Some details of its construction are known and its two round wooden galleries could probably hold 1000 people; a statue of the Goddess of Fortune stood over the entrance. It established a strong reputation as a popular venue before being burnt down in 1621; it was rebuilt in 1623 in brick but was less successful. Subsequently it was partially dismantled by the Puritans, being totally demolished in 1661.

Another **Fortune theatre** opened in 1924 in Russell Street, Covent Garden, London. The first theatre to be built in the capital after World War I, it began with plays by such authors as Galsworthy, Lonsdale, and O'Casey – many staged by J B Fagan. After World War II it became better known as a home of revue with performances by Kenneth Horne, Joyce Grenfell, and Flanders and Swann, among others; *Beyond the Fringe* was a major success in 1961. Since then several plays – notably *Sleuth* (1973) by Anthony Shaffer, *Murder at the Vicarage* (1976) by Agatha Christie, and *The Brothers Karamazov* (1981) – have been successfully presented. In 1981 attempts to stage runs of plays from the provinces and fringe theatres caused a financial crisis. *The Woman in Black*, a supernatural thriller adapted from Susan Hill's novel, opened in 1990 and was still running in 2000.

Fortuny, Mariano *See Kuppelhorizont.*

48th Street Theatre A theatre on West 48th Street, New York, which opened in 1912. Known as the **Windsor Theatre** from 1937 to 1943, it housed mostly opera and musical comedy but a few straight plays were also seen there, including *Harvey* (1944) and *Stalag 17* (1951). It was demolished in 1955.

44th Street Theatre A theatre on West 44th Street, New York, which opened as the New Weber and Fields Music Hall. Seating 1463, it housed musicals and light opera with a few classical plays having been produced in 1915. The Marx Brothers had a successful run there in 1928, while subsequent successes included plays by J B Priestley, Paul Green, and Moss Hart. A smaller theatre on the roof, known as the **Nora Bayes Theatre**, was occupied for a time by the Federal Theatre Project. Both theatres were demolished in 1945.

49th Street Theatre A theatre on West 49th Street, New York, which opened in 1921. The theatre housed both new plays and revivals of classics, notably works by Ibsen and Strindberg and productions by the Federal Theatre Project. Mei Lanfang appeared there in 1930. In 1938 it became a cinema and was later demolished.

42nd Street A major east-west street in New York which marks the traditional southern boundary of the theatre district. The block between 7th and 8th Avenues were crowded with theatres by the time of World War I. By the 1930s most of them had been converted into cinemas and by the 1970s the street had acquired a seedy reputation. After decades of discussion, improvement has finally occurred, many of the theatres being demolished and some renovated; as a result the area is once again lively with tourists.

42nd Street A musical based on the well-known movie of 1933, noted for its spectacular Busby Berkeley dance routines. First performance: New York, 1930. The success of this lavish David Merrick production showed that audiences were eager for spectacle after several years of small-scale works. The direction and choreography formed a climax to the career of Gower Champion, who died the morning of the first performance.

46th Street Theatre *See* Richard Rodgers Theatre.

Forum Theatre *See* Lincoln Center for the Performing Arts.

Fosse, Bob (1927–1987) US choreographer and director, whose sexy hip-based dance-style and gleefully cynical attitude proved highly influential. His reputation was made with the 'Steam Heat' number in *The Pajama Game* (1954) and consolidated with choreography for *Damn Yankees* (1955) and *How To Succeed in Business Without Really Trying* (1961). His style was more fully seen in shows he also directed, especially *Sweet Charity* (1966), *Pippin* (1972), and CHICAGO (1975). From 1969 he also worked in the cinema, his best-known film being the screen version of *Cabaret* (1972). The hit musical *Fosse* (1999) presents a compilation of his best work.

14th Street Theatre A theatre on West 14th Street, New York, which originally opened as the **Théâtre Français**, staging plays in French until 1871. It was then known as the Lyceum Theatre for a period and became the 14th Street Theatre in 1886. In 1932 the theatre was taken over by Eva Le Gallienne as a home for her Civic Repertory Company until 1932. The theatre was demolished in 1938.

Fox, G(eorge) L(afayette) 1825–77) US actor, who first appeared on stage at the age of seven in Boston. His New York debut came in 1850 when he joined the National Theatre under the name Lafayette Fox, remaining for several seasons and playing numerous parts. Later, moving to the Bowery Theatre, he became a celebrated pantomime performer, a reputation he maintained at the Olympic where his successes included *Humpty Dumpty* (1868), burlesques of *Hamlet* and *Macbeth* (1870), and *Wee Willie Winkie* (1870).

fox wedge A wooden wedge placed under a flat in order to compensate for any rake in the stage.

Foy, Eddie (Edwin Fitzgerald Foy; 1856–1928) US actor and entertainer. He began in vaudeville in 1869, then settled in Chicago (1888), where for six years he clowned his way through such extravanganzas as *Bluebeard Jr* (1890) and *Little Robinson Crusoe* (1893). Subsequently he starred in such musical comedies as *Up and Down Broadway* (1910) before returning to vaudeville and bringing his seven children into his act.

foyer The area of the theatre between the auditorium and the entrance; refreshments may often be purchased here. *See also* box office.

Fragson, Harry (Harry Potts; 1869–1913) Anglo-French entertainer at the piano, who became a popular café concert singer in Paris and subsequently achieved a high reputation in music hall. Famous for such songs as 'Hullo, hullo, Who's Your Lady Friend?', he was fatally shot by his father in a fit of insanity.

France, Théâtre de *See* Odéon, Théâtre National de l'.

Frank, Bruno (1887–1946) German playwright, who was the author of several popular sophisticated comedies. *Sturm im Wasserglass* (1930) was successful in Britain in an adaptation by James Bridie, while other plays include the historical drama *Zwölftausend* (Twelve Thousand; 1927).

Franklin Theatre A small theatre in Chatham Street, New York, which opened in 1835 with a season of classic comedy headed by Thomas Morton's *The School of Reform*. Although Junius Brutus Booth acted in several tragedies there (1836–37), it became well-known as a venue for melodrama and farce. In 1837 Joseph Jefferson III made his New York debut there, aged eight. The theatre did not prosper financially until 1841, when the company of the Park Theatre appeared there and *Fifteen Years of a New York Fireman's Life* had its first performance. After 1842 it was used for pantomime. The authorities closed the theatre in 1854 after a scandal involving *tableaux vivants*.

Franz, Ellen (1839–1923) German actress, who was the wife of George II, Duke of Saxe-Meiningen. Her influence was largely responsible for the Duke's interest in the theatre and his support for the famous Meininger company.

Fraser, Claude Lovat (1890–1921) British artist and stage designer, who executed designs for the Lyric Theatre in Hammersmith. His designs for *As You Like It* and *The Beggar's Opera* there in 1920, derived from the romantic styles of the 18th century, inspired a whole new school of stage design.

Frayn, Michael (1933–) British playwright and novelist, who established his reputation in the theatre with *The Two of Us* (1970). Subsequently he enjoyed success with such bitter comedies as *Alphabetical Order* (1975), *Donkeys' Years* (1976), *Clouds* (1976), and *Make and Break* (1980). *Noises Off* (1982), an ingenious parody of the world of farce, was followed by the award-winning *Benefactors* (1984). In 1998 Frayn found critical and commercial success with COPENHAGEN, an exploration of scientific responsibility. He has also won praise for his highly actable translations of Chekhov.

Frazee Theatre *See* Wallack's Theatre.

Frédérick (Antoine-Louis-Prosper Lemaître; 1800–76) French actor, who was a major exponent of Romantic drama in the popular theatres of the Boulevard du Temple. He established his reputation by sending up the villainous role of Robert Macaire in the melodrama *L'Auberge des Adrets* in 1823, the part becoming identified with him from that time on. The sequel, *Robert Macaire* (1834), was equally successful, as were subsequent performances in such plays as *Trente Ans, ou la Vie d'un joueur*, *Othello*, *Hamlet*, and *Kean, ou Désordre et génie*, which was written for him by Dumas *père*. His forceful style of acting also suited him to the plays of Victor Hugo, notably *Ruy Blas*, in which he appeared at the opening of the Théâtre de la Renaissance in 1838. Towards the end of his life, however, tastes changed and he died in poverty.

Fredro, Aleksander (1793–1876) Polish poet and playwright, who fought in the Napoleonic Wars and subsequently became famous for his well-constructed comedies in the style of Molière and Goldoni. His finest works were written early in his career as a playwright and include the comedies *Mąż i żona* (Husband and Wife; 1822), *Śluby panieńskie* (Maidens' Vows; 1833), and *Zemsta* (Vengeance; 1834), which is generally regarded as his masterpiece. After criticism by the Romantics, he ceased to write for 19 years before producing several more, less distinguished, works.

Freear, Louie (1873–1939) British comic actress, whose career encompassed Shakespeare, musical comedy, and variety. She was acclaimed in London in the musical comedy *The Gay Parisienne* (1896) and made a great hit as Fifi in *A Chinese Honeymoon* at the Strand Theatre (1901).

Freedley, George Reynolds (1904–67) US theatre historian, who founded the Theatre Collection of the New York Public Library. Having studied under George Baker at Yale, he worked with the Theatre Guild and in 1939 cofounded the Theatre Library Association; he was also connected with the management of the American National Theatre and Academy.

Freie Bühne A theatre club in Berlin, founded in 1889 by Otto Brahm. A home of naturalistic drama, it presented plays by Bjørnson, Holz, Ibsen, Hauptmann, Strindberg, Tolstoy, Zola, and others at several theatres as well as running its own literary paper; actors with the club included Agnes Sorma. In 1894 it was linked up with the Deutsches Theatre, where it continued to promote experimental drama.

Freie Volksbühne *See* Volksbühne.

French Without Tears A farce by Terence RATTIGAN. First performance: Criterion Theatre, London, 1936. Rattigan's first great success in the theatre, the play ran for 1049 performances and has since been revived many times. It revolves around a French language course arranged for candidates to the civil service at a French resort.

Fresnay, Pierre (Pierre Laudenbach; 1897–1975) French actor, who established his reputation at the Comédie-Française during the 1920s. After 1927 he appeared many times in London, succeeding Coward himself in *Conversation Piece* (opposite his wife Yvonne PRINTEMPS) in 1934. From 1937 he and his wife appeared together under their own management at the Théâtre de la Michodière in a series of popular comedies.

Fresnel spot A spotlight capable of producing a bright but soft-edged beam, frequently used in combination with other similar lighting units. It was named after the French scientist Augustin Jean Fresnel (1788–1827), who invented the type of lens on which it is based.

Freytag, Gustav (1816–95) German novelist and playwright, who was the author of several works in the tradition of the well-made play. His most successful play was *Die Journalisten* (1852); his critical writings include *Technik des Dramas*, which discusses the nature of the well-made play.

Fridolin *See* Gélinas, Gratien.

Friel, Brian (1929–) Irish playwright, born in Northern Ireland, whose work explores issues of cultural identity and collective and personal memory. His first major play, *Philadelphia, Here I Come!*, explored the factors that have driven so many Irish people into exile, a theme returned to in *The Gentle Island* and *The Faith Healer*. *The Freedom of the City* and *Volunteers* dealt directly with the contemporary Troubles in Northern Ireland, while *Translations* earned high praise for the subtle way in which it explored the cultural roots of the Anglo-Irish conflict. Friel has also translated works by Chekhov and Turgenev, influences apparent in the bittersweet DANCING AT LUGHNASA, a play widely seen as his masterpiece. He was a cofounder of the FIELD DAY THEATRE COMPANY in 1980.

Principal works:
  Philadelphia, Here I Come!: 1965.
  The Loves of Cass McGuire: 1967.
  Lovers: 1968 (double bill).
  Crystal and Fox: 1970.
  The Gentle Island: 1971.
  The Freedom of the City: 1973.
  Volunteers: 1975.
  Living Quarters: 1976.
  Aristocrats: 1979.
  Faith Healer: 1979.
  Translations: 1981.
  The Communication Cord: 1983.
  Making History: 1988.
  Dancing at Lughnasa: 1990.
  Wonderful Tennessee: 1993.
  Molly Sweeney: 1995.
  Give Me Your Answer Do: 1998.

Friml, Rudolph (1881–1972) US composer, born in Prague, whose successful operettas included *Rose-Marie* (1924). Other works for the theatre in a similar romantic vein were *The Firefly* (1912) and *The Vagabond King* (1975).

fringe theatre In Britain, any form of 'alternative' theatre that takes place outside the mainstream. The name comes from the so-called 'fringe' events that developed around the official EDINBURGH FESTIVAL in the 1950s. Fringe theatre groups range from small-scale professional companies to student and amateur societies; the first such group in Britain is usually held to have been Edinburgh's Traverse Theatre, through which C P Taylor and Tom Stoppard first emerged. Fringe drama has since become an important feature of the artistic life of London and the major metropolitan centres (equivalent to New York's off-off-Broadway). The best known fringe venues in London include the Hampstead Theatre Club, the Bush, the Gate, the Riverside Studios, and the Tricycle Theatre. Leading fringe groups include the Hull Truck theatre company, the 7:84 touring company, and the Pip Simmons theatre group. Writers who first emerged in connection with such troupes include David Hare and Caryl Churchill.

Frisch, Max (1911–91) Swiss playwright and novelist, who is regarded as one of the most significant post-war German-language dramatists. His socially challenging dramas, characterized by ironic wit and an element black farce, include *Nun singen sie wieder* (Now They Sing Again; 1945), *Die chinesische Mauer* (The Great Wall of China; 1946), *Als der Krieg zu Ende war* (When the War was Over; 1949), and *Triptychon* (1980). His most outstanding works are *Biedermann und die Brandstifter* (The FIRE RAISERS; 1953), a bitter satire on bourgeois complacency originally written for radio, and *Andorra* (1961), a controversial tragedy about anti-Semitism.

Fritellino *See* Cecchini, Pier Maria.

Frogs, The A comedy by ARISTOPHANES. First performance: Athens, 405 BC. One of Aristophanes's milder late works, the play satirizes the tragedies of the day, comparing Euripides unfavourably with Aeschylus; it anticipates the development of Middle Comedy in his last works.

Frohman, Daniel (1851–1940) US manager, who – together with his brother **Gustave Frohman** (1855–1930) – managed the Lyceum Theatre in New York with great success from 1885. Previously business manager of the Madison Square Theatre, Daniel Frohman assembled a renowned stock company at the Lyceum, presenting many acclaimed productions of plays by such authors as Pinero and H A Jones among others. Daniel was also manager of Daly's Theatre from 1899 to 1903.

Another brother, **Charles Frohman** (1860–1915), established his reputation as a successful manager with Bronson Howard's *Shenandoah* (1888) and subsequently presided over an excellent stock company at the Empire Theatre from 1893. His successful productions for the London stage included Klein's *A Night Out* (1896) and plays by J M Barrie – including *Peter Pan* (1904) – and George Edwardes; at one point he controlled five London theatres simultaneously. He was drowned when the *Lusitania* sank in 1915.

front of house Those parts of a theatre in front of the stage. These include the auditorium, foyer, bars, and offices.

Fry, Christopher (Christopher Harris, 1907–) British playwright, who is associated with the revival of poetic drama in the 1940s. Having become director of the Oxford Playhouse in 1940, he went on to enjoy great commercial success with his lively and eloquent comedies, starting with *A Phoenix Too Frequent* (1946). In 1948 THE LADY'S NOT FOR BURNING provided John Gielgud with a West End success, while Olivier was admired in the tragicomedy *Venus Observed* (1950). *The Dark Is Light Enough* (1954) was less successful despite the performance of Edith Evans and by the late 1950s Fry's elevated style had been eclipsed by the new aggressive realism of Osborne and the other Royal Court playwrights. Later works included translations of Anouilh, Giraudoux, and Ibsen, and several screenplays.

Fugard, Athol (1932–) South African playwright, director, and actor, whose plays frequently tackle issues of racialism and repression. He began his career in Cape Town, founding an experimental company there, and acted in *No Good Friday*, his first play, in 1959. He also appeared on stage in such later works as the acclaimed *Blood Knot* and established another theatre group – the Serpent Players – in Port Elizabeth in 1963, where he directed works by authors ranging from Brecht to Sophocles. He has also experimented with techniques of improvisation and collective creation in such pieces as *Sizwe Bansi Is Dead* and several of his later plays have been seen in Britain and the US, often featuring the actor James Earl Jones. His *Notebooks 1960–1977* (1984) detail his experiences in the South African theatre.

Principal works:
No Good Friday: 1959.
Ngogo: 1960.
The Blood Knot: 1961.
Hello and Goodbye: 1965.

Boesman and Lena: 1969.
The Coat: 1971.
Sizwe Bansi Is Dead : 1972.
Statements after an Arrest under the Immorality Act: 1972.
The Island: 1973.
Dimetos: 1975.
A Lesson from Aloes: 1978.
Master Harold and the Boys: 1982.
The Road to Mecca: 1985.
A Place with the Pigs: 1988.
Valley Song: 1996.
The Captain's Tiger: 1999.

Fulham Theatre *See* Grand Theatre.

Fuller, Isaac (1606–72) English scene painter, who worked in London after the Restoration, having studied in Paris. In 1669 he successfully sued the Drury Lane management in respect of his fee for painting a scene in Dryden's *Tyrannic Love*.

Fuller, Rosalinde (1892–1982) British actress, who started in the chorus of the Folies-Bergère in 1918. Subsequently she performed in revue in New York, where she appeared in her first straight part in 1921 and, the following year, played Ophelia to John Barrymore's Hamlet. She made her London debut in 1927 and went on to appear with Wolfit's Shakespearean company and in the plays of Shaw and Chekhov as well as in her own solo programmes, in which she toured the world.

Fulton Theatre *See* Helen Hayes Theatre.

Funambules, Théâtre des A theatre on the Boulevard du Temple in Paris, which opened in 1816 on the site of a former booth. Early productions were predominantly circus-type entertainments and harlequinades; later, however, Deburau appeared there as Pierrot and the theatre became known for its pantomimes, which were notable for their elaborate technical effects. The theatre was demolished in the rebuilding of Paris in 1862.

Futurism An early 20th-century movement in the theatre and the arts in general characterized by a glorification of the machine age and a rejection of the past. Developed initially by Marinetti, who coined the term Futurism in a manifesto in 1909, the movement called for a new faith in technology and dynamic action but ultimately fell from favour after being identified with fascism. It did, however, stimulate a new interest in fragmented language and narrative and challenged accepted practices in staging and lighting.

Fuzelier, Louis (1672–1752) French playwright and editor of the literary periodical *Mercure de France* (1744–52). He collaborated with Lesage, Piron, and others on numerous plays for fairground theatres and also wrote for the Opéra-Comique, the Comédie-Italienne, and the Comédie-Française.

Fyffe, Will (1885–1947) Scottish comic performer in the music hall, who began in melodrama and revue. He became immensely popular in sketches and as the singer of such songs as 'I Belong ta Glasgae'.

G

Gabrielli, Francesco (1588–c. 1636) Italian actor of the *commedia dell'arte*, who played a major role in the development of the character Scapino. He appeared with the Accesi and later became a prominent member of the Confidenti and is known to have appeared in Paris in 1624 with the Fedeli.

gaff A building temporarily converted for use as a theatre (especially in the 19th century), usually for cheap productions of music hall and melodrama, in which case it was called a **blood tub**. In Scotland the equivalent term was **geggie**.

Gaiety Theatre A theatre in the Strand, London, opened in 1864 as the **Strand Musick Hall**. Closed in 1866, it was rebuilt and, seating 2000 people, reopened in 1868 as a venue under John HOLLINGSHEAD and subsequently became famous for its burlesques, in which Nellie Farren, E W Royce, Edward Terry, and Kate Vaughan were highly acclaimed together from 1876 onwards. George Edwardes took over in 1885 with a similar programme until, in 1892, he staged *In Town*, one of the earliest examples of musical comedy and the first of many such productions at the theatre, usually featuring a famous chorus of 'Gaiety Girls'. When the Strand was widened the theatre was closed in 1903 and a new Gaiety opened close to the Aldwych, holding 1338 people. Musical comedy continued there after Edwardes died but with less success and, after diverting into straight drama in the 1920s and 1930s, the theatre closed in 1939, being demolished in 1957.

Another theatre of the same name opened in Dublin in 1871 and was used at first by touring companies from England. Later it became a venue for Irish works under the auspices of the IRISH LITERARY THEATRE (1900–01) but subsequently reverted to a largely English programme. The Gate Theatre company performed regularly at the Gaiety during World War II, after which the theatre staged both Irish and English drama. After alteration in 1955, the theatre was saved from demolition by the television presenter Eamonn Andrews and now stages a wide variety of entertainments.

A third Gaiety was opened in Manchester in 1908, in what had been a music hall, by Annie HORNIMAN as a home for the first repertory company in England. The first production, *Reaping the Whirlwind* by Allan Monkhouse, effectively founded a tradition of serious drama in Manchester; subsequent writers for the theatre included Harold Brighouse, Stanley Houghton, and St John Ervine. Lewis CASSON later took the theatre over but financial troubles led to the end of the company in 1917. The theatre became a cinema in 1921.

The **Gaiety Theatre** on Broadway, New York, opened in 1908. It housed live drama until 1932, when it became a cinema and burlesque house. Leading performers who appeared there included John Barrymore and Frank Bacon, who enjoyed great success in his own play *Lightnin'* (1918). Among other plays staged there were Lonsdale's *Aren't We All?* (1923) and Somerset Maugham's *Rain* (1926). It became a cinema, renamed the Victoria Theatre in 1943, and was demolished in the 1990s to make room for offices.

Gaîté, Théâtre de la A theatre on the Boulevard du Temple in Paris, which opened in 1764 as a venue for puppet shows. After diversifying with mime and circus-type entertainments, it was rebuilt in 1805 as a home of melodrama, especially the plays of Pixérécourt (who managed it from 1823 to 1834), and was again reconstituted (in 1862) on a new site as the Théâtre de la Musique.

galanty show *See* shadow play.

Galdós, Benito Pérez *See* Pérez Galdós, Benito.

Galileo (*Leben des Galilei*) A historical play by Bertolt BRECHT, written 1937–39. First performance: Zürich, 1943. The play draws upon Galileo's conflict with the Inquisition to explore questions of freedom, responsibility, and of personal integrity in the face of persecution. A revised English-language version was staged in Los Angeles in 1947 providing Charles Laughton with one of his most acclaimed roles. There have been numerous revivals.

Galimafré *See* Bobèche.

gallery *See* auditorium.

Galli *See* Bibiena, Ferdinando.

Gallienne, Eva Le *See* Le Gallienne, Eva.

Gallina, Giacinto (1852–97) Italian playwright, author of several plays in the Venetian dialect. Such early plays as *Le Barufe in famegia* (Family Quarrels; 1872) were influenced by Goldoni; later, however, he satirized contemporary society in several plays and ventured into tragedy with *La famegia del santolo* (The Godfather's Family; 1892), which is considered his masterpiece.

Gallo Theatre *See* New Yorker Theatre.

Galsworthy, John (1867–1933) British novelist and playwright, whose first play – THE SILVER BOX (1906) – was an immediate success. His interest in justice and moral issues reappears in such works as STRIFE (1909), JUSTICE (1910), *The Eldest Son* (1912), THE SKIN GAME (1920), and *Loyalties* (1922). His plays belong to the well-made play tradition and are rooted in the social issues of his time. He won a Nobel Prize in 1932.

Gambon, Sir Michael (1940–) British actor, born in Dublin, who made his debut in *Othello* in 1962. Since 1970 he has worked frequently with the Royal Shakespeare and National Theatre companies, while also appearing in West End productions of Ayckbourn's *The Norman Conquests* (1974), Simon Gray's *Otherwise Engaged* (1976), and other plays. In the early 1980s he played the title role in *King Lear* and Antony in *Antony and Cleopatra* at Stratford-on-Avon and the Barbican. Award-winning work of the 1980s and 1990s included Arthur Miller's *A View from the Bridge* (1987), and Jonson's *Volpone* (1995). He has also appeared in films and on television, most notably as the central character in Dennis Potter's series *The Singing Detective* (1986). In 2000 he returned to the stage as Davies the tramp in an acclaimed 40th-anniversary production of Pinter's *The Caretaker*.

Game of Love and Chance, The (*Le Jeu de l'amour et du hasard*) A comedy by Pierre MARIVAUX. First performance: Comédie-Italienne, Paris, 1730. The plot concerns the courtship of Dorante (disguised as his valet Arlequin) and Silvia (disguised as her maid Lisette). It is usually considered Marivaux's most subtle and sophisticated work.

Gammer Gurton's Needle An early English farce, probably by William STEVENSON. First performance: Christ's College, Cambridge, c. 1560. The mischievous beggar Diccon generates confusion following Gammer Gurton's loss of a needle while repairing her servant Hodge's trousers.

Ganassa, Zan (Alberto Naseli; d. c. 1583) Italian actor-manager of the *commedia dell'arte*, who led one of the first Italian companies to tour in other countries. He presented productions in Paris in 1571 and at the marriage of the King of Navarre (subsequently Henry IV) a year later; tours of Spain in the 1570s had a profound influence upon the early Spanish theatrical tradition.

Garção, Pedro António Correia (1724–72) Portuguese poet, playwright, and critic, who did much to reform Portuguese drama along classical lines. His verse comedies, *Teatro Novo* (New Theatre) and *Assembléia ou Partida* (Meeting or Parting), satirized life in contemporary Lisbon and contained much of his finest poetry.

Garcia, Victor (1934–) Argentinian director, who moved to France in 1961 and established a reputation for his innovative productions of plays by such authors as Arrabal and Jean Genet. His controversial production of García Lorca's *Yerma* (1971) involved the use of a huge trampoline. He directed Valle Inclán's *Divinas Palabras* in 1977.

Garcia de la Huerta, Vicente (1734–87) Spanish playwright, poet, and critic, who is best known as the author of the celebrated tragedy *Raquel* (1778). His critical writings were less influential, with several major writers being omitted from his 16-volume *Teatro español* (1785–86).

García Gutiérrez, Antonio (1813–84) Spanish playwright, usually remembered for the popular drama *El trovador* (The Troubadour; 1836), upon which Verdi's opera *Il trovatore* was later based. His other works include the plays *Venganza catalana* (Catalan Vengeance; 1864) and *Juan Lorenzo* (1865) and a number of *zarzuelas*.

García Lorca, Federico (1898–1936) Spanish poet and playwright, considered one of the most significant figures in modern Spanish literature. His early lyrical and experimental plays, written in a spirit of revolt against the contemporary fashion for Realism, were chiefly written for performance by the travelling theatre La Barraca, of which he was both founder and director. He is best remembered for his evocative portrayals of Andalusian peasant life and for his intense poetic tragedies treating such themes as frustrated womanhood and the conflict between love and honour. His most famous work is the trilogy *Bodas de sangre*, YERMA, and *La Casa de Bernarda Alba*. He was executed by Nationalist partisans in 1936, shortly after the outbreak of the Spanish Civil War.

Principal works:

El maleficio de la mariposa: 1920; translated as *The Butterfly's Curse*.
Mariana Pineda: 1927.
La zapatera prodigiosa: 1930; translated as *The Shoemaker's Amazing Wife*.
Bodas de sangre: 1933; translated as BLOOD WEDDING.
Yerma: 1934.
La Casa de Bernarda Alba: 1945; translated as THE HOUSE OF BERNARDA ALBA.

Garden Theatre A theatre in Madison Avenue, New York, which opened in 1890. Among its distinguished players were Sarah Bernhardt in Sardou's *La Tosca* (1891) and Ben Greet and his company in a season of Shakespeare (1910). Other productions included Gilbert's *The Mountebanks* (1893) and Hauptmann's *The Weavers* (1915). The theatre became the **Jewish Art Theatre** in 1919 and was demolished in 1925.

Gardin, Vladimir (1877–1965) Russian actor, who established his reputation in modern drama in St Petersburg under Vera Komisarjevskaya but later moved (1907) to Finland to present plays banned in Russia and toured Europe. As well as parts in the plays of Hauptmann and Andreyev, he excelled as Potrassov in Tolstoy's *The Living Corpse*, in which role he appeared in Moscow in 1912. Subsequently he appeared solely in films.

Garnier, Robert (1544–90) French playwright and lawyer, a major figure in French Renaissance drama. His plays, lyrical vehicles for his patriotic, moral, and religious ideals, consist of six tragedies on classical themes; the first French tragicomedy, *Bradamante* (published 1582), based on Ariosto's *Orlando Furioso*; and the biblical tragedy *Les Juives* (published 1583), which is generally considered to be his masterpiece.

Garrett, João Batista de Almeida (1799–1854) Portuguese poet, novelist, and playwright, who wrote the first Portuguese works influenced by the Romantic movement. He established his reputation as a playwright early in his career with such politically liberal plays as *Lucrécia* (1819) and *Catão* (1821), which led to his exile in England. Appointed Inspector-General of Theatres in 1836, his masterpiece was the tragedy *Frei Luís de Sousa* (1843).

Garrick, David (1717–79) British actor, manager, and playwright, whose new approach to acting revolutionized the theatre of his day. He was born at Hereford and educated at Lichfield, where he organized a production of *The Recruiting Officer*. In 1737 he came to London with Dr Johnson, under whom he had studied classics in Lichfield, and read for the Bar before joining his uncle's wine business. After becoming involved in the amateur theatre, he went with Giffard, manager of Goodman's Fields Theatre, to Ipswich, where he worked professionally under the name Lyddal; he made his first appearance in *Oronooko*, adapted from a novel by Aphra Behn, in about 1741. Despite his short stature he proved a revelation as Richard III and was engaged by Fleetwood at Drury Lane for the rest of the season; in the summer he went to Dublin, where he embarked on a lengthy affair with Peg WOFFINGTON.

In the long successful career that followed, Garrick played at both Covent Garden and Drury Lane, settling at the latter when he became joint patentee in 1747. His naturalistic style of acting was in marked contrast to that of contemporaries such as James Quin, who said of him: "If the young fellow is right, I and the rest of the players have been all wrong". Among his most famous roles were Hamlet, Lear, Abel Drugger, Archer in *The Beaux' Stratagem*, Bayes in *The Rehearsal*, and Sir John Brute in *The Provoked Wife*. Garrick wrote more than 40 plays, of which *Miss in her Teens* (1747) and *Bon Ton; or High Life Above Stairs* (1775) had some success; he also collaborated with George Colman the Elder on THE CLANDESTINE MARRIAGE.

His management led to at least two instances of controversy – his employment of French dancers in 1755 at a time when Britain and France were on the verge of war and his abolition of the third act admission concession in 1762 caused serious rioting and a brief retirement abroad. Summoned back by royal command, he restored his popularity with revivals of his most celebrated roles. He also imported a number of major reforms from abroad, including the removal of members of the audience from the stage itself, the concealment of lighting, and the adoption of naturalistic backdrops.

A somewhat vain man, Garrick's pageant (1769) for the Shakespeare jubilee celebrations at Stratford-on-Avon drew some malicious ribaldry when he offered pieces of his own and apparently excluded anything by Shakespeare. He and his wife, the actress **Eva Maria Veigel** (1724–1822), who often appeared as **Mlle Violetta**, finally retired in 1776 to his sumptuous mansion at Hampton Court. He was buried in Westminster Abbey.

Garrick Club A London club in Garrick Street, founded in 1831 and named after the actor David Garrick. It was established as a club for actors and educated men and included Charles Kemble, Macready, and Charles Mathews among its first members; subsequent members have included Henry Irving, Beerbohm Tree, Forbes-Robertson, Laurence Olivier, John Gielgud, and many other leading performers and writers for the theatre. The Club remains an all-male preserve. It houses a fine collection of theatrical portraits.

Garrick Theatre A theatre in Whitechapel, London, which opened in 1831 under Benjamin Conquest. Destroyed by fire in 1846, it reopened in 1854, staging popular plays at a modest standard; Beerbohm Tree made his professional debut there in 1879. The theatre closed in 1881.

A second **Garrick Theatre** was opened in Charing Cross Road, London, by W S Gilbert for the actor-manager John Hare. It was constructed partially below ground, the dress circle being on street level; a copy of Gainsborough's portrait of David Garrick was hung in the foyer. The theatre opened in 1889 with a production of Pinero's *The Profligate*. Under Hare's management both Sir Johnston Forbes-Robertson and Mrs Patrick Campbell played here, the latter being much acclaimed in *The Notorious Mrs Ebbsmith* (1895). Arthur Bourchier was manager from 1900 to 1915 and C B Cochran the lessee from 1918 to 1924. In 1935 Walter Greenwood's *Love on the Dole*, in which Wendy Hiller made her name, was staged there. A series of farces presented by Brian Rix from 1967 were also immensely popular, as was Ira Levin's thriller, *Death Trap* (1978–81). More recent productions have included Brian Friel's award-winning *Dancing at Lughnasa* (1992) and Stephen Daldry's production of *An Inspector Calls* (1995–).

The **Garrick Theatre** on West 35th Street, New York, was opened as **Harrigan's Theatre** in 1890. The theatre was later run by Richard Mansfield – who presented William Gillette, Ethel Barrymore, and others there in plays by Shaw and Clyde Fitch – and renamed the **Vieux-Colombier**. In 1919 it reopened as the Garrick with a production of Benavente's *The Bonds of Interest* by the Guild Theatre, which remained until 1925. It was demolished in 1932.

Gascoigne, George (c. 1542–77) English playwright and poet. His adaptation from the *I suppositi* of Ariosto, *The Supposes* (1566), was the first native comedy entirely in prose; Shakespeare based the subplot of *The Taming of the Shrew* directly on it. Gascoigne also translated Lodovico Dolce's *Giocasta*.

Gascon, Jean (1921–88) French-Canadian actor and director, who established his reputation with notable productions of classic plays by many European playwrights. He trained at the Vieux-Colombier in Paris before returning to Montreal and founding (1951) the Théâtre du Nouveau Monde, where he remained as artistic director until 1966. He won particular praise for his productions of Molière and Strindberg as well as for his contributions to the Stratford (Ontario) Festival (1967–74). He became director-general of the National Theatre School of Canada in 1960.

Gaskill, William (1930–) British director, who became director of the Joint Stock Company in 1973. He established his reputation as a director with the English Stage Company (1957–59 and 1965–72), later working at the National Theatre (1963–65 and 1979) and with the Royal Shakespeare Company (1961–62). His most notable productions have included plays by John Osborne at the Royal Court, a series of works by Edward Bond, and classic plays by Brecht, Farquhar, and Middleton and Rowley.

Gaspar, Enrique (1842–1902) Spanish playwright, whose plays satirizing contemporary bourgeois society helped to establish the concept of Realism in the Spanish theatre. His most successful plays include *Las personas decentes* (1890) and *La eterna cuestión* (1895).

Gassman, Vittorio (1922–2000) Italian actor-manager, who found acclaim in many productions presented by his own company, the **Teatro Popolare Italiano**, from the 1950s on. He made his debut in 1943 and enjoyed success in both comic and tragic roles in plays ranging from Alfieri's *Oreste* to Sartre's *Kean*; other major successes included performances as Sophocles's Oedipus, Ibsen's Peer Gynt, and Shakespeare's Iago, Orlando, and Othello, as well as numerous film roles.

Gassner, John Waldhorn (1903–67) US theatre critic, scholar, and playwright, born in Hungary, who established his reputation with adaptations of many major foreign works for the Theatre Guild in the 1930s. As well as translations of plays ranging from works by Sophocles to modern plays by Stefan Zweig, he also published notable studies of the theatre and collections of plays.

Gate Theatre The first London club theatre, which opened in 1925 in a converted warehouse in Floral Street, Covent Garden. In 1927 it moved to Villiers Street, near Charing Cross, where it was under the management of Norman Marshall from 1934 to 1940. In addition to plays by such authors as Lillian Hellman, Afinogenov, Cocteau, and Steinbeck, the theatre became known for its annual Gate Revue. The building was destroyed by bombs in 1941.

The **Gate Theatre** in Dublin opened in 1930 in the Rotunda Buildings as a home for a company founded by Hilton EDWARDES and Mícheál MACLIAMMÓIR in 1928. After early performances at the Peacock Theatre (*see* Abbey Theatre), the company presented plays by Shaw, Aeschylus, Goethe, and others at the Court Theatre until 1936, when a rival company under the Earl of LONGFORD took a share in the theatre, presenting its own separate programme until 1961. After World War II Lady Longford continued to run the theatre, which was closed periodically before acquiring state support in 1969 and was subsequently used by both its own resident company and other troupes. Successful productions have included numerous revivals of plays by both Irish writers and playwrights from other countries.

A third **Gate Theatre** opened above a public house in Notting Hill Gate, London, in 1979 as a venue for fringe theatre. In the 1980s it built up a reputation for lively and ambitious drama, briefly spawning an offshoot in Battersea (1982–84). From the late 1980s the Gate's director, Giles Croft, held a series of themed seasons featuring neglected classics and contemporary work from all around the world. This ambitious policy continued under the direction of Stephen Daldry (1989–92) and his successor, Laurence Boswell. The current director, Mick Gordon, has staged several highly controversial works, including Jim Allen's *Perdition* (previously cancelled by the Royal Court) in 1998. Following expansion, the theatre now seats about 112; actors and directors are still usually unpaid.

Gateway Theatre A theatre in Edinburgh, which opened in 1946 under the management of the Church of Scotland. Productions staged there included plays by a resident company as well as successful offerings by visiting troupes and a company run by Robert KEMP despite controversy between the church authorities and the theatre management. The company was closed in 1965 when the LYCEUM THEATRE was opened.

gatherer An official in the Elizabethan theatre who collected entrance money from the audience as they came into the auditorium. The money that was collected then passed either to the HOUSEKEEPERS, who had a claim to receipts from the particular area of the theatre in which the spectactor was sitting or to the owners of the building itself. *Compare* sharer.

Gatti, Armand (1924–) French playwright and film director, born in Monaco. In the 1960s Gatti produced dramas of social and political protest, inspired by such events as the Vietnam War and the execution of the anarchists Sacco and Vanzetti in the US in 1927 (*Chant publique devant deux chaises électriques*, 1966). *La Deuxième Existence du camp de Tatenberg* (1962) is based on Gatti's experiences in a Nazi concentration camp. Subsequent plays included *La passion du Général Franco* (The Passion of General Franco), which was banned until 1976. In his later years he worked mainly on COMMUNITY THEATRE projects, often involving mixed media.

Gatti's A music hall in the Westminster Bridge Road, London, opened by the brothers Carlo and Giovanni Gatti in 1865. Originally a restaurant, it was known as Gatti's-Over-the-Arches to distinguish it from another musical hall opened by the Gatti brothers in 1866, known as Gatti's-Under-the-Arches. Gatti's-Over-the-Arches seated 1183 people and saw the first London appearance of Harry Lauder, eventually closing in 1924. Gatti's-Under-the-Arches became the **Hungerford Music Hall** in 1887 and then the **Charing Cross Music Hall** before being turned into a cinema in 1910.

Gaultier-Garguille (Hugues Guéru; c. 1573–1633) French actor, who excelled in farce and also appeared, as **Fleschelles**, in serious drama. He probably performed at the

Paris fairs before appearing at the Hôtel de Bourgogne alongside Turlupin and Gros-Guillaume.

Gaussin, Jeanne-Cathérine (1711–67) French actress, who was much admired for her evocation of pathos in performances at the Comédie-Française, which she joined in 1731. She excelled in the plays of Racine, Voltaire, and especially in the comedies of La Chaussée.

Gautier, Théophile (1811–72) French poet, novelist, theatre critic, and journalist, who was a leading figure of the French Romantic movement. He defended the works of Victor Hugo and was himself the author of several melodramas and libretti for a number of ballets.

gauze An expanse of loosely woven fabric, which can be made to appear opaque when lit from behind. In the US it is referred to as a **scrim**. *See also* transparency.

Gay, John (1685–1732) English playwright and poet, whose first play, *What d'ye Call it*, was produced in 1715. He achieved his greatest success with THE BEGGAR'S OPERA, staged at Lincoln's Inn Fields in 1728. Its sequel, *Polly*, was refused a licence and was not performed until 1777. Gay also wrote several comedies, a tragedy, and the book for Handel's *Acis and Galatea* (1732).

Gay Sweatshop A British touring company founded in 1975; the UK's first (and only) professional company devoted to staging plays about gay and lesbian issues. Under the leadership of Drew Griffiths and Gerald Chapman, it toured for over a year with its first productions, the 'coming-out' revues *Mister X* and *Any Woman Can*. New work presented by Gay Sweatshop included Michelene Wandor's *Care and Control* (1977) and *Poppies* (1983) by Noel Greig, a writer-director with the company from 1977 to 1987. In 1997 it was obliged to suspend its activities owing to a withdrawal of public funding.

geggie *See* gaff.

gel A colour filter, which when placed in front of a light colours the beam. Gels were formerly made of gelatin but are now made of plastic.

Gelber, Jack (1932–) US playwright, whose first play, THE CONNECTION (1959), won several awards and was influential in the GROUP THEATRE movement. After this study of drug addiction, he wrote such plays as *The Apple* (1961), *The Cuban Thing* (1968), *Sleep* (1972), and *Barbary Shore* (1974). He is resident playwright at the American Place in New York and has also directed Wesker's *The Kitchen* (1966), Kopit's *Indians* (1968), and *Jack Gelber's New Play: Rehearsal* (1976) among other works.

Gélinas, Gratien (1909–99) French-Canadian actor, playwright, and director, who founded the famous **Théâtre de la Comédie Canadienne** in Montreal in 1958. Known as **Fridolin**, after a character in his own revues, he presented major plays by Anouilh, Marcel Dubé, and others as well as his own works, of which *'Tit-Coq* (Lil' Rooster; 1948) broke the record for the longest-running Canadian play. He was also a leading performer at the Stratford (Ontario) Festival. His last project, *La Passion de Narcisse Mondoux*, was performed some 600 times in Canada and the US.

Gelosi An early Italian *commedia dell'arte* company, founded by Flamineo Scala in Milan c. 1568. Members of the company appeared before the French Court of Henry

III in 1577 and subsequently toured many European countries. Leading actors with the Gelosi included Giovann and Isabella ANDREINI; after Isabella's death in 1604 the company was disbanded.

Gémier, Firmin (Firmin Tonnerre; 1869–1933) French actor, director, and manager, who became a leading performer on the Paris stage during the 1920s. Trained under Antoine, he had his first major success in 1896, as Ubu in Lugné-Poë's production of Jarry's *Ubu Roi*, after which he appeared in numerous roles, sometimes under his own direction. He managed the Théâtre Antoine from 1906 and founded the Théâtre Ambulant – a group travelling by rail – in 1911; during World War I he presented Shakespeare in Paris and staged extravaganzas with Gaston Baty at the Cirque d'Hiver. Subsequently he managed the Théâtre National Populaire, the Comédie des Champs-Elysées, and the Odéon, producing notable versions of plays by many foreign and contemporary playwrights and ultimately inspiring the revived TNP of Jean Vilar.

Gems, Pam (Iris Pamela Gems; 1925–) British playwright. Gems made her name on the fringe with the strongly feminist *Dusa, Fish, Stas, and Vi* (1975) before reaching a much wider audience with *Piaf* (1978), an earthy biography of the Parisian singer that eventually reached Broadway. Several of her other plays are similarly based on famous lives, notably *My Name is Rosa Luxemburg* (1976), the epic *Queen Christina* (1977), *Stanley* (1995), about the painter Stanley Spencer, and *Marlene* (1997), about Marlene Dietrich.

General Utility *See* stock company.

género chico *See* zarzuela.

Genet, Jean (1910–86) French novelist, playwright, and poet, born in Paris. An abandoned illegitimate child, he spent much of his youth in institutions and prisons in various European cities. When staged in Paris, London, and New York his five plays shocked audiences with their combination of perverse sexuality, ritualistic violence, and poetic language. In his later plays the attack on conventional society and its values became explicitly political (*Les Paravents* dealt with the contemporary situation in Algeria).

Principal works:
  Les Bonnes: 1947; translated as THE MAIDS.
  Haute Surveillance: 1949; translated as DEATHWATCH.
  Le Balcon: 1960 (published 1956); translated as THE BALCONY.
  Les Nègres: 1959; translated as THE BLACKS.
  Les Paravents: 1961; translated as *The Screens*.

Geneva A play by G B SHAW. First performance: Malvern Festival, 1938. The play considers the idea of dictators being brought before an international court of human justice to answer charges brought against them; in doing so it satirizes the helplessness of the League of Nations in dealing with Nazi Germany.

Gengenbach, Pamphilus (c. 1480–1525) German playwright, noted for his virulent attacks on the Roman Catholic church. His play *Totenfresser* (1521) was unsparing in its criticism of the Pope; his other writings include the morality play *Das Spiel von den zehn Altern* (1515).

genteel comedy A form of polite comedy popular in the early 18th century. It had much in common with both Restoration comedy, which preceded it, and sentimental comedy of the later 18th century.

Gentleman, Francis (1728–84) British actor, critic, and playwright, born in Dublin. He began as an actor in the English provinces, sometimes appearing in his own plays; subsequently he was engaged by Foote at the Haymarket. In 1770 he published *The Dramatic Censor*, a collection of judicious notices of contemporary plays.

Gentleman Dancing-Master, The A comedy by Sir William WYCHERLEY. First performance: London, c. 1671. Gerrard pretends he is Hippolita's dancing master in order to win her hand before she is married to her affected cousin.

George, Mlle (Marguerite-Josephine Weymer; 1787–1867) French actress, who was highly regarded in her day for her performances in the great tragic roles. Noted for her tempestuous manner, she first appeared at the Comédie-Française in 1802 and subsequently established her reputation in such parts as Lady Macbeth and Jocasta as well as in the historical plays of Dumas and de Vigny. Rumour had it that her many lovers included Napoleon, Talleyrand, and Metternich.

George Abbott Theatre A theatre on West 54th Street, between 7th and 8th Avenues, New York, which opened as the **Craig Theatre** in 1928. Seating 1401, it was renamed the **Adelphi Theatre** in 1934. The theatre was later taken over (1936) by the Federal Theatre Project for a period and then used for broadcasting. In 1958 it reopened for live drama as the 54th Street Theatre; it was renamed after the playwright George Abbott in 1966. The theatre was demolished in 1970.

George Dandin; ou, le Mari confondu A comedy by MOLIÈRE. First performance: Versailles, 1668. George Dandin is a rich peasant who has married the daughter of a gentleman; treated with contempt by his wife and humiliated by her parents, he blames himself for his misfortunes.

George M Cohan Theatre A theatre on Broadway, New York, which was opened by Cohan himself in 1911. Successes there included Klein and Glass's *Potash and Perlmutter* (1913), several farces, and Clemence Dane's *A Bill of Divorcement* (1921), starring Katharine Cornell. The theatre was converted into a cinema in 1933 and was demolished in 1938.

Georgian Theatre A theatre in Richmond, Yorkshire, which is one of the oldest working theatres in England. Seating 400, it opened in 1788, being renamed the Theatre Royal from 1811 to 1848, when it closed. A restored 238-seat theatre was reopened in 1963, becoming a home for amateurs and musical productions as well as a museum (from 1979).

Germanova, Maria Nikolaevna (1884–1940) Russian actress, who was much admired in intense Expressionist dramas under Nemirovich-Danchenko. She began her career at the Moscow Art Theatre in 1904 in Shakespeare; subsequently she excelled in plays by Ibsen, Maeterlinck, and Dostoevsky as well as in Andreyev's *Katerina Ivanovna* (1912), which was written for her.

Gershwin, George (1898–1937) US composer who – often in collaboration with his brother **Ira Gershwin** (Israel Gershwin; 1896–1983) as his lyricist – created a series of highly successful Broadway musicals in the 1920s and 1930s. Early successes included the song 'Swanee' and contributions to George White's *Scandals* (1920–24); subsequent full-scale productions included the jazz-oriented *Lady, Be Good!* (1924), *Oh, Kay!* (1926), *Funny Face* (1927), *Strike up the Band* (1930), *Girl Crazy* (1930), and the Pulitzer Prize-winning *Of Thee I Sing* (1931). *Porgy and Bess* (1935), his only opera, is widely performed.

After his brother's death Ira Gershwin continued to write for the stage, providing lyrics for Kurt Weill (*Lady in the Dark*: 1941) and Burton Lane (*Give the Girl a Break*: 1953) among others.

Gershwin Theatre A theatre on 51st Street and Broadway, New York, which opened in 1972 as the **Uris Theatre** with the musical *Via Galactica*. It was the first new Broadway theatre to be built in decades, the first to be incorporated into an office tower, and with 1927 seats, the largest in the city. Productions at the Uris included Sondheim's *Sweeney Todd* (1979) and the Public Theatre's version of Gilbert and Sullivan's *The Pirates of Penzance* (1981). Since it was renamed the Gershwin in 1983 productions have included Lloyd Webber's *Starlight Express* (1986) and the lavish Harold Prince-directed revival of *Show Boat* (1993).

Ghelderode, Michel de (1898–1962) Belgian playwright, who was the author of several plays notable for their combination of the comic and the grotesque. Written mostly in French, his 50 or so works – generally farcical tragedies – began with *Les Vieillards* (1919) and include amongst them *Escurial* (1927), *Barabbas* (1928), *Pantagleize* (1929), *Hop! Signor* (1935), and *Mademoiselle Jaïre* (1934). *Fastes d'enfer* (1929) provoked a riot when revived by Barrault in Paris in 1949.

Ghéon, Henri (Henri Léon Vangeon; 1875–1944) French playwright and poet, who revived medieval religious drama in the 1920s and 1930s. Many of his plays, based on biblical stories and the lives of the saints, were written for Ghéon's amateur troupe; they include *Le Pauvre sous l'escalier* (1921) and *Le Noël sur la place* (Christmas in the Market Place; 1935).

Gherardi, Evaristo (1663–1700) Italian actor of the *commedia dell'arte*, who appeared with the Comédie-Italienne in Paris. He was much admired as Arlecchino and published many of the scenarios used by the company.

ghost glide A type of trap by means of which an actor standing on a wheeled platform appears to glide across the stage as he is raised up to it through a long narrow stage cut. A variation of the ghost glide is known as the **Corsican trap** after its introduction in Boucicault's *The Corsican Brothers* (1852).

ghosts There are numerous traditions about haunted theatres, many of the best known being in Britain. The most famous instances include the reputed haunting of the Haymarket by John BUCKSTONE and the reported appearances during matinées at Drury Lane of a man in grey – believed by some to be the ghost of a man killed in a stage fight in the 18th century. Sightings of both ghosts are regarded as good omens for the play currently in production. Other British venues with similar traditions include the Adelphi Theatre, where the murdered actor William TERRISS is said to appear, the Bristol Old Vic, where Mrs SIDDONS is reported to have been sighted, and York's Theatre Royal, which lays claim to the ubiquitous unidentified shadowy figure seen during rehearsals.

Ghosts (*Gengangere*) A tragedy by Henrik IBSEN, the most controversial of all his works. First performance: Chicago, 1882. The play uses venereal disease as a symbol of collective guilt in a hypocritical society; it was widely condemned when it first appeared but is now recognized as having had a formative influence upon 20th-century Realist drama. The chief characters are the widowed Helen Alving and her son Oswald.

Ghost Sonata, The (*Spöksonaten*) A one-act play by August STRINDBERG. First performance: Intima Teatern, Stockholm, 1908. The most deeply symbolic of Strindberg's later works, the play imitates the discontinuity of a dream and anticipated much 20th-century drama.

Giacometti, Paolo (1816–82) Italian playwright, best remembered for *La morte civile* (The Outlaw; 1861), which depicts the plight of an escaped criminal who kills himself rather than disgrace his family and which remained popular in Italy for many years. His other plays include the historical drama *Elisabetta regina d'Inghilterra* (1853).

Giacosa, Giuseppe (1847–1906) Italian playwright, who wrote influential dramas in the Italian *verismo* tradition. He enjoyed considerable success with such comedies as *Una partita a scacchi* (A Game of Chess; 1871) and *La zampa del gatto* (The Cat's Paw; 1883) as well as with the historical drama *Signora di Challant* (1891), in which Bernhardt and Duse both excelled, but later turned to social dramas influenced by Ibsen. *Diritti dell'anima* (The Rights of the Soul; 1894) and other plays of the same type suffered from a lack of psychological penetration but are interesting as depictions of contemporary bourgeois society in Italy.

Gibbons' Tennis Court *See* Vere Street Theatre.

Gibbs, Mrs *See* Logan, Maria.

Gibson, William (1914–) US playwright, who is best known for the play *The Miracle Worker* (1959), based on the education of the blind and deaf Helen Keller. His other works include *Two for the Seesaw* (1958) and the book for the musical *Golden Boy* (1964).

Gide, André (1869–1951) French novelist, critic, and playwright. Gide is remembered chiefly for his semi-autobiographical stories and novels; his contribution to the theatre is of comparatively minor importance. His own plays include *Le Roi Candaule* (1901), *Saül* (1903), and *Oedipe* (1931); he also produced translations of Shakespeare, notably *Hamlet* (1946).

Giehse, Therese (1898–1975) German actress, who became a leading performer in both Munich and Zurich, appearing in premieres of many important modern dramas. Much admired for her technical virtuosity, she starred in the first productions of Ibsen's *Mutter Courage und ihre Kinder* (1941) and his adaptation of Gorky's *The Mother* (1949) as well as in plays by such authors as Dürrenmatt, Hauptmann, and O'Casey.

Gielgud, Sir John (1904–2000) British actor, a great nephew of Ellen Terry, who trained for the stage at the Royal Academy of Dramatic Art and made his debut as the Herald in *Henry V* at the Old Vic in 1921. He then worked in Fagan's Oxford Repertory Company and in London took over from Noël Coward as Nicky in *The Vortex* (1925). When he joined the Old Vic company in 1929 he began the series of great Shakespearean roles, including Hamlet, Prospero, Romeo, and Macbeth, which made him famous. In 1932 he triumphed as Joseph Schindler in Ronald Mackenzie's *Musical Chairs*, following it with another popular success in the title role of Gordon Daviot's *Richard of Bordeaux* in the West End.

In his own season at the Queen's Theatre (1937–38) his parts included Shylock and Richard II, while in 1939 he revived the most famous of all his comedy parts, John Worthing in *The Importance of Being Earnest*, having played it previously at the Lyric, Hammersmith, in 1930. He first appeared at Stratford-on-Avon in the 1950 season, playing such roles as Benedick, Lear, Cassius, and Angelo. During the years 1956–64 he was seen worldwide in his solo Shakespearean performance *The Ages of Man*, after which he reappeared in London in such contemporary plays as David Storey's *Home* (1970) and Pinter's *No Man's Land* (1975), in both of which he acted alongside Ralph Richardson. Other successes included performances in the plays of Chekhov, Congreve, Fry, Jonson, Seneca, and Sheridan. He also found praise as a director of both classical and modern plays and appeared frequently in films and on television. A fine speaker of verse who achieved a natural nobility in tragedy while also being shrewd and subtle in comedy, he remained a leading member of the profession for some 70 years. He was knighted in 1953.

Gielgud Theatre A theatre in Shaftesbury Avenue, London, that was known as the **Globe Theatre** until 1996, when it was renamed in honour of Sir John GIELGUD (and to avoid confusion with the newly opened Globe Theatre on the South Bank). Designed as a twin to the Queen's Theatre next door, the theatre opened as the Hicks (after Sir Seymour Hicks) in 1906; its first big hit was *Brewster's Millions* (1907), with Gerald Du Maurier in the leading role. Renamed the Globe in 1909, the theatre was managed by Marie Löhr and her husband Anthony Prinsep from 1918 to 1927. Subsequently, under the management of H M Tennent and then of Stoll Moss Theatres, its notable successes in comedy and light musicals have included Dodie Smith's *Call it a Day* (1935–36), Terence Rattigan's *While the Sun Shines* (1943–46), Christopher Fry's *The Lady's Not For Burning* (1949) with John Gielgud and Pamela Brown, Robert Bolt's *A Man for All Seasons* (1960), starring Paul Schofield, several plays by Alan Ayckbourn, the award-winning comedy *Daisy Pulls It Off* (1983–86), and Peter Shaffer's *Lettice and Lovage* (1987) with Maggie Smith. Productions since the theatre was renamed the Gielgud have included Peter Hall's revival of Wilde's *An Ideal Husband* (1997) and Coward's *Song at Twilight* (1999) with Vanessa and Corin Redgrave.

Giffard, Henry (c. 1695–1772) British actor and manager, who ran the Goodman's Fields Theatre from 1733 until 1737, when the Licensing Act was passed. Giffard was himself involved in the passing of the strict licensing laws, having been rewarded by Walpole for drawing his attention to the controversial play *The Golden Rump*, which provided the government with the excuse it needed to impose tighter regulation of the theatre. After 1737, Giffard continued to run the Goodman's Fields Theatre, introducing Garrick to the professional stage and subsequently moving with him to Drury Lane for a time.

Gift of the Gorgon, The A play by Peter SHAFFER. First performance: Barbican, 1992. The plot concerns the conflict between an academic keen to write the biography of his late father, a famous playwright, and his stepmother, who wishes to preserve discretion. The production, directed by Peter Hall for the Royal Shakespeare Company, starred Judi Dench and Michael Pennington. Dench later described her role as the stepmother as the most demanding of her career.

Gigaku A processional dance drama, imported to Japan from Korea in 612 AD. Consisting of a series of both comic and serious scenes performed by masked actors, the tradition was entirely replaced by the BUGAKU tradition by the 12th century.

Gilbert, Gabriel (1620–80) French playwright and poet, who was secretary to Queen Christina of Sweden. Gilbert's dramatic output consists largely of mediocre tragedies and tragicomedies; *Hippolyte* (1646) may have been used by his contemporary Jean Racine as a source for the latter's masterpiece PHÈDRE.

Gilbert, Mrs George H(enry) (Ann Hartley; 1821–1904) US actress and dancer, born in Britain, who settled with her husband in the US and made her New York debut in 1864 as Baroness Freitenhorsen in *Finesse*. Subsequently she specialized in playing comic elderly ladies, making a particular success as the Marquise de St Maur in T W Robertson's *Caste* (1867). She joined Daly's company and remained, on and off, for 30 years before going to Charles Frohman's company, her last appearance being as Granny Thompson in *Granny* (1904).

Gilbert, John (John Gibbs; 1810–89) US actor, who made his first appearance in Boston in 1828. He toured the Mississippi area until 1834 and was most admired for his performances in Boston, New York, and elsewhere as Sir Anthony Absolute in *The Rivals* and Sir Peter Teazle in *The School for Scandal*. He toured with Lester Wallack's company from 1861 until 1888.

Gilbert, Sir W(illiam) S(chwenk) (1836–1911) British playwright and lyricist, remembered for his long collaboration with the composer **Sir Arthur Sullivan** (1842–1900) on a series of light operas. Prior to meeting Sullivan, he wrote comic verses, short plays, operettas, and burlesques. His play *The Palace of Truth* was presented at the Haymarket by Buckstone in 1870, while other serious dramas, including *Pygmalion and Galatea* (1871), were also well received. His first significant collaboration with Sullivan resulted in *Trial by Jury*, which prompted Richard D'Oyly Carte to commission further work from them. HMS PINAFORE established their joint reputation and they went on to produce many subsequent works for the Opera Comique and the Savoy Theatre. Gilbert's staging of his works paid great attention to unity of effect, making him an early example of the modern director. His work with Sullivan also had an important influence on the development of the US musical.

Principal works (with Sullivan):

Thespis; or, the Gods Grown Old: 1871.
Trial by Jury: 1875.
The Sorcerer: 1877.
HMS Pinafore: 1878.
The Pirates of Penzance: 1880.
Patience: 1881.
Iolanthe: 1882.
Princess Ida: 1884.

THE MIKADO: 1885.
Ruddigore: 1887.
The Yeoman of the Guard: 1888.
The Gondoliers: 1889.
Utopia (Limited): 1893.
The Grand Duke: 1896.

Gilchrist, Connie (Constance Macdonald Gilchrist; 1865–1946) British actress, who appeared in pantomime and as a skipping-rope dancer before becoming famous in B E Woolf's play *The Mighty Dollar* in 1880. She continued with a brief career in musical comedy that ended on her marriage to the Earl of Orkney in 1889.

Gilder, (Janet) Rosamund de Kay (1891–1986) US theatre critic and administrator, who helped to found and run the Federal Theatre Project, the American National Theatre and Academy (ANTA), the Institute for Advanced Studies in Theatre Arts, and the International Theatre Institute (1948). From 1948 to 1954 she was the ANTA representative to UNESCO.

Giles, Nathaniel (fl. 1595–1634) English theatre manager, Master of the Children of the Chapel Royal from 1597 to 1634. He was responsible for the celebrated series of plays performed by the company at the Blackfriars Theatre until 1608.

Gill, Claes (1910–73) Norwegian actor, director, and author, who was admired in roles ranging from parts in the plays of Ibsen to those of Brecht, T S Eliot, and Pirandello. He was artistic adviser to the Riksteatret, the State Travelling Theatre, from 1968.

Gill, Peter (1939–) Welsh director, actor, and playwright, who began his career at the Royal Court Theatre in the 1960s, attracting attention with plays by authors ranging from D H Lawrence to Webster. In 1977 he became the first director of the Riverside Studios, where his successes included Chekhov's *The Cherry Orchard* (1978). In 1980 he joined Peter Hall as a director of the National Theatre, where he directed plays by Turgenev and Shaw among others. He directed the National's studio theatre from 1984 until 1990. His own plays include *Kick for Touch* (1983) and *Mean Tears* (1987). Recent work includes a production of *Uncle Vanya* for the Tricycle Theatre (1997).

Gilmore's Theatre *See* Daly's 63rd Street Theatre.

Gingold, Hermione (1897–1987) British actress, who appeared first as a child in 1908 and subsequently became a star of intimate revue. Revues in which she appeared included *Sweet and Low* and its sequels; other triumphs numbered amongst them plays by Coward and Stephen Sondheim's *A Little Night Music*.

Giraldi, Giovanni Battista (1504–73) Italian novelist, poet, and playwright, popularly known as **Il Cinthio**. A native of Ferrara, Giraldi was the author of *Orbecche* (1541), the earliest modern Italian tragedy to be constructed on classical lines; his other tragedies include *L'Altile* (1543), *Cleopatra* (1543), and *Epizia* (1547), which were largely based upon stories that he subsequently collected in the *Hecatommithi* (1565). His preference for a happy ending effectively created TRAGICOMEDY, while his use of romantic and chivalric material inspired such subsequent writers as Greene, Shirley, and Shakespeare.

Giraud, Giovanni (1776–1834) Italian playwright, who was the only significant writer of comedy in Italy in the period following Goldoni. His *L'aio dell'imbarazzo* (1807) was subsequently made into a comic opera by Donizetti.

Giraudoux, Jean (1882–1944) French novelist, playwright, and essayist, born in Bellac. A diplomat, he began writing for the theatre in 1928, having already published several successful novels: his first play, *Siegfried*, marked the beginning of a long collaboration with Louis JOUVET. Giraudoux's dramatic works, many of which are based on biblical stories, fairy tales, and classical mythology, are characterized by the blending of fantasy with reality, comedy with tragedy, and the supernatural with the mundane.

Principal dramatic works:
Siegfried: 1928.
AMPHITRYON 38: 1929.
Judith: 1931.
Intermezzo: 1933; translated as *The Enchanted*.
La Guerre de Troie n'aura pas lieu: 1935; translated as TIGER AT THE GATES.
Électre: 1937; translated as *Electra*.
Ondine: 1939.
La Folle de Chaillot: 1945; translated as THE *Madwoman of Chaillot*.
Pour Lucrèce: 1953; translated as DUEL OF ANGELS.

Gitana, Gertie (1888–1957) British music hall singer, who became a favourite performer at the age of 16. A chance engagement at London's Holborn Empire set her off on a bill-topping career of 30 years, singing such sentimental songs as 'Nellie Dean'.

GITIS *See* Lunacharsky State Institute of Theatre Art.

Glasgow Citizens' Theatre A flourishing Glasgow repertory company, founded in 1943 and based in the **Royal Princess's Theatre**, which was built in 1878. James BRIDIE oversaw the early years of the company, encouraging the performance of native Scottish drama; since 1969, however, the company – known for maintaining low admission prices – has presented flamboyant revivals of classic plays and built up an international reputation. Important new plays staged in the 1960s included *Armstrong's Last Goodnight* (1964) by John Arden and *A Day in the Death of Joe Egg* (1967) by Peter Nichols; the latter was one of several productions by Michael Blakemore. Outstanding productions under **Giles Havergal** (1938–), who took over in 1969, have included *Antony and Cleopatra* (1972), Goethe's *Faust* (1985), and Coward's *The Vortex* (1988). Experimental productions were also staged at the **Close Studio Theatre**, attached to the main theatre, between 1965 and 1973, when it was destroyed by fire. The theatre now has three performing spaces, seating 600, 120, and 60 people.

Glasgow Repertory Theatre A theatre company established in Glasgow in 1909. It built up a strong reputation with performances at the Royalty Theatre, Glasgow, of plays by Shaw, Chekhov, and others as well as a few native Scottish playwrights. It closed after the outbreak of World War I.

Glaspell, Susan (1876–1948) US playwright and novelist, best known for co-founding the PROVINCETOWN PLAYERS and encouraging the early work of Eugene

O'NEILL. Her own work includes *The Verge* (1921), the first fully Expressionist US play, and *Allison's House* (1931), which won the Pulitzer Prize.

glass crash A sound effect simulating the breaking of a sheet of glass, usually produced live by pouring broken glass and china from one bucket into another.

Glass Menagerie, The A drama by Tennessee WILLIAMS. First performance: New York, 1945. The play, which contains a strong element of autobiography, concerns the tensions within a Southern family. The painful drama focuses on Laura, the shy daughter with a limp, and Amanda Wingfield, the mother, who cannot deal with life effectively. The role of Amanda provided Laurette Taylor with her last major role.

Gleich, Joseph Alois (1772–1841) Austrian playwright, whose many moral comedies transformed the Viennese theatre. Writing for the Leopoldstädter and Josefstädter theatres, he wrote over 200 such plays, of which *Der Eheteufel auf Reisen* (1822) is one of the best known.

Glengarry Glen Ross A play by David MAMET. First production: National Theatre, London, 1983. The play explores the seamy side of US capitalism through its depiction of the stress-driven lives of salesmen for a dubious real-estate company. When it is announced that the two least successful members of the team will be sacked, the salesmen begin to manoeuvre against each other and a criminal conspiracy is hatched. The 1992 film starred Al Pacino and Jack Lemmon.

Globe Theatre A round wooden theatre built in 1598–99 south of the river Thames at Bankside in Southwark by Cuthbert Burbage with timber from the THEATRE at Shoreditch. It was used solely in the summer months, since only the stage and galleries were roofed. William Shakespeare was both a shareholder and an actor at the Globe, where many of his plays were staged by the Chamberlain's Men. In 1613 the theatre caught fire during a performance of *Henry VIII* and was destroyed. Rebuilt the following year with the help of public subscriptions and a royal grant, it was closed by the Puritans in 1642 and demolished two years later.

In the 1970s the US actor Sam WANAMAKER conceived the idea of building a working replica of Shakespeare's Globe as near to the original site as possible. After long years of fund raising and fighting bureaucratic obstruction, Wanamaker saw building work begin on the South Bank shortly before his death in 1993. The reconstructed **Globe Theatre** was officially opened in 1997, under the artistic direction of Mark RYLANCE. With the one addition of modern stage lighting, Shakespeare's plays are here presented and experienced in a manner as close to the original as modern scholarship can ascertain (and health and safety regulations permit).

The **Globe Theatre** in Newcastle Street, London, known together with the Opera Comique as one of the Rickety Twins on account of its somewhat ramshackle structure, was opened in 1868 on the site now occupied by Bush House. It was designed, built, and managed by Sefton Parry and had an audience capacity of 1800. Popular successes included *The Private Secretary* (1884) and *Charley's Aunt* (1893), which ran there for 1466 performances. The theatre was closed in 1902 as part of the Strand improvement scheme.

The **Globe Theatre** in Shaftesbury Avenue, London, has been known as the GIELGUD THEATRE since 1996.

See also Lunt-Fontanne Theatre; New York Theatre.

Glory A tableau, popular in Renaissance drama, in which an actor playing a god descended to the stage in a blaze of light. He was lowered on one of a series of platforms (painted to represent clouds and sky) operated by a drum-and-shaft system.

glove-puppet *See* puppet theatre.

gobo An item of lighting equipment, used to alter the shape or pattern of a light beam. It consists of a cut-out masking device and is commonly used to achieve atmospheric lighting effects.

Godber, John (1956–) British playwright. He began writing for television in 1981 and became director of the Hull Truck Theatre Company in 1984; that same year he made his reputation with the Rugby League comedy *Up N' Under*. Subsequent plays, which have been frequently revived, include the ensemble pieces *Bouncers* (1986), *Teechers* (1987), *On the Piste* (1993), and *Weekend Breaks* (1997).

Godfrey, Charles (Paul Lacey; 1851–1900) British music hall performer, who became famous as a singer of songs combining drama and pathos, exemplified by 'On Guard', the story of a Balaclava veteran. For 10 years he topped the bills performing similar pieces, interspersed with lighter songs.

gods *See* auditorium.

Godwin, Edward William (1833–86) British architect and stage designer, who lived with Ellen TERRY from 1862 and became the father of Edith and Edward Gordon CRAIG. An expert in classical architecture and costumes, his career as a theatrical designer blossomed with the Bancrofts' *The Merchant of Venice*, in which Ellen Terry returned to the stage in 1875. He published the results of his research in *The Architecture and Costume of Shakespeare's Plays*.

Goering, Reinhardt (1887–1936) German playwright, who became a leading figure in the early development of Expressionism. The highly stylized *Seeschlacht*, which is set on board a battleship during the battle of Jutland, was immensely influential through its production by Reinhardt in Berlin in 1918. Later works included an account of the death of Captain Scott.

Goethe, Johann Wolfgang von (1749–1832) German playwright, poet, novelist, scholar, and statesman, whose work in the theatre had an enormous influence on drama throughout Europe. Goethe became interested in the theatre at an early age after seeing performances of French plays in Frankfurt, where he was born; his career as a playwright is usually dated, however, from his discovery of the plays of Shakespeare, which he first read while training as a lawyer in Strasbourg. This reading inspired his first great drama, GÖTZ VON BERLICHINGEN, a major contribution to the STURM UND DRANG movement which, together with the novel *Die Leiden des jungen Werthers* (The Sorrows of Young Werther; 1774), established him as the leader of the Romantics in Germany.

In 1775 he moved to the court at Weimar, where he became prime minister and wrote and directed theatrical entertainments. In 1786 he began a two-year visit to Italy, as a result of which he rejected Romantic ideals in favour of Classicism. This was reflected in his rewriting of his prose drama IPHIGENIE AUF TAURIS along classical lines and in his subsequent plays. Having acted as an amateur in some of his plays himself, he became director (1791–1817) of a professional company at the

Court Theatre in Weimar, where Schiller also worked with him; members of the company, which became famous throughout Europe, included Iffland. Goethe's novel *Wilhelm Meisters theatrealische Sendung* (1795) is based partly on the life of the actor Friedrich Schröder. In his later years Goethe completed his masterpiece for the stage, the poetic drama FAUST, which he had been working on since the 1770s. The play encapsulates the author's philosophy of unceasing aspiration in all fields of human enterprise. Due to its great length it is often staged in its less complex original draft, known as the *Ur-Faust* (c. 1775).

Principal dramatic works:
    Götz von Berlichingen: 1773.
    Stella: 1776.
    Clavigo: 1779.
    Iphigenie auf Tauris: 1779.
    Egmont: 1787.
    Torquato Tasso: 1807.
    Faust: Part I, 1829; Part II, 1854.

Gogol, Nikolai Vasilievich (1809–52) Russian novelist and playwright, author of the first Russian plays in the Realist tradition. He is best known for the novel *Dead Souls* (1842; first successfully dramatized by Stanislavsky in 1928) but his career as a poet and actor started earlier, under the influence of his friendship with the actor Shchepkin. His masterpiece, the satirical comedy THE GOVERNMENT INSPECTOR (first seen in London in 1920), resulted in his exile in Rome (1842–48); subsequent dramas included farces and comedies. During his last years he succumbed to religious mania and depression.

Principal dramatic works:
    Revizor: 1836; translated as *The Government Inspector*.
    Marriage: 1842.
    Gamblers: 1842.
    On Leaving the Theatre After a Performance of a New Comedy: 1842.

Gold, Jimmy *See* Crazy Gang.

Golden Boy A play by Clifford ODETS. First performance: Group Theatre, New York, 1937. The plot revolves around Joe Bonaparte, a musician turned professional boxer, who becomes warped by his attempts to gain material wealth and outward success. A musical version was first staged in 1964 in New York.

Golden Theatre The usual name for the 805-seat **John Golden Theatre** on West 45th Street, New York, which opened as the **Theatre Masque** in 1927. *Tobacco Road* started its long run there in 1933. The theatre's name was changed when the actor-director John Golden (1874–1955) took it over in 1937. It has since housed a mixture of musical revues and dramas, including three Pulitzer Prize winners, *Crimes of the Heart*, *'night, Mother*, and *Glengarry Glen Ross*. *See also* Royale Theatre.

Goldfaden, Abraham (Abraham Goldenfoden; 1840–1908) Yiddish playwright and poet, who effectively founded the Yiddish theatrical tradition. He was born in Russia, acting in Ettinger's *Serkele* in 1825, but later emigrated to Poland in 1875 and then Romania, where he established the first Yiddish theatre at Jassy in 1876. Subsequently he toured Russia, Romania, and elsewhere before finally settling in New York in 1903. He was the author of almost 400 plays, including *The Recruits* (1877), *Shulamit* (1880), and *David at War* (1904).

Goldoni, Carlo (1707–93) Italian playwright, born in Venice, who played a key role in the development of the modern Italian theatrical tradition by reforming many aspects of the *commedia dell'arte*. The author of nearly 300 plays in Italian or French, he provided written parts where the actors had formerly relied upon improvisation and added a new note of realism in his characterization; in doing so he provoked opposition from many actors of the *commedia dell'arte* and his rival Carlo Gozzi. After writing numerous plays for the theatres in Venice, he moved to Paris to direct the Comédie-Italienne and produced French versions of his own works; he retired in 1764 and died in poverty following the French Revolution. His most celebrated comedies include *I pettegolezzi delle donne*, *La locandiera*, in which Duse excelled, *I rusteghi*, and *Il ventaglio*.

Principal works:

Belisario: 1734.
Il servitore di due padroni: 1743; translated as *The Servant of Two Masters*.
La vedova scaltra: 1748; translated as *The Wily Widow*.
La putta onorata: 1749.
La Pamela: 1750.
I pettegolezzi delle donne: 1750.
Il bugiardo: 1750; translated as *The Liar*.
La bottega del caffè: 1750; translated as *The Coffee House*.
Il vero amico: 1750.
La locandiera: 1753.
Il malcontenti: 1755.
Un Curioso accidente: 1757.
I rusteghi: 1760; translated as *The Boors*.
L'impresario delle Smirne: 1760; translated as *The Impresario of Smyrna*.
Le baruffe chiozzote: 1762; translated as *Squabbles in Chioggia*.
Il ventaglio: 1764; translated as *The Fan*.
Le Bourru bienfaisant: 1773; translated as *The Kindly Curmudgeon*.

Goldsmith, Oliver (1730–74) British poet, playwright, and novelist, who became one of Dr Johnson's circle. His comedy THE GOOD-NATURED MAN, rejected by Garrick, was produced by the elder Colman at Covent Garden in 1768 with some success, but it was the instantaneous triumph of SHE STOOPS TO CONQUER in 1773 that made his reputation as a dramatist. Many years after his death his novel *The Vicar of Wakefield* was also successfully adapted for the stage.

goliard A member of a troupe of wandering theatrical performers, chiefly clerics and students, common throughout Europe in medieval times. Notorious for their licentious and riotous behaviour, the goliards – who declared allegiance to the legendary Bishop Golias – presented satirical pieces that frequently criticized the Church; the authorities forbade clerics from participating in such entertainments in 1227. In the later Middle Ages the term goliard consequently became virtually synonomous with JONGLEUR and MINSTREL. Works performed by such groups included short plays (one example being the *Commedia Bile*) and poems in praise of wine and women (published as the *Carmina Burana* in the 19th century).

Gombrowicz, Witold (1904–69) Polish playwright and novelist, who spent most of his life in exile in Argentina, Germany, and France. He was the author of three notable dramas anticipating the development of the Theatre of the Absurd, *Iowna, Princess of Burgundy* (1957), *Marriage* (1963), and *Operetta* (1967), which have since been revived in several countries.

Gomersal, Edward Alexander (1788–1862) British actor, who became a leading performer at ASTLEY'S AMPHITHEATRE. He also made successful appearances in melodrama at most major provincial theatres.

Goncourt, Edmond de (1822–96) French writer who collaborated with his brother **Jules de Goncourt** (1830–70) on novels, plays, works of social history and criticism, and the famous *Journal des Goncourt*, begun in 1851. Their plays, which include *Henriette Maréchal* (1865) and dramatizations of their novels, form the least significant part of their literary output.

Gonzaga, Pietro Gottardo (Pyotr Fyodorovich; 1751–1831) Italian artist, who did much notable work for a number of Italian and Russian theatres. He moved to Russia in 1792, where he worked at theatres in Moscow and St Petersburg, designing scenery chiefly for opera and ballet. In 1817 he was asked to design a theatre at Arkhangelskoye; subsequently he went on to execute 12 influential sets of scenery in the neoclassical style for this theatre.

Goodman Memorial Theatre A 683-seat theatre in Chicago, connected physically and originally professionally to the Chicago Art Institute. It was built in memory of the playwright Kenneth Sawyer Goodman to house both an acting school and a resident professional company. It opened in 1925 but the Depression forced the company to disband. In the 1950s visiting professional players performed with students, while during the 1960s a professional company took over the theatre and student performances were presented in the adjacent Goodman Theatre Studio. The theatre's connection with the school ended in 1977, when the theatre was incorporated into the Chicago Theatre Group Inc. The company is due to move into newly renovated theatres on Chicago's Loop.

Goodman's Fields Theatre A theatre in Whitechapel, London, opened (as **Odell's Theatre**) by Thomas Odell in 1727. After the first performance, *The Recruiting Officer* by Farquhar, it was used for presentations of plays by Fielding and later taken over by Henry Giffard. Following a series of circus-type entertainments and use as a warehouse, it was destroyed by fire in 1802.

Another theatre of the same name opened early in 1732 under Giffard, who installed a distinguished company, thrived until 1737, when it lost its licence. Goodman's Fields reopened in 1740 and, later the same year, saw the professional debut of Garrick, as Richard III. It closed finally, however, in 1742 under pressure from the PATENT THEATRES.

Good-Natured Man, The A comedy by Oliver GOLDSMITH. First performance: Covent Garden, 1768. In an attempt to cure the gullible central character of his excessive good nature, his father has him arrested for debt so that he can discover who his real friends are.

Good Person of Setzuan, The (*Der gute Mensch von Sezuan*) A play by Bertolt BRECHT, written in 1938–41. First performance: Zürich, 1942. One of Brecht's most admired plays, it explores the dilemma faced by a good person in a predatory society. The play concerns Shen Te, a benevolent woman who is obliged to invent a rough male companion (impersonating him herself) as a defence against those around her.

Goodspeed Opera House A company in East Haddam, Connecticut, occupying a 200-seat theatre built in 1876 on the banks of the Connecticut River. Despite its small size, it specializes in musicals, offering mostly revivals but some new work, examples of each have transferred to Broadway.

Goodwin, Nat(haniel) (1857–1919) US actor, who made his debut in Joseph Bradford's *Law in New York* (1874) in Boston. He enjoyed great success as a mimic in New York, then formed his own farce-comedy troupe, the Froliques. In the 1890s he adopted a more serious polished style, most notably in the title role of Clyde Fitch's *Nathan Hale* (1899) and in other parts opposite his wife, Maxine Elliott; his attempts at Shakespeare, however, were failures.

Gorboduc; or, Ferrex and Porrex The first English tragedy in blank verse, written by Thomas NORTON and Thomas SACKVILLE in 1561. It was influenced by Seneca and narrates the disasters that befell Britain when Gorboduc divided the kingdom between his sons.

Gorchakov, Nicolai Mikhailovich (1899–1958) Russian producer, who became a senior administrator of the Moscow stage after experience as Stanislavsky's assistant at the Moscow Art Theatre in the 1920s. His productions of plays by Sheridan and Russian playwrights were highly praised; he later became director of the Moscow Theatre of Drama (1933–38) and of the Theatre of Satire (1941–43). He was also appointed to the Lunacharsky State Institute of Theatre Art. His many writings on the theatre provide valuable insights on Stanislavsky's methods.

Gordin, Jacob (1853–1909) Jewish playwright, born in the Ukraine, who became a prominent figure in the Yiddish theatre of New York. His many plays include Jewish adaptations of many foreign masterpieces, among them *The Jewish King Lear* (1892) and *God, Man and Devil* (1900), which was derived from Goethe's *Faust*.

Gordon-Lennox, Cosmo *See* Tempest, Dame Marie.

Goring, Marius (1912–98) British actor, who made several youthful appearances before moving into adult roles at the Old Vic, where his parts included Hamlet (1935) and Ariel (1940). Fluent in French and German, he has often played leading classical roles in those languages on the Continent. He was Richard II and Petruchio at Stratford-on-Avon in 1953 and Angelo in *Measure for Measure* for the Royal Shakespeare Company in 1962. He took over as Andrew Wyke in Peter Shaffer's *Sleuth* in 1971. Later work included *Zaïde* at the Old Vic (1982) and Jeffrey Archer's *Beyond Reasonable Doubt* (1987).

Gorky, Maxim (Alexei Maximovich Pyeshkov; 1868–1936) Russian novelist, playwright, and short-story writer, whose plays reflect his sympathy for society's outcasts. His most successful drama, THE LOWER DEPTHS, portrays life in Moscow's underworld. He was arrested for his political views in 1905 and spent the next few years as an exile in the US. Of his major dramas, which have been criticized by some for their technical shortcomings, *Somov and Others* and *Yegor Bulychov and Others* form part of an unfinished cycle of plays intended to cover Russian history from 1917 to the 1930s. He returned to Russia in 1931; his novel *The Mother* was successfully dramatized by other hands.

Principal dramatic works:

Meshchane: 1902; translated as *Scenes in the House of Bersemenov*.
Na dne: 1902; translated as *The Lower Depths*.
Dashniki: 1904; translated as *Summer Residents*.
Vragi: 1906; translated as *The Enemies*.
Vassa Zheleznova: 1906; translated as *Mother Zheleznova*.
Zykovy: 1913; translated as *The Zykovs*.
Yegor Bulychov i drugiye: 1932; translated as *Yegor Bulychov and Others*.
Dostigayev i drugiye: 1933; translated as *Dostigayev and Others*.
Yakov Bogolomov: 1941.
Somov i drugiye: unfinished; translated as *Somov and Others*.

Gorky Theatre, Grand A theatre in St Petersburg, which opened in 1919 under Alexander BLOK; it was later renamed in honour of Maxim Gorky. The theatre began with a mixed programme of Russian and foreign works before presenting various Expressionist dramas by Shaw and O'Neill amongst others. After damage in World War II, it became a venue for productions of Shakespeare, which were later repeated by the resident company in London (1966). Other successes included plays by Dostoevsky and Griboyedov, as well as Chekhov and Gogol.

Goset *See* Moscow State Jewish Theatre.

Gôt, Edmond-François-Jules (1822–1901) French actor, who joined the Comédie-Française in 1850 and later became its leader. He was highly regarded both in comedy, notably in the plays of Molière, and in classical roles.

Gottsched, Johann Christoph (1700–66) German playwright and literary critic, who did much to promote the observance of the rules of classical drama in the German theatre. With Carolina Neuber, he published the *Deutsche Schaubühne* (1740–45), a suggested repertory for the national theatre that included some adaptations by himself of French plays. Of his own dramatic works the most successful was *Der sterbende Cato* (1732), adapted from Addison's *Cato* (1713); after quarrelling with Neuber, however, he had little more to do with the theatre.

Götz von Berlichingen A play by GOETHE, his first major drama. First performance: Berlin, 1773. Inspired by Goethe's reading of Shakespeare, the play represents a deliberate rejection of the French neoclassical style. The story idealizes the career of a medieval robber baron. With its disjointed action and historical focus, it had a profound influence upon the development of the *Sturm und Drang* movement.

Gough, Michael (1917–) British actor, who began by playing small parts at the Old Vic in 1936 and, after World War II, appeared in roles ranging from Laertes in *Hamlet* (1951) to Joe in Jack Ronder's *This Year, Next Year* (1960). Among many parts for the National Theatre he played Glen in John Osborne's *Watch It Come Down* (1976) and Ernest in Ayckbourn's *Bedroom Farce* (1977). In 1986 he was Dillwyn Knox in Hugh Whitemore's *Breaking the Code*.

Gough, Robert (d. 1625) English actor, first recorded as playing a female role in Tarleton's *The Seven Deadly Sins*, with Strange's Men in about 1590. Later he was with the King's Men and was included in the 1623 Folio list of actors in Shakespeare's plays. It is thought that he may have been the original Juliet, as well as the first Portia in *The Merchant of Venice*.

Gourgaud, Françoise *See* Vestris, Madame.

Government Inspector, The (*Revizor*) A satirical comedy by Nikolai GOGOL. First performance: St Petersburg, 1836. The play exposes corrupt small-town bureaucracy through a confusion of identity that results in a petty clerk being mistaken for a government inspector; in its initial production it survived the censor only through the support of Tsar Nicholas I.

Gow, Ronald (1897–1993) British playwright, who collaborated with Walter Greenwood on an adaptation of the latter's novel *Love on the Dole*, which provided a great success for Wendy Hiller in 1935. She later married him and in 1946 played the lead in his adaptation of Hardy's *Tess of the D'Urbervilles*.

Goward, Mary Ann *See* Keeley, Robert.

Gozzi, Carlo (1720–1806) Italian playwright and poet, who resisted the attempts of Goldoni to reform the *commedia dell'arte*. He lampooned Goldoni in *L'amore delle tre melarance* (The Love of Three Oranges; 1761), which was highly popular at the time and was later made into an opera by Prokofiev; his own attempts to reform the *commedia dell'arte* were confined to the development of the FIABE, in which improvization remained a key element. Such fantasy plays as *Il corvo* (The Raven; 1761), *Il re cervo* (King Stag; 1761), and *Turandot* (1765), which was later made into an opera by Puccini, had a particularly strong influence upon writers in Germany, including Goethe and Schiller.

Grabbe, Christian Dietrich (1801–36) German poet and playwright, whose plays anticipated the Expressionist movement of the 20th century. He first became involved with the theatre in Berlin and wrote his first significant play, the satirical *Scherz, Satire, Ironie und tiefere Bedeutung*, in 1822; the more important of his later works include the tragedy *Don Juan und Faust* (1829), the experimental *Napoleon oder die Hundert Tage* (1831), and *Herzog Theodor von Gothland* (1827). He led an unhappy life and died early from alcoholism and tuberculosis.

Gracioso A comic servant character of the Spanish theatrical tradition, who was a common figure in plays of the Golden Age. Derived from BOBO, the clown of Lope de Rueda's interludes, the *Gracioso* character can in fact be traced back to ultimately Roman origins. Used for purposes of both satire and intrigue, he appeared in plays by Gil Vicente, Torres Naharro, Calderón, and Augustín de Moreto, among others.

Graham, Mary Ann (1728–87) British actress, the second wife of Richard YATES. She was at Drury Lane until 1767, then went to Covent Garden, where she was successful in a wide range of tragic parts.

Gramatica, Irma (1873–1962) Italian actress, who made her debut as a child. She won acclaim as lively young heroines in the plays of Halévy, Meilhac, and Sardou as well as for appearances in contemporary Italian plays by such authors as Giacosa and Verga; she also triumphed in Shakespearean roles, including Lady Macbeth (1938).

Her younger sister, **Emma Gramatica** (1875–1965), also began her career as an actress while still a child and gradually built up a reputation for her interpretation of roles in the realistic dramas of Ibsen, Pirandello, and Shaw, often playing in German and Spanish and touring widely. Other successes included works by D'Annunzio, Rosso di San Secondo, and Rostand.

grande See zarzuela.

Grand Guignol A style of cabaret that developed in France in the 19th century, featuring short plays based upon sensational events, including murder, rape, and hauntings. Popular in the Montmartre area of Paris at the end of the 19th century, Grand Guignol was also successfully presented in London in the early 20th century. *See also* Guignol.

grand master control A device attached to a dimmer board, allowing simultaneous changes of lighting over all or part of a set. In more recent years such control has been greatly facilitated by the introduction of computerized lighting systems.

Grand Opera House A theatre on Eighth Avenue and 23rd Street, New York, which opened as **Pike's Opera House** in 1868. It was renamed in 1869 and was used for light opera, melodrama, and the occasional classic play as well as by touring companies. It became a cinema in 1938 and was demolished in 1961.

Grand Theatre A theatre in Islington, London, which opened in 1870 as the Philharmonic Music-Hall. It staged various entertainments before being destroyed by fire in 1883. Reopened the same year, it suffered further fires in 1887 and 1900 and – renamed the **Islington Empire** in 1908 – became a venue for touring companies, pantomime, and variety until 1932, when it became a cinema.

Another theatre of the same name opened in London in 1897 and saw performances of musical comedies and shows starring Gertie Millar. It was renamed the **Fulham Theatre** in 1906 and subsequently the **Shilling Theatre** but was ultimately demolished in 1958.

Grandval, François-Charles Racot de (1710–84) French actor, who joined the Comédie-Française in 1729 and inherited the tragic roles of Dufresne. Much admired for the passion of his acting, he retired at the age of 52; his subsequent successful return to the stage ended when members of the audience, probably hired by some jealous fellow-performers, jeered him in Voltaire's *Alzire*.

Granovsky, Alexander (Abraham Ozark; 1890–1937) Jewish actor and director, who was a leading figure in the Yiddish theatre tradition in Russia in the early 20th century. He founded the Jewish Theatre Studio in St Petersburg in 1919 (later the Moscow State Jewish Theatre) and staged works by Maeterlinck and Aleichem among others; other notable successes included his adaptation of Isaac Peretz's poem *Night in the Old Market* (1925). Subsequently he directed plays for the Habimah company.

Granville-Barker, Harley (1877–1946) British actor, director, playwright, and theatre scholar, whose productions of the plays of Shaw and Shakespeare had a profound effect upon the course of 20th-century drama. He began his career as an actor, appearing with Ben Greet, Mrs Patrick Campbell, and William Poel among others, and first became associated with G B Shaw when he was chosen to play Marchbanks in the London premiere (1900) of *Candida* by the Stage Society. More Shaw premieres followed and in 1904 Granville-Barker and J E Vedrenne took over the Royal Court Theatre, where they staged a celebrated series of Shavian dramas and other new works over the next three years. As well as plays by Galsworthy, Ibsen, and Yeats the Royal Court also presented Granville-Barker's own play *The Voysey Inheritance* (1905) and attempted, until it was banned by the Lord Chamberlain, to stage his *Waste* also. Granville-Barker's other best-known play, *The Madras House*, was seen at the Duke of York's Theatre in 1910. Granville-Barker established a strong reputation as a director for his faithfulness to the text and won particular praise for his lively productions of such Shakespearean plays as *Twelfth Night* and *A Midsummer Night's Dream*, which were presented at the Savoy Theatre during 1912–14; he virtually retired from the stage, however, in 1918 after marrying a wealthy divorcée. His first wife was the actress Lillah McCarthy.

Grassi, Paolo *See* Piccolo Teatro della Città di Milano.

Grau, Jacinto (1877–1958) Spanish playwright, who made his name in the theatre with stylized dramas written under the influence of Pirandello. His most important works include *El hijo pródigo* (The Prodigal Son; 1918), *El señor de Pigmalión* (1923), and the satirical drama *El burlador que no se burla* (1930).

grave trap A rectangular trap in the centre of the stage, named after its use in the gravediggers scene in *Hamlet*.

Gray, Dulcie (Winifred Catherine Gray; 1919–) British actress, whose career has been closely associated with that of her late husband, Michael DENISON. After her debut, in Noël Coward's *Hay Fever* in 1939, she appeared at the Open Air Theatre, Regent's Park, and toured South Africa in a variety of productions. She also performed in her own play, *Love Affair,* at the Lyric, Hammersmith, in 1955, while appearances with her husband have included the title role in Shaw's *Candida* (1960) and Gina Ekdal in Ibsen's *The Wild Duck* (1970). In later years she appeared in *The School for Scandal* (1983), Graham Greene's *The Living Room* (1987), Wilde's *An Ideal Husband* (1996), and *Les Liaisons dangereuses* (2000).

Gray, 'Monsewer' Eddie *See* Crazy Gang.

Gray, Simon (1936–) British playwright and novelist, who established his reputation with his play about an academic facing a personal crisis, *Butley* (1971). Alan Bates was highly praised in the central role and has since appeared in a series of plays by Gray, notably *Otherwise Engaged* (1975), the comedy thriller *Stage Struck* (1979), *Quartermaine's Terms* (1981), and *Life Support* (1997). Gray's other works have included his first play, *Wise Child* (1967), in which Alec Guinness appeared, *Molly* (1977), starring Billie Whitelaw, *Close of Play* (1979), which featured Michael Redgrave, and *The Common Pursuit* (1988). More recent work includes *Hidden Laughter* (1990) and *Japes* (2001). He also adapted Dostoevsky's *The Idiot* for the National Theatre in 1970.

Gray, Terence (1895–1987) British theatre manager, who cofounded the Festival Theatre, Cambridge, in 1926. His reforms of staging techniques there, which included the removal of the proscenium arch and footlights and the use of multilevel staging, had enormous influence upon European theatre. His most celebrated productions included Aeschylus's *Oresteia* and various other classics; his associates at the theatre, which he left in 1933, included Maurice Evans and Flora Robson.

Graziano *See* Dottore, Il.

Grease A musical by Jim Jacobs and Warren Casey. First performance: New York, 1972 (an earlier version was staged in Chicago in 1970). Both music and plot – a high-school romance in which Sandy, a 'good' girl, goes 'bad' to get her man – offer an affectionate parody of 1950s youth culture. The show's success (3388 performances) demonstrated that there was a large youth audience potentially available for Broadway musicals. The still-more successful film version appeared in 1977.

Great Dionysia *See* Dionysia.

Great Queen Street Theatre *See* Kingsway Theatre.

Great Vance, The *See* Vance, Alfred.

Gréban, Arnoul (c. 1420–71) French playwright and organist, author of the Passion play *Mystère de la Passion*. Written in the early 1450s, it depicts the creation and fall of Adam and the life of Christ. Arnoul Gréban is believed to have collaborated with his brother Simon in the mystery play *Actes de Apôtres* (ACTS OF THE APOSTLES).

Grecian Theatre A theatre in Shoreditch, London, opened around 1830 as a concert hall. After a slow start, it became a venue for performances of Shakespeare and was enlarged in 1858 to hold 3400 people. Subsequently it diversified into pantomime and ballet under the CONQUEST family, being rebuilt in 1876 and eventually sold to the Salvation Army in 1881.

Greco-Roman drama Theatre within the Greek and Roman sphere of influence between the great age of Athenian drama and the Roman drama of the 1st century AD. Overlapping with Greek New Comedy, as exemplified in the plays of Menander, this era saw the emergence of a new generation of writers, notably Plautus and Terence, who worked from older Greek models, as well as the development of the Roman semicircular auditorium and the increasing secularization of the theatre.

Greek drama *See* Athenian drama; Greco-Roman drama; Hellenistic drama.

Green, John (fl. 1606–27) English actor, who led a company of English Comedians on the Continent in succession to Robert Browne. His name figures intermittently in annals of German theatre up to 1627.

Green, Julian (1900–98) French writer, best known for his novels. Born in Paris of US parents, he is the author of the plays *Sud* (1953), *L'Ennemi* (1954), *L'Ombre* (1956), *Demain n'existe pas* (1979), and *L'Automate* (1980), which share the sombre themes of his novels.

Green, Paul Eliot (1894–1981) US playwright, whose many plays depict rural life in North Carolina, his native state. *In Abraham's Bosom* (1926) won him a Pulitzer Prize for its condemnation of the South's decadence, while *The House of Connelly* became the inaugural production of the Group Theatre in 1931. *Tread the Green Grass* was well received in 1932 and Kurt Weill provided the music for the pacifist play *Johnny Johnson*, which was produced by Orson Welles in 1936. *The Last Colony* (1937) was the first of a series of 15 **symphonic dramas** based on episodes in US history; these were all performed outdoors and combined both amateur and professional performers.

green baize A green stage carpet, traditionally used in sets of the 18th and 19th centuries when a tragedy was to be performed.

greencoat A member of the stage-crew of the Restoration theatre. Usually dressed in green livery, the greencoats were responsible for bringing on and taking off items of furniture and detail scenery between scenes.

Greene, Graham (1904–91) British novelist and playwright, whose association with the theatre began with the stage adaptation of his novel *Brighton Rock* (1943). Subsequently he adapted his novel *The Heart of the Matter* (1950) with Basil Dean, writing his first play – *The Living Room*, a study of suicide – in 1953. Subsequent plays included *The Potting Shed* (1957), on religious themes, the comedy *The Complaisant Lover* (1959), the farcical tragedy *Carving a Statue* (1964), *The Return of A J Raffles* (1975), and *The Great Jowett* (1981).

Greene, Robert (c. 1560–92) English playwright, who is usually remembered for his attack on Shakespeare in *A Groatsworth of Wit Bought with a Million of Repentance*. His play *Friar Bacon and Friar Bungay* (1589) was an early example of romantic comedy; he may also have collaborated with Kyd and other leading contemporaries. His other plays include *Alphonsus, King of Aragon* (1587), *James IV* (1590), *A Looking Glass for London and England* (1590), and *Orlando Furioso* (1591).

green man A mythological character who often appeared dressed in green and adorned with leaves in early English folk theatre. Associated with spring and the accompanying fertility rites, he also appeared in the Morris Dance and may have provided a model for the central figure of the Robin Hood play.

green room A room in the backstage area of a theatre, set aside for the use of the cast and stage crew. It was formerly used for the reception of visitors before and after a performance.

Green Room Club A social club in Adam Street, London, founded in 1866. Established by members from the Junior Garrick Club, it traditionally includes a majority of actors and actresses in its membership.

Greenwich Theatre A theatre in Crooms Hill, London, opened as a concert hall in 1855. After a period as **Crowder's Musical Hall** from 1871, it became the Greenwich Hippodrome in 1911 and subsequently underwent a number of changes, including use as a cinema and warehouse. In 1969 it was reopened under its original name, seating 426 and incorporating a restaurant, art gallery, and jazz club; it subsequently enjoyed success with plays by Alan Ayckbourn, Coward, and Peter Nichols among others; directors there included Jonathan Miller. The theatre closed in 1998, but has since reopened as a venue for touring productions.

Greet, Sir Ben (Philip Barling; 1857–1936) British actor-manager, remembered for his performances of Shakespeare's plays for schools and in the open air. One of the cofounders of the Old Vic, where he staged 24 Shakespearean productions, he undertook several tours of the UK and the US with his own company. He was knighted in 1929.

Gregory, Augusta, Lady (1852–1932) Irish playwright, who was one of the founders of the ABBEY THEATRE. Following a meeting with W B Yeats in 1876 she dedicated herself to Irish theatre. Her best plays, written in Irish dialect, included such comedies as *Spreading the News* (1904), the tragi-comic *The Gaol Gate* (1906), and the tragedy *Dervorgilla* (1907). She provided dialect versions of Molière's plays and assisted Yeats with various works, including *The Pot of Broth* (1902) and CATHLEEN NI HOULIHAN. She also championed J M Synge and G B Shaw and brought Sean O'Casey to public notice.

Gregory, Johann Gottfried (1631–75) German Lutheran pastor, who presented various theatrical productions at the royal court in Moscow, where he was appointed in 1658. Such entertainments as *The Play of Artaxerxes* (1672) and *The Comedy of Young Tobias* (1673) were performed in a theatre at the summer palace at Preobrazhen by Russian actors trained by Gregory himself.

Grein, Jack Thomas (Jacob Thomas Grein; 1862–1935) British playwright, theatre critic, and manager, born in Holland, who did much to popularize the 'theatre of ideas' of Ibsen, Shaw, and others. His **Independent Theatre Club** presented important early productions of such plays as *Ghosts* and *Widower's Houses* despite much adverse criticism.

Grenfell, Joyce (Joyce Irene Phipps; 1910–79) British actress and writer, whose success in Farjeon's *The Little Revue* (1939) secured her appearances in several other intimate revues, notably *Sigh No More* (1945), *Tuppence Coloured* (1947), and *Penny Plain* (1951). She performed satirical monologues and songs and, after appearing in *Joyce Grenfell Requests the Pleasure* in 1954, toured the world in solo entertainments. She became a personality on radio and television and appeared in several films.

Grenier de Toulouse   *See Décentralisation Dramatique.*

Grenier-Hussenot, Les   A French theatre company founded in 1946 by the actors Jean-Pierre Grenier and Olivier Hussenot, former members of Chancerel's touring troupe. The group performed in cabarets in Paris, presenting a wide range of entertainments, from music and acrobatics to mime and satire. The company was broken up in 1957.

Gresset, Jean-Baptiste-Louis (1709–77) French poet and playwright, born in Amiens. A Jesuit teacher, Gresset was forced to leave the order as a result of his satirical poem *Vert-Vert* (1734) and other comic verses. He subsequently turned to the theatre, producing the tragedy *Édouard III* (1740) and several comedies, of which *Le Méchant* (1747), a witty study of fashionable society, was the most successful.

Grévin, Jacques (1538–70) French playwright, poet, and doctor; author of the early French tragedy, *La Mort de César* (1561), modelled on the works of Seneca. Grévin's other plays are lively satirical comedies.

Grey, Spalding (1941–) US actor and writer, a performance artist who has had great success with a series of autobiographical one-man shows, such as *Sex and Death to the Age 14* (1979) and *Swimming to Cambodia* (1985).

Gribov, Alexei Nikolayevich (1902–77) Russian actor, who became one of the most popular performers with the Moscow Art Theatre, which he joined in 1924. He was particularly acclaimed for his impersonation of peasant characters, although he also appeared as Lenin (1942) and in several classical parts.

Griboyedov, Alexander Sergeivich (1795–1829) Russian playwright and diplomat, author of the celebrated comedy *Gore ot uma* (Woe from Wit; 1822–24), which was not performed until 1831 due to its satirical comments upon contemporary Moscow society. Chatski, the hero, became a stock character of the Russian theatre and a favourite role of many actors, while several of the aphorisms in the play became popular proverbs. Having fought in the army against Napoleon, Griboyedov became Russian minister in Tehran in 1828, dying there at the hands of a mob. He also translated Molière and other French writers.

grid A framework of metal or wood over the stage area, used for the hanging of lighting equipment and scenery; it is more formally known as a **gridiron**.

Grieg, Nordahl (1902–43) Norwegian poet, novelist, and playwright, whose early experimental dramas, notably *Barrabas* (1927), treat such themes as violence and freedom. His principal works include the anti-war play *Vår ære og vår makt* (Our Honour and our Power; 1935) and *Nederflaget* (Defeat; 1937), which deals with the Paris Commune of 1871. He died in an air raid in World War II.

Grieve, William (1800–44) British scene painter, who worked as a boy at Covent Garden but became well known for his achievements at Drury Lane. Especially famed for his moonlight scenes, he once had the distinction of being called in front of the curtain after a performance in 1832. His elder brother, **Thomas Grieve** (1799–1882), was also respected as a scene painter.

Griffiths, Trevor (1935–) British playwright, whose work reflects his Marxist belief in the need for social change. Such plays as *Occupations* (1970), *The Party* (1973) and COMEDIANS have been performed by groups as diverse as the Royal Shakespeare Company and the 7:84 Theatre Company. Since the success of *Comedians* (1975), Griffiths has written mainly for television; a number of his later stage plays, such as *Oi! for England* (1982) and *Who Shall Be Happy…?* (1996) began life as television dramas. *The Gulf Between Us* (1992), a piece inspired by the Gulf War, was his first original stage work for 17 years.

Grillparzer, Franz (1791–1872) Austrian playwright, who was a leading figure of the Romantic movement. The pessimism of his 12 tragedies was a reflection of his own troubled life, in which he suffered from the early death of his father, his mother's suicide, and various unhappy love affairs. His early tragedies were modelled on classical lines, although the historical drama *König Ottokars Glück und Ende*, which was highly praised after initial opposition from the censors, drew heavily upon Schiller; *Der Traum ein Leben* was based on Calderón. After the failure of his one comedy, *Weh' dem, der lügt*, in 1838 he released no more plays for production in the theatre.

Principal works:
  Die Ahnfrau: 1817; translated as *The Ancestress*.
  Sappho: 1819.
  Das goldene Vliess: 1820.
  König Ottokars Glück und Ende: 1825.
  Des Meeres und der Liebe Wellen: 1831.
  Der Traum ein Leben: 1834; translated as *Life Is a Dream*.
  Die Jüdin von Toledo: 1888.
  Libussa: 1874.

Grimaldi, Joseph (1778–1837) British clown, commonly called **Joey**, who was born in London, the illegitimate son of the ballet master at Drury Lane. He appeared as a child at Sadler's Wells so successfully that he was taken into pantomime at Drury Lane and continued to appear at both theatres. In 1806 he was engaged at Covent Garden, where he remained for the next 17 years, transforming the English pantomime. Noted for his mastery of acrobatics and mime, he retired in 1823; all clowns are now named Joey in his honour.

Gringore, Pierre (c. 1475–1538) French actor and playwright, who wrote anti-papal pieces on behalf of Louis XII. The chief Fool with a company in Paris, he was the author of several satirical *soties*, in which he appeared himself, and the plays *Le Jeux du prince du Sots* (1511) and *Mystère de Saint-Louis*.

Gripsholm Theatre A theatre in Sweden, constructed inside a fortress built in 1535 during the time of Gustavus Vasa. Opened in 1782, the theatre survives intact, complete with various items of stage machinery and scenery.

Grock (Charles Adrien Wettach; 1880–1959) British music hall clown, born in Switzerland, who performed acrobatics at the age of 12, touring with his family group of Tyrolean singers. Subsequently he went into partnership with a clown named Brick, but after 1911 appeared as a solo act almost continuously at the London Coliseum until 1924, when he returned to the Continent. He presented an hour-long act of virtuoso musical numbers in which everything invariably went wrong.

groove A narrow channel made of wood, along which a flat could be slid on and off the stage; the groove system was eventually replaced by the carriage-and-frame system in the 19th century.

Gropius, Walter *See* Totaltheater.

Gros-Guillaume (Robert Guérin; fl. 1598–1634) French actor, who became a popular player in farce alongside Turlupin and Gaultier-Garguille at the Hôtel de Bourgogne, after appearing in the Paris fairs. A fat man, he also appeared in tragedy under the stagename **La Fleur**. Several other members of his family were also on the stage, including his son-in-law François Juvenon (c. 1623–74), who also appeared as La Fleur and inherited the tragic roles of Montfleury, and his grandson, who appeared as LA TUILLERIE.

Gros-René *See* Du Parc.

Grosses Schauspielhaus A theatre in Berlin, converted from a circus by Hans POELZIG and opened in 1919. The theatre, built for Max Reinhardt, was remarkable for its rejection of the conventional proscenium arch in favour of flexible staging and a cyclorama, with the audience of 3000 seated on three sides of the acting area. It was subsequently altered and renamed the Friedrichsstadt-Palest.

Grossman, Jan (1925–93) Czech director, who established his reputation while at the Theatre on the Balustrade in Prague, notably with the plays of Václav Havel. He took over the company in 1962 and won acclaim in the London World Theatre Seasons of 1967 and 1968, presenting Kafka's *Der Prozess* and his own *King Ubu*, adapted from Jarry. He then worked in exile until 1974, when he became director of the City Theatre in Cheb.

Grossmith, George (1847–1912) British actor, who became famous for his solo entertainments at the piano; subsequently he played principal parts in several Gilbert and Sullivan operas. Thereafter, he devoted himself mainly to performing his own sketches and songs, and wrote *Diary of a Nobody* (1892) with his brother **Weedon Grossmith** (1852–1919), who was also an actor. George's sons, **George Grossmith** (1874–1935) and **Lawrence Grossmith** (1877–1944), had distinguished acting careers, the former being associated with a number of successful revues.

Groto, Luigi (1541–85) Italian playwright and poet, often known as **Il cieco d'Adria** ('The blind man of Adria'). *Adriana* (1578) was an early version of the story that eventually provided the material for Shakespeare's *Romeo and Juliet*; other works included pastorals and comedies as well as the bloodthirsty tragedy *La Dalida* (1572).

Grotowski, Jerzy (1933–99) Polish director, who established an international reputation with his experimental productions. Having trained at the Cracow Theatre School, he became known for his emphasis on the paramount role of the actor while director of the Polish Theatre Laboratory in Wrocław during the 1960s. With this company he pioneered new ways of using movement and speech to assault the emotions; noted productions included plays by Calderón and Wyspiański (especially *Akropolis* in 1966) as well as Shakespeare. His advocacy of sparse settings and the most basic lighting effects had a strong influence on Peter Brook in Britain and the Living Theatre in the US. However, much of his later work was carried out in private, especially after he disbanded the Theatre Laboratory company in 1976. His last years were spent in France. A summary of his avant-garde ideas can be found in *Towards a Poor Theatre* (1968).

Grottesco, Teatro A movement that developed in Italy during World War I in reaction to the heroic dramas of D'Annunzio. Deriving its name from the subtitle of Chiarelli's *La maschera e il volto* (The Mask and the Face; 1916), the movement used irony and satire to explore the conflict between appearances and reality; writers of the genre included Bontempelli and Rosso di San Secondo.

groundrow A long low piece of scenery, basically a small flat, which is often painted to suggest an horizon. The upper edge can be shaped to represent mountains, waves (a **sea row** or **water row**), or other features.

Group Theatre A theatre organization founded in New York in 1931 by Harold Clurman, Cheryl Crawford, and Lee Strasberg to present serious drama outside the commercial theatre. The successor to the Theatre Guild, it established a strong reputation with plays by Paul Green, Sidney Kingsley, William Saroyan, and – above all – Clifford Odets, producing *Awake and Sing!* (1935) and *Waiting for Lefty* (1935) among other important works. The group also did much to disseminate the theories of Stanislavsky in the US before disbanding in 1941, short of money and internally split.

In 1933 another **Group Theatre** was founded in London at the Westminster Theatre to produce experimental and noncommercial drama. Under the direction of **Rupert Doone** (1904–66), it presented notable works by T S Eliot, W H Auden, and Stephen Spender, among others, often in collaboration with the composer Benjamin Britten. It closed during World War II and was briefly revived in the early 1950s.

Grove Theatre A shortlived theatre in Bedlow Street (later Madison Street), New York, which opened in 1804, with a company of then untried actors. The theatre only opened on nights when the Park Theatre was closed; it was renamed the Covent Garden Theatre after a successful pantomime presented by Signor Bologna of London's Covent Garden.

Gründgens, Gustav (1899–1963) German actor and director, who established his reputation in strong romantic parts in Berlin in the 1930s. He was particularly praised in the plays of Shaw and as Shakespeare's Hamlet (1938); subsequent successes included Mephistopheles in Goethe's *Faust* (1957–58), in which role he toured widely. After World War II he worked chiefly in Düsseldorf and Hamburg as well as in films; as a director he presented notable productions of Osborne's *The Entertainer* (1957) and plays by Brecht. His early life was the basis of Klaus Mann's controversial novel *Mephisto* (1936; dramatized 1979); he apparently committed suicide in Manila.

Grundy, Sydney (1848–1914) British playwright, who wrote numerous adaptations of French pieces, beginning with *A Little Change* at the Haymarket Theatre in 1872. *A Pair of Spectacles* (1890), from *Les Petits Oiseaux* by Labiche and Delacour, was the most successful; others include *The Silver Shield* (1885), *The New Woman* (1894), and *A Fearful Joy* (1908).

Gryphius, Andreas (1616–64) German poet and playwright, author of five tragedies remarkable for their bloodletting and horror. Typical of these was *Murdered Majesty; or, Charles Stuart, King of Great Britain* (1649), in which he depicted the recent trial and execution of Charles I; others included *Catharina von Georgien* (1647) and *Papinianus* (1659), both studies of Christian martyrs. Gryphius also wrote the early domestic drama *Cardenio und Celinde* (1647) and several comedies, of which *Horribilicribifax* (1663) is regarded as the best.

Gual, Adrià (1872–1943) Spanish playwright and director, who founded the celebrated but shortlived **Teatro Intím** in Barcelona in 1903. The company presented productions of many classic plays, ranging from works by Aeschylus to Spanish dramas, achieving high standards of acting and staging, which ultimately contributed to the revival of Spanish drama during the 1920s and 1930s. Gual's own plays included *Misteri de Dolor*.

Guare, John (1938–) US playwright, who established his reputation with *A Day for Surprises* (1965) and *The Loveliest Afternoon of the Year* (1966). Other plays have included *The House of Blue Leaves* (1970), a musical version of *The Two Gentleman of Verona* (1973), *Bosoms and Neglect* (1979), the *Lydie Breeze* trilogy (1982–86), and the extremely successful *Six Degrees of Separation* (1990).

Guarini, Giovanni Battista (1538–1612) Italian poet, playwright, and diplomat, who ranks alongside Torquato Tasso (whose post as court poet at Ferrara he inherited in 1579 as a result of Tasso's mental illness) as the creator of the Italian pastoral. His tragicomedy *Il pastor fido* (The Faithful Shepherd; 1598) was revived many times in Italy, England, and France and inspired numerous imitations. His other writings include the treatise *Compendio della poesia tragicomica* and the comedy *L'idropica*.

Guérin d'Étriché, Isaac François (c. 1636–1728) French actor, who married Armande Béjart after the death of her first husband, Molière. He was initially at the Théâtre du Marais before joining the Comédie-Française and subsequently becoming its leader. His finest roles included Harpagon in Molière's *L'Avare*.

Guerrero, María (1868–1928) Spanish actress, who became the leading national theatrical performer in Spain in the late 19th century. Acclaimed in both classical Spanish plays and in contemporary works by such authors as Benavente, Pérez Galdós, and the Álvarez Quintero brothers, she also managed her own theatre, now renamed the Teatro Nacional María Guerrero in her honour.

Guignol A character of the French puppet theatre. Probably first introduced in Lyons during the late 18th century, he was derived from the character of POLICHINELLE from the *commedia dell'arte*. He eventually lent his name to the GRAND GUIGNOL.

Guilbert, Yvette (Emma Laure Esther Guilbert; 1865–1944) French singer, who became a leading performer in French music hall. Known as '*la diseuse fin-de-siècle*', she first appeared in 1887 and soon became popular for her apparently unknowing delivery of highly *risqué* songs. Extremely thin and heavily made up, she habitually appeared in yellow with long black gloves, in which costume she was depicted in famous posters by Toulouse-Lautrec. Later in her career she sang traditional *chansons* in Europe and the US as well as appearing in many plays.

Guild Theatre *See* Virginia Theatre.

Guillot-Gorju (Bertrand Hardouin de St Jacques; 1600–48) French actor, who began his career as a barker at the Paris fairs before appearing in farce at the Hôtel de Bourgogne. He was much encouraged by Bellerose, whose daughter he married, but later retired to become a doctor.

Guimerà, Àngel (1849–1924) Spanish poet and playwright, born in Tenerife, who is generally regarded as the most significant Catalan dramatist. Inspired by the French Romantics, his early poetic historical tragedies include *Gala Placidia* (1879), and *L'ànima morta* (The Dead Soul; 1892). His later naturalist plays, of which the rural drama *Terra Baixa* (1896) is the most outstanding, portray contemporary peasant life.

Guinness, Sir Alec (1914–2000) British actor, famous for his understated introspective style. Guinness first attracted attention with the Old Vic company in the 1936–37 season, playing supporting parts in works by Shakespeare and Chekhov. He then took part in Gielgud's season at the Queen's Theatre before returning (1938) to the Old Vic to appear as Hamlet in modern dress and as Bob Acres in Sheridan's *The Rivals*. After World War II, he appeared in his own adaptation of Dostoevsky's *The Brothers Karamazov* (1946) and, during the Old Vic season from 1946–48, was highly praised in such roles as Richard II, the Fool in *King Lear*, and Abel Drugger in Jonson's *The Alchemist*. Subsequent successes included the roles of Sir Henry Harcourt-Reilly in T S Eliot's *The Cocktail Party* (1949), T E Lawrence in Terence Rattigan's *Ross* (1960), and the blind father in John Mortimer's *A Voyage Round My Father* (1981). In 1984 he returned to the stage to appear as Shylock at the Chichester Festival Theatre. His many screen successes include *The Bridge on the River Kwai*, *Kind Hearts and Coronets*, and television appearances as John Le Carré's George Smiley.

Guitry, Lucien-Germain (1860–1925) French actor and playwright, who made his stage debut in 1878. Later he undertook lengthy tours of Europe and appeared with Sarah Bernhardt, as well as managing the Théâtre de la Renaissance.

His son was the actor and playwright **Sacha Guitry** (1885–1957), who was born in St Petersburg. He wrote over 100 plays, mainly light comedies in the style of *Boulevard* theatre. He also produced such serious biographical dramas as *Pasteur* (1919), in which his father played the principal role, and wrote and directed several films. The third of his five wives was Yvonne PRINTEMPS.

Gundersen, Laura (1832–98) Norwegian actress, regarded as the first significant actress of the theatre in Norway. She first appeared at the Kristiana Theater in 1850 and excelled in the plays of Bjørnson, Ibsen, and Shakespeare.

Gunnell, Richard (d. 1634) English actor, manager, and playwright. An actor with Palsgrave's Men he took a share in the Fortune Theatre in 1618 and subsequently became manager there. In 1629, with William Blagrove, he built and then managed the Salisbury Court Theatre. His two plays are now lost.

Gurney, A R (1930–) US playwright. His *Scenes From American Life* was produced in Los Angeles in 1971 and major success followed with *The Middle Ages* (Los Angeles, 1977: New York, 1982), *The Dining Room* (1982), and *The Cocktail Hour* (1988). *Love Letters* (1988), written entirely in the form of letters sent between a man and a woman through a long relationship, has had special success; this may owe something to its inexpensive production requirements and the fact that the text can be read rather than memorized (making it easy to 'drop' stars into a production).

Gustav III (1746–92) King of Sweden (1771–92), who did much to foster the development of the Swedish theatre. He founded the Kungliga Dramatiska Teatern in 1788 and was himself the author of *Gustav Adolphs ädelmod* (Gustav Adolph's Magnanimity; 1783) and other plays.

Guthrie, Tyrone (1900–71) British actor and director, great-grandson of the actor Tyrone Power. After appearing under J B Fagan at Oxford, he worked as a director in Cambridge before presenting his first London play, THE ANATOMIST, at the Westminster Theatre in 1931. Subsequently he became famous for his productions of Shakespeare at the Old Vic, which included *Measure for Measure* (1933), with Charles Laughton and later Emlyn Williams, *Hamlet*, with Laurence Olivier (1937) and with Alec Guinness in modern dress the following year, *A Midsummer Night's Dream* (1937–38), with Robert Helpmann. He was also largely responsible for the foundation of the STRATFORD (ONTARIO) FESTIVAL, where he continued to advocate the use of the open stage, and directed major revivals of Jonson and Chekhov. The theatre in Minneapolis was named after him in 1971 (*see* Guthrie Theatre). Other important productions included Molière's *Tartuffe* (1967) with Gielgud at the Old Vic.

Guthrie Theatre A theatre in Minneapolis, Minnesota, which opened as the Minneapolis Theatre in 1963; its company quickly became perhaps the best known in the US outside New York. In 1971 the theatre, which seats 1441 and contains a seven-sided thrust stage, was renamed in honour of the company's founding director, Tyrone Guthrie. Among the productions presented there have been plays by Shakespeare, Chekhov, Arthur Miller, Molière, Rostand, and Wilder. Michael Langham succeeded Guthrie as director in 1971; subsequent directors have included Liviu Ciulei.

Gutzkow, Karl Ferdinand (1811–78) German playwright and novelist, who was the author of the celebrated Jewish play in defence of intellectual freedom, *Uriel Acosta*, written in 1847. His other writings for the stage include the satirical comedy *Das Urbild des Tartüffe* (The Model for Tartuffe; 1844).

Guys and Dolls A musical by Frank Loesser, with book by Jo Swerling and Abe Burrows. First performance: New York, 1950. This romantic tale set in a strangely innocent version of New York's gangster underworld was based on the stories of Damon Runyon; it was filmed in 1955 with Frank Sinatra, Marlon Brandon, and Jean Simmons. There have been many revivals; a 1996 production placed emphasis on the comic rather than the romantic leads.

Gwynn, Nell (1650–87) English actress, initially an orange-girl at Drury Lane. Charles Hart trained her for the stage and she made her debut in 1665 as Cydaria in Dryden's *The Indian Emperor*. Despite her limitations as an actress, she was popular in comedy and was especially acclaimed as Florimel in Dryden's *Secret Love*. She became mistress of Charles II in about 1669 and retired from the stage a year later.

Gyllenborg, Carl (1679–1746) Swedish playwright, author of some of the earliest Swedish comedy. His play *Den Swenska sprätthöken* (The Swedish Dandy; 1740) was the first native Swedish play to be presented at the Svenska Dramatiska Teatern.

Gymnase, Théâtre du A theatre in the Boulevard Bonne-Nouvelle, Paris, which opened in 1820 as a drama school. In 1830 the theatre's fortunes improved with successful productions of the plays of Eugène Scribe; later the plays of Sardou and Dumas *fils* were among notable premieres given there and the theatre established its reputation as one of the capital's most important venues for comedy and melodrama. Leading performers there have included Bernhardt and Lucien Guitry; the theatre now presents a mixed programme of drama under Marie BELL.

Gypsy A musical by Jule Styne, with lyrics by Stephen SONDHEIM and book by Arthur Laurents; the staging and choreography was by Jerome ROBBINS. First performance: New York, 1959. The plot deals with Mama Rose, who relentlessly pushes her children into the stage success she actually wants for herself. The role of Mama Rose, created for Ethel Merman, is generally considered the greatest in the American musical, while the show itself is sometimes called the greatest single work in the genre. Major revivals have starred Angela Lansbury (1974) and Tyne Daly (1989).

H

Habimah Theatre A Jewish theatre company, established in Moscow in 1917. Performing plays in Hebrew, the group began under the direction of Stanislavsky's pupil Vakhtangov; they presented his celebrated production of Ansky's *The Dybbuk* for the first time in 1922. Linked to the MOSCOW ART THEATRE, the company toured the world during the 1920s with *The Dybbuk* and plays by Calderón, Chekhov, Shakespeare, and other major playwrights. Eventually the company settled in Palestine in 1931, ultimately becoming Israel's national theatre in 1958, based in Tel Aviv. The company was reorganized in 1970 and moved into a fully-equipped National Theatre.

Hackett, J(ames) H(enry) (1800–71) US actor, who first appeared professionally in 1826 as Justice Woodcock in *Love in a Village*. He soon became celebrated for his Yankee characterizations, notably as Solomon Swop in *Jonathan in England* (1828). He also achieved a reputation for his portrayals of Falstaff and other comic Shakespearean characters, in which he appeared in both London and New York, where he was also manager of the Astor Place Opera House.

His son was the actor **James K(eteltas) Hackett** (1869–1926), who was with Daly's company in 1892, numbering Jaques in *As You Like It* among his parts. With Daniel Frohman from 1895 to 1899 he was acclaimed in romantic comedy and drama, especially as Rudolf in Hope's *The Prisoner of Zenda*; subsequent attempts at Shakespeare – his last appearance was as Macbeth in 1924 – were less successful. Having opened a theatre (later Wallack's Theatre) in New York, he staged an influential *Othello* in 1914.

Hackett, Walter (1876–1944) US playwright and manager, who became a popular producer of light comedy on the London stage, most of his productions featuring his wife, Marion Lorne. He opened the Whitehall Theatre in 1930 and later worked at the Apollo, his successes including such plays as *He Didn't Want To Do It* (1915), *The Way to Treat a Woman* (1930), and *London After Dark* (1937).

Hafner, Philipp (1731–64) Austrian playwright, whose plays effectively established the Viennese comedy of manners, the *Volksstück*. His plays, notably *Megära die förchterliche Hexe* (1755), *Der geplagte Odoardo* (1762), and *Der Furchtsame* (1764) combined literary merit with strong theatricality.

Hagen, Uta (1919–) US actress, born in Germany, who made her stage debut in Coward's *Hay Fever* (1935). In 1937 she appeared in Dennis, Massachusetts, with Eva Le Gallienne's Civic Repertory Company as Ophelia, making her New York debut a year later as Nina in Chekhov's *The Seagull*. She acted with her first husband, José

FERRER, in Maxwell Anderson's *Key Largo* (1939); later roles include Desdemona (1942–45), Blanche in *A Streetcar Named Desire* (1948), Martha in *Who's Afraid of Virginia Woolf?* (1962), and Ranevskaya in *The Cherry Orchard* (1968). Since the late 1960s she has concentrated on teaching, although she performed the title roles in *Charlotte* in 1980 and *Mrs Klein* in 1998. Her second husband was Herbert BERGHOF.

Haigh, Kenneth (1931–) British actor, who made his name as the original Jimmy Porter in John Osborne's *Look Back in Anger* (1956) in both London and New York. With the Royal Shakespeare Company his parts have included James in Harold Pinter's *The Collection* (1962) and numerous Shakespearean roles; in 1982 he played the title role in *Othello* at the Young Vic.

Haines, John Thomas (1797–1843) British playwright and actor, who was the author of numerous melodramas and nautical dramas. His dramatization of Scott's *Quentin Durward* was staged at the Coburg Theatre (later the Old Vic Theatre) in 1813; subsequently he appeared in Manchester in several of his own dramas, including *Hulme Hall; or, Manchester in Olden Times* (1828) and *The Factory Boy; or, The Love Sacrifice* (1840). Back in London he produced further nautical and domestic pieces, of which *My Poll and My Partner Joe* (1835) enjoyed the greatest success.

Haines, Joseph (d. 1701) English actor, who ran a booth at Bartholomew Fair before joining the company at Drury Lane. Noted for his practical jokes, he was a fine low comedian, singer, and dancer and became one of the first English Harlequins when he appeared in an adaptation of Molière's *Les Fourberies de Scapin*.

Hair A rock musical by Galt MacDermot, with book and lyrics by Gerome Ragni and James Rado. First performance: New York, 1967. The plot involves a young man from Oklahoma, who falls in with a group of New York Flower Children on his way to fight in the Vietnam War. The musical, which was produced under the auspices of the New York Shakespeare Festival, caused a stir with a scene in which most of the cast appeared nude (although dimly lit) at the end of the first act—the first such nudity on a Broadway stage.

Hale, Binnie (Beatrice Hale Monro; 1900–84) British actress, who made her name in the highly successful musical *No, No, Nanette* (1925) and went on to appear in many musical comedies with Jack Buchanan, Bobby Howes, and others. In 1947 she took over the Duke of York's Theatre, where she appeared in the revues *One, Two, Three* and its successor *Four, Five, Six*.

Her brother **Sonnie Hale** (Robert Hale Monro; 1902–59) was a light comedian who appeared in many musicals of the 1930s, sometimes with his wife Jessie Matthews.

Hale, Louise (Louise Closser; 1872–1933) US actress, who began her career in Detroit in 1894, toured in Augustus Thomas's *Arizona*, and was acclaimed as Prossy in Shaw's *Candida* on her New York debut in 1903. Later notable parts, before she went over to films, included Fairy Berylune in Maeterlinck's *The Blue Bird* (1910) and Mrs Atkins in O'Neill's *Beyond the Horizon* (1920).

Halévy, Ludovic *See* Meilhac, Henri.

Halevy, Mosche *See* Ohel Theatre.

Hall, Sir Peter (1930–) British director and manager, who was a founder of the Royal Shakespeare Company and subsequently head of the National Theatre (1973–88). He began his career while still at Cambridge University and then worked at the Theatre Royal, Windsor, before moving to the Arts Theatre in London, where he successfully produced plays by Anouilh and Beckett. He formed his own company in 1957 and established himself as a director at Stratford-on-Avon with his version of *Love's Labour's Lost* (1956). After further successes with Shakespearean works he was appointed managing director of the newly created RSC in 1960 and oversaw its occupation of London's Aldwych Theatre. There followed such influential and highly praised productions as *The Wars of the Roses* cycle (1963) before his resignation as managing director in 1968. Subsequently he presided over the foundation of the National Theatre (now the Royal National Theatre) and its transfer (1976) from the Old Vic to the South Bank; his successes with the National Theatre included Pinter's *No Man's Land* (1975), *Hamlet* (1975), Marlowe's *Tamburlaine the Great* (1976), Chekhov's *The Cherry Orchard* (1978), Shaffer's *Amadeus* (1979), and Wilde's *The Importance of Being Earnest* (1982). From 1980 he shared control of the Olivier and Cottesloe theatres with Peter Gill. On leaving the National Theatre in 1988 he created the Peter Hall Company, a transatlantic production company whose earlier successes included *The Merchant of Venice* (1989), with Dustin Hoffman, and *Lysistrata* (1993). In 1997 the company took up residence in the Old Vic, where Hall presented an ambitious repertoire that included plays by Beckett, Chekhov, and Granville-Barker. However, his failure to secure Arts Council backing in 1998 led Hall to disband the company and defect to the US, where he set up an American Shakespeare Company in Los Angeles. In 2000 he directed TANTALUS, a ten-hour cycle of plays about the Trojan War, in Denver, Colorado.

Hall, Willis (1929–) British playwright, whose long collaboration with Keith WATERHOUSE has resulted in a number of highly praised works for the theatre. The most significant of Hall's early (solo) works was *The Long and the Short and the Tall* (1959), about a British patrol lost in Malaya during World War II; others included the double bill *Last Day in Dreamland* and *A Glimpse of the Sea* (1959). BILLY LIAR was the first play written by Hall and Waterhouse together; among the many successful plays to follow were *England, Our England* (1962), the farce *Say Who You Are* (1965), and two adaptations of plays by Eduardo de Filippo – *Saturday, Sunday, Monday* (1973) and *Filumena* (1980). Hall's other works include the children's play *Kidnapped at Christmas* (1975) and musical adaptations of *The Wind in the Willows* (1985) and *The Water Babies* (1987).

Hallam, Lewis (1714–56) US actor, born in Britain, who emigrated with his family to the US in 1752 and installed a notable company at the Nassau Street Theatre in New York in 1753. Subsequently he toured a wide range of plays to Philadelphia, Charleston, and Jamaica.

His children included the British actress Mrs Mattocks and the US actor **Lewis Hallam** (c. 1740–1808), who became leading man with Douglass's American Company in 1758, was the earliest known US Hamlet, and won acclaim as Arsaces in the first professionally produced American play, Godfrey's *The Prince of Parthia* (1767). He took over the company in 1786 and was later associated with Hodgkinson and Dunlap in reopening the Southwark Theatre, Philadelphia, and the John Street Theatre, New York.

hall keeper *See* stage door-keeper.

halls *See* music hall.

Hallström, Per (1866–1960) Swedish playwright, poet, novelist, and critic, who was particularly noted for his translations of Shakespeare in the 1920s. His own plays included the tragedy *Bianco Capello* (1900), the comedy *Erotikon* (1908), the saga *Tusen och en natt* (A Thousand and One Nights; 1910), and several historical dramas.

ham An actor who habitually overacts, commonly from reasons of vanity, inexperience, or lack of genuine talent. The term was particularly relevant in the 19th century, when many actors favoured a ranting style of delivery.

Hamblin, Thomas Sowerby (1800–53) British actor and manager, who performed at Sadler's Wells and Drury Lane before making his US debut in 1825 at the Park Theatre, New York. In 1830 he took over the Bowery Theatre, which was burnt down three times during his tenure. In 1848 he moved to the Park Theatre, only to have this destroyed by fire the same year.

Hamlet, Prince of Denmark A revenge tragedy by William SHAKESPEARE, written c. 1600. First performance: c. 1600. The play, which is almost certainly the best-known dramatic work in the English language, centres on Hamlet's desire for vengeance following his father's murder and culminates in the death of virtually all the central characters. The text contains some of Shakespeare's finest soliloquies, including Hamlet's famous "To be or not to be". Other celebrated scenes include the appearances of the Ghost, Hamlet's dialogue with the Gravediggers, Ophelia's mad scenes, and the play-within-a-play before which Hamlet himself instructs the players about the nature of acting.

Hamlisch, Marvin (1944–) US composer whose best-known work for the stage is the score of A CHORUS LINE (1975), which received a Pulitzer Prize. His subsequent work includes the music for *They're Playing Our Song* (1979) and *The Goodbye Girl* (1993).

Hammerstein II, Oscar (1895–1960) US lyricist, whose first contribution to a musical was the book and lyrics for *Always You* (1920). Subsequently he worked in operetta with *The Desert Song* and *The New Moon*, and had a series of successes with Jerome KERN, including *Sunny* (1925), the extremely important SHOW BOAT, and *Music in the Air* (1932). In 1943 he enjoyed success with an adaptation of Bizet's *Carmen* as *Carmen Jones*. That same year saw the beginning of his collaboration with the composer Richard RODGERS on a series of highly popular and hugely influential shows. These included OKLAHOMA!, CAROUSEL, SOUTH PACIFIC, THE KING AND I, FLOWER DRUM SONG, and THE SOUND OF MUSIC.

Hammerstein's Theatre *See* Manhattan Theatre.

Hammerton, Stephen (d. c. 1648) English actor, who joined the King's Men after beginning as a boy actor at the Salisbury Court Theatre. Having played Oriana in Fletcher's *Wild Goose Chase* in 1631, he became greatly admired in female roles.

Hammond, Kay *See* Clements, Sir John (Selby).

Hampden, Walter (Walter Hampden Dougherty; 1879–1955) US actor, who began his career with Frank Benson's company and at the Adelphi Theatre in London. He returned to the US in 1907 and won acclaim in Kennedy's *The Servant in the House* (1908) and *Cyrano de Bergerac* (1923). His Shakespearean roles included Caliban, Hamlet, Macbeth, Oberon, Othello, Romeo, and Shylock. In 1925 he took over the **Colonial Theatre** and renamed it Hampden's; his productions there included *Henry V*, Benavente's *The Bonds of Interest*, and Bulwer-Lytton's *Richelieu*.

Hampshire, Susan (1942–) British actress, who is best known for her television work but has also played many classic parts on the stage. Her roles have included Kate Hardcastle in Goldsmith's *She Stoops to Conquer* (1966), Nora in Ibsen's *A Doll's House* (1972), Katherina in *The Taming of the Shrew* (1974), Ann Whitefield in Shaw's *Man and Superman* (1978), Elvira in Coward's *Blithe Spirit* (1986), Gertrude Lawrence in *Noel and Gertie* (1991), and the Countess of Marshwood in Coward's *Relative Values* (1993).

Hampstead Theatre A theatre organization founded (as the **Hampstead Theatre Club**) in 1959, which presented the London premieres of plays by Harold Pinter and Ionesco between 1959 and 1962. The club then moved to Swiss Cottage, where it presented several successful plays, including adaptations of Laurie Lee's *Cider with Rosie* (1963) and Aubrey's *Brief Lives* (1967), which transferred to the West End. Rehoused nearby in 1970, the theatre has since had further success with productions of plays by Michael Frayn, Brian Friel, and Tennessee Williams among others. The theatre building is now in a serious state of decay: there are plans to replace it with a new building nearby in 2001–02.

Hampton, Christopher (1946–) British playwright. He established his reputation with his first play, *When Did You Last See My Mother?* (1966), which was presented at the Royal Court Theatre before moving to the West End. As resident playwright at the Royal Court (1968–70), he enjoyed further success with *Total Eclipse* (1968) and *The Philanthropist* (1970) while the unconventional *Savages* (1973), concerning the kidnapping of a British diplomat in South America, provided Paul Scofield with a fine role. *Treats* (1976), *After Mercer* (1980), and *Tales from Hollywood* (1982) were among the plays that followed (several of which were performed by the National Theatre) – as well as translations of Chekhov, Ibsen, Molière, and Yasmina Reza. *Les Liaisons dangereuses* (1986), adapted from the novel by Laclos, provided him with his greatest success to date in a production by the Royal Shakespeare Company; it later became an even more successful film with Hampton's own screenplay. Subsequent works for the stage have included *White Chameleon* (1991) and the book and lyrics (with Don Black) for the Lloyd Webber musical *Sunset Boulevard* (1993).

Hampton Court Palace Theatre The oldest surviving Elizabethan theatre in England, part of the royal palace of Hampton Court in London. Plays were presented in the Great Hall of the palace from 1572 and were famed for their lavish production. Several monarchs saw plays over the Christmas period there, among them the works of Shakespeare. In 1718 George I allowed members of the public in to see productions by the company of Colley Cibber, including *Hamlet* and *Henry VIII*, although no further performances are recorded after 1731.

Hamsun, Knut (1859–1952) Norwegian novelist, poet, and playwright, who won a Nobel Prize in 1920. The comedy *Livet ivold* (In the Grip of Life; 1910) was first produced by the Moscow Art Theatre and subsequently by Reinhardt; other plays included the trilogy *Aftenrøde* (Afterglow; 1898), based on the hero Ivar Karenko, and the historical drama *Dronningen Tamara* (Queen Tamara; 1903).

Hancock, Sheila (1933–) British actress, who made her first West End appearance in Peter Coke's *Breath of Spring* (1958). She established her reputation in Charles Dyer's *Rattle of a Simple Man* (1962) and went on to appear in both straight and musical theatre, starring in the musicals *Annie* (1978) and *Sweeney Todd* (1980); she has also worked with the National and Royal Shakespeare companies as director and actress. Her parts have included Julia in Albee's *A Delicate Balance* (1969), Paulina in *The Winter's Tale* (1981), and the title roles in Webster's *The Duchess of Malfi* (1985) and Andrew Davies's *Prin* (1989). She is married to the actor John Thaw.

Handke, Peter (1942–) Austrian playwright and novelist, whose experimental work explores issues of language and communication. He first acquired a controversial reputation with his *Publikumsbeschimpfung* (Offending the Audience; 1966), in which he renounced virtually all known theatrical conventions. *Kaspar* (1968) featured a central character who is unable to speak, while *Der Ritt über den Bodensee* (1971) used only clichéd language. Other plays include *Die Unvernünftigen sterben aus* (The Foolish Ones Die Out; 1974), the monologue *A Sorrow Beyond Dreams* (1977), and *The Hour in Which We Knew Nothing of Each Other* (1994), which requires a cast of 35 (playing 300 characters) and has no dialogue at all.

Handl, Irene (1901–87) British actress, whose remarkable impact as Beer in Gerald Savory's *George and Margaret* in 1937 launched her as a comedy-character actress. Her other stage appearances included Mrs Puffin in Arthur Lovegrove's *Goodnight, Mrs Puffin* (1961), Thirza Tapper in the Chichester Festival Theatre revival of Eden Phillpotts's *The Farmer's Wife* (1967), and May in Peter Nichols's *The Freeway* (1974) at the National Theatre.

hand-prop *See* prop.

Hands, Terry (1941–) British director, who became joint artistic director of the Royal Shakespeare Company with Trevor Nunn in 1978 and chief executive in 1986. Earlier in his career he helped to found the Everyman Theatre in Liverpool, where his productions included Osborne's *Look Back in Anger* and Arrabal's *Fando and Lis*. He then became artistic director of the RSC's touring Theatregoround Company (1966) and subsequently an associate director with the main company, directing all of Shakespeare's history plays by 1980. His RSC productions of plays by other authors included Genet's *The Balcony* (1971, 1987), T S Eliot's *Murder in the Cathedral* (1972), Gorky's *The Children of the Sun* (1979), Rostand's *Cyrano de Bergerac* (1983), and Chekhov's *The Seagull* (1990). He left the RSC in 1991 but returned to direct an award-winning production of Marlowe's *Tamburlaine the Great* (1992). He has also worked widely on the Continent (especially since 1992); his foreign productions include several for the Comédie-Française (1975–78) and *Hamlet* in his own French translation (1994).

hand-worked house A theatre in which the ropes used to suspend scenery are adjusted manually rather than by means of a counterweight system. Such a theatre was formerly also referred to as a **hemp house** or **rope house**.

Hankin, Edward Charles St John (1869–1909) British playwright, author of several plays on social issues. Of his markedly cynical works, only *The Return of the Prodigal* (1905) was revived, in 1948.

Hanlon-Lees A British theatre company, comprising the six Hanlon brothers, who became famous in several countries as acrobats during the 1870s. Their spectacular displays of trickwork and mime included *Le Voyage en Suisse*, presented in Paris in 1879 and London in 1880, as well as acclaimed drunk scenes and mock disasters; the group finally disbanded during the 1890s.

Hannah Playhouse *See* Downstage Theatre.

Hannen, Nicholas (1881–1972) British actor, who scored his first London success as Nelson in Hardy's *The Dynasts* (1914). His subsequent career encompassed a wide range of parts, from comedies by Pinero and Milne to Greek tragedy and the plays of Shakespeare, Shaw, and Chekhov; he often appeared with his wife, Athene SEYLER.

Hansberry, Lorraine (1930–65) US Black playwright, who established her reputation with *A Raisin in the Sun* (1959), a study of a Black family facing disaster that proved a landmark in opening Broadway to Black authors. Her only other play to be performed before her early death was *The Sign in Sidney Brustein's Window* (1964), which is set in the Jewish community of New York.

Hansen, Christiern (16th century) Danish playwright, a major figure in the early Danish theatrical tradition. He was the author of several examples of school drama, notably *Den utro hustra* (The Unfaithful Wife) and *Dorothiae Komedie*.

Hanswurst A stock character in Viennese comedy of the 18th century. Descended from legendary German figures, he took on some of the coarser characteristics of the *zanni* of the *commedia dell'arte* and was heavily influenced by the clown Pickelhering, developed by Robert Reynolds and the English Comedians. When played by Stranitsky and Prehauser he became increasingly cunning and sophisticated and was dressed in a red jacket and blue smock decorated with a green heart. Ultimately the disruption caused by his presence in all types of plays attracted adverse criticism from Gottsched and Caroline Neuber; the character was subsequently transformed by Kurz into that of BERNADON.

happening A form of improvised theatrical event that became popular during the 1960s. Happenings were designed to appear spontaneous and to take spectators by surprise. They ranged from preplanned interruptions from the audience in the middle of a play to unannounced displays of street theatre. The fashion had largely died out by the early 1970s.

Happy Days (*Oh! Les Beaux Jours*) A play by Samuel BECKETT. First performance: New York, 1961. During this virtually one-woman play, Winnie, the central character, sinks slowly into the ground until only her head can be seen. All the while she keeps up a stream of cheerful trivial chatter. The role was interpreted by Madeleine

Renaud with great success in 1965; other actresses in the role have included Peggy Ashcroft and Billie Whitelaw.

Hardwicke, Sir Cedric (1893–1964) British actor and director. He made his debut at the Lyceum in 1912 before going on to the Birmingham Repertory Theatre, where he was acclaimed as Churdles Ash in Phillpotts's *The Farmer's Wife* in 1924. Appearances at the Malvern Festival Theatre and elsewhere won him a reputation as a Shavian actor; subsequent performances included Edward Moulton-Barrett in *The Barretts of Wimpole Street* (1930) and Dr Haggett in Emlyn Williams's *The Late Christopher Bean* (1933) as well as roles in films in the US. In 1948 he joined the Old Vic company and excelled in the plays of Shakespeare, Marlowe, and Chekhov before finally moving to New York.

Hardy, Alexandre (c. 1570–c. 1632) French playwright, who is believed to have produced more than 600 plays during the first three decades of the 17th century. Hardy wrote for several troupes of actors and was probably the first professional playwright in France. His influential plays – tragedies (notably *Marianne*, published 1625), tragicomedies, and pastorals – were written to cater for popular tastes, ignoring many of the rules and conventions of the contemporary theatre.

Hardy, Robert (1925–) British actor, whose career began at the Shakespeare Memorial Theatre in 1949. Subsequently he appeared in classic plays at the Old Vic and again at Stratford-on-Avon as well as in the US, where he played the title roles in *Henry V* and *Hamlet* in 1964. Apart from his numerous television and film roles, his stage appearances have included Shaw in Jerome Kilty's *Dear Liar* (1982) at the Mermaid, and, in 1988, Winston Churchill in the musical *Winnie* at the Victoria Palace.

Hardy, Thomas (1840–1928) British novelist, poet, and playwright, whose epic Napoleonic verse drama *The Dynasts* (1903–08) was adapted for the stage by Harley Granville-Barker in 1914. His only other play was *The Tragedy of the Queen of Cornwall* (1923), based on the Tristan and Iseult story. *Tess of the D'Urbervilles* was one of his novels successfully adapted for the stage by other hands.

Hare, Sir David (1947–) British playwright and director. Having cofounded the Portable Theatre in 1968, Hare became literary manager and resident dramatist first at the Royal Court Theatre (1969–71) and then at the Nottingham Playhouse (1973). His earlier plays, which have a sharp political edge, include *Slag*, *Knuckle*, and PLENTY, which began his long association with the National Theatre. During the 1970s and 1980s he also collaborated with Howard BRENTON, both as director of several of his plays and as co-writer of *Brassneck* and *Pravda*, a lively satire on the tabloid press. Hare was appointed an associate director of the National Theatre in 1984 and directed his first Shakespearean play, *King Lear*, there in 1986. In the early 1990s Hare added greatly to his reputation with a trilogy of plays about troubled national institutions, consisting of RACING DEMON, about the Church of England, *Murmuring Judges*, about the judiciary, and *The Absence of War*, about the Labour Party. His subsequent work includes the highly praised AMY'S VIEW, the one-man show *Via Dolorosa*, in which he also starred, and *The Blue Room*, a highly successful adaptation of Schnitzler's REIGEN.

Principal works:
Slag: 1970.
Brassneck: 1973 (with Howard Brenton).
Knuckle: 1974.
Fanshen: 1975.
Teeth 'n' Smiles: 1975.
Plenty: 1978.
A Map of the World: 1982.
Pravda: 1985 (with Howard Brenton).
The Secret Rapture: 1988.
Racing Demon: 1990.
Murmuring Judges: 1991.
The Absence of War: 1993.
Skylight: 1995.
Amy's View: 1997.
The Blue Room: 1998.
Via Dolorosa: 1998.
My Zinc Bed: 2000.

Hare, Sir John (1844–1921) British actor-manager. He made his first stage appearance at Liverpool; subsequently he made his London debut under the Bancrofts at the Prince of Wales' Theatre (later the Scala Theatre) in 1865. After several more successful appearances, he took over the Royal Court Theatre before entering into partnership with the Kendals at the St James's Theatre. In 1889 he took over the Garrick Theatre, where his greatest success was as Goldfinch in Grundy's *A Pair of Spectacles*. He was knighted in 1907.

Hare, J(ohn) Robertson (1891–1979) British actor, who became one of the team that performed the famous series of farces at the Aldwych Theatre between 1924 and 1933. He featured in 12 consecutive productions, creating such characters as Sloley-Jones in *A Cuckoo in the Nest* (1925) and Harold Twine in *Rookery Nook* (1926), both by Ben Travers. He went on to create similar characters in numerous subsequent farces and appeared in the musical *A Funny Thing Happened on the Way to the Forum* (1963); late in life he visited South Africa in John Chapman's *Oh, Clarence!* (1968).

Harlequin A central character of the HARLEQUINADE, the lover of Columbine, who was derived from the character ARLECCHINO of the Italian *commedia dell'arte*. In the English tradition the emphasis was placed upon his magical powers, especially his ability to disguise himself as a different character; he was eventually absorbed into the character of the principal boy.

harlequinade An English theatrical tradition derived ultimately from the Italian *commedia dell'arte*. Incorporating elements of music, mime, trickwork, and disguise, it revolved around the central figures of the lovers HARLEQUIN and COLUMBINE and the clown Pantaloon (*see* Pantalone). The genre first developed out of Weaver's ITALIAN NIGHT SCENES in the early 18th century; gradually, however, the fairytale element and the comic scenes featuring Pantaloon took precedence over the romantic content and led to the evolution of the PANTOMIME. The harlequinade itself was reduced to a brief epilogue and finally disappeared completely in the mid-20th century.

Harleville, Jean-François Collin d' (1755–1806) French playwright, whose moralizing comedies raised the spirits of Parisian theatregoers during the Revolution. His most successful plays included *L'Inconstant* (1786), *L'Optimiste* (1788), *Les Châteaux en Espagne* (1789), and *Le Vieux Célibataire* (1792).

Harper, Elizabeth *See* Bannister, Jack.

Harrigan, Ned (1845–1911) US actor, manager, and playwright, who formed a highly successful partnership with the female impersonator **Tony Hart** (Antony Cannon; 1855–91). From 1879 they appeared in New York in a series of plays with music, *The Mulligan Guards*, which – albeit in a simplistic manner – showed a racially and culturally mixed urban neighbourhood and are considered forerunners of musical comedy. They parted company in 1885, but Harrigan continued to revive his plays and opened a theatre in his own name (later the Garrick Theatre) in 1890.

Harrigan's Park Theatre *See* Herald Square Theatre.

Harrigan's Theatre *See* Garrick Theatre.

Harris, Sir Augustus Glossop (1852–96) British theatre manager, son of the theatre manager **Augustus Glossop Harris** (1825–73). The younger Harris acquired control of DRURY LANE in 1879, reopening it with *Henry V* and launching a spectacular series of annual pantomimes, in which he engaged the great stars of the music halls. A complete man of the theatre, he was affectionately nicknamed **Augustus Druriolanus**.

Harris, Henry (c. 1634–1704) English actor, who appeared with Davenant's company after the Restoration. He became joint manager, with Betterton, of Lincoln's Inn Fields in 1668 and subsequently a shareholder in the Dorset Garden Theatre. Among his Shakespearean roles were Aguecheek, Romeo, and Wolsey; he retired in 1681.

Harris, Julie Ann (1925–) US actress, who joined the New York-based Old Vic company in 1946 and appeared in *Henry IV, Part II* and *Oedipus*. She won acclaim in Carson McCullers's *The Member of the Wedding* (1950) and consolidated her reputation by playing Sally Bowles in *I Am a Camera* (1951). Her roles since then have included Margery Pinchwife in Wycherley's *The Country Wife* (1957), Juliet (1960), Ophelia (1964), Ann Stanley in Jay Allen's *Forty Carats* (1968), and Emily Dickinson in William Luce's *The Belle of Amherst* (1976). Later work includes *On Golden Pond* (1980) in Los Angeles and tours of *Driving Miss Daisy* (1988) and *The Gin Game* (1997).

Harris, Robert (1900–95) British actor, who first appeared in 1923 in J M Barrie's *The Will*. Important parts in a long career included Hamlet (1931) at the Old Vic, Marchbanks in Shaw's *Candida* (1937) in New York, and, in the Stratford-on-Avon season of 1946–47, Prospero and the title role in Marlowe's *Doctor Faustus*. He toured the US in 1963–64 as Sir Thomas More in Robert Bolt's *A Man for All Seasons* and later triumphed as the headmaster in Alan Bennett's *Forty Years On* (1970).

Harris, Rosemary (1930–) British actress, who made her first London appearance in *The Seven Year Itch* (1953). She played leading parts with the Bristol Old Vic company and went with the London Old Vic company to the US (1956) as Cressida in

Troilus and Cressida. Subsequent successes in Britain have included appearances at the Chichester Festival Theatre (1962), in the National Theatre's inaugural *Hamlet* (1963) as Ophelia, in Neil Simon's *Plaza Suite* (1969), and in Shaw's *Heartbreak House* (1983). In the US she excelled in such roles as Eleanor in James Goldman's *The Lion in Winter* (1966) and as Blanche Dubois in Tennessee Williams's *A Streetcar Named Desire* (1973).

Harrison, Rex (1908–90) British actor, who worked in repertory at the Liverpool Playhouse before making his London debut at the Everyman Theatre in 1930. After various West End appearances he enjoyed outstanding success in 1936, first in New York in *Sweet Aloes*, then in London in *French Without Tears*. He subsequently became a star of stage and screen on both sides of the Atlantic, specializing in refined English characters in comedies by such authors as Coward, Van Druten, and Behrman. His greatest triumph came in 1956 as Professor Higgins in the musical *My Fair Lady*, which he played for two years on Broadway before transferring to Drury Lane. Among his later appearances in London and New York were *Heartbreak House* (1983), Lonsdale's *Aren't We All?* (1984), and Barrie's *The Admirable Crichton* (1988).

His second wife was the German actress **Lilli Palmer** (Lilli Peiser; 1914–86), whose stage successes alongside him included *The Love of Four Colonels*.

His fourth wife was **Rachel Roberts** (1927–80), who appeared with him in *Platonov* and other plays; her other successes included the title role in the musical *Maggie May* (1964).

Harrison, Richard Berry (1864–1935) US Black actor, whose parents escaped from slavery to Canada, where he was brought up. Returning to Detroit, he became a teacher of elocution and drama and toured giving solo Shakespearean and other recitals. As an actor he was known for a single role, 'De Lawd' in March Connolly's *The Green Pastures* (1930), which he played nearly 2000 times.

Harris Theatre Two theatres between 7th and 8th Avenues on New York's 42nd Street used this name. One opened in 1904 as **Lew M Field's Theatre** with Victor Herbert's *It Happened in Nordland*. It underwent several name changes, being the Harris between 1911 and 1920, but became a cinema in 1930 and was torn down during the 1998 renewal of the area. The other opened as a cinema in 1914 and, as the **Chandler Theatre**, also presented such plays as Elmer Rice's *On Trial* (1914) and Glasworthy's *Justice* (1916). It was renamed the **Cohan and Harris Theatre** in 1916, and the **Sam H Harris Theatre** in 1921. John Barrymore made theatrical history there in 1922 when he played Hamlet a record 101 times. It became a cinema in 1932 and was also torn down in 1998.

Hart, Charles (d. 1683) English actor, who was a boy player of female roles with the King's Men, prior to serving as a soldier during the Commonwealth. After the Restoration he became a principal heroic actor at and shareholder in Drury Lane and trained Nell Gwynn for the stage.

Hart, Lorenz (1895–1943) US lyricist, famous for his partnership with Richard RODGERS. Their first success, the revue *The Garrick Gaieties* (1925), was followed by many hits in the 1920s and 1930s, including *A Connecticut Yankee* (1927), *Jumbo* (1935), *On Your Toes* (1936), which incorporated dance to a greater degree than any musical before it, and *The Boys from Syracuse* (1937), which was based on *The Comedy of*

Errors. Pal Joey (1940) brought a new seriousness of characterization to the musical, but was not an immediate influence owing to what many felt was unsavoury subject matter. Their last joint show was *By Jupiter* (1942).

Hart, Moss (1904–61) US playwright, whose first major success came with his play *Once in a Lifetime* (1930), upon which he collaborated with George KAUFMAN. Other collaborations with Kaufman included *Merrily We Roll Along* (1934), *You Can't Take It With You* (1936), which won a Pulitzer Prize, and *The Man Who Came to Dinner* (1939). Solo works included *Winged Victory* (1943), *Christopher Blake* (1946), *Light Up the Sky* (1948), and *The Climate of Eden* (1952). He also contributed to the musicals *As Thousands Cheer* (1933), *The Great Waltz* (1934), and *I'd Rather Be Right* (1937) and directed *Dear Ruth* (1944), *Anniversary Waltz* (1954), *My Fair Lady* (1956), and *Camelot* (1960) among other shows.

Hart, Tony *See* Harrigan, Ned.

Hart House Theatre A theatre founded by Raymond and Vincent Massey in 1919 in Toronto, Canada, as an experimental venue for the University of Toronto. Seating 500, it was used for premieres of several significant new Canadian works before closing in 1939 and being reopened in 1947 as part of the university. It gradually acquired a respected resident company and from 1966 to 1986 was under the control of the University Graduate Centre for the Study of Drama. The theatre and centre have been run by several notable professional directors, including Robert Gill and Ronald Bryden.

Hartley, Elizabeth (Elizabeth White; 1751–1824) British actress, who appeared briefly at the Haymarket in 1769 and toured the provinces before her Covent Garden debut in 1772. She combined outstanding beauty with an arresting personality – Sir Joshua Reynolds painted her several times – and she remained at Covent Garden throughout her career. In 1780 she created Lady Touchwood in Mrs Cowley's *The Belle's Stratagem*.

Hartzenbusch, Juan Eugenio (1806–80) Spanish playwright, of German extraction, whose reputation was founded on the highly popular romantic tragedy *Los amantes de Teruel* (1837). Subsequently he enjoyed some success with a number of comedies and adaptations of Spanish dramas of the Golden Age and edited the plays of Tirso de Molina, Calderón, Lope de Vega, and others.

Harvard Dramatic Club A theatre club at Harvard University, founded in 1908, originally to produce plays written by Harvard and Radcliffe students and graduates as well as foreign plays. Since 1960 it has staged productions at the Loeb Drama Center, in Cambridge, Massachusetts.

Harvey, Sir John Martin- *See* Martin-Harvey, Sir John.

Harwood, Harold Marsh (1874–1959) British playwright and manager, who achieved success with his first play, *Honour Thy Father* (1912), and consolidated it with *The Grain of Mustard Seed* (1920). Among his other works are *The Man in Possession* (1930), *The Mask* (1913), and *Billeted* (1917) – the last two written in collaboration with his wife, **F(ryniwyd) Tennyson Jesse** (1889–1958).

Harwood, John Edmund (1771–1809) US actor, who began his career at Philadelphia's Southwark Theatre, where his parts included Plagiary in Sheridan's *The Critic* and Stephano in *The Tempest*. In 1803 he had enormous success as Dennis Brulgruddery in Colman the Younger's *John Bull* and, in 1806, was again highly acclaimed as Falstaff. Latterly he played several high comedy roles.

Hasenclever, Walter (1890–1940) German playwright, poet, and novelist, whose early Expressionist dramas dealt with the themes of tyranny and revolt. His most outstanding play, *Der Sohn* (1916), which explores the relationship between a father and his son, was followed by an adaptation of *Antigone* (1917) by Sophocles and the antiwar play *Der Retter* (1919). Subsequently he turned to more conventional comedies, including *Ein besserer Herr* (A Man of Distinction; 1926), and *Ehen werden in Himmel geschlossen* (Marriages are Made in Heaven; 1928). He committed suicide in a French internment camp in 1940.

Hasenhut, Anton (1766–1841) Austrian actor, who developed the stock character THADDÄDL. He was praised by Grillparzer for his acting but fell from popularity by the 1820s, audiences having tired of conventional comedy.

Hassan A poetic drama by James Elroy FLECKER. First performance: London, 1922. This spectacular oriental drama enjoyed enormous success on its first production, complete with music by Delius and extravagant costumes and scenery, under Basil Dean at Her Majesty's Theatre. The distinguished cast was headed by Henry Ainley.

Hasse, Otto Eduard (1903–78) German actor, who trained under Reinhardt and went on to become one of Germany's leading performers, appearing first in Munich then, after World War II, in Berlin. Plays in which he triumphed ranged from Goethe's *Faust* (1945) to Jerome Kilty's *Dear Liar* (1959) and the premiere of Hochhuth's controversial *Soldaten* (1967).

Hasty Pudding Club A social club at Harvard University, founded in 1795. Since 1850 it has sponsored yearly dramatic productions; which since 1884 have been in the form of musical parodies. Many of its alumni have gone on to theatrical careers.

Hatton Garden Nursery *See* nurseries.

Hauch, Johannes Carsten (1790–1872) Danish poet, novelist, and playwright, who became a leading member of the Romantic movement in Denmark. His melancholic tragedies based on Danish historical figures include *Svend Grathe* (1841) and *Marsk Stig* (1850); others include *Søstrene paa Kinnekullen* (The Sisters of Kinnekullen; 1849).

Hauptmann, Gerhart (1862–1946) German playwright, novelist, and poet, who established his reputation in the theatre with his first play *Vor Sonnenaufgang*, which was hailed as a landmark in German naturalistic drama. Subsequent dramas dealt with such themes as heredity, psychiatry, suicide, and determinism, and were characterized by stark realism and strong social comment. His deep compassion for the poor and exploited was expressed in *Die Weber*, a historical drama written in his native Silesian dialect which portrays the despair of a group of weavers during a futile rebellion in 1844. His later work, in which he blended realism and fantasy, led to his association with Symbolism and the Romantic movement. Both his dream play *Hanneles Himmerlefahrt* and the fairy drama *Und Pippa tanzt* were successfully performed throughout Europe. Other notable works include the satirical comedy *Der Biberpelz* and *Die Atriden*, a dramatic cycle in four parts, which bitterly condemns Nazi brutality. He was awarded a Nobel Prize in 1912.

Principal works:

Vor Sonnenaufgang: 1889; translated as *Before Dawn*.
Das Friedenstest: 1890; translated as *The Coming of Peace*.
Einsame Menschen: 1891; translated as *Lonely People*.
Die Weber: 1892; translated as *The Weavers*.
Der Biberpelz: 1893; translated as *The Beaver Coat*.
Hanneles Himmelfahrt: 1893; translated as *The Assumption of Hannele*.
Florian Geyer: 1896.
Die versunkene Glocke: 1896; translated as *The Sunken Bell*.
Führman Henschel: 1898.
Der Rote Hahn: 1901; translated as *The Red Rooster*.
Rose Bernd: 1903.
Und Pippa tanzt: 1906.
Die Ratten: 1911.
Der Atriden: 1941.

Haupt- und Staatsaktionen Plays of the early native German theatrical tradition, directly descended from those presented by the English Comedians. The plays (several of which, written for performance in Vienna, survive) drew on various European sources and showed a preference for the more sensational aspects of drama, with much high rhetoric interspersed with comic scenes featuring such clowns as Pickelhering and Hanswurst. *See also Altwiener Volkstheater.*

Hauteroche, Noël-Jacques le Breton de (c. 1616–1707) French actor and playwright, who appeared at both the Théâtre du Marais and the Hôtel de Bourgogne before becoming a founder-member of the Comédie-Française in 1680. He was satirized in Molière's *L'Impromptu de Versailles* (1663) but was himself the author of several comedies in the style of Molière.

Havel, Václav (1936–) Czech playwright, essayist, and civil-rights campaigner, who became president of Czechoslavakia (1989–92) and then of the Czech Republic (1993–). In the mid-1960s he wrote a series of Absurdist satires for Prague's Theatre on the Balustrade, including *The Garden Party* (1963), *The Memorandum* (1965), and *The Increased Difficulty of Concentration* (1968). Following the Soviet invasion of 1968 his works could no longer be staged in Czechoslovakia, but such anti-totalitarian plays as *Largo Desolato* (1984) and *Temptation* (1985) continued to be seen in the West. His outspoken support for human rights led to his imprisonment in 1979–83 and again in 1989, but ensured his election to the presidency on the fall of communism in 1989.

Havergal, Giles *See* Glasgow Citizens' Theatre.

Hawthorne, Sir Nigel (1929–) British actor. He made his professional debut in 1950 but attracted little attention until 1978, when he appeared in Peter Nichols's *Privates on Parade*. Having become a household name in the television comedy *Yes, Minister* (1980–87), he returned to the theatre in 1983–84 to play the leads in *Peer Gynt* and *Tartuffe*, both for the RSC. He subsequently enjoyed West End success in

Stoppard's *Hapgood* (1988) and William Nicholson's *Shadowlands* (1989), in which he played C S Lewis. In 1992 Hawthorne triumphed in the title role of Alan Bennett's *The Madness of King George*, which subsequently toured Europe and the US and became a successful film. He returned to the West End in 1994, when he directed and starred in Colman and Garrick's *The Clandestine Marriage*.

Hawtrey, Sir Charles (1858–1923) British actor-manager, who made his debut at the Prince of Wales's Theatre in 1881. He soon went into management on his own, achieving success in 1833 with his adaptation of Von Moser's comedy *The Private Secretary*. Subsequently he acquired a fine reputation as a light comedian, whose most successful parts included Lord Goring in Wilde's *An Ideal Husband* (1895) and William in Somerset Maugham's *Home and Beauty* (1919). From 1911 he produced the annual Christmas play *Where the Rainbow Ends* with a cast of 50 child actors, one of whom was Noël Coward.

Háy, Gyula (1900–75) Hungarian playwright, who first attracted attention with *Gott, Kaiser, Bauer* (1932), which was produced by Reinhardt in Berlin. He lived in exile from Hungary for many years and was imprisoned for a time for his involvement in the 1956 rebellion. His early plays included the tragedy *Tiszazug* (1945), which was variously revived as *The Midwife*, *Haben*, and *To Have and To Hold*; later works numbered amongst them *Das Pferd* (1964), which depicted Caligula, and the anticommunist *Gaspar Varros Recht* (1965).

Hay, Ian (John Hay Beith; 1876–1952) British playwright and novelist, whose early plays *Tilly of Bloomsbury* (1919) and *A Safety Match* (1921) were adaptations of his own humorous novels. He also collaborated on various light comedies with Seymour Hicks, P G Wodehouse, Stephen King-Hall, and Anthony Armstrong.

***Hayduk* theatre** A form of Bulgarian theatre based upon stories about the *hayduks*, Bulgarian outlaws who resisted domination by Turkey until liberation in 1878. The best examples of the tradition were influenced by Byron and Schiller and included works by such authors as Iordanov, Karavelov, Velichkov, and Ivanov. In the 20th century the *hayduk* themes of nationalism and patriotism ensured frequent revivals of the genre, despite restrictions imposed by the state.

Haye, Helen (1874–1957) British actress, who had a long and highly-respected career that began at the Pier Theatre, Hastings, in 1898. After a London debut as Gertrude in *Hamlet* at His Majesty's Theatre in 1910, she appeared regularly in the West End in such parts as Mrs Pritchard in Maugham's *Caesar's Wife* (1920), Lady Sneerwell in Sheridan's *The School for Scandal* (1935), and Mrs Higgins in *Pygmalion* (1939). Her work as a teacher at the Royal Academy of Dramatic Art and elsewhere was well known.

Hayes, Helen (Helen Brown; 1900–93) US actress, who made her debut as a child in 1905. In 1907 she played the lead in Frances Hodgson Burnett's *Little Lord Fauntleroy*, making her adult debut in Kaufman and Connelly's *To the Ladies* (1922). Her subsequent roles included Cleopatra in Shaw's *Caesar and Cleopatra* (1925), Mary, Queen of Scots in Maxwell Anderson's *Mary of Scotland* (1933), Queen Victoria in Housman's *Victoria Regina* (1937), Amanda in Tennessee Williams's *The Glass Menagerie* (1941), Norma Melody in O'Neill's *A Touch of the Poet* (1958), and Mrs Antrobus in Wilder's *The Skin of Our Teeth* (1961). In 1964 she founded the Helen

Hayes Repertory Company, which presented Shakespeare readings, and from 1966–69 worked with the APA Phoenix Repertory Company in New York. An allergy to stage dust caused her retirement from the stage after 1971, although she remained active in teaching.

Hay Fever A comedy by Noël COWARD. First performance: London, 1925. The four members of the unconventional Bliss family each invite a weekend house guest unbeknown to the others; various complications ensue, leading to the disintegration of the party in the face of the family's eccentric behaviour. the play is frequently revived.

Haymarket (Theatre Royal) One of London's best-loved theatres, dating from 1720. Initially called the **Little Theatre in the Hay**, it was built on a site of an old inn but was confined at first to amateur performances. Henry Fielding became manager in 1735; in defiance of the Patent Theatres legislation then in force he staged a number of his own satires, with the result that censorship was introduced in 1737 and the theatre closed.

In 1747 Samuel Foote tried to get round the law by charging only for refreshments; after he had lost a leg in an accident brought about by a jest, the Duke of York compensated Foote by obtaining a royal patent allowing the theatre to open during the summer months. An annual licence was granted in 1777. George Colman the Elder took over the theatre in 1776, passing control to his son in 1794; when one of Foote's satires, *The Tailors*, was revived in 1805, hundreds of London tailors rioted and had to be dispersed by soldiers.

The theatre was remodelled by John Nash in 1921 with an elegant Corinthian portico on the site slightly to the south of the original building. In 1825 Madame Vestris sang 'Cherry Ripe' in John Poole's comedy *Paul Pry* and in 1833 Julia Glover caused a sensation as Falstaff in Shakespeare's *The Merry Wives of Windsor*. Benjamin Webster took over the management in 1837, producing and acting in many of his own plays; J B Buckstone was manager from 1853 to 1878, a period of outstanding success – his ghost is said still to haunt the theatre.

From 1855 it became known as the Theatre Royal; under the management of Squire and Marie Bancroft in the early 1880s, the theatre was largely rebuilt, housing the first 'picture frame' stage. Herbert Beerbohm Tree was manager from 1887 to 1896, during which time Oscar Wilde's *A Woman of No Importance* (1893) and *An Ideal Husband* (1895) were staged. Tree made sufficient profits from his productions of *Trilby* (1895), based on George Du Maurier's novel, to enable him to build Her Majesty's, a new theatre on the opposite side of the road.

In 1904 the Haymarket was again remodelled and further alterations were made in 1939–41, following which Gielgud staged a celebrated season (1944–45). Successes of the 1960s and 1970s included plays by Rattigan, N C Hunter, Enid Bagnold, and John Mortimer. More recently, the Haymarket has been noted for star revivals and for housing transfers from the Chichester Festival and other West End theatres.

The **Haymarket Theatre** in Leicester opened in 1973. Seating 752, it established its reputation almost immediately with the musicals *Cabaret* and *Joseph and the Amazing Technicolour Dreamcoat*. Productions since then have included pantomimes, revivals of classic plays, further musicals – notably *Oliver!*, *My Fair Lady*, and *Oklahoma!* – and plays by such contemporary authors as Ayckbourn, Pinter, and David Storey.

Hazlitt, William (1778–1830) British critic and essayist, who wrote numerous theatrical reviews for various periodicals, and is usually regarded as the first great critic of the British theatre. In 1817 he published *Characters of Shakespeare's Plays*, and, in the following year, *A View of the English Stage*.

Heartbreak House A comedy by G B SHAW. First performance: New York, 1920. The play, which is set among upper-class Bohemians during World War I, analyses contemporary attitudes to money, class, and morality. The young Ellie Burn rejects wealthy Boss Mangan and prepares to marry the 88-year-old Captain Shotover, an eccentric inventor. The last act features an air raid. In its depiction of an apparently doomed class Shaw's play was inspired in part by Chekhov's *The Cherry Orchard*.

Heavy Father *See* stock company.

Heavy Woman *See* stock company.

Hebbel, Friedrich (1813–63) German playwright, author of several pessimistic tragedies notable for their psychological insight. Hebbel, who was much influenced by Hegel's theories of history, excelled in the portrayal of oppressed women and established his reputation with *Judith* (1840) and *Maria Magdalena* (1844), both of which had women as their central characters. Later plays included the tragedies *Herodes und Mariamne* (1849) and *Agnes Bernauer* (1852), the *Die Nibelungen* trilogy (1861), and *Gyges und sein Ring* (1869), which was based on the legend of King Cambyses.

Hébertot, Jacques (1886–1970) French director, manager, and critic, who did much to further the performance of foreign works on the Paris stage. He acquired control of the Comédie des Champs-Élysées and the Théâtre des Champs-Élysées in 1919 and installed Jouvet as director of both before subsequently working with Baty. He concentrated on his role as a critic from 1926 to 1940 and then took over the Théâtre des Arts, renaming it the Théâtre Hébertot and presenting many major foreign dramas there.

Hedberg, Tor (1862–1931) Swedish playwright, son of a minor writer for the theatre, who wrote several plays depicting working-class life in Stockholm. His best-known works include *En Tvekamp* (A Duel; 1892), the comedy *Nattrocken* (The Dressing Gown; 1893), the tragedy *John Ulfsjerna* (1907), and *Perseus och vidundret* (Perseus and the Monster; 1917). He was director of the Kungliga Dramatiska Teatern from 1910.

Hedda Gabler A play by Henrik IBSEN, probably the most frequently performed of all his works. First performance: 1890. The play revolves around Hedda Gabler Tesman, a vindictive woman who has become bored with life and isolated from those around her. It ends with her suicide, which she sees as the only solution to her self-inflicted problems.

Hedgerow Theatre A theatre founded in 1923 in Moylan, Pennsylvania (near Philadelphia), which is the second oldest surviving repertory company in the US. The current company, which includes both professionals and students, presents a mixture of modern and classical plays, while the Hedgerow Theatre School offers a three-year course in acting.

Hedqvist, Ivan (1880–1935) Swedish actor, who was highly acclaimed in naturalistic drama. Appearing at the Svenska Teatern in Stockholm (1906–09 and 1922–25) and then with the Kungliga Dramatiska Teatern (1909–19 and 1927–32), he was much admired in Shakespearean roles and as Sophocles's Oedipus.

Heiberg, Gunnar Edvard Rode (1857–1929) Norwegian playwright, who is generally regarded as the most significant Norwegian dramatist since Ibsen. He is best remembered for his witty moralistic plays, notably *Tante Ulrikke* (1884) and *Folkeraadet* (1897), which treat contemporary and social issues. His most successful plays, *Balkonen* (The Balcony; 1894) and *Kjærlighedens Tragedie* (The Tragedy of Love; 1904) attempt to explore erotic relationships. Other works of note include *Kunstnere* (The Artists; 1893) and *Gerts Have* (Gert's Garden; 1894).

Heiberg, Johan Ludvig (1791–1860) Danish playwright and poet, who became a leading intellectual figure in Copenhagen and was the author of theoretical writing upon the Danish theatre. He was director of the Kongelige Teater for a time and created a type of popular satirical folk musical known as Danish vaudeville; his plays include *Julespøg og Nytaarsløjer* (Christmas and New Year Fun and Games; 1816), *Elverhøj* (Elfin Hill; 1828), and his masterpiece *En Sjæl efter Døden* (A Soul After Death; 1841).

His wife was the actress and playwright **Johanne Luise Heiberg** (Johanne Luise Pätges; 1812–90), who first appeared at the Kongelige Teater in 1826 and subsequently played in both tragedy and vaudeville, establishing herself as the leading Danish actress of her day. She was also herself the author of several vaudevilles.

Heijermans, Herman (1864–1924) Dutch playwright and novelist, best remembered for his socially challenging dramas treating such diverse themes as free love and anti-Semitism. His strong socialist ideals and contempt for bourgeois hypocrisy are reflected in such plays as *Op Hoop van Zegen* (The Good Hope; 1900), in which he champions the cause of exploited fisherman, and *Glück Auf* (1911), in which he expresses his concern about the working conditions of miners.

Heinrich Julius, Duke of Brunswick (1564–1613) German scholar and patron of the arts, who maintained Thomas Sackville's troupe of English Comedians at Wolfenbüttel for many years. The company often appeared in plays written by the duke himself, which combined features of the *commedia dell'arte* with the English tradition.

Heiress, The A play by Ruth and Augustus Goetz, based on the short novel *Washington Square* by Henry JAMES. First performance: New York, 1947. The plot concerns an awkward young heiress, her tyrannical father, and her money-hungry suitor; the play was filmed in 1949 with Olivia De Havilland, Montgomery Clift, and Ralph Richardson.

Held, Anna *See* Ziegfeld, Florenz.

Helen Bonfils Theatre Complex *See* Denver Performing Arts Center.

Helen Hayes Theatre There have been two Broadway theatres of this name. The first, on West 46th Street, New York, opened in 1911 as the **Fulton Theatre**. It was renamed the Helen Hayes, after the acclaimed actress, in 1955. She appeared there herself in 1958 as Nora in *A Touch of the Poet* by Eugene O'Neill; other successes included plays by Lonsdale, d'Usseau and Gow, and Kaufman and Ferber. The theatre was demolished in 1982. The current Helen Hayes Theatre is on West 44th Street, between 7th and 8th Avenues. With 579 seats, it is the smallest of the Broadway theatres. It opened in 1912 as the **Winthrop Ames Theatre** and has had many subsequent names (including **The Little Theatre**); it was used by the *New York Times* as a conference centre between 1939 and 1959 and as a media studio from 1959 to 1963. It was named after the actress in 1983. Productions seen there under its various names have included Eugene O'Neill's first Broadway play, *Beyond the Horizon* (1920), Albert Innauato's *Gemini*, which ran from 1977 to 1982, Harvey Fierstein's *Torch Song Trilogy* (1982), Craig Lucas's *Prelude to a Kiss* (1990), and a long run of Rob Becker's one-man show *Defending the Caveman* (1995).

Hellenistic drama Greek theatre of the 3rd and 4th centuries BC, specifically that outside Athens itself but within the Athenian sphere of influence. Also known as Colonial drama, it encompassed NEW COMEDY, mime, and some tragedy as well as the critical writings and collections of theatrical scholars in Alexandria. Its greatest exponents included Menander. *See also phlyax.*

Hellinger, Theatre *See* Mark Hellinger Theatre.

Hellman, Lillian (1905–84) US playwright, whose first play, THE CHILDREN'S HOUR (1934) established her reputation. Subsequent successes included *Days to Come* (1936), THE LITTLE FOXES (1939), about an avaricious Southern family, THE WATCH ON THE RHINE (1941), *The Searching Wind* (1944), *Another Part of the Forest* (1946), which she also staged, *The Autumn Garden* (1951), and *Toys in the Attic* (1960). She also adapted several novels for the stage and provided the book for Bernstein's musical *Candide* (1956).

Hello Dolly! A musical by Jerry Herman, based on Thornton Wilder's THE MATCHMAKER. First performance: New York, 1964. The title role proved a triumph for Carol CHANNING, who later toured with it. In her absence, producer David Merrick extended the original run to a record 2844 performances with replacements including Mary Martin, Ethel Merman, and Pearl Bailey. For Bailey, Merrick completely re-cast the show with Black actors, thereby encouraging a new Black audience to attend Broadway shows.

Helpmann, Sir Robert (1909–86) Australian ballet dancer, choreographer, actor, and director, who appeared in many Shakespearean and other major roles. He made his debut as a dancer in musical comedy in Sydney in 1923 and subsequently toured Australia before joining the Vic-Wells Ballet in London in 1933. In 1937 he attracted attention as an actor playing Oberon in *A Midsummer Night's Dream* at the Old Vic; subsequently he played Hamlet (1944) and Flamineo in Webster's *The White Devil* (1947) among other important roles and, in 1948, joined the company at Stratford-on-Avon. His successful roles there included Shylock, Hamlet, and King John, while back in London (and later New York) he acted with Olivier and Vivien Leigh in *Antony and Cleopatra* (1951). As a director he presented T S Eliot's *Murder in the Cathedral* in 1953, Giraudoux's *Duel of Angels* (1960), and the musical *Camelot* (1964) among other works.

Heminge, John (1556–1630) English actor, possibly born at Shottery, near Stratford-on-Avon. He was in Burbage's company at the Theatre and is credited with playing the original Falstaff. He was probably the business manager for the company and was a shareholder in the Globe and Blackfriars theatres. He is known to have appeared in several of Jonson's plays and, with Condell, was responsible for collecting the First Folio of Shakespeare's plays.

hemp house *See* hand-worked house.

Henderson, John (1747–85) British actor, born in London. He first came to attention playing Hamlet at Bath in 1772, after which he appeared as Macbeth, Richard III, Hotspur, Lear, and in other great roles. In 1777 George Colman the Elder engaged him at the Haymarket, where he made a sensational debut as Shylock. Later he transferred to Drury Lane at Sheridan's request and then to Covent Garden. In 1785 he gave readings of William Cowper's *John Gilpin*, turning it into a bestseller.

Henley, Beth (1952–) US playwright, known for her comic treatment of dysfunctional Southern families. She first came to notice with *Crimes of the Heart* (Louisville, 1979; New York, 1981) which won the Pulitzer prize. Other works include *The Miss Firecracker Contest* (1980), *The Wake of Jodie Foster* (1982), and *Impossible Marriage* (1998).

Henry, John (1738–94) US actor, born in Ireland, who made his New York debut as Aimwell in Farquhar's *The Beaux' Stratagem* (1767). He was for many years a leading actor with the American Company and was the first professional to play Sir Peter Teazle in the US. He eventually became co-manager of the company, but was supplanted by John Hodgkinson in 1792.

Henry VIII, The Famous History of the Life of King A history play by William SHAKESPEARE and (almost certainly) John FLETCHER, written c. 1613. First performance: Globe Theatre, London, 1613. The play traces the relationship of Henry VIII with Anne Boleyn and the consequent political machinations of Wolsey; it concludes with Cranmer's speech over the infant Elizabeth I. At the play's first performance the Globe Theatre was accidentally destroyed by fire.

Henry V, The Life of King A history play by William SHAKESPEARE, the last part of a trilogy on the king's youth, written c. 1599. First performance: c. 1599. Essentially a patriotic celebration of Henry V's successful reign, the play also contains elements of irony and realism that tend to be brought out in modern productions. The action takes on heroic proportions with the king's 'St Crispin's Day' speech and the great victory over the French at Agincourt. Other highlights include the death of Falstaff, the disguised king's meeting with the common soldiers, and his wooing of the French princess Katherine.

Henry IV A history play in two parts by William SHAKESPEARE, written c. 1597–98. First performance: c. 1597–98. With *Henry V* it forms a trilogy focusing on the education of the young Prince Hal, who spurns the court to spend time with the roguish Falstaff and other low companions. Scenes of political intrigue and civil war alternate with carousings in the Boar's Head Tavern, giving a broad picture of English life among all classes. Part I culminates in the defeat of Hotspur's rebellion: the more sombre Part II ends with Henry's coronation and his banishment of Falstaff – one of the most argued-over scenes in Shakespeare.

Henry Miller's Theatre A theatre on West 43rd Street, New York, which opened in 1918 with *The Fountain of Youth* by the Álvarez Quintero brothers. Although it presented *La La Lucille*, Gershwin's first full-length score, in 1919, the majority of the plays produced there were straight dramas, the most notable including Coward's *The Vortex* (1925). Sherriff's *Journey's End* (1929), Wilder's *Our Town* (1938), and Eliot's *The Cocktail Party* (1950). In 1969 it was converted into a cinema and in 1978 into a night-club.

Henry VI A history play by William SHAKESPEARE, written in three parts c. 1590–92. First performance: c. 1592. Possibly a collaboration with Greene or Nash, the trilogy depicts the disintegration of England under Henry's weak command and culminates in Henry's own murder during the Wars of the Roses. Events portrayed include the deaths of Joan of Arc, Talbot, and the Duke of Gloucester, the marriage of Henry to Margaret of Anjou, the peasant rebellion of Jack Cade, and the rise of the future Richard III. The most admired scenes include York's speech after his capture and Henry's thoughts upon civil war.

Hensel, Sophie Friederike (Sophie Friederike Sparmann; 1738–89) German actress, who distinguished herself as a performer of tragic heroines as a member of Acker-mann's company in Hamburg. Her vicious temper won her many enemies and se-verely hampered the career of her second husband, Abel Seyler.

Henshaw, James Ene (1924–) African playwright, who trained as a doctor and be-came the first internationally recognized Nigerian writer for the theatre. His plays, which typically depict people in authority facing moral dilemmas concerning bribery and corruption, include *This Is Our Chance* (1956), *A Man of Character* (1960), *Medicine for Love* (1964), and *Dinner for Promotion* (1967).

Hensler, Karl Friedrich (1761–1825) Austrian playwright, author of notable ex-amples of the *ritterdrama*. In the operatic *Das Donau eibchen* (1797) he combined the approach of the German Romantics with Austrian folklore with great success.

Henslowe, Philip (d. 1616) English theatre owner, whose notes and diaries are a valuable source of information about the theatre of the time. He built the Rose Theatre in 1587, the Fortune – in partnership with Edward Alleyn (who married his stepdaughter) – in 1600, and the Hope in 1613, becoming the most consistently suc-cessful of all Elizabethan impresarios.

Henson, Leslie (1891–1957) British actor, who scored his first success in 1915 in *Tonight's the Night*. After service in the Royal Flying Corps he appeared in *Kissing Time* (1919), the first of several long-running musicals in which he played at the Winter Garden Theatre. He also entered management with Tom Walls, presenting several of the Aldwych farces, and subsequently leased the Gaiety Theatre (1935–39), star-ring in several successful musicals. After World War II he excelled as Pepys in *And So to Bed* (1951) and Pooter in *The Diary of a Nobody* (1955).

Hepburn, Katharine (1909–) US actress, who is best known for her many film roles. She made her stage debut in 1928, early roles including Katia in *A Month in the Country* (1930). She returned to Broadway in 1939 in Philip Barry's *The Philadelphia Story*; subsequently she played Rosalind in *As You Like It* (1950) and toured Australia (1955) with the Old Vic company. In 1957 she appeared at the Shakespeare Festival in Stratford, Connecticut. In 1969 she played the title role in the musical *Coco*;

stage appearances since then have included parts in *A Matter of Gravity* (1976) and *The West Side Waltz* (1981).

Herald Square Theatre A theatre on Broadway, New York, which opened as the **Colosseum Theatre** in 1874. It was successively renamed the Criterion (1882), **Harrigan's Park Theatre** (1885), the **Park Theatre** (1889), and finally the Herald Square Theatre (1894). The opening play in 1894 was Shaw's *Arms and the Man* starring Richard Mansfield. For several years the Herald opposed the Theatrical Syndicate but eventually (1900) it became a venue for vaudeville, after the Shubert family had assumed the management. The building was demolished in 1915.

Herbert, Sir Henry (1596–1673) English public official, appointed MASTER OF THE REVELS in 1623. Brother of the poet George Herbert, he held office until the closure of theatres in 1642 but failed to reassert his powers after the Restoration in opposition to Killigrew and Davenant. His office records provide valuable information about the 17th-century theatre.

Heřczeg, Ferenc (1863–1954) Hungarian playwright and novelist, whose dramatic output consists of comedies and historical plays, notably *Pogányok* (1902), *Bizánc* (1904), and *A híd* (1925). His most successful play, *Az ezüst róka* (1921), has been performed throughout Europe.

Herlie, Eileen (1920–) British actress, born in Scotland, who established her reputation as the Queen in Cocteau's *The Eagle Has Two Heads* (1947) at the Haymarket. After further successes as Euripides's Medea (1948) and as Pinero's Mrs Tanqueray (1950) she made her New York debut as Mrs Molloy in Thornton Wilder's *The Matchmaker* (1955), subsequently remaining in the US, where her roles have included Gertrude in Gielgud's *Hamlet* (1964) and Martha in Albee's *Who's Afraid of Virginia Woolf?* (1971).

Her Majesty's Theatre A theatre in the Haymarket, London, which is the fourth built on the same site. The original theatre, called the **Queen's Theatre** (1705–14) and then the **King's Theatre** (1714–1837), opened in 1705 under the management of Vanbrugh and Congreve and became known primarily as a venue for opera. Destroyed by fire in 1789 and rebuilt in 1790–91, it became the largest opera house in England. The auditorium was subsequently remodelled (1816–18) by Nash and Repton, who also added three exterior colonnades and the Royal Opera Arcade. During its heyday as an opera house (1830–50) the theatre, which was renamed Her Majesty's in 1837, enjoyed a reputation as a highly fashionable venue but closed in 1852 after most of its patrons had defected to Covent Garden. Reopened in 1856 after Covent Garden had been burned down, Her Majesty's was itself destroyed by fire in 1867 and, when rebuilt, remained empty until it was sold in 1874. After another change of ownership in 1877 more opera was staged; there were also plays, minstrel shows, pantomimes, and even boxing. Sarah Bernhardt acted at the theatre in 1886 and 1890 but after the Christmas pantomime of 1890 Her Majesty's was again closed; when the building was demolished in 1891 only the Royal Opera Arcade was left standing. The present theatre was financed by Beerbohm Tree; it was opened in 1897 and continued (as **His Majesty's Theatre** from 1902) under Tree's acclaimed management until his death in 1917. The musical *Chu Chin Chow* (1916) ran for a record 2238 performances. There were also two seasons of Diaghilev's Ballets Russes (1926 and 1928);

other successes included Coward's *Bitter Sweet* (1929), Priestley's *The Good Companions* (1931), and Barrie's *The Boy David* (1936). Among notable post-war productions at the theatre, which reverted to the name Her Majesty's in 1952, were Robert Morley's *Edward My Son* (1947) and the musicals *Brigadoon*, *West Side Story*, and *Fiddler on the Roof*. Andrew Lloyd Webber's musical *The Phantom of the Opera* opened in 1986 and was still running in 2000.

Herman, Jerry (1933–) US composer and lyricist who, after a start off-Broadway and in revue, has had a series of successes including *Milk and Honey* (1961), HELLO DOLLY! (1964), *Mame* (1966), and *La Cage aux folles* (1983).

Hermann, David *See* Vilna Troupe.

Hernani A Romantic verse drama by Victor HUGO. First performance: Comédie-Française, Paris, 1830. On its opening night the play provoked a riot between young supporters of Romanticism and the outraged defenders of Classical decorum. The plot concerns the love of the outlaw Hernani for Doña Sol, which is brought to a tragic end by Doña Sol's guardian.

Hero-Combat play *See* mummers' play.

Herodas (c. 300 BC–250 BC) Greek playwright, one of the foremost writers of Hellenistic drama. Nine of his mime plays, which were probably intended for solo performers, survive.

heroic drama A form of theatre popular in England during the Restoration. Much influenced by French classical tragedy, heroic drama obeyed the three unities and was written in rhymed couplets. Its preoccupation with such noble themes as the conflict between love and honour (expressed most eloquently in works by John Dryden) made it vulnerable to parody; following Buckingham's satire *The Rehearsal* (1671) it was no longer found acceptable on the English stage.

Heron, Matilda (1830–77) US actress, born in Ireland, who first appeared at Philadelphia's Walnut Street Theatre in 1851 and made her New York debut as Lady Macbeth at the Bowery Theatre in 1852. Following a visit to Paris, she adapted *La Dame aux Camélias* by Dumas *fils* as *Camille* and played it with tremendous success throughout the US.

Hertz, Henrik (1798–1870) Danish poet and playwright, who wrote numerous comedies and dramas for production at the Kongeliche Teater under J L Heiberg. Of his 50 plays, only *Sparekassen* (The Savings Bank; 1836), *Sven Dyrings Hus* (The House of Sven Dyring; 1837), and *Kong Renes Datter* (King René's Daughter; 1843) have been revived.

Hevesi, Sándor (1873–1939) Hungarian director, who did much to reform the Hungarian stage after founding the Thália Society in 1904. Presenting works by contemporary Hungarian authors, the group was run on principles similar to those of Stanislavsky and Gordon Craig; subsequently Hevesi directed influential productions at the National Theatre in Budapest.

Heywood, John (1497–1578) English playwright, best known for the interlude *The Four Ps* (c. 1520), which has been described as an important bridge between medieval and Elizabethan drama. Several of his other plays, which include *The Pardoner and* *the Friar* (1519), *Johan Johan* (c. 1520), *The Play of the Wether* (1533), and *The Play of Love* (1533), exploit the possibilities of audience involvement with characters addressing them directly.

Heywood, Thomas (c. 1570–1641) English playwright and actor, possibly a relation of John Heywood. A member of both the Admiral's Men and Queen Anne's Men, he eventually succeeded Dekker as the writer of mayoral pageants for the City of London (1631–39). He claimed to have been involved in the writing of about 220 plays, of which only 35 have survived. His dramatic works ranged from studies of mythology, including a series of four plays ending with *The Iron Age* (c. 1611–c. 1613), to the masterly domestic tragedy A WOMAN KILLED WITH KINDNESS. Others include *The Wise Woman of Hogsdon* (1604), *If You Know Not Me, You Know Nobody* (1604–05), *The Rape of Lucrece* (1607), *The Fair Maid of the West* (1610 and 1631), and the lost comedy *Love's Masterpiece*. His other writing includes an *Apology for Actors* (1612).

Hibernian Roscius *See* Brooke, Gustavus Vaughan.

Hicks, Sir (Edward) Seymour (1871–1949) British actor-manager and playwright, who made his debut at the Grand Theatre, Islington in 1887. He subsequently appeared in parts as diverse as Scrooge (1901) and Valentine Brown in Barrie's *Quality Street* (1902) as well as in musical comedy, farce, and music hall; his revue *Under the Clock* (1893) was the first such entertainment seen in London. He wrote several successful plays including *Bluebell in Fairyland* (1901), which was revived annually at Christmas for many years. He also built and managed the ALDWYCH and the Hicks (now the GIELGUD) theatres, and managed DALY'S THEATRE. He often appeared with his wife, the actress Ellaline TERRISS.

Hicks Theatre *See* Gielgud Theatre.

Hilar, Karel Hugo (Karel Hugo Bakule; 1885–1935) Czech director, who became a leading figure of the Realist movement. Influenced by the theories of Stanislavsky and Gordon Craig, he worked first at the Municipal Theatre in Prague and then at the National Theatre; his greatest successes included premieres of plays by the Čapek brothers.

Hill, Aaron (1685–1750) British playwright, who was ridiculed for his *Elfrid, or the Fair Inconstant* (performed at Drury Lane in 1710) and satirized by Pope. He was briefly lessee of the Haymarket and wrote the book for Handel's opera *Rinaldo*, which he produced in 1711. His plays include *The Fatal Vision* (1716), *Athelwold* (1732), and translations from Voltaire.

Hill, Jenny (Elizabeth Pasta; 1851–96) British music hall performer, who struggled her way onto the halls through singing in East End pubs. Billed as The Vital Spark, she excelled at such melodramatic songs as 'The Little Stowaway'.

Hillberg, Emil (1852–1929) Swedish actor, who made his debut in Stockholm in 1873 as Benvolio in *Romeo and Juliet*. He formed his own shortlived experimental theatre group in 1901 and was a pioneer of naturalistic acting in the Swedish theatre. He excelled in the plays of Strindberg and Ibsen, including *The Father* and *Brand*, while other roles included Macbeth, Shylock, and Doolittle in Shaw's *Pygmalion*.

Hiller, Dame Wendy (1912–) British actress, who came to prominence after five years in repertory at Manchester as Sally in Walter Greenwood's *Love on the Dole* (1935), adapted by Ronald GOW, whom she later married. She played important roles in seasons at the Bristol Old Vic (1946), at the Old Vic in London (1955–56), and was acclaimed in New York as Isobel in Robert Bolt's *Flowering Cherry* (1959); she also appeared as Miss Tina in Michael Redgrave's adaptation of *The Aspern Papers* (1962) by Henry James. For the National Theatre she played Gunhild Borkman in Ibsen's *John Gabriel Borkman* (1975–76). In 1987 she gave a memorable performance as Lady Bracknell in Wilde's *The Importance of Being Earnest* at the Royalty. In 1988 she appeared in Alfred Uhry's Pulitzer Prize-winning *Driving Miss Daisy*.

Hilpert, Heinze (1890–1967) German director, who became a noted figure in the German Realist movement. He first attracted attention with Brückner's *Der Verbrecher* (1928) and later managed the Deutsches Theater (1939–45); other successes included several works by Zuckmayer.

Hindle Wakes A play by Stanley HOUGHTON. First performance: Aldwych Theatre, London, 1912. The working-class heroine refuses to marry her lover, a millowner's son, because she does not love him and cannot see why she should be condemned for having indulged in temporary pleasure.

Hippodrome A theatre in Leicester Square, London, which opened in 1900. Originally a circus and a venue for aquatic drama, it was briefly a music hall before becoming a home of ballet and revue in the 1920s. Musical comedy then followed, successes including works by Ivor Novello, until, in 1958 it was reorganized as a restaurant and cabaret called the **Talk of the Town**, which closed in 1982.

Hippodrome Theatre A theatre on 6th Avenue, between 43rd and 44th Streets, New York, which opened in 1905 with *A Yankee Circus on Mars*. The largest theatre in the US, it became a vaudeville house in 1923 and, in 1928, a cinema. The theatre closed in 1936 after an unsuccessful production of *Jumbo* under the owner, Billy Rose. Three years later it was demolished.

Hirsch, John Stephen (1930–89) Canadian director, born in Hungary, who won acclaim for his work at a number of venues both in Canada and elsewhere. His many ventures included a company founded to present musical comedy, the foundation of the Theatre 77 group, direction at the Manitoba Theatre Centre, and participation (with Jean Gascon) in the Stratford (Ontario) Festival. His most celebrated productions included plays by Ansky, Brecht, Chekhov, Frisch, James Reaney, and Shakespeare. He also directed plays for the New York stage and in Israel.

Hirsch, Robert Paul (1925–) French actor, who established his reputation in comic roles at the Comédie-Française, where he appeared regularly from 1948 to 1974. Noted for his idiosyncratic and highly original interpretation of such roles as Arlequin, Scapin, Tartuffe, and Bouzin in Feydeau's *Un fil à la patte* (1964), he also appeared in serious roles in such works as Dostoevsky's *Crime and Punishment* (1963).

Hirschbein, Peretz (1880–1949) Jewish actor and playwright, who founded his own Yiddish company in Odessa in 1908. The troupe performed several plays translated by Hirschbein himself as well as his celebrated studies of Jewish rural life, *The Blacksmith's Daughters* (1915) and *Green Fields* (1919).

Hirschfeld, Kurt (1902–64) German theatre manager, critic, and director, who established his reputation after moving to Zurich in 1933. There he presented influential premieres of plays by Brecht and Frisch among other important productions and did much to foster the emergence of new playwrights, including Dürrenmatt.

His Majesty's Theatre *See* Her Majesty's Theatre.

HMS Pinafore A comic opera by W S GILBERT and Sir Arthur Sullivan. first performance: London, 1878. The plot deals with a captain's daughter who loves a humble sailor despite the attentions of the First Lord of the Admiralty. All ends happily when it is found that the captain and the sailor were exchanged as babies, thus moving the sailor to a higher social station. A satire of both Italian operatic conventions and contemporary British politics, the show proved immensely successful on both sides of the Atlantic; at one time five companies were performing it simultaneously in New York.

Hoadly, Benjamin (1706–57) English physician and playwright, who with his brother **John Hoadly** (1711–76) wrote *The Contrast*, produced at Lincoln's Inn Fields in 1731, and subsequently won acclaim for the comedy *The Suspicious Husband* (1747). The success of the latter was due largely to the acting of Garrick as Ranger.

hobby horse An animal character of early folk theatre throughout Europe, usually played by an actor disguised by a wickerwork frame in the shape of a horse. A feature of the Morris Dance, mummers' play, and other ancient folk theatre traditions in England, the hobby horse possibly had its origins in primitive animal worship; later in its evolution it was reduced to a pole with a carved horse's head on top of it, a popular children's toy. *See also Mascarade*.

Hobson, Sir Harold (1904–92) British theatre critic, who consistently championed avant-garde theatre from the 1930s onwards. As critic for the *Sunday Times* from 1944 until 1976, he also paid particular attention to developments in contemporary French theatre.

Hobson's Choice A comedy by Harold BRIGHOUSE. First performance: 1915. Set in Salford in 1880, it celebrates the overthrow of Hobson, an oldfashioned tyrannical father, and his narrow middle-class attitudes by his daughter Maggie, who defies him by marrying the hapless Willie Mossop and eventually taking over her father's shoe shop. It was filmed in 1954 with Charles Laughton and John Mills.

Hochhuth, Rolf (1931–) Swiss playwright, writing in German, noted for his controversial DOCUMENTARY DRAMAS. He first achieved success in the theatre with *Der Stellvertreter* (The REPRESENTATIVE; 1963), which attacks the attitude of the Roman Catholic Church towards the Nazi persecution of the Jews during World War II. His second play, *Soldaten; Nekrolog auf Genf* (Soldiers; 1967), accused Winston Churchill of complicity in the death of the Polish leader General Sikorski and criticized his role in the bombing of Dresden in 1945. Other plays, which have generally proved less successful, include *Guerillas* (1970), *Lysistrate und Nato* (1974), and *Judith* (1984). In 1992 he caused renewed controversy with *Wessis in Weimar*, which attacked aspects of German reunification and provoked a denunciation from Helmut Kohl.

Hochwälder, Fritz (1911–86) Austrian playwright, whose early historical dramas reflect his preoccupation with the concepts of social and divine justice and interest in the unities. In *Das heilige Experiment* (The Strong Are Lonely; 1945), he examined the conflict between politics and religion in 18th-century Spanish America under Jesuit rule. Other works that deal with the themes of persecution and retribution include *Der Flüchtling* (The Fugitive; 1945) and *Der öffentliche Ankläger* (The Public Prosecutor; 1948), which is set during the French Revolution.

His later dramas, which show the influence of Grillparzer, are modern recreations of the mystery and morality plays; they include *Donadieu* (1953), the comedy *Der Unschuldige* (The Innocent Man; 1958), and *Der Befehl* (The Command; 1968).

Hock-Tuesday play An example of early English folk theatre, also called a Hocktide play or Hock play, which is presented annually in Coventry on the third Tuesday after Easter. The tradition was revived in 1575 and performances depicted the conquest of Danish invaders by the English (mounted on hobby horses) and their subsequent imprisonment by English women. Its origins probably lay in an earlier custom by virtue of which women could demand a forfeit from any man they 'hocked' (caught), the men having their turn the next day.

Hodgkinson, John (John Meadowcroft; 1767–1805) British actor, who began in the provinces before moving to the US at the instigation of John Henry. Among his early roles were Macheath, Macbeth, Jaffier, and Bob Acres. He was in management with Dunlap at the Park Theatre, New York, and achieved distinction in Dunlap's *André*. He died during a yellow fever epidemic.

Hodson, Henrietta (1841–1910) British actress and manager. Her first stage appearances were in Scotland and she became a popular burlesque actress in the provinces before coming to London in 1866. Her second husband acquired control of the Queen's Theatre, where she subsequently appeared alongside Henry Irving. In 1871 she took over the Royalty Theatre, which she ran for seven years, presenting numerous burlesques.

Hofmannsthal, Hugo von (1784–1929) Austrian playwright and poet, whose early plays rejected naturalism in favour of a more lyrical style of theatre. These plays, notably *Der Tor und der Tod* (Death and the Fool) established his reputation as a perfect stylist and colourful romantic. In the early 1900s he also adapted and modernized several classical dramas, including Euripides's *Elektra*, which deals with the theme of sexual repression, and Sophocles's *Ödipus und die Sphinx* (Oedipus and the Sphinx), a study of incest.

His most famous work, *Jedermann* (Everyman) a modernized version of an old morality play, marked the beginning of a series of dramas with social and religious implications, which finally ended with his last play, *Der Turm* (The Tower). He also achieved recognition as the librettist for Richard Strauss's operas, notably *Elektra* (1909), *Der Rosenkavalier* (1911), and *Ariadne auf Naxos* (1912), and as cofounder of the Salzburg Festival in 1920.

Principal works:

Der Tor und der Tod: 1898; translated as *Death and the Fool*.
Der Abenteurer und die Sängerin: 1898; translated as *The Adventurer and the Singer*.
Elektra: 1903.
Ödipus und die Sphinx: 1905; translated as *Oedipus and the Sphinx*.
König Ödipus: 1907; translated as *King Oedipus*.

Alkestis: 1909.
Jedermann: 1911; translated as *Everyman*.
Der Schwierige: 1921; translated as *The Difficult Man*.
Der Turm: 1925; translated as *The Tower*.

hoist *See* slote.

Holberg, Ludvig, Baron (1684–1754) Norwegian playwright, historian, and philosopher, who played a major role in the development of the theatre in Denmark and is often referred to as the 'Molière of the North'. According to tradition, he visited many European cultural centres as a young man, travelling on foot, and acquired a particular taste for the works of Plautus and Molière. On his return to Denmark he produced a series of satirical comedies, many of which he wrote and directed himself, at the first Danish-language theatre (the Danske Skueplads in Copenhagen), effectively founding the Danish theatrical comic tradition. Apart from a further six plays written after the reopening of the theatre in 1747 he retired as a playwright in 1731.

Principal works:
Den politiske Kandestøber: 1722; translated as *The Political Tinker*.
Jeppe paa Bjerget, eller den forvandlede Bonde: 1722; translated as *Jeppe of the Mountains*.
Jean de France: 1722.
Mester Gert Westphaler: 1722; translated as *The Babbling Barber*.
Den Vægelsindede: 1723; translated as *The Weathercock*.
Barselstuen: 1723; translated as *The Lying-in Room*.
Jacob von Tyboe: 1724.
Henrik og Pernille: 1724.
Den Stundesløse: 1726; translated as *The Fussy Man*.
Erasmus Montanus: 1742.

Holborn Empire A theatre in High Holborn, London, which opened in 1857 as **Weston's Music Hall**. Highly popular, it was enlarged in 1887 to hold 2500 people and renamed the **Royal Holborn**, witnessing the first appearances of Bessie Bellwood and J H Stead, among others. After a decline it was rebuilt in 1905 and reopened as the Holborn Empire. Performers who subsequently triumphed there included Albert Chevalier, Dan Leno, and Sybil Thorndike, who acted in plays by Shaw and Euripides. From 1922 to 1939 Italia CONTI presented an acclaimed annual Christmas show for children there; the building was damaged by bombs in 1940 and demolished in 1960.

Holborn Theatre Royal A theatre in High Holborn, London, opened in 1866. After initial success with *The Flying Scud* by Dion Boucicault, the theatre foundered until 1875, when – renamed the **Mirror Theatre** – a dramatization of *A Tale of Two Cities* was a success. The theatre continued (as the **Duke's Theatre**) with burlesques and other types of drama under a series of managers until destruction by fire in 1880.

Holcroft, Thomas (1745–1809) British playwright, novelist, and radical, who described his early life as a strolling player in his novel *Alwyn, or the Gentleman Comedian*. The reception of his first play, *Duplicity*, at Drury Lane in 1881 encouraged him to write a succession of comedies. Having visited Paris, he presented *The Marriage of*

Figaro by Beaumarchais at Covent Garden in 1784. His best known piece, *The Road to Ruin*, appeared in 1792 and has been frequently revived. *A Tale of Mystery* (1802), adapted from Pixérécourt, was probably the first melodrama to appear on the London stage.

Holland, George (1791–1870) British actor, who was already an experienced comedian when he went to the US and became an instant success at the Bowery Theatre, New York. He acted often in New Orleans and the South and spent six years in William Mitchell's burlesques in New York. He later joined Wallack's company, playing character parts until shortly before his death.

Hollingshead, John (1827–1904) British theatre manager, who opened the GAIETY THEATRE in 1868. There he inaugurated the matinée system and pioneered the use of electric light. For 18 years he presented burlesques, interspersed with serious new plays. In 1880 he became the first manager to stage Ibsen in London with *The Pillars of Society*.

Holloway, Joseph (1861–1944) Irish architect, theatre critic, and diarist, born in Dublin. In 1904 he was employed by Annie Horniman to renovate the building that became the original ABBEY THEATRE. Despite the conservatism of his views, he was regarded by many playwrights as a valuable guide to popular taste. Throughout his adult life he kept a copious diary, which is a valuable source of information about the Dublin theatre.

Holm, Sir Ian (Ian Holm Cuthbert; 1931–) British actor, who made his debut as a spear-carrier at Stratford-on-Avon in 1954, eventually becoming a prominent member of the Royal Shakespeare Company. His parts with the company included Troilus (1962), Henry V (1964), Lenny in Pinter's *The Homecoming* (1965), and Romeo (1967); subsequent roles included Nelson in Rattigan's *A Bequest to the Nation* (1970) and Hatch in Edward Bond's *The Sea* (1973). After a long absence from the stage, during which he concentrated on film and television work, he returned to live theatre in Harold Pinter's *Moonlight* (1993). His King Lear, given at the Royal National Theatre in 1997, is considered one of the great modern interpretations of the role.

Holt, Bland (1853–1942) British actor-manager, who emigrated with his family to Australia at an early age. He made his stage debut in Sydney in 1876; subsequently he excelled as a comedian and in melodrama and was particularly noted for his spectacular productions.

Holt, Helen Maud *See* Tree, Sir Herbert Beerbohm.

Holz, Arno (1863–1929) German novelist and playwright, who collaborated with Johannes Schlaf on the gloomy and brutal *Die Familie Selicke* (1890), which was highly influential upon the early development of naturalism. It was one of the earliest productions of the Freie Bühne and inspired numerous imitations by such authors as Gerhart Hauptmann.

Home, John (1722–1808) Scottish minister, who resigned his living after the sensational success of his tragedy *Douglas* at Edinburgh in 1756. The following year the play was produced at Covent Garden; none of his later works, however, won equal acclaim. The character of Young Norval became a favourite role of Dudley Digges,

Spranger Barry, William Betty, and John Howard Payne, while Mrs Siddons excelled as Lady Randolph.

Home, William Douglas (1912–92) British playwright and actor, whose plays consist largely of sophisticated light comedies. *The Chiltern Hundreds* (1947), starring A E Matthews, established his reputation; of the many comedies that followed the most successful included a sequel, *The Manor of Northstead* (1954), and *The Reluctant Debutante* (1955). More serious was the drama on prison life *Now Barabbas...* (1947); later successes included *The Reluctant Peer* (1964), starring Sybil Thorndike, *The Secretary Bird* (1968), *The Jockey Club Stakes* (1970), with Alastair Sim, *Lloyd George Knew My Father* (1972), with Ralph Richardson and Peggy Ashcroft, and *The Kingfisher* (1977).

Home and Beauty A farce by W Somerset MAUGHAM. First performance: London, 1919. Performed in the US as *Too Many Husbands*, the play deals with a woman who rejects two war heroes in preference for a civilian involved in black-market trading.

Homecoming, The A drama by Harold PINTER. First performance: Royal Shakespeare Company, Aldwych Theatre, 1965. The play is a savagely funny depiction of a family of men, each of whom makes a bid to possess the woman their successful brother, Teddy, has brought to stay with them. It went on to enjoy a great success on Broadway.

Hooft, Pieter Corneliszoon (1581–1647) Dutch poet and playwright, who was the author of a number of notable histories on classical themes. As well as such historical works as *Geeraedt van Velsen* (1613) and *Baeto* (1617) he wrote the pastoral *Grandida* (1605) and the comedy *Warenar* (1616).

Hope Theatre A theatre in Southwark, London, which was opened in 1613 by Philip HENSLOWE after the destruction of the rival Globe Theatre. Also used for bear and bull baiting, it was similar in design to the Swan Theatre, with a roofed stage. Early productions included Jonson's *Bartholomew Fair* (1614), although no records survive of plays being acted there after 1616. The resident company was LADY ELIZABETH'S MEN (later Prince Charles's Men). The building was demolished c. 1687.

Hopgood, Alan (1934–) Australian actor and playwright, who established a strong reputation with *And The Big Men Fly*, first presented by the Union Theatre Repertory Company in 1963. Subsequent successes have included *Private Yuk Object* (1966), set during the Vietnam War, and *Terribly, Terribly* (1968).

Hopkins, Sir Anthony (1937–) British actor, born in Wales, whose stage career began at the Library Theatre, Manchester, when he appeared in Brendan Behan's *The Quare Fellow* in 1960. He then spent seven years with the National Theatre Company at the Old Vic. In 1974 he took over from Richard Burton in the New York production of Shaffer's *Equus* and for the next 10 years he worked mainly in the US. Later he returned to the National Theatre, where he appeared as Lambert le Roux in Brenton and Hare's *Pravda* (1985), as King Lear (1987), which he played 100 times, and as Antony in *Antony and Cleopatra* (1987). The 1990s saw the emergence of Hopkins as a major film star, but he continues to make occasional appearances in the theatre.

Hopkins, Priscilla See Kemble, John Philip.

Horace A tragedy by Pierre CORNEILLE. First performance: Paris, 1640. The play is based on Livy's account of the battle between the Horatii and the Cuiratii in ancient Rome. Patriotism and honour take precedence over the ties of love between the two families.

Hordern, Sir Michael (1911–95) British actor, who made his first professional appearance in *Othello* in London in 1937. After World War II, he established his reputation at Stratford-on-Avon during the 1952 season, playing such roles as Caliban and Jaques, before going on to the Old Vic (1953–54), where he excelled as Malvolio. Subsequently he was much admired in eccentric character parts in plays by John Mortimer, Ibsen, and – with the Royal Shakespeare Company once more (1962) – Pinter and Dürrenmatt. Later successes included Stoppard's *Jumpers* (1972), Waugh's *The Ordeal of Gilbert Pinfold* (1977), *The Tempest* (1978), *The Rivals* (1983), in which he played Sir Anthony Absolute at the National Theatre, and Shaw's *You Never Can Tell* (1987). He also built up a strong reputation for his many screen and television appearances.

Horn Dance An early English folk entertainment performed annually at Abbot's Bromley in Staffordshire on the first Monday after 4 September. The male dancers wear ancient reindeer antlers and the tradition is regarded as an illustration of how primitive ritual evolved into a recognizable theatrical form.

Horniman, Annie (1860–1937) English lady of independent means who used her wealth to support various theatrical ventures, most notably financing the purchase and equipping of the ABBEY THEATRE in Dublin (1904). She had a high regard for W B Yeats, but her relationship with Lady Gregory was difficult and her attitude towards the members of the company was condescending and even hostile at times. She withdrew her backing in 1910, when the theatre remained open on the day of King Edward VII's funeral. In 1907 she invested in the GAIETY THEATRE, Manchester, and until 1921 she promoted the production there of new plays by local authors.

Horowitz, Israel (1939–) US playwright, whose first play to be produced was *The Comeback* (1957). His successes since then have included *The Indian Wants the Bronx* (1966) – a brutal one-act play about the knifing of an immigrant by two street hoodlums, *Rats* (1968), a series known collectively as *The Wakefield Plays* (1973–86), and *Park Your Car in Harvard Yard* (1991). In 1979 he founded the Gloucester Stage Company in Massachusetts, where many of his plays have been premiered.

Hostage, The A tragicomedy by Brendan BEHAN. First performance: Dublin, 1957. Seen originally in a Gaelic version, the play was successfully performed by Joan Littlewood's Theatre Workshop in 1959; the hostage of the title is an English soldier who is held prisoner in a run-down Irish brothel and eventually murdered. It includes songs and dances and speeches addressed directly to the audience; in London it became famous for Behan's speeches from the stage.

Hôtel d'Argent, Théâtre de l' *See* Argent, Théâtre de l'Hôtel d'.

Hôtel de Bourgogne, Théâtre de l' *See* Bourgogne, Théâtre de l'Hôtel de.

Hotel Paradiso (*L'Hôtel du libre échange*) A farce by Georges FEYDEAU. First performance: Paris, 1894. The play opened in London in 1956, with Alec Guinness as Boniface, whose adulterous assignation with Marcelle is interrupted by unforeseen circumstances.

Houdar de La Motte, Antoine (1672–1731) French playwright, poet, librettist, and critic, born in Paris. His tragedy *Inès de Castro* (1723) was immensely successful; he also wrote comedies, the first of which (*Les Originaux*, 1693) had such an unfavourable reception that he was discouraged from writing for the theatre for several years afterwards. In his critical works he attacked the rules of classical drama.

Houghton, (William) Stanley (1881–1913) British playwright, one of the 'Manchester School' of authors. Much influenced by Ibsen, he became famous for his realistic dramas, most of which were presented by Annie Horniman's company at the Gaiety Theatre in Manchester. The most successful of his works was the controversial HINDLE WAKES (1912), in which a poor girl unexpectedly refuses to marry her rich seducer. His other plays include *The Dear Departed* (1906) and *The Younger Generation* (1910).

housekeeper The owner of all or part of an Elizabethan theatre, who was entitled to an agreed percentage of the admission receipts in return for maintaining and paying rent for the building itself. Shakespeare was a housekeeper at the Globe Theatre but, like all other housekeepers, had no claim to playscripts or the wardrobe, unlike SHARERS.

houselights The lighting used to illuminate the auditorium, as distinct from the exit lights and those directed towards the stage.

Houseman, John (1902–88) US producer and director known for his innovative work. After directing Virgil Thompson's opera *Four Saints in Three Acts* (1934) with an all-Black cast, he joined Orson Welles to direct a famous all-Black *Macbeth* set in Haiti (1935). In 1936 he directed Mark Blitstein's musical *The Cradle Will Rock*, a show that caused problems with its left-wing politics, and in 1937 he founded the Mercury Theatre with Welles. He was a founder (1956) and first artistic director of the American Shakespeare Festival, and subsequently a founder of the Professional Theatre Group at the University of California in Los Angeles, which was later incorporated into the Mark Taper Forum. From 1972 to 1986 he was director of the Juilliard School's Drama Division, students of which were used in the ACTING COMPANY.

House of Bernarda Alba, The (*La Casa de Bernarda Alba*) A tragedy by GARCÍA LORCA, written in 1936. First performance: Madrid, 1945. The last part of the famous trilogy that also includes BLOOD WEDDING (1933) and YERMA (1934), the play deals with the mounting tension between four young women, who are confined to their house in mourning by their mother.

House of Ostrovsky *See* Maly Theatre.

Housman, Laurence (1865–1959) British playwright, brother of the poet A E Housman. The series of plays collected as VICTORIA REGINA (1935) was immensely successful in New York with Helen Hayes as the queen, but was banned (until 1937) in Britain from the public stage for its presentation of royalty. Other works included the full-length play *Prunella* (1904), which drew on the *commedia dell'arte* tradition, and the one-act series *The Little Plays of St Francis*.

Howard, Alan (1937–) British actor, who began his career at the Belgrade Theatre, Coventry, before appearing at the Royal Court Theatre in 1959 in Arnold Wesker's *Roots*. He was in the Chichester Festival season of 1962 and came to prominence for his performance as Simon in Julian Mitchell's adaptation of Ivy Compton-Burnett's *A Heritage and Its History* at the Phoenix Theatre in 1965. Since then he has excelled in many roles with the Royal Shakespeare Company, playing such parts as Hamlet (1970), Coriolanus (1977), Richard II (1980), and Nikolai Pesiakoff in Stephen Poliakoff's *Breaking the Silence* (1984). In the 1990s he appeared at the Royal National Theatre as Higgins in *Pygmalion* (1992), Macbeth (1993), Oedipus (1996), and as Lear in Peter Hall's 1997 production.

Howard, Sidney Coe (1891–1939) US playwright, who established his reputation with the comedy-drama *They Knew What They Wanted* (1924), which won a Pulitzer Prize and was later made into the musical *The Most Happy Fella*. He wrote his earliest pieces while with George Pierce Baker's Workshop '47 at Harvard and was later a cofounder of the Theatre Guild and a member of the Playwrights' Company. Other works included *Lucky Sam Carver* (1925), which concerned the love affair of a nightclub owner and a society lady, *The Silver Cord* (1926), about an obsessive relationship between a mother and her sons, and *The Ghost of Yankee Doodle* (1937), as well as the screenplay for the film *Gone With the Wind* (1939). He died in a farming accident.

Hoyt's Theatre *See* Madison Square Theatre.

Hroswitha (c. 932–83 AD) Benedictine nun from Gandersheim in Saxony, who was the author of several early Christian dramas. Her six prose plays, *Paphnutius*, *Dulcitius*, *Gallicanus*, *Callimachus*, *Abraham*, and *Sapienta*, were modelled on the style of Terence; although not originally intended for production, they have been staged several times in more recent years. The plays form an important link between the classical tradition and medieval religious drama; they are also the earliest known plays by a woman author.

Hubert, André (c. 1634–1700) French actor, who created numerous roles in Molière's plays as a member of Molière's company, to which he transferred from the Théâtre du Marais in 1664. His roles included several elderly women and character parts; he later took charge of the company's finances and management together with La Grange.

hubris In ancient Greek tragedy, an arrogant excess of pride that leads the protagonist to inevitable destruction. Heroes guilty of such presumption were portrayed as having offended the gods and thus deserving of their own downfall.

Hudson Theatre A 735-seat theatre on West 44th Street, between Broadway and 6th Avenue, New York, which opened in 1903 with *Cousin Kate* by H H Davies. Important productions there included the New York premieres of Shaw's *Man and Superman* (1905) and plays by Maugham, Henry Arthur Jones, Booth Tarkington, and Sean O'Casey. Ethel Barrymore appeared there in Mazo de la Roche's *Whiteoaks* in 1938, while further success came in 1945 with *The State of the Union* by Lindsay and Crouse. From 1934 to 1937 and again from 1949 to 1960 it was used for broadcasting. In 1968, after productions by the Actors' Studio, it was converted into a cinema. It is currently owned by and attached to the Hotel Macklowe, which uses it for conferences.

Hughes, Margaret (1643–1719) English actress, believed to be the first woman to have appeared professionally on the London stage. After her debut, as Desdemona in *The Moor of Venice* (Killigrew's version of *Othello*) at the Vere Street Theatre on 8 December 1660, she transferred to Drury Lane and then to the Dorset Garden Theatre.

Hugo, Victor (1802–85) French poet, novelist, and playwright, who emerged at the forefront of the French Romantic movement. He made his first significant contribution to the theatre with the preface to *Cromwell*, in which he championed the ideals of Romantic drama. The best of Hugo's lyrical melodramas were produced between 1830 and 1843, when the failure of *Les Burgraves* caused him to concentrate on such prose works as the novel *Les Misérables* (1862), adapted as an immensely successful musical in 1986.

Principal dramatic works:
    Cromwell: date unknown (published 1827).
    HERNANI: 1830.
    Marion de Lorme: 1831.
    Le Roi s'amuse: 1832.
    Lucrèce Borgia: 1833.
    Marie Tudor: 1833.
    Angelo, tyran de Padoue: 1835.
    RUY BLAS: 1838.
    Les Burgraves: 1843.

Huis-Clos A play by Jean-Paul SARTRE, which has also been variously translated as *Vicious Circle*, *In Camera*, and *No Exit*. First performance: Paris, 1944. The three principal characters find themselves in hell and discover that each is condemned to be tormented by the others for evermore.

Hulbert, Jack *See* Courtneidge, Dame Cicely.

Humphries, Barry (1934–) Australian actor, who came to the UK in 1959 and first appeared in London in *The Demon Barber* at the Lyric, Hammersmith. He was the original Mr Sowerberry in the musical *Oliver!* (1960), later playing Fagin in the revival (1968). He is, however, best known for his creation Dame Edna Everage, in which role he has given numerous one-man performances, including *Housewife! Superstar!* at the Apollo Theatre (1976) and *Back with a Vengeance* (1987) at the Strand.

Huneker, James Gibbons (1860–1921) US theatre critic, who did much to popularize European drama in the US. Among the notable playwrights championed by Huneker in the *Sun* and *New York Times* were Ibsen and Shaw.

Hungerford Music Hall *See* Gatti's.

Hunt, Hugh Sydney (1911–93) British director and playwright, who became artistic director at the Abbey Theatre, Dublin, in 1935 and subsequently became the first director of the Bristol Old Vic company (1945–48) and then director of the London Old Vic (1949–53), during which time he was responsible for many memorable productions, notably *Love's Labour's Lost*, *Hamlet*, *Twelfth Night*, and *Romeo and Juliet*. In 1955 he was appointed director of the Elizabethan Theatre Trust in Sydney, while on his return to the UK he became the first professor of drama at Manchester University (1961–73) and, once again, artistic director of the Abbey Theatre (1969–71). He also wrote several books on the theatre.

Hunt, (James Henry) Leigh (1784–1859) British writer and critic, whose *Critical Essays on the Performers of the London Theatre* (1808) was a collection of his reviews printed in the *News* between 1805 and 1807. He also wrote theatre criticism for the *Examiner*, which he ran with his brother until 1813, when he was imprisoned for attacking the Prince Regent. His own plays included *A Legend of Florence* (1840) and *Lovers' Amazements* (1858).

Hunter, N(orman) C(harles) (1908–71) British playwright, who established his reputation with the Chekhovian *Waters of the Moon* (1951), which provided fine roles for Edith Evans and Sybil Thorndike. Notable amongst the plays that followed were *A Day by the Sea* (1953), again starring Sybil Thorndike, *A Touch of the Sun* (1958), which featured Michael and Vanessa Redgrave, and *The Tulip Tree* (1963).

Hurry, Leslie (1909–78) British stage designer, who began his career in ballet but later produced sombre atmospheric designs for the theatre much influenced by Surrealism. His most well-known designs included those for Marlowe's *Tamburlaine the Great* (1951), Otway's *Venice Preserv'd* (1953), and Tennessee Williams's *Cat on a Hot Tin Roof* (1958).

Hutt, William (1920–) Canadian actor and director, who began his career at the Hart House Theatre in Toronto and became a leading performer and director at the Stratford (Ontario) Festival, where he first appeared in the inaugural season of 1953. He has won world acclaim for roles in the plays of Shakespeare, Molière, Marlowe, and other classic playwrights as well as in modern plays by Albee, Coward, and O'Neill. Other successes have included Caesar in Shaw's *Caesar and Cleopatra* (1969), Falstaff (1978), and the title role in Chekhov's *Uncle Vanya* (1978).

Hwang, David Henry (1957–) US playwright, many of whose works deal with immigrant or cross-cultural experiences. After off-Broadway success with *F.O.B.* (1980) and *The Dance and the Railroad* (1981), he reached Broadway with *M Butterfly* (1988), which investigates sexual, national, and racial identity. He has also provided the libretto for Phillip Glass's *The Voyage* (1992) and the book for Elton John's *Aida* (2000).

Hyde, Douglas (1860–1949) Irish playwright, scholar, poet, and first president of Eire. His main objective was the restoration of the Irish language. As a playwright and actor, he contributed to the early work of the IRISH LITERARY THEATRE; *Casadh an tSugain* (1901) was the first play in Irish ever performed on the professional stage. Several other plays in Irish followed between 1902 and 1904, often using scenarios provided by W B Yeats and Lady Gregory.

Hytner, Nicholas (1956–) British director. Hytner became an associate director at the Royal Exchange Theatre, Manchester, in 1985; his productions there included Shakespeare's *As You Like It* (1985) and Marlowe's *Edward II* (1986). In 1989 he directed the hugely successful musical MISS SAIGON at Drury Lane, a production that ran for over 10 years and transferred to Broadway. That same year he became an associate director of the Royal National Theatre (until 1997), where his productions included Alan Bennett's *The Madness of King George* (1991) and an award-winning revival of *Carousel* (1992). He has also directed opera and films.

I am a Camera A play by John VAN DRUTEN, based on *Goodbye to Berlin* by Christopher Isherwood. First performance: New York, 1951. The play depicts the decadent world of the Berlin cabaret on the eve of Hitler's rise to power. The plot is concerned with Sally Bowles, a singer, and Isherwood himself, the homosexual Englishman who admires her from afar. In 1967 it was turned into the musical CABARET.

Ibsen, Henrik (1828–1906) Norwegian playwright, who is usually regarded as the father of 20th-century drama. The son of a merchant who went bankrupt when the playwright was eight years old, he worked as a chemist's assistant before beginning to study medicine. He attempted his first plays in the 1840s, subsequently working in the theatres at Bergen and Christiania (now Oslo).

The romantic drama *Catilina* bore the influence of both Scribe and Schiller and was followed by a series of verse plays on subjects drawn from Scandinavian history, notably *The Burial Mound* and *The Vikings at Helgeland*. In 1863 he won a scholarship for *The Pretenders*, although it was the lengthy poetic drama BRAND that finally established his reputation. After leaving Norway in 1864, he lived in Italy and Germany, visiting his native land only briefly in 1874 and 1885 before returning permanently in 1891.

Brand and PEER GYNT soon became internationally recognized for their technical mastery, psychological insight, and bleakness of vision. In 1877 Ibsen wrote *Pillars of Society*, the first of the 12 prose dramas with which he would revolutionize world theatre; the plays explore issues of individual and social morality in realistic middle-class settings. Two in particular caused scandal: A DOLL'S HOUSE was seen as an attack on marriage, while GHOSTS – with its use of venereal disease as a metaphor for the collective guilt in a corrupt society – was still more controversial. AN ENEMY OF THE PEOPLE further developed the characteristic theme of an individual's resistance in a morally impoverished society, while THE WILD DUCK, *Rosmersholm*, *The Lady from the Sea*, and HEDDA GABLER highlighted Ibsen's preoccupation with isolation and obsession.

The last four plays, THE MASTER BUILDER, *Little Eyolf*, *John Gabriel Borkman*, and WHEN WE DEAD AWAKEN, saw a return to the symbolic drama of his early years, together with a focus upon the psychology of the artist that seems partly autobiographical.

Principal works:
  Catilina: 1850.
  Norma, eller en politikers kjærlighed: 1851.
  Sankthansnatten: 1853; translated as *St John's Night*.

Kjæmpehøjen: 1854; translated as *The Burial Mound*.
Fru Inger til Osteraad: 1855.
Gildet paa Solhoug: 1856; translated as *The Feast at Solhoug*.
Olaf Liljekrans: 1857.
Hæmændene paa Helgeland: 1857; translated as *The Vikings at Helgeland*.
Kjælighedens Komedie: 1873 (published 1872); translated as *Love's Comedy*.
Kongsemnerne: 1863; translated as *The Pretenders*.
Brand: 1885 (published 1866).
Peer Gynt: 1876 (published 1867).
De Unges Forbund: 1869; translated as *The League of Youth*.
Kejser og Galilæer: 1896 (published 1873); translated as *Emperor and Galilean*.
Samfundets Støtter: 1877; translated as *Pillars of Society*.
Et Dukkehjem: 1879; translated as *A Doll's House*.
Gengangere: 1882; translated as *Ghosts*.
En folkefiende: 1882; translated as *An Enemy of the People*.
Vildanden: 1886 (published 1884); translated as *The Wild Duck*.
Rosmersholm: 1886.
Fruen fra Havet: 1888; translated as *The Lady From the Sea*.
Hedda Gabler: 1890.
Bygmester Solness: 1892; translated as *The Master Builder*.
Lille Eyolf: 1894.
John Gabriel Borkman: 1896.
Naar vi Døde Vaagner: 1900; translated as *When We Dead Awaken*.

Ibsen, Lillebil (1899–1989) Norwegian dancer and actress, who married Ibsen's grandson, the film director Tancred Ibsen (1893–1978), in 1919. Having established her reputation as a dancer, she joined the Oslo Nye Teater in 1928 and attracted praise for her interpretation of comic roles, although she was also admired in Ibsen's *A Doll's House* and *Ghosts*. Later in her career she appeared at the Nationaltheatret in modern works.

Iceman Cometh, The A drama by Eugene O'NEILL. First performance: New York, 1946. The play depicts a group of disillusioned drinkers, who are roused out of their lethargy by the charismatic Hicky, only to find that their dreams cannot be realized. In what is effectively a virtuoso 20-minute monologue it is revealed that Hicky has killed his wife. The coming of death is represented by the anticipated arrival of the man who delivers the ice to the saloon. A failure in its initial production, the play revealed its stature in a 1956 revival starring Jason Robards.

Ideal Husband, An A comedy by Oscar WILDE. First performance: 1895. Mrs Cheveley, a dazzling adventuress, attempts to blackmail a politician with an incriminating letter; the threat fails when his wife recognizes her as a fellow schoolgirl who was expelled for theft.

Iden, Rosalind *See* Wolfit, Sir Donald.

Iffland, August Wilhelm (1759–1814) German actor and playwright, who was the dominant figure at the German National Theatre at Mannheim during its most successful period. He began his career under Ekhof at Gotha in 1780 and saw his first plays produced at Mannheim a year later; subsequently he established himself as a distinguished – if superficial and conservative – performer of refined comedy throughout Germany, appearing at Hamburg with Schröder and meeting Goethe in Weimar during his travels. He created Franz Moor in Schiller's *Die Räuber* in 1779 and became manager of the Berlin National Theatre in 1798, being promoted to director-general of the royal theatres in Prussia in 1811.

I Have Been Here Before A play by J B PRIESTLEY. First performance: London, 1937. One of Priestley's so-called 'time plays', it is set in a Yorkshire inn and revolves around the effect that a mysterious German doctor has on the other guests with his theories of recurring and spiralling time.

Illustre-Théâtre A French theatrical company founded in 1643, whose members included the Béjart family and Molière, who made his first stage appearance with the company. Presenting plays by Corneille, Du Ryer, and Tristan L'Hermite in the provinces, the company had been disbanded by 1645; its constitution provided the basis for that of the Comédie-Française.

Ilyinsky, Igor Vladimirovich (1901–87) Russian actor and director, who made his debut in 1918 in St Petersburg and subsequently became a leading performer under Meyerhold (1920–35) and then at the Maly Theatre. He was particularly admired in the plays of Crommelynck and Ostrovsky, while other successes included plays by Mayakovsky, Korneichuk, and Vishnevsky; he was also acclaimed as Lenin in an adaptation (1967) of John Reed's *Ten Days That Shook the World* and as the director of Sofronov's *Honesty* (1962).

Immermann, Karl (1796–1840) German director, who hoped to emulate the success of Goethe at Weimar at the theatre in Düsseldorf, of which he was director from 1834 to 1837. His attempts to improve artistic standards failed, however, to meet with public approval.

Imperial Theatre A theatre in Westminster, London, which opened in 1876 as part of the Royal Aquarium complex. Originally known as the **Royal Aquarium Theatre**, it saw the last appearance of Samuel Phelps. It changed hands in 1878, enjoying success with revivals of classic plays. Lillie Langtry became closely associated with the theatre, briefly managing it in 1882 and later rebuilding the interior (1900). The theatre failed to prosper, however, and Langtry withdrew in 1903; until 1906 it was run successfully by Lewis Waller. The interior of the theatre was later incorporated into a cinema in Canning Town and was destroyed by fire in 1931.

The 1452-seat **Imperial Theatre** on West 45th Street between Broadway and 8th Avenue in New York opened in 1923 and has been a major venue for musicals. Among them have been Gershwin's *Oh, Kay!* (1926), *On Your Toes* (1936), *Annie Get Your Gun* (1948), *Oliver* (1962), *They're Playing Our Song* (1979), *Dream Girls* (1981), and the transfer in 1990 of *Les Misérables* from the Broadway Theatre (still running in 2000).

Importance of Being Earnest, The A comedy of manners by Oscar WILDE, his last and finest play. First performance: London, 1895. Jack Worthing's friend Algernon assumes the identity of Ernest, Jack's fictitious younger brother, in order to court Jack's ward. To add to Jack's difficulties, Lady Bracknell refuses consent to his marriage to her daughter on account of his uncertain lineage. This sparkling comedy, which includes some of Wilde's wittiest dialogue, has enjoyed regular revivals. Lady Bracknell provided Edith Evans with her most famous role.

impresario A presenter of theatrical entertainments, usually of those with a strong musical element. Impresarios may include the major financial backers (or **angels**) of a production as well as those persons more immediately involved in arranging the presentation of a particular show or in managing a theatre or company. *See also choregus.*

Impromptu de Versailles, L' A comedy by MOLIÈRE. First performance: Paris, 1663. Edmé BOURSAULT, slighted by an apparent caricature of himself in LA CRITIQUE DE L'ÉCOLE DES FEMMES, had attacked Molière in a play of his own: Molière responded in this play by ridiculing Boursault and the actors of the Hôtel de Bourgogne.

improvisation A theatrical performance given without a script, relying upon an actor's ability to create his role as he performs it. An integral feature of the medieval mystery play and the *commedia dell'arte*, improvisation was reintroduced to serious drama by Stanislavsky in the 20th century, both as an aid in rehearsal and as a basis for actual performances. Improvisation became a popular technique with comedians and cabaret performers in the 1990s.

Inadmissible Evidence A play by John OSBORNE. First performance: Royal Court Theatre, 1964. In the original production Nicol Williamson brilliantly played the failing lawyer, whose monologues – expressing his feelings of disconnection from both the world at large and the individuals closest to him – form the core of the play.

Inchbald, Elizabeth (1753–1821) British playwright and actress. She married an actor, Joseph Inchbald, in 1772 and appeared with him in Bristol and elsewhere. After his death in 1779 she appeared at Covent Garden and began writing plays. George Colman the Elder produced her *A Mogul Tale, or Descent of the Balloon* at the Haymarket in 1784 and *I'll Tell You What* in 1785.

incidental music Any music written specifically for use in a theatrical production, without being an integral part of the plot itself. The most celebrated examples include numerous songs and dances for the plays of Shakespeare, instrumental tunes to accompany melodrama, and electronic music used to create atmosphere in many modern productions. Leading composers who have written such music for the stage include Beethoven, Mendelssohn, Bizet, Grieg, Sibelius, Debussy, Tchaikovsky, Vaughan Williams, Elgar, Delius, and Britten.

Incorporated Stage Society *See* Stage Society, Incorporated.

Independent Theatre Club *See* Grein, Jack Thomas.

Indipendenti, Teatro sperimentale degli An Italian theatre company, established in 1922 in a room in the old Roman baths of Virgilio Marchi. The group established a reputation for experimental productions of plays by Jarry, Wedekind, and others as well as for performances of Futurist drama.

Inge, William (1913–73) US playwright, who began as a theatre critic in 1943. His first successful play was *Come Back, Little Sheba* (1950), a study of a lonely, desolate, wife. His next play, *Picnic*, received a Pulitzer Prize in 1953; *Bus Stop* (1955) and *The*

Dark At the Top of the Stairs (1957) also won acclaim. His less successful later works included *A Loss of Roses* (1959), *Natural Affection* (1962), *Where's Daddy?* (1966), and *Summer Brave* (1962).

Ingegneri, Angelo (c. 1550–c. 1613) Italian writer on stage techniques, noted for his treatise *Della poesia rappresentativa e del modo di rappresentare le favole sceniche* (1598). In this work he places particular stress upon the correct use of stage lighting, suggesting – among other things – that the auditorium should remain in complete darkness.

In Good King Charles's Golden Days The last complete play by G B SHAW. First performance: Malvern Festival, 1939. Relying on dialogue rather than dramatic action, the play presents such historical figures as Charles II, Isaac Newton, and Nell Gwynn in conversation.

Inherit the Wind A play by Jerome Lawrence and Robert E Lee. First performance: New York, 1955. The plot, closely based on the Scopes 'Monkey trial' of 1925, concerns a Tennessee teacher who breaks a state law prohibiting the teaching of evolution. The trial becomes a cause célèbre and a personal debate between the opposing attorneys.

Innaurato, Albert (1948–) US playwright. After work at Yale University (some with Christopher DURANG) he enjoyed his first off-Broadway success with *The Transfiguration of Benno Blimpie* (New Haven, 1973; New York, 1975). The long-running Broadway comedy *Gemini* (1976) was followed by such plays as *Passione* (1980) and *Coming of Age in Soho* (1984).

inner stage An alcove at the back of the stage, concealed by a curtain, where a member of the cast can be 'discovered'. It was a common feature of the Elizabethan stage, although argument continues over its exact description.

Insect Play, The (*Ze zivota hymzu*) A play by Karel and Josef ČAPEK. First performance: Prague, 1921. This allegorical fantasy in which a tramp finds himself shrunk to the size of insects, who regard him with scorn while going about their largely materialistic business, attracted much attention outside Czechoslovakia. It has been variously seen as *And So Ad Infinitum* and *The World We Live In*.

inset A small piece of scenery placed within a larger piece in order to facilitate a rapid change of set.

Inspector Calls, An A play by J B PRIESTLEY. First performance: London, 1946. The play revolves around a mysterious police inspector, who interrupts an evening at the household of the prosperous Birling family in order to explore their various connections with a tragic suicide. Stephen Daldry's much-admired Expressionist-style revival opened at the Aldwych in 1993 and was still running in 2000.

Institute for Advance Studies in the Theatre Arts (IASTA) A US theatre organization, currently dormant, founded in New York in 1958. It enables US theatre workers to work with foreign directors and to learn foreign techniques; productions have ranged from the plays of Sophocles and Molière to Nō dramas.

interlude A brief dramatic piece – often comical in nature – that was presented in the 15th century as part of an evening's entertainment during a banquet. Such sketches were first performed in England during the reign of Henry VII, who employed a small group of professional actors for the purpose; John Heywood later developed the interlude as a distinct theatrical form but it disappeared altogether during the reign of Elizabeth I. *See also entremé; intermezzo.*

intermezzo A brief, usually comic, passage presented at banquets or between the acts of lengthy serious works in Italy during the 15th and 16th centuries. They were commonly based upon subjects taken from mythology or classical history. *See also entremé;* interlude.

International Amateur Theatre Association *See* British Theatre Association.

International Centre of Theatre Research A theatre organization founded in 1970 by Peter BROOK to provide a point of contact between actors from different nations. As well as discussing drama theory, the company has presented highly original works in Iran, Africa, Inda, the US, and elsewhere, often relying upon improvisation. In 1974 it moved to the old **Théâtre des Bouffes du Nord** in Paris, where it continues to stage a range of experimental works, as well as touring widely. The company's most celebrated production was its epic staging of the MAHAB-HARATA, first seen in 1985.

International Federation for Theatre Research A theatre organization established in London in 1955 under the aegis of the British Society for Theatre Research. Dedicated to recording and studying the theatrical tradition of its numerous member countries, it publishes a journal and coordinates research by national theatre research organizations as well as staging major conferences. It also runs its own institute at the Casa Goldoni in Venice.

International Theatre *See* Majestic Theatre.

International Theatre Institute (ITI) A theatre organization founded in Prague under the aegis of UNESCO in 1948 to promote international theatrical contacts. Based in Paris, it publishes its own journal and stages conferences; its national centres offer studying facilities and information. The ITI now has 80 national centres throughout the world, the British centre being based at Goldsmiths' College, London.

Interregnum The period between the closure of the English theatre by the Puritans in 1642 and its reopening on the coronation of Charles II in 1660. The closure order had become inevitable as the majority of those connected with the theatre had sided with the Royalists, making London's playhouses centres of intrigue against the parliamentarian cause. The performance of all plays was prohibited as offending against religious, political, and moral sensibilities and most actors and playwrights were forced to retire or return to their previous trades.

Cromwell himself had no wish to outlaw the theatre as such and allowed the performance of drama in schools and some private productions. Davenant, was one professional who found ways to continue to present theatre performances, albeit of a somewhat uncontroversial nature. Some illicit productions were staged at such venues as the Cockpit and the Red Bull, but in general the theatre lay dormant for 18 years, creating a damaging gap in a hitherto unbroken national tradition.

Intima Teatern A theatre in Stockholm, founded in 1907 as a venue for the plays of Strindberg. Over the next three years many of Strindberg's later works were performed there before the theatre (renamed the Lilla Teatern) closed in 1913.

Another theatre of the same name was opened in Engebreksplan, Stockholm, in 1911 and was eventually (1921) absorbed into the KUNGLIGA DRAMATISKA TEATERN as the Mindre Dramatiska Teatern, later the Komediteatern, and ultimately a cinema.

Intimate Theatre A theatre founded by John CLEMENTS in Palmers Green, London, in 1935. The theatre provided a mixed programme of drama on a weekly repertory basis and was the first London theatre to reopen after the outbreak of World War II.

Ionesco, Eugène (1912–94) French playwright, born in Romania, who was a pioneer of the Theatre of the ABSURD. In his first play, *The Bald Prima Donna*, Ionesco revealed his preoccupation with the failure of language as a tool for communication; subsequent plays examined the dominating presence of inanimate objects, the alienation and impotence of man, and the sterility of most social relationships. Ionesco also published a collection of essays on the theatre, *Notes et contre-notes* (1962; translated as *Notes and Counternotes*, 1964).

Principal works:

La Cantatrice chauve: 1950; translated as THE BALD PRIMA DONNA.

La Leçon: 1951; translated as THE LESSON.

Les Chaises: 1952; translated as THE CHAIRS.

Amédée ou Comment s'en débarrasser: 1954; translated as *Amédée, or How to Get Rid of It*.

Le Nouveau Locataire: 1955; translated as *The New Tenant*.

Tueur sans gages: 1959; translated as *The Killer*.

Rhinocéros: 1960; translated as RHINOCEROS.

Le Roi se meurt: 1962; translated as *Exit the King*.

Le Piéton de l'air: 1963; translated as *A Stroll in the Air*.

Le Mire: 1972.

Ion of Chios (5th century BC) Greek playwright, who was the author of several elegant tragedies. His other writings included his memoirs, the first such work recorded.

Iphigenia in Tauris A tragedy by EURIPIDES. First performance: Athens, c. 414 BC. Unlike most of his earlier works, this play has a happy ending and reveals the author as a master of romantic drama. Iphigenia is to be sacrificed to Artemis but is carried off by her to Tauris, where she subsequently saves the life of her brother Orestes and escapes with him. The story also inspired later versions by Goethe and Racine and an opera by Gluck.

Iphigenie auf Tauris A play by GOETHE, first written in a prose version in 1779 and later in verse (1786–88). First performance: (first version) Weimar, 1779; (second version) 1802. Based on the story by Euripides, the play in its later version brilliantly combined the classical plot with Goethe's personal beliefs about human redemption.

Ipsen, Bodil Louise Jensen (1889–1964) Danish actress, who became a leading interpreter of Ibsen's heroines. She made her debut at the Kongelige Teater in 1909 and later won acclaim in such roles as Nora in *A Doll's House* and Strindberg's Miss Julie.

Ireland, Kenneth *See* Pitlochry Festival Theatre.

Ireland, William Henry (1777–1835) British writer, whose Shakespearean forgeries deceived both scholars and his own father, an antiquarian book dealer, who was responsible for their publication. *Vortigern and Rowena*, which Ireland claimed to have discovered with other lost plays of Shakespeare, was produced by Sheridan at Drury Lane in 1796 before the fraud was finally exposed.

iris An adjustable diaphragm of overlapping metal leaves, by means of which the size of the area illuminated by a spotlight may be altered.

Irish Literary Theatre An organization founded in 1899 by Lady Gregory and W B Yeats to promote new Irish drama. Presenting plays by its founders among others, it moved into the Gaiety Theatre, London, in 1900, and later staged the first Gaelic play, Douglas Hyde's *Casadh an tSugáin*, in Dublin. It was taken over by the IRISH NATIONAL DRAMATIC SOCIETY in 1902.

Irish National Dramatic Society An Irish theatre company founded in 1902 by Frank and W G Fay as successor to the IRISH LITERARY THEATRE. Presenting plays by Yeats, Synge, and Padraic Colum, the company appeared in both Dublin and London (1903), leading to the foundation of the ABBEY THEATRE. A sister company in Ulster, formed in 1904, became part of the Ulster Group Theatre in 1939.

Irish Theatre *See* Provincetown Players.

iron *See* safety curtain.

Irons, Jeremy (1948–) British actor, who began his career with the Bristol Old Vic company before establishing himself as a popular leading man on both stage and screen. After a long run in the musical *Godspell* (1971–73), he appeared at the Round House as Petruchio (1975) and as Harry Thunder in O'Keeffe's *Wild Oats* (1977). In New York he appeared in Tom Stoppard's *The Real Thing* (1983) and played Hamlet at the Globe Theatre, Utah. In 1986 he starred in Aphra Behn's *The Rover* and in major Shakespearean roles at Stratford-on-Avon and the Mermaid Theatre. He is married to the actress Sinead CUSACK.

Irving, Sir Henry (John Henry Brodribb; 1838–1905) British actor-manager, who dominated the late Victorian stage. He was born at Keinton Mandeville, Somerset, but from the age of 10 lived in London. After seeing Samuel Phelps at Sadler's Wells he joined the Lyceum Theatre, Sunderland, in 1856, and then moved to Edinburgh, where he played more than 350 parts in 30 months.

He spent the next seven years touring, eventually joining the company at the St James's Theatre, London, in 1866; here he made his debut in Mrs Cowley's comedy *The Belle's Stratagem*. He then moved to the Queen's Theatre and for the first time acted with Ellen Terry. In 1870 he appeared as Digby Grant in James Albery's *The Two Roses* at the Vaudeville Theatre; in the following year he so impressed Hezekiah Bateman, the manager of the Lyceum, that he offered Irving a three year contract. With Irving's sensational success in THE BELLS, which was ideally suited to his intense and mesmeric style of acting, Bateman's ailing theatre recovered; in 1878 the Bateman management assigned the lease of the theatre to Irving, who celebrated this event with a revival of *Hamlet*, in which he defied convention by playing the central character as a victim of his own tenderness. At the same time he also secured as his leading lady Ellen Terry, with whom he was to appear in such plays as *The Merchant of Venice* (1879), *The Corsican Brothers* (1880), *Romeo and Juliet* (1882), *King Lear* (1892), and Tennyson's *Becket* (1893). From 1883 he and his company also undertook regular visits to the US and Canada, and in 1895 he was made the first theatrical knight.

Ill health and financial worries, exacerbated by a fire at his Southwark store, undermined his last years. After giving up the Lyceum he made a final US tour in 1904; during a subsequent short provincial tour he collapsed and died in the Midland Hotel, Bradford, after a performance of *Becket*. He was buried in Westminster Abbey.

His eldest son, **Henry Brodribb Irving** (1870–1919), was an actor-manager, who made his debut in Robertson's *School* in 1891. After further engagements with the companies of Ben Greet and George Alexander, he was acclaimed in 1902 in the title role of Barrie's *The Admirable Crichton* and subsequently as Hamlet in 1905. He then formed his own company and toured the world in many of his father's parts. At different times he managed the Shaftesbury, Queen's, and Savoy theatres; he was married to the actress Dorothea BAIRD.

Henry Irving's younger son, **Laurence Sidney Brodribb Irving** (1871–1914), was also an actor and playwright, who began his career under Frank Benson. As well as *Peter the Great* (1898), which he wrote for his father, and *The Unwritten Law* (1910), he was the author of several adaptations of plays by Sardou. As an actor he was highly praised in Ibsen's *The Pretenders* in 1913; he and his wife were drowned in a shipwreck in the St Lawrence.

Henry Brodribb Irving's son, **Laurence Henry Forster Irving** (1897–1988), became a stage designer and the author of a noted biography of his grandfather, *Henry Irving: the Actor and his World* (1951). As a designer he was praised for Eliot's *Murder in the Cathedral* (1935) and Priestley's *I Have Been Here Before* (1937).

Irving, Washington (1783–1859) US author, who wrote several accounts of the US stage. *The Letters of Jonathan Old Style* included a series of observations on the theatre, as did *Salmagundi* (1807). In 1826 two plays by Irving were seen, *Charles II* and *Richelieu*, both written in collaboration with John Payne. His short story 'Rip Van Winkle' was also adapted for the stage.

Irwin, May (Georgia Campbell; 1862–1928) US singer and actress, born in Canada, who began as a musical act with her sister in 1875 and subsequently became a successful burlesque artiste. She then played important supporting roles on the legitimate stage in Daly's company for some years, but returned to vaudeville in 1892 and made a spectacular hit in John J McNally's *The Widow Jones* (1895). Similar farces and musicals followed; her last major appearance was in *The 49ers* (1922).

Isaacs, Edith Juliet (1878–1956) US theatre critic, who championed the plays of such authors as G B Shaw and Robert Sherwood in her magazine *Theatre Arts* (1919–45). She also helped to found the Federal Theatre Project, the American National Theatre and Academy, and other influential theatrical ventures.

Isle of Dogs, The A play by Thomas NASHE and Ben JONSON. First performance: Swan Theatre, 1597. Now lost, the play was first presented by Pembroke's Men and led to a temporary closure of the London theatres and the imprisonment of the two authors on charges of sedition.

Islington Empire *See* Grand Theatre.

Italian night scenes An English dumb show, introduced from France in 1702 by John WEAVER. The genre was derived from the *commedia dell'arte* and featured characters from the Italian tradition in an English setting; it incorporated dancing and trickwork and gradually evolved into the HARLEQUINADE.

Italian Straw Hat, An (*Un chapeau de paille d'Italie*) A comedy by Eugène LABICHE. First performance: Paris, 1851. An English adaptation by W S Gilbert is frequently revived. The straw hat of the title is eaten by a young man's horse on the morning of his wedding; he then seeks to replace it.

ITI *See* International Theatre Institute.

Ivanov The first full-length play by Anton CHEKHOV. First performance: Alexandrinsky Theatre, St Petersburg, 1889. The play, a pessimistic drama culminating in the suicide of the central character, was a moderate success despite the inability of the troupe at the Alexandrinsky Theatre to understand the innovative naturalism of Chekhov's writing.

Ivanov, Vsevold Vyacheslavovich (1895–1963) Russian novelist and playwright, who began his career in St Petersburg as a protégé of Gorky. His Civil War plays include the Moscow Art Theatre's first Soviet play *Bronepoyezd No 14–69* (Armoured Train 14–69; 1927), a true story related by the crew of an armoured train, *Blokada* (1929), and *Golubi Mira* (1937). Other works included *Lomonosov* (1953), about a celebrated scientist.

Jack-in-the-Green *See* Robin Hood play.

jack-knife stage A method of staging in which one or more rostra are pivoted on castor wheels at one corner, thus enabling them to be swung quickly into and out of the stage area.

Jackson, Sir Barry (1879–1961) British director, manager, and playwright, whose amateur company, the **Pilgrim Players**, became professional in 1913 when he built and opened the BIRMINGHAM REPERTORY THEATRE. Jackson managed the theatre for over 20 years, presenting a wide variety of plays, including modern-dress productions of Shakespeare, masterpieces by foreign authors, and much new drama, some of which was written by Jackson himself. In 1929 he founded the MALVERN FESTIVAL as a vehicle for Shaw's plays; from 1945 to 1948 he served as a director of the Shakespeare Memorial Theatre. He was knighted in 1925.

Jackson, Glenda (1936–) British actress, who spent several years in provincial repertory companies after graduating from RADA; she made her West End debut in Bill Naughton's *Alfie* (1963). She joined the Royal Shakespeare Company in 1964 and was highly acclaimed in such leading roles as Ophelia, the Princess of France in *Love's Labours Lost*, and Charlotte Corday in Peter Weiss's *Marat/Sade*. Subsequently she combined international status as a film star with stage appearances ranging from Masha in Chekhov's *Three Sisters* (1967), Ibsen's Hedda Gabler (1975), and Shakespeare's Cleopatra (1978), to powerful performances in O'Neill's *Strange Interlude* (1985) and Brecht's *Mother Courage and her Children* (1990). Jackson's career in the theatre came to an end when she was elected as a Labour MP in 1992.

Jacobean drama English drama from the reign of James I (1603–25). Although Shakespeare was still writing plays until about 1611, the dominant figure during this period was Ben JONSON, whose bitter COMEDY OF HUMOURS reflected a new realism in the theatre. In collaboration with Inigo Jones, he was a major force in the creation of extravagant courtly masques that adopted a high scholarly tone and the inspiration for such admirers as Beaumont, Chapman, and Fletcher. The harshness underlying Jonson's satires was also a feature of Jacobean tragedy, which became obsessed with the idea of evil; through the plays of Middleton and Rowley, Tourneur, and Webster, it moved increasingly towards unsparing displays of excess and horror.

   In terms of organization, James I himself imposed strict controls upon the theatre of the day, placing all theatre companies under direct royal command; leading actors under this regime included Edward Alleyn and Richard Burbage. The period also saw the demise of the boy company, the growing influence of neoclassical theories from the Continent, increased opposition to the theatre from Puritans, and the gradual decline of audiences.

Jacobi, Sir Derek (1938–) British actor, who appeared with the National Youth Theatre and at Cambridge before making his professional debut at Birmingham in N F Simpson's *One Way Pendulum* in 1960. In 1963 he joined the National Theatre company, where he acted in plays by Shakespeare, Chekhov, Webster, Coward, and others; in 1972 he toured with the Prospect company, winning further acclaim in such roles as Oedipus, Ivanov, Hamlet, and Pericles. More recent successes have included Rostand's *Cyrano de Bergerac* (1983), the part of Alan Turing in Hugh Whitemore's *Breaking the Code* (1986), and the title roles in Anouilh's *Becket* (1991) and Chekhov's *Uncle Vanya* (1996). In 1988 he ventured into direction with Kenneth Branagh's Renaissance Theatre Company.

Jacopone da Todi (c. 1230–1306) Italian poet and playwright, who is the only writer of LAUDA known by name. He wrote nearly 90 such pieces, most of which revolved around a central *contrasto* or argument; many of them were written during his imprisonment by Pope Boniface VIII for supporting criticism of the papal elections.

Jahnn, Hans Henny (1894–1959) German playwright, novelist, and poet, whose controversial Expressionist dramas explore the ambivalent, often violent, nature of human sexuality. His major plays, in which he merges dreams with reality, include *Pastor Ephraim Magnus* (1919), *Die Krönung Richards III* (1921), *Medea* (1926), *Armut, Reichtum, Mensch und Tier* (Poverty, Wealth, Man and Beast; 1948), and *Thomas Chatterton* (1956).

Jakobsson, Jökull (1933–78) Icelandic novelist and playwright, whose realistic dramas depict life in impoverished northern communities. His plays set in Iceland include *Hart i bak* (Hard Aport; 1962) and *Songur skóarans og dóttir bakarans* (Song of the Shoemaker and the Baker's Daughter; 1978), which revolves around a small fishing village.

James, David (1839–93) British actor, who began his career in Charles Kean's company at the Princess's Theatre in 1857. Subsequently he was notable in burlesque at the Strand Theatre before assuming joint management of the Vaudeville Theatre, which he built, in 1870. Here he was particularly successful in Albery's *Two Roses* (1870) and in H J Byron's *Our Boys* (1875), which ran for 1362 performances.

James, Henry (1843–1916) US novelist, a British subject from 1915, whose first produced play was *Guy Domville* (1895). His other plays were *The High Bid* (1909), *The Outcry* (1917), and *The Other House* (1969). Among the successful plays taken from his books were *Berkeley Square* (1928) from *The Sense of the Past*, *The Heiress* (1947) from *Washington Square*, *The Innocents* (1950) from *The Turn of the Screw*, *A Boston Story* (1908) from *Watch and Ward*, and *The Spoils* (1968) from *The Spoils of Poynton* (1968).

Janauschek, Francesca Romana Maddalena (1830–1904) Czech actress, who established an international reputation as a performer of the great tragic roles. After early appearances in Prague, she spent 10 years in Frankfurt before being acclaimed in such roles as Lady Macbeth, Medea, and Mary Queen of Scots throughout Europe and in the US, where she played (in German and later in English) opposite Edwin Booth and other leading actors.

Jarry, Alfred (1873–1907) French playwright, novelist, and poet, whose farce UBU ROI was to have a profound influence on the Surrealist movement and the Theatre of the Absurd. Jarry's subsequent plays, sequels to *Ubu roi*, lacked the spirit of the original; he also wrote poems, stories, and novels and developed his theory of the absurd through 'Pataphysics, the science of imaginary solutions. His premature death was caused by alcoholism.

Principal dramatic works:
  Ubu roi: 1896.
  Ubu enchaîné: 1900.
  Ubu sur la butte: 1901.

Jarvis, Martin (1941–) British actor, who played the title role in *Henry V* for the National Youth Theatre while still at RADA. His professional career began in 1962 at Manchester and he made his London debut in Anouilh's *Poor Bitos*. Subsequent parts included Octavius in Shaw's *Man and Superman* (1966), Hamlet (1973), and Arnold Champion-Cheney in Maugham's *The Circle* (1976). In the 1980s and 1990s he appeared in a series of plays by Alan Ayckbourn, including *Woman in Mind* (1986), *Henceforward* (1988), *Man of the Moment* (1994), and *Table Manners* (1995). He has also starred in numerous radio and televison productions.

JB A verse drama by the US poet Archibald MacLeish. First performance: New York, 1958. A modern retelling of the biblical Book of Job, the play won a Pulitzer Prize.

Jeans, Isabel (1891–1985) British actress, who was highly successful in the Phoenix Society productions of 16th and 17th century plays during the 1920s, playing such parts as Cloe in Fletcher's *The Faithful Shepherdess* (1923) and Laetitia Fondlewife in Congreve's *The Old Bachelor* (1924). Her unique gift for sophisticated high comedy was brilliantly illustrated in such parts as Victoria in Maugham's *Home and Beauty* (1942) and Lady Bracknell in *The Importance of Being Earnest* (1968). She also made successful appearances in plays by Novello, Constance Collier, Sherwood, Lonsdale, Shaw, Chekhov, Anouilh, and T S Eliot.

Jefferson, Joseph (1774–1832) US actor, born in Britain, the son of a minor Drury Lane actor, he appeared in Boston in 1795 and made his New York debut as Squire Richard in Vanbrugh's *The Provok'd Husband* the following year. For upwards of 30 years he was leading actor at the Chestnut Street Theatre, Philadelphia, excelling in such comedy parts as Farmer Ashfield in Morton's *Speed the Plough*.

By his son, also **Joseph Jefferson** (1804–42), an actor and scene painter of modest ability, he was the grandfather of the third and best-known **Joseph Jefferson** (1829–1905), who made his stage debut at the age of four, performing alongside the comedy singer T D Rice. After his father died he toured with his mother and was soon playing important roles alongside such actors as John Brutus Booth. He subsequently joined Laura Keene's company and achieved great success in such parts as Pangloss in Colman the Younger's *The Heir-at-Law* and Asa Trenchard in Tom Taylor's *Our American Cousin*. With Dion Boucicault in New York he went on to play Caleb Plummer in a version of Dickens's *The Cricket on the Heath* (1859) and Salem Scudder in Boucicault's *The Octoroon* to equal acclaim before visiting Australia and then London in 1865, and attracting lasting fame in the title role of Boucicault's adaptation of Washington Irving's *Rip Van Winkle* (1865), which he continued to play throughout his career.

Jefford, Barbara (1930–) British actress, who made her debut in Brighton in 1949. Later she appeared in several seasons at Stratford-on-Avon and made her London and New York debuts as Andromache in Giraudoux's *Tiger at the Gates* (1955). She established her reputation as a classical actress while with the Old Vic company (1956–62), finding success in such plays as Shaw's *Saint Joan* (1960), and O'Neill's *Mourning Becomes Electra* (1961). During the later 1960s and 1970s she appeared with the RSC and the National Theatre Company and played a series of major Shakespearean roles with the Prospect company at the Old Vic (1977–79). Later work includes the community play *Ting Tong Mine* (1987), Volumnia in *Coriolanus* (1989), Schiller's *Wallenstein* (1993), and Lady Sneerwell in *The School for Scandal* (1995).

Jellicoe, Ann (1927–) British playwright and director, who established her reputation with *The Sport of My Mad Mother* (1958) four years after founding an open stage theatre club, The Cockpit Theatre. This brutal reflection of contemporary urban society was successfully produced at the Royal Court Theatre and was followed by the comedy *The Knack* (1961). In 1979 she founded the Colway Theatre Trust to produce large-scale community plays in Lyme Regis and other towns in the area; these have included *The Tide* (1979), *The Reckoning* (1980), and *Under the God* (1989). Her other work includes plays for children and translations of Ibsen and Chekhov.

Jennings, Alex (1957–) British actor. After training at the Bristol Old Vic and repertory work in Exeter and Manchester, he joined the Royal Shakespeare Company in 1987. The following year he made his name with an award-winning performance as Gloumov in the Old Vic's *Too Clever By Half*. Subsequent successes included Hjalmar in Ibsen's *The Wild Duck* (1990) and Captain Plume in *The Recruiting Officer* (1992). In 1994–95 he triumphed in the RSC's *Peer Gynt* and won praise in several Shakespearean roles; however, his *Hamlet* (1996–97) met with mixed reviews. In 2000 he played the title role in David Edgar's *Albert Speer* at the Royal National Theatre.

Jerome, Jerome K(lapka) (1859–1927) British humorist, novelist, and playwright, who is best known for the comic novel *Three Men in a Boat*. As well as humorous commentaries upon contemporary theatre, he was also the author of several plays, of which the most successful was *The Passing of the Third Floor Back* (1908), in which Christ – played by Forbes-Robertson to great acclaim – reappears in a boarding-house in London.

Jerrold, Douglas William (1803–57) English actor and playwright, whose early successes included the farce *Paul Pry* (1827) and the melodrama *Fifteen Years of a Drunkard's Life* (1828). Engaged by Elliston to write for the Surrey Theatre, he achieved his biggest success with BLACK-EY'D SUSAN. He went on to become manager of the Strand Theatre in 1836.

His son **William Blanchard Jerrold** (1826–84) wrote the farce *Cool as a Cucumber* (1851), performed by Charles Mathews the Younger at the Lyceum Theatre.

Jesse, F(ryniwyd) Tennyson *See* Harwood, Harold Marsh.

Jessner, Leopold (1878–1945) German director, who became a leading figure of the Expressionist movement in Berlin. His work – much influenced by Reinhardt – was particularly important for his development of the *Spieltreppe*, a form of multilevel staging that avoided the use of representational scenery which he introduced while director of the Berlin State Theatre (1919–30). His most famous production was Wedekind's *Der Marquis von Keith* (1920).

Jester *See* Court Fool.

Jesuit drama Plays written and performed by pupils of the various Jesuit colleges throughout Europe between the 16th and 18th centuries. The Jesuit Order, founded in 1534, realized the potential of drama in teaching religious ideas at an early stage and rapidly made it a regular feature of their calendar, with spectacular performances in which music, scenery, costume, and other elements were all combined. By 1750 dramatic performances were being presented at frequent intervals at nearly 300 Jesuit colleges.

The plays themselves, the subjects of which were generally taken from classical or holy writings, were initially given in Latin and adopted a high moral tone; later, however, female characters were introduced and writers drew on more varied sources for their plays, which were increasingly performed in the vernacular. By the 17th century Jesuit drama encompassed elements of opera and ballet and had acquired a reputation for sumptuousness with huge casts, large orchestras, and elaborate stage effects; eventually this extravagance contributed to the imposition of certain limitations upon such productions, which ceased altogether when the order was suppressed in 1773. Famous authors in the tradition included Scammacca and Tuccio in Italy, Avancini and Adolph in Austria, and Bidermann in Germany; pupils influenced by the form numbered amongst them Calderón, Corneille, Molière, and Voltaire.

Jesus Christ Superstar A musical by Tim RICE and Andrew LLOYD WEBBER. First performance: New York, 1970. Based upon the life of Christ and featuring extensive use of rock music, it broke all existing box-office records for a British musical. Its British run at the Palace Theatre lasted from 1972 to 1980.

Jevon, Thomas (1652–88) English actor and playwright, who excelled in low comedy. As one of the earliest English Harlequins, he appeared in Aphra Behn's *The Emperor of the Moon* in 1687 at the Dorset Garden Theatre, where he also performed in his own play *The Devil of a Wife*.

Jewish Art Theatre *See* Garden Theatre.

Jewish Drama Ensemble *See* Moscow State Jewish Theatre.

Jew of Malta, The A drama in blank verse by Christopher MARLOWE. First performance: London, c. 1590. The action, which is melodramatic and violent, focuses upon the villainous but complex Barabas and constitutes a scathing comment upon contemporary religious attitudes.

jig A short comic AFTERPIECE, which was performed in the smaller Elizabethan theatres. It consisted of rhymed verses often dealing with affairs of the day, which were sung and danced by a group of three or four actors, including a clown. A common feature of the repertory of the English Comedians, the tradition had died out by the Restoration; celebrated performers of jigs included Kempe and Tarleton.

Jim Crow *See* Rice, Thomas Dartmouth.

Jirásek, Alois (1851–1930) Czech playwright, who was the author of several plays notable for their realistic exploration of contemporary society. These included *Father* (1894); other works numbered amongst them the historical trilogy *Jan Žižka* (1903), *Jan Hus* (1911), and *Jan Roháč* (1918) and the Symbolist play *The Lantern* (1905).

Jodelet (Julian Bedeau; c. 1590–1660) French actor, brother of L'Espy, who was noted for his performances in comedy. After appearing with Montdory's company at the Théâtre du Marais, he moved to the Hôtel de Bourgogne for a time before returning to the Marais to appear in a celebrated series of farces written for him by Thomas Corneille, Scarron, and others. He always performed with his face whitened with flour; eventually he was persuaded into joining Molière's company in 1658 and appeared as the Vicomte de Jodelet in *Les Précieuses Ridicules* (1659).

Jodelle, Étienne (1532–73) French playwright and poet, who was a member of the group of seven Renaissance poets known as La Pléiade. Jodelle's *Cléopâtre captive*, one of the earliest French tragedies, and the comedy *Eugène* were first performed at the court of Henri II in 1552 or 1553; the plays were seminal works in the development of classical drama.

Jodrell Theatre *See* Kingsway Theatre.

Joey *See* Grimaldi, Joseph.

John Bull's Other Island A play by G B SHAW. First performance: Royal Court Theatre, London, 1904. Originally written for the Abbey Theatre, the play explores the differences between the English and the Irish through its two central characters and makes a case for Irish independence. The preface, written in 1906, is one of Shaw's most provocative political essays.

John F Kennedy Center for the Performing Arts *See* Kennedy Center.

John Golden Theatre A theatre on West 58th Street, New York, which was opened in 1926 and named after the actor and director **John Golden** (1874–1955). The Theatre Guild occupied the theatre for a time, producing plays by Sidney Howard and O'Neill, but in 1935 (after a brief period as the 58th Street Theatre) it was converted into a cinema. It was later used for revue (as the **Concert Theatre**) and as a television studio.

The **John Golden Theatre** on West 45th Street, New York, opened as the **Theatre Masque** in 1927. John Golden took over the theatre in 1937, opening it with *And Now Goodbye*. Since 1959 the theatre has been used for revues, which have included *At the Drop of a Hat* (1959) and *Beyond the Fringe* (1962). Other productions have been plays by Stoppard and Robert Anderson.

Johnny Jacks Play *See* mummers' play.

Johnson, Dame Celia (1908–82) British actress, who, on leaving RADA, scored early London successes in Merton Hodge's *The Wind and the Rain* (1933) and as Elizabeth Bennet in Helen Jerome's dramatization of *Pride and Prejudice* (1938). After a successful appearance in Daphne Du Maurier's *Rebecca* (1940) she made several films with Noël Coward, including the celebrated *Brief Encounter*. She returned to the stage in 1947 as Shaw's Saint Joan, subsequently starring in such modern comedies as Ayckbourn's *Relatively Speaking* (1967) and William Douglas Home's *The Dame of Sark* (1974). She also appeared for the National Theatre as Mrs Solness in Ibsen's *The Master Builder* (1964); at the Chichester Festival Theatre she played in Chekhov's *The Cherry Orchard* (1966) and was highly praised as Gertrude to the Hamlet of Alan Bates in 1971.

Johnson, Elizabeth (fl. 1790–1810) US actress, who was with the American Company in Boston and New York. At the Park Theatre, managed for a time by her husband, she played such leading Shakespearean roles as Rosalind and Imogen and became celebrated for her portrayal of elegant ladies in high comedy. She was also known for her serious portrayal of male roles, notably as Young Norval in Home's *Douglas* (1804).

Johnson, Dr Samuel (1709–84) British lexicographer, critic, and essayist. His pamphlet *A Compleat Vindication of the Licensers of the Stage* (1739) was an ironical attack on the censors, while his single tragedy *Irene* was produced by Garrick without success in 1749. His edition of Shakespeare's plays with notes and emendations was published in 1765.

Johnson, Terry (1955–) British playwright and director. Johnson worked in community theatre and with Ken Campbell's Science Fiction Theatre of Liverpool before writing his first play, *Days Here So Dark*, in 1981. He made his name with the witty *Insignificance* (1982), which imagines a meeting between Einstein, Marilyn Monroe, Joe Dimaggio, and Senator McCarthy. Subsequent plays have included *Cries from the Mammal House* (1984), *Tuesday's Child* (1986; with Kate Lock), *Imagine Drowning* (1991), *Dead Funny* (1994), and *Cleo, Camping, Emmanuelle, and Dick* (1999), a play about the lives of the 'Carry On' team.

Johnson Over Jordan A play by J B PRIESTLEY. First performance: London, 1939. The play revolves around the character of Robert Johnson, a recently deceased businessman, who reflects upon aspects of his career, his pursuit of pleasure, and his happiest memories. The part was originally played by Ralph Richardson.

Johnston, Denis (1901–84) Irish playwright and lawyer, born in Dublin. His theatrical debut, the innovative *The Old Lady Says "No!"* (1929), was first produced at the Gate Theatre in Dublin. He consolidated his reputation with a succession of plays including THE MOON IN THE YELLOW RIVER (1931) and *Strange Occurrence on Ireland's Eye* (1956), which revealed his understanding of contemporary Ireland. He was a director of the Gate Theatre, and also produced plays for the Abbey Theatre.

Johnston, Henry Erskine (1777–1845) British actor, who was extravagantly hailed as the **Scottish Roscius** when he played Hamlet at the Theatre Royal, Edinburgh in 1794. Playing Young Norval in Home's *Douglas* in full Highland costume, he caught the public imagination; in 1797 he began a five-year engagement at Covent Garden, after which he retired to obscurity.

John Street Theatre A theatre in John Street, New York, which was built of wood and painted red; under David Douglass it opened in 1767 as the first permanent New York theatre. The first production was Farquhar's *The Beaux' Stratagem*. Until the War of Independence the American Company staged many plays there, including the

New York premieres of *Macbeth*, *The Merchant of Venice*, Jonson's *Every Man in His Humour*, and Dryden's *All For Love*.

Renamed the **Theatre Royal** during the British occupation, it was used by British officers, among them the gifted scenery painter Major John André. In 1785 the American Company returned to present regular seasons, managed by the younger Hallam and John Henry. Productions included Royall Tyler's *The Contrast* (1787), Dunlap's *The Father; or, American Shandyism* (1789), John O'Keeffe's *The Poor Soldier*, Garrick's *Hamlet*, and works by Sheridan and Colman the Elder as well as Shakespeare. Among the distinguished players of the company were Thomas Wignell, Mrs Owen Morris, Joseph Jefferson I (who made his New York debut there in 1796), and the English actor John Hodgkinson. Hodgkinson became more popular than either John Henry or Hallam, who left, in 1794 and 1797 respectively. An unsuccessful season by a visiting company in 1797 prompted the American Company to return. The theatre was closed in 1798 and later sold by Hallam.

Joint Stock Company   A British touring company founded in 1974 by David HARE, Max STAFFORD-CLARK, and William GASKILL. Employing a policy of involving the playwright closely with the process of production, the group successfully staged such plays as Hare's *Fanshen* (1975), Brenton's *Epsom Downs* (1977), Stephen Lowe's *The Ragged Trousered Philanthropists* (1978), and Caryl Churchill's *A Mouthful of Birds* (1986). Joint Stock disbanded in the early 1990s; Stafford-Clark subsequently (1993) founded a new company named Out of Joint.

Jolly, George (fl. 1640–73)   English actor, who was the last notable member of the English Comedians. He returned to London after the Restoration and managed the Cockpit from 1661 to 1665, when his licence was withdrawn. Subsequently he ran the nursery attached to the patent theatres.

Jolly Boys' Play   *See* mummers' play.

Jolson, Al (Asa Yoelson; 1883–1950)   US actor and singer, best known for his work in blackface revue and musical comedy. Among the productions he appeared in were *La Belle Paree* (1911), *Whirl of Society* (1912), *Dancing Around* (1914), and *Sinbad* (1918), in which he sang 'My Mammy' and 'Swanee', his two most famous songs.

Jolson Theatre   *See* Century Theatre.

Jones, Freddie (1927–   )   British actor, who joined the Royal Shakespeare Company and first attracted attention in Peter Weiss's *Marat/Sade* (1964). He acted in the premiere of David Mercer's *Flint* (1970) at Oxford and later appeared as Mathias in a revival of Leopold Lewis's *The Bells* (1976). In 1980 he was highly praised as Sir in Ronald Harwood's *The Dresser* and subsequently played Arthur Langley in the same author's *Tramway Road* (1984).

Jones, Henry Arthur (1851–1929)   British playwright, who built up a controversial reputation with his comedies and serious plays on such themes as religious hypocrisy. Regarded in his day as a major exponent of socially relevant theatre, he is now largely forgotten because of his tendency towards the melodramatic. *The Silver King* (1882) – cowritten with Henry Herman – was his first big success, while subsequent works that were praised by Shaw and others included *The Dancing Girl* (1891), which starred

Julia Neilson, *Michael and His Lost Angel* (1896), concerning a guilt-ridden priest, and *Mrs Dane's Defence* (1900).

Jones, Inigo (1573–1652) English architect and stage designer, who studied in Italy and was influenced by the work of Parigi and Palladio. A major exponent of baroque theatre design, he was attached to Prince Henry's household in 1604 and took over production of the Court MASQUES. His long association with Jonson began in 1605 but gradually developed into a feud over the relative importance of the spoken and visual elements. After *Chloridia* in 1631, Jones engineered Jonson's dismissal. During the Civil War he fell from favour, was twice fined, and died in straitened circumstances.

Jones, James Earl (1931–) US Black actor, who made his stage debut in 1949 in Arnand d'Usseau's *Deep Are the Roots*. He had a long-running association with Joseph Papp's New York Shakespeare Festival, performing as Oberon (1961), Caliban (1962), Othello (1964), Macbeth (1966), Claudius in *Hamlet* (1972), and Lear (1973). Other successes have included Genet's *The Blacks* (1964), Fugard's *The Blood Knot* (1964), Howard Sackler's *The Great White Hope* (1967), which made him famous, *Bosman and Lena* (1970), Chekhov's *The Cherry Orchard* (1973), O'Neill's *The Iceman Cometh* (1973), Steinbeck's *Of Mice and Men* (1974), and August Wilson's *Fences* (1987), for which he won a Tony Award.

Jones, Margo (1913–55) US producer and director, whose early productions included Tennessee Williams's *You Touched Me* (1943). In 1945 she founded an experimental theatre in Dallas, Texas to present works by contemporary playwrights and avant-garde productions of older works. She directed *The Glass Menagerie* on Broadway in 1945; other presentations included Williams's *Summer and Smoke* and Maxwell Anderson's *Joan of Lorraine*.

Jones, Richard (fl. 1583–1615) English actor, who was a leading member of the English Comedians. Formerly with the Admiral's Men, he joined Robert Browne and his company in 1610 and became very popular on the Continent.

Jones, Robert Edmond (1887–1954) US stage designer and director, whose designs for Anatole France's *The Man Who Married a Dumb Wife* (1915) signalled a major reform of US stage design in general. Of his other atmospheric designs, influenced by Craig, Appia, and Copeau, the most important included those for O'Neill's *The Great God Brown* (1926) and several Shakespearean productions, notably *Hamlet* (1922).

jongleur A travelling entertainer of a type common throughout Europe during the Middle Ages. The jongleurs included both men and women who, embracing such diverse theatrical skills as acrobatics, juggling, and singing, sometimes performed only their own material (in which case they were also called *trouvères*); such entertainers usually worked as solo performers. *See also* minstrel.

Jonson, Ben (1572–1637) English playwright, regarded as second only to Shakespeare among the playwrights of his time. After training as a bricklayer and distinguishing himself in the war in Flanders, he joined Henslowe's company in 1597; shortly afterwards he narrowly escaped death for killing a fellow-actor in a duel and was imprisoned for his part in THE ISLE OF DOGS. Unsuccessful as an actor, he established his reputation as a writer with EVERY MAN IN HIS HUMOUR and went on to become the most highly regarded dramatist of the day with his numerous tragedies, comedies, and masques. However, none of the plays he wrote after a temporary exile (1616) from the theatre have remained on the stage; earlier works that have enjoyed frequent successful revivals include VOLPONE; OR, THE FOX, THE ALCHEMIST, and BARTHOLOMEW FAIR. Of his various collaborations, the most important were those with Marston and Chapman on *Eastward Ho!* (1605), which resulted in another period in prison, and the many sumptuous masques he produced with Inigo Jones. His greatest plays are memorable for their lively evocation of contemporary London and for their condemnation of human greed and materialism.

Principal works:
  The Isle of Dogs: 1597 (with Nashe).
  Every Man in his Humour: 1598.
  Every Man out of his Humour: 1599.
  Cynthia's Revels: 1600.
  The Poetaster: 1601.
  Eastward Ho!: 1605 (with Chapman and Marston).
  Sejanus: 1603.
  Volpone; or, The Fox: 1612.
  Epicoene; or, the Silent Woman: 1609.
  The Alchemist: 1610.
  Bartholomew Fair: 1614.
  Catiline: 1611.
  The Devil is an Ass: 1616.

Jordan, Dorothy (1762–1816) British actress, born in Ireland. The illegitimate daughter of an actress, she began her career (as Miss Francis) at the Crow Street Theatre in Dublin under Daly, by whom she was seduced. She subsequently joined Tate Wilkinson's company at York; as she was then pregnant, at his suggestion she adopted the name of Mrs Jordan. In 1785 Sheridan engaged her at Drury Lane as an understudy to the tragic actress Sarah Siddons, but she went on to establish her reputation playing the comic heroines of Shakespeare and breeches parts. Subsequently she excelled in the comedies of Farquhar, Congreve, and Sheridan himself. She was the mother of 15 illegitimate children, including 10 fathered by the Duke of Clarence, later William IV.

jornada A Spanish term for a division within a play, equivalent to an act.

Jōruri A dramatic narrative, chanted during a performance of the BUNRAKU puppet theatre. Named after a 15th-century ballad about a certain Princess Jōruri, these stories tended to be subordinated to the accompaniment of the three-stringed *shamisen* until the emergence of the two greatest writers of the *Jōruri*, Takemoto Gidayu (1651–1741) and Chikamatsu Monzaemon, in the 17th century. Their collaboration, resulting in a style known as 'Gidayu music', marked the most celebrated period of the Japanese puppet theatre; subsequently Japanese playwrights opted to write instead for the real actors of the *Kabuki* tradition.

Joseph, Stephen (1927–67) British director and actor, who was a tireless advocate of theatre-in-the-round. After studying in the US, he formed the Studio Theatre Company in Scarborough in 1955, touring the north of England and testing the viability of his staging ideas. In 1962 he created the country's first permanent theatre-in-the-round, the VICTORIA THEATRE, in a small converted cinema in Stoke-on-Trent. *See also* Stephen Joseph Theatre.

Journey's End A play by R C SHERRIFF. First performance: London, 1928. Set in a World War I dug-out, it concentrates on the relationship between the youthful Lieutenant Raleigh and Captain Stanhope. The actual fighting takes place offstage, but the reactions of the characters are realistically presented.

Jouvet, Louis (1887–1951) French actor and director, whose work had a profound effect upon French theatre production after World War I. He made his Paris debut in 1910 in *The Brothers Karamazov* and then joined Copeau at the Vieux-Colombier, where he excelled in plays by Shakespeare. In 1922 he became director of the Comédie des Champs-Élysées, scoring a major success with Romain's *Knock, ou le Triomphe de la médecine* in 1923. Later he became closely associated with the plays of Giraudoux and Molière. His innovations included reform of stage lighting and the use of highly evocative settings.

Joyce, James (1882–1941) Irish novelist, poet, and playwright, born in Dublin. Joyce was an outspoken champion of Ibsen; at the age of 18 his essay 'Ibsen's New Drama' was published in *The Fortnightly Review* and attracted considerable comment. His single play, *Exiles* (1919), deals with the freedoms and constraints of marriage and anticipates the complexities of his fiction.

Juell-Reimers, Johanne (1847–82) Norwegian actress, who was highly acclaimed in the plays of Ibsen and Bjørnson. Her early death cut short her promising career; her daughter was Johanne DYBWAD.

Juilliard School, The A performing arts college, the most prestigious in the US, which includes a famous drama school. It is situated in New York City on Broadway, just above the Lincoln Center.

Jujamcyn The smallest of the three New York theatrical real estate organizations, owning five Broadway theatres. Like the other such organizations, it also frequently invests in productions.

Julia, Raul (1940–94) US (Puerto Rican) actor, who had great success with both classics and musicals, many with the New York Shakespeare Festival. Roles included Orson in *Your Own Thing* (1968), Proteus in the musical version of Shakespeare's *Two Gentlemen of Verona* (1971), Macheath in *The Threepenny Opera* (1976), Guido Contini in Maury Yeston's *Nine* (1982), and *Macbeth* (1989).

Julian Eltinge Theatre *See* Empire Theatre.

Julius Caesar A play by William SHAKESPEARE, written c. 1599. First performance: c. 1599. The play traces the events surrounding the assassination of Julius Caesar and anticipates Shakespeare's major tragedies in its concentration upon the conscience-stricken Brutus and his fellow conspirators after the killing. Caesar himself dies relatively early in the play but he remains the central figure, reappearing as a corpse during Mark Antony's famous speech to the Roman mob and as a ghost before the deaths of Cassius and Brutus.

Jumpers A comedy by Tom STOPPARD. First performance: London, 1972. The play revolves around George Moore, a professor of moral philosophy, his young wife Dorothy, and her admirer Archie. George's tortuous moral arguments are paralleled by the antics of a team of acrobats (jumpers) who appear on stage.

Juno and the Paycock The second play by Sean O'CASEY. First performance: Abbey Theatre, Dublin, 1924. Set in the slums of Dublin during the civil strife of 1922, the play traces the disintegration of the Boyle family as a result of the war. A contrast is drawn between the longsuffering women of the family and their feckless vainglorious menfolk.

Justice A play by John GALSWORTHY. First performance: Savoy Theatre, 1910. The play deals with the imprisonment, persecution, and suicide of a clerk who commits forgery to rescue a woman mistreated by her husband; it allegedy inspired reform of the law relating to solitary confinement.

Juvarra, Filippo (1678–1736) Italian architect and stage designer, who designed a theatre in Rome in the Palazzo della Cancellaria for Cardinal Ottoboni. He also executed a number of designs for scenery for this theatre and worked for the queen of Poland and for Joseph I of Austria.

juvenile drama *See* toy theatre.

Juvenile Lead *See* stock company.

Kabuki The most popular form of Japanese drama, which evolved from the traditional *Nō* theatre in about 1600. Combining dialogue, music, mime, and other disparate theatrical elements, the *Kabuki* drew on plots from the JŌRURI tradition but emphasized the dominance of the actors over the musicians and playwrights. The genre encompasses various types of plays, ranging from histories to domestic dramas; it was formerly customary for a number of scenes from different pieces to be combined to make up a complete programme, which could last for a whole day. In the past, spectators at a *Kabuki* production could indulge in conversation and eating as the performance continued; such practices have, however, had to be curtailed to meet the expectations of modern audiences. The actors, who are all male, wear elaborate stylized costumes but no masks. Variations to emerge in the 20th century included the SHIMPA and the SHINGEKI, which reflected European influences.

Kachalov, Vasili Ivanovich (Vasili Ivanovich Shverubovich; 1875–1948) Russian actor, who became a leading performer at the Moscow Art Theatre. Having trained in the provinces, he was much admired in the plays of Ibsen, Shakespeare, Dostoevsky, and Leo Tolstoy (notably as the Reader in *Resurrection*) as well as in the premieres of Griboyedev's *Woe from Wit* (1906) and Ivanov's *Armoured Train 14–69* (1927).

Kagura An early form of Japanese dance drama. Based on mythological themes, the tradition was imported from China in about 540 AD.

Kahn, Florence (1877–1951) US actress, who first became known for her appearances opposite Richard MANSFIELD and later through her interpretations of Ibsen's women, whom she played throughout the US. In 1908, while playing Rebecca West in *Rosmersholm* in London, she married Max Beerbohm and virtually retired from the stage.

Kainz, Josef (1858–1910) German actor, who was noted for his distinctive voice. He first appeared with the Meininger company and later acted in Vienna, Munich, and Berlin as well as touring the US in such roles as Hamlet, Tartuffe, and Cyrano de Bergerac.

Kaiser, Georg (1878–1945) German playwright, who became a leading Expressionist writer. His major works, distinguished by their lack of plot development, stark language, and nameless characters representing general types, deal with the theme of man's regeneration through misfortune. Successful dramas include the satirical comedy *Die Bürger von Calais* (1917), *Von Morgensbis Mitternachts* (1917), and the trilogy *Die Koralle* (1917), *Gas I* (1918), and *Gas II* (1920). His condemnation of dictatorship led to his works being banned in 1933.

Kālidāsa (d. 373 AD–415 AD) Indian playwright, the most celebrated author of early Sanskrit drama. His best-known play, *Shakūntalā*, influenced Goethe and Wagner's *Der Ring des Nibelungen*.

Kalita Humphreys Theatre *See* Dallas Theatre Center.

Kameri Theatre *See* Cameri Theatre.

Kamerny Theatre A theatre in Moscow, founded in 1914 by Alexander TAÏROV. Intended for the performance of experimental dramas in contrast to the naturalistic productions of the Moscow Art Theatre, it presented numerous foreign works until Taïrov died in 1950, when the company's influence declined.

Kamińska, Ida (1899–1980) Polish-Jewish actress, who ran the **Polish State Jewish Theatre**, founded by her mother Ester Rachel Kaminska (1868–1925) in Warsaw, from 1921 to 1939. Acclaimed as an actress in the plays of Ibsen and Brecht, she reformed the theatre after World War II, renaming it after her mother and leading it on a tour of Polish cities and then through Europe before finally closing it in 1968 and moving to the US.

Kane, Sarah (1971–99) British playwright, who established a reputation as an *enfant terrible* before her suicide at the age of 27. Her first full-length play, *Blasted*, was seen at the Royal Court in 1995 and provoked outrage with scenes of rape, torture, and mutilation. Although *Phaedra's Love* (1996) and *Cleansed* (1998) were similarly bleak and brutal, *Crave* (1998) was a poetic piece about the yearning for love.

Kantor, Tadeusz (1915–90) Polish director and set designer, who established an international reputation for his work at the Stary Theatre in Cracow (1945–55) and subsequently at his own experimental Cricot 2 theatre. His most celebrated productions, several of which toured internationally, included plays by Witkiewicz and his own *Dead Class* (1975) and *Wielopole, Wielopole* (1979).

Karatygin, Vasily Andreyevich (1802–53) Russian actor, who was noted for his attention to historical accuracy in his roles. He did much background research for his performances and excelled in classical tragedy, despite his tendency towards artificiality in his acting style.

Kasperl A character of the Austrian *Altwiener Volkstheater*, derived from that of the clown HANSWURST. First played in 1764 by Laroche, he was also presented as a puppet character in the *Kasperltheater*, the Austrian equivalent of Punch and Judy.

Katayev, Valentin Petrovich (1897–1986) Russian novelist and playwright, whose socially challenging dramas criticized the morality of the NEP (New Economic Policy) period after the Russian civil war. His best-known plays included *Kvadratura Kruga* (Squaring the Circle; 1928), which is a comedy about cramped living conditions, and *The Primrose Path* (1934). Later works included dramatizations of his own novels and *Violet* (1974).

Katona, József (1791–1830) Hungarian playwright, regarded as the father of the Hungarian theatrical tradition. His celebrated five-act tragedy *Bánk Bán* (1814) depicts the dilemma faced by the regent, Bán Bánk, when the queen's brother seduces his wife and concludes in the queen's murder; it was later made into an opera by Ferenc Erkel. No other plays by Katona are known.

Kaufman, George S (1889–1961) US playwright, who wrote his first plays in collaboration with Marc Connelly. After cowriting *Merton of the Movies* (1922) and *Beggar on Horseback* (1924), he wrote *The Butter and Egg Man* (1925) and *The Cocoanuts* (1925) on his own; collaborations with **Edna Ferber** included *Dinner at Eight* (1932) and *Stage Door* (1936). He also wrote several light comedies in collaboration with Moss Hart, including *Once in a Lifetime* (1930), *Merrily We Roll Along* (1934), *You Can't Take It With You* (1936), and *The Man Who Came to Dinner* (1939). He also wrote and directed several musicals.

Kazan, Elia (1909–) US actor and director, who made his first appearance with the Group Theatre in 1935. Subsequent roles included Eddie Fuseli in Odets's *Golden Boy* (1937) and Ficzur in Molnár's *Liliom* (1940). He is best known as a director, his productions including Wilder's *The Skin of Our Teeth* (1942), Tennessee Williams's *A Streetcar Named Desire* (1947), *Cat on a Hot Tin Roof* (1955), and *Sweet Bird of Youth* (1959), and Arthur Miller's *Death of a Salesman* (1949) and *After the Fall* (1964). In 1947 he cofounded the Actors' Studio and from 1964 was involved with the Lincoln Center Repertory Company. After 1967 his work was mainly in film.

Kean, Edmund (c. 1789–1833) British actor, who was the son of a strolling player, Ann (Nance) Carey, and a minor actor, Edmund Kean (1770–92). By the age of eight he had already played small parts at Drury Lane and acquired an extravagant notion of his own importance; subsequently he toured as a strolling player, marrying an actress in 1808. In 1814 his sensational debut as Shylock at Drury Lane established an immediate reputation; his Richard III a fortnight later consolidated it. Hamlet, Othello, and Iago followed and, in 1815, he was particularly successful as Sir Giles Overreach in *A New Way to Pay Old Debts*.

Now an accepted member of society, Kean became acutely aware of his own lack of culture, which he attempted to disguise by indulging in alcoholic and other excesses. After a disappointing Lear at Drury Lane he visited the US in 1820, where again he impressed audiences with both his passionate acting and his wild behaviour. Temperamentally he was ideally suited for such roles as Macbeth, Othello, and Shylock, all of which he played with murderous intensity. In 1825 his affair with Charlotte Cox, wife of a City alderman, ended in scandal and a blackening of his public image. Kean's habitual drunkenness also resulted in several non-appearances, a gradual decline in his health, and quarrels with managers. In 1832 he played Othello to Macready's Iago, thrilling the audience but reducing himself to utter exhaustion. His final performance was again as Othello with his son, **Charles (John) Kean** (1811–68), as Iago; he died at Richmond six weeks later. His son subsequently took over the Princess's Theatre where, with his wife, the actress **Ellen Tree** (1805–80), he produced a series of historical plays, which were acclaimed for their authenticity.

Kean, Thomas (fl. 1749–50) US actor-manager, who (in partnership with Walter Murray) produced Shakespearean, Restoration, and contemporary plays – among them Gay's *The Beggar's Opera* and Congreve's *Love for Love* – in Philadelphia and New York (1749–50). He then took a touring troupe – the **Virginia Company of Com-**

edians – to Virginia, but no subsequent records exist of his activities. This was possibly the first professional US theatre company.

Keane, Doris *See* Sheldon, Edward Brewster.

Keane, John Brendan (1928–) Irish playwright and author, who established his reputation with a series of plays distinguished by strong characters and emotional situations. His works include *Sive* (1959), his first play for the stage, *The Field* (1965, later filmed), the trilogy *Values* (1973), and *The Chastitute* (1980). Since the 1970s he has mainly written novels and essays.

Kedrov, Mikhail Nikolayevich (1893–1972) Russian actor and director, who spent most of his career at the Moscow Art Theatre. Having trained under Stanislavsky, he won particular acclaim for his production of Chekhov's *Uncle Vanya* (1958) and *The Winter's Tale*.

Keeley, Robert (1793–1869) British actor, who, after experience in the provinces, was acclaimed at the Adelphi Theatre in 1819 as Jemmy Green in Pierce Egan's *Tom and Jerry*. A natural comedian, he excelled as Sairey Gamp in *Martin Chuzzlewit* by Dickens and Dogberry in *Much Ado About Nothing*.

In 1844 he took over the management of the Lyceum, in company with his wife, the actress **Mary Ann Keeley** (Mary Ann Goward; 1806–99). She made her professional debut at the Lyceum (then the English Opera House) in 1825. Later she appeared at Covent Garden, the Adelphi, and under Madame Vestris at the Olympic Theatre, usually alongside her husband. At the Adelphi she had her greatest success as Jack Sheppard in Buckstone's play of that name. She also spent two seasons at Drury Lane with Macready.

Keene, Laura (Mary Moss; c. 1826–73) British actress and manager, who began as an actress with Madame Vestris. She was seen in New York in 1851, went to Australia, and then returned to the US. She was a member of Wallack's company in New York and enjoyed success as a comedy star. In 1856 she opened her own theatre, thus becoming the first woman theatre manager, and achieved a major hit with *Our American Cousin* (1858). During the US Civil War she went on tour; it was at one of her company's performances of *Our American Cousin* at Ford's Theatre in Washington that President Lincoln was assassinated in 1865.

Keith Circuit The major VAUDEVILLE organization in the US, which at its height controlled hundreds of theatres across the country. Artists working for it had the security of knowing where they would be playing, often up to years in advance.

Kelly, Fanny (1790–1882) British actress, who made her adult acting debut in Glasgow in 1807 and was then at the Haymarket. Subsequently she played at Drury Lane for upwards of 30 years, where her parts included Ophelia to Kean's Hamlet. In 1840 she opened a theatre in Soho, later called the Royalty, where she unsuccessfully attempted to run a school for actresses.

Kelly, Hugh (1739–77) British playwright and theatre critic, whose comedy *False Delicacy* (1768) was produced at Drury Lane by Garrick in a successful effort to overshadow Goldsmith's *The Good-Natured Man* at Covent Garden. His other works include the comedy *A School for Wives* (1773).

Kelly, Jude *See* West Yorkshire Playhouse.

Kemble, John Philip (1757–1823) British actor and manager, who spent his childhood acting in the touring company of his parents, Roger Kemble (1722–1802) and Sarah Ward (d. 1807). As an actor in the provinces he built a fine reputation especially in northern England, often appearing alongside his three brothers and four sisters, the eldest of whom became famous as Sarah SIDDONS. Following two seasons at Dublin's Smock Alley Theatre, during which he fell in love with Elizabeth INCHBALD, he made his Drury Lane debut as Hamlet in 1783. His subtle performance was well received and he became identified with such great tragic roles as Coriolanus, Cato, and Alexander. He succeeded Sheridan as manager of Drury Lane and remained there until 1802, when he bought a one-sixth share in COVENT GARDEN and became the manager and leading tragedian there. In 1808 his imposition of price increases triggered the infamous OP riots. He married the actress **Priscilla Hopkins** (1755–1845) in 1787.

John's younger brother, **Stephen Kemble** (1758–1822), was also an actor and manager. His first major role was Shylock, in Dublin, but the success of his appearances on stage was often limited on account of his enormous bulk. He played Othello and even Hamlet, but is remembered as the only actor able to play Falstaff without padding. He became a prominent manager, running theatres in Edinburgh, Newcastle, and other northern towns, and was briefly manager of Drury Lane (1818).

John's youngest brother, **Charles Kemble** (1775–1854), was also an actor. He made his first stage appearance in *Macbeth*, alongside John and Sarah Siddons at the opening of Drury Lane. Initially he specialized in such parts as Richmond, Laertes, Edgar, and Mercutio but later moved on to play romantic leads. He inherited the management of Covent Garden in 1817 but only survived financially through the success of his daughter. Subsequently he toured the US. He retired in 1832 and was appointed Examiner of Plays. His wife was Maria Theresa DE CAMP.

Charles's daughter, **Fanny Kemble** (Frances Anne Kemble; 1809–93), became an actress in 1829 when she was persuaded onto the stage at Covent Garden as Juliet by her father in an effort to avert bankruptcy. For three years she filled the theatre and made several profitable tours. She also toured the US, marrying an American, Pierce Butler, in 1834. In 1848 she divorced Butler and returned to England, partnering Macready in *Macbeth*, *Othello*, and other plays. Subsequently she embarked upon a series of successful dramatic readings.

Kemp, Robert (1908–67) Scottish playwright, who wrote in both Scots and English. His varied works include such pageants as *The Saxon Saint* (1949) and *The King of Scots* (1951), history plays, which include *John Knox* (1960), and light plays, notably *The Penny Wedding* (1957). He also adapted Lyndsay's *The Thrie Estaitis* for Guthrie in 1948; his finest play was *The Other Dear Charmer* (1951), which discussed Robert Burns's affair with Mrs MacLehose.

Kempe, William (fl. 1579–1600) English comic actor, who appeared in many of Shakespeare's earlier plays. Noted as a clown, he toured Holland and Denmark, eventually joining the Chamberlain's Men in 1594 and creating such roles as Dogberry in *Much Ado About Nothing* and Peter in *Romeo and Juliet*. He did not stay long at the Globe, leaving to join Worcester's Men and to perform on the Continent. His nine days' morris dance from London to Norwich in 1600, undertaken for a bet, has passed into legend.

Kempson, Rachel *See* Redgrave, Sir Michael.

Kendal, Felicity (1946–) British actress, who grew up in India, where she toured from an early age in her parents' Shakespearean company. She made her London debut in 1967 and subsequently appeared in Ayckbourn's *The Norman Conquests* (1974) and in Frayn's *Clouds* (1978), before playing leading parts at the National Theatre, including Constanze in Peter Shaffer's *Amadeus* (1979) and Desdemona in *Othello* (1980). By this time she was a household name owing to her work in television. In the 1980s and 1990s she appeared in a series of plays by Tom Stoppard, notably *Hapgood* (1988), *Arcadia* (1993), and *Indian Ink* (1995). In 2000 she appeared in a highly successful revival of Noël Coward's *Fallen Angels*.

Kendal, W H (William Hunter Grimston; 1843–1917) British actor-manager, who began in repertory in Glasgow before coming to the Haymarket in 1866, where he met the actress **Madge Sholto Robertson** (1848–1935), whom he married in 1869. Thereafter they always acted together, going into partnership at the St James's Theatre with John Hare in 1879. Always a reliable actor, he was admired in such parts as Andrew Quick in Ernest Hendrie and Metcalfe Wood's *The Elder Miss Blossom* (1898) and Frank Maitland in Godfrey's *The Queen's Shilling* (1879). Madge Kendal was even more popular, excelling in comic roles alongside her husband, although other parts included Ophelia (1865). W H Kendal was an excellent manager, toured several times in the US and the provinces, and played through two more London seasons at the St James's in 1901 and 1905.

Kenna, Peter (1930–) Australian actor, director, and playwright, who established his reputation with *The Slaughter of St Teresa's Day* (1959). Subsequent successs have included *Talk to the Moon* (1963), *Muriel's Virtues* (1966) – which he directed, the comedy *Listen Closely* (1972), and the trilogy *A Hard God* (1973), *Furtive Love* (1978), and *An Eager Hope* (1978).

Kennedy Center An arts complex on the Potomac River in Washington, DC, first conceived in 1957 and completed in 1971 as a memorial to John F Kennedy. It houses five theatres: the 2300-seat Opera House, frequently used for touring musicals, the 1129-seat **Eisenhower Theatre** for drama, the Concert Hall, the 500-seat Terrace Theatre, and a Theatre Lab, used for children's theatre during the day and as a cabaret in the evening.

Kenny, Sean (1932–73) British stage designer, architect, and director, born in Ireland, who made a reputation for his innovative approach to stage mechanics, especially working with Joan Littlewood and Lindsay Anderson on such plays as Behan's *The Hostage* (1958). He ultimately became Art Director at the Mermaid Theatre and a prominent figure with the National Theatre. His most celebrated productions included Lionel Bart's musicals *Oliver!* and *Blitz*, in which the moving sets were controlled by a minimum number of stage crew. He was also closely associated with the Chichester Festival Theatre and designed the New London Theatre.

Kent, Jonathan (1955–) South African director, whose best-known work has been done at the ALMEIDA THEATRE in London. In 1990 he and Ian MCDIARMID became joint artistic directors of the Almeida. Kent's earlier productions for the company included Dryden's *All for Love* (1991), Euripides' *Medea* (1993), which transferred to Broadway, and *Hamlet* (1995) with Joseph Fiennes. Further acclaim followed for *Ivanov* (1997), which became the first British production of Chekhov to play in Moscow, and *Phèdre* (1998), in a much-praised version by Ted Hughes. He has also directed plays by Brecht and Corneille at the Royal National Theatre.

Kern, Jerome (1885–1945) US composer. From 1917 to 1923 he collaborated with Guy Bolton and P J Wodehouse on a series of shows for the Princess Theatre which set new standards of artistic unity for the then new American musical. The climax of his work in the 1920s was SHOW BOAT (1927), written with Oscar HAMMERSTEIN II and generally considered the first great work of the musical genre. Other successes included *Music in the Air* (1932) and *Roberta* (1935).

Kerr, Alfred (Alfred Kempner; 1867–1948) German theatre critic, who became one of the foremost advocates of naturalism in Germany. His writings, published in 1917 as *Die Welt in Drama*, supported the theories of Ibsen and Shaw among others, while later works refuted the Expressionists.

Kerr, Walter (1913–96) US critic and writer. During his long tenure with the *New York Herald Tribune* (1951–96) and the *New York Times* (1966–90) he came to be considered the best critic in his field, winning a Pulitzer Prize in 1978. Though not at his best with experimental works, he was clear, sensible, and usually kind. His volumes of criticism include *How Not to Write a Play* (1955) and *Tragedy and Comedy* (1967). His plays included an adaptation of Aristophanes' *The Birds* (1952) and a 1958 musical, *Goldilocks*, written with his wife Jean, a well-known comic writer.

Khmelev, Nikolai Pavlovich (1901–45) Russian actor and director, who eventually succeeded Nemirovich-Danchenko at the Moscow Art Theatre (1943). Earlier in his career he won acclaim in plays by Bulgakov, Chekhov, Ivanov, Maeterlinck, Pogodin, and Tolstoy at the Moscow Art Theatre, which he joined in 1919, and as director from 1937 of the Yermolova Theatre.

Kielland, Alexander (1849–1907) Norwegian novelist and playwright, whose masterpiece was the novel *Garman og Worse* (Garman and Worse; 1880), which he also adapted for the stage in 1883. Other dramatic pieces include *Tre Par* (Three Couples; 1886) and *Professoren* (The Professor; 1888).

Killigrew, Thomas (1612–83) English playwright and manager, who founded the Drury Lane Theatre in 1662. Noted for his wit, Killigrew was the author of several tragicomedies, of which the licentious drama *The Parson's Wedding* (1641), modelled on a play by Calderón, was the most successful. During the Restoration he was – with Davenant – the dominant figure in serious drama, leading a company that included Mohun, Hart, and Nell Gwynn. In 1673 he succeeded Sir Henry Herbert as Master of the Revels.

Kimberley, Charlotte (1877–1939) British theatre manageress and playwright, who ran a circuit of provincial theatres from her base at the Grand Theatre in Wolverhampton. She wrote more than 40 popular melodramas, including *Tatters* (1919) and *Kiddie o' Mine* (1921).

Kinck, Hans (1865–1926) Norwegian novelist, short-story writer, and playwright, whose works explore social problems but also highlight his love of nature and rural life. The poetic drama *Driftekaren* (The Drover; 1908) is his best-known play; others include its sequel, *Paa Rindalslægret* (At Rindal Camp; 1925)

King, Dennis (Dennis Pratt; 1897–1971) British actor and singer, who began his career in repertory at Birmingham but achieved fame in New York in 1924, when he played Jim Kenyon in *Rose Marie*. Thereafter he worked chiefly in the US; among his few London appearances were D'Artagnan in a musical version of *The Three Musketeers* (1930) and Dinsmore in Mark Reed's farcical comedy *Petticoat Fever* (1936). In New York his range of parts included Jason in Euripides's *Medea* (1947), General Burgoyne in Shaw's *The Devil's Disciple* (1950), and Bruno Mahler in Kern's *Music in the Air* (1951) as well as leading roles in the plays of Chekhov, Ibsen, and Lillian Hellmann.

King, Hetty (1883–1972) British music hall performer, who topped the bills worldwide as a male impersonator. Her most famous song was 'All the Nice Girls Love a Sailor'.

King, Tom (1730–1804) British actor, who came to Drury Lane in 1748 in *A New Way to Pay Old Debts*. After a time in the provinces he returned to Drury Lane in 1759, appearing in numerous comedy roles. In 1766 he was acclaimed as Lord Ogleby in *The Clandestine Marriage*, and in 1777 he created Sir Peter Teazle in *The School for Scandal*.

King and I, The A musical by Richard RODGERS and Oscar HAMMERSTEIN II, based on Margaret Langdon's *Anna and the King of Siam* (which is itself based on historical fact). First performance: New York, 1951. The plot concerns Anna Leonowens, an English governess who arrives in Siam to teach the King's 67 children. Although very different personalities, she and the King establish a deep rapport. Anna was played by Gertrude Lawrence in the original production, with Yul Brynner as the King. Brynner became famous in the role (especially after the 1956 film version) and revived it several times.

King John, The Life and Death of A history play by William SHAKESPEARE, written c. 1596. First performance: date unknown. A study of the political struggle between King John and the French, the play is notable chiefly for the witty character of Philip Faulconbridge, who offers sceptical comments upon politics and morality. It also explores the conflict of conscience involved when horror at John's behaviour forces his nobles into siding with their country's enemies.

King Lear A tragedy by William SHAKESPEARE, written c. 1605. First performance: London, 1606. The ageing Lear decides to divide his country between his three daughters according to the extent of their supposed love for him; this precipitates the disintegration of his whole world and his own descent into madness and death. The play is often regarded as Shakespeare's greatest because of its unremitting tragic intensity. The central role of the king, who achieves self-knowledge through suffering but only when it is too late, is widely considered the most demanding part for the older actor in world theatre.

King of Misrule *See* Misrule, Lord of.

King's Concert Rooms *See* Scala Theatre.

King's Jester *See* Court Fool.

Kingsley, Ben (1943–) British actor, who joined the Royal Shakespeare Company in 1970, his roles there including Squeers in *Nicholas Nickleby* (1980) and the title role in *Othello* (1985). In 1983 he starred in the one-man play *Edmund Kean* by Raymund FitzSimons at the Haymarket. For the National Theatre he has played Mosca in Jonson's *Volpone* and Sparkish in Wycherley's *The Country Wife* among other parts. Since winning an Oscar (1983) for his portrayal of Gandhi in the film of that name, he has worked chiefly in the cinema. In 1997 he returned to the stage in Beckett's *Waiting for Godot*.

Kingsley, Sidney (1906–95) US playwright, whose first play, *Men in White* (1933), won a Pulitzer Prize. Subsequent plays included *Dead End* (1935), *Ten Million Ghosts* (1936), *The World We Make* (1939), *The Patriots* (1943), *Detective Story* (1949), a dramatization of Arthur Koestler's *Darkness at Noon* (1951), the farce *Lunatics and Lovers* (1954), and *Nightlife* (1962).

King's Men An English theatre company, which began as the (Chamberlain's Men. Renamed in 1603 on the accession of James I, the company was resident at the Globe (and later the Blackfriars Theatre) and included Shakespeare among its members. It performed many of Shakespeare's greatest plays, usually with Richard Burbage at the head of the cast, the company's business being managed first by Heminge and Condell and later by Taylor and Lowin. The King's Men also presented plays by such authors as Beaumont and Fletcher, Jonson, Webster, Middleton, and, later, Massinger and Shirley. After the death of James I, the company appeared under the patronage of Charles I at the Cockpit-in-Court and elsewhere; it disbanded in 1642 when the theatres were closed.

King's Theatre A theatre in the Hammersmith Road, London, which opened in 1902. Touring companies, including that of Sir Donald Wolfit, used the theatre until it adopted a repertory system and ultimately became a BBC venue; it was demolished in 1963. *See also* Her Majesty's Theatre.

Kingston, Gertrude (Gertrude Konstam; 1866–1937) British actress and manager, who enjoyed a long and successful acting career before building and opening the LITTLE THEATRE in 1910 to house a repertory company. The theatre did not prosper, despite her own appearances on stage, but did much to nurture the repertory theatre system in Britain. In 1913 she acted in Shaw's *Great Catherine*, which was written for her.

Kingsway Theatre A theatre in Holborn, London, which opened in 1882 as a venue for comedy, called the **Novelty Theatre**. Renamed the **Folies-Dramatiques**, the **Jodrell Theatre**, and then the Novelty once more, it saw its first significant production in 1889 with the English premiere of Ibsen's *A Doll's House*, featuring Janet Achurch. After further changes of name (and the accidental stabbing to death of an actor in the drama *Sins of the Night*) the theatre was rebuilt by W S Penley as the **Great Queen Street Theatre**; performances during his tenure included Synge's *The Playboy of the Western World* (1907) by the Abbey Theatre company. Lena Ashwell ran the theatre for a time under its present name and was succeeded by Granville-Barker and Lillah McCarthy, who staged important works by Shaw and Arnold Bennett. In 1925 Barry Jackson brought his celebrated modern-dress *Hamlet* to the Kingsway, while in 1940 Sir Donald Wolfit staged a season of Shakespearean plays. It was bombed in World War II and demolished in 1956.

Kipphardt, Heinar (1922–82) German playwright, a leading exponent of DOCU-MENTARY DRAMA. His best-known works are *In der Sache J Robert Oppenheimer* (In the Matter of J Robert Oppenheimer; 1964), which explored the case of the black-listed US physicist, and *Joel Brand* (1965), about the Nazi period in Germany. Later works included the black comedy *Die Nacht, in der Chef geschlachtet wurde* (The Night the Boss was Slaughtered; 1967), and the documentary plays *Alexander März* (1981), about a schizophrenic poet, and *Brother Eichmann* (1983).

Kirchmayer, Thomas (1511–63) German playwright and humanist, who attacked the Roman Catholic church in several plays. Using the name **Naogeorg**, he was the author of *Pammachius* (1538), which was also performed in England in an adaptation by John Bale.

Kisfaludy, Károly (1788–1830) Hungarian poet and playwright, author of the first notable Hungarian comedies. His plays, which brought common rural characters onto the Hungarian stage for the first time, include *A Tatárok Magyarországon* (1819), *Kérök* (1819), and *Csalódások* (1828).

Kitchen, Michael (1948–) British actor, who worked with the National Youth Theatre and at the Belgrade Theatre, Coventry, before attending RADA. An actor of considerable versatility, he has often appeared with the National Theatre Company in such plays as Ayckbourn's *Bedroom Farce* (1977) and Stoppard's *Rough Crossing* (1984). With the Royal Shakespeare Company he played Mercutio in *Romeo and Juliet* and Bolingbroke in *Richard II* during 1986–87, as well as Hogarth in Nick Dear's *The Art of Success*. He has since worked mainly in television.

kitchen-sink drama A style of realistic British theatre that attracted much attention in the later 1950s. Originally intended as a derogatory description, the phrase evoked the working-class settings of such plays as John Osborne's *Look Back in Anger* (1956) and Arnold Wesker's *Roots* (1959), in contrast to the middle-class world of the West End theatre at that time.

Kivi, Alexsis (Alexsis Stenvall; 1834–72) Finnish novelist and playwright, regarded as the father of the modern Finnish theatre. His tragedy *Kullervo* (1860) established his reputation; subsequent works for the stage include his acclaimed rural comedy *Nummisuutarit* (The Village Cobblers), *Kihlaus* (The Betrothed), the biblical play *Lea*, and *Karkurit* (The Refugees).

Klaw Theatre A theatre on 45th Street, between Broadway and 8th Avenue, New York, which opened in 1921 with *Nice People* by Rachel Crothers. The Theatre Guild occupied it in 1925–26 and presented notable plays by G B Shaw; it was later renamed the **Avon Theatre** and, in the late 1930s, became a broadcasting studio. It was demolished in 1954.

Kleist, Heinrich von (1777–1811) German playwright, whose powerful and eccentric dramas are now seen as a major contribution to German Romanticism. After resigning from the Prussian army, he devoted himself to literature and led an itinerant life in several countries. While in a French prison as a suspected spy, he adapted Molière's *Amphitryon*, subsequently embarking upon his intense poetic play *Penthe-*

silea, now regarded as one of his finest works. THE BROKEN JUG was recognized as a German comic classic only after Kleist's death, while *Prinz Friedrich von Homburg*, a penetrating psychological drama, went unproduced until 1821. Depressed by lack of recognition from Goethe and others, Kleist killed himself in a suicide pact with a terminally ill woman at the age of 34.

Principal works:

Die Familie Schroffenstein: 1804.

Robert Guiskard: 1808.

Penthesilea: 1808.

Der Zerbrochene Krug: 1808; translated as *The Broken Jug* (or *The Chippit Chantie*).

Die Hermannsschlacht: 1871 (written 1808).

Käthchen von Heilbronn: 1810.

Prinz Friedrich von Homburg: 1821; translated as *The Prince of Homburg*.

Kline, Kevin (1947–) US actor, who studied at the Juilliard and performed with the Acting Company before attracting attention as the spoof matinee idol Bruce Granit in *On the Twentieth Century* (1978). His reputation was consolidated with a bravura performance as the Pirate King in the New York Shakespeare Festival's *Pirates of Penzance* in 1980. He has successfully alternated between comic and serious parts, including such Shakespearean roles as Richard III (1983), Hamlet (1986 and 1990) and Benedick (1988). He has also found success in films.

Klinger, Friedrich Maximilian (1752–1831) German playwright and novelist, whose play *Der Wirrwarr oder Sturm und Drang* (1777) inaugurated the STURM UND DRANG movement. Klinger's early plays, which included *Die Zwillinge* (The Twins; 1776), were impassioned rebellions against rationalism and owed much to the works of Shakespeare; later, however, he wrote comedies and historical tragedies of a more conventional type.

Klopstock, Friedrich Gottlob (1724–1803) German poet, who was also the author of six plays on religious and historical themes. These comprise a trilogy on German history that takes the warrior Arminius as its central character and the religious works *Der Tod Adams* (1757), *Salomo* (1769), and *David* (1772), which were influenced by Milton's *Paradise Lost*.

Knepp, Mary (d. 1677) English actress, who was trained by Killigrew and appeared in his first company at Drury Lane. She often performed in the comedies of Sir Charles Sedley, whose mistress she became, and was much admired by Samuel Pepys.

Knickerbocker Theatre A theatre on 38th Street and Broadway, New York, which opened as Abbey's Theatre in 1893 and enjoyed early success with appearances by Irving and Ellen Terry. In 1896 the theatre was taken over by Al Hayman and renamed the Knickerbocker. A number of celebrated actors and actresses appeared there, including Lillian Russell, Sarah Bernhardt, Maude Adams, and Otis Skinner. The theatre was demolished in 1930.

Knight of the Burning Pestle, The A comedy by Sir Francis BEAUMONT. First performance: c. 1607. Written for the boy company at the Blackfriars Theatre, the play satirized both the romantic 'histories' then popular and the aspirations of the middle-class audience.

Knipper-Chekhova, Olga (1870–1959) Russian actress, who married Chekhov in 1901. She was highly acclaimed as her husband's heroines – notably as Masha in *Three Sisters* – in performances at the Moscow Art Theatre, of which she was a founding member. She stayed with the company after the Revolution, making her last appearance in 1946, in Oscar Wilde's *An Ideal Husband*. Other Chekhovian roles she created included Madame Ranevskaya in *The Cherry Orchard* (1904).

Knoblock, Edward (Edward Knoblauch; 1874–1945) US playwright, later a British citizen, who became famous for his many adaptations of foreign works and novels for the stage. His most popular plays included *The Good Companions* (1931) – a version of J B Priestley's novel, and an adaptation of Vicki Blaum's *Grand Hotel* (1931) as well as his immensely successful fantasy *Kismet* (1911), which was based on a French original, and *Marie-Odile* (1915). Other works numbered amongst them *Milestones* (1912), upon which he collaborated with Arnold Bennett.

Knowles, (James) Sheridan (1784–1862) British actor and playwright, who was born in Ireland. His first work to be produced was *Caius Gracchus* (1815); later his tragedy *Virginius; or, the Liberation of Rome* was successfully produced by Macready at Covent Garden in 1820. Among his other plays were *The Hunchback* (1832) and *The Love Chase* (1837).

Knox, Teddy *See* Crazy Gang.

Koch, Esther *See* Brandes, Johann Christian.

Koch, Frederick Henry (1877–1844) US theatre scholar, who did much to promote drama education in the US university system. He was particularly noted for his influential work at the University of North Carolina and for his training of Paul Green and other significant US playwrights.

Koch, Heinrich Gottfried (1703–75) German actor-manager, who was a prominent member of Carolina Neuber's company before eventually taking over Schönemann's troupe. His finest roles were in classical comedy, although he also appeared in tragedy and was active as a scene-painter; he was acclaimed as a manager and ultimately settled his company in Leipzig.

Koltai, Ralph (1924–) German stage designer, who has spent most of his career in the British theatre. He established his reputation with his designs for the Royal Shakespeare Company, which he became associated with in 1962, for plays by Brecht and Marlowe and others as well as Shakespeare. Subsequently he found acclaim with his designs for the National Theatre, where his successes have included Ibsen's *Brand* (1978) and Shaw's *Man and Superman* (1981). In the 1980s and 1990s he worked mainly in opera and ballet. More recent work for the non-musical stage includes *Othello* (1994) in Essen, Germany, and *Timon of Athens* (1997) in Chicago.

Komisarjevskaya, Vera Fedorovna (1846–1910) Russian actress and manager, who established her reputation at the Alexandrinsky Theatre, which he joined in 1896. Sister of the director Theodore KOMISARJEVSKY, she appeared in the unsuccessful first production of Chekhov's *The Seagull* and subsequently founded her own theatre (in her own name), where she presented major dramas by Chekhov, Gorky, and Ibsen among others from 1905. Later she presented a number of Symbolist dramas, working briefly with Meyerhold, and visited the US. Her finest roles included Ibsen's Nora and Hedda Gabler.

Komisarjevskaya Theatre A theatre in St Petersburg, which was opened in 1904 by Vera KOMISARJEVSKAYA. Staging works by major Russian authors, it was directed by Meyerhold from 1906 to 1907 and saw several influential Surrealist productions. Subsequently Nikolai Evreinov and Theodore Komisarjevsky worked at the theatre until the company broke up in 1908. The theatre was reopened in 1959.

Komisarjevsky, Theodore (1882–1954) Russian director and designer, who did much to popularize the theories of Stanislavsky in Britain after emigrating from Russia in 1919. The brother of the actress Vera KOMISARJEVSKAYA, he established his reputation in Britain at the Barnes Theatre in the 1920s with his lively productions of plays by Chekhov and other Russian authors. Later he attracted further attention at the Shakespeare Memorial Theatre with such plays as *Macbeth* (1933), which featured aluminium scenery, *King Lear* (1936), and *The Taming of the Shrew* (1939). His wife, Peggy Ashcroft, appeared in many of his productions.

Komissarov, Aleksandr Mikhailovich (1904–79) Russian actor, who became a leading performer at the Moscow Art Theatre, which he joined in 1924. He was particularly admired in comic roles in the works of Beaumarchais, Sheridan, and Tolstoy but also appeared in Chekhov and Gogol. Later roles included Alyosha in Gorky's *The Lower Depths* and Bobchinsk in *The Government Inspector*.

Kongelige Teater A theatre in Copenhagen, which was first opened in 1748. In 1770 it came under royal patronage and was enlarged; rebuilt in 1874, it became famous for its productions of Ibsen's plays. A second stage (the Stærekassen) was opened in 1931.

Koonen, Alisa Georgievna (1889–1974) Russian actress, who founded the KAMERNY THEATRE in 1914 with her husband Alexander Taïrov. Having begun with the Moscow Art Theatre, she then worked under Mardzhanov before meeting Taïrov and working closely with him until 1950. Notable performances under her husband's direction included Scribe's Adrienne Lecouvreur (1919) and roles in Racine, Shakespeare, and Shaw.

Kopit, Arthur (1937–) US playwright, whose early plays included the celebrated farce *Oh Dad, Poor Dad, Mamma's Hung You In the Closet and I'm Feelin' So Sad* (1960). Other works include *The Day the Whores Came Out to Play Tennis* (1968), *Wings* (1979), the musical *Nine* (1980), and *End of the World (with Symposium to Follow)* (1984). *Phantom* (1990), a musical version of *The Phantom of the Opera* story, has toured to great effect despite being overshadowed by the Lloyd Webber version.

Korneichuk, Alexander Evdokimovich (1905–72) Russian playwright, whose plays observed all the conventions of Soviet Socialist Realism. His works range from *The Wreck of the Squadron* (1934), which depicts events from the civil war, and *Front* (1942), which was set against the German invasion of the Ukraine, to the satirical comedy *Mr Perkins's Mission to the Land of the Bolsheviks* (1944) and *Makar Dobrava* (1948).

Korsh Theatre   A theatre in Moscow, which opened in 1882. Between 1885 and 1912 it became famous for a variety of Russian and foreign productions presented by its accomplished company, which included Leonidov, Moskvin, and Orlenev. It was finally closed in 1932.

Kortner, Fritz (1892–1970)   Austrian actor and director, who became a leading performer of Expressionist drama under the direction of Jessner. Early in his career he became famous for his passionate style of delivery in such roles as Richard III and Gessler in Schiller's *Wilhelm Tell* but he later adopted a more thoughtful approach in performances of plays by Shakespeare, Ibsen, and Sophocles among others. He also appeared in films in the US and after World War II directed authoritative versions of Shakespeare and Molière as well as many German classics.

Koster and Bial's Music Hall   A theatre on West 23rd Street, New York, which was previously called **Bryant's Opera House**. Koster and Bial enlarged and reopened it in 1879 for musical shows and by 1881 it had a good reputation for light entertainment featuring famous vaudeville stars from abroad. Koster and Bial left in 1893 and it closed. Subsequently it reopened briefly as the **Bon Ton Theatre** but was demolished in 1924.

Kott, Jan (1914–)   US critic and theatre scholar, born in Poland, who has attracted much attention for his controversial writings on Shakespeare. His critical works, notably *Shakespeare, Our Contemporary* (1964), have examined such themes as sexual psychology and power politics in the plays; they had a marked impact upon the productions of Peter Brook and other directors in the 1960s and 1970s.

Kotzebue, August von (1761–1819)   German playwright, who was a prolific author of popular sentimental melodrama loosely derived from the STURM UND DRANG movement. His many well-constructed plays include lurid historical dramas, comedies, and studies of German bourgeois society; among the most successful were the melodrama *Menschenhass und Reue* (1789) and *Die Spanier in Peru* (1796), which was adapted by Sheridan as *Pizarro*. He divided his time between Germany and Russia and was director of the German theatre in St Petersburg.

Koun, Karolos (1908–87)   Greek director, who established his reputation with a series of productions of classical plays in Athens in the 1930s. Subsequently he won acclaim for plays by such modern writers as Ibsen, Tennessee Williams, and Pirandello and presented successful productions by the Greek National Theatre company in Paris and London and elsewhere. He also worked with the Royal Shakespeare Company, producing *Romeo and Juliet* in 1967.

Krannert Center for the Performing Arts   An arts centre in Urbana, Illinois, which opened in 1969. With four indoor theatres and an outdoor amphitheatre seating 560, it is one of the largest university performance centres in the US. The Great Hall is used for concerts, the Festival Theatre for opera, ballet, and modern dance, the Playhouse for drama, and the Studio Theatre for experimental theatre and music.

Krapp's Last Tape (*La Dernière Bande*)   A one-act play by Samuel BECKETT. First performance: Royal Court Theatre, 1958. In this monologue an old man listens to the tapes he recorded 30 years before, trying to recapture a fleeting love affair he had as a man in his prime: reconciling the past with the present proves both painful and comic.

Krasiński, Zygmunt (1812–59) Polish playwright and poet, author of several Romantic dramas reflecting revolutionary ideals. His plays, which were published anonymously, include *Nieboska komedia* (The Undivine Comedy; 1835), which was influenced by Goethe's *Faust* and anticipated the political upheavals of the early 20th century, and *Irydon* (not performed until 1908), which has a classical setting. Leon Schiller was among his many modern admirers.

Krasnya Presnya Theatre *See* Realistic Theatre.

Krauss, Werner (1884–1959) Austrian actor, who was widely praised in the plays of Shakespeare and in other classical roles. Seen chiefly in Berlin and Vienna, he established his reputation in a series of plays by Wedekind and later excelled in such intense parts as Macbeth and Lear, although he also won acclaim in modern dramas by Shaw and others. His committed performance in Feuchtwanger's *Jew Süss* under the Nazis led to his trial after the war.

Krejča, Otomar (1921–) Czech director, who established an international reputation with productions for the THEATRE BEHIND THE GATE, which he founded in 1965. He began his career at the Vinohrady Theatre and then worked with the National Theatre, where his successes included *Hamlet* and plays by Chekhov and Josef Topol. The Theatre Behind the Gate was closed by the authorities in 1972 and Krejča was banned from working in Czechoslovakia from 1976 until 1989. After long periods working in Germany and France, he returned to Prague and founded the Theatre Behind the Gate II in 1990. He was director of Prague's National Theatre in 1997–98.

Kristiania Theater A theatre in Oslo (formerly Kristiania or Christiania), which was founded in 1827. The first theatre was destroyed by fire in 1835 and reopened in 1837, staging an almost entirely Danish programme. The first native Norwegian works were presented after 1850, notably the plays of Bjørnson and Ibsen (who were both closely associated with the management of the theatre), and it became the focus of the national drama. In 1852 the theatre amalgamated with the rival Det Norske Teatret and ultimately, in 1899, the company transferred to the new NATIONALTHEATRET under Bjørnson.

Krleža, Miroslav (1893–1981) Croatian playwright, novelist, essayist, and poet, who was the author of several influential cycles of plays. *Legende* (1933), based upon the stories of Christ, Michelangelo, and Columbus, depicts the futile struggle to find meaning in existence; later social dramas – notably the trilogies *Golgota* (1920–23) and *The Gemblays* (1928–30) – reflect his strong nationalist and socialist views.

Krog, Helge (1889–1962) Norwegian playwright, essayist, and theatre critic, whose first play, *Det store Vi* (The Great We; 1917), criticized exploitation by the press. His later plays show the influence of Gunnar, Heiberg and Ibsen, the most successful including *Konkylien* (Happily Ever After; 1929) and *Oppbrudd* (Break-Up; 1936).

Krones, Therese (1801–30) Austrian actress, who established herself as a major actress of exceptional promise before her early death ended her career. She made her first appearance in Vienna in 1821 and attracted attention for her forceful acting and skill at improvisation, excelling in the comedies of Gleich, Meisl, Bauerle, and Raimund, especially as Youth in *Der Bauer als Millionar* (1826).

Kruczkowski, Leon (1900–62) Polish novelist and playwright, who established his reputation in the theatre with a stage adaptation of his novel *Kordian i cham* (1935), which was produced by Leon Schiller. Other works included *A Hero of Our Time* (1935), the first of several plays attacking the Nazis, and *Julius and Ethel* (1954), which defended the alleged spies, the Rosenbergs.

Kummerfeld, Karoline (1745–1815) German actress, who began her career with Ackermann's company in 1758. After falling foul of Sophie Hensel on account of her popularity she transferred to Leipzig and subsequently Gotha and Mannheim, winning the praise of Goethe, Ekhof, and Dalberg.

Kungliga Dramatiska Teatern A theatre in Stockholm, which was established in 1737. Under various names and based in a succession of buildings, the original company eventually combined with the Swedish Royal Opera in 1792 and moved into its own Kungliga Mindre Teatern in 1794. After a fire in 1825, the company transferred to the Opera House until 1863 when it acquired a new home. The present theatre opened in 1908 with a performance of one of Strindberg's plays, a studio being added in 1936 and the whole complex being renovated in 1957–60.

Kuppelhorizont An early form of cyclorama invented by **Mariano Fortuny** (1871–1949) in 1902; it consisted of a dome of reflective coloured silk.

Kurbas, Alexander Stephanovich (1887–1942) Ukrainian actor and director, a leading figure in the development of the theatre in Ukraine in the 1920s and 1930s. He was particularly active in the theatre at Kharkov, where he emphasized the influence of the director over all aspects of a production; the quality of the company he formed there was highly praised.

Kurz, Joseph Felix von (1715–84) Austrian actor, who was a leading figure in Viennese comedy of the 18th century. He was responsible for creating the stock character BERNADON, but outlived the popularity of the conventional improvised comedy in which he excelled.

Kushner, Tony (1956–) US playwright, who first gained attention with *A Bright Room Called Day* (San Francisco, 1987; New York, 1988) and created a sensation with the AIDS-inspired drama ANGELS IN AMERICA. The phantasmagoric style of that play is also seen in *Slavs* (1995). His *The Illusion* (1988) is a version of Corneille's *L'Illusion*.

Kvapil, Jaroslav (1868–1953) Czech playwright and director, who was the author of several popular plays based on folktales. As a director he presented 21 plays by Shakespeare at Prague's National Theatre between 1900 and 1918.

Kyd, Thomas (1558–94) English playwright. None of his early work survives and he remains best known for THE SPANISH TRAGEDY, which initiated the genre of the revenge tragedy. Kyd is also thought to have written a pre-Shakespearean version of *Hamlet*, now lost, and possibly to have contributed to ARDEN OF FAVERSHAM. His friendship with Marlowe led to imprisonment and torture for supposed atheism in the last year of his life.

Kynaston, Ned (Edward Kynaston; c. 1640–1706) English actor, one of the last boy actors to play female roles. He was highly acclaimed playing women at the Cockpit under Rhodes and at the Vere Street Theatre under Killigrew. He went on to play important male roles at Drury Lane, excelling as Shakespeare's Henry IV.

Kyōgen A form of Japanese farce, which was traditionally presented after or between *Nō* plays. Usually performed by the minor actors in the *Nō* production, the *Kyōgen* is customarily acted out without the use of musical accompaniment or masks and with highly stylized movements.

L

Laberius, Decimus (106 BC–42 BC) Roman nobleman, who was the author of the earliest written mime dramas. Having provoked Julius Caesar, he was forced to appear in one of his own mimes in about 45 BC in open rivalry with Publilius Syrus. Parts of 42 of his mimes have survived.

Labiche, Eugène (1815–88) French playwright, who was the author or coauthor of more than 170 light comedies and farces in the vaudeville tradition. After his first play in 1838 he wrote prolifically for some 40 years; his most successful plays included *Un chapeau de paille d'Italie* (AN ITALIAN STRAW HAT; 1851), *Le Voyage de M Perrichon* (1860), *La Poudre aux yeux* (1861), and *La Cagnotte* (1864).

Labor Stage *See* Princess Theatre.

La Calprenède, Gautier de Costes de (c. 1610–63) French novelist and playwright. His plays, tragedies and tragicomedies in the classical tradition, include *La Mort de Mithridate* (1635), *Bradamante* (1637), and *Le Comte d'Essex* (1638).

Lacey, Catherine (1904–79) British actress, whose first big success was as Leonora Yale in Mordaunt Shairp's *The Green Bay Tree* (1933). Noted for her powerful emotional acting, she went on to play Shakespearean parts at Stratford-on-Avon and the Old Vic, Clytemnestra in both Sophocles's *Electra* (1951) and Aeschylus's *Oresteia* (1961), and Elizabeth I in Schiller's *Mary Stuart* (1958). Her Agatha in Eliot's *The Family Reunion* (1939 and 1946) was also highly praised.

La Chapelle, Jean de (1655–1723) French playwright and novelist. A nobleman in the service of the Prince de Conti, he wrote four tragedies, notably *Cléopâtre* (1681), and the comedy *Les Carrosses d'Orléans*.

La Chaussée, Pierre Claude Nivelle de (1692–1754) French playwright, who was the creator of the *comédie larmoyante*, a genre of popular sentimental comedy. La Chaussée was over 40 when he began writing plays; such moralizing comedies as *La Fausse Antipathie* (1733), *Le Préjugé à la mode* (1735), and *Mélanide* (1741), which blend pathos with humour, gave rise to the bourgeois drama of Diderot and others.

Lackaye, Wilton (1862–1932) US actor, who first appeared professionally in New York in Boker's *Francesca da Rimini* in 1883. After numerous appearances alongside Fanny Davenport he went on to win acclaim in many Shakespearean and contemporary roles, including Svengali in Du Maurier's *Trilby* (1895); in 1904 he produced and played in Ibsen's *The Pillars of Society*. A highly respected actor, he was seldom absent from the stage until his retirement in 1927 and was a cofounder of the American Actors' Equity Association.

Lacy, John (d. 1681) English actor, who was a member of the first Drury Lane company. He was much admired as Falstaff and created Bayes in Buckingham's *The Rehearsal*. He wrote several plays, *The Old Troop or Monsieur Raggou* being based on his experiences during the Civil War.

Lady Elizabeth's Men An English theatre company that was formed under the patronage of James I's daughter in 1611. Members of the company appeared at Court and at the Hope under Henslowe until disbanding in 1614, then (reformed in 1622) at the Cockpit under Christoper Beeston; leading actors with the company included Nathan Field. The reformed company presented several plays by such major authors as Middleton and Rowley, Massinger, and Heywood before breaking up in 1625 because of plague.

Lady of the Camellias, The (*La Dame aux camélias*) A play by Alexandre DUMAS *fils*, also known in English as *Camille*. First performance: Paris, 1852. Adapted from Dumas's novel of the same name, the play provided the basis of Verdi's opera *La Traviata* (1853). The plot centres on the courtesan Marguerite Gautier and culminates in her death from tuberculosis in the arms of her lover. It was the source for Verdi's opera *La Traviata* (1853).

Lady's Not For Burning, The A verse play by Christopher FRY. First performance: Arts Theatre, London, 1948. Set in the Middle Ages, this romantic comedy about a young woman accused of witchcraft was widely praised at the time for its eloquent use of language. The misanthropic Thomas Mendip provided a fine role for Alec Clunes at the Arts Theatre and subsequently for John Gielgud at the Globe.

Lady Windermere's Fan A comedy by Oscar WILDE. First performance: 1892. The priggish Lady Windermere, believing her husband to be involved with Mrs Erlynne, flees to her friend Lord Darlington. When Lord Windermere discovers his wife's fan in Lord Darlington's apartments, Mrs Erlynne self-sacrificingly claims that she dropped it there, suggesting that she herself had an assignation with Darlington.

La Fleur *See* Gros-Guillaume.

La Fosse, Antoine d'Aubigny de (1653–1708) French playwright, who was born in Paris. *Manlius Capitolinus* (1698), which is generally regarded as the best of La Fosse's tragedies, was inspired by Thomas Otway's *Venice Preserv'd*.

Lagerkvist, Pär (1891–1974) Swedish poet, novelist, and playwright, who won a Nobel Prize in 1951. His Expressionist plays *Den svåra stunden* (The Difficult Hour; 1918) and *Himlens hemlighet* (The Secret of Heaven; 1921) were profoundly influenced by the writings of Strindberg and present life as without meaning or hope; of his later more optimistic works the most important include *De vises sten* (The Philosopher's Stone; 1948), *Låt människan leva* (Let Man Live; 1951), and *Barabbas* (1953).

La Grange (Charles Varlet; 1639–92) French actor, who was a prominent member of Molière's company at the Palais-Royal. He played young lovers in several plays by Molière and Racine and kept invaluable records of all the company's activities. After

Molière's death he helped to run the troupe and edited an edition of Molière's plays, published in 1682.

His wife, **Marie La Grange** (1639–1727), appeared under the stagename Marotte in plays by Molière and Rostand and eventually joined the Comédie-Française.

Lagrange-Chancel, François-Joseph de (1677–1758) French playwright and author of satirical pamphlets attacking the Duc d'Orléans. His dramatic works consist of mediocre tragedies on classical themes, notably *Ino et Mélicerte* (1713).

La Harpe, Jean-François de (1739–1803) French playwright and critic, who was the embittered author of several undistinguished tragedies. *Le Comte de Warwick* (1763) and *Mélanie* (1778) were among the best of these; far better, however, was his critical work *Cours de littérature ancienne et moderne* (1799–1805), in which he excelled in his discussion of drama of the 17th century.

Lahr, Bert (Irving Lahrheim; 1895–1967) US actor, who became a star of vaudeville and burlesque. He was very successful as the prizefighter in the musical *Hold Everything* (1928) and went on to appear in the revues *Life Begins at 8.40* (1934), *George White's Scandals of 1936* (1935), and *The Show is On* (1938). He also played in the musical *Du Barry Was a Lady* (1939), *Waiting for Godot* (1956), *Hotel Paradiso* (1957), and *A Midsummer Night's Dream* (1960). He is best remembered as the Cowardly Lion in the film *The Wizard of Oz* (1939).

La Mama Experimental Theatre Club An avant-garde theatre group founded as the **Café La Mama** in New York in 1961 by Ellen Stewart. Among the group's first productions was the musical *Hair* (1967); subsequent shows included several utilizing rock music in a similar way. Groups modelled after La Mama have been formed in the UK, Australia, Canada, South America, and throughout Europe; the **Mabou Mines** group in Nova Scotia, founded in 1970, was among the most successful.

Lamb, Charles (1775–1834) British essayist and writer. As well as contributing articles on drama to periodicals he wrote several plays, of which *Mr H* was unsuccessfully produced at Drury Lane in 1806. The following year his *Tales from Shakespeare*, written jointly with his sister **Mary Lamb** (1764–1847), was well received.

Lambs, The A supper club founded in London during the 1860s. Its members – never more than 24 in number – included such distinguished theatrical figures as Squire Bancroft and Henry Irving. A US counterpart was set up in New York in 1875 and continued long after the London club disbanded in the 1890s. The New York club went bankrupt and sold its building in 1974, but **The Lambs Theatre**, a 300-seat space in the structure, is a frequently used off-Broadway site.

LAMDA *See* London Academy of Music and Dramatic Art.

La Motte-Houdar *See* Houdar de La Motte, Antoine.

Lanchester, Elsa *See* Laughton, Charles.

Landen, Dinsdale (1932–) British actor, who toured Australia with the Old Vic company before appearing in London in Rodney Ackland's *Dead Secret* (1957). Subsequently he played Shakespearean roles at Stratford-on-Avon and at the Open Air Theatre, Regent's Park, and was John in Michael Frayn's *Alphabetical Order* (1975). For the National Theatre he appeared in such plays as Ben Travers's *Plunder* (1976 and

1978), Shaw's *The Philanderer* (1978), and Chekhov's *Uncle Vanya* (1982). Later work included Travers's *Thark* (1989), *Twelfth Night* (1991), and *The School for Scandal* (1995) at the Chichester Festival.

Lander, Mrs (Jean Margaret Davenport; 1829–1903) US actress. The daughter of a British actor-manager, she appeared with her father in New York from 1838, playing Young Norval in Home's *Douglas* and even, during her adolescence, Shylock and Sir Peter Teazle. As an adult she developed a substantial range of parts, including Marguerite in *La Dame aux camélias* by Dumas *fils* and Peg Woffington in Reade's *Masks and Faces*. She continued after her husband, General Lander, was killed in the US Civil War, until her final appearance in 1877 as Hester Prynne in her own version of Hawthorne's *The Scarlet Letter*.

Land of Heart's Desire, The A verse drama by W B YEATS. First performance: Avenue Theatre, London, 1894. Based on an old Irish legend, it tells how a fairy disguised as a child appears in the home of an elderly farmer and lures his wife away. It was first presented as part of a double bill with Shaw's *Arms and the Man*, also receiving its premiere.

Lane, Louisa *See* Drew, Mrs John.

Lane, Lupino (Henry George Lupino; 1892–1959) British actor, who made his London debut as a comedian in 1903. He went on to star in musical comedies in London and New York and also to appear in films, while in 1935 he created the character Bill Snibson in *Twenty to One*; he played the same character again with great success two years later in another musical, *Me and My Girl*, which he also produced and directed.

Lane, Nathan (1956–) US actor in comedies and musicals. He made his Broadway debut in 1982, but first became widely known for his off-Broadway performance (1989) in Terrence McNally's *The Lisbon Traviata*. Other roles include Nathan Detroit in a revival of *Guys and Dolls* (1993), Max in *Laughter on the 23rd Floor* (1993), Buzz in McNally's *Love! Valour! Compassion!* (1994), and Pseudolus in *A Funny Thing Happened on the Way to the Forum* (1996).

Lane, Sam (1804–71) British theatre manager, who managed the BRITANNIA THEATRE following the change in the licensing law in 1843. He staged both full-blooded dramas and comedies; after he died, his widow **Sara Lane** (1823–99) continued to manage the theatre, appearing annually in its famous pantomime.

Lang, (Alexander) Matheson (1879–1948) British actor-manager and playwright, born in Canada, who first appeared on stage in 1897 in Wolverhampton. Subsequently he moved to London, toured the West Indies, and then returned in 1900 to work under Vedrenne and Granville-Barker at the Royal Court in plays by Ibsen and Shaw. After scoring his first great success in Hall Caine's *The Christian* (1907), he founded his own company, and toured the world, presenting Shakespeare's plays and modern romantic drama. Subsequently he was acclaimed in the title role of *Mr Wu* (1913), a melodrama by Harry Vernon and Harold Owen, and in the Shakespearean productions of Lilian Baylis at the Old Vic Theatre.

His wife, **Nellie Britton** (Hutin Britton; 1876–1965), was the leading actress with her husband's company.

Langendijk, Pieter (1683–1756) Dutch playwright, author of several notable comedies much influenced by the works of Molière. His plays include *The Mutual Marriage Hoax* (1714), which is regarded as the finest Dutch comedy of manners of the time.

Langer, František (1888–1965) Czech playwright, whose best-known play was the comedy *The Camel Through the Needle's Eye* (1923), which was brought to Broadway by the Theatre Guild in 1929. Other works included the serious Expressionist dramas *Periphery* (1925) and *The Angel in Our Midst* (1931).

Langham, Michael (1919–) British director, who won praise for his work with the Stratford (Ontario) Festival (1956–67) and at the Guthrie Theatre (1971–78) in Minneapolis, at both of which he was successor to Guthrie himself. He presided over a fine company at Stratford (Ontario), productions ranging from Shakespeare to Marlowe, Gilbert and Sullivan, and Molière; his successes at the Guthrie Theatre included Rostand's *Cyrano de Bergerac* (1971) and Wilder's *The Matchmaker* (1976).

Langner, Lawrence (1890–1962) US patent agent and director, born in Wales, who was a cofounder of the Washington Square Players (1914) and of the Theatre Guild. He directed over 200 plays for the Theatre Guild and also founded the American Shakespeare Theatre at Stratford, Connecticut and the New York Repertory Company (1931) as well as writing several plays himself.

Langtry, Lillie (Emilie Charlotte Le Breton; 1853–1929) British actress. The daughter of the Dean of Jersey, she became known as the 'Jersey Lily'. Her fame as a beauty and as mistress of the future King Edward VII ensured a sensational response when she took to the stage. She began with small parts but eventually graduated to play Rosalind, Cleopatra, and other leading roles in England and the US with her own company.

La Noue, Jean Sauve de (1701–c. 1761) French actor and playwright, whose play *Mahomet II* (1739) provided Voltaire with the raw material for his *Mahomet, ou le fanatisme* (1742). Voltaire took steps to ensure La Noue was allowed to give the first performance of his play and subsequently arranged for him to play the title role himself at the Comédie-Française in 1742.

Lansbury, Angela (1925–) US actress, born in Britain. Having made her name in the cinema, she became a major Broadway star following her New York debut (1957) in *Hotel Paradiso*. She has found particular acclaim for her work in musicals, winning Tonys for her performances in *Mame* (1966), *Dear World* (1969), the revived *Gypsy* (1974), and Sondheim's *Sweeney Todd* (1979).

Lantern Theatre A theatre in Dublin, which opened in a cellar in 1957. In 1963 it was reopened in new premises and became well known for productions of poetic drama, Shakespeare, and works by native Irish authors, including Yeats, Padraic Colum, and O'Casey. The theatre closed in 1972 due to insurance problems stemming from the close proximity of the British Embassy.

Laplace, Pierre Antoine de (1707–93) French scholar, who translated numerous English plays into French. His *Théâtre Anglais* (1745–48) introduced many of Shakespeare's plays to French audiences for the first time.

Laporte *See* Venier, Marie.

Lapotaire, Jane (1944–) British actress, who, after working at the Bristol Old Vic, played Jessica in *The Merchant of Venice* (1970) and other parts with the National Theatre company and then joined the Royal Shakespeare Company in 1974. She had outstanding success in 1978 in the title role of Pam Gems's *Piaf* in London and, later, New York; other successes at the National Theatre have included Otway's *Venice Preserv'd* (1983) and *Antigone* (1984). In 1988 she acted in a French version of Jean-Claude Carrière's *L'Aide-Mémoire* in Paris.

Larivey, Pierre de (c. 1540–1619) French playwright, who was noted for his spirited adaptations in French of Italian comedies, collected as *Comédies facétieuses* (1579, 1611). His nine plays, of which *Les Ésprits* was the most widely known, had a strong influence upon Molière; other works include *Le Laquais, La Veuve*, and *Les Jaloux*.

Lark, The (*L'Alouette*) A *pièce costumée* by Jean ANOUILH. First performance: Paris, 1953. It was translated into English by Christopher Fry and adapted for the US stage by Lillian Hellman. This is Anouilh's interpretation of Joan of Arc's trial for heresy. Its first production in London (1955) with Dorothy Tutin was highly successful, as was the US version with Julie Harris.

Laroche, Johann (1745–1806) Austrian actor, who created the character KASPERL in 1764 in Graz. Subsequently he appeared in Vienna under Marinelli, where he became one of the leading comedians of his day.

Laroque (Pierre Regnault Petit-Jean; c. 1595–1676) French actor, who succeeded to the leadership of Montdory's company at the Théâtre du Marais. Despite his abilities as a manager the Marais eventually had to resort to staging elaborate machine plays as a result of the rivalry with the Molière and the Hôtel de Bourgogne. Players with the company during his time included Mlle Champmeslé.

Larra y Sanchez de Castro, Mariano José de (1809–37) Spanish playwright and journalist, noted for his satires on contemporary society. As well as writing theatre criticism and adapting French plays for the Spanish theatre, he wrote the play *Macías* (1834), in which he expressed his Romantic ideals. He committed suicide on being rejected by his mistress.

L'Arronge, Adolf (1838–1908) German playwright and director, who founded the Deutsches Theater in Berlin in 1883. He was responsible for assembling a fine company, later inherited by Otto Brahm, and helped reform contemporary acting styles; his plays include *Mein Leopold* (1873), *Hasemanns Töchter* (1877), and *Doktor Klaus* (1878).

La Rue, Danny (Daniel Patrick Carroll; 1928–) British female impersonator, born in Ireland, who played in the chorus of drag shows, pantomimes, and revues before achieving fame in cabaret and on television. Subsequently, he was immensely successful in spectacular pantomimes and such revues as *Danny La Rue at the Palace* (1970).

lashline *See* throwline.

Lashwood, George (1864–1942) British music hall performer, who made his London debut at the Middlesex Music Hall in 1889. Billed as 'The Beau Brummel of the

Halls' because of his elegant attire, he performed such popular songs as 'The Death and Glory Boys' and 'After the Ball'.

La Taille, Jean de (c. 1540–c. 1608) French poet, playwright, and author of the treatise *De l'art de la tragédie* (1572), in which he formulated some of the basic rules of classical tragedy, notably that of the UNITIES. His plays include the comedy *Les Corriveaux* (1574).

Laterna Magica *See* Svoboda, Josef.

La Thorillière, Françoise Lenoir de (1626–80) French actor, who performed in the provinces before first appearing at the Théâtre du Marais in 1659. Subsequently he transferred to the Palais Royal to act under Molière; after Molière's death he moved to the Hôtel de Bourgogne where he effectively delayed the formation of the Comédie-Française. He was married to Laroque's niece; his son married Biancolelli's daughter, while one daughter became the wife of Michel Baron and another married Florent Dancourt.

La Tuillerie (Jean-François Juvenon; 1650–88) French actor and playwright, grandson of Gros-Guillaume. He was best suited to tragedy and appeared at the Hôtel de Bourgogne from 1672, occasionally also playing in minor comic roles. His plays included several tragedies and farces.

lauda A form of early Italian devotional drama. The *lauda* had its roots in the hymns of praise of the 12th and 13th centuries, which evolved into religious celebrations incorporating songs and dialogue. These in turn developed into the SACRA RAPPRESENTAZIONE of the later Middle Ages. During the Renaissance the *lauda* became a part of the secular theatre, leading ultimately to the development of the oratorio.

Lauder, Sir Harry (Hugh Mackennan; 1870–1950) Scottish music hall singer and comedian. Originally a coal miner, he made his first English appearance, as an Irish comic, in 1896. He had an overnight success at Gatti's in 1900 and subsequently – dressed in a kilt and carrying a crooked walking stick – consolidated his reputation with such songs as 'Roamin' in the Gloamin'' and 'Keep Right on to the End of the Road'.

Laughton, Charles (1899–1962) US actor, born in Britain (he became a US citizen in 1940). Laughton made his professional stage debut in Gogol's *The Government Inspector* (1926) and soon gained recognition as a highly individual character actor on both sides of the Atlantic. In 1933 he appeared under Guthrie at the Old Vic, where he consolidated his reputation in such roles as Lopakhin in Chekhov's *The Cherry Orchard*, Prospero in *The Tempest*, and Angelo in *Measure for Measure*; in 1937 he became the first British actor to star at the Comédie Française, playing Sganarelle in Molière's *Le Médecin malgré lui*. Subsequently he concentrated upon his film career, although he returned to the stage in 1947, collaborating with the author upon Brecht's *Galileo* in New York. He also directed several other productions in New York (including Shaw's *Major Barbara* with himself playing Undershaft) and in Britain appeared as Richard Brough in Jane Arden's *The Party* (1958) and as Bottom and King Lear at Stratford-on-Avon (1959).

In 1961 he directed his wife, **Elsa Lanchester** (1902–87), who had appeared with him in various productions, in her one-woman show *Elsa Lanchester – Herself*.

Lavedan, Henri (1859–1940) French playwright and novelist. His dramatic output consists largely of successful comedies of manners and moralizing comedies concerned with social problems, notably *Le Prince d'Aurec* (1894) and its sequel, *Les Deux Noblesses* (1897).

Lavin, Linda (1937–) US actress, who made her New York debut in 1960. After roles off-Broadway (*The Mad Show*, 1966; *Little Murders*, 1967) and on (*Last of the Red Hot Lovers*, 1969), she starred in a popular television comedy from 1976 to 1985. Since then she has starred on Broadway in *Broadway Bound* (1986), *The Sisters Rosensweig* (1993), THE DIARY OF ANNE FRANK (1997), and *The Tale of the Allergist's Wife* (2000).

Lavinia *See* Ponti, Diana da.

Lawler, Ray (1921–) Australian playwright and actor, who became internationally known with his drama about old age, *Summer of the Seventeenth Doll* (1955), in which he also played the leading role. Subsequent plays, which included *The Unshaven Cheek* (1963), *A Breach in the Wall* (1970), and *Kid Stakes* (1976), failed to arouse equal interest.

Lawrence, D(avid) H(erbert) (1885–1930) British novelist, poet, and playwright, most of whose dramas are set against a mining background in the English Midlands. Of his eight plays, only two were produced in his lifetime. His most successful plays are *The Widowing of Mrs Holroyd* (1926), written in 1914, *A Collier's Friday Night* (1965), which was written in 1906, and *The Daughter-in-Law*, first produced in 1967 at the Royal Court.

Lawrence, Gerald (1873–1957) British actor, who began his career in Benson's Shakespearean company and later worked with Irving, playing Henry II to Irving's Becket on the night of the great actor's death. After working in the US, he directed a Shakespeare season at the Royal Court Theatre, appeared in Tree's company, and in 1912 enjoyed great success in Shaw's *Captain Brassbound's Conversion*. After World War I his appearances included the title role in Booth Tarkington's *Monsieur Beaucaire* (1923) and Juggins in Shaw's *Fanny's First Play* (1931). He was married to Lilian BRAITHWAITE (by whom he was the father of Joyce Carey) and subsequently to the US actress **Fay Davis** (1872–1945), who was much admired in Hope's *The Prisoner of Zenda* in 1895.

Lawrence, Gertrude (Gertrud Klasen; 1898–1952) British actress, who attracted attention in revues and musicals before playing her first dramatic role in 1928. Many memorable performances followed, especially as Amanda in Noël Coward's *Private Lives* (1930), which was written for her. Other Coward successes included *Tonight at 8.30* (1935–36) and *Blithe Spirit* (1945). She was also highly successful as Liza Elliot in Moss Hart's Broadway musical *Lady in the Dark* (1941) and, in her final appearance, as the English governess in *The King and I* (1951). Her autobiography, *A Star Danced*, was published in 1945.

Lawrence, Slingsby *See* Lewes, George Henry.

Lawson, Wilfrid (Wilfrid Worsnop; 1900–66) British actor, who first appeared in London in 1928 in *Sweeney Todd* at the Elephant and Castle Theatre. He was subsequently in a number of revivals of Shaw's plays with both Charles Macdona's and Barry Jackson's companies and, in 1933, made a strong impression in *Gallows Glorious* by Ronald Gow at the Shaftesbury Theatre. In 1937 he gave an outstanding performance in Priestley's *I Have Been Here Before* and was highly praised for his Doolittle in the film *Pygmalion*. Despite his notorious drinking, he later appeared successfully in Bridget Boland's *The Prisoner* (1954) and Ibsen's *Peer Gynt* (1962) among many other plays.

Laxness, Halldór Kiljan (1902–98) Icelandic novelist and playwright, whose satirical play *Silfurtunglið* (The Silver Moon; 1954); criticized US influence upon post-war Icelandic society. The most important of his other works for the stage is *Dufnavei-zlan* (The Pigeon Banquet; 1966); he was awarded a Nobel Prize in 1955.

Laye, Evelyn (1900–96) British actress, who began her stage career in Harold Owen and H M Vernon's *Mr Wu* at Brighton in 1915 and made her first appearance in London at the Gaiety Theatre in *The Beauty Spot* in 1918. She became a leading star in musical comedy, variety, pantomime, and revue between the wars, successes including *The Merry Widow* (1923), *Blue Eyes* (1927), *Bitter Sweet* (1929), and *Lights Up* (1940). She later played in such comedies as Anthony Kimmins's *The Amorous Prawn* (1959) and Marriott and Foot's *No Sex Please – We're British* (1971).

lazzo A verbal aside or comic gesture with which actors of the *commedia dell'arte* might embellish the main dialogue and action. An essential feature of the whole *commedia dell'arte* tradition, *lazzi* were mainly used to enliven the action when it flagged. The success of such interpolations as the eating of an imaginary fly or a comment upon some topical matter was considered an important measure of a performer's ability. *Compare burla.*

Leal, José da Silva Mendes (1818–86) Portuguese playwright and statesman, who was the author of several melodramas and plays tackling social issues. Such works as *Os Dois Renegados* (1839) and *Pobreza Envergonhada* (1858) were much influenced by the plays of Dumas *père* and Dumas *fils*.

Leblanc, Georgette (1867–1941) French actress and singer, who was particularly associated with the plays of Maeterlinck. She created most of Maeterlinck's heroines between 1896 and 1910, among them Aglavaine in *Aglavaine and Selysette*, which was written for her.

Lecouvreur, Adrienne (1692–1730) French actress, who became enormously popular for both her talent and her beauty after her first appearance at the Comédie-Française, in Crébillon's *Électre*, in 1717. Despite the hostility of other leading actresses, she triumphed in plays by Racine and Molière, employing a new naturalistic style. Her brief but eventful life later provided the basis for the play *Adrienne Lecouvreur* (1849) by Scribe and Legouvé, in which both Rachel and Bernhardt had great success.

Lederer Theatre Complex *See* Trinity Square Repertory Company.

Lee, Canada (Leonard Lionel Cornelius Canegata; 1907–52) US Black actor, who worked in several Black companies before coming to prominence as Bigger in Paul

Green's adaptation of Richard Wright's novel *Native Son* (1941). Later roles included Caliban in *The Tempest* (1945) and Bosola, played in whiteface make-up, in Webster's *The Duchess of Malfi* (1946).

Lee, Gypsy Rose (Rose Louise Hovick; 1914–70) US actress, who appeared as a striptease artist in burlesque on Broadway and with Ziegfeld's *Follies* (1936). The musical comedy *Gypsy* (1959) was based on her life.

Lee, Ming Cho (1930–) US scenic designer who has done extensive work for Broadway, the New York Shakespeare Festival, and the Metropolitan Opera. Productions he has designed include *Mother Courage* (1962), *The Shadow Box* (1977), and *K2* (1983).

Lee, Nathaniel (c. 1653–92) English playwright, remembered for his historical tragedies. Chief of these were *The Rival Queens; or, the Death of Alexander the Great* (1677), in the first performances of which Betterton and Mrs Barry appeared, and *The Duke of Guise* (1682), on which he collaborated with Dryden. He died insane in Bedlam.

leg A cloth or a narrow flat, also referred to as a **tail**, which is used as part of a set of borders, usually to mask the wings.

Le Gallienne, Eva (1899–1991) US actress, director, and producer, born in Britain, whose first success, as Julie in Molnár's *Liliom* (1921), led to five years of Broadway roles. In 1926 she founded the **Civic Repertory Company**, which performed major foreign works by such playwrights as Shakespeare, Molière, Goldoni, Rostand, Tolstoy, Giraudoux, and Ibsen. She herself toured in Ibsen's *A Doll's House*, *The Master Builder*, and *Hedda Gabler* from 1934 to 1935. In 1946 she cofounded the **American Repertory Theatre** with Cheryl Crawford and Margaret Webster. During the 1960s she appeared with the National Repertory Theatre in Maxwell Anderson's *Elizabeth the Queen* and Euripides' *Trojan Women*, while in 1968 she appeared in Ionesco's *Exit the King* and directed Chekhov's *The Cherry Orchard*. In 1970 she directed her own translation of this last play at the American Shakespeare Festival. Her final Broadway appearance was in 1975, in *The Royal Family*.

legitimate drama Originally, any dramatic production presented at the the the British PATENT THEATRES rather than at an unlicensed venue. Because this meant in practice plays that did not need to include musical or other interpolations in order to evade the theatre laws, the term eventually came to be used of any straight drama as opposed to a musical comedy, vaudeville show, or similar entertainment.

Legrand, Marc-Antoine (1673–1728) French actor and playwright, who was a member of the Comédie-Française. A popular performer, he specialized in comic roles and wrote a number of successful plays for the company, notably *Le Roie de Cocagne* (1718) and *Cartouche* (1721).

leg show Any theatrical entertainment in which the principal feature is the appearance of scantily-clad chorus girls. Examples include many performances of burlesque and revue.

Lehmann, Beatrix (1903–79) British actress, who first appeared at the Lyric, Hammersmith in 1924, and established her reputation in a series of performances at the

Gate Theatre Club in 1929. Subsequently she was acclaimed in such roles as Winifred in Rowley's *The Witch of Edmonton* (1936) and as Lavinia in O'Neill's *Mourning Becomes Electra* (1937). She appeared at Stratford-on-Avon in 1947, notably as Portia in *The Merchant of Venice* and Isabella in *Measure for Measure*, while later successes included performances in plays by Ustinov, Anouilh, Pinter, and T S Eliot as well as Michael Redgrave's adaptation of *The Aspern Papers* (1959).

Leicester's Men An English theatre company formed from the household of the Earl of Leicester in 1559. One of the earliest acting companies, its members included James Burbage and William Kempe; after the death of the Earl of Leicester in 1588 the company was merged with Strange's Men.

Leigh, Mike (1943–) British playwright and director, who emerged as an unconventional exponent of the technique of COLLECTIVE CREATION while at the Midlands Art Centre in Birmingham. His plays, which are arrived at almost entirely by rehearsal through improvisation, include *Bleak Moments* (1970), *Wholesome Glory* (1973), *Babies Grow Old* (1974), the celebrated black comedy *Abigail's Party* (1977), *Goose-Pimples* (1981), *Greek Tragedy* (1981), and *It's a Great Big Shame* (1993). Since the late 1980s he has worked mainly in the cinema.

Leigh, Vivien (Vivien Mary Hartley; 1913–67) British actress, who made her stage debut in 1935 in *The Masque of Virtue* by Ashley Dukes in London. Subsequently she married Laurence Olivier, having played Ophelia to his Hamlet in 1937, and secured the role of Scarlett O'Hara in the celebrated film *Gone with the Wind*. She went on to appear with Olivier in many classical and other roles, including both Shakespeare's and Shaw's Cleopatra in 1951. An actress of great beauty and strength of character, she excelled under Olivier's direction as Blanche Dubois in Tennessee Williams's *A Streetcar Named Desire* (1949) and was later admired as Viola, Lady Macbeth, and Lavinia in *Titus Andronicus* at Stratford-on-Avon (1955). After an Australian tour in 1962, she made her debut in a musical, *Tovarich*, in New York, after which she suffered increasingly from ill health.

Leighton, Margaret (1922–76) British actress, who began her career at the Birmingham Repertory Theatre. She achieved a high reputation as a stylish actress with the Old Vic company (1944–47), playing such roles as Raina in Shaw's *Arms and the Man* and Regan to Olivier's Lear. Subsequently she was Celia in Eliot's *The Cocktail Party* (1950), Rosalind, Ariel, and Lady Macbeth in the 1952 Stratford-on-Avon season, and partnered Coward in Shaw's *The Apple Cart* (1953). She also appeared in Rattigan's *Separate Tables* for nearly four years in London and New York and was then acclaimed as Beatrice to Gielgud's Benedick on Broadway (1959). She returned to England in 1967 and continued to be successful in plays by Shakespeare, Sheridan, and Ivy Compton-Burnett.

Leisewitz, Johann Anton (1752–1806) German playwright, who is best known for the fratricidal tragedy *Julius von Tarent* (1776), an example of the *Sturm und Drang* movement, which had a profound influence upon Schiller's *Die Räuber* (The Robbers; 1781). His other works include the short plays *Die Pfädung* (The Distraint; 1775) and *Der Besuch um Mitternacht* (The Midnight Visit; 1775).

Leivick, Halper (1888–1962) Jewish poet and playwright, who escaped life imprisonment in the USSR and eventually settled in the US, where he became famous for his play *The Golem* (1925), which was first produced in Moscow by the Habimah company. He published 20 prose dramas in addition to his poetry, which drew heavily upon his Soviet experiences.

Lekain, Henri-Louis (Henri-Louis Cain; 1729–78) French actor, who was praised by Voltaire as the finest player of tragedy in his day. He began as an amateur in 1748 and eventually won the support of Voltaire, who provided him with a theatre and assisted in his training. In 1750 Lekain appeared for the first time at the Comédie-Française, in Voltaire's *Brutus*, and soon established himself as a great favourite despite his short stature and harsh voice. He went on to triumph in several of Voltaire's plays, including *L'Orphelin de la Chine* and *Tancrède*, and made a number of significant reforms, banishing spectators from the stage, encouraging historical accuracy in costumes and scenery, and adopting a more natural style of delivery. He died from a chill caught after appearing as Vendôme in Voltaire's *Adélaide du Guesclin*.

Leko *See* profile spot.

Lelio *See* Andreini, Francesco; Riccoboni, Luigi.

Lemaître, Antoine-Louis-Prosper *See* Frédérick.

Lenaea A religious festival held annually (in January and February) in ancient Greece in honour of DIONYSUS. The emphasis of the various drama contests held during the festival was upon comedy, although tragedy was later added after comedy was also permitted in the City Dionysia in the 5th century BC.

Lenkom Theatre A theatre in Moscow, established as an amateur venue in 1927. The theatre later acquired professional status and became highly respected under such leading directors as Simonov, Bersenev, and Birman; in more recent years it has specialized in plays for younger audiences.

Leno, Dan (George Galvin; 1860–1904) British music hall performer, who made his first London appearance as the contortionist Little George at the age of four. He subsequently developed as a dancer and singer, and, in 1880, won the clog-dancing championship of the world at Leeds. In 1883, London saw him for the first time as Dan Leno and, from 1888 until his death, he appeared annually in the Drury Lane pantomime. He specialized in comic songs and was for a time partnered by Herbert Campbell; his best pantomime roles included Widow Twankey and Mother Goose. He died insane.

Lenoble, Eustache (1643–1711) French lawyer and writer. In 1697 the Comédie-Italienne was expelled from France for performing Lenoble's mediocre play *La Fausse Prude*, which was seen to be an attack on Louis XIV's wife, Mme de MAINTENON.

Lenoir, Charles (fl. 1610–37) French actor-manager, who led a company in the provinces before coming to Paris under the patronage of the Prince of Orange. In 1630 he and Montdory produced Pierre Corneille's first play, *Mélite*, in Paris; four years later they moved into the Théâtre du Marais but were subsequently deprived of many of their actors by Louis XIII, who ordered their transfer to the Hôtel de Bourgogne.

Lenormand, Henri-René (1882–1951) French playwright, whose pessimistic dramas were inspired by Freudian psychology. In *Les Ratés* (The Failures, 1924) the lives of a failed writer and actress end in degradation, murder, and suicide; in *Le Simoun*

(1920) the incestuous passion aroused by a daughter in her father is resolved only by her untimely death.

Lensky, Alexander Pavlovich (1847–1908) Russian actor, who championed performance of the plays of Ibsen in Russia. As director of the Maly Theatre in Moscow he did much to reform current acting practices and fostered interest in the classical repertory as well as in more natural styles of delivery.

lens spot *See* focus lamp.

Lenya, Lotte (1900–81) German actress and singer, who was closely associated with the works of Brecht and her husband Kurt Weill. Among the works in which she created major roles were *Mahagonny* (1927) and *The Threepenny Opera* (1928). She left Germany for the US during the Nazi period, later appearing in various films (including a James Bond movie) and stage shows, among them *Cabaret* (1966). She was famous for her distinctive atonal singing voice.

Lenz, Jakob Michael Reinhold (1751–92) German poet, playwright, and friend of Goethe, who played an important role in the development of the *Sturm und Drang* movement. He formulated the rules of Romantic drama in his treatise *Anmerkungen über Theater* (1774) and *Die Soldaten* (written 1774–75), which influenced Büchner's *Woyzeck*.

Leonard, Hugh (John Keyes Byrne; 1926–) Irish playwright and writer, whose dramas have won wide praise for their technical virtuosity. *The Big Birthday* (1956) attracted attention when seen at the Abbey Theatre and was followed by the equally successful *A Leap in the Dark* (1957); subsequent works included *The Passion of Peter Ginty* (1961), which was derived from Ibsen's *Peer Gynt*, and *Stephen D* (1962), which drew on the writings of James Joyce. The theme of betrayal is frequently involved; other subjects include the British-Irish relationship, as in *The Au Pair Man* (1968), and terminal illness, as in *A Life* (1978). His later plays include *Da* (1973; filmed 1984), *Moving Days* (1981), *Chamber Music* (1994), and *Magic* (1997). He has also written and adapted many works for television.

Leonidov, Leonid Mironovich (1873–1941) Russian actor and director, who became a leading performer of tragic roles at the Moscow Art Theatre. Having begun his career at the Korsch Theatre in Moscow in 1901, he won great acclaim as Dmitri Karamazov in Dostoevsky's *The Brothers Karamazov* as well as in the plays of Ibsen, Chekhov, and Gogol among others.

Leonov, Leonid Maximovich (1899–1994) Russian novelist and playwright, whose work is distinguished by intricate plot structure and detailed characterization. He wrote 12 plays, 11 of which were produced in Moscow theatres between 1936 and 1946. His best-known play is *Nashestviye* (Invasion; 1942), a story of Nazi oppression which has also been adapted for film and opera. His later dramas, which include the acclaimed *Obyknovennyy chelovek* (1940) and *Zolotaya Kareta* (1946), reveal a growing interest in moral issues.

Leopoldstädter Theater A theatre in Vienna, which was opened in 1781 by Karl MARINELLI as a venue for conventional Viennese burlesque and folk theatre. Noted performers who appeared there included Laroche and Anton Hasenhut. It was demolished in 1945.

Léotard, Jules (1830–70) French acrobat, who became an enormously popular performer in music hall. He made his first London appearance at the Alhambra in 1861 and his skill was later commemorated in the song 'The Daring Young Man on the Flying Trapeze'. The conventional practice costume of dancers and acrobats is called a leotard in his honour.

LePage, Robert (1957–) Canadian playwright, actor, and director, whose strongly visual productions frequently use the text as a pretext for his own free-form surrealistic imagery. Some of his important works are *Vinci* (1986), *Aiguilles et Opium* (1994), and *The Seven Streams of the River Ota* (1995). He was director of French language theatre at the National Arts Centre from 1989 to 1993, and in 1994 he founded the Ex Machina Company in Quebec City, which does research in theatre, puppetry, opera, dance, and music.

Lermontov, Mikhail Yurevich (1814–41) Russian poet, novelist, and playwright, who was the foremost Russian writer associated with the Romantic movement. Much influenced by Byron, he spent some time in exile in the Caucasus and, after military service, was eventually killed in a duel. His writing for the theatre comprises three plays, of which the first was *The Spaniards* (written in 1830), which criticized the Tsar and was banned. This was followed by *Menschen und Leidenschafter*, which was influenced by the *Sturm und Drang* movement, and *Masquerade* (written in 1835 and performed in 1852), which reflected his interest in Shakespeare and Byron and is regarded as his finest dramatic work.

Lerner, Alan Jay (1918–86) US lyricist, whose first works to be produced were the book and lyrics for *The Life of the Party* (1942). Subsequently he wrote the book and lyrics for such shows as *Brigadoon* (1947), *Paint Your Wagon* (1951), *My Fair Lady* (1956), *Camelot* (1960), and *Gigi* (1973, filmed in 1959), on all of which he collaborated with the composer **Frederick Loewe** (1904–88).

Lernet-Holenia, Alexander (1897–1976) Austrian poet and playwright, who revived the tradition of the *Haupt- und Staatsaktionen* with his historical plays. He was also the author of several comedies, notably *Österreichische Komödie* (1926) and the sexual fantasy *Ollapotrida* (1926).

Lesage, Alain René (1668–1747) French novelist and playwright, best known for the novel *Gil Blas de Santillane* (1715–35). During the early years of the 18th century he wrote a number of plays for the Comédie-Française; the satirical comedy *Turcaret*, his greatest success, caused considerable offence to its victims in the world of finance. Lesage subsequently became associated with the Parisian fairs, for which he produced around 100 works – vaudevilles, sketches, farces, and comic-opera libretti – often in collaboration with other writers, including Fuzelier and Piron.

Principal dramatic works:
  Crispin rival de son maître: 1707; translated as *Crispin, Rival of His Master*.
  Turcaret ou le Financier: 1709.

Lescarbot, Marc (c. 1570–1642) French playwright, whose masque *Le Théâtre de Neptune en la Nouvelle France* (1606) was the first play to be performed in Canada. A lawyer by training, he directed the masque himself at Port Royal (now Annapolis Royal in Nova Scotia).

Les Misérables A hugely successful musical by Alain BOUBLIL (book and lyrics), Claude-Michel Schönberg (music), and Herbert Kretzmer (additional lyrics). First performance: Paris, 1980. The show later enjoyed long runs in London (1984–) and New York, where it earned two Tony Awards. The plot is based on Victor Hugo's epic story (1862) of the Parisian underworld.

L'Espy (François Bedeau; d. 1663) French actor, brother of Jodelet, who was popularly known as Gorgibus after the character he created in two of Molière's plays. Like his brother he appeared at the Théâtre du Marais and at the Hôtel de Bourgogne before ultimately joining Molière's company in 1659. Subsequently he oversaw the rebuilding of the Palais-Royal in 1660.

Lesser, Anton (1952–) British actor, who since 1977 has done much notable work with the Royal Shakespeare Company. His Shakespearean performances have included Romeo (1980), Hamlet (1982), and Troilus (1985); other successes have been Edward Bond's *The Fool* (1981) and Richard Nelson's *Principia Scriptoriae* (1986).

Lessing, Gotthold Ephraim (1729–81) German playwright and theatre critic, whose writing had a lasting influence upon the German theatrical tradition. An admirer of Shakespeare, he argued for a less constrained approach to both acting and writing in such critical essays as the *Hamburgische Dramaturgie* (1767–68). As a playwright he expressed his preference for a theatre released from French conventions in such passionate and realistic dramas as the tragedy *Miss Sara Simpson*, his first major success. *Emilia Galotti* consolidated his reputation as an innovator in tragedy, while in MINNA VON BARNHELM he applied his ideas to comedy; his last play, *Nathan der Weise*, was a poetic drama.

Principal works:
  Miss Sara Simpson: 1755.
  Minna von Barnhelm: 1767.
  Emilia Galotti: 1772.
  Nathan der Weise: 1783; translated as NATHAN THE WISE.

Lesson, The (*La Leçon*) A one-act play for three characters by Eugène IONESCO. First performance: Paris, 1951. The theme is the relationship between language and reality. During the course of a lecture on linguistics, the professor becomes increasingly manic: he finally kills his student by his powerful definition of the word 'knife'.

Letourneur, Pierre (1736–88) French scholar, who is remembered for his prose versions of Shakespeare's plays. Published in 20 volumes (1776–83), Letourneur's collection was more comprehensive and his translation more accurate than previous French versions.

Levey, Barnett (1798–1837) Australian theatre manager, born in London, who went to Sydney in 1825 and in 1832 staged the first professional theatre production in Australia, when he presented *Black-Ey'd Susan* at the Royal Hotel. Subsequently he staged comedies, melodramas, and even some Shakespeare.

Levin, Hanoch (1943–) Israeli playwright and director, who has established a controversial reputation with such moving but humorous plays as *The Adventures of Solomon Grip* (1969). Other works, which lampoon such targets as bourgeois society and sexual stereotyping, include *Hefetz* (1972) and *Jacoby and Leidentahl – Temporary Title* (1973).

Levy, Benn W *See* Cummings, Constance.

Lewes, George Henry (1817–78) British writer and critic, lover of the novelist George Eliot. He was the grandson of an actor and was himself an actor for a short time; first, professionally, in Manchester, then in Charles Dickens's amateur theatricals. He wrote or adapted many plays under the names **Slingsby Lawrence** and **Frank Churchill**. He also wrote theatre criticism for the *Leader* and contributed long articles on the stage to the *Pall Mall Gazette*, which were subsequently published as *On Actors and the Art of Acting* (1875).

Lew Fields Theatre *See* Wallack's Theatre.

Lewis, Leopold David (1828–90) British playwright, whose adaptation of Erckmann-Chatrian's *Le Juif Polonais* as THE BELLS provided Irving with his most celebrated role (1871). His other plays include *The Wandering Jew* (1873) and *The Foundlings* (1881).

Lewis, Mabel Gwynedd Terry- *See* Terry-Lewis, Mabel Gwynedd.

Lewis, Matthew Gregory (1775–1818) British playwright, author of the popular gothic novel *Ambrosio; or, The Monk* (1795). He wrote numerous melodramas, including *The Castle Spectre* (1797), staged at Drury Lane, *The East Indian* (1799), and *Timour the Tartar* (1811), which was performed at Covent Garden. He died of yellow fever while returning from a visit to Jamaica.

Leybourne, George (Joe Saunders; 1842–84) British music hall performer, who became famous as a singer and *lion comique*. The success of his rendering of 'Champagne Charlie', which he sang in London for the first time at the Canterbury Music Hall, set the seal on his career. In the 1880s his popularity declined and he managed and chaired a number of minor halls, occasionally working a double act with his daughter, Florrie.

Liberty Theatre A theatre on West 42nd Street, between 7th and 8th Avenues, New York, which opened in 1904 with *The Rogers Brothers in Paris*, starring the musical comedy team for whom the theatre was built. Subsequent successes included the Black musical *Blackbirds of 1928*. In 1933 the theatre became a cinema.

Library Theatre A theatre in Manchester, which opened in the basement of the public library in 1946. A resident company was founded in 1952 and a companion theatre, the **Forum Theatre**, was added a few miles away at Wythenshawe in 1971. In more recent years the Library Theatre has been used for the presentation of contemporary drama, while the Forum is used for musicals and more commercial theatre.

licence An authorization allowing a theatre to present public performances or permitting the production of a particular work or type of entertainment. Conditions that have to be met before a venue in Britain can be licensed were stipulated in the 1843 Theatres Act, which also modified the absolute licensing powers of the LORD CHAMBERLAIN (acquired under the **Licensing Act** of 1737), and later repeated in that of 1968, which ended the Lord Chamberlain's monopoly and confirmed local authorities as the chief licensing bodies.

Licensing Acts *See* licence.

lighting The illumination of the stage by artificial light. This first became an important feature of theatrical production when indoor performances began during the Renaissance. Early methods of lighting included the use of candles, cressets, and *bozzi*. Subsequent innovations included the use of reflectors to increase the intensity of light beams, the introduction of footlights (from the 17th century), and – after much resistance from those who came to the theatre to be seen as much as they did to see – the dimming of the lights in the auditorium (customary since 1876). The development of gas lighting in the early 19th century represented a major advance despite the risks involved (*see* fires). The Chestnut Street Theatre in Philadelphia was the first to have gas installed (1816); the first British stage to be thus lit was that at the Lyceum Theatre (1817). At much the same time the first LIMELIGHTs were developed, anticipating the introduction of the modern spotlight. In 1881 the Savoy Theatre became the first public building in London to be lit throughout by electricity, the use of which had already been pioneered at the California Theatre in San Francisco in 1879. The introduction of electricity revolutionized stage lighting throughout the world by providing illumination of great power and flexibility (especially when used with irises, gobos, colour wheels, and other mechanical devices). Those who championed its use included Sir Henry Irving, André Antoine, David Belasco, and Adolphe Appia. Lighting is controlled in the modern theatre by highly sophisticated computerized dimmer boards, which can coordinate the illumination of an entire set; other recent innovations have included experiments with ultraviolet light, lasers, and holography.

Lillie, Beatrice (Constance Sylivia Munston, Lady Peel; 1898–1989) British actress and singer, born in Canada, who became one of the foremost stars of British revue and cabaret. Having started in 1914 in London as a ballad singer, she established her reputation for sophisticated comedy in André Charlot's revues during World War I, making her first US appearance in 1924. She sported a distinctive short hairstyle and specialized in Surrealistic sketches and humorous songs; among her successes were her solo show *An Evening with Beatrice Lillie* (1954) and the role of Madame Arcati in a musical version of Coward's *Blithe Spirit* (1964).

Lillo, George (1693–1739) British playwright, whose first successful play, *The London Merchant; or, the History of George Barnwell*, which was based on an old ballad, was produced at Drury Lane in 1731 and repeatedly revived over the next 100 years in several countries. His later plays include *Guilt Its Own Punishment; or, Fatal Curiosity*, which was produced at the Haymarket in 1736, and a version of ARDEN OF FAVERSHAM, which was published posthumously. His plays had an early influence on the development of domestic drama.

limelight A form of lighting, first developed in 1816, by means of which a brilliant beam could be thrown onto the stage. The beam, which could be adjusted manually in order to follow an actor or other moving object on the stage, was produced by heating a piece of lime until it became incandescent.

Lincoln Center for the Performing Arts An arts complex on the West Side of Manhattan, New York, the largest such in the world. First conceived in 1955 as a means of stabilizing a deteriorating neighbourhood, it opened in stages from 1962 to 1969. Of its various theatres, **Avery Fisher Hall** and **Alice Tully Hall** are for concerts and the 4000-seat **Metropolitan Opera House** has only rarely been used for drama, but the 2737-seat **New York State Theatre**, home to the New York City Opera and the New York City Ballet, has frequently produced operetta and musical revivals. The 1067-seat thrust-stage **Vivian Beaumont** and the 299-seat **Mitzi Newhouse** underneath it were designed for drama and opened in 1965 with the assumption that they would be used by a permanent revolving repertory company. Despite major names being involved, including Joseph PAPP, this company never found success and the theatres closed in 1977 for three years. After some years of relative neglect, the current company has enjoyed a revival with a scheme under which seats for individual productions are sold first to a base of subscribers. This has proved a success, with several plays having long runs at the Lincoln Center or transferring to Broadway. The company occasionally produces directly on Broadway when both its houses are occupied. The Lincoln Center also contains a performing arts branch of the New York Public Library, with both circulating and specialized collections.

Lincoln's Inn Fields Theatre A theatre in Portugal Street, London, which opened as a tennis-court in 1656 (as **Lisle's Tennis-Court**). In 1661 Sir William Davenant reopened it as a home for the Duke's Company, installing the first proscenium arch to be seen in a theatre in London. It was also equipped with movable scenery and saw many appearances by Thomas Betterton in *Hamlet* and other classic plays by Calderón, Dryden, and others. When the Dorset Garden Theatre opened in 1671 the company left Lincoln's Inn Fields and Killigrew took it over for a time. Reverting to a tennis-court in 1675, it was refitted by Congreve, Betterton, Mrs Bracegirdle, and Mrs Barry in 1695, and reopened with *Love for Love*. The new company moved out in 1705 after many successes and in 1714 Christopher Rich and subsequently his son John Rich restored it, presenting the first English pantomime there in 1716. Seating over 1400 people, it saw major productions of Farquhar and the first performance of Gay's *The Beggar's Opera* (1728). In 1732 Rich transferred to his new theatre in Covent Garden and Lincoln's Inn was used for various musical entertainments, as well as for a few plays produced under Giffard. After closing in 1744, the building became a barracks, an auction room, and a china warehouse, being finally demolished in 1848.

Lincoln's Men An English theatre company, formed from the household of the first Earl of Lincoln, which performed at Court during the 1570s. Disbanded in the late 1570s, a later company of the same name flourished from 1599 to 1610.

Lindberg, August (1846–1916) Swedish actor, who was closely associated with early performances of the plays of Ibsen. He created Oswald in *Ghosts* in 1883 and toured Scandinavia in many other leading roles in both Ibsen and Shakespeare, eventually joining the company at the Kungliga Dramatiska Teatern in Stockholm.

Linden Tree, The A play by J B PRIESTLEY. First performance: London, 1947. The play revolves around a family reunion at which the differences in values between the two generations become painfully clear; Lewis Casson and Sybil Thorndike appeared in the original production.

Lindsay, Howard (1889–1968) US actor, director, and playwright, whose greatest success came in 1939 with his adaptation – in collaboration with **Russel Crouse** (1893–1966) – of Clarence Day's *Life With Father*, in which Lindsay played Father. Subsequently he and Crouse shared a Pulitzer Prize for *State of the Union* (1945); other works together included *Life With Mother* (1948).

Lindsay, Robert (1949–) British actor, who worked in repertory at Manchester before taking over in the rock musical *Godspell*. As well as comic roles both on stage and on television, he has played the title role in the Manchester Royal Exchange Theatre's *Hamlet* (1984), Henry II in Anouilh's *Becket* (1991), and the title roles in *Cyrano de Bergerac* (1992) and *Richard III* (1998). His musical roles have included Bill Snibson in *Me and My Girl* (1985) and Fagin in *Oliver!* (1998).

Lindstrom, Erik (1906–74) Swedish actor, who became a leading interpreter of tragic roles at the Swedish National Theatre, where he was trained. He began his career in comedies by Sheridan, Shaw, and others but later won acclaim in such parts as Peer Gynt, Faust, Hamlet, Macbeth, and Strindberg's Gustav III.

Linsenscheinwerfer *See* focus lamp.

lion comique A popular figure of the music hall tradition in Britain, who first appeared around 1865. The *lions comiques* assumed the character of aristocratic, handsome, young men who sang such comic songs in praise of wine as 'Champagne Charlie'; leading interpreters of the role included George Leybourne and Alfred Vance.

Lipman, Maureen (1946–) British actress, who spent two years in repertory at Manchester before joining the National Theatre at the Old Vic, where her roles included Molly Molloy in Ben Hecht and Charles MacArthur's *The Front Page*. She established a reputation as a unique comedy actress in such plays as Richard Harris's *Outside Edge* (1979) and Philip King's *See How They Run* (1984). In 1987 she starred in Bernstein's *Wonderful Town*, while in 1988 she opened in a one-woman show about Joyce Grenfell, *Re: Joyce*. During the 1980s she became a household name with her appearances on television. More recent work for the stage includes *Lost in Yonkers* (1992), *The Rivals* (1996), and Alan Plater's *Peggy For You* (2000), in which she played the famous theatrical agent Peggy Ramsay.

Lisle's Tennis-Court *See* Lincoln's Inn Fields Theatre. who was born in Soho, London. Initially a strolling player, he attempted tragic roles without success until he was persuaded by Stephen Kemble to play old men and comic rustics, as which he received immediate acclaim. In 1805 George Colman the Younger presented him at the Haymarket, establishing him as a leading comedian and – while at the Olympic Theatre with Madame Vestris – the first to be paid more than a tragedian.

Lithgow, John (1945–) US actor. After work in repertory he made his New York debut in 1973 with the Long Wharf Theatre's production of David Storey's *The Changing Room*. Later that year he was seen in *My Fat Friend*. Subsequent work has included *Comedians* (1976), *Anna Christie* (1977), and *Beyond Therapy* (1982); he found particular acclaim for appearances in *M Butterfly* (1988) and a Los Angeles revival of *Who's Afraid of Virginia Woolf?* (1989).

Little Drury Lane Theatre *See* Olympic Theatre.

Little Foxes, The A play by Lillian HELLMAN. First performance: New York, 1939. This acclaimed study of a family of ruthless industrialists during the US Civil War provided a Broadway triumph for Tallulah Bankhead as Regina. Elizabeth Taylor shone in the 1980s New York revival, while the film version of 1941 starred Bette Davis.

Little Shop of Horrors A musical by Alan Menken, with book and lyrics by Howard Ashman. First performance: New York, 1982. This spoof of 1950s science-fiction movies deals with a timid man who works in a flower shop and hopes to use a strange new plant he finds to get a woman's attention. This singing and talking plant turns out to live on human blood. After a long off-Broadway run, it became one of the most produced plays in schools and theatre groups across the US.

Little Theatre A theatre in the Adelphi, London, which was opened in 1910 by the actress Gertrude KINGSTON. Seating 250, it was converted from part of a bank and, in 1911, saw the stage debut of Noël Coward in *The Goldfish*. Subsequent successes included Shaw's *Fanny's First Play* (1911) and G K Chesterton's *Magic* (1913) before it was closed due to damage from bombs in 1917. Reopened in 1920, it became a venue for revues featuring such leading performers as Cicely Courtneidge and Jack Hulbert, while plays presented there during the 1930s included *Whiteoaks* (1936) by Mazo de la Roche. It was bombed in 1941 and demolished in 1949.

The **Little Theatre** on West 44th Street, between Broadway and 8th Avenue, in New York was opened by Winthrop Ames in 1912. The theatre was subsequently enlarged and redecorated when the Shuberts took it over but later became a broadcasting studio and lecture hall. It reopened as a theatre in 1963 with a production of *Tambourines to Glory* by Langston Hughes. In 1964 the theatre's name was changed to the **Winthrop Ames Theatre** after its founder; it was then used once more for television before reopening as a theatre in 1974 with a production of Ray Aranha's *My Sister, My Sister*. Albert Innaurato's *Gemini* began a long run in 1977.

The **Little Theatre** repertory company in Bristol was founded in 1923 by the actor Rupert Harvey (1887–1954) and rapidly built a strong reputation with productions of plays by Barrie, Shaw, and local authors. Financial pressures forced the company to disband in 1934, after which their base in the Lesser Colston Hall was acquired by the **Rapier Players** (1935–61) and then handed over to the Bristol Old Vic. A new company was installed there in 1980.

Little Theatre Guild of Great Britain A British theatre organization, which was founded in 1946 to coordinate the activities of LITTLE THEATRES throughout the country. It produces publications related to the amateur theatre as well as arranging conferences and other contacts.

Little Theatre in the Hay *See* Haymarket (Theatre Royal).

Little Theatre of the Deaf (LTD) *See* National Theatre of the Deaf.

Little Theatres Small independent theatres run on an unpaid basis. Such enterprises, which often attain the highest artistic standards, include the famous MAD-

DERMARKET THEATRE in Norwich; the oldest British example is reputedly the Stockport Garrick Society, founded in 1901. The phenomenon played a major role in the development of US drama between about 1912 and 1920, when the Little Theatre Movement resulted in the opening of numerous small experimental companies; the most important included the NEIGHBORHOOD PLAYHOUSE and the WASHINGTON SQUARE PLAYERS in New York and the PROVINCETOWN PLAYERS. Notable Canadian Little Theatres from this period included the HART HOUSE THEATRE in Toronto and the French Compagnons de Saint-Laurent.

Little Tich (Harry Relph; 1868–1928) British music hall comedian, who became famous not only for his small stature (he was only four feet in height) but also for his singing and eccentric dancing in oversized boots. He appeared in the annual Drury Lane pantomime from 1891 to 1894, in the farce *Lord Tom Noddy* at the Garrick Theatre (1896), and in numerous burlesques in England and the US.

Littlewood, Joan (1914–) British director, who won renown for her direction of the THEATRE WORKSHOP company in Stratford, East London, in the 1950s and early 1960s. In 1934 she began her close collaboration with the folksinger Ewan McColl, who became her first husband, when they set up the experimental Theatre of Action in Manchester; this was later reconstituted as the **Theatre Union** and again (after World War II) as the Theatre Workshop. The company moved into the Theatre Royal, Stratford, in 1953, where Littlewood presented a programme of popular theatre for working-class audiences ranging from *Volpone*, *Mother Courage*, and *The Quare Fellow*, to *A Taste of Honey*, *Fings Ain't Wot They Used T'Be*, and OH, WHAT A LOVELY WAR! She emphasized the importance of training and rehearsal as well as improvisation around the text and ensemble acting, and was one of the first British directors to understand Brecht's ideas. Projects since 1964 have included the establishment of a theatre school in Tunisia and much work in France (from 1975).

liturgical drama (*or* ecclesiastical drama) The earliest form of medieval religious drama, consisting of plays performed in church as part of the liturgy. It developed during the 10th century from such TROPES as the famous QUEM QUAERITIS?, performed at Easter as part of the Mass. Later such episodes were expanded to tell various stories from the scriptures and were increasingly performed outside the church building. Those illustrating the Christmas story became known as **Nativity plays**, while those given at Easter were referred to as PASSION PLAYS; other performances linked to specific religious festivals included the **Epiphany play**. Ultimately, the plays became separated from the Church liturgy and were written in the vernacular; they also came to include a strong comic element, gradually evolving into the more sophisticated MYSTERY PLAY. *See also auto sacramental*; miracle play; *sacra rappresentazione*; saint play.

liturgy An obligation placed upon prominent citizens of ancient Greece, requiring selected noblemen to undertake, among other tasks, the duties of a CHOREGUS.

Livanov, Boris Nikolayevich (1904–72) Russian actor and director, who spent most of his career at the Moscow Art Theatre, which he joined in 1924. As an actor, his appearances ranged from Beaumarchais to Chekhov and Gogol, whose *Dead Souls* (adapted by Bulgakov) provided him with enormous success in the role of Nozdryov.

As a director he was particularly praised for his revival of Dostoevsky's *The Brothers Karamazov* in 1960 and for Chekhov's *The Seagull* in 1970.

Livent *See* Drabinsky, Garth.

Liverpool Playhouse The oldest surviving repertory theatre in Britain, which opened in 1911 and known as the Liverpool Repertory Theatre until 1916. Inspired by Miss Horniman's company in Manchester, the theatre was reconstructed from the old Star Theatre, where melodrama had been staged since 1866. The theatre presents a wide variety of entertainment and, in more recent years, has become famous for its productions of plays by contemporary writers, including Bennett, Pinter, and Stoppard. Actors to train with the repertory company there have included Michael Redgrave, Rex Harrison, and Ian McKellen. The main auditorium seats 762 while a smaller studio theatre – the Playhouse Upstairs – seats 120.

Living Newspaper A form of documentary theatre that developed in several countries in the early 20th century and became a major feature of the US FEDERAL THEATRE PROJECT during the 1930s. Directed initially by Elmer Rice and later by Joseph Losey and others, these productions – three of which were written by Arthur Arent – dealt with matters of immediate public concern (the invasion of Ethiopia, the plight of the farmers, the trade union movement, poverty, and the threat of syphilis) and relied upon a strong mixture of carefully documented historical fact, domestic realism, political satire, and a campaigning editorial voice.

Livings, Henry (1929–) British actor and playwright, who established his reputation while with the Theatre Workshop. His plays, chiefly comedies and farces, include *Big Soft Nellie* (1961), *Nil Carborundum* (1962), which has an RAF setting, *Eh? (1964)*, *Jonah* (1974), and *Flying Eggs and Things* (1986).

Living Stage *See* Arena Stage.

Living Theatre An off-Broadway theatre group in New York, which was founded in 1951 by Julian Beck and **Judith Malina**. Among the group's many influential avant-garde and experimental productions were Jack Gelber's *The Connection* (1959), which relied to an extent on improvisation, Jackson MacLow's *The Marrying Maiden* (1960), the outcome of which was decided by cards and dice, and a version of *Antigone* (1967) set during the Vietnam War. From 1964 to 1968 the Living Theatre toured Europe, finally disbanding in 1970.

Lloyd, Marie (Matilda Alice Victoria Wood; 1870–1922) British music hall singer, who began her career on the halls in 1885. By 1891 she was starring with Dan Leno and Little Tich in her first Drury Lane pantomime and had built up a huge popular following for her warmheartedness and her suggestive rendering of such songs as 'The Boy I Love is Up in the Gallery' and 'A Little of What You Fancy Does You Good'. She died three days after collapsing on stage at the Edmonton Empire.

Lloyd Webber, Andrew, Baron (1948–) British composer, who established his reputation in the theatre by collaborating with Tim Rice on the popular musicals *Joseph and the Amazing Technicolour Dreamcoat* (1968), JESUS CHRIST SUPERSTAR (1970), and EVITA (1976). CATS (1981), based on T S Eliot's poems, *Starlight Express* (1984), in which the cast wear roller-skates, and THE PHANTOM OF THE OPERA (1987) have all enjoyed long runs in both London and New York, making Lloyd Webber an immensely rich man: in 1997 it was estimated that his productions accounted for nearly 25% of all West End box-office takings. His more recent shows include *Sunset Boulevard* (1993), *Whistle Down the Wind* (1997), and *The Beautiful Game* (2000; book and lyrics by Ben ELTON). Lloyd Webber's production company, the **Really Useful Theatre Company**, now owns 13 of the leading London theatres.

loa A form of prologue common to Spanish drama up to the 17th century. Such introductory passages varied from brief speeches to complete short plays related to the main drama; by the 17th century they were used only before performances of *autos sacramentales* or new plays.

Lobanov, Andrei Mikhailovich (1900–59) Russian director, who established his reputation working under Reuben Simonov in the 1930s. His greatest successes included plays by Chekhov and Ostrovsky as well as productions of contemporary works; from 1945 to 1956 he worked at the Yermolova Theatre.

Lobsterscope A slotted metal disc, which produces a flickering lighting effect suggesting slow motion when rotated in front of a spotlight.

Locatelli, Basileo (d. 1650) Italian collector of *commedia dell'arte* plays. His collection, preserved in the Biblioteca Casanatense in Rome, comprises more than 100 such scenarios in two separate volumes.

Locatelli, Domenico (1613–71) Italian actor of the *commedia dell'arte*, who – under the stage name **Trivellino** – became famous in the role of Arlecchino. He spent much of his acting career in Paris.

Lodovico, Cesare Vico (1885–1968) Italian playwright, who became well-known for his works for the theatre in the *crepusolari* tradition. Such plays as *L'idiota* (1915), derived from Dostoevsky, *La donna di nessuno* (Nobody's Woman; 1919), and *L'incrinatura, o Isa, dove vai?* (The Flaw, or Isa, Where are You Going?; 1937) reflect the influence of Chekhov and explore the theme of failure of communication; he was also a noted translator of Shakespeare.

Loeb Drama Center A theatre built in 1960 for Harvard University. With one 556-seat auditorium and a 383-seat experimental space, it is used by the AMERICAN REPERTORY THEATRE and the HARVARD DRAMATIC CLUB.

Loewe, Frederick *See* Lerner, Alan Jay.

Logan, Joshua (1908–88) US author, director, and producer, who studied under Stanislavsky. Among the works he directed are *Knickerbocker Holiday* (1938), *This is the Army* (1942), *Picnic* (1953), and *The World of Suzie Wong* (1958). Works he both wrote and directed include *South Pacific* (1949), *Mister Roberts* (1948), and *Wish You Were Here* (1951).

Logan, Maria (1770–1844) British actress. She was a godchild of John PALMER and made her debut at the Haymarket in 1783. In 1787 she appeared at the Goodman's Fields Theatre, as Mrs Gibbs, under which name she continued to act after her second marriage, to George COLMAN the Younger. She also played as Drury Lane and Covent Garden, returning to the Haymarket when her husband succeeded his father as manager.

Lohenstein, Daniel Caspar von (1635–83) German playwright, who was the author of a number of violent melodramas, which were highly popular as closet drama. His plays include *Ibrahim Bassa* (1650), *Cleopatra* (1661), *Epicharis* (1665), and *Ibrahim Sultan* (1673).

Löhr, Marie (1890–1975) British actress and manager, born in Australia, who began her career in the theatre in the company of her godparents, the Kendals. Subsequently she appeared with Tree at His Majesty's, notably as Lady Teazle, and with her husband, Anthony Prinsep, went into management at the Globe Theatre (1918). They were not very successful, although Lonsdale's *Aren't We All?* (1923), in which she played Margot Tatham, was an exception. Other popular roles included Mrs Darling in Barrie's *Peter Pan* (1927), Muriel Weston in Dodie Smith's *Call It a Day* (1935), and Mary Jarrow in Esther McCracken's *Quiet Wedding* (1938).

London Academy of Music and Dramatic Art (LAMDA) A drama school in London, which was founded in 1861 by T H Yorke-Trotter. Now situated in Cromwell Road, it has its own theatre, where Peter Brook and Charles Marowitz staged their famous Theatre of Cruelty season in 1964.

London Assurance A comedy by Dion BOUCICAULT. First performance: 1841. Written under the pseudonym Lee Morton, it established Boucicault's reputation and was regularly revived throughout the late 19th century. Its first production – which starred Madame Vestris and Charles James Mathews – featured the first use of a box set. The plot hinges on a courtship between an impoverished young man and a beautiful but worldly young woman.

London Casino *See* Prince Edward Theatre.

London Coliseum A theatre in St Martin's Lane, London, which was opened by Sir Oswald Stoll as a music hall in 1904, being called simply the **Coliseum** from 1931 before reverting to its original name in recent times. Equipped with the first revolving stage in London and with an auditorium larger than either Drury Lane or Covent Garden, it failed to prosper at first. Forced to close temporarily in 1906, its fortunes revived with productions featuring such leading actresses as Ellen Terry and Sarah Bernhardt. Diaghilev's Ballets Russes appeared there for three seasons before the theatre switched to musical comedy in 1932; successful shows after World War II included *Guys and Dolls* (1953) and *The Pajama Game* (1955). The theatre then became a cinema (1961–68) before being reopened as the home of the Sadler's Wells Opera Company (now the English National Opera); it seats 2358. It was also the scene of the first stage demonstration of television (1930).

London Hippodrome *See* Hippodrome.

London Palladium A variety theatre in Argyll Street in London's West End, often the chosen venue for the Royal Variety Show. It was designed by Frank Matcham and opened in 1910 as the Palladium, with a luxurious palm court at the back of the stalls and the largest seating capacity (2306) of any London theatre. Spectacular revues were staged throughout the 1920s and Barrie's *Peter Pan* was performed annually from 1930 to 1938. The name London Palladium was used from 1934, soon after the theatre had become the home of the Crazy Gang shows, which ended in 1938 with *These Foolish Things*. Today variety, spectacular revue, and an annual pantomime maintain the

Palladium tradition and feature artistes of international renown. The longest-running show in the theatre's history to date has been *Barnum* (1981), starring Michael Crawford. A revival of *Oliver!* ran from 1994 to 1998.

London Pavilion A music hall in the Haymarket, London, which originally opened as a SONG-AND-SUPPER ROOM before being adapted as a music hall in 1861. Seating 2000 people, it saw appearances by many leading performers before demolition in 1885. It was rebuilt in the same year and continued with a typical music hall programme until 1918, when C B COCHRAN converted it for the presentation of such revues as *Blackbirds* (1926), *On With the Dance* (1925), and *One Dam Thing After Another* (1927). Variety was staged there from 1931 until 1934 when the building became a cinema, closing in 1981.

London Theatre Studio *See* Saint-Denis, Michel Jacques.

Longacre Theatre A 1090-seat theatre on West 48th Street, between Broadway and 8th Avenue, New York, which opened in 1913. It was intended for musical comedies but, straight plays were being produced there by 1925. From 1944 the theatre was used for broadcasting but it was reopened with *Ladies of the Corridor* (1953). Subsequent productions included Ionesco's *Rhinoceros* (1961), Anderson's *I Never Sang for My Father* (1968), the revue *Ain't Misbehavin'* (1978), Medoff's *Children of a Lesser God* (1980), and Horton Foote's *The Young Man from Atlanta* (1997).

Long Day's Journey Into Night A drama by Eugene O'NEILL, written in 1941. First performance: Stockholm, 1956. The play, frequently considered O'Neill's greatest, is set in 1912 and concerns James Tyrone, an actor; his sons Jamie, an alcoholic, and Edmund, who represents O'Neill; and their mother, Mary, who has become addicted to drugs owing to James's unwillingness to pay for proper care during an earlier illness.

Longepierre, Hilaire-Bernard de Roqueleyne (1659–1721) French playwright and classical scholar, born in Dijon. In his *Parallèle de Corneille et de Racine* (1686) Longepierre praised Racine, on whose great tragedies he modelled his own moderately successful plays, notably *Médée* (1694).

Longford, Sixth Earl of (Edward Arthur Henry Pakenham; 1902–61) Irish playwright and director, who became closely associated with the GATE THEATRE in Dublin in 1931. In 1936 he formed an independent company, Longford Productions, which specialized in staging classic plays at the Gate Theatre. His own plays included translations with his wife from Irish, Greek, Spanish, and French literature.

Long Wharf Theatre A theatre in New Haven, Connecticut, which opened in 1965; the main theatre has 484 seats and there is also an experimental stage with seating for 199. It houses one of the most influential companies in the US, which has successfully transferred to Broadway several times with productions that include David Storey's *The Contractor* (1970) and *The Changing Room* (1973) and Michael Cristofer's *The Shadow Box* (1977).

Lonsdale, Frederick (1881–1954) British playwright and librettist, who was the author of numerous examples of the comedy of manners, similar to those of Somerset Maugham. Among his most successful plays were *Aren't We All?* (1923), *The Last of Mrs Cheyney* (1925), and *On Approval* (1926), all of which are notable for their elegance and wit. His libretti for musical comedies include *The Maid of the Mountains* (1917), *Madame Beaucaire* (1919), and *Madame Pompadour* (1923).

Look After Lulu An adaptation by Noël COWARD of Georges FEYDEAU's farce *Occupe-toi d'Amélie*. First performance: London, 1959, with Anthony Quayle and Vivien Leigh in the leading roles. The original French version opened in Paris in 1908.

Look Back in Anger John OSBORNE's first and immensely successful play, written for George Devine's English Stage Company. First performance: Royal Court Theatre, 1956. Directed by Tony Richardson with Kenneth Haigh as Jimmy Porter, the articulate working-class antihero, who lives with Alison (Mary Ure) his middle-class girlfriend, the play voiced post-war feelings of frustration, class-consciousness, and disillusionment among the young. It inspired several other new writers (including Arnold Wesker) to write for the stage and is usually held to mark a watershed in post-war British theatre.

Loot A farce by Joe ORTON. First performance: Cambridge Arts Theatre, 1965. Much revised for its first London production in 1966, the play caused a considerable stir with its theme of police corruption and its use of a corpse as a comic device in the tradition of knockabout comedy.

Lope de Rueda *See* Rueda, Lope de.

Lope de Vega *See* Vega Carpio, Lope Félix de.

López de Ayala, Adelardo (1829–79) Spanish playwright and statesman, who began as a writer of Romantic drama but later contributed to the development of the Realist tradition in Spain. His early works include the historical plays *Un hombre de estado* (1851) and *Rioja* (1851); plays critical of contemporary society include *El tanto por ciento* (1861).

Loraine, Robert (1876–1935) British actor-manager, who became a prominent member of Ben Greet's company before achieving popularity in such dashing roles as D'Artagnan in *The Three Musketeers* (1899). Later he won acclaim in New York as John Tanner in Shaw's *Man and Superman* (1905) and flew for the RFC during World War I, returning triumphantly to the stage as Rostand's Cyrano de Bergerac in 1919. Other successful performances included Mirabell to Edith Evans's Millamant in Congreve's *The Way of the World* (1924) and the title role in Strindberg's *The Father* (1927).

Lorca, Federico García *See* García Lorca, Federico.

Lord Chamberlain A British public official, who formerly exercised complete control over the licensing and censorship of dramatic works. The influence of the Lord Chamberlain's office, dating from Tudor times, was laid down by statute in 1737; prior to that date the MASTER OF THE REVELS – a less important official – took charge of all such matters. A wave of public reaction against the liberality of the Restoration theatre had led to a demand for moral supervision of the stage and, under the 1737 act, the Lord Chamberlain was granted powers to intervene directly – without giving reasons – to curb any excess he judged to contravene prevailing moral standards; it also made him the sole licensing authority. An Examiner of Plays worked under him, inspecting copies of new dramatic works; by 1968 three English readers and one Welsh one undertook these duties in the Lord Chamberlain's office, checking for examples of indecency, profanity, impropriety, sedition, and libel. Notable Examiners over the years included George Colman the Younger and Charles Kemble.

Resistance to the Lord Chamberlain's unfettered power eventually led to its limitation in 1843. It was finally abolished in the **Theatres Act** of 1968 in the wake of the *Lady Chatterley* trial of 1960.

Lord of Misrule *See* Misrule, Lord of.

Lorne, Marion (1888–1968) US actress, who became highly popular in London in a long-running series of comedies written by her husband, Walter Hackett, and George H Broadhurst. After her first appearance in London in 1915 (following 10 years on Broadway in light drama) she had successes regularly until returning to the US in 1938, notably at the Whitehall Theatre, which Hackett opened in 1931.

LORT (League of Resident Theatres) A US organization founded in 1965 by Peter Zeisler of the GUTHRIE THEATRE; it represents over 60 resident professional companies in their negotiations with unions.

Lortel, Lucille (1905–99) US actress and producer, most famous for her work at the Theatre de Lys, in New York's Greenwich Village; her long-running production of *The Threepenny Opera* at this venue (1953–61) is frequently mentioned as having created the off-Broadway movement. In 1981 the 250-seat theatre was renamed after her (*see* Lucille Lortel Theatre).

Losey, Joseph (1909–84) US film director, whose stage production of Brecht's *Galileo* in 1947 and work with the Living Newspaper proved highly influential. Initially working as a stage manager, he was inspired by Okhlopov's experiments in the USSR to dispense with proscenium settings when he worked on the Living Newspaper project in 1936 until clashes with Hallie Flanagan forced his resignation. *Galileo*, with Charles Laughton and the author himself participating, was later turned into a film.

Lotta *See* Crabtree, Charlotte.

Loutherbourg, Philip James de (1740–1812) German artist and stage designer, who became resident scenic director at Drury Lane under Garrick (and subsequently Sheridan) in 1773. He made important innovations in the use of scenery and lighting, placing a new emphasis upon naturalistic detail, and devised machines for producing various sound effects; he also employed his skill as an artist in painting backcloths depicting romantic landscapes and experimented with the effects of perspective. He made further advances in transparencies and encouraged the use of built stuff; after his retirement from the theatre he went on to develop the EIDO-PHUSIKON.

Love for Love A comedy by William CONGREVE. First performance: 1695. Sir Sampson Legend agrees to settle the debts of his profligate son, Valentine, but expects him to sign away his inheritance in return. However, Angelica (with whom Valentine is in love) beguiles Sir Sampson and gets possession of the bond.

Love in a Village A comic opera by Isaac BICKERSTAFFE, with music by Thomas Arne and others. First performance: 1762. A rustic idyll based on *The Village Opera* (1728) by Charles Johnson, it had a major influence upon the course of English light musical drama.

Love of Four Colonels, The A comedy by Peter USTINOV. First performance: London, 1951. The plot revolves around a Sleeping Beauty in a German castle who is courted by four colonels from the British, French, Soviet, and US occupying armies; Ustinov himself acted the main role in the first production.

Love's Labour's Lost A comedy by William SHAKESPEARE, written c. 1594–95. First performance: c. 1594–95. The play satirizes the futile attempts of the young King of Navarre and three courtiers to follow a life of celibacy for three years; it contains many topical allusions that are now obscure. Largely ignored until the 20th century, it is now admired for its verbal wit and sense of humanity.

Love! Valour! Compassion! A play by Terrence MCNALLY. first performance: New York, 1994. The play follows a group of gay men, two of whom are HIV positive, through one summer at the upstate New York home of one, a well-known choreographer.

Low Comedian *See* stock company.

Lower Depths, The (*Na dne*) A play by Maxim GORKY, generally considered to be his finest. First performance: Moscow Art Theatre, 1902. Set in a derelict doss-house in Moscow, the play depicts the miserable lives led by the inhabitants with uncompromising realism. Stanislavsky's ground-breaking production was followed by a highly successful staging in Berlin (1903), where Max Reinhardt directed.

Lowin, John (1576–1653) English actor, who became an important member of the King's Men and was included in the First Folio list of Shakespearean actors. He succeeded Heminge as Falstaff and may have received advice for playing Henry VIII from Shakespeare himself. He appeared in *Sejanus* (1603) and *The Malcontent* (1604) and possibly created the roles of Bosola in *The Duchess of Malfi* and Volpone. With Taylor, he became business manager for the company and acquired a small shareholding in the Blackfriars Theatre.

Lucille La Verne Theatre *See* Princess Theatre.

Lucille Lortel Theatre A theatre on Christopher Street in Greenwich Village, New York, which opened in 1952 as the Theatre de Lys. From 1953 to 1961 Brecht's *The Threepenny Opera* was housed there; subsequent productions have included *Brecht on Brecht* (1962), Arden's *Serjeant Musgrave's Dance* (1966), David Mamet's *A Life in the Theatre* (1977), and Sam Shepard's *Buried Child* (1978), as well as *Getting Out* (1979), and *Steel Magnolias* (1987). The theatre was also known for its matinée series, which was discontinued after 1975.

Lucy Rushton's Theatre *See* New Yorker Theatre.

ludi scaenici The various dramatic entertainments presented at public games in ancient Rome. Theatrical productions were first undertaken at the **Ludi Romani** (held annually in September in honour of Jupiter), for which Livius Andronicus presented the first Latin tragedy and comedy in 240 BC. In subsequent years the type of play given at such festivals was varied to include farces and mime.

Ludlam, Charles (1943–87) US playwright, actor, producer, and director. Working mainly with his own off-off-Broadway Ridiculous Theatrical Company, he perfected a style of burlesque which was nevertheless capable of pointed artistic and social comment as well as deep feeling. His most frequently produced work is *The Mystery of Irma Vep* (1984), subtitled 'A Penny Dreadful', a multi-character gothic horror parody meant to be performed by only two actors.

Ludlow, Noah Miller (1795–1886) US actor-manager, who founded one of the first US companies in 1815. He toured widely and ran the Chatham Theatre in New York for a time. From 1835 to 1853 he comanaged the **American Theatrical Commonwealth Company** with Sol Smith as well as running several other theatres.

Ludwig, Otto (1813–65) German playwright and novelist, who established his reputation in the theatre with a psychological drama depicting provincial life, *Die Erbförster* (The Hereditary Forester; 1850). Other dramatic writings include the drama *Die Makkabäer* (1852) and studies of Shakespeare.

Lugné-Poë, Aurélien-François (1869–1940) French actor-manager and director, who succeeded Paul Fort as head of the influential Théâtre d'Art (renamed the Théâtre de l'Oeuvre) in 1893. A leading figure in the reaction against Realism, he presented important productions of plays by Maeterlinck, Ibsen, and Strindberg among others; other celebrated productions included Wilde's *Salome* (1895), the premiere of Jarry's controversial *Ubu-roi* (1896), Claudel's *L'Annonce faite à Marie* (1912), and Anouilh's *L'Hermine* (1932).

Lun *See* Rich, Christopher; Woodward, Harry.

Lunacharsky, Anatoli Vasilevich (1875–1933) Russian playwright and politician, who did much to reorganize the national theatre after the Revolution of 1917. As the first commissar for education he encouraged the writing of new propaganda plays and evolved the theory of SOCIALIST REALISM; he also ensured the continued survival of such noted venues as the Moscow Art Theatre. His own plays included *Oliver Cromwell* and *Thomas Campanella*.

Lunacharsky State Institute of Theatre Art (GITIS) A drama school in Moscow, which was founded in 1878 and renamed in 1934 in honour of Anatoli LUNACHARSKY. The oldest such establishment in Russia, it numbered Nemirovich-Danchenko among its staff; its pupils have included many future members of the Moscow Art Theatre.

Lundequist, Gerda (1871–1959) Swedish actress, who won acclaim in leading tragic roles at the Kungliga Dramatiska Teatern (1889–91) and 1906–11) and the Svenska Teatern (1891–1906). Her most successful parts included Sophocles's Antigone and Lady Macbeth.

Lunt, Alfred (1892–1977) US actor, who formed a famous acting partnership with his British wife **Lynn Fontanne** (1887–1983). Married in 1922, the Lunts appeared together regularly in sophisticated comedies by such writers as S N Behrman and Noël Coward. Notable successes included Shaw's *Arms and the Man*, Molnár's *The*

Guardsman, Coward's *Design for Living,* and Dürrenmatt's *The Visit.* Before their marriage, Alfred Lunt made his reputation in Booth Tarkington's *Clarence* (1919).

Lunt-Fontanne Theatre A 1492-seat theatre on West 46th Street, New York, which opened in 1910 as the **Globe Theatre**. Originally used for musicals, it housed a number of revues in the 1920s, including Ziegfeld's *Follies* and George White's *Scandals*. It was used as a cinema from 1931 to 1958, when it was renovated and renamed, opening with the Lunts' production of Dürrenmatt's *The Visit.* Since that time it has housed *The Sound of Music* (1959), Richard Burton's *Hamlet* (1964), Sandy Duncan's revival of the musical version of *Peter Pan* (1979), and the musical *Titanic* (1998).

Lupino, Barry (1882–1962) British actor and dancer, who was resident comedian at the Britannia Theatre, Hoxton, for some years before establishing his reputation in musicals and pantomimes, which he often wrote himself. His West End appearances included Charlie Bang in *The Millionaire Kid* (1932) and Sir John in *Me and My Girl* (1941).

His brother, **Stanley Lupino** (1894–1942), started as a variety artist but became a highly successful revue and musical comedy actor and writer. He was in several shows at the London Hippodrome and was very popular in such shows as *Love Lies* (1929) at the Gaiety and *Over She Goes* (1936) at the Saville.

Lu Pone, Patti (1949–) US actress. After study at the Julliard School, she became a founding member of The Acting Company, for which she played many parts between 1972 and 1975. She became famous in *Evita* (1979), and has since played parts in both musicals and straight plays, including Fantine in *Les Misérables* (London; 1985), Reno Sweeny in the Lincoln Center revival of *Anything Goes* (1987), Norma Desmond in Lloyd Webber's *Sunset Boulevard* (London; 1992), and Jolly in Mamet's *The Old Neighborhood* (1997).

Luscius Lanuvinus (2nd century BC) Roman playwright, chiefly remembered as a rival of Terence. He attacked Terence on a number of grounds, including plagiarism, provoking replies in several of Terence's prologues; of his own plays and translations of Menander nothing survives.

Lutèce, Théâtre de A theatre in the rue de Jussieu, Paris, which is used for the presentation of largely experimental dramas. It was a noted venue for the Theatre of the Absurd, with productions of plays by Genet, Obaldia, and others.

Luther A play by John OSBORNE. First performance: Theatre Royal, Nottingham, 1961. Another of Osborne's powerful studies of individual rebels, the play is most convincing when it portrays Luther's psychological and physiological rather than his religious struggles; in the original production Luther was played by Albert Finney.

Luzan y Claramont, Ignacio (1702–54) Spanish scholar, who was a leading figure of the Spanish neoclassical theatre. In such theoretical writings as *Poética* (1737) he attempted to translate Italian ideas into the Spanish drama and argued for rigid observance of the unities. In his later years, however, he conceded that the playwright need not follow such rules so exactly.

Luzzato, Moses Hayim (1707–47) Jewish playwright, who was born in Italy and lived in Amsterdam and was the author of plays in both Hebrew and Italian. His early plays include *Migdal Oz* (Tower of Victory); his works written after he became interested in cabbalism include the play *Tehilla Layesharim* (Praise for Uprightness) and some theatre criticism.

Lyceum Theatre A theatre in Wellington Street, London, which opened in 1771 as a venue for concerts and exhibitions. It was converted into a theatre in 1794 and eventually became the home of the Drury Lane company (1809–12) after the Theatre Royal was damaged by fire. In 1815 it was renamed the Theatre Royal English Opera House and saw appearances by Fanny Kelly and the elder Charles Mathews before destruction by fire in 1830. Re-erected close to the old site in 1834 as the Royal Lyceum and English Opera House, it was run with considerable success by Robert Keeley and then Madame Vestris and the younger Charles Mathews, notably through spectacular productions of Planché. The Convent Garden Theatre company was there from 1856 to 1859, after which Hezekiah Bateman took over. Henry Irving's performance in *The Bells* (1871) transformed the theatre's reputation overnight; subsequently Irving became the manager, triumphing in numerous performances opposite Ellen Terry, from 1878 his celebrated leading lady. This great period came to an end in 1902, when Irving made his last appearance; the theatre was then used for music hall, melodrama, and pantomime. In 1939 John Gielgud staged performances of *Hamlet* there and the theatre subsequently (1945) became a dance hall. Following major refurbishment, it reopened as a theatre in 1996 with a revival of *Jesus Christ Superstar*. The Disney musical *The Lion King* opened in 1999.

The **Lyceum Theatre** on 4th Avenue, New York, was opened in 1885 by Steele Mackaye but foundered until it was taken over by Daniel Frohman, who staged numerous successes there. It was demolished in 1902.

The 938-seat **Lyceum Theatre** on West 45th Street, between 6th Avenue and Broadway, New York, opened in 1903 with *The Proud Prince*. Barrie's *The Admirable Crichton* had its premiere there, while other significant productions included visits by Charles Wyndham's company and plays directed by Belasco. David Warfield and Ethel Barrymore appeared there to great acclaim after World War I, while later successes included Kaufman and Hart's *George Washington Slept Here* (1940), Clifford Odets's *The Country Girl* (1950), Osborne's *Look Back in Anger* (1957), Pinter's *The Caretaker* (1961), the musical *Your Arms Too Short to Box with God* (1976), and Kopit's *Wings* (1979). In the 1990s it was used by the National Actors' Theatre. It is considered to be on the 'wrong side' of Broadway and has the reputation of being a difficult house to fill.

See also ROYAL LYCEUM THEATRE.

Lycophron (b. c. 324 BC) Greek poet and playwright, who lived in Alexandria and is usually remembered for the surviving poem *Alexandra*. He was also the author of comedies and many tragedies, of which nothing remains.

lycopodium An explosive powder formerly employed to produce realistic flame effects. Derived from a type of moss, it was usually ignited in a special holder, known as a lycopodium flask.

Lyly, John (c. 1554–1606) English novelist and playwright, whose plays were performed by boy companies at Court. The most important of his elaborately written plays discussing courtly love was *Endymion, the Man in the Moon* (1588), a love story in which the title figure represented the Earl of Leicester and Cynthia Elizabeth I. Other plays included *Alexander and Campaspe* (1584), *Sappho and Phaon* (1584), *Midas*

(1589), and the witty *Mother Bombie* (1589). His most influential work, however, was his prose fiction *Euphues* (1578) and its sequel, *Euphues and his England* (1580).

Lyndsay, Sir David (1486–1554) Scottish poet and playwright, whose *An Pleasant Satyre of the Three Estates* (1552) follows a similar plot to John Skelton's *Magnyfycence*. The play criticizes the clergy and comments on aspects of Scottish politics.

Lynn, Ralph (1882–1962) British actor, famous for his performances as the affable but fatuous aristocratic heroes of numerous farces. After success in *Tons of Money* at the Shaftesbury Theatre in 1922, he consolidated his reputation in the celebrated Aldwych farces (1922–33). When the series ended he turned to films, returning to the stage in 1944 in *Is Your Honeymoon Really Necessary?*. He also starred in further farces by Ben Travers alongside his old companion Robertson Hare.

lyric The text of a song in a stage show. *Compare* book.

Lyric Players An Irish theatre company founded in 1944 by Austin Clarke for the performance of poetic drama. Appearing at the Abbey Theatre in Dublin, the group produced many plays by Clarke himself, including *The Viscount of Blarney* (1944) and *The Plot Succeeds* (1950).

The **Lyric Players** of Belfast were founded as an amateur company in 1951 and were run on similar lines to Clarke's group, presenting Irish poetic drama by Yeats and others. The company moved into its own theatre in 1952 where notable productions included Greek tragedies, Chekhov's *The Seagull* (1956), and modern works. In 1968 the group, which includes members from Northern Ireland, Eire, and England, acquired a new theatre and received a state subsidy.

Lyric Theatre A theatre in Hammersmith, London, which was opened in 1888 as the **Lyric Hall**, then redesigned and reopened in 1890 as the **Lyric Opera House**. After further rebuilding to a design by Frank Matcham, the Lyric reopened in 1895 with Lily Langtry speaking the prologue on opening night. Thereafter the theatre's reputation declined and it became known locally as 'the Blood and Flea Pit'. In 1918 Nigel Playfair renamed it the Lyric Theatre, launching a successful phase with A A Milne's *Make Believe*; John Gay's *The Beggar's Opera* ran for three and a half years from 1920 and a revival of Congreve's *The Way of the World* (1924) with Edith Evans was highly acclaimed. Ellen Terry made her final stage appearance there in Walter De La Mare's *Crossings* in 1925. After Playfair's departure in 1933, the theatre's fortunes again fluctuated; it remained closed for some time prior to 1944, when Baxter Somerville gave it a new lease of life, many of his productions – by such authors as John Mortimer and Pinter – transferring to the West End. After Somerville's death in 1963, however, the Lyric's fortunes again ebbed, and in 1966 it was closed. A new Lyric Theatre, seating 537, opened in King Street in 1979 with a production of Shaw's *You Never Can Tell*. It maintains a reputation for serious theatre and is complemented by the smaller Lyric Studio Theatre in the same building.

The **Lyric Theatre** in Shaftesbury Avenue is the oldest surviving theatre in the Avenue. It opened in 1888 with the comic opera *Dorothy* starring Marie Tempest. For some years the theatre specialized in comic operas, while Eleonora Duse made her London debut there in *La Dame aux camélias* (1892) by Dumas *fils*. Sir Johnston Forbes-Robertson became manager in 1902 and appeared alongside his wife Gertrude Elliot. In 1906 Lewis Waller took over and staged successful revivals as well as the musical *The Chocolate Soldier* (based on Shaw's *Arms and the Man*). During the 1920s and 1930s Leslie Howard, Tallulah Bankhead, Sir Alfred Lunt, and Lynn Fontanne were among those who featured in popular musicals and plays. Yvonne Arnaud appeared in *The Nutmeg Tree* in 1941, and the Lunts returned to the Lyric during World War II in a celebrated series of Rattigan plays. In 1950 *The Little Hut* with Robert Morley ran for 1261 performances. The tradition of serious theatre and popular musicals has since been maintained with such productions as *Grab Me a Gondola* (1956), Alan Bennett's *Habeas Corpus* with Alec Guinness (1973), the National Theatre production of Ayckbourn's *A Chorus of Disapproval* (1986), and *Five Guys Named Moe*, which ran for over five years from 1990.

The **Lyric Theatre** on West 42nd Street, New York, opened in 1913 with Richard Mansfield in *Old Heidelberg*. In its earlier years several of Ibsen's plays were produced there; later productions included many of Florenz Ziegfeld's musical comedies. The theatre was converted into a cinema in 1933 and torn down in 1997 during construction of the FORD THEATRE CENTER.

Lysistrata A comedy by ARISTOPHANES. First performance: Athens, 411 BC. In an attempt to end the war between Athens and Sparta the women of Athens refuse to sleep with their men until peace is declared; the play has been seen as a satire upon the recent defeats in Sicily. *Lysistrata* has enjoyed frequent modern revivals as a feminist anti-war piece, often in free adaptations.

Lyttelton Theatre One of the three theatres comprising the ROYAL NATIONAL THEATRE in London, opened in 1976. Named after the first chairman of the National Theatre Board, it seats 890 and opened with *Hamlet*, starring Albert Finney. Subsequent productions on its adjustable proscenium stage have included many new works, including plays by Ayckbourn, Pinter, Arthur Miller, and Terence Rattigan.

Lytton, Edward George Earle Bulwer- *See* Bulwer-Lytton, Edward, Lord.

Lyubimov, Yuri Petrovich (1917–) Russian director, who established his reputation with his production of Brecht's *The Good Woman of Setzuan* at the Vakhtangov Theatre after World War II. Subsequently he transferred to the Taganka Theatre and presented notable avant-garde works depending upon the techniques of COLLECTIVE CREATION. His attacks on the Soviet system of censorship provoked the authorities to strip him of his citizenship in 1984. He subsequently worked in Europe and the US, winning particular acclaim for his adaptations of Dostoevsky. He returned to Russia and the Taganka Theatre during the *glasnost* era.

Lyubimov-Lanskoy, Yevsei Osipovich (1883–1943) Russian actor and director, who played an important role in adapting the Russian stage to the new demands created by the Revolution of 1917. His productions of Bill-Belotserkovsky's *Storm* at the Trades Union Theatre in 1926 was highly influential; from 1941 he worked at the Maly Theatre.

M

Mabou Mines *See* La Mama Experimental Theatre Club.

McAnally, Ray(mond) (1926–89) Irish actor, who played many classic Irish parts at the Abbey Theatre, Dublin, between 1947 and 1963. He made his first London appearance in 1962 in Edna O'Brien's *A Cheap Bunch of Nice Flowers*, later taking over as George in Edward Albee's *Who's Afraid of Virginia Woolf?* (1964) and appearing as Macduff in *Macbeth* and Lopakhin in *The Cherry Orchard* at Chichester in 1966. In 1988 he was highly praised for his performance as G B Shaw in Hugh Whitemore's *The Best of Friends*.

Macbeth A tragedy by William SHAKESPEARE, written c. 1605–06. First performance: date unknown. One of the most celebrated plays in the English language, *Macbeth* depicts the central character's disintegration as he wins power abetted by his ambitious wife and then, struggling with both his own conscience and the forces of destiny, loses it through his use of violence. The play contains much of Shakespeare's best-known poetry and has provided many actors and actresses with their most acclaimed roles. It is believed that Shakespeare's choice of subject – the murder of a rightful Scottish king – was inspired by the recent accession of James I, whose patronage Shakespeare's company had obtained. *See also* taboos.

McBurney, Simon *See* Complicite.

McCallum, John (1914–) Australian actor, theatre manager, and producer who divided his career between Britain and Australia. Trained at RADA, he made his debut in 1934 in Brisbane, appeared with the Old Vic company from 1937 to 1940, and, after World War II, won acclaim in such varied plays as Barrie's *Peter Pan* (1956) and Lesley Storm's *Roar Like a Dove* (1957). He married Googie WITHERS in 1948, touring widely with her in many plays, including Maugham's *The Constant Wife* (1957), William Douglas Home's *The Kingfisher* (1978), and *High Spirits* (1991). He continued to play a key role in the development of the Australian theatre, encouraging the production of new plays, some of which he directed himself. From the late 1960s he was also active in the Australian television industry.

McCarter Theatre A theatre in Princeton, New Jersey, connected with Princeton University. The building was constructed in 1929 for the Triangle Club and was often used for pre-Broadway try-outs. The current company was formed in 1974 and has had success with both classics and new works.

McCarthy, Lillah (1875–1960) British actress, who is usually remembered for such Shavian roles as Nora in *John Bull's Other Island* (1905), Margaret Knox in *Fanny's First*

Play (1911), and Lavinia in *Androcles and the Lion* (1913), performed under the direction of Granville Barker, whom she married in 1906. She also appeared in Greek tragedy, Shakespeare, and Shaw in the US, which she visited with her husband in 1914, and ran the LITTLE THEATRE for a time. Other successes included performances in the plays of Barrie and Somerset Maugham as well as appearances opposite Matheson Lang (1920–21); she virtually retired on her second marriage.

McClintic, Guthrie (1893–1961) US actor, director, and producer, who directed many notable productions starring his wife, the actress Katharine Cornell. Previously associated with the companies of Jessie Bonstelle and Winthrop Ames, he attracted attention with his production of Michael Arlen's *The Green Hat* in 1925; other successes included plays by Rudolf Besier, G B Shaw, and Shakespeare, notably *Hamlet* (1936) with John Gielgud.

McCormick, F J (Peter Judge; 1891–1947) Irish actor, who spent most of his career with the Abbey Theatre company, which he joined in 1918. He appeared in over 500 plays and created many of O'Casey's characters, including Joxer Daly in *Juno and the Paycock* (1924) and Jack Clitheroe in *The Plough and the Stars* (1926).

McCowen, Alec (1925–) British actor, who began in repertory and made his London debut at the Arts Theatre as Maxim in *Ivanov* (1950). Subsequently he worked with the Old Vic and Royal Shakespeare companies, playing such roles as Richard II, Touchstone, Malvolio, and the Fool in *King Lear*. As a member of the National Theatre company he starred in Molière's *The Misanthrope* (1973) and Shaffer's *Equus* (1973), while his successes in London and New York have included the title role in Peter Luke's *Hadrian VII* (1968), Higgins in *Pygmalion* (1974), Hitler in *The Portage to San Cristobal of A H* (1982), and Gaev in *The Cherry Orchard* (1995). His remarkable one-man performances of *St Mark's Gospel* (1978), *Kipling* (1984), and *Modern Love* (1982) have also been highly praised. In 1994 he appeared as Prospero in *The Tempest*.

Maccus A character of the Roman *atellana*, whose popular appeal lay in his innate stupidity. He was the central figure of a number of plays by such authors as Novius and Pomponius, in the titles of which his name appeared; he was probably presented as a greedy peasant.

Macdermott, The Great (Gilbert Hastings Farrell; 1845–1901) British music hall singer and actor. His success in burlesque led to his career on the halls, where his biggest hit was 'We Don't Want To Fight but By Jingo! if we do'.

McDonagh, Martin (1970–) Irish playwright, born in London. His play *The Beauty Queen of Leenane* (1996), a black comedy of Irish rural life in the tradition of Synge, enjoyed great success when staged at the Royal Court by Galway's Druid Theatre Company. Two further parts of his 'Leenane Trilogy', *A Skull in Connemara* and *The Lonesome West*, were produced at the Royal Court in 1997.

McEwan, Geraldine (1932–) British actress, who made her stage debut in 1949 at the Theatre Royal, Windsor, and subsequently established her reputation in comedy. As well as appearances at the Royal Court Theatre and other notable London venues, she also acted at Stratford-on-Avon from 1958, her roles there including Ophelia and Beatrice in *Much Ado About Nothing*. In 1962 she won great praise as Lady Teazle in

Sheridan's *The School for Scandal*; she subsequently appeared in National Theatre Company productions of plays by Arden, Congreve, Feydeau, Giraudoux, Maugham, Rattigan, and Strindberg, among others. More recent successes have included Sheridan's *The Rivals* (1983), Shaffer's *Lettice and Lovage* (1988), Congreve's *The Way of the World* (1995), and Coward's *Hay Fever* (1998). Since 1988 she has also worked as an occasional director.

MacGowran, Jack (1918–73) Irish actor, who trained with the Abbey and Gate Theatres in Dublin, and appeared at both for a period of six years (1944–50). He was first seen in London as Young Covey in O'Casey's *The Plough and the Stars* (1954). His subsequent career was much associated with the plays of Samuel Beckett; he played Clov in *Endgame* (1958), Lucky in *Waiting for Godot* (1964), and devised his own solo programmes of Beckett, giving the final one in New York in 1970.

McGrath, John (1935–) British playwright, director, and founder of the 7:84 Theatre Company. He formed the company in 1971 to bring socialist theatre to the working classes, subsequently writing and directing most of its productions himself and touring various fringe venues. He formed a second company in 1973 to tour Scotland. Notable productions have included *The Cheviot, the Stag, and the Black, Black Oil* (1973), *Blood Red Roses* (1980), *The Baby and the Bathwater* (1984), *Mhàri Mhór* (1987), *Watching for Dolphins* (1991), and *The Four Estaites* (1996).

McGuinness, Frank (1953–) Irish playwright and writer. A university lecturer by profession, he made his reputation as a dramatist with *The Factory Girls* (1982) and the highly praised *Observe the Sons of Ulster Marching Towards the Somme* (1985). Subsequent successes have included *The Bread Man* (1990), the award-winning *Someone Who'll Watch Over Me* (1992), and *The Bird Sanctuary* (1994); recent work includes *Mutabilitie* (1997), about the poet Spenser in Ireland, and *Dolly West's Kitchen* (1999), set in Ireland during World War II. He has also translated works by Ibsen, Chekhov, and Brecht.

Machado, Simão (16th century) Portuguese playwright, author of two notable plays in the style of Vicente. *O Cerco de Diu* was a historical drama, while *Comedia da Pastora Alfea* was a pastoral comedy.

Machiavelli, Niccolò di Bernardo dei (1469–1527) Italian playwright and political theorist, usually remembered for the treatise *The Prince* (1513). He was also the author of several comedies in the *commedia erudita* tradition, of which *La Mandragola* (1513–20) is considered a masterpiece. *La Mandragola*, which depicts the betrayal of the heroine, has been revived several times in more recent years; other plays include *Clizia* (1525), which drew on works by Plautus.

machine play A form of spectacular dramatic entertainment presented in France during the 17th century, so called because it involved extensive use of elaborate stage machinery. Mostly presented at the Théâtre du Marais in Paris, plays belonging to the genre included Corneille's *Andromède* (1650) and Molière's *Amphitryon* (1668).

Mackay, Charles (c. 1785–1857) Scottish actor, who joined the Theatre Royal, Edinburgh in 1818. In 1819 his astonishing success as Bailie Nicol Jarvis in Isaac Pocock's adaptation of Scott's *Rob Roy* established him as a player of Scottish character parts.

McKellen, Sir Ian (1939–) British actor, who made his London debut as Godfrey in *A Scent of Flowers* by James Saunders in 1964. Four years later he established his status as a major actor when he played the title roles in *Richard II* and Marlowe's *Edward II* with the Prospect Theatre Company. In 1972 he became a founder member of the **Actors' Company** (which was controlled by the actors themselves) and, with the Royal Shakespeare Company, went on to play Faustus (1974), Romeo (1976), and a much-admired Macbeth (1977). He performed his own one-man show *Acting Shakespeare* (which he later took to the US) in Edinburgh in 1977. Subsequent triumphs have included Max in Martin Sherman's *Bent* (1979), Salieri in Shaffer's *Amadeus* (1980), Platonov in Chekhov's *Wild Honey* (1984), Iago in *Othello* (1989), the title role in *Richard III* (1990; later filmed), and Dr Stockmann in *An Enemy of the People* (1997). A leading spokesman for gay rights, he was knighted in 1991.

McKenna, Siobhán (1922–86) Irish actress, whose career began with the Gaelic Repertory Theatre in Galway in 1940. After working at the Abbey Theatre, Dublin, she made her London debut as Nora Fintry in Carroll's *The White Steed* (1947). She subsequently became well known in London, New York, and Dublin for her interpretations of the great Irish heroines in the plays of O'Casey, Synge, and others. She also appeared in the plays of Shaw, Chekhov, and Brecht, being particularly admired as Shaw's St Joan (1954), Chekhov's Madame Ranevskaya (1968), and in her own one-woman entertainment, *Here Are Ladies* (1970).

McKenna, Virginia (1931–) British actress, who began in repertory at Dundee and made her West End debut in *A Penny for a Song* in 1951. Her Shakespearean work included Perdita (1951) and Rosalind (1954); other roles included Sister Jeanne in John Whiting's *The Devils* (1961) for the Royal Shakespeare Company. In the 1960s she became well known for her film work but she later returned to the stage in the musicals *A Little Night Music* (1976), *The King and I* (1979), and *Winnie* (1988).

McKenzie, Julia (1941–) British actress and director, who came to prominence in such musical shows as *Company* (1972), *Cole* (1974), and *Side by Side by Sondheim* (1976). At the National Theatre she triumphed in *Guys and Dolls* (1982) and Sondheim's *Sweeney Todd* (1993); appearances in straight plays have included several comedies by Alan Ayckbourn, including *Woman in Mind* (1986) and *Communicating Doors* (1995).

McKern, Leo (1920–) Australian actor, who came to Britain in 1946 and has since enjoyed numerous successes on the stage and in films. With the Old Vic company he played several of the great clown parts before joining the Shakespeare Memorial Theatre company in 1952. Subsequent parts in the West End included Big Daddy in Tennessee Williams's *Cat on a Hot Tin Roof* (1958) and the Common Man in Robert Bolt's *A Man for All Seasons* (1960). He has also played the title role in Ibsen's *Peer Gynt* and Iago in *Othello* at the Old Vic, worked on television as John Mortimer's Rumpole, and appeared in Michael Frayn's adaptation of Anouilh's *Number One* (1984), Brighouse's *Hobson's Choice* (1995), and Priestley's *When We Are Married* (1996).

Mackinley, Jean Sterling *See* Williams, (Ernest George) Harcourt.

Mackintosh, Sir Cameron (1946–) British producer of musicals. He began his career as a stage hand at Drury Lane and started mounting his own productions in his early twenties. His first great triumph was the original London production of CATS

(1981); this has been followed by a series of long-running shows including *Les Misérables* (1985), *Phantom of the Opera* (1987), *Miss Saigon* (1989), *Five Guys Named Moe* (1990), and a revival of *Oliver!* (1994). The proprietor of several West End theatres, he was knighted in 1996.

Macklin, Charles (Charles McLaughlin; c. 1697–1797) British actor, born in Northern Ireland, who began his career as a strolling player. After being engaged by Christopher Rich at the Lincoln's Inn Fields Theatre in 1725, he subsequently appeared at Drury Lane as Captain Brazen in *The Recruiting Officer*. However, it was his startling interpretation of Shylock in 1741 that established him as a leading tragedian, who was later to excel in such roles as Iago and Macbeth. He also became known for his volatile nature: in 1735 he killed an actor during a quarrel over a wig and was tried for murder but conducted his own defence and managed to get the charge reduced to manslaughter. He also wrote a number of plays, of which *Love à la Mode* (1759) and *The Man of the World* (1781) were frequently revived.

MacLiammóir, Micheál (1899–1978) Irish actor, playwright, and designer, who acted as a boy in Tree's company and later (with Hilton Edwards) founded a Gaelic theatre in Galway and the GATE THEATRE, Dublin. At the Gate he designed some 300 productions and appeared as Romeo, Hamlet, and Othello among others. His London appearances included (as actor and author) Lee in *Ill Met by Moonlight* and Martin in *Where Stars Walk*, while in 1960 he had great success in his one-man celebration of Oscar Wilde, *The Importance of Being Oscar*, with which he later toured the world. He also devised two other solo performances, *I Must Be Talking to My Friends* (1963) and *Talking about Yeats* (1970).

McMahon, Gregan (1874–1941) Australian actor and director, who helped to found the influential Melbourne Repertory Company in 1911. Under his direction the company presented the first Australian productions of plays by Shaw and other notable contemporary European playwrights.

McMaster, Anew (1894–1962) Irish actor-manager, who first attracted attention in *The Scarlet Pimpernel* (1911) with Fred Terry's company. He went on to act in repertory, in the West End, and in Ireland, and in 1925 formed his own Shakespearean touring company. He was much acclaimed in many of the great leading roles, including Shylock, Hamlet, and Coriolanus.

McNally, Terrence (1939–) US playwright noted for his serious comedies, which often have gay themes. Major works, both on and off Broadway, include *Next* (1971), *Bad Habits* (1974), *The Lisbon Traviata* (1985), LOVE! VALOUR! COMPASSION! (1994), and *Master Class* (1995). He has also supplied books for musicals, including *The Rink* (1984) and *Kiss of the Spider Woman* (1991).

MacNamara, Brinsley (John Weldon; 1890–1963) Irish playwright, novelist, and short story writer, who joined the Abbey Theatre as an actor in 1910. His reputation and notoriety rest primarily upon his early fiction, but he also achieved success as a playwright, most notably with the grim drama *Margaret Gillan* (1933). He also wrote a number of successful comedies.

Macowan, Michael (1906–80) British actor and director, who gave up acting in preference for directing in 1931 and presented numerous memorable productions of contemporary plays at the Old Vic Theatre, the Shakespeare Memorial Theatre, and the Westminster Theatre (1936–39). He was also connected with the Old Vic Theatre School and was head of the London Academy of Music and Dramatic Art (1954–66).

McPherson, Conor (1972–) Irish playwright and director. Born in Dublin, McPherson founded the Fly by Night Theatre Company in the early 1990s to produce new plays, including his own *The Good Thief* (1994). Both *This Lime Tree Bower* (1996), about two Italian-Irish brothers in Dublin, and the solo play *St Nicholas* (1997), about a critic, were seen at London's Bush Theatre. The interest aroused by these plays led the Royal Court Company to commission THE WEIR (1997), which went on to enjoy huge success in London, Toronto, and New York. McPherson has since written *Dublin Carol* (2000) and *Port Authority* (2001) for the stage.

Macrae, (John) Duncan (1905–67) Scottish actor, whose successes ranged from the title role in Robert McLellan's *Jamie the Saxt* (1937) to Widow Twankey. He was frequently seen at the Edinburgh Festival, where he played in Lyndsay's *Ane Pleasant Satyre of the Thrie Estaitis* in 1948. Appearances in London included the leading part in Bridie's *Mr Bolfry* (1943), John in Ionesco's *Rhinoceros* (1960), and Harpagon in Molière's *The Miser* (1966).

Macready, William Charles (1793–1873) British actor-manager, of Anglo-Irish parentage, who became one of the most celebrated players of his day, despite his unmanageable temper and dislike of the theatre in general. When his father, an actor-manager, found himself in financial trouble, Macready reluctantly abandoned his education and became an actor, making his debut in 1810 at Birmingham, playing Romeo. In 1816 he began a five year contract at Covent Garden; subsequent appearances over the next 16 years, as Rob Roy, Hamlet, Lear, and Macbeth, established him as a distinguished tragedian second only to Kean. Other successes included Bulwer-Lytton's *The Lady of Lyons* (1838) and *Richelieu* (1839). He took over the management of Covent Garden in 1837, greatly improving the general standard of drama there and then repeated his reforms at Drury Lane. He also toured the provinces and the US, where his last visit, in 1849, culminated in the famous riot at the ASTOR PLACE OPERA HOUSE, triggered by the ill-feeling between himself and Edwin Forrest. He retired in 1851.

MacSwiney, Owen *See* Swiney, Owen.

Madách, Imre (1823–64) Hungarian playwright, poet, and philosopher, usually remembered for the tragic drama *Az ember tragédiája* (The Tragedy of Man; 1883). Taking its central characters from the story of the biblical Creation, the play became one of the most popular works in the Hungarian theatre and was much translated; other works include *The Last Days of Csák* (1886) and *Moses* (1888).

Madame Sans-Gêne A comedy by Victorien SARDOU, written in collaboration with Émile Moreau. First performance: Paris, 1893. Madame Sans-Gêne ('without constraint') is the nickname of the play's heroine, a laundress whose husband became one of Napoleon's marshals; the title role was created by Réjane.

Maddermarket Theatre A repertory theatre in Norwich, which opened in 1921. Constructed in the style of an Elizabethan playhouse, it was soon recognized as a leading venue for amateur drama under the directorship of Walter Nugent Monck

(1877–1958). Actors in productions, which change every month, are traditionally never named in programmes. It seats about 300 people.

Maddern, Minnie *See* Fiske, Minnie Maddern.

Maddox, Michael *See* Meddoks, Mikhail Egrovich.

Madison Square Theatre A theatre on 24th Street, New York, which was opened by Steele Mackaye in 1879 for his company of students to use as a repertory theatre. This failed but the theatre was successfully reopened under Daniel Frohman in 1880 with Mackaye's *Hazel Kirke*. In 1882 it was also the venue for Viola Allen's New York debut in Hugo's *The Hunchback of Notre Dame*. From 1885 Albert M Palmer took over, staging many new works, including the first English translation of Ibsen's *A Doll's House* with Beatrice Cameron and Richard Mansfield (in the 1889–90 season). Palmer was succeeded by Hoyt in 1891, who remained there until 1900. Renamed **Hoyt's Theatre** in 1905, it continued to prosper with such plays as Heijerman's *A Case of Arson* (1906). The theatre was demolished in 1908.

Madras House, The A comedy by Harley GRANVILLE-BARKER. First performance: Duke of York's Theatre, 1910. Dealing with the topic of female repression through the premarital adventures of the six Huxtable girls, it is distinguished by its natural and eloquent dialogue.

Madwoman of Chaillot, The (*La Folle de Chaillot*) A play by Jean GIRAUDOUX. First performance: Paris, 1945. A whimsical comedy with a serious underlying message, it depicts the defeat of materialism, in the form of an oil prospector and his greedy associates, by the humanitarian madwoman, Countess Aurélie.

Maeterlinck, Maurice (1862–1949) Belgian poet and playwright, who became a leading writer of Symbolist drama. Such early poetic dramas as *La Princesse Maleine* (1899), *L'Intruse* (The Intruder; 1890), and *Les Aveugles* (The Sightless; 1891) all contain elements of legend and allegory and create an oppressive dream-like atmosphere. PELLÉAS ET MÉLISANDE (1892) was his greatest success and was later used as the libretto for Debussy's opera of the same name. Other notable works included a marionette play, *La Mort de Tintagîle* (1894), *Joyzelle* (1903), the highly popular *L'Oiseau Bleu* (The Blue Bird; 1909), *Mary Magdalene* (1910), *Les Fiançailles* (The Betrothal; 1918), and *Le Bourgmestre de Stilmonde* (1918). He was awarded a Nobel Prize in 1911.

Maffei, Francesco Scipione (1675–1755) Italian playwright, author of the influential verse tragedy *Merope* (1713). Educated by the Jesuits, Maffei made use of classical and French models in his highly successful work, which had a great effect upon such playwrights as Alfieri, Lessing, and Voltaire. He also executed translations of several classical plays, collected in *Teatro italiano* (1723).

magazine batten *See* batten.

maggio A form of early Italian theatrical entertainment, which traditionally took place in May. It is known to have involved the spectacular representation of battles and other sensational events but no scripts of the genre have survived.

Magistrate, The A farce by PINERO. First performance: Royal Court Theatre, 1885. A bumbling magistrate manages to evade the police in a raid on an inn one evening, but other members of his family are brought before him in his official capacity in the morning.

Magnes (5th century BC) Greek playwright, author of early examples of Old Comedy. He is known to have won a contest in 472 BC; few fragments of his work survive.

Magnon, Jean (1620–62) French playwright and friend of Molière. Magnon wrote for the short-lived Illustre-Théâtre in the mid-1640s: his first play, *Artaxerce*, was staged by that company in 1644. He subsequently produced several other plays of mediocre quality and an encyclopedic work.

Mahabharata An adaptation of the ancient Sanskrit epic made by Peter BROOK. First performance: Avignon, 1985. The main plot concerns the feud between two clans, the Kauravas and the Pandavas. Brook's nine-hour stage version featured a multinational cast and drew on both Indian and Western dramatic traditions. It toured internationally in the mid-1980s and was widely acclaimed as one of the great theatrical experiences of the decade.

Mahelot, Laurent (fl. 1633) French stage designer, who executed designs for numerous productions at the Théâtre de l'Hôtel de Bourgogne. Notes on his settings are preserved in his *Mémoire*, which gives details of plays presented in 1633 and 1634; it is now kept in the Bibliothêque Nationale in Paris.

Maids, The (*Les Bonnes*) The first play by Jean GENET. First performance: Paris, 1947, in a production directed by Louis Jouvet. The maids, sisters Solange and Claire, take turns at impersonating their mistress in a ritual game that culminates in murder. Productions in London (1954) and New York (1955) attracted much comment and attention.

Maintenon, Madame de (Françoise d'Aubigné; 1635–1719) French noblewoman, who became the morganatic wife of Louis XIV. The widow of the playwright Paul Scarron, she exercised considerable influence over the king and caused the banishment of the Comédie-Italienne in 1697 after one of their plays had given her offence. She did, however, enjoy private theatricals and encouraged Racine to write plays for performance at her school for poor girls at Saint-Cyr; she also wrote a number of brief pieces for the same purpose herself.

Maíquez, Isidoro (1768–1820) Spanish actor, regarded as the first notable player of tragedy in Spain. Trained under Talma, he appeared as Othello in 1802 but was later caught up in political intrigues and exiled from Madrid.

Mairet, Jean (1604–86) French playwright, who was born in Besançon. His early plays, which were mainly pastoral tragicomedies, were followed by the comedy *Les Galanteries du duc d'Osonne* (1632) and his masterpiece, the Roman tragedy *Sophonisbe* (1634). This was the first French tragedy to observe the theory of the unities, which Mairet had previously discussed in the preface to *Silvanire* (1630). One of Pierre Corneille's opponents in the *querelle du* CID, he abandoned the theatre in 1640.

Maison de Molière, La *See* Comédie-Française.

Maisons de la Culture *See Décentralisation Dramatique.*

Majestic Theatre A theatre in Columbus Circle, New York, which opened as the **Cosmopolitan Theatre** in 1903 with a series of musicals. Renamed the **Park Theatre** in 1911, it saw appearances by Mrs Patrick Campbell and Herbert Tree, among others, before being turned into a cinema in 1923. Known as the **International Theatre** from 1944, the **Columbus Circle Theatre** from 1945 to 1946, and then the International once more, it eventually became a television studio and was demolished in 1954.

The current 1629-seat **Majestic Theatre** on West 44th Street, between Broadway and 8th Avenue, New York, opened in 1927. It was used for musical comedy until 1935, when the Moscow Art Players took it over to produce a series of Russian plays. After World War II it presented a series of musicals by Rodgers and Hammerstein, including *Carousel* (1945), *Allegro* (1947), *South Pacific* (1949), and *Me and Juliet* (1953). Other musicals that have played there include *The Music Man* (1957), *Camelot* (1960), and *The Wiz* (1975). Since 1987 it has been showing LLOYD WEBBER's *The Phantom of the Opera*.

Major Barbara A play by G B SHAW. First performance: Royal Court Theatre, 1905. Major Barbara, a member of the Salvation Army, is faced with having to accept money from a whisky distiller and an arms manufacturer (her father) if her work is to continue; this moral dilemma leads ultimately to her resignation and her adoption of a new mission in life.

make-up The use of cosmetics in altering an actor's physical appearance in order to suit him for a certain role or to compensate for the blanching effects of stage lighting. Dating from the earliest forms of ritual drama, the art of make-up was revolutionized by the introduction of gas and electric lighting and has now developed into a highly technical practice. The invention of greasepaint by the opera singer Ludwig Leichner (b. 1836) did much to improve standards of make-up throughout the theatre and helped to banish the harmful effects of earlier paints containing white lead. More recent innovations have included the introduction of water-based cosmetics and fluorescent colour, as well as the use of latex prosthetics for special effects.

Malade imaginaire, Le The last of Molière's comedies. First performance: Palais-Royal, 1673. The play revolves around the hypochondriac Argan, who is convinced that he is seriously ill and insists that his daughter shall marry a doctor: eventually he is persuaded to become a doctor himself. After the fourth performance of the play Molière, who had appeared in the title role, collapsed and died. English translations include *The Hypochondriac* (1981) by Alan Drury.

Malcontent, The A tragicomedy by John MARSTON, often considered his best work. First performance: 1604. The plot resembles that of *Measure for Measure*, although Marston's exposure of corruption, lust, and greed through the activities of the banished Duke (disguised as Malevole) is more harshly satiric in tone.

Malina, Judith *See* Living Theatre.

Malkovich, John (1953–) US actor and director, a founder (1975) of the STEPPENWOLF THEATRE in Chicago, with which he has been involved in over 50 productions. He made his New York debut in 1982 with Sam Shepard's *True West* and added to his reputation with Broadway productions of *Death of a Salesman* (1984) and

Lanford Wilson's *Burn This* (1987). Since the mid-1980s he has been known mainly for his film work, but he still returns regularly to the stage.

Malleson, (William) Miles (1888–1969) British actor, director, and playwright, who became famous as a somewhat eccentric comedy actor in such roles as Gobbo in *The Merchant of Venice* (1919) and Scrub in Farquhar's *The Beaux' Stratagem* (1927). Of his several original plays only *The Fanatics* (1927) had a long run, although his adaptations from Molière, including *The Miser* (in which he played the title role at the New Theatre in 1949), were more successful. Other parts included Merlyn in the musical *Camelot* (1964).

Malone, Edmond (1741–1812) British literary critic, born in Dublin, who became noted for his studies of Shakespeare. He published his *Attempt to ascertain the Order in which the Plays of Shakespeare were written* in 1778 and his own edition of Shakespeare's plays in 1790. In 1796 he was the first to denounce the forgeries of William Ireland.

Malvern Festival A major theatre festival founded at Malvern, Worcestershire, in 1929 by Barry Jackson. The festival became internationally known for its close association with the plays of G B Shaw, productions including the English premieres of *The Apple Cart* (1929), *In Good King Charles's Golden Days* (1939), and *Too True to Be Good* (1932) among others. Other successes included plays by Bridie, Drinkwater, and Priestley. The festival came to a halt during World War II, being revived briefly in 1949 and – as a festival of Elgar and Shaw – again in 1977.

Maly Theatre A theatre in Moscow, which opened in 1824 as the home of a company originally founded in 1806. The Maly (meaning small) is the oldest surviving theatre in the capital and began with productions of Shakespeare and the classics as well as of plays by such contemporary Russian playwrights as Gogol and Griboyedov. Between 1854 and 1885 many plays by Ostrovsky were performed there, meeting with such success that the theatre became popularly known as the **House of Ostrovsky**. After the Revolution the theatre continued to present contemporary Russian works, as well as revivals of the classics. In the *glasnost* era it entered a new golden age under the direction of **Lev Dodin** (1944–), who assumed control in 1983. Recent tours in the West have confirmed its reputation as perhaps the finest ensemble in the world.

Mamet, David (1947–) US playwright. In 1973 he founded the St Nicholas Theatre Company in Chicago which presented most of his early plays. He emerged as a major new voice in the US theatre with *Sexual Perversity in Chicago* (1974) and AMERICAN BUFFALO (1975), which won several awards. GLENGARRY GLEN ROSS (1983) won the Pulitzer Prize, while OLEANNA (1992) attracted much controversy with its analysis of contemporary sexual politics. Mamet's work is much concerned with the power struggles between inarticulate and emotionally repressed men. He is famous for his skill in rendering the speech patterns of such characters (not least their repetitive profanity).

Principal works:
  Duck Variations: 1971.
  Sexual Perversity in Chicago: 1973.
  American Buffalo: 1975.

A Life in the Theatre: 1976.
The Water Engine: 1977.
Lakeboat: 1980.
Edmond: 1982.
The Disappearance of the Jews: 1983.
Glengarry Glen Ross: 1984; Pulitzer Prize.
Speed-the-Plow: 1987.
The Old Neighborhood: 1991.
Oleanna: 1992.
Ricky Jay and his 52 Assistants: 1994.
Death Defying Acts: 1996.
Boston Marriage: 2000.

manager *See* producer.

Man and Superman A play by G B SHAW, written 1901–03. First performance: Royal Court Theatre, 1905. Through the relationship between Jack Tanner and the predatory Ann Whitfield, the play argues the dominance of women over men and the need for man to dedicate himself to the creation of something greater than himself; at its heart is a Shavian analysis of love and marriage as a vehicle for the 'Life Force' of creative evolution. The dream act 'Don Juan in Hell' is sometimes performed separately.

Manducus A stock character of the Roman *atellana*. He was essentially a clown with a large mouth and a hooked nose and may have represented greed or gluttony. *See also* Dossenus.

manet *See* stage direction.

Man for All Seasons, A A historical play by Robert BOLT. First performance: London, 1960. A highly acclaimed treatment of the life of Sir Thomas More and his conflict with Henry VIII, the play examines moral dilemmas and makes effective use of the doubling of roles by a Brechtian commentator called the Common Man.

Manhattan Theatre A theatre on Broadway, between 53rd and 54th streets, New York, which opened as **Hammerstein's Theatre** in 1927. It was renamed the Manhattan in 1931 and continued to be used primarily for musicals. In 1934 it became a music hall and two years later was taken over by the Federal Theatre Project, opening with *American Holiday* (1936). The theatre was thereafter used by the CBS television network which renamed it the Ed Sullivan Theatre in 1967 and purchased it in 1993.

Manhattan Theatre Club A New York theatre company, founded in 1970, that specializes in new plays. Many of its premieres have gone on to commercial runs. It has been especially successful with the plays of Terrence MCNALLY.

Manoel Theatre A theatre in Malta, which was founded in 1731. It was a popular venue for a mixed programme of opera and drama for over a century, being renamed the Royal Theatre while under British occupation. It was restored in 1957 and reopened in 1960 as the National Theatre of Malta.

Man of Mode, The   The last and best-known comedy by Sir George ETHEREGE. First performance: 1676. The plot revolves around Dorimant (modelled partly on the Earl of Rochester), who throws over two mistresses in order to pursue the heiress Harriet, and Young Bellair, who is ordered by his father to marry Harriet but loves another. Other characters include the fashionable Sir Fopling Flutter.

Manrique, Gómez (c. 1415–90) Spanish poet, soldier, diplomat, and playwright; the earliest writer in the Spanish theatrical tradition known by name. His dramas include the Nativity play *La representación del Nacimiento de Nuestro Señor* (c. 1475) and secular pieces.

Mansfield, Richard (1854–1907) US actor, born in Berlin, who began his career in the operas of Gilbert and Sullivan before establishing his reputation in New York, where he first appeared in 1882. He became one of the most popular US stars with leading roles in such plays as *Dr Jekyll and Mr Hyde* (1887), Clyde Fitch's *Beau Brummell* (1890), and Rostand's *Cyrano de Bergerac* (1898). His most admired Shakespearean parts included Richard III and Henry V; he also presented the first US productions of Shaw's *Arms and the Man* (1894) and *The Devil's Disciple* (1897) and the first English language version of Ibsen's *Peer Gynt* (1906).

His wife, **Beatrice Cameron** (1868–1940), often appeared alongside him, her most successful roles including Nora in Ibsen's *A Doll's House* (1889).

Mansfield Theatre   *See* Brooks Atkinson Theatre.

Mantell, Robert Bruce (1854–1928) US actor, born in Scotland, who became a popular star of melodrama and later attracted praise for his interpretation of Shakespearean roles. He spent some time in the US with Modjeska early in his career; later he formed his own touring company in the US and excelled in plays by such authors as Boucicault and Bulwer-Lytton.

Mantle, Robert Burns (1873–1948) US theatre critic and editor, who edited a long series of US play anthologies from 1920 until his death. He also wrote drama criticism for several leading US newspapers.

Manuel, Niklaus (1484–1530) Swiss artist, playwright, soldier, and statesman, who expressed many of the ideals of the Reformation in his writings. A native of Berne, he criticized the extravagance of the Roman Catholic church, notably in *Der Ablasskramer* (1526), in which a corrupt cleric falls victim to those he has duped.

Man Who Came to Dinner, The   A play by George S KAUFMAN and Moss HART. First performance: New York, 1939. The play revolves around an acid-tongued radio announcer (based on the critic Alexander WOOLLCOTT) who breaks his hip on tour and is forced to stay with a family in the suburbs for several weeks. During his stay he terrorizes the family with his fussiness and pomposity.

Manzoni, Alessandro (Francesco Tomaso Antonio; 1785–1873) Italian novelist and playwright, who was the author of the two romantic tragedies *Il conte di carmognola* and *Adelchi*. The plays are notable chiefly for their lyrical choruses and historical accuracy; he is usually remembered, however, for the novel *I promessi sposi* (The Betrothed).

Marais, Théâtre du A theatre in Paris, one of the earliest public theatres in France, which was opened in a converted tennis court in the Rue Vieille-du-Temple in 1634. Notable early productions there by Montdory's company included some of Corneille's comedies, his tragedy *Le Cid* (1637), and *La Mariane* by Tristan L'Hermite. Subsequently many of the actors moved to the Hôtel de Bourgogne and the Théâtre du Marais declined until Jodelet appeared there in a series of new farces. In 1644 a fire gutted the building; after the theatre was rebuilt productions continued until 1680, when the resident company (which had amalgamated with Moliére's troupe on his death in 1673) became part of the new Comédie-Française.

Marat/Sade, The (*Die Ermordung des Jean-Paul Marat, dargestellt von der Truppe des Marquis de Sade im Irrenhaus von Charenton*) A drama by Peter WEISS, the full title of which is *The Persecution and Assassination of Marat as Performed by the Inmates of the Charenton Asylum under the Direction of the Marquis de Sade*. First performance: Berlin, 1964. Peter Brook's famous production for the Royal Shakespeare Company (1964) applied many ideas derived from the Theatre of CRUELTY proclaimed by Artaud, and is often considered their definitive expression.

Marber, Patrick (1965–) British playwright, director, and actor. He made his name in the early 1990s as a comic actor on radio and television (often with the comedian Steve Coogan). His first play *Dealer's Choice*, a comedy about poker enthusiasts, won several major awards in 1995. Further acclaim followed for *Closer* (1997), a play about obsessional love in the age of the Internet, which enjoyed success in both London and New York. Plays he has directed include Dennis Potter's *Blue Remembered Hills* (1995) and a highly praised revival of Pinter's *The Caretaker* (2000).

Marble, Danforth (1810–49) US actor, who began as a silversmith before establishing himself as an actor in Yankee character roles. He was particularly successful as Sam Patch in a series of three plays based on the character and possibly written by Marble himself. He was also admired in similar roles in London and elsewhere before his early death.

Marcadé, Eustache (d. 1440) French theologian and poet, author of a lengthy early Passion play, *La Passion d'Arras*. 25 000 lines long and unremarkable in style and content, the play is nonetheless of importance as a pioneering work in this genre.

Marceau, Fèlicieu (Louis Carette; 1913–) French novelist, essayist, and playwright, whose plays are characterized by sardonic humour and an idiosyncratic style. His plays, which are all comedies, include *L'Oeuf* (The Egg; 1956), *La Bonne soupe* (1959), *L'étouffe-chrétien* (1961), and *Les cailloux* (1962).

Marceau, Marcel (1923–) French mime actor, who is regarded as the foremost performer of the art in modern times. His most famous character is Bip, a whitefaced clown dressed in a white costume with a tall black hat with a flower in it, who is descended from the traditional Pierrot figure. The character first appeared in 1946, after Marceau had completed his training with Dullin and Barrault. Other performances have included a celebrated mime drama based on Gogol's *The Overcoat*, another on the story of David and Goliath, and numerous brief sketches. He founded his own École de mimodrame de Paris at the Théâtre de la Porte-Saint-Martin in 1978.

Marcel, Gabriel (1889–1973) French philosopher and playwright, who was an early exponent of Existentialism. Converted to Roman Catholicism in 1929, Marcel examined man's alienation and frustration in such plays as *Le Coeur des autres* (1921) and *Le Chemin de Crète* (1936).

March, Fredric (Frederick McIntyre Bickle: 1897–1975) US actor, who made his first stage appearance in Baltimore in 1920 and his New York debut later that year. After time in stock companies, he went to Hollywood in 1928, where he became a major star. Later stage work included Mr Antrobus in THE SKIN OF OUR TEETH (1944), Dr Stockmann in *An Enemy of the People* (1950), and James Tyrone in LONG DAY'S JOURNEY INTO NIGHT (1956).

Marching Song A drama by John WHITING. First performance: London, 1954. Regarded by some as Whiting's finest work, this play depicts the dilemma faced by a general who, having lost in war, is forced to choose between public trial or suicide.

Mardzhanov, Konstantin Alexandrovich (1872–1933) Georgian director. Having worked with the Moscow Art Theatre from 1910 to 1913, he founded the Free Theatre, which included such influential figures as Taïrov. He then returned to Georgia, where he produced innovative productions of Shakespeare and plays by Georgian writers. In 1928 he founded a theatre in Kutaisi; this was moved to Tbilisi in 1930 and later renamed in his honour.

Maréchal, Marcel Louis-Noël (1937–) French actor and director, who established a strong reputation as one of the leading figures in French provincial theatre. His innovative productions of both Shakespeare and modern works by such authors as Audiberti and Brecht have attracted much attention; his other successes have included *Capitaine Fracasse* (1972), based on a novel by Gautier. Since 1975 he has been based in Marseilles.

Margolis, Donald (1955–) US playwright, whose work first received attention in 1989 with *The Loman Family Picnic*. His plays, which are frequently non-linear in their approach to time, also include *Sight Unseen* (1992) and *Dinner with Friends* (1999), which won the Pulitzer Prize.

Maria Stuart A historical play by Friedrich von SCHILLER. First performance: 1800. The play depicts the last three days in the life of Mary, Queen of Scots (complete with a fictional meeting with Elizabeth I) and portrays her redeeming acceptance of her fate.

Marigny, Théâtre A theatre in the Champs-Élysées, which was founded in 1850. It was run for a time by Deburau's son and later renamed the Théâtre des Champs-Élysées and the Folies-Marigny, being used for performances of vaudeville. Demolished in 1881, it was rebuilt as a music hall in 1896 and acquired its present name in 1901. It was sumptuously refurbished in 1925 and became an occasional venue for the Comédie-Française as well as the company of Jean-Louis Barrault and Madeleine Renaud (1946–56).

Marinelli, Karl (1744–1803) Austrian actor, playwright, and impresario, who was a leading figure in the tradition of Viennese folk comedy. Author of such plays as *Der Ungar in Wien* (The Hungarian in Vienna; 1773) and *Dom Juan, oder der steinerne*

Gast (1783), he installed a burlesque company at the Leopoldstädter Theater in 1781 and encouraged such influential figures as Johann Laroche and Anton Hasenhut.

Marinetti, Filippo Tommaso (1876–1944) Italian actor, novelist, poet, and playwright, who wrote in Italian and French and was effectively the founder of FUTURISM. His play *Le Roi Bombance* (1909) aroused much controversy with its use of the digestive system as an allegory of the corruption of mankind; other writings included theatrical pieces advocating Futurism and Fascist ideals.

marionette *See* puppet theatre.

Marivaux, Pierre Carlet de Chamblain de (1688–1763) French playwright, journalist, and novelist. Most of Marivaux's plays were produced by the Comédie-Italienne, who proved initially to be better interpreters of his style than the Comédie-Française. Characterized by acute psychological insight and by a subtlety of language (*marivaudage*) that causes problems for his translators, Marivaux's sophisticated romantic comedies were not fully appreciated in their time but are now admired for their powerful female characters; they had a strong influence upon Alfred de Musset among others.

Principal works:
   Arlequin poli par l'amour: 1720.
   La Surprise de l'amour: 1722.
   La Double Inconstance: 1723.
   Le Jeu de l'amour et du hasard: 1730; translated as THE GAME OF LOVE AND CHANCE.
   Les Fausses Confidences: 1737.
   L'Épreuve: 1740.

Mark Hellinger Theatre A theatre on West 51st Street, between Broadway and 8th Avenue, New York, which opened as the Hollywood Theatre, a cinema, in 1930. It became the 51st Street Theatre in 1936, when it opened with George Abbott's *Sweet River*, and in 1949 was given its present name in honour of the critic and playwright **Mark Hellinger** (1903–47), who wrote the first newspaper column on Broadway. It has mainly been used for musicals, most notably *My Fair Lady* (1956). More recent productions have included *On a Clear Day You Can See Forever* (1965), *Jesus Christ Superstar* (1971), and *Sugar Babies* (1979). It is currently leased to a church.

Mark Taper Forum A theatre in Los Angeles, built in 1967. The company of the same name was directed by **George Davison** (1933–) from 1965. The building also houses the Center Theatre Group, a non-profit-making organization created by the University of California Extension. The Forum has a pentagonal thrust stage and a semicircular auditorium seating 750; significant premieres there have included Mark Medoff's *Children of a Lesser God* (1980) and *Angels in America* (1991).

Marlowe, Christopher (1564–93) English playwright and poet, who was born in Canterbury and educated at Cambridge. Little is known of Marlowe's adult life, but there is some evidence to suggest that he may have been a government spy; he was arrested and charged with atheism and died shortly afterwards in a tavern brawl. In his brief writing career he did much to liberate English drama from the constraints of the medieval and Tudor tradition. His accomplished use of blank verse, first fully apparent in TAMBURLAINE THE GREAT, inspired numerous contemporaries, including Shakespeare. Marlowe's DR FAUSTUS made the soliloquy a means of analysing character, while his last play, EDWARD II, broke new ground in its treatment of historical subject-matter and was the first of his works to develop a range of characters. THE JEW OF MALTA may have been a model for Shakespeare's *The Merchant of Venice*. Despite the fact that some of his plays survive only in much-mangled forms, Marlowe's works were revived many times during the 20th century and have been much praised for their lyrical and theatrical qualities.

Principal works:
Tamburlaine the Great: Part I, 1587; Part II, 1588.
The Tragical History of Dr Faustus: c. 1589–92 (published 1604).
The Jew of Malta: c. 1590 (published 1633).
Edward II: c. 1591–92.

Marlowe, Julia (Sarah Frances Frost; 1866–1950) US actress, born in Britain, who established her reputation as an adult actress in New York in Mrs Lovell's *Ingomar* (1887). Subsequently she excelled in leading roles in Shakespeare (including Juliet and Lady Macbeth) and Sheridan among others and married the actor E H Sothern.

Marlowe Society A theatre group based at Cambridge University, which was founded in 1908 and dedicated to the performance of plays from the Elizabethan and Jacobean periods. The society originated from a production of Marlowe's *Dr Faustus* in 1907; notable figures connected with the group have included the poet Rupert Brooke, George Rylands, Peter Hall, and John Barton. Women have played in the society since 1934.

Marmontel, Jean-François (1723–99) French writer, who was a friend and protégé of Voltaire. Marmontel's dramatic works are the least important part of his output; his plays include the tragedies *Denys le Tyran* (1748) and *Aristomène* (1749), several comedies, and opera libretti.

Marowitz, Charles (1934–) US director and playwright. Having arrived in Britain in 1956, he worked with Peter BROOK, notably on the celebrated Theatre of Cruelty season in 1964. Subsequently he worked with the Traverse Theatre Club in Edinburgh before establishing his own **Open Space Theatre** company in London from 1968 to 1981, presenting plays by US writers, Shakespeare, and many contemporary authors. From 1982 to 1989 he was playwright-in-residence and associate director of the Los Angeles Theatre Center, which he left to found the Malibu Stage Company in 1991. His plays influenced by Artaud, include adaptations of Shakespeare and Ibsen.

Marquis Theatre A 1584-seat theatre incorporated into the Marriot Marquis Hotel on Broadway between 44th and 45th Streets. The building was controversial, as three other theatres had to be demolished to make way for it. The complex opened in 1986 with a hit revival of the 1937 musical *Me and My Girl*. Other musical productions seen there include Tyne Daly's revival of *Gypsy* (1991), Julie Andrews in *Victor/Victoria* (1995), and Bernadette Peters starring in *Annie Get Your Gun* (1999).

Marriage à la Mode A comedy by John DRYDEN. First performance: London, 1672. One of Dryden's most elegant and popular comedies, the play contrasts romantic and aristocratic ideas about love and includes some of the author's finest songs. The plot derives from the decision of Rhodophil and Doralice to embark on new love affairs after two years of marriage.

Marriage of Figaro, The (*Le Mariage de Figaro ou la Folle Journée*) A comedy by Pierre de BEAUMARCHAIS. First performance: Comédie-Française, Paris, 1784. A sequel to *The Barber of Seville* (1775), the play continues the story of Figaro and the intrigues of Count Almaviva. Figaro's complaints about social injustice led to the play being banned for three years by Louis XVI. Mozart's opera *Le nozze di Figaro* (1786) is based on this work.

Mars, Mlle (Anne-Françoise-Hippolyte Boutet; 1779–1847) French actress, who began her acting career as a child under Mlle Montansier. Noted for her beauty, she made her debut at the Comédie-Française in 1795 after being encouraged by Mlle Contat and subsequently excelled in the plays of Molière as well as in tragedy.

Marshall, Norman (1901–80) British director and manager, born in India, who became in 1926 one of the directors under Terence Gray at the Cambridge Festival Theatre. On taking over the Gate Theatre in London in 1934 he presented many challenging new plays, including works by Housman and Steinbeck. After World War II he continued to direct in London and for television and also formed his own touring company, as well as advising on the foundation of the National Theatre.

Marshall Theatre *See* Richmond Theatre.

Marston, John (c. 1575–1634) English playwright, who wrote several plays of his own as well as collaborating on others. His own plays include the tragedies *Antonio and Mellida* and *Antonio's Revenge* (both 1599), the comedy *What you Will* (1601), and his two finest works THE MALCONTENT and THE DUTCH COURTESAN. He collaborated with Jonson and Chapman on *Eastward Ho!* (1605), which angered James I and led to a brief period of imprisonment, and with Shakespeare on *Troilus and Cressida*. After another tragedy, *The Insatiate Countess* (1610), he was imprisoned once again for offending the king and took holy orders, writing no more for the theatre.

Martin, Mary (1913–90) US actress, who made her first appearance in 1938. She went to Hollywood in 1939 but returned to the stage in 1943 in the musical *One Touch of Venus*; subsequent roles included Tchao-Ou-Niang in *Lute Song* (1945–46) and Ensign Nellie Forbush in *South Pacific* (1949). A 1955 run in a musical version of *Peter Pan* was only a mild success, but Peter became one of her best-known roles after the show was done for television. Later roles included Maria in *The Sound of Music* (1959) and She in *I Do! I Do!* (1968).

Martin Beck Theatre A 1302-seat theatre on West 45th Street, between 8th and 9th Avenues, New York, which opened in 1924 with *Madame Pompadour* and was later occupied by the Theatre Guild and then the Group Theatre. Productions staged there included the US premiere of Shaw's *The Apple Cart* (1930), Hellman's *The Watch on the Rhine* (1941), O'Neill's *The Iceman Cometh* (1946), Leonard Bernstein's *Candide* (1956), and Albee's *The Ballad of the Sad Café* (1963), *A Delicate Balance* (1966), and *All Over* (1971). A revival of Hellman's *The Little Foxes* with Elizabeth Taylor in 1981 was also extremely successful. More recently there has been a series of successful musical revivals including *Guys and Dolls* (1992) and *Kiss Me Kate* (1999).

Martinelli, Drusiano (d. c. 1607) Italian actor, who was a member of the first *commedia dell'arte* company to visit England (1577). With his wife Angelica he ran the Uniti company for some time.

His brother, **Tristano Martinelli** (c. 1557–1630), was probably the first actor to play Arlecchino. He appeared with the Confidenti, the Desiosi, the Accesi, and other companies in Paris and elsewhere.

Martínez de la Rosa, Francisco (1787–1862) Spanish playwright and statesman, who was twice prime minister of Spain. After writing several insignificant neoclassical dramas he had more success with a series of comedies influenced by Moratín and then played a major role in the development of the Romantic tradition in Spain with such plays as the historical drama *Aben-Humeya* (1830) and *La conjuración de Venecia* (1830), which were modelled on the works of Victor Hugo and other French writers. Other plays include *Doña Isabel de Solís*, which was influenced by the writing of Sir Walter Scott.

Martínez Sierra, Gregorio (1881–1947) Spanish playwright and director, who was director of the influential **Teatre Eslava** in Madrid from 1917 to 1925. His own plays include *Canción da cuna* (The Cradle Song; 1910), his best known work, *El Reino de Dios* (The Kingdom of God; 1916), *Sueño de una noche de agosto* (The Romantic Young Lady; 1918), and *Triángulo* (Take Two From One; 1930). As a director he was influential for his adoption of the ideas of Adría Gual and encouragement of García Lorca, whose first play, *La maleficio de la mariposa* (The Butterfly's Curse; 1920), he produced.

Martin-Harvey, Sir John (1863–1944) British actor-manager, who spent 14 years with Irving at the Lyceum before forming his own management there in 1899 and having an immediate success as Sydney Carton in *The Only Way*, Freeman Wills's adaptation of Dickens's *A Tale of Two Cities*. He revived the play many times during his career in response to public demand, although other acclaimed parts included Count Skariatine in Charles Hannan's *A Cigarette Maker's Romance* (1901), Hamlet (1904), the title role of *Oedipus Rex* (1912), and characters in the plays of G B Shaw. Towards the end of his career he toured in many of his old Lyceum successes.

Martini, Fausto Maria (1886–1931) Italian playwright, who became a leading writer in the *crepuscolari* tradition. Such plays as *Il giglio nero* (The Black Lily; 1913) and the acclaimed *Ridi, pagliaccio!* (Laugh, Clown, Laugh!; 1919) satirize bourgeois attitudes, while *L'altra Nanetta* (The Other Nanette; 1923) reflected the influence of Pirandello. Later plays were close in style to those of the Theatre of Silence.

Martinson Hall *See* New York Shakespeare Festival.

Martoglio, Nino (1870–1921) Italian playwright, who was the author of several notable plays written in the Sicilian dialect. His most successful work was the comedy *L'aria del continente* (1915), in which attempts to impose modern standards on an island community meet with failure; he also collaborated on a number of plays with Pirandello.

Martyn, Edward (1859–1923) Irish playwright and cofounder of the IRISH LITERARY THEATRE. His plays were influenced by Ibsen and his own Catholicism.

The Heather Field (1899) typifies his interest in the conflict between an idealistic man and a ruthless woman. In 1914 he founded the the the shortlived Irish Theatre in Dublin.

Martynov, Aleksandr Evstafevich (1816–60) Russian actor, who began as a vaudeville performer before establishing his reputation as a straight actor in the plays of Gogol, Ostrovsky, and Turgenev. He was trained by Karatygin and later became one of the first actors to favour a naturalistic style of delivery.

Marylebone Music Hall A music hall in Marylebone High Street, London, which was opened in 1858 by Sam COLLINS. It was one of the most popular venues of its kind for many years but was finally closed in 1894 having fallen into disrepair.

Marylebone Theatre *See* West London Theatre.

Mascarade An early form of folk theatre that developed in the Soule region of southern France. It had several features in common with the mummers' play, including the appearance of a hobby horse.

Masefield, John (1878–1967) British poet, playwright, and novelist, whose poetic dramas were much influenced by Greek tragedy and Japanese *Nō* theatre. The plays, which are not altogether satisfactory as performance pieces, include *The Campden Wonder* (1907), based on an unsolved murder case, *The Tragedy of Nan* (1908), and *The Tragedy of Pompey the Great* (1919); he also wrote several plays on biblical themes. He became poet laureate in 1930.

mask A covering used to conceal an actor's face or head, in order to achieve some ritualistic or symbolic effect on stage. Masks were extensively used in Greek and the earlier Roman drama (partly to accentuate facial expression), in Tudor masques (when they were called **visors**), and, covering the upper part of the face, in the *commedia dell'arte*. In the modern theatre they remain an integral feature of Japanese and Chinese drama and are occasionally used elsewhere in training or for a specific stage effect as well as in mime and pantomime. *See also* disguising.

masking piece A flat or other item of scenery used to screen the backstage area or a portion of the stage from the audience's view.

Mask Theatre *See* Belfast Civic Arts Theatre.

Mason, Marshall W *See* Circle Repertory Company.

masque A form of amateur theatrical entertainment that reached its height as an elaborate dramatic spectacle in royal courts during the early 17th century. The tradition originated in the DISGUISINGS and processions of masked figures in medieval mummers' plays and probably began to develop into its later form in Italy during the 16th century. It typically involved the arrival at festive gatherings of masked revellers, who danced with the guests and presented allegorical or mythological scenes, such productions becoming increasingly spectacular in terms of costume, scenery, and machinery. The masque soon spread to France, where it inspired the development of the MASCARADE, and was ultimately revived in England, where it became a part of many royal celebrations, often staged as a compliment to the monarch or a visiting dignitary.

In 1605 Ben Jonson and Inigo Jones collaborated on the first of a series of fabulous court masques, in which their innovations included the opening ANTI-MASQUE and the **double masque**, in which performers played more than one role. Gradually, however, the literary merits of their collaborations were sacrificed to spectacle, leading to Jonson's eventual withdrawal from the partnership on acrimonious terms and the abandonment of the form to technical virtuosity alone. Charles I and his queen took part in the dances themselves and, after the theatres were closed in 1642 by the Puritans, the masque had become too closely associated with the monarchy to survive its fall. The tradition did, nonetheless, leave at least one practical legacy – the proscenium arch designed by Inigo Jones; it also had some influence upon the development of opera.

Massey, Charles (d. 1635) English actor, who joined the Admiral's Men in 1597. His plays *Malcolm, King of Scots* (1602) and *The Siege of Dunkirk* (1603) were performed by the company but are now lost. He was named as one of the lessees of the Fortune Theatre in 1618 and again in 1622.

Massey, Raymond Hart (1896–1984) US actor and director, born in Canada, who was the senior member of a famous theatrical family. He made his first appearance at the Hart House Theatre in Ibsen's *Rosmersholm* (1922) and soon attracted attention with his powerful acting, distinctive voice, and striking looks. Subsequent successes included performances in plays by O'Neill, Shaw, and Robert Emmet Sherwood, notably as Abraham Lincoln in Sherwood's *Abe Lincoln in Illinois* (1938) – his most celebrated role. He was also acclaimed in such Shakespearean parts as Brutus, Hamlet, and Prospero and was manager of the Everyman Theatre for a time; he spent the later part of his career solely in the US and enjoyed further popularity for his appearances in the television series *Dr Kildare*.

His son, **Daniel (Raymond) Massey** (1933–98), made his London debut in 1958. Among his many West End roles were Jack Absolute in *The Rivals* (1966) and John Worthing in *The Importance of Being Earnest* (1968); for the National Theatre, Robert in Harold Pinter's *Betrayal* (1978) and Jack Tanner in Shaw's *Man and Superman* (1981); and, for the Royal Shakespeare Company, Aguecheek in *Twelfth Night* (1983) and Henry Trebell in Granville Barker's *Waste* (1985). In 1987 he played Ben Stone in Stephen Sondheim's musical *Follies*.

Raymond Massey's daughter, **Anna Massey** (1937–), has also become well-known on stage and screen. She established her reputation in *The Reluctant Débutante* (1955); roles since then have included Lady Teazle (1962) and parts in the plays of Shaw, Tennessee Williams, Chekhov, and Simon Gray. In 1993 she starred with Ian Holm in Pinter's *Moonlight* and in 1995 she played Elizabeth I in a National Theatre production of Schiller's *Mary Stuart*.

Massinger, Philip (1583–1640) English playwright, who wrote about 40 plays, of which roughly half survive. A frequent collaborator with such notable contemporaries as Tourneur, Dekker, and Fletcher, he became chief dramatist of the King's Men in 1625. Best known for A NEW WAY TO PAY OLD DEBTS, he was also the author of such plays as *The Duke of Milan* (1620), *The Roman Actor* (1626), *The Great Duke of Florence* (1627), and the comedies *The City Madam* (1632) and *The Guardian* (1633).

Master Builder, The (*Bygmester Solness*) A play by Henrik IBSEN. First performance: Berlin, 1893. The play revolves around the distinguished architect Halvard Solness, who is disturbed when a young woman challenges his view of life; she also acts as a catalyst for the guilt he feels towards his own wife and for his concern that he is losing both his idealism and artistic integrity. It ends in tragedy.

Master of Santiago, The (*Le Maître de Santiago*) A play by Henri de MONTHERLANT. First performance: Paris, 1948. The hero, Don Álvaro, is reluctant to compromise his ideals in order to restore his fortunes; his daughter Mariana ultimately supports him.

Master of the Revels An English court official, who was in charge of theatrical productions at Court from the reign of Henry VII until 1737. Working under the LORD CHAMBERLAIN, he began as the organizer of various court revels until, in 1558, the current holder – Sir Thomas Cawarden – was also given powers to exercize the role of censor in the English theatre. As sole issuer of theatrical licences the Revels Office wielded great influence until its eventual abolition in 1737, when its powers passed to the Lord Chamberlain. Noted members of the Revels Office included Sir Thomas Benger, Thomas Blagrove, Sir Edmund Tilney, and Sir Henry Herbert.

mastersingers *See meistersänger.*

Matchmaker, The A play by Thorton WILDER, based on his earlier play *The Merchant of Yonkers* (1938), which was adapted from a play by Johann Nepomuk Nestroy. First performance: Edinburgh Festival, 1954. The play concerns a grain merchant who goes to a matchmaker in search of a wife, only to have her decide she wants him for herself. The play was the source of the musical HELLO DOLLY!.

Mathews, Charles (1776–1835) British actor, who became famous for his portrayal of eccentrics. Set on a stage career from an early age, Mathews first attracted attention when he and another youth paid 15 guineas to be allowed to present *Richard III* at the Richmond Theatre, in which they fought an exceptionally long duel, each refusing to be killed. After engagements at Dublin, Swansea, and elsewhere, he was taken on by George Colman the Younger at the Haymarket in 1803 and rapidly made a reputation as a comedian. Seasons at Drury Lane and Covent Garden followed, during which he appeared in such roles as Falstaff and Sir Peter Teazle. He then evolved his own one-man shows, called *Mr Mathews At Home*, in which he toured successfully for 20 years, even after being crippled in a carriage accident in 1814.

His son was the actor **Charles James Mathews** (1803–78), who with Frederick Yates replaced his father as manager of the Adelphi Theatre in 1835. He then joined Madame VESTRIS at the Olympic in his own comedy *The Humpbacked Lover* (1835). Three years later he married her and together they went into management at Covent Garden. By 1842 he was bankrupt in spite of producing over 100 plays, including *London Assurance*. He and his wife subsequently appeared at Drury Lane and the Haymarket before taking over the Lyceum in 1847. When his wife died he married the actress **Lizzie Davenport** (d. 1899) and later made a world tour.

Mathurins, Théâtre des A theatre in the rue des Mathurins, Paris, which was opened in 1906 by Sacha GUITRY. It became a popular venue for *boulevard* plays before being taken over by the Pitoëffs in 1934, subsequently being used for the presentation of plays by Ibsen, Pirandello, and Shaw amongst others. In 1939 the management changed hands again and the theatre's programme came to include numerous revivals of classic plays by such authors as Molière.

matinée A performance given during the afternoon (or, rarely, the morning), as opposed to those given in the evening. The first recorded matinée performance was given at the Olympic Theatre in New York in 1843. Many theatres offer matinées once or twice a week; they tend to attract audiences consisting of children and organized outings.

Matthews, A(lfred) E(dward) (1869–1960) British actor, who began as a call boy, stage manager, understudy, and touring actor before achieving success in innumerable West End roles in the plays of Pinero, Barrie, Galsworthy, and others. In 1910 he made his New York debut as Algernon in Wilde's *The Importance of Being Earnest*. Later in his career he was acclaimed in William Douglas Home's comedy *The Chiltern Hundreds* (1949). He repeated his success in New York, in the subsequent film, and in a sequel, *The Manor of Northstead* (1954).

Matthews, (James) Brander (1852–1929) US playwright and theatre historian, who spent his career at Columbia University. His books on the theatre greatly influenced professional critics and the general theatre-going public in the US.

Matthews, Jessie (Margaret Matthews; 1907–81) British actress, who began as a dancer in pantomime and revue and later became a popular star of musical comedy. In 1927 she triumphed in the revue *One Dam Thing After Another*, while a year later she starred in Coward's *This Year of Grace*; in 1930, she reached perhaps the height of her fame in *Ever Green*. Songs with which she became identified included 'A Room With a View' and 'My Heart Stood Still'. Subsequently she was equally successful in films and as Mrs Dale in the long-running radio serial *Mrs Dale's Diary*.

Maude, Cyril (1861–1951) British actor-manager, whose successful career began in the US in 1884. He was comanager, with Frederick Harrison, of the Haymarket from 1896 to 1905, where, with his wife Winifred EMERY as leading lady, he staged a series of distinguished productions. In 1905 he moved to the Playhouse, which he ran for 10 years. He also served as president of the Royal Academy of Dramatic Art.

Maugham, W(illiam) Somerset (1874–1965) British novelist, playwright, and short-story writer, whose works are characterized by his clear simple style and shrewd understanding of human nature. He wrote his first play in 1904 and by 1908 had four plays, including the marital comedy *Lady Frederick*, running simultaneously in London. Subsequent dramas (mostly comedies of manners) included *Our Betters* (1917), a satire on social-climbers in the US, HOME AND BEAUTY (1919), THE CIRCLE (1921), *East of Suez* (1922), which brilliantly recreated the atmosphere of an eastern city's streets, THE CONSTANT WIFE (1926), and *The Sacred Flame* (1928). He also wrote the anti-war play *For Services Rendered* (1932).

Maurstad, Alfred (1896–1967) Norwegian actor, who became a leading performer at the Nationaltheatret in Oslo, which he joined in 1931. He was particularly admired in plays by Bjørnson, Holberg, and Ibsen.

His wife, **Tordis Maurstad** (1901–), was acclaimed in powerful classical roles with the Norske Teatret. Her greatest successes included performances in works by Euripides, Sophocles, Ibsen, Strindberg, and O'Neill.

Alfred's son, **Toralv Maurstad** (1926–), found acclaim in both classical works by Shakespeare and others and contemporary plays. He appeared many times at the Oslo

Nye Teater, becoming manager there in 1967, and at the Nationaltheatret, which he managed from 1978 to 1986.

Max, (Alexandre) Édouard de (1869–1925) French actor, who was regarded as one of the finest actors of his day in both comedy and tragedy. Trained at the Paris Conservatoire under Worms, he was particularly admired in the tragedies of Racine and first appeared at the Comédie-Française in 1915.

Maxine Elliott's Theatre A theatre on 39th Street, between Broadway and 6th Avenue, New York, which was built for the actress after whom it was named and opened in 1908. Early productions included Jerome K Jerome's *The Passing of the Third Floor Back* (1909) and Synge's *The Playboy of the Western World* (1911), which provoked a riot. After 1934 the theatre was taken over by the Federal Theatre Project, which produced such plays as *Horse Eats Hat* and *Dr Faustus* directed by Orson Welles. Subsequently used for broadcasting, it was demolished in 1959.

Mayakovsky, Vladimir Vladimirovich (1893–1930) Russian poet and playwright, who became one of the leading figures of the Futurist movement. He had his first success in the theatre with the play *Vladimir Mayakovsky – A Tragedy*, which he wrote, directed, and performed in 1913. This was followed by *Misteriya-buff* (Mystery-Bouffe; 1918), in which he parodied aspects of Christianity and revealed his sympathies with the October Revolution. Of his other works the most important include the two satirical dramas *Klop* (The Bedbug), an allegory about the survival of the bourgeoisie under the new Soviet regime, and *Banya* (The Bath House), both of which were first produced by Meyerhold. He shot himself in his Moscow flat after a failed love affair.

Mayakovsky Theatre A theatre in Moscow, which opened in 1922 as the **Theatre of the Revolution**. It was used initially for propagandist drama but was later transformed under Popov as a venue for leading contemporary Russian plays by Pogodin and others. Popov was succeeded in 1943 by Okhlopkov, who produced numerous acclaimed productions, including works by Shakespeare and Brecht. The theatre continues to present a wide range of both Russian and foreign drama.

Mayfair Theatre The smallest commercial theatre in London, seating 310, which was originally the ballroom of the Mayfair Hotel. Designed by George Beech, it opened in 1963 with a revival of Pirandello's *Six Characters in Search of an Author*, with Sir Ralph Richardson and Barbara Jefford. Its longest running productions have included the popular revue *Beyond the Fringe* (1964–66) and Christopher Hampton's *The Philanthropist* (1970–73).

Mayne, Rutherford (Samuel Waddell; 1878–1967) Irish playwright and actor, born in Japan, who became a crucial figure in the ULSTER GROUP THEATRE. His early works are set in rural Ulster. His plays for the Abbey Theatre included *Peter* (1930) and *Bridgehead* (1934).

mazarine floor *See* mezzanine floor.

M Butterfly A play by David Henry HWANG. First performance: New York, 1988. The play, which is based on fact, deals with a French diplomat in the Far East who falls in love with and has a long relationship with a Chinese actress. The 'actress' is not only a spy but turns out to be a man.

Meadow Players *See* Oxford Playhouse.

Measure for Measure A comedy by William SHAKESPEARE, written c. 1604. First performance: c. 1604. One of the so-called 'problem plays', this dark comedy examines themes of sex, power, and corruption through the hypocritical behaviour of the powerful Angelo towards Isabella, who seeks to save the life of her condemned brother Claudio. The play's sombre tone and morally ambiguous characters meant that it was rarely performed until the 20th century.

mechane An item of stage machinery used in the ancient Greek theatre. It consisted of a large crane used to lower actors playing gods onto the stage, as if from the heavens. *See* deus ex machina.

Meddoks, Mikhail Egrovich (Michael Maddox; 1747–1825) Russian theatre manager, born in Britain. He enjoyed a monopoly of the theatre in Moscow from 1780 to 1795, when the theatre he built there (on the site of the present Bolshoi Theatre) was finally destroyed by fire. He arrived in Russia in 1767 and inherited his monopoly from Prince Ourusov; his company consisted of actors transferred from various notable private theatres.

Medea A tragedy by EURIPIDES. First performance: Athens, 431 BC. The play revolves around the powerful character of the enchantress Medea; the author's depiction of her as deeply wronged but treacherous and murderous – she kills all those around her, including her own children – has aroused much comment and controversy.

Medici, Lorenzo de' (1449–92) Italian poet and patron of the arts, who was virtual ruler of Florence as a member of the Medici family. Known as 'Lorenzo the Magnificent', he was the author of an example of the *sacra rappresentazione*, performed in Florence in 1499.

medieval drama European theatre of the Middle Ages. Following the decline of classical drama the theatre in Europe was reduced to the activities of MINSTRELS, JONGLEURS, and other itinerant performers; it only began to reawaken in the 10th century, when various religious houses started to employ theatrical techniques as part of the liturgy (*see* liturgical drama). At the same time the native FOLK THEATRE was beginning to gather impetus.

The earliest manifestations of medieval religious drama were the NEUME and TROPE, interpolations in the liturgy from which a tradition of Easter plays grew (*see* Quem Quaeritis?). The earliest surviving play to treat a nonliturgical theme was the vernacular *Jeu d'Adam*, performed in France in 1170; subsequently (in 1311), the Feast of Corpus Christi was made a fixed date for theatrical performances, stimulating the development of the MIRACLE PLAY and MYSTERY PLAY in England and France, the SACRA RAPPRESENTAZIONE in Italy, the AUTO SACRAMENTAL in Spain, and the *Geistliche Spiele* in Germany, where there was also the less well-known tradition of the SAINT PLAY.

Responsibility for the production of dramatic works (usually performed on open-air stages or on carts – *see* pageant) was taken up by town guilds in the late 14th century, by which time the drama of the secular tradition (including the ROBIN HOOD PLAY and MUMMERS' PLAY in England) was already well-developed. The allegorical and humorous MORALITY PLAY, borrowed from both secular and liturgical traditions, began the movement of the theatre away from the Church and foreshadowed the development of farce. Various royal courts, with their weakness for pageants and DISGUISING, fostered the development of a more rarified theatrical genre that ultimately became the MASQUE.

The foundation of the CONFRÉRIE DE LA PASSION in France in 1402, meanwhile, constituted the establishment of the first company to occupy a permanent playhouse, while the first professional actors in England were appointed by Henry VII in 1493 to perform INTERLUDES at Court in the winter and to tour the country with plays in the summer. By the 16th century the basic rules of tragedy, comedy, and farce – as well as the use of scenery – had been established, which enabled the fully mature theatre to emerge in the Renaissance. *See also* Elizabethan drama; Feast of Fools; Renaissance drama.

Medley, Matt *See* Aston, Anthony.

Medoff, Mark (1940–) US playwright, whose first play was *The Kramer* (1972). Subsequent successes were *The Wager* (1972), *When You Comin' Back, Red Ryder?* (1973), *The Conversion of Aaron Weiss* (1977), and *Children of a Lesser God* (1980), a play about deafness which reached Broadway and won a Tony Award. Later works include *The Heart Outright* (1986) and *The Homage That Follows* (1987).

Medwall, Henry (c. 1475–1514) English playwright, whose interlude *Fulgens and Lucrece* (c. 1500) was the first native comedy to show Italian influences. The play includes song contests, wrestling, and jousting as diversions from the main plot. He was also the author of the traditional allegorical play *Nature* (c. 1490–1501).

Meggs, Mary (d. 1691) English orange-seller popularly known as **Orange Moll**. A widow, Mrs Meggs was awarded the concession to sell oranges and other refreshments at Drury Lane when it opened in 1663. Pepys, to whom she retailed scandals concerning Nell Gwynn, refers to her several times in his *Diary*. After she fell into arrears she was replaced in 1682 and a legal dispute ensued that only ended when she died.

Mei Lanfang (1894–1961) Chinese actor, singer, and dancer, who is generally considered the greatest performer in the Chinese theatrical tradition. Having made his first professional appearance at the age of 14, he later became (from 1919 to 1935) the best-known performer of Peking Opera in the West, usually playing female (*dan*) roles and transforming them into central characters for the first time. His acting influenced Nemirovich-Danchenko, Stanislavsky, Brecht, and many others.

Meilhac, Henri (1831–97) French playwright, born in Paris. In collaboration with the writer **Ludovic Halévy** (1834–1908) he produced such successful comedies as *Froufrou* (1869) and libretti for Jacques Offenbach's operettas, notably *La Belle Hélène* (1864), *La Vie parisienne* (1866), and *La Grand-Duchesse de Gérolstein* (1867).

Meininger Company A theatre company founded in 1874 by George II, Duke of Saxe-Meiningen. Run by the duke and his wife with the help of the actor Ludwig Chronegk, the troupe made significant innovations in emphasizing the role of the director and the importance of good ensemble playing, particularly in crowd scenes. It was also influential in its use of historically accurate costume and scenery and experimental stage lighting. These ideas were spread throughout Europe by the company's many tours of Shakespearean and other classic works to London and other centres. Those who saw and admired the group before it ceased to tour in 1890 included Stanislavsky and Antoine; actors under the duke numbered amongst them Bassermann, Eysoldt, and Kainz.

Meisl, Karl (1775–1853) Austrian playwright, who was a leading writer for the Viennese theatre in the early 19th century. His many popular plays, which rely heavily on visual effects, include the satirical *Der lustige Fritz* (1818).

meistersänger (*or* mastersinger) A travelling poet and musician of medieval Germany. The *meistersängers* – who according to tradition were descended from 12 poets of ancient times – were trained in school groups, which were organized in the same way as craft guilds and competed regularly against each other; members passed through several grades before attaining the rank of master. Hans Sachs did much to revitalize the tradition in the 16th century, although the material, usually expressing a strong moralistic or religious sentiment, remained fairly restricted in terms of metre, melody, and subject matter. The tradition, which virtually disappeared after 1600, was especially strong in southern Germany, where the most important centre was Nürnberg.

Melbourne Theatre Company An Australian theatre company, which was founded at the University of Melbourne in 1953. It established its reputation with an early production of Ray Lawler's *Summer of the Seventeenth Doll* in 1955 and subsequently concentrated on works by leading contemporary Australian playwrights, including Alan Hopgood and Patrick White. It became the resident company at the **Russell Street Theatre** in 1966, and was directed by Tyrone Guthrie in 1970. In 1973 it moved into St Martin's Theatre and in 1977 into the Athenaeum Theatre, where productions have included a number of experimental dramas.

Mélite A comedy by Pierre CORNEILLE. First performance: Paris, 1629. Marking Corneille's debut as a playwright, *Mélite* concerns the love affairs and intrigues of the five central characters: Mélite and Tircis, Chloris and Philandre, and Éraste, whose unrequited love for Mélite drives him to revenge.

Mellon, Mrs Alfred (Sarah Jane Woolgar; 1824–1909) British actress, who made her London debut at the Adelphi Theatre in 1843. Her first successes were in burlesque, but later she was associated with Ben Webster's management in a series of domestic dramas. In 1860 she created the part of Anne Chute in Boucicault's *The Colleen Bawn*.

Mellon, Harriot (1777–1837) British actress, who was engaged by Sheridan at Drury Lane in 1795. She remained there, successfully playing comic parts, until her marriage to the banker Thomas Coutts in 1815. Five years later she married the Duke of St Albans.

Melmoth, Charlotte (1749–1823) US actress, born in Britain, who became highly popular in leading tragic roles at the Park Theatre in New York from 1793. Previously she had appeared at both Covent Garden and Drury Lane before moving to the US to join the American Company; later in her career she had further success at the Chestnut Street Theatre in Philadelphia.

Melo, Francisco Manuel de (1608–66) Portuguese statesman and playwright. His *Auto do fidalgo aprendiz* (The Apprentice Nobleman; c. 1646) was highly regarded in a time when little of value was being written for the Portuguese stage. It was modelled on the style of Vicente and itself had some influence upon Molière.

melodrama A form of drama, popular in the 19th century, in which emphasis is placed upon sensational plot rather than upon characterization or intellectual content. The term itself was derived from German opera of the 18th century, in which it meant a piece combining spoken dialogue with instrumental music to underscore the emotions. In the straight theatre melodrama signified the use of dramatic lighting and atmospheric effects, exaggerated heroes and villains, and improbable plots to achieve a desired emotional impact.

The plays of Pixérécourt – who was himself influenced by Goethe and Schiller – were among the first to be classed as melodramas and were enormously popular in both France and England, music playing a major role in their production. Later, however, the musical content became less important and by Victorian times melodrama had become a variety of straight drama, which could range from the overtly sensationalist productions of the penny gaff theatres to such dramatically poignant works as Leopold Lewis's *The Bells*, in which Irving had his first great success, *The Corsican Brothers* by Dion Boucicault, and *Uncle Tom's Cabin* by Harriet Beecher Stowe.

The genre, which at its height stimulated some of the most spectacular and involved productions ever staged, lost favour towards the end of the 19th century as audiences tired of its naivity, implausibility, and conventionally happy endings. However, some have argued that the form enjoyed an unnoticed renaissance in the 20th century through cinema and television. *See also* monodrama.

melodramma A form of musical play that was popular in Italy in the 18th century. It evolved from the pastoral, and influenced the development of opera.

Melpomene *See* Muses.

Melucha Theatre *See* Moscow State Jewish Theatre.

Melville, Walter (1875–1937) British manager and playwright, who – with his brother **Frederick Melville** (1879–1938) – managed the Lyceum Theatre for 25 years. The brothers staged many spectacular pantomimes there, as well as their own vivid and highly successful melodramas, which included *The Worst Woman in London* (1899) and *The Ugliest Woman on Earth* (1904).

Menaechmi A comedy by PLAUTUS. First performance: date unknown. The plot, which revolves around the confusion of identities between a pair of twins, provided the inspiration for plays by Hans Sachs and Carlo Goldoni and for Shakespeare's *The Comedy of Errors*.

Menander (c. 343 BC–292 BC) Greek playwright, who is now recognized as the leading exponent of Greek NEW COMEDY and consequently the father of the modern comic tradition. Menander was largely ignored by theatre historians until a number of his plays were discovered during the 20th century, the first in 1905. In contrast to such predecessors as Aristophanes, he placed a new emphasis upon the romantic content of his plays and reduced the role of the chorus. His sophisticated and realistic social comedies exerted a strong influence upon such Roman writers as

Plautus and Terence and, ultimately, upon the comedy of manners of Molière, Wilde, Coward, and others.

Reconstructions of his plays have included Gilbert Murray's *The Rape of the Locks* (1941), based on the *Perikeiromene*, and *The Arbitration* (1945), based on the *Epitrepontes*, as well as Vellacott's *The Misanthrope*, based on the *Dyskolos*. Highly acclaimed in his own time, Menander declined invitations to visit royal courts in both Egypt and Macedonia, preferring to remain in Athens; according to popular tradition he drowned while swimming in the harbour there.

Principal works (dates unknown):
Aspis.
Dyskolos.
Epitrepontes.
Heros.
Misoumenes.
Orge.
Perikeiromene.
Samia.

Mendes, Sam(uel) (1965–) British director, who was appointed director of Chichester's Minerva Theatre at the age of 23. He became nationally known with London productions of *Troilus and Cressida* (1990) and *The Rise and Fall of Little Voice* (1992), before being put in charge of the DONMAR WAREHOUSE Theatre (1992). His many acclaimed productions at the Donmar have included Mamet's *Glengarry Glen Ross* (1994), a revival of Sondheim's *Company* (1995), and David Hare's *The Blue Room* (1998). In 1999 he moved successfully into direction for the cinema.

Menken, Adah Isaacs (Dolores Adios Fuertes; 1835–68) US actress, who became famous in a stage adaptation of Byron's *Mazeppa*, which she first played in London in 1861, wearing a scanty costume and riding a horse. She later repeated the role with equal success in New York and then at Astley's Amphitheatre.

Menken, Alan (1949–) US composer, who has enjoyed great success with the lyricist **Howard Ashman** (1950–91). Their LITTLE SHOP OF HORRORS ran for years off-Broadway and led to an association with the Disney organization. After several critics praised their score for the animated film *Beauty and the Beast* as superior to most of the fare on Broadway, a live-action musical was made of it, which opened in 1994.

Men's Dramatic Ceremony *See* mummers' play.

Men Without Shadows A play by Jean-Paul SARTRE, which has also been translated as *The Victors*. First performance: Paris, 1946. The plot concerns the conflicts within a group of captured Resistance fighters, who ultimately choose to confess in the face of torture.

Mercer, David (1928–80) British playwright, whose dramas explore themes of social alienation and conflict between classes and generations. He began with a series of plays for television, before writing *Ride a Cock Horse*, his first full-length work for the stage, in 1965. Subsequent plays included *After Haggerty* (1970), about a drama critic, *Flint* (1970), about a roguish Irish priest, *Cousin Vladimir* (1978), depicting a Soviet emigré's arrival in Britain, and *No Limits to Love* (1980).

Merchant, Vivien (Vivien Thomson; 1929–82) British actress, who became well-known in the plays of her then husband, Harold Pinter, playing such roles as Sarah in *The Lover* (1963), Ruth in *The Homecoming* (1965), and Anna in *Old Times* (1971). Other roles included Lady Macbeth (1967) for the Royal Shakespeare Company and Bertha in Joyce's *Exiles* (1970).

Merchant of Venice, The A tragicomedy by William SHAKESPEARE, written c. 1596–97. First performance: date unknown. Drawing on numerous sources, the play depicts the outwitting of the Jewish usurer Shylock by the disguised Portia after he has demanded a pound of the merchant Antonio's flesh in settlement of a bond. Themes of the play include justice and mercy, religious discrimination, and the logic of the law. Since the 19th century most interest has centred on the commanding figure of Shylock, and the question of whether or not the play is anti-Semitic.

Mercier, Louis-Sébastien (1740–1814) French playwright, remembered for his bourgeois dramas in the style of Denis Diderot. These include *La Brouette du vinaigrier* (1755) and *Le Déserteur* (1782). He also produced plays on historical themes, adaptations of Shakespeare, and a *Traité du théâtre ou Nouvel Essai sur l'art dramatique* (1773), in which he developed Diderot's dramatic theories.

Mercury Theatre A theatre in Notting Hill Gate, London, which was opened in 1933 by Ashley DUKES. Seating 150, it concentrated on performances of ballet and new drama, notably T S Eliot's *Murder in the Cathedral* (1935), Auden and Isherwood's *The Ascent of F6* (1937), and O'Neill's *Days Without End* (1943). Subsequent productions included much poetic drama and children's plays. The Ballet Rambert used the theatre exclusively for some time up to 1966, after which plays were staged there by the International Theatre Club and touring companies.

Another theatre of the same name opened in Auckland, New Zealand, in 1910 as a cinema. After several changes of name, it acquired a resident company in 1968 (run by the **Auckland Theatre Trust**) and was reconstructed to provide two auditoriums. Recent years have seen an emphasis upon productions by native playwrights from New Zealand.

See also Comedy Theatre.

Mermaid Society A theatre group established in London in the 1900s to present Elizabethan and Jacobean works. Notable productions included Milton's *Comus* (1903) and Jonson's *A Hue and Cry After Cupid* (1908).

Mermaid Theatre A theatre in Puddle Dock, Blackfriars, London, that was opened in 1959 under Bernard MILES. It began as a private theatre in the garden of Miles's house in 1951, while its Elizabethan stage was first constructed in 1953 at the Royal Exchange. The new theatre of 1959, seating 500, was converted from a bombed Victorian warehouse and became an important venue for revivals of Jacobean and Elizabethan drama as well as contemporary works; notable productions in recent years have included the musical shows *Cowardy Custard* (1972), *Cole* (1974), and *Side by Side by Sondheim* (1976). In 1981 the theatre was reopened – including the Molecule Club studio theatre for children – as part of a controversial office complex and then experienced a financial crisis after a series of failures. After a year's occupation by the

Royal Shakespeare Company (1987–88), the theatre launched a new programme of commercial drama. However, a series of financial and other difficulties led to its closure in 1997; its future is now uncertain.

Merman, Ethel (Ethel Zimmermann; 1909–84) US actress, who began her career in 1928 in cabaret. Her trumpet voice and clarity of diction made her an inspiration for great composers including George Gershwin (*Girl Crazy*: 1931, her Broadway debut), Cole Porter (*Anything Goes*: 1934), Irving Berlin (*Annie Get Your Gun*: 1946; *Call Me Madam*: 1950), and Jules Styne (*Gypsy*: 1959). She also successfully took over the lead in *Hello, Dolly!* (1970).

Merrick, David (1911–2000) US producer known for his outrageous efforts to put his shows in the public eye; however, he also produced many plays of a serious nature. His hits included *Fanny* (1954), *Jamaica* (1957), *A Taste of Honey* (1960), *Hello Dolly!* (1964), *Marat/Sade* (1965), and *42nd Street* (1980).

Merry, Anne (Anne Brunton; 1768–1808) British actress. The daughter of a provincial theatre manager, she was engaged at Covent Garden in 1795, after earlier appearances in Bath. Her first husband was the dramatist Robert Merry. In 1796 she was invited by Thomas WIGNELL, who became her second husband, to the US. There she became a leading tragic actress before marrying William WARREN and dying in childbirth.

Merry Wives of Windsor, The A comedy by William SHAKESPEARE, written c. 1597. First performance: c. 1597. Probably written for performance before Elizabeth I, the play presents Falstaff's downfall at the hands of two women he pursues for their wealth. It differs from Shakespeare's other comedies by being set in Elizabethan England, rather than an imagined time and place, but retains an element of fantasy, chiefly through the mythological figure of Herne the Hunter.

Merson, Billy (William Henry Thompson; 1881–1947) British comedian and clown, who became popular for such songs as 'The Spaniard That Blighted my Life'. Later he appeared in revue and musical comedy and had a long run in *Rose Marie* at Drury Lane (1925).

mescidato A form of secular drama that developed in Italy from the religious *sacra rappresentazione*. Based on nonliturgical themes, but employing the structure of the religious drama, the *mescidato* led ultimately to the development of the pastoral towards the end of the 16th century.

Messel, Oliver Hilary Sambourne (1905–78) British stage designer, who established his reputation with his costumes and masks for Cochran's revues in the late 1920s. His early sets, which included that for Novello's *Glamorous Night* (1935), were noted for their sophistication; subsequently he developed a more romantic style. Among others, he designed sets for the plays of Wycherley, Shakespeare, Sheridan, Fry, and Anouilh.

Messenius, Johannes (1579–1636) Swedish playwright, who wrote a number of plays based on Swedish history. Six of his plays, the earliest of which is *Disa* (1611), survive.

Method, the A mainly US development of the theories of STANISLAVSKY concerning the psychology of acting. Stanislavsky's ideas were imported to the US by Richard Boleslavsky and were first explored by his Laboratory Theatre in New York during the 1920s. One of his pupils, Lee Strasberg, subsequently developed the system with the Group Theatre and, in 1947, combined with Elia Kazan and others in founding the Actors' Studio; this became the principal training centre in the Method technique. Actors trained in the approach are taught to seek out and identify with their characters' inner motivations. For this reason the Method has provoked considerable hostility. Its critics point to an inevitable tendency towards introspective mumbled speeches. It has, however, been used to good effect in many contemporary plays and even more significantly in the cinema, by such noted exponents as Marlon Brando.

Metropolitan Casino *See* Broadway Theatre.

Metropolitan Music Hall A music hall in the Edgware Road, London, which began as a concert room in an inn but was rebuilt in 1862 to seat 4000 people (named **Turnham's Grand Concert Hall**). It became the Metropolitan in 1864 and thrived until 1897, when it was again reconstructed; subsequently it declined into a venue for touring companies, wrestling, and television, being demolished in 1963.

Metropolitan Theatre A theatre on Broadway, New York, which opened in 1854 with limited success. Successively managed by Laura Keene, Burton, Boucicault (who renamed it the Winter Garden in 1859), and Edwin Booth, it saw performances from such distinguished players as Rachel, John Sleeper Clarke, Charlotte Cushman, Sothern, and the Florences. Edwin Booth made a record 100 appearances as Hamlet here in the 1864–65 season. Among other productions were dramatizations of Dickens by Boucicault, Joseph Jefferson's *Rip Van Winkle*, and works by Shakespeare and Racine. In 1867 the theatre was destroyed by fire.

Meyerhold, Vsevolod Emilievich (1874–1942) Russian actor and director, a leading exponent of experimental drama. He made his name at the Moscow Art Theatre, which he joined in 1898. A pupil of Nemirovich-Danchenko, he soon established himself as an important theorist of the avant-garde, forming his own company in 1902 and becoming assistant to Stanislavsky for a time. His development of the impersonal method known as BIO-MECHANICS led to conflict first with Stanislavsky and subsequently (1908) with Vera Komisarjevskaya. After this he led his own company in St Petersburg and further developed his ideas of theatrical **Constructivism**, which called for the use of abstract multilevel settings.

Following the Revolution of 1917 Meyerhold became the first director to stage new Soviet drama by such authors as Mayakovsky. Later, however, he fell into official disfavour for resisting the policy of Socialist Realism. In 1938 he was arrested and subsequently both he and his wife died in mysterious circumstances.

mezzanine floor (*or* mazarine floor) An area below the stage, part of the cellar, used for the manipulation of traps. In the US the term is also applied to the dress circle.

Mezzetino A character of the *commedia dell'arte*, one of the *zanni*. Costantini excelled in the role, usually dressed in red and white; in the French tradition the character was known as Mezzetin and provided one of Préville's most celebrated parts.

Michell, Keith (1928–) Australian actor and singer, who has divided his career between Australia and Britain. He made his debut in 1947 in Adelaide, then appeared at the Old Vic and the Young Vic before joining the Royal Shakespeare Company and touring Australia. He has been praised in several Shakespearean roles, among them Antony in *Antony and Cleopatra* (1956), as well as in such musicals as *Robert and Elizabeth* (1964) and *Man of La Mancha* (1968). Other successes have included Ronald Millar's *Abelard and Heloise* (1970), Rostand's *Cyrano de Bergerac*, and Shaw's *The Apple Cart*, in which he appeared while artistic director (1974–77) of the Chichester Festival. Plays since then have included *On the Rocks* (1982), *Cage aux Folles* (1984), *Aspects of Love* (1992), and *Scrooge* (1993).

Mickiewicz, Adam (1798–1855) Polish poet and playwright, who inaugurated the Romantic movement in Poland. A native of Vilna, he was deported to Russia in 1823 and subsequently lived in Italy, Germany, and France. His most celebrated play, *Dziady* (Forefather's Eve), was written in four parts and not performed until 1901, since when it has been regularly presented; its combination of patriotism and mysticism represent a unique development of Romantic drama.

Middle Comedy A style of ancient Greek comedy that developed from OLD COMEDY, specifically in the last two plays of Aristophanes. Less exuberant and more strongly plotted than earlier works, the plays of this period showed a preoccupation with social rather than political issues and prepared the way for the NEW COMEDY that succeeded it.

Middlesex Music Hall A music hall in Drury Lane, London, which was popularly known as **Old Mo**. Originally called the **Mogul Saloon**, it became a venue for music hall entertainments in 1847 and was renamed in 1851. Leading performers who appeared there for the first time included Dan Leno. It was rebuilt in 1872, 1891, and 1911, when it became the New Middlesex Theatre of Varieties seating 3000 (*see* Winter Garden Theatre).

Middleton, Thomas (c. 1570–1627) English playwright, who often worked in collaboration with his contemporaries. With William Rowley he wrote such plays as THE CHANGELING, while with Dekker he wrote *The Honest Whore* (1604–05) and *The Roaring Girl* (1610). His own plays range from comedies about London society, including *A Trick to Catch the Old One* (1605) and *A Chaste Maid in Cheapside* (1911), to the more romantic *Anything for a Quiet Life* and the satirical WOMEN BEWARE WOMEN. His political satire *A Game of Chess* (1624) was immensely popular both on stage and, after it was banned, in print.

Midsummer's Night's Dream, A A comedy by William SHAKESPEARE, written c. 1595. First performance: date unknown. One of Shakespeare's most popular works, the play combines realism with fantasy as the relationships of the fairies, ruled by Oberon and Titania, become entangled with those of the human lovers and the antics of a group of amateur actors. In the 20th century the play inspired notable productions by Max Reinhardt and Peter Brook, among others.

Mielziner, Jo (1901–76) US designer of stage sets, lighting, and costumes, born in Paris. His first designs were for the Lunts's production of Molnár's *The Guardsman* (1924). Subsequent productions included *Romeo and Juliet* (1934), *Hamlet* (1936), Maxwell Anderson's *Winterset* (1935) and *High Tor* (1937), Tennessee Williams's *The*

Glass Menagerie (1945), *A Streetcar Named Desire* (1947), and *Cat on a Hot Tin Roof* (1955), *Finian's Rainbow* (1947), *Guys and Dolls* (1950), and *The King and I* (1951).

Mikado, The A light opera with a Japanese theme by GILBERT and Sullivan. First performance: Savoy Theatre, London, 1885. The plot centres on Ko-Ko, who has been made Lord High Executioner of the town of Titipu. Nanki-Poo, son of the Mikado (emperor), disguises himself as a wandering minstrel to woo Yum-Yum, Ko-Ko's ward, whom Ko-Ko himself wishes to marry. All is complicated by the arrival of the Mikado and Nanki-Poo's chosen bride, as well as by the report of Ko-Ko's execution of the minstrel.

Although partly inspired by a contemporary enthusiasm for all things oriental, the show actually satirizes British attitudes to class and law.

Mikhoels, Salomon Mikhailovich (Salomon Michailovich Vosky; 1890–1948) Jewish actor, who became a leading performer at the Moscow State Jewish Theatre, which he managed from 1927. He began his career in St Petersburg under Granovsky; his later successes included Sholom Aleichem's *Agents* (1921) and *King Lear* (1935).

Miles, Bernard, Baron (1907–91) British actor and director, who made his debut in a minor role in *Richard III* at the New Theatre in 1930. Subsequently he was acclaimed with the Old Vic company in such roles as Iago (1942) and Face in *The Alchemist* (1947). He also created his own solo act as a West Country rustic and, in 1951, founded the MERMAID THEATRE, where his roles included Caliban and Macbeth. He opened the new Mermaid Theatre in 1959 with *Lock Up Your Daughters*, his own adaptation of Fielding's *Rape upon Rape*; subsequently he directed and played in many productions, ranging from Brecht to Shakespeare. He was knighted in 1969 and made a baron in 1979.

Miles Gloriosus A stock character of the New Comedy of ancient Greece. A boastful but cowardly soldier, he also featured in plays by the Roman writer Plautus and subsequently in the *commedia dell'arte* as Il CAPITANO. He also suggested aspects of Shakespeare's Pistol, Falstaff, and Parolles.

Miles's Musick House *See* Sadler's Wells Theatre.

Millar, Gertie (1879–1952) British musical comedy actress, who became one of the 'Gaiety Girls' of George EDWARDES in 1901, playing Cora Bellamy in *The Toreador*. She remained with Edwardes for a number of years, went to New York in *The Girls of Gottenburg* (1908), and returned to the Gaiety Theatre in *Our Miss Gibbs* (1909). Among her other shows were *The Quaker Girl* (1910), *Gipsy Love* (1912), and *Flora* (1918). After the death of her first husband, the composer Lionel Monckton, she married the Earl of Dudley.

Millar, Sir Ronald (1919–98) British actor and playwright, whose first great success was the farce *The Bride and the Bachelor* (1956), followed by the sequel *The Bride Comes Back* (1960). Earlier plays included *Murder From Memory* (1942), *Frieda* (1946), *Champagne for Delilah* (1949), and *Waiting for Gillian* (1954), based upon a novel by Nigel Balchin. After his commercial success of the late 1950s he dramatized three C P Snow novels, *The Affair* (1961), *The New Man* (1962), and *The Masters* (1963), before writing the musical *Robert and Elizabeth* (1964) about the Brownings. Subsequent plays included *Number Ten* (1967), *Abelard and Heloise* (1970), and two more adaptations of Snow's novels: *The Case in Question* (1975) and *A Coat of Varnish* (1982). He also wrote many of Margaret Thatcher's speeches.

Miller, Arthur (1915–) US playwright, who established his reputation with ALL MY SONS (1947). Subsequently DEATH OF A SALESMAN (1948) won Miller a Pulitzer Prize and recognition as a leading US playwright. His plays – most of which depict aspects of US family life – tackle such themes as illusion and reality, hypocrisy, reconciliation, and self-discovery; THE CRUCIBLE was a scathing attack on McCarthyism, while his unhappy marriage to the film star Marilyn Monroe influenced AFTER THE FALL. More recent works have failed to excite equal attention in the US, but have found an appreciative audience in Britain.

Principal works:
  All My Sons: 1947.
  Death of a Salesman: 1948.
  The Crucible: 1953.
  A VIEW FROM THE BRIDGE: 1955.
  After the Fall: 1964.
  Incident at Vichy: 1964.
  The Price: 1968.
  Playing for Time: 1981.
  Danger: Memory!: 1987.
  The Last Yankee: 1991.
  The Ride Down Mt Morgan: 1991, revised 1999.
  Broken Glass: 1994.

Miller, Henry (1860–1926) US actor, born in Britain, who made his debut in Toronto in 1878. As leading man with the Empire Theatre Stock Company he played Sydney Carton in *The Only Way* and produced and played in Vaughan Moody's *The Great Divide* (1906). His other successes included Charles Kennedy's *The Servant in the House* (1908) and Moody's *The Faith Healer* (1910). In 1916 he opened HENRY MILLER'S THEATRE in New York.

Miller, Jonathan (1934–) British director, who first attracted attention as a member of the Cambridge Footlights revue *Beyond the Fringe* in 1960. A qualified doctor of medicine, Miller first ventured into direction in 1962, when he directed Osborne's *Under Plain Cover* at the Royal Court Theatre; subsequently he directed plays in both London and New York, ranging from Sheridan's *The School for Scandal* (1968), *King Lear* (1969) with Michael Hordern, and *The Merchant of Venice* (1970) with Olivier, to Chekhov's *The Seagull* (1973). As an associated director of the National Theatre from 1973 to 1975 he continued with productions of Beaumarchais, Shakespeare, and Peter Nichols, among others, while works elsewhere have included further plays by Chekhov (notably *Three Sisters* in 1976), Ibsen, and Wilde. Since the late 1970s he has also directed a series of operas. He was artistic director of the Old Vic from 1988 to 1990. More recent productions include *King Lear* (1989) and *A Midsummer Night's Dream* (1996). He has also written books on a range of subjects and presented several television series.

Miller, Marilyn (Mary Ellen Reynolds; 1898–1936) US actress, who became a major star of musical comedy. Her greatest successes included *Sally* (1921), *Sunny* (1926), *As Thousands Cheer* (1933), and *Crazy Quilt*.

Millo, Mattei (1814–96) Romanian actor and playwright, who was the first artistic director of the Romanian National Theatre in Bucharest. His plays were largely satirical comedies lampooning contemporary society; as a director he did much to improve standards of performance.

Mills, Florence (1895–1927) US Black singer, whose vaudeville act won her a place in the New York revue *Shuffle Along* in 1922. She was brought to London by C B Cochran in his revue *Dover Street to Dixie* and later starred in *Blackbirds* (1926) both on Broadway and in London, being especially remembered for her song 'Bye Bye Blackbird'.

Mills, Sir John (Lewis Ernest Watts; 1908–) British actor, who made his debut at the London Hippodrome in 1929 and the following year played Lord Fancourt Babberley in Brandon Thomas's *Charley's Aunt* at the New Theatre. During the 1930s he played leading parts in several musicals, including Coward's *Cavalcade* (1931); in 1939 he joined the Old Vic company to play Puck in *A Midsummer Night's Dream* and Young Marlow in Goldsmith's *She Stoops to Conquer*. He made his New York debut in 1961, playing T E Lawrence in Rattigan's *Ross*. Well-known for his numerous films, he continued to appear in the theatre in plays as varied as Priestley's *The Good Companions* (1974) and Brian Clark's *The Petition* (1987). His daughters **Hayley Mills** (1946–) and **Juliet Mills** (1941–) are both actresses.

Milne, A(lan) A(lexander) (1882–1956) British novelist and playwright, best known for his Winnie-the-Pooh stories. He also wrote several light comedies, including *Mr Pim Passes By* (1919), *The Dover Road* (1923), and *The Truth about Blayds* (1923) as well as *Toad of Toad Hall* (1929), a highly successful stage adaptation of Kenneth Grahame's *The Wind in the Willows*.

Milton, Ernest (1890–1974) British actor, born in the US, who enjoyed a strong reputation in the West End following his first London appearance in 1914. He became a member of the Old Vic company in 1918 and won acclaim for Shakespearean and other classic parts, including Shylock and Macbeth. Other successes included Pirandello's *Henry IV* (1925), Ansky's *The Dybbuk* (1927), Patrick Hamilton's *Rope* (1929), Laurence Housman's *Prunella* (1930), Massinger's *A New Way To Pay Old Debts* (1944), and Hochwälder's *The Strong Are Lonely* (1955). He also appeared in two plays of his own, *Paganini* and *Timon of Athens*; he joined the Royal Shakespeare Company in 1962, appearing in plays by Middleton and Camus among others.

Milton, John (1608–74) English poet and author of the closet drama *Samson Agonistes* (1671; performed 1900). He also wrote two masques: *Comus*, on the subject of chastity, was first performed at Ludlow Castle in 1634, while *Arcades* (1633) deals with family affection. Both were probably written at the request of the musician Henry Lawes.

Milwaukee Repertory Theatre A theatre company in Milwaukee, Wisconsin, which was founded as the Fred Miller Theatre in 1954. It currently has 720-seat and 198-seat stages, as well as a cabaret.

mime (*or* dumb show) A form of theatrical performance in which no words are spoken and meaning is conveyed through movement and gesture alone. In ancient Greek and Roman drama the term had a somewhat different meaning; it was used both of comic entertainments in which the emphasis was upon physical action (including nudity and real executions in the later Roman period) and of certain literary pieces intended for reading rather than for actual performance. The former were presented by small casts who wore distinctive costumes but no masks and acted out simple, largely improvised, plots; they enjoyed great popularity and eventually overshadowed all other contemporary drama. In the 5th century AD the overt vulgarity of these productions led to the excommunication of all mime performers by the Church. Writers of the second type of mime, which was eventually absorbed by the ATELLANA, included Laberius and Publilius Syrus.

The modern silent mime show is descended from the *commedia dell'arte*, which itself borrowed from the Roman tradition. In the early 19th century Deburau established France as the leading centre for the genre; celebrated French performers in the 20th century included Jean-Louis Barrault and Marcel Marceau. Elsewhere mime is important primarily as a tool in the training of actors.

Minack Theatre An open-air theatre in Porthcurno, Cornwall, which was founded in 1933 by Miss Rowena Cade. Amateur companies presented plays at the theatre, which was carved out of a cliff, until 1939, when World War II forced its closure; it reopened in 1949 and flourished after 1959, when the Minack Theatre Society was formed. A wide variety of plays are presented there before an audience of up to 600 throughout the summer by companies from all over Britain.

Minerva Theatre *See* Chichester Festival Theatre.

Minetta Lane Theatre A 407-seat theatre in New York's Greenwich Village, constructed out of what was an old tin can factory in 1984. Plays seen at the Minetta, the largest of the Village theatres, have included Martha Clarke's avant-garde dance presentation, *The Garden of Earthly Delights* (1988), *Other People's Money* (1989), and *Travels With My Aunt* (1994).

Minna von Barnhelm A comedy by Gotthold LESSING. First performance: 1767. The play deals with the unfair dismissal of an army officer after the Seven Years' War and the effect this has upon his relationship with his fiancée. It is notable for its spirited dialogue and excellent characterization.

Minotis, Alexis (1900–90) Greek actor and director, who was closely associated with the performance of many classical Greek works as well as with the tragedies of Shakespeare and contemporary plays. He made his debut in 1925 and, after appearances in the US, joined the Greek National Theatre, for whom he directed (1939–67 and 1974–80) many plays, often acting in them himself. He also produced many productions at Epidauros and visited London in such roles as Hamlet and Oedipus. He ran his own company from 1967 to 1974, presenting mostly modern dramas.

Minskoff Theatre A 1621-seat theatre on Broadway, New York, built into an office building between 44th and 45th streets. It opened in 1973 with the musical *Irene*. Productions staged there since have included a revival of *West Side Story* (1980), the revue *Black and Blue* (1989), and Lloyd Webber's *Sunset Boulevard* (1994). It has the largest backstage area of the Broadway theatres.

minstrel A musician or other entertainer in medieval Europe. Initially the term was used solely of those performers in the service of a particular nobleman; later, however, it was also used of the travelling entertainers formerly known as JONGLEURS. The earliest minstrels emerged during the 12th century, inheriting the ancient traditions preserved by the GOLIARDs, and were usually attached to a court on a fairly permanent basis, as in the case of Richard I's **Blondel**. In the 14th and 15th centuries minstrel guilds were formed in many European towns, organizing the training of these performers and protecting their interests against their itinerant counterparts. Little of their music, which was largely improvised until the 15th century, has survived; the tradition eventually died out during the 16th century.

minstrel show A US musical entertainment featuring performers in blackface, based on an idealized picture of slave life in the Old South. In its heyday, roughly between the 1850s and 1870s, it was the most important form of musical entertainment in the US. Though at first the performers were all White, it did incorporate genuine Black material, both in the songs and in the dancing, and was thereby important in creating that mixture of African and European styles that became American popular music.

The minstrel show developed a standardized form, the best-known part being the first act, in which the performers were set in a semicircle on stage with the 'interlocutor' (master of ceremonies) in the middle and the two main comedians, Mr Tambo and Mr Bones, on the ends. This act often ended in the grand parade of the 'cakewalk'. The second act was usually a series of speciality acts and the third a burlesque, often incorporating satire on contemporary issues.

Thomas D Rice made blackfaced acts popular by the late 1830s, the minstrel show proper being created by Dan Emmett in 1843 and standardized by Edwin Cristy in the 1850s. By the time of the Civil War there were some genuinely Black companies, the most famous being that of James A Bland, but even those performers 'blacked up' with burnt cork. The minstrel show eventually declined, its US performers moving into vaudeville, its British counterparts into the music hall or touring seaside resorts. In Britain there were several idealized revivals in the 20th century, including *The Black-and-White Minstrel Show*, which was popular on television and at the Victoria Palace Theatre in the 1960s. In the US, however, a greater sensitivity to the degrading nature of blackface had consigned the form to the history books long before this.

miracle play In medieval France a SAINT PLAY dealing with events from the life of the Virgin Mary or one of the saints. In England the term was used interchangeably with MYSTERY PLAY.

Miracle Worker, The A play by William Gibson. First performance: New York, 1959, after a television version of 1957. The plot, which is based on fact, concerns the efforts of Anne Sullivan to teach the blind and deaf Helen Keller.

Mira de Amescua, Antonio (c. 1574–1644) Spanish playwright, who wrote several influential comedies and plays on religious and historical themes. His best-known work was *El esclavo del demonio* (The Devil's Slave; 1612) in which he explores the concept of damnation.

Miranda, Francisco de Sá de (1485–1558) Portuguese playwright, who wrote the earliest examples of Portuguese neoclassical drama. His two comedies *Estrangeiros* and *Vilhalpandos* were both based upon the rules of the classical drama of Italy, which he visited in the 1520s. Fragments of his tragedy *Cleopatra* survive.

Mirbeau, Octave (1848–1917) French novelist, playwright, and critic. His plays, naturalistic dramas influenced by Henry Becque, include *Les Mauvais Bergers* (1897) and the satirical *Les Affaires sont les affaires* (Business is Business; 1903).

Mirren, Helen (1946–) British actress, who began her career with the National Youth Theatre. She began her long association with the Royal Shakespeare Company in 1968 and was highly acclaimed in such roles as Ophelia (1970), Lady Macbeth (1974), and Moll Cutpurse in Middleton and Dekker's *The Roaring Girl* (1983). Contemporary works have included David Hare's *Teeth 'n' Smiles* (1975) at the Royal Court and Peter Shaffer's *The Gift of the Gorgon* in New York (1994). She was also much admired in *The Duchess of Malfi* at the Royal Exchange Theatre in 1980 and in Turgenev's *A Month in the Country* at the Albery in 1993. In the 1980s and 1990s she appeared frequently in films and on television.

Mirror Theatre *See* Holborn Theatre Royal.

Misalliance A play by G B SHAW. First performance: Duke of York's Theatre, 1910. The play, which was greeted with puzzlement at first because of its rather surreal plot, debates the relationship between parents and children and focuses on the desire of a young woman for change.

Misanthrope, Le A comedy by MOLIÈRE. First performance: Paris, 1666. The central character, Alceste, can see no good in his fellow man but remains blind to his own shortcomings. He also becomes infatuated with the hypocritical Célimène. Exasperated by polite society, he finally resolves to spend the rest of his life in solitary exile.

Miser, The (*L'Avare*) A comedy by MOLIÈRE, inspired by Plautus's *Aulularia*. First performance: Paris, 1668. Harpagon's avarice has alienated the affection of his family: he chooses for his daughter an old husband and plans to marry his son's sweetheart himself. He is ultimately forced to bow to his children's wishes.

Misrule, Lord of In the late 15th and early 16th centuries, an official commonly appointed at Court and at noble houses and colleges throughout England to preside over the Christmas festivities. Also called the **Abbot of Misrule** or **King of Misrule** (or **Abbot of Unreason** in Scotland), he reigned for a period from twelve days to three months, coordinating all the entertainment and ruling over his own mock court, in much the same way as the BOY BISHOP presided at choir schools. His function at the royal court was eventually taken over by the Master of the Revels. *See also* Feast of Fools.

Miss Julie (*Fröken Julie*) A one-act play by August STRINDBERG, written in 1888. First performance: 1889. The play depicts the tragic aftermath of a brief sexual relationship between a footman and the sensual Miss Julie, a member of a decaying aristocracy. A landmark of 19th-century NATURALISM, the play provides a savage picture of the enmity of the sexes and of human nature in general.

Miss Saigon A musical by Alain BOUBLIL (book and lyrics) and Claude-Michel Schönberg (music). First production: Drury Lane, London, 1989. A reworking of the *Madame Butterfly* story set during and after the Vietnam War, this Cameron MACK-INTOSH production ran until 1999 in London and was also successful on Broadway.

Mistinguett (Jeanne-Marie Bourgeois; 1875–1956) French actress and singer, who became a leading star of music hall, comedy, and revue in Paris between the wars. Famous for her beautiful legs and lively manner, she became the most popular performer at the Moulin Rouge and the Folies Bergère, where she was partnered by Maurice Chevalier and appeared in increasingly fabulous costumes, performing both songs and comic sketches.

Mitchell, Maggie Julia (1832–1918) US actress, much loved in the role of Fanchon in a stage adaptation of George Sand's novel *La Petite Fadette*, in which part she appeared for many years from 1861. She first attracted attention as a child at the Bowery Theatre; other adult successes included Charlotte Brontë's *Jane Eyre* and Bulwer-Lytton's *The Lady of Lyons*.

Mitchell, Warren (1926–) British actor, who made his first professional appearance at the Finsbury Park Open Air Theatre in 1950, and came to the West End in the Musical *Can-Can* (1954). Well established in television as a comedy character actor, he appeared in Johnny Speight's one-man show *The Thoughts of Chairman Alf* at the Theatre Royal, Stratford, in 1976, and subsequently in many other theatres in the UK and Australia. Other successes have included *King Lear* (1978, 1996), Arthur Miller's *Death of a Salesman* (1979), Molière's *The Miser* (1986), and Pinter's *The Homecoming* (1991).

Mitchell, William (1798–1856) British actor, who, after 15 years of experience as an actor and stage manager, emigrated to the US in 1836. He established himself as the leading producer and performer in burlesque when he took over the tiny Olympic Theatre in New York.

Mitchell's Olympic *See* Olympic Theatre.

Mitzi E Newhouse Theatre *See* Lincoln Center for the Performing Arts.

Mnouchkine, Ariane (1934–) French director, who formed the experimental Théâtre du Soleil company in Paris in 1964. Early successes included Wesker's *The Kitchen* (1967) and two epic productions about the French Revolution, *1789* (1970) and *1793* (1972), which were developed by COLLECTIVE CREATION. The company disbanded in 1976 but regrouped in 1979 to present the acclaimed *Mephisto*, about the theatre in Nazi Germany. Subsequent productions have included Hélène Cixous's epic *The King of Cambodia* (1981) and a cycle of Greek tragedies.

Moberg, (Carl Artur) Vilhelm (1898–1973) Swedish novelist and playwright, who based much of his work upon his rural upbringing. His early plays were rustic farces but his later works included *Vär ofödde son* (Our Unborn Son; 1945), which depicts the tragic consequences of an illegal abortion.

Mochalov, Pavel Stepanovich (1800–45) Russian actor, who was highly regarded as a player of tragedy despite his resistance to the reforms of Shchepkin and others. Relying on inspiration rather than technique, he was admired in the great roles of

Shakespeare and Schiller but later went out of fashion as the public rejected his romantic style of acting. His later career was blighted by alcoholism.

Modena, Gustavo (1803–61) Italian actor. The son of a comic actor, he worked in a touring company before leading his own troupe throughout Italy, appearing with great success in all types of drama. Political unrest brought him to London in the 1830s; subsequently he formed a company in Milan and, among other important innovations, introduced Shakespeare to the Italian stage.

Modjeska, Helena (Helena Opid; 1840–1909) Polish actress, who became internationally famous for her great emotional power after emigrating to the US in 1876. She also acted in London (1880–82 and 1890), where her roles included Juliet to the Romeo of Forbes-Robertson and was acknowledged as ranking with Bernhardt and Duse – particularly in the role of Lady Macbeth.

Mogul Saloon *See* Middlesex Music Hall.

Mohun, Michael (c. 1620–84) English actor, who, with Charles Hart, was the foremost actor in the first company at Drury Lane. Formerly a boy actor under Beeston, he was particularly acclaimed as Volpone, Iago, and in the plays of Nathaniel Lee.

Moiseiwitsch, Tanya (1914–) British stage designer, who began her career with designs for the Abbey Theatre in Dublin (1935–39). Subsequently she worked at the Oxford Playhouse (1941–44), the Old Vic (1944–49), the Guthrie Theatre, Minneapolis, the National Theatre, and both Stratford-on-Avon and Stratford, Ontario. Her numerous designs included many for the plays of Shakespeare, Molière, Chekhov, Jonson, Congreve, Rattigan, Brecht, John Mortimer, and Gogol as well as those for several operas.

Moissi, Alexander (1880–1935) German actor, born in Albania of Italian parents, who began his career in Prague but first attracted attention in Berlin. He was much admired in such Shakespearean roles as Romeo and Oberon under Reinhardt at the Deutsches Theater, while other successes included plays by Goethe, Ibsen, Shaw, and Schiller as well as the classical works of Sophocles and Aeschylus; in 1930 he played Hamlet in German in London at the same time as Gielgud played it in English at the neighbouring Queen's Theatre.

Molander, Olof (1892–1966) Swedish director and manager, who had a profound influence upon the national theatre while head of the Kungliga Dramatiska Teatern during the 1920s. His most important productions included both classic works and the plays of Strindberg.

Molé, François-René (1734–1802) French actor, who became highly popular in comic roles at the Comédie-Française. Despite his reputation for comedy, he also had the distinction in 1769 of being the first French Hamlet, in a version of Shakespeare's play by Ducis. Unlike most of his contemporaries he was not imprisoned during the events of 1789, but continued to appear, under the management of Mlle Montansier.

Molière (Jean-Baptiste Poquelin; 1622–73) French playwright and actor, born in Paris; he was a master of comedy whose contribution to the theatre in this genre is unsurpassed. The son of Jean Poquelin, upholsterer and *valet de chambre* to the king, Molière was educated by the Jesuits at the Collège de Clermont and subsequently studied law. Expected to take over his father's position at court, he became involved in the early 1640s with a family of actors (the BÉJARTS) and opted instead for a theatrical career.

In 1643, encouraged by Madeleine Béjart, he cofounded the ILLUSTRE-THÉÂTRE, an unsuccessful venture that culminated in his imprisonment for debt. From 1645 to 1658 he toured the provinces with a troupe of actors, performing farces inspired by the Italian *commedia dell'arte*, one of which – LE DOCTEUR AMOUREUX – was to earn the company Louis XIV's favour and a place at the Petit-Bourbon Theatre in Paris. *Les Précieuses ridicules* (1659) was Molière's first major success; it was followed by a series of comedies that revolutionized the genre, delighting his audiences, scandalizing his critics, and exasperating his rivals.

In 1661 the company moved to the Palais-Royal; the following year saw Molière's unfortunate marriage to Armande Béjart, the flirtatious young sister (or the playwright's own daughter, according to contemporary gossip) of Madeleine. Having weathered the storm aroused by *L'École des femmes* (*see Critique de l'école des femmes, La*), largely through the king's support, Molière faced an even greater outcry after the first performance of TARTUFFE at Versailles in 1664: it was five years before the final version could be staged in Paris. Meanwhile, he continued to write, act, and direct, producing four new plays in 1666 and two or three each year between 1667 and 1671. He died in February 1673, after collapsing on stage during a performance of LE MALADE IMAGINAIRE.

Molière's plays have entertained theatregoers in Paris and elsewhere for more than 300 years. Their lasting appeal may be attributed to the playwright's innate sense of comedy and to the wide range of his satirical attacks. In his hands such characters as the cuckold, the miser, the hypocrite, the social climber, the hypochondriac, and the misanthropist have provided numerous actors and actresses with their most celebrated roles.

Principal works:

L'Étourdi ou les Contretemps: 1655; translated as *The Blunderer*.
De Dépit amoureaux: 1656; translated as *The Amorous Quarrel*.
Le Docteur amoureux: 1658.
Les Précieuses ridicules: 1659; translated as *The Affected Young Ladies*.
Sganarelle ou le Cocu imaginaire: 1660.
L'École des femmes: 1662; translated as THE SCHOOL FOR WIVES.
La Critique de l'école des femmes: 1663.
*L'*IMPROMPTU DE VERSAILLES: 1663.
Tartuffe ou l'Imposteur: 1664.
Don Juan ou le Festin de pierre: 1665.
LE MISANTHROPE: 1666.
Le Médecin malgré lui: 1666; translated as *The Doctor in Spite of Himself*.
Amphitryon: 1668.
GEORGE DANDIN; OU, LE MARI CONFONDU: 1668.
L'Avare: 1668 Paris; translated as THE MISER.
Le Bourgeois Gentilhomme: 1670; translated as *The Prodigious Snob*.
Psyché: 1671 (with Pierre Corneille and Philippe Quinault).
Les Fourberies de Scapin: 1671; translated as *The Cheats of Scapin*.

Les Femmes savantes: 1672; translated as *The Blue-Stockings* (or *The Learned Ladies*). *Le Malade imaginaire*: 1673; translated as *The Imaginary Invalid* (or *The Hypochondriac*).

Molina, Tirso de *See* Tirso de Molina.

Molnár, Ferenč (Ferenč Neumann; 1878–1952) Hungarian novelist and playwright, who established an international reputation with his farces and fantasies. His works include *Az Ördög* (The Devil; 1907), *A hattyú* (The Swan; 1920), and *A vörös malom* (The Red Mill; 1923). The film and musical comedy *Carousel* (1945) was based upon his mystery play *Liliom* (1909), while *The Guardsman* (1910) provided a successful vehicle for the Lunts; other successes included *The Glass Slipper* (1924), which was based upon the story of Cinderella. Molnár became a US citizen in 1940.

Momus The god of clowns, originally the Greek god of ridicule. He appeared as a character in masques and harlequinades, and the name 'Momus' was sometimes used as an alternative name for a clown.

Monakhov, Nikolai Federovich (1875–1936) Russian actor, who served a long apprenticeship in café theatre in St Petersburg before joining Mardzhanov's Free Theatre in 1913 and attracting much attention. Subsequently he won acclaim in operetta with the Moscow Art Theatre but found his greatest success as Philip II in Schiller's *Don Carlos*.

Moncrieff, Gladys (1893–1976) Australian actress, who was particularly successful in operetta and musical comedy. Known as 'Our Glad', she became highly popular in shows by Gilbert and Sullivan as well as in native Australian productions and revivals of popular musicals.

Moncrieff, William Thomas (1794–1857) British playwright and manager, who wrote a number of melodramas and burlesques for performance in minor theatres. He also adapted several novels, especially those of Dickens. At various times he managed the Regency Theatre (later the Scala Theatre), Coburg Theatre (later the Old Vic Theatre), Vauxhall Gardens, and Astley's Amphitheatre.

Monkhouse, Allan Noble (1858–1936) British theatre critic and playwright, who was especially supportive of Annie Horniman's Gaiety Theatre. His works for the company included *Reaping the Whirlwind* (1908), *Mary Broome* (1911), and the satirical *Nothing Like Leather* (1913). His finest play, *The Conquering Hero* (1924), deals ironically with the theme of war.

monodrama A short theatrical presentation in which only one actor speaks. Such productions – often extracts from longer works – enjoyed a brief vogue in Germany in the late 18th century, performed by Johann Christian Brandes and others. In the modern theatre such pieces are normally referred to as **monologues**.

monologue *See* monodrama.

Montague, Henry James (Henry James Mann; 1844–78) US actor, who opened the Vaudeville Theatre in New York in 1870. Returning to New York in 1874 he appeared with Lester Wallack in a series of successful comedies by such authors as Clement Scott, T W Robertson, and Tom Taylor. He also founded the Lambs theatre club in 1875.

Montaland, Céline (1843–91) French actress, who established her reputation playing children at the Comédie-Française. Later in life she transferred (1860) to adult roles, the best of which included the mother in Daudet's *Jack* at the Gymnase.

Montansier, Mlle (Marguerite Brunet; 1730–1820) French actress, who became manageress of several important French theatres. After managing a theatre at Rouen she was made responsible for the theatre at Versailles, which she rebuilt in 1777. Following the Revolution she moved to Paris and established a fashionable salon; she narrowly escaped the guillotine after being accused of Royalist sympathies by Fabre d'Églantine. Subsequently she managed the Palais Royal until 1806.

Montchrétien, Antoine de (c. 1575–1621) French playwright and economist. In 1605 he fled to England after killing an adversary in a duel; he returned to France six years later but was killed during a Protestant insurrection in 1621. Montchrétien's lyrical tragedies, influenced by Garnier, include *Sophonisbe* (1596), *L'Écossaise* (1601), *David* (1601), and *Aman* (1601).

Montdory (Guillaume des Gilberts; 1594–1651) French actor-manager, who was acknowledged as the first great French actor for his performances of Corneille. After training with Valleran-Lecomte and Lenoir, he scored his first major success in Paris in 1630, in *Mélite*. Subsequently he opened the Théâtre du Marais and appeared as Rodrigue in the first production of *Le Cid*, his most celebrated tragic role. He was also acclaimed as Herod in Tristan l'Hermite's *La Mariane*, in which role he was appearing before Richelieu when he was struck down by paralysis of the tongue and had to retire.

Montfleury (Zacherie Jacob; c. 1600–67) French actor, who became a prominent figure at the Hôtel de Bourgogne. An extremely fat man, he excelled in tragedy, although he was the subject of satirical comment in *L'Impromptu de Versailles* (1663) by Molière, with whom Montfleury continued an acrimonious relationship, accusing the playwright of marrying his own daughter.

His son was the playwright **Antoine Montfleury** (1639–85), who was also involved in the rivalry with Molière. His plays, most of which were presented at the Hôtel de Bourgogne, include *L'Impromptu de l'Hôtel de Condé* (1663), which was written in reply to Molière's *L'Impromptu de Versailles*.

Montherlant, Henri de (1896–1972) French novelist and playwright, born in Paris. He became actively involved in bullfighting and other sports in his youth and extolled in his early writings physical strength, courage, and heroism. Having made his name as a novelist, he began writing for the theatre during World War II. His plays, notably *La Reine Morte* (1942), *Le maître de Santiago* (THE MASTER OF SANTIAGO; 1948), and *La Ville dont le prince est un enfant* (1951), were influenced by Corneille and Racine.

Month in the Country, A A play by Ivan TURGENEV, written in 1850 and regarded as his finest work for the theatre. First performance: 1872. Originally entitled *The Student*, the play has no single hero but explores the complex relationships between members of one household, with an emphasis on their inner motivations.

Montparnasse, Théâtre See Baty, Gaston.

Moody, William Vaughn (1869–1910) US playwright, whose first success was *The Great Divide* (1906). This and *The Faith Healer* (1909) greatly stimulated the development of US drama away from the more sentimental and melodramatic productions that had previously characterized it.

Mooney, Ria (1904–73) Irish actress, who was invited to join the Abbey Theatre company after success as an amateur in Chekhov's *The Proposal*. O'Casey chose her to play Rosie Redmond in *The Plough and the Stars* (1926), after which she toured England and the US, staying in New York for some years as assistant director with the Civic Repertory Theatre. Later, after some time with the Gate Theatre company, she returned to the Abbey as its first woman producer.

Moon for the Misbegotten, A A play by Eugene O'NEILL. First performance: 1947. First New York performance: 1957. The play, a sequel to LONG DAY'S JOURNEY INTO NIGHT, charts the continuing decline of James Tyrone Jr, who is now the owner of a farm. This was the last of O'Neill's plays to be staged during his lifetime.

Moon in the Yellow River, The A play by Denis JOHNSTON. First production: Abbey Theatre, Dublin, 1931. It explored the state of contemporary Ireland through the eyes of a German engineer. The play has been successfully presented in several languages.

Moore, Dudley (1935–) British comedy actor and musician, who was one of the quartet who appeared in the satirical revue *Beyond the Fringe* (1960) in Edinburgh, London, and New York. After starring in *Play It Again, Sam* at the Globe Theatre in 1969, he joined Peter COOK to tour in their own revue, *Behind the Fridge*. Subsequently he became well known for his screen appearances but returned to the stage to star in a Los Angeles production of *The Mikado* (1988).

Moore, Edward (1712–57) British playwright, author of the sentimental dramas *The Foundling* (1747) and *The Gamester* (1753). The latter was the result of a collaboration with David Garrick, who played the role of Beverley in it with great success at Drury Lane.

Moore, Eva *See* Esmond, Henry Vernon.

Moore, George (1852–1933) Irish novelist, poet, and playwright. His particular contribution to drama came in the 1890s when he helped to establish the IRISH LITERARY THEATRE. He also collaborated with W B Yeats on the rewriting of Edward Martyn's *The Tale of a Town* as *The Bending of the Bough* (1900); his other plays include *The Strike at Arlingford* (1893) and, also with Yeats, *Diarmuid and Grania* (1901).

Moore, Maggie (Margaret Sullivan; 1851–1926) US actress, who spent much of her career in Australia with her husband J C Williamson, notably in the much-revived comedy *Struck Oil; or, the Pennsylvanian Dutchman*. She excelled in comic roles and operetta and also appeared on tour in Britain from 1903 to 1908.

Moore, Mary *See* Wyndham, Sir Charles.

moral interlude A short dramatic entertainment that developed during the 16th century from the morality play. Although it retained the didactic purpose of the earlier form, it was notable for its development of the purely allegorical figures into more realistic characters.

morality play A type of allegorical drama, usually depicting the contest between various personified virtues and vices for the soul of a man, which gradually supplanted the mystery play during the 15th century. The earliest major example of the genre was *The Castle of Perseverance* (c. 1405); this work is also notable for the comic character Backbiter, who was introduced for purely theatrical reasons, specifically to keep the action going. The form embraced the coarse humour and grotesque detail of the mystery play and ultimately evolved into the MORAL INTERLUDE of the Tudor stage; it also played a key role in the establishment of the first troupes of professional actors. The more well-known morality plays include *Everyman* and *Magynfycence*, by John Skelton. *See also* Vice.

Moratín, Nicolás, Fernández de (1737–80) Spanish poet and playwright, author of a number of plays influenced by French neoclassical tragedy. Noted primarily as a poet, he wrote the three tragedies *Lucrecia* (1763), *Hormesinda* (1770), and *Guzmán el Bueno* (1777).

His son was **Leandro Fernández de Moratín** (1760–1828), who was the leading Spanish neoclassical playwright of his time. He was much influenced by French dramatists, especially Molière, and wrote a number of successful plays satirizing theatre criticism – including *La comedia nueva* (The New Comedy; 1792) – and marriages of convenience – as in his most celebrated work for the stage, *El sí de las niñas* (When a Girl Says Yes; 1806).

Mordvinov, Nikolai Dmitrievich (1901–66) Russian actor, who became a leading performer of tragic roles at the Mossoviet Theatre in Moscow, where he first appeared in 1940. He began his career at the Gorky State Theatre in Rostov in 1936 and later won acclaim in plays by such diverse authors as Shakespeare, Lermontov, Korneichuk, and Goldoni.

Moreto y Cabaña, Agustín (1618–69) Spanish playwright, who was the author of over 100 dramas, including several notable comedias influenced by Lope de Vega and Tirso de Molina. Trained as a lawyer, he was highly popular in his own time with such comedies as *El desdén con el desdén* (Scorn for Scorn; 1654) and *El lindo Don Diego* (1662), which was his most celebrated play.

Morgan, Charles (1894–1958) British novelist, essayist, playwright, and theatre critic of *The Times* (1926–39) in succession to A B Walkley. He was also the author of the carefully crafted plays *The Flashing Stream* (1938), *The River Line* (1952), and *The Burning Glass* (1954).

Morley, Robert (1908–92) British actor, who first appeared professionally (as an elderly pirate) in *Treasure Island* (1928). After many years in the provinces, during which he ran his own summer repertory company in Cornwall, he came to prominence in London at the Gate Theatre Club in 1936, playing the title role in *Oscar Wilde* by Leslie and Sewell Stokes. He repeated the role on Broadway in 1938. Thereafter, he appeared in numerous successes, ranging from Kaufman and Hart's *The Man Who Came to Dinner* (1941) to Alan Ayckbourn's *How the Other Half Loves* (1970). He also performed his own solo entertainments and appeared frequently on film and television; his own plays include *Goodness, How Sad!* (1938) and *Edward My Son* (1947). His son **Sheridan Morley** (1941–) is a theatre critic.

Morosco Theatre A theatre on 45th Street, New York, which opened in 1917 with *Canary Cottage* by Elmer Harris and Oliver Morosco, after whom the theatre was named. Successful productions staged there have included O'Neill's *Beyond the Horizon* (1920), George Kelly's *Craig's Wife* (1925), Coward's *Blithe Spirit* (1941), Miller's *Death of a Salesman* (1949), Tennessee Williams's *Cat on a Hot Tin Roof* (1955), and several successful transfers from the London stage, among them plays by David Storey, Simon Gray, Rattigan, and Ayckbourn. The theatre was demolished in 1982 to make way for the hotel tower which includes the Minskoff Theatre.

Morris, Clara (Clara Morrison; 1846–1925) US actress, born in Canada, who became highly popular for her spirited performances in melodrama. After extensive experience in various parts of the northern US she joined Daly's company in New York and won acclaim in Wilkie Collins's *Man and Wife* and *Article 42* (1872). Subsequently she appeared in many varied roles, attracting large audiences to such plays as *The Lady of the Camellias* by Dumas *fils*, Sardou's *Odette* (1892), and her own adaptation *Claire* (1894). Her classic parts included Lady Macbeth; later in her career she also ventured into vaudeville.

Morris Dance A rural folk dance performed in England. One of the entertainments bridging the gap between ancient ritual and recognizable folk theatre, the Morris Dance has counterparts throughout Europe and has strong associations with myth and superstition (dances being regularly performed at May Day celebrations and other notable events in the agricultural calendar). The name suggests that it may have Moorish origins. Dancers (conventionally male although female troupes now flourish) sometimes blacken their faces and conventionally dress in white, attaching bells to the legs or body and often carrying sticks or handkerchiefs; they may also be accompanied by a Fool and hobby horse and figures linked to the tradition of the Robin Hood play. *Compare* Horn Dance.

Morselli, Ercole Luigi (1882–1921) Italian playwright, who became a leading writer in the *crepuscolari* tradition. He won acclaim for his modern treatment of mythical subjects in *Orione* (1910), *Glauco* (1919), and *Belfagor* (1930).

Mortimer, John (1923–) British playwright and novelist, several of whose plays have been based upon his experiences as a barrister. The need for communication and the plight of the lonely and unsuccessful are recurrent themes. His first play, the one-act *The Dock Brief*, won the Italia Prize in 1957; other plays have included another one-act, *Lunch Hour* (1961), *The Wrong Side of the Park* (1960), *Two Stars for Comfort* (1962), *The Judge* (1967), and *Cat Among the Pigeons* (1969), which was an adaptation of a play by Feydeau. *A Voyage Round My Father* (1970) was an autobiographical play focusing upon his relationship with his blind father. Later plays include *The Lady from Maxim's* (1977) and *A Little Hotel on the Side* (1984), both based on Feydeau. He is best-known for his television series *Rumpole of the Bailey*.

Morton, Charles (1819–1904) British music hall manager, often referred to as the 'father of the halls'. Born in Hackney, he became landlord of the Canterbury Tavern in Lambeth. Here he decided to build the CANTERBURY MUSIC HALL, opening it with Sam Cowell as the first star attraction. He opened the Oxford Music Hall in 1861 and went on to run several other successful halls.

Morton, Thomas (c. 1764–1838) British playwright, who wrote a number of successful plays, including *Speed the Plough* (1798), which was famous for the character of the censorious Mrs Grundy, who never appears but is frequently referred to. Among his other comedies were *The Way to Get Married* (1796), *A Cure for the Heart-Ache* (1797), *Secrets Worth Knowing* (1798), and *The School of Reform; or, How to Rule a Husband* (1805), which enjoyed several revivals.

His son, **John Maddison Morton** (1811–91), was the author of numerous farces, many adapted from the French, the most successful being *Lend Me Five Shillings* (1846) and *Box and Cox* (1847).

Moscow Art Theatre A theatre in Moscow, which was founded in 1898 by NEMIROVICH-DANCHENKO and STANISLAVSKY. Their company soon established a controversial reputation with their naturalistic production of Chekhov's *The Seagull*, which had already proved a failure at the more conventional Alexandrinsky Theatre. Subsequently the company presented the premieres of *Uncle Vanya* (1899), *Three Sisters* (1901), *The Cherry Orchard* (1904), as well as the first production of Gorky's *The Lower Depths* (1902). After the Revolution the company toured Europe and the US (1922–23), returning to present new Soviet dramas by such playwrights as Bulgakov and Ivanov. Stanislavsky's influence on the theatre was profound; the first actors to be trained there in his style of acting included Kachalov, Olga-Knipper, and Moskvin. The company continued to tour internationally and acquired an extra new building on the Tverskoy Boulevard in 1973, in addition to an acting school. Since the mid-1980s the two theatres have operated largely independently of each other.

Moscow State Jewish Theatre A theatre founded in St Petersburg by Alexander GRANOVSKY in 1919; it is known in Yiddish as the **Melucha Theatre** and in Russian as the **Goset**. Two years later it transferred to Moscow, presenting Yiddish plays by Sholom Aleichem and acquiring a new venue seating 766. Under Salomon MIKHOELS, the theatre continued to stage a mixture of Yiddish and classic plays, including works by Shakespeare; when Mikhoels died in 1948 the company broke up until 1962, when it was resurrected as the **Jewish Drama Ensemble**.

Moskvin, Ivan Mikhailovich (1874–1946) Russian actor, who was a founding member of the Moscow Art Theatre. He played leading roles in many of the company's early productions, winning particular praise in plays by Tolstoy, Chekhov, Gorky, Gogol, Ostrovsky, and Pogodin.

Mossop, Henry (1729–74) British actor, born in Ireland. At Drury Lane he played many leading tragic parts successfully, but failed in his ill-advised attempts to play young lovers. He was resentful of Garrick and eventually returned to Dublin, where his efforts to manage the Smock Alley Theatre were disastrous; subsequently he starved to death in London.

Mossoviet Theatre A theatre in Moscow, which opened in 1923 as a venue for politically orientated drama. The earliest productions staged there included plays by Bill-Belotserkovsky; later productions under such leading directors as Lyubimov and Zavadsky have included plays by Lermontov, Shakespeare, and Shaw.

Mostel, Zero (1915–77) US actor, who began his career in cabaret and made his Broadway debut in vaudeville. Subsequent stage roles included Argan in Molière's

The Imaginary Invalid (1952), Shu Fu in Brecht's *The Good Woman of Setzuan* (1956), Leopold Bloom in *Ulysses in Night-town* (1958), John in Ionesco's *Rhinoceros* (1961), Prologus in the musical *A Funny Thing Happened on the Way to the Forum* (1962), and Tevye in the musical *Fiddler on the Roof* (1964).

Mota, Anrique da (16th century) Portuguese poet and playwright, author of several plays and collaborations with Vicente. It is not known whether any of his satirical works, which include *Farsa do Alfaiate*, were staged.

Mother Courage and Her Children (*Mutter Courage und ihre Kinder*) A play by Bertolt BRECHT, written 1938–39. First performance: Zürich, 1941. Set during the Thirty Years' War, the play explores the moral responsibility shared by an entire population in time of war, and the link between the most innocuous contribution to the war effort and the worst atrocities.

motion The PUPPET THEATRE presented by travelling puppeteers during the 16th and 17th centuries. At this time most puppet shows were based on biblical stories, although sources became increasingly varied as the tradition developed.

Moulin Rouge A dance hall in Paris, which opened in 1899. It became well known as a home of dancing, music hall, and cabaret, acquiring some notoriety for early performances of the can-can. Noted managers of the Moulin-Rouge have included Mistinguett, while posters for the dance hall by Toulouse-Lautrec were much admired and imitated elsewhere. It remains a popular tourist attraction. *See also* New York Theatre.

Mounet-Sully (Jean Sully Mounet; 1841–1916) French actor, who excelled as a player of the great tragic roles. He first appeared at the Comédie-Française in 1872 in Racine's *Andromaque*; subsequently he was consistently successful, his many triumphs including the plays of Victor Hugo.

Mountfort, William (1664–92) English actor and playwright, who appeared at the second Theatre Royal, Drury Lane. The author of such plays as *Greenwich Park* (1691) and a farcical version of *Dr Faustus* (1697), he was highly regarded for playing aristocratic roles in plays by Wycherley and others. He was murdered on the orders of one Captain Hill, in a dispute over the favours of Anne Bracegirdle. His wife was the actress Susanna PERCIVAL.

Mountview Theatre School A drama school in Crouch Hill, London, which was founded in 1947 as an amateur company. Acquiring its own small theatre, which was rebuilt after a fire in 1963, it gradually built up a strong reputation for productions of both classics and modern plays, touring widely. The drama school itself was opened in 1969 and presents regular free performances by its students in the Mountview Theatre and Judi Dench studio theatre, opened in 1971.

Mourning Becomes Electra A trilogy of plays by Eugene O'NEILL. First performance: New York, 1931. The three plays (*Homecoming*, *The Hunted*, and *The Haunted*) are an updated version of Aeschylus's *Oresteia*. Set in Puritan New England, they depict the doomed relationships between Ezra Mannon, his wife Christine, their children Orin and Lavinia, and their various lovers.

Mousetrap, The A play by Agatha CHRISTIE. First performance: Ambassador's Theatre, London, 1952. Originally written for radio, this thriller ran for 21 years before transferring to St Martin's Theatre in 1974 to continue its record-breaking unbroken run. It passed its 20 000th London performance in 2000. The original cast included Richard Attenborough and his wife Sheila Sim.

Mowatt, Anna Cora (1819–70) US playwright and actress, who was best known for *Fashion* (1845), a satirical drama that mocked the trend for affected European manners in contemporary US society. Her other plays include *Gulzara* (1841) and *Armand* (1847); as an actress she was particularly successful as Pauline in Bulwer-Lytton's *The Lady of Lyons* (1845) and later led her own company.

Mrożek, Sławomir (1930–) Polish playwright and short-story writer, the author of several satirical plays associated with the Theatre of the Absurd. His best-known work is the political satire *Tango* (1965); his other plays include *Policja* (The Police; 1958), *The Turkey Cock* (1961), *Na pełnym morzu* (Out at Sea; 1961), *Karol* (Charlie; 1962), *Striptease* (1962), *The Hunchback* (1976), and *A Summer's Day* (1983).

Mrs Warren's Profession A play by G B SHAW, written in 1893. First performance: New Haven, 1902. The play's subject, prostitution, and its onslaught upon the social conditions that make prostitution possible, caused a scandal and opposition from the censor. Acclaimed for its straightforward approach to a usually romanticized subject, it is generally considered one of Shaw's finest plays.

Much Ado About Nothing A comedy by William SHAKESPEARE, written c. 1598–99. First performance: c. 1598–99. The play is especially notable for the lively relationship between Beatrice and Benedick and for the comic pomposity of the constable, Dogberry. The central story of Claudio and Hero dates back to a Greek romance; most of the other characters are thought to have been Shakespeare's inventions.

Müller, Heiner (1929–95) German playwright, who emerged as one of East Germany's leading dramatists in the 1960s. His works range from the strongly socialist *Der Lohndrücker* (The Scab; 1950) and *Die Korrektur* (The Correction; 1958) to adapations of the classics. *Philoktet* (1968) is regarded as his best classically based play although he also wrote popular versions of *Macbeth* (1972), *Medea* (1982), and *Hamlet* (1977, 1989).

multiple setting *See* composite setting.

mummers' play A form of early English folk theatre, which probably had its roots in primitive ritual. Also known as the **Men's Dramatic Ceremony**, the mummers' play usually depicts the killing of a hero in battle and his subsequent revival at the hands of a doctor, the hero being **St George** and his opponent the **Turkish Knight** in most versions. Other characters can include a Fool, a man dressed as a woman (all parts being traditionally played by men), Father Christmas, and the doctor's assistant Johnny Jacks (hence the alternative name of **Johnny Jack's Play**). The play usually concludes with the **Quête**, a procession of characters who deliver some verse and collect money from the audience.

The earliest mummers (the name possibly being taken from the German word for mask) were street performers, who danced and enacted dumb shows at festivals throughout Europe from the 13th to the 16th centuries. The mummers' play then grew more elaborate, becoming intertwined with the early development of the masque in Italy; by the 18th century, when the first surviving contemporary accounts were written, it had numerous local variations throughout England, usually classed into three groups.

Features of the **Hero-Combat Play** include the dressing of the cast in rags or torn paper (hence the **Paper Boys' Play** of Marshfield in Avon) and the blacking of their faces, while the **Sword Play** of NE England depicts the hero's death in battle against a group of dancers. The third type, the now moribund **Wooing Ceremony** of the E Midlands was remarkable in having two women (played by men) – the Lady and Dame Jane – as central roles. Some of the more unusual extant variations include the **Pace-Egg Play** of Yorkshire, which involves a search for hidden Easter eggs, and the **Soul-Cakers Play** of Cheshire, for which special cakes are baked. The mumming tradition survives in various villages throughout the country; other alternative names by which it is known include the **Jolly Boys' Play** and the **Tipteerers' Play**.

Munday, Anthony (1560–1633) English playwright, who began as a child actor with Oxford's Men. Also active as a translator, pamphleteer, and writer of ballads and pageants, he collaborated with Chettle and probably with Shakespeare on *Sir Thomas More* (1593–95). Other plays attributed to him include *Two Italian Gentlemen; or, Fedele and Fortunio* (1584) and *John a Kent and John a Cumber* (c. 1594).

Munden, Joseph (1758–1832) British actor, who – after a long time in the provinces – moved to Covent Garden in 1790, where he succeeded John Edwin the Elder. Over the next 30 years he played a range of comic parts before transferring to Drury Lane, where he appeared with Edmund Kean.

Muni, Paul (Muni Weisenfreund; 1895–1967) US actor, who became a leading performer with the New York Jewish Art Theatre, which he joined in 1926. A famous film actor from 1929, he also enjoyed great success on stage as King McCloud in *Key Largo* (1942), Willie Loman in the London production of Arthur Miller's *Death of a Salesman* (1949), and Henry Drummond in *Inherit the Wind* (1955).

municipal theatre *See* civic theatre.

Munk, Kaj Harald Leininger (1889–1944) Danish playwright, priest, and poet, who was murdered by the Gestapo for his resistance to the German occupation of Denmark. His best known religious dramas include *En Idealist* (Herod the King; 1928), which was heavily criticized when first performed (1928) but was later praised by the critics, and *Ordet* (The Word; 1932), a miracle play. He expressed his opposition to the German occupation in such plays as *Han sidder ved Smeltediglen* (He Sits at the Melting Pot; 1938), which focuses upon the persecution of the Jews, and *Niels Ebbesen* (1942).

Murder in the Cathedral A verse drama by T S ELIOT. First performance: Canterbury Cathedral, 1935. It concerns the martyrdom of Thomas à Becket in the cathedral in 1170. Admired features of the play include the prose speeches by Becket's murderers. It promoted considerable interest in verse plays and has been revived many times.

Murdoch, James Edward (1811–93) US actor, who was highly successful in classic comedies by such authors as Aphra Behn, Sheridan, and Shakespeare. His most admired roles included Charles Surface in *The School for Scandal* (1853) and Shakespeare's Benedick, Orlando, and Mercutio; he appeared briefly in Britain in 1856.

Murphy, Arthur (1727–1805) British playwright, born in Ireland, who was the author of numerous successful comedies based on works by Molière and others, including *The Way to Keep Him* (1760) and *Three Weeks after Marriage* (1764). Of his tragedies the best were *Zenobia* (1768), *The Grecian Daughter* (1772), and *Alzuma* (1773).

Murray, Alma (1854–1945) British actress, who was much admired by Browning for her performances in some of his dramas in the 1880s and by G B Shaw, for whom she played Raina in *Arms and the Man* at the Avenue Theatre in 1894. She was also highly praised for a single performance as Beatrice in Shelley's play *The Cenci*, given in 1888.

Murray, (George) Gilbert (1866–1957) British classical scholar, poet, and philosopher, who translated numerous works of ancient Greek drama. He was particularly noted for his translations of Euripides, including versions of *Hippolytus*, *Trojan Women*, *Electra*, the *Bacchae*, and *Iphigenia in Tauris* which were successfully staged by Harley Granville-Barker. He also provided translations of Sophocles, Aeschylus, Aristophanes, and Menander.

Murray, Thomas Cornelius (1873–1959) Irish playwright, who wrote several plays reflecting Irish rural life for the Abbey Theatre. *Birthright* (1910) established him as a leading Irish writer; in 1912 he followed it with *Maurice Harte*, his best-known play. His other works include *The Briery Gap* (1917) and *Autumn Fire* (1924).

Muses A group of nine Greek goddesses, of whom three were associated with the theatre. **Melpomene**, often depicted holding a tragic mask, was the Muse connected with tragedy, **Terpsichore** with dancing and lyric poetry, and **Thalia**, usually holding a comic mask, with comedy.

musical, the A form of theatrical production in which song and dance are combined with dialogue and action. The modern musical, a largely US genre, had its roots in late 19th-century operetta and only gradually developed its own identity. In the early days it was always of a light nature, for which reason the genre was until recently known as 'musical comedy'.

The US play THE BLACK CROOK (1866) is usually considered the first production to have combined elements of ballet, melodrama, opera, and burlesque to create a distinct genre; as influential, however, were the light operettas of Gilbert and Sullivan, beginning with *HMS Pinafore* in 1878, which applied music to libretti of some literary worth.

The success of the early musical comedies inspired work by such European-born composers as Victor Herbert, Rudolf Friml, and Sigmund Romberg, who were familiar with the Viennese operetta tradition of Franz Lehár and others. These immigrants produced numerous romantic musicals for both stage and screen. The modern musical was created when this somewhat stilted tradition was infused with the vigour of American popular music, a development first apparent in the work of George M COHAN in the years after 1900. US popular song found greatness somewhat before the musical did, largely because the prominence given to the star performer held back the achievement of dramatic unity; however, the Princess Theatre musicals of Jerome

KERN (which were influenced by London's Gaiety Theatre shows) gave an early demonstration of what could be achieved. In the 1920s and 1930s the musical stage was able to offer energetic and sophisticated pieces by George GERSHWIN, RODGERS and Hart, Cole PORTER, and Irving BERLIN, which were musically magnificent and at least nominally unified in plot.

Jerome Kern's *Show Boat* signalled the next development as early as 1928, sounding a more serious note and heralding a new interest in plot as a device to carry theme, a transformation that was confirmed by Rodgers and Hammerstein's *Oklahoma!* in 1943. Thenceforth the musical showed itself capable of addressing all the subjects previously reserved for legitimate drama, the previously disparate elements of singing, dancing, and dialogue being increasingly integrated in such successes as *West Side Story* (1957) and *Fiddler on the Roof* (1964).

In the later 1960s a crisis developed as the 50-year reign of 'popular' music came to a close with the advent of rock. The musical is currently in an inchoate state artistically, even as it is tremendously successful financially. The value of the composer has decreased as emphasis has been placed on the director or the designer. At its worst this produces mere spectacle, something often associated in the US with the 'British Invasion', a term referring mainly to the works of Andrew LLOYD WEBBER; at its best, however, the contemporary musical can have a unity and seriousness never before associated with the form, though with the potential danger of pretentiousness. Off-Broadway, the period has been one of great experimentation, which has not yet resolved itself into a single musical or dramatic style – though the influence of Stephen SONDHEIM is a potential unifying factor.

Music Box A 977-seat theatre on West 45th Street, New York, which opened in 1921 with a revue by Irving Berlin, who had it built. Since then the theatre has housed a number of successful productions, including Kaufman and Ryskind's *Of Thee I Sing* (1932), Van Druten's *I Remember Mama* (1944), Inge's *Picnic* (1953), Rattigan's *Separate Tables* (1956), and Anthony Shaffer's *Sleuth* (1970). Subsequent successes have included the musical *Side by Side by Sondheim* (1977), Ira Levin's *Deathtrap* (1978), *A Few Good Men* (1989), and the British musical *Blood Brothers* (1993).

music hall A British theatrical entertainment, which flourished in the late 19th and early 20th centuries. A type of variety show, in which the programme comprised a series of 'turns' presented by singers, comedians, acrobats, dancers, and other performers, the music hall tradition had its roots in the SONG-AND-SUPPER ROOMS and taproom concerts held in London and other cities in the 18th century. The audience originally sat at tables and were encouraged to consume large amounts of alcohol; eventually, however, to avoid the restrictions imposed by the licensing act of 1751, such taverns opened their own music clubs, often housed in specially built halls, complete with a stage and conventional theatre equipment.

The Theatres Regulation Act of 1843 allowed both smoking and drinking in music halls, although they were banned from the legitimate theatre, and stimulated the growth of the phenomenon, which attracted all classes of customer from workmen to members of the royal family. Some of the most celebrated of these early venues in London included Charles Morton's Canterbury Music Hall (1852), the Holborn Empire (1857), Sam Collins's Hall in Islington Green (1863), the Alhambra (1860), the London Pavilion (1861), the Bedford (1861), Morton's Oxford Music Hall

(1861) and those run by the Gattis; noted successors numbered amongst them the Trocadero (1882), the Palace Theatre (1892), and the Tivoli (1893).

As well as presenting familiar figures from the straight theatre, the halls also threw up stars of their own making, of whom the greatest included Marie Lloyd, Dan Leno, Vesta Tilley (one of the many successful impersonators of the aristocratic male), Little Tich, Harry Lauder, Will Fyffe, George Robey, Nellie Wallace, and Harry Champion. Performers from the legitimate theatre who also built up a strong reputation in the halls included Sarah Bernhardt, Beerbohm-Tree, and Albert Chevalier, who developed the popular cockney costermonger of the halls.

Many other performers appeared in speciality acts, some of the most popular being those featuring LION COMIQUES, balladeers, graduates of the MINSTREL SHOW, and clowns. Others again owed their success entirely to a single song or other item, as in the case of James Henry Stead's dance 'The Perfect Cure'.

In 1902 drink was banned from the music hall, a move that contributed to the eventual decline of the tradition, although at the time it was at its height with new and bigger venues being built throughout the country to house increasingly spectacular shows (*see* variety). The introduction of the cinema in the 1910s finally sounded the death knell of the halls; by the end of World War II only a few venues remained open. Since then the tradition has resurfaced from time to time with popular television programmes and revivals in both the amateur and professional theatre (notably by the Players' Theatre Club).

Mussato, Albertino (1261–1329) Italian statesman, poet, and playwright, who was the author of *Ecerinis*, a tragedy criticizing the tyrant Ezzelino da Romano that was modelled upon the work of Seneca. He was originally Paduan ambassador to Pope Boniface VIII but was exiled in 1325 when he fell from political favour.

Musser, Theron (1925–) US lighting designer with literally hundreds of credits since her first Broadway show, *Long Day's Journey Into Night* (1956). Successes include *Follies* (1972), *A Little Night Music* (1973), A CHORUS LINE (1976), *Dreamgirls* (1985), and *Lost in Yonkers* (1992).

Musset, Alfred de (1810–57) French poet and playwright, a major figure of the French Romantic movement. In 1830 his first play, *La Nuit vénitienne*, opened at the Théâtre National de l'Odéon: its failure discouraged him from producing further works for public performance. Subsequently, however, he had lasting success with a series of light comedies, short plays illustrating proverbs, and the historical drama *Lorenzaccio*, written after his affair with the writer George Sand. His plays were especially significant for their blend of Romanticism with classical restraint and their use of poetic diction; *Lorenzaccio* provided Bernhardt with one of her most celebrated roles.

Principal works:

Les Caprices de Marianne: 1851 (written 1833).

Fantasio: 1866 (written 1833).

On ne badine pas avec l'amour: 1861 (written 1834); translated as *There's No Trifling With Love*.

Lorenzaccio: 1896 (written 1834).

Le Chandelier: 1848 (written 1835); translated as *The Decoy*.

Il ne faut jurer de rien: 1848 (written 1836); translated as *One Can Never Be Sure of Anything*.

Un caprice: 1847 (written 1837).

Il faut qu'une porte soit ouverte ou fermée: 1848 (written 1845); translated as *A Door Should Be Either Open or Shut*.

My Fair Lady *See Pygmalion.*

mystery play A dramatic entertainment based on a religious subject, the most important form of drama in medieval Europe. Also known as a **miracle play** in England, the mystery play derived from the earlier LITURGICAL DRAMA but was performed in the vernacular and included episodes of coarse humour and grotesque detail that may have been borrowed from folk theatre. Another name was the **Corpus Christi play**, because the plays were often performed at the feast of Corpus Christi in May or June.

As the genre developed, the plays became the responsibility of trade or craft guilds, each of which would perform a particular episode from the Bible as part of an entertainment that could last all day. These processional **bible-histories** were often acted on temporary mobile stages, usually converted wagons; they eventually made use of quite sophisticated stage production techniques and paid actors. Important surviving mystery-play cycles in England are those performed at Chester, Coventry, Lincoln, Wakefield, and York. Equivalent traditions in other countries included the AUTO SACRAMENTAL in Spain and the SACRA RAPPRESENTAZIONE in Italy.

Naevius, Gnaeus (c. 270 BC–c. 203 BC) Roman playwright, who invented both the historical play known as the PRAETEXTA and the PALLIATA. His plays in the *praetexta* form include *Romulus* and *Clastidium*, of which no more than the titles are extant; his other works included both tragedies and comedies (notably *Tarentilla*) written for contests against Livius Andronicus. He was imprisoned and possibly exiled as a result of his satirical writings.

Naharro, Bartolomé de Torres *See* Torres Naharro, Bartolomé de.

Naogeorg *See* Kirchmayer, Thomas.

Nares, Owen (1888–1943) British actor, who became a popular matinee idol. After first walking on at the Haymarket in 1908, he soon attracted a large following in such parts as Julian Beauclerc in Sardou's *Diplomacy* (1913) and Thomas Armstrong in Edward Sheldon's *Romance* (1915). His later, more substantial, roles included the Reverend Robert Carson in St John Ervine's *Robert's Wife* (1937) and Maxim de Winter in Daphne Du Maurier's *Rebecca* (1940).

Narr The Fool of the German medieval theatre, who became the central comic character of the *Fastnachtsspiel* during the 16th century. Many of his traits were later passed on to such comic figures as Jan Bouschet, Hans Stockfisch, Pickelhering, Hanswurst, and Kasperl.

Nashe, Thomas (1567–1601) English playwright and pamphleteer, who collaborated with Christopher Marlowe on *Dido, Queen of Carthage* (1587–88) and with Ben Jonson on the lost play THE ISLE OF DOGS. *Summer's Last Will and Testament* (1592), which blends comedy and masque elements, is the only surviving play wholly by him.

Nassau Street Theatre A theatre in Nassau Street, New York, which opened as the **New Theatre** in 1732; one of the first New York theatres. Its early history is unknown until 1750, when a Philadelphian company under Walter Murray and Thomas Kean opened a successful season with Cibber's adaptation of *Richard III*. In 1753, after extensive renovation by the elder Hallam, the theatre briefly prospered – opening with Steele's *The Conscious Lovers* – but closed later that same year.

Nathan, George Jean (1882–1958) US theatre critic, who did much to promote the drama of Ibsen, Shaw, Strindberg, and other European writers in the US. He also championed Eugene O'Neill, Sean O'Casey, and William Saroyan at the start of their careers and wrote over 30 books on the theatre.

Nathan the Wise (*Nathan der Weise*) A play in blank verse by Gotthold LESSING. First performance: Berlin, 1783. Lessing's last play, it argues for religious freedom through the story of a Jewish merchant and his adopted daughter in Muslim-held Jerusalem; it was subsequently acclaimed in a production by Goethe at Weimar (1801).

Nation, Théâtre de la *See* Comédie-Française.

National Concert Hall *See* Chatham Theatre.

Nationale Scene A theatre in Bergen, Norway, which was founded in 1850 at the instigation of Ole BULL. As Det Norske Teatret, it became a focus of native Norwegian drama, Ibsen becoming its first resident playwright in 1851. Bjørnson was director there from 1857 to 1859 and, after a brief closure from 1863 to 1876, subsequent notable managers included Gunnar Heiberg (1884–88) and Hans Jacob Nilsen (1934–39). It includes a small studio theatre, the Lille Scene, for experimental drama.

National Music Hall *See* Chatham Theatre.

National Operatic and Dramatic Association (NODA) A British theatre organization, which was founded in 1899. It aims to coordinate the activities of amateur theatre groups throughout Britain.

National Theatre *See* Nederlander Theatre; Royal National Theatre.

National Theatre Conference An honorary professional association consisting of 120 members of academic, community, and non-profit-making theatres in the US. The Conference seeks to share experience and ideas in the noncommercial theatre.

National Theatre of the Deaf (NTD) A US theatre organization founded in 1967 by David Hays, its director until 1996, which presents performances by signing deaf actors with simultaneous speech translation. This was highly unusual when it started: it was only the second theatre group for the deaf in the world, and has inspired many others, as well as touring extensively. Members have even played in Antarctica, making it the only theatrical organization to have played on all seven continents. It is also a training institution and has a children's theatre, the **Little Theatre of the Deaf**. Currently based in Chester, Connecticut, it was the Eugene O'Neill Theatre Center in Waterford, Connecticut, from its inception until 1983.

Nationaltheatret A theatre in Oslo, which was founded in 1899 and is now regarded as the most important theatrical venue in Norway. Bjørn Bjørnson was the theatre's first director, leading a brilliant company including Johanne Dybwad and Sofie Reimers; subsequent celebrated performers to act there included Alfred Maurstad and Tore Segelcke, who appeared during the 1930s. The theatre now includes a flourishing experimental studio, the Amfiscenen, and in the 1980s enjoyed new success under Toralv MAURSTAD.

National Youth Theatre (NYT) A British theatre organization, founded in 1955 by the director **Michael Croft** (1924–86) to promote amateur productions featuring child actors from all over Britain. Initially the company presented plays by Shakespeare, winning critical acclaim in the West End, but later diversified with such modern works as *Zigger-Zagger* by Peter Terson (1967). The company moved into the **Shaw Theatre** in London in 1971 and set up an additional professional company – the Shaw

Theatre Company – to produce plays suitable for young audiences; these have included works by Shaw, Wesker, and Barrie Keeffe. Actors with the Shaw Theatre Company have included Derek Jacobi and Helen Mirren. The NYT itself continues to present regular productions and tours widely.

Nativity play *See* liturgical drama.

naturalism A late 19th-century movement in the theatre and the arts in general that reflected a new desire to present an authentic version of real life. Naturalistic playwrights rejected theatrical and literary artifice and tended to focus on 'shocking' subjects such as divorce. The movement went beyond simple realism in its attempts to offer a 'scientific' explanation of human behaviour, usually through heredity or social environment. The main influences on the movement were Ibsen and Zola, whose *Thérèse Raquin* (1873) is often called the first naturalistic play. Other early dramas written in the naturalistic style included works by Henri Becque and Strindberg's *Miss Julie* (1888), while André Antoine applied its principles in direction at the Théâtre Libre. Elsewhere it was adopted by the Freie Bühne in Germany, by Stanislavsky in Russia, and by O'Neill in the US. Ultimately it gave way to Symbolism and other movements.

Naughton, Charlie *See* Crazy Gang.

nautical drama A form of melodrama, popular in the early 19th century, in which the central character was a 'Jolly Jack Tar' or similar nautical hero. Although distantly related to AQUATIC DRAMA, the nautical drama was enacted on an ordinary stage. Celebrated examples of the genre, many of which were performed at the Surrey Theatre, included Jerrold's *Black-Ey'd Susan* (1829) as well as parodies of the form.

Nazimova, Alla (1879–1945) Russian actress, who began her career with the Moscow Art Theatre and in St Petersburg before first appearing in the US in 1906. After success in an English-speaking version of Ibsen's *Hedda Gabler* at the Princess Theatre in New York in 1906 she became highly popular, notably in performances at her own Nazimova Theatre (later the 39th Street Theatre). After 1918 she concentrated upon films but later enjoyed further stage successes with Eva Le Gallienne's Civic Repertory Company and the Theatre Guild in plays ranging from Ibsen to Chekhov and O'Neill in the early 1930s.

Nazimova Theatre *See* 39th Street Theatre.

Nederlander Organization The second in size of the New York theatrical real-estate organizations, which controls nine theatres. It also frequently acts as a producer. Theatres in other cities have recently been sold as part of a reorganization of the company.

Nederlander Theatre A 1202-seat theatre on West 41st Street, between 7th and 8th Avenues in New York, which opened as the **National Theatre** in 1921 with Sydney Howard's *Swords*. In 1930 *Grand Hotel* was the first non-musical play to use a revolving stage and in 1936 Gertrude Lawrence and Noël Coward starred there in *Tonight at 8.30*. In 1959 the theatre was bought by Billy ROSE and reopened – as the **Billy Rose Theatre** – with a revival of Shaw's *Heartbreak House*. Productions subsequently staged there included Albee's *Who's Afraid of Virginia Woolf?* (1962), Coward's *Private Lives* (1969), and Stoppard's *Jumpers* (1974). In 1978 the theatre was purchased by a

British company and renamed the **Trafalgar Theatre**, staging works by Pinter and Brian Clark; this company left in 1980, when the theatre was acquired by the Nederlander Organization and given its present name. As the only Broadway Theatre below 42nd Street, its location is considered problematic; nevertheless, it enjoyed great success with *Rent* (1996).

Negro Ensemble Company A New York theatre company, founded by Douglas Turner Ward in 1967, with help from funds provided by the Ford Foundation. At that time the idea of a minority theatre company was unusual, and the NEC rapidly became the major Black company in the US. It has premiered many important works, notably Joseph A Walker's *The River Niger* (1972) and Charles Fuller's *A Soldier's Play* (1982), which won the Pulitzer Prize.

Neher, Caspar (1897–1962) German stage designer, who designed influential sets for early productions of Brecht's plays, including *Eduard II* (1924) and *Baal* (1926). He subsequently worked at the Deutsches Theater (1934–44) and later with the Berliner Ensemble, being particularly admired for his use of lighting.

Neidhart von Reuental (c. 1180–c. 1240) Austrian playwright and poet, who developed a new form of dramatic entertainment known as the *höfische Dorfpoesie*. The best known examples include the *Neidhartspiel*, which revolves around the central figure of a knight who, after humiliating his coarse peasant rivals, wins the love of a village girl.

Neighborhood Playhouse A theatre on Grand Street, New York, which was built in 1915. It housed a respected professional theatre company, which produced major works by such authors as Chekhov, O'Neill, Shaw, and Yeats before closing down in 1927; other productions included dance-dramas and ballets.

Neil Simon Theatre A 1334-seat theatre in New York, on West 52nd Street between Broadway and 8th Avenue. It opened as the **Alvin Theatre** in 1927 with Gershwin's *Funny Face*, the first of a successful series of musicals starring such performers as Fred Astaire and Ethel Merman. Since 1932 it has also been used for straight drama, with notable successes including works by O'Neill, Sherwood, and Stoppard; musicals continued with Sondheim's *Company* (1970), as well as *Shenandoah* (1975) and *Annie* (1977). In 1983 the current name was adopted; since then it has shown several plays by Neil Simon, including *Brighton Beach Memoirs* (1983), *Biloxi Blues* (1985), and *Laughter on the 23rd Floor* (1993), as well as a revival of *The King and I* (1996).

Neilson, (Lilian) Adelaide (1846–80) British actress, who was a millhand and barmaid before making her stage debut at Margate in 1865. She became famous as a Shakespearean actress; her Juliet, Rosalind, and Isabella were highly acclaimed at the Haymarket in 1876. She was equally popular in the US, which she visited on five occasions.

Neilson, Julia (1868–1957) British actress, who joined Tree's company in 1888 and married Fred TERRY in 1891. In management together from 1900 onwards, they established a popular reputation in such comedy melodramas as Paul Kester's *Sweet Nell of Old Drury* and Baroness Orczy's *The Scarlet Pimpernel*. After his death she appeared in Seymour Hicks's *Vintage Wine* (1934) and made a final comeback as Lady Rutven in Heron Carvic's *The Widow of Forty* (1944).

Nekrassov A play by Jean-Paul SARTRE. First performance: Paris, 1955. The central character of this political satire is the confidence trickster Georges de Valera, who assumes the identity of the Soviet minister Nekrassov. The play was first produced on the English stage in 1956.

Nemirovich-Danchenko, Vladimir Ivanovich (1859–1943) Russian director and playwright, who cofounded the MOSCOW ART THEATRE with Stanislavsky in 1898. He pioneered the development of NATURALISM in the Russian theatre after being appointed head of the Moscow Philharmonic Society's Drama Course in 1891. Subsequently working alongside Stanislavsky, he helped to select plays for production – notably Chekhov's *The Seagull* in 1898 – and directed such plays as Pogodin's *Kremlin Chimes* (1942) himself. He also founded the Moscow Musical Studio, at which he applied his ideas to musical comedy and operetta.

neoclassical drama A style of drama that flourished in Continental Europe in the 17th and 18th centuries. The style reflected contemporary interest in the classical world but owed more to the theorizing of Renaissance scholars than to actual Greek or Roman theatrical practice. Neoclassicism is now best known for its insistence on the three UNITIES, but also involved a complicated series of restrictions on characterization and action based on neo-Platonic ideas. Thus, a legitimate king was not to be shown as cowardly in battle because "Kings (in their basic nature) are brave, even if one individual was not". (This way of thinking later formed the basis of much Soviet Socialist Realism.) At its best neoclassicism stressed simplicity of form and concentration of effect, while at its worst it led to a mere stale following of the 'rules'.

Although the elements of neoclassical theory can be traced back to the 15th century, the style was only codified in 1638, when the Academie Français judged the arguments over Corneille's THE CID. The style went on to enjoy an absolute triumph on the French stage (where its greatest practitioners were Corneille and Racine) and remained a powerful influence on Continental drama until the early 19th century, when it was swept away by Romanticism. In Britain, Jonson, Dryden, and Addison were among those who responded to the interest in neoclassical theories but the movement never became established. In terms of theatre architecture neoclassicism stimulated the rejection of baroque and rococo styles and inspired attempts to invoke the grandeur of Greek and Roman temples.

Nero (37 AD–68 AD) Roman emperor (54 AD–68 AD), who prided himself upon his prowess as an actor. He appeared both as a *pantomimus* and in tragic roles and undertook a notorious acting tour of Greece; this contributed to the growing unrest that led ultimately to his downfall and suicide.

Nervo, Jimmie *See* Crazy Gang.

Nesbitt, Cathleen (1888–1982) British actress, who made her professional debut in 1910 and then went with the Irish Players to New York, where she was acclaimed in Synge's *The Well of the Saints*. Subsequently she played at the Abbey Theatre in Dublin and in London as well as returning frequently to the US. Her London credits included varied roles in plays by Webster, Dryden, Lonsdale, Zola, T S Eliot, Flecker, and Shakespeare, playing Goneril to Gielgud's Lear in 1940. Her last West End appearance was as the Dowager Lady Headleigh in Robin Maugham's *The*

Claimant (1964), and she played Mrs Higgins in a revival of *My Fair Lady* in the US when she was over 90.

Nestroy, Johann Nepomuk (1801–62) Austrian playwright and actor, who became a leading writer of comedy for the Viennese stage in the mid-19th century. Having begun as an opera singer, he became popular as a character actor and was the author of more than 80 plays satirizing contemporary bourgeois society. His plays, in which he often played the central role himself, were largely adaptations of other works and included lively parodies of Wagner and other contemporaries (of which *Judith und Holofernes* is the best known). His adaptation *Einen Jux will er sich machen* was later rewritten as THE MATCHMAKER (1954) by Thornton Wilder and provided the basis of the musical *Hello Dolly!* (1965). In 1854 he succeeded Karl Carl as director of the Leopoldstädter.

Principal works:

> *Der Zettelträger*: 1827; translated as *The Billposter*.
> *Der böse Geist Lumpazivagabundus*: 1833.
> *Das Haus der Temperamente*: 1837.
> *Die verhängnisvolle Faschingsnacht*: 1839.
> *Der Talisman*: 1840.
> *Das Mädl aus der Vorstadt*: 1841; translated as *The Girl from the Suburbs*.
> *Einen Jux will er sich machen*: 1842; translated as *The Merchant of Yonkers* (or *On the Razzle*).
> *Der Zerrissene*: 1844.
> *Der Unbedeutende*: 1846.
> *Judith und Holofernes*: 1849.

Nethersole, Olga Isabel (1870–1951) British actress and manager, who made her debut at Brighton in 1887 and enjoyed her first London success as Janet Preece in Pinero's *The Profligate* (1889). Subsequently she formed her own management and built a reputation on both sides of the Atlantic in such challenging parts as Fanny Legrand in Clyde Fitch's *Sapho* (1900), which led to her arrest in New York for indecency, and the title roles in Sudermann's *Magda* (1904) and Maeterlinck's *Mary Magdalene* (1910).

Neuber, (Frederika) Carolina (Carolina Weissenborn; 1697–1760) German actress and manager, known as Die Neuberin, whose collaboration with the critic Gottsched transformed the German theatre. Having established her reputation in breeches parts, she set up her own company and – with Gottsched – presented a largely classical repertory as opposed to the conventional farces and harlequinades. In 1739 her influential partnership with Gottsched broke up; subsequently they indulged in a series of vitriolic exchanges and Neuber's company lost popularity. In 1748 she founded a new touring troupe to present the plays of the young Lessing; this met with only limited success and she died in poverty. Her insistence on discipline and careful rehearsal are now recognized, however, as having laid the foundations of the modern German theatre.

neume A group of notes sung as an expansion of the basic melody in early church plainsong; gradually this developed into the interpolated TROPE, which is seen as the beginning of the medieval LITURGICAL DRAMA.

Neville, John (1925–) British actor and director. He worked at Birmingham and Bristol before proving himself a fine classical actor with the Old Vic company in the 1950s, his parts including Hamlet, Romeo, Othello, and Richard II. As director of the Nottingham Playhouse (1963–68), he was responsible for many interesting productions, appearing himself in such roles as Willy Loman in Miller's *Death of a Salesman* (1967). He appeared as Macheath in *The Beggar's Opera* at the Chichester Festival Theatre in 1972, then went to Canada and became director of the Citadel Theatre, Edmonton. In 1977 he played at the National Theatre in Beckett's *Happy Days*, but then returned to Canada to become director of the Neptune Theatre, Halifax, Nova Scotia. From 1983 to 1989 he was artistic director of the STRATFORD (ONTARIO) FESTIVAL. In the 1990s he appeared on the London stage again in *The School for Scandal* (1990, Royal National Theatre) and *The Dance of Death* (1995).

New Ambassadors Theatre *See* Ambassadors Theatre.

New American Museum *See* American Museum.

New Amsterdam Theatre A 1793-seat theatre on West 42nd Street, New York, which opened in 1903 with a production of *A Midsummer Night's Dream*. It housed Ziegfeld's *Follies* from 1914 to 1924 and was then used for musicals and straight plays until 1937, when it became a cinema. A studio theatre on the roof, the **Aerial Gardens Theatre**, was used for intimate revues. By the late 1980s the building was in poor condition; it was purchased by the Walt Disney Corporation in 1995, an event which is credited with sparking the revitalization of the Times Square area. It currently houses the Disney musical *The Lion King*.

New Bowery Theatre *See* Bowery Theatre.

Newcastle Playhouse A theatre in Newcastle-upon-Tyne, which was built in 1970 on the site of a previous theatre named after Flora Robson. Owned by the University of Newcastle, it became a venue for touring companies for a time. In 1978 the company was revived, since when it has staged a varied programme from Brecht to university productions in the small Gulbenkian Studio.

New Chelsea Theatre *See* Royal Court Theatre.

New Comedy A style of ancient Greek comedy that evolved from MIDDLE COMEDY during the mid-4th century BC. An early manifestation of the COMEDY OF MANNERS, the New Comedy, reached its apotheosis in the plays of Menander and exerted a strong influence upon later Roman playwrights, including Terence and Plautus.

New Drama British drama from the period 1890 to 1914, during which the influence of such writers as Ibsen, Strindberg, Maeterlinck, and Hauptmann was first felt in the UK. The movement was inaugurated by G B Shaw's first play, *Widowers' Houses* (1892), and culminated in Harley Granville-Barker's seasons at the Royal Court (1904–07); these incidentally promoted the development of new repertory theatres at Manchester, Glasgow, Liverpool, and Birmingham specifically for the performance of new and challenging works. The New Drama was most important for its introduction of socially relevant subject matter and its assertion of the function of the theatre as a forum for debate and a force for change.

New Dramatists, The A New York organization for playwrights, founded in 1947; it provides facilities for readings and workshops in a former church on 44th Street between 9th and 10th Avenues.

New English Opera House *See* Royalty Theatre.

Newes, Tilly *See* Wedekind, Frank.

Newington Butts Theatre A theatre at Newington Butts, London, which was built around 1576. The existence of the theatre was subsequently threatened by fear of the plague but is known from the writings of Henslowe to have been used for some years for performances of Marlowe, Shakespeare, and others. The site is now occupied by the Elephant and Castle traffic junction.

New London Theatre The most modern of London's West End theatres, which is equipped with a revolving stage and seats, walls, and lights that can be repositioned electrically. Designed by Sean Kenny and built on the site of the WINTER GARDEN THEATRE in Drury Lane, the New London opened in 1973 with Peter Ustinov's *The Unknown Soldier and his Wife*, followed by the rock-'n'-roll musical *Grease*. It was used as a television studio from 1977 to 1980. The theatre's original seating capacity of 907 was increased to 1102 for the Lloyd Webber musical *Cats*, which began its long run in 1981.

Newman Theatre *See* New York Shakespeare Festival.

New National Theatre *See* Chatham Theatre.

New Olympic Theatre *See* Olympic Theatre.

New Park Theatre A theatre on Broadway, New York, which opened in 1874 with Fechter in his own adaptation of a French play. In the same year John T Raymond starred in a dramatization of Mark Twain's *The Gilded Age*. Success continued with the Florences appearing in Woolf's *The Mighty Dollar* (1875) and G F Rowe in his own drama *Brass* (1876). Under Henry E Abbey from 1876, it prospered until 1882 when, on the day set for Lillie Langtry's New York debut there, the theatre was burnt down.

Mainly furnished with materials left over after the demolition of Booth's Theatre, the second **New Park Theatre** was opened in 1883 with a programme of musical drama. Subsequently Belasco became manager, presenting melodramas starring the young Minnie Maddern and others. Afterwards it became a museum.

New Royalty Theatre *See* Royalty Theatre.

New Theatre *See* Albery Theatre; Century Theatre; Nassau Street Theatre; Park Theatre.

New Theatre Comique *See* New York Theatre.

New Victoria Palace *See* Old Vic Theatre.

New Victory Theatre A 500-seat theatre on West 42nd Street, New York, between 7th and 8th Avenues, which opened (with a greater capacity) in 1902 with Lionel Barrymore in *Sag Harbor*. From 1902 until 1910 it was leased by Belasco and bore his name. *Abie's Irish Rose* transferred there in 1922 and stayed until 1928, a record-setting run. The theatre converted to a burlesque house in 1931 and to a cinema in 1942, when its name was changed to the Victory in reference to the war. The building was closed in 1992, but renovated and reopened in 1995 under the present name – the first of the 42nd Street theatres to be improved under the current plan. It has a policy of showing high-quality children's theatre from all around the world.

New Way to Pay Old Debts, A A comedy by Philip MASSINGER, written in 1625. First performance: London, c. 1632. The play is notable chiefly for the character of the scheming Sir Giles Overreach, a monstrous villain based on the extortioner Sir Giles Mompesson. Edmund Kean was the first actor to excel in the role.

New York City Center *See* City Center of Music and Drama.

New Yorker Theatre A theatre on West 54th Street, New York, which opened as the **Gallo Theatre** in 1927. The theatre reopened as the New Yorker in 1930 with Ibsen's *The Vikings* but enjoyed little success. In 1933 Billy ROSE operated it as the Casino de Paris, and in 1936 it became a British-style music hall. An important house for the Federal Theatre from 1937, it was converted into a broadcasting studio in 1942. In the late 1970s it found notoriety as Studio 54, the most glamorous and exclusive discothèque of its day. Currently it is a theatre in the form of a nightclub, showing a revival of *Cabaret*.

New York Shakespeare Festival A US theatre company, originally set up (1954) by Joseph Papp to give free Shakespeare productions in New York. Its first productions were staged at the Emmanuel Presbyterian Church, the actors getting no pay; in 1957 the Festival moved to Central Park where the **Delacorte Theatre** was built in 1962. With the acquisition of the Public Theatre in 1967, it became the largest theatrical institution in the US, sponsoring much new talent and having numerous commercial transfers, of which A CHORUS LINE is the most famous. It operates partly on a permanent subsidy from the City of New York.

The Delacorte Theatre is the Festival's permanent outdoor summer home. Most of the seats are free, given away on the day of performance. Shakespeare is the preferred playwright, but other works have been offered, including works by Molière, and musicals.

The **Public Theatre** is a complex on Lafayette Street, New York, which houses four auditoriums, having been converted from the Astor Library in 1967. The four stages opened at different times: the **Anspacher Theatre**, which seats 275, in 1967 with *Hair*; the 108-seat **Other Stage** in 1968 as a workshop for playwrights; the **Newman Theatre**, with 300 seats, in 1970 with Dennis J Reardon's *The Happiness Cage*; and the 191-seat **Martinson Hall** in 1971 with the musical *Blood*.

New York Theatre A theatre on Broadway, New York, which opened as **Lucy Rushton's Theatre** in 1865 and was used initially for the staging of popular classics. Renamed the New York Theatre in 1866, it became the home of Augustin Daly's company in 1873. Subsequently it was known as Fox's Broadway and then the **Globe Theatre**, hosting variety shows. As the **New Theatre Comique**, it was taken over by Harrigan and Hart for vaudeville in 1881. It was destroyed by fire in 1884.

Another **New York Theatre** on Broadway opened as the Olympia Music Hall in 1895 and housed primarily vaudeville until 1899, when it was renamed the New York Theatre. Both straight plays and musical comedies could be seen there until 1912, when the theatre reverted to vaudeville as the **Moulin-Rouge**. The theatre was demolished in 1935.

New Zealand Players A theatre company founded in Wellington, New Zealand, in 1953. It toured almost continuously with plays by such foreign authors as Anouilh, Shaw, and Fry as well as works by native writers, notably Bruce Mason's *The Pohutukawa Tree*. The company broke up in 1960.

Niblo's Garden A small theatre, originally called the **Sans Souci**, on Broadway, New York, which was opened in 1827 by William Niblo. Housing a successful season by the Bowery Theatre in 1828, it was renamed Niblo's Garden the following year. A fire in 1846 destroyed it but it was replaced in 1849. Enlarged in 1853, it was the venue for Rachel's last New York appearance; other notable players included Chanfrau and Charlotte Crabtree. It presented a mixed programme of drama and spectacle until 1868, when the success of Boucicault's *After Dark; or, London by Night* changed the emphasis to melodrama. Burnt down in 1872 and reopened the same year, it never re-established its popularity and was finally demolished in 1895.

Niccolini, Giambattista (1782–1861) Italian playwright, author of several openly propagandist dramas on the themes of patriotism, despotism, and political freedom. His plays include *Nabucco* (1815), based on the life of Napoleon, and the poetic *Arnaldo da Brescia* (1843), in which he criticized the papal establishment.

Nichols, Mike (Michael Igor Peschowsky; 1931–) US actor, director, and producer, born in Berlin, who began his career in cabaret with Elaine May. He directed his first production, Neil Simon's *Barefoot in the Park*, in 1961 and later directed the same author's *The Odd Couple* (1965), *Plaza Suite* (1968), and *The Prisoner of Second Avenue* (1971) to great acclaim. He also directed Murray Schisgal's *Luv* (1964), Lillian Hellman's *The Little Foxes* (1967), and Chekhov's *Uncle Vanya* (1973) with similar success. Since the late 1960s he has worked mainly in the cinema.

Nichols, Peter (1927–) British playwright, whose work has been successful both on television and on the stage. Several of his plays deal poignantly with the impact of physical suffering, the most famous being *A Day in the Death of Joe Egg* (1967), which depicts a couple's struggle to care for their severely handicapped daughter. His comedy *The National Health* (1969) contrasts hospital soap-operas on television with the reality of life on the wards, while *Forget-me-not Lane* (1971) is strongly autobiographical and *Passion Play* (1980) is a marital tragicomedy. Other works include the musical *Privates on Parade* (1977), the comedy *Born in the Gardens* (1980), *Poppy* (1982), which depicts the Chinese Opium Wars, *A Piece of My Mind* (1986), and *Blue Murder* (1995).

Nickinson, John (1808–64) Canadian theatre manager and actor, born in London. Originally a soldier, he first appeared with the Garrison Amateurs at Montreal. In 1836 he joined the Theatre Royal, Montreal and then moved to the US. At Burton's Theatre in New York, he was the original Dombey in John Brougham's dramatization of the novel by Dickens. He also appeared regularly as Haversack in Boucicault's *The Old Guard*. He formed his own company in 1852 and managed theatres in Toronto, Quebec, and Cincinatti.

Nicolet, Jean-Baptiste (c. 1728–96) French acrobat and actor, who became popular at the Paris fairs during the 1760s. Subsequently he played young lovers and the role of Harlequin in his own theatre on the Boulevard du Temple and appeared before Louis XV, renaming his theatre the Spectacle des Grands Danseurs du Roi (later the Théâtre de la Gaîté).

Nicoll, Allardyce (1894–1976) Scottish theatre historian and academic, author of numerous books on both British and world drama. He also established an important collection of theatre material at Yale University, served as Director of the Shakespeare Institute for many years, and was President of the Society for Theatre Research from 1958. His books include the six-volume *History of English Drama 1600–1900*.

Nic Shiubhlaigh, Maire (Maire Price; 1888–1958) Irish actress, one of the pioneer players of the IRISH NATIONAL DRAMATIC SOCIETY. She appeared in the first production of Yeats's *Cathleen ni Houlihan* (1902) and, at the opening of the Abbey Theatre, played Nora Burke in Synge's *In the Shadow of the Glen*. She left the company in 1905, returning for occasional guest appearances.

night scenes *See* Italian night scenes.

Nilsen, Hans Jacob (1897–1957) Norwegian actor-manager and director, who became famous for his realistic productions of plays by Holberg and Ibsen. He worked initially at the Nationaltheatret and later in Bergen and Oslo; his most notable productions included Ibsen's *Peer Gynt* (1948).

Nina Vance Alley Theatre A theatre company in Houston, Texas, one of the oldest non-profit-making companies in the US. It was founded as the **Alley Theatre** in 1947, the name changing in 1980 on the death of its founder, Nina Vance. The company's first production was Lillian Hellman's *The Children's Hour*. In 1968 it moved into a new building with two auditoriums of 824 and 296 seats. Its own productions have included a variety of classics, children's plays, and new works; since 1989 it has often brought in foreign artists.

Nō (or *Noh*) A form of Japanese theatre, which was created by the performers Kanami (1333–84) and his son ZEAMI and has since become the most important element in the classical drama of Japan. The *Nō* play reflects the ritualistic code of honour of the Samurai warriors and is performed entirely by male actors; it dates in its present form from the early 17th century. Incorporating stately dances, music, and much noble language, the plays are based upon stories taken from Buddhist scriptures, novels, poems, and other sources. They are performed on a square roofed stage, with the audience seated on two sides; little use is made of scenery. Most of the action revolves around two actors, the *shite* and the *waki*, both of whom are masked and dressed in magnificent costumes. Including the complementary KYŌGEN interludes, a *Nō* performance might last seven hours in all. European writers to have been profoundly influenced by the *Nō* tradition include W B Yeats.

Noble, Adrian (1950–) British director, who was appointed artistic director of the Royal Shakespeare Company in 1991. He began his career at the Bristol Old Vic in 1976 before joining the RSC as a resident director in 1980. His numerous Shakespearean productions include the famous Kenneth BRANAGH *Henry V* (1984) and Branagh's *Hamlet* (1992), which broke all box-office records at the RSC. Other recent work has included Sophocles' *Oedipus* plays (1991), an acclaimed *King Lear* (1993), and *The Tempest* (1998).

NODA *See* National Operatic and Dramatic Association.

Nokes, James (d. 1696) English actor, who began as a boy actor playing female roles for John Rhodes at the Cockpit before joining Davenant's company. He developed into an excellent comedian, appearing in a wide variety of parts, most notably in the title role of *Sir Martin Mar-all*, which Dryden wrote for him.

Nora Bayes Theatre *See* 44th Street Theatre.

Norman, Marsha (1947–) US playwright, who first gained public attention with *Getting Out* (1977), which deals with the emotional state of a woman released from prison. Her 1983 drama *'night, Mother*, in which a woman announces to her mother that she is going to commit suicide, won the Pulitzer Prize. She also supplied the book for the musical *The Secret Garden* (1991).

Norske Theatret A theatre in Christiana (now Oslo), Norway, which was founded in 1913 as a venue for native Norwegian drama. The theatre has had a limited impact with productions of plays written in Nynorsk, the official Norwegian language.

Northcott Theatre A repertory theatre in Exeter, which was founded in 1967 with the support of the University of Exeter and the businessman G V Northcott. The theatre, equipped with a flexible stage and seating for up to 433 (main house), presents a wide variety of drama, including modern plays, musicals, and amateur productions. There is also a studio space seating 100.

Northwestern University A university in Evanston, Illinois, just north of Chicago, whose highly regarded school of theatre is one of the oldest in the US. It has been famous for its actor training since the 1940s.

Norton, Thomas (1532–84) English lawyer and playwright, who (with Thomas Sackville) wrote GORBODUC, the first native tragedy written entirely in blank verse.

Norwid, Cyprian Kamil (1821–83) Polish poet and playwright, who contributed to the Polish Romantic movement while living in penniless exile in Paris. Ignored in his own time, he wrote a number of poetic dramas on religious and historical themes, including *Zwolon*, and several comedies tackling social issues. His sophisticated plays were first recognized as significant in the early 20th century.

Norworth, Jack (1879–1959) US comedian, who became a major star of vaudeville in both New York and London alongside his wife, the singer Nora Bayes. After their divorce in 1913 he enjoyed success in revue in London and opened a theatre (later the Belmont Theatre) in New York; he was also the composer of the popular song 'Shine on, Harvest Moon'.

Nottingham Playhouse A large theatre in Nottingham, which was opened in 1963 to replace a theatre of the same name converted from a cinema in 1948. Seating up to 766, it has been used for major plays by Brecht, Shaw, Fry, and Brenton among others, many productions subsequently transferring to London. Notable Shakespearean successes have included *King Lear* with Sir Michael Hordern and *Hamlet* with Alan Bates.

Nouveau Monde, Théâtre du A French-Canadian theatre company established in Montreal in 1951. Under the leadership of Jean Gascon it found early acclaim with productions of plays by Molière, repeating its success in Paris in 1955 and subsequently at the Stratford (Ontario) Festival. It consolidated its reputation with a wide range of Canadian and foreign plays, notably those of Marcel Dubé, presented at a succession of venues. In 1972 the company settled permanently at the Théâtre de la Comédie-Canadienne, where it presented lunchtime theatre and numerous original works. Its controversial production of *Les Fées ont soif* (The Fairies are Thirsty) by Denise Boucher in 1978 resulted in the withdrawal of its state grant. The training facility established by the company in its early days became the basis of the Canadian National Theatre School.

Nouveautés, Théâtre des A theatre on the Boulevard Poissonnière in Paris, founded in 1920 as a venue for light comedy and musicals. The earliest Parisian theatre of the name was opened in 1827 close to the Bourse but was damaged in the revolution of 1830 and finally closed after incurring official disfavour. A second Théâtre des Nouveautés opened on the Boulevard St Martin in 1866 but was destroyed by fire almost immediately; a third theatre opened in 1878 on the Boulevard des Italiens and saw the establishment of Feydeau's reputation.

Novelli, Ermete (1851–1919) Italian actor, who became a leading performer of tragic roles upon the Italian stage. Although he began in comedy, he later won great acclaim – despite his large size – in such Shakespearean roles as Othello, Lear, Macbeth, and Hamlet, all of which he delivered with great passion; other successes included Aicard's *Le Père Lebonnard*. He also ran his own theatre, La Casa di Goldoni in Rome, for a brief time in 1900 but was soon forced to close.

Novello, Ivor (David Ivor Davies; 1893–1951) British composer, actor-manager, and playwright. Novello established his reputation first as a composer with such songs as 'Keep the Home Fires Burning' during World War I. In 1921 he made his debut as an actor in Sacha Guitry's *Deburau*, after which he enjoyed success in Hollywood. He returned to the UK to star in his own drama *The Rat* (1924). Subsequent successes included a series of plays and the romantic musicals *Glamorous Night* (1935), *Careless Rapture* (1936), *Crest of the Wave* (1937), and *The Dancing Years* (1939) – all performed at Drury Lane; later musicals included *King's Rhapsody* (1949) and *Gay's the Word* (1951).

Novelty Theatre *See* Kingsway Theatre.

Nunn, Trevor (1940–) British director. He directed his first production with the Marlowe Society in Cambridge and later worked at Coventry's Belgrade Theatre before joining the RSC in 1965. Appointed the company's artistic director in 1968, he was subsequently its chief executive and joint artistic director (with Terry Hands) from 1978 to 1986. Among his important productions of the 1960s and 1970s were the first modern presentation of Tourneur's *The Revenger's Tragedy* (1966), Vanbrugh's *The Relapse* (1967), *King Lear* (1968), *The Romans* cycle (1972) of Shakespearean plays, Ibsen's *Hedda Gabler* (1975), *Macbeth* (1976), *The Comedy of Errors* (1976), and David Edgar's adaptation of *The Life and Adventures of Nicholas Nickleby* (1980). In the 1980s he directed a series of hugely successful musicals, including *Les Misérables* (1985) with the RSC and the Lloyd Webber shows *Cats* (1981), *Starlight Express* (1984), and

Aspects of Love (1989). After leaving the RSC he worked as a freelance before being appointed director of the Royal National Theatre in 1997. He was married to Janet SUZMAN from 1969 to 1986 and is now married to the actress Imogen Stubbs.

nurseries The acting schools of the Restoration theatre in London. The three main nurseries were the **Hatton Garden Nursery**, founded by Killigrew around 1662 and later installed at the Vere Street Theatre, the **Barbican Nursery**, opened by Davenant's widow in 1671, and the **Bun Hill Nursery**, founded in 1671. Actors trained in the nurseries included Joseph Haines.

Nušič, Branislav (1864–1938) Serbian playwright, who was the author of several comedies still popular in his own country. The most successful of his satires include *The Suspicious Person* (1887), *The Lady Minister* (1929), and *Power* (1938).

Nye Teater *See* Oslo Nye Teater.

O

Oakley, Annie *See* Cody, William Frederick.

Oberammergau A town in Bavaria, scene of the most famous surviving Passion play. The play was first performed in 1634; since then it has been presented every ten years in gratitude for the town's survival during the plague. It is now a major tourist attraction.

Obey, André (1892–1975) French playwright and director of the Comédie-Française. In the early 1930s he became involved with the Compagnie des Quinze, for whom he wrote *Noé* (Noah; 1931), *Le Viol de Lucrèce* (1931), and *La bataille de la Marne* (1931). His later plays include *Le Trompeur de Séville* (1937), *L'Homme de cendres* (1949), and *Lazare* (1951).

Obie awards Awards established in 1956 by New York's *Village Voice* newspaper to recognize achievement in the OFF-BROADWAY theatre. The name is a phonetic spelling of OB (off-Broadway).

Obraztsov, Sergei Vladimirovich (1901–91) Russian puppeteer, who became director of the Soviet State Puppet Theatre. A specialist in rod-puppets, he was known for his elaborate productions featuring numerous lively puppet characters.

O'Casey, Sean (1880–1964) Irish playwright, author of several major plays on the themes of Irish nationalism and life in the tenements of Dublin. His first three plays, THE SHADOW OF A GUNMAN (originally called *On the Run*), JUNO AND THE PAY-COCK, and THE PLOUGH AND THE STARS were all produced at the Abbey Theatre; for most critics these tragicomedies are his greatest and most lasting achievement. *The Plough and the Stars* provoked nationalist outrage and a riot in the theatre at its first performance; when the Abbey refused to stage his next play, THE SILVER TASSIE, on artistic grounds, O'Casey quarrelled with W B Yeats and moved to England, rarely returning to his native country thereafter. Subsequent plays, several of which were set in England and show the influence of Expressionism, were less successful despite their echoes of the superb characterization and use of comic devices in his earlier writing. At the heart of his most successful work is the concept of sacrifice for an idea and the contrast between the attitudes of men and women.

Principal works:
The Shadow of Gunman: 1923.
Juno and the Paycock: 1924.
The Plough and the Stars: 1926.
The Silver Tassie: 1929.

Within the Gates: 1934.
The Star Turns Red: 1940.
RED ROSES FOR ME: 1943.
Purple Dust: 1943.
Oak Leaves and Lavender: 1947.
Cock-a-Doodle-Dandy: 1949.
The Bishop's Bonfire: 1961.
The Drums of Father Ned: 1958.
Behind the Green Curtains: 1961.

Octagon Theatre A theatre in Bolton, which was founded in 1967 with financial support from the public. A flexible octagonal auditorium seating up to 420, it is used for a wide variety of productions, including regular presentations of Shakespeare and modern dramas, and also caters for children's theatre.

Odd Couple, The A comedy by Neil SIMON. First performance: New York, 1965. The plot deals with Felix Ungar, compulsively neat, and Oscar Madison, a slob, who decide to share an apartment after their divorces. The same problems that led to divorce appear in this new relationship. Simon rewrote the play in 1985 for two female leads. The original play spawned a successful film (1968) and a television series.

O'Dea, Jimmy (James Augustine O'Dea; 1899–1965) Irish actor, whose popular appearances in pantomime and revue included many as the rascally Biddy Mulligan. He toured England and Ireland many times and occasionally ventured into straight theatre, playing Bottom with the Gate Theatre company in 1940.

Odell's Theatre *See* Goodman's Fields Theatre.

Odéon, Théâtre National de l' A theatre in Paris, which began as the home of the Comédie-Française in 1781. Renamed the Odéon in 1795, the theatre was reconstructed in 1816, burnt down in 1818, and was again rebuilt as a venue for light comedy and operetta. Subsequently it established itself as a home for serious drama, a reputation which was further enhanced by André Antoine and Gémier in the early 20th century. In 1959 the Odéon became independent of the Comédie-Française and was renamed the **Théâtre de France**; notable directors included Jean-Louis Barrault, whose production of Genet's *Les Paravents* caused riots in 1966. The THÉÂTRE DES NATIONS was based there under Barrault, but after the student riots of 1968 (with which the theatre was identified) the Odéon reverted to its original name and again housed the Comédie-Française (1971). In 1983 it became the permanent home of the newly created THÉÂTRE DE L'EUROPE.

Odets, Clifford (1906–63) US playwright, whose first success came with the one-act play WAITING FOR LEFTY; this was produced by the Group Theatre, of which he was a founder-member. Odets joined the Communist party in 1934 and built a reputation as a theatrical radical, although towards the end of his career he turned to script writing for Hollywood. His early works are enlivened by a sense of realism, excellent characterization, and political energy; later works, including the commercially successful *The Big Knife*, suffer from an element of self-pity.

Principal works:
Waiting for Lefty: 1935.

AWAKE AND SING!: 1935.
GOLDEN BOY: 1937.
Night Music: 1940.
Clash by Night: 1941.
The Big Knife: 1949.
THE COUNTRY GIRL: 1950.
The Flowering Peach: 1954.

odeum An early roofed theatre, used by the Greeks and Romans for musical and po-
etical contests.

Oedipus at Colonus A tragedy by SOPHOCLES. First performance: Athens, 406 BC.
The sequel to OEDIPUS REX, the play was produced after the playwright's death and
depicts the redemption through suffering of the central character, now old, blind,
and in exile.

Oedipus Rex A tragedy by SOPHOCLES, often considered his masterpiece. First
performance: 429 BC. Central to the play is the incest of Oedipus when he marries
his mother Jocasta, after unwittingly murdering his father; the theme was later developed by many other playwrights and, as an instance of a pyschological phenomenon, by Freud. It was memorably revived in 1945 in London with Olivier in
the leading role.

Oehlenschläger, Adam Gottlob (1779–1850) Danish poet and playwright, who
was a prominent figure of the Romantic movement in Denmark. He drew heavily
on Norse mythology for several of his plays and was much influenced by Kotzebue,
Shakespeare, and Ewald. His most admired plays were written early in his career and
include *Sanct-Hans Aften Spil* (1802), *Aladdin* (1804), and the tragedies *Hakon Jarl hin
Rige* (1807) and *Baldur hin Gode* (1807), which reflected his meeting with Goethe at
Weimar.

Oeuvre, Théâtre de l' *See* Art, Théâtre d'; Lugné-Poë, Aurélien-François.

off-Broadway US theatre movement that developed as an alternative to the commercial theatre of Broadway during the 1950s and 1960s. The production of Tennessee Williams's *Summer and Smoke* at the Circle-in-the-Square in 1952 heralded the
emergence of a new artistically challenging theatre that rapidly spread throughout
the US, drawing on native talent and tackling difficult contemporary issues. In 1953
the great success of the Theatre de Lys production of *The Threepenny Opera* showed
that off-Broadway could be commercial in its own way. Other notable highlights included the Living Theatre's production of Jack Gelber's *The Connection* in 1959,
Albee's *The Zoo Story* (1960), and Kenneth H Brown's *The Brig* (1963). By the 1970s
many of the leading off-Broadway venues in New York had been absorbed into the
conventional Broadway tradition and truly experimental work was left to the new
OFF-OFF-BROADWAY movement.

off-Loop theatre The Chicago equivalent of OFF-BROADWAY. The 'Loop' (central
business district) of Chicago has large theatres that show musicals and dramas with
touring stars. Off-Loop refers to those many local companies, of which the STEP-
PENWOLF THEATRE is the most famous, which present challenging alternative
work. They have been an influential factor in US theatre since the 1970s.

off-off-Broadway   Technically, this term refers to any New York theatre of less than 100 seats which does not have to use union talent. However, it more usually refers to the US theatre movement that succeeded OFF-BROADWAY as a focus for serious and experimental new drama. This began in the late 1960s as off-Broadway itself became more expensive and conventional; early off-off-Broadway companies included the San Francisco Mime Troupe and the Open Theatre. Venues range from small theatres to halls and cellars, while performances may be professional or amateur.

O'Flaherty, Mrs   *See* Winstanley, Eliza.

Ohel Theatre   A Jewish theatre company, founded in Palestine in 1925. Under Moshe Halevy (1895–1974), the group was linked to the Jewish Labour Federation and began with dramatizations of stories by Peretz and biblical tales, mostly given to kibbutz audiences. Members of the group, who initially also held jobs in factories and on the fields, subsequently toured Israel and Europe but the company gradually declined after 1958, disbanding in 1969.

Ohio Roscius   *See* Aldrich, Louis.

O'Horgan, Tom (1926–)   US director. After much work off-off Broadway, he came to wider attention with his productions at the off-Broadway Café LA MAMA. He popularized then avant-garde effects in his staging of the musicals *Hair* (1968) and *Jesus Christ, Superstar* (1971), as well as the play *Lenny* (1968).

Oh, What a Lovely War!   A documentary drama with music about World War I, created by Joan LITTLEWOOD and her Theatre Workshop company. First production: Theatre Royal, Stratford East, 1963. A scathing indictment of the follies of the generals and a moving celebration of the common humanity of the soldiers on both sides, the play transferred to the West End (and Paris) later the same year, and was filmed by Richard Attenborough in 1969.

O'Keeffe, John (1747–1833)   British playwright, who began as an actor in his native Dublin but later settled in London, where he wrote a series of comic operas, farces, burlesques, and pantomimes. His plays include the farce *Tony Lumpkin in Town* (1778), *The Poor Soldier* (1783), *Peeping Tom* (1784), and *Wild Oats; or, the Strolling Gentleman* (1791).

O'Kelly, Seumas (c. 1875–1918)   Irish playwright, novelist, short-story writer, and journalist. A prolific writer, he drew repeatedly upon the rural world of his youth in his work. Several of his plays were favourably received, notably *The Shuiler's Child* (1909), which deals with the unusual theme of child desertion. *The Bribe* (1913) is also worthy of note.

Okhlopov, Nikolai Pavlovich (1900–67)   Russian actor and director, a leading figure of the experimental Soviet theatre during the 1930s. After spending four years under Meyerhold (1923–27) be became artistic director of the Realistic Theatre; there he presented innovative productions of contemporary works by such authors as Gorky and Pogodin before moving to the Vakhtangov Theatre, where his successes included Rostand's *Cyrano de Bergerac*. Subsequently he worked at the Theatre of the Revolution (later renamed the Mayakovsky Theatre), notably upon plays by Ostrovsky and Shakespeare as well as modern playwrights.

Oklahoma! A musical, based on the play *Green Grow the Rushes* by Lynn Riggs, that marked the first collaboration of Richard RODGERS and Oscar HAMMERSTEIN II. First performance: New York, 1943. The plot concerns the mutual love of Curly, a cowboy, and Laurie, a farmer's daughter, which is hindered by their own pride and the activities of Jud, a brutish hired hand. With its evident artistic seriousness and its full integration of dance, *Oklahoma!* proved a landmark in the American musical. The famous choreography was by Agnes De Mille.

Old Bachelor, The A comedy by William CONGREVE. First performance: Drury Lane, 1693. The first of Congreve's dramatic works, the play explores sexual relationships through the various marriages of Heartwell, Sylvia, Vainlove, Bellamour, Tribulation Spintext, Fondlewife, Sir Joseph Wittol, Araminta, Laetitia, and Bellinda. Betterton, Mrs Mountfort, and Mrs Bracegirdle headed the original cast.

Old Bowery Theatre *See* Bowery Theatre.

Old Comedy The earliest comic theatrical tradition of ancient Greece, which evolved during the 4th and 5th centuries BC. The Greek comic drama developed later than the tragic form (the first contest for comedy not being held until 486 BC) and was descended from primitive mime and ritual performances, especially those connected with fertility rites (as reflected by the wearing of the phallus).

Early writers of Old Comedy included Magnes and Crates; the most important figure, however, was ARISTOPHANES, whose works observe a complex set structure, incorporating satire, fantasy, poetry, obscenity, speeches on unrelated topics delivered directly to the audience, and the use of masks and a large chorus. Other masters of the genre included Ameipsas, Cratinus, and Eupolis. By the time of Aristophanes's death the tradition had given way to MIDDLE COMEDY.

Old Drury *See* Chestnut Street Theatre; Park Theatre.

Oldfield, Anne (1683–1730) English actress, discovered by Farquhar while she was working as a barmaid. For a time she was the playwright's mistress, but it was Sir John Vanbrugh's interest that led to an engagement at Drury Lane in 1699. She was admirably suited to the plays of Colley Cibber, and established her reputation playing Lady Betty Modish in *The Careless Husband* in 1704. In 1706 she succeeded Anne Bracegirdle as Millamant in *The Way of the World* and in 1707 she created the part of Silvia in *The Recruiting Officer*. She died at the height of her fame and was the first actress to be buried in Westminster Abbey.

Old Globe Theatre A theatre and company in San Diego, California. The original building was constructed in 1935 for the California Pacific International Exposition and leased from the city two years later by the San Diego Community Theatre. Over the years the organization grew and became fully professional. The current theatre, rebuilt twice after fires, contains three auditoriums, one of which is an outdoor Elizabethan-style house used for summer productions.

Old Man *See* stock company.

Oldmixon, Mrs (Georgina Sidus; c. 1763–1836) British actress. The daughter of an Oxford clergyman, she made an impressive debut at the Haymarket in 1783 and acted in London for 10 years before going to the US. She appeared with Wignell's company in Philadelphia, in ballad operas, and later at New York's Park Theatre, where she played a range of parts, including Ophelia, Mrs Candour, and the Nurse.

Old Mo *See* Middlesex Music Hall.

Old Tote Theatre A theatrical company established at a racecourse in Sydney, Australia, in 1963. It soon acquired a formidable reputation with productions of Chekhov and various classical works; directors with the company included Tyrone Guthrie, who directed a version of *Oedipus the King* by Sophocles in 1970. It also presented a number of Australian dramas before being succeeded by the Sydney Theatre Company in 1978.

Old Vic Theatre One of London's oldest surviving theatres, built in 1816–18 on a site to the south of Waterloo Bridge. Originally named the **Royal Coburg Theatre** in honour of Prince Leopold and Princess Charlotte, it quickly became established not only as the home of melodrama but as one of the sights of London on account of its looking-glass curtain. Edmund Kean gave six performances at the theatre in 1831; in 1833 the theatre was renamed the **Royal Victoria Theatre** in honour of the young Princess Victoria. In 1858 a number of people were trampled to death in a stampede in the gallery caused by a false alarm of fire and the theatre's reputation declined.

In 1871 there was a change of ownership, the interior was reconstructed, and it reopened as the **New Victoria Palace**. The name was changed again in 1880, when the theatre was taken over by the social reformer Emma Cons; after further reconstruction it reopened as the **Royal Victoria Hall and Coffee Tavern**, providing entertainment for the working classes on strict temperance lines. When Miss Cons died in 1912 her niece Lilian BAYLIS took over the management, subsequently experimenting with productions of Shakespeare at popular prices and making the Old Vic famous as the first theatre in the world to produce all the plays contained in the First Folio. The year 1931 saw the first performance of ballet, with Anton Dolin as guest artist, and the formation of the Vic-Wells Ballet Company under the direction of Ninette da Valois. In 1933 opera and ballet were transferred to the Sadler's Wells Theatre, while drama remained at the Old Vic, where the company included Gielgud, Olivier, and Richardson. Badly damaged by bombs in 1941, the theatre remained closed until 1950.

The Old Vic company was disbanded in 1963 when the National Theatre company, directed first by Olivier and later by Peter Hall, took over the theatre. The work of these two companies built up a great reputation for the Old Vic throughout the world in the post-war years. After the National Theatre company's departure in 1976, however, a less successful period ensued under the management of the Prospect Theatre company and the theatre was put up for sale. In 1982 the Old Vic was purchased by the Canadian businessman Ed Mirvish; after extensive renovation it reopened with the Tim Rice musical *Blondel*. Subscription seasons were initiated and Shakespeare plays were reintroduced along with other drama and musicals. Acclaimed productions from this period included Racine's *Andromache* (1988) directed by Jonathan Miller and an award-winning revival of *Carmen Jones* (1991). In 1996–97 the Peter Hall company took up residence and presented an ambitious mixture of new and classic plays. However, substantial losses led Mirvish to put the theatre up for sale in 1998; it was rescued by a consortium, which is now (2000) trying to raise working capital.

Old Woman *See* stock company.

Oleanna A play by David MAMET. First performance: New York, 1992. The play explores the conflict between a middle-aged academic and an insecure female student, who brings false charges of sexual harassment after he makes a foolish but innocuous remark. The controversial subject matter polarized audience responses in both New York and London (where the play was presented by Harold Pinter).

Olimpico Teatro A theatre in Vicenza, Italy, which opened in 1585 with a performance of *Oedipus Rex* by Sophocles. Famous for its neoclassical architectural features, it was designed by Palladio and completed by Scamozzi but had little effect upon subsequent Italian theatres. It is the oldest surviving theatre in Europe.

Oliver! A musical by Lionel BART, based on *Oliver Twist* by Charles Dickens. First production: Albery Theatre, London, 1960. The story follows the experiences of Oliver, an orphan, in the London underworld with Fagin and his gang. The original production, which starred Ron Moody as Fagin, ran for over 2500 performances. A film followed in 1968 and there have been two West End revivals (1983, 1994).

Olivier, Laurence (Kerr), Baron (1907–89) British actor, director, and manager, generally considered the foremost actor of the English-speaking theatre in recent times. He made his first appearance in 1922 at Stratford-on-Avon as Katharina in an all-male production of *The Taming of the Shrew* and subsequently spent some years in repertory at Birmingham, as well as playing in a number of modern plays in the West End (including Coward's *Private Lives* in 1930).

In 1935 he alternated Romeo and Mercutio with John Gielgud at the New Theatre and went on to consolidate his reputation as an exceptional interpreter of major roles with performances with the Old Vic company, among them a full-length *Hamlet* in 1937. After World War II he became a codirector of the Old Vic company at the New Theatre, where once again he confirmed his standing as a great actor, playing among other parts Richard III, Hotspur, Oedipus, and Mr Puff in Sheridan's *The Critic*.

As an actor-manager in the early 1950s his appearances included the Duke of Altair in Christopher Fry's *Venus Observed* (1950), Antony in *Antony and Cleopatra*, and Caesar in Shaw's *Caesar and Cleopatra* (1951) opposite Vivien Leigh, to whom he was at that time married. After leading a brilliant Stratford-on-Avon season in 1955 he had further spectacular West End triumphs as Archie Rice in John Osborne's *The Entertainer* (1957) and as Fred Midway in David Turner's *Semi-Detached* (1962).

He was director of the Chichester Festival Theatre from 1961 to 1963 and then became the first director of the National Theatre (1963–73), where he gave unique performances in many famous parts, including Astrov in Chekhov's *Uncle Vanya* (1963), Tattle in Congreve's *Love for Love* (1965), Othello (1965), and Shylock (1970). His many film appearances include those in *Henry V*, *Richard III*, and *Hamlet*, all of which he also produced and directed. He received a knighthood in 1947 and was created Baron Olivier of Brighton in 1970; his third wife was the actress Joan PLOWRIGHT. The **Laurence Olivier Awards** are presented annually for the best West End productions, under the auspices of the Society of London Theatre.

Olivier Theatre One of the three theatres comprising the ROYAL NATIONAL THEATRE in London. Opened in 1976 with a performance of *Tamburlaine the Great* by Marlowe, it was named in honour of Lord Olivier and, seating 1160, is used primarily for spectacular large-scale productions. Plays presented on its open stage have included works by O'Casey, Congreve, Ibsen, Bond, Shaffer, and Brenton.

Olmo, Jacob (1690–1755) Jewish playwright. His play *Eden Aruch* (c. 1720) was much influenced by *Tofteh Aruch* by Moses Zacuto.

Olympia An entertainment complex on Broadway, New York, which was opened by Oscar Hammerstein in 1895. Containing a concert hall, a music hall (which became the New York Theatre), and the Lyric Theatre, it was sold in 1898. The Lyric reopened separately as the Criterion that same year.

Olympia Music Hall *See* Standard Theatre.

Olympia Theatre A theatre off Dame Street, Dublin, which opened as a music hall in 1855. Leading English performers appeared there until 1897, when the building was reconstructed, being renamed the Empire Palace of Varieties and then the Olympia in 1922. Subsequently serious drama was presented there, including works by native Irish playwrights. After World War II the theatre housed its own resident company for several years until, in 1964, the theatre was sold; it was reorganized in 1974 as a venue for both serious dramas and variety acts. However, defects in the building itself led to the closure of the theatre until 1977, when it reopened with the musical *John, Paul, George, Ringo... and Bert.*

Olympic Theatre A theatre in the Strand, London, which was opened by Philip Astley in 1806. It was constructed largely from timber from a French sailing ship and was built in the form of a tent. Astley staged circus acts and other miscellaneous entertainments there until 1813 when R W Elliston took it over, renaming it the **Little Drury Lane Theatre** and presented plays until he was deprived of his licence as a result of the intervention of the Drury Lane management. As the Olympic Theatre it was then used for burletta and other forms of dramatic production and enjoyed considerable prosperity before being taken over by Madame Vestris in 1831. After opening with Maria Foote in *Mary Queen of Scots*, she established the theatre's reputation with a series of light entertainments and introduced Charles Mathews among others. The building was destroyed by fire in 1849 and rebuilt to seat 1750; performers who subsequently appeared there in romantic dramas included Kate Terry and Charles Wyndham. The theatre was again rebuilt in 1890 but proved unsuccessful and was demolished in 1904.

The first **Olympic Theatre** on Broadway, New York, opened in 1837 and had many changes of management before, in 1839, William Mitchell made it successful – as **Mitchell's Olympic** – as a venue for burlesque and spectacle. It was the first New York theatre to present a weekly matinée; notable productions included John Poole's *Hamlet Travestie*, burlesques of *Richard III*, Boucicault's *London Assurance*, and the opera *The Bohemian Girl*. After an outstanding season in 1847–48 with Planché's *The Pride of the Market* and Benjamin Baker's *A Glance at New York in 1848*, starring Frank Chanfrau, it eventually closed in 1850, reopening briefly to stage plays in German. The theatre was burnt down in 1854.

A second **Olympic Theatre** on Broadway opened in 1856 as **Laura Keene's Varieties** and was the first US theatre to have a female manager. In 1863 she left and, under Mrs John Wood, the theatre was renamed the Olympic. She presented the New York debuts of Mrs G H Gilbert and G F Rowe, while in 1867 G L Fox starred in *A Midsummer Night's Dream* (with scenery by Telbin), and in his pantomime *Humpty-Dumpty*, which had 483 performances. It was a home of variety from 1872 to 1880, when it was finally closed and demolished.

A **New Olympic Theatre** was opened on Broadway in 1856 by Chanfrau but failed as a venue for drama and subsequently housed minstrel shows and was renamed **Buckley's Olympic**.

Other theatres to have used the name, albeit briefly, include the Anthony Street Theatre (1812) and Wallack's Theatre (1862).

ombres chinoises *See* shadow play.

O'Neal, Frederick (1905–92) US Black actor, who made his first appearance on the professional stage as Silvius in *As You Like It* (1927). He helped found the AMERICAN NEGRO THEATRE in 1940 and made his first Broadway appearance four years later playing Frank in *Anna Lucasta* (1944), for which he won several awards. He was very active in educational work and served as president of the ACTORS' EQUITY ASSOCIATION from 1964 to 1973.

O'Neil, Nance *See* Rankin, Arthur McKee.

O'Neill, Eliza (1791–1872) Irish actress, who first appeared in her father's company at Drogheda. In 1815 she was immensely successful as Juliet at Covent Garden, where she remained for five years until her final appearance in Kotzebue's *The Stranger*. She retired on her marriage to William Becher, MP for Mallow.

O'Neill, Eugene (Gladstone) (1883–1953) US playwright, who was the son of the actor James O'Neill and wrote his first plays while recovering from tuberculosis in a sanatorium. From 1914 to 1915 he studied under George Pierce Baker at Harvard and became associated with the Provincetown Players, who produced several of his early dramas. BEYOND THE HORIZON, his first full-length play, reached Broadway and won him a Pulitzer Prize. Later plays treated such major themes as racism, human resilience, sexual passion, and family conflict, establishing him as one of the 20th century's leading dramatists, despite his somewhat uneasy command of language.

After the enormous success of MOURNING BECOMES ELECTRA, a treatment of Aeschylus's *Oresteia*, O'Neill retired from the theatre but continued to write in a more autobiographical vein. From this period came some of his finest works, notably THE ICEMAN COMETH, A MOON FOR THE MISBEGOTTEN, and LONG DAY'S JOURNEY INTO NIGHT, all of which remained unperformed for some years. His last years were blighted by Parkinson's disease, depression, and alcoholism. In the earlier part of his career he was involved with the foundation of various theatres, while the EUGENE O'NEILL THEATRE CENTER in Waterford, Connecticut, was founded and named in his honour in 1963. He was awarded a Nobel Prize in 1936.

Principal works:
  Beyond the Horizon: 1920; Pulitzer Prize.
  THE EMPEROR JONES: 1920.

ANNA CHRISTIE: 1921.
ALL GOD'S CHILLUN GOT WINGS: 1924.
DESIRE UNDER THE ELMS: 1924.
The Great God Brown: 1926.
Marco Millions: 1928.
Strange Interlude: 1928; Pulitzer Prize.
Lazarus Laughed: 1928.
The Dynamo: 1929.
Mourning Becomes Electra: 1931.
Ah, Wilderness!: 1933.
The Iceman Cometh: 1946.
A Moon for the Misbegotten: 1947.
Long Day's Journey into Night: 1956; Pulitzer Prize.
A TOUCH OF THE POET: 1957.
More Stately Mansions: 1963.

O'Neill, James (1847–1920) US actor, born in Ireland, who became a popular performer of strong romantic roles. Highly acclaimed in such adventures as *The Count of Monte Cristo* (1883) by Dumas *père*, in which he performed for over 30 years, he rivalled the success of Edwin Booth until his alcoholism and frustration as an artist led to his decline.

His second son was the celebrated playwright Eugene O'NEILL.

O'Neill, Maire (Mollie Allgood; 1887–1952) Irish actress, who was in all the Abbey Theatre's productions until 1913, coming to London in 1907 in Synge's *The Playboy of the Western World*. Later she was with the Liverpool Repertory Theatre and played a Shakespearean season at His Majesty's; subsequent triumphs included leading roles in several of O'Casey's plays.

Open Air Theatre A permanent open-air theatre in Regent's Park, London, where performances of Shakespeare were first given by Ben Greet in 1900. The idea was revived by Sydney Carroll in 1933 with a production of *Twelfth Night*. The theatre was reconstructed in 1961 and again in 1972; it has a seating capacity of 1187 and continues to present an annual summer season of Shakespeare.

Open Space Theatre *See* Marowitz, Charles.

open stage *See* thrust stage.

Open Theatre An experimental US theatre company, founded in New York in 1963 by Joseph Chaikin. The group became well known for its use of minimal staging and collective creation. The first full-length play created and produced by the group was *Viet Rock* (1966); other productions, which toured all around the world, included *The Serpent* (1968), *Terminal* (1969), *Mutation Show* (1971), and *Nightwalk* (1973). The group was disbanded in 1973.

Opera Comique A theatre built in the Aldwych, London, in 1870 and known as one of the Rickety Twins (together with the Globe Theatre, Newcastle Street). The Comédie Française and other foreign visiting companies played there, while in 1877 Richard D'Oyly Carte produced the first of several Gilbert and Sullivan operas at the theatre. Marie Tempest appeared in *The Fay o' Fire* in 1885. The theatre was closed in 1899 and demolished in 1902.

Opéra-Comique *See* Comédie-Italienne.

opposite prompt side *See* prompt side.

OP Riots *See* Covent Garden.

Orange Moll *See* Meggs, Mary.

Orange Street Theatre *See* Smock Alley Theatre.

orchestra In the Greek theatre, a circular or semicircular area in front of the main stage on which the chorus performed. Subsequently the term has been applied to the area in front of the stage where the musicians sit (*see* auditorium).

Oregon Shakespearean Festival A festival of Shakespearean drama, founded in 1935 at Ashland, Oregon. The oldest such festival in the US, it now offers a rotating repertoire in three theatres, including a 1175-seat outdoor Elizabethan stage.

Oresteia, The A trilogy of plays by AESCHYLUS, which constitutes the most complete surviving example of his work. First performance: Athens, 458 BC. Consisting of the tragedies *Agamemnon*, the *Choephori*, and the *Eumenides*, the *Oresteia* follows the pattern of thesis, antithesis, and resolution, culminating in the gods' judgement upon the murder of Clytemnestra by Orestes. The main themes are guilt and its expiation, and the relationship between vengeance and justice.

Ørjasæter, Tore (1886–1968) Norwegian poet and playwright. He is best known for the drama *Den lange bryllaupsreisa* (The Long Honeymoon; 1949), which considers the position of collaborators at the end of World War II. Other works include *Anne på torp* (Anne on the Farm; 1930) and the Expressionist play *Christophoros* (St Christopher; 1947).

Orlenev, Pavel Nikolayevich (1869–1932) Russian actor, who encouraged the adoption of naturalism outside Russia during a wide-ranging tour. Leading his own company from 1904 in conjunction with Alla Nazimova, he presented the first production in the US of Chekhov's *The Seagull* (1905) and later toured the USSR; his finest parts included the title role of Ibsen's *Brand* and Raskolnikov in Dostoevsky's *Crime and Punishment*.

Orlov, Dmitri Nikolayevich (1892–1955) Russian actor, who became highly popular in comic roles in the years after the Revolution of 1917. He enjoyed success in works by Pogodin and Simonov and influenced the theories of Meyerhold.

Orrery, Lord (Roger Boyle, First Earl of Orrery, 1621–79) English playwright, credited by Dryden with being the first to write heroic drama. His more successful surviving plays, which contain detailed stage directions, include *Mustapha* (1665) and *The Black Prince* (1667).

Orton, Joe (Joe Kingsley Orton; 1933–67) British playwright, whose black comedies shocked audiences by combining scandalous action with genteel language. Sexual perversion and official corruption are common elements throughout his plays, which began with ENTERTAINING MR SLOANE in 1964. Subsequent successes included LOOT (1966), *The Erpingham Camp* (1967), *The Ruffian on the Stair* (1967), and WHAT THE BUTLER SAW (1969). He was eventually murdered by his homosexual lover, who committed suicide.

Osborne, John (1929–94) British playwright and actor, whose extraordinarily successful play LOOK BACK IN ANGER triggered a new era in British drama. An actor in post-war repertory, Osborne drew heavily upon the conventional three-act naturalistic drama of the day in his early work, but soon began to experiment with a wide range of dramatic styles, from THE ENTERTAINER onwards. Throughout his work there runs a central preoccupation with the rebel at odds both with society and with those closest to him, expressing itself frequently in dramatic monologues of great power. Nurtured by George DEVINE at the Royal Court Theatre, he later wrote for the National Theatre and for television. *West of Suez* and subsequent plays failed to repeat the success of earlier work and Osborne had no new play on the British stage between 1976 and 1992, when *Déjà Vu*, a sequel to *Look Back in Anger*, was presented.

His first wife, the actress **Mary Ure** (1933–75), appeared in the premiere of *Look Back in Anger* and equally successfully in plays by Arthur Miller, Pinter, and Shakespeare. His second wife was Jill BENNETT.

Principal works:

Look Back in Anger: 1956.

The Entertainer: 1957.

Epitaph for George Dillon: 1958 (written with Anthony Creighton, 1955).

The World of Paul Slickey: 1959.

LUTHER: 1961.

Plays for England: The Blood of the Bambergs and *Under Plain Cover*: 1962.

INADMISSIBLE EVIDENCE: 1964.

A PATRIOT FOR ME: 1965.

A Bond Honoured: 1966.

Time Present: 1968.

Hotel in Amsterdam: 1968.

West of Suez: 1971.

A Sense of Detachment: 1973.

Watch it Come Down: 1976.

Déjà Vu: 1992.

Oscarsson, Per (1927–) Swedish actor, who won acclaim for his interpretation of intense roles in both classics and modern plays. At the Kungliga Dramatiska Teatern from 1947 to 1952 and subsequently based at Gothenburg, he found praise as Hamlet and in the plays of Strindberg and O'Neill among others. From the late 1960s onwards he worked mainly in film and television.

Oslo Nye Teater A theatre in Oslo, which opened in 1929 (as the **Nye Teater**). Although intended as a venue for native Norwegian drama, it was soon obliged to stage a more varied programme. From 1947 a new emphasis was placed upon serious drama under Axel Otto Normann. The theatre amalgamated with the Folketeatret in 1959 and, renamed the Oslo Nye Teater, eventually came under civic control; in more recent years it has enjoyed considerable success with a reduced company under the directorship of Toralv Maurstad.

Ostler, William (d. 1614) English actor, who began as a boy actor at the Blackfriars Theatre. Acclaimed in female roles, he appeared in plays by Jonson, Beaumont and Fletcher, and Webster, creating the character of Antonio in *The Duchess of Malfi*. He married the daughter of John Heminge and owned shares in the Globe and Blackfriars theatres.

Ostrovsky, Alexander Nikolayevich (1823–86) Russian playwright, whose plays in the Realist tradition linked the drama of Gogol and Chekhov. His best-known plays depict the world of the merchant class; THE BANKRUPT was banned for 13 years after it offended the traders of Moscow. Other works to find acclaim in English translation, include *The Forest* and the domestic tragedy THE STORM. *The Poor Bride* was praised for its depiction of Russian women, while *The Snow Maiden* became an opera by Rimsky-Korsakov. Most of his works were first presented at the Maly Theatre, which became known as the House of Ostrovsky.

Principal works:
Bankrot: 1849; translated as *The Bankrupt* (or *It's All in the Family*).
Bednaya nevesta: 1852.
Bednost' ne porok: 1854.
Dokhodnoye mesto: 1856.
Groza: 1859; translated as *The Storm*.
Dmitry Samozvanets: 1867.
Na vsyakogo mudretsa dovol'no prostoty: 1868.
Les: 1871; translated as *The Forest*.
Snegurochka: 1873; translated as *The Snow Maiden*.

Othello, the Moor of Venice A tragedy by William SHAKESPEARE, written c. 1602. First performance: 1604. A study of racial prejudice and sexual jealousy, the play depicts the decline of the respected Othello, a Moor, as a result of his overpowering love for Desdemona and the machinations of the malignant Iago. Based upon an Italian model, the play has been much discussed for its use of a 'double time scheme', by which events lasting several weeks are compressed into two days; it has been greatly admired for its richly poetic language.

Other Place A studio theatre established in 1974 at Stratford-on-Avon by the Royal Shakespeare Company; it is used for small-scale productions of classic and new plays as well as works not often seen today, such as Ford's *Perkin Warbeck* (1975). A production of *Hamlet* starring Ben Kingsley was particularly acclaimed in 1975. It has also staged premieres of plays by many leading contemporary authors, including Christopher Hampton's *Les Liaisons Dangereuses* (1985).

Other Stage *See* New York Shakespeare Festival.

O'Toole, Peter (1932–) British actor, born in Ireland, who began his career at the Bristol Old Vic in 1955. During the 1960 Stratford-on-Avon season his roles included Petruchio and a celebrated Shylock, while in 1963 he played Hamlet in the National Theatre's inaugural production at the Old Vic. After establishing a new reputation in major film roles, he returned to the London stage as Macbeth in a notorious production at the Haymarket Theatre in 1980. Subsequently he played in three Shaw revivals, as Tanner in *Man and Superman* (1983), as Higgins in *Pygmalion* (1984), and as King Magnus in *The Apple Cart* (1986). Recent work has included two successful plays by Keith Waterhouse, *Jeffrey Bernard is Unwell* (1989), in which he played the inebriated title character, and *Our Song* (1992).

Otto, Teo (1904–68) German stage designer, who attracted attention with his designs for the plays of Brecht. He worked on the premieres of both *Mutter Courage and ihre Kinder* (1941) and *Der gute Mensch von Sezuan* (1943) in Zurich; other successes included his designs for plays by Frisch and Goethe's *Faust* (1957).

Otway, Thomas (1652–85) English playwright and poet, who is best known for the blank-verse tragedy VENICE PRESERV'D (1682). The most successful of his plays in his own lifetime, however, was the farce *The Cheats of Scapin*, which was based on Molière. Several of his finest plays were written for Elizabeth Barry, with whom Otway was hopelessly in love; they included *Alcibiades* (1675) – a rhyming tragedy, and *The Orphan; or, the Unhappy Marriage* (1680), which was a blank verse domestic tragedy. Other works included *Don Carlos* (1676), *The Soldier's Fortune* (1680), and a sequel – *The Atheist; or, the Second Part of the Soldier's Fortune* (1683); he also adapted plays by Racine.

OUDS *See* Oxford University Dramatic Society.

Ouest, Comédie de l' *See Décentralisation Dramatique.*

Our Town A drama by Thornton WILDER. First performance: New York, 1938. Set in smalltown New England, the play revolves around Emily Webb and George Gibbs, following the course of their lives from childhood, through their marriage, to Emily's early death. It was famous for its then unusual non-literal staging, using a bare stage and no props. The play won a Pulitzer Prize.

out-of-town tryout The once-usual US practice of staging the first performance of new plays and (especially) musicals in cities other than New York – most commonly Boston, New Haven, or Philadelphia – thus allowing any needed changes to be made away from the eyes of the New York press. As productions have become increasingly elaborate, this practice has become rare; it has been replaced to some extent by the use of regional theatres to develop new works.

Ouville, Antoine Le Metel d' (c. 1590–1657) French playwright, elder brother of Boisrobert. Having established his reputation with *L'Esprit follet* (1638–39), based on a play by Calderón, he went on to adapt other Spanish works for the French stage.

Owens, John Edmond (1823–86) US actor, born in London, who excelled in comic and Yankee roles in both New York and London. He appeared widely as Sholon Shingle in Joseph S Jones's *The People's Lawyer*, while other successes included eccentric characters in plays by H J Byron, Colman the Younger, and Dion Boucicault.

Oxberry, William (1784–1824) British actor, who broke his indentures with a printer to work in the theatre. After work in the provinces he appeared unsuccessfully at Covent Garden, then toured Scotland before returning to London to appear in minor roles at the Lyceum, Drury Lane, and the Haymarket. He wrote the farce *The Actress of All Work* (1819) and founded the *Dramatic Mirror*.

His son was the actor **William Henry Oxberry** (1808–52), whose theatrical publications included *Oxberry's Weekly Budget* (1843–44). A popular actor in burlesque, he was also the author of several plays, notably *Matteo Falcone; or, the Brigand and His Son* (1836).

Oxford Music Hall A music hall opened by Charles Morton in 1861 in an old galleried tavern at the corner of Oxford Street and Tottenham Court Road, London. It was a leading venue during the heyday of the music hall, was twice destroyed by fire and rebuilt, and was replaced by a new building in 1893. Charles Cochran produced Bruce Bairnsfather's *The Better 'Ole* there in 1918; three years later it became the New Oxford Theatre. Sacha Guitry, Yvonne Printemps, Duse, and the Old Vic company all appeared there before the theatre closed in 1926.

Oxford Playhouse A repertory theatre in Beaumont Street, Oxford, which was opened in 1938 by Eric Dance to replace an earlier theatre adapted by J B Fagan as a home for his famous Oxford company. In 1956 the theatre won financial support from the Arts Council and from the actor Richard Burton. The **Meadow Players**, under Frank Hauser's direction, reopened the theatre with Giraudoux's *Electra* and remained for 17 years. In 1961 Oxford University acquired the lease and, in 1966, Richard Burton and his wife, Elizabeth Taylor, starred in an OUDS production of Marlowe's *Dr Faustus* to raise funds for an extension. A new Oxford Playhouse Company (known as **Anvil Productions**) was installed in 1974, their regular work being interspersed with university productions and visits from outside companies. Continuing financial crises led to a period of closure in the 1990s, since when the Playhouse has re-emerged as a leading venue for touring companies. A new production company was formed in 1999.

Oxford's Men An English theatre company formed from the household of the Earl of Oxford around 1492. Based in the provinces, the company caused controversy in 1547 when it performed during public mourning for Henry VIII; reformed in 1580 it later performed at the Theatre until a scandal provoked by a brawl resulted in its return to the provinces. In 1584 young members of the group appeared at Blackfriars and at Court. The company disbanded in 1602.

Oxford University Dramatic Society (OUDS) A theatre club founded at Oxford University in 1885 by Arthur Bourchier and other undergraduates. The society has built up a strong reputation over the years for its performances of Shakespeare and the classics; its productions, some of which have been presented outdoors, are often directed by professionals. Until 1939, professional actresses played all the female roles. A subsidiary society, Friends of the OUDS, staged successful productions from 1940 to 1946. The OUDS now has its base at the Oxford Playhouse, from which it also organizes tours and a festival of drama.

Oyono-Mbia, Guillaume (c. 1940–) African playwright, born in French Cameroon. His popular comedies deal with contemporary African themes but make use of the conventions of classical European comedy; they include *Trois Prétendants, un mari* (Three Suitors, One Husband; 1964) and *Notre Fille ne se mariera pas* (Our Daughter Will Never Get Married; 1971).

P

Pace-Egg Play *See* mummers' play.

Pacino, Al(fredo) (1940–) US actor. Although famous for his movie roles, Pacino started on the stage and has consistently returned to it. His early off-Broadway work included *The Indian Wants the Bronx* (1968) and *Does a Tiger Wear a Necktie?* (1969). He later appeared in AMERICAN BUFFALO on Broadway (1981 and 1983) and has played Antony in *Julius Caesar* for the New York Shakespeare Festival (1988). In 2000 he was appointed a co-president of the ACTORS' STUDIO.

Pacuvius, Marcus (220 BC–c. 130 BC) Roman artist and playwright, one of the first great writers of Latin tragedies. The nephew of Quintus Ennius, he is known to have written one play in the *praetexta* tradition, *Paullus*, and about 12 plays based on Greek originals; only the titles of these works survive. He was noted in his own time for the elegance of his style and his free treatment of Greek models.

Page, Anthony (1935–) British director. Page began acting and directing at Oxford University, later training at the Neighborhood Playhouse in New York. From 1958 he worked at London's Royal Court Theatre, becoming joint artistic director in 1964–65, when his productions included the English premiere of *Waiting for Godot*. Subsequent productions have included *Uncle Vanya* (1970) at the Royal Court, *King Lear* for the American Shakespeare Festival (1975), Shaw's *Heartbreak House* (1984) on Broadway, and an award-winning version of Ibsen's *A Doll's House* (1996) seen in both London and New York. He has also directed for the cinema and (particularly) for television.

Page, Geraldine (1924–87) US actress, who made her New York debut in 1945. Her performance as Alma Winemiller in Tennessee Williams's *Summer and Smoke* (1954) was her first big success; later the same year she excelled as Marcelline in *The Immoralist* (based on Gide's novel) and Lizzie Curry in N Richard Nash's *The Rainmaker*. Subsequent triumphs included performances in Williams's *Sweet Bird of Youth* (1959), Chekhov's *Three Sisters* (1964), Hellman's *The Little Foxes* (1974), Ayckbourn's *Absurd Person Singular* (1974), and Williams's *Clothes for a Summer Hotel* (1980). Her last role was in Coward's *Blithe Spirit* on Broadway.

pageant A medieval festivity, originally consisting of a procession of decorated carts, each organized by a different town guild. Later the term was also used of the speeches or short dramatic entertainments given in the open-air in honour of a visiting dignitary, such performances being repeated at various sites throughout the town during the course of the celebration.

Later still, the term was used of masques of the Tudor period, and more specifically of the stages themselves, which were made of canvas and wood; these were sometimes still capable of movement.

A third application of the word was made in the early 20th century, when processional open-air entertainments celebrating the history of a town or some historical anniversary became popular. Such productions combined amateur and professional talent and were often staged with other attractions. Similar pageants focusing on the history of a particular theatre have also been staged at professional venues.

pageant lantern A unit of lighting producing a narrow beam; it is capable of being used as either a spotlight or a footlight. In the US it is usually referred to as a **projector unit**.

Paige, Elaine (1952–) British actress and singer, whose first adult successes included the rock musical *Hair* (1969), *Jesus Christ Superstar* (1972), and the leading role in *Grease* (1973). Her performance as Eva Peron in Lloyd Webber's *Evita* (1978) won her several awards and she went on to star in the musicals *Cats* (1981) and *Chess* (1986). In the 1990s she took the title role in Pam Gems's *Piaf* (1993) and made her debut in classical drama as Célimène in Peter Hall's production of *The Misanthrope* (1998). She also enjoyed a major triumph on Broadway in Lloyd Webber's *Sunset Boulevard* (1995).

Palace Theatre A theatre in Shaftesbury Avenue, London, which was originally intended as a home for English opera. It opened, as the **Royal English Opera House**, in 1891 with Sullivan's *Ivanhoe*; later in the year Sarah Bernhardt appeared there. The theatre was subsequently sold and reopened as the Palace Theatre of Varieties in 1892. Marie Tempest made her first appearance in variety there in 1906 and in 1910 the great Russian ballerina Anna Pavlova also made her debut there. Renamed the Palace Theatre in 1911 it staged the first Royal Command Variety Performance. In 1925 *No, No, Nanette* starring Binnie Hale ran for 655 performances and during World War II Jack Hulbert and Cicely Courtneidge starred in a succession of musical comedies. Post-war successes have included *The Song of Norway* (1946), Novello's *King's Rhapsody* (1949), *The Sound of Music* (1961–67), and *Jesus Christ Superstar* (1972–80). The Royal Shakespeare Company's musical *Les Misérables* transferred from the Barbican Theatre to the Palace in 1985 and was still running in 2000.

Another **Palace Theatre** was opened in Manchester in 1891 as a venue for touring companies. Specializing initially in music hall and variety, it was reconstructed in 1913 and has been used for more varied productions following the closure of the Manchester Opera House. It was extensively renovated in 1978–80, since when notable performances there have included *Jesus Christ Superstar* (1981) and operas staged by the Royal Opera and other touring companies as well as pantomime and straight drama.

A third **Palace Theatre** opened in Watford in 1908 as a music hall and became a repertory theatre in 1932. Seating 667, it is used for productions by touring companies and for pre-West End runs; notable productions under the management of Michael Attenborough have included plays by Tennessee Williams, Pinter, Osborne, and Simon Gray. The auditorium was renovated in 1981.

The **Palace Theatre** on Broadway, New York, seats 1358 and opened as a vaudeville house in 1913. It rapidly became the most prestigious such vanue in the country, to the point that 'playing the Palace' meant that one had attained the height of the profession. With the death of vaudeville in the early 1930s the theatre was transformed into a cinema. After 1965 it reverted to live theatre, housing mainly musicals; the most successful of these have included *Sweet Charity* (1966), *Applause* (1970), *La Cage aux folles* (1983), and Disney's *Beauty and the Beast* (1994).

Palais-Royal, Théâtre du A theatre in Paris, which was originally the private theatre of Cardinal Richelieu. After expensive rebuilding, the theatre opened to the public in 1641; after Richelieu's death a year later it was used for Court productions until 1660, when it was handed over to Molière. Again rebuilt in 1670, it was the scene of Molière's death in 1673, after which it was taken over by Lully as a concert hall. It burnt down in 1781 and underwent several reconstructions, eventually becoming the home of the Comédie-Française. Another Palais-Royal, opened in 1831, housed productions of notable farces by Labiche, Bernard, and others during the 19th century; in 1958 Barrault installed his company there. It is now used chiefly for the presentation of comedies and *Boulevard* plays.

Palaprat, Jean de Bigot (1650–1721) French playwright, born in Toulouse. He wrote a number of comedies in collaboration with David-Augustin de Brueys, notably *Le Grondeur* (1691) and *Le Muet* (1691). Palaprat's own plays were less successful.

Palitzsch, Peter (1918–) German director. He became one of the leading directors with the Berliner Ensemble in the 1950s and directed the first production of Brecht's *Der aufhaltsame Aufstieg des Arturo Ui* (1959). Subsequent productions included a version of the Royal Shakespeare Company's cycle *The Wars of the Roses* (1967) and contemporary works by Tankred Dorst and Martin Walser. In the 1970s and 1980s he was associated with the theatres in Stuttgart and Frankfurt-am-Main while also working as a freelance director throughout Europe. In 1992 he was one of a group of directors brought in to rescue the Berliner Ensemble from collapse.

Palladio, Andrea (Andrea di Pietro; 1508–80) Italian architect, whose work had a major influence upon later architects and the design of all types of public buildings throughout Europe. His use of classical styles, in such buildings as the Teatro Olimpico, and his discussion of them in his *Quattro libri dell'architettura* (1570) had a particularly profound effect in England, where his followers included Inigo Jones.

Palladium *See* London Palladium.

Pallenberg, Max (1877–1934) Austrian actor, who was closely associated with Reinhardt's productions. He was particularly popular in comic roles, which included the Barker in Molnár's *Liliom* and Shweik in Piscator's adaptation of Hašek's famous novel.

palliata (*or crepidata*) A form of Roman comedy, translated from or written in imitation of Greek New Comedy. Initially the *palliata*, named after the *pallium* (a Greek cloak), was faithful to the original Greek model in terms of both plot and characters; under Plautus, however, it became a lively and distinct Roman form. Other writers of the *palliata* included Terence, Naevius, and Sextus Turpilius; it was eventually superseded by the TOGATA.

Palmer, John (1742–98) British actor, who began as a strolling player. Subsequently he was employed by Foote at the Haymarket, after which Garrick engaged him at Drury Lane. In 1777 he created Joseph Surface in *The School for Scandal*; other roles included comic characters in Shakespeare. Palmer opened the Royalty Theatre in 1787, but failed to get a licence and was forced to close. He died suddenly on stage in Liverpool.

Palmer, Lilli *See* Harrison, Rex.

Palmer's Theatre *See* Wallack's Theatre.

Palsgrave's Men *See* Admiral's Men.

Pandora's Box (*Die Büchse der Pandora*) A play by Frank WEDEKIND, written in 1894. First performance: 1905. A sequel to EARTH SPIRIT, the play presents Lulu's decline and her violent death at the hands of Jack the Ripper as an inevitable consequence of her sexuality; the two plays were later made into an opera by Alban Berg as *Lulu*.

Panopticon of Science and Art, Royal *See* Alhambra.

panorama A length of painted canvas, depicting a distant landscape or other view, which is unfurled across the back of the stage between two cylinders so as to present a continually changing scene.

Pantalone A character of the *commedia dell'arte*, an elderly, cunning, but frequently deceived Venetian merchant. Bearded and distinguished by his large nose, he was conventionally dressed in red and black and gradually evolved into the Pantaloon of the English harlequinade. He is traditionally the father and guardian of Columbine and is implacably opposed to her association with Harlequin.

pantomime An English theatrical form, derived from the HARLEQUINADE. Traditionally a Christmas entertainment with a special appeal for younger audiences, the pantomime inherited its fairytale and comic elements from the harlequinade, which was gradually absorbed by the new form and disappeared altogether in the 20th century. The modern pantomime is distantly related to the *ballets-pantomimes* staged in France during the 18th century, which were themselves a somewhat inaccurate imitation of a Roman tradition, also called pantomime, that comprised a popular dumb show performed by a single masked dancer (*see pantomimus*).

Pantomime as it is now understood first emerged as a distinctive English form under John Rich and others. Together with music, trickwork, audience participation, topical references, dancing, and transformation scenes, features of the genre conventionally include the playing of the PRINCIPAL BOY by a woman and the casting of a man as the DAME, while the productions themselves are often exceedingly lavish and may run for several weeks. The music hall provided a supply of popular singers and comedians for the pantomime, which in recent times has also recruited performers familiar from television appearances.

The most popular traditional pantomimes include *Cinderella*, *Aladdin*, *Red Riding Hood*, *Babes in the Wood*, *The Sleeping Beauty*, *Mother Goose*, *Jack and the Beanstalk*, and

Dick Whittington. The term pantomime has also been used of mime and of melodrama (when performed as a dumb show).

pantomimus A dancer in dumb shows of the ancient Roman tradition, in which he played all the roles. He wore a number of different masks and performed his dance to musical accompaniment; noted *pantomimi*, who remained popular with audiences throughout the history of the Roman Empire, included Bathyllus, Paris, and Pylades.

Paper Boys' Play *See* mummers' play.

Papp, Joseph (Joseph Papirofsky; 1921–91) US director and producer, who in 1954 founded the NEW YORK SHAKESPEARE FESTIVAL, with which his name became virtually synonymous. From 1973 until 1980 he was also the director of the Vivian Beaumont and Mitzi E Newhouse theatres at the LINCOLN CENTER FOR THE PERFORMING ARTS. In 1980 his production of *The Pirates of Penzance* was a huge success and transferred to the Uris Theatre, helping to relieve his financial pressures. Because of the great influence of the Festival he was, at his height, the most influential figure in US theatre.

Pappus A stock character of the Roman *atellana*. Probably depicted as a gullible old man, he was the central character of several plays, which exploited the comic possibilities presented by his incompetence.

parade A short dramatic entertainment that developed in France during the 18th century. *Parades* were performed outside booths at fairgrounds in order to entice passers-by into paying to see a play; they incorporated features of the *commedia dell'arte* and were later revived by Beaumarchais and other writers in the late 18th century.

paradiso A piece of stage machinery, by means of which a group of actors representing various angels or other supernatural characters might be lowered to or raised from the stage in a copper dome. The device was originally designed by **Filippo Brunelleschi** (1377–1446) and remained in use until the 18th century. *See also* Glory.

parallel *See* rostrum.

Parigi, Giulio (1590–1636) Italian scene designer, a pupil of Buontalenti. Together with his son **Alfonso Parigi** (d. 1656) he did much to disseminate Italian concepts of scenery throughout Europe, having a particular influence upon the masques of Inigo Jones.

Paris (d. 67 AD) A noted *pantomimus* of ancient Rome, whose popularity eventually provoked the jealousy of Nero, who had him executed. Another celebrated performer of the same name was executed by Domitian in 83 AD.

Paris, Théâtre de A theatre in Paris, which opened in 1891 as the Nouveau Théâtre. Under Réjane and subsequently Léon Volterra it acquired a reputation for performances of plays by Verneuil, Sacha Guitry, and Marcel Pagnol, among others. A smaller auditorium, the Théâtre Moderne, was added in 1958.

Parker, Louis Napoleon (1852–1944) British playwright and pageant organizer, who produced and directed a number of civic pageants during the Edwardian period and in London during World War I. His most successful plays were *Rosemary* (1896), upon which he collaborated with Murray Carson, *Pomander Walk* (1911), and *Disraeli* (1911).

Park Lane Theatre *See* Daly's 63rd Street Theatre.

Park Theatre A theatre in Park Row, New York, which was nicknamed the **Old Drury** in recognition of its importance as the earliest significant venue in the US. It opened in 1798 under Hallam and Hodgkinson, initially as the **New Theatre**, with *As You Like It*. At first it enjoyed only limited success despite its good company, but subsequently its reputation grew under Stephen Price's management (from 1808). In 1809, he produced the first American play, *The Indian Princess; or, La Belle Sauvage* by J N Barker; in this year he also added John Howard Payne to the company. Barker's use of foreign actors, however, caused the decline of the stock company and after 1818 its members simply provided support for such touring stars as Edmund Kean.

After rebuilding (caused by fire) in 1821, the theatre emerged as the most important venue in the US, with appearances by almost every leading contemporary actor. Closed between 1829 and 1834, the theatre presented the debut of Jean Davenport Lander, the child prodigy, in 1837; her later roles there included Sir Peter Teazle in *The School for Scandal*, Shylock in *The Merchant of Venice*, and Richard III. After Price's death in 1840 the company left and the theatre was sold (1841). Apart from such notable productions as Boucicault's *London Assurance* in 1841 and an appearance by Macready in 1843, the theatre's fortunes never recovered; Hamblin took over in 1848 but that same year the theatre was burnt down and was not rebuilt.

Another **Park Theatre** was erected in 1863 in Brooklyn, New York, and was successfully managed by F B Conway until 1871. When Conway left it became a venue for touring companies and was the last New York theatre to support visiting stars with its own stock company. Burnt down in 1908, it was never rebuilt.

See also Curtain Theatre; Herald Square Theatre; Majestic Theatre; Pitlochry Festival Theatre.

Parsons, Estelle (1927–) US actress, who made her New York debut in *Happy Hunting* (1956). Broadway roles include Myrtle in Tennessee Williams's *The Seven Descents of Myrtle* (1968), Catherine in *And Miss Reardon Drinks a Little* (1971), the title role in *Miss Margarida's Way* (1977), Ruth in the New York Shakespeare Festival's *The Pirates of Penzance* (1982), and Winnie in the Lincoln Center's production of Beckett's *Happy Days* (1996).

Pasadena Playhouse A theatre in Pasadena, California, one of the first community theatres in the US. It was founded in 1918 by the Pasadena Community Playhouse Association and opened in its 820-seat home in 1925. In 1928 a College of Theatre Arts was founded there. The playhouse, which was highly regarded for its productions of Shakespeare and of new plays, closed in 1970.

Pasco, Richard (1926–) British actor, who first appeared at the Q Theatre in Goldsmith's *She Stoops to Conquer*. Subsequently he developed into a fine classical actor and worked with most of the principal companies, including the English Stage Company and the Royal Shakespeare Company. His many performances have included Thomas à Becket in T S Eliot's *Murder in the Cathedral* (1972), alternation with Ian Richardson as Richard II and Bolingbroke in *Richard II* (1973), and the title character in *Timon of Athens* (1980). Since joining the National Theatre company in 1987 his work has included David Hare's *Racing Demon* (1990) and *The Absence of War* (1993) as well as the award-winning revival of Priestley's *An Inspector Calls* (1992).

Pashennaya, Vera Nikolayevna (1887–1962) Russian actress, who became a leading performer first at the Maly Theatre (1905–22) and then with the Moscow Art Theatre. She was noted for her intelligent and forceful interpretation of roles in the plays of Gorky, Schiller, Shakespeare, Sofronov, and Tolstoy among others.

paso A brief comic interlude common to drama in Spain during the 16th century. Originated by Lope de Rueda, such pieces were based on events from daily life and anticipated the development of the ENTREMÉ; written in simple language, they usually featured popular characters from the *commedia dell'arte*.

Paso, Alfonso (1926–) Spanish playwright, who became Spain's most successful writer for the commercial theatre in the 1960s and 1970s. He began writing in collaboration with his father and was briefly associated with the more controversial writer Alfonso Sastre; his plays include many unsophisticated comedies and thrillers.

Pasquati, Giulio (16th century) Italian actor of the *commedia dell'arte*, who was famous as Pantalone. He appeared with the Gelosi and was instrumental in causing the company to be invited to France in 1577.

Pasquino A character of the *commedia dell'arte*, one of the *zanni*. As a satirical valet he also featured in the Comédie-Italienne, called Pasquin.

pass door A door linking the backstage areas and the auditorium, for the use of theatre staff.

Passion play A genre of medieval liturgical drama, depicting the events surrounding the Crucifixion. Traditionally performed on Good Friday, the Passion play was popular throughout Europe from the 14th century until the Reformation and was often presented in the open air. The most famous surviving example is that given every ten years at OBERAMMERGAU.

Pastor, Tony (Antonio Pastor; 1837–1908) US entertainer, who made his first appearance as a child with Barnum, travelling in circuses and minstrel shows as a clown and singer. He is credited with inventing VAUDEVILLE at Tony Pastor's Opera House in New York, which he took over in 1865. By 1881 his 14th Street Theatre on Broadway was the leading house for the genre.

pastoral A genre of drama, popular from the 15th to the 17th centuries, that evoked an idealized world of rustic shepherds and nymphs free from the corruption of contemporary urban existence. It evolved in Italy from an older poetic tradition and was typified by Tasso's *Aminta* (1573). This and the works of Guarini, Poliziano, Epicuro, Cinthio, and Beccari were subsequently much imitated in France and, to a lesser extent, in England, where writers of pastorals included Fletcher, Lyly, Daniel, and the creators of the Stuart masques. The genre also had a marked influence upon Shakespeare's *As You Like It*. In France, Mairet's *Silvie* (1626) was the supreme example, although the allegorical depiction of rural pleasures later also became an element of the comedies of Corneille and many others.

'Pataphysics *See* Jarry, Alfred.

patent theatres The Theatres Royal, Drury Lane and Covent Garden, which were granted Letters Patent by Charles II in 1662, thus acquiring a monopoly of the theatre within the city of Westminster. The privileges were given specifically to Thomas Killigrew, who managed Drury Lane, and William Davenant, who ran Lincoln's Inn Fields (the patent eventually being inherited by the Dorset Garden company before reaching Covent Garden). The restrictions placed upon other theatres were gradually eroded and reinterpreted as referring only to straight drama; they were ultimately lifted in 1843, although both Drury Lane and Covent Garden still operate under the terms of the original charters.

Patriot for Me, A A play by John OSBORNE about the political intrigue and scandal that surrounded the career of Alfred Redl, an officer in the Austro-Hungarian Army at the turn of the century. First performance: Royal Court Theatre, 1965. It was heavily censored by the Lord Chamberlain and received its first performance as a club production, with Maximilian Schell as Redl. A successful revival took place in 1983, with Alan Bates in the leading role.

Pavilion *See* Anthony Street Theatre; Chatham Theatre.

Pavilion Music Hall *See* London Pavilion.

Pavilion Theatre A theatre in the Whitechapel area of London, which was built in 1828 and known as the 'Drury Lane of the East'. It was rebuilt after a fire in 1856, and again in 1874. Morris Abrahams, who became manager in 1871, and then Isaac Cohen successfully attracted a large Jewish audience; after bomb damage in World War II the theatre was demolished in 1961.

Pavy, Salathiel (1590–1603) English child-actor, who appeared frequently at the Blackfriars Theatre, where he became famous. He acted in Jonson's *Cynthia's Revels* and *The Poetaster* and was praised by the author for his playing of old men; he died at the age of 13.

Paxinou, Katina (Katina Konstantopoulou; 1900–73) Greek actress, who was closely associated with the productions of her husband Alexis MINOTIS. She made her first stage appearance in 1924 and was seen in the US (1930) before joining the Greek National Theatre in 1932. There she excelled in such roles as Clytemnestra in the plays of Sophocles and Aeschylus, as well as in modern works by O'Neill and Ibsen, notably as Mrs Alving in *Ghosts* (1934–40). She also triumphed in Shakespearean roles opposite her husband and in plays by García Lorca, Christopher Fry, and Euripides.

Payne, Ben Iden (1881–1976) British actor and director, who was first associated with Benson's company (1899) and later with Miss Horniman's theatre in Manchester. He then moved to the US (1913–34), where he was active both as an actor and as a lecturer in drama. Subsequently he became director of the Shakespeare Memorial Theatre, a post which he occupied until 1943 when he returned to the US. In 1950 he established a summer Shakespeare Festival at Balboa Park, San Diego.

Payne, John Howard (1791–1852) US actor and playwright, who had his first play successfully presented in New York at the age of 14. Subsequently he toured to great acclaim in such roles as Hamlet and Romeo, appearing in Britain in 1813 and then in Paris, where he became friendly with Talma and began a long association with the

Comédie-Française. Of his many plays the most successful was the tragedy *Brutus; or, the Fall of Tarquin* (1818) starring Edmund Kean; others included adaptations of Pixérécourt's melodramas and collaborations with Washington Irving. He was briefly manager of Sadler's Wells, consequently spending a year in prison for debt, and from 1842 was US consul in Tunis. His libretto for the opera *Clari, the Maid of Milan* (1823) included the popular song 'Home Sweet Home'.

Peace, The A comedy by ARISTOPHANES. First performance: Athens, 421 BC. The plot revolves around a farmer who travels to heaven on the back of a dung-beetle and discovers that the gods have forsaken mankind; it was intended as an appeal for peace between Athens and Sparta.

Peacock Theatre *See* Abbey Theatre.

Pedrolino A character of the *commedia dell'arte*, one of the *zanni*. Pellesini ex-celled in the role, which gradually evolved from being that of a simple honest ser-vant, conventionally dressed in white, to the pathetic lover PIERROT of the Comédie-Italienne. He was usually played without a mask, but with his face whitened.

Peele, George (c. 1558–97) English playwright, one of the University Wits. His *The Arraignment of Paris* (1581) contributed to the development of romantic comedy, while *The Old Wives' Tale* (1590) elevated farce to a more sophisticated level. His other works include the patriotic *Edward I* (1591) and the biblical drama *The Love of King David and Fair Bathsabe* (1587). Peele may also have contributed to Shakespeare's *Titus Andronicus* and collaborated with Greene.

Peer Gynt A poetic drama by Henrik IBSEN, published in 1867. First performance: Oslo, 1876. Consolidating the success of *Brand*, which preceded it, the play is a crit-ical examination of the Norwegian character and draws heavily upon folklore and legend. The title character is a selfish fantasist who drifts irresponsibly through life under the illusion that he is 'being himself'. The incidental music for the first pro-duction was composed by Grieg.

Peking Opera The most important genre of Chinese drama. The form has ancient roots but only became established as the main theatrical tradition of China in the 19th century. Combining elements of music, dialogue, and acrobatics, the plays fea-ture virtuous protagonists who experience numerous melodramatic adventures be-fore finally triumphing over evil.

The plots are derived from a variety of mythological and literary sources, with plays being divided into *weu* (civil) and *wu* (military) forms. Productions are pre-sented on a bare square stage with minimal use of props, the meaning of which has been long established by convention.

The actors are trained to achieve their effects with great economy of movement. Each performer usually specializes in one of four main roles – the male characters (*sheng*), female characters (*dan*), large males with painted faces (*jing*), and comedi-ans (*chou*) – or in certain subdivisions of them. Female roles were traditionally played by men, the greatest such interpreter being Mei Lanfang, although women have been permitted in these roles since 1911. Lines are generally delivered in a falsetto voice with orchestral accompaniment; performers are expected to develop the basic storyline themselves, the script being normally little more than an outline (as in the European *commedia dell'arte*). Costumes, like most other aspects of the Peking Opera, obey convention in terms of colour, ornamentation, and headwear; make-up is similarly dictated by tradition with certain colours suggesting specific temperaments.

Along with *hua ju*, a form of modern spoken drama influenced by Western models, the Peking Opera remains China's best known and most popular form of theatre, despite a period during the Cultural Revolution (1967–72) when all such productions were prohibited.

Pelléas et Mélisande A play by Maurice MAETERLINCK. First performance: Paris, 1893. A somewhat enigmatic love story based on medieval legend, the play was a big success in both New York and London with Mrs Patrick Campbell as Mélisande and with incidental music by Fauré. In 1904 Sarah Bernhardt partnered her, playing Pelléas. It later became an opera by Debussy.

Pellesini, Giovanni (c. 1526–1612) Italian actor of the *commedia dell'arte*, who played the role of Pedrolino. He led his own company for a time before joining the Confidenti, of which he subsequently became the director.

Pellico, Silvio (1789–1854) Italian patriot and playwright. His plays include several classical tragedies, notably *Francesca da Rimini* (1815), which were much influenced by Alfieri and Foscolo; the part of Francesca herself later provided a favourite role for Adelaide Ristori. He is now mainly remembered for his memoirs describing his imprisonment for political offences.

Pellio, Titus Publilius (2nd century BC) Roman actor, who became famous for his performances in the plays of Plautus. He is known to have appeared in the *Menaechmi*, the *Stichus*, the *Bacchides*, and the *Epidecus*.

Pemán y Pemartín, José Mariá (1898–1981) Spanish poet and playwright, whose best-known play was *El divino impaciente* (A Saint in a Hurry; 1935). A staunch Catholic and royalist, he also enjoyed success with such plays as *La santa vivreina* (1939) and *Callados como muertos* (Silent as the Dead; 1952).

Pembroke's Men An English theatre company formed from the household of the Earl of Pembroke around 1592. The company was closely associated with the plays of Shakespeare, notably *Titus Andronicus* and the later parts of *Henry VI*, until 1594, when he joined the Chamberlain's Men. In 1597 Pembroke's Men moved into the Swan Theatre, where their production of the controversial *The Isle of Dogs* by Jonson and Nashe led to their dissolution, actors from the company joining the Admiral's Men and other troupes.

Penço de la Vega, Joseph (1650–1703) Jewish playwright, author of the first printed Hebrew play. Printed in Amsterdam in 1673 and later reprinted in Leghorn in 1770, *Asiré Hatiqva* is a morality play probably written for a religious festival.

Penkethman, William (d. 1725) British actor, who at one time travelled the provinces with a peepshow and ran fairground booths. He appeared in comedy at Drury Lane under Christopher Rich and specialized in playing masked harlequins. Colley Cibber wrote for him the characters of Don Lewis in *Love Makes a Man* (1701) and Trappanti in *She Would and She Would Not* (1702).

Penley, William Sydney (1852–1912) British actor-manager, who made his stage debut at the Royal Court Theatre in 1871. He became an accomplished farceur and light opera singer, achieving outstanding success in such parts as the title role in Hawtrey's *The Private Secretary* (1884) and, most notably, Lord Fancourt Babberley in *Charley's Aunt* (1892), which he played for 1466 consecutive performances.

Pennington, Michael (1943–) British actor. He was a member of the Royal Shakespeare Company in 1964–65 and again from 1974 to 1981, when his roles included Berowne, Angelo, and Hamlet. In 1986 he was a cofounder (with Michael Bogdanov) of the ENGLISH SHAKESPEARE COMPANY, with whom he toured internationally until 1993. He also directed productions of *Twelfth Night* in Tokyo (1993) and Chicago (1996). Other recent work has included Granville Barker's *Waste* (1997), Chekhov's *The Seagull* (1997), and de Filippo's *Filumena* (1998), all at the Old Vic with Peter Hall's company.

Penny for a Song, A A comedy by John WHITING. First performance: London, 1951. A study of eccentricity and a satire upon the nature of war, it is set in Britain during the Napoleonic Wars. A revised version was successfully presented by the Royal Shakespeare Company in 1962.

penny plain, twopence coloured *See* toy theatre.

Penthouse Theatre A theatre-in-the-round at the University of Washington, Seattle. Built in 1940 by Glenn Hughes, it was the first theatre-in-the-round in the world.

People Show A British touring company founded in London in 1966 to present experimental drama. Relying upon the techniques of collective creation, the company aims for an effect of spontaneity and has dispensed with the use of a director or writer; its multidisciplinary performance works have toured successfully throughout Europe and the US.

People's National Theatre *See* Price, (Lilian) Nancy.

Pepper's ghost A stage effect by means of which a transparent 'ghost' can be presented alongside real actors. Developed by John Henry Pepper (1821–1900), the effect is achieved by reflecting the image of a live actor walking in the pit onto an inclined sheet of glass positioned on the stage.

Pepys, Samuel (1633–1703) English administrator, diarist, and playgoer. His famous *Diary* provides a vivid picture of the Restoration theatre. A friend of many actors and actresses, notably Mary Knepp, he recorded invaluable comments on the theatre during the 1660s, as well as much backstage gossip.

perch A small raised platform behind the proscenium arch, used for the manipulation of additional lighting units.

Percival, Susanna (1667–1703) English actress, wife of William MOUNTFORT. She was very popular as a performer of breeches parts and was admired by Colley Cibber, among others, in such plays as Buckingham's *The Rehearsal* and Dryden's *Marriage à la Mode*.

Percy, Esmé (Saville) (1887–1957) British actor and director, who worked in Benson's company and for Annie Horniman at Manchester. In 1913 he formed his own touring company, producing plays by Shaw and Wilde – including the first staging of *Man and Superman* in its entirety. After World War I he became general producer and a leading performer with Macdona's Shaw Repertory Company; his roles included Dobelle in Denis Johnston's *The Moon in the Yellow River* (1934) and Matthew Skipps in Fry's *The Lady's Not for Burning* (1949). His last months were spent with the English Stage Company at the Royal Court Theatre.

Peretz, Isaac Leib (1852–1915) Jewish poet and playwright, living in Poland, who is regarded as one of the fathers of Yiddish literature. He tried to combine the elements of traditional Judaism with modern secular trends in such plays as *The Golden Chain* and *Bei Nacht oifn alten Mark* (Night in the Old Market; 1925).

Peréz, Cosmé (c. 1585–1673) Spanish actor, whose comic roles included several *Gracioso* characters. He was especially popular in *entreméses* by Cervantes and Quiñones de Benavente as Juan Rana and is known to have appeared before the Spanish court in 1665.

Pérez Galdós, Benito (1843–1920) Spanish novelist and playwright, whose quest for realism and an honest portrayal of contemporary society is reflected in such plays as *Realidad* (Reality; 1892) and *Electra* (1901); the latter provoked much controversy with its discussion of hypocrisy within the Church. Many of his plays show the influence of Ibsen and Zola.

Performance Group A US theatre company founded in New York in 1967 by Richard Schechner. The group experimented with environmental theatre, new training techniques, and the relationship between actor and audience, presenting innovative productions of Brecht and Shakespeare among others. In 1970 the group reformed as the Wooster Group under the direction of Spalding Gray and Elizabeth LeCompte.

periaktoi The earliest known examples of scenery, as used in the ancient Greek and Roman theatre. They probably consisted of painted prisms, which could be revolved to suggest a change in setting and also helped to project sound from the stage into the auditorium. They were reintroduced on the Renaissance stage, when they were known as **telari**.

Pericles, Prince of Tyre A romance by William SHAKESPEARE, written c. 1608. First performance: c. 1608. Possibly containing passages by another playwright, the play was based on a Greek story and depicts the separation and ultimate reunion of Pericles with his wife Thaisa and his daughter Marina. Marina survives an attempt to kill her and a stay in a brothel in Mytilene, where she remains untouched on account of her beauty and virtue, before the joyful meeting with her long-lost father. The uneven quality of the first half of the play has led to suggestions that it has been reconstructed from memory.

Perkins, Osgood (1892–1937) US actor, who won acclaim in both comic and serious roles in a wide range of productions. He established his reputation in Hecht and MacArthur's *The Front Page* in 1928, while subsequent successes included roles in plays by Chekhov and Molière; he also appeared alongside the Lunts in Coward's *Point Valentine* (1935) and briefly in Rachel Crothers's *Susan and God* (1937).

Persians, The A tragedy by AESCHYLUS, regarded as the earliest surviving drama of the Western theatre. First performance: Athens, c. 472 BC. The play depicts the defeat of the Persians at Salamis in 480 BC and was, unlike much of his other surviving work, probably not part of a tetralogy.

Peruzzi, Baldassare (1481–1536) Italian architect and artist, who executed early perspective scenes for the theatre. He was the first artist to employ perspective in such designs for the stage; his pupils included Serlio.

Peter Pan A play by J M BARRIE, adapted from his novel *The Little White Bird*. First performance: 1904. With Nina Boucicault as the first Peter Pan, the boy who never grows up, the play – a children's fantasy adventure – has remained a popular item in the theatrical repertory, especially at Christmas. Copyright fees on the play pass automatically to the Great Ormond Street Children's Hospital in London, as stipulated by the author. In the US it is often performed in a musical version created in 1954 for Mary Martin.

Peters, Bernadette (1948–) US actress and singer, who made her debut in 1967 and first gained attention in the off-Broadway *Dames at Sea* (1968). Other major roles include Mabel in Jerry Herman's *Mack and Mabel* (1974), Dot in Sondheim's *Sunday in the Park with George* (1984), the Witch in his *Into the Woods* (1987), and the title role in the 1999 revival of *Annie Get Your Gun*.

Petit-Bourbon, Salle du A theatre in Paris, which was first used as a venue for professional performances in 1577. The Gelosi and other noted Italian companies appeared there, later being joined by Molière's company, which performed some of the great playwright's early works there. When the theatre was threatened with demolition in 1668 Molière's troupe moved to the Palais-Royal, taking much of the scenery designed by Torelli and others as well as much of the equipment with them.

Petri, Olaus (1493–1552) Swedish humanist and churchman, who was the author of the first Swedish vernacular play, *Tobiae Comedia* (1550). Chancellor to Gustavus Vasa and a leading figure of the Reformation in Sweden, he was the subject of Strindberg's play *Mäster Olof* (1872).

Petrified Forest, The A play by Robert SHERWOOD. First performance: New York, 1935. The play, an allegory of Fascism, examines the destructive force of evil in a world where good men are helpless and power remains with the criminals.

Phantom of the Opera, The A musical by Andrew LLOYD WEBBER, with words by Charles Hart and Richard Stilgoe. First performance: London, 1986. This version of Gaston Leroux's story about a demented composer haunting the nether regions of the Paris Opéra proved immediately popular despite its lack of suspense or mystery, owing mainly to the lush score and Michael Crawford's performance as the Phantom. The show was still running in 2000.

Phèdre A tragedy by Jean RACINE. First performance: Paris, 1677. Based on Euripides's *Hippolytus*, the play is generally considered to be Racine's greatest work. The plot concerns Phèdre's passion for Hippolyte, son of her husband Thésée, and culminates in Hippolyte's death and Phèdre's suicide. English translations include a version by Ted Hughes (1998).

Phelps, Samuel (1804–78) British actor and manager, who became an actor in 1826 and played in the provinces for 11 years, establishing himself as a fine tragedian. In 1837 Ben Webster engaged him at the Haymarket, where he opened successfully as Shylock. Subsequently he joined Macready's Covent Garden company, appearing as Othello to Macready's Iago. In 1843 he took over Sadler's Wells; during the next 18 years he produced numerous Shakespeare plays, restoring many of the texts to their original versions and appearing in such roles as Lear and Bottom. He continued to act in the provinces and other London theatres after he gave up management, usually in Shakespeare or dramatizations of Scott's novels.

Pherecrates (5th century BC) Greek playwright, author of several examples of Old Comedy. He won his first victory in a drama contest around 437 BC; many fragments of his plays survive.

Philanderer, The A play by G B SHAW, written in 1893. First performance: London, 1905. The play examines love and marriage through the relationships of the three central characters, Charteris, Julia, and Grace. Through its satire on feminism and 'Ibsenism' – two causes that he supported – Shaw demonstrated his capacity for self-criticism; the play failed to find a producer for many years.

Philemon (c. 368 BC–c. 264 BC) Greek playwright, who was regarded in his own time as the equal of Menander. He was the author of 97 moralistic comedies, of which only fragments survive; Plautus was amongst the Roman playwrights much influenced by his writing.

Philipe, Gérard (1922–59) French actor, who became highly popular in romantic roles following his first major success, in the title role of *Caligula* (1945) by Camus. He then embarked upon a successful film career before returning to the stage in 1951, when he joined Jean Vilar's Théâtre National Populaire. He was particularly admired in Corneille's *Le Cid*, Musset's *Lorenzaccio*, Hugo's *Ruy Blas*, and Shakespeare's *Richard II* among other plays; following his early death he was buried in the costume he wore in *Le Cid*.

Philippides (c. 4th–3rd century BC) Greek playwright, author of several examples of New Comedy. His excitement at winning a dramatic competition as an old man is said to have precipitated his death.

Philips, Ambrose (1674–1749) English poet and playwright, for whom the nickname 'Namby-Pamby' was coined with reference to his insipid verses. His translation of Racine's *Andromaque*, entitled *The Distrest Mother*, was received with great acclaim at Drury Lane in 1712; two other tragedies, *The Briton* (1722) and *Humfrey, Duke of Gloucester* (1723), were less successful.

Philips, Katherine (1632–64) English poet and playwright, known as 'the matchless Orinda'. Her *Pompey* (1663) was the first play by a woman to be professionally produced on the London stage.

Phillipin *See* Villiers, Claude Deschamps de.

Phillips, Augustine (d. 1605) English actor, who appeared in Tarleton's *Seven Deadly Sins* in about 1590 and later joined the Chamberlain's Men (1594). He acted in Jonson's early plays and is in the First Folio list of Shakespearean players; he was also an original shareholder in the Globe Theatre.

Phillips, Robin (1942–) British director and actor, who began his career at the Bristol Old Vic in 1959 and was subsequently praised for his work as artistic director (1974–80) of the Stratford (Ontario) Festival. He has also worked at the Chichester Festival Theatre (1962–64 and 1971–72), the Oxford Playhouse (1964–65), with the Royal Shakespeare Company (1965–67 and 1970), at Exeter's Northcott Theatre (1967–68), at the Greenwich Theatre (1973), and at the Citadel Theatre in Edmonton, Canada (1990–95). His most celebrated productions have included plays by Congreve, Coward, Shakespeare, O'Neill, and Shaw, starring such leading performers as Maggie Smith and Peter Ustinov.

Phillips, Siân (1935–) British actress. Phillips began as a child actress on Welsh radio and television before studying at RADA. Her early London appearances included the title roles in *Hedda Gabler* (1959) and *The Duchess of Malfi* (1960) for the Royal Shakespeare Company. She has played in a series of Shaw comedies including *Man and Superman* (1966), *You Never Can Tell* (1979), and *Major Barbara* (1982). Musical work includes *Pal Joey* (1980), *Gigi* (1985), *A Little Night Music* (1995) at the Royal National Theatre, and *Marlene* (1996), in which she toured as Marlene Dietrich. She has also appeared regularly in films and on television. She was married to Peter O'Toole from 1960 to 1979.

Phillips, Stephen (1864–1915) British playwright, poet, and actor. In 1900 his *Herod*, staged by Tree, was widely thought to signify the dawn of a new era of poetic drama. *Paolo and Francesca* (1902) and *Ulysses* (1902) were similarly acclaimed, but the failure of *Nero* (1906) effectively ruined his reputation.

Phillip Street Theatre A theatre in Sydney, Australia, which was used for a series of successful revues beginning in 1954. Relying heavily upon Australian writers and performers, a more varied programme was staged at a new venue, the Phillip Theatre, from 1961 until 1974, when the series finally came to an end.

Phillpotts, Eden (1862–1960) British novelist and playwright, whose most successful work for the stage was the rustic comedy *The Farmer's Wife* (1916). His other plays include *Devonshire Cream* (1924), *Jane's Legacy* (1925), and *Yellow Sands* (1926), which was written in collaboration with his daughter, **Adelaide Eden**.

Philocles (5th century BC) Greek playwright, nephew of Aeschylus. No fragments of his tragedies survive, although he is believed to have defeated Sophocles in one drama contest.

Philoctetes A tragedy by SOPHOCLES. First performance: Athens, 409 BC. The plot revolves around the central character, a famous archer, who has been cast away on a desert island and fears he may never escape.

phlyax A form of mime play or farce popular in the Greco-Roman world. It developed from Middle Comedy and was much performed in southern Italy during the 3rd and 4th centuries BC. Writers of the form, which usually comprised various burlesques, included **Rhinthon of Tarentum** (4th century BC); eventually the form was absorbed into the ATELLANA. It is now known mainly from vase paintings of the period.

Phoenix Arts Centre A theatre in Leicester (originally the Phoenix Theatre) that opened in 1963 with Thornton Wilder's *The Matchmaker*. It was erected on a short-term basis pending building of a larger theatre but proved so popular, particularly with young people, that it continued in use; its range of activities was subsequently extended to concerts, dance, art exhibitions, and films. The centre reopened after refurbishment in 1988; it is now affiliated to De Montfort University.

Phoenix Society A British theatre group founded in London in 1919 under the aegis of the Stage Society. Dedicated to the performance of early English drama, the society presented 26 influential productions of major plays from the period between 1919 and 1925, enthusiastically supported by such notable theatre figures as Edith Craig, Allan Wade, and Norman Wilkinson, while Sir Thomas Beecham arranged the music for Fletcher's *The Faithful Sherpherdess* in 1923.

Phoenix Theatre A theatre in Charing Cross Road, London, which was built on the site of a former music hall, the Alcazar. The opening production, in 1930, was *Private Lives* by Noël Coward with the author, Gertrude Lawrence, and Laurence Olivier in the cast. Coward scored another hit in 1936 with a programme of one-act plays under the title *Tonight at 8.30*. During World War II John Gielgud successfully revived William Congreve's *Love for Love* (1943) there and in 1945 Cicely Courtneidge enjoyed a long run in *Under the Counter*. Subsequent productions have included plays by Thornton Wilder, Rattigan, John Osborne, Brecht, and Chekhov, while in 1968 a musical drama based on Geoffrey Chaucer's *Canterbury Tales* ran for over 2000 performances. More recent successes have included Tom Stoppard's *Night and Day* (1978), Simon Gray's *The Common Pursuit* (1988), and the musical *Blood Brothers*, which opened in 1993 and was still running in 2000.

In New York the name **Phoenix Theatre** referred to a company (now disbanded) and the two buildings it occupied. The first building, on 12th Street, was founded as Maurice Schwartz's **Yiddish Art Theatre**. In 1953, after some time as a cinema, it was reopened for the new company as the Phoenix with Sidney Howard's *Madam, Will You Walk?* The company, an important non-profit-making theatre for 30 years, moved in 1961 to a smaller house on East 74th Street, the name of which was also changed to the Phoenix. There it presented such important plays as Ionesco's *Exit the King* (1961), Kopit's *Oh Dad, Poor Dad...* (1972), and Marsha Norman's *Getting Out*, as well as Mary Rodger's musical *Once Upon a Mattress*. In 1972 it was reorganized as the New Phoenix Repertory Company, continuing under this name until it was disbanded in 1983. The original theatre on 12th Street presented burlesque from 1961 to 1965 and was then renamed the **Eden Theatre**; it enjoyed success with *Oh, Calcutta!* (1969) and the musical *Grease* (1972) before it was renamed the Entermedia and enlarged to house a variety of events in 1977. The Phoenix Theatre on East 74th Street became the **Eastside Playhouse** in 1968 and housed both plays and musicals before concentrating on light opera.

See also Cockpit.

Phrynichus (c. 6th-5th century BC) Greek playwright, a contemporary of Aeschylus. His tragedies included a controversial account of the capture of Miletus and *Phoenissae*, which was based on events following the battle of Salamis; he won drama contests in 512 BC and 476 BC. Another Greek writer of the same name flourished in Athens in the 5th century BC, winning two victories for his plays, which were examples of Old Comedy; many fragments of his writings survive.

Piaf, Edith (Giovanna Gassion; 1915–63) French singer, who became a celebrated star of French cabaret and music hall. Adopting the name *piaf* (French slang for sparrow) on account of her diminutive stature, she became famous for her distinctive raw singing voice and resilient personality. She appeared throughout France and in the US, being much admired by Cocteau and other influential figures. Her life, which was marred by an unhappy childhood, failed marriages, alcoholism, and addiction to drugs, provided the basis for the play *Piaf* (1980) by Pam Gems, in which Jane Lapotaire won great acclaim.

Picard, Louis-Benoît (1769–1828) French playwright, actor, and manager, who was born in Paris. His comedies of manners, which gently satirized bourgeois society, were immensely popular during the Napoleonic era. *La Petite Ville* (1801; adapted as *The Merry Widow*), is probably his best-known and most popular play; others include *Médiocre et rampant* (1797), *Les Provinciaux à Paris* (1802), *La Vieille Tante* (1811), and *Les Deux Philibert* (1816).

Piccadilly Theatre A theatre close to Piccadilly Circus that was the first in London to be fully air-conditioned. It was built in 1928 on the site of derelict stables and opened with *Blue Eyes*, a romantic musical starring Evelyn Laye. The Piccadilly's early history was not one of spectuacular success; in 1960 the theatre was acquired and improved by the Albery family, who installed the air-conditioning. Since then successful runs have included Edward Albee's *Who's Afraid of Virginia Woolf?* (1964), Robert Bolt's *Vivat! Vivat Regina!*, transferred from Chichester in 1970, Willy Russell's very popular *Educating Rita* (1980), one of several Royal Shakespeare Company transfers, and the musical *Spend, Spend, Spend* (1999).

Piccolo Teatro della Città di Milano An Italian theatre company founded in 1947, the first permanent regional troupe (*see* Teatro Stabile) to be established in Italy. Organized by the director Giorgio STREHLER and the actor-director **Paolo Grassi** (1919–81), the company established a reputation for high artistic standards with productions of Shakespeare, Goldoni, Brecht, and others and quickly built up a large audience in Milan, its leading performers including Marcello Moretti (1910–61). The model for many similar Italian companies, the group has toured internationally in a wide range of productions. It was run solely by Strehler from 1973 until 1992, when he resigned following allegations that he had mismanaged an EU grant.

Pickelhering *See* Reynolds, Robert.

Pickup, Ronald (1940–) British actor. After training at RADA he appeared at the Royal Court in 1964–65 and then at the National Theatre until 1973, where his roles included Rosalind in an all-male *As You Like It* (1967) and the title role in *Richard II* (1972). Subsequent stage work has included Ayckbourn's *The Norman Conquests* (1974), Beckett's *Play* (1976), Chekhov's *Uncle Vanya* (1982) and *The Cherry Orchard* (1989), and Hare's *Amy's View* (1997). He has also appeared frequently on television.

Pierrot   A character of the French Comédie-Italienne and the English harlequinade, derived from that of PEDROLINO in the Italian *commedia dell'arte*. Traditionally dressed in a loose white suit with a large hat and whitened face, Pierrot owed his later development to Deburau and others, who exaggerated the melancholic side of his nature and made him an increasingly pathetic figure. After disappearing from the harlequinade, he was reintroduced into the English theatre through the dumb play *L'Enfant Prodigue* in 1891, his costume subsequently being adopted by numerous concert parties at British holiday resorts (*see* pierrot troupes). In France he was further developed by Marcel Marceau in his creation of the mime character Bip.

pierrot troupes   Theatrical companies established in Britain in the late 19th and early 20th centuries in which a group of performers assumed collectively the white costume of the traditional PIERROT character. Such troupes were inspired by the success of the mime play *L'Enfant prodigue* (1891), which was based on a Pierrot figure, and included singers, dancers, and comedians, performing at various seaside holiday resorts and elsewhere. The most successful groups included the **Co-Optimists**, who played in London under **Davy Burnaby** (1881–1949) in the 1920s.

Pigott-Smith, Tim (1946–)   British actor, who worked in repertory before joining the Royal Shakespeare Company in 1972 and becoming established as a television star. He played Colin in Michael Frayn's *Benefactors* (1984) at the Vaudeville Theatre and portrayed many characters in a one-man show, *Bengal Lancer* (1985), at the Lyric, Hammersmith. At the National Theatre in 1987–88 he was Octavius in *Antony and Cleopatra*, Iachimo in *Cymbeline*, and Leontes in *The Winter's Tale*. He was artistic director of the Compass Theatre company in 1989–92. Recent work has included directing a revival of *The Royal Hunt of the Sun* (1989) and starring in an open-air *Hamlet* (1994).

Pike's Opera House   *See* Grand Opera House.

Pike Theatre   A small experimental theatre in Dublin, which was opened by Alan Simpson in 1953. Among his productions there were the premieres of Brendan Behan's *The Quare Fellow* (1954) and Beckett's English version of *Waiting for Godot* (1955), and many contemporary plays by international authors, including Tennessee Williams's *The Rose Tattoo* (1957), which led to Simpson's arrest on obscenity charges. The size of the theatre made it inviable and after Simpson's last production, J B McGowan's *God's Child* (1959), the theatre was eventually sold.

Pilgrim Players   *See* Browne, E Martin; Jackson, Sir Barry.

Pillars of Society (*Samfundets Støtter*)   A play by Henrik IBSEN. First performance: Copenhagen, 1877. The first of Ibsen's revolutionary series of social dramas, it depicts the guilt suffered by a public figure whose reputation is founded on a lie.

Pinero, Sir A(rthur) W(ing) (1855–1934)   British playwright, who began his career as an actor in 1874. He was encouraged to write by Sir Henry Irving; his earliest play to be staged was *£200 a Year* (1877), but it was not until his series of farces written for the Royal Court Theatre in the 1880s that he achieved real popularity. Pinero was especially influenced by the realism of T W Robertson, by the well-made plays of Eugene Scribe, and by the social dramas of Ibsen, as is apparent in his 'thesis' plays of the late 1880s and 1890s. The innovative THE SECOND MRS TANQUERAY was particularly well received, with Mrs Patrick Campbell in the leading role; following TRELAWNY OF THE 'WELLS' and *The Gay Lord Quex*, however, his work was progressively less successful.

Principal works:

THE MAGISTRATE: 1885.
The Schoolmistress: 1886.
DANDY DICK: 1887.
The Profligate: 1889.
The Cabinet Minister: 1890.
The Second Mrs Tanqueray: 1893.
The Notorious Mrs Ebbsmith: 1895.
Trelawny of the 'Wells': 1898.
The Gay Lord Quex: 1899.

pin spot A spotlight capable of throwing a very small, precise beam of light onto the stage.

Pinter, Harold (Harold Da Pinta; 1930–) British playwright, who began as an actor before emerging as one of the most original and distinctive dramatists of the last 50 years. His first play, the one-act THE ROOM, established the atmosphere of menace that was to characterize most of his subsequent work, while THE CARETAKER marked him out as a leading contemporary writer. The drama and the comedy of his plays frequently arise from a struggle for dominance in which language is more usually a weapon than a tool for communication; the term Pinteresque is now commonly used for dialogue that conceals as much as it reveals and is punctuated frequently by portentous pauses. The plays *No Man's Land* (1974) and *Betrayal* (1978) moved into rather different territory, the first revealing a new preoccupation with the nature of memory and the second being more a comedy of manners than of menace. In the 1980s Pinter's plays were mainly short parables on political themes. *Moonlight* (1993) was his first full-length work for 15 years. Pinter has written successfully for radio, television, and cinema and has also directed at the National Theatre and in the West End. His first wife was the actress Vivien MERCHANT, with whom he sometimes appeared in his own plays.

Principal works:

The Room: 1957.
THE BIRTHDAY PARTY: 1957.
THE DUMB WAITER: 1957.
A Slight Ache: 1958.
The Caretaker: 1959.
The Homecoming: 1964.
Silence: 1968.
Old Times: 1970.
No Man's Land: 1974.
Betrayal: 1978.
Family Voices: 1980.
A Kind of Alaska: 1982.
One for the Road: 1984.
Mountain Language: 1988.

Party Time: 1991.
Moonlight: 1993.
Ashes to Ashes: 1996.
Celebration: 2000.

pipe *See* batten.

pipe batten *See* batten.

Pip Simmons Theatre Group A British theatre company, which was founded in London in 1968 to present experimental drama. Named after its founder, the group employed the techniques of collective creation and performed works based on such diverse sources as Chaucer, Lewis Carroll, Dostoevsky, and Edgar Allan Poe. The company broke up in 1973 but was immediately reformed by Simmons on an international basis. It finally disbanded in 1986. Simmons, who is now based in Sweden, continues to direct and to write and lecture on theatre.

Pirandello, Luigi (1867–1936) Italian playwright, actor, novelist, critic, and short-story writer, who first established his reputation on the stage with *Right You Are (If You Think So)*, a dramatization of one of his early short stories. His most important dramas, which deal chiefly with the absurdity of human existence and the relativity of truth, include the tragedy *Henry IV*, which examines the uneasy relationship between sanity and madness, and SIX CHARACTERS IN SEARCH OF AN AUTHOR, which is the first part of a trilogy that also includes *Each in His Own Way* and *Tonight We Improvise*.

Regarded as one of the best interpreters of the period between the two world wars, he attempted to portray the degeneration of middle-class values and broke away from the conventional dramatic techniques that had stunted Italian theatre in the early 20th century. After his wife's confinement in a mental home in 1919 he founded his own company; for many years the leading lady in his plays was **Marta Abba** (1900–88). He was awarded a Nobel Prize in 1934.

Principal works:
  Così è (se vi pare): 1917; translated as *Right You Are (If You Think So)*.
  Il giuoco delle parti: 1918; translated as *The Rules of the Game*.
  Sei personaggi in cerca d'autore: 1922; translated as *Six Characters in Search of an Author*.
  Enrico IV: 1922; translated as *Henry IV*.
  L'uomo dal fiore in boca : 1923; translated as *The Man With a Flower in his Mouth*.
  Ciascuno a suo modo: 1924; translated as *Each in His Own Way*.
  Lazzaro: 1929; translated as *Lazarus*.
  Questa sera si recita a soggetto: 1929; translated as *Tonight We Improvise*.
  Come tu mi vuoi: 1930; translated as *As You Desire Me*.

Piron, Alexis (1689–1773) French playwright and poet, who made his name at the fairground theatres with monologues, comic operas, and farces, notably *Arlequin Deucalion* (1722). His first play written for the official stage was produced at the Comédie-Française in 1728. Piron's comedy *La Métromanie* (1738) enjoyed considerable success; *Gustave Wasa* (1734) was the best of his tragedies. A licentious poem penned in his youth prevented his election to the Académie Française in 1753.

Piscator, Erwin (1893–1966) German director, who played a key role in the development of EPIC THEATRE, being one of the first directors to use filmstrips and cartoons in conjunction with live actors. A pupil of Reinhardt, he was a close associate of Brecht, whom he greatly influenced, and a member of the Communist party, believing in the theatre as a tool for propaganda and social reform. His early Expressionist productions, notably Brecht's *The Good Soldier Schweik* (1927) and Elm Welk's *Gervitter über Gottland* (1927) provoked his dismissal from the Volksbühne. He then opened his own theatre (1927–29), where he staged revolutionary versions of Brecht, Tolstoy, and Toller; subsequently he moved to New York where he influenced such notable figures as Arthur Miller and Tennessee Williams. In 1962 he returned to Berlin to the Freie Volksbühne where he directed documentary dramas. His influence was also profound upon the Living Theatre in the US and the Theatre Workshop in Britain.

Pisistratus (d. 528 BC) Ruler of Athens, who did much to reorganize the early theatre in Greece. He made extensive changes to the DIONYSIA and founded contests for dithyrambs and tragedies.

Pistoia, Il *See* Caminelli, Antonio.

pit *See* auditorium.

Pit *See* Barbican Centre.

Pitlochry Festival Theatre A theatre at Pitlochry in Scotland, established by John Stewart (founder of Glasgow's **Park Theatre**) in 1951 for summer seasons of plays in repertory. It was originally housed in a marquee but then transferred to a semi-permanent structure (1953–80) and finally to the present theatre, specially built on a new riverside site. The annual festival itself includes the production of six or seven plays as well as concerts and exhibitions.

Pitoëff, Georges (1887–1939) French actor, director, and playwright, born in Russia, who founded his own company in 1924. Having begun his career in Russia in association with such figures as Stanislavsky and Meyerhold, he joined Copeau's company in France in 1921 (after a period in Switzerland). He subsequently presented his own productions at the Théâtre des Arts and then at the Mathurins. These included influential versions of plays by such foreign playwrights as Chekhov, Pirandello, Shakespeare, and Shaw as well as much contemporary French drama.

His wife, **Ludmilla Pitoëff** (1896–1951), took over the company upon her husband's death and led it on an acclaimed tour of the US and Canada. As an actress she was much praised in plays by Ibsen and Shaw among others.

Their son, **Sacha Pitoëff** (1920–), began his career with Barsacq's Compagnie des Quatre Saisons and then worked in his parents' company. He founded his own troupe in 1949 and produced numerous plays by foreign playwrights, including several from Japan, often appearing in them himself with great success.

Pitt, Charles Isaac Mungo (1768–1833) British playwright and manager, who was the illegitimate son of Charles Dibdin. He wrote several successful plays and pantomimes and became the manager of Sadler's Wells. He also wrote *History of the London Theatres* (1826).

Pixérécourt, Guilbert de (1773–1844) French playwright, who wrote the first melodramas for the Parisian *Boulevard* theatres and introduced the genre to the English stage through translations of his early works. A prolific writer, he was known as 'the Corneille of the boulevards' and wrote over 100 plays. His melodramas were a successful blend of violence, spectacle, and sentimentality, culminating in the inevitable triumph of virtue over vice; they had a major influence on the Romantic drama that was to follow. He was also a director of the Théâtre de la Gaîté; when it burned down in 1835 he retired from the theatre.

Principal works:

VICTOR OU L'ENFANT DE LA FORÊT: 1798.
Coelina ou l'Enfant du mystère: 1800; translated as *A Tale of Mystery*.
Marguerite d'Anjou: 1810.
Valentine ou la Séduction: 1821.
Le Château de Loch-Leven: 1822.
Latude ou Trente-cinq Ans de captivité: 1834.

Place, The *See* Royal Shakespeare Company.

Placide, Henry (1799–1870) US actor, who became one of the most admired performers in classic comedy in Colman the Younger's *The Heir at Law* (1823) at New York's Park Theatre and as Sir Peter Teazle in Sheridan's *The School for Scandal*. Several other members of his family were also well-known upon the US and Canadian stage.

Plain Dealer, The A comedy by Sir William WYCHERLEY. First performance: c. 1674. Manly, the misanthropic plain dealer, returns from war to find that his fiancée, to whom he entrusted money, has secretly married his best friend; he brings about her disgrace and finally marries the faithful Fidelia.

Planché, James Robinson (1796–1880) British playwright and theatrical designer of Huguenot descent, who wrote numerous burlesques, extravaganzas, melodramas, and pantomimes for the London stage. His most popular works included the melodrama *The Vampire; or, the Bride of the Isles* (1820), in which a VAMP TRAP was first used, and the burlesque *The Island of Jewels* (1849), which was produced at the Lyceum Theatre. As a designer he was responsible for the first authentically-costumed version of Shakespeare's *King John*, directed by Charles Kean in 1823. He was also active in arguing for copyright protection of theatrical works.

Planchon, Roger (1931–) French director, actor, and playwright, who has done much to transfer the focus of the French theatre from Paris to the provinces through his work in Villeurbanne, near Lyon. Much influenced by Artaud, Vilar, and – above all – Brecht, he opened a small theatre in Lyon itself in 1950 and moved to Villeurbanne in 1957, subsequently becoming head of the local *centre dramatique* (1959) and concentrating on attracting a popular audience. In general he rejected the French classical theatre in favour of such authors as Adamov and Brecht and built up a huge audience, although he also attracted much critical attention with his savage interpretations of such works as Marlowe's *Edward II*, Molière's *George Dandin*, and Shakespeare's *Henry IV, Parts I and II*.

In 1972 his company was renamed the THÉÂTRE NATIONAL POPULAIRE in recognition of its achievement. Subsequently he adopted a less prominent role with the group, concentrating on writing his own dramas, which include *Bleus, blancs, rouges* (1967), *Le Cochon noir* (1974), and *Gilles de Rais* (1976), and on writing and directing films. Planchon's more recent productions for the company include *Andromaque* (1987) and Pinter's *No Man's Land* (1994).

platform stage *See* thrust stage.

Plato (427 BC–348 BC) Greek philosopher, whose major works were written in dialogue form; they also include various comments on the role of theatre in society. He burned his own early dramatic writings when he became convinced that drama and poetry could exercise a destructive influence upon the community through their appeal to the emotions rather than the intellect. Nonetheless, in such dialogues as the *Protagoras* and the *Phaedo* there is ample evidence of his mastery of dramatic technique and feeling for characterization as well as for poetic language. His views, which favoured strict censorship and the harnessing of drama for the good of the state, prompted important responses from Aristotle.

Plato Comicus (c. 5th–4th century BC) Greek playwright, a contemporary of Aristophanes. Few fragments of his plays, with which he won several contests, survive.

platt The plot or synopsis of a play as used by the stage crew in the Elizabethan theatre. Surviving examples include details of exits and entrances and lists of props.

Plautus, Titus Maccus (c. 254 BC–184 BC) Roman playwright, author of numerous major comedies that have had a profound influence upon subsequent comic drama. Although the most popular playwright of his day, Plautus's life remains obscure, little being known beyond the tradition that he spent his youth in the theatre and, after losing the fortune earned from his writing in business, was obliged to work in a grain mill. Most of his 150 plays, of which about 21 probably by him survive, were loosely based upon works of Greek Old Comedy; they are characterized by complex plots, lively language, and much ribald and often outrageous farce. Among the more influential of his plays were the AMPHITRUO, which Dryden imitated in his *Amphitryon*, the *Aulularia*, upon which Molière based his *L'Avare*, and the MENAECHMI, which provided the inspiration for Shakespeare's *The Comedy of Errors*; in the 20th century several of the plays were successfully combined in the musical *A Funny Thing Happened on the Way to the Forum*.

Principal works (some dates unknown):
   Amphitruo.
   Aulularia.
   Bacchides.
   Captivi.
   Cistellaria: 204 BC.
   Menaechmi.
   MILES GLORIOSUS: 204 BC.
   Mostellaria.
   Pseudolus: 191 BC.
   Rudens.
   Stichus: 200 BC.
   Truculentus.

playbill A theatre programme giving details of a particular performance, or a **poster** advertising the show in production or a forthcoming attraction. The first play-bills to appear in Britain were produced at Drury Lane and Covent Garden in 1737.

Playboy of the Western World, The An ironic comedy by J M SYNGE, which is generally regarded as his masterpiece. First performance: Abbey Theatre, Dublin, 1907. A young man, Christy Mahon, arrives fearfully in a Mayo village, claiming that he has killed his domineering father. Christy is welcomed as a hero by the local women until his supposedly dead father turns up in pursuit of him. The play's irreverent treatment of Irish peasant life provoked violent riots when it was first staged at the Abbey Theatre.

Players' Club A gentleman's club founded in New York in 1888 by Edwin Booth, who was also its first president. Like his successors, Joseph Jefferson and John Drew, he died in office. Subsequent presidents have included Walter Hampden (1928–55) and Alfred Drake (1970–78). Lynne Redgrave became the first woman president in 1994. The club has a fine library and an extensive theatrical collection.

Players' Theatre A theatre club situated under the railway arches in Villiers Street, Charing Cross, London. It was opened as **Playroom Six** in New Compton Street in 1927 and was reopened (as the Players' Theatre) in 1936 in King Street, Covent Garden, in what was once Evans's song-and-supper rooms. Here began the nightly Victorian burlesque and music hall performances called *Late Joys* for which the theatre, having moved to Villiers Street in 1946, is now famous. In 1953 the theatre staged the premiere of Sandy Wilson's musical comedy *The Boy Friend*. During redevelopment of the area in 1987 the club went into temporary exile at the Duchess Theatre, Catherine Street. It returned to renovated premises under the arches in 1990.

Playfair, Sir Nigel (1874–1934) British actor-manager and director, who was noted for his management of the Lyric Theatre, Hammersmith, from 1918 to 1934. His greatest successes there included Drinkwater's *Abraham Lincoln* (1919), Gay's *The Beggar's Opera* (1920), Congreve's *The Way of the World* (1924), and Wilde's *The Importance of Being Earnest* (1930). As an actor he appeared in the first productions of plays by Shaw and in many productions at the Lyric. He also collaborated in the translation and production at the Regent Theatre of *The Insect Play* (1923) by the Čapek brothers.

Playhouse A theatre on the Embankment near Charing Cross, London, which was opened by Cyril Maude in 1907. It replaced the **Royal Avenue Theatre** (built 1882), which had housed the premiere of Shaw's *Arms and the Man* (1894). In 1905 six people died when the neighbouring Charing Cross station partially collapsed on it; after the theatre was rebuilt Maude and his wife, Winifred Emery, appeared in many distinguished productions until 1915. Frank Curzon took over in 1917, with Gladys Cooper as his leading lady; she later ran the theatre on her own, presenting several of Somerset Maugham's plays, including *The Letter* (1927). Nancy Price ran her People's National Theatre company at the Playhouse prior to World War II but, in 1951, it became a BBC studio and was not reclaimed as a theatre until 1987, when it reopened with a new musical, *Girl Friends*. It has since presented a series of farces by Ray Cooney, who bought the theatre in 1992, as well as new dramas and classic revivals.

Playhouse Theatre A theatre on West 48th Street, between Broadway and 6th Avenue, New York, which opened in 1911. Both classical and modern plays were housed there, the most important including Broadhurst's *Bought and Paid For* (1911), the US premiere of Shaw's *Major Barbara* (1915), Robert Sherwood's *The Road to Rome* (1927), Rice's *Street Scene* (1929), Tennessee Williams's *The Glass Menagerie* (1945), and Gibson's *The Miracle Worker* (1959). The theatre was demolished in 1968.

Playroom Six *See* Players' Theatre.

Playwrights' Horizons An important non-profit-making New York organization that sponsors playwrights and new plays, a great many of which have gone on to commercial runs. It was founded by Robert Moss in 1971 and has been run by Andre Bishop since 1974. New plays that it has sponsored include three Pulitzer Prize winners, *Sunday in the Park with George* (1984), *Driving Miss Daisy* (1988), and *The Heidi Chronicles* (1989). It also took a lead in redeveloping 42nd Street's THEATRE ROW, where it currently has two spaces, of 175 and 75 seats.

Playwrights' Theatre *See* Provincetown Players.

Plenty A play by David HARE. First performance: National Theatre Company, Lyttleton Theatre, 1978. The play explores the predicament of Susan Traherne, a wartime Resistance heroine disillusioned by the complacency of post-war British society. The play was poorly received on its first run but is now seen as a modern classic; it was filmed in 1985 and has enjoyed several revivals.

Plinge, Walter A fictitious name used on British playbills to disguise the fact that the same actor is playing two roles. The name dates from about 1900 and was possibly that of the landlord of a public house near the Lyceum Theatre; the US equivalent is **George Spelvin**, which is also sometimes used for animals.

Plough and the Stars, The A play by Sean O'CASEY. First performance: Abbey Theatre, Dublin, 1926. Set during the 1916 Easter Rising, the play details the effects of the violence upon the inhabitants of Dublin's slums. Although its unromantic depiction of the struggle provoked riots at its first performance, the play was soon recognized as a classic and went on to become the Abbey's most frequently revived play.

Plough Monday The first Monday after Twelfth Night, when an early example of FOLK THEATRE was traditionally performed in certain English villages. Linked to ancient rural ritual, it involves the blessing of a plough and a collection; it may have inspired the development of the Wooing Ceremony (*see* mummers' play). The ritual is now usually carried out on the first Saturday after Plough Monday.

Plowright, Joan (1929–) British actress, who made her first appearance at the Grand Theatre, Croydon, in 1951. Subsequently she was acclaimed for her work at the Royal Court Theatre with the English Stage Company, especially as Margery Pinchwife in the 1956 revival of Wycherley's *The Country Wife*. Contemporary roles have included Jean Rice in Osborne's *The Entertainer* (1957) opposite OLIVIER, whom she married in 1961. She was the original Beatie in Wesker's *Roots* (1959) and has played many leading roles with the National Theatre Company. Other successes have included de Filippo's *Saturday, Sunday, Monday* (1973) and *Filumena* (1977), the Chichester Festival production of *The Way of the World* at the Haymarket (1984), and *Uncle Vanya* (1988). In 1988 she made her debut as a director with the play *Married*

Love for Kenneth Branagh's Renaissance Company. She has subsequently worked mainly in films.

Plummer, Christopher (1929–) Canadian actor, who has appeared in a wide variety of stage roles, ranging from comedy to Shakespearean tragedy, as well as in films. He began his career in the theatre in Ottawa and established his reputation in such Shakespearean roles as Henry V (1956), Hamlet (1957), Richard III (1961), Antony (1967), and Iago (1981); other successes have included Shaffer's *The Royal Hunt of the Sun* (1965), plays by Anouilh, Chekhov, and Neil Simon, Pinter's *No Man's Land* (1994), and a one-man show *Barrymore* (1997). His daughter **Amanda Plummer** has also had a successful career in the theatre.

Plymouth Theatre A theatre on West 45th Street, New York, which opened in 1917. Among the productions seen there were the premiere in English of Ibsen's *The Wild Duck* (1918), Maxwell Anderson's *What Price Glory?* (1924), Sherwood's *Abe Lincoln in Illinois* (1938), Shaw's *Don Juan in Hell* (1952), Neil Simon's *Plaza Suite* (1969), Peter Shaffer's *Equus* (1974), and the Royal Shakespeare Company's *Nicholas Nickleby* (1981). Recent productions include *The Heidi Chronicles* (1989), *Dancing at Lughnasa* (1991), and the musical version of *Jekyll and Hyde* (1997).

Pocock, Isaac (1782–1835) British playwright, who became popular for his many farces and melodramas. He followed *Yes or No*, staged at the Haymarket in 1808, with *Hit or Miss* (1810), in which the elder Mathews had great success. His most famous piece was the melodrama *The Miller and His Men* (1813); often revived, it became a toy theatre favourite. His dramatizations of Scott's novels included *Rob Roy* (1818).

Poel, William (William Pole; 1852–1934) British actor and director, who attracted much attention for his interest in recreating the theatre of Shakespeare's day. After training as an actor under Charles James Mathews, he founded the influential ELIZ-ABETHAN STAGE SOCIETY in 1894 and over the next 11 years presented works by most of the early British dramatists, ranging from *Twelfth Night* (1895) to the long-forgotten morality play *Everyman*. All were distinguished by their unfashionably austere settings and use of a stage approximating to that of the typical Elizabethan theatre.

Poelzig, Hans (1869–1936) German architect, who designed the Grosses Schaupiel-haus in Berlin for Max Reinhardt. Seating 3000 on three sides of a flexible stage, it profoundly influenced subsequent theatre design and hastened the decline of the proscenium arch.

poetic drama Any play in which the dialogue is written mainly in verse. Although most early plays were written in verse – Shakespeare being the acknowledged master of its use – the term poetic drama is usually reserved for works written since the Restoration, at which time it became usual for comedies to be written in prose and tragedies in verse. The great neoclassical works of Corneille and Racine were written in rhyming couplets, as were the tragedies of Dryden and his successors on the English stage. The Romantic period saw a self-conscious attempt to revive the Shakespearean tradition of poetic drama in the early works of Goethe and Schiller. However, the plays of the English Romantic poets Coleridge, Byron, Keats, and Shelley fail to fuse poetry with theatricality and veer constantly towards closet drama. Although new verse dramas continued to be presented during the 19th century, the tradition had become wholly artificial in most European countries. In the 1880s and 1890s Ibsen – himself the author of the poetic masterpieces *Brand* and *Peer Gynt* – led the revolution that made prose the normal medium for serious contemporary drama. Since then the dominance of prose has rarely been challenged. Among 20th-century poets to write effectively for the stage were W B Yeats, whose work drew on Japanese *Nō* traditions, and T S Eliot, who introduced free verse in his plays of the 1930s and 1940s. After World War II there was a brief fashion for verse drama in Britain, when Eliot, Christopher Fry, and other writers enjoyed success in the West End. In the US impetus was also added by performances given under the aegis of the Federal Theatre Project and the Poets' Theatre of Cambridge, Massachusetts.

Pogodin, Nikolai Fedorovich (Nikolai Fedorovich Stukalov; 1902–62)   Russian playwright, who began to write for the stage during the 1930s. His early plays, which deal chiefly with the working man's struggle to overcome economic and personal difficulty, include *Ten'* (Tempo; 1930) and *Poem About an Axe* (1931). Other major works include *Aristokraty* (Aristocrats; 1934) and a historical trilogy on the life of Lenin – *Chelovek s ruzhiem* (The Man with the Gun; 1937), *Kremlevskiye kuranty* (Kremlin Chimes; 1942), and *Tret'aya pateticheskaya* (The Third Pathétique; 1958).

Poisson, Paul (1658–1735)   French actor, the son of BELLEROCHE, who inherited several of his father's comic roles as well as his stutter. He joined the Comédie-Française in 1686 and was married to the actress **Marie-Angélique de L'École** (1657–1756), who was the stepdaughter of Du Croisy and the author of various pieces on Molière.

Their son **Philippe Poisson** (1682–1743) had a short career as an actor but later wrote several popular plays, as did their daughter **Madeleine-Angélique Poisson** (1684–1770), author of the tragedy *Habis* (1714). Their other son **François Arnould Poisson** (1696–1753) became an actor with the Comédie-Française, also inheriting his grandfather's stutter and excelling in comic roles.

Poliakoff, Stephen (1952–)   British playwright. He emerged as a leading writer for the contemporary stage in the mid-1970s with such works as *Hitting Town* (1975), *City Sugar* (1975), and *Strawberry Fields* (1977), about a neo-Nazi sect. Subsequent plays have included *Breaking the Silence* (1984), based on the life of his own grandfather, *Coming in to Land* (1987), which starred Maggie Smith as a Polish emigrant, *Playing with Trains* (1989), *Sienna Red* (1992), *Blinded by the Sun* (1996), one of several plays to discuss the role of modern science, and *Talk of the City* (1998). He has also written and directed for television and the cinema.

Polichinelle   A character of the French Comédie-Italienne, derived from the character of PULCINELLA in the Italian *commedia dell'arte*. A hunchback similar to Pulcinella in appearance, he was cunning and witty in the French version and anticipated the subsequent development of the English character Punch (*see* Punch and Judy).

Polish State Jewish Theatre   *See* Kamińska, Ida.

Politis, Fotos (1890–1934)   Greek director, who did much to make the Greek National Theatre, founded in 1930, an important centre of European drama. He emphasized revivals of classical plays but also encouraged the application to them of modern experimental staging techniques.

Poliziano, Angelo (Angelo Ambrogini; 1454–94) Italian scholar, also known as Politian, who was the author of the first major play written in the vernacular. His *Favola d'Orfeo* (1472) shared features of the *sacra rappresentazione* but was based upon mythological rather than biblical material and anticipated the development of the pastoral.

Polotsky, Simeon (Samuil Yemelyanovich Petrovsky-Sitnianovich; 1629–80) Russian monk, poet, and playwright, whose plays initiated school drama in Russia. His two plays, the *Comedy-Parable of the Prodigal Son* and *Nebuchadnezzar the King, the Golden Calf, and the Three Youths Unconsumed in the Fiery Furnace*, were given elaborate productions at the royal court, where Polotsky was tutor to the tsar's children.

Polus (4th century BC) Greek tragic actor, traditionally believed to have taught Demosthenes elocution. Acting in *Electra* by Sophocles, he reputedly carried his own son's ashes in an urn in a particular scene in order to make his grief on stage seem more convincing.

Ponsard, François (1814–67) French playwright, who led a reaction against Romantic drama and advocated a return to the classical tradition. His first play, the tragedy *Lucrèce* (1843), enjoyed considerable success; it was followed by a number of other dramas and comedies, notably *Charlotte Corday* (1850), *Horace et Lydie* (1850), *L'Honneur et l'argent* (1853), and *Le Lion amoureux* (1866).

Ponti, Diana da (fl. 1582–1605) Italian actress of the *commedia dell'arte*, who appeared under the stagename **Lavinia**. She acted with the Confidenti and the Gelosi before forming her own troupe – possibly the Desiosi – and is known to have appeared in France in 1601.

Pope, Jane (1742–1818) British actress, who began her career at Drury Lane as Corinna in Vanbrugh's *The Confederacy* in 1759. She gradually took over the roles associated with Kitty Clive and, in 1765, played Beatrice to Garrick's Benedick in *Much Ado About Nothing*. She also appeared in the first production of *The Clandestine Marriage* (1766) and created Mrs Candour and Tilburina in Sheridan's plays.

Pope, Thomas (d. 1604) English actor, an original shareholder in the Globe and Curtain theatres, who is in the First Folio list of actors in Shakespeare's plays. He joined the Chamberlain's Men on their formation and probably inherited Kempe's roles as a clown.

Popov, Alexei Dmitrevich (1892–1961) Russian director, who won acclaim for his work at the Red Army Theatre after establishing his reputation at the Moscow Art Theatre (1912–18) and the Vakhtangov Theatre (from 1973). His most influential productions included Pogodin's *Poem About an Axe* (1931) at the Theatre of the Revolution (later the Mayakovsky Theatre), *Romeo and Juliet* (1936), *The Taming of the Shrew* (1938) at Moscow's Red Army Theatre, and *A Midsummer Night's Dream* (1940); later successes were Gogol's *The Government Inspector* (1951) and Pogodin's *Kremlin Chimes* (1956). He also helped to found the International Federation for Theatre Research in 1955.

His son, **Andrei Alexeyevich Popov** (1918–), became artistic director of the Red Army Theatre in 1963 after his father's death. As an actor, he was praised in plays by Gogol, Shakespeare, and Tolstoy among others.

Porgy and Bess A work with music by George Gershwin, lyrics by Ira Gershwin, and book by Du Bose Heyward, based on his play. First performance: New York, 1935. Set on Catfish Row in Charleston, South Carolina, it deals with the love of Porgy, a disabled beggar, for Bess; this is complicated by her brutal former lover and her addiction to drugs. Controversy as to whether it was an opera, a 'folk opera', or a musical led to the original production closing at a loss; it is now recognized as a masterpiece.

Porta, Giambattista Della *See* Della Porta, Giambattista.

portal opening *See* false proscenium.

Porter, Cole (1892–1964) US composer, famous for his wittily salacious lyrics and langorous love ballads; he also supplied music for about 20 popular stage shows. Beginning with *See America First* (1916), his best-known productions included *Wake Up and Dream* (1929), *The Gay Divorce* (1932), *Anything Goes* (1934), *Kiss Me Kate* (1948), which is loosely based on *The Taming of the Shrew*, and *Silk Stockings* (1955). Performers who appeared in his shows include Fred Astaire, Mary Martin, Ethel Merman, and Alfred Drake.

Porter, Eric (1928–95) British actor, who made his professional debut at Stratford-on-Avon in 1945. Subsequently he gained experience with Wolfit's company and at the Birmingham Repertory Theatre before triumphing as Bolingbroke in *Richard II* and Fainall in Congreve's *The Way of the World* in Gielgud's 1952–53 season at the Lyric, Hammersmith. He subsequently appeared in numerous important parts at the Old Vic and Stratford-on-Avon and elsewhere, being acclaimed in such roles as Shylock (1965), King Lear (1968), and Malvolio (1976). He also established a wide reputation as a television actor.

Porter, Mary Ann (d. 1765) British actress, who began acting as a child. She was taught by Betterton and made her first recorded appearance in 1699 at Lincoln's Inn Fields. Over the next 40 years she became a highly respected tragic actress, excelling as Belvidera in *Venice Preserv'd*.

Porter's Hall A theatre built near Blackfriars, London, by Philip Rosseter and Philip Kingman in 1615 to house the combined Queen's Revels and Lady Elizabeth's companies. However, their licence was revoked before the theatre (also called the **Puddle Wharf Theatre**) was complete, and although some early performances may have taken place, there is no evidence of use after 1618.

Porte-Saint-Martin, Théâtre de la A theatre in Paris, which was erected in 1782 as a new home for the company from the Paris Opéra. After a period of disuse (1794–1802), the theatre established itself as a venue for performances of the plays of Pixérécourt and prospered from appearances by Frédérick and Mlle Dorval in *Trente Ans, ou la vie d'un joueur* (1827) and other plays. During the 1830s the theatre consolidated its reputation with plays by Dumas *père* and Hugo before controversy surrounding Balzac's *Vautrin* (1840) caused the theatre's closure. Subsequently it was used for more sentimental pieces and occasional revivals, being destroyed during a riot in 1870 and then rebuilt on a smaller scale. Sarah Bernhardt ran the theatre during the 1880s with some success, after which Rostand's *Cyrano de Bergerac* restored it to its former glory. From 1936 to 1978 it concentrated on musical comedy, eventually being taken over by Marcel Marceau.

Portman, Eric (1903–69) British actor, who first came to London in 1923 playing Shakespearean roles. He joined the Old Vic company in 1927 and was acclaimed as Undershaft in Shaw's *Major Barbara* at Wyndham's (1929). Subsequently he played important parts in many plays and films, to all of which he brought remorseless energy and integrity, most notably in works by Terence Rattigan, J B Priestley, Graham Greene, O'Neill, and Robert Bolt.

Portman Theatre *See* West London Theatre.

Porto-Riche, Georges de (1849–1930) French playwright, whose psychological studies of the 'eternal triangle' of wife, husband, and lover established a genre known as the *théâtre d'amour*. *La Chance de Françoise*, produced at the Théâtre Libre in 1889, was followed by *Amoureuse* (1891), *Le Passé* (1897), and *Le Vieil Homme* (1911), which are generally considered to be his finest plays.

Posset, Jean *See* Sackville, Thomas, First Earl of Dorset.

poster *See* playbill.

Potier des Cailletières, Charles Gabriel (1774–1838) French actor, highly regarded in his own day as a performer of comic roles. He achieved fame after appearing at the Théâtre des Variétés in Paris in 1809, later enjoying further success at the Palais-Royal.

Pouget, Madeleine de *See* Beauchâteau.

Poulsen, Emil (1842–1911) Danish actor, who – with his brother **Olaf Poulsen** (1849–1923) – won acclaim in the plays of Shakespeare and in many native Scandinavian dramas. They both excelled in plays by Holberg and Ibsen, while Olaf was particularly admired as Falstaff and other comic characters in Shakespeare.

Emil's sons, **Adam Poulsen** (1879–1969) and **Johannes Poulsen** (1881–1938), were connected respectively with the Dagmarteatret and the Kongelige Teater.

Powell, George (1668–1714) British actor, who originated numerous leading roles at Drury Lane, including Bellamour in Congreve's *The Old Bachelor* and Lothario in Rowe's *The Fair Penitent*. Noted for his volatile temper, he left Drury Lane on the advent of Wilks. The most successful of his own plays was *The Imposture Defeated; or a Trick to Cheat the Devil* (1697).

Powell, Martin (fl. 1710–13) British puppeteer. He became famous for his puppet shows in Bath and in London's Covent Garden Piazza, satirizing Italian opera.

Power, Tyrone (David Powell; 1797–1841) Irish actor, who became successful in such stage Irish parts as Sir Lucius O'Trigger in Sheridan's *The Rivals*. He also appeared in comedies and farces of his own, including *St Patrick's Eve* (1832) and *O'Flannigan and the Fairies* (1836). He left the Haymarket for a tour of the US in 1840 but was drowned on the way home.

He was the great-grandfather of the US actor **Tyrone Power** (1914–58), who made his first stage appearance, as a page in *Hamlet*, in 1931. Although primarily famous as a film star, he found success on the US stage in such roles as Benvolio in

Romeo and Juliet (1935), de Poulengy in Shaw's *Saint Joan* (1936), and Gettner in Fry's *The Dark Is Light Enough* (1955).

Pradon, Jacques (1644–98) French playwright, sometimes incorrectly referred to as Nicolas Pradon. Having enjoyed some success with his first play, *Pyrame et Thisbé* (1674), he wrote *Phèdre et Hippolyte* (1677), which was timed to coincide with Racine's PHÈDRE, a version of the same legend. The latter opened just two days before Pradon's inferior play and was undeservedly eclipsed by it.

praetexta A subdivision of Roman *fabula*, comprising serious dramas based on mythological or contemporary themes. The genre was invented by Naevius, while noted writers included Accius, Ennius, Pacuvius, and possibly Seneca. Few examples survive.

Praga, Marco (1862–1929) Italian playwright and novelist, who was a leading writer in the *verismo* tradition. His plays satirize such targets as bourgeois complacency and were much influenced by contemporary French drama; the most successful of his works included *Mater dolorosa* (1888), based on a novel by Girolamo Rovetta, *La moglie ideale* (The Ideal Wife; 1890), in which Duse was highly acclaimed, and *La Porta chiusa* (The Closed Door; 1913). He was also a director of the Stabile Milanese company for a time and promoted the early career of Pirandello.

Pratinus of Phlius (c. 540–470 BC) Greek playwright, author of the earliest satyrplays. He is believed to have written more than 30 such pieces, as well as 18 tragedies.

Pray, Malvina *See* Florence, William Jermyn.

Prehauser, Gottfried (1699–1769) Austrian actor, who inherited the part of HANSWURST from Stranitsky in 1725. An experienced performer with travelling companies, Prehauser further developed the role, making him a more recognizably Viennese creation; after Prehauser's death Hanswurst fell from favour on the Viennese stage.

prelude A brief theatrical entertainment occasionally presented in British theatres in the late 18th century. Preludes usually consisted of a satirical sketch discussing current theatrical issues and were presented at the opening of a new theatre or at the start of a theatre season.

Present Laughter A comedy by Noël COWARD. First performance: London, 1943. The plot revolves around an actor (first played by Coward himself), who maintains an unconventional household with the help of his separated but still adoring wife. As his love life becomes intolerably complicated, he realizes that his wife remains more important to him than his casual flirtations.

Prestes, Antônio (d. 1587) Portuguese playwright, regarded in his own time as being of the same stature as Gil Vicente. His seven surviving plays comprise six comedies and a morality play, the *Auto de Ave Maria*.

Preston, Thomas (fl. 1570) English playwright, about whom little is known beyond the fact that he wrote *Cambyses King of Persia* (c. 1570). A popular early tragicomedy written in a bombastic style, the play marks the transition of the morality play into the Elizabethan historical drama.

Préville (Pierre-Louis Dubus; 1721–99) French actor, who excelled as a player in comedy after joining the Comédie-Française in 1753. He inherited many of the roles of François Poisson and was particularly popular in the plays of Marivaux, Boursault, and as Beaumarchais's Figaro.

Price, Maire *See* Nic Shiubhlaigh, Maire.

Price, (Lilian) Nancy (1880–1970) British actress and manager, who joined Benson's company in 1899 and first won attention as Calypso in Stephen Phillips's *Ulysses* in 1902. Admired in a variety of roles, she also founded the **People's National Theatre** company (1930) and went on to produce numerous significant plays, among them the Čapeks's *The Insect Play* and Hsiung's *Lady Precious Stream* at the Little Theatre in London. She retired in 1952.

Priestley, J(ohn) B(oynton) (1894–1984) British novelist, journalist, and playwright, who wrote many successful plays in a wide variety of styles. The West Riding farce WHEN WE ARE MARRIED, in which he originally played a leading role, and AN INSPECTOR CALLS are possibly his best-known dramas. He also wrote a series of experimental Expressionist plays reflecting his preoccupation with the nature of Time: I HAVE BEEN HERE BEFORE, TIME AND THE CONWAYS, and JOHNSON OVER JORDAN. *Laburnum Grove* (1933) and *Eden End* were among his best comedies. Among his many adaptations was a dramatization of his first commercially successful novel, *The Good Companions* (1929) on which he collaborated with Edward Knoblock.

Principal works:
DANGEROUS CORNER: 1932.
Laburnum Grove: 1933.
I Have Been Here Before: 1937.
Time and the Conways: 1937.
When We Are Married: 1938.
Johnson over Jordan: 1939.
An Inspector Calls: 1946.
THE LINDEN TREE: 1947.

Prime Minister of Mirth *See* Robey, Sir George.

Prince, Hal (Harold Prince: 1928–) US producer and director, whose first success was *The Pajama Game* (1954). Since then he has directed or produced many hits, including *Damn Yankees* (1955), *West Side Story* (1957), *A Funny Thing Happened on the Way to the Forum* (1963), *Fiddler on the Roof* (1964), *Cabaret* (1966), and Stephen Sondheim's *Company* (1970), *Follies* (1971), *A Little Night Music* (1973), *Pacific Overtures* (1976), and *Sweeney Todd* (1979). More recent successes include *The Phantom of the Opera* (1987). In the 1980s and 1990s he concentrated on directing, including operas.

Prince Charles's Men An English theatre company founded in 1616 by Alleyn. Usually referred to as the Prince's Men, the company enjoyed the patronage of the future Charles I and performed at the Porter's Hall, the Hope, the Cockpit, the Curtain, and the Red Bull theatres between 1616 and 1625. On Charles's coronation the company was broken up, several of the actors joining the King's Men; in 1631 the name was revived for a new company that came under the patronage of the future Charles II and performed regularly at the Salisbury Court and Fortune theatres until 1642.

Prince Edward Theatre A 1647-seat theatre in Old Compton Street, housing the third largest stage in London. It opened in 1930 but was reconstructed in 1936 as a cabaret-restaurant and renamed the **London Casino**. Closed in 1940, it later became the Queensbury All-Services Club. Post-war productions included Ivor Novello's *The Dancing Years* (1947) and an annual pantomime. In 1954 the theatre became a cinema, but in 1974 there followed a period of stage shows alternating with films. In 1978, on the opening of *Evita*, the theatre reverted to its original name. In recent years it has staged a series of blockbuster musicals, including *Martin Guerre* (1996–98) and the Abba spectacular *Mamma Mia!* (from 1999).

Prince Henry's Men *See* Admiral's Men.

Prince of Wales' Theatre A 1133-seat theatre in Coventry Street, London, which has a long record of successful revues and musicals. The present building is the second theatre on the site. The first was financed by the profits made on a burlesque, *The Colonel*, at an earlier Prince of Wales' Theatre in Tottenham Street (later the Scala Theatre). Opening in 1884 as the **Prince's Theatre**, it enjoyed early success with Charles Hawtrey's farce *The Private Secretary*, with Beerbohm Tree in the title role. Lillie Langtry made several appearances at the theatre in 1885–86 and in 1886 the theatre's name was changed to the Prince of Wales' Theatre. Mrs Patrick Campbell, Sir Johnston Forbes-Robertson, and Marie Tempest all played here in ensuing years. From 1918 to 1926 André Charlot, then the lessee, presented a series of revues. For a short time in 1930 Edith Evans took over as manager. Later, under the control of Charles Clore, and then of Alfred Esdaile, the policy became one of revues only.

In 1937 the theatre was rebuilt and reopened with *Les Folies de Paris et Londres*. There was a short-lived return to mixed entertainment in the 1940s, which included Sid Field's success in *Harvey* (1949), but thereafter revue, musical comedy, and the occasional farce held sway. *The Danny La Rue Show* was presented from 1973. Recent musical revivals include *South Pacific* (1988), *Annie Get Your Gun* (1992), and *West Side Story* (1999). There are plans to rename the theatre after its former owner Lord (Bernard) Delfont.

Princess's Theatre A theatre in Oxford Street, London; it opened as a concert hall in 1840, was remodelled as an opera house in 1842, and was then used for drama. Macready, Fanny Kemble, the Cushman Sisters, and other leading players appeared there, but it was under the management of Charles Kean with his magnificent Shakespearean productions from 1851 to 1859 that the theatre, now called the **Royal Princess's Theatre**, achieved its highest distinction. In the 1860s Augustus Harris presented Irving there, while under George Vining's management the melodramas of Dion Boucicault, especially *The Streets of London* (1864), were highly successful – as was Charles Warner who caused a sensation as Coupeau in Charles Reade's *Drink* in 1879. In 1880 the old theatre was rebuilt, opening with Edwin Booth as Hamlet. From 1881 to 1886 Wilson Barrett attracted large audiences with such melodramas as *The Silver King*, but the theatre then declined. The theatre finally closed in 1902, becoming a warehouse and being demolished in 1931. *See also* Glasgow Citizens' Theatre.

Princess Theatre A theatre in Melbourne, Australia, opened in 1886 on the site of an older theatre. It was much admired for its decor and has since been used as a venue for a wide variety of entertainments, including opera.

The **Princess Theatre** on West 49th Street in New York opened in 1913 with a series of one-act plays. With 299 seats it was one of the smallest of the Broadway houses and had trouble finding suitable productions. From 1915 to 1919, it became well known for the Princess Theatre Musicals, an influential series of intimate shows with music by Jerome KERN. Since the small house made spectacle impossible, these musicals developed the integration of plot, character, and song that became the hallmark of the mature American musical. The Provincetown Players appeared there in 1920–21, while important premieres included Maxwell Anderson's *The White Desert* (1922). In 1928 the theatre was renamed the **Lucille La Verne Theatre**; a year later it became the **Assembly Theatre** and then a cinema. In 1937 it reopened briefly as a home for live drama as the **Labor Stage**; shows presented included *Pins and Needles*, a revue developed by the union for garment-district workers which went on to a long run elsewhere. From 1944 to 1947 it was known as the **Theatre Workshop** but then reverted to use as a cinema, being demolished in 1955.

Prince's Theatre *See* Prince of Wales' Theatre; Shaftesbury Theatre.

principal boy The traditional hero of the English pantomime, conventionally played by a female. The playing of the principal boy – a role which was in part derived from that of Harlequin – by a woman may have its roots in ancient ritual and subsequently in the popularity of actresses playing BREECHES PARTS. Famous principal boys include Nellie Stewart, Fay Compton, and more recently such popular singers as Lulu.

Printemps, Yvonne (1895–1977) French actress and singer, who became a leading star of musical theatre. She began her career in revue in Paris, performing at the Folies-Bergère and the Palais-Royal, and then married (1919) Sacha Guitry, in whose plays she frequently appeared. Later she married the actor Pierre Fresnay, acting with him in such successes as *O Mistress Mine* (1936) by Ben Travers. Other notable performances included Guitry's *Mozart* (1926) and Coward's *Conversation Piece* (1934); from 1937 she also ran the Théâtre de la Michodière.

Pritchard, Hannah (Hannah Vaughan; 1711–68) British actress, who began her career as a strolling player. She first appeared at Drury Lane in 1732, after which she built a reputation as an excellent comic actress, being particularly admired as Rosalind in *As You Like It* and Beatrice in *Much Ado About Nothing*. In 1748 Garrick engaged her at Drury Lane once more and installed her husband as treasurer. Over the next 21 years she added leading tragic roles to her celebrated comedy parts, including a notable Lady Macbeth, which she performed many times between 1748 and her retirement in 1768, by which time she had put on a great deal of weight.

Private Lives A comedy by Noël COWARD. First performance: London, 1930. The play follows the fortunes of a divorced couple and their new partners who find they are all honeymooning in the same hotel; the eccentric original pair finally reunite, rejecting their conventional spouses. The original cast was led by Coward himself, with Gertrude Lawrence as Amanda.

producer The person who organizes the financial and managerial aspects of a production. In Britain, the term was formerly used to mean the person in overall control of a production, including the direction of the cast and the interpretation of the play. The US term director was officially adopted for this person in 1956.

Professor Taranne (*Le Professeur Taranne*) A play by Arthur ADAMOV. First performance: Lyons, 1953 (produced by Roger Planchon). The plot, based on a dream, deals with the problems of a university professor accused of obscene behaviour. A powerful example of the Theatre of the ABSURD, the play reflects the influence of Kafka.

profile board A small section of wood and canvas attached to a flat in order to alter its shape for scenic purposes.

profile spot A spotlight capable of throwing a bright, clean-edged beam onto the stage; it is generally known in the US by the tradename **Leko**.

projector A projection unit used to create atmospheric lighting on stage. Special effects projectors, known in the US as **sciopticons**, are capable of producing complex mobile patterns of light suggesting such phenomena as stormy skies, snow, and fire. Projection from a computer display is increasingly supplanting the traditional use of slides or transparencies.

projector unit *See* pageant lantern.

Proletkult Theatre *See* Trades Unions Theatre.

prologue A brief scene or speech given at the beginning of a performance. In the ancient Greek theatre, the term referred to any part of the play before the first entrance of the chorus. The plays of Euripides were sometimes criticized for using this as an expository rather than a truly dramatic device. In Elizabethan times an introductory speech of this kind was usually known as a chorus. During the Restoration, the prologue was a short rhyming poem containing witty comments upon contemporary affairs.

promenade A development of theatre-in-the-round, in which the audience, which usually remains standing, is invited to accompany the actors from one area of an auditorium to another in order to follow the action.

Prometheus Bound A tragedy by AESCHYLUS. First performance: c. 460 BC. The first part of a tetralogy (neither of the other parts survives), it condemns tyrannical rule and shows the influence of Sophocles. It revolves around the central character of Prometheus, who has been bound to a rock for stealing fire from heaven but remains defiant.

prompt corner An area immediately behind the proscenium arch in which the prompter sits. In Britain the prompt corner is traditionally downstage left, while in the US it is usually downstage right. On the Continent and in most opera houses the prompter occupies a prompt box situated at the front of the stage and concealed by a hood.

prompter The person employed to provide an actor who forgets his words with the correct line; in his own copy of the play he may also keep a record of all the moves settled on during rehearsals. In Elizabethan times these duties were fulfilled by the BOOK-HOLDER.

prompt side (PS) A term used in the British theatre to denote the side of the stage (stage left) where the prompter usually sits. The other side of the stage is conventionally referred to as the **opposite prompt side** (OP).

prop Any inanimate item that appears on the stage, with the exception of the scenery, furniture, costumes, and various pieces of technical equipment. More formally referred to as stage properties, these articles are ultimately the responsibility of the stage manager. Props that are carried onto the stage by the actors themselves are known as **hand-props**.

proscenium The long, narrow acting area of the ancient Greek theatre. Originally referred to as the *proskenion*, it denoted the space between the orchestra and the SKENE. In the modern theatre the word is often used to mean the proscenium arch.

proscenium arch The wall and opening that divides the stage from the auditorium in most theatres built between the 17th and 20th centuries. The name comes from the *proscenium* of the ancient Greeks. The earliest proscenium arch was that erected at the Teatro Farnese in 1618. Early theatres often had a forestage area for acting in front of the arch; by the 19th century most theatres had dispensed with this and the proscenium arch developed as an elaborate 'frame' for the scene presented on the stage. Many modern theatre designs have, however, dropped the proscenium arch in favour of a more open stage plan.

proscenium border A border situated immediately upstage of the proscenium arch, referred to in the US (together with other short masking cloths) as a **teaser**.

proscenium doors In the Restoration theatre, one (or more) pairs of doors set into the proscenium arch, providing actors with access to and from the forestage. By the 19th century they were only used for actors to take their bow at the end of a performance, becoming known as **call doors**.

Prospect Theatre Company A British theatre company, founded in Oxford in 1961. Originally called Prospect Productions, the company moved under **Toby Robertson** (Sholto David Maurice Robertson; 1928–) to the Arts Theatre, Cambridge in 1964; from here it toured successfully in classic plays until 1969. In 1977 it transferred to the Old Vic Theatre in London, being renamed the Old Vic company in 1979. Its most acclaimed productions included Shakespeare's *Richard II* (1968), Marlowe's *Edward II* (1969), Turgenev's *A Month in the Country* (1975), *Antony and Cleopatra* (1977), Shaw's *Saint Joan* (1977), and *Hamlet* (1978); actors with the company included Ian McKellen, Dorothy Tutin, Alec McCowen, Eileen Atkins, Derek Jacobi, Peter O'Toole (who was much criticized for his Macbeth in 1980), and Timothy West, who was artistic director when the company was disbanded in 1980 on the loss of its state grant.

protagonist The principal actor in ancient Greek drama. The role of the protagonist developed from that of the actor who led the chorus during the performance of dithyrambs; according to tradition, this was as a result of an innovation by Thespis. A second and third actor (the **deuteragonist** and the **tritagonist**) were added for the plays of Euripides and Sophocles.

Provincetown Players An organization of US actors and playwrights founded in 1916. The group began at the **Wharf Theatre** in Providence, Rhode Island, and later moved to the **Playwrights' Theatre** in Greenwich Village, New York, before settling into their own Provincetown Playhouse in the same district in 1918. The most famous of the playwrights they helped to launch was Eugene O'Neill, with productions of *The Hairy Ape* and *The Emperor Jones* among other works. The group disbanded in 1921, but the Playwrights' Theatre prospered under Kenneth MacGowan and others until demolition in 1930, being renamed the **Irish Theatre** in 1929. The Provincetown Playhouse has since played host to many companies, housing the US premieres of Albee's *The Zoo Story* and Beckett's *Krapp's Last Tape* in 1960 and the long run of Charles Busch's *Vampire Lesbians of Sodom* from 1985 to 1990.

Provoked Wife, The   A comedy by Sir John VANBURGH. First performance: Drury Lane, 1697. The play explores the predicament of Lady Brute in her unfortunate marriage and debates her obligation to remain faithful to her drunken husband.

Pryce, Jonathan (1947–)   British actor, who was with the Everyman Theatre Company at Liverpool (where he also directed on occasions) before achieving great success as Gethin Price in Trevor Griffiths's *Comedians* (1975) at Nottingham Playhouse and the Old Vic. His major roles since then have included Hamlet (1980) at the Royal Court, Macbeth (1986) at Stratford-on-Avon and the Barbican, and Astrov in Michael Frayn's version of Chekhov's *Uncle Vanya* (1988) at the Vaudeville. He subsequently starred in the musicals *Miss Saigon* (1989) and *Oliver!* (1994) while also building a career in films.

Public Theatre   *See* New York Shakespeare Festival.

Publilius Syrus (1st century BC)   Roman playwright, author of early mime dramas. Originally a slave, he was judged superior to Laberius, and was highly regarded as a performer in his own pieces; of his works only a number of aphorisms have survived.

Puddle Wharf Theatre   *See* Porter's Hall.

Pulcinella   A character of the *commedia dell'arte*, one of the *zanni*. Possibly first played by Fiorillo, Pulcinella was a hunchback with a hooked nose and little intellect and probably inherited many of his traits from the Roman MACCUS. In the French Comédie-Italienne he became POLICHINELLE, while in England he evolved into the irascible Punch (*see* Punch and Judy).

Punch and Judy   The central tradition of the English puppet theatre. Traditionally presented by a single puppeteer in a small booth made of striped cloth, the Punch and Judy show has Italian and French origins. The character of Punch, a crafty hunchback with a large nose, vicious temper, and high voice – achieved by means of a small diaphragm (a **swazzle**) placed in the operator's mouth – was derived from that of POLICHINELLE; his wife Judy (sometimes called Joan) first appeared around 1688. Other characters in the show include the Baby, the dog TOBY, the Hangman, the Crocodile, and the Devil. Originally the puppets were marionettes, but by the early 19th century almost all Punch and Judy puppeteers favoured the use of glove puppets. Equivalents of Punch and Judy in other countries include shows featuring the Austrian character KASPERL and the Russian Petrushka.

Punch and Judy Theatre   A theatre on West 49th Street, New York, which opened in 1914 with Harold Chapin's *The Marriage of Columbine*. In 1926 the theatre was renamed the **Charles Hopkins Theatre**, reopening with Karel Čapek's *The Makropulos Secret*. In 1933 it was converted into a cinema.

Punch's Playhouse *See* Strand Theatre.

puppet theatre A form of dramatic entertainment in which the characters are represented by puppets. Traditionally made of wood and manipulated by hand (**glove puppets**) or by means of rods, wire, or string (in which case they are technically **marionettes**), puppets have been used since ancient times. In Western countries, puppets have usually been a street or fairground attraction and are now mainly associated with children's entertainment. In India, Japan, Java, and elsewhere in the Far East, however, they have a role in serious mainstream theatre. *See also Jōruri*; motion; shadow play.

Purim play A tradition of Jewish drama, performed during the festival of Purim in mid-March. With its roots in the 14th century, the genre comprised lively musical comedies with elements borrowed from Italian carnival. Such entertainments became popular throughout Europe in the 17th century and contributed to the development of a distinctly Jewish theatre. Later the tradition was also influenced by the *commedia dell'arte* and, in Germany, by the English Comedians. Most plays in the form were based on the Old Testament story of Esther and Haman, which the festival of Purim commemorates. The Purim play declined in the 18th century after it grew too licentious for the Jewish religious authorities. It was cleaned up in Germany by the so-called Haskala groups before finally disappearing upon the establishment of a fresh Yiddish theatrical tradition.

Pushkin, Alexander Sergeivich (1799–1837) Russian poet and playwright, whose most significant work for the theatre was the historical drama *Boris Godunov*. Best known for his poetry, Pushkin began writing drama while still a boy and particularly admired the plays of Shakespeare, which exercized a strong influence upon his one great dramatic work. Intended as the first of a series of major dramas on Russian themes, *Boris Godunov* (completed in 1825 but not staged until 1870) reflected the troubled political atmosphere of the time and is notable for its combination of poetry and colloquial language; it was later turned into an opera by Mussorgsky. Pushkin's short play *Mozart and Salieri* (1837) was set to music by Rimsky-Korsakov. Other works include a one-act version of the Don Juan story (1837).

Pushkin Theatre A theatre in St Petersburg, opened in 1824 as the **Alexandrinsky Theatre**. After enjoying early success with appearances by Karatygin, it presented a varied programme of ballet, opera, and melodrama for many years before achieving new acclaim with the Realist dramas of Strindberg and others. The conventional approach of the company led, however, to the failure of Chekhov's *The Seagull* in 1896 and it was not until the arrival of Meyerhold that the theatre's fortunes revived. Subsequent directors have included Lunacharsky and Radlov; the theatre (given its present name in 1937) has enjoyed success with plays by Chekhov, Lermontov, Shakespeare, and others, while the company has established a strong reputation for the quality of its acting.

Another theatre of the same name was founded in Moscow in 1951 and achieved early success with Sukhovo-Kobylin's *Krechinsky's Wedding*. Since then it has won attention with productions of plays by Ostrovsky, Oscar Wilde, and others, notably under the direction of Tumanov (1953–61).

Pygmalion   One of the most popular plays by G B SHAW, written in 1912. First performance: Vienna, 1913. The plot, concerning the social transformation of the cockney flower-seller, Eliza Doolittle, by the professor of linguistics, Henry Higgins, provided the basis for the musical *My Fair Lady* and for a film starring Wendy Hiller and Leslie Howard. The musical version was first staged in New York in 1956 and provided a major success for Rex Harrison, with famous sets by Cecil Beaton.

Pylades (1st century BC)   A noted *pantomimus* of ancient Rome, who was responsible for the introduction of the mime dance tradition from his native Greece. His success in tragic roles drew audiences away from straight tragedy.

Q Theatre A theatre on the north side of the River Thames at Kew Bridge, London, which was converted from the former Prince's Hall by Jack de Leon. It opened in 1924 with a revival of Gertrude Jennings's *The Young Person in Pink*. For upwards of 30 years he produced revivals of West End hits and many new plays there, including Frederick Knott's *Dial M for Murder* and Philip King's *See How They Run*. Unable to meet the requirements of the licensing authority, the theatre closed in 1956.

Quaglio, Lorenzo (1730–1804) Italian artist, who was the eldest member of a notable family of scene designers for various European court theatres. Lorenzo and his brother, **Giuseppe Quaglio** (1747–1828), executed numerous influential neoclassical designs, eventually settling in Germany, where succeeding generations of the family were active in designing scenery until the late 19th century.

Quality Street A play by J M BARRIE. First performance: London, 1902. The play is a Regency period romance in which a young woman, disappointed in her lover after a long absence, woos him again in the disguise of an imaginary niece.

Quare Fellow, The A tragicomedy by Brendan BEHAN. First performance: Dublin, 1954. First seen in a Gaelic verison, the play was highly acclaimed when performed by Joan Littlewood's Theatre Workshop in 1958; it depicts events in an Irish prison on the eve of a hanging, with both bitterness and humour.

Quartermaine, Leon (1876–1967) British actor, who made his London debut in Forbes-Robertson's company in 1901. Throughout his long career he played a wide range of parts, from the Emperor in Shaw's *Androcles and the Lion* to Ishak in Flecker's *Hassan* and Osborne in R C Sherriff's *Journey's End*. He was also admired for performances during Gielgud's season at the Haymarket (1944) and as a member of the Stratford-on-Avon company.

Quayle, Sir Anthony (1913–89) British actor, who made his professional debut in 1931 and spent the next eight years in supporting roles at the Old Vic and elsewhere. After World War II he reappeared as Jack Absolute in Sheridan's *The Rivals* (1945) and then went to Stratford-on-Avon (1948) as actor and director. Over the following eight years he played several major roles, including Iago, Falstaff, and Othello. In New York in 1956 he starred in Marlowe's *Tamburlaine the Great*; subsequently he made numerous film appearances, but also triumphed on stage in such parts as Eddie in Arthur Miller's *A View from the Bridge* (1956) and Andrew Wyke in Anthony Shaffer's *Sleuth* (1970). In 1984 he launched a touring company (Compass Productions), opening with his own production of Colman and Garrick's *The Clandestine Marriage*, in which he played Lord Ogleby.

Queen Anne's Men An English theatre company formed in 1603 from members of Oxford's and Worcester's Men. Usually referred to as the Queen's Men, the company included Christopher Beeston and Thomas Heywood; it performed at the Curtain and Red Bull theatres until 1616, when it moved to the Cockpit. It was disbanded in 1619.

Queen Elizabeth's Men An English theatre company founded in 1583. Usually known as the Queen's Men and performing at inns as well as at the Theatre, Curtain, and Rose theatres, it enjoyed considerable success through the popularity of such members as Richard Tarleton. It was disbanded in 1594.

Queen Henrietta's Men An English theatre company, founded in 1625 on the coronation of Charles I and Henrietta Maria. Usually referred to as the Queen's Men, the company was led by Christopher Beeston and performed numerous plays by James Shirley and others at the Cockpit from 1625 to 1636. Inigo Jones also designed scenery for their appearances at Court. An outbreak of the plague forced the company's dissolution in 1636, although a new company of the same name performed at Salisbury Court from 1637 to 1647.

Queen's Theatre A theatre in Long Acre, London, originally called **St Martin's Hall**. Converted into a theatre in 1867 and in its day the largest theatre in London next to Drury Lane and the opera houses, Queen's enjoyed a brief period of popularity. Actors there including Henry Irving and Ellen Terry. Renamed the National in 1877 it was finally closed in 1878 and later demolished.

In 1907 a new **Queen's Theatre** was opened in Shaftesbury Avenue as a twin to the Globe Theatre, but was not immediately successful. In 1913 the management introduced tango teas, for which patrons paid half a crown for dancing, a dress parade, and afternoon tea. The comedy *Potash and Perlmutter* (1914) was the Queen's Theatre's first real success; this was followed in 1916 by a sequel, *Potash and Perlmutter in Society*. Among subsequent notable productions were Bernard Shaw's *The Apple Cart* (1929), with Cedric Hardwicke and Edith Evans, *The Barretts of Wimpole Street* (1930), and, in 1937, a brilliant season of plays by Shakespeare and others featuring John Gielgud and Peggy Ashcroft. Bombed in 1940, the theatre remained derelict for nearly 20 years; it reopened in 1959 with a modern exterior but with the original style largely retained inside, seating 989. It has a strong reputation for drama and comedy, as well as such musicals as *Stop the World, I Want to Get Off* (1961) and *Wonderful Town!* (1986). Recent hits include Maggie Smith in Alan Bennett's *The Lady in the Van* (1999). *See also* Her Majesty's Theatre.

Quem Quaeritis? The most famous example of a TROPE in the liturgy of the early medieval church. Consisting of a brief exchange concerning the events surrounding the Resurrection, the *Quem Quaeritis?* evolved during the 10th century and was gradually embellished with extra scenes and comic characters as an early development of LITURGICAL DRAMA.

Questors Theatre A theatre at Ealing in West London that is the headquarters of a prominent group of amateurs, founded in 1929 by **Alfred Emmett**. The building itself, financed through fund-raising appeals, opened in 1964. At one period the group staged annual festivals of new drama, introducing the plays of James Saunders (including *Next Time I'll Sing to You* in 1962). In 1946 it became one of the founder-members of the Little Theatre Guild of Great Britain.

Quête *See* mummers' play.

Quick, John (1748–1831) British actor, who worked in the provinces before being engaged by Foote at the Haymarket. He then transferred to Covent Garden, where he remained for the rest of his career playing clowns, rustics, and comic servants, notably in plays by Shakespeare and Sheridan. He was much admired by George III.

quick-change room A dressing-room or convenient recess situated close to the stage, where actors may make rapid adjustments to their costume and make-up when so required.

Quilley, Denis (1927–) British actor, who began his career at the Birmingham Repertory Theatre and came to London to replace Richard Burton in Fry's *The Lady's Not for Burning* (1949). Subsequently he worked with the Old Vic and Young Vic companies; in 1955 he had his first leading West End role, in the musical *Wild Thyme*. He has subsequently combined musical and straight theatre, appearing with distinction in O'Neill's *Long Day's Journey into Night* for the National Theatre (1971), Peter Nichols's *Privates on Parade* (1977), Ira Levin's *Deathtrap* (1978), Sondheim's *Sweeney Todd* (1980, 1993), the musical *La Cage aux Folles* (1986), *The Merry Wives of Windsor* (1995), and *Waiting for Godot* (1997).

Quin, James (1693–1766) British actor, who first appeared on stage in Dublin in 1712 and made a success deputizing as Bajazet in Rowe's *Tamerlane* at Drury Lane in 1714. He then joined John Rich at Lincoln's Inn Fields, playing leading Shakespearean roles, including Falstaff, for which he was particularly renowned. Subsequently he went on to Covent Garden and thence to Drury Lane, where he was often at loggerheads with Macklin. He was nicknamed 'Bellower' Quin because of his bombastic declamatory style.

Quinault, Abraham-Alexis *See* Dufresne.

Quinault, Philippe (1635–88) French playwright, born in Paris. The son of a baker, he began writing for the theatre while in the service of Tristan L'Hermite. Quinault's sentimental comedies were his most successful works – *Le Comédie sans comédie* (1655) and *La Mère coquette* (1665) are notable examples. He also wrote tragedies, the most famous being *Astrate roi de Tyr* (1664), which was criticized by Boileau, libretti for Lully's operas, and lyrics in collaboration with Pierre Corneille and Molière.

Quiñones de Benavente, Luis (c. 1593–1651) Spanish playwright, a contemporary of Lope de Vega. His comedies, several of which revolved around the character of Juan (based on a character from Cervantes), influenced the development of the *loa* and the *entremé*.

Quintero, José Benjamin (1924–99) US director, born in Panama, who cofounded the CIRCLE-IN-THE-SQUARE, where his successes included O'Neill's *The Iceman Cometh* (1956), Behan's *The Hostage* (1958), and *Our Town* (1959). A specialist in the plays of O'Neill, and a major contributor to the rediscovery of his works, he directed the US premiere of *Long Day's Journey Into Night* at the Helen Hayes Theatre in 1956 and the premiere of *A Moon for the Misbegotten* in Spoleto, Italy, in 1958. Other O'Neill productions included *Desire Under the Elms* (1963), *Marco Millions* (1964), and *Anna Christie* (1977).

Quintero, Serafín Álvarez *See* Álvarez Quintero, Serafín.

Rabe, David (1940–) US playwright, whose first play to be produced in New York was *The Basic Training of Pavlo Hummel*, which was presented at the New York Shakespeare Festival in 1971. This play, together with *Sticks and Bones* (1971) and *Streamers* (1976), formed a trilogy on issues relating to the Vietnam War and earned several awards. His other works include *In the Boom Boom Room* (1973) and *Hurlyburly* (1984), as well as several screenplays and novels.

Rabémananjara, Jacques (1913–) Malagasy playwright, poet, and politician. A leading figure in the movement for Malagasy independence in the 1940s and 1950s, he also established a reputation as a dramatist with a series of eloquent – though rarely acted – plays on political and historical themes. Written in French, his most admired works include *Agapes des Dieux* (Feasts of the Gods), published in 1962, and *Les Dieux Malgaches* (The Gods of Madagascar), published in 1964.

Racan, Honorat de Bueil, Seigneur de (1589–1670) French poet and playwright, whose play *Les Bergeries* (1620) is considered to be one of the finest pastoral comedies in the French theatre. A disciple of François de Malherbe, Racan served at the court of Henri IV and in the army before retiring to his château in Touraine.

Rachel (Élisa Félix; 1820–58) French actress, of poor Jewish parentage, who rose to become one of the most celebrated of all tragic actresses. She sang in the streets of Lyons and Paris as a child and, after training at the Théâtre Molière and the Conservatoire, appeared for the first time at the Comédie-Française in 1838. Despite her slight figure, she gave performances of great energy and went on to triumph in the title roles of Racine's *Phèdre* (1843) and Scribe and Legouvé's *Adrienne Lecouvreur* (1848), as well as in classical plays by Corneille and others. She came to dominate the Comédie-Française and toured widely, becoming notorious for her many love affairs; her early death was caused by consumption brought on by physical exhaustion.

Racine, Jean (1639–99) French playwright, who made an unequalled contribution to the development of French classical tragedy. Orphaned at an early age, he was educated by the Jansenists at Port-Royal, where he developed an interest in Greek and Latin literature and a talent for writing poetry. After studying at the University of Paris and a brief taste of ecclesiastical life in Languedoc, he eventually opted for a career in the theatre, contrary to the wishes of his relatives.

His first two plays were produced by Molière at the Palais-Royal, but Racine's decision to move *Alexandre le Grand* to the Hôtel de Bourgogne and his enticement of his mistress Mlle du Parc from Molière's company turned the friendship to hostility. *Andromaque* was the first of a series of great poetic tragedies, differing from those of his rival Pierre Corneille in that Racine's heroes and heroines are motivated by passion rather than duty: Corneille is said to have portrayed men as they should be, Racine to have shown them as they are. This period of Racine's career also saw the production of his only comedy, *Les Plaideurs*, which was inspired by Aristophanes's *Wasps*.

The success of PHÈDRE, the last of Racine's tragedies to be publicly performed in his lifetime, was marred by the popularity of an inferior play by PRADON, written deliberately in competition with Racine's masterpiece; he subsequently retired from the theatre, devoting himself to family life and to his new position as historiographer-royal. This break with the world of drama enabled him to renew his connections with the Jansenists of Port-Royal. His last two plays, commissioned by Madame de Maintenon for the young ladies of her school at Saint-Cyr, were not staged in public until after his death: ATHALIE in 1716 and *Esther* in 1721. Racine's masterly characterizations and poetic powers have ensured constant revivals of his plays throughout modern times.

Principal works:
La Thébaïde ou les Frères ennemies: 1664.
Alexandre le Grand: 1665.
Andromaque: 1667; translated as *Andromache*.
Les Plaideurs: 1668; translated as *The Litigants*.
Britannicus: 1669.
Bérénice: 1670.
BAJAZET: 1672.
Mithridate: 1673.
Iphigénie: 1674.
Phèdre: 1677; translated as *Phaedra*.
Esther: 1689.
Athalie: 1691; translated as *Athaliah*.

Racing Demon A play by David HARE. First production: Royal National Theatre, 1990. The play explores the state of the contemporary Church of England through the plight of the Rev. Lionel Espy, an old-fashioned liberal faced with his own dwindling faith and the challenge of a young fundamentalist rival. With *Murmuring Judges* (1991), about the judiciary, and *The Absence of War* (1993), about the Labour Party, it forms a trilogy about British institutions in the 1990s.

RADA *See* Royal Academy of Dramatic Art.

Radio City Music Hall An auditorium within the Rockefeller Center in New York that seats 5888, making it the largest theatre in the world when it opened in 1932. It was built as a variety theatre but soon began to present newly released films together with live stage shows featuring the famous Rockettes dancers. By the 1970s this formula was failing, owing partly to the shortage of films suitable to accompany live family entertainment. Today the landmark Art Deco auditorium has been renovated; the theatre is now a major concert house offering a spectacular stage show at Christmas.

Radius A British Christian organization, founded in 1929 to coordinate religious drama in Britain. Originally known as the Religious Drama Society of Great Britain, it promotes the use of drama by all denominations and encourages new writing on religious themes. An associated organization, **Sesame**, organizes drama involving the mentally and physically handicapped.

Radlov, Sergei Ernestovich (1892–1958) Russian actor and director, who emerged as a leading interpreter of the plays of Shakespeare. Having worked under Meyerhold, he later developed Expressionist staging techniques and experimented with opera. His best-known success was the Moscow State Jewish Theatre production of *King Lear*; other notable productions included plays by Ibsen and Ostrovsky.

Raimund, Ferdinand (Jakob Raimann; 1790–1836) Austrian playwright and actor, who was the author of several popular Viennese comedies in which he usually appeared himself. Highly acclaimed as a comic actor, he enjoyed enormous success with such farces as *Der Barometermacher auf der Zauberinsel* (1823) and *Der Alpenkönig und der Menschenfeind* (1828). However, he allowed a note of bitterness to enter his writing (a result of his dissatisfaction with both his audience and his own private life) and later attempted less successfully to imitate Shakespeare and Calderón. *Der Verschwender* (The Prodigal; 1834) restored his reputation but the rivalry of Nestroy eventually led to his suicide.

rain machine A mechanical device, by means of which the sound effect of falling rain, waves, or hail may be produced live. It usually consists of a large cylinder containing dried peas, beans, or marbles, which is revolved by hand.

Raisin, Jean-Baptiste (1655–93) French actor, who appeared as a child alongside his sister **Cathérine Raisin** (1649–1701) and brother **Jacques Raisin** (1653–1703). He excelled in comedy and later appeared with success at the Hôtel de Bourgogne, together with his wife **Françoise Pitel de Longchamp** (1661–1721); in 1680 they both joined the Comédie-Française.

Raisin in the Sun, A A play by Lorraine HANSBERRY. First performance: New York, 1958. A drama about a Black Chicago family's struggles, it revolves around Walter Lee, a chauffeur, and his wife Ruth, who plan to move into an all-White area. The first production was a theatrical landmark, the play being the first by a Black woman author on Broadway and one of the first to offer a non-exotic view of Blacks to a mainly White audience. It was made into a film in 1961 with several original cast members, including Sidney Poitier, Ruby Dee, and Claudia McNeil.

rake The slope of the auditorium or stage floor downwards towards the footlights. Stages in older theatres were frequently raked for reasons of perspective, but most modern theatres have level stages with raked seating for the audience.

Ralph Roister Doister A doggerel verse comedy in five acts, written by Nicholas UDALL c. 1534. First performance: Eton College, c. 1534. The first true English comedy, it was modelled on the plays of Plautus and Terence and follows the central character's unsuccessful courtship of Dame Christian Custance.

Rame, Franca (1929–) Italian actress, playwright, and manager, known chiefly for collaborations with her former husband Dario FO. As the child of travelling players, she absorbed techniques of improvisation and physical comedy that inform most of her work. After marrying Fo in 1954 she helped him to establish the left-wing company La Comune (1970). Her best-known solo works are the feminist monologues collected as *Tutto casa, letto e chiesa* (All Home, Bed, and Church; 1978) and the autobiographical *Rape* (1983). She wrote the marital comedy *The Open Couple* (1987) with Fo shortly before their separation.

Ramsay, Allan (1686–1758) Scottish poet, originally an Edinburgh wigmaker, whose pastoral *The Gentle Shepherd* won acclaim when adapted as a ballad opera with Scottish tunes. In 1730 it was successfully produced at Drury Lane as *Patie and Peggy; or, the Fair Foundling*. Ramsay attempted to open a theatre in Edinburgh in 1736 but was thwarted by the licensing laws.

Ranch, Hieronymus Justesen (16th century) Danish playwright, author of an early example of Danish school drama. *Karrig Niding* (The Miser) is one of the few surviving plays of the period based on Danish sources.

Randall, Harry (1860–1932) British comic actor, who succeeded Dan Leno as dame in the annual Drury Lane pantomime in 1903. Previously he was associated for 10 years with the Grand Theatre, Islington, where he first played Mother Hubbard in 1893.

Randall, Tony (1920–) US actor, who made his New York debut in Piscator's production of *The Caucasian Chalk Circle* in 1941. After service in World War II, he appeared on Broadway in small parts, gaining attention in *Inherit the Wind* (1955). He then had a long career in film and television, notably in the series version of SIMON'S THE ODD COUPLE. In 1989 he took over the lead in *M Butterfly*. He founded (1991) the National Actors' Theatre to bring the concept of classical repertory to Broadway, and has acted in several of its productions.

Rankin, Arthur McKee (1841–1914) Canadian actor-manager, a leading performer of melodrama and native Canadian plays. He began his career as an amateur and later made his reputation in Philadelphia, subsequently touring in melodrama with his wife, the actress **Kitty Blanchard** (1847–1911). His greatest successes included Joaquín Miller's *The Danites* (1877) and *The Canuck* (1890), his own adaptation of a French-Canadian novel. He was also seen in plays in London and elsewhere with the actress **Nance O'Neil** (Gertrude Lamson; 1874–1965), whose most acclaimed roles included Juliet and Marguerite Gautier in *Camille* by Dumas *fils*. He was the grandfather of Lionel BARRYMORE.

Rapier Players *See* Little Theatre.

Rastell, John (d. 1536). English playwright, brother-in-law of Sir Thomas More and father-in-law of John Heywood. He was probably the author of *Calisto and Meliboea*, adapted from LA CELESTINA by de Rojas, and *The Dialogue of Gentleness and Nobility*; both were performed in about 1527. He may also have written the interlude *The Play of the Four Elements* (c. 1517).

Rattigan, Sir Terence (1911–77) British playwright, whose well-constructed plays demonstrate the author's command of stagecraft. FRENCH WITHOUT TEARS established his reputation as a writer of excellent middle-class comedies. Of the plays that followed, the most successful included the war drama FLARE PATH, but it was not until THE WINSLOW BOY in 1946 that Rattigan was recognized as a writer of serious drama. THE BROWNING VERSION consolidated this reputation; subsequent works tackling similarly intense themes included THE DEEP BLUE SEA, about adultery and suicide, SEPARATE TABLES, and ROSS. *Cause Célèbre* depicted events surrounding a real murder trial. He was also responsible for creating the fictional character 'Aunt Edna', who represented the conventional unadventurous theatregoer of the 1950s. Rattigan's reputation was eclipsed in the era of the Angry Young Men and the political 1960s and 1970s, but recent years have seen a revival of interest in his work.

Principal works:
French Without Tears: 1936.
Flare Path: 1942.
While the Sun Shines: 1943.
The Winslow Boy: 1946.
The Browning Version: 1948.
The Deep Blue Sea: 1952.
Separate Tables: 1954.
Ross: 1960.
A Bequest to the Nation: 1970.
Cause Célèbre: 1977.

Räuber, Die   The first play by Friedrich von SCHILLER, written in 1781. First performance: Mannheim, 1782. Written when Schiller was only 22 years old, the play, a controversial attack upon tyranny, was a major development in the STURM UND DRANG movement and established the author's reputation. As *The Robbers* it was highly influential in English translations.

Raucourt, Mlle (Françoise-Marie-Antoinette-Josèphe Saucerotte; 1756–1815)   French actress, who was much admired in tragic roles at the Comédie-Française until her notorious private life obliged her to leave Paris for a time. Marie-Antoinette engineered her return but she later fell foul of Madame Vestris and was imprisoned during the Revolution.

Ravenscroft, Edward (fl. 1671–97)   English playwright, whose most successful work, the farce *The London Cuckolds* (1681), was performed annually on Lord Mayor's Day at both Drury Lane and Covent Garden for 70 years. He wrote numerous other plays, drawing on various sources, including *The Careless Lovers* (1673), which was based on Molière, *The Wrangling Lovers* (1676), *The Anatomist; or, the Sham Doctor* (1696), also based on Molière, and a version of *Titus Andronicus* (1686).

Raymond, John T (John O'Brien; 1836–87)   US actor, who became a highly successful performer of comic roles in both classic and contemporary plays. A member of Laura Keene's company from 1861, he excelled in such plays as Tom Taylor's *Our American Cousin*, Goldsmith's *She Stoops to Conquer*, and Sheridan's *The School for Scandal*. His most famous parts, however, were those of Colonel Mulberry Sellers in Mark Twain's *The Gilded Age* (1874) and Ichabod Crane in an adaptation of Washington Irving's *The Legend of Sleepy Hollow* (1879).

Raynal, Paul (1885–1971)   French playwright, who made his name in 1920 with *Le Maître de son coeur*, a psychological drama. He went on to write plays modelled on classical tragedy, including *Le Tombeau sous l'Arc de Triomphe* (1924: translated as *The Unknown Warrior*, 1928), which contrasts the lives of soldiers and civilians during

World War I and is his most famous work. Later plays include *La Francerie* (1933) and *Le Matériel humain* (1947).

Reade, Charles (1814–84) British novelist and playwright, whose first play, *Masks and Faces* (1852), was based on the relationship between Garrick and Peg Woffington and was written in collaboration with Tom Taylor. Subsequent successes included *Gold* (1853), *The Courier of Lyons* (1854), which was made famous by Irving as *The Lyons Mail*, and *Drink* (1879), in which Charles Warner collaborated with him. A number of Reade's novels were also successfully dramatized.

Realism A theatre movement of the late 19th century, in which the artificial conventions of subject matter, plot, and dialogue then prevailing were rejected in favour of a more faithful depiction of real-life situations and characters. The movement also had important implications for acting styles, scenery, and make up. Key figures in the movement, which revolutionized the contemporary theatre, included Ibsen, Shaw, and Stanislavsky; ultimately it inspired the more extreme approach of NATURALISM.

Realistic Theatre A small theatre in Moscow, founded in 1921 as part of the MOSCOW ART THEATRE. Also called the **Krasnya Presnya Theatre**, it enjoyed particular success with experimental productions under Okhlopkov from 1930, staging works by contemporary writers until it closed after failing to amalgamate with Taïrov's company at the Kamerny Theatre in 1938.

Really Useful Theatre Company *See* Lloyd Webber, Andrew, Baron.

Reaney, James Crerar (1926–) Canadian playwright, poet, and novelist. His first play *The Killdeer* (1959) was written for an Ontario college; subsequent works have ranged from the melodramatic *The Sun and the Moon* (1965) to *Colours in the Dark* (1967), which combined autobiographical and historical detail. His best-known work is the trilogy *The Donnellys* (1973–75), which follows the story of an immigrant Irish family. He has also worked extensively with children's theatre, with productions including a 1994 Stratford Festival version of *Alice Through the Looking Glass*.

Rebhun, Paul (c. 1500–46) German playwright, remembered for the biblical play *Suzanna* (1535). The play, the writing of which was much influenced by Luther, combined features of both medieval and Renaissance drama.

Recital Theatre *See* Daly's 63rd Street Theatre.

Recruiting Officer, The A comedy by George FARQUHAR. First performance: London, 1706. Drawing upon Farquhar's own experience as a recruiting officer, the play revolves around the adventures of Captain Plume and his disreputable associate Sergeant Kite, who tricks recruits into signing up for the army.

Red Army Theatre A theatre in Moscow, founded in 1919 from troupes organized to entertain the armed forces. Also known (until 1990) as the **Central Theatre of the Soviet Army**, the company established a strong reputation under Zavadsky and then Alexei Popov, who directed it from 1937 to 1961, and moved into a specially built star-shaped theatre in 1940. As well as contemporary Russian works, the company staged plays by Shakespeare and other foreign playwrights.

Red Bull Theatre A theatre in Upper Street, Clerkenwell, in London, which began as an inn where plays were presented from time to time in the courtyard. In 1605 it became a permanent theatrical venue and the home of Queen Anne's Men; it was subsequently reconstructed in 1625 but declined in reputation, probably being used for the presentation of more sensational drama. During the Commonwealth the theatre staged occasional shows without permission; actors who appeared there included Killigrew and Mohun. It was demolished during the 1660s.

Rederykers *See* Chambers of Rhetoric.

Redgrave, Sir Michael (1908–85) British actor, who began his career in repertory at the Liverpool Playhouse in 1934 and made his London debut as Ferdinand in *Love's Labour's Lost* at the Old Vic in 1936. The following year he played important parts in Gielgud's Queen's Theatre season, including Bolingbroke in *Richard II*. A subtle and intelligent actor, he reached the height of his career after World War II, playing such roles as Macbeth (1947), Crocker-Harris in Terence Rattigan's *The Browning Version* (1948), and Shylock, Antony, and Lear at Stratford-on-Avon (1953). Subsequently he was much admired as H J in his own dramatization of Henry James's *The Aspern Papers* (1959), in the title role of Chekhov's *Uncle Vanya* (1961) at Chichester and the National Theatre, and as Hobson in *Hobson's Choice* (1963) before ill health limited his appearances. Later roles included the part of the father in John Mortimer's *A Voyage Round My Father* (1972), in which he toured overseas.

He was married to the actress **Rachel Kempson** (1910–) and their elder daughter, **Vanessa Redgrave** (1937–), also became a major star of stage and films, making her first London appearance in N C Hunter's *A Touch of the Sun* in 1958. Later she was acclaimed in performances over several seasons at Stratford-on-Avon, notably as Rosalind, Katharina, and Imogen. Her other successes of the 1960s and 1970s included Nina in Chekhov's *The Seagull* (1964), the title role in Muriel Spark's *The Prime of Miss Jean Brodie* (1966), Gilda in Noël Coward's *Design for Living* (1973), and Shakespeare's Cleopatra. More recent work has included a revival of O'Neill's *A Touch of the Poet* (1988), Shaw's *Heartbreak House* (1992), and Ibsen's *John Gabriel Borkman* (1996). Vanessa Redgrave has also aroused controversy with her involvement in Marxist political activity. From 1962 to 1967 she was married to the director Tony RICHARDSON: their daughters are the actresses Natasha and Joely Richardson.

Sir Michael Redgrave's other children, **Corin Redgrave** (1939–) and **Lynn Redgrave** (1943–), are also known as performers on stage and screen. Corin Redgrave starred in several West End productions in the early 1970s but then gave up acting to become a full-time political activist. He returned to stage and screen in the 1990s. In 1999 he starred with his sister Vanessa and his wife Kikha Markham in an acclaimed revival of Coward's *Song at Twilight*. Lynn Redgrave made her professional debut as Helena in *A Midsummer Night's Dream* (1962) before joining the National Theatre Company (1963–66). In 1973 she moved to the US, where she appeared on Broadway, in touring productions, and on television. In 1990 she returned to the West End to appear in a much-publicized production of Chekhov's *Three Sisters* with her sister Vanessa and her niece Natasha Richardson. From 1996 she toured successfully with *Shakespeare for My Father*, a one-woman show based on her relationship with Sir Michael Redgrave.

Red Lion Inn A tavern in Stepney, London, where plays were staged in the late 16th century.

Red Roses for Me A play by Sean O'CASEY. First performance: Dublin, 1943. The play is largely based upon O'Casey's experiences during the 1913 General Strike in Dublin, adapted to provide a contemporary anti-fascist moral. It is usually considered the best of his later works.

Rees, Roger (1944–) British actor, who attracted attention after joining the Royal Shakespeare Company in 1967. Among his parts have been Hamlet, Charles Courtley in Boucicault's *London Assurance*, and the title role in the much-acclaimed *Nicholas Nickleby* (1980). Other successes have included Terry Johnson's *Cries from the Mammal House* (1984) and Tom Stoppard's *Hapgood* (1988). He has been an associate director of the Bristol Old Vic since 1986.

reflector A spotlight or floodlight in which the lamp and metal reflector exist as one unit.

Regency Theatre *See* Scala Theatre.

Regent Theatre A theatre in King's Cross, London, that opened as a music hall called the **Euston Palace** in 1900. Nigel Playfair took it over in 1924, renaming it the Regent Theatre and opening with Arnold Bennett's *Body and Soul*. Later that year Barry Jackson presented Rutland Boughton's musical drama *The Immortal Hour*; subsequent successes included John Gielgud and Gwen Ffrangcon-Davies in *Romeo and Juliet* (1974). Among other interesting productions were plays by Shaw, the Čapeks' *The Insect Play*, and John Drinkwater's *Robert E Lee*. The theatre was also used by the Phoenix Society for revivals of classic plays and by several other notable groups before it became a cinema in 1935.

Regnard, Jean-François (1655–1709) French playwright, whose witty comedies continued the tradition established by Molière. After an adventurous early life he settled down to write, collaborating with Dufresny on plays for the Comédie-Italienne. His best-known and most successful plays were produced by the Comédie-Française; these include *Attendez-moi sous l'orme* (1694), *La Sérénade* (1694), *Le Joueur* (1696), and *Le Légataire universel* (1708).

Rehan, Ada (Ada Crehan; 1860–1916) US actress, born in Ireland, who became a leading performer with Augustin Daly's company in both New York and London (from 1879). Previously with Mrs John Drew's troupe in Philadelphia and other companies, she excelled in comic roles in many classic plays, among the most notable being Katharina in *The Taming of the Shrew* (1887) and Lady Teazle in Sheridan's *The School for Scandal*. She retired in 1905 after her style of acting fell from fashion.

rehearsal A meeting of director, cast, and others at which every aspect of a show can be worked upon in order to bring the production to performance standard. In medieval times there were few rehearsals and emphasis was placed upon an actor's skill at improvisation; in the 19th century, however, they became widely accepted practice.

Rehearsal, The A comedy by George Villiers, Duke of BUCKINGHAM. First performance: Drury Lane, London, 1671. This burlesque of heroic drama – especially that of Dryden – effectively ended the genre and inspired numerous imitations, notably Sheridan's *The Critic*. The central character, Bayes, was intended to represent Dryden himself.

Reid, Beryl (1920–96) British actress, who established herself as a comedienne in revue, pantomime, and variety; she moved into straight theatre after being cast with great success in Frank Marcus's *The Killing of Sister George* in 1965. Subsequent roles included Madame Arcadi in Coward's *Blithe Spirit* (1970), the Nurse in *Romeo and Juliet* (1974) for the National Theatre, Lady Wishfort in Congreve's *The Way of the World* (1978) for the Royal Shakespeare Company, and Mrs Candour in Sheridan's *The School for Scandal* (1983). She also enjoyed great success in Peter Nichols's *Born in the Gardens* (1979).

Reid, Kate (1930–93) Canadian actress, born in England, who made her London debut as Lizzie in N Richard Nash's *The Rainmaker* in 1956. She has since appeared mainly in Canada and the US, often in leading Shakespearean parts. Her New York roles included Caitlin Thomas in Sidney Michael's *Dylan* (1964) and Esther Franz in Arthur Miller's *The Price* (1968), in which part she also appeared in London in 1969. She worked frequently with the American Shakespeare Company and with the Shaw Festival in Ontario, as well as gaining good notices as Big Mama in the 1974 revival of *Cat On A Hot Tin Roof* and as Linda Loman in the 1985 Broadway revival of *Death of a Salesman*.

Reigen A play by Arthur SCHNITZLER, written 1896–97. First performance: Budapest, 1912. The play, which is notable for its cynical wit, presents a 'round dance' of sexual liaisons involving a recurring set of characters in late 19th-century Vienna. It was greeted with riots on its first performance in Austria in 1921. There have been two film versions (as *La Ronde*) and several English translations and adaptations, most recently David Hare's *The Blue Room* which caused a sensation at London's Donmar Warehouse in 1998.

Reimers, Arnoldus (1844–99) Norwegian actor, husband of Johanne Juell-Reimers; he appeared for many years at the Kristiania Theater, being particularly admired in the plays of Ibsen.

His sister was the actress **Sofie Reimers** (1853–1932), who was especially popular in the comedies of Holberg and Wessel. She first appeared at the National Scene in Bergen, transferring later to the Kristiania Theater and then the Nationaltheatret in 1899.

Reinhardt, Max (Max Goldmann; 1873–1943) Austrian director, actor, and manager, who became the first leading international director, dominating the Berlin stage and profoundly influencing the theatre in Britain, the US, and many other countries. He began as an actor (1890–1900), specializing in playing older men and establishing himself as a leading performer under Otto Brahm at the Deutsches Theater in Berlin. He then ventured into direction, scoring his first major success in 1903 with Gorky's *The Lower Depths* and subsequently also directing at the Neues Theater am Schiffbauerdamm, where his productions in a variety of styles included works by Hofmannsthal, Lessing, Shakespeare, and Schiller.

His production in 1910 of *Oedipus Rex* by Sophocles inspired a revival of interest in Greek classical drama and was toured through 10 European capitals, while his series of Shakespearean productions (1913–14) also had a major impact. At the same time he demonstrated his versatility with successful versions of contemporary plays by Ibsen, Strindberg, and Wedekind among others and encouraged the performance of new drama at the Berlin Voksbühne (1915–20).

Although he was equally adept at using such restricted acting spaces as that at the Kammerspiele, he is usually remembered for his spectacular productions at such huge venues as London's Olympia and the Grosses Schauspielhaus, as well as for those at the Deutsches Theater (which he bought in 1906 and where he installed his own acting school), controlling massive casts with supreme skill. He also worked at a number of important festivals, founding the Salzburg Festival in 1920 and directing there regularly until 1934.

The Nazis deprived him of the ownership of his theatres in 1933 and from 1938 Reinhardt worked in the US, where his productions included a film of his famous version of *A Midsummer Night's Dream* (first given in 1905 and later reinterpreted by him many times).

Réjane (Gabrielle-Charlotte Réju; 1857–1920) French actress, who became one of the most popular performers of comedy in Paris during the 1890s and 1900s. She began her career in 1875 at the Théâtre du Vaudeville and specialized in comic roles in fairly inconsequential plays; her few performances in dramas of major significance included the title role in Sardou's *Madame Sans-Gêne* (1895).

Relapse, The A comedy by Sir John VANBRUGH. First performance: Drury Lane, 1697. Colley Cibber's *Love's Last Shift* (1696) partly suggested the plot although Vanbrugh rejected Cibber's sentimentality in his frank exploration of marriage. The most memorable character in the play, Lord Foppington, was based on Cibber's fop Sir Novelty Fashion.

Renaissance, Théâtre de la A theatre in Paris, opened on the site of the Théâtre de la PORTE-SAINT-MARTIN in 1873. After staging dramas by Zola and others it diversified with the farces of Feydeau and Labiche until Sarah Bernhardt took it over in the 1890s. Notable successes under her included plays by Rostand and Musset as well as earlier works by Racine and Dumas *fils*; subsequently Gémier and Lucien Guitry ensured the theatre's continued prosperity for some years before a long period of decline set in. After 1956 the theatre was restored and used for staging a new contemporary programme.

An earlier theatre of the same name opened in Paris in 1826 and was used for plays by Hugo and Dumas *père*, scoring its greatest success with Frédérick in Hugo's *Ruy Blas* (1838); it closed in 1841.

Renaissance drama European drama of the period roughly between the 15th and 17th centuries, when the rediscovery of classical drama combined with a revival of intellectual aspirations effectively laid the foundations of the modern theatre. Although the theatre was initially considered too vulgar for the attention of the serious scholar, the rediscovery of such classical playwrights as Plautus, Euripides, and Seneca (as well as such theorists as Aristotle) inspired imitators in Italy and later throughout Europe. The first important Renaissance tragedy based on classical lines was Trissino's *Sophonisba*, written in 1515 and performed in 1562. Cinthio, Rucellai, Aretino, Speroni, Groto, and Tasso were among other early writers of tragedy in Italy, while those in other countries included Étienne Jodelle in France, Cristóbel de

Virués, Juan de la Cueva, and Cervantes in Spain, and Marlowe, Kyd, and Shakespeare in England (*see* Elizabethan drama).

The development of a revived comic tradition during this era was more complicated, with elements from the classical theatre being combined with features of the mystery play, morality play, and liturgical drama of the Middle Ages. Ariosto was a key figure in the early emergence of the COMMEDIA ERUDITA, which, together with the early COMMEDIA DELL'ARTE, established the popularity of two very different types of comedy. Elsewhere Grévin and Larivey were among those who revolutionized comedy in France, while in Spain Torres Naharro distinguished between two national comic styles, the *comedia a noticia* (later popularized by Lope de Vega) and the *comedia a fantasía*; in England Shakespeare and Jonson were unmatched.

The influence of Renaissance thought also extended to theatre design, with the period witnessing the building of the first permanent playhouses, much influenced by the theories of Vitruvius. Classical staging techniques, including the use of *periaktoi*, were also revived and led to the introduction of new scenic devices (as well as the study of perspective) in theatres designed by Sangallo, Serlio, Palladio, Scamozzi, and Aleotti among others. France saw the establishment of its first permanent theatre, the Théâtre de l'Hôtel de Bourgogne, in 1548, although stages in Britain and Spain remained generally uncovered until well into the 17th century and owed much of their design to their origins in inn-yard performances. The period also witnessed early experiments with stage lighting. *See also* interlude; masque; pastoral; *sacra rappresentazione*.

Renaissance Theatre Company *See* Branagh, Kenneth.

Renaud, Madeleine-Lucie (1903–94) French actress, who became a leading performer of French classical comedy, notably under the direction of her husband, Jean-Louis BARRAULT. She began her career at the Comédie-Française, being particularly admired in the plays of Molière, Marivaux, and Musset, before marrying Barrault in 1940. Subsequently (1946) they founded their own Compagnie Renaud-Barrault, with which Renaud appeared throughout France and abroad in plays by Anouilh, Beckett, Chekhov, Claudel, Kafka, and many others.

Rent A rock musical by Jonathan Larson, who died the night before its first preview in New York in 1996. The plot is an updating of Puccini's *La Bohème* set in New York's East Village. The play, which won the Pulitzer Prize, is an unusual example of rock music used for traditional Broadway musical purposes.

repertory A group of plays or other productions that are prepared by a company for presentation on different nights of the week or on a weekly basis. Formerly standard practice, it is now more common in both Britain and the US for companies to present RUNS of a single play, thus maximising the commercial return from a hit and avoiding the dangers of exhaustion and under-rehearsal. *See also* Repertory Theatre Movement.

Repertory Theatre Movement The development, during the 20th century, of a theatrical tradition whereby various British theatres offered a series of their own productions in quick succession, independent of touring companies. High standards of production, the promotion of new plays by British writers, and a responsiveness to the multiplicity of interests in the community around it are all now considered part of such a theatre's responsibility. Beginning at the end of the 19th century as a reaction to the dominance of the actor-manager and the long run, the movement flourished particularly in the provinces. In 1907 Annie Horniman established the first English repertory theatre company in Manchester; by 1914 similar companies had been established at Glasgow, Liverpool, Birmingham, and Bristol, some financed by wealthy entrepreneurs and others by shareholders. Such theatres generally presented new productions each week and provided an excellent training ground for young actors.

The opening of the Belgrade Theatre in Coventry (1958) signalled a revival of interest in the system but the number of regional repertory theatres operating in Britain has since fallen to about 50.

Representative, The (*Der Stellvertreter*) A documentary drama by Rolf HOCHHUTH. First performance: Berlin, 1963. Seen in the US as *The Deputy*, this embittered criticism of papal inaction during the massacre of the Jewish population in Nazi-occupied Europe inspired a revival of German drama in the 1960s. It also effectively founded the DOCUMENTARY DRAMA movement, despite its inordinate length and wealth of detail.

Republic Theatre A theatre on 42nd Street, between Seventh and Eighth avenues, New York, which opened in 1900 with James A Herne's *Sag Harbor*. In 1902 it was taken over by David Belasco and renamed the Belasco Theatre. It reverted, however, to its original name in 1910; from 1931 it was a burlesque house until, in 1942, it became a cinema.

République, Théâtre de la *See* Comédie-Française.

Resistible Rise of Arturo Ui, The (*Der aufhaltsame Aufstieg des Arturo Ui*) A play by Bertolt BRECHT. First performance: Berlin, 1957. Brecht wrote this parable about the violent career of a gangster in prewar Chicago soon after arriving in the US in 1941, but it was not staged until after his death. The rise of the ruthless title character parallels that of Hitler and the Nazis.

Restoration drama English drama from the coronation of Charles II in 1660 to around the end of the 17th century. The period saw the revival of the English theatrical tradition following its interruption by the INTERREGNUM. The theatre became the province of the Court and the upper classes and was reorganized under the PATENT THEATRES system.

Initially plays dating to the period before the closure of the theatres in 1642 provided the basic fare, but the development of the COMEDY OF MANNERS from the mid-1660s represented the beginning of a new and genuinely original phase in English drama. Aphra Behn, George Etherege, Thomas Shadwell, William Wycherley, Congreve, and Vanbrugh were among the leading playwrights for the Restoration stage. Although it is for comedy that the period is now usually celebrated, other features of the period included the now largely forgotten HEROIC DRAMA of Dryden and others. The only significant Restoration writer of tragedy was Thomas Otway, whose *Venice Preserv'd*, harked back to Jacobean models.

Popular performers of the day included Nell Gwynn, Mrs Barry, and Anne Bracegirdle – who were among the first females to be allowed upon the English stage – and Thomas Betterton.

return A flat or cloth used to mask off any backstage area not screened by a tormentor or other parts of the set.

Reumert, Poul (1883–1968) Danish actor, who became the most celebrated actor in Denmark of his day. Closely associated with the Kongelige Teater from 1911, he was particularly admired in the plays of Molière as well as in contemporary Scandinavian drama.

Reuter, Christian (1665–c. 1712) German playwright, noted for his attacks on bourgeois values. His early comedies include *L'Honnête Femme, oder Die ehrliche Frau zu Plissine* (1695) and *La maladie et la mort de l'honnête femme, das ist: Der ehrlichen Frau Schlampampe Krankheit und Tod* (1696), which satirized his landlady and resulted in his imprisonment. Later works include a further attack on his landlady and a satire upon the aristocracy.

Revels Office *See* Master of the Revels.

Revenger's Tragedy, The A tragedy in blank verse first published in 1607, possibly by Cyril TOURNEUR although Thomas MIDDLETON is favoured as the author by some scholars. First performance: London, c. 1607. Vindice uses the skull of his beloved to poison the Duke who has murdered her, but then becomes involved in a wider conspiracy culminating in scenes of violent mayhem.

revenge tragedy A genre of English tragedy popular during Elizabethan and Jacobean times. The essentials of the revenge tragedy were derived from classical models by Seneca and include ghosts, murder, madness, and intrigue as embellishments of a central theme of revenge, often of the bloodiest kind. Shakespeare's *Hamlet* is much the most sophisticated example of the genre but remains typical in its concluding carnage; other notable plays include Shakespeare's *Titus Andronicus*, Kyd's *The Spanish Tragedy* (c. 1585–89), Tourneur's *The Revenger's Tragedy* (1607), and Webster's *The Duchess of Malfi* (1614).

reverberator An early lighting unit, used to light the apron in the Restoration theatre. It was a forerunner of the modern floodlight.

Revolution, Theatre of the *See* Mayakovsky Theatre.

revolving stage A stage equipped with a turntable, allowing a large part of the acting area to revolve, thus revealing one or more new sets in succession. The first complete revolving stage was constructed at Osaka in Japan in 1758; the first British example was installed at the London Coliseum in 1904.

revue A musical entertainment in which a team of performers presents a programme of unrelated songs, dances, and sketches in quick succession. Revues are usually enlivened with an element of satire or topicality and are distantly descended from the satirical tradition of French street performers in the Middle Ages.

Such shows were first presented at the Théâtre de la Porte-Saint-Martin in Paris in the late 19th century and later became highly popular at the Folies-Bergère and elsewhere. The first English revue was Seymour Hicks's *Under the Clock* (1893), while the first on Broadway was *The Passing Show* (1894). An emphasis upon large-scale spectacle was a feature of many subsequent revues, notably Ziegfeld's *Follies*, which became the longest-running annual revue (1907–57) and achieved wide fame for its fabulously costumed chorus girls and celebrity acts.

In Britain C B Cochran and André Charlot had similar success in the 1920s with somewhat smaller-scale shows (known as 'intimate' revues) featuring such talents as Noël Coward, Gertrude Lawrence, and Jack Buchanan; many of these later transferred to the US where they won equal acclaim. Subsequent intimate revues, which created such stars as Jack Hulbert and Cicely Courtneidge, included *Sweet and Low* (1943) at the Ambassadors Theatre and a series of productions at the Gate Theatre. Back in the US George White also concentrated on a more intimate version of Ziegfeld's *Follies*, presenting his own successful annual *Scandals* revue, which concentrated more on comedy than upon spectacle; stars of such productions included Ed Wynn, Eddie Cantor, and W C Fields.

In the 1950s a surreal element was introduced by the choreographer John Cranko in *Cranks* (1955) and by such revues as *Pieces of Eight* (1959), which included contributions by Harold Pinter and N F Simpson; new stars of the genre that emerged included Joyce Grenfell, Kenneth Williams, and Flanders and Swann. However, the success of the highly satirical *Beyond the Fringe* (1961) by the Cambridge Footlights Club, led to a boom in satire and the genre's virtual desertion of the stage for television, where greater topicality was possible. The same era also saw the end of the conventional spectacular revue (which had become hugely expensive to present) and of a third variety of revue, the *Revuedeville* of the Windmill Theatre and elsewhere, the distinguishing feature of which was the frequent appearance of nudes. *Compare* music hall; Pierrot troupes; vaudeville.

Rey de Artieda, Andrés (1549–1613) Spanish playwright, remembered for the tragedy *Los amantes* (The Lovers; 1581). Based upon tales from Boccaccio, this was one of the earliest treatments in Spain of the theme of tragic love.

Reynolds, Frederick (1764–1841) British playwright, whose first play, *Werter* (based on Goethe's novel), was presented at Covent Garden in 1786. Subsequently he wrote a number of comedies, notably *The Dramatist* (1789) and *How to Grow Rich* (1793). His dog drama *The Caravan; or, the Driver and his Dog* (1803) was immensely popular when staged at Drury Lane, chiefly for its scene featuring a dog saving a child from drowning.

Reynolds, Robert (fl. 1610–40) English actor, who became immensely popular in Germany as the clown **Pickelhering**, many of whose characteristics were later assimilated into the stock German comic figure of HANSWURST. He appeared as one of the English Comedians with Robert Browne and John Green, succeeding the latter in 1627 as leader of the troupe.

Reza, Yasmina (1960–) French playwright, director, and actress. Of part-Iranian descent, she worked as an actress from the late 1970s before making her name with the play *Conversations après un enterrement* (1987; translated as *Conversations After a Burial*), a dry comedy about family relationships that won numerous awards. Her international breakthrough came with the intellectual comedy ART (1994), which has enjoyed huge success in London, New York, and elsewhere. Subsequent work has included *L'Homme du hasard* (1997; translated as *An Unexpected Man*) and *Trois Versions de la vie* (2000; translated as *Life × 3*).

Rhinoceros (*Rhinocéros*) A play by Eugène IONESCO. First performance: Paris, 1960. The central character (played by Olivier in the first London production) watches with increasing concern as all his friends turn into rhinoceroses; he wonders whether to do the same or to make a stand in defence of mankind. The play is an absurdist satire on conformity.

rhinthonica A form of Roman *fabula*, comprising burlesques of earlier Greek tragedies. Named after the Greek playwright **Rhinthon of Tarentum** (4th century BC), who also wrote plays in the PHLYAX tradition, the form was especially popular among Greeks in southern Italy and scenes from it appear on numerous vases of the period.

Rhodes, John (b. 1606) English theatre manager and bookseller, who was appointed Keeper of the Cockpit in 1644 and reopened it with a small company that included Betterton and Kynaston in 1660. However, his licence was withdrawn when the patent theatres opened.

Riccoboni, Luigi (1676–1753) Italian actor-manager and writer on the theatre, who ran his own *commedia dell'arte* company for many years. Popularly known as **Lélio**, he revived the Comédie-Italienne in Paris, using written scripts, as well as twice visiting London. His books on the theatre include his *Histoire du théâtre italien*.

Rice, Elmer (Elmer Reizenstein; 1892–1967) US playwright, whose first play, *On Trial* (1914), introduced the innovation of the flashback. Of his other works the most influential was THE ADDING MACHINE (1923); others included STREET SCENE (1929), *Counsellor-at-Law* (1931), *We, The People* (1933), *Judgement Day* (1934), *Between Two Worlds* (1934), *American Landscape* (1938), *Flight to the West* (1940), *A New Life* (1942), the fantasy *Dream Girl* (1945), and *Cue for Passion* (1958). In 1936 he helped found the Playwright's Producing Company.

Rice, John (b. 1596) English actor, who, as a boy, played female roles and appeared in 1610 in a water-pageant with Richard Burbage. He later joined the King's Men and appeared in Shakespeare's plays. He is also known to have acted in *The Duchess of Malfi* but eventually probably retired to take Holy Orders.

Rice, Thomas Dartmouth (1808–60) US vaudeville performer, who was popularly known as **Jim Crow**, after the character he created in his most famous act. His adoption of blackface make-up in the 1820s inspired the development of the minstrel show, while the success of the Jim Crow character led to appearances throughout the US and in London (1836).

Rice, Sir Tim (1944–) British lyricist, who established his reputation with three successful musicals written in collaboration with Andrew LLOYD WEBBER: *Joseph and the Amazing Technicolor Dreamcoat* (1968), JESUS CHRIST SUPERSTAR (1970), and EVITA (1976). Subsequent work includes *Blondel* (1983, music by Stephen Oliver), CHESS (1984, music by Benny Andersson and Bjorn Ulvaeus), *Heathcliff* (1995, music by John Farrar), and *Aida* (1998, music by Elton John). He also supplied lyrics for the Disney film musicals *Beauty and the Beast* (music by Alan Menken) and *The Lion King* (music by Elton John), both of which were later staged (1994, 1997).

Rich, Christopher (d. 1714) British theatre manager, who acquired control of Drury Lane in 1693. He cut salaries and reduced his expenses at every opportunity, causing Betterton and most of his company to withdraw. When the Lord Chamberlain forced Rich to close the theatre, he removed to Lincoln's Inn Fields, but died before he was able to reopen the theatre there.

His son, **John Rich** (1681–1761), was an actor and succeeded his father at Lincoln's Inn Fields. He was a successful Harlequin, appearing as **Lun**, and contributed greatly to the establishment of the English pantomime. As a manager his outstanding success was *The Beggar's Opera*, which provided him with the funds to build the first theatre at COVENT GARDEN.

Richard II, The Tragedy of King A history play by William SHAKESPEARE, written c. 1595. First performance: c. 1595. The play details the downfall of the ineffectual Richard II at the hands of the pragmatic Bolingbroke; the deposition scene was omitted in early performances for fear of offending Elizabeth I. The play is especially notable for its excellent characterization and for Richard's soliloquies in prison, in which he realizes his faults and thus meets his death with a new dignity.

Richard III, The Tragedy of King A history play by William SHAKESPEARE, written 1592–93. First performance: c. 1593. Drawing on Holinshed, Hall, and Sir Thomas More, the plot traces the process by which the deformed but defiant Richard seizes the throne and is then himself killed in battle by Richmond, later Henry VII. One of the most celebrated roles in the theatre, Richard III – who is depicted as a savage, brilliant, and highly complex character – has provided such actors as Kean, Garrick, Olivier, and Anthony Sher with one of their greatest successes.

Richard Rodgers Theatre A 1342-seat theatre on West 46th Street, New York, which opened as Chanin's 46th Street Theatre in 1925 and was renamed the 46th Street Theatre later that year. Under this name it had major successes, almost entirely with musicals, including *Good News* (1925), *Anything Goes* (1935), *Finian's Rainbow* (1947), *Guys and Dolls* (1950), *How to Succeed in Business Without Really Trying* (1962), and *Chicago* (1975). Although none of his shows has ever played there, the theatre's name was changed to honour the composer in 1990. Hits since then have included *Lost in Yonkers* (1991) and a revival of *Chicago* (1996).

Richards, Elizabeth Rebecca *See* Edwin, John.

Richardson, Ian (1934–) British actor, who was one of the founder members of the Royal Shakespeare Company in 1961. His roles with the company have included Edmund in Peter Brook's production of *King Lear* (1964), Ford in *The Merry Wives of Windsor* (1964), Coriolanus (1967), and Richard II (1973). On Broadway he appeared as Higgins in a revival of *My Fair Lady* (1976) and in a dramatic version of *Lolita* (1981); other roles have included Marat in Weiss's *Marat/Sade* (1964), Vindice in Tourneur's *The Revenger's Tragedy* (1966), Tanner in Shaw's *Man and Superman* (1979), and Harpagon in Molière's *The Miser* (1995). He is also well known for his television work.

Richardson, Sir Ralph (1902–83) British actor, who made his debut as Lorenzo in *The Merchant of Venice* in 1921, worked with the Birmingham Repertory Theatre, and came to London in Eden Phillpotts's *Yellow Sands* in 1926. After success in Barry Jackson's modern-dress productions of classic plays at the Royal Court and seasons at the Old Vic and Malvern he became a leading West End actor, establishing his reputation especially in the plays of Priestley and Shakespeare. He was joint-director of the Old Vic company during the legendary seasons (1944–47) at the New Theatre, when his stature as a great actor was confirmed with performances as Falstaff, Vanya, Peer Gynt, Cyrano, and Inspector Goole in *An Inspector Calls*. His unique ability to blend pathos with eccentric good humour ensured his continued popularity in roles as varied as Dr Sloper in *The Heiress* in 1949, Prospero (1951), Timon of Athens (1956), Jim Cherry in Bolt's *Flowering Cherry* (1957), Bottom (1964), Shylock (1967), Dr Rance in Orton's *What the Butler Saw* (1968), Jack in David Storey's *Home* (1970), Hirst in Pinter's *No Man's Land* (1975), and Cecil in William Douglas Home's *The Kingfisher* (1977). He was also a distinguished actor in films. Richardson gave his final stage performance as Alberto in Eduardo de Filippo's *Inner Voices* at the National Theatre in the year he died.

Richardson, Tony (Cecil Antonio Richardson; 1928–91) British director, who established his reputation at the Royal Court Theatre with his direction of Osborne's *Look Back in Anger* (1956) and *The Entertainer* (1958). Similarly successful were Ionesco's *The Chairs* (1957) and initial forays into Shakespeare – notably *Othello* with Paul Robeson – at Stratford-on-Avon (1958). His acclaimed staging of Osborne's *Luther* (1961) was subsequently seen on Broadway, as were productions of Brecht and Ibsen. Vanessa REDGRAVE, to whom he was then married, appeared successfully in his version of Chekhov's *The Seagull* (1964), while Nicol Williamson won great acclaim in his *Hamlet* (1969): his later work was carried out mainly in the US. Richardson also directed for the cinema.

His daughters by Vanessa Redgrave are the actresses **Natasha Richardson** (1963–) and **Joely Richardson** (1965–). Natasha made her adult debut in *The Seagull* in 1985, won several awards for playing the title role in *Anna Christie* (1990, 1992), and starred to huge acclaim in the New York revival of *Cabaret* (1998). Joely made her London debut in 1989 and has since appeared mainly in films and on television.

Richelieu, Armand-Jean du Plessis de, Cardinal (1585–1642) French statesman, who was the chief minister of Louis XIII and a patron of the arts. His private theatre, which housed Montdory's company, became one of the first professional public playhouses in France (*see* Palais-Royal, Théâtre du). He also encouraged several notable playwrights, including Corneille, Boisrobert, and Rotrou.

Richepin, Jean (1849–1926) French poet and playwright, born in Algeria. His first collection of poetry, *La chanson des gueux* (1876), brought him a month's imprisonment for its vulgar language. He wrote several successful plays, notably *Nana Sahib* (1883), written for Sarah Bernhardt, *Par le glaive* (1892), and *Le Chemineau* (1897).

Richmond Hill Theatre A theatre in Charlton Street, New York, which staged its first play in 1831. Headed by Mrs Duff, the resident company gave two successful seasons until a plague outbreak forced its closure. Productions included revivals and Sheridan Knowles's *The Hunchback*, which boldly opened on the same night as the Park Theatre's first performance of it in 1832. The theatre reopened with a season of Italian opera; subsequently it was managed by Mrs Hamblin and staged the New York debut of James E Murdoch. Between 1845 and 1848 it presented circus and variety shows, being briefly known as the **Tivoli Gardens**. It was demolished in 1849.

Richmond Theatre A theatre in Richmond, Virginia, which was built in the 1700s but burned down in 1811, claiming 72 lives. Rebuilt and opened as the **Marshall Theatre** in 1818, it staged the first US appearance of the elder Booth in 1821 and Edwin

Forrest in 1841. Joseph Jefferson III was manager between 1854 and 1856. Again destroyed by fire in 1862, it was replaced by a very grand theatre, called the New Richmond, in 1863. It became the leading theatre of the Southern states before demolition in 1896.

riciniata A form of early Roman *fabula*, comprising a mime play. It was named after the *ricinium*, the hood worn by the actors during the performance.

Rickman, Alan (1946–) British actor, who first attracted attention during the 1978 season at Stratford-on-Avon, when his roles included Angelo in *Measure for Measure*. Subsequently he appeared at the Royal Court Theatre in Chekhov's *The Seagull* and, in 1985, enjoyed success as Le Vicomte de Valmont in Christopher Hampton's *Les Liaisons Dangereuses*. The early 1990s saw Rickman's emergence as a film star. His more recent work for the stage includes *Hamlet* (1992) and a poorly received *Antony and Cleopatra* (1998, with Helen Mirren).

Rideau Vert, Théâtre du A Montreal company founded in 1949 by Mercedes Palomino and Yvette Brind'Amour, who remained its artistic director until her death in 1992. Its first production, a French translation of Hellman's *The Children's Hour*, was followed by many years of repertory. In 1968 its production of Michel Tremblay's *Les Belles-Soeurs* changed the face of Canadian theatre with its critical view of society and its use of the *joual* dialect. The company has maintained an adventurous reputation, touring both at home and abroad. Guillermo de Andrea is the current director.

Riders to the Sea A tragedy by J M SYNGE. First performance: Abbey Theatre, Dublin, 1904. The play concerns an old woman, Maurya, and her fatalistic acceptance of the implacable force of nature after losing all her menfolk at sea; it was adapted as an opera by Vaughan Williams in 1937.

Rifbjerg, Klaus (1931–) Danish poet, novelist, and playwright, who is the author of several plays tackling such themes as human identity and the nature of theatre. His works include *Hva skal vi lave?* (What Shall We Make?; 1963), *Voks* (Wax; 1968), *År* (A Year; 1970), which is set during the German occupation of Denmark, and *All Quiet on the Kitchen Front* (1984). He has also written some 20 plays for radio.

Rigg, Dame Diana (1938–) British actress, whose parts with the Royal Shakespeare Company, which she joined after working in repertory, have included Philipe Trincante in John Whiting's *The Devils* (1961), Cordelia in *King Lear* (1962), and Viola in *Twelfth Night* (1966). For the National Theatre Company she was Dottie in Tom Stoppard's *Jumpers* (1972), Lady Macbeth (1972), and Célimène in Molière's *The Misanthrope* (1973). Among her many leading roles of the 1980s were Hesione Hushabye in Shaw's *Heartbreak House* (1983) and Phyllis Stone in Sondheim's *Follies* (1987). More recently she won major awards for her performances in Euripides' *Medea* (1993) and Brecht's *Mother Courage and Her Children* (1995); she also found acclaim in Albee's *Who's Afraid of Virginia Woolf?* (1996) and Racine's *Phèdre* (1998). She is also well known for her television and film appearances.

Ring An octagonal building in Blackfriars Road, London, built in 1783 as the Surrey Chapel and later used as a boxing ring. Robert Atkins brought the Bankside Players to the venue in *Henry V* in 1936, subsequently presenting *Much Ado about Nothing* and *The Merry Wives of Windsor* in celebrated theatre-in-the-round productions in 1937. The building was demolished after the World War II.

Ring Round the Moon (*L'Invitation au château*) A *pièce brillante* by Jean ANOUILH. First performance: Théâtre de l'Atelier, Paris, 1947; Christopher Fry's English translation appeared in 1950. The central characters of the play are identical twins – one cunning and cynical, the other sincere and romantic – and their matchmaking aristocratic aunt.

rise-and-sink A former method of changing an entire set, by means of which the upper half of the scenery on the stage rises into the flies and the lower half sinks into the cellar, revealing a new set behind.

Ristori, Adelaide (1822–1906) Italian actress, who became famous as a performer of tragic roles and was regarded by some as ranking with Sarah Bernhardt. She first appeared on stage as a child and was subsequently acclaimed in the title role of Schiller's *Maria Stuart* at the age of 18. She became leading lady with the Campagnia Reale Sarda and in 1855 her performances in Paris rivalled those of Rachel – Dumas *père* was amongst those deeply impressed by her passionate delivery in such plays as Goldoni's *La Locandiera* and Alfieri's *Mirra*. She also acted in Britain and the US, sometimes performing in romantic melodrama.

Ritchard, Cyril (1898–1977) British actor, director, and comedian, born in Australia, who became a leading star in the revues of Herbert Farjeon. He also appeared with success in Coward's revue *Sigh No More* (1945) and in plays by Congreve, Vanbrugh, and Shakespeare; he spent the last 20 years of his career in the US.

Ritterdrama A theatrical genre associated with the STURM UND DRANG movement of the late 18th century in Germany. It was distinguished by its passion for all things medieval, depicting jousting, battles, and other displays of chivalry and romance. Productions of such plays, which were initially inspired by the historical dramas of Goethe and Klinger, were enacted with authentic historical settings and costume. The genre fell from favour by the end of the century.

Ritz Theatre *See* Walter Kerr Theatre.

Rivals, The A classic comedy by SHERIDAN. First performance: 1775. Captain Absolute, in love with Mrs Malaprop's niece, Lydia Languish, assumes the character of an ensign to appeal to her romantic notion of marrying a penniless young officer, rather than an heir to a baronetcy. Set in fashionable Bath, the play is now mainly remembered for Mrs Malaprop and her linguistic foibles.

Rivas, Duke of *See* Saavedra Remírez de Baquedano, Ángel.

Riverside Studios An arts centre in Hammersmith, London, where both classic and contemporary plays were performed by resident and visiting companies. Originally a foundry, then film studios and a television centre, the arts centre opened in 1976 under the direction of Peter Gill; successes included the Joint Stock Company's *The Ragged Trousered Philanthropist* (1978), Chekhov's *The Cherry Orchard* (1978), *Julius Caesar* (1980), and several seasons of works by Samuel Beckett. In the 1980s the theatre was taken over by United British Actors, a company organized by Albert Finney, Glenda Jackson, Harold Pinter, Diana Rigg, and Maggie Smith.

Rix, Brian, Baron (1924–) British actor-manager, who began his career with Wolfit's company in 1942. He then joined the White Rose Players at Harrogate and played in farce for the first time. After World War II he toured in Colin Morris's army farce *Reluctant Heroes*, bringing it to the Whitehall Theatre in 1950. It ran for four years and was the first of a series of long-running farces at that theatre and at the Garrick that established him as a leading comic actor. He retired in 1977 to work in theatre management and for MENCAP, a charity for the mentally handicapped (he became its general secretary in 1980 and chairman in 1988). In 1993 he resigned as chairman of the Arts Council's drama panel in protest at cuts to regional grants.

Robards Jr, Jason (1922–98) US actor, who made his stage debut in 1947. In 1956 he was praised in O'Neill's *The Iceman Cometh* and *Long Day's Journey Into Night*, in which he played James. His successes since then have included Manley Halliday in Budd Schulberg's *The Disenchanted* (1958), Julian Berniers in Lillian Hellman's *Toys in the Attic* (1960), Murray Burns in Herb Gardner's *A Thousand Clowns* (1962), and O'Neill's *Hughie* (1964), *A Moon for the Misbegotten* (1973), and *A Touch of the Poet* (1977).

Robbins, Jerome (1918–98) US director and choreographer, who began as a dancer in London. Successful works he choreographed included *On the Town* (1944), *Call Me Madam* (1950), *The King and I* (1951), *The Pajama Game* (1954), *Peter Pan* (1954), *West Side Story* (1957), *Gypsy* (1959), and *Fiddler on the Roof* (1964). After *Fiddler* he concentrated on ballet as one of the directors of the New York City Ballet (with George Ballanchine). *Jerome Robbins' Broadway*, an evening of selections from his Broadway shows, won the Tony Award for best musical of 1989.

Roberts, Rachel *See* Harrison, Rex.

Robert S Marx Theatre *See* Cincinnati Playhouse in the Park.

Robertson, Agnes Kelly (1833–1916) British actress, born in Scotland, where she first appeared as a child. She made her London debut at the Princess's Theatre with Charles Kean's company in 1851. After accompanying her lover Dion BOUCICAULT to the US, she became very popular as the heroine in a succession of his plays. She eventually retired in 1896. Her four children included 'Dot' and Nina Boucicault.

Robertson, T(homas) W(illiam) (1829–71) British playwright, brother of Madge KENDAL. After training with his father as an actor, he scored his first success as a playwright with *David Garrick*, which was produced at the Haymarket in 1864. SOCIETY, produced by the Bancrofts at the Prince of Wales' Theatre in 1865, introduced the type of realistic CUP-AND-SAUCER DRAMA with which his name is associated. Subsequent triumphs, which were often staged under his own direction, paved the way for the realistic settings of much 20th-century drama; CASTE is the most frequently revived of his plays.

Principal works:
David Garrick: 1864.
Society: 1865.
Ours: 1866.
Caste: 1867.
Play: 1868.

School: 1869.

Robertson, Toby *See* Prospect Theatre Company.

Robeson, Paul (1898–1976) US Black actor and singer, who made his first stage appearance in 1921. He established his reputation with the Provincetown Players in 1924 when he played Jim Harris in O'Neill's *All God's Chillun Got Wings*. He went on to triumph as Brutus Jones in O'Neill's *The Emperor Jones* (1930), while subsequent successes included *Show Boat* (1928), in which he sang 'Ole Man River', *Othello* (1930, 1943, 1959), and O'Neill's *The Hairy Ape* (1931). His career was blighted by hostility aroused by his Communist sympathies and his support for Black causes.

Robey, Sir George (George Edward Wade; 1869–1954) British music hall comedian and actor, known as the **Prime Minister of Mirth**. He made his West End debut at the Oxford Music Hall in 1891 and was subsequently acclaimed for such comic characters as The Mayor of Mudcumdyke and Daisy Dilwater and as dames in pantomimes. In 1916 he was in the first of many successful revues, *The Bing Boys Are Here*, at the Alhambra. In 1932 he extended his range, playing Menelaus in A P Herbert's *Helen* at the Adelphi, and in 1935 scored a remarkable triumph as Falstaff in *Henry IV* at His Majesty's.

Robin Hood play A tradition of rural English FOLK THEATRE, in which the adventures of the legendary outlaw and his followers were celebrated at various country festivals. The character of Robin Hood seems to have blurred with that of **Jack-in-the-Green**, a somewhat enigmatic figure in English folk festivities, who may have originated in pre-Christian ritual. Such pieces were the work of various minstrels and were presented on May Day and other key dates in the agricultural calendar together with morris dances and other simple entertainments. The genre was also a feature of court festivities in Tudor times and was eventually absorbed into pantomime.

Robins, Elizabeth (1862–1952) US actress, who became a leading interpreter of the plays of Ibsen upon the London stage, having made her first appearance there in 1889. As well as winning acclaim in such roles as Hedda Gabler (1891) and Hilda in *The Master Builder*, she promoted the British premieres of many of Ibsen's works by such troupes as Grein's Independent Theatre.

Robinson, (Esmé Stuart) Lennox (1886–1958) Irish playwright, whose first play, *The Clancy Name*, was successfully staged in 1908 at the Abbey Theatre, of which he became manager in 1910. His plays range in theme from politics to social comedy. He experimented with Symbolism and Expressionism and the influence of Pirandello is evident in the innovative form of *Church Street* (1934).

Robinson, Mary (1758–1800) British actress, who was imprisoned with her husband for debt before being engaged by Garrick at Drury Lane in 1776. In 1778 she triumphed as Perdita in *The Winter's Tale* and captivated the Prince of Wales (later George IV), eventually becoming his mistress. In 1782, however, she was crippled by rheumatic fever; thereafter she enjoyed a second career as a popular poet.

Robinson, Richard (d. 1648) English actor, who probably began as a boy actor in female roles at the Blackfriars Theatre and later joined the King's Men. He appeared in plays by Webster, Jonson, and Shakespeare, and was included in the dedicatory list prefacing the Beaumont and Fletcher Folio of 1647.

Robson, Dame Flora (1902–84) British actress, who made her debut in Clemence Dane's *Will Shakespeare* on leaving the Royal Academy of Dramatic Art in 1921. She then appeared in repertory at Oxford but failed to attract any attention until 1931, when she won great acclaim as Abbie Putnam in O'Neill's *Desire Under the Elms* and Mary Paterson in Bridie's *The Anatomist*. She consolidated her reputation in numerous classical parts – including comedy – at the Old Vic. She later appeared in films and went to New York as Ellen Creed in Reginald Denham and Edward Percy's *Ladies in Retirement* (1940). Among her other outstanding successes were Gwendolen Fairfax in *The Importance of Being Earnest* (1933), Lady Macbeth (1948), Lady Cicely Wayneflete in *Captain Brassbound's Conversion* (1948), Lesley Storm's *Black Chiffon* (1949), Miss Giddens in *The Innocents* (1952), and Miss Tina in *The Aspern Papers* (1959), the latter two being adaptations from Henry James.

Robson, Frederick (1821–64) British actor, who toured the provinces before achieving fame at the Grecian Theatre, where he sang and appeared in farces. He had three years as principal comedian at the Queen's Theatre, Dublin, but returned to London to the Olympic Theatre in 1853, becoming joint-manager there in 1857.

Rodgers, Richard (1902–79) US composer, who first with Lorenz HART and then with Oscar HAMMERSTEIN II contributed enormously to the development of the American musical. His hits with Hart included *A Connecticut Yankee* (1927), *The Boys from Syracuse* (1937), and the ground-breaking *Pal Joey* (1940). However, it was the musicals written with Hammerstein that truly revolutionized the form, by integrating the various elements of music, dialogue, character, and action, and establishing the ability of the genre to treat serious themes. Especially noted at the time was their use of dance to further plot and character development. Their partnership began with the classic OKLAHOMA! (1943) and continued with CAROUSEL, *Allegro* (1947), SOUTH PACIFIC (1949), which won a Pulitzer Prize, and THE KING AND I (1951). Their later works, which included FLOWER DRUM SONG (1958) and THE SOUND OF MUSIC (1959), were on a lower artistic level and led to a decline in their reputation; however, recent revivals have shown the genuine tension and depth of their best works. After Hammerstein's death in 1959 Rodgers collaborated with Stephen Sondheim and even tried writing his own lyrics, but these projects found little success.

Rodríguez Buded, Ricardo (1926–) Spanish playwright, the author of several influential and realistic dramas on social themes. His best-known works include *La madriguera* (The Warren; 1960) and *El Charlatán* (1962).

Rogers, Paul (1917–) British actor, who worked with the Bristol Old Vic company after World War II before appearing at the Old Vic in London, where he played many leading Shakespearean roles, including Henry VIII (1953) and King Lear (1958). He also played Sir Claude Mulhammer in *The Confidential Clerk* (1953) and Lord Claverton in *The Elder Statesman* (1958), both by T S Eliot, and Max in Pinter's *The Homecoming* (1965) for the Royal Shakespeare Company. More recent successes have included *The Importance of Being Earnest* (1982) at the National Theatre, Shaw's *The Apple Cart* (1986) at the Haymarket, and *King Lear* (1989).

Rojas, Fernando de (c. 1465–1541) Spanish writer, author of the dialogue novel LA CELESTINA (1499). His authorship of the work was uncertain for many years, partly as a result of his own efforts to hide the fact; this may have been because of similarities between the situation of the heroine Melibea and that of de Rojas himself as the offspring of unwilling Jewish converts to Christianity.

Rojas Villandrando, Agustín de (1572–c. 1635) Spanish actor and playwright, best known for the dialogue novel *El viaje entretenido* (The Pleasant Voyage; 1603) in which he depicts the Spanish theatre of the period. A member of a touring company of actors, he was also the author of several of the best examples of the Spanish *loa*.

Rojas Zorrilla, Francisco de (1607–48) Spanish playwright, a contemporary of Calderón, who developed the *comedia de figurón*, in which the action revolves around an eccentric central character. His best-known play is *Del rey abajo, ninguno* (Below the King, No One; 1650), which concerns the dilemma of a country nobleman who suspects that he has been cuckolded by the king but dares not complain.

Rolland, Romain (1866–1944) French novelist, playwright, and essayist, born in Burgundy. His works for the theatre included three tragedies, notably *Aërt* (1898), a series of plays on the French Revolution, and the treatise *Le Théâtre du peuple* (1903). Rolland is chiefly remembered, however, for the novel cycle *Jean-Christophe* (1904–12). He was awarded a Nobel Prize in 1915.

Rollenhagen, Georg (1542–1609) German churchman and playwright, who was the author of three plays dealing with biblical subjects, intended for performance in schools.

His son **Gabriel Rollenhagen** (1583–1619) was a lawyer and playwright, who adapted the tale of Euryalus and Lucretia in *Amantes amentes* (1609).

Roller, Andrei Adamovich (Andreas Leongard; 1805–91) Russian scene designer, who trained in various European countries before moving to St Petersburg in 1834. There he worked in several theatres, designing numerous influential Romantic sets with atmospheric lighting effects. Later in his career he helped to restore the Winter Palace after a fire.

roll-out A loose flap of canvas cut into a piece of scenery through which a performer can roll onto the stage, thus effecting an unexpected entrance. *See also* trickwork.

Romains, Jules (Louis-Henri-Jean Farigoule; 1885–1972) Fench poet, novelist, and playwright. His best-known plays are his three satirical farces of the mid-1920s – the two *Monsieur Le Trouhadec* comedies, which follow the adventures of a geography teacher, and the internationally successful *Knock* – in which Louis Jouvet participated as actor and producer. *Knock*, which revolves around the character of a cunning quack doctor, was successfully staged in Britain in a translation by Granville-Barker. Outside the theatre, Romains is remembered from the novel cycle *Les Hommes de bonne volonté* (1932–47; translated as *Men of Good Will*).

Principal works:

  L'Armée dans la ville: 1911.

  Cromedeyre-le-Vieil: 1920.

  Monsieur Le Trouhadec saisi par la débauche: 1923.

  Knock, ou le Triomphe de la médecine: 1923; translated as *Dr Knock*, 1925; filmed 1932.

Le Mariage de Monsieur Le Trouhadec: 1925.
Le Dictateur: 1926.
Donogoo: 1930.

Roman drama The theatrical tradition of ancient Rome, which first developed in the 3rd century BC from the older Greek theatre. Most early Roman drama consisted of translations and adaptations of Greek plays; notable exponents included PLAUTUS and TERENCE. The theatres themselves were initially temporary and based on Greek designs, but later more elaborate buildings were constructed from stone. The Greek chorus largely disappeared during Roman times and masks and costumes were extensively employed. In the later stages of the Roman era drama became more spectacular and bawdy in content and comedy was the dominant form. Eventually audiences declined and serious drama became an intellectual preoccupation for the few, of whom SENECA was one of the most significant. Christian opposition finally resulted in the closure of the theatres in the 6th century AD. *See also fabula.*

Romanoff and Juliet A comedy by Peter USTINOV. First performance: London, 1956. A parallel to Shakespeare's *Romeo and Juliet*, it concerns a love affair between the son of a Soviet diplomat and the daughter of a US diplomat; Ustinov himself appeared in the first production.

Romans in Britain, The A play by Howard BRENTON. First performance: National Theatre, London, 1980. An anti-imperialist parable based on the Roman conquest of Britain, the play aroused considerable controversy by linking the Roman occupation to the presence of British forces in Northern Ireland; a scene featuring male rape led to a widely publicized (and eventually abandoned) court case.

Romashov, Boris Sergeivich (1895–1958) Russian playwright, who was the author of several popular dramas depicting events during and after the Russian Civil War. These included *The Fiery Bridge* (1929) and *Fighters* (1934); other works were *Meringue Pie* (1925), which attacked bourgeois values, and *Shine, Stars!* (1942), which was based on the battle for Moscow in World War II.

Romeo and Juliet A tragedy by William SHAKESPEARE, written c. 1595. First performance: c. 1596. The plot, which is based on an old Italian story, traces the destruction of the young lovers Romeo and Juliet as a result of animosity between their two families, the Montagues and the Capulets. In Shakespeare's hands this becomes a means to expose a whole society, as the innocent love of the two central characters is contrasted with the pride of their parents and the worldly preoccupations of such figures as Mercutio and the Nurse. The balcony scene, in which the two lovers secretly meet, remains one of the most well-known in world theatre.

Rondiris, Dimitrios (1899–1981) Greek director, who became well known for his work with the Greek National Theatre, which he joined in the 1930s after studying with Max Reinhardt in Vienna. His modern production of Sophocles' *Electra* in 1936 heralded a long series of celebrated festivals of classic plays; other important productions included *Hamlet* (in 1939). In 1957 he founded a theatre in Piraeus.

Rookery Nook A farce by Ben TRAVERS. First performance: Aldwych Theatre, London, 1926. The second and best-known of the Aldwych farces, it consolidated the author's reputation and has been much revived; it originally ran for 409 performances.

Room, The A one-act play by Harold PINTER. First performance: Bristol, 1957. This, Pinter's first play, set the style he was to follow with increasing mastery in subsequent works; the enigmatic action takes place in a dreary bed-sitting room, which seems to be a refuge from a menacing world beyond.

Roots The second and most optimistic play in Arnold WESKER's trilogy about the Jewish Kahn family. First performance: Belgrade Theatre, Coventry, 1959, directed by John Dexter. Joan Plowright played Beatie Bryant, the girl who returns to her family in rural Norfolk determined to pass on the new ideas she has learnt from her boyfriend Ronnie Kahn (one of the characters in *Chicken Soup with Barley*). When Ronnie abandons her, she at last discovers a voice of her own.

rope-house *See* hand-worked house.

Roscius Gallus, Quintus (c. 120 BC–62 BC) Roman actor, considered the foremost comic actor of his time. He was praised by Cicero, being defended by him in a lawsuit, and was given honours by the dictator Sulla. He excelled in the plays of Plautus, Terence, and others and did much to enhance the social status of actors. His name later became identified with any acting of quality.

Rose, Billy (William Samuel Rosenberg; 1899–1966) US producer, impresario, and lyricist. After working as a songwriter in the 1920s, he turned to producing in 1930 and became well known for his brash showmanship; productions included Rodgers and Hart's *Jumbo* (1935), *Carmen Jones* (1943), and a famous 'aquacade' for the 1939–40 New York World's Fair. In the 1950s he owned two theatres, the Ziegfeld and the National, which was named after him in 1959. His will set up a foundation which has funded the important theatre collection of the New York Public Library at the Lincoln Center.

Rosencrantz and Guildenstern are Dead A play by Tom STOPPARD. First performance: Edinburgh Festival, 1966. Two minor characters from Shakespeare's *Hamlet* pass their time in talk while the tragic events of the drama take place off stage. The play is an ingenious and witty exploration of the themes of identity and fate in the tradition of Beckett and Pirandello.

Rosenplüt, Hans (c. 1400–c. 1470) German playwright and poet, popularly known as *der Schnepperer* (the chatterbox). A native of Nuremberg, he was the first important author of the *Fastnachtsspiel* tradition; his satirical writings include *Des Türken Vasnachtspil* (1456).

Rose Tattoo, The A play by Tennessee WILLIAMS. First performance: New York, 1950. The play concerns an Italian American woman who is troubled by her dead husband's infidelity until she meets a rugged truck driver. It was filmed in 1955 with Anna Magnani and Burt Lancaster.

Rose Theatre An Elizabethan theatre built by Philip Henslowe on Bankside, London in 1587. In 1592 Strange's Men, with Edward Alleyn as the leading actor, appeared there. In between closures on account of outbreaks of plague various other companies used the theatre, including the Admiral's Men, until they removed to the Fortune in 1600. The Rose, an octagonal partly-thatched building, remained open until the lease expired in 1605 and was then pulled down. In 1989 part of the foundation was discovered during building work. Following a campaign by prominent actors and directors, this was preserved; an exhibition centre opened on the site in 1999.

Rosimond (Claude la Roze; c. 1640–86) French actor and playwright. After appearances at the Théâtre du Marais he worked at the Palais-Royal and was briefly considered a possible successor to Molière. He wrote only one more play, however, after joining the company.

Ross A play by Terence RATTIGAN. First performance: London, 1960. It explores the last years of T E Lawrence, who – in a bid to escape the demands of public attention – joined the RAF at a junior rank under the name of Ross; Alec Guinness was highly acclaimed in the title role in the original production.

Ross, W G (d. 1876) British music hall performer, born in Scotland, who became an overnight success at the Cyder Cellars in the 1840s with 'Sam Hall', a grisly ballad of a condemned murderer. When, however, the novelty of 'Sam Hall' wore off, Ross fell from favour and died in obscurity.

Rosseter, Philip (c. 1575–1623) English musician and manager, under whose direction children from several disbanded companies appeared together before royalty and at the Whitefriars Theatre (1609–14). In 1615 he began the building of Porter's Hall, presenting several plays there before it was suppressed.

Rossi, Ernesto Fortunato Giovanni Maria (1827–96) Italian actor, who was highly regarded in tragic roles, especially those of Shakespeare. He appeared in Italy opposite Adelaide Ristori with success and later moved with her to Paris (1855), where he was acclaimed in such roles as Othello, Hamlet, and King Lear; he was less popular, however, with English-speaking audiences.

Rosso di San Secondo, Pier Maria (1887–1956) Italian novelist and playwright, who wrote several plays in the *grottesco* tradition. Such plays as *Marionette, che passione!* (1917), in which the actors play puppets, reflect the influence of Chiarelli and Pirandello and tackle such themes as the contrast between fantasy and reality. Others include a series based on the myth of Persephone, notably *La Scala* (The Ladder; 1926) and *Il ratto di Proserpina* (The Rape of Persephone; 1954).

Rostand, Edmond (1868–1918) French Romantic playwright and poet, who rejected the naturalist and Symbolist movements of the late 19th century. Born in Marseilles, he made his name with the comedy *Les Romanesques* (1894). This was followed by *La Princesse lointaine* (1895), *La Samaritaine* (1897), the immensely successful heroic comedy CYRANO DE BERGERAC, and the tragedy *L'Aiglon* (1900), in which Sarah Bernhardt played the central role of Napoleon's son. The allegory *Chantecler* (1910) was Rostand's last complete play, *La Dernière Nuit de Don Juan* being left unfinished at his death.

rostrum A platform of varying dimensions, used to provide different levels of staging, or a complete temporary stage. Known in the US as **parallels**, rostra are usually collapsible, thus facilitating transport and storage.

Roswitha *See* Hroswitha.

Rotimi, Ola (Emmanuel Gladstone Olawole; 1938–) Nigerian playwright, who is the author of several plays based upon African history. His first plays, *To Stir the God* *of Iron* (1963) and *Our Husband Has Gone Mad Again* (1965), were written in the US; later works include an adaptation of *Oedipus Rex* by Sophocles and *If* (1973), which was set against the background of the Nigerian Civil War.

Rotrou, Jean de (1609–50) French playwright, who was a friend and rival of Pierre Corneille. Rotrou's early plays, the first of which was produced at the Hôtel de Bourgogne in 1628, brought him to the attention of Cardinal de Richelieu. Inspired by classical and Spanish literature, he wrote prolifically during his short career, producing comedies, tragicomedies, and tragedies, notably *Le Véritable Saint-Genest* (1646), *Venceslas* (1647), and *Cosroès* (1649). He spent his latter years in his native Dreux, where he held an administrative post; he died there during a plague in 1650.

Rotunda A building that once stood in Albion Place, off Blackfriars Road, London, erected to house a collection of stuffed animals and curios in 1790. It degenerated into a penny waxwork show, but by 1829 some form of entertainment was being given there, perhaps an early form of music hall. An attempt to run it as the Globe Theatre in 1833 was a failure and it resorted to music hall and boxing, being renamed the **Britannia Music Hall**. It was closed down in about 1882 after an illegal cockfight.

Roundabout Theatre Company An important non-profit-making company in New York, founded in a converted supermarket basement in 1968. From 1995 to 1999 it was housed in the Criterion Center on Broadway between 44th and 45th Streets and, in 2000 it is set to move into the **American Airlines Theatre** (formerly the **Selwyn**) on the renovated 42nd Street. Several of its shows have transferred to commercial theatres.

Round House A circular 19th-century railway building in Chalk Farm Road, Camden Town, London, which was converted into a theatre in 1968, opening with Peter Brook's experimental in-the-round production *Themes on The Tempest*. Its foundation was largely the work of Arnold Wesker, who occupied it with his **Centre 42** arts group (founded in 1960) until it was licensed as a theatre. It became the venue for many unusual and interesting productions, varying from the nude revue *Oh, Calcutta!* (1970) to Howard Brenton's *Epsom Downs* (1977). There were also seasons by leading provincial companies, particularly the Royal Exchange Theatre, Manchester, which presented Vanessa Redgrave in Ibsen's *Lady from the Sea* (1979) and Helen Mirren in Webster's *The Duchess of Malfi* (1981). Financial pressures forced the theatre, which was reconstructed in 1979, to close in 1984. It has since reopened as a venue for live music and other events.

Rousseau, Jean-Jacques (1712–78) French philosopher and writer, born in Geneva. His contribution to the theatre is of minor importance, consisting of the opera *Le Devin du village* (1752) and the comedy *Narcisse* (1753). In his *Lettre à d'Alembert contre les spectacles* (1758), however, Rousseau attacked the proposed establishment of a theatre in Geneva, condemning the potentially dangerous influences of drama and criticizing the plays of Molière.

Rover, The A play by Aphra BEHN. First performance: 1678. The plot concerns the adventures of a band of exiled English cavaliers, notably the dissolute Willmore, a character probably based on the Earl of Rochester.

Rovetta, Gerolamo (1851–1910) Italian novelist and playwright, author of many plays in the VERISMO tradition. His plays, which are somewhat marred by a profusion of irrelevant detail, include *La trilogia di Dorina* (1889), *I dishonesti* (1892), and the historical drama *Romanticismo* (1901), which is generally considered his finest work.

Rowe, George Fawcett (1834–89) US actor, who was highly successful in leading roles in romantic dramas during the 1860s and 1870s in both New York and London. His most famous part was Digby Grant in James Albery's *Two Roses* (1872); later in life he was also admired in an adaptation of Dickens's *David Copperfield* and in his own version for the stage of James Fenimore Cooper's *The Last of the Mohicans*.

Rowe, Nicholas (1674–1718) English playwright and poet laureate, who wrote several tragedies much admired in their day. Such early works as *The Ambitious Stepmother* (1700) and *Tamerlane* (1702) were written along conventional neoclassical lines. His more emotional later works, including *The Fair Penitent* (1703), *The Tragedy of Jane Shore* (1714), and *The Tragedy of Lady Jane Grey* (1715), provided bravura roles for Sarah Siddons among others.

Rowley, Samuel (c. 1517–1624) English playwright and actor, whose dramatic works included two biblical plays and one concerning Richard III, none of which have survived. His one surviving play is *When You See Me, You Know Me* (1603-05), which was based on Henry VIII's reign.

Rowley, William (c. 1585–c. 1637) English actor and playwright, who specialized in clown parts. Although he wrote several plays himself, he is usually remembered for his collaboration with such writers as Dekker, Ford, Fletcher, Webster, and Middleton, with whom he wrote THE CHANGELING among others.

Royal Academy of Dramatic Art (RADA) The leading British stage school, founded in 1904 at His Majesty's Theatre by Beerbohm Tree. Later the same year RADA moved to Gower Street, where it still has presmises. **Sir Kenneth Barnes** (1878–1957) was its principal from 1909 to 1955 while G B Shaw was an important early supporter. The school has trained such leading actors as Sir John Gielgud, Alan Bates, Glenda Jackson, and Kenneth Branagh. Its three theatres – the Vanbrugh (founded 1954), the GBS, and Studio 14 – are all currently being redeveloped.

Royal Adelphi Theatre *See* Adelphi Theatre.

Royal Alexandria Theatre A 1500-seat theatre in Toronto, built in 1907. It was North America's first 'fireproof' theatre and one of the first with air conditioning. The largest and grandest in Toronto, it was used by several stock companies and for Broadway tryouts. In 1963 the impresario Ed Mirvish bought and refurbished it, as a showcase for both touring productions and Canadian works; in 1986 his son David became executive producer, using it as a Toronto forum for important Canadian companies. Since 1989 it has been the Toronto home of blockbuster musicals, including *Les Misérables*.

Royal Alfred Theatre *See* West London Theatre.

Royal Amphitheatre of Arts *See* Astley's Amphitheatre.

Royal Aquarium Theatre *See* Imperial Theatre.

Royal Arctic Theatre A tradition of theatre that flourished aboard ships of the British Royal Navy in Canada during the 19th century. Performed either on board the icebound vessels themselves or in temporary buildings erected nearby, the first plays were presented around 1819 and are known to have included Garrick's *Miss in Her Teens*. The tradition, in which officers and men played both male and female roles, was revived 30 years later with comedies, harlequinades, and even Shakespeare's *Hamlet* (1852). The last such performances, which often involved quite elaborate staging, were seen in 1875–76.

Royal Artillery Theatre A theatre in Woolwich, London, converted from the Barracks Chapel in 1863 to house amateur shows by members of the Royal Artillery. After a fire it reopened in 1905 as a professional theatre and became a useful venue for first class touring companies. It was damaged in World War II and finally closed in 1954.

Royal Avenue Theatre *See* Playhouse.

Royal Brunswick Theatre *See* Royalty Theatre.

Royal Circus *See* Surrey Theatre.

Royal Coburg Theatre *See* Old Vic Theatre.

Royal Court Theatre A small theatre in Sloane Square, London, which first became famous for its adventurous productions in the early 20th century. An earlier theatre of this name, a converted Dissenters' Chapel on the south side of the square, opened in 1870, originally called the **New Chelsea** and then the **Belgravia**, but was closed in 1887 and demolished as part of improvements to the square. The present building, designed by Walter Emden and W R Crewe, was constructed nearby on the east side of the square and opened as the Royal Court Theatre in 1888 under the joint management of Mrs John Wood and Arthur Chudleigh.

The partnership of J S Leigh, J E Vedrenne, and Granville-Barker in 1904–07 saw the production of 32 plays by 17 authors, including Ibsen, Yeats, and Shaw. Ten plays by Shaw were premiered, establishing the theatre's avant-garde reputation. Subsequently, under Barry Jackson's managership (1924–28), Eden Phillpotts's *The Farmer's Wife* ran for almost three years. In the early 1930s the theatre was closed and became a cinema for a short time; it was bombed in 1940. Reopened in 1952, its next major success was Laurier Lister's revue *Airs on a Shoestring* (1954), which ran for 772 performances. In 1956 the theatre was taken over by the English Stage Company, whose artistic director George Devine introduced a number of epoch-making plays by new writers, of which John Osborne's *Look Back in Anger* (1956) and Arnold Wesker's *Chips with Everything* (1962) were among the most important. In 1969 the staging of Edward Bond's *Saved* provoked a cause célèbre and led to a prosecution. A small experimental theatre, the **Theatre Upstairs** was added that same year.

During the 1970s the Royal Court was associated with the political plays of David Hare, Caryl Churchill, and others. Famous productions of more recent years have included Timberlake Wertenbaker's *Our Country's Good* (1988), Ariel Dorfman's *Death and the Maiden* (1991), David Mamet's *Oleanna* (1993), and Sarah Kane's much-reviled *Blasted* (1995). In 1996 the Royal Court closed for major rebuilding and the company moved its base to the Ambassadors Theatre. Its productions there included Conor McPherson's *The Weir* (1996), which is still running (2000) in the West

End and on Broadway, having become the Royal Court's most successful ever play. The Sloane Square theatre reopened with McPherson's *Dublin Carol* in 2000.

Royal English Opera House *See* Palace Theatre.

Royale Theatre A 1076-seat theatre on West 45th Street, New York, which opened in 1927. A number of musicals and straight plays, including Mae West's *Diamond Lil* (1928), were staged there before it became a broadcasting studio in 1936; it was re-named the **John Golden Theatre** from 1934 to 1940. After 1940 it reverted to live drama. Important plays opening there included Tennessee Williams's *The Night of the Iguana* (1961) and Frank Gilroy's *The Subject Was Roses* (1964), although its greatest success to date is the musical *Grease*, which moved there in 1972 and ran to 1980. Recent shows included David Mamet's *Speed the Plow* (1988), Herb Gardner's *Conversations With My Father* (1992), and Yasmina Reza's *Art* (1998).

Royal Exchange Theatre A theatre in Manchester, constructed inside the Victorian Royal Exchange in 1976. The impetus for the building of the theatre came from the success of Michael Elliott's 69 Theatre Company (founded in 1959 as the 59 Theatre Company) and its need for a permanent base in Manchester. Initially the company occupied a temporary theatre within the Exchange before the new structure – a suspended seven-sided theatre-in-the-round – opened in 1976 with Sheridan's *The Rivals*. The prestige of the company grew rapidly with a range of classic and contemporary plays, major successes including works by Chekhov, Ibsen, Webster, and Ronald Harwood. In 1984 the company made its first national tour, culminating in roof-top performances of *Hamlet* at London's Barbican Centre. The theatre was badly damaged by an IRA bomb in 1996 but reopened with a revival of *Hindle Wakes* in 1998.

Royal Holborn *See* Holborn Empire.

Royal Hunt of the Sun, The A play by Peter SHAFFER. First performance: Chichester Festival, 1964. Set in Inca Peru, the play depicts the clash of cultures resulting from the arrival of the Spanish conquistadors and culminates in the murder of the Inca King Atahualpa on the orders of the Spanish leader, Pizarro.

Royal Lyceum Theatre A 773-seat theatre in Edinburgh; it opened (as the Lyceum Theatre) in 1883 and is now considered a showpiece of late Victorian architecture. The Lyceum initially served as a venue for touring companies, notably that of Henry Irving. Eventually, in 1964, it acquired its own resident company – the **Edinburgh Civic Theatre Company**, later renamed the Royal Lyceum Theatre Company. Since then it has been used for presentations of both classic and modern plays, with an emphasis on work by Scottish authors, notably under Bill BRYDEN in the early 1970s. The current artistic director is Kenny Ireland. During August each year the theatre is used for Edinburgh Festival productions.

Royal National Theatre A theatre complex on the South Bank of the Thames in London, containing the OLIVIER THEATRE, the LYTTELTON THEATRE, and the COTTESLOE THEATRE. The idea of a National Theatre was first aired in 1848 but the project was not taken up seriously until 1907, when the Shakespeare Memorial National Theatre Committee was established. In 1944 a site was offered on the South Bank and Denys Lasdun was appointed to design the complex. A National Theatre

Board was set up in 1962, Sir Laurence Olivier being appointed artistic director of the newly created National Theatre Company; he was succeeded by Peter Hall in 1975. In 1976 the company moved to the South Bank from its temporary home at the Old Vic Theatre, the National Theatre itself opening later that year. The three theatres opened as each in turn was completed: the Lyttelton in March 1976, the Olivier in October 1976, and the Cottesloe in March 1977. There is a small experimental National Theatre Studio at the Old Vic Annexe, from which plays are transferred periodically to the Cottlesloe. The Royal National Theatre complex includes foyer space for live music and exhibitions, bookshops, restaurant and buffet facilities, and a car park. Plays are presented in repertory and range from Shakespeare and the classics to new (and sometimes controversial) drama. The prefix Royal was added in 1988 at about the time that Hall was succeeded by Richard Eyre. Trevor Nunn took over as artistic director in 1997.

Royal Opera House *See* Covent Garden (Royal Opera House).

Royal Princess's Theatre *See* Glasgow Citizens' Theatre; Princess's Theatre.

Royal Shakespeare Company (RSC) A British theatre company, founded in 1960 when the company at the SHAKESPEARE MEMORIAL THEATRE in Stratford-on-Avon was reorganized. Under Peter Hall, the RSC quickly established itself with its *Wars of the Roses* cycle of Shakespeare's plays in 1963 and other productions performed at Stratford and also at the Aldwych Theatre (and briefly the Arts Theatre in 1962) in London. As well as Shakespeare, the company has presented modern plays and other classics and toured internationally, its members including many of Britain's leading theatrical figures.

From 1965 to 1971 the company also included **Theatregoround**, a subsidiary touring group that presented plays at various smaller venues. In 1968 Hall was succeeded by Trevor Nunn, who opened **The Place** in London as a venue for smaller-scale productions in 1971 (later transferred to the OTHER PLACE in Stratford). During the 1970s the company also staged acclaimed productions in London at the Warehouse (opened in 1977) and annually at the Theatre Royal in Newcastle-upon-Tyne; in 1978 Terry Hands joined as joint artistic director. In 1982 the RSC transferred its London operations to the new Barbican Centre. The 1980s and 1990s saw mounting financial pressures, only partly offset by the company's conquest of Broadway and the West End with such musical shows as *Nicholas Nickleby* and *Les Misérables* (the Stephen King adaptation *Carrie* was, by contrast, a notorious flop). The company also presents plays by Shakespeare's contemporaries at the Elizabethan-style Swan Theatre in Stratford. The current artistic director is Adrian Noble (since 1991).

Royal Shakespeare Theatre The Stratford-on-Avon home of the Royal Shakespeare Company, formerly called the SHAKESPEARE MEMORIAL THEATRE. The present name of the theatre dates from 1961, when the newly-constituted RSC gave its inaugural season under the direction of Peter Hall. Plays from the Shakespearean repertory are performed annually from March through to the following January; highlights in an outstanding record of interesting productions have included John Barton's adaptation in 1963 of the *Henry VI* trilogy and *Richard III* as *The Wars of the Roses* and Peter Brook's startling *A Midsummer Night's Dream* in 1970. New cycles of Shakespeare's histories were presented in 1988 and 2000. *See also* Swan Theatre.

Royal Soho Theatre *See* Royalty Theatre.

Royal Standard Music Hall *See* Victoria Palace Theatre.

royalty *See* copyright.

Royalty Theatre A theatre in Well Street, London, which was opened by John Palmer and John Bannister in 1787 with *As You Like It* and Garrick's *Miss in Her Teens*. It was almost immediately forced to close by the intervention of the patent theatres; later it was used for burlesque and pantomime. As the **East London Theatre** from 1813, it had limited success but burned down in 1826. Reopening as the **Royal Brunswick Theatre** in 1828, it collapsed three days later during a rehearsal, killing 15 people.

Another **Royalty Theatre** was opened in Dean Street, London, in 1840. A small theatre, designed for Fanny Kelly and her acting school, it had to have the original stage machinery removed since it proved too noisy. After closing in 1849, it was successively renamed the **Royal Soho Theatre**, the **New English Opera House**, and the **New Royalty Theatre**. Thereafter it flourished with melodrama and (in 1875) the debut of the Gilbert and Sullivan partnership with *Trial by Jury*. Subsequently it established a reputation for modern drama with plays by Ibsen, Shaw, and Brandon Thomas. Other notable productions included William Poel's version of *Measure for Measure* (1893), revivals of Maeterlinck's *Pelléas and Mélisande* and Sudermann's *Magda* (both 1900), Galsworthy's *The Pigeon* (1912), the premiere of Maugham's *Caesar's Wife* (1919) with Fay Compton, and Sean O'Casey's *Juno and the Paycock* (1925). Long runs were also enjoyed by John Drinkwater's *Bird in Hand* (1928) and Priestley's *I Have Been Here Before* (1938), which was the last great success before, damaged by bombs in World War II, the theatre was demolished (1955).

A third **Royalty Theatre** was opened in Portugal Street, London, on the site of the STOLL THEATRE in 1960. It opened with Dürrenmatt's *The Visit*, starring Alfred Lunt and Lynn Fontanne but less than a year later became a cinema and did not reopen as a theatre until 1970, when the all-male revue *Birds of a Feather* was staged. The erotic revue *Oh, Calcutta!* (1970) ran for four years, while another success was the US musical *Bubbling Brown Sugar* (1977). In 1981 the Royalty became a television studio but was later acquired by Stoll Moss Theatres Ltd as a venue for plays, concerts, and business conferences. In 1987 the newly-formed Royalty Theatre Company launched a programme of revivals of late 19th and 20th century plays. It also enjoyed success with a stage version of *Winnie-the-Pooh* (1987). However, drama productions ceased in the 1990s.

Royal Victoria Hall and Coffee Tavern *See* Old Vic Theatre.

Royal Victoria Theatre *See* Old Vic Theatre.

Rozewicz, Tadeusz (1921–) Polish poet and playwright, who emerged as one of Poland's leading contemporary writers for the theatre in the 1960s. His experimental plays, some of which are very fragmentary in form, include *Card Index* (1960), *Laocoon Group* (1962), the tragicomedy *White Wedding* (1975), and *The Trap* (1982).

Rozov, Victor Sergeyevich (1913–) Russian playwright, actor, and director, who originally trained as an actor at Moscow's Theatre of the Revolution (1934–38). During World War II he set up a children's theatre in Alma-Ata, Kazakhstan, and later returned to Moscow where he became director of the Theatre of the Central House of Culture for Railwaymen. Many of his plays deal with the issues facing the younger generation after World War II; the best known outside Russia is *Vecho Zhivye* (Alive Forever; 1957), which was filmed as *The Cranes are Flying*. Later works include *The Nest of the Woodgrouse* (1978) and *The Little Cabin* (1982), both of which ran into censorship problems.

RSC *See* Royal Shakespeare Company.

Rucellai, Giovanni (1475–1525) Italian playwright, who wrote tragedies based on classical models. A friend of Trissino, by whom he was influenced, he was the author of *Oreste* (1514) – an unfinished tragedy borrowing from Euripides, and *Rosmunda* (1516), which took a medieval story as its subject.

Rueda, Lope de (c. 1505–65) Spanish actor-manager and playwright, who was one of the most prominent figures in the early Spanish theatre. His plays, written for his own company, were noted for their natural dialogue and influenced Cervantes. He was also the author of the first examples of the brief interludes known as PASOS; longer works influenced by Italian models included *Eufemia*, *Los enganados*, and *Prendas de amor*.

Ruggeri, Ruggero (1871–1953) Italian actor, who became famous in strong romantic roles. A noted member (1891–99) of Novelli's company and later of Pirandello's troupe, he gave passionate performances in such roles as Hamlet, Iago, Aligi in D'Annunzio's *La figlia di Jorio* (1904) as well as in the plays of Pirandello, but resisted any attempts to modernize his old-fashioned acting style.

Ruggle, George (1575–1622) English playwright, who is thought to have been the author of the comedy *Ignoramus* (1615), a popular satire on the law profession written in Latin and English. Based upon Della Porta's *La Trappolaria* (1596), it was subsequently translated fully into English as *Ignoramus; or, the Academical Lawyer* (1662).

Ruiz de Alarcón y Mendoza, Juan (c. 1581–1639) Spanish playwright, born in Mexico, whose well-constructed plays are notable for their strong characterization and concern with moral issues. A hunchback, who suffered much ridicule in the plays of Lope de Vega and others, he wrote a number of comedies set in Madrid, of which *La verdad Sospechosa* discussed impulsive lying, *Las paredes oyen* took as its hero a much-slandered hunchback, and *La prueba* criticized ingratitude.

run A series of performances of a single play on successive nights, the length of which is commonly regarded as an indication of a play's success. The record for the world's longest run is held by Agatha Christie's *The Mousetrap*, which ran for 21 years at the Ambassadors Theatre before transferring to St Martin's Theatre in 1974. The 20 000th performance was given in 2000. The world's longest-running comedy was *No Sex Please We're British*, which opened in 1971 and closed in 1987.

Rundhorizont *See* cyclorama.

runway A narrow extension of the stage over the pit or into the auditorium, along which a performer can walk.

RUR A play by Karel Čapek. First performance: Prague, 1921. A warning of the dangers inherent in a society dominated by technology, *RUR* – short for Rossum's Universal Robots – was much influenced by German Expressionism and incorporated elements of revue; it also introduced the word 'robot' into the language.

Rural Dionysia Religious festivals held annually (in December) in ancient Greece in honour of DIONYSUS, shortly before the Lenaea and the City Dionysia. These local festivals probably included drama contests featuring both new plays and revivals of better-known older works.

Russell, Fred (Thomas Frederick Parnell; 1862–1957) British ventriloquist, who made his first music hall appearance in 1896. With his cheeky doll, Coster Joe, he toured the world for 40 years and was a founder of the Variety Artists' Federation.

Russell, George William *See* AE.

Russell, Willy (1947–) British playwright, whose plays draw heavily upon his Liverpool background. They include a musical about the Beatles, *John, Paul, George, Ringo... and Bert* (1974), *One for the Road* (1976), *Stags and Hens* (1978), and the hugely successful *Educating Rita* (1980, later filmed), which depicts the relationship between a disenchanted university tutor and a working-class mature student. In 1983 his acclaimed musical BLOOD BROTHERS, highlighting the gulf between rich and poor in contemporary Britain, transferred from the Liverpool Playhouse to the West End. Plays since then have included the highly popular *Shirley Valentine* (1986), which also became a successful film, and *Dancing through the Dark* (1989).

Russell Street Theatre *See* Melbourne Theatre Company.

Rutebeuf (c. 1245–c. 1285) French poet and jongleur, who wrote comic monologues and witty poems characterized by biting satire. Little is known of his life and it is possible that the name Rutebeuf was a pseudonym. He was the author of one of the earliest miracle plays, *Le Miracle de Théophile*, in which the Virgin Mary intervenes to save a priest who has sold his soul to the devil.

Rutherford, Dame Margaret (1892–1972) British actress, who began her career at the Old Vic in 1925. 15 years later, with much provincial repertory experience behind her, she enjoyed success as Bijou Furze in M J Farrell and John Perry's *Spring Meeting* (1938). The following year she excelled as Miss Prism in Gielgud's production of *The Importance of Being Earnest* and from then on specialized in playing quirky yet shrewd middle-aged ladies. Among her other roles were Madame Arcati in Coward's *Blithe Spirit* (1941), the headmistress in John Dighton's *The Happiest Days of Your Life* (1948), Lady Wishfort in Congreve's *The Way of the World* (1953), and Mrs Candour in Sheridan's *The School for Scandal* (1962). She appeared in many films, notably as Agatha Christie's Miss Marple.

Ruy Blas A verse drama by Victor HUGO. First performance: Paris, 1838. The valet and poet Ruy Blas enters the Spanish court in the guise of his master's cousin; he wins the love of the queen and is appointed prime minister, but commits suicide when his true identity is revealed.

Ruzzante, Il *See* Beolco, Angelo.

Ryga, George (1932–87) Canadian playwright, who is best known for *The Ecstacy of Rita Joe* (1967), which depicts the tragic death of a Red Indian girl; like most of his other plays, this included folksongs and dances. His other works ranged from *Noth-*

ing But a Man (1966), which recounts the life of García Lorca, to the controversial *Captives of the Faceless Drummer* (1971), which explores the theme of urban violence.

Rylance, Mark (1960–) British actor and director, who trained at RADA before joining the Glasgow Citizen's Theatre in 1980. He subsequently played Hamlet (1988) and Romeo (1989) for the RSC and won an Olivier award for his Benedict in *Much Ado About Nothing* (1994). In 1996 he was appointed artistic director of the recreated GLOBE THEATRE on London's South Bank; his roles there have included Henry V (1997), Bassanio (1998), and Cleopatra (1999).

S

Saavedra Remírez de Baquedano, Ángel, Duke of Rivas (1791–1865) Spanish poet, playwright, and statesman, who was one of the founders of the Romantic movement in Spain. Influenced by Victor Hugo, he was the author of *Don Álvaro, o la fuerza del sino* (1835), which was the first great Romantic drama of the Spanish theatre. Other plays included several unremarkable costume dramas.

Sabbattini, Nicola (1574–1654) Italian stage designer, who wrote the influential theatrical treatise *Pratica di fabricar scene e machine ne'teatri* (1638), which included details of contemporary stage lighting. He was also the designer of a theatre at Pesaro.

Sacchi, Antonio (1708–88) Italian actor of the *commedia dell'arte*, who appeared in the role of Truffaldino. He led his own touring company, performing in Venice and throughout Europe, and presented plays by both Gozzi and Goldoni, who wrote *Il servitore di due padrone* (The Servant of Two Masters; 1746) especially for him.

Sachs, Hans (1494–1576) German playwright, a leading figure among the *meistersängers* and subsequently the central character in Wagner's opera *Die Meistersinger von Nürnberg*. A cobbler by trade, he wrote numerous rustic comic plays of the *Fastnachtsspiel* tradition as well as many moralistic tragedies and comedies. He is known to have directed the actors himself and to have installed them in what was effectively the country's first theatre.

Sackville, Thomas (fl. 1590–1613) English actor, who toured Europe with the English Comedians before forming his own group, which enjoyed the patronage of the Duke of Brunswick from 1596 to 1613. Speaking a mixture of English, German, and Dutch, he created the popular clown **Jan Bouschet** (or **Jean Posset**).

Sackville, Thomas, First Earl of Dorset (1536–1608) English poet and playwright, who collaborated with Thomas Norton in writing GORBODUC, the first English tragedy in blank verse. He is generally assumed to have written the last two acts; his other writings included poems for *A Mirror for Magistrates* (1563).

sacra rappresentazione A form of early Italian religious drama, equivalent to the mystery play in England and France and the *auto sacramental* in Spain. Incorporating the LAUDA and derived from the earlier liturgical drama, the *sacra rappresentazione* developed chiefly in Florence and consisted of dramatic re-enactments of biblical stories. Writers of such pieces included Feo Belcari, Savonarola, and Lorenzo de' Medici. Eventually it became increasingly secular in form and was absorbed into the more classically orientated drama of the 15th century.

saddle-iron A flat metal strip, known in the US as a **sill-iron**, which is fastened across the bottom of any flat with a large opening in it to give it greater rigidity.

Sá de Miranda, Francisco de See Miranda, Francisco de Sá de.

Sadler's Wells Theatre A theatre in Finsbury, north-east London, built in 1927–31 on a site that in the 17th century was a popular spa. The original Sadler's Wells was the wooden Musick House erected in 1683 by Thomas Sadler, in whose grounds a medicinal well had been discovered; under subsequent ownership, however, the place was badly neglected. In 1746 a local builder, Thomas Rosoman, built a new stone theatre and restored its popularity. For 10 years from 1772, it was managed by Thomas King, who had been associated with the Drury Lane Theatre and brought with him a fashionable audience. Joseph Grimaldi played at the Wells between 1781 and 1828, while in 1804 Edmund Kean appeared as a young boy in one of the nautical spectacles that caused the theatre to be renamed the **Aquatic Theatre** for a time. A false alarm of fire in 1807 resulted in the deaths of 20 people.

In 1844 Sadler's Wells was let to Samuel Phelps and Mary Warner, who presented no less than 34 of Shakespeare's plays there. After 1871, however, the theatre degenerated into a skating rink, a pickle factory, and then a boxing arena; it was closed in 1878. Revived briefly by Mrs Bateman and her daughter Kate, it later became a house of melodrama and a music hall, before closing again in 1906. Lilian Baylis opened the current building in 1931 in co-ordination with the Old Vic Theatre, but from 1934 onwards the Wells became devoted solely to opera and ballet. Its ballet company transferred to Covent Garden in 1946, where it formed the nucleus of the Royal Ballet in 1956. Similarly, the resident Sadler's Wells Opera Company moved to the **Coliseum** in 1968, becoming the English National Opera in 1974. The theatre continued to be used by touring and foreign companies. In the late 1990s Sadler's Wells underwent a multimillion-pound redevelopment programme, re-opening as a high-tech state-of-the-art dance theatre in 1999. The original well is concealed under a trap door at the rear of the stalls.

Sadovsky, Prov Mikhailovich (Prov Mikhailovich Yermilov; 1818–72) Russian actor, who began his career in Tula as a child and later appeared at the Maly Theatre in Moscow. He was particularly successful giving realistic performances in the plays of Ostrovsky.

safety curtain A fireproof curtain, also known as an **iron**, designed to reduce the risk of a fire in the stage area spreading to the auditorium. The first safety curtain in Britain was installed at Drury Lane in 1794.

sainete A short comic entertainment given between the acts of full-length dramas in Spain, chiefly during the 17th century. Such interludes featured music, urban themes, and some satirical content; notable authors included Ramón de la Cruz in the 18th century. The tradition, which foreshadowed the *género chico* of the 19th century (*see zarzuela*), has been revived periodically in modern Spanish drama.

Saint-Denis, Michel Jacques (1897–1971) French director and actor, who founded the celebrated Compagnie des Quinze in 1930. The nephew of Jacques Copeau, he trained under him at the Vieux-Colombier before founding the Compagnie des Quinze and working with it as both director and actor in notable productions of plays by such authors as André Obey. After the company was broken up in 1936 he worked in London with such actors as Olivier and Gielgud on major plays by Shakespeare, Chekhov, García Lorca, and others and founded the **London Theatre Studio** (1936–39) to further drama study. After World War II he taught drama and directed at the Old Vic, founded the Centre Dramatique de l'Est in Strasbourg, and worked with the Vivian Beaumont Theatre Project in New York. Subsequently he collaborated (from 1962) with the Royal Shakespeare Company on plays by Brecht and others and also worked in Canada.

Sainte-Beuve, Charles-Augustin (1804–69) French theatre critic, who was famous for his 'Monday articles', written for several leading French journals. He championed the plays of Victor Hugo (becoming the lover of Hugo's wife) and much admired the actor Molé.

Saint-Étienne, Comédie de *See Décentralisation Dramatique*.

St George *See* mummers' play.

St George's Theatre A London theatre modelled on Elizabethan lines, complete with balconied stage, in a former church in Tufnell Park. It was founded by the actor George Murcell in 1976 with the aim of presenting Shakespearean plays in a form resembling their original productions. There is a strong emphasis on educational work and schools make up a large part of the audiences.

Saint-Germain fairground *See* fair.

Sainthill, Loudon (1919–69) Australian stage designer, born in Tasmania, who became famous for his romantic settings for the plays of both Shakespeare and modern playwrights. He worked at the Shakespeare Memorial Theatre and the Old Vic, his most acclaimed designs including those for *The Tempest* (1951), *Pericles* (1958), *Othello* (1959), Tennessee Williams's *Orpheus Descending* (1959), and Wilde's *A Woman of No Importance* (1953).

St James's Theatre A London theatre in King Street, St James's. It was built by the famous tenor John Braham (1777–1856) to designs by Samuel Beazley and opened in 1835 with the burletta *Agnes Sorel*. In spite of attempts by succeeding managements who presented opera, French companies, burlesques, dramas, and magic shows, as well as appearances by such stars as Rachel, Fanny Kemble, Ristori, and Louisa Herbert, the theatre did not achieve stability until the joint management of Hare and the Kendals in 1879. In 1891 George Alexander began a celebrated period of management that established the St James's as the criterion of distinguished elegant theatre until his death in 1918. His productions included Wilde's *Lady Windermere's Fan* (1892) and *The Importance of Being Earnest* (1895); Pinero's *The Second Mrs Tanqueray* (1893) and *His House in Order* (1906); Anthony Hope's *The Prisoner of Zenda* (1896); and Stephen Phillips's *Paolo and Francesca* (1902). Gilbert Miller took over the lease in 1918 and subsequent notable productions included Lonsdale's *The Last of Mrs Cheyney* (1925), Emlyn Williams's *The Late Christopher Bean* (1933), and Turgenev's *A Month in the Country* (1943). After World War II, first John Clements then Laurence Olivier staged highly acclaimed seasons, while in 1954 Terence Rattigan's *Separate Tables* began a two year run. In spite of a vigorous campaign to save it, the theatre was sold to a building speculator in 1957 and eventually replaced by an office block.

St James Theatre A theatre on West 44th Street between Broadway and 8th Avenue, New York, which opened as **Erlanger's Theatre** in 1927. In 1932 it was renamed the St James. Plays staged there have included Margaret Webster's *Richard II* (1937), *Hamlet* (1938), and *Twelfth Night* (1940), all with Maurice Evans, as well as Osborne's *Luther* (1963). However, it is best known as a musical house, with such historic productions as *Oklahoma!* (1943), *The King and I* (1951), *Flower Drum Song* (1958), *Hello Dolly!* (1964), *Barnum* (1980), *My One and Only* (1983), and *Tommy* (1993).

Saint Joan A play by G B SHAW, often regarded as his finest. First performance: New York, 1923. Based on the life and death of Joan of Arc, the play discusses nationalism, Protestantism, and the notion of sainthood. Joan's death is depicted as the inevitable conclusion of her rebellion against the feudal state and the spiritual authority of the Church. In the ironic epilogue, a dream sequence, a visitor from 1923 tells Joan of her impending canonization; however, when she speaks of returning to earth, the offer is firmly declined. Shaw's point is that saints are much easier to deal with dead than alive.

Saint-Laurent fairground *See* fair.

St Martin's Hall *See* Queen's Theatre.

St Martin's Theatre One of the smaller London theatres, planned as a twin to the Ambassadors Theatre but not completed until 1916. C B Cochran was the theatre's first lessee and manager (1916–20); subsequently the theatre experimented with matinée performances, known as 'The Playbox Theatre' (1923–24). In the 1920s plays by Clemence Dane and John Galsworthy were presented, another major success being Arnold Ridley's *The Ghost Train* (1925). Thereafter a mixed selection of plays was staged, including many transfers from other theatres. A homegrown success was Anthony Shaffer's *Sleuth* (1970), with Anthony Quayle, which ran for three years before being transferred to the Garrick Theatre. Agatha Christie's *The Mousetrap* was transferred from the Ambassadors Theatre in March 1974 and can still be seen here.

St Martin's Theatre in Melbourne, Australia, was founded in 1931 as the Melbourne Little Theatre and run on an amateur basis. It acquired its present name in 1962 and was noted for productions of Australian plays, especially works by Hal Porter. The theatre failed to prosper commercially and since 1973 it has been leased to the Melbourne Theatre Company.

saint play In medieval Europe, a type of play dramatizing episodes in the lives of such saints as Nicholas and Paul. The plays were performed in England and France by laymen and clergy alike, despite the fact that they were not directly connected with the liturgy.

Saint's Day A drama by John WHITING. First performance: London, 1951. Characterized by dark humour, this controversial study of senile violence anticipated the challenging drama of the late 1950s at the Royal Court Theatre and elsewhere.

Salacrou, Armand (1899–1989) French playwright and journalist, born in Rouen. After a number of unsuccessful Surrealist plays he found favour with the public and critics with the comedy *Atlas-Hôtel*, produced at the Théâtre de l'Atelier. His subsequent works include the farcical *Histoire de rire*, the historical drama *La Terre est ronde*, and *Les Nuits de la colère*, which centres on the activities of the Resistance in German-occupied Chartres.

Principal works:
  Atlas-Hôtel: 1931.
  L'Inconnue d'Arras: 1935; translated as *The Unknown Woman of Arras*.
  Un homme comme les autres: 1936.
  La Terre est ronde: 1938.
  Histoire de rire: 1939; translated as *No Laughing Matter*.
  Les Nuits de la colère: 1946; translated as *Nights of Wrath*.
  L'Archipel Lenoir: 1947; translated as *The Honour of the Family*.
  Une femme trop honnête: 1956.
  Boulevard Durand: 1961.

Salisbury Court Theatre The last London theatre to be built before the Civil War, erected south of Fleet Street. It was used by the King's Men (1629–31), Princes Charles's Men (1631–35), and Queen Henrietta's Men (1637–42). Players attempted clandestine performances there during the Commonwealth, but the theatre was wrecked by soldiers in 1649. Refurbished by Beeston after the Restoration, various companies, including Rhodes's and Davenant's, performed there until its destruction in the Great Fire of 1666.

Salle des Machines A large theatre in the Tuileries, Paris, built in 1660 as a venue for entertainments celebrating the marriage of Louis XIV. Designed by Vigarani, it was subsequently used for elaborate stage productions, notably under the influence of Servandony, and was briefly the home of the Comédie-Française in the 1770s.

Salles, Aurélia de (16th century) French actress, the first woman known by name to appear on the French stage. She is recorded as having appeared on stage with a company in Mâcon in 1581.

Salmacida Spolia A masque by Sir William DAVENANT. First performance: 1640. Designed by Inigo Jones and celebrating the reign of Charles I, this was the last court masque to be staged in England and included Charles himself and Queen Henrietta Maria amongst its participants.

Salom, Jaime (1925–) Spanish playwright, who established a reputation initially as a writer of comedies but subsequently won acclaim for serious dramas. *La casa de las Chivas* (1968) recalls the Spanish Civil War, while *Los delfines* (The Dauphins; 1969) examines the society; later works include *El corto vuello del gallo* (1980).

Salomé A tragedy by Oscar WILDE. First performance: Paris, 1896. A version of the story of the beheading of John the Baptist at the request of Salomé, who is portrayed as a dissipated neurotic, it was banned in England until 1931. The title role was written for Sarah Bernhardt.

saltica A form of Roman *fabula*. It consisted of a play in which the chorus sang the text and the PANTOMIMUS mimed the action.

Saltikov-Shchedrin, Mikhail Evgrapovich (1826–89) Russian novelist and playwright, noted for his satirical writings on Tsarist Russia. His play *The Death of*

Pazukhin, not performed until 1901, was a typical attack on official corruption; it was later revived by the Moscow Art Theatre (1914).

Salvini, Tommaso (1829–1915) Italian actor, who became famous for his playing of Othello in Italian. Having first appeared on stage at the age of 14 he was trained by Gustavo Modena and went on to establish his reputation opposite Adelaide Ristori in Alfieri's *Oreste* (1848). He was also fairly successful as Hamlet (in which role he appeared many times) but enjoyed his greatest success as a particularly forceful Othello in 1856, later repeating the role in many countries (in 1886 to the Iago of Edwin Booth). Other Shakespearean roles included Macbeth (1876) and Lear (1884). His habit of long study of the parts he was to play is referred to with approval by Stanislavsky in his influential book *My Life in Art*.

Sam H Harris Theatre *See* Harris Theatre.

Samson, Joseph-Isidore (1793–1871) French actor, who – as a teacher at the Conservatoire – trained Rachel in the French classical tradition. He was himself highly popular as an actor at the Odéon (1819–26) and subsequently at the Comédie-Française and the Palais-Royal and influenced the revival of French tragedy.

Sam S Shubert Theatre *See* Shubert Theatre.

San Diego National Shakespeare Festival *See* Old Globe Theatre.

San Francisco Mime Theatre A US theatre company founded in 1959 to present political dramas and adaptations of *commedia dell'arte* sketches in San Francisco parks. The group wrote their own sketches after 1970, drawing on such varied sources as minstrel shows, vaudeville, melodrama, spy films, and television detective series. It has made extensive world tours since the 1980s.

Sanger's Grand National Amphitheatre *See* Astley's Amphitheatre.

Sans Pareil *See* Adelphi Theatre.

Sans Souci A theatre established by Charles Dibdin in the Strand, London in 1791. Five years later he moved to new premises off Leicester Square, opening with a topical show, *The General Election*. He gave three performances a week there during the winter months until 1804. The theatre then continued to be used for a variety of theatrical entertainments before becoming a warehouse and a hotel; it was demolished in 1898. *See also* Niblo's Garden.

Saracen's Head Inn A tavern in Islington in London, where plays were staged in the 16th century. One of the earliest such theatrical venues, it was much altered in the early 17th century.

Sarat, Agnan (d. 1613) French actor, who won fame when an old man as the leading comedian with Valleran-Lecomte's company. Earlier in his career (1578) he brought his own company to Paris and installed it at the Hôtel de Bourgogne for a time before returning to the provinces.

Sardi's A restaurant on 44th Street, New York, between 7th and 8th Avenues, noted for its theatrical clientele. In the heyday of Broadway it was the favoured location for opening night parties.

Sardou, Victorien (1831–1908) French playwright, whose WELL-MADE PLAYS are characterized by complicated plots and spectacular theatrical effects. His first play was a failure, but after the success of *Les Pattes de Mouche* in 1860 he wrote prolifically, producing 20 plays during the next six years and some 50 more before his death. Sardou's works were very popular in their time but were subsequently attacked by critics, notably George Bernard Shaw, who dismissed them as 'sardoodledom'. His most popular dramas included *Fédora* (1882), *La Tosca* (1887), and MADAME SANS-GÊNE (1893).

Sarment, Jean (Jean Bellemère; 1897–1976) French playwright and actor; his melancholy comedies, which have been likened to those of Alfred de Musset, explore the conflict between illusion and reality. They include *Le Pêcheur d'ombres* (The Fisher of Shadows; 1921), *Le Mariage d'Hamlet* (1922), *Je suis trop grand pour moi* (1924), *Léopold le Bien-Aimé* (1927), *Bobard* (1930), and *Le Discours des prix* (1934).

Saroyan, William (1908–81) US playwright and novelist, who began his theatrical career in management at the Lyceum Theatre (1941). After the Theatre Guild staged his one-act play *My Heart's in the Highlands* (1939), he went on to enjoy a huge critical and commercial success with THE TIME OF YOUR LIFE (1939). Later plays, which include *Love's Old Sweet Song* (1940), *Hello, Out There* (1942), *Get Away, Old Man* (1943), *The Cave Dwellers* (1957), and *Sam, The Highest Jumper of Them All* (1960), proved much less popular. His works are notable for their innovative structure and elements of fantasy.

Sarrazin, Maurice (1925–72) French director, who founded one of the most important companies established under the *Décentralisation Dramatique* policy. Le Grenier de Toulouse, founded in 1945, began as an amateur organization and established its reputation with its production of Shakespeare's *The Taming of the Shrew*; subsequently it also presented much new drama.

Sarthou, Jacques (1920–) French actor and director, who founded his own company in 1952 to present drama to working-class audiences throughout France. He established his reputation as an actor in Vilar's production of T S Eliot's *Murder in the Cathedral* in 1945; plays presented by his own company included works by Giraudoux, Hugo, Molière, and Musset.

Sartre, Jean-Paul (1905–80) French novelist, playwright, and philosopher, who began writing for the theatre during World War II. His plays, which are generally pessimistic, use the conventions of melodrama to explore moral conflicts and expound his existentialist philosophy. *Les Mouches* was a reworking of the story of Orestes, *Le Diable et le bon Dieu* was based on Goethe, and *Kean* was an adaptation of Dumas *père's* play. Sartre also wrote a number of film scenarios, notably *L'Engrenage*, which was adapted for the theatre in 1969. In 1964 he refused a Nobel Prize.

Principal dramatic works:
 Les Mouches: 1953.
 HUIS-CLOS: 1944; translated as *In Camera*.
 Morts sans sépulture: 1946; translated as MEN WITHOUT SHADOWS.
 La Putain respectueuse: 1946.
 Les Mains sales: 1948.
 Le Diable et le bon Dieu: 1951.

Kean: 1953.
NEKRASSOV: 1955.
Les Séquestrés d'Altona: 1959; translated as ALTONA.

Sastre, Alfonso (1926–) Spanish playwright and novelist, whose first play *Escuadra hacia la muerte* (The Condemned Squad; 1953) was banned by the authorities for its anti-militarist content. His earlier plays, which were seldom performed in his native country because of his political stance, included *La mordaza* (1954), *Muerte en el barrio* (Death in the Neighbourhood; 1955), *La cornada* (The Death Thrust; 1960), *En la red* (1960), about Algeria's struggle for independence, *The Banquet* (1965), and *Exercises in Terror* (1970). When he returned to the theatre after an interval of some years, his plays were more experimental and non-linear in form; these late works include *No Laughing Matter* (1979) and *Tragicomedy of the Gypsy Celestina* (1984).

Satin Slipper, The (*Le Soulier de satin*) A play by Paul CLAUDEL, written in 1924 and regarded as his best. First performance: Comédie-Française, Paris, 1943. Set in the late 16th century, the play centres on two lovers who resist their earthly passion in order to attain spiritual salvation. Its action ranges across continents and oceans.

satire A form of comedy in which vice and folly are exposed to ridicule. A satirical element was, according to Aristotle, part of the earliest classical tradition, notably through the inclusion of songs making fun of unpopular public figures; indeed, it has been suggested that the use of masks in comedy was a means of allowing an actor to make such criticisms without being identified.

Aristophanes was the first great writer of satirical comedy, his targets including the army, national leaders, contemporary thinkers, and fellow playwrights. Satire was an element in the medieval mystery play and became more prominent in the 16th-century morality plays, which often attacked Church abuses. By the time of Shakespeare satire had become an essential feature of the main comic tradition in European drama. In England it enjoyed a particular vogue in the reign of James I, with Jonson as the leading satirist of the era. Subsequently it added extra piquancy to the comedies of Molière, whose targets included greed, snobbery, and quack doctors, and to the English Restoration comedies, which attacked the excesses of fashion. In 18th-century Britain satire became increasingly political in nature. One of the most notorious uses of satire to lampoon politicians occurred in Gay's *The Beggar's Opera* (1728), which attacked Sir Robert Walpole's government so virulently that parliament was persuaded to tighten controls on the theatre in 1737.

In Western Europe and North America the 20th century saw the gradual freeing of comedy from such bonds and consequently a new role for satirical drama as a scourge of political and social ills. Most modern democratic societies have learnt to absorb satire and to regard it as a creative force, highlighting faults and challenging complacency.

Satire, Theatre of A theatre in Moscow, founded in 1924 as a home of revue. It soon developed a programme of satire and comedy, notably under Gorchakov and subsequently Pluchek, who diversified with productions of plays by Shaw, Gogol, and others. In the 1960s the resident company was rehoused in a larger theatre nearby.

satyr-play A farcical entertainment of the ancient Greek theatre, comprising an obscene burlesque on legendary themes. It was usually the work of the same author who wrote the trilogy of tragedies with which it was performed at the Dionysia. The satyr-play always included a chorus of satyrs, borrowed from the cult of DIONYSUS, who appeared as half human and half beast. The first writer of the satyr-play in Athens was, by tradition, Pratinus of Phlius; subsequent practitioners of the form included Euripides (author of *Cyclops*, the only intact surviving satyr-play), Aeschylus, and Sophocles. Aristotle claimed that Greek tragedy was directly descended from the satyr-play.

Saunders, James (1925–) British playwright, who established his reputation with *Next Time I'll Sing to You* (1962), a one-act play about the hermit Alexander James Mason. Other well-received one-acters have included *Alas, Poor Fred* (1959), the Absurdist *Who Was Hilary Maconochie?* (1963), *Savoury Meringue* (1971), and *Birdsong* (1979). Among his full-length plays have been *A Scent of Flowers* (1964), depicting events following a suicide, the children's play *The Travails of Sancho Panza* (1969), *The Island* (1975), *Bodies* (1977), a very successful drama in which couples meet again after changing partners years previously, *The Girl in Melanie Klein* (1980), and *Fall* (1984). Saunders also collaborated with Iris Murdoch on a dramatization of her novel *The Italian Girl* (1967).

Saunderson, Mary (d. 1712) English actress, wife of Thomas Betterton. One of the first women to appear on the English stage, she excelled as Ianthe in *The Siege of Rhodes* by Davenant and was admired by Pepys and many others.

Saurin, Bernard-Joseph (1706–81) French playwright and lawyer, son of the mathematician Joseph Saurin. His dramatic works include the comedy *Les Moeurs du temps* (1759), the tragedies *Spartacus* (1760) and *Blanche et Guiscard* (1763) – inspired by James Thomson's *Tancred and Sigismunda* – and *Beverley* (1768), a *drame bourgeois* based on Edward Moore's *The Gamester*.

Saved A play by Edward BOND. First performance: Royal Court Theatre, 1965. The Lord Chamberlain's refusal to grant this play a licence helped to accelerate the abolition of theatre censorship. The original controversy centred on the casual stoning to death of a baby in its pram, a deliberately shocking image that was meant to show the moral vacuum in modern capitalist society. The play depicts the aimless and alienated lives of a group of young people in South London.

Saville Theatre A theatre in Shaftesbury Avenue, London, built in 1931; the front elevation is distinguished by a frieze in bas-relief entitled *Drama through the Ages* by the sculptor Gilbert Bayes. It opened with H F Maltby and Clifford Grey's musical play *For the Love of Mike* and for the next few years pursued a successful policy of musical comedy and revue. Among interesting plays staged there later were Shaw's *Geneva* (1938) and Priestley's *Johnson over Jordan* (1939). John Clements staged a two-year season of classical plays from 1955, while subsequent productions included Ustinov's *Photo Finish* (1962) and the musical *Pickwick* (1963); actors who have appeared there include Emlyn Williams, the Redgraves, Paul Scofield, and Laurence Olivier. The theatre was converted into twin cinemas in 1970.

Savoy Theatre A theatre in the Strand in London, built specifically for the production of Gilbert and Sullivan comic operas. It was financed by Richard D'Oyly Carte and was the first theatre in the world to be lit by electricity. It opened in 1881 with *Patience*, which was followed by *Iolanthe* (1882), *Princess Ida*, *The Sorcerer*, and *Trial by Jury* (all 1884), THE MIKADO (1885), *Ruddigore* (1887), *The Yeomen of the Guard* (1888), *The Gondoliers* (1889), and *Utopia Limited* (1893). After a row over the expenses incurred for *The Gondoliers*, Gilbert and Sullivan became estranged and their last joint production, *The Grand Duke* (1896), was a failure. Subsequently the theatre was run by J E Vedrenne and Harley Granville-Barker, who presented a series of Shakespeare plays. Henry Brodribb Irving was lessee for nine years from 1910, playing Hamlet there in 1917. Later successes included Sherriff's *Journey's End* (1929) and, after the theatre was converted into a two-tier auditorium, revivals of Gilbert and Sullivan. A wartime success was *The Man Who Came to Dinner* (1941), with Robert Morley; subsequent triumphs have included William Douglas-Home's long-running comedy *The Secretary Bird* (1968), Michael Frayn's *Noises Off* (1982), and the Royal Shakespeare Company's *Kiss Me Kate* (1988). The theatre was badly damaged by fire in 1990 but has since been restored.

Scala, Flamineo (fl. 1600–21) Italian actor-manager, popularly known as **Flavio**. He was an important member of the Confidenti *commedia dell'arte* group and was the author of a collection of scenarios entitled *Il teatro delle favole rappresentative* (1611).

Scala Theatre A theatre in Tottenham Street, London, which opened as the **King's Concert Rooms** in 1772. Converted into a theatre in 1802, it underwent several changes of management and name during the first half of the 19th century, becoming in turn the **Tottenham Street Theatre**, the **Regency**, the **West London**, and the **Fitzroy Theatre**. A rival of the patent theatres, its reputation had sunk so low that it was widely referred to as the **Dust Hole**, when Marie Wilton (later, Lady Bancroft) took it over in 1865. She renamed it the Prince of Wales's and transformed it into one of the most respected theatres in town, introducing the new CUP-AND-SAUCER DRAMAS of T W Robertson. The theatre did not long survive the Bancrofts' departure in 1880 after 14 successful years. It was ultimately demolished and replaced by a new Scala Theatre which opened in 1905 with J R Fyffe's *The Conquerors*. In spite of one or two respectable runs, including W G Wills's *A Royal Divorce* (1906) and Matheson Lang in *The Purple Mask* (1918), the theatre had little success. It was often given over to amateur shows, dance exhibitions, and films. After World War II, occasional seasons were staged by the D'Oyly Carte opera company and it was used for Christmas revivals of *Peter Pan*. It was demolished in 1972.

Scammacca, Ortensio (1562–1648) Italian playwright, one of the leading writers of Jesuit drama in Italy. He was the author of about 50 plays in the tradition, in all of which the religious content is paramount.

Scamozzi, Vincenzo (1552–1616) Italian architect, whose numerous influential buildings included several theatres. He was a pupil of Andrea Palladio and completed work on the Teatro Olimpico in Vicenza following Palladio's death in 1580; other important theatres included the court theatre at Sabbioneta (1588–90) with its horseshoe-shaped auditorium. ·

Scapino A character of the *commedia dell'arte*, one of the *zanni*. A cowardly rogue, Scapino (conventionally dressed in green and white) was first played by Gabrielli; the character later evolved into the cunning and unprincipled Scapin of the Comédie-Italienne, as portrayed in Molière's *Les Fourberies de Scapin* (1671).

Scaramuccia A character of the *commedia dell'arte*, one of the *zanni*. Initially similar to Il CAPITANO in character, Scaramuccia was transformed by Fiorillo (who played the role without a mask and dressed in black) into the comic valet Scaramouche of the Comédie-Italienne.

Scarron, Paul (1610–60) French playwright, poet, and novelist, born in Paris. Partially paralysed by rheumatism, he began writing for the theatre in 1643, producing two farces for Jodelet and other plays inspired by Spanish works. In 1652 he married Françoise d'Aubigné (Madame de MAINTENON), the future wife of Louis XIV. Scarron is also remembered for his burlesques, notably *Virgile travesti* (1648), and for the unfinished *Le Roman comique*, a novel based on the adventures of a company of strolling players.

scenario A synopsis of a dramatic work, first used of the loose plots of the *commedia dell'arte*. It is now more commonly used of musical entertainments or films.

scene A subdivision of an act, usually comprising a distinct episode in a single setting.

scene dock A part of the backstage area of a theatre used for the storage of scenery. Sometimes known in Britain as a **scene bay**, it is usually situated close to the stage itself.

scene of releave (*or* scene of relief) A scenic view, usually suggesting three dimensions, revealed by the opening of a pair of shutters. A feature of the Restoration stage, the illusion was achieved by extensive use of cut-out scenery.

scenery Any of the various flats, cloths, and other scenic pieces used to suggest a particular location or context on stage. Although there were a few isolated examples of the use of scenery in classical drama (*see periaktoi*) and during the Middle Ages (with elaborate 'mansions' constructed to represent the entrance to hell, for instance), it was not until the Renaissance that it became an essential element in dramatic production. Such distinguished theatrical designers as Peruzzi, Serlio, and Scamozzi in this period introduced wings, the use of perspective designs, and the distinction between sets suitable for different types of drama.

The 18th century saw a preference for neoclassical designs as well as a growing taste for naturalistic and historically accurate scenery; this culminated in the 19th century in elaborately realistic sets and props and the use of the BOX SET. Scenery designs in the last hundred years have ranged from the completely naturalistic to the entirely abstract, but have often favoured economical and intimate sets rather than spectacular ones. Notable designers over the years have included Inigo Jones, Giacomo Torelli, the Bibiena family, David Garrick, Philippe James de Loutherbourg, William Capon, André Antoine, Paul Fort, Lugné-Poë, Stanislavsky, Adolphe Appia, Gordon Craig, Max Reinhardt, Beerbohm Tree, Cecil Beaton, Sean Kenny, and Ralph Koltai.

Schechner, Richard (1934–) US director and critic, who worked with the East End Players in Provincetown, Massachusetts and the Free Southern Theatre before founding the PERFORMANCE GROUP in 1967. For them he produced and directed such plays as *Dionysus in '69* (1968), adapted from Euripides, *Macbeth* (1969), and Brecht's *Mother Courage and Her Children* (1975). He resigned as head of the group in 1970, since when he has written much on drama theory. He has been editor of *The Tulane Drama Review* and its successor, *The Drama Review*, since 1962 and is the founder of the performance studies department at New York University.

Schelandre, Jean de (c. 1584–1635) French playwright and poet, born into a noble Protestant family of German origin. He is remembered for the tragedy *Tyre et Sidon*, which first appeared in 1608 and was remodelled 20 years later as a tragicomedy, with a celebrated preface by François Ogier.

Schicksaltragödie A German theatrical genre, also known as **fate drama**, which became popular in the early 19th century. Its distinguishing feature was the inevitability of the central character's downfall at the hands of destiny, conventionally through his killing his own father or committing some other similar crime. Writers of the genre included Zacharias Werner and Franz Grillparzer.

Schiller, Friedrich von (1759–1805) German playwright and poet, a major figure of the German Romantic movement. After the success of the anonymously published play DIE RÄUBER (The Robbers), a major contribution to the STURM UND DRANG movement, he deserted from the army and became resident playwright at the theatre in Mannheim. He then concentrated for a time on historical and academic writing but was persuaded by his friend Goethe (who first met him in Weimar in 1787) to embark upon a series of historical tragedies, notably the WALLENSTEIN trilogy. Goethe produced several of these last plays, written before Schiller's early death from tuberculosis; all his works were translated into English at an early stage. His plays were remarkable for their lyrical beauty, while his last works anticipated the development of Expressionism.

Principal works:
  Die Räuber: 1782.
  Kabale und Liebe: 1784.
  DON CARLOS, INFANT VON SPANIEN: 1787.
  Wallenstein: 1800.
  MARIA STUART: 1801.
  Die Jungfrau von Orleans: 1801.
  Die Braut von Messina: 1803.
  WILHELM TELL: 1804.

Schiller, Leon (Leon de Schildenfeld; 1887–1954) Polish director and designer, who became a leading figure in the Polish theatre after World War I. Influenced by both Gordon Craig and Stanislavsky, he founded the celebrated left-wing Bogusławski Theatre in 1924, directing there such plays as Krasiński's *The Undivine Comedy* (1926). In 1930 a production of Brecht's *Die Dreigroschenoper* (1930) led to the closing down of his theatre. Subsequently he worked in Lwów and in Sofia, was interned in Auschwitz (until 1941), and revived liturgical dramas from the Middle Ages. After World War II he took over at Łódź, where his productions included *The Tempest*.

Schlegel, Johann Elias von (1719–49) German playwright and diplomat, who played an important role in the development of a German national theatre. His early comedies were based on the French tradition, while such tragedies as *Hermann* (1743) reflected the influence of his teacher Gottsched; later, however, he revealed his admiration for Shakespeare in such essays as *Vergleichung Shakespeares und Andreas Gryphius* (1741).

His nephew, **August Wilhelm von Schlegel** (1767–1845), was a critic and the author of several plays, an early history of the stage, and still-performed adaptations of Shakespeare, Dante, Cervantes, and Calderón. With Tieck he established a model for subsequent Romantic criticism.

Schmeltzl, Wolfgang (c. 1505–c. 1557) Viennese playwright and schoolteacher, author of several plays on biblical themes. Such works as *Der verlorene Sohn* (The Prodigal Son; 1540), *Judith* (1542), and *David and Goliath* (1545), were influenced by Paul Rebhun and were all written in the vernacular.

Schnitzler, Arthur (1862–1931) Austrian playwright and novelist, whose plays analysed the decadence of Viennese society in the 1890s. Under the fashionable influence of Freud, Schnitzler explored the problems connected with anti-Semitism, honour, marriage, love, and ultimately sex. The flirtatious young man and the sweet naive girl are recurrent figures throughout his drama, being introduced in his first work, *Anatol* (1893) – a series of seven dramatic sketches – and reappearing in *Liebelei* (1896). REIGEN caused a sensation with its depiction of ten casual sexual exchanges and was unperformed from 1921 to 1982. Of his historical plays, *Der grüne Kakadu* is set during the French Revolution and *Der Schleier der Beatrice* describes an Italian Renaissance city on the night before its downfall.

Principal works:

Anatol: 1893.

Liebelei: 1895.

Freiwild: 1896.

Das Vermächtnis: 1897.

Der grüne Kakadu: 1899; translated as *The Green Cockatoo*.

Der Schleier der Beatrice: 1899.

Reigen: 1900; translated as *The Round Dance*; filmed as *La Ronde*.

Der einsame Weg: 1903; translated as *The Lonely Way*.

Zurischenspiel: 1904.

Das Weite Land: 1911; translated as *Undiscovered Country*.

Professor Bernhardi: 1912.

Schönberg, Claude Michel *See* Boublil, Alain.

Schönemann, Johann Friedrich (1704–82) German actor and director, in whose company, formed in 1740, several major German theatrical figures appeared. He established his own troupe after performing in Carolina Neuber's company and was at his best in comedy; members of his celebrated company included Ackermann, Ekhof (who took control after Schönemann ruined himself in horsedealing), and Sophia Schröder.

Schönherr, Karl (1867–1943) Austrian playwright, poet, and short-story writer, whose plays depict the problems faced by the peasant classes. His best-known naturalistic plays, written in dialect, are *Erde* (Earth; 1907), *Glaube and Heimat* (Faith and Homeland; 1910), and *Der Kampf* (1920). Many of his works were first performed at the Burgtheater and Deutsches Volkstheater in Vienna.

school drama Plays written for performance by pupils at colleges and schools throughout Europe during the Renaissance. Although many of the plays were written in Latin, including most of those produced at Jesuit colleges (*see* Jesuit drama), the tradition also encompassed plays in the vernacular. English examples included *Ralph Roister Doister*, presented at Eton or Winchester, and *Gammer Gurton's Needle*, given at Christ's College, Cambridge. *See also* Westminster Play.

School for Scandal, The A classic comedy by SHERIDAN. First performance: 1777. Joseph Surface, abetted by Lady Sneerwell, circulates malign rumours about his brother, Charles, while himself attempting to seduce the young ward of Sir Peter Teazle. Their uncle, returning from abroad, disguises himself to test the characters of his nephews. The play has enjoyed numerous successful revivals.

School for Wives, The (*L'École des femmes*) A comedy by MOLIÈRE. First performance: Paris, 1662. Agnès is raised by Arnolphe, who hopes to marry her but fears a clever wife. Horace falls in love with Agnès and confides in Arnolphe; the latter's subsequent attempts to prevent the union of the young lovers end in failure. *See also Critique de l'école des femmes, La*; *Impromptu de Versailles, L'*.

Schouwburg *See* Campen, Jacob van.

Schreyvogel, Josef (1768–1832) Austrian director, who became the leading theatrical figure in Vienna in 1814. As director of the Burgtheater, the Kärntnertor, and the Theater an der Wien, he staged a wide variety of plays and championed the works of Grillparzer.

Schröder, Sophia Carlotta (Sophia Carlotta Biereichel; 1714–92)   German actress, who became a leading actress with Ackermann's company after first achieving fame with Schönemann's troupe. Ackermann himself became her second husband and she retained financial control of the company after his death.

By her first marriage she was the mother of the actor and director **Friedrich Ludwig Schröder** (1744–1816), who began his career as a child in Ackermann's company. He was trained by Ekhof, whose roles he inherited, and later excelled in comedy at Ackermann's National Theatre in Hamburg. Although he was constantly at loggerheads with his mother over the financial control of the company, he went on to present influential productions of Goethe, Lessing, and Shakespeare. He continued to renovate conventional German acting practices after moving to the Burgtheater in Vienna in 1782. Later he took over Ackermann's old company once more, producing minor works by Iffland and Kotzebue.

Schröder, Sophie (1781–1868) Austrian actress, who became a leading performer noted for the grace and restraint of her acting at the Burgtheater in Vienna. Directed by Schreyvogel, she excelled in plays by Goethe, Kleist, Schiller, Shakespeare, and Grillparzer, most notably in the title role of his *Sappho* (1818).

Schuch, Franz (c. 1716–64) Austrian actor, who was much admired for his refined comic interpretations. He led his own company of travelling players; members of his troupe included Johann Brandes, Ekhof, and Döbbelin, who settled the company in Berlin after Schuch's death.

Schuster, Ignaz (1779–1835) Austrian actor, who became a highly popular comic performer with the Leopoldstädter company in Vienna, first appearing with it in 1801. He established his reputation in 1813 as Staberl in *Die Bürger in Wien* by Bäuerle; subsequently he was especially successful as the same character in pieces written by Karl Carl.

Schwartz, Evgenyi Lvovich *See* Shwartz, Evgenyi Lvovich.

Schwartz, Maurice (1889–1960) Jewish actor and director, born in Russia, who began his professional career in New York. Following success with the plays of Peretz Hirschbein and Sholom Aleichem, he toured Europe and later opened a shortlived theatre specifically for Jewish plays in New York. In 1926 he opened the more successful Yiddish Art Theatre, which became a national focus for Jewish drama; the company later visited South America and Palestine and eventually worked (1959) in Israel.

Science Fiction Theatre of Liverpool *See* Campbell, Ken.

sciopticon *See* projector.

scissor cross *See* stage direction.

Scofield, Paul (1922–) British actor, who made his debut at the Westminster Theatre in 1940. Subsequently he played leading roles in repertory at Birmingham before joining Barry Jackson's Stratford-on-Avon company in 1946. In 1955 he led the company on a tour of the USSR, playing Hamlet; later successes at Stratford included Peter Brook's *King Lear* (1962) and *The Government Inspector* (1965). At the Globe Theatre he scored an outstanding success in Anouilh's *Ring Round the Moon* (1950); since then he has been highly praised in parts ranging from the seedy agent in the musical *Expresso Bongo* (1958) to Chekhov's Vanya (1970), Prospero (1974), and Salieri in Shaffer's *Amadeus* at the National Theatre (1979). In 1986 he gave a witty performance in Herb Gardner's *I'm Not Rappaport* at the Apollo Theatre. After a lengthy absence from the stage he made a triumphant return in the title role of Ibsen's *John Gabriel Borkman* (1996) at the ROYAL NATIONAL THEATRE.

Scott, Clement William (1841–1904) British theatre critic, who, as drama critic for the *Daily Telegraph* (1872–97) and editor of *The Theatre* (1877–97), tried to prevent the development of the new drama of Ibsen and others. His own attempts at playwriting were of little account, with the exception of *Diplomacy* (1878), which he adapted from Sardou in collaboration with B C Stephenson.

Scott, Sir Walter (1771–1832) Scottish novelist, poet, and playwright, whose novels inspired numerous stage adaptations. His own dramatic works, none of which were especially remarkable, included *The House of Aspen*, produced at the Surrey Theatre in 1829, and *Auchindrane*, produced at Edinburgh in 1830. Of the many stage interpretations of his novels and narrative poems, some of the more important were those of *Rob Roy* (several versions), *The Heart of Midlothian* (used by Dion Boucicault for *The Trial of Effie Deans*), *Montrose* (adapted by Thomas Dibdin), *Ivanhoe*, *Kenilworth*, and *Quentin Durward*. Scott himself collaborated on a Covent Garden production of *Guy Mannering* in 1816; other works, notably *The Bride of Lammermoor*, were turned into grand operas.

Scottish National Players A Scottish theatre company founded in Glasgow in 1921. The company toured during the summer to areas of Scotland where drama was rarely presented and encouraged native Scottish writing; writers whose plays were performed by the group before it was broken up in 1947 included John Brandane, James Bridie, and Robert Kemp. In 1926 and 1927 it was directed by Tyrone Guthrie.

Scottish Roscius *See* Johnston, Henry Erskine.

Scribe, (Augustin-)Eugène (1791–1861) French playwright, whose skilfully constructed plays were characteristic of the WELL-MADE PLAY. His output consists of some 350 works, including vaudevilles, comedies, historical dramas, and opera libretti, many of which were written in collaboration. Scribe began writing for the theatre in 1810 and made his name with the vaudeville *Encore une nuit de la Garde Nationale*. The popularity of his works was immense but shortlived, their superficial characterization and contrived plots being widely disparaged by the latter half of the 19th century. *Adrienne Lecouvoeur* was his most successful play and provided Rachel, Bernhardt, and others with a much acclaimed role.

Principal works:

Encore une nuit de la Garde Nationale: 1815.
L'Ours et le pacha: 1820.
Le Mariage de raison: 1826.
Bertrand et Raton: 1833.
Le Verre d'eau: 1840; translated as *A Glass of Water; or, Great Events from Trifling Causes Spring* (or *The Queen's Favourite*).
Une chaîne: 1841.
Adrienne Lecouvreur: 1849.

scrim *See* gauze.

scruto Thin strips of wood attached to a piece of canvas and used to conceal a trap or an opening in the scenery through which an actor may make an unexpected entrance.

Scudéry, Georges de (1601–67) French playwright, who was the brother of the writer Madeleine de Scudéry, many of whose novels were published in his name. Having abandoned a military career, he produced numerous tragedies, tragicomedies, and comedies characterized by high rhetoric and inventive plots. They include *La Mort de César* (1635), *Le Trompeur puni* (1631), *La Comédie des comédiens* (1635), which depicted Montdory's company, and *L'Amour tyrannique* (1638). Scudéry was also one of Pierre Corneille's adversaries in the *'querelle du Cid'*.

Seagull, The A play by Anton CHEKHOV. First performance: Alexandrinsky Theatre, St Petersburg, 1896. The first performance was a disaster, the actors failing to come to terms with the play's revolutionary naturalism; when, however, this story of disappointed love, aspiring artists, and suicide was revived at Stanislavsky's Moscow Art Theatre in 1898 it created a sensation and established Chekhov's reputation.

sea row *See* groundrow.

Seattle Repertory Theatre A company in Seattle, the most important in the US North-West; it was founded in 1969 and housed in a theatre built in 1963 for an earlier troupe. The current company is very active in the community and won a Tony Award in 1990.

Sebastian, Mihail (1907–45) Romanian playwright and novelist, whose promising career was cut short by his death in a road accident. His best play was the brilliant comedy *Ultima oră* (Stop Press; 1948); others include *Jocul-de-a-vacanţa* (Holiday Games; 1938), and *Steaua fără nume* (The Nameless Star; 1944).

Second City A Chicago company that specializes in improvisational theatre, founded in 1959; it is the best known such company in the US. Its comedic style has been highly influential, with many actors who played there going on to fame in television and film. A second company in Toronto has also had great success.

Second Mrs Tanqueray, The A play by PINERO. First performance: 1893. Mrs Tanqueray reveals that she has had an affair with the man whom her stepdaughter is intending to marry, thus sacrificing her own good name in order to protect the girl. Mrs Patrick Campbell was the first to play the central role.

Sedaine, Michel-Jean (1719–97) French playwright, who is remembered for his masterpiece *Le Philosophe sans le savoir* (1765; translated as *The Duel*, 1772), an excellent example of the *drame bourgeois*. Sedaine began writing in 1750, having previously worked as a stonemason. His other works consist of libretti for comic operas, notably *Le Roi et le fermier* (1762), *Rose et Colas* (1764), and *Richard Coeur de Lion* (1784), and the comedy *La Gageure imprévue* (1768).

Sedley, Sir Charles (c. 1639–1701) English playwright and man of letters, whose comedy of manners *The Mulberry Garden* (1668) was influenced by both Molière and Etherege. His *Bellamira; or, the Mistress* (1687), based on Terence's *Eunuchus*, is also worthy of note.

Sedley-Smith, William Henry (1806–72) US actor, manager, and playwright, born in Wales, who became a leading performer in light comedy on the US stage. He established his reputation with his melodrama *The Drunkard; or, the Fallen Sword*, which was first presented at the Boston Museum (where he was stage manager from 1843 to 1860) in 1844. A tract against the evils of drink, it enjoyed long runs in the 1850s; after Sedley-Smith's death it was revived as a comic parody of melodrama, running in Los Angeles from 1933 to 1959.

Segelcke, Tore (1901–79) Norwegian actress, who became a leading performer in the plays of Ibsen at the Nationaltheatret, where she first appeared in 1928. Earlier in her career she was seen at the Norske Theatret in Oslo (1921) and in Bergen (1924–28); her finest roles included Nora in *A Doll's House* as well as parts in the plays of Shakespeare and contemporary playwrights.

segment stage A method of staging based on the use of one or more large wedge-shaped rostra pivoted on castor wheels at the upstage apex.

Selwyn Theatre *See* American Airlines Theatre.

Semenova, Ekaterina Semenovna (1786–1849) Russian actress, who was noted for her beautiful voice, being regarded as the finest Russian actress of her day. She was trained by Dmitrevsky and excelled in the tragedies of Ozerov, Racine, Shakespeare, and Schiller.

Seneca, Lucius Annaeus (c. 4 BC–65 AD) Roman playwright, statesman, and philosopher, whose nine extant tragedies are the only surviving drama of the period of the Roman Empire. His plays were written to be read and present certain difficulties when they are staged; unlike earlier Roman works, however, they were original plays and not adaptations of Greek plots, despite their indebtedness to Euripides and Aeschylus. Notable for the brutality of some scenes – significantly Seneca was Nero's tutor for a time – and usually based upon the Stoic concept of the conflict between passion and reason, the tragedies were much admired during the Renaissance. In England they had a profound influence on early revenge tragedy, finding echoes in the plays of Shakespeare, Jonson, Webster, and others. Typical features include the use of stereotyped characters, supernatural elements, and melodramatic plots. Other writings included the political satire *The Pumpkinification of the Divine Claudius*. After Seneca's suicide under pressure from Nero little of any worth was written for the Roman stage.

Principal dramatic works (dates unknown):
  Agamemnon.
  Hercules Furens.
  Hercules Oetaeus.
  Medea.
  Oedipus.
  Phaedra.
  Phoenissae.
  Thyestes.
  Troades.

sentimental comedy A form of moralizing comedy in which there is a strong element of pathos. Especially popular with audiences of the 17th and 18th centuries, the genre was epitomized in England by the plays of Steele and in France by the COMÉDIE LARMOYANTE.

Separate Tables A play by Terence RATTIGAN. First performance: London, 1954. Subdivided as *Table by the Window* and *Table Number Seven*, it is set in the dining-room of a small provincial hotel. The play explores the problems faced by individual guests in terms of their emotional inadequacy and the isolation sometimes caused by social conventions.

Serban, Andrei (1943–) Romanian director. After leaving Romania in the 1960s he worked under Peter Brook before taking up a position at La Mama in New York. He remained in the US for the next 20 years, winning particular acclaim for such productions as the musical *The Umbrellas of Cherbourg* (1979) and plays by Chekhov. During this period he worked extensively at the American Repertory Theatre in Cambridge, Massachusetts, being especially known for avant-garde productions of the classics. After the Romanian revolution he returned to his homeland to become general manager of the National Theatre in Bucharest (1990–93).

Serious Money A play by Caryl CHURCHILL. First performance: Royal Court Theatre, London, 1987. The play is set in the City of London during the boom year that followed deregulation in 1986. Although intended as a Jonsonian satire on the crazed greed of the times, the play found a keen following among City workers, with many firms making block bookings for their staff. It transferred successfully to the West End and subsequently ran on Broadway.

Serjeant Musgrave's Dance A play by John ARDEN. First performance: Royal Court Theatre, London, 1959. Set in a northern mining town in the late 19th century, the play follows an army deserter's attempts to exact revenge for the death of a fellow-soldier; the language of the play is remarkable for its combination of heightened prose and ballad forms.

Serlio, Sebastiano (1475–1554) Italian architect and artist, who designed much influential perspective scenery. A pupil of Peruzzi and an admirer of Vitruvius, he detailed his theories concerning scenery and lighting in his treatise *The Second Book of Architecture* (1545), in which he distinguished between sets suitable for tragedy, comedy, and fantasy.

Serrau, Jean-Marie (1915–73) French actor and director, who became famous for his productions of important new works for the stage in the 1950s and 1960s. As well as the plays of Brecht, he championed the Theatre of the Absurd and the avant-garde movement, presenting many experimental works at his own Théâtre de Babylone and Théâtre de la Tempête and elsewhere; other productions included several notable works by little-known African playwrights.

Servandony, Jean-Nicolas (1695–1766) French architect, noted for his early neo-classical theatre designs. He was trained in Rome but later worked on theatres and designed scenery throughout Europe.

Sesame *See* Radius.

set A collective term for the scenery, props, and lighting used to suggest the location or context of a play. *See also* box set; curtain set.

set piece A flat shaped to represent a particular object on stage, usually standing by itself; the term is also used of BUILT STUFF.

Settle, Elkanah (1648–1724) English playwright, whose early works were drolls staged at various London fairs. When his tragedy *Cambyses, King of Persia* was successfully produced by Betterton at Lincoln's Inn Fields in 1666, he went on to write further bombastic heroic dramas, notably *The Empress of Morocco* (1671), which threatened to overshadow Dryden. It was also notable for being the first playtext to be published with scenic engravings. His later plays, however, failed to attract the same success.

Seven Against Thebes A tragedy by AESCHYLUS. First performance: Athens, 469 BC. Set in Thebes during an attack by a neighbouring state, it is thought to be the third part of a tetralogy, the other parts of which have not survived.

7:84 Theatre Company A British theatre group founded in 1971 by the playwright John MCGRATH to present politically orientated drama. The name of the group was derived from the statistic that 84 per cent of Britain's wealth is reputedly owned by seven per cent of the population. Plays presented by the company have included many by McGrath himself as well as works by John Arden and David Edgar.

Seyler, Abel (1730–1801) German theatre manager, who inherited the leadership of Ackermann's company in Hamburg and later ran his own travelling company. He was married to the actress Sophie HENSEL and his career suffered greatly from the effects her evil temper had upon various hosts and patrons; he did, however, enjoy periods of success when Ekhof joined his troupe and when working under Iffland at Gotha.

Seyler, Athene (1889–1990) British actress, who won the Bancroft Gold Medal at RADA in 1908 and made her first professional appearance a year later. Her sharp sense of comedy and style suited her perfectly to such parts as Cynthia in Congreve's *The Double Dealer* (1916), Lady Fidget in Wycherley's *The Country Wife* (1924), and roles in other Restoration comedies as well as those of Shakespeare and Wilde. In 1937 she played Prossy in Shaw's *Candida* and took part in Gielgud's Queen's Theatre season, playing Mrs Candour in Sheridan's *The School for Scandal*. Subsequent successes included Vita Louise in Mary Chase's *Harvey* (1949) and Martha Brewster in Joseph Kesselring's *Arsenic and Old Lace* (1966), after which she retired from the stage. Her husband was the actor Nicholas Thomas HANNEN.

Seymour, William Gorman (1855–1933) US actor. The son of theatrical parents, he made his debut as a child of two and subsequently appeared alongside most of the leading performers of the day, including Edwin Booth and Joseph Jefferson. In 1871 he joined the Globe Theatre in Boston, where he appeared with Edwin Forrest; subsequently he also managed several theatres and worked under Charles Frohman. His personal library eventually formed the basis of a theatre collection at Princeton University.

Seyrig, Delphine (1932–90) French actress, born in Lebanon, who became one of the leading performers on the Paris stage. Acclaimed for her subtle use of movement as well as for her distinctive voice, she first attracted attention as Nina in Chekhov's *The Seagull*; subsequently she triumphed in plays by Pinter, Pirandello, Stoppard, and Turgenev among many others. She appeared in several well-known French films of the 1960s and 1970s.

Shadow of a Gunman, The The first play by Sean O'CASEY. First performance: Abbey Theatre, Dublin, 1923. The central character, Donal Davoreen, is caught up in the conflict between Irish Republicans and the British army; the play explores ideas of patriotism, deception, and self-knowledge.

shadow play A form of puppet theatre (usually silent) in which the audience watch the shadows cast on a screen by two-dimensional puppets. Although usually associated with the theatre of the Far East (especially that of Java and Bali), the tradition has enjoyed periods of popularity in Western Europe – notably in Greece, where many plays featured the comic character Karaghiozis, and in 18th-century France, where it was known as ***ombres chinoises***. In England a form of shadow play called the **galanty show** was popular for a time in the late 19th century in conjunction with PUNCH AND JUDY shows. Countries with a continuing tradition of shadow theatre include Turkey and India. Figures are mounted on rods or manoeuvred by wires.

Shadwell, Thomas (c. 1642–92) English playwright, a rival of John Dryden whom he succeeded as poet laureate in 1689. His plays include the comedies *The Sullen Lovers* (1668), which was based upon Molière's *Les Fâcheux*, *Epsom Wells* (1672), which was influenced by Jonson, *The Virtuoso* (1676), which satirized the Royal Society, *The Squire of Alsatia* (1688), and *Bury Fair* (1689). He also adapted Shakespeare's drama *The Tempest* as the opera *The Enchanted Island* (1674) and *Timon of Athens* as *The Man-Hater* (1678).

Shaffer, Sir Peter (1926–) British playwright, who has won acclaim for dramas ranging from traditional farce to intense psychological studies. He established his reputation with FIVE FINGER EXERCISE (1958), which was followed by *The Private Ear* and *The Public Eye*, two one-act plays staged as a double bill in 1962. The ambitious historical epic THE ROYAL HUNT OF THE SUN (1964) was well received, as was the farce *Black Comedy* (1965), in which the characters behave as if they are in an unlit room. His other works have included the one-act play *White Lies* (1967), the psychological drama EQUUS (1973), the highly successful AMADEUS (1979), the comedy *Lettice and Lovage* (1988), and THE GIFT OF THE GORGON (1992).

His brother, **Anthony Shaffer** (1926–), also enjoyed considerable success with the ingenious thriller SLEUTH (1970), although such later plays as *Murderer* (1975) attracted less attention.

Shaftesbury Theatre The first theatre to be built on London's Shaftesbury Avenue. It opened in 1888 with *As You Like It*, Johnston Forbes-Robertson playing Orlando. None of the early productions, which included Italian operas, were successful, but the theatre's fortunes were restored with the introduction to England of the first US musical comedy, *The Belle of New York*, which opened in 1898. Other musical comedies followed, including the all-Black cast play *In Dahomey* (1903). In 1909 Cicely Courtneidge appeared in *The Arcadians*, a musical play which ran for over two years. Subsequently musical comedy alternated with opera, farce, and light comedy until the theatre was destroyed by bombs in 1941.

A second **Shaftesbury Theatre** opened as the New Prince's Theatre (later simply the **Prince's Theatre**) at the northern end of Shaftesbury Avenue in 1911. In 1916 Seymour Hicks took over and presented musicals and light opera – a policy that was continued from 1919 by C B Cochran, who forged an association between the theatre and the D'Oyly Carte Opera Company that was to last for over 40 years. Plays were interspersed with ballet and opera through the 1920s and 1930s and included a notable performance by Sarah Bernhardt in Louis Verneuil's *Daniel* (1921), Sybil Thorndike and Henry Ainley in *Macbeth* (1926), and Gershwin's *Funny Face* (1928), starring the Astaires and Leslie Henson. Less frequent successes after World War II included appearances by Maurice Chevalier (1952) and *Antony and Cleopatra* (1953), starring Michael Redgrave and Peggy Ashcroft. In 1962 the theatre was refurbished, reopening as the Shaftesbury Theatre with the musical *How to Succeed in Business Without Really Trying*. This success was later consolidated by *Hair* (1968), which ran for nearly 2000 performances until part of the ceiling collapsed in 1973. Public outcry saved the theatre from redevelopment and in 1983 Ray Cooney's Theatre of Comedy company purchased it and presented the first of a series of farces. Productions by outside companies continued to appear there, notably the Sondheim musical *Follies*, which opened in l987. Recent productions have included the award-winning musicals *The Kiss of the Spider Woman* (1992) and *Rent* (1998).

Shakespeare, William (1564–1616) English playwright and actor, author of two long narrative poems, the most famous of all sonnet sequences, and 37 plays, generally considered the finest body of work in world drama. Little is known about his life, which has consequently been the subject of much conjecture. He was born in Stratford-on-Avon and married Anne Hathaway in 1582; a daughter, Susanna, was born in 1583 and twins, Hamnet (d. 1596) and Judith, in 1585. In 1588 Shakespeare moved to London and became well-known as an actor; by 1592 he had begun to write for the stage, although the dating of his early plays is notoriously imprecise. By 1595 he was a shareholder in the Chamberlain's Men, who later became the King's Men; he finally retired to Stratford a wealthy man in 1610.

The success of his first historical tetralogy (written 1590–92) quickly established his reputation and encouraged him to diversify into other types of drama. His initial experiments with comedy (1593–95), which ranged from the broad farce of THE COMEDY OF ERRORS to the courtly LOVE'S LABOUR'S LOST, culminated in such masterpieces as A MIDSUMMER'S NIGHT'S DREAM and TWELFTH NIGHT, while his growing interest in characterization found full expression in the first of his major tragedies, ROMEO AND JULIET, and the two parts of HENRY IV. The series (1600–06) of tragedies that followed, notably HAMLET, OTHELLO, KING LEAR, and MACBETH, are usually considered the summit of his achievement and have remained in performance all over the world ever since; they provide many of the most challenging and rewarding roles in the theatre. The comedies that Shakespeare wrote during this period, notably MEASURE FOR MEASURE, show a similar preoccupation with the darker side of human nature. The final phase in Shakespeare's writing (from about 1608) produced the so-called 'last plays' or 'romances'. These sophisticated dramas, culminating in the author's farewell to the stage in THE TEMPEST, reflect a more serene view of life and unite many of the disparate elements of the plays that preceded them.

The first comprehensive collection of Shakespeare's plays was published in 1623 and is known as the First Folio; it also includes an invaluable list of contemporary performers who appeared in them.

Principal dramatic works with dates of composition:

HENRY VI: c. 1590–92 (in three parts).

RICHARD III: c. 1592–93.

The Comedy of Errors: c. 1592–93.

TITUS ANDRONICUS: c. 1592–93.

THE TWO GENTLEMEN OF VERONA: c. 1592–93.

THE TAMING OF THE SHREW: c. 1593.

Love's Labour's Lost: c. 1594–95.

Romeo and Juliet: c. 1595.

RICHARD II: c. 1595.

A Midsummer Night's Dream: c. 1595.

KING JOHN: c. 1596.

THE MERCHANT OF VENICE: c. 1596–97.

Henry IV: c. 1597–98 (in two parts).

THE MERRY WIVES OF WINDSOR: C. 1597.

MUCH ADO ABOUT NOTHING: C. 1598–99.

HENRY V: C. 1599.

JULIUS CAESAR: C. 1599.

AS YOU LIKE IT: C. 1599–1600.

Twelfth Night: c. 1600–01.

Hamlet: c. 1600–01.

TROILUS AND CRESSIDA: C. 1602.

Othello: c. 1603.

ALL'S WELL THAT ENDS WELL: C. 1603–04.

Measure for Measure: c. 1604.

King Lear: c. 1605.

Macbeth: c. 1605–06.

TIMON OF ATHENS: C. 1605–07.

ANTONY AND CLEOPATRA: C. 1606–07.

CORIOLANUS: C. 1607–08.

PERICLES: C. 1608.

CYMBELINE: C.1610.

THE WINTER'S TALE: C. 1610–11.

The Tempest: c. 1611.

HENRY VIII: C. 1613 (with Fletcher).

THE TWO NOBLE KINSMEN: C. 1613–14 (with Fletcher).

Shakespeare Memorial Theatre A theatre at Stratford-on-Avon. The first build-ing was built by public subscription in 1879, on land beside the river given by Charles Edward Flower, a member of the local brewing family. A controversial Gothic-style redbrick building criticized for its somewhat bleak interior, it was the home of the annual festival of Shakespeare's plays from 1886 to 1926. It was then de-stroyed by fire and the current theatre, designed by Elizabeth Scott, was opened on the same site in 1932 (again with help from the Flower family). Despite fresh criti-cism of its design, the theatre grew in prominence under successive directors, in-cluding W Bridges-Adams (who increased the month-long season to five months), Ben Iden Payne, Barry Jackson (who encouraged the use of a large team of directors and brought in new young actors of the calibre of Paul Scofield and Peter Brook to Stratford), and Anthony Quayle, whose productions featured such stars as John Gielgud and Peggy Ashcroft. Glen Byam Shaw succeeded Quayle in 1956, oversee-ing further successful international tours and consolidating the theatre's reputation. In 1961 Peter Hall took over, forming the Royal Shakespeare Company and renam-ing the theatre itself the ROYAL SHAKESPEARE THEATRE.

Shakhovsky, Alexander Alexandrovich (1777–1846) Russian playwright, who is credited with having founded the vaudeville tradition in Russia. The first of his witty entertainments of the type was presented at the Hermitage Theatre in 1795 and in-fluenced many notable contemporary writers.

Shank, John (d. 1636) English actor, listed in the First Folio as an actor in Shake-speare's plays. He is thought to have succeeded Armin as chief clown with the King's Men. He played in several of Beaumont and Fletcher's works and was Hilario in Massinger's *The Picture*. Latterly, he bought shares in the Globe and Blackfriars theatres and was possibly concerned with the training of boy-apprentices.

sharer Any member of an Elizabethan theatre company who shared in the ownership of scripts and costumes. The sharer had a claim to any profits made; those who also had an interest in the building itself were called HOUSEKEEPERS.

sharing system A financial arrangement commonly agreed in English theatres in the early 18th century. The system involved the sharing of a night's profits equally among the company, with the manager receiving up to five shares in all. It was, however, vulnerable to the activities of corrupt managements and was eventually superseded by the payment of set salaries. *See also* benefit.

Shaw, Fiona (Fiona Wilson; 1958–) British actress, born in Ireland, who made her debut at the Octagon Theatre, Bolton in 1982. In the later 1980s she played a series of leading roles for the Royal Shakespeare Company, including Mme de Volanges in *Les Liaisons dangereuses* (1985), Katharina in *The Taming of the Shrew* (1987), and Portia in *The Merchant of Venice* (1987). Subsequent work has included an award-winning performance in the Royal National Theatre's *Machinal* (1993), May in Deborah Warner's controversial staging of Beckett's *Footfalls* (1993), Richard II at the National (1995), and the title character in *The Prime of Miss Jean Brodie* (1998).

Shaw, George Bernard (1856–1950) Irish playwright, director and critic, born in Dublin, who won a Nobel Prize in 1925 and is considered one of the great theatrical figures of the 20th century. Shaw moved to London in 1876, where he became a founder member of the Fabian Society and worked for a time as a music critic and novelist. He then became drama critic for the *Saturday Review* (1895–98). His admiration for Ibsen and his own interest in seeing a new relevant social drama led him to write plays himself.

His first play, WIDOWERS' HOUSES (1892), was a well-received comedy expressing his socialist views; thereafter he attempted a broader human comedy whose enduring qualities established his reputation. A series of 10 plays was presented by Harley GRANVILLE-BARKER and John VEDRENNE at the ROYAL COURT THEATRE (1904–07); they also staged later Shavian works at the Savoy Theatre, supporting his treatment of subjects previously banned by the censor, including prostitution, religion, and sexual politics. Occasionally Shaw's preoccupation with the intellectual content of his drama hampers its theatrical effectiveness, but in his best plays his eloquence and wit carry the action; many of his works have been revived time and time again. Of his 50 plays, Shaw considered BACK TO METHUSELAH (1922) his best, although other critics have singled out HEARTBREAK HOUSE and SAINT JOAN (1923). He was also noted for the lengthy prefaces to his plays, in which he further expounded his views on a wide variety of topics. Several of his early plays were first published in 1898 under the title *Plays Pleasant and Unpleasant*.

Principal dramatic works:
Widowers' Houses: 1892.
THE DEVIL'S DISCIPLE: 1897.
MRS WARREN'S PROFESSION: 1902 (written 1893).
THE PHILANDERER: 1905 (written 1893).
ARMS AND THE MAN: 1894.

CANDIDA: 1895.
YOU NEVER CAN TELL: 1900.
CAPTAIN BRASSBOUND'S CONVERSION: 1900.
MAN AND SUPERMAN: 1901–03.
JOHN BULL'S OTHER ISLAND: 1904.
MAJOR BARBARA: 1905.
THE DOCTOR'S DILEMMA: 1906.
CAESAR AND CLEOPATRA: 1906.
MISALLIANCE: 1910.
FANNY'S FIRST PLAY: 1911.
PYGMALION: 1913.
ANDROCLES AND THE LION: 1913.
Heartbreak House: 1920.
Back to Methuselah: 1922.
Saint Joan: 1923.
THE APPLE CART: 1929.
TOO TRUE TO BE GOOD: 1932.
GENEVA: 1938.
IN GOOD KING CHARLES'S GOLDEN DAYS: 1939.

Shaw, Glen Alexander Byam *See* Byam Shaw, Glen Alexander.

Shaw Festival A major theatre festival founded at Niagara-on-the-Lake in Canada in 1962 by the playwright **Brian Doherty** (1906–74). Initially it was devoted exclusively to the plays of G B Shaw, but it now includes productions of plays by his contemporaries and later writers influenced by him. It has the second largest repertory company in North America, with three stages and a season running from April to November.

Shawn, Wallace (1943–) US playwright, actor, and director, who has worked extensively with the New York Shakespeare Festival and with La Mama. His play *My Dinner With André* (1980) went unperformed at first, but became a well-known film with the author himself starring. Subsequent plays, including *Aunt Dan and Lemon* (1985) and *The Designated Mourner* (1996), are known for their challenging refusal to take easy sides on artistic and political issues.

Shaw Theatre *See* National Youth Theatre.

Shchepkin, Mikhail Semenovich (1788–1863) Russian actor, who began as an amateur in comic roles in Kursk and was later released from serfdom and became a leading theatrical figure in Moscow. He first appeared at the Maly Theatre in Moscow in 1822, subsequently winning much praise for his interpretation of roles in the plays of Gogol and Griboyedov, as well as in comic parts in Molière and Shakespeare. He was also highly influential in fostering interest in realism in the Russian theatre, anticipating the reforms of Stanislavsky.

Shchukin, Boris Vasilievich (1894–1939) Russian actor, who became a leading performer at the Vakhtangov Theatre. He was particularly admired in Russian plays by such authors as Afinogenov, Gorky, and Pogodin, whose Lenin he was the first to portray.

Sheldon, Edward Brewster (1886–1946) US playwright, who was recognized as a leading exponent of Realism in the US with his first play, *Salvation Nell*, in 1908. Of the plays that followed, the most successful included *The Nigger* (1909), which tackled the problem of race, and *Romance* (1913), in which **Doris Keane** (1881–1945) was highly acclaimed as an Italian opera singer. He was also the author of several noted collaborations and translations.

Shelley, Percy Bysshe (1792–1822) British poet, who wrote several verse plays. His lyrical drama *Prometheus Unbound* and his burlesque *Oedipus Tyrannus; or, Swellfoot the Tyrant* were published in 1820. His gothic tragedy *The Cenci* (1819) was first performed in 1886 and has enjoyed several successful revivals, despite some obvious flaws in the play's construction.

Shepard, Sam (Samuel Shepard Rogers; 1943–) US playwright and actor, whose early works included the one-act plays *Cowboys* (1964), *Chicago* (1965), and *Icarus's Mother* (1965). His first full-length play, *La Turista*, has been followed by a series of avant-garde works exploring the myths of machismo, rock music, and the American West. He also writes, directs, and stars in films.

Principal works:
  La Turista: 1966.
  Operation Sidewinder: 1970.
  The Tooth of Crime: 1972.
  The Curse of the Starving Class: 1977.
  Buried Child: 1978; Pulitzer Prize.
  True West: 1980.
  Fool for Love: 1983.
  A Lie of the Mind: 1986.
  Simpatico: 1994.
  Eyes for Consuela: 1998.

Sher, Sir Antony (1951–) British actor, born in South Africa, who made his London debut in Willy Russell's musical *John, Paul, Ringo…and Bert* (1974). In 1975 he attracted much attention at Edinburgh in Gogol's *The Government Inspector*. After joining the Royal Shakespeare Company in 1982, he won much praise as the Fool in *King Lear*, Molière's *Tartuffe*, and an unforgettable Richard III, which brought comparisons with Olivier, and toured to Australia. He played the drag queen Arnold Beckoff in Harvey Fierstein's *Torch Song Trilogy* (1985) and – at Stratford-on-Avon in 1987 – Shylock, Malvolio, and Vendice in Tourneur's *The Revenger's Tragedy*. More recent parts have included the title role in Brecht's *The Resistible Rise of Arturo Rui* (1991), the artist Stanley Spencer in *Stanley* (1996), and Leontes in *A Winter's Tale* (1998).

Sheridan, Mark (Fred Shaw; 1867–1918) British comic singer, who became famous in music hall for such songs as 'I Do Like to be Beside the Seaside' and 'Who Were You With Last Night?'; he was also known for conducting the audience in chorus songs with his baggy umbrella. Sheridan toured with his own burlesque company during World War I; he shot himself while depressed.

Sheridan, Richard Brinsley (1751–1861) British playwright, theatre manager, and politician. Sheridan was born in Dublin, the son of an actor and the writer Frances Chamberlaine (1724–66). The success of his early plays, notably THE RIVALS, enabled him to buy Garrick's share in DRURY LANE and to take over the management there in 1776. After *A Trip to Scarborough*, his adaptation of THE RELAPSE, he presented his brilliant comedy of manners THE SCHOOL FOR SCANDAL to universal acclaim. The burlesque THE CRITIC followed in 1779. That same year Sheridan entered parliament and gained a reputation as a fine orator. The destruction of Drury Lane by fire in 1809 compounded his financial difficulties and ended his career in the theatre. He was buried in Westminster Abbey.

Principal works:
  The Rivals: 1775.
  St Patrick's Day; or, The Scheming Lieutenant: 1775.
  The Duenna: 1775.
  A Trip to Scarborough: 1777.
  The School for Scandal: 1777.
  Robinson Crusoe; or, Harlequin Friday: 1781.
  The Critic; or, a Tragedy Rehears'd: 1799.
  Pizarro: 1799.

Sheridan Square Playhouse *See* Circle Repertory Company.

Sherlock Holmes A play by the US actor and author William Gillette (1855–1937). First performance: Buffalo, 1899. Loosely based on three of Conan Doyle's popular stories, it introduced the detective play to the US stage; Gillette himself appeared for many years in the role of the fictional hero.

Sherman Theatre A university theatre in Cardiff, South Wales, which opened in 1973. It presents a mixed programme in each of its two auditoriums, one of which is the STUDIO THEATRE, based on productions by its resident company. It is the headquarters of the Welsh Drama Company and the Welsh Dance Company.

Sherriff, R(obert) C(edric) (1896–1975) British playwright and novelist, best known for his play JOURNEY'S END (1928), which realistically portrayed events in a World War I dugout and established his reputation. His other plays include *Badger's Green* (1930), which was a rustic comedy about cricket, *Home at Seven* (1950), a psychological drama about amnesia, *The White Carnation* (1953), *The Long Sunset* (1955), and *The Telescope* (1957).

Sherwood, Robert Emmet (1896–1955) US playwright, whose first successful play was *The Road to Rome* (1927), an anti-war piece based on Hannibal's crossing of the Alps. Subsequently he was praised for such plays as *The Queen's Husband* (1928), *Reunion in Vienna* (1931), which starred the Lunts, and THE PETRIFIED FOREST. The pessimistic *Idiot's Delight* (1936) won a Pulitzer Prize, as did *Abe Lincoln in Illinois* (1938) and *There Shall Be No Night* (1940). Later works included *Small War on Murray Hill* (1957).

She Stoops to Conquer A comedy by Oliver GOLDSMITH. First performance: 1773. Tony Lumpkin directs Young Marlow and his friend to the Hardcastles' house, having led them to believe it is an inn. There they treat Hardcastle as the landlord and his daughter Kate as one of the servants. The play has enjoyed frequent revivals.

She Would if She Could A comedy by George ETHEREGE. First performance: 1668. When Sir Oliver and Sir Joshua, seeking opportunity for dissipation, bring their families to London, both Sir Oliver's wife and Sir Joshua's two nieces embark on intrigues; finally all parties come together at the Bear Tavern.

Shields, Arthur (1900–70) Irish actor, who was with the Abbey Theatre company for 23 years. His roles there included Denis in Lennox Robinson's *The White-Headed Boy* (1916) and leading parts in Synge's *The Playboy of the Western World* and O'Casey's *The Plough and the Stars*. After 1941 he concentrated on films.

Shields, Ella (1879–1952) British music hall singer, born in the US, who became famous as a male impersonator. Best known of all her songs was 'Burlington Bertie', which was written by her husband.

Shiels, George (1886–1949) Irish playwright, who from 1921 onwards had plays regularly staged at the Abbey Theatre. Having established his reputation with such satirical comedies as *Paul Twyning* (1922), he went on to find success with his more serious plays, which included *The Passing Day* (1936), *The Rugged Path* (1940), and *The Summit* (1941).

Shifrin, Nisson Ambramovich (1892–1959) Russian stage designer, who was particularly noted for his designs for the plays of Shakespeare. Some of his most admired designs, which made use of lavish tapestries, were executed for Popov at the Red Army Theatre, the most successful including *A Midsummer Night's Dream* (1940). He also designed productions of several modern Soviet plays.

Shilling Theatre *See* Grand Theatre.

Shimpa A Japanese theatre movement, which developed from the KABUKI tradition in the early 20th century. Meaning the 'new school', *Shimpa* challenged many of the conventions associated with *Kabuki* productions and allowed women to appear on stage. Most *Shimpa* plays were sentimental melodramas.

Shingeki A Japanese theatre movement that flourished in the early 20th century. Meaning the 'new drama', *Shingeki* included translations of works by noted European and US writers; the movement revived after World War II, providing an outlet for new Japanese writers as well as major contemporary foreign works.

Shirley, James (1596–1666) English playwright, who was a prolific writer of comedy. His 40 plays reflect the influence of both Jonson and Fletcher and were revived after the Restoration. His comedies of manners included *The Witty Fair One* (1628), *Hyde Park* (1632), *The Gamester* (1633), and *The Lady of Pleasure* (1635); among his other plays was the revenge tragedy *The Traitor* (1631). He wrote for the King's Men and many of his plays were performed in private theatres.

Shoemaker's Holiday, The A comedy by Thomas DEKKER. First performance: London, 1599. The play presents a romantic picture of harmony among London tradesmen and tells of the rise of Simon Eyre from master shoemaker to Lord Mayor.

showboat A floating theatre of the type once common on the Mississippi, Ohio, and other major US rivers. The first showboat, the *Floating Palace*, was built for William Chapman in 1831 and was typical in providing a variety of melodramas and sentimental plays; other floating companies also offered nautical dramas, vaudeville, and even equestrian dramas. The Civil War caused an interruption in the tradition but the showboats reappeared in 1878 when Captain A B French launched his *New Sensation*. The last showboat, the *Dixie Queen*, was launched in 1939.

Show Boat A musical with words by Oscar HAMMERSTEIN II and music by Jerome KERN, based on a novel by Edna Ferber. First performance: New York, 1927. A tale of life on a Mississippi show boat, it included such songs as 'Ol' Man River' and 'Only Make Believe'. Its treatment of race relations showed that the musical could deal with serious subjects. It was filmed in 1929, again in 1936 (with Paul Robeson), and again in 1951.

Shtraukh, Maxim Maximovich (1900–74) Russian actor and director, who became famous for his character roles at the Proletkult Theatre (later the Trades Unions Theatre). He also appeared under Meyerhold at the Mayakovsky Theatre and at the Maly Theatre; his successes included impersonations of Lenin in Korneichuk's *Truth* (1937), Vishnevsky's *The Unforgettable 1919* (1949), and several films.

Shubert Organization The largest of the New York theatrical real-estate and producing organizations, founded by the Shubert brothers Lee (1875–1953), Sam (1876–1905), and Jacob (1880–1965). It owns 16 Broadway theatres, plus a half-interest in the Music Box, as well as owning or controlling theatres in Boston, Chicago, Los Angeles, Philadelphia, and Washington, DC.

Shubert Theatre The more familiar name of the 1504-seat Sam S Shubert Theatre, on West 44th Street, New York, which opened in 1918 with *Hamlet*, starring Forbes-Robertson. It is probably the most famous musical house in the US, but a number of straight plays have been staged there successfully, including several produced by the Theatre Guild. Among the musicals are *Bloomer Girl* (1944), *Paint Your Wagon* (1951), *Stop the World – I Want to Get Off* (1962), *Promises, Promises* (1968), *A Little Night Music* (1973), and *A Chorus Line* (1975).

Shumsky, Yakov Danilovich (d. 1812) Russian actor, who was a founding member of the country's first professional acting company. He was highly popular playing old women, most notably in *The Minor* (1782) by Fonvizin, and in comic roles in the plays of Holberg and Molière.

Shusherin, Yakov Emelyanovich (1753–1813) Russian actor, who was highly regarded in a variety of roles, ranging from the neoclassical dramas of Sumarokov and Lessing to plays in the *comédie-larmoyante* style. He appeared with the companies of Meddocks and Dmitrevsky and won royal approval in plays written by Catherine the Great herself.

Shuter, Ned (Edward Shuter; 1728–76) British actor, praised by Garrick as the greatest comic genius he had known. After making his debut at Richmond in 1744 he moved to Drury Lane, where he created, among other characters, Old Hardcastle, Sir Anthony Absolute, and Justice Woodcock in Bickerstaffe's *Love in a Village*.

Shwartz, Evgenyi Lvovich (1896–1958) Russian actor and playwright, who was the author of several popular plays for young people. *The Dragon* (1944), a lively and provocative political satire, was his most successful work; others included several based on fairytales, among them *Red Riding Hood* (1937) and *The Snow Queen* (1938).

Siddons, Sarah (Sarah Kemble; 1755–1831) British actress, the eldest child of Roger Kemble (1722–1802) and Sarah Ward (d. 1807), whose touring company was well-known. She disappointed her parents by marrying William Siddons (1744–1808), an actor in their company, when she was 18. In 1745 she was invited by Garrick to Drury Lane but her debut in *The Merchant of Venice* was unsuccessful and she returned to the provinces. Sheridan recalled her to Drury Lane in 1782 and her performance in Garrick's *Isabella* established her as the leading tragic actress of her day, winning acclaim for her beauty and her noble manner. Other memorable parts included the title role in Rowe's *Jane Shore* and Belvidera in *Venice Preserv'd*; later in her career she excelled in Shakespearean roles, notably as Lady Macbeth, although she never attempted comedy. In 1802 she and her brother, John Philip KEMBLE, took over Covent Garden, where she appeared regularly until 1812.

Sierra, Gregorio Martínez *See* Martínez Sierra, Gregorio.

sightline An imaginary line extending from any particular seat in the auditorium to the stage, used to determine what the audience can see of the set and the wings.

Sigurjónsson, Jóhan (1880–1919) Icelandic playwright, who wrote in Icelandic and Danish. His play *Fjalla-Eyvindur* (Eyvind of the Hills; 1911), a tragedy based upon an Icelandic love story, was an outstanding success in Scandinavia, Germany, England, and the US; subsequent plays included *Galdra-Loftur* (Loftur the Sorceror; 1915).

Silence, Theatre of A theatrical theory developed in the 1920s, which emphasized the use of long significant pauses to convey meaning or emotion. Major works employing the technique (also called the **Théâtre de l'Inexprimé**) include plays by Maeterlinck and Jean-Jacques Bernard.

sill-iron *See* saddle-iron.

Silva, António José da (1705–39) Portuguese playwright, born in Brazil, who wrote several lively comedies, notably *A Vida do Grande D Quixote* (1733) and *As Guerras Do Alecrim e da Mangerona* (1737). A Jew, he died at the hands of the Inquisition.

Silver Box, The A play by John GALSWORTHY. First performance: Royal Court Theatre, 1906. The play depicts the contrasting treatment given by the law to two men, one rich and one poor, who are both accused of theft.

Silver King, The A melodrama by Henry Arthur JONES and Henry Herman. First performance: 1882. A young Englishman, wrongfully accused of murder, flees the country; having made a fortune in the US, he returns to avenge himself.

Silver Tassie, The A play by Sean O'CASEY. First performance: London, 1929. Through the experiences of the soldier Harry Heegan, O'Casey discusses the corruption of human nature by war. Owing mainly to O'Casey's adoption of an Expressionist style in the second act, the Abbey Theatre rejected the play. This prompted the author to leave Ireland altogether.

Silvia (Zanetta-Rosa-Giovanna Benozzi; c. 1701–58) Italian actress, who became the leading lady at the Comédie-Italienne after arriving in Paris in 1716. She was especially admired as heroines in the plays of Marivaux.

Sim, Alastair (1900–76) Scottish actor, who began a theatrical career when almost 30 years of age. He was soon recognized as a superbly idiosyncratic comedian, both on stage and in films, after appearing as Ponsonby in Hubert Griffith's *Youth at the Helm* (1934). Subsequently he starred in and directed many plays by James Bridie, including *Mr Bolfry* (1943 and 1956) and *Dr Angelus* (1947). He also played Captain Hook in *Peter Pan* on five occasions, excelled as Lord Ogleby in Colman the Elder's *The Clandestine Marriage* (1966), and was highly praised in revivals of Pinero's farces, notably as Mr Posket in *The Magistrate* (1969) and as the Dean in *Dandy Dick* (1973).

Simmons, Pip *See* Pip Simmons Theatre Group.

Simon, John (1925–) US theatre critic, born in Yugoslavia, who has reviewed for *New York Magazine* since 1968. Although he has caused controversy with his vitriolic negative notices, which include what are felt to be personal attacks, he is also respected for his knowledge, especially of the classics.

Simon, (Marvin) Neil (1927–) US playwright, who began by writing for television. His first full-length Broadway show, *Come Blow Your Horn*, was written in collaboration with his brother, Daniel; since then he has won great popularity for his witty studies of modern relationships, with emphasis on urban Jewish characters. His semi-autobiographical plays of the 1980s and 1990s were more serious and won him greater critical respect, with *Lost in Yonkers* winning a Pulitzer Prize. Other works include the books for several musicals.

Principal works:

Come Blow Your Horn: 1961.
Little Me: 1962.
BAREFOOT IN THE PARK: 1963.
THE ODD COUPLE: 1965 (revised for female leads 1985).
Sweet Charity: 1966.
Promises, Promises: 1968.
Plaza Suite: 1968.
The Last of the Red Hot Lovers: 1969.
The Prisoner of Second Avenue: 1971.
The Sunshine Boys: 1972.
CALIFORNIA SUITE: 1976.
They're Playing Our Song: 1978.
BRIGHTON BEACH MEMOIRS: 1983.
Biloxi Blues: 1985.
Broadway Bound: 1986.
Lost in Yonkers: 1991.
Laughter on the 23rd Floor: 1993.
London Suite: 1995.
The Dinner Party: 2000.

Simonov, Konstantin Mikhailovich (1915–79) Russian journalist, novelist, poet, and playwright, whose plays have been widely translated and performed in the West. War and the need for peace are predominant themes. *Russkiye Lyndi* (1942) was highly acclaimed when seen as *The Russians* at the Old Vic in 1943; subsequent works included *A Fellow from Our Town* (1942), *Wait for Me* (1943), *The Russian Question* (1947), and the comedy *A Good Name* (1953).

Simonov, Reuben Nikolaivich (1899–1968) Russian actor and director. He established his reputation as an actor with the Moscow Art Theatre, which he joined in 1920, and went on to win particular acclaim as Rostand's Cyrano de Bergerac. He made his name as a director with a production of Sholokhov's *Virgin Soil Upturned* and subsequently became the foremost director at the Vakhtangov Theatre. His greatest successes included plays by Gorky and Pogodin.

Simonson, Lee (1888–1967) US stage designer, who became famous for his designs for modern plays produced by the Theatre Guild, of which he was a founding member. His most celebrated contributions included his designs for O'Neill's *Dynamo* (1929) and for plays by Masefield, Shaw, and Strindberg.

Simov, Victor Andreyevich (1858–1935) Russian stage designer, who spent most of his career with the Moscow Art Theatre. He dominated the designs of all the organization's early productions, attracting much praise for his work on the plays of Chekhov, Gorky, Shakespeare, and Tolstoy; later designs included those for Ivanov's *Armoured Train 14–69* (1927).

Simpson, Edmund Shaw (1784–1848) US actor and manager, a leading performer at the Park Theatre in New York from 1809. He became highly popular there alongside Cooke, Kean, and the elder Booth in such plays as *Richard III*; however, in 1833 he was forced by injury to turn to fulltime management of the theatre, relinquishing it only a short time before his death.

Simpson, N(orman) F(rederick) (1919–) British playwright, whose surreal comedies are characterized by brilliant verbal humour. His first success, *A Resounding Tinkle* (1957), was followed by the highly praised *One-Way Pendulum* (1959), which concerns a man who builds a model of the Old Bailey in his living-room and finds himself in the dock. Later plays included *The Cresta Run* (1965) and *Was He Anyone?* (1972).

simultaneous-scene setting *See* composite setting.

Sinclair, Arthur (Francis Quinton McDonnell; 1883–1951) Irish actor, who began at the Abbey Theatre in 1904 in Yeats's *On Baile's Strand* and made his London debut in Lady Gregory's *Spreading the News* (1905). He appeared in numerous comic Irish roles on both sides of the Atlantic, notably in plays by Shaw, Synge, O'Casey, and Lennox Robinson.

Sinden, Sir Donald (1923–) British actor, who began his career entertaining the troops during World War II and then spent two seasons at Stratford-on-Avon before making his London debut in *Richard II* in 1947. He came to prominence in Ruth and Augustus Goetz's *The Heiress* (1949) and then went into films, before returning to Stratford in 1963, where he was outstanding as Richard Plantagenet in a Shakespeare trilogy, *The Wars of the Roses*. A virtuoso performer with a sonorous and unmistakable voice, he has alternated between classics and modern comedies, his parts including Lord Foppington in Vanbrugh's *The Relapse* (1967), Gilbert in Ray Cooney and John Chapman's *Not Now, Darling* (1968), the title role in *Henry VIII* (1969), Lear

(1977), Sir Percy Blakeney in *The Scarlet Pimpernel* (1985), and Polonius in *Hamlet* (1994). He is also well known for his many television appearances.

Singspiele *See* ballad opera.

siparium *See* curtain.

Six Characters in Search of an Author (*Sei personaggi in cerca d'autore*) A drama by Luigi PIRANDELLO. First performance: Rome, 1921. The most celebrated of Pirandello's plays, it explores the nature of theatrical illusion by introducing six characters who have been 'rejected' by the author who created them; they attempt to take control of their fate despite confusion over their identity and the presence of actors who attempt to take over their roles.

69 Theatre Company *See* Royal Exchange Theatre.

Sjöberg, Alf (1903–80) Swedish director, actor, and manager, who did much work in the theatre before winning acclaim as a director in cinema. As well as the plays of Shakespeare, he directed notable productions of works by Brecht, Ibsen, García Lorca, and Arthur Miller; his most famous film productions included Strindberg's *Miss Julie* (1959) and *The Father* (1969).

Skelton, John (c. 1460–1529) English poet and playwright, whose *Magnyfycence* (c. 1515–18) is a morality play offering moral instruction to the young Henry VIII. None of his other dramatic works survive.

skene In the ancient Greek theatre, a building behind the *proscenium* which was used as a dressing-room. Actors portraying gods probably appeared on the roof of this building and were lowered from it to the stage below.

Skin Game, The A play by John GALSWORTHY. First performance: London, 1920. The play depicts the conflict of interests and values between a genteel aristocratic family and their newly prosperous neighbours; both parties are morally compromised by events, which end in tragedy.

Skinner, Otis (1858–1942) US actor, who first appeared on stage in 1877. He made his New York debut two years later and then worked with Augustin Daly and Modjeska. Acclaimed in plays by Sheridan, he won further praise in *Your Humble Servant* (1910) and *Mr Antonio* (1916), which were both written for him by Booth Tarkington. His greatest success, however, was as Hajj in Knoblock's *Kismet* (1911). From 1926 to 1933 he appeared in various Shakespearean roles, including Shylock and Falstaff.

His daughter, **Cornelia Otis Skinner** (1902–79), appeared with her father and was known as a singer and writer.

Skin of Our Teeth, The A play by Thorton WILDER. First performance: New York, 1942. In this, the most experimental and Expressionistic of Wilder's plays, a single family experiences the history of the world from the Ice Age on. The moral is that mankind has survived thus far by the skin of its teeth.

Skuszanka, Krystyna (1924–) Polish director, who attracted international attention for work at the People's Theatre in Nowa Huta. Such productions as Gozzi's *Turandot* (1956) and *The Tempest* (1959) were well received when seen in Paris; subsequently she worked at the Polski Theatre in Warsaw, the Wrocław Theatre, and Cracow's Słowacki Theatre, frequently alongside her husband Jósef SZAJNA.

sky border *See* border.

sky cloth *See* cloth.

Slade, Julian (Penkivil) (1930–) British composer and playwright, who was the author (with Dorothy Reynolds) of the book, music, and lyrics for the popular musical *Salad Days* (1954). Other successes have included musical versions of *The Comedy of Errors* (1954), *Vanity Fair* (1963), *Winnie the Pooh* (1970), and *Dear Brutus* (1985).

slapstick Originally, the bat wielded by Harlequin. A slapstick consists of two strips of wood bound together, which when struck against another object – usually one of the other characters on the stage – produces a convincing slapping noise. Slapsticks have also been employed in music hall, vaudeville, and by clowns. The term is now used of any boisterous physical comedy.

Sleeping Clergyman, A A play by James BRIDIE. First performance: Malvern Festival, 1933. The play explores the conflict between good and evil through three generations of one family.

Sleuth A thriller by Antony SHAFFER. First performance: London, 1970. The play revolves around two central characters, both writers of murder stories, who act out their plots with one another until reality and fiction blur and the audience can no longer tell which is which.

slips A British term used in the early 19th century to denote those seats at the ends of the upper tiers of an auditorium. Its use has been retained at Covent Garden.

slip stage *See* wagon stage.

Sloman, Charles (1808–70) British music hall performer, whose reputation was made in the song-and-supper rooms. He specialized in the improvisation of verses on subjects suggested by the audience. He also wrote songs for Sam Cowell and served as chairman at the Middlesex Music Hall; he died in the workhouse.

slote A mechanical device, comprising an arrangement of metal rails and weights, by means of which actors or scenery can be raised to or lowered from the stage, often through traps. The slote was developed in the early 19th century; in the US it is usually referred to as a **hoist**.

Słowacki, Juliusz (1809–49) Polish poet and playwright, a leading figure of the Polish Romantic movement. After being exiled in 1831 he lived mostly in Paris, where he was a rival of Mickiewicz. He saw Kean's *Richard III* in London and was subsequently much influenced by Shakespeare in such plays as *Horsztyński* and his masterpiece *Kordian* (written in 1833 and first performed in 1899). Other works include adaptations of Calderón, notably *Il principe constante*, further tragedies – including *The Silver Dream of Salomé* and *Samuel Zborowski* – the comedy *Fantazy*, and *Lilla Weneda*, which drew on mythological material. His poetic dramas were rediscovered by Leon Schiller in the early 20th century.

Sly, William (d. 1608) English actor, who is known to have appeared in Tarleton's *Seven Deadly Sins* in about 1590, with Strange's Men. He is in the First Folio list of actors of Shakespeare's plays and may have been the first Osric. He joined the Chamberlain's Men in 1594, eventually becoming a shareholder in the Globe and Blackfriars theatres.

SM *See* stage manager.

Smith, Albert (1816–60) British playwright and performer, noted for his one-man entertainments. After having a drama produced at the Surrey Theatre in 1842, he embarked upon a series of extravaganzas and adaptations, mainly for the Keeleys at the Lyceum. In 1850, following an Indian tour, he wrote and performed *The Overland Mail*, with scenery by William Roxby Beverley. It proved highly popular and was followed by the similar *The Ascent of Mont Blanc* and *China*.

Smith, Anna Devere (1950–) US playwright and performer who has developed a style combining monodrama and documentary; she examines social turmoil by interviewing the people involved and portraying them herself. Successes include *Fires in the Mirror* (1991), about racial and religious tensions in a Brooklyn neighbourhood, and *Twilight: Los Angeles* (1994), which treated the Watts riots in Los Angeles.

Smith, Dodie (Dorothy Gladys Smith; 1896–1990) British playwright and novelist, who used the pseudonym C L Anthony until 1935. She established her reputation with the play *Autumn Crocus* (1931); her other plays include *Service* (1932), *Touch Wood* (1934), *Call It A Day* (1935), and *Dear Octopus* (1938), her most successful work, in which the family is depicted as "that dear Octopus from whose tentacles we never quite escape". The play ran until the theatres were closed in 1939 and re-opened in 1940.

Smith, Edward Tyrrell (1804–77) British theatre manager, noted for his often reckless support for a variety of theatrical ventures. He rented Drury Lane in 1852 and ran it for seven years, opening successfully with *Uncle Tom's Cabin*; his involvement with less remunerative productions, however, eventually ruined him. His introduction of 'morning performances' anticipated the modern matinée.

Smith, Dame Maggie (Margaret Natalie Smith; 1934–) British actress, who appeared at Oxford before making her professional debut in New York in the revue *New Faces of '56*. She then joined the Old Vic company, being much admired in Shaffer's *The Private Ear* and *The Public Eye* at the Globe, before transferring in 1963 to the National Theatre company, in which she played Desdemona to Olivier's Othello and Silvia in Farquhar's *The Recruiting Officer* among many leading parts. Since then she has demonstrated the diversity of her talent in such roles as Amanda in *Private Lives* (1972), Cleopatra, Millamant in *The Way of the World*, Virginia Woolf in Edna O'Brien's *Virginia* (1981), Lady Macbeth, and Nadia in Ronald Harwood's *Interpreters* (1985). Her more recent successes have included Peter Shaffer's *Lettice and Lovage* (1987), Lady Bracknell in *The Importance of Being Earnest* (1993), and the title role in Alan Bennett's *The Lady in the Van* (1999). She has also appeared in many films and television productions.

Smith, Oliver (1918–94) US stage designer and producer, noted for his works on both ballets and straight drama. His designs for musicals have won much praise, particularly those for *On the Town* (1944), *Brigadoon* (1947), *Paint Your Wagon* (1951), *Pal Joey* (1952), *My Fair Lady* (1956), *West Side Story* (1957), *Flower Drum Song* (1958), *The Sound of Music* (1959), and *Camelot* (1960).

Smith, Sol(omon) Franklin (1801–69) US actor and manager, who became a powerful figure in the early development of US drama in the South and West in collaboration with Noah Ludlow. Their **American Theatrical Commonwealth Company** was highly successful and inspired the building of permanent theatres. Smith also appeared in comic roles at the Park Theatre and elsewhere as did his son, **Marc(us) Smith** (1829–74).

Smith, William (d. 1696) English actor in Betterton's company at Dorset Garden, where he appeared as the original Sir Fopling Flutter in *The Man of Mode* and created Otway's Pierre in *Venice Preserv'd* and Chamont in *The Orphan*. He retired owing to his unpopularity with some young nobles, but later returned to the theatre and died on stage.

Smith, William (1730–1819) British actor, known as 'Gentleman Smith'. Through the influence of Spranger Barry he was engaged for the 1753 season at Covent Garden, where he stayed for 20 years. He joined Garrick at Drury Lane in 1774, first appearing as Richard III and later creating the role of Charles Surface in *The School for Scandal* (1777). He retired in 1788 to live the life of a sporting country gentleman at Bury St Edmunds.

Smith, William Henry Sedley- *See* Sedley-Smith, William Henry.

Smithson, Harriet (1800–54) Anglo-Irish actress, daughter of the manager of the Waterford and Kilkenny theatre circuit. She began her stage career at the Crow Street Theatre, Dublin, and arrived at Drury Lane in 1818. Subsequently she played several Shakespearean roles alongside Edmund Kean. In 1828 she was received ecstatically with Macready in Paris, where she married Berlioz, the composer, in 1833. They separated in 1840 and she died in poverty.

Smock Alley Theatre A theatre in Dublin opened by John Ogilby in 1662 with Fletcher's *Wit Without Money*. Also known as the **Orange Street Theatre**, it survived collapses in 1671 and again in 1701 to become the only public theatre in the city from 1701 to 1733. Appearances by David Garrick and Peg Woffington were highly popular, while R B Sheridan's father, Thomas Sheridan (1719–88), ran the theatre from 1744 to 1758. The theatre was wrecked during his production of Voltaire's *Mahomet* (1754) and later saw a succession of managers before being closed by Richard Daly; it was demolished in 1815.

Smoktunovsky, Innokenti Mikhailovich (1925–94) Russian actor, who became one of the leading performers in the post-war Soviet theatre. He began his career with the Gorky Theatre company in St Petersburg, later appearing in London (1966) and at the Maly Theatre; his most successful roles included Prince Myshkin in a version of Dostoevsky's *The Idiot* (1957) and a filmed Hamlet.

Snow, Sophia (1745–86) British actress, daughter of the trumpeter Valentine Snow. She appeared at Drury Lane on her marriage to Robert BADDELEY and excelled as

Shakespearean heroines. Famed for her beauty, she was also a popular singer until her extravagance and addiction to laudanum ruined her career.

soccus A soft low-heeled shoe worn by the comic actor in the classical Greek or Roman theatre. It was later more commonly referred to as a 'sock'. *See also cothurnus*.

Socialist Realism A government-enforced movement in the theatre and other arts of the USSR in the 1920s and 1930s. Developed by Lunacharsky and others, Socialist Realism reflected the ideals of the Revolution of 1917, advocating the treatment of themes relevant to the common people in a realistic style. As well as new works, classics were also reinterpreted to achieve the same end. Soon, however, the movement became almost totally subservient to the Soviet government's propagandist aims. Notable early figures closely associated with the ideals of Socialist Realism included Gorky and Mayakovsky.

sociétés joyeuses Amateur theatre companies that flourished in France during medieval times. Such groups consisted largely of young men who presented ribald tales in their own locality following the decline of the comic theatrical tradition of religious houses; they represented the earliest origins of secular drama in France.

Society The first of T W ROBERTSON's important realistic comedies. First performance: 1865. A father and son attempt to buy their introduction into high society; when Sydney Daryl – the gentleman approached – declines to cooperate, the son attempts in vain to ruin him.

Society for Theatre Research A British theatre organization founded in 1948 at the Old Vic Theatre to coordinate research in the theatre in Britain. As well as publishing a journal, the society arranges lectures, conservation of theatre artefacts and records, and contributed to the foundation of the national Theatre Museum, where it is now based. It also helped to found the International Federation for Theatre Research and has a US counterpart, the American Society for Theatre Research.

Society of London Theatre *See* West End.

soggetto, commedia a *See commedia dell'arte*.

Soleil, Théâtre du A French theatre company founded in Paris in 1964 as a workers' cooperative under Ariane MNOUCHKINE. The society experimented with the techniques of collective creation and established its reputation with several epic productions on historical themes. In 1972 it moved into dilapidated premises in a former military base, the **Cartoucherie de Vincennes**, which became a popular venue and home for several other experimental companies. Subsequent works have included a highly praised cycle of Greek tragedies in the 1980s.

Somi, Leone Ebreo di (1527–92) Jewish playwright and writer on stage techniques. His *Dialogues on Stage Affairs* (c. 1565) describes in detail contemporary lighting practices, including the positioning of lights and the achievement of atmospheric effects.

Sønderby, Knut (1909–66) Danish novelist, essayist, and playwright, whose plays exposed the underlying insecurity of fashionable society in the 1920s. He dramatized his novel *En Kvinde er overflødig* (A Woman is Superfluous; 1936) very successfully; other triumphs included *Krista* (1947) and *Kvindernes Oprør* (The Woman's Uprising; 1955).

Sondheim, Stephen (1930–) US composer and lyricist, whose first contribution to the theatre was the incidental music for *Girls of Summer* (1956). He went on to write the lyrics for WEST SIDE STORY (1957), GYPSY (1959), and *Do I Hear a Waltz?* (1965), but has since written both words and music. His intellectually sophisticated works are frequently organized around a single dominating idea, for example a painting by Seurat in *Sunday in the Park With George* and fairy tales in *Into the Woods*. They give a portrait of modern American life that is simultaneously scathing and sympathetic.

Principal works:
A Funny Thing Happened on the Way to the Forum: 1962.
COMPANY: 1970.
Follies: 1971.
A Little Night Music: 1973.
Pacific Overtures: 1976.
SWEENEY TODD: 1979.
Merrily We Roll Along: 1981.
Sunday in the Park With George: 1984; Pulitzer Prize.
Into the Woods: 1986.
Assassins: 1991.
Passion: 1994.

son et lumière A type of theatrical entertainment that is usually presented outdoors, with considerable use of lasers, floodlighting, and recorded sound effects. Staged in castles or similar spectacular sites, such productions conventionally consist of re-enactments of episodes of local history. The earliest *son et lumière* performances were staged in France in the 1950s.

song-and-supper rooms Venues for musical entertainment that became popular in London and elsewhere in the early 19th century and preceded the development of the MUSIC HALL. Customers sat at tables and were served with food and drink while varied programmes of comic songs and monologues were presented free. The most famous of these venues, Evans's, was typical, being based initially in the cellar of a tavern; it was eventually enlarged as a music hall proper. Such venues were themselves descended from earlier clubs of a similar type, of which the most celebrated included the **Coal Hole** and the **Cyder Cellars**.

Sonnenfels, Josef von (1733–1817) Austrian director, who oversaw the reformation of the Viennese stage after becoming director of the Burgtheater (1776). A disciple of Gottsched, he supported the suppression of Hanswurst and popular farce and introduced a programme of serious drama; after his death his reforms were continued by Schreyvogel.

Sophocles (496 BC–406 BC) Greek playwright and administrator, born at Colonus near Athens, who was the author of over 100 plays, of which seven tragedies and fragments of a satyr-play survive. Known for his dancing while still a boy, he defeated Aeschylus in the Dionysia in 468 BC and went on to win a further 18 drama contests.

His intricate tragedies, of which OEDIPUS REX has proved the most lasting, dwell upon the conquest of suffering and are especially notable for their development of character.

Sophocles developed many of Aeschylus' ideas, introducing a third actor and limiting the role of the chorus to one of commentary upon the main action. His theories about drama led to the use of the PERIAKTOI as an early scenic device; they also had a profound influence upon Aristotle and many subsequent playwrights, including Seneca, Corneille, Dryden, and T S Eliot.

Principal works:

Ajax: 450 BC.

ANTIGONE: C. 442 BC.

Oedipus Rex: 429 BC.

TRACHINIAE: C. 425 BC.

ELECTRA: 409 BC.

PHILOCTETES: 409 BC.

OEDIPUS AT COLONUS: 401 BC.

Sophron of Syracuse (5th century BC) Greek playwright, author of several mime plays. Although none of his works survive, he is believed to have influenced the writings of Plato, Theocritus, and Herodas.

Sorano, Daniel (1920–62) French actor, who was much admired in both classical French comedy and in the plays of Shakespeare and his contemporaries. He began his career with Sarrazin's Grenier de Toulouse company and subsequently found acclaim in Paris with leading roles in the plays of Molière. He then joined the Théâtre National Populaire and excelled in further Molière classics as well as in plays by Beaumarchais, Brecht, Hugo, and Marivaux, and as Shakespeare's Richard III and Shylock. After his premature death the Grenier de Toulouse occupied (1965) a theatre named in his memory.

Sorge, Reinhard Johannes (1892–1916) German poet and playwright, who pioneered Expressionism in his first play *Der Bettler* (The Beggar; 1912), which utilized symbolic sets and a series of tableaux on its first production (1917) under Reinhardt. His later mystical and religious dramas included *König David* and *Der Sieg des Christos*. He died in the Battle of the Somme.

Sorma, Agnes (Agnes Zaremba; 1865–1927) German actress, who established her reputation as a player of young girls at the Deutsches Theater in Berlin in the 1880s. Subsequently she excelled as Juliet, Ophelia, and Desdemona and in plays by Grillparzer, Goldoni, Hauptmann, Sudermann, and Ibsen, notably as Nora in *A Doll's House*, in which role she appeared in several countries.

Sosnitsky, Ivan Ivanovich (1794–1871) Russian actor, who was admired for his refined interpretations of young men in plays by Griboyedov and others. A pupil of Dmitrevsky, he later successfully introduced a note of realism and satire to his performances.

Sothern, Edward Askew (1826–81) British actor, born in Liverpool. After appearances in the provinces, he joined Lester Wallack's company in New York but did not meet with success until he played Lord Dundreary in Tom Taylor's *Our American*

Cousin at Laura Keene's Theatre in 1858. He repeated the role at the Haymarket in 1861 and continued to appear as Dundreary in sketches and monologues throughout his career. Other roles included the lead in T W Robertson's *David Garrick*.

Of his three sons on the stage, **Edward Hugh Sothern** (1859–1933) was the most successful, playing similar comic roles to those of his father and also some romantic parts. In 1904 he joined Frohman at the Lyceum Theatre in New York; later he formed his own company, presenting plays by Shakespeare and by his second wife, Julia MARLOWE, with whom he often appeared. He donated most of his company's property to the Shakespeare Memorial Theatre in 1924.

sotie A theatrical tradition of medieval France. Performers (called *sots*) presented light and amusing satirical entertainments while dressed in the costume of the medieval fool. The *sots* could be amateurs or belong to permanent troupes. Several written examples of the form survive, notably those of Pierre Gringore. The *sotie* was eventually prohibited in the 16th century due to its strong satirical element.

soubrette A class of minor female roles in comedy, typically those of flirtatious lady's maids.

Soul-Cakers Play *See* mummers' play.

sound effects The production of any special noises required by a play script. These are usually, but not always, engineered offstage. Those most commonly required include various weather effects, the sound of animals, warfare, doors, traffic, and bells. In more recent years extensive use has been made of recorded sound effects, although many are still produced live. *See also* glasscrash; rain machine; thunder run; thundersheet; wind machine.

Sound of Music, The A musical with book by Howard LINDSAY and Russel Crouse, music by Richard RODGERS, and lyrics by Oscar HAMMERSTEIN II. First performance: New York, 1959. Set in Austria in 1938, the plot concerns a young nun, Maria, who becomes governess to the children of an Austrian captain, with whom she falls in love. She later helps the family to flee the country after the Nazi takeover. It was filmed in 1965 with Julie Andrews and Christopher Plummer.

Southerne, Thomas (1660–1746) English playwright of Irish parentage, who provided prologues and epilogues for some of Dryden's plays. He wrote several moderately successful comedies of manners but his two best plays were tragedies based on the novels of Aphra Behn, *The Fatal Marriage; or, the Innocent Adultery* (1694) and *Oroonoko* (1696). His other tragedies include *The Loyal Brother; or, the Persian Prince* (1682) and *The Spartan Dame* (1719).

South London Music Hall The third music hall to be built in London, opened in 1856. Connie Gilchrist and Florrie Forde appeared here early in their careers and the chairman, Bob Courtney, was one of the most famous in London. The theatre remained in use (as the Shoreditch Empire) until it was bombed in World War II.

South Pacific A musical with music by Richard RODGERS and lyrics by Oscar HAMMERSTEIN II and Joshua LOGAN. First performance: New York, 1949. The story takes place on a Pacific island during World War II and revolves around Nellie, a navy nurse, who falls in love with a French planter. Both the Broadway and London productions starred Mary Martin.

South Street Theatre *See* Southwark Theatre.

Southwark Theatre The first permanent theatre in Philadelphia, which was built by David Douglass for his American Company in 1766. Made of timber and brick and painted red, it opened with Vanbrugh's *The Provoked Wife*. In 1767 the theatre (sometimes called the **South Street Theatre**) staged the first professional production of an American play, Godfrey's *The Prince of Parthia*. Closed during the War of Independence, it reopened briefly in 1778 and was temporarily used again by the American Company in 1784. Plays were performed there until it was damaged by fire in 1821. It was demolished in 1912.

Soviet Army, Central Theatre of the *See* Red Army Theatre.

Sovremennik Theatre A theatre founded in Moscow in 1958 by a troupe of young performers assembled by YEFREMOV from various venues in the city. The group established a strong reputation with productions of plays by John Osborne and Edward Albee as well as contemporary Soviet writers, placing an emphasis upon humanist themes. In 1975 it presented Shakespeare for the first time.

Soya (Carl Erik Soya-Jensen; 1896–1983) Danish short-story writer and playwright, whose plays include the naturalistic *Parasitterne* (The Parasites; 1929) and *Hvem er jeg?* (Who Am I?; 1931), which is considered his finest. He also wrote a tetralogy (1940–48): *Brudstykker af et Mønster* (Fragments of a Pattern), *To Traade* (Two Threads), *30 Aars Henstand* (30 Years' Respite), and *Frit Valg* (Free Choice), which explore themes of justice and retribution.

Soyinka, Wole (Akinwande Oluwole; 1934–) Nigerian poet, novelist, literary critic, and playwright, who won a Nobel Prize in 1986. He studied in Britain as a young man and began his association with the theatre when he became one of the writers at the Royal Court Theatre in 1958. His verse play *The Dance of the Forests* was performed at the Nigerian Independence celebrations (1960), since when he has become Africa's leading dramatist.

   His plays reflect the experiences of modern West African society (in particular his own Yoruba tribal history) and adopt a deeply satirical perspective. His political commitments led to his imprisonment from 1967 to 1969 and exile until 1975. His subsequent opposition to the military regime obliged him to remain abroad to escape treason charges in 1997–98. He is important for his foundation (1960) of a national Nigerian theatre, The Masks, which later became the Orisun Theatre and is also head of the Nigerian branch of the International Theatre Institute.

Principal dramatic works:
   The Swamp Dwellers: 1957.
   The Lion and the Jewel: 1957.
   The Dance of the Forests: 1960.
   The Road: 1965.
   Kongi's Harvest: 1966.
   Madmen and Specialists: 1970.
   Death and the King's Horseman: 1975.

Opera Wonyosi: 1977.
A Play for Giants: 1985.
The Beatification of Area Boy: 1995.

Spanish Tragedy, The   A tragedy in blank verse by Thomas KYD. First performance: London, c. 1585–89. Set in Spain, the play focuses on the plight of Hieronimo, who, following the murder of his son and his failure to secure legal justice, becomes drawn into a bloody revenge dispute.

Speaight, Robert William   (1904–76) British actor, who made his professional debut at Liverpool in 1926, coming to the Arts Theatre, London, in 1927 in Avery Hopwood's adaptation of *The Duchess of Elba*. He then had a long run in R C Sherriff's *Journey's End* (1929) and joined the Old Vic company (1931), where he played King John, Malvolio, and Cassius among other roles. In 1935 he played Becket in T S Eliot's *Murder in the Cathedral*, a part with which he became identified and repeated in numerous revivals. Other successes included appearances in Wilder's *A Life in the Sun* (1955) and Bolt's *A Man for All Seasons* (1962).

spectacle theatres   The earliest playhouses to be built in Europe, dating from the late 16th century. Distinguished by their elaborate ornamentation, these included the Teatro Olimpico, Teatro Farnese, and Sabbioneta Court Theatre in Italy, the only surviving examples.

spectatory   *See* auditorium.

Speed the Plough   A play by Thomas MORTON. First performance: 1798. The main plot concerns the return of Sir Philip Blandford, who mistakenly believes he has killed his own brother; however, the play is remembered chiefly for the unseen character of Mrs Grundy, who became a symbol of middle-class propriety.

Spelvin, George.   *See* Plinge, Walter.

Speroni, Sperone   (1500–88) Italian playwright, remembered as the author of the bloodthirsty tragedy *Canace* (1543). The violence of this play provoked considerable unrest when it was first presented in Padua.

Sperr, Martin   (1944–) German playwright and director, who led a revival of the folk theatre form in the 1960s. His most successful works include *Landshuter Erzählungen* (Tales from Landshut; 1967) and *Koralle Meier* (1970), which concerns the relationship between a small town and a nearby concentration camp.

spieltreppe   *See* Jessner, Leopold.

spot bar   *See* batten.

spotlight   A lighting unit capable of producing a bright narrow beam. Spotlights are often equipped with such devices as barn door shutters and colour-wheels; these are one of the standard lighting units of the modern stage.

Spring Awakening   (*Frühlings Erwachen*) The first play by Frank WEDEKIND, written in 1891. First performance: Berlin, 1906. An attack on sexual repression, the play concerns a tragic love affair between two 14 year-olds; parental disapproval leads to an abortion and the deaths of the lovers. It was considered too outrageous to be seen publicly in Britain until 1963.

Spring '71 (*Le Printemps '71*) A play by Arthur ADAMOV. First performance: Paris, 1961. Influenced by the epic theatre of Brecht, the play presents a history of the Paris Commune of 1871 and attempts to draw contemporary political lessons.

Staberl A character of the Viennese comic theatrical tradition, related to the clowns Hanswurst and Kasperl. Usually depicted as a jovial but scheming umbrella-maker, Chrysostomos Staberl was first played by Ignaz Schuster in Bäuerle's *Bürger von Wien* (1813) and was then seen in a lengthy series of popular comedies.

stabile, teatro *See teatro stabile*.

Stadt Theatre *See* Bowery Theatre.

Stafford-Clark, Max (1941–) British director, who was artistic director of the Royal Court Theatre from 1979 until 1993. Stafford-Clark was associated with the Traverse Theatre in Edinburgh from 1968 until 1974, when he became artistic director of the JOINT STOCK COMPANY. His productions at the Royal Court included Caryl Churchill's *Top Girls* (1982) and *Serious Money* (1987), and Timberlake Wertenbaker's *Our Country's Good* (1988). In 1993 he formed a new touring company, Out of Joint; his productions for the troupe have included Mark Ravenhill's controversial *Shopping and Fucking* (1996).

stage cloth Any painted canvas or other floor covering laid over the stage-floor.

stage crew Theatre staff who undertake duties backstage, including the building and setting of scenery, the supply of props, and the control of the lighting and sound effects. They are under the direction of the stage manager.

stage direction An instruction, given in the script or by the director, telling an actor to move to a particular area of the stage, or the stage manager to provide a particular stage effect. Traditionally such directions are given in relation to the actor's view from the stage as he looks into the auditorium, so that what appears to the audience to be on the left-hand side, for example, is conventionally referred to as 'stage right'. Any movement towards the audience is labelled **downstage**, while those away from the audience are **upstage**; the area in the middle of the stage is called **centrestage**. Stage directions that an actor should move **above** an object on the stage indicate that the actor should be upstage of it; **below** denotes that he or she should be downstage of it. **Exit** indicates that an actor should leave the stage, while **enter** denotes that he should come onto it; **manet**, now little used, indicates that he or she should remain on the stage. The direction **cross** indicates that an actor should move from one side of the stage to the other, while **scissor cross** requires two actors to exchange positions on opposite sides of the stage.

stage door An entrance at the back of a theatre, through which actors and other theatre staff have access to the backstage area from outside the building. It is also traditionally the place where admirers of particular performers await the reappearance of the cast as they leave the theatre after a show.

stage door-keeper An employee of a theatre, who is responsible for ensuring that no unauthorized person obtains access to the theatre via the stage door.

stage-keeper The person responsible in the Elizabethan theatre for ensuring that the stage itself was kept in a reasonable condition for performances.

stage lighting *See* lighting.

stage manager (SM) The person in charge of the stage crew and responsible for ensuring that all goes smoothly both on the stage and backstage during a performance. Before the position of the director was developed in the 20th century the stage manager was also often in charge of rehearsals. He is usually helped by an **assistant stage manager** (ASM), who sometimes also acts as prompter.

Stage Society, Incorporated A British theatre organization founded in London in 1899 to present rarely performed experimental dramas. The society played at West End venues at times when they were not being used for more commercial productions, usually on Sunday nights. The first production was Shaw's *You Never Can Tell* (1899), while later successes included Shaw's *Mrs Warren's Profession* (1902), which had previously been refused a licence for public performance. Plays by Gorky, Wedekind, Tolstoy, Pirandello, James Joyce, Cocteau, and others, have also been performed. Many of these transferred to the commercial stage. Later in its life the society presented classic plays and encouraged the foundation of the Phoenix Society, despite the fact that it faced mounting financial pressures itself.

In 1926 it amalgamated with the **Three Hundred Club**, founded in 1923, after which its productions included works by D H Lawrence and García Lorca. Notable theatrical figures associated with the Stage Society included the directors Granville-Barker, Michel Saint-Denis, and Allan Wade as well as such performers as Peggy Ashcroft, Edith Evans, and Laurence Olivier; Theodore Komisarjevsky made influential innovations in scenery in connection with the society's productions. The society was disbanded during World War II.

Stagnelius, Erik Johan (1793–1823) Swedish poet and playwright, author of several notable Romantic dramas. His highly poetic plays, several of which tackle the relationship between eroticism and religious feeling, include *Martyrerna* (1821) and *Bacchanterna* (1822), which were his only dramatic works published during his lifetime.

stalls *See* auditorium.

Standard Theatre A theatre in Shoreditch, London, which originated as part of the Royal Standard Public House and Pleasure Garden, where entertainment was offered in the early 1830s. It housed a circus ring, which was also used for plays and concerts, and was rebuilt in 1866 after a fire. It reopened as the New Standard Theatre, managed by John Douglass, who retained a first class company, staged fine pantomimes, and attracted visiting stars. The Melville brothers took over in 1888 and continued a similar policy until 1907, when the theatre became the **Olympia Music Hall**. It changed to a cinema in 1926 and was demolished following bomb damage in 1940.

The **Standard Theatre** on Broadway, New York, opened as the **Eagle Theatre** in 1875 as a variety house. Renamed the Standard, it was the venue in 1879 for the New York debut of Gilbert and Sullivan's *HMS Pinafore*; other productions were Bret

Harte's *M'liss; An Idyll of Red Mountain, Patience,* which ran for the whole 1881 season, and *Iolanthe* (1882). Burnt down in 1883, it reopened the following year as a home of light opera. However in 1896, under William A Brady (who renamed it the Manhattan Theatre), the bill switched to straight drama. From 1901 to 1906 the theatre housed a successful company led by Minnie Fiske. It was demolished in 1909.

Standing, John (Sir John Ronald Leon; 1934–) British actor, the son of a baronet and actress Kay Hammond. After his first London appearance as Mr Charlton in *The Darling Buds of May* (1959), he emerged as a fine comedy actor in such elegant roles as Algernon in Wilde's *The Importance of Being Earnest* (1968) and Elyot in Coward's *Private Lives* (1973). His appearances at the National Theatre have included Freddy Malone in Ben Travers's *Plunder* (1978) and Turai in Tom Stoppard's *Rough Crossing* (1984); in the 1990s he appeared in plays ranging from Turgenev's *A Month in the Country* (1994) to Dennis Potter's *Son of Man* (1995).

Stanfield, Clarkson (1793–1867) British marine painter and scenic designer, the son of an actor. He worked as a scene painter in Edinburgh and the Coburg Theatre (*see* Old Vic Theatre) before moving to Drury Lane. His theatre work diminished as he became increasingly successful as an easel-painter, although he did later paint at Covent Garden for Macready.

Stanislavsky, Konstantin (Konstantin Sergeyevich Alekseyev; 1863–1938) Russian director and actor, who founded the Moscow Art Theatre and first developed the principles that were later adopted as the basis of the METHOD theory of acting. Having begun his career as an amateur actor, he subsequently trained under the Komisarjevskys and directed major plays by Leo Tolstoy and Dostoevsky before establishing the Moscow Art Theatre with Nemirovich-Danchenko in 1898.

That same year he produced his famous version of Chekhov's *The Seagull,* in which he pioneered an intense psychological approach and a new naturalism in terms of acting, setting, and costume. A celebrated series of Chekhov's works followed, all characterized by subtle control of atmosphere and simplicity of delivery; most including Stanislavsky himself in the cast. Other productions included plays by Shakespeare, Ostrovsky, and, in 1902, Gorky's *The Lower Depths.*

Later he experimented with Formalism and Symbolism, notably through the plays of Maeterlinck and Andreyev, before concentrating upon teaching. His revolutionary theories concerning the psychology of acting, which have had a fundamental effect upon 20th-century drama, were summed up in 1936 in AN ACTOR PREPARES and other essays.

Stapleton, (Lois) Maureen (1925–) US actress, who made her New York debut in Synge's *The Playboy of the Western World* (1946). She established her reputation as Serafina in Tennessee Williams's *The Rose Tattoo* (1951); subsequent successes have included Ann in *Richard III,* Elisabeth Proctor in Miller's *The Crucible* (1953), Masha in Chekhov's *The Seagull* (1954), Lady Torrence in Williams's *Orpheus Descending* (1957), Carrie in Lillian Hellman's *Toys in the Attic* (1960), Amanda Wingfield in Williams's *The Glass Menagerie* (1965), Evy Meara in Simon's *The Gingerbread Lady* (1970), and Birdie Hubbard in Hellman's *The Little Foxes* (1981). Her work since then has been mainly in film and television.

Star Theatre A theatre on Broadway, New York, which was opened in 1861 as Wallack's Theatre by the elder James Wallack and was later run by his son Lester Wallack (1864–81). The theatre then staged plays in German until it was reopened as the Star in 1882. In 1883 this was the venue for Irving's New York debut with Ellen Terry and his Lyceum company. Managed by H E Abbey, the theatre won acclaim for modern plays; distinguished players who appeared there included Edwin Booth, Mary Anderson, Modjeska, Bernhardt, and Wilson Barrett. The building was demolished in 1901.

star trap A circular trap consisting of wooden segments divided into the shape of a star that spring open to allow an actor to make a sudden entrance onto the stage.

Staunton, Imelda (1956–) British actress, who made her debut in 1976 as Goldoni's *Mistress of the Inn* at the Swan Theatre, Worcester. In 1982 she joined the National Theatre where her roles included Lucy Lockit in *The Beggar's Opera* and Miss Adelaide in *Guys and Dolls*. In 1985 she won awards in Ayckbourn's *A Chorus of Disapproval* at the National and in Emlyn Williams's *The Corn is Green* at the Old Vic. She has also appeared with the Royal Shakespeare Company (1986–87) and in *Uncle Vanya* at the Vaudeville Theatre (1988). Her musical work includes Sondheim's *Into the Woods* (1990). More recently she has appeared mainly in films and on television.

Stead, James Henry (d. 1886) British music hall performer, who delivered songs at breathtaking speed, accompanied by frenzied acrobatic dancing. His most famous song was 'The Perfect Cure', which he first performed in 1861. He died in poverty after the novelty of his act had worn off.

Steadman, Alison (1946–) British actress. She worked in repertory before making her name in the title role of *Abigail's Party* (1977), a play by her then-husband Mike LEIGH. Subsequent stage work has included *Uncle Vanya* (1979), *Tartuffe* for the RSC (1985), *Cat on a Hot Tin Roof* for the National Theatre (1988), an award-winning performance in *The Rise and Fall of Little Voice* (1992), and *The Provok'd Wife* (1997). She has also appeared regularly on British television.

Steaming A play by Nell Dunn. First performance: Theatre Royal, Stratford, 1981. Set in a Turkish bath with an all-female cast, the play caused a considerable stir at first with its nudity, but was soon recognized as a sympathetic examination of women's issues.

Steele, Sir Richard (1672–1729) English essayist and playwright, of Anglo-Irish parentage. His first comedy, *The Funeral; or, Grief à la Mode* (1701), was followed by *The Lying Lover* (1703) and *The Tender Husband* (1705), all of which attempted to curb the excesses of earlier Restoration drama. A co-patentee of Drury Lane, he devoted most of his time to writing and editing *The Spectator*, *The Tatler*, and *The Theatre* (1719–20), which was the first English theatre paper. His final comedy, *The Conscious Lovers*, was adapted from Terence and successfully produced at Drury Lane in 1722.

Steele, Tommy (Thomas Hicks; 1936–) British singer and actor, who began as a pop idol of the 1950s but later became a star of variety and musical comedy. As well as such shows as *Half-a-Sixpence* (1963), *Singin' in the Rain* (1983), and *Some Like it Hot* (1992), he has also ventured into straight theatre, playing Tony Lumpkin in *She Stoops to Conquer* in 1960 and Truffaldino in Goldoni's *The Servant of Two Masters* in 1968.

Stein, Peter (1937–) German director, who became famous with a controversial Marxist version of Goethe's *Torquato Tasso* staged at Bremen in 1969. He subsequently established a theatre collective at the Schaubühne in West Berlin. His widely acclaimed (and much-rehearsed) productions there included Bond's *Saved* (1967) and plays by Aeschylus, Gorky, Ibsen, and Shakespeare, several of which have been seen in other countries. In 1982 he supervised the Schaubühne's transfer to a larger building, where productions included a highly successful staging of Chekhov's *Three Sisters* (1984). After leaving the Schaubühne in 1987, Stein spent several years concentrating on opera production; he also became director of theatre at the Salzburg Festival (from 1990). He is now based in Rome but continues to direct work in several European languages: recent productions have included a seven-hour Russian version of the *Oresteia* presented at the Edinburgh Festival (1994) and *Uncle Vanya* in Italian (1996).

Steinbeck, John (1902–68) US novelist, who adapted his own novels *Of Mice and Men* (1937) and *The Moon Is Down* (1942) for the stage. The Rodgers and Hammerstein musical *Pipe Dream* (1955) was based on his novel *Sweet Thursday*. Among his other works to be dramatized were *Tortilla Flats* (1938) and *Burning Bright* (1950). He won a Nobel Prize in 1962.

Stephen Joseph Theatre A theatre in Scarborough, North Yorkshire. The original Stephen Joseph Theatre in the Round was established by JOSEPH in the Public Library in 1955. Alan Ayckbourn, who became artistic director in 1970, has had most of his plays premiered at the theatre since 1959. It moved to a new 300-seat building in 1976 and to a still larger venue in 1995–96; this has both a 400-seat theatre-in-the-round and a normal auditorium seating 150. Despite its association with Ayckbourn, the new theatre soon ran into serious financial problems and had to be rescued by a local government grant in 1997.

Stephens, Sir Robert (1931–95) British actor, who made his name at the Royal Court Theatre in the 1950s, when he appeared in several works by John Osborne. He joined Olivier's National Theatre company in 1963, winning particular acclaim as the Inca king Atahuallpa in Shaffer's *The Royal Hunt of the Sun* (1964). Successes of the 1970s included National Theatre productions of *Armstrong's Last Goodnight* (1978) and Ibsen's *Brand* (1978), but his career was subsequently blighted by alcoholism. He enjoyed a major return to form in the early 1990s, when he gave towering performances of Lear (1992) and Falstaff (1993) for the RSC.

Stephens was married to the actress Maggie SMITH from 1967 to 1975. Their son Toby Stephens (1969–) is also an actor; his work has included an award-winning performance as Coriolanus (1994) for the RSC and Hippolytus in Racine's *Phèdre* (1998; with Diana Rigg).

Steppenwolf Theatre A company in Chicago, founded in 1976 by an ensemble of actors including Gary Sinese, John MALKOVICH, and Laurie Metcalf. Although it has presented a wide variety of works, it is best known for modern plays performed in an intensely physical style. Several of its productions have attracted national attention, especially its version of Steinbeck's *The Grapes of Wrath*, which won the 1990 Tony Award for best play. The current theatre, which opened in 1991, has 500- and 200-seat auditoriums.

stereopticon *See* projector.

Stern, Ernst (1876–1954) German stage designer, born in Bucharest, who became famous for his designs for many of Reinhardt's productions. He was much admired for his work on the plays of Aeschylus, Goethe, and Shakespeare as well as contemporary plays by such authors as Ibsen and Noël Coward; he also executed several designs for Shakespearean productions by Donald Wolfit's company.

Sternhagen, Frances (1930–) US actress, who made her stage debut in provincial summer theatre in 1948 and, after work with the Arena Stage, made her New York debut off-Broadway in *Thieves' Carnival* in 1955. She did much work with the Phoenix Theatre but her best-known roles have been Ethel Theyer in *On Golden Pond* (1979) and the lead in *Driving Miss Daisy* (1988). Her Lavinia in the 1995 revival of *The Heiress* was much acclaimed.

Sternheim, Carl (1878–1942) German playwright, who satirized German bourgeois society in a number of grotesque comedies. His best-known work is *Die Hose* (The Knickers; 1911), the first in a series of plays that follows a bourgeois family's decline; it was banned for some years after its first production by Reinhardt. Other plays include *Bürger Schippel* (Citizen Schippel; 1913), *Der Snob* (1914), and *Die Marquise von Arcis* (1919), which was highly successful in its English translation as *The Mask of Virtue* (1935), starring Vivien Leigh.

Stevenson, Juliet (1956–) British actress, who trained at RADA and made her debut with the Royal Shakespeare Company in *The Tempest* (1978) at Stratford-on-Avon. Within a few years she graduated to such leading roles as Isabella in *Measure for Measure* (1983) and Rosalind in *As You Like It* (1985). With the National Theatre in 1987–89 she was highly acclaimed in the title roles of Lorca's *Yerma* and Ibsen's *Hedda Gabler*. More recently she has played a torture victim in Ariel Dorfman's *Death and the Maiden* (1992), the title role in *The Duchess of Malfi* (1995), Grusha in *The Caucasian Chalk Circle* (1997), and Amanda in Coward's *Private Lives* (1998). She has also appeared in films.

Stevenson, William (1521–75) English playwright. He is generally assumed to have written GAMMER GURTON'S NEEDLE during his time as a fellow of Christ's College, Cambridge, thereby helping to establish the basis of native comedy within the formal framework of Plautus and Terence.

Stewart, Nellie (1858–1931) Australian actress, who became a leading performer of comic opera in the late 19th century. Having made her acting debut as a child, she enjoyed a long singing career before returning to straight drama with great success in Kester's *Sweet Nell of Drury Lane* (1902). Subsequent successes included Sheldon's *Romance* and Romeo to the Juliet of her daughter **Nancy Stewart** (1892–1973).

stichomythia A form of dialogue in which actors exchange a series of rapid single lines, usually for comic effect or to create a mood of tension. The device was first developed in classical Greek verse drama.

Stiernhielm, Georg Olofson (1598–1672) Swedish poet and playwright, often referred to as 'the father of Swedish poetry'. His dramatic writing comprises a number of masques written for the royal court, notably *Then Fåoangne Cupido* (Cupid Captured; 1649).

Stirling, Fanny (Mary Anne Kehl; 1815–95) British actress, who first appeared under the name Fanny Clifton at the Coburg Theatre (now the Old Vic) in 1832. Subsequent London appearances included two seasons with Macready. She was particularly successful in such parts as Mrs Candour in *The School for Scandal*, Mrs Malaprop in *The Rivals*, and the Nurse in *Romeo and Juliet*.

stock company In the 18th and 19th centuries, a troupe organized to perform a limited repertory at a particular theatre or group of theatres. It was usually led by the **Tragedian** and the **Low Comedian**; other actors would be recruited to fill the roles of **Juvenile Lead**, **Old Man**, **Old Woman**, **Heavy Father**, **Heavy Woman**, **General Utility**, **Walking Lady**, **Walking Gentleman**, **Supernumerary**, and other lesser characters. The system ended with the advent of professional touring companies in the late 19th century.

Stoll Theatre A theatre in Kingsway, London, which was opened as the London Opera House by the elder Oscar Hammerstein in a bid to rival Covent Garden. Early productions were failures and in 1917 Oswald Stoll turned it into a cinema. It became a theatre again in 1941 and for 10 years housed revivals of such musicals as *Rose Marie* and *The Student Prince*, as well as spectacular ice shows. Subsequently it presented ballet and opera seasons as well as the long-running musical *Kismet* (1955). Its final show was a five-week season of the Stratford-on-Avon *Titus Andronicus*, starring Laurence Olivier and Vivien Leigh. It closed in 1957 and was replaced by an office block and the ROYALTY THEATRE, which opened in 1960.

Stoppard, Sir Tom (Tom Straussler; 1937–) British playwright, born in Czechoslovakia, whose distinctive combination of satire, verbal dexterity, and structural ingenuity has produced many award-winning plays. His first play, ROSENCRANTZ AND GUILDENSTERN ARE DEAD, brought him instant recognition as a writer in the tradition of the Theatre of the Absurd. *The Real Inspector Hound* and *After Magritte* were successful one-act plays, the former revolving around two drama critics who become fatally linked to the murder mystery they are reviewing. JUMPERS and *Travesties* consolidated his reputation for inventive discussion of complex intellectual issues, while the musical play *Every Good Boy Deserves Favour* showed a new political seriousness in its depiction of a dissident in a Soviet psychiatric hospital. *The Real Thing* was a marital tragicomedy, while *Hapgood* worked variations upon the conventional spy-thriller. More recent work has included ARCADIA, *Indian Ink*, and *The Invention of Love*, about the poet and scholar A E Housman. Other works have included adapations of Schnitzler's *Das Weite Land* and *Liebelei* as *Undiscovered Country* (1979) and *Dalliance* (1986) respectively, and of Nestroy's *Einen Jux will er sich machen* as *On the Razzle* (1981).

Principal works:
Rosencrantz and Guildenstern are Dead: 1966.
The Real Inspector Hound: 1968.
After Magritte: 1970.
Jumpers: 1972.
Travesties: 1974.

Dirty Linen: 1976.
New Found Land: 1976.
Every Good Boy Deserves Favour: 1977.
Night and Day: 1978.
Dogg's Hamlet: 1979.
Cahoot's Macbeth: 1979.
The Real Thing: 1982.
Hapgood: 1988.
ARCADIA: 1993.
Indian Ink: 1995.
The Invention of Love: 1997.

Storey, David (1933–) British novelist and playwright, whose first play, *The Restoration of Arnold Middleton*, was staged at the Royal Court Theatre, London, in 1967 to immediate acclaim. This was followed by *In Celebration* (1969), which depicted a 40th wedding anniversary party, and *The Contractor* (1970), the action of which centres on the erection of a marquee for a wedding reception. Both *Home* (1970), an examination of life in a mental institution and *The Changing Room* (1971), about the members of a rugby league team, enjoyed success on Broadway. Subsequent plays have included *Cromwell* (1973), *Life Class* (1974), *Mother's Day* (1976), *Sisters* (1978), *Early Days* (1980), *Phoenix* (1984), *The March on Russia* (1989), and *Stages* (1992).

Storm, The (*Groza*) A play by Alexander OSTROVSKY, regarded as his masterpiece. First performance: 1859. Set in a small town on the Volga, the play depicts the tragic love and suicide of the young wife of a merciless trader. English versions were presented in New York in 1900 and London in 1929.

Storm and Stress *See Sturm und Drang.*

Strand Musick Hall *See Gaiety Theatre.*

Strand Theatre A theatre in the Strand in London, which opened in 1832 after several years' use without a licence. It staged burlesque and melodrama before reopening in 1833 under Fanny Kelly and housing a theatre school. It was again reopened in 1836 by Douglas Jerrold, who presented popular adaptations of the novels of Dickens; subsequent successes under William Farren included a version of Goldsmith's *The Vicar of Wakefield* (1848). In 1850 the theatre was renamed **Punch's Playhouse** but failed to prosper until 1858, when burlesques by H J Byron were successfully staged. The theatre was altered in 1865, closed in 1882, and then reopened with classical comedies and revivals of H J Byron. The theatre closed for good in 1905 and was demolished to make way for the Aldwych underground station.

Another **Strand Theatre** was opened in 1905 as a companion to the Aldwych Theatre on the opposite corner of Catherine Street and the Aldwych. Originally called the Waldorf Theatre, it was leased to the US impresarios the Shubert brothers and began with a season of Italian opera, which alternated with plays performed by Eleanora Duse and her company. Beerbohm Tree, H B Irving, and Cyril Maude all played at the theatre in its early years. In 1909 the name was changed to the Strand; two years later it became the **Whitney Theatre**, after the US manager F C Whitney (who purchased the building); however, in 1913 it reverted to the Strand. Under Louis Mayer's directorship (1913–16) the theatre scored its first major success, Vernon and

Owen's *Mr Wu*, with Matheson Lang. José Levy, who took over in 1916, was followed in 1919 by Arthur Bourchier. Among a number of popular Bourchier productions was R L Stevenson's *Treasure Island* (1922), which was revived each Christmas until 1926, and again in 1929. Fred Terry and Julia Neilson presented a season of plays from 1928, including *The Scarlet Pimpernel*. During the 1930s the Strand presented several musical farces as well as 1066 and All That (1935). Donald Wolfit gave lunchtime performances of Shakespeare throughout the London blitz (1940–41) and in 1942 *Arsenic and Old Lace* began its run of 1337 performances. Notable productions of the 1950s and 1960s were *Sailor Beware* (1955) and *A Funny Thing Happened on the Way to the Forum* (1963), starring Frankie Howerd. The theatre was completely refurbished in the early 1970s. Subsequent successes have included the farce *No Sex Please – We're British* (1971–82) and the musical *Buddy*, which opened in 1995 and is still running (2001).

Strange's Men An English theatre company, first recorded performing at Court in 1582. Closely associated for some years with the Admiral's Men, the company appeared at the Theatre (1590–91) and included Shakespeare among its members; subsequently it performed at the Rose Theatre (1592–93) in several of Shakespeare's plays as well as in works by Greene, Marlowe, and others. After 1594 the company moved to the provinces, although several members left to join the Chamberlain's Men.

Stranitsky, Joseph Anton (1676–1726) Austrian actor, who played a key role in the creation of the stock comic character HANSWURST. He developed the role while performing with his own troupe at their home in the Kärntnertortheater in Vienna and made him the central figure in numerous comic plays.

Strasberg, Lee (1901–82) US director, producer, and teacher born in Austria-Hungary, who began as an assistant stage manager at the Garrick Theatre in 1924. He went on to direct plays for the GROUP THEATRE, which he cofounded in 1931, before becoming director of the ACTORS' STUDIO in 1950. There he trained several generations of actors in the METHOD while also directing such successes as Chekhov's *Three Sisters* (1965), the premiere of Odets's *The Silent Partner* (1972), Paul Zindel's *The Effect of Gamma Rays on Man-In-the-Moon Marigolds* (1973), and O'Neill's *Long Day's Journey into Night* (1973).

Stratford (Ontario) Festival A major theatre festival founded in Stratford, Ontario, in Canada in 1953, specifically for the production of the plays of Shakespeare. Under Tyrone Guthrie and Tanya Moiseiwitsch the festival rapidly acquired a strong reputation and a permanent theatre was erected in 1957, arousing great interest with its semicircular auditorium and intimate atmosphere.

Michael Langham succeeded Guthrie in 1956 and, like his predecessor, presented notable foreign stars alongside a well-respected resident Canadian company; actors associated with the festival have included Alec Guinness, Gratien Gélinas, Christopher Plummer, William Hutt, Paul Scofield, Jessica Tandy, and Maggie Smith. As well as Shakespeare, the company has presented plays by such authors as Marlowe, Molière, and Shaw; contemporary works have also been presented and the company has travelled widely. A second theatre, the **Avon Theatre**, was opened in 1963 and an experimental venue, the **Third Stage**, was added in 1971.

Jean Gascon and John Hirsch succeeded Langham in 1967 and Gascon was sole director from 1969 to 1974, encouraging the performance of European classics; the company had presented all of Shakespeare's plays by 1978. Robin Phillips took over in 1975, emphasizing the native Canadian aspects of the festival and making many reforms; the subsequent directors have been John Hirsch (1981–85), John Neville (1986–89), David William (1990–93) and Richard Monette (1994–).

The festival is currently faced with cutbacks in its government funding, resulting in some feeling that productions have been 'dumbed down' to ensure larger audiences. Nevertheless, it remains a vital institution – the largest repertory theatre in North America, with 500 performances on three stages in a 27-week season.

Strattis (4th century BC) Greek playwright, author of several examples of Old Comedy. Fragments of his satirical writings on contemporary figures survive.

Stratton, Eugene (Eugene Augustus Ruhlmann; 1861–1918) British music hall singer, born in the US, who came to London in 1881 and had a brilliant career as a coon singer. He performed such sentimental songs as 'Lily of Laguna' and 'Little Dolly Day Dream'.

Strauss, Botho (1945–) German playwright, poet, and novelist, whose enigmatic work made him the most heatedly discussed German dramatist of the 1980s and 1990s. He was appointed resident playwright at the Berlin Schaubühne in 1970 and won several awards with his first play *Die Hypochonder* (The Hypochondriac, 1971). Subsequent plays, which are noted for their disconnected narratives and menacing atmosphere, include *Gross und Klein* (Great and Small, 1978), *Der Park* (The Park, 1983), *Schlüsschor* (1991), *Das Gleichagewicht* (Equilibrium, 1994), and the epic *Die Ahnlichen* (1998).

Streater, Robert (1624–80) English artist, one of the earliest known English scene painters. Several times praised by John Evelyn, 'His Majesty's Sergeant Painter' worked at the Court theatre in Whitehall and was particularly praised for the sumptuous scenes for Dryden's *The Conquest of Granada* (1670–71).

Streetcar Named Desire, A A Pulitzer Prize-winning play by Tennessee WILLIAMS. First performance: Broadway, 1947, directed by Elia Kazan, with Jessica Tandy as the precocious but neurotic Blanche DuBois. Blanche's mental disintegration in the face of her brother-in-law Stanley's brutality is the central theme of the play. Stanley was played by the young Marlon Brando.

Street Scene A play by Elmer RICE. First performance: New York, 1929. The play takes place on a hot summer night in a New York neighbourhood near the East River, where poor and rich live in proximity. It is an ensemble play with a large cast and several interweaving plots, the main one dealing with an adulterous wife who is shot dead by her husband. A musical version by Kurt WEILL was staged in 1947.

Strehler, Giorgio (1921–97) Italian director, who cofounded the PICCOLO TEATRO DELLA CITTÀ DI MILANO in 1947 and remained associated with it for 45 years. The establishment of this important regional company began the TEATRO STABILE movement in Italy. Strehler's numerous productions for the troupe included works by Shakespeare and Brecht as well as Italian playwrights. From 1968 to 1972 he also directed the Gruppo Teatro e Azione, a company committed to more directly political theatre. In the early 1980s he was chiefly responsible for establishing the EC-funded THÉÂTRE DE L'EUROPE in Paris and became its first head. He was obliged to resign from the Piccolo Teatro in 1997, owing to allegations of financial mismanagement.

Strife A play by John GALSWORTHY. First performance: London, 1909. The play vividly dramatizes the struggle between management and working men during a prolonged strike, depicting with sympathy the suffering it causes.

strike To remove an item of scenery or other object from the stage, or the entire set itself.

Strindberg, (Johann) August (1849–1912) Swedish playwright and novelist, whose best-known plays are characterized by his compulsive interest in the conflict between the sexes. Strindberg's unsettled childhood influenced much of his writing, which frequently demonstrates his emotional instability. After early experiments with historical dramas and farces influenced by his reading of Ibsen, he adopted an increasingly embittered tone culminating in the misogynistic drama THE FATHER, which he wrote during the first (1877–91) of his three unhappy marriages (to the actress Siri von Essen).

MISS JULIE and THE CREDITORS were equally savage and pessimistic in their view of sexual relationships and constitute a landmark in the Scandinavian theatre with their naturalistic dialogue. After the failure of his second marriage (1893–94) to the Austrian journalist Frida Uhl, Strindberg underwent a complete mental breakdown; subsequently (as well as becoming interested in alchemy) he exchanged his naturalistic approach for a more Symbolist style and widened the scope of his drama. Works of this prolific period include the lengthy mystical play *To Damascus* and *The Dance of Death* and A DREAM PLAY, which anticipated the development of Expressionism.

In 1904 his third marriage, to the Norwegian actress Harriet Bosse, ended in divorce; at the same time Strindberg became more closely involved with the Intima Teatern in Stockholm, where such late dramas (sometimes called the Chamber Plays) as THE GHOST SONATA, *The Storm*, and *The Burnt House* were first performed. His works are regularly revived on the international stage and remain influential for their sexual subject matter, their exploration of the unconscious mind, and their technical virtuosity.

Principal works:

Mäster Olof: 1890 (written 1872).

Lycko-Pers Resa: 1883.

Fadren: 1887; translated as *The Father*.

Fröken Julie: 1889; translated as *Miss Julie*.

Fordringsägare: 1890; translated as *The Creditors*.

Advent: 1898.

Folksungagen: 1899; translated as *The Saga of the Folkungs*.

Gustaf Vasa: 1899.

Erik XIV: 1899.

Gustaf Adolph: 1899.

Brott och Brott: 1899; translated as *Crimes and Crimes*.

Påsk: 1900; translated as *Easter*.

Till Damaskus: 1900.

Dödsdansen I–II: 1905 (written 1901); translated as *The Dance of Death*.

Kronbruden: 1901; translated as *The Crown Bride*.
Ett drömspel: 1905 (written 1902); translated as *A Dream Play*.
Spöksonaten: 1908 (written 1907); translated as *The Ghost Sonata*.
Oväder: 1907; translated as *The Storm*.
Brända tomten: 1907; translated as *The Burnt House*.
Pelikanen: 1907; translated as *The Pelican*.

strip light *See* batten.

striptease *See* burlesque.

Stritch, Elaine (1926–) US actress, who made her first stage appearance in 1944. Her successes since then have included Regina Giddens in Lillian Hellman's *The Little Foxes* (1947), Sally Adams in *Call Me Madam* (1953), Grace in Inge's *Bus Stop* (1955), Martha in Albee's *Who's Afraid of Virginia Woolf?* (1963), and a starring role in Sondheim's *Company* (1970). She made her London debut in Coward's *Sail Away* (1961). Following much work in British television, she returned to the stage in Toronto and New York as Parthy in the Harold Price revival of *Show Boat* (1993) and as Claire in the 1996 revival of Albee's *A Delicate Balance*.

stroboscope A unit of lighting, capable of producing rapid flashes of light that create the illusion of slow motion on the stage.

Strømsted, Liv (1922–) Norwegian actress, who became a leading performer at the Nationaltheatret in Oslo. She found acclaim in a wide range of plays, from the tragedies of Shakespeare to dramas by Brecht and Ibsen, notably *The Master Builder*, *Peer Gynt*, and *A Doll's House*.

Student Prince, The An operetta by Sigmund Romberg, based on the play *Old Heidelberg* by Wilhelm Meyer-Foerster. First performance: New York, 1924. The plot revolves around a prince studying in Heidelberg and his romance with a barmaid.

Studio Arena Theatre A US company founded as the Buffalo Community Theatre in 1927. By 1965 they were a completely professional troupe specializing in contemporary US drama. Among the many premieres given by the group have been Albee's *Box Mao Box* (1968), Truman Capote's *Other Voices, Other Rooms* (1973), and Paul Giovanni's *The Crucifer of Blood* (1978). Its theatre school, which opened in 1929, is the oldest continually operating school attached to a resident theatre; it is now affiliated with the State University of New York at Buffalo.

Studio Theatre A small flexible auditorium attached to the Sherman Theatre in Cardiff, Wales. Opened in 1973 (as the **Arena**) and seating 163, it is used as a venue for both experimental professional companies and amateurs.

Sturdza-Bulandra, Lucia (1873–1961) Romanian actress, who – with her husband – founded a noted company in 1914. Highly acclaimed in a wide range of parts, she and her husband led the company until 1943, noted successes including Zamfirescu's *Miss Anastasia* (1928). Upon her husband's death she became manager of the Municipal Theatre, which was subsequently renamed the Bulandra Theatre in her honour.

Sturm und Drang (Storm and Stress) A German theatrical movement of the later 18th century that anticipated many aspects of Romanticism. Taking Shakespeare as their model, such writers as the young Goethe and Schiller reacted fiercely against NEOCLASSICAL DRAMA, tackling such themes as social injustice in highly emotional terms. The movement's philosophy was largely derived from Rousseau's writings, and took its name from the title of a play by Klinger (1776). The form was highly influential upon the development of MELODRAMA and spawned a subsidiary genre, the RITTERDRAMA.

Stuyvesant Theatre *See* Belasco Theatre.

Sudakov, Ilya Kayovleivich (1890–1969) Russian actor and director, who began his career at the Moscow Art Theatre. After success with such plays as Ivanov's *Armoured Train 14–69* (1927) and Afinogenov's *Fear* (1935), he moved to the Maly Theatre (1937) and finally to the Gogol Theatre in Moscow. Notable productions after World War II included Chekhov's *Uncle Vanya* (1947) and Alexei Tolstoy's *The Road to Calvary* (1957).

Suddenly Last Summer A play by Tennessee WILLIAMS. First performance: New York, 1958. The plot concerns the evil Mrs Venable, who, in an attempt to hide the truth about her son's death – and what that reveals about his life – tries to force a lobotomy on her young cousin, who witnessed everything. The play was filmed in 1959 with Katherine Hepburn, Elizabeth Taylor, and Montgomery Clift.

Sudermann, Hermann (1857–1928) German novelist, playwright, and pioneer of Realism in Germany. His brilliant dramatic technique transformed otherwise superficial treatments of the problems facing contemporary Berlin society; his most famous play – *Heimat* (Magda; 1893) – was performed worldwide with such leading ladies as Sarah Bernhardt, Eleonora Duse, Mrs Patrick Campbell, and Minnie Maddern Fiske. He also wrote historical and biblical plays but was better known for such dramas of intrigue as *Es lebe das Leben!* (The Joy of Living; 1902) and *Der gute Ruf* (A Good Reputation; 1913).

Sud-Est, Centre Dramatique du *See Décentralisation Dramatique.*

Suett, Richard (1755–1805) British actor, usually known as 'Dicky' Suett. An actor from the age of 14, as a member of Foote's company at the Haymarket, he was eminently successful playing Shakespearean clowns. Admired by George III, he was noted for his practical jokes and collection of wigs.

Sukhovo-Kobylin, Alexander Vasilievich (1817–1903) Russian playwright, who wrote three dramas depicting the changing nature of contemporary Russian society. A nobleman, he was imprisoned while writing his first play, the comedy *Svad'ba Krechinskogo* (Krechinsky's Wedding; 1855), after being implicated in the death of his mistress and thereafter suffered from the attentions of the censor. Together with his other two plays, the satires *Delo* (The Case; 1881) and *Smert' Tarel'kina* (Tarelkin's Death; 1900), this play was much influenced by Gogol and Saltikov-Shchedrin.

Sullivan, Sir Arthur *See* Gilbert, Sir W(illiam) S(chwenk).

Sullivan, (Thomas) Barry (1821–91) British actor, who gained a reputation in Ireland before touring the provinces and managing a theatre in Aberdeen for three years. In 1852 he played Hamlet at the Haymarket, subsequently joining Phelps at Sadler's Wells and touring the US and Australia. In 1879 he played opposite Helen Faucit at the inaugural performance in the Memorial Theatre, Stratford-on-Avon.

Sumarokov, Alexei Petrovich (1718–77) Russian playwright and poet, known as the 'Racine of the North'. His neoclassical dramas drew heavily on Russian history and include several comedies and nine tragedies as well as an adaptation of *Hamlet*. He encouraged the foundation of the first professional acting company in Russia and was director of the Russian Theatre in St Petersburg from 1756 to 1761.

Summer and Smoke A play by Tennessee WILLIAMS. First performance: New York, 1948. The plot concerns a spinster, Alma, and the local rebel, John; at the beginning of the play John pursues Alma, who will have nothing to do with him, but by the end of the play Alma pursues John, who has since become the town doctor and turns her down.

Sumner, John (1924–) British director, who became a leading figure in post-war Australian theatre. He was closely associated with the Melbourne Theatre Company from 1959, having previously directed the premiere of Ray Lawler's *Summer of the Seventeenth Doll* (1955) for the Union Theatre Repertory Company. Other significant productions included several other plays by Lawler.

Supernumerary *See* stock company.

Suppliant Women, The A tragedy by AESCHYLUS. First performance: Athens, c. 460 BC. The first part of a tetralogy, it depicts the adventures of Danaus and reflects the threat to contemporary Athens presented by various neighbours. Another tragedy of the same name was written by EURIPIDES (date unknown) but this has a different theme.

Surrey Music Hall *See* Winchester Music Hall.

Surrey Theatre A theatre in Blackfriars Road, London, converted by Elliston in 1809 from an amphitheatre known as the **Royal Circus**, originally opened in 1782. He incorporated ballets in all his productions to overcome the Patent Act, but without much success and he relinquished the theatre to Thomas Dibdin after five years. However, Elliston returned as manager in 1827 and had an outstanding success with Douglas Jerrold's *Black-Ey'd Susan* (1829); later managements established the theatre as a home of popular melodrama. It was burned down in 1865, but was rapidly rebuilt and after George Conquest took over in 1880 it became famous for sensational dramas and pantomime. When he died the theatre suffered a decline; it was demolished in 1934.

Susie *See* Toby.

Sussex's Men An English theatre company formed by the Earl of Sussex in 1569. The company played at Court, in the provinces, and at the Rose Theatre under Henslowe, performing Shakespeare's *Titus Andronicus* and other works. It dissolved following the Earl's death in 1593.

Sutherland, Efua (1924–96) Ghanaian playwright, who did much to popularize theatre in Ghana. She founded the Experimental Theatre Players in 1958 and the

Ghana Drama Studio in Accra in 1960, as well as being very active as a teacher of drama. Her own plays included *Edufa* (1957), which is an adaptation of *Alcestis* by Euripides, *Foriwa* (1967), *The Marriage of Anansewa* (1975), and plays for children.

Suzman, Janet (1939–) British actress and director, born in South Africa, who has found repeated acclaim in both Shakespearean and modern drama. She joined the Royal Shakespeare Company in 1962; early successes included performances as Portia, Ophelia, and Rosalind as well as roles in plays by Willis Hall and Pinter. In 1972 she was high praised as Shakespeare's Cleopatra, while subsequent successes included Athol Fugard's *Hello and Goodbye* (1973), Masha in Chekhov's *Three Sisters* (1976), the title role in Ibsen's *Hedda Gabler* (1977), Clytemnestra and Helen in *The Greeks* (1980), and Racine's *Andromache* (1987). In 1987 she returned to South Africa to direct a much-praised *Othello* in Johannesburg. She has since directed a number of plays including *Death of a Salesman* (1993) and, in Johannesburg again, the Brecht adaptation *The Good Woman of Sharkville* (1996). She was married to Trevor NUNN from 1969 to 1986.

Svoboda, Josef (1920–) Czech stage designer, who has attracted much attention for his work as head designer (since 1951) of the National Theatre in Prague. His innovative and highly influential designs for theatres in other countries have included his abstract set for Ostrovsky's *The Storm* (1966) and Chekhov's *Three Sisters* (1967), both seen at London's National Theatre. Other notable productions have included Gogol's *The Government Inspector* (1948), *Hamlet* (1959), and Dostoevsky's *The Idiot* (1970). He is also widely known for his development of the **Laterna Magika**, a method by which cinematic projections and live performances are combined. In 1973 he founded a group specifically to present such productions.

Swann, Donald *See* Flanders, Michael.

Swanston, Eliard (d. 1651) English actor, who became well known as a member of the King's Men from 1624. His roles ranged from Othello to Chapman's Bussy d'Ambois. He was also involved in the business management of the company; during the Civil War he worked as a jeweller and supported the Parliamentarians.

Swan Theatre The fourth Elizabethan playhouse to be built in London, erected on Bankside by Francis Langley in about 1595. Its design is known to theatre historians owing to a sketch made by a Dutch visitor, Johanne de Witt. The theatre was first let to Pembroke's Men but their production of the satirical play *The Isle of Dogs* (1597) caused the suspension of dramatic performances there for some months. Various sporting contests and exhibitions also took place in the late 1590s, while Lady Elizabeth's Men, led by Henslowe, performed for two years there before moving to the Hope in 1614. Middleton's *A Chaste Maid in Cheapside* was produced in 1611 and it is possible that Prince Charles's Men appeared there a few years later; after 1621 it seems to have been used for prize fights and, by 1632 it was derelict.

The **Swan Theatre** at Stratford-on-Avon was designed by Michael Reardon, who was not uninfluenced by de Witt's drawing, and built in the shell of the old SHAKE-SPEARE MEMORIAL THEATRE. Here the Royal Shakespeare Company tends to produce plays from the apocryphal Shakespearean canon or works that he might have influenced, or been influenced by. The theatre opened in 1986 with *The Two Noble Kinsmen*; subsequent productions have included Thomas Heywood's *The Fair Maid* *of the West*, Aphra Behn's *The Rover*, Ben Jonson's *The New Inn*, and a cycle of Shakespeare's history plays (2000). Edward Bond's *Restoration* was the first contemporary play to be staged there (1988).

swazzle *See* Punch and Judy.

Sweeney Todd A musical by Stephen SONDHEIM, with book by Hugh Wheeler. First performance: New York, 1979. The plot is based on the early Victorian legend of Sweeney Todd, the 'demon barber of Fleet Street', who cut the throats of his customers and gave their bodies to a Mrs Lovett, who baked them into meat pies. Previous treatments of the tale tended towards burlesque, but Sondheim's version is genuinely dark, even if it has moments of ghoulish humour. The show has little spoken dialogue, bringing the effect close to opera.

Sweet Bird of Youth A play by Tennessee WILLIAMS. First performance: New York, 1959. Chance, a Hollywood drifter, brings the Princess Kosmonopolous back to his hometown, only to meet with serious trouble from the father of a girl he had once seduced.

Świnarski, Konrad (1930–75) Polish director, who had attracted a wide reputation before his early death in an air crash. After training with the Berliner Ensemble he presented the premiere of Weiss's *Marat/Sade* (1963) and subsequently worked in Cracow, where he took over the Stary Theatre in 1969. His innovative productions included such works as Krasiński's *The Undivine Comedy* (1965) and plays by Shakespeare, while his production of Mickiewicz's *Forefathers' Eve* was seen in London in 1975; among his last works was Mayakovsky's *The Bed Bug*.

Swinbourne, Charlotte Elizabeth *See* Vandenhoff, George.

Swiney, Owen (1675–1754) British actor and manager, born in Wexford, Ireland, who appeared with the Drury Lane company in 1700 and also acted as Christopher Rich's manager. He leased the Haymarket in 1705, where he was forced to stage opera due to the licensing laws, and managed Drury Lane for a brief period before returning to the Haymarket. He left the country to escape creditors in 1710 and did not return for 20 years, when he called himself **MacSwiney**. He was the constant companion of Peg Woffington.

Sword Play *See* mummers' play.

Sydney Opera House A distinctive theatre and operatic complex on the harbour front in Sydney, Australia, designed by Jorn Utzon and opened in 1973. It houses four separate auditoriums, of which one (seating 500) is used for straight dramatic productions. The Old Tote Theatre company was resident there for a time until the formation of the Sydney Theatre Company, which was installed there in 1980.

Symbolism A late 19th-century movement in the theatre and the arts in general which constituted a reaction against Realism. It involved the deliberate use of highly stylized language, decor, and acting styles in an attempt to convey the inner significance of life, as opposed to superficial realities. The first Symbolist dramas were created by Paul Fort and subsequently Lugné-Poë at the Théâtre d'Art in the late 1890s. The plays of Maeterlink, Claudel, Strindberg, Yeats, and O'Neill were all to varying degrees influenced by the movement.

symphonic drama *See* Green, Paul Eliot.

Syndicate *See* Theatrical Syndicate.

Synge, J(ohn) M(illington) (1871–1909) Irish playwright, born in Dublin, whose plays are noted for his understanding of character and his poetic use of language. Educated at Trinity College, Dublin, he spent some years travelling in Europe before settling in Paris. In 1896 he met W B Yeats, who persuaded him into visiting the Aran Islands off Galway, where he spent every summer between 1898 and 1902. He recounted his experiences in *The Aran Islands*; his work as a dramatist began after 1902, when he joined the Irish National Dramatic Society. All of his six plays explore life in remote rural communities with irreverence and ironic humour; however, they angered nationalists, who felt that they misrepresented the Irish people and Catholicism and offended decency. Synge's early death deprived the Abbey Theatre of its first great dramatist; such masterpieces as THE PLAYBOY OF THE WESTERN WORLD are constantly revived.

Principal works:
  In the Shadow of the Glen: 1903.
  RIDERS TO THE SEA: 1904.
  The Well of the Saints: 1905.
  The Playboy of the Western World: 1907.
  The Tinker's Wedding: 1908.
  DEIRDRE OF THE SORROWS: 1910.

Syrus, Publilius *See* Publilius Syrus.

Szajna, Józef (1922–) Polish director and set designer, who became famous for his work at the People's Theatre in Nowa Huta (of which he was director from 1963 to 1966) and subsequently at the Studio Theatre in Warsaw. As well as classic plays by Goethe and Shakespeare, he has also staged numerous contemporary Polish dramas, many of which have been influenced by his experiences in Auschwitz. Productions seen in the UK have included *Macbeth* (1970).

Szigligeti, Ede (1814–78) Hungarian playwright, who became the first professional Hungarian writer for the stage. Closely associated with the National Theatre of Hungary, as both secretary and then director, he contributed over 100 plays, including such histories as *The Captivity of Ferenc Rákóczi II* (1848), comedies, and folk dramas.

Tabarin (Antoine Girard; d. 1626) French actor, who was highly popular in booths on the Pont Neuf and the Place Dauphine in Paris, where he gave performances designed to attract customers for his brother Mondor, a quack doctor. He performed farcical pieces much influenced by the Italian *commedia dell'arte* and was famous for his wide-brimmed hat, which he manipulated into numerous forms.

tabernaria *See togata.*

tableau A grouping of motionless actors assembled to achieve a particular visual effect. The practice was especially popular in the 19th century, notably in imitation of famous paintings, and was also used in the nude *tableaux vivants* of the earlier 20th century.

taboos Many of the superstitions associated with the theatre are common throughout the world. Some have a sound basis in commonsense, particularly those surrounding the use of unreliable props (real flowers, for instance, should never appear on stage) and the conduct of rehearsals (a good dress rehearsal is considered unlucky because it can create a false sense of security). Others that are more enigmatic include the taboos prohibiting the presence in the theatre of peacock feathers, whistling in the dressing-room, the wishing of good luck to an actor before he goes on, and the many superstitions linked to *Macbeth* – probably a consequence of the element of black magic involved in the play and the long history of mishaps in its production. The tradition that no actor should wear green on stage dates from the time when limelight, which itself cast a greenish hue, was in use, making performers in that colour seem to disappear.

tabs *See curtain.*

Tadema, Sir Lawrence Alma- *See Alma-Tadema, Sir Lawrence.*

Taganka Theatre A theatre in Moscow, properly called the **Theatre of Drama and Comedy**, which was established in 1946. Seating 600 people, it began with a lengthy programme of modern Soviet works but diversified from the 1960s with avant-garde productions of Brecht, Weiss, Gorky, Molière, and Shakespeare.

Tagore, Rabindranath (1861–1941) Indian poet, philosopher, and playwright, who wrote in Bengali and has been widely translated into English. His sympathy for the rural poor and his love of the Bengali countryside are common themes throughout his work. Among his best-known plays are *Visarjana* (Sacrifice; 1890), *Dakaghan*

(The Post Office; 1913), and *Rakta-Karabi* (Red Oleanders; 1924); later works include the dance play *Chitrangada* (1936).

tail *See* leg.

Taïrov, Alexander Yakovlevich (Aleksandr Kornblit; 1885–1950) Russian director, who founded the celebrated KAMERNY THEATRE in Moscow in 1914 and was the leading director there until his death. His productions were remarkable for their combination of various types of performance, including ballet and music hall, and reflected his opposition to the theories of Stanislavsky. Although influenced by Meyerhold in his preference for highly theatrical drama, he nonetheless upheld Stanislavsky's ideas about the importance of the actor, emphasizing the physical aspects of the actors' presence and demanding long rehearsals. He used strongly symbolic – often Cubist – sets and insisted upon the director's overall control. Productions included both classics and plays by contemporary playwrights, including Shaw and O'Neill. After the Revolution of 1917 he gradually adapted to the demand for Socialist Realism in the theatre; successes from this later period included Vishnevsky's *An Optimistic Tragedy* (1935) and *Madame Bovary* (1939). His wife was Alisa Koonen, the leading actress at the Kamerny Theatre.

Tale of Mystery, A A melodrama by Thomas HOLCROFT, adapted from Pixérécourt's *Coelina, ou l'Enfant de mystère*. First performance: 1802. The play revolves around the wicked Count Romaldo, who plots a murder in order to marry a wealthy heiress; it effectively inaugurated melodrama in Britain.

Talfourd, Sir Thomas Noon (1795–1854) British playwright, theatre critic, and lawyer, who was also the author of several verse tragedies in the French style. *Ion* (1836) was a personal success for Macready when produced at Covent Garden; *The Athenian Captive* (1838) and *Glencoe* (1840) were less popular. As a member of parliament he became identified with the Copyright Act of 1833.

Talk of the Town *See* Hippodrome.

Talma, François-Joseph (1763–1826) French actor-manager, who spent his childhood in England before training as an actor in Paris under Molé and others. He made his first appearance as a professional actor at the Comédie-Française in 1787 in Voltaire's *Mahomet*. In 1789 his passionate interpretation of Chénier's antimonarchical *Charles IX* caused an uproar and the closure of the theatre. His reputation established, he went on to form his own company at the Théâtre de la Révolution and to produce realistically staged and costumed versions of plays by Corneille, Shakespeare, and others. In 1799 the Comédie-Française was reunited at Talma's theatre and, with Napoleon's approval, he set about reforming the national theatre and establishing himself as the foremost player of tragedy in his day.

Tamayo y Baus, Manuel (1829–98) Spanish playwright, who wrote numerous plays in both the Romantic and Realist traditions. Early in his career he wrote such popular dramas as the patriotic *La ricahembra* (1854), which was influenced by Schiller, and the historical drama *La locura de amor* (The Insanity of Love; 1855). Later he turned to social issues in such works as *Lances de honor* (1863) and *Los hombres de bien* (1870). Other plays include *Lo positivo* (Materialism; 1862) and (under the name

Joaquín Estebánez) *Un drama nuevo* (A New Play; 1867), a tragedy set in Elizabethan England, which is considered his finest play.

Tamburlaine the Great A drama in blank verse by Christopher MARLOWE, written in two parts. First performance: London, 1587–88. The play's grandiose rhetoric influenced many contemporaries. Tamburlaine's rise from shepherd to imperial ruler typifies the vaunting confidence of the Renaissance period, but his subsequent fall reveals Marlowe's interest in characterization. Notable scenes include the deaths of the Turkish ruler Bajazet and his wife in a cage and Tamburlaine's own demise after his beloved Zenocrate has died.

Taming of the Shrew, The A comedy by William SHAKESPEARE, written c. 1593. First performance: date unknown. Ostensibly a broad comedy of love and marriage, the play comments, through the enforced subservience of Katherina (the 'Shrew') by Petruchio, upon the role of women in society. Features of the play include the framing device according to which the main action is a play-within-a-play presented to a drunken tinker, Christopher Sly, and Katherina's long final speech on the subject of marital obedience.

Tandy, Jessica (1909–94) US actress, born in Britain, who first appeared in London in 1927. She made her New York debut in G B Stern's *The Matriarch* (1930) and then returned to London, where she played Ophelia to Gielgud's Hamlet (1934) and appeared in Rattigan's *French Without Tears* (1936). She played for a season with the Old Vic company, mainly in Shakespearean roles, and then returned to New York to play Kay in Priestley's *Time and the Conways* and to triumph as Blanche in Williams's *A Streetcar Named Desire* (1947). Subsequently she was acclaimed alongside her second husband, Hume CRONYN, in such plays as N C Hunter's *A Day By the Sea* (1955), Chekhov's *Three Sisters* (1963), and Miller's *Death of a Salesman* (1963). They also appeared in plays by Dürrenmatt, Albee, and Beckett, as well as *The Gin Game* (1977) and *Foxfire* (1982). Her first husband was the film actor Jack Hawkins.

Tantalus An epic cycle of plays about the Trojan War, devised by John BARTON and staged by Peter HALL. First production: Denver Center for the Performing Arts, Colorado, 2000. Some 15 years in gestation, the project was held back by a series of financial, artistic, and logistic problems that culminated in Barton disowning Hall's production because of cuts to the text. The ten-hour epic, which featured an Anglo-American cast, toured Britain in 2001.

Tapping, Florence (Florence Cowell; 1852–1926) British actress, daughter of the music hall star Sam COWELL. As a child she toured with the Wyndhams in the US, then worked in the companies of Kate Vaughan, Ben Greet, and the Kendals, and was in Miss Horniman's company at Manchester. She rejoined this company in 1916 for a revival of Houghton's *Hindle Wakes*.

Tardieu, Jean (1903–95) French poet and playwright. Several of his short dramatic works, such as *Conversation-Sinfonietta* (1951) and *La Sonate et les trois messieurs* (1955), explore the relationship between music and language. He also wrote burlesque sketches and experimental plays in the absurdist tradition, notably *Les Amants du métro* (1952), *La Serrure* (1955), and *Le Guichet* (1955). In the 1950s and 1960s he was head of the French broadcasting service's experimental drama studios.

Tarkington, (Newton) Booth (1869–1946) US novelist and playwright, whose most famous play was *Monsieur Beaucaire*, which he adapted from his own novel in 1901. His other plays include *Your Humble Servant* (1910), *Mr Antonio* (1916), *Clarence* (1919), and *Tweedles* (1923).

Tarleton, Richard (d. 1588) English actor, who was considered the finest player of rustic clowns of his day. Short in stature and described as flat-nosed and having a squint, he is thought to have inspired the character of Bottom in Shakespeare's *A Midsummer Night's Dream* and the description of Yorick in *Hamlet*. He joined Queen Elizabeth's Men in 1583 and became a great favourite of Elizabeth I until jokes about Sir Walter Raleigh and the Earl of Leicester provoked his dismissal from the Court. None of his own roles are known for certain and it is thought that much of his clowning was composed on an extemporaneous basis. He popularized the JIG – of which he was the finest interpreter – and composed ballads; he was also credited with several lost plays and numerous jestbooks (including many certainly by later writers).

Tarragon Theatre A Toronto theatre company founded in 1971 by Bill Glassco and his wife Jane Gordon. Important for its sponsoring of Canadian plays, it not only shows works originally written in English, but often produces translations of French-Canadian dramatists.

Tartuffe; ou, l'Imposteur A comedy by MOLIÈRE. First performance: Versailles, 1664. A satirical attack on religious hypocrisy, the play was banned in Paris until 1669. Tartuffe gains entrance to the household of Orgon through exaggerated displays of false piety and takes advantage of his host's gullibility: he is finally unmasked when he attempts to seduce Orgon's wife.

Tasso, Torquato (1544–95) Italian poet and playwright, usually remembered for the epic poem *Gerusalemme liberata* (1581). His play *L'Aminta* (1573) was one of the earliest of all pastoral dramas and inspired numerous imitations, including passages in *Love's Labour's Lost*. His other dramatic works include the early romantic tragedy *Torrismondo* (1587) and the comedy *Intrighi d'amore*.

Taste of Honey, A A play by Shelagh Delaney. First performance: Theatre Workshop, London, 1958. The plot, which revolves around the pregnant and rebellious Jo, celebrates working-class values and female independence.

Tate, Harry (Ronald Macdonald Hutchison; 1872–1940) British comedian, born in Scotland, who began as a mimic at the Camberwell Empire in 1895. He developed his sketch 'Motoring' into one of the most famous comic acts on the halls and followed it with a series of similar sporting sketches.

Tate, Nahum (1652–1715) English poet and playwright, born in Ireland, usually remembered for his eccentric versions of the plays of Shakespeare. His most notorious adaptation was that of *King Lear* (1681), in which he omitted the Fool altogether and allowed Cordelia to marry Edgar; it remained the most performed version of the play until 1838. His other Shakespearean adaptations included *The Sicilian Usurper* (1681), from *Richard II*, and *The Ingratitude of a Common-Wealth* (1681), from *Coriolanus*. He became poet laureate in 1692.

Tavistock House Theatre A private theatre created by Charles Dickens at his house in Tavistock Square, London. Albert Smith's burletta *Guy Fawkes* was the inaugural performance; subsequently the first productions of *The Lighthouse* (1855) – in which Dickens played the lighthouse-keeper – and *The Frozen Deep* (1857), both by Dickens's friend Wilkie Collins, were given there.

Tavistock Repertory Company A nonprofessional theatre company founded in Bloomsbury, London, in 1932; in 1952 it moved to new premises in Islington, where it established a strong reputation with the London premieres of plays by Tennessee Williams, Arrabal, and John Whiting among others. Their home venue was opened as the **Tower Theatre** in 1953; the company continues to present about 18 productions there each year and also mounts regular foreign tours.

Taylor, C(ecil) P(hilip) (1929–81) Scottish playwright, whose works were mainly performed in regional theatres, notably the Traverse Theatre, Edinburgh. Although his plays were often political, the dominant theme throughout his work is the value of simple honesty. This is apparent in *Allergy*, a comic one-act play attributing political failure to human weakness, and in his most highly acclaimed play, *Good*. First staged in 1981 by the Royal Shakespeare Company at the Warehouse, it examines the self-deception behind a progressive German professor's decision to work at Auschwitz.

Despite Taylor's strong reputation, relatively few of his plays appeared in West End theatres. Among those that did were *Good*, *Schippel* (as *The Plumber's Progress*, 1975), and *And a Nightingale Sang...* (1979).

Principal works:
Happy Days Are Here Again: 1965.
Of Hope and Glory: 1965.
Allergy: 1966.
Bread and Butter: 1966.
Passion Play: 1971.
The Black and White Minstrels: 1972.
Next Year in Tel Aviv: 1973.
Schippel: 1974.
Gynt!: 1975.
Walter: 1977.
And A Nightingale Sang...: 1979.
Good: 1981.
Bring Me Sunshine, Bring Me Smiles: 1982.

Taylor, Joseph (c. 1585–1652) English actor, who was a shareholder in the Blackfriars Theatre and was named in the First Folio list of Shakespearean players. He joined the King's Men in 1619, later becoming (with John Lowin) the company's business manager. He appeared as Hamlet, Ferdinand in *The Duchess of Malfi*, and in other parts created by Richard Burbage; he also acted in plays by Jonson, Massinger, and Beaumont and Fletcher.

Taylor, Laurette (Laurette Cooney; 1884–1946) US actress, who made her stage debut as a child. She was subsequently acclaimed in the title role of *Peg o' My Heart* (1912), a play by her second husband John Manners. In 1938 she returned to the stage as Miss Midget in Sutton Vane's *Outward Bound*; shortly before her death she won further praise in Tennessee Williams's *The Glass Menagerie* (1945–46).

Taylor, Tom (1817–80) British playwright, journalist, and amateur actor, who was the author of around 100 dramatic pieces. His best-known works include *Masks and Faces* (1852, with Charles Reade), which was based on the life of Peg Woffington, *Still Waters Run Deep* (1855), *Our American Cousin* (1858), in which Sothern triumphed as Lord Dundreary, and *The Ticket-of-Leave Man* (1863). As an actor he often took part in the amateur productions presented by Dickens.

Taymore, Julie (1952–) US director and designer, who has developed a striking visual style incorporating puppetry and elements of non-Western theatre. Her first New York work was *The Haggada* for the New York Shakespeare Festival (1980), but wider notice came when *Juan Darien: A Carnival Mass* (1988) was revived at the Lincoln Center in 1996. *The Green Bird* (1996) gained the attention of the Disney Corporation, which hired her to direct the stage version of *The Lion King* (1997) to startling effect.

Tchehov or **Tchekhov** *See* Chekhov, Anton (Pavlovich).

Tearle, (George) Osmund (1852–1901) British actor, who made his first appearance in Liverpool in 1869. Two years later he performed Hamlet for the first time at Warrington. He made his London debut at the Gaiety Theatre in 1875. Later he spent five years in the US at Wallack's Theatre; in 1888, on his return to Britain, he formed a Shakespearean company that toured the country.

His son was the actor **Sir Godfrey Seymour Tearle** (1884–1953), who made his stage debut in his father's company at the age of nine. After initial success in romantic dramas, he played Othello (1921) and Hamlet (1931) without distinction; later, having been acclaimed in Charles Morgan's *The Flashing Stream* (1938) and Emlyn Williams's *The Light of Heart* (1940), he was praised in numerous Shakespearean roles at the Shakespeare Memorial Theatre.

teaser *See* proscenium border.

Teatro Campesino *See* Chicano Theatre.

Teatro Chicano *See* Chicano Theatre.

Teatro de la Esperanza *See* Chicano Theatre.

Teatro de la Gente *See* Chicano Theatre.

Teatro de los Barrios *See* Chicano Theatre.

Teatro del Piojo *See* Chicano Theatre.

Teatro Eslava *See* Martínez Sierra, Gregorio.

Teatro Farnese An elaborate theatre in Parma, Italy, designed by Giovanni Aleotti. Begun in 1619 and opened in 1628, the theatre was one of the first to have a stage framed by a proscenium arch; in front of this there was a further open space, which could also be used by the actors. The building has survived but is now rarely used for dramatic performances.

Teatro Intím *See* Gual, Adriá.

Teatro Popolare Italiano *See* Gassman, Vittorio.

teatro por horas *See zarzuela.*

Teatro sperimentale degli Indipendenti *See* Indipendenti, Teatro sperimentale degli.

teatro stabile Any one of the professional regional companies founded in Italy in the later half of the 20th century. The establishment of *teatri stabili* throughout the country marked the first attempt to form permanent troupes in the Italian theatrical tradition; leading companies to emerge in this phase included the PICCOLO TEATRO DELLA CITTÀ DI MILANO.

technical rehearsal A rehearsal, usually held shortly before the first public performance, at which all the technical aspects of a production are run through.

Teirlinck, Herman (1879–1967) Belgian playwright, who became one of the leading writers associated with the Vlaamse Volkstoneel in Antwerp, writing in Flemish. *The Slow-Motion Film* (1922) inaugurated Flemish Expressionism; other significant works included a revived miracle play, the experimental *Man Without a Body* (1925), and *De Oresteia* (1946). He also imported the ideas of Appia and Gordon Craig and published much theoretical work on the theatre as well as teaching drama and founding the Flemish National Theatre.

telari *See periaktoi.*

Telbin, William (1813–73) British scene painter, who worked extensively in the provinces before joining Macready at Drury Lane. Later he painted sets at Covent Garden and the Lyceum.

His son, **William Lewis Telbin** (1846–1931), was for many years scene designer at the Theatre Royal, Manchester and collaborated with Hawes Craven on sets for Henry Irving at the Lyceum.

Téllez, Fray Gabriel *See* Tirso de Molina.

Tempest, Dame Marie (Mary Susan Etherington; 1864–1942) British actress, who made her stage debut in 1885 in Suppé's comic opera *Boccaccio*. She enjoyed great success as Kitty Carol in *The Red Hussar* (1889) and subsequently starred in operetta in the US before returning to London in 1895 to appear in musicals and, after 1900, in straight comedy. She triumphed as Kitty in *The Marriage of Kitty* (1902), adapted from Thackeray by her second husband **Cosmo Gordon-Lennox** (1869–1921), and as Judith Bliss in *Hay Fever* (1925), specially written for her by Noël Coward. She was also admired in St John Ervine's *The First Mrs Fraser* (1929), Kaufman and Ferber's *Theatre Royal* (1934), and Dodie Smith's *Dear Octopus* (1938).

Tempest, The The last play written wholly by William SHAKESPEARE. First performance: Whitehall, 1611. It revolves around the enchanter Prospero, formerly the Duke of Milan, who lives in exile upon a remote island with his daughter Miranda. Using his magical arts, he shipwrecks his enemies on the island, brings them to a sense of repentance, and arranges a dynastic marriage for Miranda. Other characters include the spirit Ariel and the brutish Caliban. Prospero's final speech has been frequently interpreted as Shakespeare's own farewell to the stage. The island theme can be seen as reflecting contemporary interest in the recently discovered but largely un-known New World.

Tennyson, Alfred, Lord (1809–92) British poet laureate and playwright, author of several undistinguished poetic dramas. Of those produced by Irving – *Queen Mary* (1876), *The Cup* (1881), *The Foresters* (1892), and *Becket* (1893) – only the last enjoyed any success. *The Falcon* (1879), produced by the Kendals at the St James's Theatre, and *The Promise of May* (1882) were both failures. Another play, *Harold*, remained unacted until 1928.

Terence (Publius Terentius Afer; c. 190 BC–159 BC) Roman playwright, six of whose plays – examples of the PALLIATA – survive. His verse comedies were based upon those of Menander and other writers of Greek New Comedy and are notable for their attention to structure and characterization. His early plays have a strong farcical el-ement, which is less marked in his later, more thoughtful and sentimental, work; all his writing is, however, distinguished by his pure and elegant style. Born a slave and probably of African descent, Terence was overshadowed during his lifetime by Plau-tus. However, he was much admired during the Renaissance and after as a model for contemporary playwrights, influencing Udall, Shakespeare, Molière, and Steele among many others. *See also* Terence-stage.

Principal works:
Andria: 166 BC.
Hecyra: 165 BC.
Heauton Timorumenos: 163 BC.
Eunuchus: 161 BC.
Phormio: 161 BC.
Adelphi: 160 BC.

Terence-stage A form of staging used for performances of the plays of Terence dur-ing the Renaissance. Woodcuts from the period indicate that the plays were presented in a two-storey building with tiered seating and a large apron; entrances were made through arches on the lower level. Eventually the Terence-stage contributed to the development of the proscenium arch and the adoption of the horseshoe-shaped au-ditorium.

Terpsichore See Muses.

Terriss, William (William Charles James Lewin; 1847–97) British actor, who began in minor roles in Birmingham. In 1873 he achieved fame in Hannah Cowley's *The Belle's Stratagem* at the Strand Theatre. His biggest triumph, however, came in 1878 at the Royal Court Theatre when he appeared opposite Ellen Terry in W G Wills's *Olivia*. He joined Irving at the Lyceum in 1880 and later became famous in melo-drama at the Adelphi Theatre. It was outside the stagedoor of this theatre that he was stabbed to death by a deranged actor.

His daughter was the actress **Ellaline Terriss** (1871–1971), who was born in the Falkland Islands. She made her stage debut at the Haymarket in 1888 and later ap-peared at the Criterion Theatre with Wyndham. She was acclaimed in several plays by her husband, Seymour HICKS, and in J M Barrie's *Quality Street* (1902). She also appeared in music hall and entertained the troops in World War I.

Terry, Benjamin (1818–96) British actor and manager, who married the actress Sarah Ballard (1817–92) and became the progenitor of a great theatrical family. With their 11 children they toured the provinces for some years before joining Charles KEAN's company at the Princess's Theatre in London.

Their eldest daughter was **Kate Terry** (1844–1924), who began her career as an actress at the age of eight, playing Prince Arthur in Charles Kean's production of *King John*. She was highly acclaimed when she played Cordelia at the age of 14 and, in 1861, Ophelia at the Lyceum. She caused a further sensation at the Adelphi when she appeared in Charles Reade's dramatization of Tennyson's poem *Dora*, but left the stage in 1867 on her marriage to Arthur Lewis. Her youngest daughter was the actress Mabel TERRY-LEWIS, and another daughter became the mother of John GIELGUD.

Benjamin Terry's second daughter, **Ellen (Alice) Terry** (1847–1928), also began her acting career with Charles Kean's company at the Princess's Theatre, appearing as Mamillius in *The Winter's Tale* and then touring for several seasons and joining the company at the Haymarket (1861). The first of her three marriages, to the painter G F Watts in 1864, was shortlived and she returned to the stage to appear with Irving in *The Taming of the Shrew*. She then retired for a time, living with the designer E W Godwin and having two children, Edith and Edward Gordon CRAIG. She returned to the theatre as a lively Portia in the Bancrofts' production of *The Merchant of Venice* at the Prince of Wales' Theatre in 1875, and three years later became Irving's leading lady at the Lyceum. A legendary partnership lasting 25 years ensued and she won great fame playing Shakespearean heroines and major roles in contemporary dramas. She took over the management of the Imperial Theatre in 1903 and in 1906 was the original Lady Cicely Wayneflete – which Shaw wrote for her – in *Captain Brassbound's Conversion*. The following year, however, she virtually retired from the stage to travel in the US and Australia, lecturing on Shakespeare. Her autobiography was published in 1908.

Benjamin Terry's third daughter, **Marion Terry** (1856–1930), first appeared on stage at the age of 16 and soon established a reputation in such plays as *Much Ado about Nothing*, Bulwer-Lytton's *Money*, and W S Gilbert's *Engaged*. She went on to work in the companies of Tree, the Bancrofts, Irving, Forbes-Robertson, and Alexander, creating the role of Mrs Erlynne in Wilde's *Lady Windermere's Fan* in 1892. Other successes included Barrie's *Quality Street* (1902) and Maugham's *Our Betters* (1923).

Florence Terry (1855–96), Benjamin Terry's fourth daughter, also appeared on stage at an early age and later acted at the Lyceum alongside other members of her family. She inherited several of Ellen Terry's roles, notably Olivia in an adaptation of *The Vicar of Wakefield*, but retired on her marriage to a lawyer in 1882.

Fred Terry (1863–1933) was the youngest of Benjamin Terry's children and made his debut with the Bancrofts in 1880. He became a popular romantic actor in such parts as Sir Percy Blakeney in Baroness Orczy's *The Scarlet Pimpernel* (1905) and Sir John Manners in Paul Kester's *Dorothy o' the Hall* (1906), often appearing in partnership with his wife, Julia NEILSON.

Terry, Daniel (1789–1829) British actor, who toured the provinces in Stephen Kemble's company and became friends with Sir Walter Scott before making his London debut at the Haymarket in 1812. After appearances at Covent Garden and Drury Lane, he purchased the Adelphi Theatre in partnership with Frederick Yates, but retired within two years.

Terry, Edward (1844–1912) British actor and manager. After establishing a reputation in the provinces in eccentric comedy roles he came to the Surrey Theatre in London in 1867 in Thomas J Williams's *A Cure for the Fidgets*. He soon became one of the leading actors in burlesque, first at the Strand Theatre, then at the Gaiety, where he remained until 1884. He opened his own theatre, Terry's, in 1887, and had an enormous success there the following year as Richard Phenyl in Pinero's *Sweet Lavender*, which he frequently revived in tours at home and abroad.

Terry, Megan (Marguerite Duffy; 1932–) US playwright, who was a founding member of the OPEN THEATRE (1963) and has been called 'the mother of American feminist drama'. Her first play to be produced was *Beach Grass* (1933), which was followed by *Ex-Miss Copper Queen on a Set of Pills* (1963), her first play to be produced in New York. Since then her plays, which are fiercely critical of modern US society, have included *Keep Tightly Closed in a Cool Dry Place* (1965), the musical *Viet Rock* (1966), *Approaching Simone* (1970), *Nightwalk* (1973), which was written in collaboration with Sam Shepard, *Hothouse* (1974), and *The Gloaming, Oh My Darling* (1984).

Terry-Lewis, Mabel Gwynedd (1872–1957) British actress, daughter of Kate TERRY. She began her career with Hare's company in 1895 and eventually established her reputation in such plays as Pinero's *The Gay Lord Quex* (1899) and, the following year, Shaw's *You Never Can Tell*. She left the stage on her marriage in 1904, but made a comeback in 1920, playing such ladies of quality as Dona Filomena in the Álvarez Quinteros' *A Hundred Years Old* (1928) and Lady Bracknell in Wilde's *The Importance of Being Earnest* (1930).

Terson, Peter (1932–) British playwright, who became closely associated with the National Youth Theatre after it staged his best-known play, *Zigger-Zagger*, about a young football fan, in 1967. His first play, *Make the Angels Weep*, and his popular dramatization of Arnold Bennett's *Clayhanger* were produced at the Victoria Theatre, Stoke-on-Trent, where he was briefly resident dramatist (1964).

Following the success of *Zigger-Zagger* his plays concentrated on the problems of youth and on examinations of modern British society. Of his other works the most successful include the semi-documentary *The 1861 Whitby Lifeboat Disaster* (1970), a dramatization of Melville's *Moby Dick*, and *Strippers* (1984).

tetralogy In ancient Greece, a series of dramatic entertainments, comprising a **trilogy** of tragedies followed by a satyr-play, all written by the same playwright for performance in drama contests. Initially the satyr-play shared the same theme as the preceding trilogy; the only surviving such trilogy is THE ORESTEIA by Aeschylus.

Thacker, David (1950–) British director. He began his career in 1974 as a stage manager at the Theatre Royal, York, and subsequently directed there and at several other regional theatres. From 1984 to 1993 he was the artistic director of the Young Vic Theatre, where his productions included Ibsen's *An Enemy of the People* (1988) and several plays by Arthur Miller, including *The Last Yankee* (1993). Thacker became a director-in-residence for the RSC in the mid-1990s, with productions including a modern-dress *The Merchant of Venice* (1994).

Thaddädl A stock character of Viennese comedy, descended from the *commedia dell'arte*. A high-voiced foolish youth, Thaddädl was the creation of Anton HASEN-HUT but was too ridiculous to enjoy more than temporary popularity.

Thalia *See* Muses.

Thalia Theatre *See* Bowery Theatre.

Theater an der Wien A theatre in Vienna, which opened as a venue for the old-fashioned folk comedy of Kasperl and Thaddädl after such entertainment was banished from the Burgtheater. Noted managers of the theatre included Mozart's librettist Emanuel Schikaneder (1751–1812). In the 20th century it became a home of operetta and musicals.

Theatr Clwyd A civic theatre at Mold in North Wales, housing three auditoria and a resident company, that opened in 1976 with a production of *Macbeth*. At the same time David Cregan's *Arthur* was staged in its studio theatre, called the Emlyn Williams, after the playwright. The main auditorium is now named after Sir Anthony Hopkins. There is also a film theatre and a very large exhibition concourse. Recent productions have included *King Lear* starring Nicol Williamson (2001).

Theatre, the The first purpose-built public playhouse in England, designed and constructed by James Burbage in 1576. Situated in Shoreditch, just outside the limits of the City of London, the Theatre was used by such companies as Leicester's Men and the Queen's Men as well as the Chamberlain's Men, with whom Richard Burbage was the leading actor. Together with premieres of *Hamlet* and other great plays, there were also exhibitions and competitions at swordplay and athletics. In 1598, being unable to agree terms with Giles Alleyn, the landlord, for renewal of the lease, the Burbages dismantled the circular wooden structure and used the materials in the construction of a new playhouse, the Globe, on Bankside.

Théâtre Antoine A theatre in the Boulevard de Strasbourg, Paris, which opened in 1866. Existing under various names until renamed the Théâtre Antoine in 1896, it flourished under Antoine himself until 1906 when Gémier took over with similar success. It became a centre of existentialist drama after World War II.

Theatre Behind the Gate A theatre in Prague, Czech Republic, founded by Otomar Krejča in 1965. It opened with the resident playwright Josef Topol's *Cat on the Rails* and became the home of a famous company, which toured internationally in 1969. Krejča lost his post there in 1971 and the theatre closed a year later.

Théâtre d'Art *See* Art, Théâtre d'.

Théâtre de Complicité *See* Complicite.

Théâtre de l'Atelier *See* Atelier, Théâtre de l'.

Théâtre de l'Europe A project established by the European Parliament in 1983 as a symbol of the continent's common theatrical tradition. Productions by leading companies from all the member states of the EU are staged at the Odéon in Paris in the original languages; touring productions are also funded. The scheme was principally the idea of Giorgio STREHLER, who became its first director.

Théâtre de l'Hôtel d'Argent *See* Argent, Théâtre de l'Hôtel d'.

Théâtre de l'Hôtel de Bourgogne *See* Bourgogne, Théâtre de l'Hôtel de.

Théâtre de l'Inexprimé *See* Silence, Theatre of.

Theatre de Lys *See* Lucille Lortel Theatre.

Théâtre des Nations A major theatre festival first organized by UNESCO in 1954 at the Théâtre Sarah-Bernhardt (now the **Théâtre de la Ville**). Companies from 50 countries appeared at the festival between 1955 and 1965, after which Barrault took over its management until the riots of 1968 disrupted its organization. Since then it has been revived on an irregular basis in various countries.

Théâtre du Nouveau Monde *See* Nouveau Monde, Théâtre du.

Théâtre du Rideau Vert *See* Rideau Vert, Théâtre du.

Théâtre du Vieux-Colombier *See* Vieux-Colombier, Théâtre du.

Théâtre Français *See* 14th Street Theatre.

Théâtre-Français *See* Comédie-Française.

Theatregoround *See* Royal Shakespeare Company.

Theatre Guild A US production company founded in New York in 1919. Initially based at the Garrick Theatre, it soon attracted attention with its productions of non-commercial US and foreign drama and eventually moved into its own Guild Theatre in 1925. Among its most influential early productions were G B Shaw's *Heartbreak House* (1920), Molnár's *Liliom* (1921), Andreyev's *He Who Gets Slapped* (1922), Ibsen's *Peer Gynt* (1923), and Rice's *The Adding Machine* (1923). It had triumphs in the early 1930s with plays by Shaw, Chekhov, Marlowe, and O'Neill, but it was close to bankruptcy by the early 1940s, being rescued by the spectacular success of the musical *Oklahoma!* (1943). Notable performers with the group included Helen Hayes, the Lunts, and Alla Nazimova. The Guild came under the aegis of the American National Theatre and Academy in 1950.

Theatre in Education (TIE) A form of educational theatre for young people that originated in Britain in 1965 at the Belgrade Theatre, Coventry; TIE companies are now widespread in Britain, Australia, and in parts of Canada and the US. A distinguishing feature of most TIE has been its innovative use of audience participation. Programmes range from 'full participation' (in which children make decisions alongside the actor-teachers, who remain in role throughout) to 'semi-participation' (in which children may quiz characters about their behaviour). Subject matter ranges from social history to racism and drug dependency. Many teams are based permanently in one place and receive funding from their local education authority.

theatre-in-the-round A form of staging in which the audience is seated on all sides of a central acting space. Although many early theatrical traditions necessarily involved such an arrangement, it was not until the 20th century that it was deliberately developed in preference to more conventional layouts based upon a proscenium arch. Theatre-in-the-round encourages inventive, often symbolic staging and the audience's intimate identification with the action; as it is impossible to use elaborate artificial sets, the emphasis is thrown upon the performers themselves. It was first employed in the 1930s by Okhlopkov in the USSR and by Robert Atkins at the Ring in Britain, but it was only fully realized in the 1950s, initially through experimental productions in the US. The first permanent venue of the kind was the Penthouse Theatre in Seattle, built in 1940; later noted venues adapted for theatre-in-the-round have included the Circle-in-the-Square in New York, the Arena Stage in Washington DC, the Stephen Joseph Theatre in Scarborough, the Royal Exchange Theatre in Manchester, and André Villiers's Théâtre en Rond de Paris. *See also* promenade.

Théâtre-Italien *See* Comédie-Italienne.

Théâtre Libre A theatre club in Paris, founded in 1887 by André Antoine to present contemporary drama. Early productions included influential naturalistic performances of adaptations of Zola and works by Hauptmann, Ibsen, Strindberg, and others. The society was dissolved in 1896 chiefly as a result of financial pressures.

Theatre Masque *See* John Golden Theatre.

Theatre Museum A museum housing material relating to the British theatre; it was founded in 1974 as a department of the Victoria and Albert Museum and moved to its own building in Covent Garden, London, in 1987. The museum covers drama, opera, ballet, music hall, and pop music. Prompt scripts, costumes, posters, props, stage designs, engravings, paintings, photographs, and a variety of ephemera all have their place; the main galleries trace the history of the theatre, while short-term exhibitions focus on special topics.

Théâtre National Populaire (TNP) A French theatre institution established (with government support) to bring drama to large and socially diverse audiences. The first organization of this name was founded by Gémier in 1920; this staged performances by visiting companies for mainly working-class audiences at the Palais de Chaillot, Paris, until 1934. The TNP at the Palais de Chaillot was revived by Jean Vilar in 1951, this time with its own company, which undertook tours from 1956. As well as introducing innovations in the handling of bookings and publicity, it built up a strong reputation for its economical interpretations of both classic plays and works by such contemporaries as Jarry and Brecht. From 1963 Vilar's work was continued by Georges Wilson. The TNP declined in popularity somewhat after the implementation of the DÉCENTRALISATION DRAMATIQUE policy and finally closed in 1972, when both name and subsidy passed to a group based in Lyon under Planchon.

Theatre of Cruelty *See* Cruelty, Theatre of.

Theatre of Drama and Comedy *See* Taganka Theatre.

Theatre of Fact *See* documentary theatre.

Theatre of Satire *See* Satire, Theatre of.

Theatre of Silence *See* Silence, Theatre of.

Theatre of the Absurd *See* Absurd, Theatre of the.

Theatre of the Baltic Fleet A theatre founded in St Petersburg in 1934 utilizing actors serving with the Soviet navy. Performances, which are given on board ship and in various home ports, have included such patriotic dramas as Vishnevsky's *At the Walls of Leningrad* (1943) and other pieces chiefly on military and naval themes.

Theatre of the Revolution *See* Mayakovsky Theatre.

Theatre Row A name sometimes given to 42ND STREET between 9th and 10th Avenues in New York City: the block is currently home to several off-off Broadway companies, the most famous of which is PLAYWRIGHTS' HORIZONS. This part of 42nd Street had become somewhat unsavoury by the late 1970s; its renovation in 1978–79 foreshadowed the later rehabilitation of the wider area in the mid-1990s.

Theatre Royal A title granted to the theatres in COVENT GARDEN and DRURY LANE under Letters Patent in 1662. Since then the title has also been adopted by notable theatres at Bath, Brighton, Bury St Edmunds, Exeter, Lincoln, Manchester, Newcastle-upon-Tyne, Norwich, Nottingham, and York.

   See also Adelphi Theatre; Astley's Amphitheatre; Bristol Old Vic; Haymarket (Theatre Royal); John Street Theatre.

Theatre Royal (Stratford East) A theatre in Stratford East, London, which was opened by W Charles Dillon with Bulwer Lytton's *Richelieu* in 1884. For two years Dillon produced revivals of famous plays there, but when he left the theatre concentrated on pantomime and touring melodramas. Twice-nightly variety was established in 1927, followed by an unsuccessful return to melodrama. From 1946 to 1949 David Horne presented seasons of plays with only modest success, and for a brief spell in 1952 the theatre became the Palace of Varieties. The advent of Joan Littlewood's THEATRE WORKSHOP company in 1953 brought a change of fortune to the Theatre Royal such productions as Shelagh Delaney's *A Taste of Honey*, Brendan Behan's *The Hostage*, and Frank Norman and Lionel Bart's musical *Fings Ain't Wot They Used T' Be*, went on to successful West End runs. The Stage Sixty Company occupied the theatre from 1964, but Joan Littlewood returned for another six years in 1967. In the 1980s and 1990s the theatre continued its lively policy of mixing new plays with occasional classic revivals, achieving a major success with Nell Dunn's *Steaming* (1981) and presenting several new works by Asian writers. The theatre was expanded and refurbished in 2000.

Theatres Act *See* licence.

Théâtres Nationaux *See Décentralisation Dramatique*.

théâtre total A theory of drama that advocates the absolute control of the director over all aspects of a production; this may extend to the text itself. Jean-Louis Barrault is the best-known director to have worked in this way.

Theatre Union *See* Littlewood, Joan.

Theatre Upstairs *See* Royal Court Theatre.

Theatre Virginia A theatre in Richmond, Virginia, founded in 1955 as the **Virginia Museum Theatre** under the auspices of the Virginia Museum. In 1984, still using the museum facilities, it became a separate entity under the new name. It is well known for its annual 'New Voices' programme for young playwrights.

Theatre Workshop A theatre company founded in Kendal in 1945. Under the leadership of Joan LITTLEWOOD, the company toured Britain and Europe before settling at the Theatre Royal, Stratford East, in London (1952). There it rapidly established a strong reputation with productions ranging from *Twelfth Night* (1953) to Hašek's *The Good Soldier Schweik* (1956); many of these were also seen at leading foreign venues – including the Théâtre des Nations in Paris and the Moscow Art Theatre. The company concentrated on plays with a strong left-wing bias but nonetheless enjoyed lengthy West End runs with such works as *The Hostage* (1958) by Brendan Behan and *A Taste of Honey* (1958) by Shelagh Delaney. In 1963 the company's own documentary drama OH, WHAT A LOVELY WAR! provided another major success. The company then dispersed for a time before regrouping in 1967 and finally disbanding in 1973. *See also* Princess Theatre.

Theatr Gwynedd A theatre in Bangor, established by the University College of North Wales in 1974. It presents a mixed programme of drama, dance, opera, concerts, films, and pantomime in both English and Welsh. The resident company, **Cwmni Theatr Cymru**, stages and tours Welsh language productions with financial support from the Welsh Arts Council.

Theatrical Commonwealth A troupe of actors who, under Thomas Twaits, left the Park Theatre, New York, in 1813 after falling out with the management and took over a converted circus on Broadway. They disbanded upon the death of Mrs Twaits (a member of the company) one season later, having staged excellent productions of *As You Like It*, Sheridan's *The School for Scandal*, and Frederick Reynolds's *The Virgin of the Sun*.

Theatrical Syndicate An association of US businessmen, formed in 1896 to rationalize theatre organization nationwide, that came to exert a virtual monopoly over the profession. Its members included the booking agency Klaw and Erlanger and the theatre owners Al Hayman and Charles Frohman. They controlled most municipal theatres in the US until opposition from Mrs Fiske, Sarah Bernhardt, Belasco, and the Shubert brothers, broke their monopoly in the 1910s.

Theocritus (c. 310 BC–250 BC) Greek playwright, one of the leading writers of Hellenistic drama. A native of Syracuse, he probably spent much of his life in Egypt where he wrote several pastoral *Idylls* and the mime play *Adoniazusae*, translated into English by Matthew Arnold.

Theognis (5th century BC) Greek poet and playwright, usually remembered for his love poems addressed to one Cyrnus. His plays, however, were so frosty in tone that – according to Aristophanes – they caused the rivers to freeze in Thrace when they were performed in Athens.

Théophile de Viau (1590–1626) French poet and playwright, born in Clairac. A Huguenot and free-thinker, Théophile was imprisoned for his suspected collaboration in *Le Parnasse satirique*, a collection of licentious verse, and died soon after his release. His single contribution to the theatre was the tragedy *Pyrame et Thisbé* (published 1623), which was unjustly criticized by Boileau and is now acknowledged as a fine example of baroque tragedy.

Theoric Fund A grant organized by the state in ancient Athens to enable the poorest citizens to afford a visit to the theatre during the festival of Dionysus. The practice was eventually discontinued in 338 BC.

Thérèse Raquin A play by Émile ZOLA, based on his novel of the same name (1867). First performance: 1873. The eponymous heroine has an adulterous affair with Laurent, the friend of her husband Camille, whom the lovers conspire to drown. Haunted by guilt and fear, Thérèse and Laurent ultimately commit suicide in front of Camille's paralysed mother. The play helped to set the fashion for theatrical NATURALISM.

Thesiger, Ernest (1879–1961) British actor, who started with George Alexander's company in 1909. Subsequently he worked with Hawtrey and Tree before appearing in Walter Ellis's farce *A Little Bit of Fluff* (1915), which ran for three years. In 1920 he had an unexpected success in Barrie's *Mary Rose* and went on to establish himself as an excellent actor of high comedy. He played the Dauphin in *Saint Joan* – the first of many Shavian roles which delighted the author – in 1924 and was also acclaimed in supporting roles in the plays of Shakespeare.

Thespis (6th century BC) Greek poet and playwright, usually credited with being the founder of the acting profession. A native of Attica, he was reputedly the first to introduce an actor alongside the chorus and to give him a distinct narrative role. He was the winner of the very first drama contest held during the Dionysia (534 BC) and led his own travelling company; the word thespian, taken from his name, now denotes anything theatrical.

Thieves' Carnival (*Le Bal des voleurs*) A *pièce rose* by Jean ANOUILH. First performance: Paris, 1938. Lady Hurf knowingly admits into her home three confidence tricksters posing as Spanish grandees; the plot centres on the romantic involvement of two of the men with Lady Hurf's nieces. The play was first performed in English in 1952.

Third Stage *See* Stratford (Ontario) Festival.

39th Street Theatre A theatre on West 39th Street, New York, which opened as the **Nazimova Theatre** in 1910 with the New York premiere of Ibsen's *Little Eyolf*. It reopened as the 39th Street Theatre in 1911 with *Green Stockings* and saw appearances by John Barrymore and Walter Hampden among others. It was demolished in 1925.

This Happy Breed A play by Noël COWARD. First performance: London, 1943. The play, an episodic and somewhat sentimental history of a suburban family between the wars, extols British middle-class values.

Thomas, Augustus (1857–1934) US playwright and manager, whose plays were among the first to be based solely upon US material. His best known work is *The Copperhead* (1918); other plays include *Alabama* (1891), *A Man of the World* (1883), *The Burglar* (1889), and *In Mizzoura* (1893).

Thomas, (Walter) Brandon (1857–1914) British playwright, actor, and composer of music-hall songs, who is usually remembered for his farce CHARLEY'S AUNT, first performed in London in 1892 and revived many times since. It was made into a musical, *Where's Charley?* (1948), and has also been filmed; Thomas himself sometimes appeared in the transvestite leading role.

Thomassin *See* Vicentini, Tommaso Antonio.

Thompson Shelterhouse *See* Cincinnati Playhouse in the Park.

Thorndike, Dame (Agnes) Sybil (1882–1976) British actress, who began her career in the theatre with Ben Greet's Pastoral Players in 1904. While in repertory with Annie Horniman's company at Manchester (from 1908), she met and married Lewis Casson, with whom she later appeared in various jointly managed productions, including several plays by J B Priestley. During World War I she was in Lilian Baylis's Old Vic company and afterwards consolidated her reputation in Gilbert Murray's versions of Euripides, playing such roles as Hecuba in *The Trojan Women* (1919) and the title role in *Medea* (1920). Probably her most famous part was the heroine of Shaw's *St Joan*, which she first played in 1924; subsequent successes included Volumnia in *Coriolanus* at the Old Vic (1938) and Miss Moffat in Emlyn Williams's *The Corn is Green* (1938). She toured mining towns and villages with a mainly Shakespearean repertoire during World War II and gave her last performance in London as Abby in Joseph Kesselring's *Arsenic and Old Lace* (1966). She returned to the stage for the last time in 1969 for the opening of a theatre named after her in Leatherhead.

Thorne, Charles Robert (1840–83) US actor, son of theatrical parents, who began his career as a child and later became very popular in leading romantic roles. As a member of the Union Square Theatre company from 1871, he appeared successfully in numerous melodramas, also performing in London in 1874; his last appearance was in Boucicault's *The Corsican Brothers* (1883).

Thorne, Thomas (1841–1918) British actor-manager, who came from a large family with theatre connections. He first appeared at his father's theatre in Margate but later moved to London where he played at the Strand Theatre (1864–70). Subsequently he opened the Vaudeville Theatre with Henry Montague and David James, serving as sole manager from 1882 to 1892.

Three Hundred Club *See* Stage Society, Incorporated.

Threepenny Opera, The (*Die Dreigroschenoper*) A musical play by Bertolt BRECHT with music by Kurt WEILL. First performance: Berlin, 1928. Derived from Gay's *The Beggar's Opera*, it has as its central theme the corruption of good men by evil values and provided Brecht with his first major success in the theatre. The central story of the marriage, imprisonment, and eventual pardon of the robber Macheath was used by the author to satirize European society before World War II.

Three Sisters (*Tri sestry*) A play by Anton CHEKHOV. First performance: Moscow Art Theatre, 1901. Regarded as one of Chekhov's finest plays, it sympathetically depicts the various longings of three sisters – Irina, Masha, and Olga – living a dreary life in the provinces. Instead of realizing their dream of returning to Moscow, they face disappointment in love and work and the destruction of their illusions.

throwline Any rope used to secure flats or other pieces of scenery by tying them together; also referred to in the US as a **lashline**.

thrust stage A stage that projects into the auditorium, with seating arranged on three sides of it. Such stages, also called **open stages**, resemble the **platform stage** of the Elizabethan and Restoration theatre and thus facilitate revivals of plays from that period.

Thunder Rock A play by the US dramatist Robert Ardrey. First performance: New York, 1939. Set in a lighthouse, the play centres on a young intellectual's attempt to face up to the approaching World War through the challenges presented by the ghosts of shipwrecked sailors.

thunder run A series of wooden channels mounted on a wall in the backstage area of some 18th-century theatres; a cannon ball was rolled down them to create a noise resembling that of thunder. Such runs were eventually superseded by thunder-sheets.

thundersheet A large sheet of iron or thin wood suspended from the flies; when shaken it produces a noise resembling thunder. In the modern theatre such sheets have often been replaced by audio recordings.

Ticket-of-Leave Man, The A melodrama by Tom TAYLOR, adapted from *Léonard* by Edouard Brisbarre and Eugène Nus. First performance: 1863. A young man falls in with bad company and is imprisoned for a crime of which he is innocent; he subsequently helps a detective (the first ever presented on stage) to bring the guilty to book. The play had a strong influence upon subsequent writers of melodrama.

Tidings Brought to Mary, The (*L'Annonce faite à Marie*) A play in the style of a medieval mystery by Paul CLAUDEL. First performance: Paris, 1912. Based on an earlier work, *La Jeune Fille Violaine* (written 1892), the play centres on the innocent young Violaine, who miraculously cures a leper but contracts the disease herself, and her evil sister Mara.

Tieck, (Johann) Ludwig (1773–1853) German poet, novelist, and playwright, who was a leading figure of the German Romantic movement. His writings for the stage include such Romantic tragedies as *Karl von Berneck* (1797) and several influential plays based on fairytales, including *Ritter Blaubart* (Bluebeard; 1796), *Der gestiefelte Kater* (Puss-in-Boots; 1797), and *Die verkehrte Welt* (The World Upside-Down; 1798). As director of the Court Theatre in Dresden, he attempted to produce historically authentic versions of Shakespeare and also assisted in Schlegel's translations of Shakespeare's plays.

Tiger at the Gates (*La Guerre de Troie n'aura pas lieu*) A play by Jean GIRAUDOUX. First performance: Paris, 1935. Christopher Fry's translation, with Michael Redgrave as Hector, opened in London in 1955. A retelling of the events preceding the Trojan War, the play centres on the conflict between patriotism and pacifism.

Tilley, Vesta (Matilda Alice Powles; 1864–1952) British music hall singer, who first appeared at St George's Hall, Nottingham (where her father was chairman) in 1868. She established a reputation as a fine male impersonator, coming to the Royal Holborn, London, in 1878 as 'The Great Little Tilley'. By 1880 she was billed as 'The London Idol' and so she remained for another 40 years, singing such songs as 'Burlington Bertie' and 'After the Ball'. She visited the US several times and appeared at Daly's,

New York, in a musical comedy, *My Lady Molly*, as well as touring in a comedy, *Algy*, which was based on one of her numbers. She was also popular in pantomime at Drury Lane.

Tillinger, John (1939–) US director, especially at the Long Wharf Theatre and at the Manhattan Theatre Club, who has premiered works by, among others, Terrence McNally and A E Gurney.

Tilney, Sir Edmund (d. 1610) English public official, MASTER OF THE REVELS from 1579. Despite the fact that his tenure of office saw the greatest period of Elizabethan and Jacobean drama, Tilney did little in pursuit of his duties beyond the basic censorship of plays.

Time and the Conways A play by J B PRIESTLEY. First performance: London, 1937. The first and third acts present a family party in 1919 while the second act, set in 1937, contrasts reality with the aspirations expressed 20 years before. It is one of several plays by Priestley to explore the nature of time.

Time of Your Life, The A play by William SAROYAN. First performance: New York, 1939. A group of eccentrics meet to talk about life and philosophy in a bar in San Francisco. The play, which was very successful, won a Pulitzer Prize which Saroyan refused. It was filmed in 1948 with James Cagney and William Bendix.

Times Square An open area in Manhattan, New York, where Broadway crosses 7th Avenue in the heart of the theatre district. Times Square is strictly speaking between 45th and 43rd Streets, although the entire open area up to 47th Street is popularly so-called. The name is also used to mean the whole district, especially when evoking its sleazier aspects.

Times Square Theatre A theatre on West 42nd Street, New York, which opened in 1920 with *The Mirage*. Successful productions there included *Charlot's Revue of 1924*, Anita Loos's *Gentlemen Prefer Blondes* (1926), and Coward's *Private Lives* (1931). The theatre was converted into a cinema after 1933. It is now empty; in the current renovation of 42nd Street it is uncertain if it will continue as a theatre or serve some other purpose.

Timoneda, Joan (c. 1520–c. 1583) Spanish playwright, poet, and novelist, who published plays by Alonso de la Vega, Lope de Vega, and many others. His own dramatic works include imitations of Plautus, comedies, and five *autos sacramentales*.

Timon of Athens A tragedy by William SHAKESPEARE, written c. 1605–07. First recorded performance: 1678 (adapted by Thomas Shadwell). The play revolves around Timon, a generous Greek lord who becomes disillusioned after his friends refuse to help him when his wealth runs out: he eventually dies alone in bitter self-imposed exile. The play seems to represent an experiment with the tragic form, with little character development except for Timon himself and a loose plot; some argue that the play as it survives is still in a draft stage.

Tipteerers' Play *See* mummers' play.

tireman An official of the Elizabethan theatre, who organized all matters relating to the wardrobe. He also arranged seating for the audience on the stage and in some theatres had responsibility for the lights.

Tirso de Molina (Fray Gabriel Téllez; c. 1571–1648) Spanish playwright, who was much influenced by the plays of Lope de Vega and wrote numerous secular works as well as four *autos sacramentales* and religious pieces. His 80 surviving plays include the tragedies *El condenado por desconfiado* (c. 1624) and *El Burlador de Sevilla y Convidado de Piedra* (1630), which introduced the character of DON JUAN; other works are notable for his interest in psychology as well as his understanding of female characters and his clever handling of clowns.

'Tis Pity She's a Whore A tragedy by John FORD. First performance: c. 1627. The play concerns the incestuous relationship between Giovanni and his sister Annabella, which so deranges him that he murders her and stabs her husband, only to be killed himself.

Titinius (2nd century BC) Roman playwright, noted for his plays in the *togata* tradition. Fragments of his work and 15 titles survive; he was probably much influenced by the works of Menander.

Titus Andronicus The first tragedy by William SHAKESPEARE, written c. 1592–93. First performance: c. 1592–93. This bloody tale of revenge and madness revolves around Titus, a victorious Roman general whose daughter Lavinia is raped and mutilated. His two sons are then executed on false charges. Titus exacts his vengeance when he tricks his enemy Tamora into eating a pie in which her two sons have been baked. The play is much cruder than Shakespeare's later Roman tragedies but was popular for many years, largely as a result of the violence of many of the scenes.

Tivoli A music hall in the Strand, London, opened in 1890. From 1891 until 1914 it was a thriving centre of the London music hall, presenting such great stars as Marie Lloyd under the management of Charles Morton. The Tivoli Cinema was erected on the site in 1923.

Tivoli Gardens *See* Richmond Hill Theatre.

Toby The name of the live dog that traditionally accompanies performers of the British PUNCH AND JUDY show. Usually a terrier, Toby wears a ruff and sits on the ledge of the booth while the entertainment takes place; after the show the dog collects money from the audience in a small bag.

In the US theatre **Toby** was a stock character of the travelling tent-shows and showboats of the early 20th century. The character was usually portrayed as a simple country bumpkin who triumphs over the evil 'city slicker'; the role called for an excellent gymnast and spawned a female counterpart called **Susie**. The last Toby appeared in 1962.

togata (or *tabernaria*) A form of Roman *fabula*, that evolved from the PALLIATA in the 2nd century BC. More satirical than its predecessor, the *togata* consisted of bawdy lampoons of the lower classes. Writers of the form included Afranius, Atta, and Titinius; none of their plays survive intact.

Toller, Ernst (1893–1939) German Expressionist poet and playwright. His communist sympathies were reflected in such plays as *Die Wandlung* (The Inner Change; 1919) and *Masse-Mensch* (Masses and Man; 1920) and led to his imprisonment in 1919. His early dramas, noted for their symbolic characters and elements of unreality, deal chiefly with the recurring themes of martyrdom and revolt, as in *Die Maschinenstürmer* (The Machine Wreckers; 1922) and *Feuer aus den Kesseln* (Draw the Fires!; 1930), which deals with the Kiel mutiny of 1917. Other major works include *Hinkemann* (1923), *Hoppla, wir leben* (Hoppla!; 1927) and *Die blinde Göttin* (The Blind Goddess; 1932). He committed suicide in New York on the outbreak of World War II.

Tolstoy, Count Alexei Konstantinovich (1817–75) Russian poet, playwright, and diplomat; distantly related to Leo Tolstoy, he was the author of a celebrated historical trilogy, first performed in St Petersburg in 1898. Consisting of *Smert' Ioanna Groznogo* (The Death of Ivan the Terrible), *Tsar Fedor Ivanovich*, and *Tsar Boris*, the trilogy has been much revived since censorship of it was lifted.

Tolstoy, Alexsei Nikolaivich (1882–1945) Russian poet, novelist, and playwright, who wrote a number of plays in support of the new regime following the Revolution of 1917. As well as several historical dramas, his plays include *The Road to Victory* (1939), which numbers both Lenin and Stalin amongst the characters.

Tolstoy, Count Leo Nikolaivich (1828–1910) Russian writer, author of novels successful in stage adaptations and several plays. His early dramatic writings consisted of a number of unfinished comedies written in the 1850s; later, however, he broke new ground with such plays as *The First Distiller* and the tragedy *The Power of Darkness*, in which he made peasant characters the centre of the action. *The Fruits of Enlightenment* was a satirical comedy on social issues, attacking the rural gentry, while *The Living Corpse* (or *Redemption*) and *Light Shining in the Darkness*, which were both left unfinished, criticized the contemporary marriage laws and class differences respectively. Of his novels, *Anna Karenina* and *War and Peace* have been the most successful in the theatre.

Principal dramatic works:
  Pervy vinokur: 1887; translated as *The First Distiller*.
  Vlast tmi: 1888; translated as *The Power of Darkness*.
  Plodi prosveshcheniya: 1891; translated as *The Fruits of Enlightenment*.
  Zhivoi trup: 1911 (written 1900); translated as *The Living Corpse* (or *Redemption*).
  I svet vo tme tsvetit: never performed; translated as *Light Shining in the Darkness*.

Tom Thumb the Great A satirical burlesque by Henry FIELDING. First performance: 1730. Tom Thumb, whose diminutive stature represents a mockery of the grandiose central characters of contemporary heroic tragedy, is betrothed to Princess Huncamunca; although he overcomes an infamous rival, Lord Grizzle, he himself gets eaten by a cow.

Tony Award The Antoinette Perry Award, which was named after the chairman of the board and secretary of the American Theatre Wing and was first bestowed in 1947. The award is given for 'distinguished achievement' in the US theatre, reflecting Perry's own dedication to the highest standards of quality. Following the change in the character of Broadway, and its current intense focus on the musical, there is some discussion of opening the Tony Awards to off-Broadway as well.

Toole, John Laurence (1830–1906) British actor, who made his first professional appearances in the provinces under the name John Lavers. In 1856 he appeared at the Lyceum; over the next nine years he was seen in a variety of parts at the Adelphi Theatre, notably in plays by Dickens. He appeared frequently at the Gaiety Theatre, toured in the US, and managed the Folly Theatre (later the Charing Cross Theatre), renaming it Toole's Theatre in 1879.

Too True to be Good A play by G B SHAW. First performance: Boston, 1932. Through the play's 10 characters, who include a thinly disguised T E Lawrence, Shaw analyses the workings of capitalism and a wide range of other topics with varying degrees of success. The play's basic theme is the moral bankruptcy of mankind.

top drop *See* border.

Top Girls A play by Caryl CHURCHILL. First performance: Royal Court Theatre, London, 1982. The play, which has an all-female cast, explores the role of women in today's society through the character of Marlene, a successful career woman; in one famous scene she attends a party given for her by a group of women from other periods of history.

Topol, Chaim (1934–) Israeli actor, producer, and director, who is best known for his performances as Tevye in the musical *Fiddler on the Roof* (1967, 1983, 1990, 1994, 1998; filmed 1971). Earlier in his career he founded a highly popular satirical theatre in Tel Aviv and he has appeared in various countries in plays by Brecht, Brendan Behan, Ionesco, and Shakespeare among others. He has appeared frequently at the Cameri Theatre in Tel Aviv since 1965. In 1988 he reappeared in London's West End in *Ziegfeld*.

Torch Theatre A small repertory theatre at Milford Haven in Pembrokeshire, Wales, which houses a resident company. It is also equipped for film shows and exhibitions and sometimes presents visiting companies in opera and dance.

Torelli, Achille (1841–1922) Italian playwright, who pioneered drama on social themes in the Italian theatre. *I mariti* (1867) established his reputation, exploring the relationship of two married couples; subsequent equally influential plays included *La moglie* (1868) and *L'ultima convegno* (1898).

Torelli, Giacomo (1608–78) Italian stage designer, known as 'the Great Magician' for his many inventions of stage devices. A pupil of Giambattista Aleotti (at whose Teatro Farnese he installed what was probably the first set of wings ever used), he did his most important work at the Teatro Novissimo in Venice (1641–45) and at Molière's Théâtre du Petit-Bourbon, most notably for Corneille's *Andromède* (1650). His innovations included the CARRIAGE-AND-FRAME SYSTEM and an early revolving stage.

tormentor A narrow flat or curtain used to mask the wings; it is usually black or grey in colour.

Toronto Workshop Productions (TWP) One of Canada's first alternative companies, founded in 1959 by George Luscomb, a former member of Joan Littlewood's Theatre Workshop in London. The company philosophy stressed training, ensemble acting, and COLLECTIVE CREATION; it opened the way for many similar companies before disbanding in 1988.

Torres Naharro, Bartolomé de (c. 1485–c. 1524) Spanish playwright, regarded as the founder of the comic theatrical tradition in Spain. His plays, which were mostly written in Rome, were collected in the *Propalladia* (1517) and foreshadowed the development of the *comedia* of the Golden Age, notably in the case of *Himenea*, which was based on *La Celestina*. As a drama theorist, he also distinguished between the *comedia a noticia* and the *comedia a fantasía* as separate genres, the former relating to realistic dramas and the latter to those based on fantasy.

Tortoriti, Giuseppe (fl. late 17th century) Italian actor of the *commedia dell'arte*, who began in the role of Pasquariello but later became famous as Scaramuccia. He appeared with the Duke of Modena's company in London (1678–79) and with the Comédie-Italienne before unsuccessfully attempting to lead his own touring company.

Totaltheater A theatre designed by **Walter Gropius** for Piscator in 1926 but never built. The theatre would have seated an audience of 2000 and have included a proscenium arch with a rotating forestage and various ambitious adaptations to facilitate the use of film projection and other special effects. It foreshadowed the development of the flexible stages of the modern era.

Tottenham Street Theatre *See* Scala Theatre.

Touch of the Poet, A A play by Eugene O'NEILL, written c. 1940. First performance: Stockholm, 1957. The play examines the conflict between Con Melody, an immigrant father, and his American-born son. It was intended to be part of a cycle of 11 plays about a single family, examining the mercenary and self-destructive aspects of the national psyche.

touring company A theatre company that presents plays at a series of different venues, often part of a set circuit based on a particular city or theatre. Touring companies in Britain have burgeoned since the disappearance of the stock companies and the demise of the repertory system. Companies usually travel by road and may present a wide variety of works – some politically orientated or in the tradition of fringe theatre – at both large and small venues. Surviving on slender government subsidies, they comprise a significant part of many professional theatre programmes. Formerly many West End hits were also extensively toured before expense brought the practice to an end.

Tourneur, Cyril (1575–1626) English playwright, whose life is largely shrouded in obscurity. He is usually credited with writing THE REVENGER'S TRAGEDY (1607), which conveys a deeply pessimistic view of human nature, although some recent scholarship attributes it to Thomas Middleton. He was also the author of *The Nobleman* (1607), now lost, and *The Atheist's Tragedy* (1611).

Tovstonogov, Georgyi Alexandrovich (1915–89) Georgian director, known for his innovative productions of many classic plays. He began his career in Tbilisi, Georgia, in 1931 and subsequently worked at the Lenkom Theatre in Moscow and the Gorky and Pushkin Theatres in St Petersburg. His best-known productions, several of which were seen internationally, included Dostoevsky's *The Idiot* (1957), Arbuzov's *It Happened in Irkutz* (1959), Shteyn's *The Ocean* (1961), Chekhov's *Three Sisters* (1964), Shakespeare's *Henry IV* (1969), Gogol's *The Government Inspector* (1972), the Tolstoy adaptation *The Story of a Horse* (1975), which ran on Broadway, and Sukhovo-Kobylin's *Tarelkin's Death* (1984).

Tower Theatre *See* Tavistock Repertory Company.

Toys in the Attic A play by Lillian HELLMAN. First performance: New York, 1950. The plot concerns two elderly spinsters living in New Orleans and their struggle to take care of their brother. The play was filmed in 1963 with Geraldine Page and Dean Martin.

toy theatre A miniature theatre made of cardboard, complete with actors and scenery imitating that used in contemporary productions. Popular in several European countries during the 19th century, toy theatres are now a valuable source of information about the sets of the period. In Britain sheets of figures and scenery from about 300 plays for use in the toy theatre (or **juvenile drama**) were available in both **penny plain** and **twopence coloured** forms.

trabeata A form of Roman *fabula*, closely related to the TOGATA. It was named after the *trabea*, a robe worn by Roman knights, who were apparently the main characters in the play. Originated by Melissus, no examples of the form have survived.

Trachiniae A tragedy by SOPHOCLES. First performance: Athens, c. 425 BC. The play studies the impact of suffering through the tormented relationship of Heracles and his wronged wife Deianeira, which ends in both their deaths.

Trades Unions Theatre A theatre in Moscow, originally called the **Proletkult Theatre**, founded shortly after the Revolution of 1917 to present plays on proletarian themes. Sergei Eisenstein worked there from 1921 to 1923, directing plays by Ostrovsky and Tretyakov before switching to films; later it enjoyed acclaim under Alexei Dikie before finally closing in 1936.

Trafalgar Square Theatre *See* Duke of York's Theatre.

Trafalgar Theatre *See* Nederlander Theatre.

Tragedian *See* stock company.

tragédie-Bourgeoise *See* drame.

tragedy A form of drama characterized by its serious tone and unhappy ending. Tragedy, which means 'goat-song' (probably after the prize given to the winning playwright at the DIONYSIA), was first developed in ancient Greece from the earlier tradition of the DITHYRAMB. The practice of Aeschylus, Euripides, Sophocles, and others – subsequently codified by ARISTOTLE – established a number of basic ground rules, stipulating for instance that the central characters should come from the upper echelons of society and that their downfall, usually culminating in their death, should be caused by a combination of their own flaws and the workings of fate. The closet plays of Seneca helped to transmit Greek ideas about tragedy to Renaissance scholars and thence to the Elizabethan theatre of Marlowe and Shakespeare, in which the poetic possibilities of the form were fully realized. Subsequently the theories of Aristotle provided the main impetus for the neoclassical tragedies of Racine and Corneille. During the 18th and 19th centuries the requirement for characters to come from the upper classes was relaxed and the form splintered into various subdivisions, including melodrama, domestic and social drama, and tragicomedy. In the late 19th century many of the preoccupations of tragedy were revived in the dramas of Ibsen, Strindberg, and Chekhov.

Tragical History of Dr Faustus, The *See Dr Faustus, The Tragical History of.*

tragicomedy A form of drama combining elements of both comedy and tragedy. Although experimented with by Plautus, the form first emerged as a distinct genre in the Renaissance. Ignoring the unities and other classical conventions, it capitalized upon the more sensational aspects of tragedy while borrowing the happy ending typical of comedy; the central characters were conventionally of noble but not royal status. Writers of the form in its early stages of development included Giraldi, Dolce, Garnier, Alexandre Hardy, and Corneille. Several of Shakespeare's plays are also frequently described as tragicomedies. The form disappeared as a separate genre in the 18th century but many of its features have re-emerged in the plays of such authors as Ibsen, Beckett, and Pinter.

transformation scene A convention of the English PANTOMIME, in which a rapid and spectacular change of scenery is effected by means of falling flaps and other devices. Use of a RISE-AND-SINK or of SCRUTO could facilitate the effect, while other methods of achieving it included the **fan effect**, which involved the removal of scenery by collapsing it sideways in the manner of a folding fan. In the modern theatre transformation scenes are often effected by means of transparencies.

transparency An expanse of gauze or other thin fabric, which when painted with transparent dyes and lit from the front appears to be a normally painted cloth; when lit from behind, however, the gauze becomes transparent, revealing whatever lies behind it.

Transpontine melodrama Popular melodrama that was performed south of the Thames in mid-19th-century London, playing at such theatres as the Old Vic and the Surrey. The term was originally intended to be insulting but was later used as a generic description of any sensational melodrama.

trap A trapdoor cut into the stage floor or scenery to allow performers to make sudden unexpected entrances. They are also sometimes used to change scenery or stage equipment. *See also* bristle trap; cauldron trap; corner trap; footlights trap; ghost glide; grave trap; slote; star trap; vamp trap.

Traveller Without Luggage, The (*Le Voyageur sans bagage*) A *pièce noire* by Jean ANOUILH. First performance: Paris, 1937. The central character is an ex-soldier suffering from amnesia. On learning with disgust of his dishonourable youth, he contrives to adopt a new identity. The play provided Anouilh with his first major success.

Travers, Ben (1886–1980) British playwright, whose particular genius was for farce. Beginning with A CUCKOO IN THE NEST (1925), he wrote a series of plays that became known as the 'Aldwych farces' because they were first performed in the Ald-

wych Theatre. ROOKERY NOOK (1926), *Thark* (1927), and *Plunder* (1928) are among
the most famous, while later farces include *Banana Ridge* (1939) and *The Bed Before
Yesterday* (1975). He also wrote two volumes of autobiography.

Traverse Theatre A studio theatre in Edinburgh, the first of its kind in Britain, that
developed out of the International Festival of 1963. The original theatre, situated in
the Lawnmarket, had a stage positioned between two opposite banks of seats. The
company moved to a larger and more flexible space in the Grassmarket in 1969 and
then to its own purpose-built theatre in Cambridge Street in 1992. Committed to the
production of new and experimental work, it has premiered many modern plays, including Berkoff's *East* and John Byrne's *The Slab Boys*. It achieved the status of a public (as opposed to a club) theatre in 1988.

Travesties A comedy by Tom STOPPARD. First performance: London, 1974. The play
makes ingenious capital out of the fact that Lenin, James Joyce, and the dadaist Tristan Tzara were all living in Zürich during the same period of World War I. Events are
seen through the eyes of Henry Carr, a somewhat obtuse official at the British con-
sulate, who fails to see the revolutionary significance of what is taking place around
him. The play is famous for its brilliant wit and intricate structure.

Tree, Ellen *See* Kean, Edmund.

Tree, Sir Herbert Beerbohm (1853–1917) British actor-manager of mixed European
descent. He made his professional debut in 1878 and nine years later took over the
Comedy Theatre. After a number of successes, he moved to the more prestigious Haymarket, where he remained for 10 years, scoring a personal triumph as Svengali in
an adaptation of George Du Maurier's *Trilby*. The success of these years enabled him
to build HER MAJESTY'S THEATRE, which opened in 1897 with a series of magnificent Shakespearean productions. He was also acclaimed for his interpretations of Professor Higgins in *Pygmalion* opposite Mrs Patrick Campbell, and as Nero, Herod,
Beethoven, and Fagin. Tree also founded (1904) the Royal Academy of Dramatic Art.
He was knighted in 1909. His wife **Helen Maud Holt** (1863–1937) was his leading lady
in many productions. *See also* Beerbohm, Sir Max.

tree border *See* border.

Trelawny of the 'Wells' A comedy by PINERO. First performance: 1898. Rose
Trelawny breaks off her engagement to Arthur Gower to return to the stage, but finds
it impossible to deliver unnatural stage dialogue. A sentimental comedy, the play
ends with her triumph in a realistic play and her reunion with Arthur.

Tremblay, Michel (1942–) French-Canadian playwright, who established a controversial reputation with his use in his first play, *Les Belles-soeurs* (1968), of mixed
English and French, as spoken in Quebec. Later plays, which explore both Quebec's
mixed culture and the nature of sexual identity, include *En pièces détachées* (1969),
La Duchesse de Langlais (1970), *Hosanna* (1973), which depicts a transvestite's suffering, *Bonjour, Bonjour* (1974), *Carmen of the Boulevards* (1976), *Albertine in Five Times*
(1984), *Le Vrai Monde?* (1986), and *For the Pleasure of Seeing Her Again* (1998).

Trenev, Konstantin Andreievich (1884–1945) Russian playwright and short-story
writer, whose works remain popular in his own country. His best-known play is

Lyubov Yarovaya (1926), which depicts the conflict of loyalties facing a young teacher; it was performed with great success by the Moscow Art Theatre at the 1937 World Exhibition in Paris. Other plays included *Pugachevshchina* (1924), which depicts a peasant revolt in the 18th century, *On the Banks of the Neva* (1937), and *Anna Luchinina* (1941).

Tretyakov, Sergei Mikhailovich (1892–1939) Russian poet and playwright, best known for the play *Roar, China!* (1926), which recounts the clashes that took place between British imperialists and the Chinese in 1924. His other propagandist plays include *Are You Listening, Moscow?* and *Gas Masks*, on both of which he collaborated with Sergei Eisenstein. Later he helped to popularize the plays of Brecht in the USSR.

Trevelyan, Hilda (Hilda Tucker; 1880–1959) British actress. She made her stage debut as a child but her first serious engagement (1898) was understudying the part of Avonia Bunn – a part she later played many times – in Pinero's *Trelawny of the 'Wells'* at the Royal Court Theatre. She came to be associated particularly with the plays of J M Barrie, creating the role of Wendy in *Peter Pan* in 1904.

trickwork The use of traps and other mechanical devices to create illusions on stage, as practised particularly in the 19th-century British theatre. The success of such popular tricks as the roll-out and the leap trickwork depended upon both the acrobatic skills of the performers and the meticulous preparation of the machinery.

Tricycle Theatre A theatre and company in Kilburn, north London. Founded in 1980, the company presents mainly new plays, with a bias towards multicultural work and women's drama. It also offers entertainments and workshops for children. Recent productions include *The Colour of Justice* (1999), a dramatization of the Stephen Lawrence enquiry that later transferred to the West End.

trilogy *See* tetralogy.

Trinity Square Repertory Company A US theatre company founded in 1964 in Providence, Rhode Island. The company soon established a reputation for its productions of contemporary US drama and moved into a permanent home in the Lederer Theatre Complex in 1973. It also runs training courses and produces a summer repertory programme.

Trissino, Giangiorgio (1478–1550) Italian writer, author of the influential tragedy *Sofonisba* (1562), written c. 1514. His use of classical Greek models, observation of the unities of time and action, and employment of blank verse in this play set the pattern for much subsequent Italian tragedy. His other plays include the verse comedy *I simillimi*, based on Plautus.

Tristan l'Hermite (François l'Hermite; c. 1601–55) French playwright, poet, and gambler, who was a pioneer of French classical drama. Tristan's first play was the tragedy *La Mariane* (1636), based on Herod's jealousy for his wife, which enjoyed considerable success, rivalling that of Pierre Corneille's *Le Cid*. His other works include the tragedies *La Mort de Sénèque* (1644) and *La Mort de Crispe* (1645) and the comedy *Le Parasite* (1654).

tritagonist *See* protagonist.

Triumph of Horus, The A play written in Egypt around 3200 BC. The oldest surviving written drama in the world, it recounts a ritual battle between Horus, the son of Osiris, and his evil uncle, Set. The play, which was performed as part of a religious ceremony, survives in an ancient papyrus account. It was revived in translation in Britain in 1971.

Trivellino *See* Locatelli, Domenico.

Trocadero Palace of Varieties A music hall in Windmill (now Great Windmill) Street, London, which occupied the site of a tennis court built in 1744. Opened by Robert Bignell in 1851 as the **Argyll Rooms** for various kinds of entertainment, it met with scant success and was closed in 1878. Bignell reopened it in 1882 as the Trocadero Palace, and in 1886 Charles Coburn drew large audiences for 14 months singing 'Two Lovely Black Eyes'. Music hall continued until 1894, when the property was reopened as a restaurant (1896). In the 1920s C B Cochran staged a celebrated nightly cabaret in the Grill Room, remaining there until 1946. The property subsequently became a shopping centre.

Troepolskaya, Tatiana Mikhailovna (d. 1774) Russian actress, one of the first women to join a professional company in Russia. She excelled as heroines in the tragedies of Sumarokov.

Troilus and Cressida A tragicomedy by William SHAKESPEARE, written c. 1602. First performance: date unknown. Set against the background of the Trojan War, the play is a sardonic examination of the ideals of romance and chivalry and was little performed before the 20th century. Based on Homer and on Chaucer's *Troilus and Criseyde*, it is notable for its frank discussion of sexual desire and its apparent rejection, through the foul-mouthed Thersites, of the concepts of love and honour.

Trojan Women, The A tragedy by EURIPIDES. First performance: Athens, 415 BC. Of all Euripides' works, this play, relating the fate of Cassandra, Hecuba, and other characters after the fall of Troy, was his fiercest condemnation of war. It is thought to reflect the prolonged conflict then being continued between Sicily and Athens.

trope In the early Middle Ages, a brief passage inserted into the mass to illustrate the meaning of a particular service or festival. The earliest recorded trope, a natural development of the NEUME, was inserted in a 10th-century Easter service at the Monastery of St Martial at Limoges. Subsequently such tropes evolved into rudimentary plays, the earliest form of LITURGICAL DRAMA.

Troupes Permanentes *See Décentralisation Dramatique.*

trouvère *See* jongleur.

truck *See* boat truck.

Tuccio, Stefano (1540–97) Italian playwright, born in Sicily, who was a major writer of Jesuit drama. His plays, written for the Jesuit college at Messina, include *Juditha* (1564) and a trilogy, consisting of *Christus Natus*, *Christus Patiens*, and *Christus Judex*, which was one of the earliest such works written in the vernacular.

Tuke, Sir Samuel (d. 1674) English courtier, who (at the prompting of Charles II) wrote the tragicomedy *The Adventures of Five Hours*, based on a play by Calderón. It was performed at Lincoln's Inn Fields in 1663 and was praised by Samuel Pepys.

tumbler A batten used in rolling up canvas scenery, specifically to prevent it from becoming creased.

Tune, Tommy (1939–) US performer, choreographer, and director, known for his string-bean physique and his imaginative theatricality. His first Broadway choreography was one dance number in Michael Bennett's *Seesaw* (1973). He came into his own with *The Best Little Whorehouse in Texas* (1978) and later directed a straight play, Caryl Churchill's *Cloud Nine*, off-Broadway (1981). His later productions are noted for their seamless flow of action; they include *Nine* (1982), *My One and Only* (1983), in which he also starred, *Grand Hotel* (1989), and *Will Rogers' Follies* (1991).

Turgenev, Ivan Sergeivich (1818–83) Russian novelist and playwright, best known as a dramatist for *Mesiats v derevne* (A MONTH IN THE COUNTRY; written in 1850 and staged in 1872). This play, which anticipated Chekhov, was the first Russian psychological drama and Turgenev's final work for the stage, which he abandoned in the face of opposition from the censor. His earlier plays include the satirical comedies *Bezdenezhe* (Insolvency), *Gde tonko, tam i rvyotsa* (Where It's Thin It Breaks), *Kholostiak* (The Bachelor), and *Privubtsialka* (A Provincial Lady).

Turkish Knight *See* mummers' play.

Turlupin (Henri Legrand; c. 1587–1637) French actor, who was highly popular in farce at the Hôtel de Bourgogne alongside Gaultier-Garguille and Gros-Guillaume. He also appeared in tragedy, using the stagename **Belleville**.

Turnham's Grand Concert Hall *See* Metropolitan Music Hall.

Turpio, Ambivius (2nd century BC) Roman actor, who created numerous roles in the plays of Terence. He also appeared in works by Caecilius Statius.

Tutin, Dame Dorothy (1930–) British actress, who, after working at Bristol and at the Old Vic, came to prominence as Rose in Graham Greene's *The Living Room* (1953) and Sally Bowles in *I Am a Camera* (1954). She subsequently found acclaim in many parts with the Royal Shakespeare and National Theatre companies, notably Hedvig in *The Wild Duck*, Portia, Viola, Cressida, Juliet, Sister Jeanne in Whiting's *The Devils* (1961), Desdemona, Rosalind, Kate in Pinter's *Old Times* (1971), and Peter Pan (1971–72). Later work has included *The Cherry Orchard* (1978), Rattigan's *The Deep Blue Sea* (1981), Pinter's *A Kind of Alaska* (1985), *Henry VIII* (1991), and Shaw's *Getting Married* (1993).

Twaits, William (d. 1814) US actor, born in Britain, who excelled in farce and comedy first in Britain and then in the US. His most successful roles included Shakespeare's Polonius, Dogberry, Launcelot Gobbo, and the First Gravedigger, in which parts he was highly popular at such venues as the Chestnut Street Theatre in Philadelphia and the Park Theatre in New York.

Twelfth Night; or, What You Will A comedy by William SHAKESPEARE, written 1600–01. First performance: c. 1602. Probably written as a Christmas entertainment, the play is the last and finest of Shakespeare's romantic comedies, with characters including the disguised Viola, the lovelorn Orsino, and the rascally Sir Toby Belch. Its use of the imagery of war, storms, and madness and the anguish of the duped Malvolio are often seen as anticipating the series of great tragedies that was to follow.

Twentieth Century Theatre *See* Bijou Theatre.

two-fold *See* book flat.

Two Gentlemen of Verona, The A comedy by William SHAKESPEARE, written c. 1592–93. First recorded performance: 1672. The first and least successful of Shakespeare's romantic comedies, the play was derived from Jorge de Montemayor's prose romance *Diana* and focuses on the conflicting demands of love and friendship through the relationship of Valentine and Proteus.

Two Noble Kinsmen, The A tragicomedy by John FLETCHER and William SHAKESPEARE, written c. 1613. First performance: c. 1619. Probably Shakespeare's last play, it is based on Chaucer's *Knight's Tale* and follows the contest by tournament between Palamon and Arcite for the hand of Emilia, the whole event being presided over by Theseus. It has been suggested that Shakespeare wrote the first and fifth acts and Fletcher most of the remainder.

Tyl, Josef Kajetán (1808–50) Czech playwright and actor, who is commonly regarded as the father of the modern Czech theatre. He wrote his first play, the folk comedy *The Fair*, for his own company in 1834; the play includes verses that later became the Czech national anthem. He was famous for his patriotic plays arguing for Czech independence, notably *The Bagpiper of Strakonice* (1847), *The Bloody Trial, or the Miners of Kutná Hora* (1848), and *Jan Hus* (1848).

Tyler, Royall (1757–1826) US playwright, who wrote the first US comedy – *The Contrast* – in 1787. Influenced by the works of such English writers as Goldsmith and Sheridan, it introduced the stock rural Yankee character, whose simple native honesty triumphs over foreign affectation. His later plays were less successful.

Tynan, Kenneth (Peacock) (1927–80) British theatre critic, who wrote for *The Observer* (1954–58 and 1960–63) and *The New Yorker* (1958–60) and was closely associated with the National Theatre (1963–69). He was a noted supporter of the new drama of Osborne and others in the 1950s and of the more political playwrights that succeeded in the 1960s. As such he was in constant conflict with the censors; he was also the main force behind the popular nude revue *Oh, Calcutta!* (1969).

Tyrone Guthrie Theatre *See* Guthrie Theatre.

Ubu roi A satirical farce by Alfred JARRY. First performance: Paris, 1896. The loathsome Père Ubu, a caricature of one of Jarry's schoolmasters, is the embodiment of stupidity, greed, and cruelty; this ferocious attack on bourgeois society proved a source of inspiration to many playwrights of the 1950s and 1960s.

Udall, Nicholas (1505–56) English playwright, chiefly remembered for RALPH ROISTER DOISTER, the earliest known comedy in English; it was written for the boys of Eton school, of which he was headmaster. None of his other dramatic pieces have survived intact.

Ulster Group Theatre A small repertory theatre established in Ulster Hall, Bedford Street, Belfast, in 1932. Known first as the Little Theatre and then the Playhouse, it was renamed in 1940 when an organization of amateur groups took it over. Eventually this organization acquired professional status and built a reputation for productions of plays by such writers as James Bridie, St John Ervine, George Shiels, and Joseph Tomelty; actors at the theatre have included Colin Blakely and J G Devlin. After surviving a period in decline in the late 1950s it concentrated on comedy until 1972, when it was closed for four years due to the sectarian conflict in Northern Ireland. Re-equipped in 1976, it reopened in 1978 as a venue for amateur groups.

Unamuno y Jugo, Miguel de (1864–1936) Spanish writer and philosopher of Basque descent. As a playwright he was best known for *Sombras de sueño* (Dream Shadows; 1930); his other works for the theatre included *Abel Sánchez* (1917), based on his own novel, and *El hermano Juan* (Brother Juan; 1929), an adaptation of the Don Juan legend. One of his short stories was later dramatized by Julio de Hoyos as *Nada menos que todo un hombre* (Nothing Less Than a Total Man).

Uncle Vanya A play by Anton CHEKHOV. First performance: Moscow Art Theatre, 1899. A reworking of his earlier unsuccessful play *The Wood Demon* (1899), it depicts the sense of purposelessness in the lives of the inhabitants of a large house in the countryside. The roles of Vanya, his niece Sonya, and their companions – an elderly professor and his wife – have provided many leading performers with rewarding roles.

Underhill, Cave (c. 1634–c. 1710) British actor, noted as a comedian. His most famous parts included Codpate in Shadwell's *Epsom Wells* and Sir Sampson Legend in *Love for Love*. In 1681 he created the role of Blunt in Aphra Behn's *The Rover*.

Under Milk Wood A 'play for voices' by Dylan Thomas. First stage performance: London, 1956. Although written originally as a radio play, this depiction of life in the

Welsh town of Llaregub has often been presented on stage. It is popular for its rich humour and eloquent language.

understudy An actor who learns the part of another, so that he is able to replace the latter in the case of an emergency.

Underwood, John (c. 1590–1624) English actor, who appeared as a boy in Jonson's *Cynthia's Revels* and *The Poetaster* at the Blackfriars Theatre. He was with the King's Men from 1608 and is in the First Folio list of Shakespearean actors. He held shares in the Blackfriars, Globe, and Curtain theatres.

Union Square Theatre A theatre in Union Square, New York, which opened in 1871. It was managed by A M Palmer and had one of the best stock companies in the US, presenting such plays as John Oxenford's *The Two Orphans* (1874) and *La Dame aux Camélias* by Dumas *fils*; after 1885, when Palmer and the company left, it housed travelling companies. In 1888 it was burned down and rebuilt as a vaudeville house. In 1936, after it had been used as a cinema, it was demolished.

Union Theatre *See* Chatham Theatre.

Uniti An Italian *commedia dell'arte* company, which drew on actors from a number of other troupes to present special performances. In its various forms its directors included Drusiano MARTINELLI, while Silvio FIORILLO numbered amongst its actors.

unities, the The convention that a play should observe consistency of time, place, and action, as developed in Italy in the 16th century and first codified by Jean MAIRET in 1630. According to the proponents of this view, a play should represent a single action taking place in a single day in the same setting. A strong influence upon classical French tragedy, the concept of the unities was derived, somewhat inaccurately, from the theories of Aristotle. It was widely influential elsewhere on the Continent but did not take root in England.

Unity Theatre A communist theatre in London, founded by a left-wing amateur group in a hall near King's Cross in 1936. It moved to permanent premises in Goldington Street, St Pancras, in 1937, and introduced the Living Newspaper technique of presenting current issues in documentary style. Among other productions were the first Brecht play to be staged in London, O'Casey's *The Star Turns Red* (1940), and Adamov's *Spring '71* (1962). Fire destroyed the theatre in 1975.

The Unity Theatre in Glasgow was a similarly motivated amateur company formed in 1941. Having won acclaim for its production of Gorky's *The Lower Depths*, which was seen at London's Unity Theatre in 1945, it became a professional company. It continued to play in Glasgow as well as touring Scotland, achieving an outstanding success with Robert MacLeish's *The Gorbals Story* (1948). Financial insecurity led to the company's disbandment in the early 1950s.

university drama departments The study of the history, theory, and practice of drama as the basis of a degree course was first undertaken in the US, specifically at the Carnegie Institute of Technology in Pittsburgh (1914). In Britain the first such department was established at Bristol University in 1946; Manchester, Hull, and Birmingham followed during the early 1960s and expansion continued into the mid-1970s. Most departments have their own studio theatres or access to larger campus theatres, which in their turn have made important contributions to the cultural life of their surrounding communities. Vocational training is rarely provided (that being the province of the drama schools) but extensive practical work is usually undertaken and many graduates at universities throughout the world go on to become successful actors, directors, designers, and administrators both in the theatre and in the media.

University Wits The name later given to a group of Elizabethan playwrights noted for their educated wit and their wild behaviour. They included Greene, Nashe, Marlowe, and Peele among other graduates of Oxford and Cambridge.

Unreason, Abbot of *See* Misrule, Lord of.

Unruh, Fritz von (1885–1970) German playwright and poet, who resigned his commission in the cavalry following Reinhardt's successful production of his patriotic play *Offiziere* in 1911. Throughout World War I he served in the army, but soon after he became known for his strongly pacifist views, as expressed in the Expressionist plays *Ein Geschlecht* (One Generation; 1917) and *Platz* (1920).

upper circle *See* auditorium.

upstage *See* stage direction.

Urban, Joseph (1872–1933) US theatre architect and stage designer, born in Austria, who became famous for his sets for Ziegfeld's *Follies*. Other designs included sets for opera in Boston and for Shakespearean productions in New York. As an architect, he designed the innovative Ziegfeld Theatre in New York.

Ure, Mary *See* Osborne, John.

Uris Theatre *See* Gershwin Theatre.

Ustinov, Sir Peter (1921–) British actor, playwright, director, and stage designer of Russian descent, who trained under Saint-Denis and made early appearances at the Players' Theatre, London, in his own sketches. After serving in World War II, during which five of his plays – including *House of Regrets* (1942) and *The Banbury Nose* (1944) – were produced, he returned to the stage as Petrovich in Dostoevsky's *Crime and Punishment* (1946) and Sergeant Dohda in Eric Linklater's *Love in Albania* in 1949. He then embarked upon a successful film career, and for the next 30 years appeared in the theatre only in his own plays; the most successful of these included THE LOVE OF FOUR COLONELS (1951) and ROMANOFF AND JULIET (1956). He played Lear at Stratford, Ontario, in 1979 and in 1983 appeared as Ludwig in his own play *Beethoven's Tenth*. In the 1980s and 1990s he mounted several acclaimed opera and ballet productions. As well as being a highly versatile man of the theatre, he has acquired a reputation as a brilliant raconteur and mimic.

V

Vadstena Theatre A private theatre in Vadstena, Sweden, established in 1826. Although the last professional performance was in 1878, it survives as a venue for amateurs.

Vakhtangov, Eugene V (1883–1922) Russian actor and director, who became a leading director of the Moscow Art Theatre, initially as a pupil of Stanislavsky. With his own studio group, the Third Workshop, he mounted an acclaimed production of *Macbeth* in 1921, with himself in the leading role. The group thrived on a combination of the naturalism of Stanislavsky and the experimentalism of Meyerhold. Vakhtangov's work for the theatre culminated in a highly praised version of Gozzi's *Turandot*, presented after his early death at the height of his fame. The Third Workshop was subsequently renamed the Vakhtangov Theatre. He also founded (1918) the Habimah Theatre, famous for its production of Ansky's *The Dybbuk* (1922).

Vakhtangov Theatre A studio theatre in Moscow, originally known as the Third Workshop, established in 1921 as part of the MOSCOW ART THEATRE. Founded by Eugene V Vakhtangov, who did some of his best work there, it was later used for productions directed by such notable figures as Akimov, Meyerhold, Popov, and Zavadsky, of which *Hamlet* (1932) and plays by Gorky attracted the most attention. Okhlopkov and Shchukin staged plays by Pogodin with success, while after World War II a series of both modern and – under Reuben and Yevgenyi Simonov – Shakespearean works were presented.

Valle-Inclán, Ramón María del (1866–1936) Spanish novelist, poet, and playwright, who was the author of a number of avant-garde dramas. These ranged from the children's play *La cabeza del dragón* (The Dragon's Head; 1918) and the Carlist poetic drama *Voces de gesta* (Epic Voices; 1912) to the highly satirical *La marquese Rosalinda* (1913) and *Divinas palabras* (Divine Words; 1920). His targets included the oppression of the poor, the extravagance of the rich, and the decadence of high society; several of his plays anticipated the Theatre of the Absurd.

Valleran-Lecomte (fl. 1590–c. 1615) French actor-manager, who presented various plays in Bordeaux, Strasbourg, Frankfurt, and elsewhere before establishing his own company. Acting plays by Alexandre Hardy and others, his company appeared at the Hôtel de Bourgogne and undertook several tours. Performers with the company included Marie Venier and Agnan Sarat; Valleran-Lecomte himself appeared in farce and in *commedia dell'arte* roles. He also ran a training school for young actors.

Valli, Romolo (1925–80) Italian actor and manager, who became highly popular in character parts. He first attracted attention while at the Piccolo Teatro della Città di Milano, excelling in such plays as Goldoni's *La locandiera* and as Malvolio in *Twelfth Night*. In 1954 he founded his own Compagnia dei Giovanni (later I Giovani del Teatro Elisio), with whom he won acclaim in plays by Fabbri and Pirandello. He died in a car accident.

vamp trap A trap, more formally called a vampire trap, by means of which an actor, passing through two spring flaps, can appear to walk through a solid piece of scenery. It acquired its name from Planché's play *The Vampire*, in which it was first used in 1820.

Vanbrugh, Sir John (1664–1726) English playwright and architect, whose first successful comedy, THE RELAPSE; or, Virtue in Danger, was produced in 1696. THE PROVOKED WIFE followed in 1697 at Lincoln's Inn Fields; other plays and translations were less successful, although *The Confederacy* (1705) enjoyed many revivals. It was originally produced by Betterton at the Queen's Theatre (on the site of Her Majesty's), which Vanbrugh himself had designed. His unfinished play *A Journey to London* was completed by Cibber as *The Provoked Husband* (1728).

Vanbrugh, Violet (Violet Augusta Barnes; 1867–1942) British actress, who began her career at Margate and subsequently worked in the Kendals' company and with Irving. She had particular success as Queen Katharine in *Henry V* (1910) opposite her husband, Arthur BOURCHIER, and often appeared as a leading lady under his management. Other acclaimed roles included Lady Macbeth and several modern parts.

Her sister was the actress **Dame Irene Vanbrugh** (Irene Barnes; 1872–1949), who made her London debut in *Alice in Wonderland* in 1888. She became a leading lady in the companies of Tree, Alexander, and Hare, and, during a 13-year connection with Charles Frohman at the Duke of York's Theatre under the direction of her husband, the younger Dion BOUCICAULT, proved herself a superb exponent of the plays of Pinero and Barrie. Her most celebrated roles included the very first Gwendolen Fairfax in *The Importance of Being Earnest* (1895) and Sophie Fullgarney in *The Gay Lord Quex* (1899). The Vanbrugh Theatre of the Royal Academy of Dramatic Art was named in honour of the two sisters by their brother, Sir Kenneth Barnes.

Vance, Alfred (Alfred Peck Stevens; 1839–88) British music hall performer, known as **The Great Vance**. After appearing at the St James's Theatre, London, he went on the halls in a blackfaced double act with his brother. In 1864 he switched to singing broad cockney songs; later he became a popular *lion comique*. He died on stage at the Sun Music Hall in Knightsbridge.

Vance, Nina *See* Nina Vance Alley Theatre.

Vančura, Antonín (1882–1939) Czech playwright, who – with his brother, the novelist **Vladislav Vančura** (1891–1942) – was associated with the Free Theatre. Antonín, writing as **Jiří Mahen**, wrote *Heaven, Hell, Paradise* (1919), *Progeny* (1921), and *The Deserter* (1924), all depicting contemporary turmoil in Central Europe. He committed suicide in 1939. Vladislav's best-known plays were *Teacher and Pupil* (1927) and *The Sick Girl* (1928). He died in a concentration camp.

Vandenhoff, George (1813–85) US actor, born in Britain, who settled in the US after appearing successfully as Hamlet at the Park Theatre in New York in 1842 and became a popular leading man. Previously at Covent Garden in London, he returned here in 1853 to appear as Hamlet once more and then retired. Overcoming his dislike for the theatre, he came out of retirement briefly in 1878 to appear as Wolsey in *Henry VIII* opposite Geneviève Ward.

His sister, **Charlotte Elizabeth Vaudenhoff** (Mrs Swinbourne; 1818–60), was much admired playing such roles as Juliet, Cordelia, and Antigone. She also created the parts of Lydia in Sheridan Knowles's *The Love Chase* (1837) and Parthenia in Mrs Lovell's *Ingomar* (1851).

Vanderbilt Theatre A theatre on 48th Street, New York, which opened in 1921 with O'Neill's *Anna Christie*. Subsequent triumphs were somewhat rare but included a revival of Wilde's *The Importance of Being Earnest* (1939); it was then converted into a broadcasting studio and was demolished in 1954.

Van Druten, John (1901–57) London-born playwright and novelist, who became a US citizen in 1944; he emigrated to the US when his first play, *Young Woodley* (1925) – a study of adolescence – was banned in Britain. Later plays include such popular light comedies as *The Voice of the Turtle* (1943) and *Bell, Book and Candle* (1950). He is now best known for his I AM A CAMERA (1951), based on *Goodbye to Berlin*, Christopher Isherwood's portrait of Berlin between the wars; it was later turned into the musical CABARET (1966).

Van Itallie, Jean-Claude (1936–) US playwright, born in Belgium, who wrote his first produced play, *War*, in 1963. Since then he has written works for such avant-garde theatres as the Café La Mama and the Open Theatre, including *American Hurrah!* (1966), *The Serpent* (1968), and *Mystery Play* (1973); he has also adapted several plays by Chekhov. He was writer-in-residence at the McCarter Theatre in Princeton from 1972 to 1976. His 1983 play, *The Tibetan Book of the Dead*, foreshadowed his current interest in Eastern culture and mysticism; he now lectures on the healing power of the theatre for his own Shantigar Foundation and at Esalen.

Variétés, Théâtre des A theatre in Paris, opened in 1807 and still surviving in substantially its original condition. Partially altered in 1823, it was used for a wide range of productions, including revues, the plays of Dumas *père*, and vaudeville.

An earlier theatre of the same name was founded in the Boulevard du Temple in 1779.

variety In Britain, a tradition of entertainment that developed from MUSIC HALL in the late 19th century. Variety represented the later, less spontaneous, period of the halls, with the audience being seated as in an ordinary theatre and with the older continuous bills being replaced by twice-nightly programmes; these often included elaborately staged extracts from ballets and plays. *See also* vaudeville.

Variety Artistes' Federation *See* British Actors' Equity Association.

Varius Rufus, Lucius (c. 74 BC–14 BC) Roman playwright, a friend of both Virgil and Horace. His tragedy *Thyestes* (29 BC), now lost, was considered the equal of any Greek tragedy.

Varro, Marcus Terentius (116 BC–27 BC) Roman scholar, poet, and satirist, author of several theatrical pieces, all of which are lost. His works are thought to have included examples of closet drama and *didascaliae* as well as histories of the theatre.

Vasconcelos, Jorge Ferreira de (1515–85) Portuguese writer, author of several dialogue novels. These included *Eufrósina*, *Ulissipo*, and *Aulegrafia*, which were all intended for reading aloud rather than for actual performance.

vaudeville A mainly US tradition of popular musical entertainment. The name is thought to derive from French *vaux-de-vire* (songs of the Vire, a region of Normandy) or *vaux des villes* (songs of the cities). The term *vaudeville* was applied (by Boileau) to certain satirical ballads in the 17th century and later to dumb shows in the booth theatres of Paris. These were presented as musical entertainments in order to circumvent the Comédie-Française's monopoly of straight drama. The most famous writers of these dramas included Lesage and Favart, whose works foreshadowed the development of popular farce and light opera in the 19th century.

In the mid-19th century the word vaudeville came to be applied to variety entertainments for the first time, particularly in the US. Roughly equivalent to the MUSIC HALL in Britain, US vaudeville developed in beer halls throughout the country; typical programmes comprised a mixture of songs, comic sketches, and various dance, magic, and acrobatic acts, usually about a dozen in number (although the US tradition sometimes included more diverse elements than was customary on the other side of the Atlantic). Following the opening of a vaudeville theatre in New York by Tony Pastor in 1881 the tradition became steadily more respectable, attracting family audiences. Successful chains of vaudeville theatres were subsequently set up, the most celebrated venue being the Palace Theatre on Broadway. US vaudeville stars included Lew Dockstader, Jimmy Durante, W C Fields, Bert Lahr, Bert Williams, Weber and Fields, Jack Norworth, Lillian Russell, Ed Wynn, and many others.

By 1932, when the Palace Theatre finally closed, vaudeville had gone into decline with the arrival of radio and the cinema (although for a time films were presented as part of vaudeville programmes with some success). Many of its most popular stars subsequently deserted the medium for the screen.

Vaudeville, Théâtre du A theatre in the rue de Chartres, Paris, opened in 1792 as a home for actors formerly with the Comédie-Italienne. The company provoked official hostility with the satirical element in its work, but later concentrated on less contentious historical pieces. In 1838 the troupe moved to the Place de la Bourse, then (in 1869) to the Chaussée d'Autin, which became a cinema in 1927.

Vaudeville Theatre An elegant theatre in London's Strand where Sir Henry Irving once played, now known for its musical and comedy productions. The Vaudeville was built in 1870 by C J Phipps but has been reconstructed twice since, in 1891 and again in 1925. Sir Seymour Hicks, his wife Ellaline Terriss, and Sir Charles Hawtrey all acted here in the early 1900s; its first big success was H J Byron's *Our Boys* (1875), which ran for 1362 performances. From 1915 André Charlot presented a long series of revues here, while in the post-World War II years its greatest success was the record-breaking Julian Slade musical *Salad Days*, which opened in 1954 and ran until 1960. In 1969 Peter Saunders purchased the theatre from the Gatti family, who had owned it since 1892. Subsequent hits have included John Chapman and Ray Cooney's farce

Move Over Mrs Markham (1970), Agatha Christie's *A Murder is Announced* (1977), a revival of Chekhov's *Uncle Vanya* (1988), Alan Ayckbourn's *Time of My Life* (1993), and Shelagh Stephenson's *The Memory of Water* (1999) with Alison Steadman.

Vaughan, Hannah *See* Pritchard, Hannah.

Vaughan, Kate (Catherine Candelon; c. 1852–1903) British actress and dancer. She made her debut as a dancer on the music hall stage in 1870 and played a prominent part in burlesque at the Gaiety Theatre (1876–83); in 1886 she gave up dancing to organize a comedy company and appeared in plays by Sheridan and others.

Vauthier, Jean (1910–92) Belgian playwright. His best-known plays feature the character Captain Bada, a grotesque anarchic figure who first appeared in *Capitaine Bada* (1952). Barrault was acclaimed in the role in *Le Personnage combattant* (1956), and Bada is also the central figure in *Le Sang* (1970). Other works include an adaptation of Machiavelli's *La Mandragora* (1952), radically reworked versions of plays by Shakespeare and Euripides, and *Island of Birds* (1992).

Vauxhall An area in London on the south side of the river where, in 1660, a complex of pleasure gardens was opened. They reached a peak of popularity in the 18th century, being renowned as a venue for concerts, fireworks, dances, and occasional spectacular dramas and operettas. They were closed in 1859, having acquired a reputation for low behaviour and disorder.

Vauxhall Garden and Theatre An open-air theatre opened in 1808 in the grounds of Vauxhall Garden on 4th Avenue, New York. It was destroyed in a fire a short time after opening and was not replaced until 1838. The new theatre had several successful seasons in the 1840s and was demolished in 1855.

Vazov, Ivan Minchev (1850–1921) Bulgarian poet, novelist, and playwright, whose strongly patriotic works remain extremely popular in Bulgaria. His most successful play *Khushove* (1894) depicts Romania's struggle for liberation; other plays included *Kam Propast* (Towards the Abyss; 1907), *Borislav* (1909), and a series of dramas set in medieval Bulgaria.

Vedrenne, John Eugene (1867–1930) British theatre manager, whose most important work was done in conjunction with Harley Granville-Barker at the Royal Court Theatre (1904–07) and the Savoy Theatre (1907). Together they presented many major new works by G B Shaw and others.

Vega, Ventura de la (Buenaventura José Mariá Vega y Cárdenas; 1807–65) Spanish playwright, author of plays in a variety of styles, the most successful being the drama *El hombre del mundo* (A Man of the World; 1845). Less successful works include a tragedy, a history, comedies, and translations of French plays.

His son, **Ricardo de la Vega** (1841–1910), wrote several notable examples of the *género chico*, notably *La canción de la Lola* (Lola's Song; 1880).

Vega Carpio, Lope Félix de (1562–1635) Spanish playwright and poet, considered the most influential figure in the Golden Age of Spanish literature. He sailed with the Armada in 1588 and was famous for his many passionate love affairs, which continued after his ordination as a priest in 1614; he claimed to be the author of 1500 plays, although only 470 or so now survive.

His drama, which established the ground rules for the Spanish *comedia* for many years to come, reflects his belief in the contemporary honour code and in the divine right of kings; in form it ranges from tragicomedy to farce and lives of the saints. His earlier works were written for the open-air theatres of Madrid; subsequently, however, he also wrote plays, generally pastorals and mythological dramas, for performance at the royal court, thus influencing the development of the *zarzuela*. He was also the author of notable *autos sacramentales* and of the treatise *Arte neuvo de hacer comedias* (New Art of Writing Plays; c. 1609), in which he analysed the nature of drama.

Principal works:

Castelvines y Monteses: c. 1608.
Fuenteovejuna: c. 1612; translated as *The Sheep-Well*.
Peribáñez y el comedador de Ocaña: 1614.
El perro del hortelano: c. 1615.
La dama boba: 1617.
El villano en su rincón: 1617.
La selva sin amor: 1629; translated as *The Loveless Forest*.
El mejor alcalde, el rey: 1635; translated as *The King the Best Magistrate*.
Por la puente, Juana: 1635.
El caballero de Olmedo: 1641.

Veigel, Eva Maria *See* Garrick, David.

Vélez de Guevara, Luis (1579–1644) Spanish playwright, poet, and novelist, who was a distinguished follower of Lope de Vega. His 400 lively plays include examples of the *comedia* and the *entremé*, *autos sacramentales*, and versions of Lope de Vega's works; his novel *El diablo cojuelo* (The Crippled Devil; 1641) was highly influential in an adaptation by Alain Lesage as *Le Diable boileux* (1707).

Velten, Johannes (1640–92) German actor, whose touring company was eventually inherited by Carolina Neuber, Schönemann, Koch, Ackermann, and Schröder. Under Velten the company became well known for its high theatrical standards, performing plays by Molière and Shakespeare among others; unlike many companies of the day it avoided improvisation.

Venice Preserv'd; or, a Plot Discovered A tragedy by Thomas OTWAY. First performance: London, 1682. It tells of the secret marriage of Jaffier to a senator's daughter, Belvedira, and of his subsequent downfall; in the original production the leading roles were played by Betterton and Mrs Barry. It is one of the few Restoration tragedies still revived.

Venice Theatre *See* Century Theatre.

Venier, Marie (Marie Vernier; fl. 1590–1627) French actress, one of the first women to appear on the Parisian stage. The daughter of an actor-manager, she became the leading lady with Valleran-Lecomte's company at the Hôtel de Bourgogne; subsequently she and her actor-husband **Laporte** (Mathieu de Febvre; 1572–c. 1626) were criticized for appearing without permission at the Hôtel d'Argent.

Venne, Lottie (1852–1928) British actress, who first made a name for herself in burlesque. She was a clever mimic and a popular performer in George Edwardes's musical comedies, but in her later years specialized in playing older ladies in straight comedy, being especially admired as Mrs Malaprop in *The Rivals* (1910).

Vere Street Theatre A theatre converted from a tennis court – Gibbon's Tennis Court – in Clare Market, London, where actors attempted to perform after the closure of theatres in 1642. Davenant used it to stage 'music and instruction', thus evading the law. Following the Restoration, Killigrew reopened it with *Henry IV, Part I* and remained there until moving to Drury Lane in 1663. Vere Street was then used as an acting school until 1671; it burnt down in 1809.

Verfremdungseffekt *See* alienation effect.

Verga, Giovanni (1840–1922) Italian novelist and playwright, born in Sicily, who became a notable writer in the *verismo* tradition with his tragedies of Sicilian life. His most important works were all produced after his return to Sicily in the 1880s; these include *Cavalleria rusticana* (Rustic Chivalry; 1884), later an opera by Mascagni, *La Lupa* (The She-Wolf; 1896), about sexual psychology, *La caccia al lupo* (The Wolf-Hunt; 1901), and *In portieria* (In the Porter's Lodge; 1885).

Vergerio, Pier Paolo (1370–1445) Italian playwright, remembered as the author of the Latin comedy *Paulus* (c. 1390). The play, influenced by Terence, depicts the moral dilemma of the central character when faced with a choice between leading a studious or degenerate life.

verismo A movement in the theatre and the arts in general that developed in Italy in the late 19th century. Based on the principles of NATURALISM, as popularized by Zola and Balzac, the movement inspired many plays on political and social themes and set in working-class surroundings. Writers associated with the *verismo* tradition included the Sicilian novelists Luigi Capuana and Giovanni Verga and the playwrights D'Annunzio, Giacosa, and Pirandello. The movement was suppressed by the Fascists in the 1920s but was revived after World War II.

Verneuil, Louis (Louis-Collin Barbie de Bocage; 1893–1952) French actor and playwright, who became a leading writer of plays in the *Boulevard* tradition. His best-known play was *Ma Cousine de Varsovie*, while Sarah Bernhardt herself made her last appearance in his *Daniel* (1921). He subsequently spent some years in films, before eventually committing suicide.

Versailles The principal residence of the French royal family until the Revolution and the scene of numerous theatrical entertainments. Although many performances were presented during the time of Louis XIV, a purpose-built stage was not installed there until 1768, when Louis XV had a well-equipped, oval-shaped theatre built in the north wing. The theatre was then used for banquets as well as for plays by Racine, Voltaire, and others; during the Revolution it became a meeting place for the Jacobins. Since then it has hosted further banquets, plays, and concerts, being restored to its original condition in the 1950s. Another theatre at Versailles, built in 1777 by Mlle Montansier, was abandoned in 1886.

Verulamium A Roman town in southern England (now St Albans), which was the site of a 2nd-century theatre. It is believed that it was used for sporting events as well as for mime and dancing before being rebuilt in the 3rd century. It was not used after 400 AD and was rediscovered in 1847.

Vestris, Françoise (Françoise Gourgaud; 1743–1804) French actress, who was a noted member of the Comédie-Française, where she appeared with her brother Dugazon. She was acclaimed as tragic heroines in the plays of Belloy, Chénier, and Voltaire.

Vestris, Madame (Lucy Elizabeth Bartolozzi; 1797–1856) British actress and manager, whose first husband, the French ballet dancer Armand Vestris, left her in 1820. She established herself as an actress in 1817 in burlesque at Drury Lane. After several seasons in Paris, she became a popular performer at both Drury Lane and Covent Garden. In 1830 she took over the Olympic Theatre, where she remained for nine years, introducing numerous reforms. In 1838 she married Charles James Mathews; together they managed Covent Garden and the Lyceum for a short period.

Vezin, Herman (1829–1910) British actor, born in Philadelphia. After appearances at York, he played Pembroke in *King John* at the Princess's Theatre in London. He became manager of the Surrey Theatre in 1859 and came to the fore playing the major tragic parts. He was subsequently engaged by Phelps at Sadler's Wells and by Irving at the Lyceum; his last appearance was under Tree in 1909.

His wife was the Australian actress **Jane Elizabeth Vezin** (Jane Elizabeth Thomson; 1827–1902), who came to England in 1857 and was immediately acclaimed at Sadler's Wells; she later excelled in numerous Shakespearean roles.

Vian, Boris (1920–59) French novelist and playwright, whose works (influenced by Alfred Jarry) blend satire and poetic fantasy with nightmare and violence. *Les Bâtisseurs d'empire, ou le Schmürz* (1959; translated as *The Empire Builders*, 1962), Vian's most successful play, depicts the decline of bourgeois values. War and militarism are the targets of *L'Équarrissage pour tous* (1950) and *Le Goûter des généraux* (1963; translated as *The Generals' Tea-Party*, 1967).

Viau, Théophile de *See* Théophile de Viau.

Vice A character of the English morality play, notable as an early clown figure. In his original form he was portrayed as the cynical servant of the Devil. He is thought to have influenced certain characteristics of Shakespeare's Falstaff.

Vicente, Gil (c. 1465–c. 1536) Portuguese playwright and poet, regarded as the most distinguished writer of drama in the Portuguese tradition. His 44 surviving plays – some written in Spanish – include *autos sacramentales*, tragicomedies, comedies, and farces. Many of these were intended for performance at the royal court, where he occupied the post of court poet from 1502 to 1536. His earliest plays were chiefly eclogues written in imitation of Encina; these gradually developed into a distinctive type of morality play, the best examples of which are those making up his *Barcas* trilogy. In their approach to religious and social issues, these works had a profound effect upon subsequent Spanish drama.

Vicente's romantic comedies – written after 1520 and modelled upon the plays of Bartolomé de Torres Naharro – were also highly influential, as were his many farces. The allegorical fantasies of his last years are notable for their satirical content and their use of sophisticated stage devices familiar from the mummers' tradition.

Principal works:

Auto da Alma: c. 1517.

Barca do Inferno: 1517.

Barca do Purgatório: 1518.

Barca do Glória: 1519.

Farsa de Inês Pereira: 1523.

Vicentini, Tommaso Antonio (1682–1739) Italian actor, who began in tragedy but later became famous as Arlecchino in the *commedia dell'arte* under the stagename **Thomassin**. In 1716 he moved to Paris with the younger Riccoboni; there he appeared at the Palais-Royal and the Hôtel de Bourgogne with great success, being noted for his acrobatic skills. He was much acclaimed in the plays of Marivaux, some of which may have been written specifically for him as well as for Silvia.

Victoria Palace Theatre A theatre opposite Victoria Station, London, which was once the capital's most popular music hall. It began as a venue for entertainment attached to the Royal Standard tavern, being known successively as Moy's Music-Hall and (from 1863) the **Royal Standard Music Hall**. Following the construction of the railway station, the Standard was rebuilt in 1886 and finally demolished in 1910. The Victoria Palace opened in 1911 with a variety bill and over the next decade all the leading music hall stars appeared there. Revues were presented in 1929–34 and in 1934 (renamed the Victoria Palace Theatre) it staged Walter Reynolds's infamous patriotic play YOUNG ENGLAND, which quickly acquired cult status. Seymour Hicks took over the management for a season in 1935, reviving some of his earlier productions, while later successes included revues and the musical comedy *Me and My Girl* (1937–39). The home of the Crazy Gang from 1947 to 1962 and then of the Black and White Minstrels, the Victoria Palace next played host to a stage version of the popular 'Carry On' films. Since then its musical tradition has continued with revivals of *Annie*, *High Society*, and other favourites, as well as *Buddy*, a show based on the songs of Buddy Holly, which ran here from 1989 to 1994.

Victoria Regina A group of one-act plays by Laurence HOUSMAN depicting the court of Queen Victoria. First performance: Gate Theatre, London, 1935. Banned by the censor owing to the depiction of royalty, they were originally presented privately and only received a public performance in Britain after the intervention of Edward VIII.

Victoria Theatre A theatre-in-the-round at Stoke-on-Trent, established by Stephen Joseph in a converted cinema in 1962. Under its artistic director, Peter Cheeseman, the resident company maintained close links with the neighbourhood, producing plays and musicals concerned with local history, including *The Jolly Potters* (1964), *The Knotty* (1966), and *Plain Jos* (1980). At one time Peter Terson was the theatre's playwright-in-residence. The theatre closed when a new purpose-built theatre-in-the-round was constructed for the company at nearby Newcastle-under-Lyme; this opened in 1986 as the **New Victoria Theatre**. *See also* Gaiety Theatre; Old Vic Theatre.

Victor ou l'Enfant de la forêt A melodrama by Guilbert de PIXÉRÉCOURT, based on a novel by François-Guillaume Ducray-Duminil. First performance: Paris, 1798.

The hero, Victor, is faced with a moral dilemma – in order to protect his adopted father he must kill his real father, a bandit.

Viertel, Berthold (1885–1955) Austrian poet, actor, and director, who established his reputation under Reinhardt after joining the Deutsches Theater in Berlin in 1922. After success with Hebbel's *Judith* he won acclaim in Bronnen's *Vatermord* and founded his own company, Die Truppe. Subsequently he worked in London and the US before returning to Germany to direct the Berliner Ensemble (1949); his last years were spent at the Vienna Burgtheater.

Vieux-Colombier *See* Garrick Theatre.

Vieux-Colombier, Théâtre du A theatre erected near the Abbey of St Germain, Paris, in the early 19th century and used as a venue for touring companies. In 1913 Jacques Copeau and Louis Jouvet established its reputation with a series of experimental productions of serious contemporary dramas, altering the interior to place the audience on three sides of the stage. Notable productions included the plays of Molière, Shakespeare (especially *Twelfth Night*), and other 17th-century writers as well as works by Gide, Musset, and Romains. After four years as a cinema (1926–30) the theatre became the home of the Compagnie des Quinze, who staged the plays of Obey there; subsequently it housed productions of Eliot, García Lorca, Sartre, and Vilar before finally closing in 1972.

View from the Bridge, A A drama (originally a one-act play but later rewritten in three acts) by Arthur MILLER. First performance: New York, 1955. The plot revolves around Eddie Carbone, a longshoreman who secretly desires his wife's niece; these feelings erupt when the niece announces her engagement and leads to tragedy.

Vigarani, Gaspare (1586–1663) Italian architect and stage designer, who built and equipped the Salle des Machines in Paris in 1660. Previously he had worked in Modena before being given charge of the entertainments at the marriage of Louis XIV. Jealous of Torelli, he destroyed many of the devices invented by his rival for the Petit-Bourbon after Torelli's death.

His son, **Carlo Vigarani** (d. 1693), was also a stage designer, who contributed to the building of the Salle des Machines. He also developed machinery for Louis XIV's entertainment *Les Plaisirs de l'île enchantée* in 1664 and worked on operatic productions.

Vigny, Alfred de (1797–1863) French poet, novelist, and playwright, a major figure of the Romantic movement. His first dramatic works, adaptations of Shakespeare, were followed by the historical drama *La Maréchale* (1831), *Quitte pour la peur* (1833), and the immensely successful *Chatterton* (1835); this, his final contribution to the theatre, is generally considered to be his masterpiece.

Vilar, Jean (1912–71) French actor, director, and manager, who was the founder of the Théâtre National Populaire. Having trained as manager to Charles Dullin, he established his reputation as a director in Paris and elsewhere during World War II (founding the Compagnie des Sept in 1943) and subsequently won acclaim for his long association with the AVIGNON FESTIVAL, which he founded in 1947. In his characteristically large-scale productions he favoured the use of sparse settings and strong movement, paying great attention to costume and lighting; he also helped to promote the theatre in remote areas of France as well as presenting productions elsewhere in Europe. He was appointed director of the Théâtre National Populaire in Paris in 1951 and remained in the post for 12 years. As an actor he appeared in his own version of Eliot's *Murder in the Cathedral* in 1945; other successes included plays by Aristophanes, Brecht, Büchner, and Molière. In his later years he also directed operas.

Vildrac, Charles (Charles Messager; 1882–1971) French poet and playwright, whose plays include *Le Paquebot Tenacity* (The SS Tenacity; 1920), *Michel Auclair* (1922), *Madame Béliard* (1925), and *La Brouille* (1930). The first and last of these, both of which deal with rivalry and conflict between friends of very different characters, are regarded as Vildrac's finest dramatic works.

Ville, Théâtre de la *See* Théâtre des Nations.

Villiers, Claude Deschamps de (1600–81) French actor and playwright, who became highly successful in farce under the stagename **Philippin**. He appeared with Lenoir and Montdory at the Théâtre du Marais and subsequently at the Hôtel de Bourgogne with his wife; his plays had some influence on Molière, who satirized him in *L'Impromptu de Versailles*.

Villiers, George *See* Buckingham, George Villiers, Second Duke of.

Villiers, Jean de (1648–1701) French actor, who appeared as a child with the Raisin family before joining Molière at the Palais-Royal in 1672. Subsequently he moved to the Hôtel de Bourgogne and ultimately to the Comédie-Française, where he continued to excel in comedy. His wife was the actress Cathérine Raisin.

Vilna Troupe Russian theatre company, founded in 1916 by **David Hermann** (1876–1930) as the Union of Yiddish Dramatic Artists to perform contemporary Yiddish dramas. After early success with *Landsleute* by Sholom Asch the company transferred to Warsaw in 1917; from this new base it toured internationally with its best-known work, Ansky's *The Dybbuk*. In 1924 the company moved to Vienna but then split into two groups – one moving to the US and the other to Romania before returning to Warsaw in 1927.

Vincennes, Cartoucherie de *See* Soleil, Théâtre du.

Violetta, Mlle *See* Garrick, David.

Virginia Company of Comedians *See* Kean, Thomas.

Virginia Museum Theatre *See* Theatre Virginia.

Virginia Theatre A 1214-seat theatre on West 52nd Street, between Broadway and 8th Avenue in New York. Built for the THEATRE GUILD, it opened in 1925 as the **Guild Theatre** with Shaw's *Caesar and Cleopatra*. In 1950 it became a venue for experimental theatre presented by the American National Theatre and Academy, being renamed first the ANTA Playhouse and then, in 1954, the **ANTA Theatre**. Three years later it began housing commercial productions, including MacLeish's *J. B.* (1958), Robert Bolt's *A Man for All Seasons* (1961), Peter Shaffer's *The Royal Hunt of the Sun* (1965), and the revue *Bubbling Brown Sugar* (1975). In 1981 it was acquired by Jujamcyn Theatres and renamed the Virginia. Productions since then have included a 1983 revival of *On Your Toes*, the muscials *City of Angels* (1989) and *Jelly's Last Jam* (1992), and the long-running revue *Smoky Joe's Café* (1995).

Virués, Cristóbal de (c. 1550–c. 1614) Spanish playwright. He was the author of the five neoclassical tragedies *Elisa Dido*, *Atila furioso*, *Le gran Semíramis*, *La cruel Casandra*, and *La infeliz Marcela*.

Visconti, Luchino (1906–76) Italian director and stage designer, who won equal acclaim in the theatre and the cinema. He began his career in Paris and established his reputation in the theatre when he presented various European classics at the Teatro Eliseo in Rome after World War II. Subsequent productions (many of which were presented by the Paolo Stoppa-Rina Morelli company) included plays by such writers as Anouilh, Chekhov, Jean Cocteau, Arthur Miller, and Tennessee Williams, on several of which he worked alongside Franco Zeffirelli. Among his later works were notable versions of *A Streetcar Named Desire* and Pinter's *Old Times*, as well as several Verdi operas.

Visé, Jean Donneau de (1638–1710) French playwright and theatre critic, who co-founded the periodical *Le Mercure galant* in 1672. His comments on Molière's *L'École des femmes* (1662) precipitated a heated pamphlet war; de Visé's play *Zélinde* (1663) was subsequently written in response to Molière's own *Critique de l'École des femmes*, while he also wrote a malicious play in reply to Molière's *L'Impromptu de Versailles* in the same year. Later, however, de Visé's play *La Mère coquette* (1665) was performed by Molière's company and de Visé published admiring reviews of Molière's *Le Misanthrope*.

Vishnevsky, Vsevolod Vitalevich (1900–51) Russian playwright, noted for his epic dramas on political themes. His most successful play, *Optimisticheskaya Tragediya* (The Optimistic Tragedy; 1932), was first presented by Taïrov at the Kamerny Theatre. During the siege of Leningrad he wrote *Raskinulos' morye shirokoye* (At the Walls of Leningrad; 1942) with Kron and Azarov; he is also remembered for the pro-Stalinist play *Nezabyvaemyy 1919* (The Unforgettable 1919; 1949).

visor *See* mask.

Vitez, Antoine (1930–90) French actor and director, born in Russia, who emerged as a leading Marxist director during the 1960s. His early work in Marseilles and Caen was much influenced by Brecht and was later seen at a variety of venues in and around Paris; successful productions included Sophocles' *Electra* as well as plays by Brecht and Claudel. Following the upheaval of 1968 he was attached to the Conservatoire, later taking control of the Théâtre National de Chaillot in 1981.

Vitrac, Roger (1899–1952) French poet and playwright, who was involved with Dadaism and the Surrealist movement. His first two plays, *Les Mystères de l'amour* (1927) and *Victor ou les Enfants au pouvoir* (1928), were produced at the Théâtre Alfred Jarry. *Victor* enjoyed two successful revivals, the second of which was directed by Jean Anouilh in 1962. Among Vitrac's other plays are *Le Coup de Trafalgar* (1934), *Le Camelot* (1936), *Les Demoiselles du large* (1938), and *Le Sabre de mon père* (1951).

Vitruvius Pollio, Marcus (1st century BC) Roman architect and engineer, author of the treatise *De Architectura*. The fifth book of this treatise discusses the building of theatres and had a profound effect upon theatre architecture of the Renaissance.

Vivian Beaumont Theatre *See* Lincoln Center for the Performing Arts.

Vlaamse Volkstoneel A Belgian theatre company, founded after World War I to present Expressionist drama. During the 1920s it established a strong reputation with productions of plays by Herman Tierlinck (1879–1967) and others.

Vokes, Frederick Mortimer (1846–88) British actor, the eldest of the pantomime act known as The Vokes Children, formed in 1861 and later called The Vokes Family. His sister, **Jessie Catherine Biddulph Vokes** (1851–84), looked after the troupe's business. **Victoria Vokes** (1853–94) made her stage debut at the age of two, while **Rosina Vokes** (1854–94) was carried on as a baby. From 1869 the family monopolized the Drury Lane pantomimes for 10 years.

Volkov, Feodor Grigoryevich (1729–63) Russian actor, who was a leading member of the first professional acting company in Russia, which he joined in 1756. He studied under Dmitrevsky after appearing before the Tsar in 1752 and later became Sumarokov's leading actor. His involvement in the overthrow of Peter III won him the job of arranging the celebrations for Catherine the Great's coronation; however, a chill contracted while he was doing this, hastened his death.

Volksbühne An organization founded in Berlin in 1890 (as the **Freie Volksbühne**) to bring drama to working-class audiences. In 1914 it opened its own theatre in the Bülowplatz; subsequently over 300 subsidiary organizations were founded throughout Germany in the 1920s and 1930s. The movement was suppressed by the Nazis but resurfaced after the war in both East and West Germany. The original Volksbühne in East Berlin was rebuilt and opened again in 1954; it was subsequently reorganized by Benno Besson between 1969 and 1979. In West Berlin Erwin Piscator oversaw the building of a new Volksbühne theatre in 1963. The two companies combined on German reunification in 1990.

Volpone; or, The Fox A satirical comedy by Ben JONSON. First performance: 1606. Set in Venice, the play depicts Volpone's exploitation of the greed of those around him as he pretends to be a rich man with no heirs and a terminal illness. He is ultimately undone by his treacherous servant, Mosca.

Voltaire (François-Marie Arouet; 1694–1778) French philosopher, novelist, playwright, poet, and historian, who was one of the most influential writers of the 18th century. Born in Paris and educated by the Jesuits, he soon established his reputation as a wit. He wrote his first play, the tragedy *Oedipe*, during a spell of imprisonment in the Bastille (1717–18); its success brought him fame and fortune. From 1726 to 1729 he lived in exile in England, where he was impressed by English literature in general and the works of Shakespeare in particular: on his return to France he produced a number of plays on Shakespearean lines, notably *Zaïre*.

The scandal that followed the publication of Voltaire's *Lettres philosophiques* (1734), in which French institutions were unfavourably compared with the intellectual, philosophical, and political life of England, caused their author to take refuge at Cirey in Champagne. There he lived with Madame du Châtelet and continued to write successful tragedies, notably *Alzire*, *Mahomet*, and *Mérope*, and historical and scientific works. His contributions to the genres of sentimental comedy and the *drame bourgeois*, such as *L'Enfant prodigue* and *Nanine*, were less popular. After the death of Madame du Châtelet in 1749 Voltaire moved to Berlin and ultimately settled in Switzerland, where he wrote the comedy *L'Écossaise* and the spectacular tragedy *Tancrède*. He returned to Paris in 1778 for the first performance of *Irène* and died two months later.

Principal dramatic works:

> *Oedipe*: 1718.
> *Brutus*: 1730.
> *Eriphyle*: 1732.
> *Zaïre*: 1732.
> *Le Mort de César*: 1735.
> *Alzire*: 1736.
> *L'Enfant prodigue*: 1736.
> *Mahomet ou le Fanatisme*: 1741.
> *Mérope*: 1743.
> *Nanine*: 1749.
> *L'Orphelin de la Chine*: 1755.
> *Tancrède*: 1760.
> *L'Écossaise*: 1760.
> *Irène*: 1778.

Vondel, Joost van den (1587–1679) Dutch playwright and poet, whose best plays were written after he was 60 years old. His early work, notably *Het Pascha* (The Passover; 1612), shows the influence of such Roman authors as Seneca and Virgil and his own intense religious faith; later, he wrote plays based on Old Testament stories and modelled on classical Greek lines. The most important examples of these later works include *Jeptha* (1659) and the trilogy *Lucifer* (1654), *Adam in ballingschap* (1664), and *Noah* (1667). Through adaptations by Gryphius he also influenced German baroque drama.

Vortex, The A play by Noël COWARD. First performance: London, 1924. In the original production, which established the author's reputation, Coward himself played the drug-addicted son who compels his adulterous mother to confront reality.

Vos, Jan (c. 1620–67) Dutch playwright, author of several popular neoclassical tragedies. He was particularly important for his innovatory use of scenery and stage machinery.

Voysey Inheritance, The A play by Harley GRANVILLE-BARKER. First performance: Royal Court Theatre, 1905. The play depicts the dilemma faced by Edward Voysey on inheriting his father's business, which he finds to be deep in debt owing to illegal speculation with clients' funds.

VTO *See* All-Russian Theatrical Society.

W

Wade, Allan (1881–1954) British actor, manager, and director, who was a founder of the Phoenix Society and its principal director. In 1906 he became assistant to Harley Granville-Barker at the Royal Court; three years later he arranged the first English tour of the Abbey Theatre players. His dramatic writings include translations of Giradoux's *Intermezzo* and Cocteau's *The Infernal Machine*.

Wagner, (Wilhelm) Richard (1813–83) German composer, whose attempts to reform the conventional opera house had a major influence upon theatre design. His work on the Festpielhaus at Bayreuth, opened in 1876, renewed interest in sightlines and prompted the replacement of traditional box and gallery arrangements.

Wagner, Robin (1933–) US stage designer who made his debut in 1953 with the Golden Gate Theatre in his native San Francisco. He subsequently worked off-Broadway and at the Arena Stage, making his Broadway debut with a production of *The Great White Hope* in 1968. Thereafter he became one of the US theatre's busiest and most respected designers. Major shows include *Hair* (1968), *A Chorus Line* (1975), *42nd Street* (1980), *Dreamgirls* (1983), *City of Angels* (1989), and *Angels in America* (1993).

wagon stage A method of staging in which one or more boat trucks are used to enable rapid changes of scene; it is referred to as a **slip stage** in the US.

Waiting for Godot (*En attendant Godot*) A two-act play by Samuel BECKETT, written in French, 1949. First performance: Théâtre de Babylone, Paris, 1953. Despite the bewilderment it initially caused critics and audiences, the play rapidly gained the status of a modern classic. Two tramps, Vladimir and Estragon, wait in vain for the arrival of the mysterious Godot, who they believe will give purpose to their lives. In their efforts to divert themselves from the prospect of total meaninglessness they devise various physical and verbal games and exploit the interruptions of a passing master and his slave. The enigmatic symbolism of the play has been much debated. In 1999 an international poll of theatre professionals voted it the most significant play of the century.

Waiting for Lefty A one-act play by Clifford ODETS. First performance: Group Theatre, New York, 1935. The play shows the poverty of a group of taxi drivers as they wait in a union hall for Lefty, their union leader. At the end it is revealed that he has been killed by management thugs; an impassioned appeal is made to the audience – treated as members also waiting in the hall – for a strike. The play is a plea for the rejection of capitalist values.

waits The nightwatchmen of medieval England, who gradually became a part of the national theatrical tradition. Originally sounding out the hours by playing upon a musical instrument, waits later joined into groups to provide the music for plays in the Elizabethan theatre or became attached to a household or town as resident musicians (unlike minstrels who travelled from one venue to another). The last waits disappeared in the early 19th century with the foundation of the police force, by which time their activities were largely confined to performing festive music in the streets at Christmas.

Wakefield Master The unidentified author or reviser of the Towneley cycle of mystery plays, of which five complete dramas survive. Written in the early 15th century, the plays are considered the finest examples of their kind in terms of both wit and style.

Wakhevitch, Georges (1907–84) French designer for the stage and cinema, born in Odessa, Georgia. He began his career in the theatre under Lugné-Poë at the Théâtre de l'Oeuvre after working in the French cinema. His much-acclaimed sets included those for *Macbeth* in Marseilles and for plays by Anouilh, Claudel, and others at such venues as the Théâtre de l'Atelier, Paris, and the Comédie-Française. As an art director of the cinema he worked in Hollywood and throughout Europe.

Waldis, Burkard (c. 1490–c. 1556) German playwright, who wrote dramas attacking the Roman Catholic Church during the Reformation. Formerly a Franciscan monk, he became widely known for his reworking of the parable of the prodigal son in his anti-Catholic play *Vom verlorenen Sohn* (1527).

Waldorf Theatre A theatre on West 50th Street, between 6th and 7th Avenues, New York, which opened in 1926. The theatre housed live drama – notably plays by Gorky, Chekhov, and J B Priestley – until 1933, when it was turned into a cinema and subsequently demolished. *See also* Strand Theatre.

Walker, George F (1947–) Canadian playwright and director, whose first play was performed in 1971 at Toronto's Factory Lab, where he subsequently became playwright-in-residence (1971–76) and artistic director (1978–79). His plays treat themes of evil and oppression with dark humour and are often modelled on Hollywood B-movies. Among the best known are his *Power Plays* trilogy (1984) and *Love and Anger* (1990). He has also adapted Turgenev's *Father and Sons* as *Nothing Sacred* (1988).

Walking Gentleman *See* stock company.

Walking Lady *See* stock company.

Walkley, Alfred Bingham (1855–1926) British theatre critic, satirized by Shaw as Mr Trotter in *Fanny's First Play* (1911). He was drama critic of *The Times* from 1900 to 1926; his writings were published in a number of volumes between 1892 and 1925.

walk-on A role in which an actor appears on stage but has no lines to deliver.

Wall, Max (1908–90) British variety comedian noted especially for his eccentric physical routines. He began performing as a boy and made his West End debut in the *London Review* of 1925. During the 1920s and 1930s, he toured internationally, becoming well known for his mournful appearance and sardonic quips. His first straight role was the title character in Jarry's *Ubu roi* (1956); others included appearances in Osborne's *The Entertainer* (1974) and Beckett's *Waiting for Godot* (1981).

Wallace, Edgar (1875–1932) British novelist, journalist, and playwright, who wrote several successful detective dramas, most being adapted from his own fiction. Among his most popular plays were *The Ringer* (1936), *On the Spot* (1930), and *The Case of the Frightened Lady* (1931).

Wallace, Nellie (Eleanor Jane Wallace; 1870–1948) British music hall performer, who first appeared as a child clog dancer in 1882 and later as part of an act called the Three Sisters Wallace. She became highly popular singing such songs as 'My Mother Said Always Look Under the Bed' and 'Three Cheers for the Red, White, and Blue' and was one of the few successful female pantomime dames. At the London Palladium she starred in several revues.

Wallack, Henry John (1790–1870) US actor, born in London, who emigrated to the US in 1818 and appeared in leading roles on both sides of the Atlantic. He took over the Chatham Theatre in 1826 and ran the Manchester Theatre Royal for a time; his most popular roles included Sir Peter Teazle in Sheridan's *The School for Scandal* (1847) and Falstaff (1858).

His younger brother, **James William Wallack** (1791–1864), was an actor and manager; he divided his time between England and the US for 20 years, winning praise in both romantic and tragic roles. WALLACK'S LYCEUM, New York, which he opened in 1852, became a leading US venue. Subsequently (1861) he also opened the Star Theatre on Broadway.

Henry John Wallack's son, also **James William Wallack** (1818–73), trained under his father before joining his uncle's company at New York's National Theatre, where he excelled in such leading roles as Macbeth and Richard III. Subsequent successes included the parts of Fagin in an adaptation of Dickens's *Oliver Twist* (1867) and Mathias in Lewis's *The Bells* (1872).

The elder James Wallack's son, **Lester Wallack** (1820–88), began his career in Britain but later moved to the US, where he triumphed in both romantic and comic roles. Acclaimed in the plays of Shakespeare and Sheridan in particular, he managed the Star Theatre from 1861 to 1881 and then transferred to a new Wallack's Theatre, where his productions included plays by T W Robertson and Shakespeare.

Wallack's Lyceum A theatre on Broadway, New York, which opened in 1850 as Brougham's Lyceum, housing burlesque and farce. Subsequently the elder James Wallack became manager (1852) and renamed it Wallack's Lyceum. It prospered, with a good stock company producing both classic and modern material, until 1859 when Wallack retired. After reopening in 1861 as the **Broadway Music Hall**, it was renamed the Olympic and then the Broadway Theatre. It was the venue for Florence's pirated adaptation of Robertson's *Caste* in 1867 and demolished two years later.

Wallack's Theatre A theatre on Broadway, New York, which was built by the actors James Wallack (1795–1864) and his son Lester Wallack (1820–88), opening in 1861. It saw appearances by Lillie Langtry but failed to prosper; it was taken over by Palmer in 1888 as **Palmer's Theatre** but soon returned to its original name and closed in 1915, despite giving the first US production of Shaw's *Androcles and the Lion*.

A second **Wallack's Theatre**, on West 42nd Street, between 7th and 8th Avenues, New York, opened as the **Lew Fields Theatre** in 1904. The theatre changed names in 1906, when it became James Hackett's Theatre. In 1911 it became the **Harris Theatre**, in 1920 the **Frazee Theatre**, and in 1924, it finally became Wallack's Theatre. It became a cinema in 1931.

Wallenstein A major historical trilogy by Friedrich von SCHILLER, completed in 1799. First performance: date unknown. Inspired by Schiller's study at Jena of the history of the Netherlands and of the Thirty Years' War, the trilogy interprets the career of the Austrian general Wallenstein as an example of the corrupting influence of power. Usually considered Schiller's dramatic masterpiece, it was translated into English by Coleridge in 1800.

Waller, Emma (1820–99) US actress, born in Britain. She became a leading performer of classic drama in the US after making her debut there in 1857 as Ophelia. Subsequent successes included Lady Macbeth, Scott's *Guy Mannering*, and Sheridan Knowles's *The Hunchback*, as well as the roles of Hamlet and Iago.

Waller, Lewis (William Waller Lewis; 1860–1915) British actor-manager, who began his career in Tree's company and was subsequently idolized in picturesque romantic parts. He entered management at the Haymarket in 1895 and later ran the Comedy Theatre (1902), the Imperial (1903–06), and the Lyric (1906–10). As an actor he was acclaimed as Hotspur and Henry V as well as in the title roles of such plays as Conan Doyle's *Brigadier Gerard* and Booth Tarkington's *Monsieur Beaucaire*.

Walls, Tom (1883–1949) British actor and manager, who began in a pierrot troupe at Brighton. Subsequently he made his name in musical comedy before going into management. In 1922, with Leslie Henson, he produced the farce *Tons of Money* with great success; there followed the great series of 'Aldwych farces' by Ben Travers, in which he played such roles as Clive Popkiss in *Rookery Nook* (1926) and Freddy Malone in *Plunder* (1929). In the 1930s he starred in films and indulged his passion for horseracing, winning the Derby in 1932.

Walnut Street Theatre A theatre in Philadelphia, built in 1809. It is the oldest in the US and one of the oldest in the English-speaking world not to have had major structural changes. Initially the home of a circus, it has been used as a theatre since 1811; it was the first theatre to offer a version of air-conditioning (from 1855) and was owned by Edwin Booth for a brief period after 1865. The theatre was designated a National Landmark in 1964. From 1941 to 1969 it was owned by the Shubert Organization and was frequently used for pre-Broadway tryouts. It was remodelled in 1970 to seat 1052 people and served as the base for the Philadelphia Drama Guild from 1971 to 1980. Reorganized in 1983 as the Walnut Street Theatre Corporation, it now offers a well-attended five-play subscription series.

Walser, Karl (1877–1943) Swiss stage designer, who became famous for his work in Berlin before World War I. His successes there under Reinhardt included *A Midsummer Night's Dream* (1905), with its revolving stage, and Wedekind's *Frühlings Erwachen* (1906) at the Kammerspiele.

Walter, Eugene (1874–1941) US playwright, whose early plays anticipated the social subjects of modern US drama. His 16 plays ranged from the three melodramas

Paid in Full (1908), *The Easiest Way* (1909), and *Fine Feathers* (1913), to a dramatization of John Fox's *The Trail of the Lonesome Pine* (1912).

Walter Kerr Theatre A 936-seat theatre on 48th Street, New York, which opened as The Ritz in 1921 with John Drinkwater's *Mary Stuart*. Plays by such authors as Sutton Vane and Ashley Dukes followed and in 1937 the theatre was taken over by the Federal Theatre Project. It was then used for broadcasting. It reopened briefly as a theatre in the 1970s, but had more success after it was again remodelled and adopted its current name in 1990. Major productions since then include *Angels in America* (1993), *Love! Valour! Compassion!* (1994), and *The Beauty Queen of Leenane* (1997).

Walton, Tony (1934–) US stage designer, born in Britain. His major shows include *Pippin* (1972), *Chicago* (1975), *Grand Hotel* (1989), and *Will Rogers Follies* (1991). Since 1997 he has also directed, especially off-Broadway.

Waltz of the Toreadors, The (*La Valse des toréadors*) A *pièce grinçante* by Jean ANOUILH. First performance: Paris, 1952. The play depicts a marriage in which love has died and the husband's unconsummated passion for a young girl, with whom he once danced the Waltz of the Toreadors.

Wanamaker, Sam (1919–93) US actor, director, and producer, who became well known for his work in Britain. His successes included Odets's *Winter Journey* (1952) and *The Big Knife* (1954), N Richard Nash's *The Rainmaker* (1956), and the British premieres of Inge's *Bus Stop* and Tennessee Williams's *The Rose Tattoo* (both staged at Liverpool's New Shakespeare Theatre where he was manager from 1957 to 1959). He also excelled in performances with the Royal Shakespeare Company but is most remembered for leading the campaign (from 1970) to rebuild the Elizabethan GLOBE THEATRE near its original site on Bankside in London. Work upon the new Globe began in earnest in 1988 and was completed shortly after his death.

His daughter is the British actress **Zoë Wanamaker** (1950–). She made her professional debut in *A Midsummer Night's Dream* in 1970 and then spent several years in provincial repertory before joining the RSC in 1976. Her work with the company has included Viola in *Twelfth Night* (1983), the title character in *Mother Courage and Her Children* (1984), and Desdemona in *Othello* (1989). More recent work includes *The Crucible* (1990) for the Royal National Theatre, Amanda in *The Glass Menagerie* (1995), A R Gurney's *Sylvia* (1996), in which she played a dog, and an award-winning performance in Sophocles' *Electra* (1997). She is also well known on British television.

Warburton, John (1682–1759) British antiquarian, whose manuscript collection of some 60 unpublished Elizabethan and Jacobean plays was unique. All but three were mistakenly destroyed by his servant, who used them to wrap pies; according to Warburton himself the greatest losses were works by Massinger, Ford, and Dekker.

Warchus, Matthew (1967–) British director, who made his name as a freelance while still in his twenties. His earlier productions included *Henry V* (1994) for the RSC and a highly praised *Volpone* (1995) at the National, one of several Ben Jonson plays that he has directed. He is now particularly associated with the work of Yasmina Reza, having enjoyed success in both London and New York with her *Art* (1996) and *An Unexpected Man* (1998). Other work on Broadway has included Sam Shepard's *True West* (2000) and a revival of Sondheim's *Follies* (2001).

Ward, Fannie (Fannie Buchanan; 1872–1952) US actress, who became a leading performer of light comedy on the London stage, following her first appearance there in 1894. Subsequently she divided her time between London and New York, also appearing in variety during the late 1920s.

Ward, Dame Geneviève Teresa (1838–1922) British actress, born in the US, who began her career as a singer but later won acclaim in such roles as Lady Macbeth and Portia. The first actress to be created DBE, she also appeared in plays by Sophocles, Sheridan Knowles, and Otway in Paris, New York, and London, where she managed the Lyceum Theatre for a time and scored a great success with *Forget-Me-Not* by Herman Merivale and F C Grove. She also acted opposite Henry Irving and with Frank Benson's company with great success.

Warde, Frederick Barkham (1851–1935) US actor, born in Britain, who established his reputation after joining Booth's Theatre in New York in 1870. Acclaimed in Shakespeare and other well-established plays, he remained in the city for three years and then toured widely, never attempting modern works.

wardrobe The items of costume required for a particular production, or the larger collection of stage clothes permanently housed in a theatre. Many theatres have a full-time wardrobe master or mistress who supervises all matters relating to costume.

Warehouse *See* Donmar Warehouse Theatre.

Warfield, David (1866–1951) US actor, who established a reputation in musical comedy and burlesque before winning acclaim as an actor under Belasco in Klein's *The Auctioneer* (1901). Subsequently he won even greater praise in Klein's *The Music Master* (1904), in which he appeared widely for three years. He also appeared in plays by Belasco and as Shakespeare's Shylock before retiring in 1924.

Warner, Charles (Charles John Lickfold; 1846–1909) British actor, whose father was in the Sadler's Wells company. After his London debut as Romeo in 1864, he became a supporting actor at Drury Lane and scored his first success in H J Byron's *Daisy Farm*. Later he was acclaimed in the same author's *Our Boys* (1875). He subsequently appeared at the Adelphi Theatre in melodrama. He committed suicide while on a tour of the US.

Warner, Deborah (1959–) British director. She founded her own Kick Theatre Company in 1980 and established her reputation with productions of *Woyzeck* (1981, 1983), *King Lear* (1985), and *Coriolanus* (1986). As a resident director with the RSC (1987–89) she won particular acclaim with her *Titus Andronicus* (1987). She has formed a strong association with the actress Fiona SHAW, who starred in her acclaimed *Electra* (1988), *The Good Person of Setzuan* (1989), *Hedda Gabler* (1991), and an adaptation of Eliot's *The Waste Land* (1997). More controversial was Shaw's casting in the title role of *Richard II* (1995); a production of Beckett's *Footfalls* (1994) also caused uproar by departing from the original text.

Warren, William (1767–1832) US actor, born in Britain, who emigrated to the US in 1796 to join Thomas Wignell in Philadelphia. Eventually he took over the Chestnut Street Theatre, presiding over the debut of Edwin Forrest in 1820 and attracting praise himself in such roles as Sir Toby Belch in *Twelfth Night* and Sir Peter Teazle in

Sheridan's *The School for Scandal*. His three wives included the actress Mrs Merry and Joseph Jefferson's sister-in-law, by whom he had six children.

Of these, the most famous in the theatre was **William Warren** (1812–88), who became a leading performer at the Boston Museum, where he first appeared in 1847. He was especially admired in comic roles in Shakespeare and Sheridan, but also in contemporary plays by such authors as T W Robertson.

Washington Square Players A US theatre group founded in New York in 1914. The group produced its first full-length plays in 1916, the most influential being Chekhov's *The Seagull*, Ibsen's *Ghosts*, and Shaw's *Mrs Warren's Profession*. The group broke up in 1918 but not before it had inspired the foundation of the Theatre Guild; associates of the group included Lee Simonson and Katharine Cornell.

Washington Square Theatre A theatre on West 4th Street in Greenwich Village, New York, which was used by the Lincoln Center Repertory Company before they moved to the Vivian Beaumont Theatre. It opened in 1964 with Miller's *After the Fall*. When the Lincoln Center company moved to their permanent home in 1965, the musical *Man of La Mancha* was housed at the Washington Square. In 1968 the production closed and the theatre was demolished.

Wasserstein, Wendy (1950–) US playwright, known for her serio-comic studies of modern American women and their situation. Her first play, *Uncommon Women and Others* (1977) was based on her college experiences. Other works include *Isn't it Romantic?* (1991), *The Heidi Chronicles* (1989), for which she received the Pulitzer Prize, *The Sisters Rosensweig* (1992), and *An American Daughter* (1997).

Waste A tragedy by Harley GRANVILLE-BARKER. First performance: London, 1907. The play deals with the topics of illicit love and suicide; the Lord Chamberlain refused to license it for public production because the plot involves an abortion.

Watch on the Rhine, The A play by Lillian HELLMAN. First performance: New York, 1941. The play depicts the deadly conflict between a German underground worker and a Nazi sympathizer, who meet in America; as such it foreshadowed US involvement in World War II.

Waterhouse, Keith (1929–) British playwright, novelist, and journalist. His first work for the theatre was an adaptation, with Willis HALL, of his novel *Billy Liar* (1960). Further collaborations with Hall followed, including *All Things Bright and Beautiful* (1963), *Who's Who* (1972), and adaptations of de Filippo's *Saturday, Sunday, Monday* (1973) and *Filumena* (1977). His plays without Hall include the award-winning *Jeffrey Bernard is Unwell* (1989), which starred Peter O'Toole as the famously inebriated columnist, *Bookends* (1990), and *Our Song* (1992).

water row *See* groundrow.

Waters, Ethel (1900–77) Black US actress, who first appeared in cabaret and vaudeville. She became a leading star of revue, with successes including Berlin's *As Thousands Cheer* (1933). Her straight roles included parts in Dubose Heyward's *Mamba's Daughters* (1939) and Carson McCullers's *The Member of the Wedding* (1950).

Watt, Joachim von (1484–1551) Austrian playwright, author of the early Viennese farce *Gallus pugnans* (1514). The play depicts a trial at which cocks and hens argue over the difference between the sexes and over cockfighting.

Way of the World, The A comedy by William CONGREVE. First performance: 1700. A stylish comedy of sexual liaisons, the play revolves around the efforts of the gallant Mirabell and the witty Millamant to secure Lady Wishfort's consent to their union. The play's failure led to Congreve's retirement from the theatre, but it is now recognized as his most sophisticated, serious, and brilliantly constructed work.

Weaver, John (1673–1760) British dancing master, who was actively associated with London theatres from 1702, when he produced a balletic mime at Drury Lane. He went on to produce a series of ITALIAN NIGHT SCENES, which contributed to the development of pantomime.

Webb, John (1611–72) English architect and scene painter, who became a pupil of Inigo Jones in 1628. He painted scenery for plays staged by Davenant, beginning with *The Siege of Rhodes* (1656), his designs for which were based on contemporary engravings.

Weber and Fields A popular US comedy act, one of the best-loved turns in US vaudeville and burlesque. **Joseph Weber** (1867–1942) and **Lew Fields** (1867–1941) had such success with their slapstick act that eventually they formed their own company (1885), presenting their own burlesques at the former Broadway Music-Hall. Later in their careers Weber took up direction while Fields appeared in musical comedy; he was the father of the playwright Joseph Fields.

Webster, Benjamin Nottingham (1797–1882) British actor, manager, and playwright. He began by playing Harlequin and other small parts in the provinces. After appearing at Drury Lane and the Olympic Theatre, he established himself as a leading comedian at Covent Garden, the Haymarket, and the Adelphi, where he created many roles in contemporary comedies. He became lessee of the Haymarket in 1837, of the Adelphi in 1844, and took over the Princess's Theatre in 1869. He was the author of numerous comedies and farces and as an actor was particularly acclaimed as Triplet in *Masks and Faces* by Tom Taylor and Charles Reade.

His great grand-daughter was the actress and director **Margaret Webster** (1905–72), who began with the Cassons' company in 1924 and later joined Gielgud's Old Vic company (1929). After appearing with Gielgud again in Ronald Mackenzie's *Musical Chairs* (1932) and Gordon Daviot's *Richard of Bordeaux* (1933), she established herself as a notable director, working chiefly in the US, where Paul Robeson's *Othello* (1943) was one of her major successes. She was a cofounder of the **American Repertory Company** and led her own Shakespearean touring company from 1948 to 1950. In England in the 1950s she directed *The Merchant of Venice* at Stratford-on-Avon, *Measure for Measure* at the Old Vic, and, in 1960, Noël Coward's *Waiting in the Wings* at the Duke of York's Theatre.

Webster, John (c. 1580–1634) English playwright, who collaborated with Thomas Dekker, John Ford, William Rowley, and John Heywood, as well as writing four extant plays known to be entirely his own. His two tragedies, THE WHITE DEVIL and THE DUCHESS OF MALFI, have been revived many times in recent years. Webster's plays are notable for their rich imagery, intricate plotting, and gruesome violence; their sympathetic treatment of complex female characters has also aroused comment.

Wedekind, Frank (1864–1918) German playwright and actor, whose bizarre and grotesque dramas, influenced by Strindberg, aroused both admiration and considerable controversy. His political poems led to his imprisonment in 1899, while his plays, peopled with clowns, harlots, and charlatans, contain violent attacks on bourgeois hypocrisy and warn of the dangers of sexual repression.

His preoccupation with sex and death forms the core of such plays as SPRING AWAKENING, which anticipated Expressionism, and the two 'Lulu Tragedies', EARTH SPIRIT and PANDORA'S BOX. Of his other works the most important include *Der Marquis von Keith*, first seen in an influential production by Jessner, and *Such is Life*. His wife, **Tilly Newes** (Mathilde Newes; 1886–1970), appeared in many of his plays.

Principal works:
  Frühlings Erwachen: 1906 (written 1891); translated as *Spring Awakening*.
  Erdgeist: 1902 (written 1893); translated as *Earth Spirit*.
  Die Büchse der Pandora: 1905 (written 1894); translated as *Pandora's Box*.
  Der Marquis von Keith: 1901.
  König Nicolò, oder So ist das Leben: 1902; translated as *Such is Life*.
  Schloss Wetterstein: 1917; translated as *Castle Wetterstein*.

Wehr Theatre *See* Milwaukee Repertory Theatre.

Weigel, Helene (1900–71) Austrian actress and manager closely associated with the plays of Bertolt BRECHT, who became her husband in 1928. She began her career in intense dramas by Büchner and others in Frankfurt, later appearing under Jessner in Berlin (from 1923). During this period she became well known for playing working-class women. She won particular acclaim in Brecht's *Mann ist Mann* (1928) and his adaptation of Gorky's *The Mother* (1932), but after this she and her husband left Germany to escape the Nazis, not returning until 1948. On their return they founded the celebrated BERLINER ENSEMBLE, with Weigel playing such roles as Mother Courage. After Brecht's death in 1956 she ran the company alone, consolidating her fame as the leading exponent of the ALIENATION EFFECT theory of acting.

Weill, Kurt (1900–50) German composer, who became famous for his collaborations with Brecht on such plays as *The Threepenny Opera* (1928) and *The Rise and Fall of the City of Mahagonny* (1927). Subsequently he worked in the US, his musicals including *Lady in the Dark* (1941) and *One Touch of Venus* (1943). His wife was Lotte LENYA.

Weir, The A play by Conor MCPHERSON. First performance: Duke of York's, London, 1997. The play, which is set in a bar room in rural Ireland, consists of the ghost stories told by three regulars and a young woman from Dublin. Commissioned and produced by the Royal Court Theatre, it became the most successful play in the company's history, with long runs in both London and New York.

Weise, Christian (1642–1702) German playwright, author of a number of minor tragedies and more influential comedies. His later comedies were important for their depiction of bourgeois society for the first time in German drama and for their interest in characterization.

Weiss, Peter Ulrich (1916–82) German-born playwright and novelist, whose works were translated and performed worldwide in the 1960s and 1970s. Most of his plays are documentary dramas (*see* living newspaper) with a strong political message. The MARAT/SADE, his first play, was an instant international success; his reputation established, he went on to write *The Investigation*, based on the 1964 Frankfurt War Crimes Trial, which ran simultaneously in 14 German theatres. In 1966 a translated version was produced by Peter Brook in London and New York.

Recurrent themes are war and suffering, as in *Song of the Lusitanian Bogey*, which discussed the anticolonial uprising in Angola, *Vietnam Discourse*, and *How Mr Mockingpott was Relieved of his Sufferings*, in which the protagonists are two clowns. Other notable works include the allegory *The Insurance*, with human and animal characters, and *Trotsky in Exile*, in which Trotsky is presented as both physically and mentally exiled from his people.

Principal works:

Die Verfolgung und Ermodung Jean Paul Marats dargestellt durch die Schauspielgruppe des Hospizes zu Charenton unter Anleitung des Herrn de Sade: 1964.

Die Ermittlung: 1965; translated as *The Investigation*.

Der Turm: 1967; translated as *The Tower*.

Gesang vom lusitanischen Popanz: 1968; translated as *Song of the Lusitanian Bogey*.

Viet Nam Diskurs: 1968; translated as *Vietnam Discourse*.

Herrn Mockingpott das Leiden ausgetrieben wird: 1968; translated as *How Mr Mockingpott was Relieved of his Sufferings*.

Die Versicherung: 1969; translated as *The Insurance*.

Trotzki in Exil: 1970; translated as *Trotsky in Exile*.

Hölderlin: 1971.

Wekworth, Manfred (1929–) German director, who established his reputation with the Berliner Ensemble in the 1950s. He collaborated successfully with Brecht on the latter's adaptations of Gorky's *The Mother* and Shakespeare's *Coriolanus* among other plays but later resigned from the company (1971) when he felt that it was moving away from its founder's ideals. He then worked with the National Theatre in London and elsewhere before returning to the Berliner Ensemble as its manager in 1977.

Welfare State International A British theatre company, founded in 1968 to present experimental drama. The group employs the techniques of COLLECTIVE CREATION and is noted for its highly unconventional productions, which usually include elements of carnival, feasting, fireworks, and social dancing. In the 1990s it became increasingly rooted in Ulverston, Cumbria, where it now holds three public festivals a year. The group also organizes private ceremonies for rites of passage such as betrothals, baby namings, and funerals.

Welles, Orson (1915–85) US director, actor, and writer. After making his debut in Dublin in Feuchtwanger's *Jew Süss* (1933), he toured in such roles as Mercutio in *Romeo and Juliet*, Marchbanks in Shaw's *Candida*, and Octavius in Besier's *The Barretts of Wimpole St*. Subsequently he directed a controversial all-Black *Macbeth* (1936) and collaborated with **John Houseman** (1902–88) on the Federal Theatre Project, for which he directed an acclaimed *Dr Faustus* (1937), and the MERCURY THEATRE (1937); he also established his reputation in the cinema. Later stage roles included an appearance in his own musical version of Verne's *Around the World in 80 Days* (1946), Othello (1951), Lear (1956), and Ahab in his own adaptation of *Moby Dick* (1955, 1962). He also directed Ionesco's *Rhinoceros* in London (1960).

well-made play A play in which the effect depends upon a cleverly constructed plot rather than upon characterization. Initially used in France in the early 19th century as a compliment to a playwright's skill, the term (in French *pièce bien faite*) was later applied pejoratively to any play with an artificial or formulaic plot. In this sense it was used as a term of ridicule by Zola and G B Shaw. Writers of such works included the prolific Sardou and Scribe in France and Wilkie Collins, Henry Arthur Jones, and Arthur Pinero in Britain. Ultimately the well-made play provoked the development of naturalism.

Werfel, Franz (1890–1945) Austrian novelist, poet, and playwright. After service in World War I he developed passionate antimilitarist views which are reflected in all his work. In the 1920s he emerged as a leading writer of the Expressionist movement with such plays as *Bocksgesang* (The Goat Song; 1921) and the historical tragedy *Juarez und Maximilian* (1924). *Der We der Verheissung* (1936) depicted the persecution of the Jews in the early years of Nazism and in 1938 he fled Austria, eventually settling in the US, where he died. His last play was the the comedy *Jacobowsky und der Oberst* (Jacobowsky and the Colonel; 1940).

Wergeland, Henrik Arnold (1808–45) Norwegian poet and playwright. His early works for the stage were such farces as *Ah!* (1827), *Phantasmer* (1829), and *Harlequin Virtuos* (1830). Subsequently he came under the influence of Shakespeare's plays, as reflected in the tragedy *Sinclars Død* (The Death of Sinclair; 1828) and the comedy *Opium* (1828). An ardent nationalist, he gave full rein to his exuberant imagination in such late plays as *Den indinske Cholera* (Indian Cholera; 1835) and *Barnemordersken* (The Child Murderess; 1835).

Werner, Zacharias (1768–1823) German playwright and priest, who founded the German SCHICKSALSTRAGÖDIE with his one-act play *Der vierundzwanzigste Februar* (1810). Later poetic dramas, including *Das Kreuz an der Ostsee* (1806) and *Martin Luther* (1807), had a strong religious content.

Wertenbaker, Timberlake (c.1955–) British playwright, born in the US and brought up in France. Her early plays include *Case to Answer* (1980) and *New Anatomies* (1981). She began her productive association with the Royal Court Theatre when she became its resident playwright in 1984–85. Plays for the Royal Court have included *The Grace of Mary Travers* (1985) and *Our Country's Good* (1988), an award-winning drama based on Thomas Keneally's novel *The Playmaker* (1988), *Three Birds Alighting on a Field* (1991), and *Credible Witness* (2001). In 1988 the RSC presented *The Love of the Nightingale*, a reworking of the Greek legend of Philomel. She has also translated work by Sophocles, Euripides, Marivaux, and Anouilh.

Wesker, Arnold (1932) British playwright, of Jewish parentage, whose East-End background provides a recurring theme in his plays. His first critical success was CHICKEN SOUP WITH BARLEY (1958). This became the first part of a trilogy, completed by ROOTS and *I'm Talking About Jerusalem*, which charted the history of a family from 1936 to 1959. In subsequent plays he continued to develop the theme of beleaguered idealism and that of the exile, especially the Jew, within a hostile society. In 1961 he took a leading role in setting up Centre 42; he then acquired the ROUND HOUSE in London but steady financial backing never materialized and the Centre was formally wound up in 1970. His later works have not generally found the commercial and critical success of his first five plays.

Principal works:

Chicken Soup with Barley: 1958.
Roots: 1959.
The Kitchen: 1959.
I'm Talking About Jerusalem: 1960.
CHIPS WITH EVERYTHING: 1962.
The Four Seasons: 1965.
Their Very Own and Golden City: 1966.
The Friends: 1970.
The Old Ones: 1972.
The Wedding Feast: 1974.
The Merchant: 1976.
Caritas: 1981.
One More Ride on the Merry Go Round: 1981.
Sullied Hands: 1981.
Mothers: 1982.
Annie Wobbler: 1983.
Whatever Happened to Betty Lemon: 1986.
Beorhtel's Hill: 1989.
Blood Libel: 1991.
Break My Heart: 1997.

Wessel, Johan Herman (1742–85) Danish poet and playwright, born in Norway, who is remembered for the play *Kierlighed uden Strømper* (Love Without Stockings; 1772). This parody of French neoclassicism curtailed the current popularity of such drama in Denmark.

West, Mae (1892–1980) US actress and singer, who enjoyed notoriety both on stage – chiefly in musical comedy and revue – and in the cinema. After making her debut as a child, she cultivated a provocative and flamboyant stage persona. In constant conflict with the censors, she was confined in prison on one occasion (1926), only to emerge with her greatest success, *Diamond Lil*, in 1928. Other stage triumphs included *Catherine was Great* (1944) and a revival of *Diamond Lil* in London in 1948.

West, Timothy (1934–) British actor and director. Having begun in stage management, he made his London debut in 1959 and joined the RSC in 1964. During his lengthy association with the PROSPECT THEATRE COMPANY in the 1960s and 1970s, he appeared as Bolingbroke in *Richard II* (1968), Robert Hand in Joyce's *Exiles* (1970), and Enobarbus in *Antony and Cleopatra* (1977). After Prospect was renamed the Old Vic Company in 1980 he was briefly its artistic director (until 1981). He has also played Sir Thomas Beecham in *Beecham* (1980, 1983, 1984), Stalin in *Master Class* (1983, 1984), James Tyrone in *Long Day's Journey into Night* (1991; Royal National Theatre), Falstaff in the *Henry IV* plays (1997), and Gloucester in *King Lear* (1997; Royal

National Theatre). He also appears regularly on British television. His wife is the actress Prunella Scales.

Westcott, Sebastian (d. 1582) English theatre manager, Master of the Children of St Paul's. Under his direction the company performed regularly, not only at Court, but also in their own cathedral courtyard or school hall.

West End The commercial theatre district in London, situated west of the City of London between Oxford Street and the Thames; most of the theatres are in Shaftesbury Avenue, Aldwych, St Martin's Lane, Charing Cross Road, and the Strand. It first developed in the late 17th century around the Lincoln's Inn Fields Theatre and Drury Lane. The **Society of London Theatre** (SOLT; formerly the Society of West End Theatre) is a forum for the managers of the 45 or so theatres that are situated in central London. The term 'West End' is used to denote the commercial theatre in London in the same general way that 'Broadway' is used in the US.

West London Theatre A London theatre that opened in 1832 as the Royal Pavilion West, just off the Edgware Road. Its name was changed to the **Portman Theatre** in 1835, the Royal West London in 1836, and the **Marylebone Theatre** in 1837. Melodramas, farces, and the occasional classic were staged at low prices; noted performers included Macready and T W Robertson, who made his debut there. After rebuilding in 1868 it opened as the **Royal Alfred Theatre**, but reverted to its former name five years later; it then became the West London Music Hall (1893–95) and eventually the Royal West London Theatre. Charles Warner played there in 1896, but it gradually declined, finally becoming a cinema. It was bombed in 1941 and burnt down in 1962. *See also* Scala Theatre.

Westminster Play A drama presented annually at Westminster School in London since 1560. The only example of a largely unbroken tradition of SCHOOL DRAMA in Britain, the Westminster Play is performed in Latin and is usually chosen from the plays of Plautus, Terence, or other classical authors. Until the 1920s it was presented in the ancient College Hall. There was a break in performances – which were frequently attended by members of the royal family – during the Civil War but the tradition was revived upon the Restoration, with such child actors as Barton Booth appearing in a set cycle of plays comprising the *Adelphi*, *Andria*, *Phormio*, and *Eunuchus* (which was replaced for a time by Plautus' *Trinummus* and then *Rudens* in 1926). After a break in World War II, the Westminster Play was revived on a biennial basis in 1954 in Little Dean's Yard in the open air, the performers appearing in contemporary dress and with few props. In recent years the cycle of plays has been varied to include other Roman classics.

Westminster Theatre A theatre in Palace Street, London, which opened in 1931 after several years' use as a cinema. It opened with James Bridie's *The Anatomist*, produced by Tyrone Guthrie; plays by Ibsen, Shaw, Eliot, and others followed. From 1938 to 1940 J B Priestley directed the Mask Theatre here; productions included his own play *Music at Night* (1939). From 1943 to 1945 the theatre was managed by Robert Donat, whose production of Oscar Wilde's *An Ideal Husband* (1943) ran for 266 performances. Subsequent successes included Lesley Storm's *Black Chiffon* (1949) and *Dial M for Murder* (1952). The Moral Re-Armament Movement controlled the theatre from 1960, its productions mostly written by Peter Howard and Alan Thornhill, with a regular Christmas play for children. In 1966 the Westminster was closed for re-building as part of an arts centre; it staged regular revivals in the 1970s and 1980s but has not been used for theatre since 1991. A campaign has begun to prevent its demolition.

Weston, Thomas (1737–76) British actor. The son of the head chef to George II, he joined some strolling players and eventually appeared at Bartholomew Fair. Foote spotted his talent as a comedian and engaged him at the Haymarket; from 1760 he appeared regularly there and at Drury Lane.

Weston's Music Hall *See* Holborn Empire.

Westray, Mrs Anthony (d. 1836) British actress, who went to the US in 1792 with her second husband, John Simpson, to play at the Park Theatre, New York. Her three daughters by her first husband – Ellen, Juliana, and Elizabeth – all became actresses in due course.

West Side Story A musical by Arthur Laurents, with music by Leonard BERNSTEIN, lyrics by Stephen SONDHEIM, and choreography by Jerome ROBBINS. First perfor-mance: New York, 1957. Set in the slums of New York, it updates the story of *Romeo and Juliet* to the world of feuding inner-city gangs. The show introduced the vigor-ous modern-dance style that has since become a hallmark of US musicals.

West Yorkshire Playhouse A theatre and company in Leeds, Yorkshire. It began life as the Leeds Playhouse in 1970, with premises in a converted sports hall on the Leeds University campus. Work on a purpose-built theatre began in 1986 and was completed by 1990. The Playhouse has two auditoriums – the Quarry, seating 750, and the Courtyard, seating 350. Under the artistic direction of **Jude Kelly** the com-pany has established an international reputation, with several productions trans-ferring to the West End or touring overseas. It is now the largest repertory company outside London apart from the RSC at Stratford-on-Avon. In 1998 Ian McKellen joined the company.

Wharf Theatre *See* Cruger's Wharf Theatre; Provincetown Players.

What Every Woman Knows A play by J M BARRIE. First performance: London, 1908. A social comedy revolving around the resourceful wife of a promising politician, the play shows some sympathy with feminist views; it was highly successful in both Lon-don and New York.

What the Butler Saw A comedy by Joe ORTON. First performance: 1969. This par-ody of farce takes place in the surgery of Dr Prentice, a specialist in mental health. It shocked its first audiences with its unrestrained discussion of sexual perversions, the police, and the private parts of Sir Winston Churchill.

Whelan, Albert (Albert Waxman; 1875–1961) Australian singer, who became a leading performer in British music hall. He first appeared (at the Empire) in 1901 and – immaculately dressed – became the first performer to adopt his own signature tune (*Lustige Brüder*).

When We Are Married A play by J B PRIESTLEY. First performance: London, 1938. Three well-respected Yorkshire couples, on the anniversary of their joint wedding day, discover that they are not legally married. As a result they are faced with new personal choices.

When We Dead Awaken The last play by Henrik IBSEN. First performance: Oslo, 1900. Through the central figure of Rubek, a sculptor, Ibsen makes his final analysis of the relationship between the creative artist and life itself.

White, George (George Weitz; 1890–1968) US dancer, producer, and director, who became famous for his series of revues, *George White's Scandals*, which lasted through 13 editions until 1939. His other shows included *Runnin' Wild* (1923), *Manhattan Mary* (1927), and *Flying High* (1930).

White, Patrick (1912–90) Australian novelist and playwright, born in Britain, who won a Nobel Prize in 1973. White first achieved international acclaim with the publication of his novel *Boss* (1957); of his plays the most significant are *The Ham Funeral* (1961), *The Season at Sarsaparilla* (1961), *A Cheery Soul* (1962), and *Night on Bald Mountain* (1964). Others include the comedy *Return to Abyssinia* (1946), *Big Toys* (1977), *Signal Driver* (1981), and *Netherwood* (1983).

White Devil, The A tragedy in blank verse by John WEBSTER. First performance: London, 1612. The play centres on the Venetian aristocrat Vittoria Corombona, whose courage and intelligence earn her much sympathy in spite of her treachery and infidelity. None of the major characters are noted for their virtue but all are distinguished by their intense and self-destructive passions; the play is remembered for its rich poetry, copious bloodshed, and use of ghosts and dumb shows.

White-eyed Kaffir *See* Chirgwin, George H.

Whitefriars Theatre A theatre near Blackfriars, London, converted from the refectory of a dissolved monastery and leased in 1605 by Michael Drayton and Thomas Woodford. First used by the Children of His Majesty's Revels, it later became the home of an amalgamated company called the Children of the Queen's Revels (1610). At least one important play, Ben Jonson's *Epicoene*, was written for this company. The theatre, later used by Lady Elizabeth's Men, declined after 1614 and seems to have been abandoned by 1629.

Whitehall Theatre A theatre situated at the Trafalgar Square end of Whitehall, London, built in 1930. Decorated internally in black and silver, it made its name as a home of modern comedy under Walter Hackett before switching to revue during World War II. Subsequently the success of R F Delderfield's *Worm's Eye View* (1945) heralded a new phase of farce, for which the Whitehall was to become famous under the management (1950–67) of Brian Rix. Major successes of this period were *Reluctant Heroes* (1950) and *Uproar in the House* (1967). The impresario Paul Raymond then staged his long-running revue *Pyjama Tops* (1969–74), London's first all-nude production, buying the lease in 1971. Later successes included John Wells's spoof on the Thatcher household *Anyone for Denis?* (1981). The theatre changed ownership in 1985 and reopened after restoration in 1986. Subsequent productions have included a stage version of Irvine Welsh's *Trainspotting* (1995) and *Puppetry of the Penis* (2000), featuring "the ancient art of genital origami".

Whitelaw, Billie (1932–) British actress who made her London debut as Victoire in Feydeau's *Hotel Paradiso* in 1956; she went on to play important parts with the National and Royal Shakespeare companies. Her biggest successes have included Maggie in Harold Brighouse's *Hobson's Choice* (1965), Clare in David Mercer's *After Haggerty* (1971), Eleanor in Peter Nichols's *Passion Play* (1981), and Nelly Mann in Christopher Hampton's *Tales from Hollywood* (1983). She is also known for her long association with the works of Samuel Beckett, including *Play* (1963), *Not I* (1973, 1975), *Happy Days* (1979), and a trilogy of plays presented in New York (1984) and London (1986).

Whitemore, Hugh (1936–) British playwright, who first attracted attention with the play *Stevie* (1977), about the poet Stevie Smith. Successes since then have included *Pack of Lies* (1983), about a notorious British spy case of the 1960s, *Breaking the Code* (1986), about the World War II codebreaker and computer pioneer Alan Turing, and *A Letter of Resignation* (1997), about the private and public troubles of Harold Macmillan. He has also written many television and film screenplays.

Whiting, John (1917–63) British playwright, who first achieved success with the comedy A PENNY FOR A SONG (1951). In the same year his award-winning play SAINT'S DAY was staged at the Arts Theatre. His other works include MARCHING SONG (1954), *The Gates of Summer* (1956), and THE DEVILS (1961), which was produced very successfully by the Royal Shakespeare Company. Whiting also translated a play by Anouilh as *The Traveller Without Luggage* in 1959; his last work, presented posthumously, was *Conditions of Agreement* (1965). After his premature death an annual award scheme for promising young playwrights was set up in his memory. Winners have included Edward Bond and Tom Stoppard.

Whitley, James Augustus (c. 1724–81) British provincial actor-manager, born in Ireland. He began at the Smock Alley Theatre and later developed a strong Midlands circuit, appearing regularly at Manchester, Stamford, and Nottingham, where he built the first Theatre Royal.

Whitney Theatre *See* Strand Theatre.

Whittle, Charles (1874–1947) British music hall singer, who made his first London appearance in 1899. He was best known for the song 'Let's All Go Down the Strand'.

Who's Afraid of Virginia Woolf? A play by Edward ALBEE. First performance: New York, 1962. The play, which established Albee's reputation, revolves around the obsessive love-hate relationship of George, a history professor, and his wife. The film version provided rewarding roles for Richard Burton and Elizabeth Taylor.

Widowers' Houses The first play by G B SHAW, written 1885–87. First performance: London, 1892. A young doctor, Harry Trench, falls in love with Blanche Sartorius, whose wealth is derived from the ownership of slums; the play presents his conflict of conscience as inevitable in a capitalist system. Originally a collaboration with the critic William Archer, the play caused a stir with its rejection of conventional romantic drama, its echoes of Ibsen, and its presentation of Socialist arguments.

Wied, Gustav (1858–1914) Danish playwright, who became famous for the four humorous one-act plays collected as *Adel, Gejstlighed, Borger og Bonde* (Nobility, Clergy,

Burgher, and Peasant; 1897). Longer plays included *Danesmus* (Dancing Mice; 1905) and *Ranke Viljer* (2 × 2 = 5; 1906); he committed suicide shortly after the outbreak of World War I.

Wieth, Mogens (1919–62) Danish actor, who became a leading performer of classical roles at the Kongelige Teater in Copenhagen, where he first appeared in 1939. As well as Shakespearean tragic heroes, he played leading roles in plays by Ibsen, Wilde, and many others and made guest appearances in London before his early death.

Wignell, Thomas (1735–1803) US actor, who founded a celebrated company, consisting largely of English performers, at the Chestnut Street Theatre in Philadelphia in the 1790s. Previously he had attracted much praise as leading man with the American Company, which he joined in 1774, and had also presented Royall Tyler's *The Contrast*, the first native US comedy, in 1879. His famous company included amongst its members James Fennell, Mrs Oldmixon, and Mrs Merry, to whom Wignell was briefly married.

Wild Duck, The A play by Henrik IBSEN. First performance: 1884. The play revolves around the photographer Hjalmar Ekdal; when his sanity is threatened by the suggestion that his beloved daughter Hedvig is not in fact his, she responds by shooting herself. The duck of the title is kept captive in the family's attic and appears to symbolize the various self-delusions of the characters.

Wilde, Oscar (Fingal O'Flahertie Wills) (1854–1900) Irish playwright, whose first major success in the theatre came with George Alexander's production of LADY WINDERMERE'S FAN at the St James's Theatre in 1892. Lionized by society for his elegance and wit, he followed this success with two more sentimental drawing-room comedies, A WOMAN OF NO IMPORTANCE (1893) and AN IDEAL HUSBAND (1895), before reverting to the true comedy of manners in his masterpiece, THE IMPORTANCE OF BEING EARNEST, which remains one of the most frequently revived plays in the English language. SALOMÉ, banned in London, was performed by Sarah Bernhardt in Paris in 1896. In 1895 he was imprisoned for homosexual acts; the hardships he suffered over the next two years broke his health and contributed to his death in straitened circumstances in Paris.

Principal dramatic works:
Lady Windermere's Fan: 1892.
A Woman of No Importance: 1893.
An Ideal Husband: 1895.
The Importance of Being Earnest: 1895.
Salomé: 1896.

Wilder, Thornton (1897–1975) US playwright, best known for his evocation of small-town America in OUR TOWN and his use of various non-naturalistic conventions. Of his other plays, *The Long Christmas Dinner* was later made into an opera and THE MATCHMAKER provided the basis for the musical HELLO DOLLY!. Other dramatic works included translations of Obey's *Le Viol de Lucrèce* (as *Lucrece*; 1932), Ibsen's *A Doll's House* (1937), and an adaptation of Euripides' *Alcestis* (as *A Life in the Sun*; 1955).

Principal works:
  The Trumpet Shall Sound: 1927.
  The Long Christmas Dinner: 1931.
  Our Town: 1938.
  THE SKIN OF OUR TEETH: 1942.
  The Matchmaker: 1954.
  Three Plays for Bleeker Street: 1962.

Wildgans, Anton (1881–1932) Austrian poet, playwright, and director of the Burgtheater, Vienna (1921–22 and 1930–31). Wildgans first received acclaim with the production of such tragic plays as *Armut* (1914), *Liebe* (1916), and *Dies Irae* (1919), but is now probably best remembered for his poetry.

Wilhelm Tell The last complete play by Friedrich von SCHILLER. First performance: 1804. Probably the most popular of all Schiller's plays, it explores the ethics of using violence against tyranny.

Wilkinson, Norman (1882–1934) British artist, who achieved particular success with his set and costume designs for Granville-Barker's productions at the Savoy Theatre, especially those for *Twelfth Night* (1912) and *A Midsummer Night's Dream* (1914). Later he worked for Nigel Playfair, C B Cochran, the Phoenix and Stage Societies, and for the Shakespeare Memorial Theatre.

Wilkinson, Tate (1739–1803) British actor-manager. He began his career with Garrick at Drury Lane, where his imitations of other actors were much admired. Foote then took him to Dublin where he was well received, although his subsequent appearances in London were not a success. Consequently, his major contribution to the theatre was his masterly control of York and the northern circuit, which lasted for some 30 years. Wilkinson grew rather eccentric in later life and was satirized by Foote in *The Minor* (1760) and by Charles Mathews.

Wilks, Robert (1665–1732) British actor and manager, born in Ireland. After establishing his reputation in Dublin, he was engaged by Christopher Rich at Drury Lane in 1692 to replace William Mountfort. In 1709 Wilks became one of the famous triumvirate managing Drury Lane, with Colley Cibber and Thomas Doggett. As an actor he excelled in the plays of Cibber and Farquhar.

Willard, E(dward) S(mith) (1853–1915) British actor, who began his career at Weymouth in 1869, coming to London in 1875 in Thomas Morton's *A Roland for an Oliver*. From 1881–86 he was with Wilson Barrett's company, in which he was acclaimed in such melodramatic roles as Captain Skinner in Henry Arthur Jones and Henry Herman's *The Silver King* (1882). At the Haymarket in 1886 he played James Ralston in Charles Young's *Jim the Penman*, the play with which he launched his own management of the Shaftesbury Theatre in 1889.

Williams, Bert (Egbert Austin Williams; 1876–1922) Black US actor, born in the Bahamas, who began his career in a minstrel show. Later he appeared in a double act with the comedian George Walker in New York and, in 1903, they produced an all-Black musical comedy there entitled *In Dahomey*, the first of a series of such shows. He did much to raise the dignity of Black performers, his appearances in revue being the first in which a 'Negro' was unquestionably on the same star level as the

Whites. Williams formed an all-Black actors' society in 1906 and – after Walker's death – appeared in Ziegfeld's *Follies*, performing his own songs.

Williams, Bransby (Bransby William Pharez; 1870–1961) British actor and music hall performer. He spent some years in stock companies before taking to the halls, where he became famous for his renderings of characters from Dickens. In the 1920s he acted in several plays, reviving, for instance, Irving's part in *The Lyons Mail*. His monologues included 'The Green Eye of the Little Yellow God'.

Williams, (George) Emlyn (1905–87) Welsh actor, director, and playwright, who made many successful appearances in his own plays. He established himself as a leading character actor in the 1930s and 1940s and was highly acclaimed as the maniacal Danny in *Night Must Fall*, his first great success as a playwright.

His plays often depict life in his native Wales, most memorably in the semi-autobiographical THE CORN IS GREEN, which remains his best-known work. Of his many subsequent plays, the most popular included *The Wind of Heaven*, in which Christ is reincarnated as a Welsh boy. He also adapted works by Ibsen and Turgenev and was much acclaimed for his readings from Dickens and Dylan Thomas. Other successes as an actor included Angelo in *Measure for Measure* (1937), Rattigan's *The Winslow Boy* (1940), Shylock and Iago (1956), Robert Ardrey's *Shadow of Heroes* (1958), Robert Bolt's *A Man For All Seasons* (1962), and Alan Bennett's *Forty Years On* (1969).

Principal works:
  A Murder Has Been Arranged: 1930.
  Spring 1600: 1934.
  Night Must Fall: 1935.
  He Was Born Gay: 1937.
  The Corn is Green: 1938.
  The Light of Heart: 1940.
  The Morning Star: 1941.
  The Druid's Rest: 1944.
  The Wind of Heaven: 1945.
  Trespass: 1947.
  Accolade: 1950.
  Someone Waiting: 1953.
  Beth: 1958.

Williams, (Ernest George) Harcourt (1880–1957) British actor and director. As a young man he appeared with such leading performers as Ellen Terry, George Alexander, and Henry Irving, with whom he toured the US. He excelled in the plays of Shakespeare and Shaw and developed the theories of Granville-Barker in his Shakespearean productions at the Old Vic Theatre, of which he became a director in 1929.

His wife was the actress **Jean Sterling Mackinlay** (1882–1958), who promoted children's theatre in Britain and became famous for her Christmas shows.

Williams, Kenneth (1926–88) British comic actor, who made his London debut in *Peter Pan* in 1952. Subsequently he appeared in plays, revues, and pantomime, his roles including Maxime in Feydeau's *Hotel Paradiso* (1956) and Julian in Peter Shaffer's *The Public Eye* (1962). His flamboyant style and mastery of comic voices was also exploited in numerous radio shows and films.

Williams, Michael (1935–2001) British actor, who came to London from the Nottingham Playhouse in Keith Waterhouse and Willis Hall's *Celebration* (1961). In 1963 he began a long association with the Royal Shakespeare Company, his numerous parts including Petruchio (1967), Henry V (1971), and the title role in Brecht's *Schweyk in the Second World War* (1976). Opposite his wife, Judi Dench, he played Bob in Hugh Whitemore's *Pack of Lies* (1983) and was George in Ray Cooney's *Two into One* (1984). From the late 1980s he worked mainly in television.

Williams, Peter Vladimirovich (1902–47) Russian stage designer, who became famous for his work at the Moscow Art Theatre. His most admired designs included those for *The Pickwick Club* (1934), based on Dickens, and Alexei Tolstoy's *The Death of Ivan the Terrible* (1946).

Williams, Tennessee (Thomas Lanier Williams; 1911–83) US playwright, born in Columbus, Mississippi, and brought up in St Louis from the age of 12. After graduating in 1938 he won a Theatre Guild prize for four one-act plays (*American Blues*); six years later he established his reputation with THE GLASS MENAGERIE, which was largely based upon his own family background. Thereafter his reputation soared and a number of his plays, which often tackle the extremes of human behaviour, were successfully filmed. His plays typically depict the frustration of aspiring central characters in a society that suffocates ambition. His *Memoirs* (1975) disclosed his homosexuality and his breakdown in 1969.

Principal works:
  Battle of Angels: 1940.
  The Glass Menagerie: 1945; filmed 1950.
  A STREETCAR NAMED DESIRE: 1947; filmed 1952.
  Summer and Smoke: 1948; filmed 1961.
  The Rose Tattoo: 1951; filmed 1956.
  Camino Real: 1953.
  CAT ON A HOT TIN ROOF: 1955; filmed 1958.
  Orpheus Descending: 1957 (new version of *Battle of Angels*).
  Suddenly Last Summer: 1958; filmed 1959.
  Sweet Bird of Youth: 1959; filmed 1963.
  Period of Adjustment: 1959.
  The Night of the Iguana: 1962; filmed 1964.
  The Milk Train Doesn't Stop Here Any More: 1962.
  Slapstick Tragedy: 1966.
  Two Character Play: 1967.
  In the Bar of a Tokyo Hotel: 1969.
  Clothes for a Summer Hotel: 1980.

Williamson, David (1942–) Australian playwright, who established his reputation with the award-winning plays *The Removalists* (1972) and *Don's Party* (1973). He has adapted a number of his plays for the cinema, including *Travelling North* (1979), and has also written expressly for film and television. His more recent works include *Emerald City* (1987), *Siren* (1990), *Money and Friends* (1992), and *Dead White Males* (1995).

Williamson, Nicol (1938–) British actor, who began in repertory at Dundee before making his first London appearance in Henry Chapman's *That's Us* in 1961. He subsequently played in many productions at the Royal Court Theatre, including the part of Bill Maitland in John Osborne's *Inadmissible Evidence* (1964). He was highly praised as Hamlet at the Round House in 1969 and later played Coriolanus (1973) and Macbeth (1974) with the Royal Shakespeare Company. Later work for the stage has included Osborne's *The Entertainer* (1983), Stoppard's *The Real Thing* (1985), *Jack* (1994), a one-man show about John Barrymore, and *King Lear* (2001).

William Street Theatre A theatre in New York, which was opened around 1790 for entertainments staged by amateurs. Productions presented there included Dodsley's *The King and the Miller of Mansfield*, Lillo's *The London Merchant*, Dunlop's farce *The Soldier's Return*, and a pantomime version of *Robinson Crusoe*. It was also used for shadow shows.

Will's Coffee House A meeting place for critics and other playgoers in Covent Garden, London during and after the Restoration. Also known as the Rose Tavern, it was a favourite haunt of many notable wits and literary figures, including John Dryden.

Wilson, August (1945–) US Black playwright, whose works chronicle the Black experience in the US from the early 20th century onwards. His plays are known for their rich roles – *Fences* offering an especially strong part to James Earle Jones – and the opportunity they provide for ensemble acting.

Principal works:
Jitney (one-act version): 1982 (two-act version, 1998).
Ma Rainey's Black Bottom: 1984.
Fences: 1985, Pulitzer Prize.
Joe Turner's Come and Gone: 1986.
The Piano Lesson: 1987, Pulitzer Prize.
Two Trains Running: 1990.
Seven Guitars: 1995.
King Hedley II: 1999.

Wilson, Georges (1921–) French actor, director, and manager, who succeeded Jean Vilar as manager of the Théâtre National Populaire in 1963. Earlier in his career he worked with the Grenier-Hussenot company before joining Vilar's group in 1952 and excelling in leading roles in plays by Jarry and Musset among others. As manager he promoted the plays of Brecht, Brendan Behan, and Edward Bond before the troupe broke up in 1972. Since then he has worked at the Avignon Festival and elsewhere as well as directing for the cinema.

Wilson, Lanford (1937–) US playwright. His works, frequently premiered by the CIRCLE REPERTORY COMPANY, combine a Chekhovian sense of interweaving characters with a 1960s counterculture sensibility. He made his reputation with *The Madness of Lady Bright* and *The Rimers of Eldrich* in 1965. Subsequent works have included *Lemon Sky* (1968), *The Hot -l Baltimore* (1973), *The Fifth of July* (1973), the Pulitzer Prize-winning *Talley's Folly* (1980), *Angels Falls* (1982), *Burn This* (1987), and *Redwood Curtain* (1991).

Wilson, Robert (c. 1550–c. 1600) English actor and playwright, who in 1583 co-founded Queen Elizabeth's Men. His three surviving works are loosely constructed morality plays in which personified virtues and vices play the leading parts, as in his *Three Ladies of London* (1584).

Wilson, Robert (1941–) US playwright, designer, and actor, who has achieved great success with a genre of his own creation. Sometimes called 'operas', because of their heavy use of music, his works combine slow ritualistic action, minimal text, and vivid non-realistic stage pictures, the effect being something like a living sur-realistic painting. Besides his own works, the best known of which are *Deafman Glance* (1970), *The Life and Times of Joseph Stalin* (1973), *Einstein on the Beach* (1975; with Philip Glass), and *The Civil Wars* (1984; with Philip Glass), he has also success-fully applied these techniques to classic theatre and opera.

Wilson, Sandy (Alexander Galbraith Wilson; 1924–) British composer and play-wright, who established his reputation writing songs for revues but whose major suc-cess was THE BOY FRIEND (1953). His later musicals include *The Buccaneer* (1956), *Valmouth* (1958), which is based on Ronald Firbank's novel, *Divorce Me, Darling* (1965), *The Clapham Wonder* (1978), and *Aladdin* (1979).

Wilton, Marie Effie *See* Bancroft, Squire.

Wilton's Music Hall A music hall in Whitechapel, London, which began in 1850 as the music room of a public house. A new music hall was built behind the pub and opened in 1858, remaining active until 1887. An official preservation order was later made, when it was recognized as the earliest surviving music hall building in Lon-don.

Winchester Music Hall The first concert room in a pub (opened in the 1830s in Southwark, London) to be called a music hall. It was known as the **Surrey Music Hall** from 1848 until 1856, when its name was changed to the Winchester. It was destroyed by fire in 1861, but rebuilt and later remodelled as a theatre (1872), before being de-molished in 1878.

wind machine A mechanical device consisting of a large drum, which rubs against a stretch of canvas when rotated, producing a sound effect resembling that of wind. In many modern theatres such machines have been superseded by audio recordings.

Windmill Theatre The only London theatre to remain open during the whole of World War II, its slogan being 'We never closed'. Originally a cinema built in 1910, it took its name from a windmill which stood on the site up to the late 18th century. After an unsuccessful opening as a theatre in 1931 films were reintroduced until the manager, Vivian Van Damm, inaugurated (1932) a programme of non-stop variety called *Revuedeville*. This proved extremely popular and the Windmill became cele-brated for its tableaux of scantily clad girls. Subsequently many comedians, includ-ing Jimmy Edwards, Harry Secombe, and Tony Hancock, began their careers here. The Windmill was closed in 1964 and reconstructed as a cinema; in 1974 it was pur-chased by Paul Raymond, who revived the policy of nude revues. It closed again in 1981 for conversion into a theatre-restaurant.

Windsor Theatre *See* 48th Street Theatre.

wings The offstage areas on either side of the main acting space. The term is also used of the flats used to screen these areas from the audience's view.

Winslow Boy, The A drama by Terence RATTIGAN. First performance: London, 1946. Based on an actual case, the play depicts a father's attempts to clear the reputation of his son – a cadet at a naval college – after he has been accused of petty theft. The play was a big success in both London and New York, and has enjoyed several revivals.

Winstanley, Eliza (1818–82) Australian actress and writer, also known as Mrs O'Flaherty, who was born in England but made her debut in Australia in 1834. She was highly acclaimed in melodrama and also made successful appearances in Britain and the US, acting with Charles Kean's company for several years.

Winter, William (1836–1917) US theatre critic, who exercised enormous influence with his reviews for the *Albion* (1861–65) and then the *New York Times* (1865–1909). He followed the majority opinion in most matters but failed to appreciate the importance of such notable figures as Sarah Bernhardt, Ibsen, and Shaw.

Winter Garden Theatre A 1482-seat theatre on Broadway, between 50th and 51st Streets, New York, which opened in 1911 and was Al Jolson's home base throughout the 1920s. It is used primarily for musicals, with notable productions including *West Side Story* (1957), *Funny Girl* (1964), *Mame* (1966), *Pacific Overtures* (1976), and *42nd Street* (1980). In 1985 *Cats* began its record-setting run, which lasted until 2000.

The **Winter Garden Theatre** in Drury Lane, London, opened as the New Middlesex Theatre of Varieties on the site of the MIDDLESEX MUSIC HALL in 1911. Music hall and touring revues held the stage until 1919, when the theatre was acquired by George Grossmith and Edward Laurillard, refurbished, renamed the Winter Garden, and reopened with Guy Bolton and P G Wodehouse's musical *Kissing Time*. A series of successful musicals under various managements followed, ending with Gracie Fields in the revue *Walk This Way* (1932). Following World War II Joan Temple's *No Room at the Inn* (1946) and Agatha Christie's *Witness for the Prosecution* (1953) had long runs, while such plays as Shaw's *The Devil's Disciple* (1956), starring Tyrone Power, and O'Neill's *The Iceman Cometh* (1958) transferred there from the Arts Theatre. The Winter Garden was demolished in 1960 and in 1973 the NEW LONDON THEATRE opened on the site.

Winter's Tale, The A romance by William SHAKESPEARE, written c. 1610–11. First performance: c. 1611. Based upon Robert Greene's *Pandosto*, the play is Shakespeare's last treatment of sexual jealousy and depicts the consequences of Leontes' mistaken belief that his queen Hermione has had a love affair with his friend, Polixenes, King of Bohemia. The play is remarkable for its disjointed time scheme (one break covering 16 years) and for the final scene, in which the 'statue' of Hermione, long believed dead, comes to life. It also contains the famous stage direction requiring the character Antigonus to exit 'pursued by a bear'. It was revived by Garrick as *Florizel and Perdita* during the Restoration.

Winthrop Ames Theatre *See* Little Theatre.

Withers, Googie (Georgette Lizette Withers; 1917–) British actress, who started her stage career as a child and signed her first film contract at the age of 17. Her roles have included such parts as Georgie in Clifford Odets's *Winter Journey* (1952) and Hester Collyer in Terence Rattigan's *The Deep Blue Sea* (1955) as well as characters in plays by Noël Coward, J B Priestley, Shakespeare, Chekhov, Wilde, and Ionesco. With her husband, the actor John MCCALLUM, she has played often in Australia and New Zealand, returning to England at intervals, sometimes to appear at the Chichester Festival Theatre.

Witkiewicz, Stanisław Ignacy (1885–1939) Polish writer, artist, and philosopher, who wrote over 40 grotesque comedies, which remained virtually unknown and unperformed during his lifetime. It was not until the 1960s that he was rediscovered and came to be regarded as a major forerunner of the Theatre of the Absurd. Among his most important works are the plays *The Water Hen*, *The Crazy Locomotive*, *The Shoemakers*, and the tragedy *The Pragmatists*, written in 1918. Witkiewicz committed suicide when Poland was invaded by the Germans.

Woffington, Peg (Margaret Woffington; c. 1714–60) British actress, born in Dublin of Irish parentage. She first went on the stage with a children's company, making a brief appearance at the Haymarket. Subsequently she appeared at Dublin's Smock Alley Theatre, where she played Ophelia and was a notable Silvia in *The Recruiting Officer*, although it was as Sir Harry Wildair in Farquhar's *The Constant Couple* that she established her reputation as a performer of breeches parts. In 1740 she repeated the role with phenomenal success at Covent Garden. After a quarrel with John Rich she transferred to Drury Lane and lived with Garrick for a time. Famed for her beauty, she was particularly admired as Millamant in *The Way of the World* and Lady Betty Modish in Colley Cibber's *The Careless Husband*. Off the stage she was also celebrated for her tempestuous relations with other actresses.

Wolf, Friedrich (1888–1953) German playwright, who was the author of several notable Realist dramas exposing political and social injustice. *Kolonne Hund* (1926) espoused the cause of poverty-stricken coal miners while *Cyankali* (Potassium Cyanide; 1929) criticized the contemporary anti-abortion laws. His later Marxist plays were more politically outspoken, *Matrosen von Cattaro* (The Sailors of Cattaro; 1930) depicting a naval mutiny and *Tai Yang erwacht* (1931) taking a stand against Fascism; *Professor Mamlock* (1935) decried the persecution of the Jews by the Nazis.

Wolfe, George C (1954–) US writer and director, who first gained attention with his book and lyrics for *The Colored Museum*, written in 1985 and performed at the New York Shakespeare Festival in 1987. He consolidated his reputation with *Jelly's Last Jam* in 1991. In 1993 he was appointed head of the New York Shakespeare Festival, in which capacity he has produced and directed many shows, as well as developing the well-received revue *Bring on da Noise, Bring On da Funk* (1996).

Wolff, Pius Alexander (1782–1828) German actor, who played many leading roles in the plays of Goethe at Weimar. He and his wife, also an actress in the company, eventually left and became established favourites in Berlin.

Wolfit, Sir Donald (Donald Woolfitt; 1902–68) British actor-manager, who began in Shakespearean roles, then joined Matheson Lang at the New Theatre (1924). He played seasons at the Old Vic and at Stratford-on-Avon and, in 1937, formed his own Shakespearean company; this undertook lengthy tours of the provinces for many years thereafter, only occasionally visiting the capital. He twice visited the US after World War II. Wolfit's outstanding parts were Shylock, Volpone, Richard III, a masterly King Lear, and Solness in Ibsen's *The Master Builder*. In 1951 he returned to the Old Vic as Marlowe's Tamburlaine.

Woman Killed with Kindness, A A domestic tragedy by Thomas HEYWOOD. First performance: London, 1603. The infidelity of Mrs Frankford is discovered by her husband, who refrains from killing her lover but cannot forgive her for dishonouring their marriage. She eventually dies of remorse.

Woman of No Importance, A A comedy by Oscar WILDE. First performance: 1893. Lord Illingworth dismisses his former mistress Mrs Arbuthnot as "a woman of no importance", unaware that Gerald, the young man he decides to employ as his secretary, is in fact their son. When he tries to seduce Gerald's fiancée, Mrs Arbuthnot reveals the truth.

Women Beware Women A tragedy by Thomas MIDDLETON. First performance: London, c. 1621. Set in Renaissance Italy, the play explores the sexual decadence of the central characters and is notable for its understanding of female psychology.

women's theatre Drama for and by women that gives particular prominence to feminist issues. With the development of the Women's Liberation movement in the late 1960s, a number of US groups were founded to promote opportunities for women in all aspects of the theatre and to present experimental drama with a feminist message. Celebrated groups of this kind include the It's All Right To Be a Woman Theatre in New York, which specializes in improvisation; British counterparts have included The Monstrous Regiment, Mrs Worthington's Daughters, and the Sphinx Theatre Company (formerly the Women's Theatre Group).

Wood, Charles Gerald (1932–) British playwright, whose first work *Cockade* (1963) – a triple bill comprising *Prisoner and Escort*, *John Thomas*, and *Spare* – was the first of several to reflect his experiences in the army. Subsequent plays have included the farce *Meals on Wheels* (1965), *Fill the Stage With Happy Hours* (1966), the war plays *Dingo* (1967) and *H* (1969), *Welfare* (1970), *Veterans* (1972), *Jingo* (1975), and *Has 'Washington' Legs?* (1978), *Red Star* (1984), and *Across From the Garden of Allah* (1986). He has also adapted several plays by Pirandello and written for the cinema.

Wood, John (1930–) British actor, who was president of OUDS before joining the Old Vic company in 1954 and making his West End debut in Tennessee Williams's *Camino Real* (1957). He was admired as Guildenstern in Stoppard's *Rosencrantz and Guildenstern are Dead* in New York (1967) and subsequently – after further acclaim in Joyce's *Exiles* (1970) – gave a series of highly praised performances with the Royal Shakespeare Company, his parts including Brutus, Sherlock Holmes, and Henry Carr in Stoppard's *Travesties*. After success in Ira Levin's *Deathtrap* (1978) he joined the National Theatre, appearing as Richard III (1979) and Salieri in Shaffer's *Amadeus* (1981). In 1988 he returned to Stratford-on-Avon to play Prospero in *The Tempest*. Subsequent work has included Ibsen's *The Master Builder* (1989) and *King Lear* (1990).

Wood, William Burke (1779–1861) US actor, born in Montreal, who was the first native American to play a significant part in the development of the national theatre. He was manager with William Warren of the Chestnut Street Theatre in

Philadelphia for many years and also wrote a diary giving valuable information about the theatre of his day. As an actor he was particularly admired in comedy, although he also appeared in tragedy and promoted the performance of new US drama.

Wood's Museum *See* Daly's Theatre.

Woodward, Harry (1717–77) British actor, who began performing as a child. In 1729 he joined John Rich at Lincoln's Inn Fields, where he later appeared in *The Beggar's Opera*. Subsequently he played comedy roles at Drury Lane and Covent Garden, appearing as **Lun** junior, and spent a year at the Smock Alley Theatre with Sheridan in 1747. He also wrote several pantomimes for Garrick. In 1777 he created the role of Captain Absolute in *The Rivals*.

Wooing Ceremony *See* mummers' play.

Woollcott, Alexander (1887–1943) US theatre critic and playwright, who worked for the *New York Times*, the *New York Herald*, the *Sun*, and the *New York World*. Although his light and amusing style proved widely popular, his reviews prompted several New York theatres to attempt to ban him in 1915; later in his career he entirely failed to perceive any merit in the plays of O'Neill. He also collaborated with Moss Hart and George S Kaufman on *The Channel Road* (1929) and *The Dark Tower* (1932). Woollcott was lampooned as the pompous Sheridan Whiteside in Kaufman's play *The Man Who Came to Dinner* (1939), but later toured in the role himself to great success.

Woolgar, Sarah Jane *See* Mellon, Mrs Alfred.

World Theatre Season A major theatre festival for foreign drama founded in London by Peter Daubeny in 1964. Hosted by the Aldwych Theatre, it welcomed such celebrated companies as the Comédie-Française, the Abbey Theatre company, and the Moscow Art Theatre, as well as famous companies from Austria, Belgium, Czechoslovakia, Germany, Greece, India, Israel, Italy, Japan, Poland, Spain, South Africa, Sweden, Turkey, Uganda, and the US. The last of these annual seasons was in 1973, with one revival in 1975.

Worms, Gustave-Hippolyte (1836–1910) French actor, who excelled as young lovers at both the Comédie-Française and in Russia, where he remained for several years. He was successful in both comedy and tragedy, most notably – as Don Carlos – with Sarah Bernhardt in Hugo's *Hernani* (1877) and in the plays of Dumas *fils* as well as in earlier works.

Worth, Irene (1916–) US actress, who made her stage debut in 1942 in Margaret Kennedy's *Escape Me Never*. She first appeared on the New York stage in 1943 and subsequently (1951) joined the London Old Vic company, excelling as Desdemona and Portia and in *A Midsummer Night's Dream*. Working mainly in Britain until 1959, she won further acclaim in plays by N C Hunter, Betti, Feydeau, Schiller, and Graham Greene. After success in the US in Lillian Hellman's *Toys in the Attic* (1960) she returned to Britain to join the Royal Shakespeare Company. There she began a collaboration with the director Peter Brook; her roles with him included Goneril in *King Lear*, Dr Zahnd in Dürrenmatt's *The Physicists*, and the lead in Ted Hughes's experimental piece *Orghast*, staged in Iran in 1971. She has played modern roles, including Winnie in Beckett's *Happy Days* (1979) and Ella in Ibsen's *John Gabriel Borkman* (1980), more recently she appeared in *The Bay at Nice* and *Wrecked Eggs* (both 1986) by David Hare, played Grandma Kurnitz in Neil Simon's *Lost in Yonkers* (1991), and toured in her own one-woman play *Irene Worth's Portrait of Edith Wharton* (1994).

Woyzeck A play by Georg BÜCHNER, left unfinished at his death in 1937. First performance: Vienna, 1913. A pessimistic story of an illiterate soldier's descent into madness and suicide, it provided the basis of the opera *Wozzeck* (1925) by Alban Berg and has enjoyed many successful revivals since World War II.

Wycherley, Sir William (1640–1716) English playwright, noted for his savage moralistic comedies, which are amongst the finest examples of Restoration drama. His first play, *Love in a Wood; or, St James's Park* (1671), was followed by an adaptation from Calderón, THE GENTLEMAN DANCING-MASTER (1672); his biggest success, however, came in 1675 with THE COUNTRY WIFE, which was later revived at Drury Lane as *The Country Girl* by Garrick in 1766. His fourth play, THE PLAIN DEALER, was inspired by Molière's *Le Misanthrope*.

Wyndham, Sir Charles (Charles Culverwell; 1837–1919) British actor-manager, born in Liverpool, whose first appearance on the London stage was in 1862. Trained in medicine, Wyndham served as a surgeon during the US Civil War. From 1865 onwards he began to acquire a reputation in comedy roles on both sides of the Atlantic; he also had a shortlived spell in management at the Queen's Theatre (1868), after which he returned to the US. Following his success in Bronson Howard's *Saratoga* in 1870, he became manager of the Criterion Theatre in 1876, where he remained for 23 years. In 1886 he excelled in T W Robertson's *David Garrick*. In 1899 he opened WYNDHAM'S THEATRE; subsequently he opened the New Theatre (*see* Albery Theatre) in 1903. Wyndham was knighted in 1902. Following the death of his first wife in 1916, he married his leading lady, **Mary Moore** (1869–1931), widow of James Albery.

Wyndham's Theatre A theatre in the Charing Cross Road, London, which was opened in 1899 and named after the actor-manager Sir Charles Wyndham. The first production, a revival of T W Robertson's *David Garrick*, was followed by *Cyrano de Bergerac* and Henry Arthur Jones's *Mrs Dane's Defence*, which ran for over 200 performances. Gerald Du Maurier joined the management in 1910 and enjoyed considerable success as an actor there. In the period 1926–32 Wyndham's was widely known for its productions of the plays of Edgar Wallace. Post-war successes include *The Boy Friend*, which ran for a record-breaking 2078 performances in the 1950s, Ronald Millar's *Abelard and Heloise* (1970–72), *Godspell* (1972–74), and *Side by Side by Sondheim* (1976–77). More recent successes have included Dario Fo's *Accidental Death of an Anarchist* (1980), which ran for 622 performances, and Yasmin Reza's *Art*, which opened in 1996 and is still running. From 1978 until 1987 the theatre was managed by Ian Albery, a great-grandson of the actress Mary Moore (Mrs James Albery, later Lady Wyndham).

Wynn, Ed (Edwin Leopold Wynn; 1886–1966) US comedian, who began in vaudeville when he was 15. He consolidated his reputation as a comic when he appeared in a ridiculous costume in the *Ed Wynn Carnival* revue of 1921; subsequently he starred in Ziegfeld's *Follies* and other revues and musical comedy.

Wynyard, Diana (Dorothy Isobel Cox; 1906–64) British actress, whose first big success was as Charlotte Brontë in Clemence Dane's *Wild Decembers* (1933). After further acclaim as Belinda Warren in Joyce Carey's *Sweet Aloes* (1934), she appeared in many West End comedies, at Stratford-on-Avon, and opposite Gielgud in *The Winter's Tale* (1951) and *Much Ado About Nothing* (1952). She appeared with the National Theatre company at the Old Vic until shortly before her death. She also excelled in plays by Coward, Lillian Hellman, and Tennessee Williams.

Wyspiański, Stanisław (1869–1907) Polish playwright, artist, poet, director, and stage designer, who studied art in France and Italy and wrote 16 plays. Four of these are poetic dramas with classical settings, notably *The Return of Ulysses* (1907); of the remaining 12, which deal largely – often in allegorical form – with the problems of Poland and its people, *The Legion* (1900), *The Wedding* (1901), *Akropolis* (1903), and *November Light* (1904) are the most important. As a director he aroused interest with his unusual production of *Hamlet* (1901), in which the Ghost became the central character.

Y

Yablochkina, Alexandra Alexandrovna (1868–1964) Russian actress, who spent most of her career at the Maly Theatre, where she first performed in 1888. Between her first appearance at the age of six and her last at the age of 94, she played numerous celebrated roles from the plays of Shakespeare, Gorky, Korneichuk, and Wilde; from 1916 she was chairman of the All-Russian Theatrical Society.

Yakovlev, Alexei Semenovich (1773–1817) Russian actor, who established a reputation as a strong – if unpredictable – performer of leading roles with the St Petersburg Imperial Theatre company. A pupil of Dmitrevsky, he supported a more realistic approach to drama but suffered from his weakness for drink and his reliance on inspiration.

Yale Repertory Theatre A theatre at Yale University, founded by Robert Brustein in 1966. The company moved off-campus in 1968 to a church with a stage; this was renovated in 1975 to create a 491-seat theatre. From 1979 until 1991 the company was managed by Lloyd Richards, Stan Wojewodski taking over in 1992. It has offered a wide variety of classics and new plays, including Aeschylus' *Prometheus Bound*, Eric Bentley's *Are You Now or Have You Ever Been...?*, Kopit's *Wings*, and works by Edward Bond and Athol Fugard.

Yanshin, Mikhail Mikhailovich (1902–76) Russian actor and director, who established his reputation with the Moscow Art Theatre, which he joined in 1924. Acclaimed in plays be Bulgakov, Chekhov, Ostrovosky, and Sheridan, he later became director of the Gypsy Theatre (1937–41) and subsequently (1950) producer of the Stanislavsky Theatre in Moscow.

Yates, Frederick Henry (1795–1842) British actor and manager, who was persuaded to begin his stage career by Charles Mathews. He played Shakespearean roles in Edinburgh, including Bolingbroke to Edmund Kean's Richard II, before making his Covent Garden debut as Iago in 1819. Subsequently he took over the Adelphi Theatre in partnership with Daniel Terry. His wife was the actress **Elizabeth Brunton** (1799–1860).

Yates, Richard (1706–96) British actor, noted for his performances of Shakespearean clowns. With Ned Shuter he set up a booth in Bartholomew Fair, playing Pantaloon to his partner's Harlequin. He later appeared at Covent Garden and Drury Lane, where he created the role of Sir Oliver Surface in *The Rivals* in 1777. His second wife was the actress Mary Ann GRAHAM.

Yavorov, Peio (Peyo Kracholov; 1877–1914) Bulgarian poet, playwright, and pioneer of Symbolism in Bulgarian poetry. His output as a dramatist included the tragedies *V Polite na Vitosha* (In the Foothills of Mount Vitosha; 1911) and *Kogato Gram Udari* (When the Thunder Rolls; 1912), which told the life-story of the Macedonian leader Gotse Delchev. He committed suicide on the death of his wife.

Yeats, W(illiam) B(utler) (1865–1939) Irish poet and playwright, one of the founders of the ABBEY THEATRE. Yeats wrote some 30 plays, beginning with the verse dramas THE LAND OF HEART'S DESIRE (1894) and *The Countess Cathleen* (1899). Dedicated to the development of a distinct Irish drama, and hostile to the prevailing canons of realism, he drew extensively upon Irish legend and the aristocratic Japanese *Nō* theatre for his plays. In addition to his roles as playwright, director, and manager of the Abbey Theatre, Yeats also championed his fellow Irishmen J M Synge and Sean O'Casey, although he subsequently fell out with the latter after rejecting *The Silver Tassie* for production. He was awarded a Nobel Prize in 1923.

Principal works:
  The Land of Heart's Desire: 1894.
  The Countess Cathleen: 1899.
  CATHLEEN NI HOULIHAN: 1902.
  On Baile's Strand: 1904.
  Deirdre: 1906.
  At The Hawk's Well: 1917.
  The Only Jealousy of Emer: 1919.
  The Dreaming of the Bones: 1919.
  The Player Queen: 1919.
  Calvary: 1920.
  The Words Upon the Window Pane: 1930.
  Purgatory: 1938.
  The Death of Cuchulain: 1949.

Yefremov, Oleg Nikolayevich (1927–) Russian actor and director, who became famous for his work with young actors and audiences at the Sovremennik Theatre in Moscow. He installed a company of young performers there in 1958 and presented with them a variety of modern Soviet and European dramas. In 1971 he succeeded Livanov as head of the Moscow Art Theatre; when this divided in the mid-1980s, he remained artistic director of the company based in the original building (now known as the Moscow Chekhov Art Theatre).

Yerma A tragedy by GARCÍA LORCA. First performance: Madrid, 1934. The second part of a famous trilogy of folk tragedies, the other parts being BLOOD WEDDING (1933) and THE HOUSE OF BERNARDA ALBA (1945), the play depicts the suffering of a childless gypsy woman who finally murders her sterile husband.

Yermolova, Maria Nikolaievna (1853–1928) Russian actress, who became a leading performer of tragic roles at the Maly Theatre. Much admired by Stanislavsky, she excelled in such parts as Lady Macbeth, Joan of Arc, and Phèdre both before and after the Revolution of 1917. The Yermolova Theatre, founded in 1930, was named in her honour.

Yermolova Theatre A studio theatre in Moscow, founded in 1930 and named after the actress Maria Nikolaievna YERMOLOVA. In 1937 it amalgamated with the Khmelev Studio and enjoyed success with Khmelev's productions of Russian works and Shakespeare. Notable performances have included the premiere of the Dosto-evsky adaptation *Crime and Punishment* (1956).

Yeston, Maury (1945–) US composer and lyricist, whose first success was *Nine* (1983). Other works include *Grand Hotel* (1989) and *Phantom* (1992), another version of *The Phantom of the Opera* story. *Titanic* (1997) is an excellent example of a new style of Broadway composing, in which there is very little dialogue, the effect being of an opera written in a popular music vocabulary.

Yevreinov, Nikolai *See* Evreinov, Nikolai Nikolaivich.

Yiddish Art Theatre *See* Phoenix Theatre.

York, Susannah (Susannah Fletcher; 1942–) British actress, who has appeared worldwide in parts ranging from Amanda in Coward's *Private Lives* (Australia) to the title role in Ibsen's *Hedda Gabler* (US) and Ann Whitfield in Shaw's *Man and Super-man* (Dublin); she has also appeared with Barrault's company in Paris. In spite of a busy film career, she has played regularly in London in productions as diverse as *Peter Pan* (1977) and Clare Boothe Luce's *The Women* (1986). In 1992 she directed Wilde's *Salomé* at the Traverse Theatre in Edinburgh. Recent stage work has included *The Merry Wives of Windsor* (1997) for the RSC and Wilde's *An Ideal Husband* (1998).

You Can't Take It With You A comedy by George S KAUFMAN and Moss HART. First performance: New York, 1936. The plot deals with the eccentric and free-spirited Sycamores and the complications that occur when Alice falls in love with the son of a rich stuffy family. The play, which won a Pulitzer Prize, offers gentle but pointed criticism of America's fixation with success.

You Never Can Tell A play by G B SHAW, written 1895–97. First performance: Strand Theatre, London, 1900. A cheerful domestic comedy, the play explores the theme of love through the relationships of husband and wife, parents and children, and lovers. The setting is a hotel in an English seaside town, where a waiter plays a leading role.

Young, Charles Mayne (1777–1856) British actor, born in London. Having made his debut in 1798, in Liverpool, he played leading parts at Manchester, Edinburgh, and, again, at Liverpool. Invited to the Haymarket by Charles Mathews in 1820, he was much acclaimed as Hamlet and acknowledged as a leading tragedian. Later tri-umphs included his performances as Cassius to John Philip Kemble's Brutus at Covent Garden and appearances with Kean at Drury Lane.

Young American Roscius *See* Cowell, Joseph Leathley.

Young England A play by Walter Reynolds. First performance: London, 1934. In-tended as a patriotic celebration, it was received as a riotous parody and gained huge popularity as the butt of audience humour and mockery.

Young Roscius *See* Betty, William Henry West.

Young Vic Theatre A theatre opened in London in 1970 on a bombsite close to the Old Vic Theatre in Lambeth, specifically to offer good theatre to young audiences at low prices. It was founded by Frank Dunlop and officially opened by Dame Sybil Thorndike, the first production being *Scapino*, an adaptation from Molière. Initially under the management of the National Theatre, the Young Vic became independent in 1974. It has a seating capacity of 500 and a small studio theatre seating 114. Michael Bogdanov was its director from 1978 to 1980 and David Thacker from 1984 to 1993.

Yovkov, Yordan Stefanovich (1880–1937) Bulgarian short-story writer, novelist, and playwright, whose plays are chiefly concerned with Balkan peasant life. He wrote about the effects of war in *Albena* (1930) and *Boryana* (1932); his best-known play was the comedy about a poor vet's marriage into a rich family *Milionerut* (The Millionaire; 1930).

Yubani, Zef (1910–58) Albanian actor, who became a leading performer at the Üsküdar Migjeni Theatre. He was highly acclaimed in parts ranging from Molière's Harpagon to Ibsen's Stockman.

Yurka, Blanche (Blanche Jurka; 1893–1974) US actress, who first appeared in New York in 1907. She played Gertrude to John Barrymore's Hamlet in 1922 and later appeared in various plays by Ibsen, including *The Wild Duck* (1928), *Hedda Gabler* (1929), *The Lady from the Sea* (1929), and *The Vikings* (1930). She toured the US in a solo production from 1936 to 1938, performing scenes from great plays. She went on to play Mrs Antrobus in Wilder's *The Skin of Our Teeth* (1958) and Miss Moffat in a revival of Emlyn Williams's *The Corn Is Green* (1961).

Z

Zabłocki, Franciszek (1754–1821) Polish playwright, author of satirical comedies largely based on French models. Typical of his works was the verse comedy *Sarmatyzm* (1785), the plot of which was also explored by Fredro and Mickiewicz.

Zacconi, Ermete (1857–1948) Italian actor, who became a leading performer of plays of the *verismo* tradition. He formed his own company in 1894 and pioneered performances of the plays of Ibsen in Italian as well as translating major works by Hauptmann, Tolstoy, and Strindberg. He was also much admired in Shakespearean roles, particularly as Hamlet.

Zacuto, Moses (1625–97) Jewish playwright, much influenced by Vondel. His plays include *Yesod Olam*, which was first presented in Italy, and *Tofteh Aruch*, performed in Ferrara in about 1700.

Zadek, Peter (1926–) German director, who established his reputation while working at Bremen in the mid-1960s. Here he produced politically committed re-interpretations of the classics as well as new plays by Dorst and Forte, a policy he continued at the Bochum Theatre in the 1970s. He also found success with his adaptations of several novels by Hans Fallada. His Shakespeare productions have included *Hamlet* (1977), *The Merchant of Venice* (1988), and *Measure for Measure* (1990). He was head of the Deutsches Schauspielhaus, Hamburg, from 1985 to 1989 and a director of the Berliner Ensemble from 1992 to 1995.

Zakhava, Boris Evgenevich (1898–1976) Russian actor and director, who established his reputation as Timur in Vakhtangov's production of Gozzi's *Turandot* (1922). Subsequently he joined Meyerhold's company and directed plays by Dostoevsky, Gorky, Ostrovsky, and Shakespeare before taking charge of the Shchukin School of Acting in Moscow.

Zangwill, Israel (1864–1926) British novelist, playwright, and poet, who was regarded as the most important Anglo-Jewish writer of his day. He first came to notice with novels about Jewish ghetto life in London; his best-known play, *The Melting Pot* (1908), deals with the assimilation of the US immigrant population.

zanni The servant characters of the *commedia dell'arte*, several of which were later developed into major roles of the English harlequinade. Wearing masks and specializing in slapstick humour, the *zanni* included ARLECCHINO, BRIGHELLA, Columbina (*see* Columbine), MEZZETINO, PANTALONE, PASQUINO, PEDROLINO, PULCINELLA, SCAPINO, and SCARAMUCCIA.

zarzuela A form of musical play first developed in Spain during the 17th century. Consisting of narrative passages combined with music and dances, the *zarzuela* (named after the royal palace of La Zarzuela near Madrid) usually took a mythological or heroic subject as its theme. Writers of notable examples included Lope de Vega and Calderón; the form was later revived in the 19th century by Ramón de la Cruz and others, who introduced plots based on everyday life. Gradually it became divided into the *género chico* (or *teatro por horas*), a one-act comedy, and the *grande*, a serious musical play akin to opera.

Zavadsky, Yuri Alexeivich (1894–1977) Russian director and actor, who trained under Vakhtangov before ultimately taking over the Gorky State Theatre in Rostov. His highly-acclaimed lyrical productions there included plays by Gorky and Shakespeare; later in his career he also worked at the Mossoviet Theatre. His pupils included Grotowski.

Zeami (1363–1443) Japanese playwright and actor, who played a key role in the development of the Nō play. The son of the actor Kanami, Zeami appeared in his father's company at the court of the shogun Yoshimitsu while still a child; after his father's death in 1384 he continued the transformation of the *Nō* drama into the complex and aristocratic tradition still performed in modern times. He wrote about 200 plays (of which 124 survive) in the genre and was the author of immensely influential theatrical treatises setting out the nature and structure of the *Nō* play, delineating the role of the actor and discussing the symbolic and spiritual content. His most celebrated plays include *Matsukaze*, which is typical of the main body of his work.

Zeffirelli, Franco (1923–) Italian director and stage designer. He began his career working in collaboration with VISCONTI and subsequently became famous as a director and designer of operas, films, and classic plays. His greatest successes have included *Romeo and Juliet* (1960) at the Old Vic, *Othello* (1961) at Stratford-on-Avon, and *Hamlet* (1964) at the Old Vic, as well as plays by Albee, Eduardo De Filippo, Dumas *fils*, and Arthur Miller. His best-known films include versions of *The Taming of the Shrew* (1967), *Romeo and Juliet* (1968), and *Hamlet* (1991).

Ziegfeld, Florenz (1867–1932) US producer, who first staged the famous *Ziegfeld Follies* in 1907. Modelled on the shows at the Folies-Bergère in Paris, the *Follies* represented the height of revue, with lavish costumes, beautiful girls, and spectacular sets; it ran in a continuous series until 1932 and then periodically until 1957. Ziegfeld also produced such musicals as *Show Boat* (1927) at his own Ziegfeld Theatre, as well as a number of straight plays.

His first wife was the actress **Anna Held** (1873–1918), a star of musical comedy, and his second was **Billie Burke** (Ethelbert Appleton Burke; 1884–1970), who was also popular in light comedy.

Ziegfeld Theatre A theatre on 6th Avenue and 54th Street, New York, which opened in 1927 with the musical *Rio Rita*. After successes with plays by Coward and Ziegfeld's *Follies*, the theatre was used as a cinema from 1932, when Ziegfeld died, to 1944, when Billy Rose reopened it. It was used for broadcasting from 1955 to 1963 but returned to live theatre for four years before it was demolished in 1967.

Ziegler, Clara (1844–1909) German actress, who established herself as a popular performer of tragic roles in both Leipzig and Munich. Her finest performances included leading roles in the plays of Euripides, Grillparzer, and Schiller, as well as Shakespeare's Romeo. Her house and library later provided the basis of a theatre museum in Munich.

Zipprodt, Patricia (1925–99) US costume designer for plays, ballet, and opera, whose first Broadway work was for *Visit to a Small Planet* (1957). Other major shows included *Fiddler on the Roof* (1962), *Cabaret* (1966), *1776* (1968), *Chicago* (1975), *Brighton Beach Memoirs* (1983), and the 1985 revival of *Sweet Charity*.

Zola, Émile (1840–1902) French novelist and playwright, leader of the naturalist movement in 19th-century literature (*see* naturalism). Remembered chiefly for his novels, Zola made a comparatively small, but not insignificant, contribution to the theatre. He wrote several plays, of which the most successful was THÉRÈSE RAQUIN (1873), based on his novel, and his critical works *Le Naturalisme au théâtre* (1878) and *Nos auteurs dramatiques* (1881) had an important influence on the development of naturalistic drama in the plays of Henry Becque and André Antoine's Théâtre Libre.

Zorrilla, Francisco de Rojas *See* Rojas Zorrilla, Francisco de.

Zorrilla y Moral, José (1817–93) Spanish poet and playwright, the author of several dramas in the Romantic tradition. His plays include *Don Juan Tenorio* (1844), a popular version of the DON JUAN story, and the historical plays *El zapatero y el rey* (The Cobbler and the King; 1840) and *Traidor, inconfeso y mártir* (1849).

Zuckmayer, Carl (1896–1977) German playwright, poet, and novelist, whose first success in the theatre came with the play *Der fröhliche Weinberg* (The Merry Vineyard; 1925), a lively rustic comedy set in his native Rhineland. His finest drama was *Der Hauptmann von Köpenick* (The Captain of Kopernich; 1930), a satire on German militarism. Following the rise of Nazism, Zuckmayer left Germany to live variously in Austria, Switzerland, and the US; his other important works include *Das Teufels General* (The Devil's General; 1946) and such late works as *Das Kalte Licht* (The Cold Light; 1956) and *Der Rattenfänger* (The Pied Piper; 1974).

Zweig, Stefan (1881–1942) Austrian poet, novelist, and playwright. Zweig, who came from a wealthy Jewish background, established his reputation in the theatre with *Jeremias* (Jeremiah; 1917), which expressed his pacifist beliefs. Later works included satires upon the hypocrisy of public figures and an adaptation of Jonson's *Volpone* (1926); after leaving Austria in the 1930s, he eventually settled in Brazil, where he committed suicide.